Place-of-Service Codes for Professional Claims

Listed below are place-of-service codes and descriptions. These codes should be used on [...] entity where service(s) were rendered. Check with individual payers (eg, Medicare, Medi[...] reimbursement policies regarding these codes. If you would like to comment on a code(s[...] your request to posinfo@cms.hhs.gov.

Place of Service Code(s)	Place of Service Name	Place of Service Description
01	Pharmacy	A facility or location where drugs and other medically related items and services are sold, dispensed, or otherwise provided directly to patients. (effective 10/1/05)
02	Unassigned	N/A
03	School	A facility whose primary purpose is education.
04	Homeless shelter	A facility or location whose primary purpose is to provide temporary housing to homeless individuals (eg, emergency shelters, individual or family shelters).
05	Indian Health Service freestanding facility	A facility or location, owned and operated by the Indian Health Service, that provides diagnostic, therapeutic (surgical and nonsurgical), and rehabilitation services to American Indians and Alaska Natives who do not require hospitalization.
06	Indian Health Service provider-based facility	A facility or location, owned and operated by the Indian Health Service, that provides diagnostic, therapeutic (surgical and nonsurgical), and rehabilitation services rendered by, or under the supervision of, physicians to American Indians and Alaska Natives admitted as inpatients or outpatients.
07	Tribal 638 freestanding facility	A facility or location owned and operated by a federally recognized American Indian or Alaska Native tribe or tribal organization under a 638 agreement that provides diagnostic, therapeutic (surgical and nonsurgical), and rehabilitation services to tribal members who do not require hospitalization.
08	Tribal 638 provider-based facility	A facility or location owned and operated by a federally recognized American Indian or Alaska Native tribe or tribal organization under a 638 agreement that provides diagnostic, therapeutic (surgical and nonsurgical), and rehabilitation services to tribal members admitted as inpatients or outpatients.
9-10	Unassigned	N/A
11	Office	Location, other than a hospital, skilled nursing facility, military treatment facility, community health center, state or local public health clinic, or intermediate care facility, where the health professional routinely provides health examinations, diagnosis, and treatment of illness or injury on an ambulatory basis.
12	Home	Location, other than a hospital or other facility, where the patient receives care in a private residence.
13	Assisted living facility	Congregate residential facility with self-contained living units providing assessment of each resident's needs and on-site support 24 hours a day, seven days a week, with the capacity to deliver or arrange for services including some health care and other services. (effective 10/1/03)
14	Group home	A residence, with shared living areas, where clients receive supervision and other services such as social and/or behavioral services, custodial service, and minimal services (eg, medication administration) (effective 4/1/04)
15	Mobile unit	A facility or unit that moves from place to place and is equipped to provide preventive, screening, diagnostic, and/or treatment services.
16	Temporary lodging	A short-term accommodation such as a hotel, camp ground, hostel, cruise ship, or resort where the patient receives care, and which is not identified by any other POS code. (effective 4/1/08)
17-19	Unassigned	N/A
20	Urgent care facility	Location, distinct from a hospital emergency department, an office, or a clinic, whose purpose is to diagnose and treat illness or injury for unscheduled, ambulatory patients seeking immediate medical attention.
21	Inpatient hospital	A facility, other than psychiatric, that primarily provides diagnostic, therapeutic (both surgical and nonsurgical), and rehabilitation services by, or under, the supervision of physicians to patients admitted for a variety of medical conditions..
22	Outpatient hospital	A portion of a hospital that provides diagnostic, therapeutic (both surgical and nonsurgical), and rehabilitation services to sick or injured persons who do not require hospitalization or institutionalization.
23	Emergency room—hospital	A portion of a hospital where emergency diagnosis and treatment of illness or injury is provided.
24	Ambulatory surgical center	A freestanding facility, other than a physician's office, where surgical and diagnostic services are provided on an ambulatory basis.
25	Birthing center	A facility, other than a hospital's maternity facilities or a physician's office, that provides a setting for labor, delivery, and immediate postpartum care as well as immediate care of newborn infants.
26	Military treatment facility	A medical facility operated by one or more of the uniformed services. Military treatment facility also refers to certain former US Public Health Service facilities now designated as uniformed service treatment facilities.
27-30	Unassigned	N/A
31	Skilled nursing facility	A facility that primarily provides inpatient skilled nursing care and related services to patients who require medical, nursing, or rehabilitative services but does not provide the level of care or treatment available in a hospital.

32	Nursing facility	A facility that primarily provides to residents skilled nursing care and related services for the rehabilitation of injured, disabled, or sick persons, or, on a regular basis, health-related care services above the level of custodial care to other than mentally retarded individuals.
33	Custodial care facility	A facility that provides room, board, and other personal assistance services, generally on a long-term basis, and does not include a medical component.
34	Hospice	A facility, other than a patient's home, in which palliative and supportive care for terminally ill patients and their families are provided.
35-40	Unassigned	N/A
41	Ambulance—land	A land vehicle specifically designed, equipped, and staffed for lifesaving and transporting the sick or injured.
42	Ambulance—air or water	An air or water vehicle specifically designed, equipped, and staffed for lifesaving and transporting the sick or injured.
43-48	Unassigned	N/A
49	Independent clinic	A location, not part of a hospital and not described by any other place-of-service code, that is organized and operated to provide preventive, diagnostic, therapeutic, rehabilitative, or palliative services to outpatients only. (effective 10/1/03)
50	Federally qualified health center	A facility located in a medically underserved area that provides Medicare beneficiaries preventive primary medical care under the general direction of a physician.
51	Inpatient psychiatric facility	A facility that provides inpatient psychiatric services for the diagnosis and treatment of mental illness on a 24-hour basis, by or under the supervision of a physician.
52	Psychiatric facility— partial hospitalization	A facility for the diagnosis and treatment of mental illness that provides a planned therapeutic program for patients who do not require full-time hospitalization but who need broader programs than are possible from outpatient visits to a hospital-based or hospital-affiliated facility.
53	Community mental health center	A facility that provides the following services: outpatient services, including specialized outpatient services for children, the elderly, individuals who are chronically ill, and residents of the community mental health center's mental health services area who have been discharged from inpatient treatment at a mental health facility; 24-hour-a-day emergency care services; day treatment, other partial hospitalization services, or psychosocial rehabilitation services; screening for patients being considered for admission to state mental health facilities to determine the appropriateness of such admission; and consultation and education services.
54	Intermediate care facility/mentally retarded	A facility that primarily provides health-related care and services above the level of custodial care to mentally retarded individuals but does not provide the level of care or treatment available in a hospital or skilled nursing facility.
55	Residential substance abuse treatment facility	A facility that provides treatment for substance (alcohol and drug) abuse to live-in residents who do not require acute medical care. Services include individual and group therapy and counseling, family counseling, laboratory tests, drugs and supplies, psychological testing, and room and board.
56	Psychiatric residential treatment center	A facility or distinct part of a facility for psychiatric care that provides a total 24-hour therapeutically planned and professionally staffed group living and learning environment.
57	Nonresidential substance abuse treatment facility	A location that provides treatment for substance (alcohol and drug) abuse on an ambulatory basis. Services include individual and group therapy and counseling, family counseling, laboratory tests, drugs and supplies, and psychological testing. (effective 10/1/03)
58-59	Unassigned	N/A
60	Mass immunization center	A location where providers administer pneumococcal pneumonia and influenza virus vaccinations and submit these services as electronic media claims or paper claims or by using the roster billing method. This generally takes place in a mass immunization setting, such as a public health center, pharmacy, or mall but may include a physician office setting.
61	Comprehensive inpatient rehabilitation facility	A facility that provides comprehensive rehabilitation services under the supervision of a physician to inpatients with physical disabilities. Services include physical therapy, occupational therapy, speech pathology, social or psychological services, and orthotics and prosthetics services.
62	Comprehensive outpatient rehabilitation facility	A facility that provides comprehensive rehabilitation services under the supervision of a physician to outpatients with physical disabilities. Services include physical therapy, occupational therapy, and speech pathology services.
63-64	Unassigned	N/A
65	End-stage renal disease treatment facility	A facility, other than a hospital, that provides dialysis treatment, maintenance, and/or training to patients or caregivers on an ambulatory or home-care basis.
66-70	Unassigned	N/A
71	Public health clinic	A facility maintained by either state or local health departments that provides ambulatory primary medical care under the general direction of a physician. (effective 10/1/03)
72	Rural health clinic	A certified facility located in a rural, medically underserved area that provides ambulatory primary medical care under the general direction of a physician.
73-80	Unassigned	N/A
81	Independent laboratory	A laboratory certified to perform diagnostic and/or clinical tests independent of an institution or a physician's office.
82-98	Unassigned	N/A
99	Other place of service	Other place of service not identified above.

current procedural terminology

cpt® 2010

Professional Edition

Michelle Abraham, BS
Michael Beebe
Joyce A. Dalton
Desiree D. Evans, AAS
Rejina L. Glenn
Gloria Green, BA
DeHandro Hayden, BS

Elizabeth Lumakovska, MPA, RHIT
Janette Meggs, RHIA
Marie L. Mindeman, BA, RHIT
Karen E. O'Hara, BS, CCS-P
Mary R. O'Heron, RHIA, CCS-P
Danielle Pavloski, BS, RHIT, CCS-P
Marjorie C. Rallins, DPM

Dan Reyes
Desiree Rozell, MPA
Lianne Stancik, RHIT
Peggy Thompson, MS, RHIA, CCS
Susan Tracy, MA, RHIT
Ada Walker, CCA
Arletrice Watkins, MHA, RHIA

AMA
AMERICAN
MEDICAL
ASSOCIATION

Executive Vice President, Chief Executive Officer: Michael D. Maves, MD, MBA
Chief Operating Officer: Bernard L. Hengesbaugh
Senior Vice President, Publishing and Business Services: Robert A. Musacchio, PhD
Vice President and General Manager, Publishing: Frank J. Krause
Vice President, Business Operations: Vanessa Hayden
Publisher, Physician Practice Solutions: Jay T. Ahlman
Senior Acquisitions Editor: Elise Schumacher
Director of Marketing, Business Marketing and Communication: Pam Palmersheim
Director of Sales, Business Products: J.D. Kinney
Manager, Book and Product Development and Production: Nancy Baker
Director, Production and Manufacturing: Jean Roberts
Manager, Marketing and Strategic Planning: Erin Kalitowski
Senior Developmental Editor: Lisa Chin-Johnson
Production Manager: Rosalyn Carlton
Senior Production Coordinator: Boon Ai Tan
Senior Print Coordinator: Ronnie Summers
Production Specialist: Mary Ann Albanese
Marketing Manager: Leigh Adams

Professional ISBN: 978-1-60359-119-5
ISSN: 0276-8283

To purchase additional CPT products, contact the American Medical Association Customer Service
at 800 621-8335.

To request a license for distribution of products containing or reprinting CPT codes and/or guidelines,
please see our Web site at *www.ama-assn.org/go/cpt* or contact the American Medical Association CPT
Intellectual Property Services, 515 N. State Street, Chicago, Illinois 60654, 312 464-5022.

AC36:EP054110:10/09
AC36:EP888810:10/09

Foreword

Current Procedural Terminology (CPT®), Fourth Edition, is a listing of descriptive terms and identifying codes for reporting medical services and procedures performed by physicians. The purpose of the terminology is to provide a uniform language that will accurately describe medical, surgical, and diagnostic services, and will thereby provide an effective means for reliable nationwide communication among physicians, patients, and third parties. *CPT 2010* is the most recent revision of a work that first appeared in 1966.

CPT descriptive terms and identifying codes currently serve a wide variety of important functions in the field of medical nomenclature. The CPT codebook is useful for administrative management purposes such as claims processing and for the development of guidelines for medical care review. The uniform language is also applicable to medical education and outcomes, health services, and quality research by providing a useful basis for local, regional, and national utilization comparisons. The CPT codebook is the most widely accepted nomenclature for the reporting of physician procedures and services under government and private health insurance programs. In 2000, the CPT code set was designated by the Department of Health and Human Services as the national coding standard for physician and other health care professional services and procedures under the Health Insurance Portability and Accountability Act (HIPAA). This means that for all financial and administrative health care transactions sent electronically, the CPT code set will need to be used.

The changes that appear in this revision have been prepared by the CPT Editorial Panel with the assistance of physicians representing all specialties of medicine, and with important contributions from many third-party payers and governmental agencies.

The American Medical Association trusts that this revision will continue the usefulness of its predecessors in identifying, describing, and coding medical, surgical, and diagnostic services.

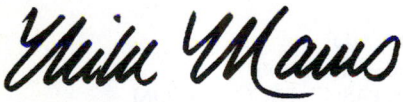

Michael D. Maves, MD, MBA
Executive Vice President, CEO

Acknowledgments

Publication of the annual CPT codebook represents many challenges and opportunities. From reconciling the many differences of opinion about the best way to describe a procedure, to the last details on placement of a semicolon, many individuals and organizations devote their energies and expertise to the preparation of this revision.

The editorial staff wishes to express sincere thanks to the many national medical specialty societies, health insurance organizations and agencies, and individual physicians and other health professionals who have made contributions.

Thanks are due to Robert A. Musacchio, PhD, Sr VP, American Medical Association; Claudia Bonnell, Blue Cross and Blue Shield Association; Nelly Leon-Chisen, American Hospital Association; Jeannette Thornton, America's Health Insurance Plans; and Sue Bowman, RHIA, American Health Information Management Association, for their invaluable assistance for enhancing the CPT code set.

For their assistance in development of the CPT Category II codes:

Ronald A. Gabel, MD
Darryl T. Gray, MD, ScD
Robert S. Haskey, MD
Susan M. Nedza, MD
Gregory Pawlson, MD, MPH
Sylvia Publ, RHIA, MBA

Phil Renner, MBA
Sam J. W. Romeo, MD, MBA
Paul M. Schyve, MD
Sharon Sprenger, RHIA, PHQ, MPA
Sally Turbyville, MA

We recognize the following people for efforts in working with the Physician Consortium for Performance Improvement and other quality measurement organizations:

Mark Antman, DDS, MBA
Heidi Bossley, MSN, MBA
Joseph Gave, MPH
Kendra Hanley, MS
Erin Kaleba, MPH
Karen S. Kmetik, PhD

Shannon Sims, MD, PhD
Beth Tapper, MA, MPH
Sheila Teasdale, MMed Sci FBCS
Samantha Tierney, MPH
E. ChynaWilcoxson, BS
Temaka Williams, MPH, MBA

AMA CPT Editorial Panel

Chair
William T. Thorwarth, Jr, MD, FACR*

Vice-Chair
Peter A. Hollmann, MD*

Albert E. Bothe, Jr, MD, FACS†
Joel F. Bradley, Jr, MD
Kenneth P. Brin, MD, PhD
Boyd R. Buser, DO, FACOFP
Patrick J. Cafferty, MPAS, PA-C*
Jeffrey W. Cozzens, MD, FACS
Richard Duszak, Jr, MD, FACR†
David A. Ellington, MD†
Helene M. Fearon, PT
Robert Haskey, MD
M. Bradford Henley, MD, MBA
Joseph V. Messer, MD, MACC†
Andrea H. McGuire, MD, MBA
Antonio E. Puente, PhD†
Kenneth B. Simon, MD, MBA*
Stanley W. Stead, MD, MBA*
Mark S. Synovec, MD
J. Martin Tucker, MD*
Richard W. Waguespack, MD

Secretary
Marie L. Mindeman, BA, RHIT

*Member of the CPT Executive Committee
†New Panel Member June 2008 and November 2008
‡New Advisors

AMA CPT Advisory Committee

Academy of Pharmaceutical Physicians and Investigators
Grant P. Bagley, MD
American Academy of Allergy, Asthma and Immunology
Donald W. Aaronson, MD
American Academy of Child & Adolescent Psychiatry
David I. Berland, MD
American Academy of Dermatology
Dirk M. Elston, MD
American Academy of Facial Plastic and Reconstructive Surgery
Edward H. Farrior, MD, FACS
American Academy of Family Physicians
Robert J. Carr, Jr, MD‡
American Academy of Neurology
Marc Nuwer, MD, PhD
American Academy of Ophthalmology
Michael X. Repka, MD
American Academy of Orthopaedic Surgeons
Richard J. Friedman, MD, FACSC
American Academy of Otolaryngic Allergy
Paul T. Fass, MD, FACS
American Academy of Otolaryngology-Head and Neck Surgery
Joseph E. Leonard, MD, FACS
American Academy of Pain Medicine
Eduardo M. Fraifeld, MD
American Academy of Pediatrics
Richard A. Molteni, MD
American Academy of Physical Medicine and Rehabilitation
Francis P. Lagattuta, MD
American Academy of Sleep Medicine
Samuel A. Fleishman, MD
American Association for Clinical Chemistry
Robert L. Murray, JD, PhD
American Association for Thoracic Surgery
Kirk R. Kanter, MD

American Association of Clinical Endocrinologists
Eric A. Orzek, MD, FACP, FACE
American Association of Hip and Knee Surgeons
Richard Iorio, MD
American Association of Neurological Surgeons
R. Patrick Jacob, MD
American Association of Neuromuscular and Electrodiagnostic Medicine
Kyle W. Ruffing, MD
American Association of Public Health Physicians
Arvind K. Goyal, MD, MPH, FAAFP, FACPM
American Clinical Neurophysiology Society
Marc Nuwer, MD, PhD
American College of Allergy, Asthma, and Immunology
Gary N. Gross, MD
American College of Cardiology
Robert N. Piana, MD, FACC‡
American College of Chest Physicians
Steve G. Peters, MD
American College of Emergency Physicians
Kenneth L. DeHart, MD, FACEP
American College of Gastroenterology
Daniel C. DeMarco, MD, FACG‡
American College of Medical Genetics
David B. Flannery, MD
American College of Medical Quality
Joel Grossman, MD
American College of Nuclear Physicians
Gary L. Dillehay, MD, FACNP, FACR
American College of Obstetricians and Gynecologists
Jordan G. Pritzker, MD, MBA, FACOG
American College of Occupational and Environmental Medicine
Lee S. Glass, MD
American College of Physicians
R. Scott Hanson, MD, MPH
American College of Preventive Medicine
Ryung Suh, MD, MPP, MBA, MPH
American College of Radiation Oncology
Carl C. Van Wey, MD‡
American College of Radiology
Daniel Picus, MD, FACR, RCC‡
American College of Rheumatology
Robert J. Lloyd, MD
American College of Surgeons
Linda M. Barney, MD, FACS‡
American Dental Association
Anthony M. Spina, DDS, MD‡
American Gastroenterological Association
Joel V. Brill, MD, AGAF, FASGE, FACG, CHCQM
American Geriatric Society
Robert A. Zorowitz, MD, MBA
American Institute of Ultrasound in Medicine
Harvey L. Nisenbaum, MD
American Medical Directors Association
Dennis L. Stone, MD, MBA
American Medical Group Association
David E. Hooper, MD
American Orthopaedic Association
Blair C. Filler, MD
American Orthopaedic Foot and Ankle Society
Walter J. Pedowitz, MD
American Osteopathic Association
Judith A. O'Connell, DO, FAAO
American Psychiatric Association
David K. Nace, MD
American Roentgen Ray Society
Mark D. Alson, MD

CPT® Assistant references within *CPT® Professional 2010*

When using your *CPT® Professional* codebook you will notice the symbol "➲" located next to many codes throughout the body of the book. This symbol has been included to indicate that the AMA has published in-depth information in *CPT® Assistant* on that particular code.

Example	+ 34808	Endovascular placement of iliac artery occlusion device (List separately in addition to code for primary procedure) ➲ *CPT Assistant* Dec 00:1, Sep 02:3

This reference indicates that in the ***CPT Assistant*** newsletter December 2000 issue, page 1 and September 2002 issue, page 3, there is material that will assist you in understanding the application of this code.

From the authors of CPT®—the AMA—this monthly newsletter responds to real-world coding issues and helps resolve differences in opinion between physicians and third-party payers. Reviewed by an editorial board composed of some of the most respected physician and nonphysician coding experts in the country, *CPT Assistant* is the AMA's official communication tool for circulating accurate information and guidance on CPT codes and issues.

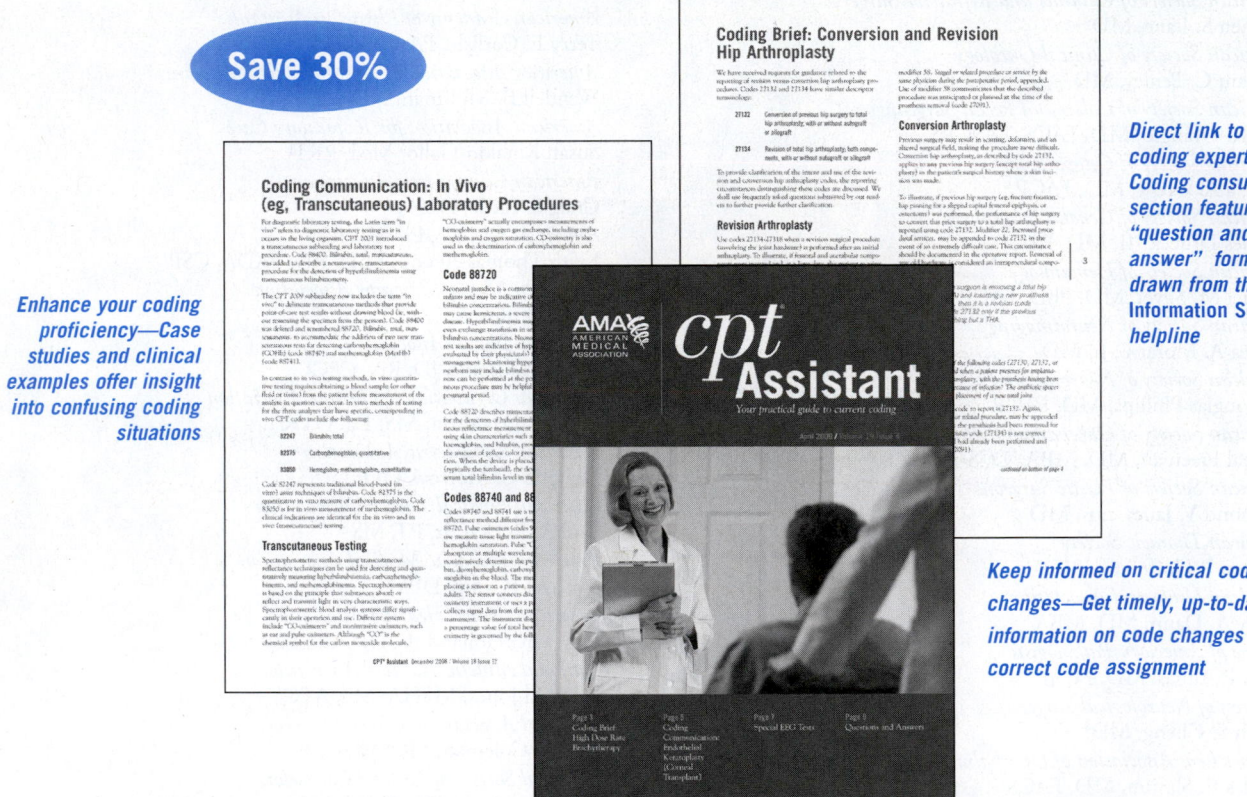

Save 30%

Enhance your coding proficiency—Case studies and clinical examples offer insight into confusing coding situations

Direct link to AMA coding experts— Coding consultation section features a "question and answer" format drawn from the CPT Information Services helpline

Keep informed on critical code changes—Get timely, up-to-date information on code changes and correct code assignment

E-mail **cptasstsample@ama-assn.org** to request a free sample issue, and an issue will be e-mailed to you promptly.

Subscribe today and save 30 percent!

You'll receive 12 or 24 monthly issues, special report bulletins, a frequently asked questions/answers bonus issue and the ability to earn CEU credits toward AAPC certification. Call (800) 621-8335 to order.

Order #: CA492605

Price		**AMA member price**	
~~$199~~	$139.30/one year	~~$149~~	$104.30/one year
~~$299~~	$209.30/two years	~~$205~~	$143.50/two years

AMERICAN MEDICAL ASSOCIATION

Contents

Introduction

Current Procedural Terminology (CPT®), Fourth Edition, is a set of codes, descriptions, and guidelines intended to describe procedures and services performed by physicians and other health care providers. Each procedure or service is identified with a five-digit code. The use of CPT codes simplifies the reporting of services.

Inclusion of a descriptor and its associated five-digit code number in the CPT codebook is based on whether the procedure is consistent with contemporary medical practice and is performed by many practitioners in clinical practice in multiple locations. Inclusion in the CPT codebook does not represent endorsement by the American Medical Association (AMA) of any particular diagnostic or therapeutic procedure. Inclusion or exclusion of a procedure does not imply any health insurance coverage or reimbursement policy

The CPT code set is published annually in the late summer or early fall as both electronic data files and books. The release of CPT data files on the Internet typically precedes the book by several weeks. In any case, January 1 is the effective date for use of the update of the CPT code set. The interval between the release of the update and the effective date is considered the implementation period and is intended to allow physicians and other providers, payers, and vendors to incorporate CPT changes into their systems. The exceptions to this schedule of release and effective dates are CPT Category III and vaccine product codes, which are released twice a year on January 1 or July 1 with effective dates for use six months later, and CPT Category II codes. Changes to the CPT code set are meant to be applied prospectively from the effective date.

The main body of the material is listed in six sections. Each section is divided into subsections with anatomic, procedural, condition, or descriptor subheadings. The procedures and services with their identifying codes are presented in numeric order with one exception—the entire **Evaluation and Management** section (99201-99499) appears at the beginning of the listed procedures. These items are used by most physicians in reporting a significant portion of their services.

Section Numbers and Their Sequences

Evaluation and Management 99201-99499
Anesthesiology 00100-01999, 99100-99140
Surgery 10021-69990
Radiology (Including Nuclear Medicine
    and Diagnostic Ultrasound) 70010-79999
Pathology and Laboratory 80048-89356
Medicine
  (except Anesthesiology) 90281-99199, 99500-99602

The first and last code numbers and the subsection name of the items appear at the top margin of most pages (eg, "11010-11306 Surgery/Integumentary System"). The continuous pagination of the CPT codebook is found on the lower margin of each page along with explanation of any code symbols that are found on that page.

Instructions for Use of the CPT Codebook

Select the name of the procedure or service that accurately identifies the service performed. Do not select a CPT code that merely approximates the service provided. If no such specific code exists, then report the service using the appropriate unlisted procedure or service code. In surgery, it may be an operation; in medicine, a diagnostic or therapeutic procedure; in radiology, a radiograph. Other additional procedures performed or pertinent special services are also listed. When necessary, any modifying or extenuating circumstances are added. Any service or procedure should be adequately documented in the medical record.

It is important to recognize that the listing of a service or procedure and its code number in a specific section of this book does not restrict its use to a specific specialty group. Any procedure or service in any section of this book may be used to designate the services rendered by any qualified physician or other qualified health care professional.

Instructions, typically included as parenthetical notes with selected codes, indicate that a code should not be reported with another code or codes. These instructions are intended to prevent errors of significant probability and are not all inclusive. For example, the code with such instructions may be a component of another code and therefore it would be incorrect to report both codes even when the component service is performed. These instructions are not intended as a listing of all possible code combinations that should not be reported, nor to indicate all possible code combinations that are appropriately reported. When reporting codes for services provided, it is important to assure the accuracy and quality of coding through verification of the intent of the code by use of the related guidelines, parenthetical instructions, and coding resources, including *CPT Assistant* and other publications resulting from collaborative efforts of the American Medical Association with medical specialty societies (ie, *Clinical Examples in Radiology*).

Format of the Terminology

The CPT code set has been developed as stand-alone descriptions of medical procedures. However, some of the procedures in the CPT codebook are not printed in their entirety but refer back to a common portion of the procedure listed in a preceding entry. This is evident when an entry is followed by one or more indentations. This is done in an effort to conserve space.

Example

25100   Arthrotomy, wrist joint; with biopsy

25105   with synovectomy

Note that the common part of code 25100 (the part before the semicolon) should be considered part of code 25105. Therefore, the full procedure represented by code 25105 should read:

25105   Arthrotomy, wrist joint; with synovectomy

Requests to Update the CPT Nomenclature

The effectiveness of the CPT nomenclature depends on constant updating to reflect changes in medical practice. This can only be accomplished through the interest and timely suggestions of practicing physicians, medical specialty societies, state medical associations, and other organizations and agencies. Accordingly, the AMA welcomes correspondence, inquiries, and suggestions concerning old and new procedures, as well as other matters such as codes and indices.

To submit a suggestion to add, delete, or revise procedures contained in the CPT codebook, please contact:

CPT Editorial Research & Development
American Medical Association
515 North State Street
Chicago, Illinois 60654

Coding change request forms are available at the AMA's CPT web site: www.ama-assn.org/ama/pub/category/3866.html.

All proposed changes of the CPT codebook will be considered by the CPT Editorial Panel with consultation of appropriate medical specialty societies.

Guidelines

Specific guidelines are presented at the beginning of each of the six sections. These guidelines define items that are necessary to appropriately interpret and report the procedures and services contained in that section. For example, in the **Medicine** section, specific instructions are provided for handling unlisted services or procedures, special reports, and supplies and materials provided. Guidelines also provide explanations regarding terms that apply only to a particular section. For instance, **Radiology Guidelines** provide a definition of the unique term, "radiological supervision and interpretation." While in **Anesthesia,** a discussion of reporting time is included.

Add-on Codes

Some of the listed procedures are commonly carried out in addition to the primary procedure performed. These additional or supplemental procedures are designated as add-on codes with the symbol ✚ and they are listed in **Appendix D** of the CPT codebook. Add-on codes in *CPT 2010* can be readily identified by specific descriptor nomenclature that includes phrases such as "each additional" or "(List separately in addition to primary procedure)."

The add-on code concept in *CPT 2010* applies only to add-on procedures or services performed by the same physician. Add-on codes describe additional intra-service work associated with the primary procedure (eg, additional digit[s], lesion[s], neurorrhaphy[s], vertebral segment[s], tendon[s], joint[s]).

Add-on codes are always performed in addition to the primary service or procedure and must never be reported as a stand-alone code. All add-on codes found in the CPT codebook are exempt from the multiple procedure concept (see the modifier 51 definition in **Appendix A**).

Modifiers

A modifier provides the means to report or indicate that a service or procedure that has been performed has been altered by some specific circumstance but not changed in its definition or code. Modifiers also enable health care professionals to effectively respond to payment policy requirements established by other entities. The judicious application of modifiers obviates the necessity for separate procedure listings that may describe the modifying circumstance. Modifiers may be used to indicate to the recipient of a report that:

- A service or procedure had both a professional and technical component.
- A service or procedure was performed by more than one physician and/or in more than one location.
- A service or procedure was increased or reduced.
- Only part of a service was performed.
- An adjunctive service was performed.
- A bilateral procedure was performed.
- A service or procedure was provided more than once.
- Unusual events occurred.

Example

A physician providing diagnostic or therapeutic radiology services, ultrasound, or nuclear medicine services in a hospital would add modifier 26 to report the professional component.

73090 with modifier 26 = Professional component only for an X-ray of the forearm

Example

Two surgeons may be required to manage a specific surgical problem. When two surgeons work together as primary surgeons performing distinct part(s) of a procedure, each surgeon should report his/her distinct operative work by adding modifier 62 to the procedure code and any associated code(s) for that procedure as long as both surgeons continue to work together as primary surgeons. Each surgeon should report the co-surgery once using the same procedure code. Modifier 62 would be applicable. For instance, a neurological surgeon and an otolaryngologist are working as co-surgeons in performing transphenoidal excision of a pituitary neoplasm.

The first surgeon would report:

61548 62 = Hypophysectomy or excision of pituitary tumor, transnasal or transseptal approach, nonstereotactic + two surgeons modifier

AND the second surgeon would report:

61548 62 = Hypophysectomy or excision of pituitary tumor, transnasal or transseptal approach, nonstereotactic + two surgeons modifier

If additional procedure(s) (including add-on procedure[s]) are performed during the same surgical session, separate code(s) may also be reported with modifier 62 added. It should be noted that if a co-surgeon acts as an assistant in the performance of additional procedure(s) during the same surgical session, those services may be reported using separate procedure code(s) with modifier 80 or modifier 82 added, as appropriate. A complete listing of modifiers is found in **Appendix A.**

Place of Service and Facility Reporting

Some codes have specified places of service (eg, evaluation and management codes are specific to a setting). Other services and procedures may have instructions specific to the place of service (eg, therapeutic, prophylactic, and diagnostic injections and infusions). The CPT code set is designated for reporting physician and qualified health care professional services. It is also the designated code set for reporting services by organizational or facility providers (eg, hospitals) in specific circumstances. Facilities are entities that may report services in addition to the physician or qualified health care professional for the same service. For example, a physician may report a procedure performed in the outpatient department of the hospital and the hospital may report the same procedure. The CPT codebook uses the term *facility* to describe such providers and the term *nonfacility* to describe services where no facility reporting may occur. Services provided in the home by an agency are facility services. Services provided in the home by a physician or qualified health care professional who is not a representative of the agency are nonfacility services.

Unlisted Procedure or Service

It is recognized that there may be services or procedures performed by physicians or other qualified health care professionals that are not found in the CPT codebook. Therefore, a number of specific code numbers have been designated for reporting unlisted procedures. When an unlisted procedure number is used, the service or procedure should be described (see specific section guidelines). Each of these unlisted procedural code numbers (with the appropriate accompanying topical entry) relates to a specific section of the book and is presented in the guidelines of that section.

In some cases alternative coding and procedural nomenclature as contained in other code sets may allow appropriate reporting of a more specific code. CPT references to use an unlisted procedure code do not preclude the reporting of an appropriate code that may be found in other code sets.

Results, Testing, Interpretation, and Report

Results are the technical component of a service. Testing leads to results; results lead to interpretation. Reports are the work product of the interpretation of test results. Certain procedures or services described in CPT involve a technical component (eg, tests) which produce "results" (eg, data, images, slides). For clinical use, some of these results require interpretation. Some CPT descriptors specifically require interpretation and reporting to report that code.

Special Report

A service that is rarely provided, unusual, variable, or new may require a special report. Pertinent information should include an adequate definition or description of the nature, extent, and need for the procedure and the time, effort, and equipment necessary to provide the service.

Code Symbols

A summary listing of additions, deletions, and revisions applicable to the CPT codebook is found in **Appendix B.** New procedure numbers added to the CPT codebook are identified throughout the text with the symbol ● placed before the code number. In instances where a code revision has resulted in a substantially altered procedure descriptor, the symbol ▲ is placed before the code number. The symbols ► ◄ are used to indicate new and revised text other than the procedure descriptors. These symbols indicate CPT Editorial Panel actions. The AMA reserves the right to correct typographical errors and make stylistic improvements.

CPT add-on codes are annotated by the symbol ✚ and are listed in **Appendix D.** The symbol ⊘ is used to identify codes that are exempt from the use of modifier 51 but have not been designated as CPT add-on procedures or services. A list of codes exempt from modifier 51 usage is included in **Appendix E.** The symbol ⊙ is used to identify codes that include moderate sedation (see **Appendix G**). The symbol ⁄ is used to identify codes for vaccines that are pending FDA approval (see **Appendix K**).

Resequenced codes that are not placed numerically are identified with the # symbol, and a reference placed numerically (eg, **Code is out of numerical sequence. See…**) as a navigational alert to direct the user to the location of the out-of-sequence code (see **Appendix N**). Resequencing is utilized to allow placement of related concepts in appropriate locations within the families of codes regardless of the availability of numbers for sequential numerical placement.

Alphabetical Reference Index

This codebook features an expanded alphabetical index that includes listings by procedure and anatomic site. Procedures and services commonly known by their eponyms or other designations are also included.

CPT 2010 in Electronic Formats

CPT 2010 procedure codes and descriptions are available on CD-ROM as data files and electronic software. Data files are available in ASCII and EBCDIC formats and can be imported into any billing and claims reporting software that accepts a text (.TXT) file format. *CPT 2010 Electronic Professional* software, with *Netter's Atlas of Human Anatomy for CPT Coding*, provides access to the entire *CPT 2010 Professional Edition* codebook on your desktop. Easy-to-use and fully searchable, this invaluable software contains all of the favorite *CPT Professional* features plus CPT codes and quick linking access between CPT codes, guidelines, modifiers, appendices, index, and more. For more information call (800) 621-8335 or visit *www.amabookstore.com*.

References to AMA Resources

The symbols ➲ and ➲ appear after many codes throughout this codebook and indicate that the AMA has published reference material regarding that particular code.

The symbol ➲ refers to the *CPT Assistant* monthly newsletter and *CPT Changes: An Insider's View*, an annual book with all of the coding changes for the current year. The symbol ➲ refers to the quarterly newsletter *Clinical Examples in Radiology*.

Example

36598 Contrast injection(s) for radiologic evaluation of existing central venous access device, including fluoroscopy, image documentation and report
➲ *CPT Changes: An Insider's View* 2006
➲ *Clinical Examples in Radiology* Winter 2006:15

(For placement of centrally inserted non-tunneled central venous catheter, without subcutaneous port or pump, age 5 years or older, use 36556)

In this example, the green reference symbol indicates that in the 2006 edition of *CPT Changes: An Insider's View* material is available that may assist in understanding the application of the code. The red reference symbol indicates that the 2006 issue of *Clinical Examples in Radiology* (page 15) should be consulted.

Subscriptions to *CPT Assistant* and *Clinical Examples in Radiology* can be purchased by calling the AMA's Unified Service Center at (800) 621-8335. Individual back issues are available for purchase and immediate download at *www.amabookstore.com*.

An archive software product with every issue of *CPT Assistant* is also available. *CPT Assistant Archives 1990-2008* provides convenient access to 20 years of *CPT Assistant* newsletter articles on your desktop. Search past issues of the AMA's authoritative coding newsletter by keyword, phrase, CPT code number, newsletter issue, article index, or codebook table of contents. This product offers simple search capabilities and a complete historical CPT code list from 1990-2008 that references when a code was added, deleted, and/or revised. Call (800) 621-8335 or visit *www.amabookstore.com* for more information.

Current and past editions of *CPT Changes: An Insider's View* can be purchased by calling the AMA's Unified Service Center at (800) 621-8335 or visiting *www.amabookstore.com*.

Additionally, an archives software product with all content from past and present editions of *CPT Changes: An Insider's View* is available. *CPT Changes Archives 2000-2010* provides access to current and historical CPT code and guideline changes on your computer desktop. Search by keyword, phrase, CPT code number, edition, and CPT codebook table of contents. For more information, call (800) 621-8335 or visit *www.amabookstore.com*.

Illustrated Anatomical and Procedural Review

It is essential that coders have a thorough understanding of medical terminology and anatomy to code accurately. The following section reviewing the basics of vocabulary and anatomy can be used as a quick reference to help you with your coding. It is not intended as a replacement for up-to-date medical dictionaries and anatomy texts, which are essential tools for accurate coding.

Prefixes, Suffixes, and Roots

Although medical terminology may seem complex, many medical terms can be broken into component parts, which makes them easier to understand. Many of these terms are derived from Latin or Greek words, but some include the names of physicians.

Prefixes are word parts that appear at the beginning of a word and modify its meaning; suffixes are found at the end of words. By learning what various prefixes and suffixes mean, it is possible to decipher the meaning of a word quickly. The following lists are a quick reference for some common prefixes and suffixes.

Numbers

Prefix	Meaning	Example
mono-, uni-	one	monocyte, unilateral
bi-	two	bilateral
tri-	three	triad
quadr-	four	quadriplegia
hex-, sex-	six	hexose
diplo-	double	diplopia

Surgical Procedures

Suffix	Meaning	Example
-centesis	puncture a cavity to remove fluid	amniocentesis
-ectomy	surgical removal (excision)	appendectomy
-ostomy	a new permanent opening	colostomy
-otomy	cutting into (incision)	tracheotomy
-orrhaphy	surgical repair/suture	herniorrhaphy
-opexy	surgical fixation	nephropexy
-oplasty	surgical repair	rhinoplasty
-otripsy	crushing, destroying	lithotripsy

Conditions

Prefix	Meaning	Example
ambi-	both	ambidextrous
aniso-	unequal	anisocoria
dys-	bad, painful, difficult	dysphoria
eu-	good, normal	euthanasia
hetero-	different	heterogeneous
homo-	same	homogeneous
hyper-	excessive, above	hypergastric
hypo-	deficient, below	hypogastric
iso-	equal, same	isotonic
mal-	bad, poor	malaise
megalo-	large	megalocardia

Conditions (continued)

Suffix	Meaning	Example
-algia	pain	neuralgia
-asthenia	weakness	myasthenia
-emia	blood	anemia
-iasis	condition of	amebiasis
-itis	inflammation	appendicitis
-lysis	destruction, break down	hemolysis
-lytic	destroy, break down	hemolytic
-oid	like	lipoid
-oma	tumor	carcinoma
-opathy	disease of	arthropathy
-orrhagia	hemorrhage	menorrhagia
-orrhea	flow or discharge	amenorrhea
-osis	abnormal condition of	tuberculosis
-paresis	weakness	hemiparesis
-plasia	growth	hyperplasia
-plegia	paralysis	paraplegia
-pnea	breathing	apnea

Directions and Positions

Prefix	Meaning	Example
ab-	away from	abduction
ad-	toward	adduction
ecto, exo-	outside	ectopic, exocrine
endo-	within	endoscope
epi-	upon	epigastric
infra-	below, under	infrastructure
ipsi-	same	ipsilateral
meso-	middle	mesopexy
meta-	after, beyond, transformation	metastasis
peri-	surrounding	pericardium
retro-	behind, back	retroversion
trans-	across, through	transvaginal

Word	Meaning
anterior or ventral	at or near the front surface of the body
posterior or dorsal	at or near the back surface of the body
superior	above
inferior	below
lateral	side

Directions and Positions (continued)

Word	Meaning
distal	farthest from center
proximal	nearest to center
medial	middle
supine	face up or palm up
prone	face down or palm down
sagittal	vertical body plane, divides the body into equal right and left sides
transverse	horizontal body plane, divides the body into top and bottom sections
coronal	vertical body plane, divides the body into front and back sections

Additional References

For best coding results, you will need to use other reference materials in addition to your coding books. These references include a medical dictionary and one or more anatomy books that can be purchased from the American Medical Association by calling 800 621-8335.

Medical Dictionaries

Stedman's CPT® Dictionary, 2nd ed.
Chicago, IL: American Medical Association, 2009.
OP300609

Merriam-Webster's Medical Desk Dictionary.
Springfield, Mass: Merriam Webster.
OP941493

Stedman's Medical Dictionary. 27th ed.
Baltimore, Md: Williams & Wilkins; 2000.
OP982900

Anatomy References

Kirschner, CG. *Netter's Atlas of Anatomy for CPT® Coding, 2nd ed.*
Chicago, Ill: American Medical Association; 2005
OP490609

Kirschner, CG. *Netter's Atlas of Human Anatomy for CPT® and ICD-9-CM Coding Series: Musculoskeletal.*
Chicago, Ill: American Medical Association
OP492206

Netter, FH. *Atlas of Human Anatomy.* 3rd ed.
East Hanover, NJ: Novartis; 2003.
OP936798

Lists of Illustrations

To further aid coders in properly assigning CPT codes, the codebook contains a number of anatomical and procedural illustrations.

Anatomical Illustrations

Twenty-nine anatomical illustrations are located on the following pages.

Procedural Illustrations

Procedural illustrations are placed throughout the codebook and are associated with the following specific CPT codes.

CPT Code(s)	Illustration Title
33517-33530	Coronary Artery Bypass—Combined Arterial-Venous Grafting
33517-33530	Coronary Artery Bypass—Sequential Combined Arterial-Venous Grafting
33979	Insertion of Implantable Single Ventricle Assist Device
34802	Endovascular Repair of Abdominal Aortic Aneurysm
35371-35372	Thromboendarterectomy
35473	Transluminal Balloon Angioplasty
35571	Bypass Graft, Vein
35600	Harvest of Upper Extremity Artery
36002	Injection Procedure (eg, Thrombin) for Percutaneous Treatment of Extremity Pseudoaneurysm
36555-36556	Insertion of Non-Tunneled Centrally Inserted Central Venous Catheter
36557-36558	Insertion of Tunneled Central Venous Catheter
36570-36571, 36576, 36578	Implantable Venous Access Port
36821	Arteriovenous Anastomosis, Direct
36822	Insertion of Cannulas for Prolonged Extracorporeal Circulation Membrane Oxygenation (ECMO)
36825-36830	Arteriovenous Fistula
37700	Ligation and Division of Long Saphenous Vein
38230	Bone Marrow Harvesting for Transplantation
43235	Upper Gastrointestinal Endoscopy
43260	Endoscopic Retrograde Cholangiopancreatography (ERCP)
43280	Laparoscopic Fundoplasty
43324	Nissen Fundoplasty
43846	Gastric Bypass for Morbid Obesity
44127	Enterectomy, Resection for Congenital Atresia
44140	Colectomy, Partial
44160	Colectomy With Removal of Terminal Ileum and Ileocolostomy
45378	Colonoscopy
45383, 45385	Colonoscopy With Lesion Ablation or Removal
46020	Placement of Seton
46250-46262-	Hemorrhoidectomy Procedure
47562	Laparoscopic Cholecystectomy
49320	Laparoscopy
50020	Drainage of Renal Abscess
50060-50075	Nephrolithotomy With Calculus Removal
50392	Introduction of Catheter Into Renal Pelvis
50545	Laparoscopic Radical Nephrectomy
50546	Laparoscopic Nephrectomy
50590	Lithotripsy
50605	Indwelling Ureteral Stent
50820	Ureteroileal Conduit
50947	Laparoscopic Ureteroneocystostomy
51798	Measurement of Postvoiding
51990	Laparoscopic Sling Suspension Urinary Incontinence

CPT Code(s)	Illustration Title
52005	Cystourethroscopy With Ureteral Catheterization
52601	Transurethral Resection of Prostate, Complete
52648	Contact Laser Vaporization of Prostate
54692	Laparoscopic Orchiopexy
57106	Vaginectomy, Partial Removal of Vaginal Wall
57111	Vaginectomy, Complete Removal of Vaginal Wall (Radical Vaginectomy)
58563	Hysteroscopy
59001	Amniocentesis, Therapeutic Amniotic Fluid Reduction
59150	Laparoscopic Treatment of Ectopic Pregnancy
59400-59410	Vaginal Delivery
59510-59515	Cesarean Delivery
60512	Posterior View of the Pharynx
60650	Laparoscopic Adrenalectomy
61700	Intracranial Aneurysm, Intracranial Approach
61867-61868, 61885	Placement of Cranial Neurostimulator
62223	Cerebrospinal Fluid (CSF) Shunt (Ventricular Peritoneal)
62362	Intrathecal or Epidural Drug Infusion Pump Implantation
63005	Lumbar Laminectomy
63650	Percutaneous Implantation of Neurostimulator Electrodes
63655	Placement of Neurostimulator Electrodes Through Laminectomy
61885, 64573	Implantation Neurostimulator Electrodes, Cranial Nerve (Vagal Nerve Stimulation)
64581	Incisional Implantation of Sacral Nerve Neurostimulator
64612-64614	Chemodenervation of Extremity
65450	Cryotherapy of Lesion on Cornea
67027	Intravitreal Drug Delivery System
67107	Repair of Retinal Detachment
67311	Extraocular Muscles of Right Eye
67311-67312	Strabismus Surgery—Horizontal Muscles
67314-67316	Strabismus Surgery—Vertical Muscles
67320	Transposition Procedure
67335	Strabismus Surgery—Adjustable Sutures
67820-67825	Trichiasis
68761	Closure of Lacrimal Punctum by Plug
68815	Probing of Nasolacrimal Duct
69433-69436	Tympanostomy
69635-69646	Tympanoplasty
69930	Cochlear Device Implantation
69990	Operating Microscope
72275	Epidurography
75600-75630	Aortography
75660-75680	Angiography, Carotid Artery
75820-75822	Venography
77057	Screening Mammography

Figure 1A
Body Planes — 3/4 View

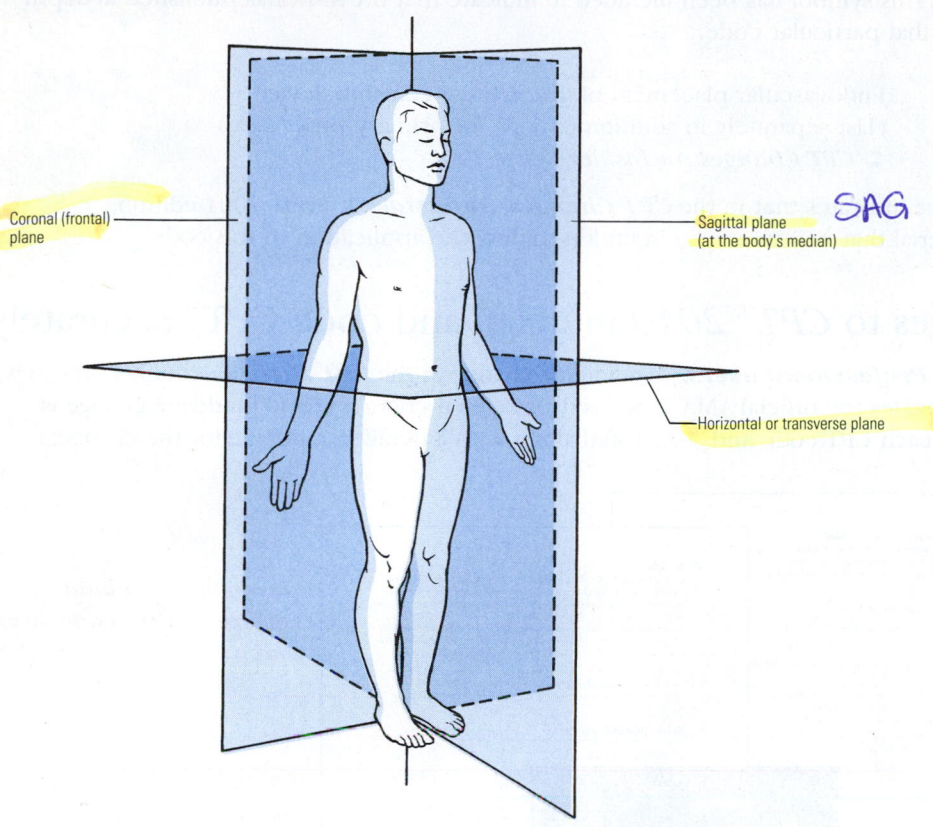

Coronal (frontal) plane

Sagittal plane (at the body's median)   *SAG*

Horizontal or transverse plane

Figure 1B
Body Aspects — Side View

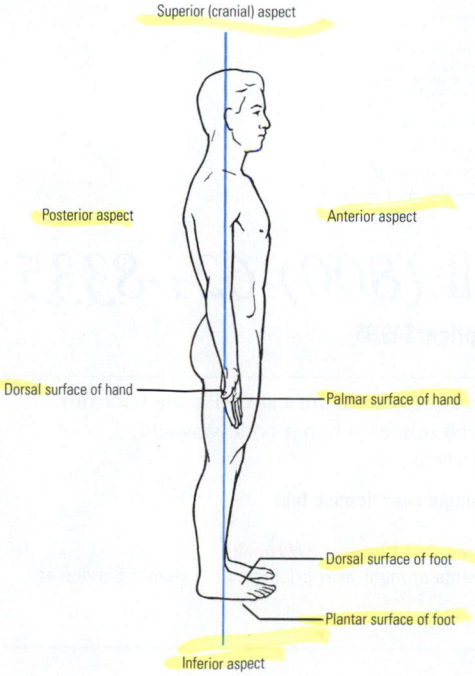

Superior (cranial) aspect

Posterior aspect

Anterior aspect

Dorsal surface of hand

Palmar surface of hand

Dorsal surface of foot

Plantar surface of foot

Inferior aspect

Figure 1C
Body Planes — Front View

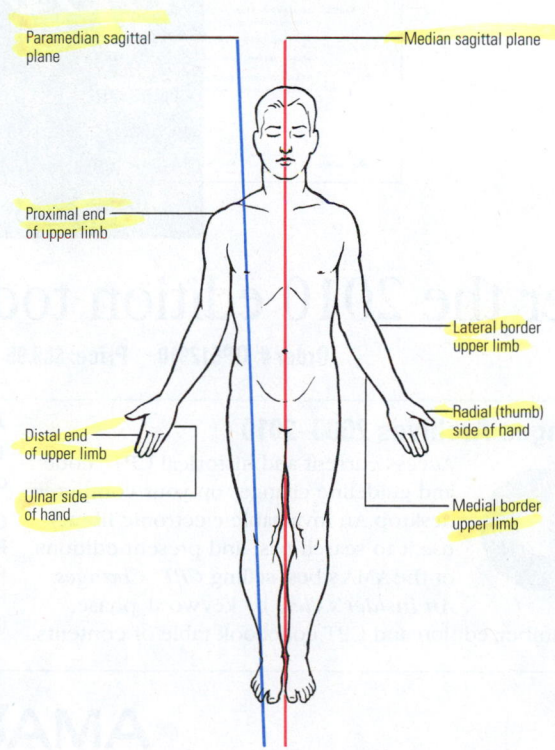

Paramedian sagittal plane

Median sagittal plane

Proximal end of upper limb

Lateral border upper limb

Radial (thumb) side of hand

Distal end of upper limb

Ulnar side of hand

Medial border upper limb

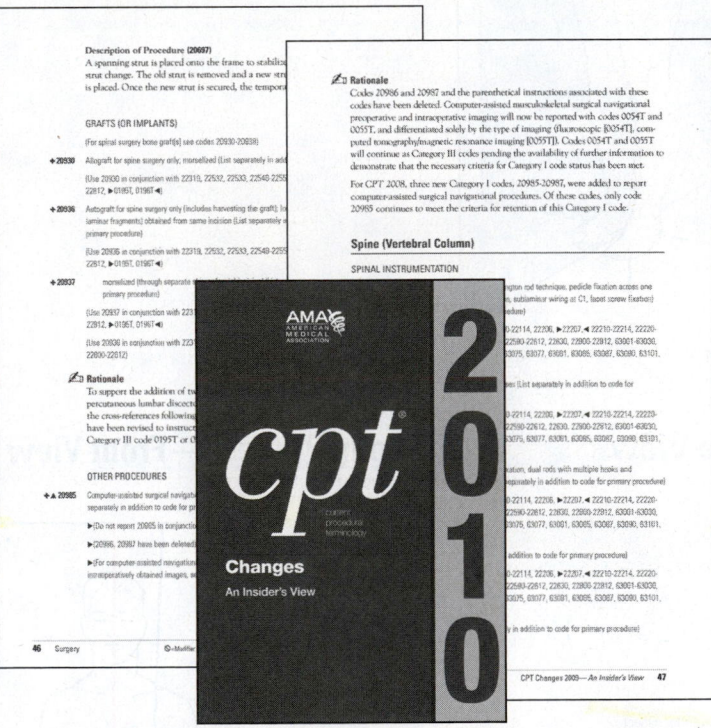

Evaluation and Management (E/M) Services Guidelines

Evaluation and Management

Evaluation and Management (E/M) Services Guidelines

In addition to the information presented in the Introduction, several other items unique to this section are defined or identified here.

Classification of Evaluation and Management (E/M) Services

The E/M section is divided into broad categories such as office visits, hospital visits, and consultations. Most of the categories are further divided into two or more subcategories of E/M services. For example, there are two subcategories of office visits (new patient and established patient) and there are two subcategories of hospital visits (initial and subsequent). The subcategories of E/M services are further classified into levels of E/M services that are identified by specific codes. This classification is important because the nature of physician work varies by type of service, place of service, and the patient's status.

The basic format of the levels of E/M services is the same for most categories. First, a unique code number is listed. Second, the place and/or type of service is specified, eg, office consultation. Third, the content of the service is defined, eg, comprehensive history and comprehensive examination. (See "Levels of E/M Services," page 3, for details on the content of E/M services.) Fourth, the nature of the presenting problem(s) usually associated with a given level is described. Fifth, the time typically required to provide the service is specified. (A detailed discussion of time is provided on page 4.)

Definitions of Commonly Used Terms

Certain key words and phrases are used throughout the E/M section. The following definitions are intended to reduce the potential for differing interpretations and to increase the consistency of reporting by physicians in differing specialties. E/M services may also be reported by other qualified health care professionals who are authorized to perform such services within the scope of their practice.

►New and Established Patient

Solely for the purposes of distinguishing between new and established patients, **professional services** are those face-to-face services rendered by a physician and reported by a specific CPT code(s). A new patient is one who has not received any professional services from the physician or another physician of the same specialty who belongs to the same group practice, within the past three years.

An established patient is one who has received professional services from the physician or another physician of the same specialty who belongs to the same group practice, within the past three years.

In the instance where a physician is on call for or covering for another physician, the patient's encounter will be classified as it would have been by the physician who is not available.

No distinction is made between new and established patients in the emergency department. E/M services in the emergency department category may be reported for any new or established patient who presents for treatment in the emergency department.

The decision tree on page 2 is provided to aid in determining whether to report the E/M service provided as a new or an established patient encounter.

Chief Complaint

A chief complaint is a concise statement describing the symptom, problem, condition, diagnosis, or other factor that is the reason for the encounter, usually stated in the patient's words.

►Concurrent Care and Transfer of Care◄

►Concurrent care is the provision of similar services (eg, hospital visits) to the same patient by more than one physician on the same day. When concurrent care is provided, no special reporting is required. Transfer of care is the process whereby a physician who is providing management for some or all of a patient's problems relinquishes this responsibility to another physician who explicitly agrees to accept this responsibility and who, from the initial encounter, is not providing consultative services. The physician transferring care is then no longer providing care for these problems though he or she may continue providing care for other conditions when appropriate. Consultation codes should not be reported by the physician who has agreed to accept transfer of care before an initial evaluation but are appropriate to report if the decision to accept transfer of care cannot be made until after the initial consultation evaluation, regardless of site of service.◄

⊙=Moderate sedation +=Add-on code ✗=FDA approval pending #=Resequenced code ➋➊=See p xiii for details

Decision Tree for New vs Established Patients

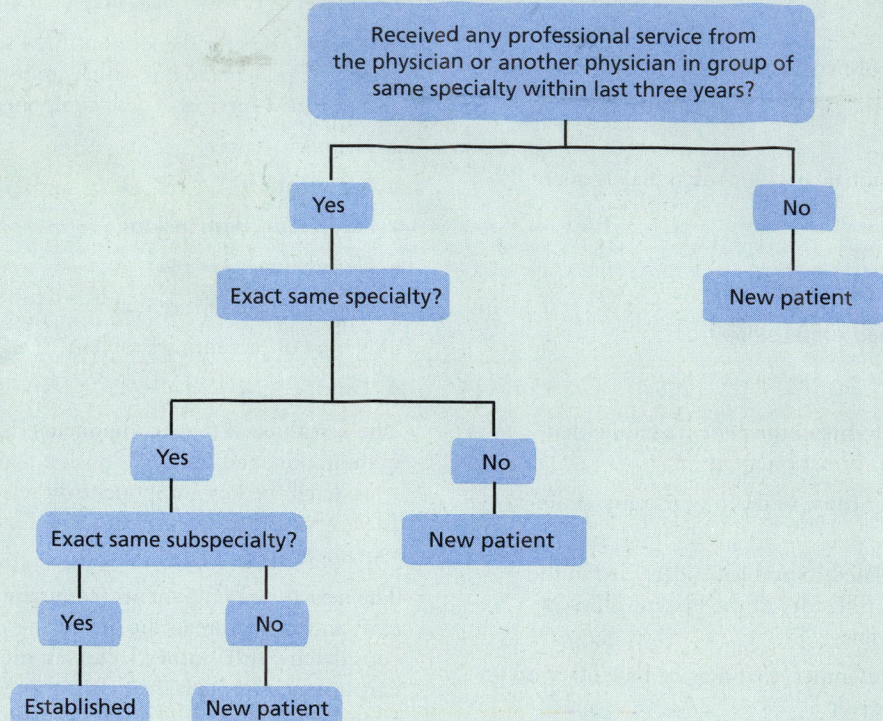

Counseling

Counseling is a discussion with a patient and/or family concerning one or more of the following areas:

- Diagnostic results, impressions, and/or recommended diagnostic studies
- Prognosis
- Risks and benefits of management (treatment) options
- Instructions for management (treatment) and/or follow-up
- Importance of compliance with chosen management (treatment) options
- Risk factor reduction
- Patient and family education

(For psychotherapy, see 90804-90857)

Family History

A review of medical events in the patient's family that includes significant information about:

- The health status or cause of death of parents, siblings, and children
- Specific diseases related to problems identified in the Chief Complaint or History of the Present Illness, and/or System Review
- Diseases of family members that may be hereditary or place the patient at risk

History of Present Illness

A chronological description of the development of the patient's present illness from the first sign and/or symptom to the present. This includes a description of location, quality, severity, timing, context, modifying factors, and associated signs and symptoms significantly related to the presenting problem(s).

Levels of E/M Services

Within each category or subcategory of E/M service, there are three to five levels of E/M services available for reporting purposes. Levels of E/M services are **not** interchangeable among the different categories or subcategories of service. For example, the first level of E/M services in the subcategory of office visit, new patient, does not have the same definition as the first level of E/M services in the subcategory of office visit, established patient.

The levels of E/M services include examinations, evaluations, treatments, conferences with or concerning patients, preventive pediatric and adult health supervision, and similar medical services, such as the determination of the need and/or location for appropriate care. Medical screening includes the history, examination, and medical decision-making required to determine the need and/or location for appropriate care and treatment of the patient (eg, office and other outpatient setting,

emergency department, nursing facility). The levels of E/M services encompass the wide variations in skill, effort, time, responsibility, and medical knowledge required for the prevention or diagnosis and treatment of illness or injury and the promotion of optimal health. Each level of E/M services may be used by all physicians.

The descriptors for the levels of E/M services recognize seven components, six of which are used in defining the levels of E/M services. These components are:

- History
- Examination
- Medical decision making
- Counseling
- Coordination of care
- Nature of presenting problem
- Time

The first three of these components (history, examination, and medical decision making) are considered the **key** components in selecting a level of E/M services. (See "Determine the Extent of History Obtained," page 11.)

The next three components (counseling, coordination of care, and the nature of the presenting problem) are considered **contributory** factors in the majority of encounters. Although the first two of these contributory factors are important E/M services, it is not required that these services be provided at every patient encounter.

Coordination of care with other providers or agencies without a patient encounter on that day is reported using the case management codes.

The final component, time, is discussed in detail on page 8.

Any specifically identifiable procedure (ie, identified with a specific CPT code) performed on or subsequent to the date of initial or subsequent E/M services should be reported separately.

The actual performance and/or interpretation of diagnostic tests/studies ordered during a patient encounter are not included in the levels of E/M services. Physician performance of diagnostic tests/studies for which specific CPT codes are available may be reported separately, in addition to the appropriate E/M code. The physician's interpretation of the results of diagnostic tests/studies (ie, professional component) with preparation of a separate distinctly identifiable signed written report may also be reported separately, using the appropriate CPT code with modifier 26 appended.

The physician may need to indicate that on the day a procedure or service identified by a CPT code was performed, the patient's condition required a significant separately identifiable E/M service above and beyond other services provided or beyond the usual preservice

and postservice care associated with the procedure that was performed. The E/M service may be caused or prompted by the symptoms or condition for which the procedure and/or service was provided. This circumstance may be reported by adding modifier 25 to the appropriate level of E/M service. As such, different diagnoses are not required for reporting of the procedure and the E/M services on the same date.

Nature of Presenting Problem

A presenting problem is a disease, condition, illness, injury, symptom, sign, finding, complaint, or other reason for encounter, with or without a diagnosis being established at the time of the encounter. The E/M codes recognize five types of presenting problems that are defined as follows:

Minimal: A problem that may not require the presence of the physician, but service is provided under the physician's supervision.

Self-limited or minor: A problem that runs a definite and prescribed course, is transient in nature, and is not likely to permanently alter health status OR has a good prognosis with management/compliance.

Low severity: A problem where the risk of morbidity without treatment is low; there is little to no risk of mortality without treatment; full recovery without functional impairment is expected.

Moderate severity: A problem where the risk of morbidity without treatment is moderate; there is moderate risk of mortality without treatment; uncertain prognosis OR increased probability of prolonged functional impairment.

High severity: A problem where the risk of morbidity without treatment is high to extreme; there is a moderate to high risk of mortality without treatment OR high probability of severe, prolonged functional impairment.

Past History

A review of the patient's past experiences with illnesses, injuries, and treatments that includes significant information about:

- Prior major illnesses and injuries
- Prior operations
- Prior hospitalizations
- Current medications
- Allergies (eg, drug, food)
- Age appropriate immunization status
- Age appropriate feeding/dietary status

Social History

An age appropriate review of past and current activities that includes significant information about:

- Marital status and/or living arrangements

- Current employment
- Occupational history
- Use of drugs, alcohol, and tobacco
- Level of education
- Sexual history
- Other relevant social factors

System Review (Review of Systems)

An inventory of body systems obtained through a series of questions seeking to identify signs and/or symptoms that the patient may be experiencing or has experienced. For the purposes of the CPT codebook the following elements of a system review have been identified:

- Constitutional symptoms (fever, weight loss, etc)
- Eyes
- Ears, nose, mouth, throat
- Cardiovascular
- Respiratory
- Gastrointestinal
- Genitourinary
- Musculoskeletal
- Integumentary (skin and/or breast)
- Neurological
- Psychiatric
- Endocrine
- Hematologic/lymphatic
- Allergic/immunologic

The review of systems helps define the problem, clarify the differential diagnosis, identify needed testing, or serves as baseline data on other systems that might be affected by any possible management options.

Time

The inclusion of time in the definitions of levels of E/M services has been implicit in prior editions of the CPT codebook. The inclusion of time as an explicit factor beginning in *CPT 1992* is done to assist physicians in selecting the most appropriate level of E/M services. It should be recognized that the specific times expressed in the visit code descriptors are averages and, therefore, represent a range of times that may be higher or lower depending on actual clinical circumstances.

Time is **not** a descriptive component for the emergency department levels of E/M services because emergency department services are typically provided on a variable intensity basis, often involving multiple encounters with several patients over an extended period of time. Therefore, it is often difficult for physicians to provide accurate estimates of the time spent face-to-face with the patient.

Studies to establish levels of E/M services employed surveys of practicing physicians to obtain data on the amount of time and work associated with typical E/M services. Since "work" is not easily quantifiable, the codes must rely on other objective, verifiable measures that correlate with physicians' estimates of their "work." It has been demonstrated that physicians' estimations of **intraservice** time (as explained on the next page), both within and across specialties, is a variable that is predictive of the "work" of E/M services. This same research has shown there is a strong relationship between intraservice time and total time for E/M services. Intraservice time, rather than total time, was chosen for inclusion with the codes because of its relative ease of measurement and because of its direct correlation with measurements of the total amount of time and work associated with typical E/M services.

Intraservice times are defined as **face-to-face** time for office and other outpatient visits and as **unit/floor** time for hospital and other inpatient visits. This distinction is necessary because most of the work of typical office visits takes place during the face-to-face time with the patient, while most of the work of typical hospital visits takes place during the time spent on the patient's floor or unit.

Face-to-face time (office and other outpatient visits and office consultations): For coding purposes, face-to-face time for these services is defined as only that time that the physician spends face-to-face with the patient and/or family. This includes the time in which the physician performs such tasks as obtaining a history, performing an examination, and counseling the patient.

Physicians also spend time doing work before or after the face-to-face time with the patient, performing such tasks as reviewing records and tests, arranging for further services, and communicating further with other professionals and the patient through written reports and telephone contact.

This **non-face-to-face** time for office services—also called pre- and postencounter time—is not included in the time component described in the E/M codes. However, the pre- and post-face-to-face work associated with an encounter was included in calculating the total work of typical services in physician surveys.

Thus, the face-to-face time associated with the services described by any E/M code is a valid proxy for the total work done before, during, and after the visit.

▶*Unit/floor time (hospital observation services, inpatient hospital care, initial inpatient hospital consultations, nursing facility):* For reporting purposes, intraservice time for these services is defined as unit/floor time, which includes the time that the physician is present on the patient's hospital unit and at the bedside rendering services for that patient. This includes the time in which the physician establishes and/or reviews the patient's chart, examines the patient, writes notes, and communicates with other professionals and the patient's family.◀

In the hospital, pre- and post-time includes time spent off the patient's floor performing such tasks as reviewing pathology and radiology findings in another part of the hospital.

This pre- and postvisit time is not included in the time component described in these codes. However, the pre- and postwork performed during the time spent off the floor or unit was included in calculating the total work of typical services in physician surveys.

Thus, the unit/floor time associated with the services described by any code is a valid proxy for the total work done before, during, and after the visit.

Unlisted Service

An E/M service may be provided that is not listed in this section of the CPT codebook. When reporting such a service, the appropriate unlisted code may be used to indicate the service, identifying it by "Special Report," as discussed in the following paragraph. The "Unlisted Services" and accompanying codes for the E/M section are as follows:

99429   **Unlisted preventive** medicine service

99499   **Unlisted evaluation and management** service

Special Report

An unlisted service or one that is unusual, variable, or new may require a special report demonstrating the medical appropriateness of the service. Pertinent information should include an adequate definition or description of the nature, extent, and need for the procedure and the time, effort, and equipment necessary to provide the service. Additional items that may be included are complexity of symptoms, final diagnosis, pertinent physical findings, diagnostic and therapeutic procedures, concurrent problems, and follow-up care.

Clinical Examples

Clinical examples of the codes for E/M services are provided to assist physicians in understanding the meaning of the descriptors and selecting the correct code. The clinical examples are listed in Appendix C. Each example was developed by physicians in the specialties shown.

The same problem, when seen by physicians in different specialties, may involve different amounts of work. Therefore, the appropriate level of encounter should be reported using the descriptors rather than the examples.

The examples have been tested for validity and approved by the CPT Editorial Panel. Physicians were given the examples and asked to assign a code or assess the amount of time and work involved. Only examples that were rated consistently have been included in Appendix C.

Instructions for Selecting a Level of E/M Service

▶Identify the category and subcategory of service codes available for reporting E/M services shown in the subsection opener (pages 1-3).◀

Review the Reporting Instructions for the Selected Category or Subcategory

Most of the categories and many of the subcategories of service have special guidelines or instructions unique to that category or subcategory. Where these are indicated, eg, "Inpatient Hospital Care," special instructions will be presented preceding the levels of E/M services.

Review the Level of E/M Service Descriptors and Examples in the Selected Category or Subcategory

The descriptors for the levels of E/M services recognize seven components, six of which are used in defining the levels of E/M services. These components are:

- History
- Examination
- Medical decision making
- Counseling
- Coordination of care
- Nature of presenting problem
- Time

The first three of these components (ie, history, examination, and medical decision making) should be considered the **key** components in selecting the level of E/M services. An exception to this rule is in the case of visits that consist predominantly of counseling or coordination of care (see numbered paragraph 3, page 8).

The nature of the presenting problem and time are provided in some levels to assist the physician in determining the appropriate level of E/M service.

Determine the Extent of History Obtained

The extent of the history is dependent upon clinical judgment and on the nature of the presenting problems(s). The levels of E/M services recognize four types of history that are defined as follows:

Problem focused: Chief complaint; brief history of present illness or problem.

Expanded problem focused: Chief complaint; brief history of present illness; problem pertinent system review.

Detailed: Chief complaint; extended history of present illness; problem pertinent system review extended to include a review of a limited number of additional systems; **pertinent** past, family, and/or social history **directly related to the patient's problems.**

Comprehensive: Chief complaint; extended history of present illness; review of systems that is directly related to the problem(s) identified in the history of the present illness plus a review of all additional body systems; **complete** past, family, and social history.

The comprehensive history obtained as part of the preventive medicine E/M service is not problem-oriented and does not involve a chief complaint or present illness. It does, however, include a comprehensive system review and comprehensive or interval past, family, and social history as well as a comprehensive assessment/history of pertinent risk factors.

Determine the Extent of Examination Performed

The extent of the examination performed is dependent on clinical judgment and on the nature of the presenting problem(s). The levels of E/M services recognize four types of examination that are defined as follows:

Problem focused: A limited examination of the affected body area or organ system.

Expanded problem focused: A limited examination of the affected body area or organ system and other symptomatic or related organ system(s).

Detailed: An extended examination of the affected body area(s) and other symptomatic or related organ system(s).

Comprehensive: A general multisystem examination or a complete examination of a single organ system. **Note:** The comprehensive examination performed as part of the preventive medicine E/M service is multisystem, but its extent is based on age and risk factors identified.

For the purposes of these CPT definitions, the following body areas are recognized:

- Head, including the face
- Neck
- Chest, including breasts and axilla
- Abdomen
- Genitalia, groin, buttocks
- Back
- Each extremity

Table 1
Complexity of Medical Decision Making

Number of Diagnoses or Management Options	Amount and/or Complexity of Data to be Reviewed	Risk of Complications and/or Morbidity or Mortality	Type of Decision Making
minimal	minimal or none	minimal	**straightforward**
limited	limited	low	**low complexity**
multiple	moderate	moderate	**moderate complexity**
extensive	extensive	high	**high complexity**

For the purposes of these CPT definitions, the following organ systems are recognized:

- Eyes
- Ears, nose, mouth, and throat
- Cardiovascular
- Respiratory
- Gastrointestinal
- Genitourinary
- Musculoskeletal
- Skin
- Neurologic
- Psychiatric
- Hematologic/lymphatic/immunologic

Determine the Complexity of Medical Decision Making

Medical decision making refers to the complexity of establishing a diagnosis and/or selecting a management option as measured by:

- The number of possible diagnoses and/or the number of management options that must be considered
- The amount and/or complexity of medical records, diagnostic tests, and/or other information that must be obtained, reviewed, and analyzed
- The risk of significant complications, morbidity, and/or mortality, as well as comorbidities, associated with the patient's presenting problems(s), the diagnostic procedure(s), and/or the possible management options

Four types of medical decision making are recognized: straightforward, low complexity, moderate complexity, and high complexity. To qualify for a given type of decision making, two of the three elements in Table 1 must be met or exceeded.

Comorbidities/underlying diseases, in and of themselves, are not considered in selecting a level of E/M services *unless* their presence significantly increases the complexity of the medical decision making.

Select the Appropriate Level of E/M Services Based on the Following

1. For the following categories/subcategories, **all of the key components,** ie, history, examination, and medical decision making, must meet or exceed the stated requirements to qualify for a particular level of E/M service: office, new patient; hospital observation services; initial hospital care; office consultations; initial inpatient consultations; emergency department services; initial nursing facility care; domiciliary care, new patient; and home, new patient.

2. For the following categories/subcategories, **two of the three key components** (ie, history, examination, and medical decision making) must meet or exceed the stated requirements to qualify for a particular level of E/M services: office, established patient; subsequent hospital care; subsequent nursing facility care; domiciliary care, established patient; and home, established patient.

3. When counseling and/or coordination of care dominates (more than 50%) the physician/patient and/or family encounter (face-to-face time in the office or other outpatient setting or floor/unit time in the hospital or nursing facility), then **time** may be considered the key or controlling factor to qualify for a particular level of E/M services. This includes time spent with parties who have assumed responsibility for the care of the patient or decision making whether or not they are family members (eg, foster parents, person acting in loco parentis, legal guardian). The extent of counseling and/or coordination of care must be documented in the medical record.

Evaluation and Management

Office or Other Outpatient Services

The following codes are used to report evaluation and management services provided in the physician's office or in an outpatient or other ambulatory facility. A patient is considered an outpatient until inpatient admission to a health care facility occurs.

To report services provided to a patient who is admitted to a hospital or nursing facility in the course of an encounter in the office or other ambulatory facility, see the notes for initial hospital inpatient care (page 12) or initial nursing facility care (page 20).

For services provided by physicians in the emergency department, see 99281-99285.

For observation care, see 99217-99220.

For observation or inpatient care services (including admission and discharge services), see 99234-99236.

New Patient

99201 **Office or other outpatient visit** for the evaluation and management of a new patient, which requires these 3 key components:

- **A problem focused history;**
- **A problem focused examination;**
- **Straightforward medical decision making.**

Counseling and/or coordination of care with other providers or agencies are provided consistent with the nature of the problem(s) and the patient's and/or family's needs.

Usually, the presenting problem(s) are self limited or minor. Physicians typically spend 10 minutes face-to-face with the patient and/or family.

➤ *CPT Assistant* Winter 91:11, Spring 92:13, 24, Summer 92:1, 24, Spring 93:34, Summer 93:2, Fall 93:9, Spring 95:1, Summer 95:4, Fall 95:9, Jul 98:9, Sep 98:5, Jun 99:8, Feb 00:3, 9, 11, Aug 01:2, Oct 04:11, Mar 05:11, Apr 05:1, May 05:1, Jun 05:11, Dec 05:10, Feb 06:14, May 06:1, Jun 06:1, Aug 06:12, Oct 06:15, Apr 07:11, Sep 07:1, Nov 08:10, Mar 09:3

99202 **Office or other outpatient visit** for the evaluation and management of a new patient, which requires these 3 key components:

- **An expanded problem focused history;**
- **An expanded problem focused examination;**
- **Straightforward medical decision making.**

Counseling and/or coordination of care with other providers or agencies are provided consistent with the nature of the problem(s) and the patient's and/or family's needs.

Usually, the presenting problem(s) are of low to moderate severity. Physicians typically spend 20 minutes face-to-face with the patient and/or family.

➤ *CPT Assistant* Winter 91:11, Spring 92:13, 24, Summer 92:1, 24, Spring 93:34, Summer 93:2, Fall 93:9, Spring 95:1, Summer 95:4, Fall 95:9, Jul 98:9, Sep 98:5, Feb 00:11, Aug 01:2, Apr 02:14, Oct 04:10, Apr 05:1, 3, Jun 05:11, Dec 05:10, May 06:1, Jun 06:1, Oct 06:15, Apr 07:11, Sep 07:1, Mar 09:3

99203 **Office or other outpatient visit** for the evaluation and management of a new patient, which requires these 3 key components:

- **A detailed history;**
- **A detailed examination;**
- **Medical decision making of low complexity.**

Counseling and/or coordination of care with other providers or agencies are provided consistent with the nature of the problem(s) and the patient's and/or family's needs.

Usually, the presenting problem(s) are of moderate severity. Physicians typically spend 30 minutes face-to-face with the patient and/or family.

➤ *CPT Assistant* Winter 91:11, Spring 92:14, 24, Summer 92:1, 24, Spring 93:34, Summer 93:2, Fall 93:9, Spring 95:1, Summer 95:4, Fall 95:9, Jul 98:9, Sep 98:5, Feb 00:11, Aug 01:2, Apr 02:14, Oct 04:10, Feb 05:9, Apr 05:1, 3, Jun 05:11, Dec 05:10, May 06:1, Jun 06:1, Oct 06:15, Apr 07:11, Sep 07:1, Mar 09:3

99204 **Office or other outpatient visit** for the evaluation and management of a new patient, which requires these 3 key components:

- **A comprehensive history;**
- **A comprehensive examination;**
- **Medical decision making of moderate complexity.**

Counseling and/or coordination of care with other providers or agencies are provided consistent with the nature of the problem(s) and the patient's and/or family's needs.

Usually, the presenting problem(s) are of moderate to high severity. Physicians typically spend 45 minutes face-to-face with the patient and/or family.

➤ *CPT Assistant* Winter 91:11, Spring 92:14, 24, Summer 92:1, 24, Spring 93:34, Summer 93:2, Fall 93:9, Spring 95:1, Summer 95:4, Fall 95:9, Jul 98:9, Sep 98:5, Feb 00:11, Aug 01:2, Apr 02:14, May 02:1, Oct 04:10, Apr 05:1, 3, Jun 05:11, Dec 05:10, May 06:1, Jun 06:1, Oct 06:15, Apr 07:11, Sep 07:1, Mar 09:3

99205 **Office or other outpatient visit** for the evaluation and management of a new patient, which requires these 3 key components:

- **A comprehensive history;**
- **A comprehensive examination;**
- **Medical decision making of high complexity.**

Counseling and/or coordination of care with other providers or agencies are provided consistent with the nature of the problem(s) and the patient's and/or family's needs.

Usually, the presenting problem(s) are of moderate to high severity. Physicians typically spend 60 minutes face-to-face with the patient and/or family.

➲ *CPT Assistant* Winter 91:11, Spring 92:14, 24, Summer 92:1, 24, Spring 93:34, Summer 93:2, Fall 93:9, Spring 95:1, Summer 95:4, Fall 95:9, Jul 98:9, Sep 98:5, Feb 00:11, Aug 01:2, Apr 02:2, May 02:1, Oct 04:10, Apr 05:1, 3, Jun 05:11, Dec 05:10, May 06:1, Jun 06:1, Oct 06:15, Apr 07:11, Sep 07:1, Mar 09:3

Established Patient

99211 **Office or other outpatient visit** for the evaluation and management of an established patient, that may not require the presence of a physician. Usually, the presenting problem(s) are minimal. Typically, 5 minutes are spent performing or supervising these services.

➲ *CPT Assistant* Winter 91:11, Spring 92:14, 24, Summer 92:1, 24, Spring 93:34, Summer 93:2, Fall 93:9, Spring 95:1, Summer 95:4, Fall 95:9, Oct 96:10, Feb 97:9, May 97:4, Jul 98:9, Sep 98:5, Oct 99:9, Feb 00:11, Aug 01:2, Jan 02:2, Oct 04:10, Feb 05:15, Mar 05:11, Apr 05:1,3, May 05:1, Jun 05:11, Nov 05:1, Dec 05:10, Feb 06:14, May 06:1, Jun 06:1, Jul 06:19, Oct 06:15, Nov 06:21, Apr 07:11, Jul 07:1, Sep 07:1, Dec 07:9, Mar 08:3, Aug 08:13, Mar 09:3

99212 **Office or other outpatient visit** for the evaluation and management of an established patient, which requires at least 2 of these 3 key components:

- **A problem focused history;**
- **A problem focused examination;**
- **Straightforward medical decision making.**

Counseling and/or coordination of care with other providers or agencies are provided consistent with the nature of the problem(s) and the patient's and/or family's needs.

Usually, the presenting problem(s) are self limited or minor. Physicians typically spend 10 minutes face-to-face with the patient and/or family.

➲ *CPT Assistant* Winter 91:11, Spring 92:14, 24, Summer 92:1, 24, Spring 93:34, Summer 93:2, Fall 93:9, Spring 95:1, Summer 95:4, Fall 95:9, Jul 98:9, Sep 98:5, Feb 00:11, Jun 00:11, Aug 01:2, Jan 02:2, May 02:3, Apr 04:14, Oct 04:10, Apr 05:1, 3 Jun 05:11, Dec 05:10, May 06:1, Jun 06:1,11, Sep 06:8, Oct 06:15, Apr 07:11, Jul 07:1, Sep 07:1, Mar 08:3, Mar 09:3

99213 **Office or other outpatient visit** for the evaluation and management of an established patient, which requires at least 2 of these 3 key components:

- **An expanded problem focused history;**
- **An expanded problem focused examination;**
- **Medical decision making of low complexity.**

Counseling and coordination of care with other providers or agencies are provided consistent with the nature of the problem(s) and the patient's and/or family's needs.

Usually, the presenting problem(s) are of low to moderate severity. Physicians typically spend 15 minutes face-to-face with the patient and/or family.

➲ *CPT Assistant* Winter 91:11, Spring 92:14,24, Summer 92:1,24, Spring 93:34, Summer 93:2, Fall 93:9, Spring 95:1, Summer 95:4, Fall 95:9, Jan 97:10, Jul 98:9, Sep 98:5, Aug 01:2, May 02:3, Oct 03:5, Apr 04:14, Oct 04:10, Mar 05:11, Apr 05:1,3, Jun 05:11, Dec 05:10, May 06:1, Jun 06:1,11, Sep 06:8, Oct 06:15, Apr 07:11, Jul 07:1, Sep 07:1, Mar 08:3, Mar 09:3

99214 **Office or other outpatient visit** for the evaluation and management of an established patient, which requires at least 2 of these 3 key components:

- **A detailed history;**
- **A detailed examination;**
- **Medical decision making of moderate complexity.**

Counseling and/or coordination of care with other providers or agencies are provided consistent with the nature of the problem(s) and the patient's and/or family's needs.

Usually, the presenting problem(s) are of moderate to high severity. Physicians typically spend 25 minutes face-to-face with the patient and/or family.

➲ *CPT Assistant* Winter 91:11, Spring 92:15,24, Summer 92:1,24, Spring 93:34, Summer 93:2, Fall 93:9, Spring 95:1, Summer 95:4, Fall 95:9, May 97:4, Jul 98:9, Sep 98:5, Aug 01:2, Jan 02:2, May 02:1-2, Oct 03:5, Apr 04:14, Oct 04:10, Apr 05:1,3, Jun 05:11, Dec 05:10, May 06:1, Jun 06:1,11, Sep 06:8, Oct 06:15, Apr 07:11, Jul 07:1, Sep 07:1, Mar 08:3, Mar 09:3

99215 **Office or other outpatient visit** for the evaluation and management of an established patient, which requires at least 2 of these 3 key components:

- **A comprehensive history;**
- **A comprehensive examination;**
- **Medical decision making of high complexity.**

Counseling and/or coordination of care with other providers or agencies are provided consistent with the nature of the problem(s) and the patient's and/or family's needs.

Usually, the presenting problem(s) are of moderate to high severity. Physicians typically spend 40 minutes face-to-face with the patient and/or family.

➲ *CPT Assistant* Winter 91:11, Spring 92:15,24, Summer 92:1,24, Spring 93:34, Summer 93:2, Fall 93:9, Spring 95:1, Summer 95:4, Fall 95:9, Jan 97:10, Jul 98:9, Sep 98:5, Aug 01:2, Jan 02:2, May 02:1,3, Apr 04:14, Oct 04:10, Mar 05:11, Apr 05:1,3, Jun 05:11, Dec 05:10, May 06:1, Jun 06:1,11, Sep 06:8, Oct 06:15, Apr 07:11, Jul 07:1, Sep 07:1, Mar 08:3, Mar 09:3

Hospital Observation Services

The following codes are used to report evaluation and management services provided to patients designated/admitted as "observation status" in a hospital. It is not necessary that the patient be located in an observation area designated by the hospital.

If such an area does exist in a hospital (as a separate unit in the hospital, in the emergency department, etc.), these codes are to be utilized if the patient is placed in such an area.

For definitions of key components and commonly used terms, please see **Evaluation and Management Services Guidelines.**

Typical times have not yet been established for this category of services.

Observation Care Discharge Services

Observation care discharge of a patient from "observation status" includes final examination of the patient, discussion of the hospital stay, instructions for continuing care, and preparation of discharge records. For observation or inpatient hospital care including the admission and discharge of the patient on the same date, see codes 99234-99236 as appropriate.

99217   **Observation care discharge** day management (This code is to be utilized by the physician to report all services provided to a patient on discharge from "observation status" if the discharge is on other than the initial date of "observation status." To report services to a patient designated as "observation status" or "inpatient status" and discharged on the same date, use the codes for Observation or Inpatient Care Services [including Admission and Discharge Services, 99234-99236 as appropriate.])

➡ *CPT Assistant* Nov 97:2, Mar 98:1, May 98:3, Sep 98:5, Sep 00:3, May 05:1, Nov 05:10, Sep 06:8, Dec 06:14

Initial Observation Care

New or Established Patient

The following codes are used to report the encounter(s) by the supervising physician with the patient when designated as "observation status." This refers to the initiation of observation status, supervision of the care plan for observation and performance of periodic reassessments. For observation encounters by other physicians, see Office or Other Outpatient Consultation codes (99241-99245).

To report services provided to a patient who is admitted to the hospital after receiving hospital observation care services on the same date, see the notes for initial hospital inpatient care (page 12). For a patient admitted to the hospital on a date subsequent to the date of observation status, the hospital admission would be reported with the appropriate Initial Hospital Care code (99221-99223). For a patient admitted and discharged from observation or inpatient status on the same date, the services should be reported with codes 99234-99236 as appropriate. Do not report observation discharge (99217) in conjunction with a hospital admission.

When "observation status" is initiated in the course of an encounter in another site of service (eg, hospital emergency department, physician's office, nursing facility) all evaluation and management services provided by the supervising physician in conjunction with initiating "observation status" are considered part of the initial observation care when performed on the same date. The observation care level of service reported by the supervising physician should include the services related to initiating "observation status" provided in the other sites of service as well as in the observation setting.

Evaluation and management services on the same date provided in sites that are related to initiating "observation status" should **not** be reported separately.

These codes may not be utilized for post-operative recovery if the procedure is considered part of the surgical "package." These codes apply to all evaluation and management services that are provided on the same date of initiating "observation status."

99218   **Initial observation care,** per day, for the evaluation and management of a patient which requires these 3 key components:

- **A detailed or comprehensive history;**
- **A detailed or comprehensive examination; and**
- **Medical decision making that is straightforward or of low complexity.**

Counseling and/or coordination of care with other providers or agencies are provided consistent with the nature of the problem(s) and the patient's and/or family's needs.

Usually, the problem(s) requiring admission to "observation status" are of low severity.

➡ *CPT Assistant* Spring 93:34, Fall 95:9, Nov 97:2, Mar 98:1, Sep 98:5, Sep 00:3, Jan 03:10, Aug 04:11, May 05:1, Nov 05:10, Sep 06:8, Dec 06:14

99219   **Initial observation care,** per day, for the evaluation and management of a patient, which requires these 3 key components:

- **A comprehensive history;**
- **A comprehensive examination; and**
- **Medical decision making of moderate complexity.**

Counseling and/or coordination of care with other providers or agencies are provided consistent with the nature of the problem(s) and the patient's and/or family's needs.

Usually, the problem(s) requiring admission to "observation status" are of moderate severity.

→ *CPT Assistant* Spring 93:34, Fall 95:16, Nov 97:2, Mar 98:1, Sep 98:5, Sep 00:3, Jan 03:10, Aug 04:11, Nov 05:10, Sep 06:8, Dec 06:14

99220 **Initial observation care,** per day, for the evaluation and management of a patient, which requires these 3 key components:

- **A comprehensive history;**
- **A comprehensive examination; and**
- **Medical decision making of high complexity.**

Counseling and/or coordination of care with other providers or agencies are provided consistent with the nature of the problem(s) and the patient's and/or family's needs.

Usually, the problem(s) requiring admission to "observation status" are of high severity.

→ *CPT Assistant* Spring 93:34, Fall 95:16, Nov 97:2, Mar 98:1, Sep 98:5, Sep 00:3, Jan 03:10, Aug 04:11, Nov 05:10, Sep 06:8, Dec 06:14

Hospital Inpatient Services

The following codes are used to report evaluation and management services provided to hospital inpatients. Hospital inpatient services include those services provided to patients in a "partial hospital" setting. These codes are to be used to report these partial hospitalization services. See also psychiatry notes in the full text of the CPT codebook.

For definitions of key components and commonly used terms, please see **Evaluation and Management Services Guidelines.** For Hospital Observation Services, see 99218-99220. For a patient admitted and discharged from observation or inpatient status on the same date, the services should be reported with codes 99234-99236 as appropriate.

Initial Hospital Care

New or Established Patient

The following codes are used to report the first hospital inpatient encounter with the patient by the admitting physician.

For initial inpatient encounters by physicians other than the admitting physician, see initial inpatient consultation codes (99251-99255) or subsequent hospital care codes (99231-99233) as appropriate.

For admission services for the neonate (28 days of age or younger) requiring intensive observation, frequent interventions, and other intensive care services, see 99477.

When the patient is admitted to the hospital as an inpatient in the course of an encounter in another site of service (eg, hospital emergency department, observation status in a hospital, physician's office, nursing facility) all evaluation and management services provided by that physician in conjunction with that admission are considered part of the initial hospital care when performed on the same date as the admission. The inpatient care level of service reported by the admitting physician should include the services related to the admission he/she provided in the other sites of service as well as in the inpatient setting.

Evaluation and management services on the same date provided in sites that are related to the admission "observation status" should **not** be reported separately. For a patient admitted and discharged from observation or inpatient status on the same date, the services should be reported with codes 99234-99236 as appropriate.

99221 **Initial hospital care,** per day, for the evaluation and management of a patient, which requires these 3 key components:

- **A detailed or comprehensive history;**
- **A detailed or comprehensive examination; and**
- **Medical decision making that is straightforward or of low complexity.**

Counseling and/or coordination of care with other providers or agencies are provided consistent with the nature of the problem(s) and the patient's and/or family's needs.

Usually, the problem(s) requiring admission are of low severity. Physicians typically spend 30 minutes at the bedside and on the patient's hospital floor or unit.

→ *CPT Assistant* Winter 91:11, Spring 92:14, 24, Summer 92:10, 24, Fall 92:1, Spring 93:34, Spring 95:1, Fall 95:9, Jul 96:11, Sep 96:10, Nov 97:2, Mar 98:1, Sep 98:5, Jan 02:2-3, Apr 03:26, Apr 04:14, Aug 04:11, May 05:1, Sep 06:8, Jul 07:12

99222 **Initial hospital care,** per day, for the evaluation and management of a patient, which requires these 3 key components:

- **A comprehensive history;**
- **A comprehensive examination; and**
- **Medical decision making of moderate complexity.**

Counseling and/or coordination of care with other providers or agencies are provided consistent with the nature of the problem(s) and the patient's and/or family's needs.

Usually, the problem(s) requiring admission are of moderate severity. Physicians typically spend 50 minutes at the bedside and on the patient's hospital floor or unit.

→ *CPT Assistant* Winter 91:11, Spring 92:14, 24, Summer 92:10, 24, Fall 92:1, Spring 93:34, Spring 95:1, Fall 95:9, Jul 96:11, Sep 96:10, Nov 97:2, Mar 98:1, Sep 98:5, Jan 02:2-3, Apr 03:26, Apr 04:14, Aug 04:11, Sep 06:8, Jul 07:12

99223 **Initial hospital care,** per day, for the evaluation and management of a patient, which requires these 3 key components:

- **A comprehensive history;**
- **A comprehensive examination; and**
- **Medical decision making of high complexity.**

Counseling and/or coordination of care with other providers or agencies are provided consistent with the nature of the problem(s) and the patient's and/or family's needs.

Usually, the problem(s) requiring admission are of high severity. Physicians typically spend 70 minutes at the bedside and on the patient's hospital floor or unit.

➔ *CPT Assistant* Winter 91:11, Spring 92:14, 24, Summer 92:10, 24, Fall 92:1, Spring 93:34, Spring 95:1, Fall 95:9, Jul 96:11, Sep 96:10, Nov 97:2, Mar 98:1, Sep 98:5, Jan 02:2-3, Apr 03:26, Apr 04:14, Aug 04:11, Sep 06:8, Jul 07:12

Subsequent Hospital Care

All levels of subsequent hospital care include reviewing the medical record and reviewing the results of diagnostic studies and changes in the patient's status (ie, changes in history, physical condition and response to management) since the last assessment by the physician.

99231 **Subsequent hospital care,** per day, for the evaluation and management of a patient, which requires at least 2 of these 3 key components:

- **A problem focused interval history;**
- **A problem focused examination;**
- **Medical decision making that is straightforward or of low complexity.**

Counseling and/or coordination of care with other providers or agencies are provided consistent with the nature of the problem(s) and the patient's and/or family's needs.

Usually, the patient is stable, recovering or improving. Physicians typically spend 15 minutes at the bedside and on the patient's hospital floor or unit.

➔ *CPT Assistant* Winter 91:11, Spring 92:14, 24, Summer 92:10, 24, Fall 92:1, Spring 93:34, Spring 95:1, Fall 95:16, Nov 97:2, Sep 98:5, Jan 99:10, Nov 99:5, Aug 01:2, Jan 02:2-3, Apr 04:14, Aug 04:11, Mar 05:11, May 05:1, May 06:1, 16, Jul 06:4, Mar 07:9, Jul 07:1, Mar 09:3

99232 **Subsequent hospital care,** per day, for the evaluation and management of a patient, which requires at least 2 of these 3 key components:

- **An expanded problem focused interval history;**
- **An expanded problem focused examination;**
- **Medical decision making of moderate complexity.**

Counseling and/or coordination of care with other providers or agencies are provided consistent with the nature of the problem(s) and the patient's and/or family's needs.

Usually, the patient is responding inadequately to therapy or has developed a minor complication. Physicians typically spend 25 minutes at the bedside and on the patient's hospital floor or unit.

➔ *CPT Assistant* Winter 91:11, Spring 92:14, 24, Summer 92:10, 24, Fall 92:1, Spring 93:34, Spring 95:1, Fall 95:16, Nov 97:2, Sep 98:5, Jan 99:10, Nov 99:5, Jan 00:11, Aug 01:2, Apr 04:14, Aug 04:11, May 06:1, 16, Jul 06:4, Mar 07:9, Jul 07:1, Mar 09:3

99233 **Subsequent hospital care,** per day, for the evaluation and management of a patient, which requires at least 2 of these 3 key components:

- **A detailed interval history;**
- **A detailed examination;**
- **Medical decision making of high complexity.**

Counseling and/or coordination of care with other providers or agencies are provided consistent with the nature of the problem(s) and the patient's and/or family's needs.

Usually, the patient is unstable or has developed a significant complication or a significant new problem. Physicians typically spend 35 minutes at the bedside and on the patient's hospital floor or unit.

➔ *CPT Assistant* Winter 91:11, Spring 92:14, 24, Summer 92:10, 24, Fall 92:1, Spring 93:34, Spring 95:1, Fall 95:16, Nov 97:2, Sep 98:5, Jan 99:10, Nov 99:5, Aug 01:2, Apr 04:14, Aug 04:11, May 06:1, 16, Jul 06:4, Mar 07:9, Jul 07:1, Mar 09:3

Observation or Inpatient Care Services (Including Admission and Discharge Services)

The following codes are used to report observation or inpatient hospital care services provided to patients admitted and discharged on the same date of service. When a patient is admitted to the hospital from observation status on the same date, the physician should report only the initial hospital care code. The initial hospital care code reported by the admitting physician should include the services related to the observation status services he/she provided on the same date of inpatient admission.

When "observation status" is initiated in the course of an encounter in another site of service (eg, hospital emergency department, physician's office, nursing facility) all evaluation and management services provided by the supervising physician in conjunction with initiating "observation status" are considered part of the initial observation care when performed on the same date. The observation care level of service should include the services related to initiating "observation status" provided in the other sites of service as well as in the observation setting when provided by the same physician.

For patients admitted to observation or inpatient care and discharged on a different date, see codes 99218-99220 and 99217, or 99221-99223 and 99238, 99239.

99234 **Observation or inpatient hospital care,** for the evaluation and management of a patient including admission and discharge on the same date, which requires these 3 key components:

- **A detailed or comprehensive history;**
- **A detailed or comprehensive examination; and**
- **Medical decision making that is straightforward or of low complexity.**

Counseling and/or coordination of care with other providers or agencies are provided consistent with the nature of the problem(s) and the patient's and/or family's needs.

Usually the presenting problem(s) requiring admission are of low severity.

➲ *CPT Assistant* Nov 97:2, Mar 98:2, May 98:1, Sep 98:5, Jan 00:11, Sep 00:3, Jan 02:2, Jun 02:10, Jan 03:10, May 05:1, Nov 05:10, Sep 06:8, Dec 06:14

99235 **Observation or inpatient hospital care,** for the evaluation and management of a patient including admission and discharge on the same date, which requires these 3 key components:

- **A comprehensive history;**
- **A comprehensive examination; and**
- **Medical decision making of moderate complexity.**

Counseling and/or coordination of care with other providers or agencies are provided consistent with the nature of the problem(s) and the patient's and/or family's needs.

Usually the presenting problem(s) requiring admission are of moderate severity.

➲ *CPT Assistant* Nov 97:2, Mar 98:2, May 98:1, Sep 98:5, Jan 00:11, Sep 00:3, Jan 02:2, Jun 02:10, Jan 03:10, Nov 05:10, Sep 06:8, Dec 06:14

99236 **Observation or inpatient hospital care,** for the evaluation and management of a patient including admission and discharge on the same date, which requires these 3 key components:

- **A comprehensive history;**
- **A comprehensive examination; and**
- **Medical decision making of high complexity.**

Counseling and/or coordination of care with other providers or agencies are provided consistent with the nature of the problem(s) and the patient's and/or family's needs.

Usually the presenting problem(s) requiring admission are of high severity.

➲ *CPT Assistant* Nov 97:2, Mar 98:2, May 98:1, Sep 98:5, Jan 00:11, Sep 00:3, Jan 02:2, Jun 02:10, Jan 03:10, Nov 05:10, Sep 06:8, Dec 06:14

Hospital Discharge Services

The hospital discharge day management codes are to be used to report the total duration of time spent by a physician for final hospital discharge of a patient. The codes include, as appropriate, final examination of the patient, discussion of the hospital stay, even if the time spent by the physician on that date is not continuous, instructions for continuing care to all relevant caregivers, and preparation of discharge records, prescriptions and referral forms. For a patient admitted and discharged from observation or inpatient status on the same date, the services should be reported with codes 99234-99236 as appropriate.

99238 **Hospital discharge day management;** 30 minutes or less

➲ *CPT Assistant* Fall 92:1, Spring 93:4, Nov 97:4, Mar 98:3, 11, May 98:2, Jan 99:10, Jan 02:2, Aug 04:11, May 05:1, Sep 06:8

99239 more than 30 minutes

➲ *CPT Assistant* Nov 97:4, Mar 98:3, 11, May 98:2, Jan 99:10, Jan 02:2, Aug 04:11, Sep 06:8

(These codes are to be utilized by the physician to report all services provided to a patient on the date of discharge, if other than the initial date of inpatient status. To report services to a patient who is admitted as an inpatient and discharged on the same date, see codes 99234-99236 for observation or inpatient hospital care including the admission and discharge of the patient on the same date. To report concurrent care services provided by a physician[s] other than the attending physician, use subsequent hospital care codes [99231-99233] on the day of discharge.)

(For Observation Care Discharge, use 99217)

(For observation or inpatient hospital care including the admission and discharge of the patient on the same date, see 99234-99236)

(For Nursing Facility Care Discharge, see 99315, 99316)

(For discharge services provided to newborns admitted and discharged on the same date, use 99463)

Consultations

▶A consultation is a type of evaluation and management service provided by a physician at the request of another physician or appropriate source to either recommend care for a specific condition or problem or to determine whether to accept responsibility for ongoing management of the patient's entire care or for the care of a specific condition or problem.◀

A physician consultant may initiate diagnostic and/or therapeutic services at the same or subsequent visit.

▶A "consultation" initiated by a patient and/or family, and not requested by a physician or other appropriate source (eg, physician assistant, nurse practitioner, doctor of chiropractic, physical therapist, occupational therapist, speech-language pathologist, psychologist, social worker, lawyer, or insurance company), is not reported using the consultation codes but may be reported using the office visit, home service, or domiciliary/rest home care codes as appropriate.

The written or verbal request for consult may be made by a physician or other appropriate source and documented in the patient's medical record by either the consulting or requesting physician or appropriate source. The consultant's opinion and any services that were ordered or performed must also be documented in the patient's medical record and communicated by written report to the requesting physician or other appropriate source.◀

If a consultation is mandated (eg, by a third-party payer) modifier 32 should also be reported.

Any specifically identifiable procedure (ie, identified with a specific CPT code) performed on or subsequent to the date of the initial consultation should be reported separately.

If subsequent to the completion of a consultation the consultant assumes responsibility for management of a portion or all of the patient's condition(s), the appropriate **Evaluation and Management** services code for the site of service should be reported. In the hospital or nursing facility setting, the consulting physician should use the appropriate inpatient consultation code for the initial encounter and then subsequent hospital or nursing facility care codes. In the office setting, the physician should use the appropriate office or other outpatient consultation codes and then the established patient office or other outpatient services codes.

▶To report services provided to a patient who is admitted to a hospital or nursing facility in the course of an encounter in the office or other ambulatory facility, see the notes for Initial Hospital Inpatient Care (page 16) or Initial Nursing Facility Care (page 24).◀

For definitions of key components and commonly used terms, please see **Evaluation and Management Services Guidelines.**

Office or Other Outpatient Consultations

New or Established Patient

▶The following codes are used to report consultations provided in the physician's office or in an outpatient or other ambulatory facility, including hospital observation services, home services, domiciliary, rest home, or emergency department (see the preceding consultation definition above). Follow-up visits in the consultant's office or other outpatient facility that are initiated by the physician consultant or patient are reported using the appropriate codes for established patients, office visits (99211-99215), domiciliary, rest home (99334-99337), or home (99347-99350). If an additional request for an opinion or advice regarding the same or a new problem is received from another physician or other appropriate source and documented in the medical record, the office consultation codes may be used again. Services that constitute transfer of care (ie, are provided for the management of the patient's entire care or for the care of a specific condition or problem) are reported with the appropriate new or established patient codes for office or other outpatient visits, domiciliary, rest home services, or home services.◀

99241   **Office consultation** for a new or established patient, which requires these 3 key components:

- **A problem focused history;**
- **A problem focused examination; and**
- **Straightforward medical decision making.**

Counseling and/or coordination of care with other providers or agencies are provided consistent with the nature of the problem(s) and the patient's and/or family's needs.

Usually, the presenting problem(s) are self limited or minor. Physicians typically spend 15 minutes face-to-face with the patient and/or family.

➔ *CPT Assistant* Winter 91:11, Spring 92:4, 23-24, Summer 92:12, Spring 93:4, Spring 95:1, Oct 97:1, Sep 98:5, Jun 99:10, Apr 00:10, Aug 01:3, Jan 02:2, Jul 02:2, Sep 02:11, May 05:1, Dec 05:10, Jan 06:46, May 06:1, 16, Jun 06:1, Sep 06:8, Jan 07:28, Apr 07:11, Jul 07:1, May 08:13, Nov 08:10

99242   **Office consultation** for a new or established patient, which requires these 3 key components:

- **An expanded problem focused history;**
- **An expanded problem focused examination; and**
- **Straightforward medical decision making.**

Counseling and/or coordination of care with other providers or agencies are provided consistent with the nature of the problem(s) and the patient's and/or family's needs.

Usually, the presenting problem(s) are of low severity. Physicians typically spend 30 minutes face-to-face with the patient and/or family.

➔ *CPT Assistant* Winter 91:11, Spring 92:4, 23-24, Summer 92:12, Spring 93:2, 34, Spring 95:1, Oct 97:1, Sep 98:5, Aug 01:3, Jan 02:2, Jul 02:2, Sep 02:11, Dec 05:10, May 06:1, 16, Jun 06:1, Sep 06:8, Apr 07:11, Jul 07:1; *CPT Changes: An Insider's View* 2000

99243 **Office consultation** for a new or established patient, which requires these 3 key components:

- A detailed history;
- A detailed examination; and
- Medical decision making of low complexity.

Counseling and/or coordination of care with other providers or agencies are provided consistent with the nature of the problem(s) and the patient's and/or family's needs.

Usually, the presenting problem(s) are of moderate severity. Physicians typically spend 40 minutes face-to-face with the patient and/or family.

➔ *CPT Assistant* Winter 91:11, Spring 92:4, 23-24, Summer 92:12, Spring 93:2, 34, Spring 95:1, Oct 97:1, Sep 98:5, Aug 01:3, Jan 02:2, Jul 02:2, Sep 02:11, Oct 03:5, Dec 05:10, May 06:1, 16, Jun 06:1, Sep 06:8, Apr 07:11, Jul 07:1

99244 **Office consultation** for a new or established patient, which requires these 3 key components:

- A comprehensive history;
- A comprehensive examination; and
- Medical decision making of moderate complexity.

Counseling and/or coordination of care with other providers or agencies are provided consistent with the nature of the problem(s) and the patient's and/or family's needs.

Usually, the presenting problem(s) are of moderate to high severity. Physicians typically spend 60 minutes face-to-face with the patient and/or family.

➔ *CPT Assistant* Winter 91:11, Spring 92:3, 23-24, Summer 92:12, Spring 93:2, 34, Spring 95:1, Oct 97:1, Sep 98:5, Aug 01:3, Jan 02:2, Jul 02:2, Sep 02:11, Oct 03:5, Dec 05:10, May 06:1, 16, Jun 06:1, Sep 06:8, Apr 07:11, Jul 07:1

99245 **Office consultation** for a new or established patient, which requires these 3 key components:

- A comprehensive history;
- A comprehensive examination; and
- Medical decision making of high complexity.

Counseling and/or coordination of care with other providers or agencies are provided consistent with the nature of the problem(s) and the patient's and/or family's needs.

Usually, the presenting problem(s) are of moderate to high severity. Physicians typically spend 80 minutes face-to-face with the patient and/or family.

➔ *CPT Assistant* Winter 91:11, Spring 92:4, 23-24, Summer 92:12, Spring 93:2, 34, Spring 95:1, Oct 97:1, Sep 98:5, Aug 01:2, Jan 02:2, Jul 02:2, Sep 02:11, Dec 05:10, May 06:1, 16, Jun 06:1, Sep 06:8, Apr 07:11, Jul 07:1

Inpatient Consultations

New or Established Patient

▶The following codes are used to report physician consultations provided to hospital inpatients, residents of nursing facilities, or patients in a partial hospital setting. Only one consultation should be reported by a consultant per admission. Subsequent services during the same admission are reported using subsequent hospital care codes (99231-99233) or subsequent nursing facility care codes (99307-99310), including services to complete the initial consultation, monitor progress, revise recommendations, or address a new problem. Use subsequent hospital care codes (99231-99233) or subsequent nursing facility care codes (99307-99310) to report transfer of care services (see page 25, Concurrent Care and Transfer of Care definitions).

When an inpatient consultation is performed on a date that a patient is admitted to a hospital or nursing facility, all evaluation and management services provided by the consultant related to the admission are reported with the inpatient consultation service code (99251-99255). If a patient is admitted after an outpatient consultation (office, emergency department, etc), and the patient is not seen on the unit on the date of admission, only report the outpatient consultation code (99241-99245). If the patient is seen by the consultant on the unit on the date of admission, report all evaluation and management services provided by the consultant related to the admission with either the inpatient consultation code (99251-99255) or with the initial inpatient admission service code (99221-99223). Do not report both an outpatient consultation and inpatient consultation for services related to the same inpatient stay. When transfer of care services are provided on a date subsequent to the outpatient consultation, use the subsequent hospital care codes (99231-99233) or subsequent nursing facility care codes (99307-99310).◀

99251 **Inpatient consultation** for a new or established patient, which requires these 3 key components:

- A problem focused history;
- A problem focused examination; and
- Straightforward medical decision making.

Counseling and/or coordination of care with other providers or agencies are provided consistent with the nature of the problem(s) and the patient's and/or family's needs.

Usually, the presenting problem(s) are self limited or minor. Physicians typically spend 20 minutes at the bedside and on the patient's hospital floor or unit.

➔ *CPT Assistant* Winter 91:11, Spring 92:16, 23-24, Summer 92:12, Spring 93:34, Spring 95:1, Oct 97:1, Sep 98:5, Aug 01:3, Sep 02:11, May 05:1, May 06:1, 16, Jun 06:1, Jul 06:19, Jul 07:1; *CPT Changes: An Insider's View* 2007

99252   **Inpatient consultation** for a new or established patient, which requires these 3 key components:

- **An expanded problem focused history;**
- **An expanded problem focused examination; and**
- **Straightforward medical decision making.**

Counseling and/or coordination of care with other providers or agencies are provided consistent with the nature of the problem(s) and the patient's and/or family's needs.

Usually, the presenting problem(s) are of low severity. Physicians typically spend 40 minutes at the bedside and on the patient's hospital floor or unit.

➲ *CPT Assistant* Winter 91:11, Spring 92:16, 23-24, Summer 92:12, Summer 93:34, Spring 95:1, Oct 97:1, Sep 98:5, Aug 01:4, Sep 02:11, May 06:1, 16, Jun 06:1, Jul 06:19, Jul 07:1; *CPT Changes: An Insider's View* 2007

99253   **Inpatient consultation** for a new or established patient, which requires these 3 key components:

- **A detailed history;**
- **A detailed examination; and**
- **Medical decision making of low complexity.**

Counseling and/or coordination of care with other providers or agencies are provided consistent with the nature of the problem(s) and the patient's and/or family's needs.

Usually, the presenting problem(s) are of moderate severity. Physicians typically spend 55 minutes at the bedside and on the patient's hospital floor or unit.

➲ *CPT Assistant* Winter 91:11, Spring 92:16, 23-24, Summer 92:12, Summer 93:34, Spring 95:1, Oct 97:1, Sep 98:5, Aug 01:4, Sep 02:11, May 06:1,16, Jun 06:1, Jul 06:19, Jul 07:1; *CPT Changes: An Insider's View* 2007

99254   **Inpatient consultation** for a new or established patient, which requires these 3 key components:

- **A comprehensive history;**
- **A comprehensive examination; and**
- **Medical decision making of moderate complexity.**

Counseling and/or coordination of care with other providers or agencies are provided consistent with the nature of the problem(s) and the patient's and/or family's needs.

Usually, the presenting problem(s) are of moderate to high severity. Physicians typically spend 80 minutes at the bedside and on the patient's hospital floor or unit.

➲ *CPT Assistant* Winter 91:11, Spring 92:16, 23-24, Summer 92:12, Summer 93:34, Spring 95:1, Oct 97:1, Sep 98:5, Aug 01:4, Sep 02:11, May 06:1, 16, Jun 06:1, Jul 06:19, Jul 07:1; *CPT Changes: An Insider's View* 2007

99255   **Inpatient consultation** for a new or established patient, which requires these 3 key components:

- **A comprehensive history;**
- **A comprehensive examination; and**
- **Medical decision making of high complexity.**

Counseling and/or coordination of care with other providers or agencies are provided consistent with the nature of the problem(s) and the patient's and/or family's needs.

Usually, the presenting problem(s) are of moderate to high severity. Physicians typically spend 110 minutes at the bedside and on the patient's hospital floor or unit.

➲ *CPT Assistant* Winter 91:11, Spring 92:16, 23-24, Summer 92:12, Summer 93:34, Spring 95:1, Oct 97:1, Sep 98:5, Aug 01:4, Sep 02:11, May 06:1,16, Jun 06:1, Jul 06:19, Jul 07:1; *CPT Changes: An Insider's View* 2007

Emergency Department Services

New or Established Patient

The following codes are used to report evaluation and management services provided in the emergency department. No distinction is made between new and established patients in the emergency department.

An emergency department is defined as an organized hospital-based facility for the provision of unscheduled episodic services to patients who present for immediate medical attention. The facility must be available 24 hours a day.

For critical care services provided in the emergency department, see Critical Care notes and 99291, 99292.

For evaluation and management services provided to a patient in an observation area of a hospital, see 99217-99220.

For observation or inpatient care services (including admission and discharge services), see 99234-99236.

99281   **Emergency department visit** for the evaluation and management of a patient, which requires these 3 key components:

- **A problem focused history;**
- **A problem focused examination; and**
- **Straightforward medical decision making.**

Counseling and/or coordination of care with other providers or agencies are provided consistent with the nature of the problem(s) and the patient's and/or family's needs.

Usually, the presenting problem(s) are self limited or minor.

➲ *CPT Assistant* Winter 91:11, Spring 92:24, Summer 92:18, Spring 93:34, Spring 95:1, Feb 96:3, Sep 98:5, Jan 00:11, Feb 00:11, Sep 00:3, Apr 02:14, Jul 02:2, Nov 05:10, Feb 06:14, Dec 06:14, Dec 07:13

99282 **Emergency department visit** for the evaluation and management of a patient, which requires these 3 key components:

■ An expanded problem focused history;

■ An expanded problem focused examination; and

■ Medical decision making of low complexity.

Counseling and/or coordination of care with other providers or agencies are provided consistent with the nature of the problem(s) and the patient's and/or family's needs.

Usually, the presenting problem(s) are of low to moderate severity.

➲ *CPT Assistant* Winter 91:11, Spring 92:24, Summer 92:18, Spring 93:34, Spring 95:1, Summer 95:1, Feb 96:3, Sep 98:5, Jan 00:11, Feb 00:11, Sep 00:3, Apr 02:14, Jul 02:2, Nov 05:10, Feb 06:14, Dec 06:14, Dec 07:13

99283 **Emergency department visit** for the evaluation and management of a patient, which requires these 3 key components:

■ An expanded problem focused history;

■ An expanded problem focused examination; and

■ Medical decision making of moderate complexity.

Counseling and/or coordination of care with other providers or agencies are provided consistent with the nature of the problem(s) and the patient's and/or family's needs.

Usually, the presenting problem(s) are of moderate severity.

➲ *CPT Assistant* Winter 91:11, Spring 92:24, Summer 92:18, Spring 93:34, Spring 95:1, Summer 95:1, Feb 96:3, Sep 98:5, Jan 00:11, Feb 00:11, Sep 00:3, Apr 02:14, Jul 02:2, Nov 05:10, Feb 06:14, Dec 06:14, Dec 07:13

99284 **Emergency department visit** for the evaluation and management of a patient, which requires these 3 key components:

■ A detailed history;

■ A detailed examination; and

■ Medical decision making of moderate complexity.

Counseling and/or coordination of care with other providers or agencies are provided consistent with the nature of the problem(s) and the patient's and/or family's needs.

Usually, the presenting problem(s) are of high severity, and require urgent evaluation by the physician but do not pose an immediate significant threat to life or physiologic function.

➲ *CPT Assistant* Winter 91:11, Spring 92:24, Summer 92:18, Spring 93:34, Spring 95:1, Summer 95:1, Feb 96:3, Sep 98:5, Jan 00:11, Feb 00:11, Sep 00:3, Apr 02:14, Jul 02:2, Nov 05:10, Feb 06:14, Dec 06:14, Dec 07:13

99285 **Emergency department visit** for the evaluation and management of a patient, which requires these 3 key components within the constraints imposed by the urgency of the patient's clinical condition and/or mental status:

■ A comprehensive history;

■ A comprehensive examination; and

■ Medical decision making of high complexity.

Counseling and/or coordination of care with other providers or agencies are provided consistent with the nature of the problem(s) and the patient's and/or family's needs.

Usually, the presenting problem(s) are of high severity and pose an immediate significant threat to life or physiologic function.

➲ *CPT Assistant* Winter 91:11, Spring 92:24, Summer 92:18, Spring 93:34, Spring 95:1, Summer 95:1, Feb 96:3, Aug 98:8, Sep 98:5, Nov 99:23, Jan 00:11, Feb 00:11, Sep 00:3, Apr 02:14, Jul 02:2, Sep 02:11, Mar 05:11, Nov 05:10, Feb 06:14, Dec 06:14, Dec 07:13; *CPT Changes: An Insider's View* 2000

Other Emergency Services

In physician directed emergency care, advanced life support, the physician is located in a hospital emergency or critical care department, and is in two-way voice communication with ambulance or rescue personnel outside the hospital. The physician directs the performance of necessary medical procedures, including but not limited to: telemetry of cardiac rhythm; cardiac and/or pulmonary resuscitation; endotracheal or esophageal obturator airway intubation; administration of intravenous fluids and/or administration of intramuscular, intratracheal or subcutaneous drugs; and/or electrical conversion of arrhythmia.

99288 **Physician direction of** emergency medical systems (EMS) emergency care, advanced life support

➲ *CPT Assistant* Summer 92:18, May 05:1, Nov 07:5

(99289 has been deleted. To report, use 99466)

(99290 has been deleted. To report, use 99467)

Critical Care Services

Critical care is the direct delivery by a physician(s) of medical care for a critically ill or critically injured patient. A critical illness or injury acutely impairs one or more vital organ systems such that there is a high probability of imminent or life threatening deterioration in the patient's condition. Critical care involves high complexity decision making to assess, manipulate, and support vital system function(s) to treat single or multiple vital organ system failure and/or to prevent further life threatening deterioration of the patient's condition. Examples of vital organ system failure include, but are not limited to: central nervous system failure, circulatory failure, shock, renal, hepatic, metabolic, and/or respiratory failure.

Although critical care typically requires interpretation of multiple physiologic parameters and/or application of advanced technology(s), critical care may be provided in life threatening situations when these elements are not present. Critical care may be provided on multiple days, even if no changes are made in the treatment rendered to the patient, provided that the patient's condition continues to require the level of physician attention described above.

Providing medical care to a critically ill, injured, or post-operative patient qualifies as a critical care service only if both the illness or injury and the treatment being provided meet the above requirements. Critical care is usually, but not always, given in a critical care area, such as the coronary care unit, intensive care unit, pediatric intensive care unit, respiratory care unit, or the emergency care facility.

Inpatient critical care services provided to infants 29 days through 71 months of age are reported with pediatric critical care codes 99471-99476. The pediatric critical care codes are reported as long as the infant/young child qualifies for critical care services during the hospital stay through 71 months of age. Inpatient critical care services provided to neonates (28 days of age or younger) are reported with the neonatal critical care codes 99468 and 99469. The neonatal critical care codes are reported as long as the neonate qualifies for critical care services during the hospital stay through the 28th postnatal day. The reporting of the pediatric and neonatal critical care services is not based on time or the type of unit (eg, pediatric or neonatal critical care unit) and it is not dependent upon the type of provider delivering the care. To report critical care services provided in the outpatient setting (eg, emergency department or office), for neonates and pediatric patients up through 71 months of age, see the critical care codes 99291, 99292. If the same physician provides critical care services for a neonatal or pediatric patient in both the outpatient and inpatient settings on the same day, report only the appropriate neonatal or pediatric critical care code 99468-99472 for all critical care services provided on that day. Also report 99291-99292 for neonatal or pediatric critical care services provided by the physician providing critical care at one facility but transferring the patient to another facility. Critical care services provided by a second physician of a different specialty not reporting a per day neonatal or pediatric critical care code can be reported with codes 99291-99292. For additional instructions on reporting these services, see the Neonatal and Pediatric Critical Care section and codes 99468-99476.

Services for a patient who is not critically ill but happens to be in a critical care unit are reported using other appropriate E/M codes.

Critical care and other E/M services may be provided to the same patient on the same date by the same physician.

The following services are included in reporting critical care when performed during the critical period by the physician(s) providing critical care: the interpretation of cardiac output measurements (93561, 93562), chest X-rays (71010, 71015, 71020), pulse oximetry (94760, 94761, 94762), blood gases, and information data stored in computers (eg, ECGs, blood pressures, hematologic data [99090]); gastric intubation (43752, 91105); temporary transcutaneous pacing (92953); ventilatory management (94002-94004, 94660, 94662); and vascular access procedures (36000, 36410, 36415, 36591, 36600). Any services performed that are not included in this listing should be reported separately.

Codes 99291, 99292 should be reported for the physician's attendance during the transport of critically ill or critically injured patients older than 24 months of age to or from a facility or hospital. For physician transport services of critically ill or critically injured pediatric patients 24 months of age or younger, see 99466, 99467.

The critical care codes 99291 and 99292 are used to report the total duration of time spent by a physician providing critical care services to a critically ill or critically injured patient, even if the time spent by the physician on that date is not continuous. For any given period of time spent providing critical care services, the physician must devote his or her full attention to the patient and, therefore, cannot provide services to any other patient during the same period of time.

Time spent with the individual patient should be recorded in the patient's record. The time that can be reported as critical care is the time spent engaged in work directly related to the individual patient's care whether that time was spent at the immediate bedside or elsewhere on the floor or unit. For example, time spent on the unit or at the nursing station on the floor reviewing test results or imaging studies, discussing the critically ill patient's care with other medical staff or documenting critical care services in the medical record would be reported as critical care, even though it does not occur at the bedside. Also, when the patient is unable or lacks capacity to participate in discussions, time spent on the floor or unit with family members or surrogate decision makers obtaining a medical history, reviewing the patient's condition or prognosis, or discussing treatment or limitation(s) of treatment may be reported as critical care, provided that the conversation bears directly on the management of the patient.

Time spent in activities that occur outside of the unit or off the floor (eg, telephone calls whether taken at home, in the office, or elsewhere in the hospital) may not be reported as critical care since the physician is not immediately available to the patient. Time spent in activities that do not directly contribute to the treatment of the patient may not be reported as critical care, even if they are performed in the critical care unit (eg, participation in administrative meetings or telephone calls to discuss other patients). Time spent performing separately reportable procedures or services should not be included in the time reported as critical care time. No physician may report remote real-time interactive video-conferenced critical care services (0188T, 0189T) for the period in which any physician reports 99291-99292.

Code 99291 is used to report the first 30-74 minutes of critical care on a given date. It should be used only once per date even if the time spent by the physician is not continuous on that date. Critical care of less than 30 minutes total duration on a given date should be reported with the appropriate E/M code.

Code 99292 is used to report additional block(s) of time, of up to 30 minutes each beyond the first 74 minutes. (See the following table.)

The following examples illustrate the correct reporting of critical care services:

Total Duration of Critical Care	Codes
less than 30 minutes	appropriate E/M codes
30-74 minutes (30 minutes - 1 hr. 14 min.)	99291 X 1
75-104 minutes (1 hr. 15 min. - 1 hr. 44 min.)	99291 X 1 AND 99292 X 1
105-134 minutes (1 hr. 45 min. - 2 hr. 14 min.)	99291 X 1 AND 99292 X 2
135 - 164 minutes (2 hr. 15 min. - 2 hr. 44 min.)	99291 X 1 AND 99292 X 3
165 - 194 minutes (2 hr. 45 min. - 3 hr. 14 min.)	99291 X 1 AND 99292 X 4
195 minutes or longer (3 hr. 15 min. - etc.)	99291 and 99292 as appropriate (see illustrated reporting examples above)

99291   **Critical care, evaluation and management** of the critically ill or critically injured patient; first 30-74 minutes

➥ CPT Assistant Summer 92:18, Summer 93:1, Summer 95:1, Jan 96:7, Apr 97:3, Dec 98:6, Nov 99:3, Apr 00:6, Sep 00:1, Dec 00:15, Jul 02:2, Feb 03:15, Oct 03:2, Aug 04:7, 10, Oct 04:14, May 05:1, Jul 05:15, Nov 05:10, Jul 06:4, Dec 06:13, Nov 07:5, Jan 09:5, Mar 09:3

+ 99292   each additional 30 minutes (List separately in addition to code for primary service)

➥ CPT Assistant Summer 92:18, Summer 93:1, Summer 95:1, Jan 96:7, Apr 97:3, Dec 98:6, Nov 99:3, Apr 00:6, Sep 00:1, Dec 00:15, Feb 03:15, Oct 03:2, Aug 04:10, Oct 14:14, Jul 05:15, Nov 05:10, Jul 06:4, Dec 06:13, Nov 07:5, Jan 09:5, Mar 09:3

(Use 99292 in conjunction with 99291)

(99293 has been deleted. To report, use 99471)

(99294 has been deleted. To report, use 99472)

(99295 has been deleted. To report, use 99468)

(99296 has been deleted. To report, use 99469)

(99298 has been deleted. To report, use 99478)

(99299 has been deleted. To report, use 99479)

(99300 has been deleted. To report, use 99480)

Nursing Facility Services

The following codes are used to report evaluation and management services to patients in nursing facilities (formerly called skilled nursing facilities [SNFs], intermediate care facilities [ICFs], or long-term care facilities [LTCFs]).

These codes should also be used to report evaluation and management services provided to a patient in a psychiatric residential treatment center (a facility or a distinct part of a facility for psychiatric care, which provides a 24-hour therapeutically planned and professionally staffed group living and learning environment). If procedures such as medical psychotherapy are provided in addition to evaluation and management services, these should be reported in addition to the evaluation and management services provided.

Nursing facilities that provide convalescent, rehabilitative, or long term care are required to conduct comprehensive, accurate, standardized, and reproducible assessments of each resident's functional capacity using a Resident Assessment Instrument (RAI). All RAIs include the Minimum Data Set (MDS), Resident Assessment Protocols (RAPs), and utilization guidelines. The MDS is the primary screening and assessment tool; the RAPs trigger the identification of potential problems and provide guidelines for follow-up assessments.

Physicians have a central role in assuring that all residents receive thorough assessments and that medical plans of care are instituted or revised to enhance or maintain the residents' physical and psychosocial functioning. This role includes providing input in the development of the MDS and a multi-disciplinary plan of care, as required by regulations pertaining to the care of nursing facility residents.

Two major subcategories of nursing facility services are recognized: Initial Nursing Facility Care and Subsequent Nursing Facility Care. Both subcategories apply to new or established patients.

For definitions of key components and commonly used terms, please see **Evaluation and Management Services Guidelines.**

(For care plan oversight services provided to nursing facility residents, see 99379-99380)

Initial Nursing Facility Care

New or Established Patient

When the patient is admitted to the nursing facility in the course of an encounter in another site of service (eg, hospital emergency department, physician's office), all evaluation and management services provided by that physician in conjunction with that admission are considered part of the initial nursing facility care when performed on the same date as the admission or readmission. The nursing facility care level of service reported by the admitting physician should include the services related to the admission he/she provided in the other sites of service as well as in the nursing facility setting.

Hospital discharge or observation discharge services performed on the same date of nursing facility admission or readmission may be reported separately. For a patient discharged from inpatient status on the same date of nursing facility admission or readmission, the hospital discharge services should be reported with codes 99238, 99239 as appropriate. For a patient discharged from observation status on the same date of nursing facility admission or readmission, the observation care discharge services should be reported with code 99217. For a patient admitted and discharged from observation or inpatient status on the same date, see codes 99234-99236.

(For nursing facility care discharge, see 99315, 99316)

▲ 99304 Initial nursing facility care, per day, for the evaluation and management of a patient, which requires these 3 key components:

- A detailed or comprehensive history;
- A detailed or comprehensive examination; and
- Medical decision making that is straightforward or of low complexity.

Counseling and/or coordination of care with other providers or agencies are provided consistent with the nature of the problem(s) and the patient's and/or family's needs.

Usually, the problem(s) requiring admission are of low severity. Physicians typically spend 25 minutes at the bedside and on the patient's facility floor or unit.
➔ CPT Changes: An Insider's View 2006, 2008, 2010

▲ 99305 Initial nursing facility care, per day, for the evaluation and management of a patient, which requires these 3 key components:

- A comprehensive history;
- A comprehensive examination; and
- Medical decision making of moderate complexity.

Counseling and/or coordination of care with other providers or agencies are provided consistent with the nature of the problem(s) and the patient's and/or family's needs.

Usually, the problem(s) requiring admission are of moderate severity. Physicians typically spend 35 minutes at the bedside and on the patient's facility floor or unit.
➔ CPT Changes: An Insider's View 2006, 2008, 2010

▲ 99306 Initial nursing facility care, per day, for the evaluation and management of a patient, which requires these 3 key components:

- A comprehensive history;
- A comprehensive examination; and
- Medical decision making of high complexity.

Counseling and/or coordination of care with other providers or agencies are provided consistent with the nature of the problem(s) and the patient's and/or family's needs.

Usually, the problem(s) requiring admission are of high severity. Physicians typically spend 45 minutes at the bedside and on the patient's facility floor or unit.
➔ CPT Changes: An Insider's View 2006, 2008, 2010

Subsequent Nursing Facility Care

All levels of subsequent nursing facility care include reviewing the medical record and reviewing the results of diagnostic studies and changes in the patient's status (ie, changes in history, physical condition, and response to management) since the last assessment by the physician.

▲ 99307 Subsequent nursing facility care, per day, for the evaluation and management of a patient, which requires at least 2 of these 3 key components:

- A problem focused interval history;
- A problem focused examination;
- Straightforward medical decision making.

Counseling and/or coordination of care with other providers or agencies are provided consistent with the nature of the problem(s) and the patient's and/or family's needs.

Usually, the patient is stable, recovering, or improving. Physicians typically spend 10 minutes at the bedside and on the patient's facility floor or unit.
➔ CPT Assistant May 06:16, May 06:1, Jun 06:1, Jul 06:19, Mar 07:9, Jul 07:1; CPT Changes: An Insider's View 2006, 2008, 2010

▲ 99308 Subsequent nursing facility care, per day, for the evaluation and management of a patient, which requires at least 2 of these 3 key components:

- An expanded problem focused interval history;
- An expanded problem focused examination;
- Medical decision making of low complexity.

Counseling and/or coordination of care with other providers or agencies are provided consistent with the nature of the problem(s) and the patient's and/or family's needs.

Usually, the patient is responding inadequately to therapy or has developed a minor complication. Physicians typically spend 15 minutes at the bedside and on the patient's facility floor or unit.

➲ *CPT Assistant* May 06:16, May 06:1, Jun 06:1, Jul 06:19, Mar 07:9, Jul 07:1; *CPT Changes: An Insider's View* 2006, 2008, 2010

▲ 99309   Subsequent nursing facility care, per day, for the evaluation and management of a patient, which requires at least 2 of these 3 key components:

■ **A detailed interval history;**

■ **A detailed examination;**

■ **Medical decision making of moderate complexity.**

Counseling and/or coordination of care with other providers or agencies are provided consistent with the nature of the problem(s) and the patient's and/or family's needs.

Usually, the patient has developed a significant complication or a significant new problem. Physicians typically spend 25 minutes at the bedside and on the patient's facility floor or unit.

➲ *CPT Assistant* May 06:16, May 06:1, Jun 06:1, Jul 06:19, Mar 07:9, Jul 07:1; *CPT Changes: An Insider's View* 2006, 2008, 2010

▲ 99310   Subsequent nursing facility care, per day, for the evaluation and management of a patient, which requires at least 2 of these 3 key components:

■ **A comprehensive interval history;**

■ **A comprehensive examination;**

■ **Medical decision making of high complexity.**

Counseling and/or coordination of care with other providers or agencies are provided consistent with the nature of the problem(s) and the patient's and/or family's needs.

The patient may be unstable or may have developed a significant new problem requiring immediate physician attention. Physicians typically spend 35 minutes at the bedside and on the patient's facility floor or unit.

➲ *CPT Assistant* May 06:16, May 06:1, Jun 06:1, Jul 06:19, Mar 07:9, Jul 07:1; *CPT Changes: An Insider's View* 2006, 2008, 2010

Nursing Facility Discharge Services

The nursing facility discharge day management codes are to be used to report the total duration of time spent by a physician for the final nursing facility discharge of a patient. The codes include, as appropriate, final examination of the patient, discussion of the nursing facility stay, even if the time spent by the physician on

that date is not continuous. Instructions are given for continuing care to all relevant caregivers, and preparation of discharge records, prescriptions and referral forms.

99315   Nursing facility discharge day management; 30 minutes or less

➲ *CPT Assistant* Nov 97:5-6, Sep 98:5, May 02:19, Nov 02:11, May 05:1

99316   more than 30 minutes

➲ *CPT Assistant* Nov 97:5-6, Sep 98:5, May 02:19, Nov 02:11

Other Nursing Facility Services

▲ 99318   Evaluation and management of a patient involving an annual nursing facility assessment, which requires these 3 key components:

■ **A detailed interval history;**

■ **A comprehensive examination; and**

■ **Medical decision making that is of low to moderate complexity.**

Counseling and/or coordination of care with other providers or agencies are provided consistent with the nature of the problem(s) and the patient's and/or family's needs.

Usually, the patient is stable, recovering, or improving. Physicians typically spend 30 minutes at the bedside and on the patient's facility floor or unit.

➲ *CPT Changes: An Insider's View* 2006, 2008, 2010

(Do not report 99318 on the same date of service as nursing facility services codes 99304-99316)

Domiciliary, Rest Home (eg, Boarding Home), or Custodial Care Services

The following codes are used to report evaluation and management services in a facility which provides room, board and other personal assistance services, generally on a long-term basis. They also are used to report evaluation and management services in an assisted living facility.

The facility's services do not include a medical component.

For definitions of key components and commonly used terms, please see **Evaluation and Management Services Guidelines**.

(For care plan oversight services provided to a patient in a domiciliary facility under the care of a home health agency, see 99374-99375)

(For care plan oversight services provided to a patient in a domiciliary facility under the individual supervision of a physician, see 99339, 99340)

New Patient

99324   Domiciliary or rest home visit for the evaluation and management of a new patient, which requires these 3 key components:

- ■ **A problem focused history;**
- ■ **A problem focused examination; and**
- ■ **Straightforward medical decision making.**

Counseling and/or coordination of care with other providers or agencies are provided consistent with the nature of the problem(s) and the patient's and/or family's needs.

Usually, the presenting problem(s) are of low severity. Physicians typically spend 20 minutes with the patient and/or family or caregiver.

➡ *CPT Assistant* Jan 06:1, Jun 06:1; *CPT Changes: An Insider's View* 2006

99325   Domiciliary or rest home visit for the evaluation and management of a new patient, which requires these 3 key components:

- ■ **An expanded problem focused history;**
- ■ **An expanded problem focused examination; and**
- ■ **Medical decision making of low complexity.**

Counseling and/or coordination of care with other providers or agencies are provided consistent with the nature of the problem(s) and the patient's and/or family's needs.

Usually, the presenting problem(s) are of moderate severity. Physicians typically spend 30 minutes with the patient and/or family or caregiver.

➡ *CPT Assistant* Jan 06:1, Jun 06:1; *CPT Changes: An Insider's View* 2006

99326   Domiciliary or rest home visit for the evaluation and management of a new patient, which requires these 3 key components:

- ■ **A detailed history;**
- ■ **A detailed examination; and**
- ■ **Medical decision making of moderate complexity.**

Counseling and/or coordination of care with other providers or agencies are provided consistent with the nature of the problem(s) and the patient's and/or family's needs.

Usually, the presenting problem(s) are of moderate to high severity. Physicians typically spend 45 minutes with the patient and/or family or caregiver.

➡ *CPT Assistant* Jan 06:1, Jun 06:1; *CPT Changes: An Insider's View* 2006

99327   Domiciliary or rest home visit for the evaluation and management of a new patient, which requires these 3 key components:

- ■ **A comprehensive history;**
- ■ **A comprehensive examination; and**
- ■ **Medical decision making of moderate complexity.**

Counseling and/or coordination of care with other providers or agencies are provided consistent with the nature of the problem(s) and the patient's and/or family's needs.

Usually, the presenting problem(s) are of high severity. Physicians typically spend 60 minutes with the patient and/or family or caregiver.

➡ *CPT Assistant* Jan 06:1, Jun 06:1; *CPT Changes: An Insider's View* 2006

99328   Domiciliary or rest home visit for the evaluation and management of a new patient, which requires these 3 key components:

- ■ **A comprehensive history;**
- ■ **A comprehensive examination; and**
- ■ **Medical decision making of high complexity.**

Counseling and/or coordination of care with other providers or agencies are provided consistent with the nature of the problem(s) and the patient's and/or family's needs.

Usually, the patient is unstable or has developed a significant new problem requiring immediate physician attention. Physicians typically spend 75 minutes with the patient and/or family or caregiver.

➡ *CPT Assistant* Jan 06:1, Jun 06:1; *CPT Changes: An Insider's View* 2006

Established Patient

99334   Domiciliary or rest home visit for the evaluation and management of an established patient, which requires at least 2 of these 3 key components:

- ■ **A problem focused interval history;**
- ■ **A problem focused examination;**
- ■ **Straightforward medical decision making.**

Counseling and/or coordination of care with other providers or agencies are provided consistent with the nature of the problem(s) and the patient's and/or family's needs.

Usually, the presenting problem(s) are self-limited or minor. Physicians typically spend 15 minutes with the patient and/or family or caregiver.

➡ *CPT Assistant* Jan 06:1, Jun 06:1, Jul 07:1; *CPT Changes: An Insider's View* 2006

99335   Domiciliary or rest home visit for the evaluation and management of an established patient, which requires at least 2 of these 3 key components:

- ■ **An expanded problem focused interval history;**
- ■ **An expanded problem focused examination;**
- ■ **Medical decision making of low complexity.**

Counseling and/or coordination of care with other providers or agencies are provided consistent with the nature of the problem(s) and the patient's and/or family's needs.

Usually, the presenting problem(s) are of low to moderate severity. Physicians typically spend 25 minutes with the patient and/or family or caregiver.

➜ *CPT Assistant* Jan 06:1, Jun 06:1, Jul 07:1; *CPT Changes: An Insider's View* 2006

99336 Domiciliary or rest home visit for the evaluation and management of an established patient, which requires at least 2 of these 3 key components:

- **A detailed interval history;**
- **A detailed examination;**
- **Medical decision making of moderate complexity.**

Counseling and/or coordination of care with other providers or agencies are provided consistent with the nature of the problem(s) and the patient's and/or family's needs.

Usually, the presenting problem(s) are of moderate to high severity. Physicians typically spend 40 minutes with the patient and/or family or caregiver.

➜ *CPT Assistant* Jan 06:1, Jun 06:1, Jul 07:1; *CPT Changes: An Insider's View* 2006

99337 Domiciliary or rest home visit for the evaluation and management of an established patient, which requires at least 2 of these 3 key components:

- **A comprehensive interval history;**
- **A comprehensive examination;**
- **Medical decision making of moderate to high complexity.**

Counseling and/or coordination of care with other providers or agencies are provided consistent with the nature of the problem(s) and the patient's and/or family's needs.

Usually, the presenting problem(s) are of moderate to high severity. The patient may be unstable or may have developed a significant new problem requiring immediate physician attention. Physicians typically spend 60 minutes with the patient and/or family or caregiver.

➜ *CPT Assistant* Jan 06:1, Jun 06:1, Jul 07:1; *CPT Changes: An Insider's View* 2006

Domiciliary, Rest Home (eg, Assisted Living Facility), or Home Care Plan Oversight Services

(For instructions on the use of 99339, 99340, see introductory notes for 99374-99380)

(For care plan oversight services for patients under the care of a home health agency, hospice, or nursing facility, see 99374-99380)

(Do not report 99339, 99340 for time reported with 98966-98969, 99441-99444)

99339 Individual physician supervision of a patient (patient not present) in home, domiciliary or rest home (eg, assisted living facility) requiring complex and multidisciplinary care modalities involving regular physician development and/or revision of care plans, review of subsequent reports of patient status, review of related laboratory and other studies, communication (including telephone calls) for purposes of assessment or care decisions with health care professional(s), family member(s), surrogate decision maker(s) (eg, legal guardian) and/or key caregiver(s) involved in patient's care, integration of new information into the medical treatment plan and/or adjustment of medical therapy, within a calendar month; 15-29 minutes

➜ *CPT Assistant* Jan 06:1, Dec 06:4, Mar 07:11, Sep 08:3; *CPT Changes: An Insider's View* 2006

99340 30 minutes or more

➜ *CPT Assistant* Jan 06:1, Dec 06:4, Mar 07:11, Sep 08:3; *CPT Changes: An Insider's View* 2006

(Do not report 99339, 99340 for patients under the care of a home health agency, enrolled in a hospice program, or for nursing facility residents)

Home Services

The following codes are used to report evaluation and management services provided in a private residence.

For definitions of key components and commonly used terms, please see **Evaluation and Management Services Guidelines.**

(For care plan oversight services provided to a patient in the home under the care of a home health agency, see 99374-99375)

(For care plan oversight services provided to a patient in the home under the individual supervision of a physician, see 99339, 99340)

New Patient

99341 **Home visit** for the evaluation and management of a new patient, which requires these 3 key components:

- **A problem focused history;**
- **A problem focused examination; and**
- **Straightforward medical decision making.**

Counseling and/or coordination of care with other providers or agencies are provided consistent with the nature of the problem(s) and the patient's and/or family's needs.

Usually, the presenting problem(s) are of low severity. Physicians typically spend 20 minutes face-to-face with the patient and/or family.

➲ *CPT Assistant* Winter 91:11, Spring 92:24, Summer 92:12, Spring 93:34, Spring 95:1, Jun 97:6, Nov 97:6-8, Oct 98:6, Oct 03:7, May 05:1, Jan 06:1

99342   **Home visit** for the evaluation and management of a new patient, which requires these 3 key components:

- **An expanded problem focused history;**
- **An expanded problem focused examination; and**
- **Medical decision making of low complexity.**

Counseling and/or coordination of care with other providers or agencies are provided consistent with the nature of the problem(s) and the patient's and/or family's needs.

Usually, the presenting problem(s) are of moderate severity. Physicians typically spend 30 minutes face-to-face with the patient and/or family.

➲ *CPT Assistant* Winter 91:11, Spring 92:24, Summer 92:12, Spring 93:34, Spring 95:1, Jun 97:6, Nov 97:6-8, Oct 98:6, Jan 06:1

99343   **Home visit** for the evaluation and management of a new patient, which requires these 3 key components:

- **A detailed history;**
- **A detailed examination; and**
- **Medical decision making of moderate complexity.**

Counseling and/or coordination of care with other providers or agencies are provided consistent with the nature of the problem(s) and the patient's and/or family's needs.

Usually, the presenting problem(s) are of moderate to high severity. Physicians typically spend 45 minutes face-to-face with the patient and/or family.

➲ *CPT Assistant* Winter 91:11, Spring 92:24, Summer 92:12, Spring 93:34, Spring 95:1, Jun 97:6, Nov 97:6-8, Oct 98:6, Jan 06:1

99344   **Home visit** for the evaluation and management of a new patient, which requires these 3 key components:

- **A comprehensive history;**
- **A comprehensive examination; and**
- **Medical decision making of moderate complexity.**

Counseling and/or coordination of care with other providers or agencies are provided consistent with the nature of the problem(s) and the patient's and/or family's needs.

Usually, the presenting problem(s) are of high severity. Physicians typically spend 60 minutes face-to-face with the patient and/or family.

➲ *CPT Assistant* Nov 97:6-8, Oct 98:6, Jan 06:1

99345   **Home visit** for the evaluation and management of a new patient, which requires these 3 key components:

- **A comprehensive history;**
- **A comprehensive examination; and**
- **Medical decision making of high complexity.**

Counseling and/or coordination of care with other providers or agencies are provided consistent with the nature of the problem(s) and the patient's and/or family's needs.

Usually, the patient is unstable or has developed a significant new problem requiring immediate physician attention. Physicians typically spend 75 minutes face-to-face with the patient and/or family.

➲ *CPT Assistant* Nov 97:6-8, Oct 98:6, Jan 06:1

Established Patient

99347   **Home visit** for the evaluation and management of an established patient, which requires at least 2 of these 3 key components:

- **A problem focused interval history;**
- **A problem focused examination;**
- **Straightforward medical decision making.**

Counseling and/or coordination of care with other providers or agencies are provided consistent with the nature of the problem(s) and the patient's and/or family's needs.

Usually, the presenting problem(s) are self limited or minor. Physicians typically spend 15 minutes face-to-face with the patient and/or family.

➲ *CPT Assistant* Nov 97:6-8, Oct 98:6, May 05:1, Jan 06:1, Jul 07:1

99348   **Home visit** for the evaluation and management of an established patient, which requires at least 2 of these 3 key components:

- **An expanded problem focused interval history;**
- **An expanded problem focused examination;**
- **Medical decision making of low complexity.**

Counseling and/or coordination of care with other providers or agencies are provided consistent with the nature of the problem(s) and the patient's and/or family's needs.

Usually, the presenting problem(s) are of low to moderate severity. Physicians typically spend 25 minutes face-to-face with the patient and/or family.

➲ *CPT Assistant* Nov 97:6-8, Oct 98:6, Jan 06:1, Jul 07:1

99349   **Home visit** for the evaluation and management of an established patient, which requires at least 2 of these 3 key components:

- **A detailed interval history;**
- **A detailed examination;**
- **Medical decision making of moderate complexity.**

Counseling and/or coordination of care with other providers or agencies are provided consistent with the nature of the problem(s) and the patient's and/or family's needs.

Usually, the presenting problem(s) are moderate to high severity. Physicians typically spend 40 minutes face-to-face with the patient and/or family.

→ *CPT Assistant* Nov 97:6-8, Oct 98:6, Jan 06:1, Jul 07:1

99350   **Home visit** for the evaluation and management of an established patient, which requires at least 2 of these 3 key components:

- **A comprehensive interval history;**
- **A comprehensive examination;**
- **Medical decision making of moderate to high complexity.**

Counseling and/or coordination of care with other providers or agencies are provided consistent with the nature of the problem(s) and the patient's and/or family's needs.

Usually, the presenting problem(s) are of moderate to high severity. The patient may be unstable or may have developed a significant new problem requiring immediate physician attention. Physicians typically spend 60 minutes face-to-face with the patient and/or family.

→ *CPT Assistant* Nov 97:6-8, Oct 98:6, Oct 03:7, Jan 06:1, Jul 07:1

Prolonged Services

Prolonged Physician Service With Direct (Face-To-Face) Patient Contact

Codes 99354-99357 are used when a physician provides prolonged service involving direct (face-to-face) patient contact that is beyond the usual service in either the inpatient or outpatient setting. This service is reported in addition to the designated evaluation and management services at any level and any other physician services provided at the same session as evaluation and management services. Appropriate codes should be selected for supplies provided or procedures performed in the care of the patient during this period.

Codes 99354-99355 are used to report the total duration of face-to-face time spent by a physician on a given date providing prolonged service, even if the time spent by the physician on that date is not continuous. Codes 99356-99357 are used to report the total duration of unit time spent by a physician on a given date providing prolonged service to a patient, even if the time spent by the physician on that date is not continuous.

Code 99354 or 99356 is used to report the first hour of prolonged service on a given date, depending on the place of service.

Either code should be used only once per date, even if the time spent by the physician is not continuous on that date. Prolonged service of less than 30 minutes total duration on a given date is not separately reported because the work involved is included in the total work of the evaluation and management codes.

Code 99355 or 99357 is used to report each additional 30 minutes beyond the first hour, depending on the place of service. Either code may also be used to report the final 15-30 minutes of prolonged service on a given date. Prolonged service of less than 15 minutes beyond the first hour or less than 15 minutes beyond the final 30 minutes is not reported separately.

The use of the time based add-on codes requires that the primary evaluation and management service have a typical or specified time published in the CPT codebook.

The following examples illustrate the correct reporting of prolonged physician service with direct patient contact in the office setting:

Total Duration of Prolonged Services	Code(s)
less than 30 minutes (less than 30 minutes)	Not reported separately
30-74 minutes (30 minutes - 1 hr. 14 min.)	99354 X 1
75-104 minutes (1 hr. 15 min. - 1 hr. 44 min.)	99354 X 1 AND 99355 X 1
105 or more (1 hr. 45 min. or more) 30 minutes	99354 X 1 AND 99355 X 2 or more for each additional

+ **99354**   Prolonged physician service in the office or other outpatient setting requiring direct (face-to-face) patient contact beyond the usual service; first hour (List separately in addition to code for office or other outpatient **Evaluation and Management** service)

→ *CPT Assistant* Spring 94:30, 32, May 97:3, Sep 98:5, Sep 00:2, Jul 01:2, May 05:1, Nov 05:10, Jun 08:12, Sep 08:3; *CPT Changes: An Insider's View* 2009

(Use 99354 in conjunction with 99201-99215, 99241-99245, 99324-99337, 99341-99350, 90809, 90815)

+ **99355**   each additional 30 minutes (List separately in addition to code for prolonged physician service)

→ *CPT Assistant* Spring 94:30, 32, May 97:3, Sep 98:5, Sep 00:2, Jul 01:2, Nov 05:10, Jun 08:12, Sep 08:3; *CPT Changes: An Insider's View* 2009

(Use 99355 in conjunction with 99354)

+ **99356**   Prolonged physician service in the inpatient setting, requiring unit/floor time beyond the usual service; first hour (List separately in addition to code for inpatient **Evaluation and Management** service)

➤ *CPT Assistant* Spring 94:30, 32, Apr 97:3, May 97:3, Sep 98:5, Sep 00:2, Jul 01:2, Nov 05:10, Jun 08:12, Sep 08:3; *CPT Changes: An Insider's View* 2009

(Use 99356 in conjunction with 99221-99233, 99251-99255, 99304-99310, 90822, 90829)

+ 99357   each additional 30 minutes (List separately in addition to code for prolonged physician service)

➤ *CPT Assistant* Spring 94:34, Apr 97:3, May 97:3, Sep 98:5, Sep 00:2, Jul 01:2, Nov 05:10, Jun 08:12, Sep 08:3; *CPT Changes: An Insider's View* 2009

(Use 99357 in conjunction with 99356)

Prolonged Physician Service Without Direct (Face-To-Face) Patient Contact

►Codes 99358 and 99359 are used when a physician provides prolonged service not involving direct (face-to-face) care that is beyond the usual non-face-to-face component of physician service time.

This service is to be reported in relation to other physician services, including evaluation and management services at any level. This prolonged service may be reported on a different date than the primary service to which it is related. For example, extensive record review may relate to a previous evaluation and management service performed earlier and commences upon receipt of past records. However, it must relate to a service or patient where direct (face-to-face) patient care has occurred or will occur and relate to ongoing patient management. A typical time for the primary service need not be established within CPT code set.

Codes 99358 and 99359 are used to report the total duration of non-face-to-face time spent by a physician on a given date providing prolonged service, even if the time spent by the physician on that date is not continuous. Code 99358 is used to report the first hour of prolonged service on a given date regardless of the place of service. It should be used only once per date.◀

Prolonged service of less than 30 minutes total duration on a given date is not separately reported.

Code 99359 is used to report each additional 30 minutes beyond the first hour regardless of the place of service. It may also be used to report the final 15 to 30 minutes of prolonged service on a given date.

Prolonged service of less than 15 minutes beyond the first hour or less than 15 minutes beyond the final 30 minutes is not reported separately.

►Do not report 99358-99359 for time spent in medical team conferences, on-line medical evaluations, care plan oversight services, anticoagulation management, or other non-face-to-face services that have more specific codes and no upper time limit in the CPT code set. Codes 99358-99359 may be reported when related to other

non-face-to-face services codes that have a published maximum time (eg, telephone services).◀

▲ **99358**   **Prolonged evaluation and management service** before and/or after direct (face-to-face) patient care; first hour

➤ *CPT Assistant* Spring 94:34, Nov 98:3, Sep 00:3, Nov 05:10, Jun 08:12, Sep 08:3; *CPT Changes: An Insider's View* 2010

+▲ 99359   each additional 30 minutes (List separately in addition to code for prolonged physician service)

➤ *CPT Assistant* Spring 94:34, Sep 00:3, Nov 05:10, Jun 08:12, Sep 08:3; *CPT Changes: An Insider's View* 2010

(Use 99359 in conjunction with 99358)

Physician Standby Services

Code 99360 is used to report physician standby service that is requested by another physician and that involves prolonged physician attendance without direct (face-to-face) patient contact. The physician may not be providing care or services to other patients during this period. This code is not used to report time spent proctoring another physician. It is also not used if the period of standby ends with the performance of a procedure subject to a "surgical" package by the physician who was on standby.

Code 99360 is used to report the total duration of time spent by a physician on a given date on standby. Standby service of less than 30 minutes total duration on a given date is not reported separately.

Second and subsequent periods of standby beyond the first 30 minutes may be reported only if a full 30 minutes of standby was provided for each unit of service reported.

99360   **Physician standby service,** requiring prolonged physician attendance, each 30 minutes (eg, operative standby, standby for frozen section, for cesarean/high risk delivery, for monitoring EEG)

➤ *CPT Assistant* Spring 94:32, Apr 97:10, Aug 97:18, Nov 97:8, Nov 99:5-6, Aug 00:3, Sep 00:3, May 05:1, Nov 05:10, Nov 06:23, Mar 08:14

(For hospital mandated on call services, see 99026, 99027)

(99360 may be reported in addition to 99460, 99465 as appropriate)

(Do not report 99360 in conjunction with 99464)

Case Management Services

Case management is a process in which a physician or another qualified health care professional is responsible for direct care of a patient and, additionally, for coordinating, managing access to, initiating, and/or supervising other health care services needed by the patient.

(99361, 99362 have been deleted. To report, see 99366-99368)

Anticoagulant Management

Anticoagulant services are intended to describe the outpatient management of warfarin therapy, including ordering, review, and interpretation of International Normalized Ratio (INR) testing, communication with patient, and dosage adjustments as appropriate.

When reporting these services, the work of anticoagulant management may not be used as a basis for reporting an evaluation and management (E/M) service or care plan oversight time during the reporting period. Do not report these services with 98966-98969, 99441-99444 when telephone or on-line services address anticoagulation with warfarin management. If a significant, separately identifiable E/M service is performed, report the appropriate E/M service code using modifier 25.

These services are outpatient services only. When anticoagulation therapy is initiated or continued in the inpatient or observation setting, a new period begins after discharge and is reported with 99364. Do not report 99363-99364 with 99217-99239, 99291-99292, 99304-99318, 99471-99480 or other code(s) for physician review, interpretation, and patient management of home INR testing for a patient with mechanical heart valve(s).

Any period less than 60 continuous outpatient days is not reported. If less than the specified minimum number of services per period are performed, do not report the anticoagulant management services (99363-99364).

99363 Anticoagulant management for an outpatient taking warfarin, physician review and interpretation of International Normalized Ratio (INR) testing, patient instructions, dosage adjustment (as needed), and ordering of additional tests; initial 90 days of therapy (must include a minimum of 8 INR measurements)
➜ CPT Assistant Sep 07:1; CPT Changes: An Insider's View 2007

99364 each subsequent 90 days of therapy (must include a minimum of 3 INR measurements)
➜ CPT Assistant Sep 07:1; CPT Changes: An Insider's View 2007

Medical Team Conferences

Medical team conferences include face-to-face participation by a minimum of three qualified health care professionals from different specialties or disciplines (each of whom provide direct care to the patient), with or without the presence of the patient, family member(s), community agencies, surrogate decision maker(s) (eg, legal guardian), and/or caregiver(s). The participants are actively involved in the development, revision, coordination, and implementation of health care services needed by the patient. Reporting participants shall have performed face-to-face evaluations or treatments of the patient, independent of any team conference, within the previous 60 days.

Physicians may report their time spent in a team conference with the patient and/or family present using evaluation and management (E/M) codes (and time as the key controlling factor for code selection when counseling and/or coordination of care dominates the service). These introductory guidelines do not apply to services reported using E/M codes (see E/M services guidelines). However, the physician must be directly involved with the patient, providing face-to-face services outside of the conference visit with other providers or agencies.

Reporting participants shall document their participation in the team conference as well as their contributed information and subsequent treatment recommendations.

No more than one individual from the same specialty may report 99366-99368 at the same encounter.

Individuals should not report 99366-99368 when their participation in the medical team conference is part of a facility or organizational service contractually provided by the organizational or facility provider.

The team conference starts at the beginning of the review of an individual patient and ends at the conclusion of the review. Time related to record keeping and report generation is not reported. The reporting participant shall be present for all time reported. The time reported is not limited to the time that the participant is communicating to the other team members or patient and/or family. Time reported for medical team conferences may not be used in the determination of time for other services such as care plan oversight (99374-99380), home, domiciliary, or rest home care plan oversight (99339-99340), prolonged services (99354-99359), psychotherapy, or any E/M service. For team conferences where the patient is present for any part of the duration of the conference, nonphysician qualified health care professionals report the team conference face-to-face code 99366.

Medical Team Conference, Direct (Face-to-Face) Contact With Patient and/or Family

99366 **Medical team conference** with interdisciplinary team of health care professionals, face-to-face with patient and/or family, 30 minutes or more, participation by nonphysician qualified health care professional
➜ CPT Changes: An Insider's View 2008

(Team conference services of less than 30 minutes duration are not reported separately)

(For team conference services by a physician with patient and/or family present, see Evaluation and Management services)

Medical Team Conference, Without Direct (Face-to-Face) Contact With Patient and/or Family

99367   **Medical team conference** with interdisciplinary team of health care professionals, patient and/or family not present, 30 minutes or more; participation by physician

➲ *CPT Changes: An Insider's View* 2008

99368   participation by nonphysician qualified health care professional

➲ *CPT Changes: An Insider's View* 2008

(Team conference services of less than 30 minutes duration are not reported separately)

(99371-99373 have been deleted. To report telephone evaluation and management services, see 99441-99443)

Care Plan Oversight Services

Care plan oversight services are reported separately from codes for office/outpatient, hospital, home, nursing facility or domiciliary, or non-face-to-face services. The complexity and approximate physician time of the care plan oversight services provided within a 30-day period determine code selection. Only one physician may report services for a given period of time, to reflect that physician's sole or predominant supervisory role with a particular patient. These codes should not be reported for supervision of patients in nursing facilities or under the care of home health agencies unless they require recurrent supervision of therapy.

The work involved in providing very low intensity or infrequent supervision services is included in the pre- and post-encounter work for home, office/outpatient and nursing facility or domiciliary visit codes.

(For care plan oversight services of patients in the home, domiciliary, or rest home (eg, assisted living facility) under the individual supervision of a physician, see 99339, 99340)

(Do not report 99374-99380 for time reported with 98966-98969, 99441-99444)

99374   **Physician supervision** of a patient under care of home health agency (patient not present) in home, domiciliary or equivalent environment (eg, Alzheimer's facility) requiring complex and multidisciplinary care modalities involving regular physician development and/or revision of care plans, review of subsequent reports of patient status, review of related laboratory and other studies, communication (including telephone calls) for purposes of assessment or care decisions with health care professional(s), family member(s), surrogate decision maker(s) (eg, legal guardian) and/or key caregiver(s) involved in patient's care, integration of new information into the medical treatment plan and/or adjustment of medical therapy, within a calendar month; 15-29 minutes

➲ *CPT Assistant* Summer 94:9, Nov 97:8-9, May 05:1, Dec 06:4, Mar 07:11, Mar 08:6, Sep 08:3; *CPT Changes: An Insider's View* 2002

99375   30 minutes or more

➲ *CPT Assistant* Summer 94:9, Nov 97:8-9, Dec 06:4, Mar 07:11, Mar 08:6, Sep 08:3

99377   **Physician supervision** of a hospice patient (patient not present) requiring complex and multidisciplinary care modalities involving regular physician development and/or revision of care plans, review of subsequent reports of patient status, review of related laboratory and other studies, communication (including telephone calls) for purposes of assessment or care decisions with health care professional(s), family member(s), surrogate decision maker(s) (eg, legal guardian) and/or key caregiver(s) involved in patient's care, integration of new information into the medical treatment plan and/or adjustment of medical therapy, within a calendar month; 15-29 minutes

➲ *CPT Assistant* Nov 97:8-9, Dec 06:4, Mar 07:11, Sep 08:3; *CPT Changes: An Insider's View* 2001, 2002

99378   30 minutes or more

➲ *CPT Assistant* Nov 97:8-9, Dec 06:4, Mar 07:11, Mar 08:6, Sep 08:3

99379   **Physician supervision** of a nursing facility patient (patient not present) requiring complex and multidisciplinary care modalities involving regular physician development and/or revision of care plans, review of subsequent reports of patient status, review of related laboratory and other studies, communication (including telephone calls) for purposes of assessment or care decisions with health care professional(s), family member(s), surrogate decision maker(s) (eg, legal guardian) and/or key caregiver(s) involved in patient's care, integration of new information into the medical treatment plan and/or adjustment of medical therapy, within a calendar month; 15-29 minutes

➲ *CPT Assistant* Dec 06:4, Mar 08:6, Sep 08:3; *CPT Changes: An Insider's View* 2002

99380   30 minutes or more

➲ *CPT Assistant* Nov 97:8-9, Dec 06:4, Mar 08:6, Sep 08:3

Preventive Medicine Services

The following codes are used to report the preventive medicine evaluation and management of infants, children, adolescents, and adults.

The extent and focus of the services will largely depend on the age of the patient.

If an abnormality is encountered or a preexisting problem is addressed in the process of performing this preventive medicine evaluation and management service, and if the problem or abnormality is significant enough to require additional work to perform the key components of a problem-oriented E/M service, then the appropriate

Office/Outpatient code 99201-99215 should also be reported. Modifier 25 should be added to the Office/Outpatient code to indicate that a significant, separately identifiable evaluation and management service was provided by the same physician on the same day as the preventive medicine service. The appropriate preventive medicine service is additionally reported.

An insignificant or trivial problem/abnormality that is encountered in the process of performing the preventive medicine evaluation and management service and which does not require additional work and the performance of the key components of a problem-oriented E/M service should not be reported.

The "comprehensive" nature of the Preventive Medicine Services codes 99381-99397 reflects an age and gender appropriate history/exam and is **not** synonymous with the "comprehensive" examination required in Evaluation and Management codes 99201-99350.

Codes 99381-99397 include counseling/anticipatory guidance/risk factor reduction interventions which are provided at the time of the initial or periodic comprehensive preventive medicine examination. (Refer to codes 99401-99412 for reporting those counseling/anticipatory guidance/risk factor reduction interventions that are provided at an encounter separate from the preventive medicine examination.)

Vaccine/toxoid products, immunization administrations, ancillary studies involving laboratory, radiology, other procedures, or screening tests (eg, vision, hearing, developmental) identified with a specific CPT code are reported separately. For immunization administration and vaccine risk/benefit counseling, see 90465-90474. For vaccine/toxoid products, see 90476-90749.

New Patient

99381 **Initial comprehensive preventive medicine** evaluation and management of an individual including an age and gender appropriate history, examination, counseling/anticipatory guidance/risk factor reduction interventions, and the ordering of laboratory/diagnostic procedures, new patient; infant (age younger than 1 year)

➲ *CPT Assistant* Winter 91:11, Spring 93:14, 34, Spring 95:1, Aug 97:1, Jul 98:9, Sep 98:5, Nov 98:3-4, May 02:1, May 05:1, Aug 05:15, Oct 06:15, Mar 09:3; *CPT Changes: An Insider's View* 2002, 2009

99382 early childhood (age 1 through 4 years)

➲ *CPT Assistant* Winter 91:11, Spring 93:14, 34, Spring 95:1, Aug 97:1, Jul 98:9, Sep 98:5, Nov 98:3-4, May 02:1, Aug 05:15, Oct 06:15; *CPT Changes: An Insider's View* 2009

99383 late childhood (age 5 through 11 years)

➲ *CPT Assistant* Winter 91:11, Spring 93:14, 34, Spring 95:1, Aug 97:1, Jul 98:9, Sep 98:5, Nov 98:3-4, May 02:1, Aug 05:15, Oct 06:15; *CPT Changes: An Insider's View* 2009

99384 adolescent (age 12 through 17 years)

➲ *CPT Assistant* Winter 91:11, Spring 93:14, 34, Spring 95:1, Aug 97:1, Jul 98:9, Sep 98:5, Nov 98:3-4, May 02:1, Aug 05:15, Oct 06:15; *CPT Changes: An Insider's View* 2009

99385 18-39 years

➲ *CPT Assistant* Winter 91:11, Spring 93:14, 34, Spring 95:1, Aug 97:1, Jul 98:9, Sep 98:5, Nov 98:3-4, May 02:1, Aug 05:15, Oct 06:15; *CPT Changes: An Insider's View* 2009

99386 40-64 years

➲ *CPT Assistant* Winter 91:11, Spring 93:14, 34, Spring 95:1, Aug 97:1, Jul 98:9, Sep 98:5, Nov 98:3-4, May 02:1, Aug 05:15, Oct 06:15; *CPT Changes: An Insider's View* 2009

99387 65 years and older

➲ *CPT Assistant* Winter 91:11, Spring 93:14, 34, Spring 95:1, Aug 97:1, Jul 98:9, Sep 98:5, Nov 98:3-4, May 02:1, Aug 05:15, Oct 06:15; *CPT Changes: An Insider's View* 2009

Established Patient

99391 **Periodic comprehensive preventive medicine** reevaluation and management of an individual including an age and gender appropriate history, examination, counseling/anticipatory guidance/risk factor reduction interventions, and the ordering of laboratory/diagnostic procedures, established patient; infant (age younger than 1 year)

➲ *CPT Assistant* Winter 91:11, Spring 93:14, 34, Spring 95:1, Aug 97:1, Jul 98:9, Sep 98:5, Nov 98:3-4, May 02:1, May 05:1, Aug 05:15, Oct 06:15, Mar 09:3; *CPT Changes: An Insider's View* 2002, 2009

99392 early childhood (age 1 through 4 years)

➲ *CPT Assistant* Winter 91:11, Spring 93:14, 34, Spring 95:1, Aug 97:1, Jul 98:9, Sep 98:5, Nov 98:3-4, May 02:1, Aug 05:15, Oct 06:15; *CPT Changes: An Insider's View* 2009

99393 late childhood (age 5 through 11 years)

➲ *CPT Assistant* Winter 91:11, Spring 93:14, 34, Spring 95:1, Aug 97:1, Jul 98:9, Sep 98:5, Nov 98:3-4, May 02:1, Aug 05:15, Oct 06:15; *CPT Changes: An Insider's View* 2009

99394 adolescent (age 12 through 17 years)

➲ *CPT Assistant* Winter 91:11, Spring 93:14, 34, Spring 95:1, Aug 97:1, Jul 98:9, Sep 98:5, Nov 98:3-4, May 02:1, Aug 05:15, Oct 06:15; *CPT Changes: An Insider's View* 2009

99395 18-39 years

➲ *CPT Assistant* Winter 91:11, Spring 93:14, 34, Spring 95:1, Aug 97:1, Jul 98:9, Sep 98:5, Nov 98:3-4, May 02:1, Aug 05:15, Oct 06:15, Mar 08:3; *CPT Changes: An Insider's View* 2009

99396 40-64 years

➲ *CPT Assistant* Winter 91:11, Spring 93:14, 34, Spring 95:1, Aug 97:1, Jul 98:9, Sep 98:5, Nov 98:3-4, May 02:1, Aug 05:15, Oct 06:15; *CPT Changes: An Insider's View* 2009

99397 65 years and older

➲ *CPT Assistant* Winter 91:11, Spring 93:14, 34, Spring 95:1, Aug 97:1, Jul 98:9, Sep 98:5, Nov 98:3-4, May 02:1, Aug 05:15, Oct 06:15; *CPT Changes: An Insider's View* 2009

Counseling Risk Factor Reduction and Behavior Change Intervention

New or Established Patient

These codes are used to report services provided face-to-face by a physician or other qualified health care professional for the purpose of promoting health and preventing illness or injury. They are distinct from evaluation and management (E/M) services that may be reported separately when performed. Risk factor reduction services are used for persons without a specific illness for which the counseling might otherwise be used as part of treatment.

Preventive medicine counseling and risk factor reduction interventions will vary with age and should address such issues as family problems, diet and exercise, substance use, sexual practices, injury prevention, dental health, and diagnostic and laboratory test results available at the time of the encounter.

Behavior change interventions are for persons who have a behavior that is often considered an illness itself, such as tobacco use and addiction, substance abuse/misuse, or obesity. Behavior change services may be reported when performed as part of the treatment of condition(s) related to or potentially exacerbated by the behavior or when performed to change the harmful behavior that has not yet resulted in illness. Any E/M services reported on the same day must be distinct, and time spent providing these services may not be used as a basis for the E/M code selection. Behavior change services involve specific validated interventions of assessing readiness for change and barriers to change, advising a change in behavior, assisting by providing specific suggested actions and motivational counseling, and arranging for services and follow-up.

For counseling groups of patients with symptoms or established illness, use 99078.

Health and Behavior Assessment/Intervention services (96150-96155) should not be reported on the same day.

Preventive Medicine, Individual Counseling

99401   **Preventive medicine counseling** and/or risk factor reduction intervention(s) provided to an individual (separate procedure); approximately 15 minutes
➲ *CPT Assistant* Aug 97:1, Jan 98:12, May 05:1, Aug 07:9

99402   approximately 30 minutes
➲ *CPT Assistant* Aug 97:1, Jan 98:12, May 05:1

99403   approximately 45 minutes
➲ *CPT Assistant* Aug 97:1, Jan 98:12, May 05:1

99404   approximately 60 minutes
➲ *CPT Assistant* Aug 97:1, Jan 98:12, May 05:1

Behavior Change Interventions, Individual

99406   Smoking and tobacco use cessation counseling visit; intermediate, greater than 3 minutes up to 10 minutes
➲ *CPT Assistant* Jan 08:1; *CPT Changes: An Insider's View* 2008

99407   intensive, greater than 10 minutes
➲ *CPT Assistant* Jan 08:1; *CPT Changes: An Insider's View* 2008

(Do not report 99407 in conjunction with 99406)

99408   Alcohol and/or substance (other than tobacco) abuse structured screening (eg, AUDIT, DAST), and brief intervention (SBI) services; 15 to 30 minutes
➲ *CPT Changes: An Insider's View* 2008

(Do not report services of less than 15 minutes with 99408)

99409   greater than 30 minutes
➲ *CPT Changes: An Insider's View* 2008

(Do not report 99409 in conjunction with 99408)

(Do not report 99408, 99409 in conjunction with 99420)

(Use 99408, 99409 only for initial screening and brief intervention)

Preventive Medicine, Group Counseling

99411   **Preventive medicine counseling** and/or risk factor reduction intervention(s) provided to individuals in a group setting (separate procedure); approximately 30 minutes
➲ *CPT Assistant* Aug 97:1, Jan 98:12, Sep 98:5, May 05:1

99412   approximately 60 minutes
➲ *CPT Assistant* Aug 97:1, Jan 98:12, Sep 98:5, May 05:1, Aug 07:9

Other Preventive Medicine Services

99420   **Administration and interpretation** of health risk assessment instrument (eg, health hazard appraisal)
➲ *CPT Assistant* May 05:1

99429   **Unlisted preventive** medicine service
➲ *CPT Assistant* Sep 98:5, May 05:1

(99431 has been deleted. To report, use 99460)

(99432 has been deleted. To report, use 99461)

(99433 has been deleted. To report, use 99462)

(99435 has been deleted. To report, use 99463)

(99436 has been deleted. To report, use 99464)

(99440 has been deleted. To report, use 99465)

Non-Face-to-Face Physician Services

Telephone Services

Telephone services are non-face-to-face evaluation and management (E/M) services provided by a physician to a patient using the telephone. These codes are used to report episodes of care by the physician initiated by an established patient or guardian of an established patient. If the telephone service ends with a decision to see the patient within 24 hours or next available urgent visit appointment, the code is not reported; rather the encounter is considered part of the preservice work of the subsequent E/M service, procedure, and visit. Likewise if the telephone call refers to an E/M service performed and reported by the physician within the previous seven days (either physician requested or unsolicited patient follow-up) or within the postoperative period of the previously completed procedure, then the service(s) are considered part of that previous E/M service or procedure. (Do not report 99441-99443 if reporting 99441-99444 performed in the previous seven days.)

(For telephone services provided by a qualified nonphysician health care professional, see 98966-98968)

99441   Telephone evaluation and management service provided by a physician to an established patient, parent, or guardian not originating from a related E/M service provided within the previous 7 days nor leading to an E/M service or procedure within the next 24 hours or soonest available appointment; 5-10 minutes of medical discussion
➔ *CPT Assistant* Mar 08:6; *CPT Changes: An Insider's View* 2008

99442   11-20 minutes of medical discussion
➔ *CPT Assistant* Mar 08:6; *CPT Changes: An Insider's View* 2008

99443   21-30 minutes of medical discussion
➔ *CPT Assistant* Mar 08:6; *CPT Changes: An Insider's View* 2008

(Do not report 99441-99443 when using 99339-99340, 99374-99380 for the same call[s])

(Do not report 99441-99443 for anticoagulation management when reporting 99363-99364)

On-Line Medical Evaluation

An on-line electronic medical evaluation is a non-face-to-face evaluation and management (E/M) service by a physician to a patient using Internet resources in response to a patient's on-line inquiry. Reportable services involve the physician's personal timely response to the patient's inquiry and must involve permanent storage (electronic or hard copy) of the encounter. This service is reported only once for the same episode of care during a seven-day period, although multiple physicians could report their

exchange with the same patient. If the on-line medical evaluation refers to an E/M service previously performed and reported by the physician within the previous seven days (either physician requested or unsolicited patient follow-up) or within the postoperative period of the previously completed procedure, then the service(s) are considered covered by the previous E/M service or procedure. A reportable service encompasses the sum of communication (eg, related telephone calls, prescription provision, laboratory orders) pertaining to the on-line patient encounter.

(For an on-line medical evaluation provided by a qualified nonphysician health care professional, use 98969)

99444   Online evaluation and management service provided by a physician to an established patient, guardian, or health care provider not originating from a related E/M service provided within the previous 7 days, using the Internet or similar electronic communications network
➔ *CPT Changes: An Insider's View* 2008

(Do not report 99444 when using 99339-99340, 99374-99380 for the same communication[s])

(Do not report 99444 for anticoagulation management when reporting 99363, 99364)

Special Evaluation and Management Services

The following codes are used to report evaluations performed to establish baseline information prior to life or disability insurance certificates being issued. This service is performed in the office or other setting, and applies to both new and established patients. When using these codes, no active management of the problem(s) is undertaken during the encounter.

If other evaluation and management services and/or procedures are performed on the same date, the appropriate E/M or procedure code(s) should be reported in addition to these codes.

Basic Life and/or Disability Evaluation Services

99450   **Basic life** and/or disability examination that includes:

- Measurement of height, weight, and blood pressure;
- Completion of a medical history following a life insurance pro forma;
- Collection of blood sample and/or urinalysis complying with "chain of custody" protocols; and
- Completion of necessary documentation/certificates.

➔ *CPT Assistant* Summer 95:14, Sep 98:5, May 05:1

Work Related or Medical Disability Evaluation Services

99455   **Work related** or medical disability examination by the treating physician that includes:

- **Completion of a medical history commensurate with the patient's condition;**
- **Performance of an examination commensurate with the patient's condition;**
- **Formulation of a diagnosis, assessment of capabilities and stability, and calculation of impairment;**
- **Development of future medical treatment plan; and**
- **Completion of necessary documentation/certificates and report.**

➔ *CPT Assistant* Summer 95:14, Sep 98:5, May 05:1

99456   **Work related** or medical disability examination by other than the treating physician that includes:

- **Completion of a medical history commensurate with the patient's condition;**
- **Performance of an examination commensurate with the patient's condition;**
- **Formulation of a diagnosis, assessment of capabilities and stability, and calculation of impairment;**
- **Development of future medical treatment plan; and**
- **Completion of necessary documentation/certificates and report.**

➔ *CPT Assistant* Summer 95:14, Sep 98:5

(Do not report 99455, 99456 in conjunction with 99080 for the completion of Workman's Compensation forms)

Newborn Care Services

The following codes are used to report the services provided to newborns (birth through the first 28 days) in several different settings. Use of the normal newborn codes is limited to the initial care of the newborn in the first days after birth prior to home discharge.

Evaluation and Management (E/M) services for the newborn include maternal and/or fetal and newborn history, newborn physical examination(s), ordering of diagnostic tests and treatments, meetings with the family, and documentation in the medical record.

When delivery room attendance services (99464) or delivery room resuscitation services (99465) are required, report these in addition to normal newborn services Evaluation and Management codes.

For E/M services provided to newborns who are other than normal, see codes for hospital inpatient services (99221-99233) and neonatal intensive and critical care services (99466-99469, 99477-99480). When normal

newborn services are provided by the same physician on the same date that the newborn later becomes ill and receives additional intensive or critical care services, report the appropriate E/M code with modifier 25 for these services in addition to the normal newborn code.

Procedures (eg, 54150, newborn circumcision) are not included with the normal newborn codes, and when performed, should be reported in addition to the newborn services.

When newborns are seen in follow-up after the date of discharge in the office or outpatient setting, see 99201-99215, 99381, 99391 as appropriate.

99460   Initial hospital or birthing center care, per day, for evaluation and management of normal newborn infant

➔ *CPT Changes: An Insider's View* 2009

99461   Initial care, per day, for evaluation and management of normal newborn infant seen in other than hospital or birthing center

➔ *CPT Changes: An Insider's View* 2009

99462   Subsequent hospital care, per day, for evaluation and management of normal newborn

➔ *CPT Changes: An Insider's View* 2009

99463   Initial hospital or birthing center care, per day, for evaluation and management of normal newborn infant admitted and discharged on the same date

➔ *CPT Changes: An Insider's View* 2009

(For newborn hospital discharge services provided on a date subsequent to the admission date, see 99238, 99239)

Delivery/Birthing Room Attendance and Resuscitation Services

99464   Attendance at delivery (when requested by the delivering physician) and initial stabilization of newborn

➔ *CPT Changes: An Insider's View* 2009

(99464 may be reported in conjunction with 99460, 99468, 99477)

(Do not report 99464 in conjunction with 99465)

99465   Delivery/birthing room resuscitation, provision of positive pressure ventilation and/or chest compressions in the presence of acute inadequate ventilation and/or cardiac output

➔ *CPT Changes: An Insider's View* 2009

►(99465 may be reported in conjunction with 99460, 99468, 99477)◄

(Do not report 99465 in conjunction with 99464)

(Procedures that are performed as a necessary part of the resuscitation [eg, intubation, vascular lines] are reported separately in addition to 99465. In order to report these procedures, they must be performed as a necessary component of the resuscitation and not as a convenience before admission to the neonatal intensive care unit)

Inpatient Neonatal Intensive Care Services and Pediatric and Neonatal Critical Care Services

Pediatric Critical Care Patient Transport

The following codes (99466, 99467) are used to report the physical attendance and direct face-to-face care by a physician during the interfacility transport of a critically ill or critically injured pediatric patient 24 months of age or younger. For the purpose of reporting codes 99466 and 99467, face-to-face care begins when the physician assumes primary responsibility of the pediatric patient at the referring hospital/facility, and ends when the receiving hospital/facility accepts responsibility for the pediatric patient's care. Only the time the physician spends in direct face-to-face contact with the patient during the transport should be reported. Pediatric patient transport services involving less than 30 minutes of face-to-face physician care should not be reported using codes 99466, 99467. Procedure(s) or service(s) performed by other members of the transporting team may not be reported by the supervising physician.

For the definition of the critically ill or critically injured pediatric patient and the list of services included in critical care, see the **Neonatal and Pediatric Critical Care Services** section. Any services performed, which are not listed, may be reported separately.

The direction of emergency care to transporting staff by a physician located in a hospital or other facility by two-way communication is not considered direct face-to-face care and should not be reported with 99466, 99467. Physician-directed emergency care through outside voice communication to transporting staff personnel is reported with 99288.

Emergency department services (99281-99285), initial hospital care (99221-99223), critical care (99291, 99292), initial date neonatal intensive (99477) or critical care (99468) are only reported after the patient has been admitted to the emergency department, the inpatient floor, or the critical care unit of the receiving facility. If inpatient critical care services are reported in the referring facility prior to transfer to the receiving hospital, use the critical care codes (99291, 99292).

Code 99466 is used to report the first 30 to 74 minutes of direct face-to-face time with the transport pediatric patient and should be reported only once on a given date. Code 99467 is used to report each additional 30 minutes provided on a given date. Face-to-face services of less than 30 minutes should not be reported with these codes.

99466   **Critical care** services delivered by a physician, face-to-face, during an interfacility transport of critically ill or critically injured pediatric patient, 24 months of age or younger; first 30-74 minutes of hands-on care during transport

    ➲ *CPT Changes: An Insider's View* 2009

+ 99467   each additional 30 minutes (List separately in addition to code for primary service)

    ➲ *CPT Changes: An Insider's View* 2009

(Use 99467 in conjunction with 99466)

(Critical care of less than 30 minutes total duration should be reported with the appropriate E/M code)

Inpatient Neonatal and Pediatric Critical Care

The same definitions for critical care services apply for the adult, child, and neonate.

Codes 99468, 99469 are used to report services provided by a physician directing the inpatient care of a critically ill or infant 28 days of age or younger. They represent care starting with the date of admission (99468) and subsequent day(s) (99469) that the neonate remains critical. These codes may be reported only by a single physician and only once per day, per patient.

The initial day neonatal critical care code (99468) can be used in addition to 99464 or 99465 as appropriate, when the physician is present for the delivery (99464) or resuscitation (99465) is required. Other procedures performed as a necessary part of the resuscitation (eg, endotracheal intubation [31500]) are also reported separately when performed as part of the pre-admission delivery room care. In order to report these procedures separately, they must be performed as a necessary component of the resuscitation and not simply as a convenience before admission to the neonatal intensive care unit.

Codes 99471-99476 are used to report services provided by a physician directing the inpatient care of a critically ill infant or young child from 29 days of postnatal age through five years of age. They represent care starting with the date of admission (99471, 99475) and subsequent day(s) (99472, 99476) the infant or child remains critical. These codes may be reported only by a single physician and only once per day, per patient in a given setting. Service for the critically ill or critically injured child older than five years of age would be reported with critical care codes (99291, 99292).

The pediatric and neonatal critical care codes include those procedures listed for the critical care codes (99291, 99292). In addition, the following procedures are also included (and not separately reported) in the pediatric and neonatal critical care service codes (99468-99472, 99475, 99476), the intensive care services codes (99477-99480), and the pediatric critical care patient transport codes (99466, 99467):

Invasive or non-invasive electronic monitoring of vital signs

Vascular access procedures

    Peripheral vessel catheterization (36000)

    Other arterial catheters (36140, 36620)

    Umbilical venous catheters (36510)

    Central vessel catheterization (36555)

    Vascular access procedures (36400, 36405, 36406)

    ►Vascular punctures (36420, 36600)◄

    Umbilical arterial catheters (36660)

Airway and ventilation management

    Endotracheal intubation (31500)

    Ventilatory management (94002-94004)

    Bedside pulmonary function testing (94375)

    Surfactant administration (94610)

    Continuous positive airway pressure (CPAP) (94660)

Monitoring or interpretation of blood gases or oxygen saturation (94760-94762)

Transfusion of blood components (36430, 36440)

Oral or nasogastric tube placement (43752)

Suprapubic bladder aspiration (51100)

Bladder catheterization (51701, 51702)

Lumbar puncture (62270)

Any services performed which are not listed above may be reported separately.

When a neonate or infant is not critically ill but requires intensive observation, frequent interventions, and other intensive care services, the Continuing Intensive Care Services codes (99477-99480) should be used to report these services.

To report critical care services provided in the outpatient setting (eg, emergency department or office) for neonates and pediatric patients of any age, see the Critical Care codes 99291, 99292. If the same physician provides critical care services for a neonatal or pediatric patient in both the outpatient and inpatient settings on the same day, report only the appropriate Neonatal or Pediatric Critical Care codes 99468-99476 for all critical care services provided on that day. Critical care services provided by a second physician of a different specialty not reporting a per-day neonatal or pediatric critical care code can be reported with 99291, 99292.

When critical care services are provided to neonates or pediatric patients less than five years of age at two separate institutions by a physician from a different group on the same date of service, the physician from the referring institution should report their critical care services with the critical care codes (99291, 99292) and the receiving institution should report the appropriate

global admission code (99468, 99471, 99475, 99476) for the same date of service.

Critical care services to a pediatric patient six years of age or older are reported with the critical care codes 99291, 99292.

Critical care services to a neonate or pediatric patient provided in an outpatient environment are reported with the critical care codes 99291, 99292.

Critical care services provided by a second physician of a different specialty not reporting a 24-hour global code can be reported with the critical care codes 99291, 99292.

No physician may report remote real-time videoconferenced critical care (0188T, 0189T) when neonatal or pediatric intensive or critical care services (99468-99476) are reported.

99468   **Initial inpatient neonatal critical care,** per day, for the evaluation and management of a critically ill neonate, 28 days of age or younger
    ➔ *CPT Changes: An Insider's View* 2009

99469   **Subsequent inpatient neonatal critical care,** per day, for the evaluation and management of a critically ill neonate, 28 days of age or younger
    ➔ *CPT Changes: An Insider's View* 2009

99471   **Initial inpatient pediatric critical care,** per day, for the evaluation and management of a critically ill infant or young child, 29 days through 24 months of age
    ➔ *CPT Changes: An Insider's View* 2009

99472   **Subsequent inpatient pediatric critical care,** per day, for the evaluation and management of a critically ill infant or young child, 29 days through 24 months of age
    ➔ *CPT Changes: An Insider's View* 2009

99475   **Initial inpatient pediatric critical care,** per day, for the evaluation and management of a critically ill infant or young child, 2 through 5 years of age
    ➔ *CPT Changes: An Insider's View* 2009

99476   **Subsequent inpatient pediatric critical care,** per day, for the evaluation and management of a critically ill infant or young child, 2 through 5 years of age
    ➔ *CPT Changes: An Insider's View* 2009

Initial and Continuing Intensive Care Services

Code 99477 represents the initial day of inpatient care for the child who is not critically ill but requires intensive observation, frequent interventions, and other intensive care services. Codes 99478-99480 are used to report subsequent day services provided by a physician directing the continuing intensive care of the low birth weight (LBW 1500-2500 grams) present body weight infant, very low birth weight (VLBW less than 1500 grams) present body weight infant, or normal (2501-5000 grams) present body weight newborn who does not meet the definition of critically ill but continues to require intensive observation, frequent interventions, and other intensive care services. These services are for infants and neonates who are not critically ill but continue to require intensive cardiac and respiratory monitoring, continuous and/or frequent vital sign monitoring, heat maintenance, enteral and/or parenteral nutritional adjustments, laboratory and oxygen monitoring, and constant observation by the health care team under direct physician supervision. Codes 99477-99480 may be reported by only one physician and only once per day, per patient. These codes include the same procedures that are outlined in the **Pediatric Critical Care Services** section and these services should not be separately reported.

For the subsequent care of the sick neonate younger than 28 days of age but more than 5000 grams who does not require intensive or critical care services, use codes 99231-99233.

99477 **Initial hospital care,** per day, for the evaluation and management of the neonate, 28 days of age or younger, who requires intensive observation, frequent interventions, and other intensive care services

➲ *CPT Assistant* Jan 08:8, Jul 08:10, Mar 09:3; *CPT Changes: An Insider's View* 2008

(For the initiation of inpatient care of the normal newborn, use 99460)

(For the initiation of care of the critically ill neonate, use 99468)

(For initiation of inpatient hospital care of the ill neonate not requiring intensive observation, frequent interventions, and other intensive care services, see 99221-99223)

99478 **Subsequent intensive care,** per day, for the evaluation and management of the recovering very low birth weight infant (present body weight less than 1500 grams)

➲ *CPT Changes: An Insider's View* 2009

99479 **Subsequent intensive care,** per day, for the evaluation and management of the recovering low birth weight infant (present body weight of 1500-2500 grams)

➲ *CPT Changes: An Insider's View* 2009

99480 **Subsequent intensive care,** per day, for the evaluation and management of the recovering infant (present body weight of 2501-5000 grams)

➲ *CPT Changes: An Insider's View* 2009

Other Evaluation and Management Services

99499 **Unlisted evaluation and management** service

➲ *CPT Assistant* Apr 96:11, Mar 05:11, May 05:1, Jan 06:46, Sep 06:8, Jan 07:30

Anesthesia Guidelines

Anesthesia

Anesthesia Guidelines

Services involving administration of anesthesia are reported by the use of the anesthesia five-digit procedure code (00100-01999) plus modifier codes (defined under "Anesthesia Modifiers" later in these Guidelines).

The reporting of anesthesia services is appropriate by or under the responsible supervision of a physician. These services may include but are not limited to general, regional, supplementation of local anesthesia, or other supportive services in order to afford the patient the anesthesia care deemed optimal by the anesthesiologist during any procedure. These services include the usual preoperative and postoperative visits, the anesthesia care during the procedure, the administration of fluids and/or blood and the usual monitoring services (eg, ECG, temperature, blood pressure, oximetry, capnography, and mass spectrometry). Unusual forms of monitoring (eg, intra-arterial, central venous, and Swan-Ganz) are not included.

Items used by all physicians in reporting their services are presented in the **Introduction.** Some of the commonalities are repeated in this section for the convenience of those physicians referring to this section on **Anesthesia.** Other definitions and items unique to anesthesia are also listed.

To report moderate (conscious) sedation provided by a physician also performing the service for which conscious sedation is being provided, see codes 99143-99145.

For the procedures listed in Appendix G, when a second physician other than the health care professional performing the diagnostic or therapeutic services provides moderate (conscious) sedation in the facility setting (eg, hospital, outpatient hospital/ambulatory surgery center, skilled nursing facility), the second physician reports the associated moderate sedation procedure/service 99148-99150; when these services are performed by the second physician in the nonfacility setting (eg, physician office, freestanding imaging center), codes 99148-99150 would not be reported. Moderate sedation does not include minimal sedation (anxiolysis), deep sedation, or monitored anesthesia care (00100-01999).

To report regional or general anesthesia provided by a physician also performing the services for which the anesthesia is being provided, see modifier 47 in Appendix A.

Time Reporting

Time for anesthesia procedures may be reported as is customary in the local area. Anesthesia time begins when the anesthesiologist begins to prepare the patient for the induction of anesthesia in the operating room (or in an equivalent area) and ends when the anesthesiologist is no longer in personal attendance, that is, when the patient may be safely placed under postoperative supervision.

Physician's Services

Physician's services rendered in the office, home, or hospital; consultation; and other medical services are listed in the section titled **Evaluation and Management Services** (99201-99499 series) found on page 1. "Special Services and Reporting" (99000-99091 series) are listed in the **Medicine** section.

Materials Supplied by Physician

Supplies and materials provided by the physician (eg, sterile trays, drugs) over and above those usually included with the office visit or other services rendered may be listed separately. Drugs, tray supplies, and materials provided should be listed and identified with 99070 or the appropriate supply code.

Separate or Multiple Procedures

When multiple surgical procedures are performed during a single anesthetic administration, the anesthesia code representing the most complex procedure is reported. The time reported is the combined total for all procedures.

Special Report

▶A service that is rarely provided, unusual, variable, or new may require a special report. Pertinent information should include an adequate definition or description of the nature, extent, and need for the procedure and the time, effort, and equipment necessary to provide the service.◀

Anesthesia Modifiers

All anesthesia services are reported by use of the anesthesia five-digit procedure code (00100-01999) plus the addition of a physical status modifier. The use of other optional modifiers may be appropriate.

Physical Status Modifiers

Physical Status modifiers are represented by the initial letter 'P' followed by a single digit from 1 to 6 as defined in the following list:

P1: A normal healthy patient

P2: A patient with mild systemic disease

P3: A patient with severe systemic disease

P4: A patient with severe systemic disease that is a constant threat to life

P5: A moribund patient who is not expected to survive without the operation

P6: A declared brain-dead patient whose organs are being removed for donor purposes

These six levels are consistent with the American Society of Anesthesiologists (ASA) ranking of patient physical status. Physical status is included in the CPT codebook to distinguish among various levels of complexity of the anesthesia service provided.

Example: 00100-P1

Qualifying Circumstances

More than one qualifying circumstance may be selected.

Many anesthesia services are provided under particularly difficult circumstances, depending on factors such as extraordinary condition of patient, notable operative conditions, and/or unusual risk factors. This section includes a list of important qualifying circumstances that significantly affect the character of the anesthesia service provided. These procedures would not be reported alone but would be reported as additional procedure numbers qualifying an anesthesia procedure or service.

+ 99100   Anesthesia for patient of extreme age, younger than 1 year and older than 70 (List separately in addition to code for primary anesthesia procedure)

(For procedure performed on infants younger than 1 year of age at time of surgery, see 00326, 00561, 00834, 00836)

+ 99116   Anesthesia complicated by utilization of total body hypothermia (List separately in addition to code for primary anesthesia procedure)

+ 99135   Anesthesia complicated by utilization of controlled hypotension (List separately in addition to code for primary anesthesia procedure)

+ 99140   Anesthesia complicated by emergency conditions (specify) (List separately in addition to code for primary anesthesia procedure)

(An emergency is defined as existing when delay in treatment of the patient would lead to a significant increase in the threat to life or body part.)

Anesthesia

Head

00100   Anesthesia for procedures on salivary glands, including biopsy
→ *CPT Assistant* Feb 97:4, Nov 99:6, Feb 06:9, Mar 06:15, Nov 07:8

00102   Anesthesia for procedures involving plastic repair of cleft lip
→ *CPT Assistant* Nov 99:6; *CPT Changes: An Insider's View* 2000

00103   Anesthesia for reconstructive procedures of eyelid (eg, blepharoplasty, ptosis surgery)
→ *CPT Assistant* Nov 99:6; *CPT Changes: An Insider's View* 2000

00104   Anesthesia for electroconvulsive therapy

00120   Anesthesia for procedures on external, middle, and inner ear including biopsy; not otherwise specified

00124   otoscopy
→ *CPT Assistant* Nov 99:7

00126   tympanotomy

00140   Anesthesia for procedures on eye; not otherwise specified

00142   lens surgery

00144   corneal transplant

00145   vitreoretinal surgery
→ *CPT Changes: An Insider's View* 2001

00147   iridectomy

00148   ophthalmoscopy

00160   Anesthesia for procedures on nose and accessory sinuses; not otherwise specified

00162   radical surgery

00164   biopsy, soft tissue

00170   Anesthesia for intraoral procedures, including biopsy; not otherwise specified

00172   repair of cleft palate

00174   excision of retropharyngeal tumor

00176   radical surgery

00190   Anesthesia for procedures on facial bones or skull; not otherwise specified
→ *CPT Changes: An Insider's View* 2001

00192   radical surgery (including prognathism)

00210   Anesthesia for intracranial procedures; not otherwise specified

00211   craniotomy or craniectomy for evacuation of hematoma
→ *CPT Changes: An Insider's View* 2009

00212   subdural taps

00214   burr holes, including ventriculography
→ *CPT Assistant* Nov 99:7; *CPT Changes: An Insider's View* 2000

00215   cranioplasty or elevation of depressed skull fracture, extradural (simple or compound)
→ *CPT Changes: An Insider's View* 2001

00216   vascular procedures

00218   procedures in sitting position

00220   cerebrospinal fluid shunting procedures

00222   electrocoagulation of intracranial nerve

Neck

00300   Anesthesia for all procedures on the integumentary system, muscles and nerves of head, neck, and posterior trunk, not otherwise specified
→ *CPT Assistant* Nov 99:7, Mar 06:15

00320   Anesthesia for all procedures on esophagus, thyroid, larynx, trachea and lymphatic system of neck; not otherwise specified, age 1 year or older
→ *CPT Changes: An Insider's View* 2003

00322   needle biopsy of thyroid

(For procedures on cervical spine and cord, see 00600, 00604, 00670)

00326   Anesthesia for all procedures on the larynx and trachea in children younger than 1 year of age
→ *CPT Changes: An Insider's View* 2003

(Do not report 00326 in conjunction with 99100)

00350   Anesthesia for procedures on major vessels of neck; not otherwise specified

00352   simple ligation
→ *CPT Assistant* Nov 07:8

(For arteriography, use 01916)

Thorax (Chest Wall and Shoulder Girdle)

00400   Anesthesia for procedures on the integumentary system on the extremities, anterior trunk and perineum; not otherwise specified
→ *CPT Assistant* Mar 06:15, Nov 07:8

00402   reconstructive procedures on breast (eg, reduction or augmentation mammoplasty, muscle flaps)

00404   radical or modified radical procedures on breast

00406   radical or modified radical procedures on breast with internal mammary node dissection

00410   electrical conversion of arrhythmias

00450   Anesthesia for procedures on clavicle and scapula; not otherwise specified

00452   radical surgery

00454   biopsy of clavicle

00470   Anesthesia for partial rib resection; not otherwise specified

00472   thoracoplasty (any type)

00474   radical procedures (eg, pectus excavatum)
➔ *CPT Assistant* Nov 07:8

Intrathoracic

00500   Anesthesia for all procedures on esophagus
➔ *CPT Assistant* Mar 06:15, Nov 07:8

00520   Anesthesia for closed chest procedures; (including bronchoscopy) not otherwise specified
➔ *CPT Assistant* Nov 99:7; *CPT Changes: An Insider's View* 2000

00522   needle biopsy of pleura

00524   pneumocentesis

00528   mediastinoscopy and diagnostic thoracoscopy not utilizing 1 lung ventilation
➔ *CPT Assistant* Nov 99:7; *CPT Changes: An Insider's View* 2000, 2003, 2004

(For tracheobronchial reconstruction, use 00539)

00529   mediastinoscopy and diagnostic thoracoscopy utilizing 1 lung ventilation
➔ *CPT Assistant* Jun 04:3; *CPT Changes: An Insider's View* 2004

00530   Anesthesia for permanent transvenous pacemaker insertion
➔ *CPT Changes: An Insider's View* 2001

00532   Anesthesia for access to central venous circulation

00534   Anesthesia for transvenous insertion or replacement of pacing cardioverter-defibrillator
➔ *CPT Changes: An Insider's View* 2001

(For transthoracic approach, use 00560)

00537   Anesthesia for cardiac electrophysiologic procedures including radiofrequency ablation
➔ *CPT Changes: An Insider's View* 2001

00539   Anesthesia for tracheobronchial reconstruction
➔ *CPT Changes: An Insider's View* 2003

00540   Anesthesia for thoracotomy procedures involving lungs, pleura, diaphragm, and mediastinum (including surgical thoracoscopy); not otherwise specified

00541   utilizing 1 lung ventilation
➔ *CPT Changes: An Insider's View* 2003

(For thoracic spine and cord anesthesia procedures via an anterior transthoracic approach, see 00625-00626)

00542   decortication

00546   pulmonary resection with thoracoplasty

00548   intrathoracic procedures on the trachea and bronchi
➔ *CPT Assistant* Nov 97:10

00550   Anesthesia for sternal debridement
➔ *CPT Changes: An Insider's View* 2001

00560   Anesthesia for procedures on heart, pericardial sac, and great vessels of chest; without pump oxygenator
➔ *CPT Changes: An Insider's View* 2002

00561   with pump oxygenator, younger than 1 year of age
➔ *CPT Changes: An Insider's View* 2005

(Do not report 00561 in conjunction with 99100, 99116, and 99135)

00562   with pump oxygenator, age 1 year or older, for all non-coronary bypass procedures (eg, valve procedures) or for re-operation for coronary bypass more than 1 month after original operation
➔ *CPT Changes: An Insider's View* 2009

00563   with pump oxygenator with hypothermic circulatory arrest
➔ *CPT Changes: An Insider's View* 2001

00566   Anesthesia for direct coronary artery bypass grafting; without pump oxygenator
➔ *CPT Changes: An Insider's View* 2001, 2009

00567   with pump oxygenator
➔ *CPT Changes: An Insider's View* 2009

00580   Anesthesia for heart transplant or heart/lung transplant
➔ *CPT Assistant* Nov 07:8

Spine and Spinal Cord

00600   Anesthesia for procedures on cervical spine and cord; not otherwise specified
➔ *CPT Assistant* Mar 06:15, May 07:9, Nov 07:8

(For percutaneous image-guided spine and spinal cord anesthesia procedures, see 01935, 01936)

00604   procedures with patient in the sitting position
➔ *CPT Changes: An Insider's View* 2001

00620   Anesthesia for procedures on thoracic spine and cord; not otherwise specified
➔ *CPT Assistant* Mar 07:9

00622   thoracolumbar sympathectomy
> *CPT Assistant* Mar 07:9

00625   Anesthesia for procedures on the thoracic spine and cord, via an anterior transthoracic approach; not utilizing 1 lung ventilation
> *CPT Assistant* Mar 07:9; *CPT Changes: An Insider's View* 2007

00626   utilizing 1 lung ventilation
> *CPT Assistant* Mar 07:9; *CPT Changes: An Insider's View* 2007

(For anesthesia for thoracotomy procedures other than spinal, see 00540-00541)

00630   Anesthesia for procedures in lumbar region; not otherwise specified

00632   lumbar sympathectomy

00634   chemonucleolysis

00635   diagnostic or therapeutic lumbar puncture
> *CPT Changes: An Insider's View* 2001

00640   Anesthesia for manipulation of the spine or for closed procedures on the cervical, thoracic or lumbar spine
> *CPT Changes: An Insider's View* 2003

00670   Anesthesia for extensive spine and spinal cord procedures (eg, spinal instrumentation or vascular procedures)
> *CPT Assistant* Nov 07:8; *CPT Changes: An Insider's View* 2001

Upper Abdomen

00700   Anesthesia for procedures on upper anterior abdominal wall; not otherwise specified
> *CPT Assistant* Mar 06:15, Nov 07:8

00702   percutaneous liver biopsy

00730   Anesthesia for procedures on upper posterior abdominal wall

00740   Anesthesia for upper gastrointestinal endoscopic procedures, endoscope introduced proximal to duodenum
> *CPT Assistant* Nov 99:7; *CPT Changes: An Insider's View* 2000

00750   Anesthesia for hernia repairs in upper abdomen; not otherwise specified

00752   lumbar and ventral (incisional) hernias and/or wound dehiscence

00754   omphalocele

00756   transabdominal repair of diaphragmatic hernia

00770   Anesthesia for all procedures on major abdominal blood vessels

00790   Anesthesia for intraperitoneal procedures in upper abdomen including laparoscopy; not otherwise specified

00792   partial hepatectomy or management of liver hemorrhage (excluding liver biopsy)
> *CPT Changes: An Insider's View* 2001

00794   pancreatectomy, partial or total (eg, Whipple procedure)

00796   liver transplant (recipient)

(For harvesting of liver, use 01990)

00797   gastric restrictive procedure for morbid obesity
> *CPT Assistant* Nov 07:8; *CPT Changes: An Insider's View* 2002

Lower Abdomen

00800   Anesthesia for procedures on lower anterior abdominal wall; not otherwise specified
> *CPT Assistant* Mar 06:15, Nov 07:8

00802   panniculectomy

00810   Anesthesia for lower intestinal endoscopic procedures, endoscope introduced distal to duodenum
> *CPT Assistant* Nov 99:7; *CPT Changes: An Insider's View* 2000

00820   Anesthesia for procedures on lower posterior abdominal wall

00830   Anesthesia for hernia repairs in lower abdomen; not otherwise specified

00832   ventral and incisional hernias

(For hernia repairs in the infant 1 year of age or younger, see 00834, 00836)

00834   Anesthesia for hernia repairs in the lower abdomen not otherwise specified, younger than 1 year of age
> *CPT Changes: An Insider's View* 2003

(Do not report 00834 in conjunction with 99100)

00836   Anesthesia for hernia repairs in the lower abdomen not otherwise specified, infants younger than 37 weeks gestational age at birth and younger than 50 weeks gestational age at time of surgery
> *CPT Changes: An Insider's View* 2003

(Do not report 00836 in conjunction with 99100)

00840   Anesthesia for intraperitoneal procedures in lower abdomen including laparoscopy; not otherwise specified

00842   amniocentesis

00844   abdominoperineal resection

00846   radical hysterectomy

00848   pelvic exenteration

00851   tubal ligation/transection
> *CPT Changes: An Insider's View* 2002

00860   Anesthesia for extraperitoneal procedures in lower abdomen, including urinary tract; not otherwise specified

00862   renal procedures, including upper one-third of ureter, or donor nephrectomy

00864   total cystectomy

00865   radical prostatectomy (suprapubic, retropubic)

00866   adrenalectomy

00868   renal transplant (recipient)

(For donor nephrectomy, use 00862)

(For harvesting kidney from brain-dead patient, use 01990)

00870   cystolithotomy

00872   Anesthesia for lithotripsy, extracorporeal shock wave; with water bath

00873   without water bath

00880   Anesthesia for procedures on major lower abdominal vessels; not otherwise specified

00882   inferior vena cava ligation

Perineum

(For perineal procedures on integumentary system, muscles and nerves, see 00300, 00400)

00902   Anesthesia for; anorectal procedure
> *CPT Assistant* Mar 06:15; *CPT Changes: An Insider's View* 2001

00904   radical perineal procedure

00906   vulvectomy

00908   perineal prostatectomy

00910   Anesthesia for transurethral procedures (including urethrocystoscopy); not otherwise specified

00912   transurethral resection of bladder tumor(s)

00914   transurethral resection of prostate

00916   post-transurethral resection bleeding

00918   with fragmentation, manipulation and/or removal of ureteral calculus
> *CPT Assistant* Nov 99:8, Apr 09:8; *CPT Changes: An Insider's View* 2000

00920   Anesthesia for procedures on male genitalia (including open urethral procedures); not otherwise specified
> *CPT Changes: An Insider's View* 2001

00921   vasectomy, unilateral or bilateral
> *CPT Changes: An Insider's View* 2003

00922   seminal vesicles

00924   undescended testis, unilateral or bilateral

00926   radical orchiectomy, inguinal

00928   radical orchiectomy, abdominal

00930   orchiopexy, unilateral or bilateral

00932   complete amputation of penis

00934   radical amputation of penis with bilateral inguinal lymphadenectomy

00936   radical amputation of penis with bilateral inguinal and iliac lymphadenectomy

00938   insertion of penile prosthesis (perineal approach)

00940   Anesthesia for vaginal procedures (including biopsy of labia, vagina, cervix or endometrium); not otherwise specified

00942   colpotomy, vaginectomy, colporrhaphy, and open urethral procedures
> *CPT Changes: An Insider's View* 2001, 2002

00944   vaginal hysterectomy

00948   cervical cerclage

00950   culdoscopy

00952   hysteroscopy and/or hysterosalpingography
> *CPT Assistant* Nov 99:8; *CPT Changes: An Insider's View* 2000

Pelvis (Except Hip)

01112   Anesthesia for bone marrow aspiration and/or biopsy, anterior or posterior iliac crest
> *CPT Assistant* Mar 06:15; *CPT Changes: An Insider's View* 2001

01120   Anesthesia for procedures on bony pelvis

01130   Anesthesia for body cast application or revision

01140   Anesthesia for interpelviabdominal (hindquarter) amputation

01150   Anesthesia for radical procedures for tumor of pelvis, except hindquarter amputation

01160   Anesthesia for closed procedures involving symphysis pubis or sacroiliac joint

01170   Anesthesia for open procedures involving symphysis pubis or sacroiliac joint

01173   Anesthesia for open repair of fracture disruption of pelvis or column fracture involving acetabulum
> *CPT Assistant* Jun 04:3-4; *CPT Changes: An Insider's View* 2004

01180   Anesthesia for obturator neurectomy; extrapelvic

01190   intrapelvic
> *CPT Assistant* Nov 07:8

Upper Leg (Except Knee)

01200   Anesthesia for all closed procedures involving hip joint
> *CPT Assistant* Mar 06:15, Nov 07:8

01202   Anesthesia for arthroscopic procedures of hip joint

01210   Anesthesia for open procedures involving hip joint; not otherwise specified

01212   hip disarticulation

01214   total hip arthroplasty
> *CPT Changes: An Insider's View* 2001, 2002

01215   revision of total hip arthroplasty
➔ *CPT Changes: An Insider's View* 2001, 2002

01220   Anesthesia for all closed procedures involving upper two-thirds of femur

01230   Anesthesia for open procedures involving upper two-thirds of femur; not otherwise specified

01232   amputation

01234   radical resection

01250   Anesthesia for all procedures on nerves, muscles, tendons, fascia, and bursae of upper leg

01260   Anesthesia for all procedures involving veins of upper leg, including exploration

01270   Anesthesia for procedures involving arteries of upper leg, including bypass graft; not otherwise specified

01272   femoral artery ligation

01274   femoral artery embolectomy
➔ *CPT Assistant* Nov 07:8

Knee and Popliteal Area

01320   Anesthesia for all procedures on nerves, muscles, tendons, fascia, and bursae of knee and/or popliteal area
➔ *CPT Assistant* Mar 06:15, Nov 07:8

01340   Anesthesia for all closed procedures on lower one-third of femur

01360   Anesthesia for all open procedures on lower one-third of femur

01380   Anesthesia for all closed procedures on knee joint

01382   Anesthesia for diagnostic arthroscopic procedures of knee joint
➔ *CPT Changes: An Insider's View* 2003

01390   Anesthesia for all closed procedures on upper ends of tibia, fibula, and/or patella

01392   Anesthesia for all open procedures on upper ends of tibia, fibula, and/or patella

01400   Anesthesia for open or surgical arthroscopic procedures on knee joint; not otherwise specified
➔ *CPT Changes: An Insider's View* 2003

01402   total knee arthroplasty
➔ *CPT Changes: An Insider's View* 2002

01404   disarticulation at knee

01420   Anesthesia for all cast applications, removal, or repair involving knee joint

01430   Anesthesia for procedures on veins of knee and popliteal area; not otherwise specified

01432   arteriovenous fistula

01440   Anesthesia for procedures on arteries of knee and popliteal area; not otherwise specified

01442   popliteal thromboendarterectomy, with or without patch graft

01444   popliteal excision and graft or repair for occlusion or aneurysm
➔ *CPT Assistant* Nov 07:8

Lower Leg (Below Knee, Includes Ankle and Foot)

01462   Anesthesia for all closed procedures on lower leg, ankle, and foot
➔ *CPT Assistant* Mar 06:15, Nov 07:8

01464   Anesthesia for arthroscopic procedures of ankle and/or foot
➔ *CPT Changes: An Insider's View* 2003

01470   Anesthesia for procedures on nerves, muscles, tendons, and fascia of lower leg, ankle, and foot; not otherwise specified

01472   repair of ruptured Achilles tendon, with or without graft

01474   gastrocnemius recession (eg, Strayer procedure)

01480   Anesthesia for open procedures on bones of lower leg, ankle, and foot; not otherwise specified

01482   radical resection (including below knee amputation)
➔ *CPT Changes: An Insider's View* 2001

01484   osteotomy or osteoplasty of tibia and/or fibula

01486   total ankle replacement

01490   Anesthesia for lower leg cast application, removal, or repair

01500   Anesthesia for procedures on arteries of lower leg, including bypass graft; not otherwise specified

01502   embolectomy, direct or with catheter

01520   Anesthesia for procedures on veins of lower leg; not otherwise specified

01522   venous thrombectomy, direct or with catheter
➔ *CPT Assistant* Nov 07:8

Shoulder and Axilla

Includes humeral head and neck, sternoclavicular joint, acromioclavicular joint, and shoulder joint.

01610   Anesthesia for all procedures on nerves, muscles, tendons, fascia, and bursae of shoulder and axilla
➔ *CPT Assistant* Mar 06:15, Nov 07:8

01620   Anesthesia for all closed procedures on humeral head and neck, sternoclavicular joint, acromioclavicular joint, and shoulder joint

---

01622   Anesthesia for diagnostic arthroscopic procedures of shoulder joint

> *CPT Changes: An Insider's View* 2003

01630   Anesthesia for open or surgical arthroscopic procedures on humeral head and neck, sternoclavicular joint, acromioclavicular joint, and shoulder joint; not otherwise specified

> *CPT Changes: An Insider's View* 2003

►(01632 has been deleted. To report, see 01630, 01638)◄

01634   shoulder disarticulation

01636   interthoracoscapular (forequarter) amputation

01638   total shoulder replacement

01650   Anesthesia for procedures on arteries of shoulder and axilla; not otherwise specified

01652   axillary-brachial aneurysm

01654   bypass graft

01656   axillary-femoral bypass graft

01670   Anesthesia for all procedures on veins of shoulder and axilla

01680   Anesthesia for shoulder cast application, removal or repair; not otherwise specified

01682   shoulder spica

> *CPT Assistant* Nov 07:8

Upper Arm and Elbow

01710   Anesthesia for procedures on nerves, muscles, tendons, fascia, and bursae of upper arm and elbow; not otherwise specified

> *CPT Assistant* Mar 06:15, Nov 07:8

01712   tenotomy, elbow to shoulder, open

01714   tenoplasty, elbow to shoulder

01716   tenodesis, rupture of long tendon of biceps

01730   Anesthesia for all closed procedures on humerus and elbow

01732   Anesthesia for diagnostic arthroscopic procedures of elbow joint

> *CPT Changes: An Insider's View* 2003

01740   Anesthesia for open or surgical arthroscopic procedures of the elbow; not otherwise specified

> *CPT Changes: An Insider's View* 2003

01742   osteotomy of humerus

01744   repair of nonunion or malunion of humerus

01756   radical procedures

01758   excision of cyst or tumor of humerus

01760   total elbow replacement

01770   Anesthesia for procedures on arteries of upper arm and elbow; not otherwise specified

01772   embolectomy

01780   Anesthesia for procedures on veins of upper arm and elbow; not otherwise specified

01782   phleborrhaphy

> *CPT Assistant* Nov 07:8

Forearm, Wrist, and Hand

01810   Anesthesia for all procedures on nerves, muscles, tendons, fascia, and bursae of forearm, wrist, and hand

> *CPT Assistant* Mar 06:15, Nov 07:8

01820   Anesthesia for all closed procedures on radius, ulna, wrist, or hand bones

01829   Anesthesia for diagnostic arthroscopic procedures on the wrist

> *CPT Changes: An Insider's View* 2003

01830   Anesthesia for open or surgical arthroscopic/endoscopic procedures on distal radius, distal ulna, wrist, or hand joints; not otherwise specified

> *CPT Changes: An Insider's View* 2003

01832   total wrist replacement

01840   Anesthesia for procedures on arteries of forearm, wrist, and hand; not otherwise specified

01842   embolectomy

01844   Anesthesia for vascular shunt, or shunt revision, any type (eg, dialysis)

01850   Anesthesia for procedures on veins of forearm, wrist, and hand; not otherwise specified

01852   phleborrhaphy

01860   Anesthesia for forearm, wrist, or hand cast application, removal, or repair

> *CPT Assistant* Nov 07:8

Radiological Procedures

(01905 has been deleted. To report, see 01935, 01936)

01916   Anesthesia for diagnostic arteriography/venography

> *CPT Assistant* Nov 07:8; *CPT Changes: An Insider's View* 2002

(Do not report 01916 in conjunction with therapeutic codes 01924-01926, 01930-01933)

01920 Anesthesia for cardiac catheterization including coronary angiography and ventriculography (not to include Swan-Ganz catheter)

01922 Anesthesia for non-invasive imaging or radiation therapy

01924 Anesthesia for therapeutic interventional radiological procedures involving the arterial system; not otherwise specified

➡ *CPT Changes: An Insider's View* 2002

01925 carotid or coronary

➡ *CPT Changes: An Insider's View* 2002

01926 intracranial, intracardiac, or aortic

➡ *CPT Changes: An Insider's View* 2002

01930 Anesthesia for therapeutic interventional radiological procedures involving the venous/lymphatic system (not to include access to the central circulation); not otherwise specified

➡ *CPT Changes: An Insider's View* 2002

01931 intrahepatic or portal circulation (eg, transvenous intrahepatic portosystemic shunt[s] [TIPS])

➡ *CPT Assistant* Apr 08:3; *CPT Changes: An Insider's View* 2002, 2008

01932 intrathoracic or jugular

➡ *CPT Changes: An Insider's View* 2002

01933 intracranial

➡ *CPT Changes: An Insider's View* 2002

01935 Anesthesia for percutaneous image guided procedures on the spine and spinal cord; diagnostic

➡ *CPT Assistant* Apr 08:3; *CPT Changes: An Insider's View* 2008

01936 therapeutic

➡ *CPT Assistant* Apr 08:3; *CPT Changes: An Insider's View* 2008

Burn Excisions or Debridement

01951 Anesthesia for second- and third-degree burn excision or debridement with or without skin grafting, any site, for total body surface area (TBSA) treated during anesthesia and surgery; less than 4% total body surface area

➡ *CPT Assistant* Mar 06:15; *CPT Changes: An Insider's View* 2001, 2002

01952 between 4% and 9% of total body surface area

➡ *CPT Changes: An Insider's View* 2001, 2002

+ 01953 each additional 9% total body surface area or part thereof (List separately in addition to code for primary procedure)

➡ *CPT Changes: An Insider's View* 2001

(Use 01953 in conjunction with 01952)

Obstetric

01958 Anesthesia for external cephalic version procedure

➡ *CPT Assistant* Jun 04:5-6; *CPT Changes: An Insider's View* 2004

01960 Anesthesia for vaginal delivery only

➡ *CPT Assistant* Dec 01:3; *CPT Changes: An Insider's View* 2002

01961 Anesthesia for cesarean delivery only

➡ *CPT Changes: An Insider's View* 2002, 2003

01962 Anesthesia for urgent hysterectomy following delivery

➡ *CPT Changes: An Insider's View* 2002, 2003

01963 Anesthesia for cesarean hysterectomy without any labor analgesia/anesthesia care

➡ *CPT Changes: An Insider's View* 2002, 2003

01965 Anesthesia for incomplete or missed abortion procedures

➡ *CPT Changes: An Insider's View* 2006

01966 Anesthesia for induced abortion procedures

➡ *CPT Changes: An Insider's View* 2006

01967 Neuraxial labor analgesia/anesthesia for planned vaginal delivery (this includes any repeat subarachnoid needle placement and drug injection and/or any necessary replacement of an epidural catheter during labor)

➡ *CPT Assistant* Dec 01:3; *CPT Changes: An Insider's View* 2002

+ 01968 Anesthesia for cesarean delivery following neuraxial labor analgesia/anesthesia (List separately in addition to code for primary procedure performed)

➡ *CPT Assistant* Dec 01:3; *CPT Changes: An Insider's View* 2002, 2003

(Use 01968 in conjunction with 01967)

+ 01969 Anesthesia for cesarean hysterectomy following neuraxial labor analgesia/anesthesia (List separately in addition to code for primary procedure performed)

➡ *CPT Assistant* Dec 01:3; *CPT Changes: An Insider's View* 2002, 2003

(Use 01969 in conjunction with 01967)

Other Procedures

01990 Physiological support for harvesting of organ(s) from brain-dead patient

➡ *CPT Assistant* Mar 06:15, Nov 07:8

01991 Anesthesia for diagnostic or therapeutic nerve blocks and injections (when block or injection is performed by a different provider); other than the prone position

➡ *CPT Changes: An Insider's View* 2003

01992   prone position
> ➲ *CPT Changes: An Insider's View* 2003

(Do not report 01991 or 01992 in conjunction with 99143-99150)

▶(When regional intravenous administration of local anesthetic agent or other medication in the upper or lower extremity is used as the anesthetic for a surgical procedure, report the appropriate anesthesia code. To report a Bier block for pain management, use 64999)◀

(For intra-arterial or intravenous therapy for pain management, see 96373, 96374)

01996   Daily hospital management of epidural or subarachnoid continuous drug administration
> ➲ *CPT Assistant* Feb 97:5, Nov 97:10, May 99:6; *CPT Changes: An Insider's View* 2003

(Report code 01996 for daily hospital management of continuous epidural or subarachnoid drug administration performed after insertion of an epidural or subarachnoid catheter)

01999   Unlisted anesthesia procedure(s)
> ➲ *CPT Assistant* Feb 97:4, Feb 06:9, Mar 06:15, Jan 07:30, Nov 07:8

Notes

⊙=Moderate sedation ✚=Add-on code ✗=FDA approval pending #=Resequenced code ➡➡=See p xiii for details

Surgery Guidelines

Surgery Guidelines

Items used by all physicians in reporting their services are presented in the **Introduction.** Some of the commonalities are repeated here for the convenience of those physicians referring to this section on **Surgery.** Other definitions and items unique to Surgery are also listed.

Physicians' Services

Physicians' services rendered in the office, home, or hospital, consultations, and other medical services are listed in the section entitled **Evaluation and Management Services** (99201-99499) found in the front of the book, beginning on page 9. "Special Services and Reports" (99000 series) is presented in the **Medicine** section.

CPT Surgical Package Definition

The services provided by the physician to any patient by their very nature are variable. The CPT codes that represent a readily identifiable surgical procedure thereby include, on a procedure-by-procedure basis, a variety of services. In defining the specific services "included" in a given CPT surgical code, the following services are always included in addition to the operation per se:

- Local infiltration, metacarpal/metatarsal/digital block or topical anesthesia

- Subsequent to the decision for surgery, one related Evaluation and Management (E/M) encounter on the date immediately prior to or on the date of procedure (including history and physical)

- Immediate postoperative care, including dictating operative notes, talking with the family and other physicians

- Writing orders

- Evaluating the patient in the postanesthesia recovery area

- Typical postoperative follow-up care

Follow-Up Care for Diagnostic Procedures

Follow-up care for diagnostic procedures (eg, endoscopy, arthroscopy, injection procedures for radiography) includes only that care related to recovery from the diagnostic procedure itself. Care of the condition for which the diagnostic procedure was performed or of other concomitant conditions is not included and may be listed separately.

Follow-Up Care for Therapeutic Surgical Procedures

Follow-up care for therapeutic surgical procedures includes only that care which is usually a part of the surgical service. Complications, exacerbations, recurrence, or the presence of other diseases or injuries requiring additional services should be separately reported.

Materials Supplied by Physician

Supplies and materials provided by the physician (eg, sterile trays/drugs), over and above those usually included with the procedure(s) rendered are reported separately. List drugs, trays, supplies, and materials provided. Identify as 99070 or specific supply code.

Reporting More Than One Procedure/Service

When a physician performs more than one procedure/service on the same date, same session or during a post-operative period (subject to the "surgical package" concept), several CPT modifiers may apply (see Appendix A for definition).

Separate Procedure

Some of the procedures or services listed in the CPT codebook that are commonly carried out as an integral component of a total service or procedure have been identified by the inclusion of the term "separate procedure." The codes designated as "separate procedure" should not be reported in addition to the code for the total procedure or service of which it is considered an integral component.

However, when a procedure or service that is designated as a "separate procedure" is carried out independently or considered to be unrelated or distinct from other procedures/services provided at that time, it may be reported by itself, or in addition to other procedures/services by appending modifier 59 to the specific "separate procedure" code to indicate that the procedure is not considered to be a component of another procedure, but is a distinct, independent procedure. This may represent a different session, different procedure or surgery, different site or organ system, separate incision/excision, separate lesion, or separate injury (or area of injury in extensive injuries).

Unlisted Service or Procedure

A service or procedure may be provided that is not listed in this edition of the CPT codebook. When reporting such a service, the appropriate "Unlisted Procedure" code may be used to indicate the service, identifying it by "Special Report" as discussed in the section below. The "Unlisted Procedures" and accompanying codes for **Surgery** are as follows:

15999	Unlisted procedure, excision pressure ulcer
17999	Unlisted procedure, skin, mucous membrane and subcutaneous tissue
19499	Unlisted procedure, breast
20999	Unlisted procedure, musculoskeletal system, general
21089	Unlisted maxillofacial prosthetic procedure
21299	Unlisted craniofacial and maxillofacial procedure
21499	Unlisted musculoskeletal procedure, head
21899	Unlisted procedure, neck or thorax
22899	Unlisted procedure, spine
22999	Unlisted procedure, abdomen, musculoskeletal system
23929	Unlisted procedure, shoulder
24999	Unlisted procedure, humerus or elbow
25999	Unlisted procedure, forearm or wrist
26989	Unlisted procedure, hands or fingers
27299	Unlisted procedure, pelvis or hip joint
27599	Unlisted procedure, femur or knee
27899	Unlisted procedure, leg or ankle
28899	Unlisted procedure, foot or toes
29799	Unlisted procedure, casting or strapping
29999	Unlisted procedure, arthroscopy
30999	Unlisted procedure, nose
31299	Unlisted procedure, accessory sinuses

31599	Unlisted procedure, larynx
31899	Unlisted procedure, trachea, bronchi
32999	Unlisted procedure, lungs and pleura
33999	Unlisted procedure, cardiac surgery
36299	Unlisted procedure, vascular injection
37501	Unlisted vascular endoscopy procedure
37799	Unlisted procedure, vascular surgery
38129	Unlisted laparoscopy procedure, spleen
38589	Unlisted laparoscopy procedure, lymphatic system
38999	Unlisted procedure, hemic or lymphatic system
39499	Unlisted procedure, mediastinum
39599	Unlisted procedure, diaphragm
40799	Unlisted procedure, lips
40899	Unlisted procedure, vestibule of mouth
41599	Unlisted procedure, tongue, floor of mouth
41899	Unlisted procedure, dentoalveolar structures
42299	Unlisted procedure, palate, uvula
42699	Unlisted procedure, salivary glands or ducts
42999	Unlisted procedure, pharynx, adenoids, or tonsils
43289	Unlisted laparoscopy procedure, esophagus
43499	Unlisted procedure, esophagus
43659	Unlisted laparoscopy procedure, stomach
43999	Unlisted procedure, stomach
44238	Unlisted laparoscopy procedure, intestine (except rectum)
44799	Unlisted procedure, intestine
44899	Unlisted procedure, Meckel's diverticulum and the mesentery
44979	Unlisted laparoscopy procedure, appendix
45499	Unlisted laparoscopy procedure, rectum
45999	Unlisted procedure, rectum
46999	Unlisted procedure, anus
47379	Unlisted laparoscopic procedure, liver
47399	Unlisted procedure, liver
47579	Unlisted laparoscopy procedure, biliary tract
47999	Unlisted procedure, biliary tract
48999	Unlisted procedure, pancreas
49329	Unlisted laparoscopy procedure, abdomen, peritoneum and omentum
49659	Unlisted laparoscopy procedure, hernioplasty, herniorrhaphy, herniotomy

49999	Unlisted procedure, abdomen, peritoneum and omentum
50549	Unlisted laparoscopy procedure, renal
50949	Unlisted laparoscopy procedure, ureter
51999	Unlisted laparoscopy procedure, bladder
53899	Unlisted procedure, urinary system
54699	Unlisted laparoscopy procedure, testis
55559	Unlisted laparoscopy procedure, spermatic cord
55899	Unlisted procedure, male genital system
58578	Unlisted laparoscopy procedure, uterus
58579	Unlisted hysteroscopy procedure, uterus
58679	Unlisted laparoscopy procedure, oviduct, ovary
58999	Unlisted procedure, female genital system (nonobstetrical)
▲ **59897**	Unlisted fetal invasive procedure, including ultrasound guidance, when performed
59898	Unlisted laparoscopy procedure, maternity care and delivery
59899	Unlisted procedure, maternity care and delivery
60659	Unlisted laparoscopy procedure, endocrine system
60699	Unlisted procedure, endocrine system
64999	Unlisted procedure, nervous system
66999	Unlisted procedure, anterior segment of eye
67299	Unlisted procedure, posterior segment
67399	Unlisted procedure, ocular muscle
67599	Unlisted procedure, orbit
67999	Unlisted procedure, eyelids
68399	Unlisted procedure, conjunctiva
68899	Unlisted procedure, lacrimal system
69399	Unlisted procedure, external ear
69799	Unlisted procedure, middle ear
69949	Unlisted procedure, inner ear
69979	Unlisted procedure, temporal bone, middle fossa approach

Special Report

▶A service that is rarely provided, unusual, variable, or new may require a special report. Pertinent information should include an adequate definition or description of the nature, extent, and need for the procedure, and the time, effort, and equipment necessary to provide the service.◀

Surgical Destruction

Surgical destruction is a part of a surgical procedure and different methods of destruction are not ordinarily listed separately unless the technique substantially alters the standard management of a problem or condition. Exceptions under special circumstances are provided for by separate code numbers.

Surgery

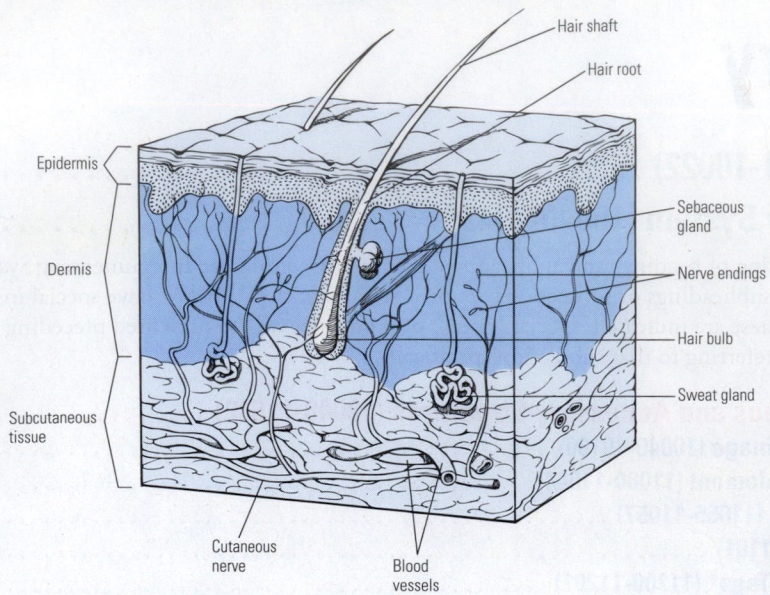

Hair shaft

Hair root

Epidermis

Dermis

Sebaceous gland

Nerve endings

Hair bulb

Subcutaneous tissue

Sweat gland

Cutaneous nerve

Blood vessels

Surgery

Least envasive to most envasive (handwritten)

General

10021 Fine needle aspiration; without imaging guidance
→ *CPT Assistant* Aug 02:10, Mar 05:11; *CPT Changes: An Insider's View* 2002
→ *Clinical Examples in Radiology* Fall 08:4

10022 with imaging guidance   *w/ X-Ray* (handwritten)
→ *CPT Assistant* Nov 02:1, Jun 07:10; *CPT Changes: An Insider's View* 2002
→ *Clinical Examples in Radiology* Summer 05:1, 6, Summer 08:5, Fall 08:2, 3, 4

►(For placement of percutaneous localization clip during breast biopsy, use 19295)◄

(For radiological supervision and interpretation, see 76942, 77002, 77012, 77021)

(For percutaneous needle biopsy other than fine needle aspiration, see 20206 for muscle, 32400 for pleura, 32405 for lung or mediastinum, 42400 for salivary gland, 47000, 47001 for liver, 48102 for pancreas, 49180 for abdominal or retroperitoneal mass, 60100 for thyroid, 62267 for nucleus pulposus, intervertebral disc, or paravertebral tissue, 62269 for spinal cord)

(For evaluation of fine needle aspirate, see 88172, 88173)

Integumentary System

Skin, Subcutaneous, and Accessory Structures

(handwritten) simple ... complicated / packing

Incision and Drainage

(For excision, see 11400, et seq)

10040 Acne surgery (eg, marsupialization, opening or removal of multiple milia, comedones, cysts, pustules)
→ *CPT Assistant* Fall 92:10, Feb 08:8

10060 Incision and drainage of abscess (eg, carbuncle, suppurative hidradenitis, cutaneous or subcutaneous abscess, cyst, furuncle, or paronychia); simple or single

10061 complicated or multiple   *(w/ packing)* (handwritten)

10080 Incision and drainage of pilonidal cyst; simple
→ *CPT Assistant* Fall 92:13, Dec 06:15, May 07:5

10081 complicated
→ *CPT Assistant* Fall 92:13, Dec 06:15, May 07:5

(For excision of pilonidal cyst, see 11770-11772)

10120 Incision and removal of foreign body, subcutaneous tissues; simple

10121 complicated *(handwritten scribble)*
→ *CPT Assistant* Spring 91:7, Dec 06:15

(To report wound exploration due to penetrating trauma without laparotomy or thoracotomy, see 20100-20103, as appropriate)

(To report debridement associated with open fracture(s) and/or dislocation(s), use 11010-11012, as appropriate)

10140 Incision and drainage of hematoma, seroma or fluid collection
→ *CPT Changes: An Insider's View* 2002

(If imaging guidance is performed, see 76942, 77012, 77021)

10160 Puncture aspiration of abscess, hematoma, bulla, or cyst
→ *CPT Changes: An Insider's View* 2002

(If imaging guidance is performed, see 76942, 77012, 77021)

10180 Incision and drainage, complex, postoperative wound infection

(For secondary closure of surgical wound, see 12020, 12021, 13160)

Excision—Debridement

(For dermabrasions, see 15780-15783)

(For nail debridement, see 11720-11721)

(For burn(s), see 16000-16035)

11000 Debridement of extensive eczematous or infected skin; up to 10% of body surface
→ *CPT Assistant* May 99:10

(For abdominal wall or genitalia debridement for necrotizing soft tissue infection, see 11004-11006)

+ 11001 each additional 10% of the body surface, or part thereof (List separately in addition to code for primary procedure)
→ *CPT Assistant* May 99:10; *CPT Changes: An Insider's View* 2009

(Use 11001 in conjunction with 11000)

11004 Debridement of skin, subcutaneous tissue, muscle and fascia for necrotizing soft tissue infection; external genitalia and perineum
→ *CPT Changes: An Insider's View* 2005

(handwritten notes at bottom)
Aspiration - Removal w/ needle
Penrose = packing   gauze
19% 11000 / 11001   21% 11000 / 11001 / 11001
12% / 11000 / 11001

11005 abdominal wall, with or without fascial closure
➲ *CPT Changes: An Insider's View* 2005

Debridement of Abdominal Wall
11005

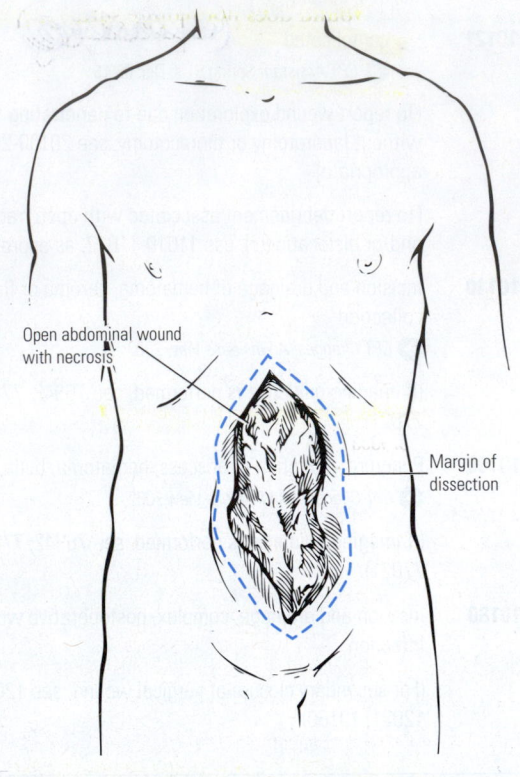

Open abdominal wound with necrosis

Margin of dissection

11006 external genitalia, perineum and abdominal wall, with or without fascial closure
➲ *CPT Changes: An Insider's View* 2005

+ 11008 Removal of prosthetic material or mesh, abdominal wall for infection (eg, for chronic or recurrent mesh infection or necrotizing soft tissue infection) (List separately in addition to code for primary procedure)
➲ *CPT Changes: An Insider's View* 2005, 2008

(Use 11008 in conjunction with 10180, 11004-11006)

(Do not report 11008 in conjunction with 11000-11001, 11010-11044)

(Report skin grafts or flaps separately when performed for closure at the same session as 11004-11008)

(When insertion of mesh is used for closure, use 49568)

(If orchiectomy is performed, use 54520)

(If testicular transplantation is performed, use 54680)

11010 Debridement including removal of foreign material associated with open fracture(s) and/or dislocation(s); skin and subcutaneous tissues
➲ *CPT Assistant* Mar 97:2, Apr 97:10, Aug 97:6, Oct 03:10

11011 skin, subcutaneous tissue, muscle fascia, and muscle
➲ *CPT Assistant* Mar 97:2, Apr 97:10, Aug 97:6

11012 skin, subcutaneous tissue, muscle fascia, muscle, and bone
➲ *CPT Assistant* Mar 97:2, Apr 97:10, Aug 97:6, Oct 03:10

11040 Debridement; skin, partial thickness
➲ *CPT Assistant* Fall 93:21, May 96:6, Feb 97:7, Aug 97:6, Jun 05:1,10, Oct 07:15

11041 skin, full thickness
➲ *CPT Assistant* Fall 93:21, May 96:6, Feb 97:7, Aug 97:6, Jun 05:1,10, Oct 07:15

11042 skin, and subcutaneous tissue
➲ *CPT Assistant* Winter 92:10, May 96:6, Feb 97:7, Aug 97:6, Jun 05:1,10, Oct 07:15

11043 skin, subcutaneous tissue, and muscle
➲ *CPT Assistant* May 96:6, Feb 97:7, Apr 97:11, Aug 97:6, Dec 99:10, Jun 05:1,10, Oct 07:15

11044 skin, subcutaneous tissue, muscle, and bone
➲ *CPT Assistant* Fall 93:21, Mar 96:10, May 96:6, Feb 97:7, Apr 97:11, Aug 97:6, Jun 05:1,10, Oct 07:15

(Do not report 11040-11044 in conjunction with 97597-97602)

Paring or Cutting

(To report destruction, see 17000-17004)

11055 Paring or cutting of benign hyperkeratotic lesion (eg, corn or callus); single lesion
➲ *CPT Assistant* Nov 97:11, Jan 99:11

11056 2 to 4 lesions
➲ *CPT Assistant* Nov 97:11, Jan 99:11

11057 more than 4 lesions
➲ *CPT Assistant* Nov 97:11, Jan 99:11, May 99:10

Biopsy

During certain surgical procedures in the integumentary system, such as excision, destruction, or shave removals, the removed tissue is often submitted for pathologic examination. The obtaining of tissue for pathology during the course of these procedures is a routine component of such procedures. This obtaining of tissue is not considered a separate biopsy procedure and is not separately reported. The use of a biopsy procedure code (eg, 11100, 11101) indicates that the procedure to obtain tissue for pathologic examination was performed independently, or was unrelated or distinct from other procedures/services provided at that time. Such biopsies are not considered components of other procedures when performed on different lesions or different sites on the same date, and are to be reported separately.

(For biopsy of conjunctiva, use 68100; eyelid, use 67810)

11100 Biopsy of skin, subcutaneous tissue and/or mucous membrane (including simple closure), unless otherwise listed; single lesion
➲ *CPT Assistant* Fall 94:20, Mar 97:12, Jun 97:12, Apr 00:7, Nov 02:6, Jul 04:5, Oct 04:4, Nov 06:1, Feb 08:1; *CPT Changes: An Insider's View* 2004

+ 11101   each separate/additional lesion (List separately in addition to code for primary procedure)
> *CPT Assistant* Fall 94:20, Apr 00:6, Apr 00:7, Nov 02:6, Jul 04:5, Oct 04:4, Nov 06:1, Feb 08:1

(Use 11101 in conjunction with 11100)

Removal of Skin Tags

Removal by scissoring or any sharp method, ligature strangulation, electrosurgical destruction or combination of treatment modalities, including chemical destruction or electrocauterization of wound, with or without local anesthesia.

11200   Removal of skin tags, multiple fibrocutaneous tags, any area; up to and including 15 lesions
> *CPT Assistant* Winter 90:3, Nov 97:11-12, Nov 02:11

+ 11201   each additional 10 lesions, or part thereof (List separately in addition to code for primary procedure)
> *CPT Assistant* Winter 90:3, Nov 97:11-12, Nov 02:11; *CPT Changes: An Insider's View* 2009

(Use 11201 in conjunction with 11200)

(handwritten: add on code)

Removal of Skin Tags
11200, 11201

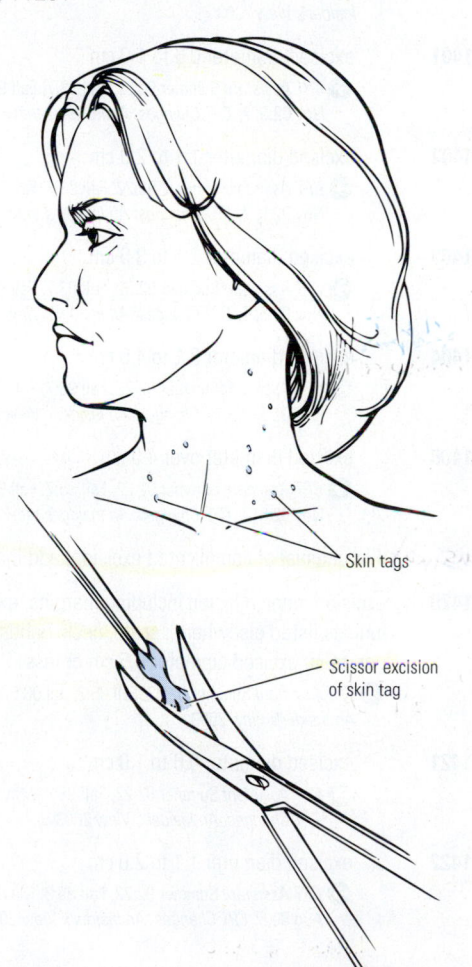

Skin tags

Scissor excision of skin tag

Shaving of Epidermal or Dermal Lesions

Shaving is the sharp removal by transverse incision or horizontal slicing to remove epidermal and dermal lesions without a full-thickness dermal excision. This includes local anesthesia, chemical or electrocauterization of the wound. The wound does not require suture closure.

11300   Shaving of epidermal or dermal lesion, single lesion, trunk, arms or legs; lesion diameter 0.5 cm or less
> *CPT Assistant* Feb 00:11, Nov 02:11, Feb 08:1

11301   lesion diameter 0.6 to 1.0 cm
> *CPT Assistant* Feb 00:11, Feb 08:1

11302   lesion diameter 1.1 to 2.0 cm
> *CPT Assistant* Feb 00:11, Feb 08:1

11303   lesion diameter over 2.0 cm
> *CPT Assistant* Feb 00:11, Feb 08:1

11305   Shaving of epidermal or dermal lesion, single lesion, scalp, neck, hands, feet, genitalia; lesion diameter 0.5 cm or less
> *CPT Assistant* Feb 00:11, Feb 08:1

11306   lesion diameter 0.6 to 1.0 cm
> *CPT Assistant* Feb 00:11, Feb 08:1

11307   lesion diameter 1.1 to 2.0 cm
> *CPT Assistant* Feb 00:11, Feb 08:1

11308   lesion diameter over 2.0 cm
> *CPT Assistant* Feb 00:11, Feb 08:1

11310   Shaving of epidermal or dermal lesion, single lesion, face, ears, eyelids, nose, lips, mucous membrane; lesion diameter 0.5 cm or less
> *CPT Assistant* Feb 00:11, Feb 08:1

11311   lesion diameter 0.6 to 1.0 cm
> *CPT Assistant* Feb 00:11, Feb 08:1

11312   lesion diameter 1.1 to 2.0 cm
> *CPT Assistant* Feb 00:11, Feb 08:1

11313   lesion diameter over 2.0 cm
> *CPT Assistant* Feb 00:11, Feb 08:1

Measuring and Coding the Removal of a Lesion

Measuring lesion removal.
A. Example: excision, malignant lesion of the back, 1.0 cm. Code 11606.

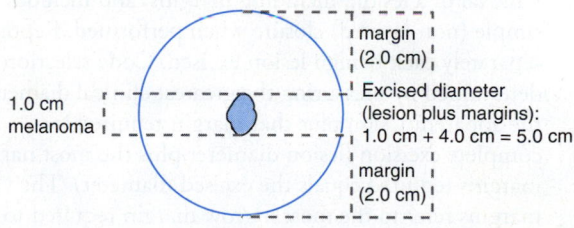

1.0 cm melanoma

margin (2.0 cm)

Excised diameter (lesion plus margins): 1.0 cm + 4.0 cm = 5.0 cm

margin (2.0 cm)

B. Example: Excision of benign lesion of the neck, 1.0 cm by 2.0 cm. Code 11423.

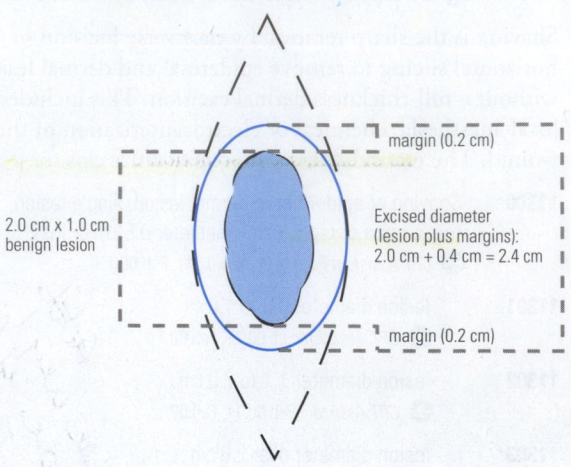

margin (0.2 cm)

2.0 cm x 1.0 cm
benign lesion

Excised diameter
(lesion plus margins):
2.0 cm + 0.4 cm = 2.4 cm

margin (0.2 cm)

C. Example: Excision, malignant lesion of the nose, 0.9 cm. Code 11642.

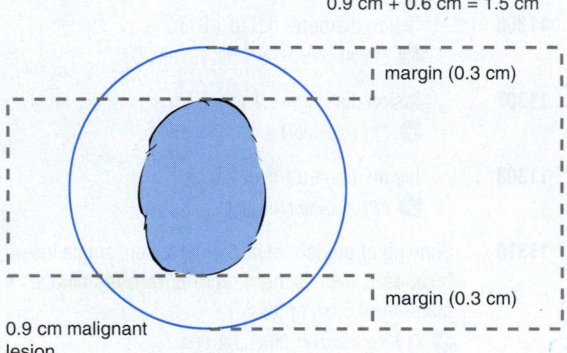

Excised diameter
(lesion plus margins):
0.9 cm + 0.6 cm = 1.5 cm

margin (0.3 cm)

margin (0.3 cm)

0.9 cm malignant
lesion

Excision—Benign Lesions

Excision (including simple closure) of benign lesions of skin (eg, neoplasm, cicatricial, fibrous, inflammatory, congenital, cystic lesions), includes local anesthesia. See appropriate size and area below. For shave removal, see 11300 et seq, and for electrosurgical and other methods see 17000 et seq.

Excision is defined as full-thickness (through the dermis) removal of a lesion, including margins, and includes simple (non-layered) closure when performed. Report separately each benign lesion excised. Code selection is determined by measuring the greatest clinical diameter of the apparent lesion plus that margin required for complete excision (lesion diameter plus the most narrow margins required equals the excised diameter). The margins refer to the most narrow margin required to

adequately excise the lesion, based on the physician's judgment. The measurement of lesion plus margin is made prior to excision. The excised diameter is the same whether the surgical defect is repaired in a linear fashion, or reconstructed (eg, with a skin graft).

►The closure of defects created by incision, excision, or trauma may require intermediate or complex closure. Repair by intermediate or complex closure should be reported separately. For excision of benign lesions requiring more than simple closure, ie, requiring intermediate or complex closure, report 11400-11446 in addition to appropriate intermediate (12031-12057) or complex closure (13100-13153) codes. For reconstructive closure, see 15002-15261, 15570-15770. For excision performed in conjunction with adjacent tissue transfer, report only the adjacent tissue transfer code (14000-14302). Excision of lesion (11400–11446) is not separately reportable with adjacent tissue transfer. See page 58 for the definition of *intermediate* or *complex* closure.◄

11400   Excision, benign lesion including margins, except skin tag (unless listed elsewhere), trunk, arms or legs; excised diameter 0.5 cm or less

➲ *CPT Assistant* Summer 92:22, Fall 93:7, Fall 95:3, May 96:11, Aug 00:5, Nov 02:5, 7, Aug 06:10, Jul 08:5; *CPT Changes: An Insider's View* 2003

11401   excised diameter 0.6 to 1.0 cm

➲ *CPT Assistant* Summer 92:22, Fall 93:7, Fall 95:3, May 96:11, Nov 02:5, 7; *CPT Changes: An Insider's View* 2003

11402   excised diameter 1.1 to 2.0 cm

➲ *CPT Assistant* Summer 92:22, Fall 93:7, Fall 95:3, May 96:11, Nov 02:5, 7; *CPT Changes: An Insider's View* 2003

11403   excised diameter 2.1 to 3.0 cm

➲ *CPT Assistant* Summer 92:22, Fall 93:7, Fall 95:3, May 96:11, Nov 02:5, 7; *CPT Changes: An Insider's View* 2003

11404   excised diameter 3.1 to 4.0 cm

➲ *CPT Assistant* Summer 92:22, Fall 93:7, Fall 95:3, May 96:11, Nov 02:5, 7; *CPT Changes: An Insider's View* 2003

11406   excised diameter over 4.0 cm

➲ *CPT Assistant* Summer 92:22, Fall 93:7, Fall 95:3, May 96:11, Nov 02:5, 7; *CPT Changes: An Insider's View* 2003

(extensive) (For unusual or complicated excision, add modifier 22)

11420   Excision, benign lesion including margins, except skin tag (unless listed elsewhere), scalp, neck, hands, feet, genitalia; excised diameter 0.5 cm or less

➲ *CPT Assistant* Summer 92:22, Fall 95:3, Jul 08:5; *CPT Changes: An Insider's View* 2003

11421   excised diameter 0.6 to 1.0 cm

➲ *CPT Assistant* Summer 92:22, Fall 95:3, May 96:11; *CPT Changes: An Insider's View* 2003

11422   excised diameter 1.1 to 2.0 cm

➲ *CPT Assistant* Summer 92:22, Fall 95:3, May 96:11, Aug 00:5; *CPT Changes: An Insider's View* 2003

11423   excised diameter 2.1 to 3.0 cm
➜ *CPT Assistant* Summer 92:22, Fall 95:3, May 96:11;
CPT Changes: An Insider's View 2003

11424   excised diameter 3.1 to 4.0 cm
➜ *CPT Assistant* Summer 92:22, Fall 95:3, May 96:11;
CPT Changes: An Insider's View 2003

11426   excised diameter over 4.0 cm
➜ *CPT Assistant* Summer 92:22, Fall 95:3, May 96:11;
CPT Changes: An Insider's View 2003

(For unusual or complicated excision, add modifier 22)

11440   Excision, other benign lesion including margins, except skin tag (unless listed elsewhere), face, ears, eyelids, nose, lips, mucous membrane; excised diameter 0.5 cm or less
➜ *CPT Assistant* Summer 92:22, Fall 95:3, May 96:11, Jul 08:5;
CPT Changes: An Insider's View 2003

11441   excised diameter 0.6 to 1.0 cm
➜ *CPT Assistant* Summer 92:22, Fall 95:3, May 96:11;
CPT Changes: An Insider's View 2003

11442   excised diameter 1.1 to 2.0 cm
➜ *CPT Assistant* Summer 92:22, Fall 95:3, May 96:11,
Aug 00:5, Jun 08:14; *CPT Changes: An Insider's View* 2003

11443   excised diameter 2.1 to 3.0 cm
➜ *CPT Assistant* Summer 92:22, Fall 95:3, May 96:11;
CPT Changes: An Insider's View 2003

11444   excised diameter 3.1 to 4.0 cm
➜ *CPT Assistant* Summer 92:22, Fall 95:3, May 96:11;
CPT Changes: An Insider's View 2003

11446   excised diameter over 4.0 cm
➜ *CPT Assistant* Summer 92:22, Fall 95:3, May 96:11,
Aug 06:10, Jul 08:5; *CPT Changes: An Insider's View* 2003

(For unusual or complicated excision, add modifier 22)

(For eyelids involving more than skin, see also 67800 et seq)

11450   Excision of skin and subcutaneous tissue for hidradenitis, axillary; with simple or intermediate repair

11451   with complex repair

11462   Excision of skin and subcutaneous tissue for hidradenitis, inguinal; with simple or intermediate repair

11463   with complex repair

11470   Excision of skin and subcutaneous tissue for hidradenitis, perianal, perineal, or umbilical; with simple or intermediate repair

11471   with complex repair

(When skin graft or flap is used for closure, use appropriate procedure code in addition)

(For bilateral procedure, add modifier 50)

Excision—Malignant Lesions

Excision (including simple closure) of malignant lesions of skin (eg, basal cell carcinoma, squamous cell carcinoma, melanoma) includes local anesthesia. (See appropriate size and body area below.) For destruction of malignant lesions of skin, see destruction codes 17260-17286.

Excision is defined as full-thickness (through the dermis) removal of a lesion including margins, and includes simple (non-layered) closure when performed. Report separately each malignant lesion excised. Code selection is determined by measuring the greatest clinical diameter of the apparent lesion plus that margin required for complete excision (lesion diameter plus the most narrow margins required equals the excised diameter). The margins refer to the most narrow margin required to adequately excise the lesion, based on the physician's judgment. The measurement of lesion plus margin is made prior to excision. The excised diameter is the same whether the surgical defect is repaired in a linear fashion, or reconstructed (eg, with a skin graft).

▶The closure of defects created by incision, excision, or trauma may require intermediate or complex closure. Repair by intermediate or complex closure should be reported separately. For excision of malignant lesions requiring more than simple closure, ie, requiring intermediate or complex closure, report 11600-11646 in addition to appropriate intermediate (12031-12057) or complex closure (13100-13153) codes. For reconstructive closure, see 15002-15261, 15570-15770. For excision performed in conjunction with adjacent tissue transfer, report only the adjacent tissue transfer code (14000-14302). Excision of lesion (11600–11646) is not separately reportable with adjacent tissue transfer. See page 58 for the definition of *intermediate* or *complex* closure.◀

When frozen section pathology shows the margins of excision were not adequate, an additional excision may be necessary for complete tumor removal. Use only one code to report the additional excision and re-excision(s) based on the final widest excised diameter required for complete tumor removal at the same operative session. To report a re-excision procedure performed to widen margins at a subsequent operative session, see codes 11600-11646, as appropriate. Append modifier 58 if the re-excision procedure is performed during the postoperative period of the primary excision procedure.

11600 Excision, malignant lesion including margins, trunk, arms, or legs; excised diameter 0.5 cm or less

> ⟹ CPT Assistant Fall 95:3, May 96:11, Nov 02:5, Oct 04:4, Feb 08:8; CPT Changes: An Insider's View 2003

Measuring and Coding the Removal of a Lesion
11600

Example: Excision, malignant lesion, 0.4 cm. Code 11600.

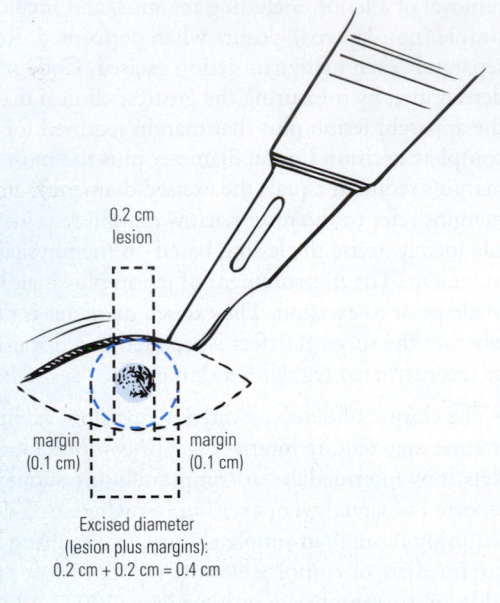

margin (0.1 cm)   margin (0.1 cm)

0.2 cm lesion

Excised diameter
(lesion plus margins):
0.2 cm + 0.2 cm = 0.4 cm

11601 excised diameter 0.6 to 1.0 cm

> ⟹ CPT Assistant Fall 95:3, May 96:11, Nov 02:5; CPT Changes: An Insider's View 2003

11602 excised diameter 1.1 to 2.0 cm

> ⟹ CPT Assistant Fall 95:3, May 96:11, Nov 02:5, Feb 08:8; CPT Changes: An Insider's View 2003

11603 excised diameter 2.1 to 3.0 cm

> ⟹ CPT Assistant Fall 95:3, May 96:11, Nov 02:5, Feb 08:8; CPT Changes: An Insider's View 2003

11604 excised diameter 3.1 to 4.0 cm

> ⟹ CPT Assistant Fall 95:3, May 96:11, Nov 02:5, Feb 08:8; CPT Changes: An Insider's View 2003

11606 excised diameter over 4.0 cm

> ⟹ CPT Assistant Fall 91:6, Fall 95:3, May 96:11, Nov 02:5, Feb 08:8; CPT Changes: An Insider's View 2003

11620 Excision, malignant lesion including margins, scalp, neck, hands, feet, genitalia; excised diameter 0.5 cm or less

> ⟹ CPT Assistant Fall 95:3, Nov 02:5, Oct 04:4, Feb 08:8; CPT Changes: An Insider's View 2003

11621 excised diameter 0.6 to 1.0 cm

> ⟹ CPT Assistant Fall 95:3, May 96:11, Nov 02:5, Feb 08:8; CPT Changes: An Insider's View 2003

11622 excised diameter 1.1 to 2.0 cm

> ⟹ CPT Assistant Fall 95:3, May 96:11, Nov 02:5, Feb 08:8; CPT Changes: An Insider's View 2003

11623 excised diameter 2.1 to 3.0 cm

> ⟹ CPT Assistant Fall 95:3, May 96:11, Nov 02:5, Feb 08:8; CPT Changes: An Insider's View 2003

11624 excised diameter 3.1 to 4.0 cm

> ⟹ CPT Assistant Fall 95:3, May 96:11, Nov 02:5, Feb 08:8; CPT Changes: An Insider's View 2003

11626 excised diameter over 4.0 cm

> ⟹ CPT Assistant Fall 95:3, May 96:11, Nov 02:5, Feb 08:8; CPT Changes: An Insider's View 2003

11640 Excision, malignant lesion including margins, face, ears, eyelids, nose, lips; excised diameter 0.5 cm or less

> ⟹ CPT Assistant Fall 95:3, May 96:11, Nov 02:5, Oct 04:4, Feb 08:8; CPT Changes: An Insider's View 2003

11641 excised diameter 0.6 to 1.0 cm

> ⟹ CPT Assistant Fall 95:3, May 96:11, Feb 08:8; CPT Changes: An Insider's View 2003

11642 excised diameter 1.1 to 2.0 cm

> ⟹ CPT Assistant Fall 95:3, May 96:11, Feb 08:8; CPT Changes: An Insider's View 2003

11643 excised diameter 2.1 to 3.0 cm

> ⟹ CPT Assistant Fall 95:3, May 96:11, Feb 08:8; CPT Changes: An Insider's View 2003

11644 excised diameter 3.1 to 4.0 cm

> ⟹ CPT Assistant Fall 95:3, May 96:11, Feb 08:8; CPT Changes: An Insider's View 2003

11646 excised diameter over 4.0 cm

> ⟹ CPT Assistant Fall 95:3, May 96:11, Feb 08:8; CPT Changes: An Insider's View 2003

(For eyelids involving more than skin, see also 67800 et seq)

Nails

(For drainage of paronychia or onychia, see 10060, 10061)

11719 Trimming of nondystrophic nails, any number

> ⟹ CPT Assistant Nov 97:12, Dec 02:4

Lateral Nail View
11719-11765

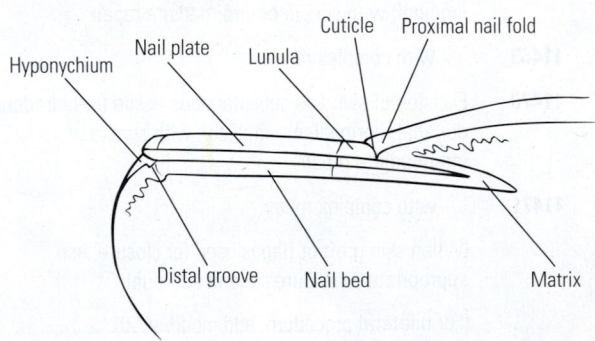

Hyponychium   Nail plate   Lunula   Cuticle   Proximal nail fold

Distal groove   Nail bed   Matrix

11720 Debridement of nail(s) by any method(s); 1 to 5
➜ *CPT Assistant* Nov 96:3, Dec 02:4

11721 6 or more
➜ *CPT Assistant* Nov 96:3, Dec 02:4

11730 Avulsion of nail plate, partial or complete, simple; single
➜ *CPT Assistant* Mar 96:10, Dec 02:4, Dec 03:11

+ 11732 each additional nail plate (List separately in addition to code for primary procedure)
➜ *CPT Assistant* Dec 02:4

(Use 11732 in conjunction with 11730)

11740 Evacuation of subungual hematoma
➜ *CPT Assistant* Dec 02:4

11750 Excision of nail and nail matrix, partial or complete (eg, ingrown or deformed nail), for permanent removal;
➜ *CPT Assistant* Dec 02:4

11752 with amputation of tuft of distal phalanx
➜ *CPT Assistant* Dec 02:4

(For skin graft, if used, use 15050)

11755 Biopsy of nail unit (eg, plate, bed, matrix, hyponychium, proximal and lateral nail folds) (separate procedure)
➜ *CPT Assistant* Mar 96:11, Dec 02:4, Oct 04:14; *CPT Changes: An Insider's View* 2002

11760 Repair of nail bed
➜ *CPT Assistant* Dec 02:4

11762 Reconstruction of nail bed with graft
➜ *CPT Assistant* Dec 02:4

11765 Wedge excision of skin of nail fold (eg, for ingrown toenail)
➜ *CPT Assistant* Dec 02:4

Dorsal Nail View
11719-11765

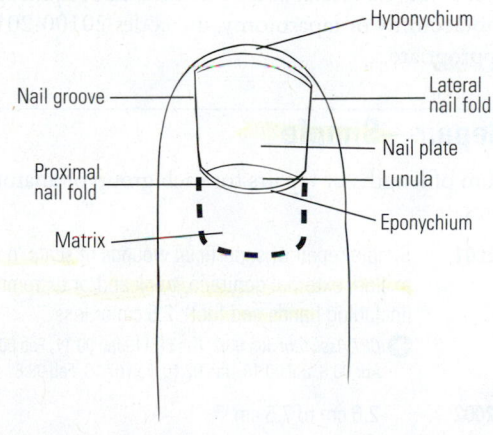

Hyponychium
Nail groove
Lateral nail fold
Nail plate
Proximal nail fold
Lunula
Matrix
Eponychium

Pilonidal Cyst

11770 Excision of pilonidal cyst or sinus; simple

11771 extensive

11772 complicated

(For incision of pilonidal cyst, see 10080, 10081)

Introduction

11900 Injection, intralesional; up to and including 7 lesions
➜ *CPT Assistant* Sep 96:5, May 98:10, Nov 99:8, Feb 00:11, Sep 04:12

11901 more than 7 lesions
➜ *CPT Assistant* Sep 96:5, May 98:10, Nov 99:8, Feb 00:11, Sep 04:12

(11900, 11901 are not to be used for preoperative local anesthetic injection)

(For veins, see 36470, 36471)

(For intralesional chemotherapy administration, see 96405, 96406)

11920 Tattooing, intradermal introduction of insoluble opaque pigments to correct color defects of skin, including micropigmentation; 6.0 sq cm or less

11921 6.1 to 20.0 sq cm

+ 11922 each additional 20.0 sq cm, or part thereof (List separately in addition to code for primary procedure)
➜ *CPT Changes: An Insider's View* 2009

(Use 11922 in conjunction with 11921)

11950 Subcutaneous injection of filling material (eg, collagen); 1 cc or less

11951 1.1 to 5.0 cc

11952 5.1 to 10.0 cc

11954 over 10.0 cc

11960 Insertion of tissue expander(s) for other than breast, including subsequent expansion
➜ *CPT Assistant* Winter 91:2

(For breast reconstruction with tissue expander(s), use 19357)

11970 Replacement of tissue expander with permanent prosthesis
➜ *CPT Assistant* Aug 05:1

11971 Removal of tissue expander(s) without insertion of prosthesis
➜ *CPT Assistant* Jun 05:11

11975 Insertion, implantable contraceptive capsules

11976 Removal, implantable contraceptive capsules

11977 Removal with reinsertion, implantable contraceptive capsules

11980 Subcutaneous hormone pellet implantation (implantation of estradiol and/or testosterone pellets beneath the skin)
➜ *CPT Assistant* Nov 99:8; *CPT Changes: An Insider's View* 2000

11981 Insertion, non-biodegradable drug delivery implant
➜ *CPT Changes: An Insider's View* 2002

11982 Removal, non-biodegradable drug delivery implant
➔ *CPT Changes: An Insider's View* 2002

11983 Removal with reinsertion, non-biodegradable drug delivery implant
➔ *CPT Changes: An Insider's View* 2002

Repair (Closure)

Use the codes in this section to designate wound closure utilizing sutures, staples, or tissue adhesives (eg, 2-cyanoacrylate), either singly or in combination with each other, or in combination with adhesive strips. Wound closure utilizing adhesive strips as the sole repair material should be coded using the appropriate E/M code.

Definitions

The repair of wounds may be classified as Simple, Intermediate, or Complex.

Simple repair is used when the wound is superficial; eg, involving primarily epidermis or dermis, or subcutaneous tissues without significant involvement of deeper structures, and requires simple one layer closure. This includes local anesthesia and chemical or electrocauterization of wounds not closed.

Intermediate repair includes the repair of wounds that, in addition to the above, require layered closure of one or more of the deeper layers of subcutaneous tissue and superficial (non-muscle) fascia, in addition to the skin (epidermal and dermal) closure. Single-layer closure of heavily contaminated wounds that have required extensive cleaning or removal of particulate matter also constitutes intermediate repair.

Complex repair includes the repair of wounds requiring more than layered closure, viz., scar revision, debridement (eg, traumatic lacerations or avulsions), extensive undermining, stents or retention sutures. Necessary preparation includes creation of a defect for repairs (eg, excision of a scar requiring a complex repair) or the debridement of complicated lacerations or avulsions. Complex repair does not include excision of benign (11400-11446) or malignant (11600-11646) lesions.

Instructions for listing services at time of wound repair:

1. The repaired wound(s) should be measured and recorded in centimeters, whether curved, angular, or stellate.

2. When multiple wounds are repaired, add together the lengths of those in the same classification (see above) and from all anatomic sites that are grouped together into the same code descriptor. For example, add together the lengths of intermediate repairs to the trunk and extremities. Do not add lengths of repairs from different groupings of anatomic sites (eg, face and extremities). Also, do not add together lengths of different classifications (eg, intermediate and complex repairs).

When more than one classification of wounds is repaired, list the more complicated as the primary procedure and the less complicated as the secondary procedure, using modifier 51.

3. Decontamination and/or debridement: Debridement is considered a separate procedure only when gross contamination requires prolonged cleansing, when appreciable amounts of devitalized or contaminated tissue are removed, or when debridement is carried out separately without immediate primary closure. (For extensive debridement of soft tissue and/or bone, see 11040-11044.)

(For extensive debridement of soft tissue and/or bone, not associated with open fracture(s) and/or dislocation(s) resulting from penetrating and/or blunt trauma, see 11040-11044.)

(For extensive debridement of subcutaneous tissue, muscle fascia, muscle, and/or bone associated with open fracture(s) and/or dislocation(s), see 11010-11012.)

4. Involvement of nerves, blood vessels and tendons: Report under appropriate system (Nervous, Cardiovascular, Musculoskeletal) for repair of these structures. The repair of these associated wounds is included in the primary procedure unless it qualifies as a complex wound, in which case modifier 51 applies.

Simple ligation of vessels in an open wound is considered as part of any wound closure.

Simple "exploration" of nerves, blood vessels or tendons exposed in an open wound is also considered part of the essential treatment of the wound and is not a separate procedure unless appreciable dissection is required. If the wound requires enlargement, extension of dissection (to determine penetration), debridement, removal of foreign body(s), ligation or coagulation of minor subcutaneous and/or muscular blood vessel(s) of the subcutaneous tissue, muscle fascia, and/or muscle, not requiring thoracotomy or laparotomy, use codes 20100-20103, as appropriate.

Repair—Simple

Sum of lengths of repairs for each group of anatomic sites.

12001 Simple repair of superficial wounds of scalp, neck, axillae, external genitalia, trunk and/or extremities (including hands and feet); 2.5 cm or less
➔ *CPT Assistant* Jun 96:7, Feb 98:11, Jan 00:11, Feb 00:10, Apr 00:8, Jul 00:10, Jan 02:10, Feb 07:10, Feb 08:8

12002 2.6 cm to 7.5 cm
➔ *CPT Assistant* Feb 00:10, Jan 02:10, Feb 08:8

12004 7.6 cm to 12.5 cm
➔ *CPT Assistant* Feb 00:10, Jan 02:10, Feb 08:8

12005 12.6 cm to 20.0 cm
➔ *CPT Assistant* Feb 00:10, Jan 02:10, Feb 08:8

12006   20.1 cm to 30.0 cm
➜ *CPT Assistant* Feb 98:11, Feb 00:10, Jan 02:10, Feb 08:8

12007   over 30.0 cm
➜ *CPT Assistant* Feb 00:10, Jan 02:10, Feb 08:8

12011   Simple repair of superficial wounds of face, ears, eyelids, nose, lips and/or mucous membranes; 2.5 cm or less
➜ *CPT Assistant* Feb 00:10, May 00:8, Jan 02:10, Feb 08:8

12013   2.6 cm to 5.0 cm
➜ *CPT Assistant* Feb 00:10, Jan 02:10, Feb 08:8

12014   5.1 cm to 7.5 cm
➜ *CPT Assistant* Feb 00:10, Jan 02:10, Feb 08:8

12015   7.6 cm to 12.5 cm
➜ *CPT Assistant* Feb 00:10, Jan 02:10, Feb 08:8

12016   12.6 cm to 20.0 cm
➜ *CPT Assistant* Feb 00:10, Jan 02:10, Feb 08:8

12017   20.1 cm to 30.0 cm
➜ *CPT Assistant* Feb 00:10, Jan 02:10, Feb 08:8

12018   over 30.0 cm
➜ *CPT Assistant* Feb 00:10, Jan 02:10, Feb 07:10, Feb 08:8

12020   Treatment of superficial wound dehiscence; simple closure   *non-healing*
➜ *CPT Assistant* Feb 00:10, Jan 02:10, Feb 08:8

12021   with packing
➜ *CPT Assistant* Feb 00:10, Jan 02:10, Feb 08:8

(For extensive or complicated secondary wound closure, use 13160)

Repair—Intermediate

Sum of lengths of repairs for each group of anatomic sites.

12031   Repair, intermediate, wounds of scalp, axillae, trunk and/or extremities (excluding hands and feet); 2.5 cm or less
➜ *CPT Assistant* Sep 97:11, Feb 00:10, Apr 00:8, Jan 02:10, Aug 06:1, Feb 07:10; *CPT Changes: An Insider's View* 2009

12032   2.6 cm to 7.5 cm
➜ *CPT Assistant* May 96:6, Jun 96:8, Feb 00:10, Jan 02:10, Feb 07:10; *CPT Changes: An Insider's View* 2009

12034   7.6 cm to 12.5 cm
➜ *CPT Assistant* Fall 91:6, Feb 00:10, Jan 02:10, Feb 07:10; *CPT Changes: An Insider's View* 2009

12035   12.6 cm to 20.0 cm
➜ *CPT Assistant* Feb 00:10, Jan 02:10, Feb 07:10; *CPT Changes: An Insider's View* 2009

12036   20.1 cm to 30.0 cm
➜ *CPT Assistant* Feb 00:10, Jan 02:10, Feb 07:10; *CPT Changes: An Insider's View* 2009

12037   over 30.0 cm
➜ *CPT Assistant* Feb 00:10, Jan 02:10, Feb 07:10; *CPT Changes: An Insider's View* 2009

12041   Repair, intermediate, wounds of neck, hands, feet and/or external genitalia; 2.5 cm or less
➜ *CPT Assistant* Sep 97:11, Feb 00:10, Apr 00:8, Jan 02:10, Feb 07:10; *CPT Changes: An Insider's View* 2009

12042   2.6 cm to 7.5 cm
➜ *CPT Assistant* Feb 00:10, Apr 00:9, Jan 02:10, Feb 07:10; *CPT Changes: An Insider's View* 2009

12044   7.6 cm to 12.5 cm
➜ *CPT Assistant* Feb 00:10, Jan 02:10, Feb 07:10; *CPT Changes: An Insider's View* 2009

12045   12.6 cm to 20.0 cm
➜ *CPT Assistant* Feb 00:10, Jan 02:10, Feb 07:10; *CPT Changes: An Insider's View* 2009

12046   20.1 cm to 30.0 cm
➜ *CPT Assistant* Feb 00:10, Jan 02:10, Feb 07:10; *CPT Changes: An Insider's View* 2009

12047   over 30.0 cm
➜ *CPT Assistant* Feb 00:10, Jan 02:10, Feb 07:10; *CPT Changes: An Insider's View* 2009

12051   Repair, intermediate, wounds of face, ears, eyelids, nose, lips and/or mucous membranes; 2.5 cm or less
➜ *CPT Assistant* Sep 97:11, Feb 00:10, Apr 00:8, Jan 02:10, Feb 07:10; *CPT Changes: An Insider's View* 2009

12052   2.6 cm to 5.0 cm
➜ *CPT Assistant* Feb 00:10, Aug 00:9, Jan 02:10, Feb 07:10, Jul 08:5; *CPT Changes: An Insider's View* 2009

12053   5.1 cm to 7.5 cm
➜ *CPT Assistant* Feb 00:10, Jan 02:10, Feb 07:10; *CPT Changes: An Insider's View* 2009

12054   7.6 cm to 12.5 cm
➜ *CPT Assistant* Feb 00:10, Jan 02:10, Feb 07:10; *CPT Changes: An Insider's View* 2009

12055   12.6 cm to 20.0 cm
➜ *CPT Assistant* Feb 00:10, Jan 02:10, Feb 07:10; *CPT Changes: An Insider's View* 2009

12056   20.1 cm to 30.0 cm
➜ *CPT Assistant* Feb 00:10, Jan 02:10, Feb 07:10; *CPT Changes: An Insider's View* 2009

12057   over 30.0 cm
➜ *CPT Assistant* Feb 00:10, Jan 02:10, Feb 07:10; *CPT Changes: An Insider's View* 2009

Repair—Complex

Reconstructive procedures, complicated wound closure.

Sum of lengths of repairs for each group of anatomic sites.

(For full thickness repair of lip or eyelid, see respective anatomical subsections)

13100   Repair, complex, trunk; 1.1 cm to 2.5 cm
➜ *CPT Assistant* Sep 97:11, Dec 98:5, Nov 99:9-10, Feb 00:10, Apr 00:8

(For 1.0 cm or less, see simple or intermediate repairs)

13101   2.6 cm to 7.5 cm
> *CPT Assistant* Dec 98:5, Nov 99:9-10, Feb 00:10, Apr 00:9

+ 13102   each additional 5 cm or less (List separately in addition to code for primary procedure)
> *CPT Assistant* Nov 99:9-10, Feb 00:10, Apr 00:9; *CPT Changes: An Insider's View* 2000

(Use 13102 in conjunction with 13101)

13120   Repair, complex, scalp, arms, and/or legs; 1.1 cm to 2.5 cm
> *CPT Assistant* Sep 97:11, Apr 99:11, Nov 99:9-10, Feb 00:10, Apr 00:8

(For 1.0 cm or less, see simple or intermediate repairs)

13121   2.6 cm to 7.5 cm
> *CPT Assistant* Dec 98:5, Nov 99:9-10, Feb 00:10

+ 13122   each additional 5 cm or less (List separately in addition to code for primary procedure)
> *CPT Assistant* Nov 99:10; *CPT Changes: An Insider's View* 2000

(Use 13122 in conjunction with 13121)

13131   Repair, complex, forehead, cheeks, chin, mouth, neck, axillae, genitalia, hands and/or feet; 1.1 cm to 2.5 cm
> *CPT Assistant* Fall 93:7, Sep 97:11, Dec 98:5, Nov 99:10, Feb 00:10, Apr 00:8

(For 1.0 cm or less, see simple or intermediate repairs)

13132   2.6 cm to 7.5 cm
> *CPT Assistant* Fall 93:7, Dec 98:5, Nov 99:10, Dec 99:10, Feb 00:10, Apr 00:9, Aug 00:9

+ 13133   each additional 5 cm or less (List separately in addition to code for primary procedure)
> *CPT Assistant* Fall 93:7, Feb 00:10, Apr 00:9; *CPT Changes: An Insider's View* 2000

(Use 13133 in conjunction with 13132)

13150   Repair, complex, eyelids, nose, ears and/or lips; 1.0 cm or less
> *CPT Assistant* Sep 97:11, Dec 98:5, Nov 99:10, Feb 00:10, Apr 00:8

(See also 40650-40654, 67961-67975)

13151   1.1 cm to 2.5 cm
> *CPT Assistant* Dec 98:5, Nov 99:10, Feb 00:10

13152   2.6 cm to 7.5 cm
> *CPT Assistant* Dec 98:5, Nov 99:10, Feb 00:10

+ 13153   each additional 5 cm or less (List separately in addition to code for primary procedure)
> *CPT Assistant* Nov 99:10, Feb 00:10; *CPT Changes: An Insider's View* 2000

(Use 13153 in conjunction with 13152)

13160   Secondary closure of surgical wound or dehiscence, extensive or complicated
> *CPT Assistant* Sep 97:11, Dec 98:5, Apr 00:8

(For packing or simple secondary wound closure, see 12020, 12021)

Adjacent Tissue Transfer or Rearrangement

For full thickness repair of lip or eyelid, see respective anatomical subsections.

►Codes 14000-14302 are used for excision (including lesion) and/or repair by adjacent tissue transfer or rearrangement (eg, Z-plasty, W-plasty, V-Y plasty, rotation flap, random island flap, advancement flap). When applied in repairing lacerations, the procedures listed must be performed by the surgeon to accomplish the repair. They do not apply to direct closure or rearrangement of traumatic wounds incidentally resulting in these configurations. Undermining alone of adjacent tissues to achieve closure, without additional incisions, does not constitute adjacent tissue transfer, see complex repair codes 13100-13160. The excision of a benign lesion (11400-11446) or a malignant lesion (11600-11646) is not separately reportable with codes 14000-14302.◄

Skin graft necessary to close secondary defect is considered an additional procedure. For purposes of code selection, the term "defect" includes the primary and secondary defects. The primary defect resulting from the excision and the secondary defect resulting from flap design to perform the reconstruction are measured together to determine the code.

14000   Adjacent tissue transfer or rearrangement, trunk; defect 10 sq cm or less
> *CPT Assistant* Sep 96:11, Jul 99:3, Jul 00:10, Jan 06:47, Dec 06:15, Jul 08:5

14001   defect 10.1 sq cm to 30.0 sq cm
> *CPT Assistant* Aug 96:8, Jul 99:3, Jan 06:47, Dec 06:15, Jul 08:5

14020   Adjacent tissue transfer or rearrangement, scalp, arms and/or legs; defect 10 sq cm or less
> *CPT Assistant* Jul 99:3, Jan 06:47, Dec 06:15, Jul 08:5

14021   defect 10.1 sq cm to 30.0 sq cm
> *CPT Assistant* Jul 99:3, Jan 06:47, Dec 06:15, Jul 08:5

14040   Adjacent tissue transfer or rearrangement, forehead, cheeks, chin, mouth, neck, axillae, genitalia, hands and/or feet; defect 10 sq cm or less
> *CPT Assistant* Jul 99:3, Jul 00:10, Jan 06:47, Dec 06:15, Jul 08:5

14041   defect 10.1 sq cm to 30.0 sq cm
> *CPT Assistant* Jul 99:3, Jan 06:47, Dec 06:15, Jul 08:5

14060   Adjacent tissue transfer or rearrangement, eyelids, nose, ears and/or lips; defect 10 sq cm or less
> *CPT Assistant* Fall 93:7, Jul 99:3, Jan 06:47, Dec 06:15, Jul 08:5

14061   defect 10.1 sq cm to 30.0 sq cm
> *CPT Assistant* Jul 99:3, Jan 06:47, Dec 06:15, Jul 08:5

(For eyelid, full thickness, see 67961 et seq)

Adjacent Tissue Repairs
14000-14061

Repair of primary and secondary defects requires assignment of a code based upon the repair location and the approximate description (as demonstrated below) of the area repaired.

A. Advancement Flap

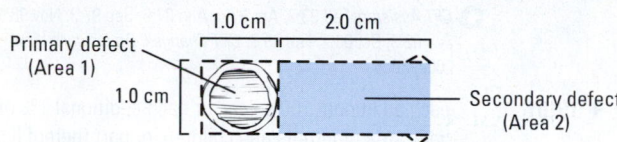

Area 1: 1.0 cm x 1.0 cm = 1.0 sq cm
Area 2: 1.0 cm x 2.0 cm = 2.0 sq cm
(Area 1) + (Area 2) = 1.0 sq cm + 2.0 sq cm = 3.0 sq cm

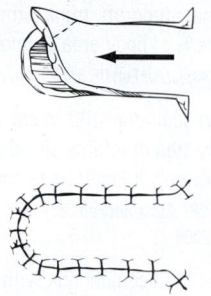

B. Rotation Flap

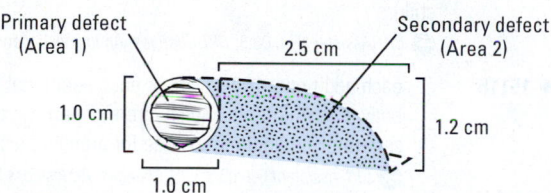

Area 1: 1.0 cm x 1.0 cm = 1.0 sq cm
Area 2: 2.5 cm x 1.2 cm = 3.0 sq cm
(Area 1) + (Area 2) = 1.0 sq cm + 3.0 sq cm = 4.0 sq cm

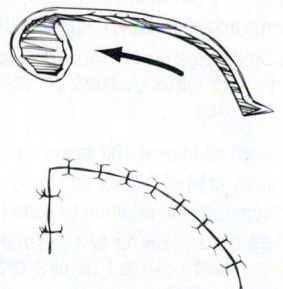

▶(14300 has been deleted. To report, see 14301, 14302)◀

 ● **14301** Adjacent tissue transfer or rearrangement, any area; defect 30.1 sq cm to 60.0 sq cm

➲ *CPT Changes: An Insider's View* 2010

+ ● **14302** each additional 30.0 sq cm, or part thereof (List separately in addition to code for primary procedure)

➲ *CPT Changes: An Insider's View* 2010

▶(Use 14302 in conjunction with 14301)◀

14350 Filleted finger or toe flap, including preparation of recipient site

➲ *CPT Assistant* Jan 06:47, Jul 08:5

Skin Replacement Surgery and Skin Substitutes

Identify by size and location of the defect (recipient area) and the type of graft or skin substitute; includes simple debridement of granulation tissue or recent avulsion.

When a primary procedure such as orbitectomy, radical mastectomy, or deep tumor removal requires skin graft for definitive closure, see appropriate anatomical subsection for primary procedure and this section for skin graft or skin substitute.

Use codes 15002-15005 for initial wound recipient site preparation.

Use codes 15100-15261 for autologous skin grafts. For autologous tissue-cultured epidermal grafts, use codes 15150-15157. For harvesting of autologous keratinocytes and dermal tissue for tissue-cultured skin grafts, use code 15040. Procedures are coded by recipient site. Use codes 15170-15176 for acellular dermal replacement.

Repair of donor site requiring skin graft or local flaps is to be added as an additional procedure.

Codes 15002-15005 describe burn and wound preparation or incisional or excisional release of scar contracture resulting in an open wound requiring a skin graft. Codes 15100-15431 describe the application of skin replacements and skin substitutes. The following definition should be applied to those codes that reference "100 sq cm or 1% of body area of infants and children" when determining the involvement of body size: The measurement of 100 sq cm is applicable to adults and children age 10 and older; percentages of body surface area apply to infants and children younger than the age of 10.

These codes are not intended to be reported for simple graft application alone or application stabilized with dressings (eg, by simple gauze wrap). The skin substitute/graft is anchored using the surgeon's choice of fixation. When services are performed in the office, the supply of the skin substitute/graft should be reported separately. Routine dressing supplies are not reported separately. When square centimeters are indicated, this refers to 1 sq cm up to the stated amount. Add-on codes begin with the next sq cm (eg, 130 sq cm would be coded using a code for the first 100 sq cm and an add-on code for the next 30 sq cm). Use modifier 58 for staged application procedure(s).

(For microvascular flaps, see 15756-15758)

[handwritten: dead sea] *[handwritten: notes & add on codes]*

Surgical Preparation

15002 Surgical preparation or creation of recipient site by excision of open wounds, burn eschar, or scar (including subcutaneous tissues), or incisional release of scar contracture, trunk, arms, legs; first 100 sq cm or 1% of body area of infants and children
➔ *CPT Changes: An Insider's View* 2007

+ 15003 each additional 100 sq cm, or part thereof, or each additional 1% of body area of infants and children (List separately in addition to code for primary procedure)
➔ *CPT Changes: An Insider's View* 2007, 2009

(Use 15003 in conjunction with 15002)

15004 Surgical preparation or creation of recipient site by excision of open wounds, burn eschar, or scar (including subcutaneous tissues), or incisional release of scar contracture, face, scalp, eyelids, mouth, neck, ears, orbits, genitalia, hands, feet and/or multiple digits; first 100 sq cm or 1% of body area of infants and children
➔ *CPT Changes: An Insider's View* 2007

+ 15005 each additional 100 sq cm, or part thereof, or each additional 1% of body area of infants and children (List separately in addition to code for primary procedure)
➔ *CPT Changes: An Insider's View* 2007, 2009

(Use 15005 in conjunction with 15004)

(Report 15002-15005 in conjunction with code for appropriate skin grafts or replacements [15050-15261, 15330-15336]. List the graft or replacement separately by its procedure number when the graft, immediate or delayed, is applied)

(For excision of benign lesions, see 11400-11471)

(For excision of malignant lesions, see 11600-11646)

(For excision to prepare or create recipient site with dressings or materials not listed in 15040-15431, use 15002-15005 only)

(For excision with immediate skin grafting, use 15002-15005 in conjunction with 15050-15261)

(For excision with immediate allograft skin placement, use 15002-15005 in conjunction with 15300-15336 and 15360-15366)

(For excision with immediate xenogeneic dermis placement, use 15002-15005 in conjunction with 15400-15421)

Grafts

Autograft/Tissue Cultured Autograft

15040 Harvest of skin for tissue cultured skin autograft, 100 sq cm or less
➔ *CPT Assistant* Aug 06:10, Oct 06:1, Feb 08:3; *CPT Changes: An Insider's View* 2006

15050 Pinch graft, single or multiple, to cover small ulcer, tip of digit, or other minimal open area (except on face), up to defect size 2 cm diameter
➔ *CPT Assistant* Apr 97:4, Sep 97:2, Nov 98:6

15100 Split-thickness autograft, trunk, arms, legs; first 100 sq cm or less, or 1% of body area of infants and children (except 15050)
➔ *CPT Assistant* Fall 93:7, Apr 97:4, Aug 97:6, Sep 97:3, Nov 98:6, Sep 02:3, Oct 06:1, Feb 08:3; *CPT Changes: An Insider's View* 2002, 2006

+ 15101 each additional 100 sq cm, or each additional 1% of body area of infants and children, or part thereof (List separately in addition to code for primary procedure)
➔ *CPT Assistant* Apr 97:4, Nov 98:6, Sep 02:3, Feb 08:3; *CPT Changes: An Insider's View* 2002

(Use 15101 in conjunction with 15100)

15110 Epidermal autograft, trunk, arms, legs; first 100 sq cm or less, or 1% of body area of infants and children
➔ *CPT Assistant* Feb 08:3; *CPT Changes: An Insider's View* 2006

+ 15111 each additional 100 sq cm, or each additional 1% of body area of infants and children, or part thereof (List separately in addition to code for primary procedure)
➔ *CPT Assistant* Feb 08:3; *CPT Changes: An Insider's View* 2006

(Use 15111 in conjunction with 15110)

15115 Epidermal autograft, face, scalp, eyelids, mouth, neck, ears, orbits, genitalia, hands, feet, and/or multiple digits; first 100 sq cm or less, or 1% of body area of infants and children
➔ *CPT Assistant* Feb 08:3; *CPT Changes: An Insider's View* 2006

+ 15116 each additional 100 sq cm, or each additional 1% of body area of infants and children, or part thereof (List separately in addition to code for primary procedure)
➔ *CPT Assistant* Feb 08:3; *CPT Changes: An Insider's View* 2006

(Use 15116 in conjunction with 15115)

15120 Split-thickness autograft, face, scalp, eyelids, mouth, neck, ears, orbits, genitalia, hands, feet, and/or multiple digits; first 100 sq cm or less, or 1% of body area of infants and children (except 15050)
➔ *CPT Assistant* Apr 97:4, Aug 97:6, Sep 97:3, Nov 98:6, Jan 99:4, Sep 02:3, Feb 08:3, Jul 08:5; *CPT Changes: An Insider's View* 2002, 2006

+ 15121 each additional 100 sq cm, or each additional 1% of body area of infants and children, or part thereof (List separately in addition to code for primary procedure)
➔ *CPT Assistant* Apr 97:4, Aug 97:6, Sep 97:3, Nov 98:6, Jan 99:4, Sep 02:3, Feb 08:3; *CPT Changes: An Insider's View* 2002

(Use 15121 in conjunction with 15120)

(For eyelids, see also 67961 et seq)

15130 Dermal autograft, trunk, arms, legs; first 100 sq cm or 1% of body area of infants and children
➔ *CPT Assistant* Feb 08:3; *CPT Changes: An Insider's View* 2006

+ 15131   each additional 100 sq cm, or each additional 1% of body area of infants and children, or part thereof (List separately in addition to code for primary procedure)

➔ *CPT Assistant* Feb 08:3; *CPT Changes: An Insider's View* 2006

(Use 15131 in conjunction with 15130)

15135   Dermal autograft, face, scalp, eyelids, mouth, neck, ears, orbits, genitalia, hands, feet, and/or multiple digits; first 100 sq cm or less, or 1% of body area of infants and children

➔ *CPT Assistant* Feb 08:3; *CPT Changes: An Insider's View* 2006

+ 15136   each additional 100 sq cm, or each additional 1% of body area of infants and children, or part thereof (List separately in addition to code for primary procedure)

➔ *CPT Changes: An Insider's View* 2006

(Use 15136 in conjunction with 15135)

15150   Tissue cultured epidermal autograft, trunk, arms, legs; first 25 sq cm or less

➔ *CPT Assistant* Oct 06:1, Feb 08:3; *CPT Changes: An Insider's View* 2006

+ 15151   additional 1 sq cm to 75 sq cm (List separately in addition to code for primary procedure)

➔ *CPT Assistant* Oct 06:1, Feb 08:3; *CPT Changes: An Insider's View* 2006

(Do not report 15151 more than once per session)

(Use 15151 in conjunction with 15150)

+ 15152   each additional 100 sq cm, or each additional 1% of body area of infants and children, or part thereof (List separately in addition to code for primary procedure)

➔ *CPT Assistant* Oct 06:1, Feb 08:3; *CPT Changes: An Insider's View* 2006

(Use 15152 in conjunction with 15151)

15155   Tissue cultured epidermal autograft, face, scalp, eyelids, mouth, neck, ears, orbits, genitalia, hands, feet, and/or multiple digits; first 25 sq cm or less

➔ *CPT Assistant* Oct 06:1, Feb 08:3; *CPT Changes: An Insider's View* 2006

+ 15156   additional 1 sq cm to 75 sq cm (List separately in addition to code for primary procedure)

➔ *CPT Assistant* Oct 06:1, Feb 08:3; *CPT Changes: An Insider's View* 2006

(Do not report 15156 more than once per session)

(Use 15156 in conjunction with 15155)

+ 15157   each additional 100 sq cm, or each additional 1% of body area of infants and children, or part thereof (List separately in addition to code for primary procedure)

➔ *CPT Assistant* Oct 06:1, Feb 08:3; *CPT Changes: An Insider's View* 2006

(Use 15157 in conjunction with 15156)

Acellular Dermal Replacement

15170   Acellular dermal replacement, trunk, arms, legs; first 100 sq cm or less, or 1% of body area of infants and children

➔ *CPT Assistant* Oct 06:1, Feb 08:3; *CPT Changes: An Insider's View* 2006

+ 15171   each additional 100 sq cm, or each additional 1% of body area of infants and children, or part thereof (List separately in addition to code for primary procedure)

➔ *CPT Assistant* Oct 06:1, Feb 08:3; *CPT Changes: An Insider's View* 2006

(Use 15171 in conjunction with 15170)

15175   Acellular dermal replacement, face, scalp, eyelids, mouth, neck, ears, orbits, genitalia, hands, feet, and/or multiple digits; first 100 sq cm or less, or 1% of body area of infants and children

➔ *CPT Assistant* Oct 06:1, Feb 08:3; *CPT Changes: An Insider's View* 2006

+ 15176   each additional 100 sq cm, or each additional 1% of body area of infants and children, or part thereof (List separately in addition to code for primary procedure)

➔ *CPT Assistant* Oct 06:1, Feb 08:3; *CPT Changes: An Insider's View* 2006

(Use 15176 in conjunction with 15175)

15200   Full thickness graft, free, including direct closure of donor site, trunk; 20 sq cm or less

➔ *CPT Assistant* Aug 96:11, Aug 97:6, Sep 97:3, Feb 08:3, Mar 08:14; *CPT Changes: An Insider's View* 2002

+ 15201   each additional 20 sq cm, or part thereof (List separately in addition to code for primary procedure)

➔ *CPT Assistant* Apr 97:4, Aug 97:6, Sep 97:3, Feb 08:3, Mar 08:14; *CPT Changes: An Insider's View* 2002, 2009

(Use 15201 in conjunction with 15200)

15220   Full thickness graft, free, including direct closure of donor site, scalp, arms, and/or legs; 20 sq cm or less

➔ *CPT Assistant* Apr 97:4, Aug 97:6, Sep 97:3, Aug 98:9, Feb 08:3, Mar 08:14; *CPT Changes: An Insider's View* 2002

+ 15221   each additional 20 sq cm, or part thereof (List separately in addition to code for primary procedure)

➔ *CPT Assistant* Apr 97:4, Aug 97:6, Sep 97:3, Aug 98:9, Feb 08:3, Mar 08:14; *CPT Changes: An Insider's View* 2002, 2009

(Use 15221 in conjunction with 15220)

15240   Full thickness graft, free, including direct closure of donor site, forehead, cheeks, chin, mouth, neck, axillae, genitalia, hands, and/or feet; 20 sq cm or less

➔ *CPT Assistant* Apr 97:4, Aug 97:6, Sep 97:3, Nov 00:10, Feb 08:3, Mar 08:14; *CPT Changes: An Insider's View* 2002

(For finger tip graft, use 15050)

(For repair of syndactyly, fingers, see 26560-26562)

+ 15241   each additional 20 sq cm, or part thereof (List separately in addition to code for primary procedure)

➔ *CPT Assistant* Apr 97:4, Aug 97:6, Sep 97:3, Feb 08:3, Mar 08:14; *CPT Changes: An Insider's View* 2002, 2009

(Use 15241 in conjunction with 15240)

15260   Full thickness graft, free, including direct closure of donor site, nose, ears, eyelids, and/or lips; 20 sq cm or less

➔ *CPT Assistant* Fall 91:7, Fall 93:7, Apr 97:4, Aug 97:6, Sep 97:3, Jul 99:3, Feb 08:3, Mar 08:14; *CPT Changes: An Insider's View* 2002

+ 15261   each additional 20 sq cm, or part thereof (List separately in addition to code for primary procedure)

➔ *CPT Assistant* Fall 91:7, Apr 97:4, Aug 97:6, Sep 97:3, Feb 08:3, Mar 08:14; *CPT Changes: An Insider's View* 2002, 2009

(Use 15261 in conjunction with 15260)

(For eyelids, see also 67961 et seq)

(Repair of donor site requiring skin graft or local flaps, to be added as additional separate procedure)

Allograft/Tissue Cultured Allogeneic Skin Substitute

Application of a non-autologous human skin graft (ie, homograft) from a donor to a part of the recipient's body to resurface an area damaged by burns, traumatic injury, soft tissue infection and/or tissue necrosis or surgery.

15300   Allograft skin for temporary wound closure, trunk, arms, legs; first 100 sq cm or less, or 1% of body area of infants and children

➔ *CPT Assistant* Oct 06:1; *CPT Changes: An Insider's View* 2006

+ 15301   each additional 100 sq cm, or each additional 1% of body area of infants and children, or part thereof (List separately in addition to code for primary procedure)

➔ *CPT Assistant* Oct 06:1; *CPT Changes: An Insider's View* 2006

(Use 15301 in conjunction with 15300)

15320   Allograft skin for temporary wound closure, face, scalp, eyelids, mouth, neck, ears, orbits, genitalia, hands, feet, and/or multiple digits; first 100 sq cm or less, or 1% of body area of infants and children

➔ *CPT Assistant* Oct 06:1; *CPT Changes: An Insider's View* 2006

+ 15321   each additional 100 sq cm, or each additional 1% of body area of infants and children, or part thereof (List separately in addition to code for primary procedure)

➔ *CPT Assistant* Oct 06:1; *CPT Changes: An Insider's View* 2006

(Use 15321 in conjunction with 15320)

Allograft, Skin
15300-15321

Application of allograft skin (homograft) from a healthy cadaveric donor is applied to a part of the patient's body to resurface an area damaged by burns, traumatic injury, or surgery.

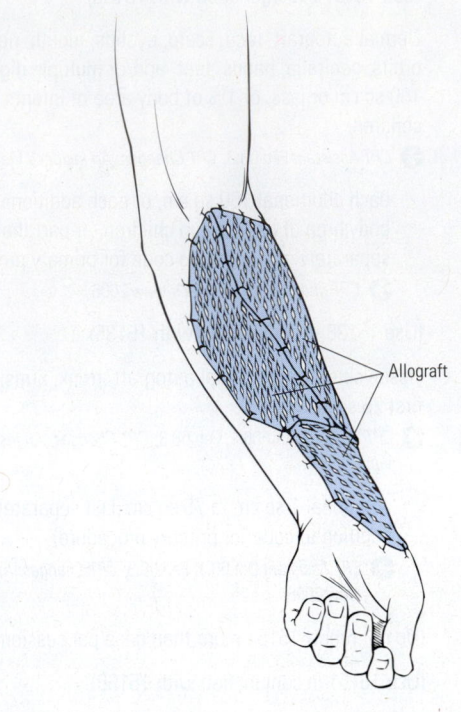

Allograft

15330   Acellular dermal allograft, trunk, arms, legs; first 100 sq cm or less, or 1% of body area of infants and children

➔ *CPT Changes: An Insider's View* 2006

+ 15331   each additional 100 sq cm, or each additional 1% of body area of infants and children, or part thereof (List separately in addition to code for primary procedure)

➔ *CPT Changes: An Insider's View* 2006

(Use 15331 in conjunction with 15330)

15335   Acellular dermal allograft, face, scalp, eyelids, mouth, neck, ears, orbits, genitalia, hands, feet, and/or multiple digits; first 100 sq cm or less, or 1% of body area of infants and children

➔ *CPT Changes: An Insider's View* 2006

+ 15336   each additional 100 sq cm, or each additional 1% of body area of infants and children, or part thereof (List separately in addition to code for primary procedure)

➔ *CPT Changes: An Insider's View* 2006, 2007

(Use 15336 in conjunction with 15335)

15340   Tissue cultured allogeneic skin substitute; first 25 sq cm or less

➔ *CPT Assistant* Oct 06:1; *CPT Changes: An Insider's View* 2006

+ 15341   each additional 25 sq cm, or part thereof (List separately in addition to code for primary procedure)

➔ *CPT Assistant* Oct 06:1; *CPT Changes: An Insider's View* 2006, 2009

(Use 15341 in conjunction with 15340)

(Do not report 15340, 15341 in conjunction with 11040-11042, 15002-15005)

15360   Tissue cultured allogeneic dermal substitute, trunk, arms, legs; first 100 sq cm or less, or 1% of body area of infants and children

➔ *CPT Assistant* Oct 06:1, Feb 08:3; *CPT Changes: An Insider's View* 2006

+ 15361   each additional 100 sq cm, or each additional 1% of body area of infants and children, or part thereof (List separately in addition to code for primary procedure)

➔ *CPT Assistant* Oct 06:1, Feb 08:3; *CPT Changes: An Insider's View* 2006

(Use 15361 in conjunction with 15360)

15365   Tissue cultured allogeneic dermal substitute, face, scalp, eyelids, mouth, neck, ears, orbits, genitalia, hands, feet, and/or multiple digits; first 100 sq cm or less, or 1% of body area of infants and children

➔ *CPT Assistant* Oct 06:1, Feb 08:3; *CPT Changes: An Insider's View* 2006

+ 15366   each additional 100 sq cm, or each additional 1% of body area of infants and children, or part thereof (List separately in addition to code for primary procedure)

➔ *CPT Assistant* Oct 06:1; *CPT Changes: An Insider's View* 2006, 2007

(Use 15366 in conjunction with 15365)

Xenograft

Application of a non-human skin graft or biologic wound dressing (eg, porcine tissue or pigskin) to a part of the recipient's body following debridement of the burn wound or area of traumatic injury, soft tissue infection and/or tissue necrosis, or surgery.

15400   Xenograft, skin (dermal), for temporary wound closure, trunk, arms, legs; first 100 sq cm or less, or 1% of body area of infants and children

➔ *CPT Assistant* Apr 97:4, Sep 97:3, Nov 98:6, Jan 99:4, Apr 01:10, Nov 03:15, Jan 06:1, Aug 06:10, Oct 06:1; *CPT Changes: An Insider's View* 2006

Xenograft, Skin
15400-15401

non-human

Application of porcine skin graft following excision of the burn wound and/or surgical preparation of the site

most of times (swine

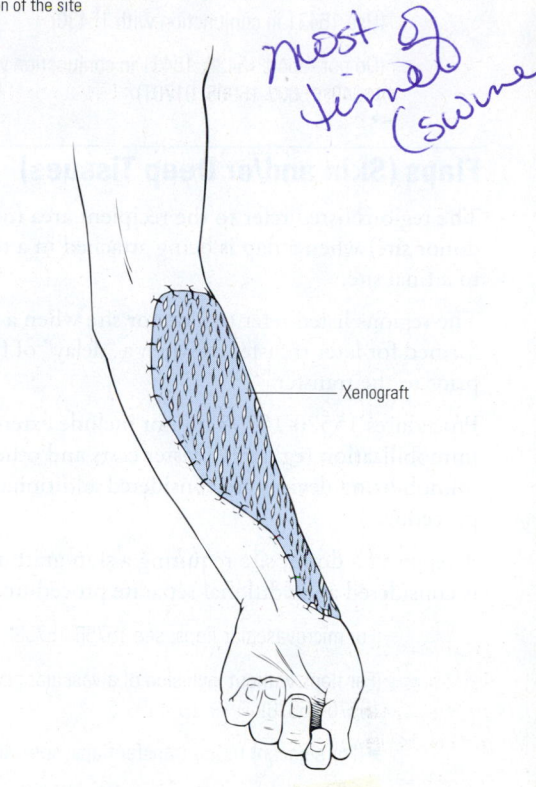

Xenograft

+ 15401   each additional 100 sq cm, or each additional 1% of body area of infants and children, or part thereof (List separately in addition to code for primary procedure)

➔ *CPT Assistant* Nov 98:6, Jan 99:4, Jan 06:1; *CPT Changes: An Insider's View* 2006

(Use 15401 in conjunction with 15400)

15420   Xenograft skin (dermal), for temporary wound closure, face, scalp, eyelids, mouth, neck, ears, orbits, genitalia, hands, feet, and/or multiple digits; first 100 sq cm or less, or 1% of body area of infants and children

➔ *CPT Changes: An Insider's View* 2006

+ 15421   each additional 100 sq cm, or each additional 1% of body area of infants and children, or part thereof (List separately in addition to code for primary procedure)

➔ *CPT Changes: An Insider's View* 2006

(Use 15421 in conjunction with 15420)

15430   Acellular xenograft implant; first 100 sq cm or less, or 1% of body area of infants and children

➔ *CPT Changes: An Insider's View* 2006

+ 15431   each additional 100 sq cm, or each additional 1% of body area of infants and children, or part thereof (List separately in addition to code for primary procedure)

→ *CPT Changes: An Insider's View* 2006

(Use 15431 in conjunction with 15430)

(Do not report 15430, 15431 in conjunction with 11040-11042, 15002-15005, 0170T)

Flaps (Skin and/or Deep Tissues)

The regions listed refer to the recipient area (not the donor site) when a flap is being attached in a transfer or to a final site.

The regions listed refer to a donor site when a tube is formed for later transfer or when a "delay" of flap occurs prior to the transfer.

Procedures 15570-15738 do not include extensive immobilization (eg, large plaster casts and other immobilizing devices are considered additional separate procedures).

A repair of a donor site requiring a skin graft or local flaps is considered an additional separate procedure.

(For microvascular flaps, see 15756-15758)

(For flaps without inclusion of a vascular pedicle, see 15570-15576)

▶(For adjacent tissue transfer flaps, see 14000-14302)◀

15570   Formation of direct or tubed pedicle, with or without transfer; trunk

→ *CPT Assistant* Nov 02:7

15572   scalp, arms, or legs

15574   forehead, cheeks, chin, mouth, neck, axillae, genitalia, hands or feet

15576   eyelids, nose, ears, lips, or intraoral

15600   Delay of flap or sectioning of flap (division and inset); at trunk

→ *CPT Assistant* Nov 99:10

15610   at scalp, arms, or legs

15620   at forehead, cheeks, chin, neck, axillae, genitalia, hands, or feet

15630   at eyelids, nose, ears, or lips

15650   Transfer, intermediate, of any pedicle flap (eg, abdomen to wrist, Walking tube), any location

(For eyelids, nose, ears, or lips, see also anatomical area)

▶(For revision, defatting or rearranging of transferred pedicle flap or skin graft, see 13100-14302)◀

(Procedures 15732-15738 are described by donor site of the muscle, myocutaneous, or fasciocutaneous flap)

15731   Forehead flap with preservation of vascular pedicle (eg, axial pattern flap, paramedian forehead flap)

→ *CPT Changes: An Insider's View* 2007

(For muscle, myocutaneous, or fasciocutaneous flap of the head or neck, use 15732)

Axial Pattern Forehead Flap
15731

Reconstruction of a nasal defect with a forehead flap based on the left supratrochlear vessels

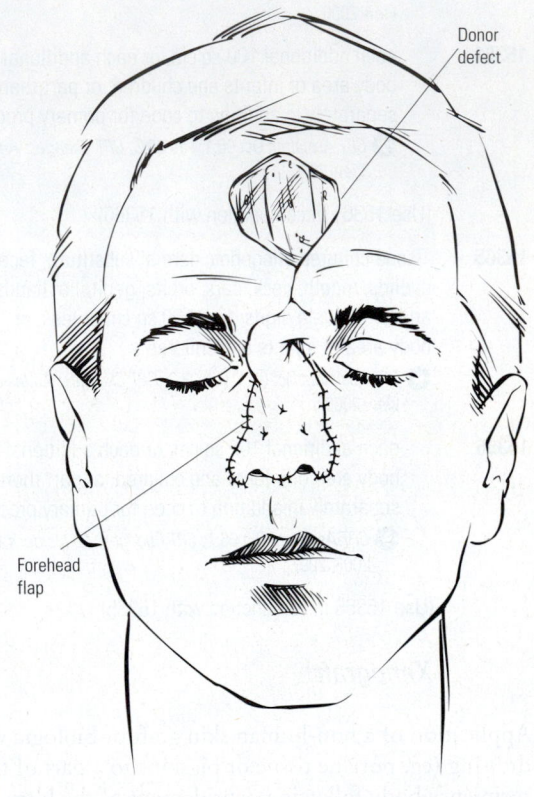

Donor defect

Forehead flap

15732   Muscle, myocutaneous, or fasciocutaneous flap; head and neck (eg, temporalis, masseter muscle, sternocleidomastoid, levator scapulae)

→ *CPT Changes: An Insider's View* 2002

(For forehead flap with preservation of vascular pedicle, use 15731)

15734   trunk

15736   upper extremity

15738   lower extremity

→ *CPT Assistant* Sep 03:15

Other Flaps and Grafts

▶Code 15740 describes a cutaneous flap, transposed into a nearby but not immediately adjacent defect, with a pedicle that incorporates an axial vessel into its design. The flap is typically transferred through a tunnel underneath the skin and sutured into its new position. The donor site is closed directly.

Neurovascular pedicle procedures are reported with 15750. This code includes not only skin but also a functional motor or sensory nerve(s). The flap serves to reinnervate a damaged portion of the body dependent on touch or movement (eg, thumb).◀

Repair of donor site requiring skin graft or local flaps should be reported as an additional procedure.

15740   Flap; island pedicle
  ➔ *CPT Assistant* Mar 04:11, Sep 04:12, Oct 04:15

15750   neurovascular pedicle

  ▶(For random island flaps, V-Y subcutaneous flaps and other flaps from adjacent areas, see 14000-14302)◀

15756   Free muscle or myocutaneous flap with microvascular anastomosis
  ➔ *CPT Assistant* Apr 97:5, Nov 97:12, Nov 98:6; *CPT Changes: An Insider's View* 2003

  (Do not report code 69990 in addition to code 15756)

15757   Free skin flap with microvascular anastomosis
  ➔ *CPT Assistant* Apr 97:5, Nov 98:6

  (Do not report code 69990 in addition to code 15757)

15758   Free fascial flap with microvascular anastomosis
  ➔ *CPT Assistant* Apr 97:5, Nov 98:6

  (Do not report code 69990 in addition to code 15758)

15760   Graft; composite (eg, full thickness of external ear or nasal ala), including primary closure, donor area
  ➔ *CPT Assistant* Sep 97:3

15770   derma-fat-fascia
  ➔ *CPT Assistant* Sep 97:3

15775   Punch graft for hair transplant; 1 to 15 punch grafts
  ➔ *CPT Assistant* Sep 97:3

15776   more than 15 punch grafts
  ➔ *CPT Assistant* Sep 97:3

  (For strip transplant, use 15220)

Other Procedures

15780   Dermabrasion; total face (eg, for acne scarring, fine wrinkling, rhytids, general keratosis)
  ➔ *CPT Assistant* Apr 03:27

15781   segmental, face

15782   regional, other than face

15783   superficial, any site (eg, tattoo removal)
  ➔ *CPT Assistant* Apr 03:27

15786   Abrasion; single lesion (eg, keratosis, scar)

+ 15787   each additional 4 lesions or less (List separately in addition to code for primary procedure)

  (Use 15787 in conjunction with 15786)

15788   Chemical peel, facial; epidermal

15789   dermal

15792   Chemical peel, nonfacial; epidermal

15793   dermal

15819   Cervicoplasty

15820   Blepharoplasty, lower eyelid;
  ➔ *CPT Assistant* Feb 04:11, May 04:12, Feb 05:16

15821   with extensive herniated fat pad
  ➔ *CPT Assistant* Feb 04:11, May 04:12, Feb 05:16

15822   Blepharoplasty, upper eyelid;
  ➔ *CPT Assistant* Feb 04:11, May 04:12, Feb 05:16

15823   with excessive skin weighting down lid
  ➔ *CPT Assistant* Sep 00:7, Feb 04:11, May 04:12, Feb 05:16

  (For bilateral blepharoplasty, add modifier 50)

15824   Rhytidectomy; forehead

  (For repair of brow ptosis, use 67900)

15825   neck with platysmal tightening (platysmal flap, P-flap)

15826   glabellar frown lines

15828   cheek, chin, and neck

15829   superficial musculoaponeurotic system (SMAS) flap

  (For bilateral rhytidectomy, add modifier 50)

15830   Excision, excessive skin and subcutaneous tissue (includes lipectomy); abdomen, infraumbilical panniculectomy
  ➔ *CPT Changes: An Insider's View* 2007

  ▶(Do not report 15830 in conjunction with 12031, 12032, 12034, 12035, 12036, 12037, 13100, 13101, 13102, 14000-14001, 14302)◀

15832   thigh

15833   leg

15834   hip

15835   buttock

15836   arm

15837   forearm or hand

15838   submental fat pad

15839   other area

  (For bilateral procedure, add modifier 50)

15840   Graft for facial nerve paralysis; free fascia graft (including obtaining fascia)

  (For bilateral procedure, add modifier 50)

15841   free muscle graft (including obtaining graft)

▲=Revised code   ●=New code   ▶◀=Contains new or revised text   ⊘=Modifier 51 exempt

15842   free muscle flap by microsurgical technique
> *CPT Changes: An Insider's View* 2001

(Do not report code 69990 in addition to code 15842)

15845   regional muscle transfer

(For intravenous fluorescein examination of blood flow in graft or flap, use 15860)

(For nerve transfers, decompression, or repair, see 64831-64876, 64905, 64907, 69720, 69725, 69740, 69745, 69955)

+ 15847   Excision, excessive skin and subcutaneous tissue (includes lipectomy), abdomen (eg, abdominoplasty) (includes umbilical transposition and fascial plication) (List separately in addition to code for primary procedure)
> *CPT Changes: An Insider's View* 2007

(Use 15847 in conjunction with 15830)

(For abdominal wall hernia repair, see 49491-49587)

(To report other abdominoplasty, use 17999)

15850   Removal of sutures under anesthesia (other than local), same surgeon
> *CPT Assistant* Spring 93:34, Nov 97:22

15851   Removal of sutures under anesthesia (other than local), other surgeon
> *CPT Assistant* Spring 93:34, Nov 97:22

15852   Dressing change (for other than burns) under anesthesia (other than local)

15860   Intravenous injection of agent (eg, fluorescein) to test vascular flow in flap or graft
> *CPT Changes: An Insider's View* 2002

15876   Suction assisted lipectomy; head and neck

15877   trunk
> *CPT Assistant* Oct 99:10, Feb 05:14

15878   upper extremity

15879   lower extremity

Pressure Ulcers (Decubitus Ulcers)

15920   Excision, coccygeal pressure ulcer, with coccygectomy; with primary suture

15922   with flap closure

15931   Excision, sacral pressure ulcer, with primary suture;

15933   with ostectomy

15934   Excision, sacral pressure ulcer, with skin flap closure;

15935   with ostectomy

15936   Excision, sacral pressure ulcer, in preparation for muscle or myocutaneous flap or skin graft closure;
> *CPT Assistant* Nov 98:6-7

15937   with ostectomy

(For repair of defect using muscle or myocutaneous flap, use code(s) 15734 and/or 15738 in addition to 15936, 15937. For repair of defect using split skin graft, use codes 15100 and/or 15101 in addition to 15936, 15937)

15940   Excision, ischial pressure ulcer, with primary suture;

15941   with ostectomy (ischiectomy)

15944   Excision, ischial pressure ulcer, with skin flap closure;

15945   with ostectomy

15946   Excision, ischial pressure ulcer, with ostectomy, in preparation for muscle or myocutaneous flap or skin graft closure
> *CPT Assistant* Nov 98:6-7, Jun 02:10, Jan 03:23

(For repair of defect using muscle or myocutaneous flap, use code(s) 15734 and/or 15738 in addition to 15946. For repair of defect using split skin graft, use codes 15100 and/or 15101 in addition to 15946)

15950   Excision, trochanteric pressure ulcer, with primary suture;

15951   with ostectomy

15952   Excision, trochanteric pressure ulcer, with skin flap closure;

15953   with ostectomy

15956   Excision, trochanteric pressure ulcer, in preparation for muscle or myocutaneous flap or skin graft closure;
> *CPT Assistant* Nov 98:6-7

15958   with ostectomy
> *CPT Assistant* Nov 98:6-7

(For repair of defect using muscle or myocutaneous flap, use code(s) 15734 and/or 15738 in addition to 15956, 15958. For repair of defect using split skin graft, use codes 15100 and/or 15101 in addition to 15956, 15958)

15999   Unlisted procedure, excision pressure ulcer

(For free skin graft to close ulcer or donor site, see 15002 et seq)

Burns, Local Treatment

Procedures 16000-16036 refer to local treatment of burned surface only. Codes 16020-16030 include the application of materials (eg, dressings) not described in codes 15100-15431.

List percentage of body surface involved and depth of burn.

For necessary related medical services (eg, hospital visits, detention) in management of burned patients, see appropriate services in **Evaluation and Management** and **Medicine** sections.

For the application of skin grafts or skin substitutes, see codes 15100-15650.

16000   Initial treatment, first degree burn, when no more than local treatment is required

> *CPT Assistant* Aug 97:6

Calculation of Total Body Surface Area (TBSA) Burn 16000

Calculation of the percentage of a body burned is achieved by dividing the total body surface area into 9% or multiples of 9% segments. In the infant or child, the "rule" deviates because of the large surface area of the child's head.

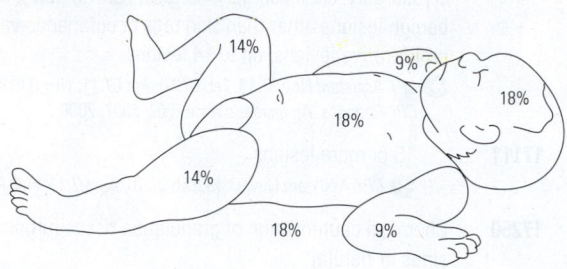

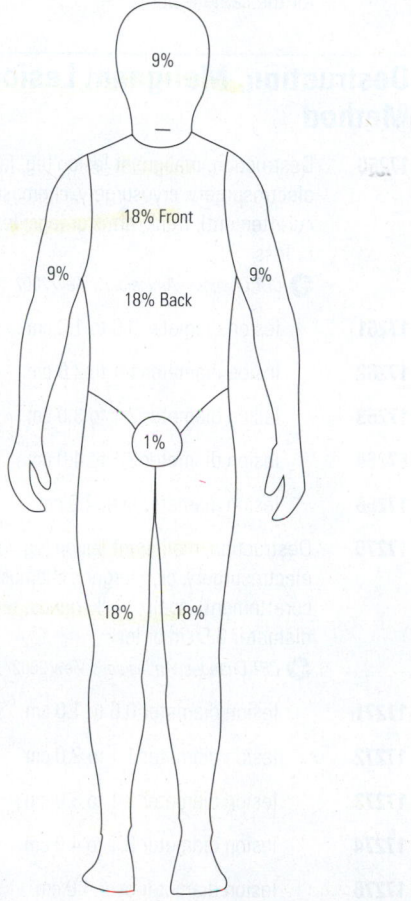

16020   Dressings and/or debridement of partial-thickness burns, initial or subsequent; small (less than 5% total body surface area)

> *CPT Assistant* Aug 97:6; *CPT Changes: An Insider's View* 2006

16025   medium (eg, whole face or whole extremity, or 5% to 10% total body surface area)

> *CPT Assistant* Aug 97:6, Jun 08:14; *CPT Changes: An Insider's View* 2006

16030   large (eg, more than 1 extremity, or greater than 10% total body surface area)

> *CPT Assistant* Aug 97:6, Jun 08:14; *CPT Changes: An Insider's View* 2006

16035   Escharotomy; initial incision   *(black skin)*

> *CPT Assistant* Aug 97:6; *CPT Changes: An Insider's View* 2001

+ 16036   each additional incision (List separately in addition to code for primary procedure)

> *CPT Changes: An Insider's View* 2001

(Use 16036 in conjunction with 16035)

(For debridement, curettement of burn wound, see 16020-16030)

Destruction

Destruction means the ablation of benign, premalignant or malignant tissues by any method, with or without curettement, including local anesthesia, and not usually requiring closure.

Any method includes electrosurgery, cryosurgery, laser and chemical treatment. Lesions include condylomata, papillomata, molluscum contagiosum, herpetic lesions, warts (ie, common, plantar, flat), milia, or other benign, premalignant (eg, actinic keratoses), or malignant lesions.

> (For destruction of lesion(s) in specific anatomic sites, see 40820, 46900-46917, 46924, 54050-54057, 54065, 56501, 56515, 57061, 57065, 67850, 68135)
>
> ▶(For laser treatment for inflammatory skin disease, see 96920-96922)◀
>
> (For paring or cutting of benign hyperkeratotic lesions (eg, corns or calluses), see 11055-11057)
>
> (For sharp removal or electrosurgical destruction of skin tags and fibrocutaneous tags, see 11200, 11201)
>
> (For cryotherapy of acne, use 17340)
>
> (For initiation or follow-up care of topical chemotherapy (eg, 5-FU or similar agents), see appropriate office visits)
>
> (For shaving of epidermal or dermal lesions, see 11300-11313)

Destruction, Benign or Premalignant Lesions

17000   Destruction (eg, laser surgery, electrosurgery, cryosurgery, chemosurgery, surgical curettement), premalignant lesions (eg, actinic keratoses); first lesion

> *CPT Assistant* Winter 90:3, Nov 97:12, Jun 99:10, May 06:19, Feb 07:10; *CPT Changes: An Insider's View* 2002, 2007

+ 17003   second through 14 lesions, each (List separately in addition to code for first lesion)

> *CPT Assistant* Nov 97:12, Jun 99:10, May 06:19, Feb 07:10

(Use 17003 in conjunction with 17000)

(For destruction of common or plantar warts, see 17110, 17111)

⊘ **17004** Destruction (eg, laser surgery, electrosurgery, cryosurgery, chemosurgery, surgical curettement), premalignant lesions (eg, actinic keratoses), 15 or more lesions

➡ *CPT Assistant* Nov 97:12, Nov 98:7, Jun 99:10, Mar 03:21, Feb 07:10; *CPT Changes: An Insider's View* 2002, 2007

(Do not report 17004 in conjunction with 17000-17003)

Destruction, Benign or Premalignant Lesions
17004

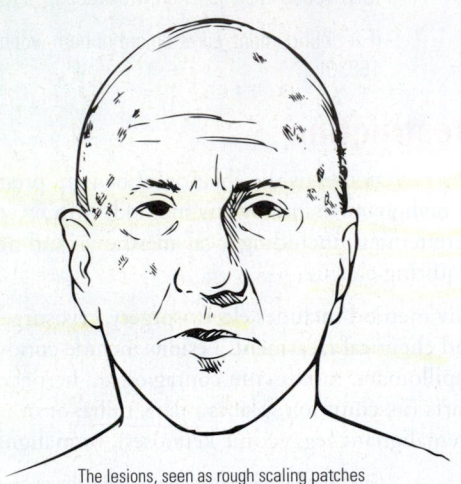

The lesions, seen as rough scaling patches scattered over the face, scalp, and ears, are destroyed by cryosurgery or other surgical means.

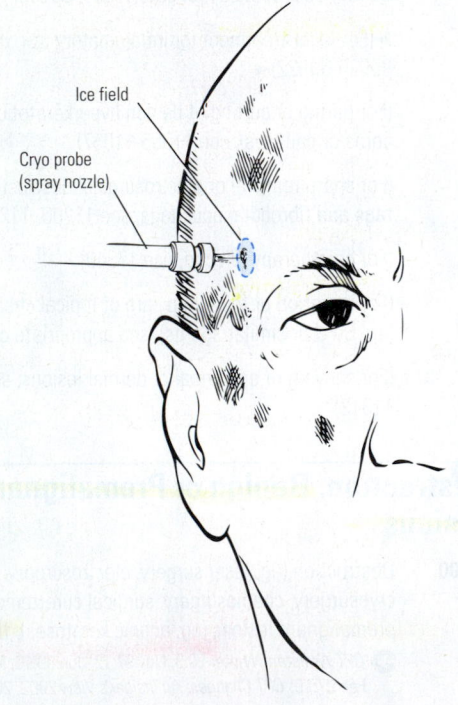

Ice field

Cryo probe
(spray nozzle)

17106 Destruction of cutaneous vascular proliferative lesions (eg, laser technique); less than 10 sq cm

➡ *CPT Assistant* Winter 90:3, Apr 07:11, Jun 08:14

17107 10.0 to 50.0 sq cm

➡ *CPT Assistant* Winter 90:3, Apr 07:11, Jun 08:14

17108 over 50.0 sq cm

➡ *CPT Assistant* Winter 90:3, Apr 07:11, Jun 08:14

17110 Destruction (eg, laser surgery, electrosurgery, cryosurgery, chemosurgery, surgical curettement), of benign lesions other than skin tags or cutaneous vascular proliferative lesions; up to 14 lesions

➡ *CPT Assistant* Nov 97:13, Feb 07:10, Apr 07:11, Nov 08:10; *CPT Changes: An Insider's View* 2002, 2007, 2008

17111 15 or more lesions

➡ *CPT Assistant* Nov 97:13, Feb 07:10, Apr 07:11, Nov 08:10

17250 Chemical cauterization of granulation tissue (proud flesh, sinus or fistula)

(17250 is not to be used with removal or excision codes for the same lesion)

Destruction, Malignant Lesions, Any Method

17260 Destruction, malignant lesion (eg, laser surgery, electrosurgery, cryosurgery, chemosurgery, surgical curettement), trunk, arms or legs; lesion diameter 0.5 cm or less

➡ *CPT Changes: An Insider's View* 2002

17261 lesion diameter 0.6 to 1.0 cm

17262 lesion diameter 1.1 to 2.0 cm

17263 lesion diameter 2.1 to 3.0 cm

17264 lesion diameter 3.1 to 4.0 cm

17266 lesion diameter over 4.0 cm

17270 Destruction, malignant lesion (eg, laser surgery, electrosurgery, cryosurgery, chemosurgery, surgical curettement), scalp, neck, hands, feet, genitalia; lesion diameter 0.5 cm or less

➡ *CPT Changes: An Insider's View* 2002

17271 lesion diameter 0.6 to 1.0 cm

17272 lesion diameter 1.1 to 2.0 cm

17273 lesion diameter 2.1 to 3.0 cm

17274 lesion diameter 3.1 to 4.0 cm

17276 lesion diameter over 4.0 cm

17280 Destruction, malignant lesion (eg, laser surgery, electrosurgery, cryosurgery, chemosurgery, surgical curettement), face, ears, eyelids, nose, lips, mucous membrane; lesion diameter 0.5 cm or less

➡ *CPT Changes: An Insider's View* 2002

17281 lesion diameter 0.6 to 1.0 cm

17282 lesion diameter 1.1 to 2.0 cm

17283	lesion diameter 2.1 to 3.0 cm
17284	lesion diameter 3.1 to 4.0 cm
17286	lesion diameter over 4.0 cm

Mohs Micrographic Surgery

Mohs micrographic surgery is a technique for the removal of complex or ill-defined skin cancer with histologic examination of 100% of the surgical margins. It requires a single physician to act in two integrated but separate and distinct capacities: surgeon and pathologist. If either of these responsibilities is delegated to another physician who reports the services separately, these codes should not be reported. The Mohs surgeon removes the tumor tissue and maps and divides the tumor specimen into pieces, and each piece is embedded into an individual tissue block for histopathologic examination. Thus a tissue block in Mohs surgery is defined as an individual tissue piece embedded in a mounting medium for sectioning.

If repair is performed, use separate repair, flap, or graft codes. If a biopsy of a suspected skin cancer is performed on the same day as Mohs surgery because there was no prior pathology confirmation of a diagnosis, then report diagnostic skin biopsy (11100, 11101) and frozen section pathology (88331) with modifier 59 to distinguish from the subsequent definitive surgical procedure of Mohs surgery.

> (If additional special pathology procedures, stains or immunostains are required, use 88311-88314, 88342)

> (Do not report 88314 in conjunction with 17311-17315 for routine frozen section stain (eg, hematoxylin and eosin, toluidine blue) performed during Mohs surgery. When a nonroutine histochemical stain on frozen tissue is utilized, report 88314 with modifier 59)

> (Do not report 88302-88309 on the same specimen as part of the Mohs surgery)

17311   Mohs micrographic technique, including removal of all gross tumor, surgical excision of tissue specimens, mapping, color coding of specimens, microscopic examination of specimens by the surgeon, and histopathologic preparation including routine stain(s) (eg, hematoxylin and eosin, toluidine blue), head, neck, hands, feet, genitalia, or any location with surgery directly involving muscle, cartilage, bone, tendon, major nerves, or vessels; first stage, up to 5 tissue blocks

> ➔ CPT Changes: An Insider's View 2007

+ 17312   each additional stage after the first stage, up to 5 tissue blocks (List separately in addition to code for primary procedure)

> ➔ CPT Changes: An Insider's View 2007

> (Use 17312 in conjunction with 17311)

17313   Mohs micrographic technique, including removal of all gross tumor, surgical excision of tissue specimens, mapping, color coding of specimens, microscopic examination of specimens by the surgeon, and histopathologic preparation including routine stain(s) (eg, hematoxylin and eosin, toluidine blue), of the trunk, arms, or legs; first stage, up to 5 tissue blocks

> ➔ CPT Changes: An Insider's View 2007

+ 17314   each additional stage after the first stage, up to 5 tissue blocks (List separately in addition to code for primary procedure)

> ➔ CPT Changes: An Insider's View 2007

> (Use 17314 in conjunction with 17313)

+ 17315   Mohs micrographic technique, including removal of all gross tumor, surgical excision of tissue specimens, mapping, color coding of specimens, microscopic examination of specimens by the surgeon, and histopathologic preparation including routine stain(s) (eg, hematoxylin and eosin, toluidine blue), each additional block after the first 5 tissue blocks, any stage (List separately in addition to code for primary procedure)

> ➔ CPT Changes: An Insider's View 2007

> (Use 17315 in conjunction with 17311-17314)

Other Procedures

17340	Cryotherapy (CO_2 slush, liquid N_2) for acne
17360	Chemical exfoliation for acne (eg, acne paste, acid)
17380	Electrolysis epilation, each 30 minutes

> (For actinotherapy, use 96900)

17999   Unlisted procedure, skin, mucous membrane and subcutaneous tissue

> ➔ CPT Assistant Dec 98:9, May 99:11, Jun 05:11, Nov 08:10

Breast

Incision

19000   Puncture aspiration of cyst of breast;

> ➔ CPT Assistant Fall 94:18, Apr 05:6, Nov 08:10

+ 19001   each additional cyst (List separately in addition to code for primary procedure)

> ➔ CPT Assistant Fall 94:18, Apr 05:6

> (Use 19001 in conjunction with 19000)

> (If imaging guidance is performed, see 76942, 77021, 77031, 77032)

19020   Mastotomy with exploration or drainage of abscess, deep

> ➔ CPT Assistant Apr 05:6

19030   Injection procedure only for mammary ductogram or galactogram

> ➔ CPT Assistant Jul 04:8, Apr 05:6

> (For radiological supervision and interpretation, see 77053, 77054)

Excision

Excisional breast surgery includes certain biopsy procedures, the removal of cysts or other benign or malignant tumors or lesions, and the surgical treatment of breast and chest wall malignancies. Biopsy procedures may be percutaneous or open, and they involve the removal of differing amounts of tissue for diagnosis.

Breast biopsies are reported using codes 19100-19103. The open excision of breast lesions (eg, lesions of the breast ducts, cysts, benign or malignant tumors), without specific attention to adequate surgical margins, with or without the preoperative placement of radiological markers, is reported using codes 19110-19126. Partial mastectomy procedures (eg, lumpectomy, tylectomy, quadrantectomy, or segmentectomy) describe open excisions of breast tissue with specific attention to adequate surgical margins.

Partial mastectomy procedures are reported using codes 19301 or 19302 as appropriate. Documentation for partial mastectomy procedures includes attention to the removal of adequate surgical margins surrounding the breast mass or lesion.

Total mastectomy procedures include simple mastectomy, complete mastectomy, subcutaneous mastectomy, modified radical mastectomy, radical mastectomy, and more extended procedures (eg, Urban type operation). Total mastectomy procedures are reported using codes 19303-19307 as appropriate.

Excisions or resections of chest wall tumors including ribs, with or without reconstruction, with or without mediastinal lymphadenectomy, are reported using codes 19260, 19271, or 19272. Codes 19260-19272 are not restricted to breast tumors and are used to report resections of chest wall tumors originating from any chest wall component. (For excision of lung or pleura, see 32310 et seq)

(To report bilateral procedure, report modifier 50 with the procedure code)

19100 Biopsy of breast; percutaneous, needle core, not using imaging guidance (separate procedure)

➜ *CPT Assistant* Spring 93:35, Fall 94:18, Apr 96:8, Mar 97:4, Nov 97:24, Nov 98:7, Jan 01:10, May 02:18, Apr 05:6, Dec 06:10, Nov 08:10; *CPT Changes: An Insider's View* 2001

(For fine needle aspiration, use 10021)

(For image guided breast biopsy, see 19102, 19103, 10022)

19101 open, incisional

➜ *CPT Assistant* Spring 93:35, Fall 94:19, Nov 97:24, Jan 01:8, May 02:18, Apr 05:6; *CPT Changes: An Insider's View* 2001

19102 percutaneous, needle core, using imaging guidance

➜ *CPT Assistant* Jan 01:10, May 02:18, Apr 05:6, Nov 08:10; *CPT Changes: An Insider's View* 2001

➜ *Clinical Examples in Radiology* Summer 05:1, 2, Fall 08:3

(For placement of percutaneous localization clip, use 19295)

19103 percutaneous, automated vacuum assisted or rotating biopsy device, using imaging guidance

➜ *CPT Assistant* Jan 01:10, May 02:18, Apr 03:7, Apr 05:6, Nov 08:10; *CPT Changes: An Insider's View* 2001

➜ *Clinical Examples in Radiology* Fall 08:3

(For imaging guidance performed in conjunction with 19102, 19103, see 76942, 77012, 77021, 77031, 77032)

(For placement of percutaneous localization clip, use 19295)

19105 Ablation, cryosurgical, of fibroadenoma, including ultrasound guidance, each fibroadenoma

➜ *CPT Changes: An Insider's View* 2007

(Do not report 19105 in conjunction with 76940, 76942)

(For adjacent lesions treated with 1 cryoprobe insertion, report once)

19110 Nipple exploration, with or without excision of a solitary lactiferous duct or a papilloma lactiferous duct

➜ *CPT Assistant* Apr 05:6

19112 Excision of lactiferous duct fistula

➜ *CPT Assistant* Apr 05:6

19120 Excision of cyst, fibroadenoma, or other benign or malignant tumor, aberrant breast tissue, duct lesion, nipple or areolar lesion (except 19300), open, male or female, 1 or more lesions

➜ *CPT Assistant* Feb 96:9, Nov 97:14, Jan 01:8, May 01:10, Apr 05:6, 13; *CPT Changes: An Insider's View* 2001, 2007

19125 Excision of breast lesion identified by preoperative placement of radiological marker, open; single lesion

➜ *CPT Assistant* Fall 94:18, Mar 98:10, Jan 01:8, Apr 05:6, Mar 09:10; *CPT Changes: An Insider's View* 2001

+ 19126 each additional lesion separately identified by a preoperative radiological marker (List separately in addition to code for primary procedure)

➜ *CPT Assistant* Fall 94:18, Mar 98:10, Jan 01:8, Apr 05:6; *CPT Changes: An Insider's View* 2001

(Use 19126 in conjunction with 19125)

19260 Excision of chest wall tumor including ribs

➜ *CPT Assistant* Apr 05:6, 7

19271 Excision of chest wall tumor involving ribs, with plastic reconstruction; without mediastinal lymphadenectomy

➜ *CPT Assistant* Apr 05:6, 7

19272 with mediastinal lymphadenectomy

➜ *CPT Assistant* Apr 05:6, 7

(Do not report 19260, 19271, 19272 in conjunction with 32100, 32422, 32503, 32504, 32551)

Introduction

19290 Preoperative placement of needle localization wire, breast;

➲ *CPT Assistant* Fall 94:19, Apr 05:6

➲ *Clinical Examples in Radiology* Fall 05:01

+ 19291 each additional lesion (List separately in addition to code for primary procedure)

➲ *CPT Assistant* Fall 94:19, Apr 05:6

(Use 19291 in conjunction with 19290)

(For radiological supervision and interpretation, see 76942, 77031, 77032)

+▲ 19295 Image guided placement, metallic localization clip, percutaneous, during breast biopsy/aspiration (List separately in addition to code for primary procedure)

➲ *CPT Assistant* Jan 01:10, Apr 05:6, Nov 08:10; *CPT Changes: An Insider's View* 2001, 2010

➲ *Clinical Examples in Radiology* Fall 08:2, 3

►(Use 19295 in conjunction with 10022, 19102, 19103)◄

19296 Placement of radiotherapy afterloading expandable catheter (single or multichannel) into the breast for interstitial radioelement application following partial mastectomy, includes imaging guidance; on date separate from partial mastectomy

➲ *CPT Assistant* Apr 05:6-8, Nov 05:15, Apr 09:3; *CPT Changes: An Insider's View* 2005, 2009

+ 19297 concurrent with partial mastectomy (List separately in addition to code for primary procedure)

➲ *CPT Assistant* Apr 05:6-8, Nov 05:15, Apr 09:3; *CPT Changes: An Insider's View* 2005, 2009

(Use 19297 in conjunction with 19301 or 19302)

⊙ 19298 Placement of radiotherapy afterloading brachytherapy catheters (multiple tube and button type) into the breast for interstitial radioelement application following (at the time of or subsequent to) partial mastectomy, includes imaging guidance

➲ *CPT Assistant* Apr 05:6-7, 9, 16, Nov 05:15, Apr 09:3; *CPT Changes: An Insider's View* 2005

Mastectomy Procedures

19300 Mastectomy for gynecomastia

➲ *CPT Assistant* Feb 07:4; *CPT Changes: An Insider's View* 2007

19301 Mastectomy, partial (eg, lumpectomy, tylectomy, quadrantectomy, segmentectomy);

➲ *CPT Assistant* Feb 07:4, Dec 07:8, Sep 08:5; *CPT Changes: An Insider's View* 2007

19302 with axillary lymphadenectomy

➲ *CPT Assistant* Feb 07:4, Dec 07:8, Sep 08:5; *CPT Changes: An Insider's View* 2007

(For placement of radiotherapy afterloading balloon/brachytherapy catheters, see 19296-19298)

19303 Mastectomy, simple, complete

➲ *CPT Assistant* Feb 07:4; *CPT Changes: An Insider's View* 2007

(For immediate or delayed insertion of implant, see 19340, 19342)

(For gynecomastia, use 19300)

19304 Mastectomy, subcutaneous

➲ *CPT Assistant* Feb 07:4, Dec 07:7, 8; *CPT Changes: An Insider's View* 2007

(For immediate or delayed insertion of implant, see 19340, 19342)

19305 Mastectomy, radical, including pectoral muscles, axillary lymph nodes

➲ *CPT Assistant* Feb 07:4, Sep 08:5; *CPT Changes: An Insider's View* 2007

(For immediate or delayed insertion of implant, see 19340, 19342)

19306 Mastectomy, radical, including pectoral muscles, axillary and internal mammary lymph nodes (Urban type operation)

➲ *CPT Assistant* Feb 07:4, Sep 08:5; *CPT Changes: An Insider's View* 2007

(For immediate or delayed insertion of implant, see 19340, 19342)

19307 Mastectomy, modified radical, including axillary lymph nodes, with or without pectoralis minor muscle, but excluding pectoralis major muscle

➲ *CPT Assistant* Feb 07:4, Sep 08:5; *CPT Changes: An Insider's View* 2007

(For immediate or delayed insertion of implant, see 19340, 19342)

Repair and/or Reconstruction

(To report bilateral procedure, report modifier 50 with the procedure code)

19316 Mastopexy

➲ *CPT Assistant* Jan 03:7, Apr 05:6

19318 Reduction mammaplasty

➲ *CPT Assistant* Jan 03:7, Apr 05:6

19324 Mammaplasty, augmentation; without prosthetic implant

➲ *CPT Assistant* Apr 05:6

19325 with prosthetic implant

➲ *CPT Assistant* Apr 05:6

(For flap or graft, use also appropriate number)

19328 Removal of intact mammary implant

➲ *CPT Assistant* Apr 05:6

19330 Removal of mammary implant material

➲ *CPT Assistant* Nov 01:11, Apr 05:6

19340 Immediate insertion of breast prosthesis following mastopexy, mastectomy or in reconstruction

➲ *CPT Assistant* Aug 96:8, Apr 05:6, Aug 05:1

19342 Delayed insertion of breast prosthesis following mastopexy, mastectomy or in reconstruction

➔ *CPT Assistant* Aug 96:8, Apr 05:6, Aug 05:1

(For supply of implant, use 99070)

(For preparation of custom breast implant, use 19396)

19350 Nipple/areola reconstruction

➔ *CPT Assistant* Aug 96:11, Apr 05:6

19355 Correction of inverted nipples

➔ *CPT Assistant* Apr 05:6

19357 Breast reconstruction, immediate or delayed, with tissue expander, including subsequent expansion

➔ *CPT Assistant* Winter 91:2, Apr 05:6, Aug 05:1

19361 Breast reconstruction with latissimus dorsi flap, without prosthetic implant

➔ *CPT Assistant* Apr 05:6, Aug 05:1; *CPT Changes: An Insider's View* 2007

(For insertion of prosthesis, use also 19340)

19364 Breast reconstruction with free flap

➔ *CPT Assistant* Aug 96:8, Nov 98:7, Apr 05:6, Aug 05:1

(Do not report code 69990 in addition to code 19364)

(19364 includes harvesting of the flap, microvascular transfer, closure of the donor site, and inset shaping the flap into a breast)

19366 Breast reconstruction with other technique

➔ *CPT Assistant* Aug 96:8, Nov 98:7, Apr 05:6

(For operating microscope, use 69990)

(For insertion of prosthesis, use also 19340 or 19342)

19367 Breast reconstruction with transverse rectus abdominis myocutaneous flap (TRAM), single pedicle, including closure of donor site;

➔ *CPT Assistant* Nov 98:7, Apr 05:6, Aug 05:1

19368 with microvascular anastomosis (supercharging)

➔ *CPT Assistant* Nov 98:7, Apr 05:6, Aug 05:1

(Do not report code 69990 in addition to code 19368)

19369 Breast reconstruction with transverse rectus abdominis myocutaneous flap (TRAM), double pedicle, including closure of donor site

➔ *CPT Assistant* Oct 00:3, Apr 05:6, Aug 05:1

19370 Open periprosthetic capsulotomy, breast

➔ *CPT Assistant* Aug 96:8, Apr 05:6

19371 Periprosthetic capsulectomy, breast

➔ *CPT Assistant* Aug 96:8, Nov 01:11, Apr 05:6

19380 Revision of reconstructed breast

➔ *CPT Assistant* Apr 05:6

19396 Preparation of moulage for custom breast implant

➔ *CPT Assistant* Jan 03:7, Apr 05:6

Other Procedures

19499 Unlisted procedure, breast

➔ *CPT Assistant* Apr 05:6

➔ *Clinical Examples in Radiology* Fall 08:4

Musculoskeletal System* (20000-29999) 86

The following is a listing of headings and subheadings that appear within the Musculoskeletal System section of the CPT codebook. The subheadings or subsections denoted with asterisks (*) below have special instructions unique to that section. Where these are indicated, special "notes" or guidelines will be presented preceding those procedural terminology listings, referring to that subsection specifically.

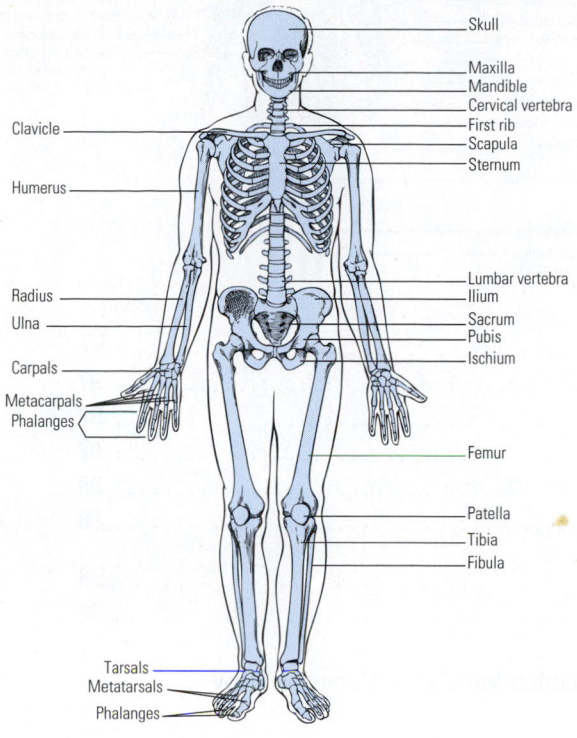

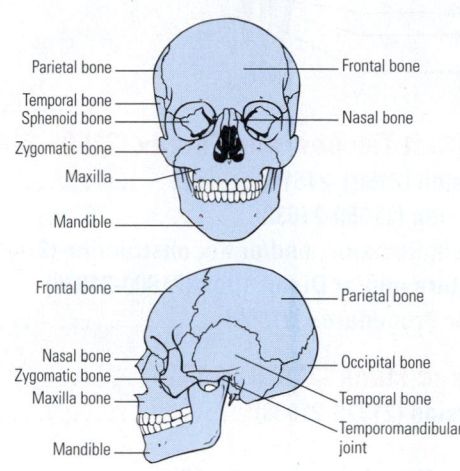

Musc 20000

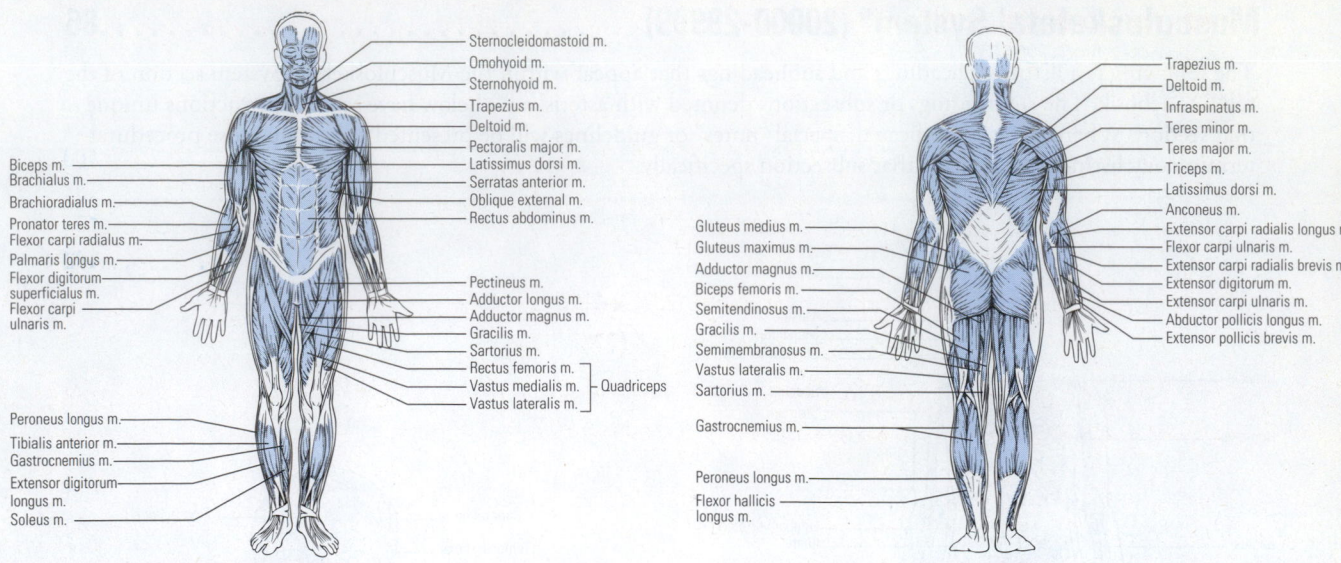

Thoracic Vertebra—Superior View

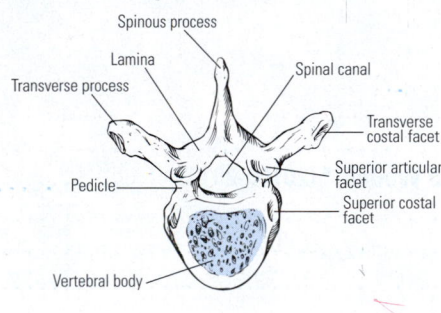

Lumbar Vertebra—Superior View

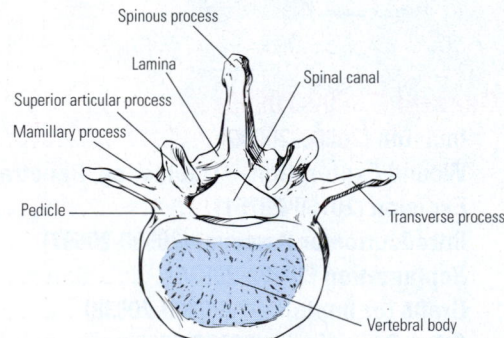

Lumbar Vertebrae—Lateral View

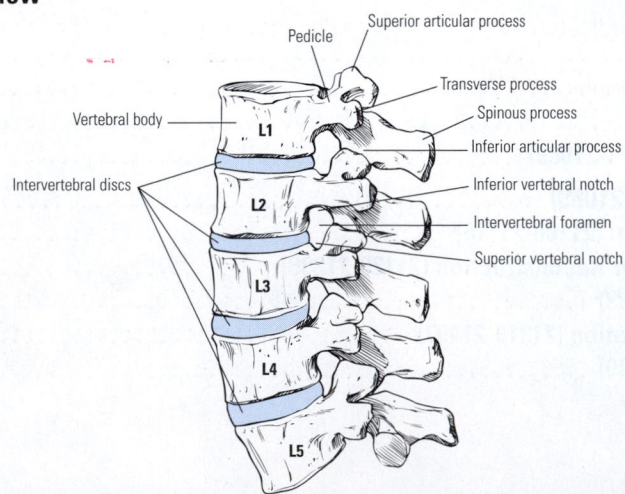

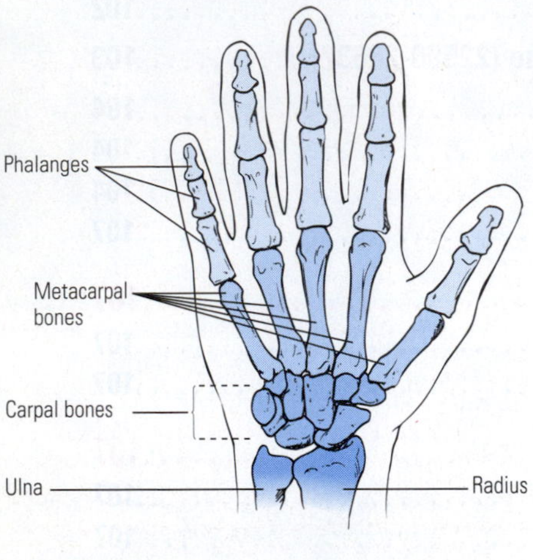

Phalanges

Metacarpal bones

Carpal bones

Ulna

Radius

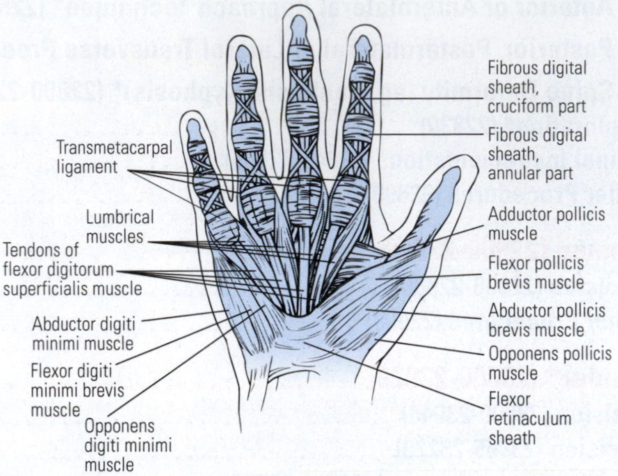

Fibrous digital sheath, cruciform part

Fibrous digital sheath, annular part

Transmetacarpal ligament

Lumbrical muscles

Tendons of flexor digitorum superficialis muscle

Abductor digiti minimi muscle

Flexor digiti minimi brevis muscle

Opponens digiti minimi muscle

Adductor pollicis muscle

Flexor pollicis brevis muscle

Abductor pollicis brevis muscle

Opponens pollicis muscle

Flexor retinaculum sheath

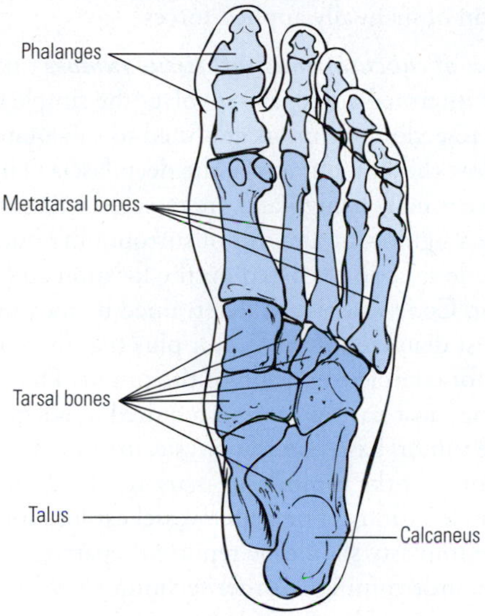

Phalanges

Metatarsal bones

Tarsal bones

Talus

Calcaneus

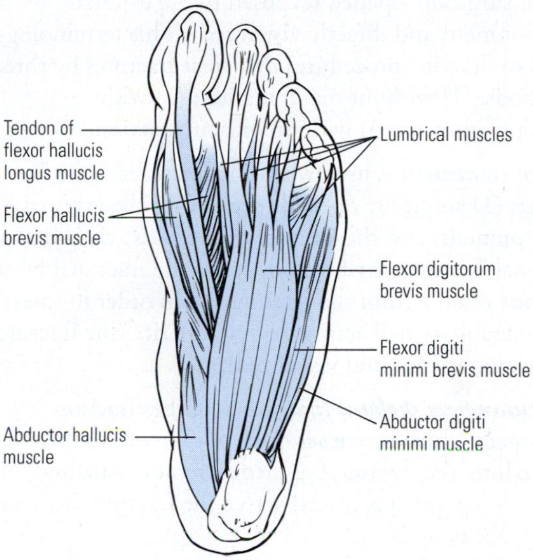

Tendon of flexor hallucis longus muscle

Flexor hallucis brevis muscle

Abductor hallucis muscle

Lumbrical muscles

Flexor digitorum brevis muscle

Flexor digiti minimi brevis muscle

Abductor digiti minimi muscle

Musculoskeletal System

Cast and strapping procedures appear at the end of this section.

The services listed below include the application and removal of the first cast or traction device only. Subsequent replacement of cast and/or traction device may require an additional listing.

Definitions

The terms "closed treatment," "open treatment," and "percutaneous skeletal fixation" have been carefully chosen to accurately reflect current orthopaedic procedural treatments.

Closed treatment specifically means that the fracture site is not surgically opened (exposed to the external environment and directly visualized). This terminology is used to describe procedures that treat fractures by three methods: (1) without manipulation; (2) with manipulation; or (3) with or without traction.

Open treatment is used when the fractured bone is either: (1) surgically opened (exposed to the external environment) and the fracture (bone ends) visualized and internal fixation may be used; or (2) the fractured bone is opened remote from the fracture site in order to insert an intramedullary nail across the fracture site (the fracture site is not opened and visualized).

Percutaneous skeletal fixation describes fracture treatment which is neither open nor closed. In this procedure, the fracture fragments are not visualized, but fixation (eg, pins) is placed across the fracture site, usually under X-ray imaging.

The type of fracture (eg, open, compound, closed) does not have any coding correlation with the type of treatment (eg, closed, open, or percutaneous) provided.

The codes for treatment of fractures and joint injuries (dislocations) are categorized by the type of manipulation (reduction) and stabilization (fixation or immobilization). These codes can apply to either open (compound) or closed fractures or joint injuries.

Skeletal traction is the application of a force (distracting or traction force) to a limb segment through a wire, pin, screw, or clamp that is attached (eg, penetrates) to bone.

Skin traction is the application of a force (longitudinal) to a limb using felt or strapping applied directly to skin only.

External fixation is the usage of skeletal pins plus an attaching mechanism/device used for temporary or definitive treatment of acute or chronic bony deformity.

Codes for obtaining autogenous bone grafts, cartilage, tendon, fascia lata grafts or other tissues through separate incisions are to be used only when the graft is not already listed as part of the basic procedure.

Re-reduction of a fracture and/or dislocation performed by the primary physician may be identified by the addition of the modifier 76 to the usual procedure number to indicate "Repeat Procedure or Service by Same Physician." (See Appendix A guidelines.)

Codes for external fixation are to be used only when external fixation is not already listed as part of the basic procedure.

All codes for suction irrigation have been deleted. To report, list only the primary surgical procedure performed (eg, sequestrectomy, deep incision).

Manipulation is used throughout the musculoskeletal fracture and dislocation subsections to specifically mean the attempted reduction or restoration of a fracture or joint dislocation to its normal anatomic alignment by the application of manually applied forces.

▶*Excision of subcutaneous soft tissue tumors* (including simple or intermediate repair) involves the simple or marginal resection of tumors confined to subcutaneous tissue below the skin but above the deep fascia. These tumors are usually benign and are resected without removing a significant amount of surrounding normal tissue. Code selection is based on the location and size of the tumor. Code selection is determined by measuring the greatest diameter of the tumor plus that margin required for complete excision of the tumor. The margins refer to the most narrow margin required to adequately excise the tumor, based on the physician's judgment. The measurement of the tumor plus margin is made at the time of the excision. Appreciable vessel exploration and/or neuroplasty should be reported separately. Extensive undermining or other techniques to close a defect created by skin excision may require a complex repair which should be reported separately. Dissection or elevation of tissue planes to permit resection of the tumor is included in the excision.

Excision of fascial or subfascial soft tissue tumors (including simple or intermediate repair) involves the resection of tumors confined to the tissue within or below the deep fascia, but not involving the bone. These tumors are usually benign, are often intramuscular, and are resected without removing a significant amount of surrounding normal tissue. Code selection is based on size and location of the tumor. Code selection is determined by measuring the greatest diameter of the tumor plus that margin required for complete excision of the tumor. The margins refer to the most narrow margin required to adequately excise the tumor, based on the physician's judgment. The measurement of the tumor plus margin is made at the time of the excision. Appreciable vessel exploration and/or neuroplasty should be reported separately. Extensive undermining or other techniques to close a defect created by skin excision may require a complex repair which should be reported separately. Dissection or elevation of tissue planes to permit resection of the tumor is included in the excision.

Digital (ie, fingers and toes) subfascial tumors are defined as those tumors involving the tendons, tendon sheaths, or joints of the digit. Tumors which simply abut but do not breach the tendon, tendon sheath, or joint capsule are considered subcutaneous soft tissue tumors.

Radical resection of soft tissue tumors (including simple or intermediate repair) involves the resection of the tumor with wide margins of normal tissue. Appreciable vessel exploration and/or neuroplasty repair or reconstruction (eg, adjacent tissue transfer[s], flap[s]) should be reported separately. Extensive undermining or other techniques to close a defect created by skin excision may require a complex repair which should be reported separately. Dissection or elevation of tissue planes to permit resection of the tumor is included in the excision. Although these tumors may be confined to a specific layer (eg, subcutaneous, subfascial), radical resection may involve removal of tissue from one or more layers. Radical resection of soft tissue tumors is most commonly used for malignant tumors or very aggressive benign tumors. Code selection is based on size and location of the tumor. Code selection is determined by measuring the greatest diameter of the tumor plus that margin required for complete excision of the tumor. The margins refer to the most narrow margin required to adequately excise the tumor, based on the physician's judgment. The measurement of the tumor plus margin is made at the time of the excision. For radical resection of tumors of cutaneous origin, (eg, melanoma) see 11600-11646.

Radical resection of bone tumors (including simple or intermediate repair) involves the resection of the tumor with wide margins of normal tissue. Appreciable vessel exploration and/or neuroplasty and complex bone repair or reconstruction (eg, adjacent tissue transfer[s], flap[s]) should be reported separately. Extensive undermining or other techniques to close a defect created by skin excision may require a complex repair which should be reported separately. Dissection or elevation of tissue planes to permit resection of the tumor is included in the excision. It may require removal of the entire bone if tumor growth is extensive (eg, clavicle). Radical resection of bone tumors is usually performed for malignant tumors or very aggressive benign tumors. If surrounding soft tissue is removed during these procedures, the radical resection of soft tissue tumor codes should not be reported separately. Code selection is based solely on the location of the tumor, **not** on the size of the tumor or whether the tumor is benign or malignant, primary or metastatic.◀

General

Incision

20000 Incision of soft tissue abscess (eg, secondary to osteomyelitis); superficial

20005 deep or complicated

Wound Exploration—Trauma (eg, Penetrating Gunshot, Stab Wound)

20100-20103 relate to wound(s) resulting from penetrating trauma. These codes describe surgical exploration and enlargement of the wound, extension of dissection (to determine penetration), debridement, removal of foreign body(s), ligation or coagulation of minor subcutaneous and/or muscular blood vessel(s), of the subcutaneous tissue, muscle fascia, and/or muscle, not requiring thoracotomy or laparotomy. If a repair is done to major structure(s) or major blood vessel(s) requiring thoracotomy or laparotomy, then those specific code(s) would supersede the use of codes 20100-20103. To report simple, intermediate, or complex repair of wound(s) that do not require enlargement of the wound, extension of dissection, etc, as stated above, use specific Repair code(s) in the **Integumentary System** section.

20100 Exploration of penetrating wound (separate procedure); neck
> *CPT Assistant* Jun 96:7, Aug 96:10, Sep 06:13

20101 chest
> *CPT Assistant* Jun 96:7, Sep 06:13

20102 abdomen/flank/back
> *CPT Assistant* Jun 96:7, Sep 06:13

20103 extremity
> *CPT Assistant* Jun 96:7, Aug 96:10, Sep 06:13

Excision

20150 Excision of epiphyseal bar, with or without autogenous soft tissue graft obtained through same fascial incision

(For aspiration of bone marrow, use 38220)

20200 Biopsy, muscle; superficial

20205 deep

20206 Biopsy, muscle, percutaneous needle
> *Clinical Examples in Radiology* Summer 08:5

(If imaging guidance is performed, see 76942, 77012, 77021)

(For fine needle aspiration, use 10021 or 10022)

(For evaluation of fine needle aspirate, see 88172-88173)

(For excision of muscle tumor, deep, see specific anatomic section)

20220 Biopsy, bone, trocar, or needle; superficial (eg, ilium, sternum, spinous process, ribs)
> *CPT Assistant* Winter 92:17, Jul 98:4
> *Clinical Examples in Radiology* Summer 08:5

20225   deep (eg, vertebral body, femur)

> *CPT Assistant* Winter 92:17, Jul 98:4; *CPT Changes: An Insider's View* 2002

(For bone marrow biopsy, use 38221)

(For radiologic supervision and interpretation, see 77002, 77012, 77021)

20240   Biopsy, bone, open; superficial (eg, ilium, sternum, spinous process, ribs, trochanter of femur)

> *CPT Assistant* Winter 92:17, Jul 98:4, Aug 04:11, Aug 05:13; *CPT Changes: An Insider's View* 2004

20245   deep (eg, humerus, ischium, femur)

> *CPT Assistant* Winter 92:17, Jul 98:4

20250   Biopsy, vertebral body, open; thoracic

> *CPT Assistant* Winter 92:17, Jul 98:4

20251   lumbar or cervical

> *CPT Assistant* Winter 92:17, Jul 98:4

(For sequestrectomy, osteomyelitis or drainage of bone abscess, see anatomical area)

Introduction or Removal

(For injection procedure for arthrography, see anatomical area)

20500   Injection of sinus tract; therapeutic (separate procedure)

20501   diagnostic (sinogram)

(For radiological supervision and interpretation, use 76080)

(For contrast injection[s] and radiological assessment of gastrostomy, duodenostomy, jejunostomy, gastro-jejunostomy, or cecostomy [or other colonic] tube including fluoroscopic imaging guidance, use 49465)

20520   Removal of foreign body in muscle or tendon sheath; simple

20525   deep or complicated

20526   Injection, therapeutic (eg, local anesthetic, corticosteroid), carpal tunnel

> *CPT Assistant* Mar 02:7; *CPT Changes: An Insider's View* 2002

20550   Injection(s); single tendon sheath, or ligament, aponeurosis (eg, plantar "fascia")

> *CPT Assistant* Jan 96:7, Jun 98:10, Mar 02:7, Aug 03:14, Sep 03:13, Dec 03:11, Jan 09:6; *CPT Changes: An Insider's View* 2002, 2003, 2004

(For injection of Morton's neuroma, see 64455, 64632)

20551   single tendon origin/insertion

> *CPT Assistant* Mar 02:7, Sep 03:13; *CPT Changes: An Insider's View* 2002, 2004

20552   Injection(s); single or multiple trigger point(s), 1 or 2 muscle(s)

> *CPT Assistant* Mar 02:7, May 03:19, Sep 03:11; *CPT Changes: An Insider's View* 2002, 2003, 2004

20553   single or multiple trigger point(s), 3 or more muscle(s)

> *CPT Assistant* Mar 02:7, May 03:19, Sep 03:11, Jun 08:8; *CPT Changes: An Insider's View* 2002, 2003

(If imaging guidance is performed, see 76942, 77002, 77021)

Trigger Point Injection
20552, 20553

Insertion of needle into muscle trigger point for injection of therapeutic agent

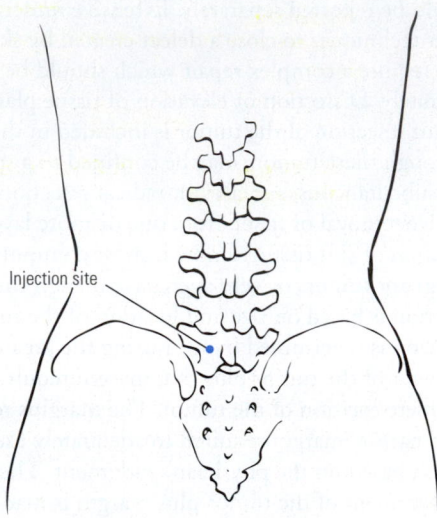

Injection site

Cross section through the body wall at level of lumbar vertebra

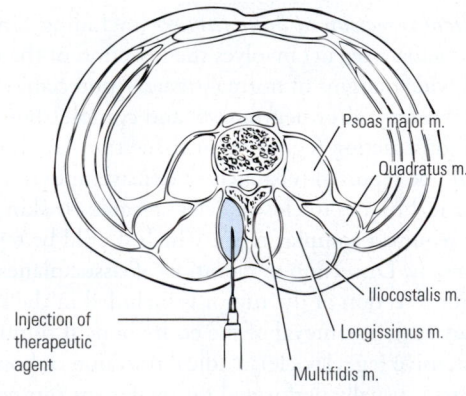

Psoas major m.

Quadratus m.

Iliocostalis m.

Longissimus m.

Multifidis m.

Injection of therapeutic agent

20555   Placement of needles or catheters into muscle and/or soft tissue for subsequent interstitial radioelement application (at the time of or subsequent to the procedure)

> *CPT Assistant* Feb 08:8; *CPT Changes: An Insider's View* 2008

(For placement of devices into the breast for interstitial radioelement application, see 19296-19298)

(For placement of needles, catheters, or devices into muscle or soft tissue of the head and neck, for interstitial radioelement application, use 41019)

(For placement of needles or catheters for interstitial radioelement application into prostate, use 55875)

(For placement of needles or catheters into the pelvic organs or genitalia [except prostate] for interstitial radioelement application, use 55920)

▶(For interstitial radioelement application, see 77776-77778, 77785-77787)◀

(For imaging guidance, see 76942, 77002, 77012, 77021)

20600 Arthrocentesis, aspiration and/or injection; small joint or bursa (eg, fingers, toes)

➔ *CPT Assistant* Dec 07:10; *CPT Changes: An Insider's View* 2003

20605 intermediate joint or bursa (eg, temporomandibular, acromioclavicular, wrist, elbow or ankle, olecranon bursa)

➔ *CPT Assistant* Dec 07:10; *CPT Changes: An Insider's View* 2003

20610 major joint or bursa (eg, shoulder, hip, knee joint, subacromial bursa)

➔ *CPT Assistant* Spring 92:8, Mar 01:10, Apr 04:15, Jul 06:1, Dec 07:10, Jul 08:9

(If imaging guidance is performed, see 76942, 77002, 77012, 77021)

Arthrocentesis, Aspiration, or Injection of Major Joint or Bursa
20610

Insertion of needle into major joint or bursa for injection of therapeutic or diagnostic agent, aspiration, or arthrocentesis

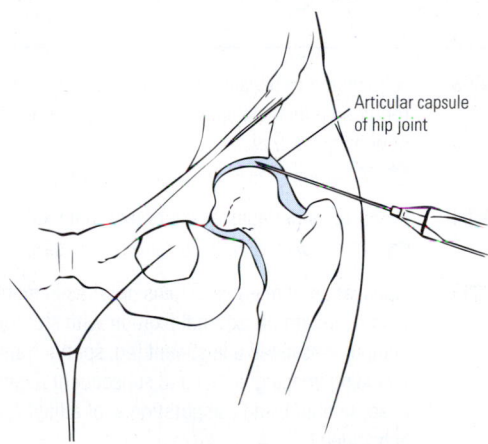

Articular capsule of hip joint

20612 Aspiration and/or injection of ganglion cyst(s) any location

➔ *CPT Changes: An Insider's View* 2003

(To report multiple ganglion cyst aspirations/injections, use 20612 and append modifier 59)

20615 Aspiration and injection for treatment of bone cyst

20650 Insertion of wire or pin with application of skeletal traction, including removal (separate procedure)

20660 Application of cranial tongs, caliper, or stereotactic frame, including removal (separate procedure)

➔ *CPT Assistant* Jun 96:10, Nov 97:14, Jan 06:46, Dec 06:10, Feb 08:8, Jul 08:10; *CPT Changes: An Insider's View* 2008

20661 Application of halo, including removal; cranial

➔ *CPT Assistant* Nov 97:14

20662 pelvic

20663 femoral

20664 Application of halo, including removal, cranial, 6 or more pins placed, for thin skull osteology (eg, pediatric patients, hydrocephalus, osteogenesis imperfecta), requiring general anesthesia

➔ *CPT Assistant* Nov 97:14

Halo Application for Thin Skull Osteology
20664

A cranial halo is placed on the head of a child whose skull is unusually thin due to congenital or developmental problems.

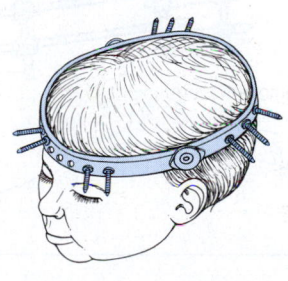

20665 Removal of tongs or halo applied by another physician

20670 Removal of implant; superficial (eg, buried wire, pin or rod) (separate procedure)

➔ *CPT Assistant* Dec 07:7, Dec 07:8

20680 deep (eg, buried wire, pin, screw, metal band, nail, rod or plate)

➔ *CPT Assistant* Spring 92:11

20690 Application of a uniplane (pins or wires in 1 plane), unilateral, external fixation system

➔ *CPT Assistant* Winter 90:4, Winter 92:11, Fall 93:21, Oct 99:5, Jan 04:27, Jun 05:12, Oct 07:7, Jan 08:4, Feb 08:9; *CPT Changes: An Insider's View* 2008

Uniplane External Fixation System
20690

The following figures are examples of types of stabilization devices. Codes 20690 and 20692 describe the placement of types of external fixation devices. The method of stabilization depends upon fracture grade (degree of soft tissue injury/skin integrity disruption), type (eg, comminuted, spiral, impacted), and location (eg, extremity, pelvis).

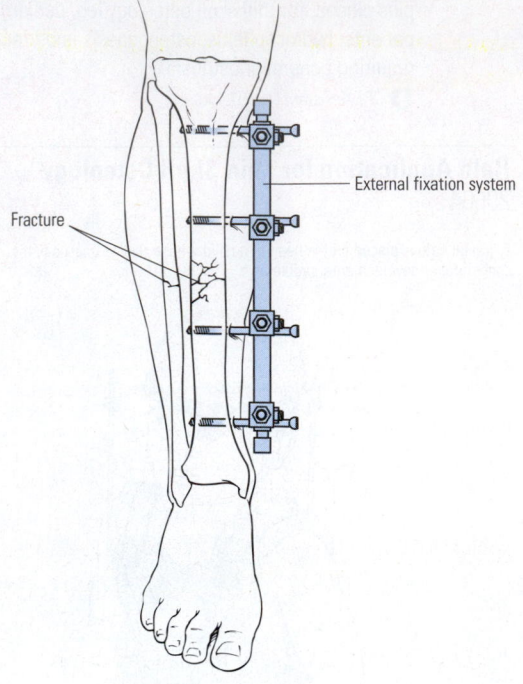

Fracture

External fixation system

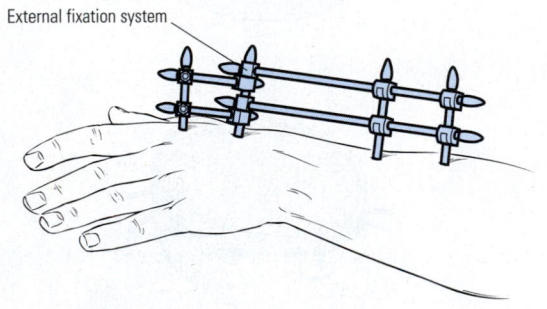

External fixation system

20692 Application of a multiplane (pins or wires in more than 1 plane), unilateral, external fixation system (eg, Ilizarov, Monticelli type)

➲ *CPT Assistant* Winter 90:4, Fall 93:21, Oct 99:5, Jul 00:11, Feb 08:9; *CPT Changes: An Insider's View* 2008

Multiplane External Fixation System
20692

The following figure is an example of a type of multiplane stabilization device. Codes 20690 and 20692 describe the placement of types of external fixation devices. The method of stabilization depends upon fracture grade (degree of soft tissue injury/skin integrity disruption), type (eg, comminuted, spiral, impacted), and location (eg, extremity, pelvis).

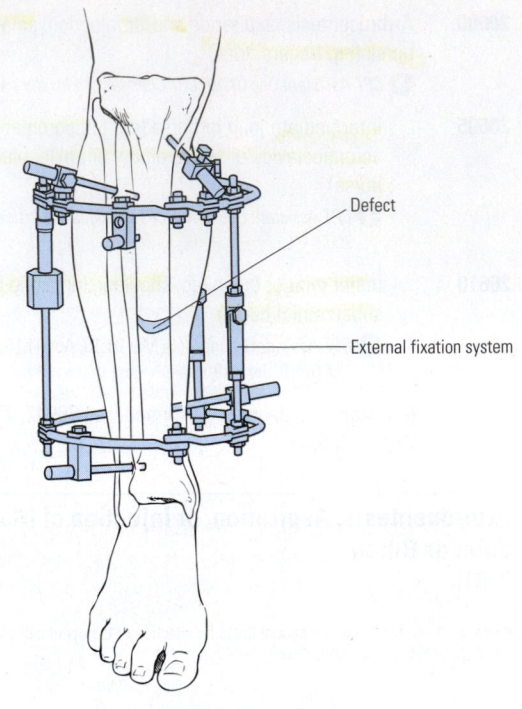

Defect

External fixation system

20693 Adjustment or revision of external fixation system requiring anesthesia (eg, new pin[s] or wire[s] and/or new ring[s] or bar[s])

➲ *CPT Assistant* Fall 93:21, Oct 99:5, Jul 00:11

20694 Removal, under anesthesia, of external fixation system

➲ *CPT Assistant* Winter 92:10, Fall 93:21, Oct 99:5, Jul 00:11

20696 Application of multiplane (pins or wires in more than 1 plane), unilateral, external fixation with stereotactic computer-assisted adjustment (eg, spatial frame), including imaging; initial and subsequent alignment(s), assessment(s), and computation(s) of adjustment schedule(s)

➲ *CPT Changes: An Insider's View* 2009

(Do not report 20696 in conjunction with 20692, 20697)

⊘ **20697** exchange (ie, removal and replacement) of strut, each

➲ *CPT Changes: An Insider's View* 2009

(Do not report 20697 in conjunction with 20692, 20696)

Replantation

20802　Replantation, arm (includes surgical neck of humerus through elbow joint), complete amputation

(To report replantation of incomplete arm amputation, see specific code[s] for repair of bone[s], ligament[s], tendon[s], nerve[s], or blood vessel[s] with modifier 52)

20805　Replantation, forearm (includes radius and ulna to radial carpal joint), complete amputation

(To report replantation of incomplete forearm amputation, see specific code[s] for repair of bone[s], ligament[s], tendon[s], nerve[s], or blood vessel[s] with modifier 52)

20808　Replantation, hand (includes hand through metacarpophalangeal joints), complete amputation

(To report replantation of incomplete hand amputation, see specific code[s] for repair of bone[s], ligament[s], tendon[s], nerve[s], or blood vessel[s] with modifier 52)

20816　Replantation, digit, excluding thumb (includes metacarpophalangeal joint to insertion of flexor sublimis tendon), complete amputation

➔ *CPT Assistant* Oct 96:11

(To report replantation of incomplete digit amputation, excluding thumb, see specific code[s] for repair of bone[s], ligament[s], tendon[s], nerve[s], or blood vessel[s] with modifier 52)

20822　Replantation, digit, excluding thumb (includes distal tip to sublimis tendon insertion), complete amputation

(To report replantation of incomplete digit amputation, excluding thumb, see specific code[s] for repair of bone[s], ligament[s], tendon[s], nerve[s], or blood vessel[s] with modifier 52)

20824　Replantation, thumb (includes carpometacarpal joint to MP joint), complete amputation

(To report replantation of incomplete thumb amputation, see specific code[s] for repair of bone[s], ligament[s], tendon[s], nerve[s], or blood vessel[s] with modifier 52)

20827　Replantation, thumb (includes distal tip to MP joint), complete amputation

(To report replantation of incomplete thumb amputation, see specific code[s] for repair of bone[s], ligament[s], tendon[s], nerve[s], or blood vessel[s] with modifier 52)

(To report replantation of complete leg amputation, see specific code[s] for repair of bone[s], ligament[s], tendon[s], nerve[s], or blood vessel[s] with modifier 52)

(To report replantation of incomplete leg amputation, see specific code[s] for repair of bone[s], ligament[s], tendon[s], nerve[s], or blood vessel[s] with modifier 52)

20838　Replantation, foot, complete amputation

(To report replantation of incomplete foot amputation, see specific code[s] for repair of bone[s], ligament[s], tendon[s], nerve[s], or blood vessel[s] with modifier 52)

Grafts (or Implants)

Codes for obtaining autogenous bone, cartilage, tendon, fascia lata grafts, or other tissues through separate skin/fascial incisions should be reported separately unless the code descriptor references the harvesting of the graft or implant (eg, includes obtaining graft).

Do not append modifier 62 to bone graft codes 20900-20938.

(For spinal surgery bone graft[s] see codes 20930-20938)

20900　Bone graft, any donor area; minor or small (eg, dowel or button)

➔ *CPT Assistant* Dec 00:15; *CPT Changes: An Insider's View* 2008

20902　major or large

➔ *CPT Assistant* Dec 00:15; *CPT Changes: An Insider's View* 2008

20910　Cartilage graft; costochondral

➔ *CPT Changes: An Insider's View* 2008

20912　nasal septum

➔ *CPT Changes: An Insider's View* 2008

(For ear cartilage, use 21235)

20920　Fascia lata graft; by stripper

➔ *CPT Assistant* Aug 99:5, Jan 05:8; *CPT Changes: An Insider's View* 2008

20922　by incision and area exposure, complex or sheet

➔ *CPT Assistant* Jan 05:8; *CPT Changes: An Insider's View* 2008

20924　Tendon graft, from a distance (eg, palmaris, toe extensor, plantaris)

➔ *CPT Changes: An Insider's View* 2008

20926　Tissue grafts, other (eg, paratenon, fat, dermis)

➔ *CPT Assistant* Summer 91:12, Aug 99:5, Nov 99:10, May 06:16; *CPT Changes: An Insider's View* 2008

+ 20930　Allograft for spine surgery only; morselized (List separately in addition to code for primary procedure)

➔ *CPT Assistant* Feb 96:6, Mar 96:4, Sep 97:8, Nov 99:10, Feb 02:6, Jan 04:27, Dec 07:1, Feb 08:8; *CPT Changes: An Insider's View* 2008

(Use 20930 in conjunction with 22319, 22532, 22533, 22548-22558, 22590-22612, 22630, 22800-22812, 0195T, 0196T)

+ 20931　structural (List separately in addition to code for primary procedure)

➔ *CPT Assistant* Feb 96:6, Feb 02:6, Feb 05:15, Feb 08:8; *CPT Changes: An Insider's View* 2008

(Use 20931 in conjunction with 22319, 22532-22533, 22548-22558, 22590-22612, 22630, 22800-22812)

+ 20936　Autograft for spine surgery only (includes harvesting the graft); local (eg, ribs, spinous process, or laminar fragments) obtained from same incision (List separately in addition to code for primary procedure)

➔ *CPT Assistant* Feb 96:6, Sep 97:8, Feb 02:6, Feb 08:8; *CPT Changes: An Insider's View* 2008

(Use 20936 in conjunction with 22319, 22532, 22533, 22548-22558, 22590-22612, 22630, 22800-22812, 0195T, 0196T)

+ 20937   morselized (through separate skin or fascial incision) (List separately in addition to code for primary procedure)
→ *CPT Assistant* Feb 96:6, Sep 97:8, Dec 99:2, Feb 02:6, Feb 08:8; *CPT Changes: An Insider's View* 2008

(Use 20937 in conjunction with 22319, 22532, 22533, 22548-22558, 22590-22612, 22630, 22800-22812, 0195T, 0196T)

+ 20938   structural, bicortical or tricortical (through separate skin or fascial incision) (List separately in addition to code for primary procedure)
→ *CPT Assistant* Feb 96:6, Mar 96:5, Sep 97:8, Feb 02:6, Feb 08:8; *CPT Changes: An Insider's View* 2008

(Use 20938 in conjunction with 22319, 22532, 22533, 22548-22558, 22590-22612, 22630, 22800-22812)

(For needle aspiration of bone marrow for the purpose of bone grafting, use 38220)

Other Procedures

20950   Monitoring of interstitial fluid pressure (includes insertion of device, eg, wick catheter technique, needle manometer technique) in detection of muscle compartment syndrome
→ *CPT Assistant* Sep 07:10

20955   Bone graft with microvascular anastomosis; fibula
→ *CPT Assistant* Apr 97:4

20956   iliac crest
→ *CPT Assistant* Apr 97:4

20957   metatarsal
→ *CPT Assistant* Apr 97:4

20962   other than fibula, iliac crest, or metatarsal
→ *CPT Assistant* Apr 97:4

(Do not report code 69990 in addition to codes 20955-20962)

20969   Free osteocutaneous flap with microvascular anastomosis; other than iliac crest, metatarsal, or great toe
→ *CPT Assistant* Apr 97:4

20970   iliac crest
→ *CPT Assistant* Apr 97:4

20972   metatarsal
→ *CPT Assistant* Apr 97:4

20973   great toe with web space
→ *CPT Assistant* Apr 97:4

(Do not report code 69990 in addition to codes 20969-20973)

(For great toe, wrap-around procedure, use 26551)

⊘ **20974**   Electrical stimulation to aid bone healing; noninvasive (nonoperative)
→ *CPT Assistant* Sep 96:11, Nov 00:8

⊘ **20975**   invasive (operative)
→ *CPT Assistant* Nov 00:8

20979   Low intensity ultrasound stimulation to aid bone healing, noninvasive (nonoperative)
→ *CPT Assistant* Nov 99:10, Nov 00:8; *CPT Changes: An Insider's View* 2000

⊙ **20982**   Ablation, bone tumor(s) (eg, osteoid osteoma, metastasis) radiofrequency, percutaneous, including computed tomographic guidance
→ *CPT Changes: An Insider's View* 2004

(Do not report 20982 in conjunction with 77013)

+ 20985   Computer-assisted surgical navigational procedure for musculoskeletal procedures, image-less (List separately in addition to code for primary procedure)
→ *CPT Changes: An Insider's View* 2008, 2009

(Do not report 20985 in conjunction with 61795)

(20986, 20987 have been deleted)

(For computer-assisted navigational procedures with image guidance based on pre-operative and intraoperatively obtained images, see 0054T, 0055T)

20999   Unlisted procedure, musculoskeletal system, general
→ *CPT Assistant* Sep 03:13

Head

Skull, facial bones, and temporomandibular joint.

Incision

(For drainage of superficial abscess and hematoma, use 20000)

(For removal of embedded foreign body from dentoalveolar structure, see 41805, 41806)

21010   Arthrotomy, temporomandibular joint

(To report bilateral procedure, report 21010 with modifier 50)

Excision

● **21011**   Excision, tumor, soft tissue of face or scalp, subcutaneous; less than 2 cm
→ *CPT Changes: An Insider's View* 2010

● **21012**   2 cm or greater
→ *CPT Changes: An Insider's View* 2010

● **21013**   Excision, tumor, soft tissue of face and scalp, subfascial (eg, subgaleal, intramuscular); less than 2 cm
→ *CPT Changes: An Insider's View* 2010

● **21014**   2 cm or greater
→ *CPT Changes: An Insider's View* 2010

▲ **21015**   Radical resection of tumor (eg, malignant neoplasm), soft tissue of face or scalp; less than 2 cm
   ➲ *CPT Changes: An Insider's View* 2010

   (To report excision of skull tumor for osteomyelitis, use 61501)

● **21016**   2 cm or greater
   ➲ *CPT Changes: An Insider's View* 2010

21025   Excision of bone (eg, for osteomyelitis or bone abscess); mandible

21026   facial bone(s)

21029   Removal by contouring of benign tumor of facial bone (eg, fibrous dysplasia)

21030   Excision of benign tumor or cyst of maxilla or zygoma by enucleation and curettage
   ➲ *CPT Assistant* Nov 03:9; *CPT Changes: An Insider's View* 2003

21031   Excision of torus mandibularis

21032   Excision of maxillary torus palatinus

21034   Excision of malignant tumor of maxilla or zygoma
   ➲ *CPT Assistant* Nov 03:9; *CPT Changes: An Insider's View* 2003

21040   Excision of benign tumor or cyst of mandible, by enucleation and/or curettage
   ➲ *CPT Assistant* Nov 03:9; *CPT Changes: An Insider's View* 2003

   (For enucleation and/or curettage of benign cysts or tumors of mandible not requiring osteotomy, use 21040)

   (For excision of benign tumor or cyst of mandible requiring osteotomy, see 21046-21047)

21044   Excision of malignant tumor of mandible;

21045   radical resection

   (For bone graft, use 21215)

21046   Excision of benign tumor or cyst of mandible; requiring intra-oral osteotomy (eg, locally aggressive or destructive lesion(s))
   ➲ *CPT Assistant* Nov 03:9; *CPT Changes: An Insider's View* 2003

21047   requiring extra-oral osteotomy and partial mandibulectomy (eg, locally aggressive or destructive lesion(s))
   ➲ *CPT Assistant* Nov 03:9; *CPT Changes: An Insider's View* 2003

21048   Excision of benign tumor or cyst of maxilla; requiring intra-oral osteotomy (eg, locally aggressive or destructive lesion(s))
   ➲ *CPT Assistant* Nov 03:9; *CPT Changes: An Insider's View* 2003

21049   requiring extra-oral osteotomy and partial maxillectomy (eg, locally aggressive or destructive lesion(s))
   ➲ *CPT Assistant* Nov 03:9; *CPT Changes: An Insider's View* 2003

21050   Condylectomy, temporomandibular joint (separate procedure)

   (For bilateral procedures, report 21050 with modifier 50)

21060   Meniscectomy, partial or complete, temporomandibular joint (separate procedure)

   (For bilateral procedures, report 21060 with modifier 50)

21070   Coronoidectomy (separate procedure)

   (For bilateral procedures, report 21070 with modifier 50)

Manipulation

21073   Manipulation of temporomandibular joint(s) (TMJ), therapeutic, requiring an anesthesia service (ie, general or monitored anesthesia care)
   ➲ *CPT Assistant* Feb 08:9; *CPT Changes: An Insider's View* 2008

   (For TMJ manipulation without an anesthesia service [ie, general or monitored anesthesia care], see 97140, 98925-98929, 98943)

   (For closed treatment of temporomandibular dislocation, see 21480, 21485)

Head Prosthesis

Codes 21076-21089 describe professional services for the rehabilitation of patients with oral, facial, or other anatomical deficiencies by means of prostheses such as an artificial eye, ear, or nose or intraoral obturator to close a cleft. Codes 21076-21089 should only be used when the physician actually designs and prepares the prosthesis (ie, not prepared by an outside laboratory).

   (For application or removal of caliper or tongs, see 20660, 20665)

21076   Impression and custom preparation; surgical obturator prosthesis

21077   orbital prosthesis

21079   interim obturator prosthesis
   ➲ *CPT Assistant* Winter 90:5, Sep 06:13, Dec 06:10

21080   definitive obturator prosthesis
   ➲ *CPT Assistant* Winter 90:5, Sep 06:13, Dec 06:10

21081   mandibular resection prosthesis
   ➲ *CPT Assistant* Winter 90:5, Sep 06:13, Dec 06:10

21082   palatal augmentation prosthesis
   ➲ *CPT Assistant* Winter 90:5, Sep 06:13, Dec 06:10

21083   palatal lift prosthesis
   ➲ *CPT Assistant* Winter 90:5, Sep 06:13, Dec 06:10

21084   speech aid prosthesis
   ➲ *CPT Assistant* Winter 90:5, Sep 06:13, Dec 06:10

21085   oral surgical splint
   ➲ *CPT Assistant* Winter 90:5, Sep 06:13, Dec 06:10

21086   auricular prosthesis
   ➲ *CPT Assistant* Winter 90:5, Sep 06:13, Dec 06:10

21087   nasal prosthesis
   ➲ *CPT Assistant* Winter 90:5, Sep 06:13, Dec 06:10

21088   facial prosthesis
       ➲ *CPT Assistant* Winter 90:5, Sep 06:13, Dec 06:10

Other Procedures

21089   Unlisted maxillofacial prosthetic procedure
       ➲ *CPT Assistant* Winter 90:5, Sep 06:13, Dec 06:10

Introduction or Removal

21100   Application of halo type appliance for maxillofacial fixation, includes removal (separate procedure)

21110   Application of interdental fixation device for conditions other than fracture or dislocation, includes removal
       ➲ *CPT Assistant* Mar 97:10

     (For removal of interdental fixation by another physician, see 20670-20680)

21116   Injection procedure for temporomandibular joint arthrography

     (For radiological supervision and interpretation, use 70332. Do not report 77002 in conjunction with 70332)

Repair, Revision, and/or Reconstruction

     (For cranioplasty, see 21179, 21180 and 62116, 62120, 62140-62147)

21120   Genioplasty; augmentation (autograft, allograft, prosthetic material)

21121   sliding osteotomy, single piece

21122   sliding osteotomies, 2 or more osteotomies (eg, wedge excision or bone wedge reversal for asymmetrical chin)

21123   sliding, augmentation with interpositional bone grafts (includes obtaining autografts)

21125   Augmentation, mandibular body or angle; prosthetic material

21127   with bone graft, onlay or interpositional (includes obtaining autograft)

21137   Reduction forehead; contouring only

21138   contouring and application of prosthetic material or bone graft (includes obtaining autograft)

21139   contouring and setback of anterior frontal sinus wall

21141   Reconstruction midface, LeFort I; single piece, segment movement in any direction (eg, for Long Face Syndrome), without bone graft

21142   2 pieces, segment movement in any direction, without bone graft

21143   3 or more pieces, segment movement in any direction, without bone graft

21145   single piece, segment movement in any direction, requiring bone grafts (includes obtaining autografts)

21146   2 pieces, segment movement in any direction, requiring bone grafts (includes obtaining autografts) (eg, ungrafted unilateral alveolar cleft)

21147   3 or more pieces, segment movement in any direction, requiring bone grafts (includes obtaining autografts) (eg, ungrafted bilateral alveolar cleft or multiple osteotomies)

21150   Reconstruction midface, LeFort II; anterior intrusion (eg, Treacher-Collins Syndrome)

21151   any direction, requiring bone grafts (includes obtaining autografts)

21154   Reconstruction midface, LeFort III (extracranial), any type, requiring bone grafts (includes obtaining autografts); without LeFort I

21155   with LeFort I

21159   Reconstruction midface, LeFort III (extra and intracranial) with forehead advancement (eg, mono bloc), requiring bone grafts (includes obtaining autografts); without LeFort I

21160   with LeFort I

21172   Reconstruction superior-lateral orbital rim and lower forehead, advancement or alteration, with or without grafts (includes obtaining autografts)

     (For frontal or parietal craniotomy performed for craniosynostosis, use 61556)

21175   Reconstruction, bifrontal, superior-lateral orbital rims and lower forehead, advancement or alteration (eg, plagiocephaly, trigonocephaly, brachycephaly), with or without grafts (includes obtaining autografts)

     (For bifrontal craniotomy performed for craniosynostosis, use 61557)

21179   Reconstruction, entire or majority of forehead and/or supraorbital rims; with grafts (allograft or prosthetic material)

21180   with autograft (includes obtaining grafts)

     (For extensive craniectomy for multiple suture craniosynostosis, use only 61558 or 61559)

21181   Reconstruction by contouring of benign tumor of cranial bones (eg, fibrous dysplasia), extracranial

21182   Reconstruction of orbital walls, rims, forehead, nasoethmoid complex following intra- and extracranial excision of benign tumor of cranial bone (eg, fibrous dysplasia), with multiple autografts (includes obtaining grafts); total area of bone grafting less than 40 sq cm

21183   total area of bone grafting greater than 40 sq cm but less than 80 sq cm
       ➲ *CPT Changes: An Insider's View* 2002

21184   total area of bone grafting greater than 80 sq cm
       ➲ *CPT Changes: An Insider's View* 2002

     (For excision of benign tumor of cranial bones, see 61563, 61564)

21188   Reconstruction midface, osteotomies (other than LeFort type) and bone grafts (includes obtaining autografts)

21193   Reconstruction of mandibular rami, horizontal, vertical, C, or L osteotomy; without bone graft
➲ *CPT Assistant* Apr 96:11

21194   with bone graft (includes obtaining graft)
➲ *CPT Assistant* Apr 96:11

21195   Reconstruction of mandibular rami and/or body, sagittal split; without internal rigid fixation
➲ *CPT Assistant* Apr 96:11

21196   with internal rigid fixation
➲ *CPT Assistant* Apr 96:11, Mar 97:11

Reconstruction of Mandibular Rami
21196

The mandibular ramus is reconstructed to lengthen, set back, or rotate the mandible.

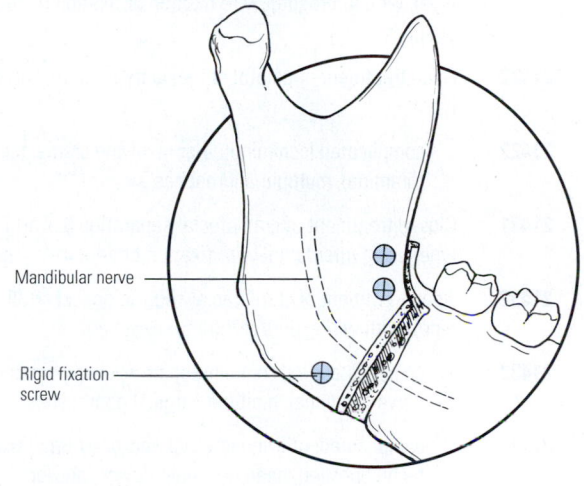

Mandibular nerve

Rigid fixation screw

21198   Osteotomy, mandible, segmental;
➲ *CPT Changes: An Insider's View* 2001

21199   with genioglossus advancement
➲ *CPT Changes: An Insider's View* 2001

(To report total osteotomy of the maxilla, see 21141-21160)

21206   Osteotomy, maxilla, segmental (eg, Wassmund or Schuchard)

21208   Osteoplasty, facial bones; augmentation (autograft, allograft, or prosthetic implant)

21209   reduction

21210   Graft, bone; nasal, maxillary or malar areas (includes obtaining graft)

(For cleft palate repair, see 42200-42225)

21215   mandible (includes obtaining graft)

21230   Graft; rib cartilage, autogenous, to face, chin, nose or ear (includes obtaining graft)

21235   ear cartilage, autogenous, to nose or ear (includes obtaining graft)

(To report graft augmentation of facial bones, use 21208)

21240   Arthroplasty, temporomandibular joint, with or without autograft (includes obtaining graft)

21242   Arthroplasty, temporomandibular joint, with allograft

21243   Arthroplasty, temporomandibular joint, with prosthetic joint replacement

21244   Reconstruction of mandible, extraoral, with transosteal bone plate (eg, mandibular staple bone plate)

21245   Reconstruction of mandible or maxilla, subperiosteal implant; partial

21246   complete

21247   Reconstruction of mandibular condyle with bone and cartilage autografts (includes obtaining grafts) (eg, for hemifacial microsomia)

21248   Reconstruction of mandible or maxilla, endosteal implant (eg, blade, cylinder); partial

21249   complete

(To report midface reconstruction, see 21141-21160)

21255   Reconstruction of zygomatic arch and glenoid fossa with bone and cartilage (includes obtaining autografts)

21256   Reconstruction of orbit with osteotomies (extracranial) and with bone grafts (includes obtaining autografts) (eg, micro-ophthalmia)

21260   Periorbital osteotomies for orbital hypertelorism, with bone grafts; extracranial approach

21261   combined intra- and extracranial approach

21263   with forehead advancement

21267   Orbital repositioning, periorbital osteotomies, unilateral, with bone grafts; extracranial approach

21268   combined intra- and extracranial approach

21270   Malar augmentation, prosthetic material

(For malar augmentation with bone graft, use 21210)

21275   Secondary revision of orbitocraniofacial reconstruction

21280   Medial canthopexy (separate procedure)

(For medial canthoplasty, use 67950)

21282   Lateral canthopexy

21295   Reduction of masseter muscle and bone (eg, for treatment of benign masseteric hypertrophy); extraoral approach

21296   intraoral approach

Other Procedures

21299   Unlisted craniofacial and maxillofacial procedure

Fracture and/or Dislocation

(For operative repair of skull fracture, see 62000-62010)

(To report closed treatment of skull fracture, use the appropriate Evaluation and Management code)

21310 Closed treatment of nasal bone fracture without manipulation

21315 Closed treatment of nasal bone fracture; without stabilization

21320 with stabilization

21325 Open treatment of nasal fracture; uncomplicated

21330 complicated, with internal and/or external skeletal fixation

21335 with concomitant open treatment of fractured septum

21336 Open treatment of nasal septal fracture, with or without stabilization

21337 Closed treatment of nasal septal fracture, with or without stabilization

21338 Open treatment of nasoethmoid fracture; without external fixation

21339 with external fixation

21340 Percutaneous treatment of nasoethmoid complex fracture, with splint, wire or headcap fixation, including repair of canthal ligaments and/or the nasolacrimal apparatus

21343 Open treatment of depressed frontal sinus fracture

21344 Open treatment of complicated (eg, comminuted or involving posterior wall) frontal sinus fracture, via coronal or multiple approaches

21345 Closed treatment of nasomaxillary complex fracture (LeFort II type), with interdental wire fixation or fixation of denture or splint

21346 Open treatment of nasomaxillary complex fracture (LeFort II type); with wiring and/or local fixation

21347 requiring multiple open approaches

21348 with bone grafting (includes obtaining graft)

21355 Percutaneous treatment of fracture of malar area, including zygomatic arch and malar tripod, with manipulation

21356 Open treatment of depressed zygomatic arch fracture (eg, Gillies approach)

21360 Open treatment of depressed malar fracture, including zygomatic arch and malar tripod

21365 Open treatment of complicated (eg, comminuted or involving cranial nerve foramina) fracture(s) of malar area, including zygomatic arch and malar tripod; with internal fixation and multiple surgical approaches

21366 with bone grafting (includes obtaining graft)

21385 Open treatment of orbital floor blowout fracture; transantral approach (Caldwell-Luc type operation)

21386 periorbital approach

21387 combined approach

21390 periorbital approach, with alloplastic or other implant

21395 periorbital approach with bone graft (includes obtaining graft)

21400 Closed treatment of fracture of orbit, except blowout; without manipulation

21401 with manipulation

21406 Open treatment of fracture of orbit, except blowout; without implant

21407 with implant

21408 with bone grafting (includes obtaining graft)

21421 Closed treatment of palatal or maxillary fracture (LeFort I type), with interdental wire fixation or fixation of denture or splint

21422 Open treatment of palatal or maxillary fracture (LeFort I type);

21423 complicated (comminuted or involving cranial nerve foramina), multiple approaches

21431 Closed treatment of craniofacial separation (LeFort III type) using interdental wire fixation of denture or splint

21432 Open treatment of craniofacial separation (LeFort III type); with wiring and/or internal fixation

21433 complicated (eg, comminuted or involving cranial nerve foramina), multiple surgical approaches

21435 complicated, utilizing internal and/or external fixation techniques (eg, head cap, halo device, and/or intermaxillary fixation)

(For removal of internal or external fixation device, use 20670)

21436 complicated, multiple surgical approaches, internal fixation, with bone grafting (includes obtaining graft)

21440 Closed treatment of mandibular or maxillary alveolar ridge fracture (separate procedure)

21445 Open treatment of mandibular or maxillary alveolar ridge fracture (separate procedure)

21450 Closed treatment of mandibular fracture; without manipulation

21451 with manipulation

21452 Percutaneous treatment of mandibular fracture, with external fixation

21453 Closed treatment of mandibular fracture with interdental fixation
  ⟶*CPT Assistant* Dec 07:7, Dec 07:8

21454 Open treatment of mandibular fracture with external fixation

21461   Open treatment of mandibular fracture; without interdental fixation

21462   with interdental fixation

21465   Open treatment of mandibular condylar fracture

21470   Open treatment of complicated mandibular fracture by multiple surgical approaches including internal fixation, interdental fixation, and/or wiring of dentures or splints
➔ *CPT Assistant* Nov 02:10

21480   Closed treatment of temporomandibular dislocation; initial or subsequent

21485   complicated (eg, recurrent requiring intermaxillary fixation or splinting), initial or subsequent

21490   Open treatment of temporomandibular dislocation

(For interdental wire fixation, use 21497)

21495   Open treatment of hyoid fracture

(For laryngoplasty with open reduction of fracture, use 31584)

(To report treatment of closed fracture of larynx, use the applicable Evaluation and Management codes)

21497   Interdental wiring, for condition other than fracture
➔ *CPT Assistant* Mar 97:10

Other Procedures

21499   Unlisted musculoskeletal procedure, head

(For unlisted craniofacial or maxillofacial procedure, use 21299)

Neck (Soft Tissues) and Thorax

(For cervical spine and back, see 21920 et seq)

(For injection of fracture site or trigger point, use 20550)

Incision

(For incision and drainage of abscess or hematoma, superficial, see 10060, 10140)

21501   Incision and drainage, deep abscess or hematoma, soft tissues of neck or thorax;

(For posterior spine subfascial incision and drainage, see 22010-22015)

21502   with partial rib ostectomy

21510   Incision, deep, with opening of bone cortex (eg, for osteomyelitis or bone abscess), thorax

Excision

(For bone biopsy, see 20220-20251)

21550   Biopsy, soft tissue of neck or thorax

(For needle biopsy of soft tissue, use 20206)

21552   ▶Code is out of numerical sequence. See 21550-21632◀

21554   ▶Code is out of numerical sequence. See 21550-21632◀

▲ **21555**   Excision, tumor, soft tissue of neck or anterior thorax, subcutaneous; less than 3 cm
➔ *CPT Assistant* Oct 02:11; *CPT Changes: An Insider's View* 2010

#● **21552**   3 cm or greater
➔ *CPT Changes: An Insider's View* 2010

▲ **21556**   Excision, tumor, soft tissue of neck or anterior thorax, subfascial (eg, intramuscular); less than 5 cm
➔ *CPT Changes: An Insider's View* 2010

#● **21554**   5 cm or greater
➔ *CPT Changes: An Insider's View* 2010

▲ **21557**   Radical resection of tumor (eg, malignant neoplasm), soft tissue of neck or anterior thorax; less than 5 cm
➔ *CPT Changes: An Insider's View* 2010

● **21558**   5 cm or greater
➔ *CPT Changes: An Insider's View* 2010

21600   Excision of rib, partial

(For radical resection of chest wall and rib cage for tumor, use 19260)

(For radical debridement of chest wall and rib cage for injury, see 11040-11044)

21610   Costotransversectomy (separate procedure)

21615   Excision first and/or cervical rib;

21616   with sympathectomy

21620   Ostectomy of sternum, partial

21627   Sternal debridement

(For debridement and closure, use 21750)

21630   Radical resection of sternum;

21632   with mediastinal lymphadenectomy

Repair, Revision, and/or Reconstruction

(For superficial wound, see **Integumentary System** section under Repair—Simple)

21685   Hyoid myotomy and suspension
➔ *CPT Assistant* Aug 04:11; *CPT Changes: An Insider's View* 2004

21700   Division of scalenus anticus; without resection of cervical rib

21705   with resection of cervical rib

21720   Division of sternocleidomastoid for torticollis, open operation; without cast application

(For transection of spinal accessory and cervical nerves, see 63191, 64722)

21725   with cast application

21740   Reconstructive repair of pectus excavatum or carinatum; open
> *CPT Changes: An Insider's View* 2003

21742   minimally invasive approach (Nuss procedure), without thoracoscopy
> *CPT Changes: An Insider's View* 2003

21743   minimally invasive approach (Nuss procedure), with thoracoscopy
> *CPT Changes: An Insider's View* 2003

21750   Closure of median sternotomy separation with or without debridement (separate procedure)
> *CPT Changes: An Insider's View* 2002

Fracture and/or Dislocation

21800   Closed treatment of rib fracture, uncomplicated, each

21805   Open treatment of rib fracture without fixation, each

21810   Treatment of rib fracture requiring external fixation (flail chest)

21820   Closed treatment of sternum fracture

21825   Open treatment of sternum fracture with or without skeletal fixation

(For sternoclavicular dislocation, see 23520-23532)

Other Procedures

21899   Unlisted procedure, neck or thorax

Back and Flank

Excision

21920   Biopsy, soft tissue of back or flank; superficial

21925   deep

(For needle biopsy of soft tissue, use 20206)

▲ **21930**   Excision, tumor, soft tissue of back or flank, subcutaneous; less than 3 cm
> *CPT Changes: An Insider's View* 2010

● **21931**   3 cm or greater
> *CPT Changes: An Insider's View* 2010

● **21932**   Excision, tumor, soft tissue of back or flank, subfascial (eg, intramuscular); less than 5 cm
> *CPT Changes: An Insider's View* 2010

● **21933**   5 cm or greater
> *CPT Changes: An Insider's View* 2010

▲ **21935**   Radical resection of tumor (eg, malignant neoplasm), soft tissue of back or flank; less than 5 cm
> *CPT Changes: An Insider's View* 2010

● **21936**   5 cm or greater
> *CPT Changes: An Insider's View* 2010

Spine (Vertebral Column)

Cervical, thoracic, and lumbar spine.

Within the spine section, bone grafting procedures are reported separately and in addition to arthrodesis. For bone grafts in other Musculoskeletal sections, see specific code(s) descriptor(s) and/or accompanying guidelines.

To report bone grafts performed after arthrodesis, see 20930-20938. Do not append modifier 62 to bone graft codes 20900-20938.

Example:

Posterior arthrodesis of L5-S1 for degenerative disc disease utilizing morselized autogenous iliac bone graft harvested through a separate fascial incision.

Report as 22612 and 20937.

Within the spine section, instrumentation is reported separately and in addition to arthrodesis. To report instrumentation procedures performed with definitive vertebral procedure(s), see 22840-22855. Instrumentation procedure codes 22840-22848 and 22851 are reported in addition to the definitive procedure(s). Modifier 62 may not be appended to the definitive or add-on spinal instrumentation procedure code(s) 22840-22848 and 22850-22852.

Example:

Posterior arthrodesis of L4-S1, utilizing morselized autogenous iliac bone graft harvested through separate fascial incision, and pedicle screw fixation.

Report as 22612, 22614, 22842, and 20937.

Vertebral procedures are sometimes followed by arthrodesis and in addition may include bone grafts and instrumentation.

When arthrodesis is performed in addition to another procedure, the arthrodesis should be reported in addition to the original procedure with modifier 51 (multiple procedures). Examples are after osteotomy, fracture care, vertebral corpectomy, and laminectomy. Bone grafts and instrumentation are never performed without arthrodesis.

Example:

Treatment of a burst fracture of L2 by corpectomy followed by arthrodesis of L1-L3, utilizing anterior instrumentation L1-L3 and structural allograft.

Report as 63090, 22558-51, 22585, 22845, and 20931.

When two surgeons work together as primary surgeons performing distinct part(s) of a single reportable procedure, each surgeon should report his/her distinct operative work by appending modifier 62 to the single definitive procedure code. If additional procedure(s) (including add-on procedure[s]) are performed during the same surgical session, separate code(s) may be reported by each co-surgeon, with modifier 62 appended (see Appendix A).

Example:

A 42-year-old male with a history of posttraumatic degenerative disc disease at L3-4 and L4-5 (internal disc disruption) underwent surgical repair. Surgeon A performed an anterior exposure of the spine with mobilization of the great vessels. Surgeon B performed anterior (minimal) discectomy and fusion at L3-4 and L4-5 using anterior interbody technique.

Report surgeon A: 22558 append modifier 62, 22585 append modifier 62
Report surgeon B: 22558 append modifier 62, 22585 append modifier 62, 20931

> (Do not append modifier 62 to bone graft code 20931)

> (For injection procedure for myelography, use 62284)

> (For injection procedure for discography, see 62290, 62291)

> (For injection procedure, chemonucleolysis, single or multiple levels, use 62292)

> ►(For injection procedure for facet joints, see 64490-64495, 64622-64627)◄

> (For needle or trocar biopsy, see 20220-20225)

Incision

22010   Incision and drainage, open, of deep abscess (subfascial), posterior spine; cervical, thoracic, or cervicothoracic
➔ *CPT Changes: An Insider's View* 2006

22015   lumbar, sacral, or lumbosacral
➔ *CPT Changes: An Insider's View* 2006

> (Do not report 22015 in conjunction with 22010)

> (Do not report 22015 in conjunction with instrumentation removal, 10180, 22850, 22852)

> (For incision and drainage of abscess or hematoma, superficial, see 10060, 10140)

Excision

For the following codes, when two surgeons work together as primary surgeons performing distinct part(s) of partial vertebral body excision, each surgeon should report his/her distinct operative work by appending modifier 62 to the procedure code. In this situation, modifier 62 may be appended to the procedure code(s) 22100-22102, 22110-22114 and, as appropriate, to the associated additional vertebral segment add-on code(s) 22103, 22116 as long as both surgeons continue to work together as primary surgeons.

> (For bone biopsy, see 20220-20251)

> (To report soft tissue biopsy of back or flank, see 21920-21925)

> (For needle biopsy of soft tissue, use 20206)

> (To report excision of soft tissue tumor of back or flank, use 21930)

22100   Partial excision of posterior vertebral component (eg, spinous process, lamina or facet) for intrinsic bony lesion, single vertebral segment; cervical

22101   thoracic

22102   lumbar

> (For insertion of posterior spinous process distraction devices, see 0171T, 0172T)

+ 22103   each additional segment (List separately in addition to code for primary procedure)
➔ *CPT Assistant* Feb 96:6

> (Use 22103 in conjunction with 22100, 22101, 22102)

22110   Partial excision of vertebral body, for intrinsic bony lesion, without decompression of spinal cord or nerve root(s), single vertebral segment; cervical

22112   thoracic

22114   lumbar

+ 22116   each additional vertebral segment (List separately in addition to code for primary procedure)
➔ *CPT Assistant* Feb 96:6

> (Use 22116 in conjunction with 22110, 22112, 22114)

> (For complete or near complete resection of vertebral body, see vertebral corpectomy, 63081-63091)

> (For spinal reconstruction with bone graft (autograft, allograft) and/or methylmethacrylate of cervical vertebral body, use 63081 and 22554 and 20931 or 20938)

> (For spinal reconstruction with bone graft (autograft, allograft) and/or methylmethacrylate of thoracic vertebral body, use 63085 or 63087 and 22556 and 20931 or 20938)

> (For spinal reconstruction with bone graft (autograft, allograft) and/or methylmethacrylate of lumbar vertebral body, use 63087 or 63090 and 22558 and 20931 or 20938)

> (For spinal reconstruction following vertebral body resection, use 63082 or 63086 or 63088 or 63091, and 22585)

> (For harvest of bone autograft for vertebral reconstruction, see 20931 or 20938)

> (For cervical spinal reconstruction with prosthetic replacement of resected vertebral bodies, see codes 63081 and 22554 and 20931 or 20938 and 22851)

> (For thoracic spinal reconstruction with prosthetic replacement of resected vertebral bodies, see codes 63085 or 63087 and 22556 and 20931 or 20938 and 22851)

> (For lumbar spinal reconstruction with prosthetic replacement of resected vertebral bodies, see codes 63087 or 63090 and 22558, and 20931 or 20938 and 22851)

> (For osteotomy of spine, see 22210-22226)

Osteotomy

To report arthrodesis, see codes 22590-22632. (Report in addition to code[s] for the definitive procedure with modifier 51.)

To report instrumentation procedures, see 22840-22855. (Report in addition to code[s] for the definitive procedure[s].) Do not append modifier 62 to spinal instrumentation codes 22840-22848 and 22850-22852.

To report bone graft procedures, see 20930-20938. (Report in addition to code[s] for the definitive procedure[s].) Do not append modifier 62 to bone graft codes 20900-20938.

For the following codes, when two surgeons work together as primary surgeons performing distinct part(s) of an anterior spine osteotomy, each surgeon should report his/her distinct operative work by appending modifier 62 to the procedure code. In this situation, modifier 62 may be appended to the procedure code(s) 22210-22214, 22220-22224 and, as appropriate, to associated additional segment add-on code(s) 22216, 22226 as long as both surgeons continue to work together as primary surgeons.

Spinal osteotomy procedures are reported when a portion(s) of the vertebral segment(s) is cut and removed in preparation for re-aligning the spine as part of a spinal deformity correction. For excision of an intrinsic lesion of the vertebra without deformity correction, see 22100-22116. For decompression of the spinal cord and/or nerve roots, see 63001-63308.

The three columns are defined as anterior (anterior two-thirds of the vertebral body), middle (posterior third of the vertebral body and the pedicle), and posterior (articular facets, lamina, and spinous process).

22206   Osteotomy of spine, posterior or posterolateral approach, 3 columns, 1 vertebral segment (eg, pedicle/vertebral body subtraction); thoracic
➔ *CPT Assistant* Feb 08:9; *CPT Changes: An Insider's View* 2008

(Do not report 22206 in conjunction with 22207)

22207   lumbar
➔ *CPT Assistant* Feb 08:9; *CPT Changes: An Insider's View* 2008

(Do not report 22207 in conjunction with 22206)

+ 22208   each additional vertebral segment (List separately in addition to code for primary procedure)
➔ *CPT Assistant* Feb 08:9; *CPT Changes: An Insider's View* 2008

(Use 22208 in conjunction with 22206, 22207)

(Do not report 22206, 22207, 22208 in conjunction with 22210-22226, 22830, 63001-63048, 63055-63066, 63075-63091, 63101-63103, when performed at the same level)

22210   Osteotomy of spine, posterior or posterolateral approach, 1 vertebral segment; cervical

22212   thoracic
➔ *CPT Assistant* Dec 07:1

22214   lumbar
➔ *CPT Assistant* Dec 07:1

+ 22216   each additional vertebral segment (List separately in addition to primary procedure)
➔ *CPT Assistant* Dec 07:1

(Use 22216 in conjunction with 22210, 22212, 22214)

22220   Osteotomy of spine, including discectomy, anterior approach, single vertebral segment; cervical
➔ *CPT Assistant* Feb 02:4

22222   thoracic
➔ *CPT Assistant* Feb 02:4

22224   lumbar
➔ *CPT Assistant* Feb 02:4

+ 22226   each additional vertebral segment (List separately in addition to code for primary procedure)
➔ *CPT Assistant* Feb 96:6, Feb 02:4

(Use 22226 in conjunction with 22220, 22222, 22224)

(For vertebral corpectomy, see 63081-63091)

Fracture and/or Dislocation

To report arthrodesis, see codes 22590-22632. (Report in addition to code[s] for the definitive procedure with modifier 51.)

To report instrumentation procedures, see 22840-22855. (Report in addition to code[s] for the definitive procedure[s].) Do not append modifier 62 to spinal instrumentation codes 22840-22848 and 22850-22852.

To report bone graft procedures, see 20930-20938. (Report in addition to code[s] for the definitive procedure[s].) Do not append modifier 62 to bone graft codes 20900-20938.

For the following codes, when two surgeons work together as primary surgeons performing distinct part(s) of open fracture and/or dislocation procedure(s), each surgeon should report his/her distinct operative work by appending modifier 62 to the procedure code. In this situation, modifier 62 may be appended to the procedure code(s) 22318-22327 and, as appropriate, the associated additional fracture vertebrae or dislocated segment add-on code 22328 as long as both surgeons continue to work together as primary surgeons.

22305   Closed treatment of vertebral process fracture(s)

22310   Closed treatment of vertebral body fracture(s), without manipulation, requiring and including casting or bracing

22315 Closed treatment of vertebral fracture(s) and/or dislocation(s) requiring casting or bracing, with and including casting and/or bracing, with or without anesthesia, by manipulation or traction

(For spinal subluxation, use 97140)

22318 Open treatment and/or reduction of odontoid fracture(s) and or dislocation(s) (including os odontoideum), anterior approach, including placement of internal fixation; without grafting

➲ *CPT Assistant* Nov 99:11; *CPT Changes: An Insider's View* 2000

22319 with grafting

➲ *CPT Assistant* Nov 99:11; *CPT Changes: An Insider's View* 2000

22325 Open treatment and/or reduction of vertebral fracture(s) and/or dislocation(s), posterior approach, 1 fractured vertebra or dislocated segment; lumbar

➲ *CPT Assistant* Sep 97:8

22326 cervical

➲ *CPT Assistant* Sep 97:8

22327 thoracic

➲ *CPT Assistant* Sep 97:8

+ 22328 each additional fractured vertebra or dislocated segment (List separately in addition to code for primary procedure)

➲ *CPT Assistant* Feb 96:6

(Use 22328 in conjunction with 22325-22327)

(For treatment of vertebral fracture by the anterior approach, see corpectomy 63081-63091, and appropriate arthrodesis, bone graft and instrument codes)

(For decompression of spine following fracture, see 63001-63091; for arthrodesis of spine following fracture, see 22548-22632)

Manipulation

(For spinal manipulation without anesthesia, use 97140)

22505 Manipulation of spine requiring anesthesia, any region

➲ *CPT Assistant* Mar 97:11, Jan 99:11

Vertebral Body, Embolization or Injection

⊙▲ **22520** Percutaneous vertebroplasty, 1 vertebral body, unilateral or bilateral injection; thoracic

➲ *CPT Assistant* Mar 01:2, Oct 06:13; *CPT Changes: An Insider's View* 2001, 2010

⊙▲ **22521** lumbar

➲ *CPT Assistant* Mar 01:2, Oct 06:13; *CPT Changes: An Insider's View* 2001, 2010

+ 22522 each additional thoracic or lumbar vertebral body (List separately in addition to code for primary procedure)

➲ *CPT Assistant* Mar 01:2, Oct 06:13; *CPT Changes: An Insider's View* 2001

(Use 22522 in conjunction with 22520, 22521 as appropriate)

(For radiological supervision and interpretation, see 72291, 72292)

Percutaneous Vertebroplasty
22520

Augmentation of a vertebral fracture is achieved by percutaneous injections of polymethylmethacrylate under fluoroscopic guidance.

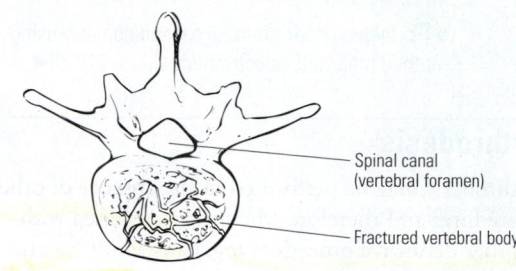

Spinal canal (vertebral foramen)

Fractured vertebral body

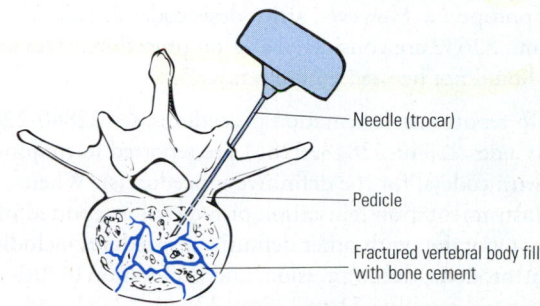

Needle (trocar)

Pedicle

Fractured vertebral body filled with bone cement

22523 Percutaneous vertebral augmentation, including cavity creation (fracture reduction and bone biopsy included when performed) using mechanical device, 1 vertebral body, unilateral or bilateral cannulation (eg, kyphoplasty); thoracic

➲ *CPT Changes: An Insider's View* 2006

➲ *Clinical Examples in Radiology* Winter 06:14

22524 lumbar

➲ *CPT Changes: An Insider's View* 2006

➲ *Clinical Examples in Radiology* Winter 06:14

+ 22525 each additional thoracic or lumbar vertebral body (List separately in addition to code for primary procedure)

➲ *CPT Changes: An Insider's View* 2006

➲ *Clinical Examples in Radiology* Winter 06:14

(Do not report 22525 in conjunction with 20225 when performed at the same level as 22523-22525)

(Use 22525 in conjunction with 22523, 22524)

(For radiological supervision and interpretation, see 72291, 72292)

⊙ **22526**   Percutaneous intradiscal electrothermal annuloplasty, unilateral or bilateral including fluoroscopic guidance; single level

> *CPT Assistant* Sep 07:10; *CPT Changes: An Insider's View* 2007

⊙+ **22527**   1 or more additional levels (List separately in addition to code for primary procedure)

> *CPT Assistant* Sep 07:10; *CPT Changes: An Insider's View* 2007

(Do not report codes 22526, 22527 in conjunction with 77002, 77003)

▶(For percutaneous intradiscal annuloplasty using method other than electrothermal, use 22899)◀

Arthrodesis

Arthrodesis may be performed in the absence of other procedures and therefore when it is ==combined with another definitive procedure (eg, osteotomy, fracture care, vertebral corpectomy or laminectomy), modifier 51 is== appropriate. However, arthrodesis codes 22585, 22614, and 22632 are considered add-on ==procedure codes and should not be used with modifier 51.==

To report instrumentation procedures, see 22840-22855. (Codes 22840-22848, 22851 are reported in conjunction with code[s] for the definitive procedure[s]. When instrumentation reinsertion or removal is reported in conjunction with other definitive procedures including arthrodesis, decompression, and exploration of fusion, append modifier 51 to 22849, 22850, 22852, and 22855.) To report exploration of fusion, use 22830. (When exploration is reported in conjunction with other definitive procedures, including arthrodesis and decompression, append modifier 51 to 22830.) Do not append modifier 62 to spinal instrumentation codes 22840-22848 and 22850-22852.

To report bone graft procedures, see 20930-20938. (Report in addition to code[s] for the definitive procedure[s].) Do not append modifier 62 to bone graft codes 20900-20938.

Lateral Extracavitary Approach Technique

22532   Arthrodesis, lateral extracavitary technique, including minimal discectomy to prepare interspace (other than for decompression); thoracic

> *CPT Changes: An Insider's View* 2004

22533   lumbar

> *CPT Changes: An Insider's View* 2004

+ **22534**   thoracic or lumbar, each additional vertebral segment (List separately in addition to code for primary procedure)

> *CPT Changes: An Insider's View* 2004

(Use 22534 in conjunction with 22532 and 22533)

Anterior or Anterolateral Approach Technique

Procedure codes 22554-22558 are for SINGLE interspace; for additional interspaces, use 22585. A vertebral interspace is the non-bony compartment between two adjacent vertebral bodies, which contains the intervertebral disc, and includes the nucleus pulposus, annulus fibrosus, and two cartilagenous endplates.

For the following codes, when two surgeons work together as primary surgeons performing distinct part(s) of an anterior interbody arthrodesis, each surgeon should report his/her distinct operative work by appending modifier 62 to the procedure code. In this situation, modifier 62 may be appended to the procedure code(s) 22548-22558 and, as appropriate, to the associated additional interspace add-on code 22585 as long as both surgeons continue to work together as primary surgeons.

22548   Arthrodesis, anterior transoral or extraoral technique, clivus-C1-C2 (atlas-axis), with or without excision of odontoid process

> *CPT Assistant* Spring 93:36, Feb 96:7, Sep 97:8, Sep 00:10, Feb 02:4

(For intervertebral disc excision by laminotomy or laminectomy, see 63020-63042)

Arthrodesis (Anterior Transoral Technique)
22548

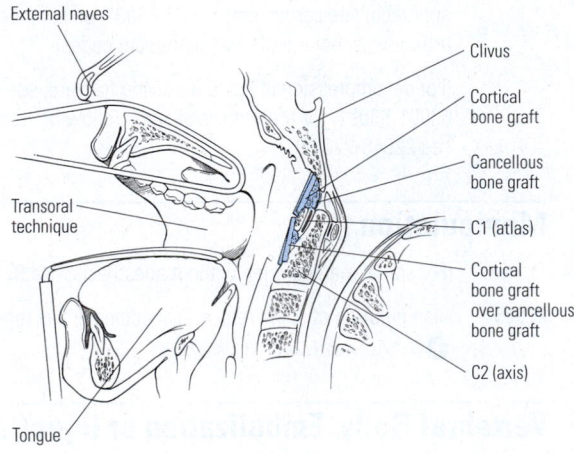

22554   Arthrodesis, anterior interbody technique, including minimal discectomy to prepare interspace (other than for decompression); cervical below C2

> *CPT Assistant* Spring 93:36, Sep 97:8, Sep 00:10, Jan 01:12, Feb 02:4

22556   thoracic

> *CPT Assistant* Spring 93:36, Jul 96:7, Sep 97:8, Sep 00:10, Feb 02:4

Anterior Approach for Cervical Fusion
22554

An example of an exposure technique used to reach anterior cervical vertebrae for spinal procedures (eg, discectomy, arthrodesis, spinal instrumentation)

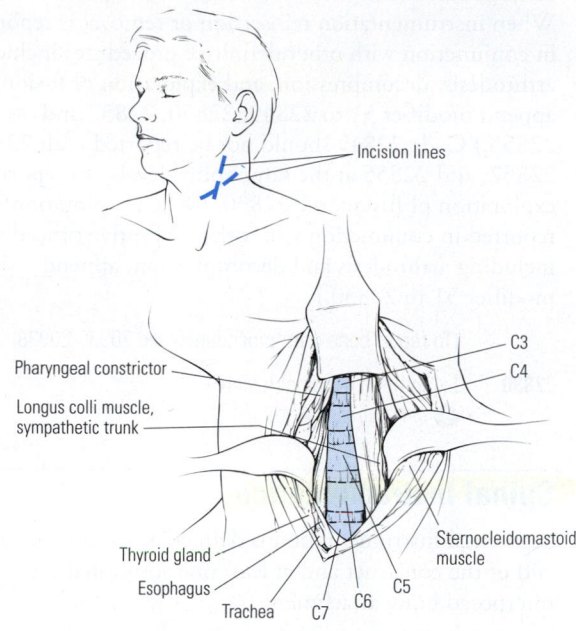

Incision lines

Pharyngeal constrictor

Longus colli muscle, sympathetic trunk

C3
C4

Thyroid gland

Esophagus

Trachea   C7   C6   C5

Sternocleidomastoid muscle

22558   lumbar

> *CPT Assistant* Spring 93:36, Mar 96:6, Jul 96:7, Sep 97:8, Sep 00:10, Feb 02:4

Anterior Approach for Lumbar Fusion (Anterior Retroperitoneal Exposure)
22558

An example of an exposure technique used to reach anterior lumbar vertebrae for spinal procedures (eg, discectomy, arthrodesis, spinal instrumentation)

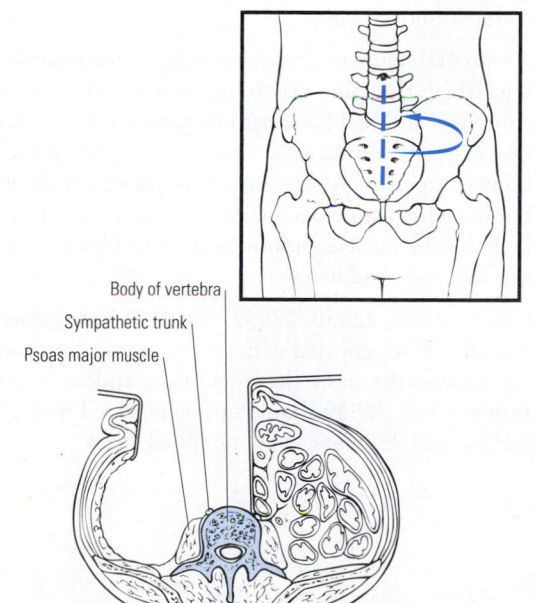

Incision line and approach to lumbar spine

Body of vertebra

Sympathetic trunk

Psoas major muscle

+ 22585   each additional interspace (List separately in addition to code for primary procedure)

> *CPT Assistant* Spring 93:36, Feb 96:6, Mar 96:6, Sep 97:8, Sep 00:10, Feb 02:4, Apr 08:11

(Use 22585 in conjunction with 22554, 22556, 22558)

Posterior, Posterolateral or Lateral Transverse Process Technique

To report instrumentation procedures, see 22840-22855. (Report in addition to code[s] for the definitive procedure[s].) Do not append modifier 62 to spinal instrumentation codes 22840-22848 and 22850-22852.

To report bone graft procedures, see 20930-20938. (Report in addition to code[s] for the definitive procedure[s].) Do not append modifier 62 to bone graft codes 20900-20938.

A vertebral segment describes the basic constituent part into which the spine may be divided. It represents a single complete vertebral bone with its associated articular processes and laminae. A vertebral interspace is the non-bony compartment between two adjacent vertebral bodies which contains the intervertebral disc, and includes the nucleus pulposus, annulus fibrosus, and two cartilagenous endplates.

22590   Arthrodesis, posterior technique, craniocervical (occiput-C2)

> *CPT Assistant* Spring 93:36, Sep 97:8

22595   Arthrodesis, posterior technique, atlas-axis (C1-C2)

> *CPT Assistant* Spring 93:36, Sep 97:8

22600   Arthrodesis, posterior or posterolateral technique, single level; cervical below C2 segment

> *CPT Assistant* Spring 93:36, Sep 97:8

22610   thoracic (with or without lateral transverse technique)

> *CPT Assistant* Spring 93:36, Sep 97:8

22612   lumbar (with or without lateral transverse technique)

> *CPT Assistant* Spring 93:36, Mar 96:7, Sep 97:8,11, Apr 08:11, Jul 08:7

+ 22614   each additional vertebral segment (List separately in addition to code for primary procedure)

> *CPT Assistant* Feb 96:6, Mar 96:7

(Use 22614 in conjunction with 22600, 22610, 22612)

22630   Arthrodesis, posterior interbody technique, including laminectomy and/or discectomy to prepare interspace (other than for decompression), single interspace; lumbar

> *CPT Assistant* Spring 93:36, Sep 97:8, Nov 99:11, Dec 99:2, Jan 01:12; *CPT Changes: An Insider's View* 2000

+ 22632   each additional interspace (List separately in addition to code for primary procedure)

> *CPT Assistant* Feb 96:6, Sep 97:8, Dec 99:2

(Use 22632 in conjunction with 22630)

Spine Deformity (eg, Scoliosis, Kyphosis)

To report instrumentation procedures, see 22840-22855. (Report in addition to code[s] for the definitive procedure[s].) Do not append modifier 62 to spinal instrumentation codes 22840-22848 and 22850-22852.

To report bone graft procedures, see 20930-20938. (Report in addition to code[s] for the definitive procedure[s].) Do not append modifier 62 to bone graft codes 20900-20938.

A vertebral segment describes the basic constituent part into which the spine may be divided. It represents a single complete vertebral bone with its associated articular processes and laminae.

For the following codes, when two surgeons work together as primary surgeons performing distinct part(s) of an arthrodesis for spinal deformity, each surgeon should report his/her distinct operative work by appending modifier 62 to the procedure code. In this situation, modifier 62 may be appended to procedure code(s) 22800-22819 as long as both surgeons continue to work together as primary surgeons.

22800 Arthrodesis, posterior, for spinal deformity, with or without cast; up to 6 vertebral segments

22802 7 to 12 vertebral segments
➔ *CPT Assistant* Mar 96:10

22804 13 or more vertebral segments

22808 Arthrodesis, anterior, for spinal deformity, with or without cast; 2 to 3 vertebral segments
➔ *CPT Assistant* Feb 02:4

22810 4 to 7 vertebral segments
➔ *CPT Assistant* Mar 96:10, Sep 97:8, Feb 02:4

22812 8 or more vertebral segments
➔ *CPT Assistant* Feb 02:4

22818 Kyphectomy, circumferential exposure of spine and resection of vertebral segment(s) (including body and posterior elements); single or 2 segments
➔ *CPT Assistant* Nov 97:14

22819 3 or more segments
➔ *CPT Assistant* Nov 97:14

(To report arthrodesis, see 22800-22804 and add modifier 51)

Exploration

To report instrumentation procedures, see 22840-22855. (Codes 22840-22848 and 22851 are reported in conjunction with code[s] for the definitive procedure[s]. When instrumentation reinsertion or removal is reported in conjunction with other definitive procedures including arthrodesis, decompression, and exploration of fusion, append modifier 51 to 22849, 22850, 22852 and 22855.) Code 22849 should not be reported with 22850, 22852, and 22855 at the same spinal levels. To report exploration of fusion, see 22830. (When exploration is reported in conjunction with other definitive procedures, including arthrodesis and decompression, append modifier 51 to 22830.)

(To report bone graft procedures, see 20930-20938)

22830 Exploration of spinal fusion
➔ *CPT Assistant* Sep 97:11

Spinal Instrumentation

Segmental instrumentation is defined as fixation at each end of the construct and at least one additional interposed bony attachment.

Non-segmental instrumentation is defined as fixation at each end of the construct and may span several vertebral segments without attachment to the intervening segments.

Insertion of spinal instrumentation is reported separately and in addition to arthrodesis. Instrumentation procedure codes 22840-22848 and 22851 are reported in addition to the definitive procedure(s). Do not append modifier 62 to spinal instrumentation codes 22840-22848 and 22850-22852.

To report bone graft procedures, see 20930-20938. (Report in addition to code[s] for definitive procedure[s].) Do not append modifier 62 to bone graft codes 20900-20938.

A vertebral segment describes the basic constituent part into which the spine may be divided. It represents a single complete vertebral bone with its associated articular processes and laminae. A vertebral interspace is the non-bony compartment between two adjacent vertebral bodies, which contains the intervertebral disc, and includes the nucleus pulposus, annulus fibrosus, and two cartilagenous endplates.

Codes 22849, 22850, 22852, and 22855 are subject to modifier 51 if reported with other definitive procedure(s), including arthrodesis, decompression, and exploration of fusion. Code 22849 should not be reported with 22850, 22852, and 22855 at the same spinal levels.

+ 22840 Posterior non-segmental instrumentation (eg, Harrington rod technique, pedicle fixation across 1 interspace, atlantoaxial transarticular screw fixation, sublaminar wiring at C1, facet screw fixation) (List separately in addition to code for primary procedure)

> *CPT Assistant* Feb 96:6, Jul 96:10, Sep 97:8, Nov 99:12, Feb 02:6; *CPT Changes: An Insider's View* 2000, 2008

(Use 22840 in conjunction with 22100-22102, 22110-22114, 22206, 22207, 22210-22214, 22220-22224, 22305-22327, 22532, 22533, 22548-22558, 22590-22612, 22630, 22800-22812, 63001-63030, 63040-63042, 63045-63047, 63050-63056, 63064, 63075, 63077, 63081, 63085, 63087, 63090, 63101, 63102, 63170-63290, 63300-63307)

(For insertion of posterior spinous process distraction devices, see 0171T, 0172T)

Non-Segmental Spinal Instrumentation
22840

Fixation at each end of the construct

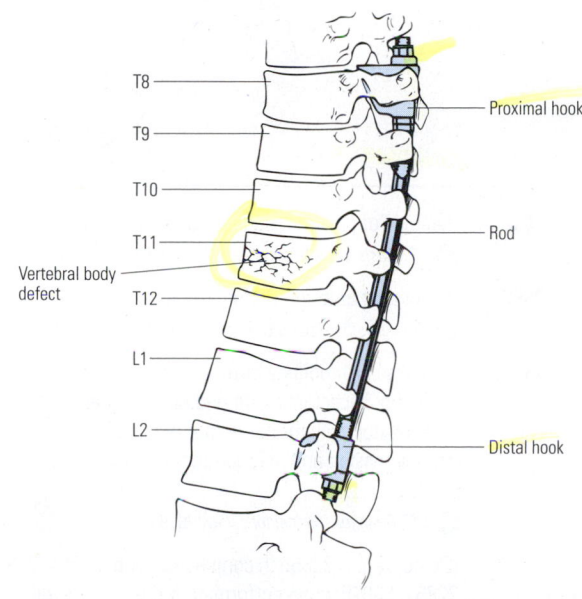

T8 —
T9 —
T10 —
T11 —
Vertebral body defect —
T12 —
L1 —
L2 —
Proximal hook
Rod
Distal hook

+ 22841 Internal spinal fixation by wiring of spinous processes (List separately in addition to code for primary procedure)

> *CPT Assistant* Feb 96:6, Sep 97:8, Feb 02:6; *CPT Changes: An Insider's View* 2008

(Use 22841 in conjunction with 22100-22102, 22110-22114, 22206, 22207, 22210-22214, 22220-22224, 22305-22327, 22532, 22533, 22548-22558, 22590-22612, 22630, 22800-22812, 63001-63030, 63040-63042, 63045-63047, 63050-63056, 63064, 63075, 63077, 63081, 63085, 63087, 63090, 63101, 63102, 63170-63290, 63300-63307)

+ 22842 Posterior segmental instrumentation (eg, pedicle fixation, dual rods with multiple hooks and sublaminar wires); 3 to 6 vertebral segments (List separately in addition to code for primary procedure)

> *CPT Assistant* Feb 96:6, Mar 96:7, Sep 97:8, Feb 02:6; *CPT Changes: An Insider's View* 2008

(Use 22842 in conjunction with 22100-22102, 22110-22114, 22206, 22207, 22210-22214, 22220-22224, 22305-22327, 22532, 22533, 22548-22558, 22590-22612, 22630, 22800-22812, 63001-63030, 63040-63042, 63045-63047, 63050-63056, 63064, 63075, 63077, 63081, 63085, 63087, 63090, 63101, 63102, 63170-63290, 63300-63307)

+ 22843 7 to 12 vertebral segments (List separately in addition to code for primary procedure)

> *CPT Assistant* Feb 96:6, Sep 97:8, Feb 02:6; *CPT Changes: An Insider's View* 2008

(Use 22843 in conjunction with 22100-22102, 22110-22114, 22206, 22207, 22210-22214, 22220-22224, 22305-22327, 22532, 22533, 22548-22558, 22590-22612, 22630, 22800-22812, 63001-63030, 63040-63042, 63045-63047, 63050-63056, 63064, 63075, 63077, 63081, 63085, 63087, 63090, 63101, 63102, 63170-63290, 63300-63307)

+ 22844 13 or more vertebral segments (List separately in addition to code for primary procedure)

> *CPT Assistant* Feb 96:6, Sep 97:8, Feb 02:6; *CPT Changes: An Insider's View* 2008

(Use 22844 in conjunction with 22100-22102, 22110-22114, 22206, 22207, 22210-22214, 22220-22224, 22305-22327, 22532, 22533, 22548-22558, 22590-22612, 22630, 22800-22812, 63001-63030, 63040-63042, 63045-63047, 63050-63056, 63064, 63075, 63077, 63081, 63085, 63087, 63090, 63101, 63102, 63170-63290, 63300-63307)

Segmental Spinal Instrumentation
22842-22844

Fixation at each end of the construct and at least one additional interposed bony attachment

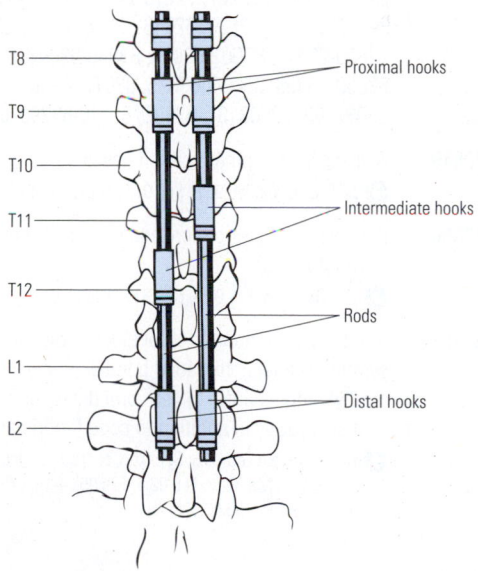

T8 —
T9 —
T10 —
T11 —
T12 —
L1 —
L2 —
Proximal hooks
Intermediate hooks
Rods
Distal hooks

+ 22845   Anterior instrumentation; 2 to 3 vertebral segments (List separately in addition to code for primary procedure)
➔ *CPT Assistant* Feb 96:6, Mar 96:10, Jul 96:7, 10, Sep 97:8, Feb 02:6; *CPT Changes: An Insider's View* 2008

(Use 22845 in conjunction with 22100-22102, 22110-22114, 22206, 22207, 22210-22214, 22220-22224, 22305-22327, 22532, 22533, 22548-22558, 22590-22612, 22630, 22800-22812, 63001-63030, 63040-63042, 63045-63047, 63050-63056, 63064, 63075, 63077, 63081, 63085, 63087, 63090, 63101, 63102, 63170-63290, 63300-63307)

+ 22846   4 to 7 vertebral segments (List separately in addition to code for primary procedure)
➔ *CPT Assistant* Feb 96:6, Sep 97:8, Feb 02:6; *CPT Changes: An Insider's View* 2008

(Use 22846 in conjunction with 22100-22102, 22110-22114, 22206, 22207, 22210-22214, 22220-22224, 22305-22327, 22532, 22533, 22548-22558, 22590-22612, 22630, 22800-22812, 63001-63030, 63040-63042, 63045-63047, 63050-63056, 63064, 63075, 63077, 63081, 63085, 63087, 63090, 63101, 63102, 63170-63290, 63300-63307)

+ 22847   8 or more vertebral segments (List separately in addition to code for primary procedure)
➔ *CPT Assistant* Feb 96:6, Sep 97:8, Feb 02:6; *CPT Changes: An Insider's View* 2008

(Use 22847 in conjunction with 22100-22102, 22110-22114, 22206, 22207, 22210-22214, 22220-22224, 22305-22327, 22532, 22533, 22548-22558, 22590-22612, 22630, 22800-22812, 63001-63030, 63040-63042, 63045-63047, 63050-63056, 63064, 63075, 63077, 63081, 63085, 63087, 63090, 63101, 63102, 63170-63290, 63300-63307)

+ 22848   Pelvic fixation (attachment of caudal end of instrumentation to pelvic bony structures) other than sacrum (List separately in addition to code for primary procedure)
➔ *CPT Assistant* Feb 96:6, Sep 97:8, Feb 02:6; *CPT Changes: An Insider's View* 2008

(Use 22848 in conjunction with 22100-22102, 22110-22114, 22206, 22207, 22210-22214, 22220-22224, 22305-22327, 22532, 22533, 22548-22558, 22590-22612, 22630, 22800-22812, 63001-63030, 63040-63042, 63045-63047, 63050-63056, 63064, 63075, 63077, 63081, 63085, 63087, 63090, 63101, 63102, 63170-63290, 63300-63307)

22849   Reinsertion of spinal fixation device
➔ *CPT Assistant* Feb 96:6, Sep 97:8, Feb 02:6, Nov 02:3

22850   Removal of posterior nonsegmental instrumentation (eg, Harrington rod)
➔ *CPT Assistant* Feb 96:6, Sep 97:8, Feb 02:6

+ 22851   Application of intervertebral biomechanical device(s) (eg, synthetic cage(s), threaded bone dowel(s), methylmethacrylate) to vertebral defect or interspace (List separately in addition to code for primary procedure)
➔ *CPT Assistant* Feb 96:6, Sep 97:8, Nov 99:12, Dec 99:2, May 00:11, Mar 01:2, Feb 02:6, Feb 05:14-15; *CPT Changes: An Insider's View* 2002, 2008

(Use 22851 in conjunction with 22100-22102, 22110-22114, 22206, 22207, 22210-22214, 22220-22224, 22305-22327, 22532, 22533, 22548-22558, 22590-22612, 22630, 22800-22812, 63001-63030, 63040-63042, 63045-63047, 63050-63056, 63064, 63075, 63077, 63081, 63085, 63087, 63090, 63101, 63102, 63170-63290, 63300-63307)

(For insertion of posterior spinous process distraction devices, see 0171T, 0172T)

Spinal Prosthetic Devices
22851

Application of prosthetic device

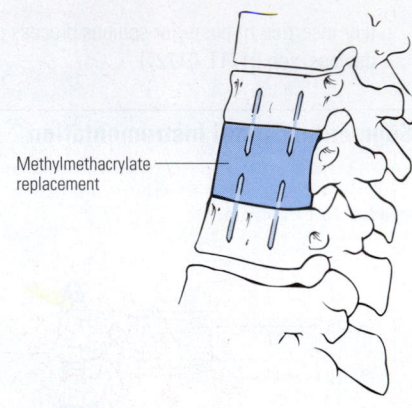

Methylmethacrylate replacement

22852   Removal of posterior segmental instrumentation
➔ *CPT Assistant* Feb 96:6, Sep 97:8, Feb 02:6, May 06:16

22855   Removal of anterior instrumentation
➔ *CPT Assistant* Feb 96:6, Sep 97:8, Feb 02:6, Nov 02:2

22856   Total disc arthroplasty (artificial disc), anterior approach, including discectomy with end plate preparation (includes osteophytectomy for nerve root or spinal cord decompression and microdissection), single interspace, cervical
➔ *CPT Changes: An Insider's View* 2009

(Do not report 22856 in conjunction with 22554, 22845, 22851, 63075 when performed at the same level)

(Do not report 22856 in conjunction with 69990)

(For additional interspace cervical total disc arthroplasty, use 0092T)

22857   Total disc arthroplasty (artificial disc), anterior approach, including discectomy to prepare interspace (other than for decompression), single interspace, lumbar
➔ *CPT Changes: An Insider's View* 2007, 2009

(Do not report 22857 in conjunction with 22558, 22845, 22851, 49010 when performed at the same level)

(For additional interspace, use Category III code 0163T)

22861   Revision including replacement of total disc arthroplasty (artificial disc), anterior approach, single interspace; cervical
➔ *CPT Changes: An Insider's View* 2009

(Do not report 22861 in conjunction with 22845, 22851, 22864, 63075 when performed at the same level)

(Do not report 22861 in conjunction with 69990)

(For additional interspace revision of cervical total disc arthroplasty, use 0098T)

22862   lumbar
➔ *CPT Assistant* Jun 07:1; *CPT Changes: An Insider's View* 2007, 2009

(Do not report 22862 in conjunction with 22558, 22845, 22851, 22865, 49010 when performed at the same level)

(For additional interspace, use Category III code 0165T)

22864   Removal of total disc arthroplasty (artificial disc), anterior approach, single interspace; cervical
➔ *CPT Changes: An Insider's View* 2009

(Do not report 22864 in conjunction with 22861, 69990)

(For additional interspace removal of cervical total disc arthroplasty, use 0095T)

22865   lumbar
➔ *CPT Assistant* Jun 07:1; *CPT Changes: An Insider's View* 2007, 2009

(Do not report 22865 in conjunction with 49010)

(For additional interspace, see Category III code 0164T)

(22856-22865 include fluoroscopy when performed)

(For decompression, see 63001-63048)

Other Procedures

22899   Unlisted procedure, spine
➔ *CPT Assistant* May 00:11, Sep 00:10, Jul 06:19

Abdomen

Excision

▲ **22900**   Excision, tumor, soft tissue of abdominal wall, subfascial (eg, intramuscular); less than 5 cm
➔ *CPT Changes: An Insider's View* 2010

● **22901**   5 cm or greater
➔ *CPT Changes: An Insider's View* 2010

● **22902**   Excision, tumor, soft tissue of abdominal wall, subcutaneous; less than 3 cm
➔ *CPT Changes: An Insider's View* 2010

● **22903**   3 cm or greater
➔ *CPT Changes: An Insider's View* 2010

● **22904**   Radical resection of tumor (eg, malignant neoplasm), soft tissue of abdominal wall; less than 5 cm
➔ *CPT Changes: An Insider's View* 2010

● **22905**   5 cm or greater
➔ *CPT Changes: An Insider's View* 2010

Other Procedures

22999   Unlisted procedure, abdomen, musculoskeletal system

Shoulder

The area known as the shoulder is made up of the clavicle, scapula, humerus head and neck, sterno-clavicular joint, acromioclavicular joint, and shoulder joint.

Incision

23000   Removal of subdeltoid calcareous deposits, open
➔ *CPT Changes: An Insider's View* 2002, 2003

(For arthroscopic removal of bursal deposits, use 29999)

23020   Capsular contracture release (eg, Sever type procedure)

(For incision and drainage procedures, superficial, see 10040-10160)

23030   Incision and drainage, shoulder area; deep abscess or hematoma

23031   infected bursa

23035   Incision, bone cortex (eg, osteomyelitis or bone abscess), shoulder area

23040   Arthrotomy, glenohumeral joint, including exploration, drainage, or removal of foreign body
➔ *CPT Assistant* Nov 98:8

23044   Arthrotomy, acromioclavicular, sternoclavicular joint, including exploration, drainage, or removal of foreign body
➔ *CPT Assistant* Nov 98:8

Excision

23065   Biopsy, soft tissue of shoulder area; superficial

23066   deep

(For needle biopsy of soft tissue, use 20206)

23071   ►Code is out of numerical sequence. See 23065-23220◄

23073   ►Code is out of numerical sequence. See 23065-23220◄

▲ **23075**   Excision, tumor, soft tissue of shoulder area, subcutaneous; less than 3 cm
➔ *CPT Assistant* Summer 92:22, Nov 98:8; *CPT Changes: An Insider's View* 2010

#● **23071**   3 cm or greater
➔ *CPT Changes: An Insider's View* 2010

▲ **23076**   Excision, tumor, soft tissue of shoulder area, subfascial (eg, intramuscular); less than 5 cm
➔ *CPT Assistant* Summer 92:22; *CPT Changes: An Insider's View* 2010

23190
Ostectomy of scapula, partial (eg, superior medial angle)

23195
Resection, humeral head

(For replacement with implant, use 23470)

▲ **23200** Radical resection of tumor; clavicle
→ *CPT Changes: An Insider's View* 2010

▲ **23210** scapula
→ *CPT Changes: An Insider's View* 2010

▲ **23220** Radical resection of tumor, proximal humerus
→ *CPT Assistant* Nov 98:8; *CPT Changes: An Insider's View* 2010

▶(23221, 23222 have been deleted)◀

Introduction or Removal

(For arthrocentesis or needling of bursa, use 20610)

(For K-wire or pin insertion or removal, see 20650, 20670, 20680)

23330 Removal of foreign body, shoulder; subcutaneous
→ *CPT Assistant* Aug 99:3

23331 deep (eg, Neer hemiarthroplasty removal)
→ *CPT Assistant* Aug 99:3

23332 complicated (eg, total shoulder)
→ *CPT Assistant* Jun 96:10, Nov 98:8, Aug 99:3

23350 Injection procedure for shoulder arthrography or enhanced CT/MRI shoulder arthrography
→ *CPT Assistant* Jul 01:3; *CPT Changes: An Insider's View* 2002
→ *Clinical Examples in Radiology* Spring 05:5, Spring 09:6, 7

(For radiographic arthrography, radiological supervision and interpretation, use 73040. Fluoroscopy [77002] is inclusive of radiographic arthrography)

(When fluoroscopic guided injection is performed for enhanced CT arthrography, use 23350, 77002, and 73201 or 73202)

(When fluoroscopic guided injection is performed for enhanced MR arthrography, use 23350, 77002, and 73222 or 73223)

(For enhanced CT or enhanced MRI arthrography, use 77002 and either 73201, 73202, 73222, or 73223)

(To report biopsy of the shoulder and joint, see 29805-29826)

Repair, Revision, and/or Reconstruction

23395 Muscle transfer, any type, shoulder or upper arm; single

23397 multiple

23400 Scapulopexy (eg, Sprengels deformity or for paralysis)

23405 Tenotomy, shoulder area; single tendon
→ *CPT Assistant* Nov 98:8

23406 multiple tendons through same incision
→ *CPT Assistant* Nov 98:8

\# ● **23073** 5 cm or greater
→ *CPT Changes: An Insider's View* 2010

▲ **23077** Radical resection of tumor (eg, malignant neoplasm), soft tissue of shoulder area; less than 5 cm
→ *CPT Changes: An Insider's View* 2010

● **23078** 5 cm or greater
→ *CPT Changes: An Insider's View* 2010

23100 Arthrotomy, glenohumeral joint, including biopsy
→ *CPT Assistant* Nov 98:8

23101 Arthrotomy, acromioclavicular joint or sternoclavicular joint, including biopsy and/or excision of torn cartilage
→ *CPT Assistant* Nov 98:8

23105 Arthrotomy; glenohumeral joint, with synovectomy, with or without biopsy
→ *CPT Assistant* Nov 98:8

23106 sternoclavicular joint, with synovectomy, with or without biopsy

23107 Arthrotomy, glenohumeral joint, with joint exploration, with or without removal of loose or foreign body

23120 Claviculectomy; partial

(For arthroscopic procedure, use 29824)

23125 total

23130 Acromioplasty or acromionectomy, partial, with or without coracoacromial ligament release
→ *CPT Assistant* Aug 01:11

23140 Excision or curettage of bone cyst or benign tumor of clavicle or scapula;

23145 with autograft (includes obtaining graft)

23146 with allograft

23150 Excision or curettage of bone cyst or benign tumor of proximal humerus;

23155 with autograft (includes obtaining graft)

23156 with allograft

23170 Sequestrectomy (eg, for osteomyelitis or bone abscess), clavicle

23172 Sequestrectomy (eg, for osteomyelitis or bone abscess), scapula

23174 Sequestrectomy (eg, for osteomyelitis or bone abscess), humeral head to surgical neck

23180 Partial excision (craterization, saucerization, or diaphysectomy) bone (eg, osteomyelitis), clavicle
→ *CPT Assistant* Nov 98:9

23182 Partial excision (craterization, saucerization, or diaphysectomy) bone (eg, osteomyelitis), scapula
→ *CPT Assistant* Nov 98:9

23184 Partial excision (craterization, saucerization, or diaphysectomy) bone (eg, osteomyelitis), proximal humerus
→ *CPT Assistant* Nov 98:9

23410 Repair of ruptured musculotendinous cuff (eg, rotator cuff) open; acute
➔ *CPT Assistant* Aug 01:11, Feb 02:11; *CPT Changes: An Insider's View* 2003

23412 chronic
➔ *CPT Assistant* Feb 02:11

(For arthroscopic procedure, use 29827)

23415 Coracoacromial ligament release, with or without acromioplasty

(For arthroscopic procedure, use 29826)

23420 Reconstruction of complete shoulder (rotator) cuff avulsion, chronic (includes acromioplasty)
➔ *CPT Assistant* Feb 02:11, Oct 05:23

23430 Tenodesis of long tendon of biceps

(For arthroscopic biceps tenodesis, use 29828)

23440 Resection or transplantation of long tendon of biceps

23450 Capsulorrhaphy, anterior; Putti-Platt procedure or Magnuson type operation

(To report arthroscopic thermal capsulorrhaphy, use 29999)

23455 with labral repair (eg, Bankart procedure)
➔ *CPT Assistant* Nov 98:8

(For arthroscopic procedure, use 29806)

23460 Capsulorrhaphy, anterior, any type; with bone block

23462 with coracoid process transfer

(To report open thermal capsulorrhaphy, use 23929)

23465 Capsulorrhaphy, glenohumeral joint, posterior, with or without bone block
➔ *CPT Assistant* Nov 98:8

(For sternoclavicular and acromioclavicular reconstruction, see 23530, 23550)

23466 Capsulorrhaphy, glenohumeral joint, any type multi-directional instability
➔ *CPT Assistant* Nov 98:8

23470 Arthroplasty, glenohumeral joint; hemiarthroplasty
➔ *CPT Assistant* Nov 98:8

23472 total shoulder (glenoid and proximal humeral replacement (eg, total shoulder))
➔ *CPT Assistant* Jun 96:10, Nov 98:8

(For removal of total shoulder implants, see 23331, 23332)

(For osteotomy, proximal humerus, use 24400)

23480 Osteotomy, clavicle, with or without internal fixation;

23485 with bone graft for nonunion or malunion (includes obtaining graft and/or necessary fixation)

23490 Prophylactic treatment (nailing, pinning, plating or wiring) with or without methylmethacrylate; clavicle

23491 proximal humerus
➔ *CPT Assistant* Nov 98:8

Fracture and/or Dislocation

23500 Closed treatment of clavicular fracture; without manipulation

23505 with manipulation

23515 Open treatment of clavicular fracture, includes internal fixation, when performed
➔ *CPT Assistant* Jan 08:4; *CPT Changes: An Insider's View* 2008

23520 Closed treatment of sternoclavicular dislocation; without manipulation

23525 with manipulation

23530 Open treatment of sternoclavicular dislocation, acute or chronic;

23532 with fascial graft (includes obtaining graft)

23540 Closed treatment of acromioclavicular dislocation; without manipulation

23545 with manipulation

23550 Open treatment of acromioclavicular dislocation, acute or chronic;

23552 with fascial graft (includes obtaining graft)

23570 Closed treatment of scapular fracture; without manipulation

23575 with manipulation, with or without skeletal traction (with or without shoulder joint involvement)

23585 Open treatment of scapular fracture (body, glenoid or acromion) includes internal fixation, when performed
➔ *CPT Assistant* Oct 04:10; *CPT Changes: An Insider's View* 2009

23600 Closed treatment of proximal humeral (surgical or anatomical neck) fracture; without manipulation

23605 with manipulation, with or without skeletal traction

23615 Open treatment of proximal humeral (surgical or anatomical neck) fracture, includes internal fixation, when performed, includes repair of tuberosity(s), when performed;
➔ *CPT Assistant* Jan 08:4; *CPT Changes: An Insider's View* 2008

23616 with proximal humeral prosthetic replacement
➔ *CPT Changes: An Insider's View* 2008

23620 Closed treatment of greater humeral tuberosity fracture; without manipulation
➔ *CPT Assistant* Nov 98:8

23625 with manipulation

23630 Open treatment of greater humeral tuberosity fracture, includes internal fixation, when performed
➔ *CPT Assistant* Nov 98:8; *CPT Changes: An Insider's View* 2008

23650 Closed treatment of shoulder dislocation, with manipulation; without anesthesia

23655 requiring anesthesia

23660 Open treatment of acute shoulder dislocation
➔ CPT Assistant Feb 96:5

(Repairs for recurrent dislocations, see 23450-23466)

23665 Closed treatment of shoulder dislocation, with fracture of greater humeral tuberosity, with manipulation
➔ CPT Assistant Nov 98:8

23670 Open treatment of shoulder dislocation, with fracture of greater humeral tuberosity, includes internal fixation, when performed
➔ CPT Assistant Nov 98:8; CPT Changes: An Insider's View 2008

23675 Closed treatment of shoulder dislocation, with surgical or anatomical neck fracture, with manipulation

23680 Open treatment of shoulder dislocation, with surgical or anatomical neck fracture, includes internal fixation, when performed
➔ CPT Changes: An Insider's View 2008

Manipulation

23700 Manipulation under anesthesia, shoulder joint, including application of fixation apparatus (dislocation excluded)
➔ CPT Assistant Jan 99:10, Apr 05:14

Arthrodesis

23800 Arthrodesis, glenohumeral joint;
➔ CPT Assistant Nov 98:8

23802 with autogenous graft (includes obtaining graft)

Amputation

23900 Interthoracoscapular amputation (forequarter)

23920 Disarticulation of shoulder;

23921 secondary closure or scar revision

Other Procedures

23929 Unlisted procedure, shoulder

Humerus (Upper Arm) and Elbow

The elbow area includes the head and neck of the radius and olecranon process.

Incision

(For incision and drainage procedures, superficial, see 10040-10160)

23930 Incision and drainage, upper arm or elbow area; deep abscess or hematoma

23931 bursa
➔ CPT Assistant Nov 98:8

23935 Incision, deep, with opening of bone cortex (eg, for osteomyelitis or bone abscess), humerus or elbow

24000 Arthrotomy, elbow, including exploration, drainage, or removal of foreign body
➔ CPT Assistant Nov 98:8-9

24006 Arthrotomy of the elbow, with capsular excision for capsular release (separate procedure)

Excision

24065 Biopsy, soft tissue of upper arm or elbow area; superficial

24066 deep (subfascial or intramuscular)

(For needle biopsy of soft tissue, use 20206)

24071 ►Code is out of numerical sequence. See 24065-24155◄

24073 ►Code is out of numerical sequence. See 24065-24155◄

▲ **24075** Excision, tumor, soft tissue of upper arm or elbow area, subcutaneous; less than 3 cm
➔ CPT Changes: An Insider's View 2002, 2010

#● **24071** 3 cm or greater
➔ CPT Changes: An Insider's View 2010

▲ **24076** Excision, tumor, soft tissue of upper arm or elbow area, subfascial (eg, intramuscular); less than 5 cm
➔ CPT Changes: An Insider's View 2010

#● **24073** 5 cm or greater
➔ CPT Changes: An Insider's View 2010

▲ **24077** Radical resection of tumor (eg, malignant neoplasm), soft tissue of upper arm or elbow area; less than 5 cm
➔ CPT Changes: An Insider's View 2010

● **24079** 5 cm or greater
➔ CPT Changes: An Insider's View 2010

24100 Arthrotomy, elbow; with synovial biopsy only

24101 with joint exploration, with or without biopsy, with or without removal of loose or foreign body

24102 with synovectomy

24105 Excision, olecranon bursa

24110 Excision or curettage of bone cyst or benign tumor, humerus;

24115 with autograft (includes obtaining graft)

24116 with allograft

24120 Excision or curettage of bone cyst or benign tumor of head or neck of radius or olecranon process;

24125 with autograft (includes obtaining graft)

24126 with allograft

24130 Excision, radial head

(For replacement with implant, use 24366)

⊙=Moderate sedation ✚=Add-on code ✔=FDA approval pending #=Resequenced code ➔🔴=See p xiii for details

24134   Sequestrectomy (eg, for osteomyelitis or bone abscess), shaft or distal humerus

24136   Sequestrectomy (eg, for osteomyelitis or bone abscess), radial head or neck

24138   Sequestrectomy (eg, for osteomyelitis or bone abscess), olecranon process

24140   Partial excision (craterization, saucerization, or diaphysectomy) bone (eg, osteomyelitis), humerus
➲ *CPT Assistant* Nov 98:9

24145   Partial excision (craterization, saucerization, or diaphysectomy) bone (eg, osteomyelitis), radial head or neck
➲ *CPT Assistant* Nov 98:9

24147   Partial excision (craterization, saucerization, or diaphysectomy) bone (eg, osteomyelitis), olecranon process
➲ *CPT Assistant* Nov 98:9

24149   Radical resection of capsule, soft tissue, and heterotopic bone, elbow, with contracture release (separate procedure)
➲ *CPT Assistant* Nov 96:4

(For capsular and soft tissue release only, use 24006)

▲ **24150**   Radical resection of tumor, shaft or distal humerus
➲ *CPT Changes: An Insider's View* 2010

►(24151 has been deleted)◄

▲ **24152**   Radical resection of tumor, radial head or neck
➲ *CPT Changes: An Insider's View* 2010

►(24153 has been deleted)◄

24155   Resection of elbow joint (arthrectomy)

Introduction or Removal

(For K-wire or pin insertion or removal, see 20650, 20670, 20680)

(For arthrocentesis or needling of bursa or joint, use 20605)

24160   Implant removal; elbow joint

24164   radial head

24200   Removal of foreign body, upper arm or elbow area; subcutaneous

24201   deep (subfascial or intramuscular)
➲ *CPT Assistant* Nov 98:8

24220   Injection procedure for elbow arthrography

(For radiological supervision and interpretation, use 73085. Do not report 77002 in conjunction with 73085)

(For injection for tennis elbow, use 20550)

Repair, Revision, and/or Reconstruction

24300   Manipulation, elbow, under anesthesia
➲ *CPT Changes: An Insider's View* 2002

(For application of external fixation, see 20690 or 20692)

24301   Muscle or tendon transfer, any type, upper arm or elbow, single (excluding 24320-24331)

24305   Tendon lengthening, upper arm or elbow, each tendon
➲ *CPT Assistant* Nov 98:8

24310   Tenotomy, open, elbow to shoulder, each tendon
➲ *CPT Assistant* Nov 98:8

24320   Tenoplasty, with muscle transfer, with or without free graft, elbow to shoulder, single (Seddon-Brookes type procedure)

24330   Flexor-plasty, elbow (eg, Steindler type advancement);

24331   with extensor advancement

24332   Tenolysis, triceps
➲ *CPT Changes: An Insider's View* 2002

24340   Tenodesis of biceps tendon at elbow (separate procedure)

24341   Repair, tendon or muscle, upper arm or elbow, each tendon or muscle, primary or secondary (excludes rotator cuff)
➲ *CPT Assistant* Nov 96:4

24342   Reinsertion of ruptured biceps or triceps tendon, distal, with or without tendon graft
➲ *CPT Assistant* Nov 96:4

24343   Repair lateral collateral ligament, elbow, with local tissue
➲ *CPT Changes: An Insider's View* 2002

24344   Reconstruction lateral collateral ligament, elbow, with tendon graft (includes harvesting of graft)
➲ *CPT Changes: An Insider's View* 2002

24345   Repair medial collateral ligament, elbow, with local tissue
➲ *CPT Changes: An Insider's View* 2002

24346   Reconstruction medial collateral ligament, elbow, with tendon graft (includes harvesting of graft)
➲ *CPT Changes: An Insider's View* 2002

(24350-24356 have been deleted. To report, see 24357-24359)

24357   Tenotomy, elbow, lateral or medial (eg, epicondylitis, tennis elbow, golfer's elbow); percutaneous
➲ *CPT Assistant* Jan 08:4; *CPT Changes: An Insider's View* 2008

24358   debridement, soft tissue and/or bone, open
➲ *CPT Assistant* Jan 08:4; *CPT Changes: An Insider's View* 2008

24359   debridement, soft tissue and/or bone, open with tendon repair or reattachment
➔ *CPT Assistant* Jan 08:4; *CPT Changes: An Insider's View* 2008

(Do not report 24357-24359 in conjunction with 29837, 29838)

24360   Arthroplasty, elbow; with membrane (eg, fascial)
➔ *CPT Assistant* Nov 98:8

24361   with distal humeral prosthetic replacement

24362   with implant and fascia lata ligament reconstruction

24363   with distal humerus and proximal ulnar prosthetic replacement (eg, total elbow)

24365   Arthroplasty, radial head;

24366   with implant

24400   Osteotomy, humerus, with or without internal fixation

24410   Multiple osteotomies with realignment on intramedullary rod, humeral shaft (Sofield type procedure)

24420   Osteoplasty, humerus (eg, shortening or lengthening) (excluding 64876)

24430   Repair of nonunion or malunion, humerus; without graft (eg, compression technique)

24435   with iliac or other autograft (includes obtaining graft)

(For proximal radius and/or ulna, see 25400-25420)

24470   Hemiepiphyseal arrest (eg, cubitus varus or valgus, distal humerus)

24495   Decompression fasciotomy, forearm, with brachial artery exploration

24498   Prophylactic treatment (nailing, pinning, plating or wiring), with or without methylmethacrylate, humeral shaft
➔ *CPT Assistant* Nov 98:8

Fracture and/or Dislocation

24500   Closed treatment of humeral shaft fracture; without manipulation

24505   with manipulation, with or without skeletal traction

24515   Open treatment of humeral shaft fracture with plate/screws, with or without cerclage

24516   Treatment of humeral shaft fracture, with insertion of intramedullary implant, with or without cerclage and/or locking screws
➔ *CPT Assistant* Feb 96:4; *CPT Changes: An Insider's View* 2003

24530   Closed treatment of supracondylar or transcondylar humeral fracture, with or without intercondylar extension; without manipulation

24535   with manipulation, with or without skin or skeletal traction

24538   Percutaneous skeletal fixation of supracondylar or transcondylar humeral fracture, with or without intercondylar extension
➔ *CPT Assistant* Winter 92:10

24545   Open treatment of humeral supracondylar or transcondylar fracture, includes internal fixation, when performed; without intercondylar extension
➔ *CPT Changes: An Insider's View* 2008

24546   with intercondylar extension
➔ *CPT Changes: An Insider's View* 2008

24560   Closed treatment of humeral epicondylar fracture, medial or lateral; without manipulation

24565   with manipulation

24566   Percutaneous skeletal fixation of humeral epicondylar fracture, medial or lateral, with manipulation

24575   Open treatment of humeral epicondylar fracture, medial or lateral, includes internal fixation, when performed
➔ *CPT Changes: An Insider's View* 2008

24576   Closed treatment of humeral condylar fracture, medial or lateral; without manipulation

24577   with manipulation

24579   Open treatment of humeral condylar fracture, medial or lateral, includes internal fixation, when performed
➔ *CPT Changes: An Insider's View* 2008

(To report closed treatment of fractures without manipulation, see 24530, 24560, 24576, 24650, 24670)

(To report closed treatment of fractures with manipulation, see 24535, 24565, 24577, 24675)

24582   Percutaneous skeletal fixation of humeral condylar fracture, medial or lateral, with manipulation

24586   Open treatment of periarticular fracture and/or dislocation of the elbow (fracture distal humerus and proximal ulna and/or proximal radius);

24587   with implant arthroplasty

(See also 24361)

24600   Treatment of closed elbow dislocation; without anesthesia

24605   requiring anesthesia

24615   Open treatment of acute or chronic elbow dislocation

24620   Closed treatment of Monteggia type of fracture dislocation at elbow (fracture proximal end of ulna with dislocation of radial head), with manipulation

24635   Open treatment of Monteggia type of fracture dislocation at elbow (fracture proximal end of ulna with dislocation of radial head), includes internal fixation, when performed
➔ *CPT Changes: An Insider's View* 2008

24640   Closed treatment of radial head subluxation in child, nursemaid elbow, with manipulation

24650   Closed treatment of radial head or neck fracture; without manipulation

24655   with manipulation

24665   Open treatment of radial head or neck fracture, includes internal fixation or radial head excision, when performed;
➔ *CPT Changes: An Insider's View* 2008

24666   with radial head prosthetic replacement
➔ *CPT Changes: An Insider's View* 2008

24670   Closed treatment of ulnar fracture, proximal end (eg, olecranon or coronoid process[es]); without manipulation
➔ *CPT Changes: An Insider's View* 2008

24675   with manipulation
➔ *CPT Changes: An Insider's View* 2008

24685   Open treatment of ulnar fracture, proximal end (eg, olecranon or coronoid process[es]), includes internal fixation, when performed
➔ *CPT Changes: An Insider's View* 2008

(Do not report 24685 in conjunction with 24100-24102)

Arthrodesis

24800   Arthrodesis, elbow joint; local

24802   with autogenous graft (includes obtaining graft)

Amputation

24900   Amputation, arm through humerus; with primary closure

24920   open, circular (guillotine)

24925   secondary closure or scar revision

24930   re-amputation

24931   with implant

24935   Stump elongation, upper extremity

24940   Cineplasty, upper extremity, complete procedure

Other Procedures

24999   Unlisted procedure, humerus or elbow

Forearm and Wrist

Radius, ulna, carpal bones, and joints.

Incision

25000   Incision, extensor tendon sheath, wrist (eg, deQuervains disease)
➔ *CPT Assistant* Nov 98:8

(For decompression median nerve or for carpal tunnel syndrome, use 64721)

25001   Incision, flexor tendon sheath, wrist (eg, flexor carpi radialis)
➔ *CPT Changes: An Insider's View* 2002

25020   Decompression fasciotomy, forearm and/or wrist, flexor OR extensor compartment; without debridement of nonviable muscle and/or nerve
➔ *CPT Changes: An Insider's View* 2002

25023   with debridement of nonviable muscle and/or nerve

(For decompression fasciotomy with brachial artery exploration, use 24495)

(For incision and drainage procedures, superficial, see 10060-10160)

(For debridement, see also 11000-11044)

25024   Decompression fasciotomy, forearm and/or wrist, flexor AND extensor compartment; without debridement of nonviable muscle and/or nerve
➔ *CPT Changes: An Insider's View* 2002

25025   with debridement of nonviable muscle and/or nerve
➔ *CPT Changes: An Insider's View* 2002

25028   Incision and drainage, forearm and/or wrist; deep abscess or hematoma

25031   bursa
➔ *CPT Assistant* Nov 98:9

25035   Incision, deep, bone cortex, forearm and/or wrist (eg, osteomyelitis or bone abscess)

25040   Arthrotomy, radiocarpal or midcarpal joint, with exploration, drainage, or removal of foreign body

Excision

25065   Biopsy, soft tissue of forearm and/or wrist; superficial

25066   deep (subfascial or intramuscular)
➔ *CPT Assistant* Nov 98:8

(For needle biopsy of soft tissue, use 20206)

25071   ▶Code is out of numerical sequence. See 25065-25240◀

25073   ▶Code is out of numerical sequence. See 25065-25240◀

▲ **25075**   Excision, tumor, soft tissue of forearm and/or wrist area, subcutaneous; less than 3 cm
➔ *CPT Changes: An Insider's View* 2002, 2010

#● **25071**   3 cm or greater
➔ *CPT Changes: An Insider's View* 2010

▲ **25076**   Excision, tumor, soft tissue of forearm and/or wrist area, subfascial (eg, intramuscular); less than 3 cm
➔ *CPT Changes: An Insider's View* 2010

#● **25073**   3 cm or greater
➔ *CPT Changes: An Insider's View* 2010

▲ **25077**   Radical resection of tumor (eg, malignant neoplasm), soft tissue of forearm and/or wrist area; less than 3 cm
➔ *CPT Changes: An Insider's View* 2010

● **25078**   3 cm or greater
➔ *CPT Changes: An Insider's View* 2010

25085 Capsulotomy, wrist (eg, contracture)

25100 Arthrotomy, wrist joint; with biopsy

25101 with joint exploration, with or without biopsy, with or without removal of loose or foreign body

25105 with synovectomy

25107 Arthrotomy, distal radioulnar joint including repair of triangular cartilage, complex

25109 Excision of tendon, forearm and/or wrist, flexor or extensor, each
➔ *CPT Changes: An Insider's View* 2007

25110 Excision, lesion of tendon sheath, forearm and/or wrist

25111 Excision of ganglion, wrist (dorsal or volar); primary

25112 recurrent

(For hand or finger, use 26160)

25115 Radical excision of bursa, synovia of wrist, or forearm tendon sheaths (eg, tenosynovitis, fungus, Tbc, or other granulomas, rheumatoid arthritis); flexors

25116 extensors, with or without transposition of dorsal retinaculum

(For finger synovectomies, use 26145)

25118 Synovectomy, extensor tendon sheath, wrist, single compartment;

25119 with resection of distal ulna

25120 Excision or curettage of bone cyst or benign tumor of radius or ulna (excluding head or neck of radius and olecranon process);

(For head or neck of radius or olecranon process, see 24120-24126)

25125 with autograft (includes obtaining graft)

25126 with allograft

25130 Excision or curettage of bone cyst or benign tumor of carpal bones;

25135 with autograft (includes obtaining graft)

25136 with allograft

25145 Sequestrectomy (eg, for osteomyelitis or bone abscess), forearm and/or wrist

25150 Partial excision (craterization, saucerization, or diaphysectomy) of bone (eg, for osteomyelitis); ulna

25151 radius

(For head or neck of radius or olecranon process, see 24145, 24147)

▲ **25170** Radical resection of tumor, radius or ulna
➔ *CPT Changes: An Insider's View* 2010

25210 Carpectomy; 1 bone

(For carpectomy with implant, see 25441-25445)

25215 all bones of proximal row

25230 Radial styloidectomy (separate procedure)

25240 Excision distal ulna partial or complete (eg, Darrach type or matched resection)

(For implant replacement, distal ulna, use 25442)

(For obtaining fascia for interposition, see 20920, 20922)

Introduction or Removal

(For K-wire, pin or rod insertion or removal, see 20650, 20670, 20680)

25246 Injection procedure for wrist arthrography

(For radiological supervision and interpretation, use 73115. Do not report 77002 in conjunction with 73115)

(For foreign body removal, superficial use 20520)

25248 Exploration with removal of deep foreign body, forearm or wrist

25250 Removal of wrist prosthesis; (separate procedure)

25251 complicated, including total wrist

25259 Manipulation, wrist, under anesthesia
➔ *CPT Assistant* Jan 04:27, Jun 05:12; *CPT Changes: An Insider's View* 2002

(For application of external fixation, see 20690 or 20692)

Repair, Revision, and/or Reconstruction

25260 Repair, tendon or muscle, flexor, forearm and/or wrist; primary, single, each tendon or muscle

25263 secondary, single, each tendon or muscle

25265 secondary, with free graft (includes obtaining graft), each tendon or muscle

25270 Repair, tendon or muscle, extensor, forearm and/or wrist; primary, single, each tendon or muscle

25272 secondary, single, each tendon or muscle

25274 secondary, with free graft (includes obtaining graft), each tendon or muscle
➔ *CPT Changes: An Insider's View* 2002

25275 Repair, tendon sheath, extensor, forearm and/or wrist, with free graft (includes obtaining graft) (eg, for extensor carpi ulnaris subluxation)
➔ *CPT Changes: An Insider's View* 2002

25280 Lengthening or shortening of flexor or extensor tendon, forearm and/or wrist, single, each tendon

25290 Tenotomy, open, flexor or extensor tendon, forearm and/or wrist, single, each tendon

25295 Tenolysis, flexor or extensor tendon, forearm and/or wrist, single, each tendon
➔ *CPT Assistant* Apr 97:11, Aug 98:10

25300 Tenodesis at wrist; flexors of fingers

25301 extensors of fingers

25310 Tendon transplantation or transfer, flexor or extensor, forearm and/or wrist, single; each tendon
➔ *CPT Assistant* Jun 02:11

25312 with tendon graft(s) (includes obtaining graft), each tendon

25315 Flexor origin slide (eg, for cerebral palsy, Volkmann contracture), forearm and/or wrist;

25316 with tendon(s) transfer

25320 Capsulorrhaphy or reconstruction, wrist, open (eg, capsulodesis, ligament repair, tendon transfer or graft) (includes synovectomy, capsulotomy and open reduction) for carpal instability
➔ *CPT Changes: An Insider's View* 2003

25332 Arthroplasty, wrist, with or without interposition, with or without external or internal fixation
➔ *CPT Assistant* Nov 96:5, Jan 05:8

(For obtaining fascia for interposition, see 20920, 20922)

(For prosthetic replacement arthroplasty, see 25441-25446)

25335 Centralization of wrist on ulna (eg, radial club hand)

25337 Reconstruction for stabilization of unstable distal ulna or distal radioulnar joint, secondary by soft tissue stabilization (eg, tendon transfer, tendon graft or weave, or tenodesis) with or without open reduction of distal radioulnar joint

(For harvesting of fascia lata graft, see 20920, 20922)

25350 Osteotomy, radius; distal third

25355 middle or proximal third

25360 Osteotomy; ulna

25365 radius AND ulna

25370 Multiple osteotomies, with realignment on intramedullary rod (Sofield type procedure); radius OR ulna

25375 radius AND ulna

25390 Osteoplasty, radius OR ulna; shortening

25391 lengthening with autograft

25392 Osteoplasty, radius AND ulna; shortening (excluding 64876)

25393 lengthening with autograft

25394 Osteoplasty, carpal bone, shortening
➔ *CPT Changes: An Insider's View* 2002

25400 Repair of nonunion or malunion, radius OR ulna; without graft (eg, compression technique)

25405 with autograft (includes obtaining graft)
➔ *CPT Changes: An Insider's View* 2002

25415 Repair of nonunion or malunion, radius AND ulna; without graft (eg, compression technique)

25420 with autograft (includes obtaining graft)
➔ *CPT Changes: An Insider's View* 2002

25425 Repair of defect with autograft; radius OR ulna

25426 radius AND ulna

25430 Insertion of vascular pedicle into carpal bone (eg, Hori procedure)
➔ *CPT Changes: An Insider's View* 2002

25431 Repair of nonunion of carpal bone (excluding carpal scaphoid (navicular)) (includes obtaining graft and necessary fixation), each bone
➔ *CPT Changes: An Insider's View* 2002

25440 Repair of nonunion, scaphoid carpal (navicular) bone, with or without radial styloidectomy (includes obtaining graft and necessary fixation)
➔ *CPT Changes: An Insider's View* 2002

25441 Arthroplasty with prosthetic replacement; distal radius
➔ *CPT Assistant* Jan 05:8-9

25442 distal ulna
➔ *CPT Assistant* Jan 05:8-9

25443 scaphoid carpal (navicular)
➔ *CPT Assistant* Jan 05:8-9; *CPT Changes: An Insider's View* 2002

25444 lunate
➔ *CPT Assistant* Jan 05:8, 10

25445 trapezium
➔ *CPT Assistant* Jan 05:8, 10

25446 distal radius and partial or entire carpus (total wrist)
➔ *CPT Assistant* Jan 05:8, 11

25447 Arthroplasty, interposition, intercarpal or carpometacarpal joints
➔ *CPT Assistant* Nov 98:8, Jan 05:8, 11-12

(For wrist arthroplasty, use 25332)

25449 Revision of arthroplasty, including removal of implant, wrist joint

25450 Epiphyseal arrest by epiphysiodesis or stapling; distal radius OR ulna

25455 distal radius AND ulna

25490 Prophylactic treatment (nailing, pinning, plating or wiring) with or without methylmethacrylate; radius

25491 ulna

25492 radius AND ulna

Fracture and/or Dislocation

(For application of external fixation in addition to internal fixation, use 20690 and the appropriate internal fixation code)

25500 Closed treatment of radial shaft fracture; without manipulation

25505 with manipulation

25515 Open treatment of radial shaft fracture, includes internal fixation, when performed
➔ *CPT Changes: An Insider's View* 2008

▲ = Revised code   ● = New code   ▶◀ = Contains new or revised text   ⊘ = Modifier 51 exempt

25520 Closed treatment of radial shaft fracture and closed treatment of dislocation of distal radioulnar joint (Galeazzi fracture/dislocation)
➔ *CPT Changes: An Insider's View* 2002

25525 Open treatment of radial shaft fracture, includes internal fixation, when performed, and closed treatment of distal radioulnar joint dislocation (Galeazzi fracture/ dislocation), includes percutaneous skeletal fixation, when performed
➔ *CPT Changes: An Insider's View* 2008

25526 Open treatment of radial shaft fracture, includes internal fixation, when performed, and open treatment of distal radioulnar joint dislocation (Galeazzi fracture/ dislocation), includes internal fixation, when performed, includes repair of triangular fibrocartilage complex
➔ *CPT Changes: An Insider's View* 2002, 2008

25530 Closed treatment of ulnar shaft fracture; without manipulation
➔ *CPT Assistant* Apr 02:14

25535 with manipulation

25545 Open treatment of ulnar shaft fracture, includes internal fixation, when performed
➔ *CPT Assistant* Fall 93:23, Oct 99:5; *CPT Changes: An Insider's View* 2008

25560 Closed treatment of radial and ulnar shaft fractures; without manipulation

25565 with manipulation

25574 Open treatment of radial AND ulnar shaft fractures, with internal fixation, when performed; of radius OR ulna
➔ *CPT Assistant* Fall 93:23, Oct 99:5; *CPT Changes: An Insider's View* 2008

25575 of radius AND ulna
➔ *CPT Changes: An Insider's View* 2008

25600 Closed treatment of distal radial fracture (eg, Colles or Smith type) or epiphyseal separation, includes closed treatment of fracture of ulnar styloid, when performed; without manipulation
➔ *CPT Assistant* Oct 07:7; *CPT Changes: An Insider's View* 2007

25605 with manipulation
➔ *CPT Assistant* Oct 07:7

(Do not report 25600, 25605 in conjunction with 25650)

25606 Percutaneous skeletal fixation of distal radial fracture or epiphyseal separation
➔ *CPT Changes: An Insider's View* 2007

(Do not report 25606 in conjunction with 25650)

(For percutaneous treatment of ulnar styloid fracture, use 25651)

(For open treatment of ulnar styloid fracture, use 25652)

25607 Open treatment of distal radial extra-articular fracture or epiphyseal separation, with internal fixation
➔ *CPT Assistant* Oct 07:7; *CPT Changes: An Insider's View* 2007

(Do not report 25607 in conjunction with 25650)

(For percutaneous treatment of ulnar styloid fracture, use 25651)

(For open treatment of ulnar styloid fracture, use 25652)

25608 Open treatment of distal radial intra-articular fracture or epiphyseal separation; with internal fixation of 2 fragments
➔ *CPT Assistant* Oct 07:7; *CPT Changes: An Insider's View* 2007

(Do not report 25608 in conjunction with 25609)

25609 with internal fixation of 3 or more fragments
➔ *CPT Assistant* Oct 07:7; *CPT Changes: An Insider's View* 2007

(Do not report 25608, 25609 in conjunction with 25650)

(For percutaneous treatment of ulnar styloid fracture, use 25651)

(For open treatment of ulnar styloid fracture, use 25652)

25622 Closed treatment of carpal scaphoid (navicular) fracture; without manipulation

25624 with manipulation

25628 Open treatment of carpal scaphoid (navicular) fracture, includes internal fixation, when performed
➔ *CPT Changes: An Insider's View* 2008

25630 Closed treatment of carpal bone fracture (excluding carpal scaphoid [navicular]); without manipulation, each bone

25635 with manipulation, each bone

25645 Open treatment of carpal bone fracture (other than carpal scaphoid [navicular]), each bone
➔ *CPT Changes: An Insider's View* 2002

25650 Closed treatment of ulnar styloid fracture
➔ *CPT Assistant* Oct 07:7

(Do not report 25650 in conjunction with 25600, 25605, 25607-25609)

25651 Percutaneous skeletal fixation of ulnar styloid fracture
➔ *CPT Changes: An Insider's View* 2002

25652 Open treatment of ulnar styloid fracture
➔ *CPT Assistant* Oct 07:7; *CPT Changes: An Insider's View* 2002

25660 Closed treatment of radiocarpal or intercarpal dislocation, 1 or more bones, with manipulation

25670 Open treatment of radiocarpal or intercarpal dislocation, 1 or more bones

25671 Percutaneous skeletal fixation of distal radioulnar dislocation
➔ *CPT Changes: An Insider's View* 2002

25675 Closed treatment of distal radioulnar dislocation with manipulation

25676 Open treatment of distal radioulnar dislocation, acute or chronic

25680 Closed treatment of trans-scaphoperilunar type of fracture dislocation, with manipulation

25685	Open treatment of trans-scaphoperilunar type of fracture dislocation	
25690	Closed treatment of lunate dislocation, with manipulation	
25695	Open treatment of lunate dislocation	

Arthrodesis

25800   Arthrodesis, wrist; complete, without bone graft (includes radiocarpal and/or intercarpal and/or carpometacarpal joints)

➔ *CPT Assistant* Nov 98:8

25805   with sliding graft

25810   with iliac or other autograft (includes obtaining graft)

25820   Arthrodesis, wrist; limited, without bone graft (eg, intercarpal or radiocarpal)

➔ *CPT Assistant* Nov 98:8

25825   with autograft (includes obtaining graft)

25830   Arthrodesis, distal radioulnar joint with segmental resection of ulna, with or without bone graft (eg, Sauve-Kapandji procedure)

➔ *CPT Assistant* Nov 98:8

Amputation

25900   Amputation, forearm, through radius and ulna;

25905   open, circular (guillotine)

25907   secondary closure or scar revision

25909   re-amputation

25915   Krukenberg procedure

25920   Disarticulation through wrist;

25922   secondary closure or scar revision

25924   re-amputation

25927   Transmetacarpal amputation;

25929   secondary closure or scar revision

25931   re-amputation

Other Procedures

25999   Unlisted procedure, forearm or wrist

Hand and Fingers

Incision

26010   Drainage of finger abscess; simple

26011   complicated (eg, felon)

26020   Drainage of tendon sheath, digit and/or palm, each

26025   Drainage of palmar bursa; single, bursa

➔ *CPT Assistant* Nov 98:8

26030   multiple bursa

➔ *CPT Assistant* Nov 98:8

26034   Incision, bone cortex, hand or finger (eg, osteomyelitis or bone abscess)

➔ *CPT Assistant* Nov 98:8

26035   Decompression fingers and/or hand, injection injury (eg, grease gun)

26037   Decompressive fasciotomy, hand (excludes 26035)

(For injection injury, use 26035)

26040   Fasciotomy, palmar (eg, Dupuytren's contracture); percutaneous

➔ *CPT Assistant* Nov 98:8

26045   open, partial

(For fasciectomy, see 26121-26125)

26055   Tendon sheath incision (eg, for trigger finger)

26060   Tenotomy, percutaneous, single, each digit

26070   Arthrotomy, with exploration, drainage, or removal of loose or foreign body; carpometacarpal joint

➔ *CPT Assistant* Nov 98:10

26075   metacarpophalangeal joint, each

26080   interphalangeal joint, each

Excision

26100   Arthrotomy with biopsy; carpometacarpal joint, each

26105   metacarpophalangeal joint, each

26110   interphalangeal joint, each

26111   ▶Code is out of numerical sequence. See 26100-26262◀

26113   ▶Code is out of numerical sequence. See 26100-26262◀

▲ **26115**   Excision, tumor or vascular malformation, soft tissue of hand or finger, subcutaneous; less than 1.5 cm

➔ *CPT Changes: An Insider's View* 2002, 2010

#● **26111**   1.5 cm or greater

➔ *CPT Changes: An Insider's View* 2010

▲ **26116**   Excision, tumor, soft tissue, or vascular malformation, of hand or finger, subfascial (eg, intramuscular); less than 1.5 cm

➔ *CPT Changes: An Insider's View* 2002, 2010

#● **26113**   1.5 cm or greater

➔ *CPT Changes: An Insider's View* 2010

▲ **26117**   Radical resection of tumor (eg, malignant neoplasm), soft tissue of hand or finger; less than 3 cm

➔ *CPT Changes: An Insider's View* 2010

● **26118**   3 cm or greater

➔ *CPT Changes: An Insider's View* 2010

26121   Fasciectomy, palm only, with or without Z-plasty, other local tissue rearrangement, or skin grafting (includes obtaining graft)

26123 Fasciectomy, partial palmar with release of single digit including proximal interphalangeal joint, with or without Z-plasty, other local tissue rearrangement, or skin grafting (includes obtaining graft);
➡ *CPT Assistant* Jan 05:8

+ 26125 each additional digit (List separately in addition to code for primary procedure)
➡ *CPT Assistant* Jan 05:8

(Use 26125 in conjunction with 26123)

(For fasciotomy, see 26040, 26045)

26130 Synovectomy, carpometacarpal joint

26135 Synovectomy, metacarpophalangeal joint including intrinsic release and extensor hood reconstruction, each digit

26140 Synovectomy, proximal interphalangeal joint, including extensor reconstruction, each interphalangeal joint

26145 Synovectomy, tendon sheath, radical (tenosynovectomy), flexor tendon, palm and/or finger, each tendon
➡ *CPT Assistant* Nov 98:8

(For tendon sheath synovectomies at wrist, see 25115, 25116)

26160 Excision of lesion of tendon sheath or joint capsule (eg, cyst, mucous cyst, or ganglion), hand or finger
➡ *CPT Changes: An Insider's View* 2002

(For wrist ganglion, see 25111, 25112)

(For trigger digit, use 26055)

26170 Excision of tendon, palm, flexor or extensor, single, each tendon
➡ *CPT Changes: An Insider's View* 2007

(Do not report 26170 in conjunction with 26390, 26415)

26180 Excision of tendon, finger, flexor or extensor, each tendon
➡ *CPT Assistant* Nov 98:8; *CPT Changes: An Insider's View* 2007

(Do not report 26180 in conjunction with 26390, 26415)

26185 Sesamoidectomy, thumb or finger (separate procedure)

26200 Excision or curettage of bone cyst or benign tumor of metacarpal;

26205 with autograft (includes obtaining graft)

26210 Excision or curettage of bone cyst or benign tumor of proximal, middle, or distal phalanx of finger;

26215 with autograft (includes obtaining graft)

26230 Partial excision (craterization, saucerization, or diaphysectomy) bone (eg, osteomyelitis); metacarpal

26235 proximal or middle phalanx of finger

26236 distal phalanx of finger

▲ **26250** Radical resection of tumor, metacarpal
➡ *CPT Assistant* Nov 98:8; *CPT Changes: An Insider's View* 2010

►(26255 has been deleted)◄

▲ **26260** Radical resection of tumor, proximal or middle phalanx of finger
➡ *CPT Assistant* Nov 98:8; *CPT Changes: An Insider's View* 2010

►(26261 has been deleted)◄

▲ **26262** Radical resection of tumor, distal phalanx of finger
➡ *CPT Assistant* Nov 98:8; *CPT Changes: An Insider's View* 2010

Introduction or Removal

26320 Removal of implant from finger or hand

(For removal of foreign body in hand or finger, see 20520, 20525)

Repair, Revision, and/or Reconstruction

26340 Manipulation, finger joint, under anesthesia, each joint
➡ *CPT Assistant* Nov 02:10; *CPT Changes: An Insider's View* 2002

(For application of external fixation, see 20690 or 20692)

26350 Repair or advancement, flexor tendon, not in zone 2 digital flexor tendon sheath (eg, no man's land); primary or secondary without free graft, each tendon
➡ *CPT Assistant* Nov 98:8; *CPT Changes: An Insider's View* 2002

26352 secondary with free graft (includes obtaining graft), each tendon

26356 Repair or advancement, flexor tendon, in zone 2 digital flexor tendon sheath (eg, no man's land); primary, without free graft, each tendon
➡ *CPT Assistant* Nov 98:8, Dec 98:9, Dec 08:6; *CPT Changes: An Insider's View* 2002, 2004

26357 secondary, without free graft, each tendon
➡ *CPT Changes: An Insider's View* 2004

26358 secondary, with free graft (includes obtaining graft), each tendon

26370 Repair or advancement of profundus tendon, with intact superficialis tendon; primary, each tendon
➡ *CPT Assistant* Nov 98:8, Dec 08:6

26372 secondary with free graft (includes obtaining graft), each tendon
➡ *CPT Assistant* Nov 98:8

26373 secondary without free graft, each tendon
➡ *CPT Assistant* Nov 98:8

26390 Excision flexor tendon, with implantation of synthetic rod for delayed tendon graft, hand or finger, each rod
➡ *CPT Assistant* Nov 98:8; *CPT Changes: An Insider's View* 2002

26392 Removal of synthetic rod and insertion of flexor tendon graft, hand or finger (includes obtaining graft), each rod
➡ *CPT Assistant* Nov 98:8; *CPT Changes: An Insider's View* 2002

26410 Repair, extensor tendon, hand, primary or secondary; without free graft, each tendon
➡ *CPT Assistant* Nov 98:8

26412 with free graft (includes obtaining graft), each tendon
➡ *CPT Assistant* Nov 98:8

26415   Excision of extensor tendon, with implantation of synthetic rod for delayed tendon graft, hand or finger, each rod
> *CPT Assistant* Nov 98:8; *CPT Changes: An Insider's View* 2002

26416   Removal of synthetic rod and insertion of extensor tendon graft (includes obtaining graft), hand or finger, each rod
> *CPT Assistant* Nov 99:12; *CPT Changes: An Insider's View* 2000, 2002

26418   Repair, extensor tendon, finger, primary or secondary; without free graft, each tendon
> *CPT Assistant* Nov 98:8, Dec 99:10, Dec 00:14

26420   with free graft (includes obtaining graft) each tendon

26426   Repair of extensor tendon, central slip, secondary (eg, boutonniere deformity); using local tissue(s), including lateral band(s), each finger
> *CPT Assistant* Nov 98:8; *CPT Changes: An Insider's View* 2002

26428   with free graft (includes obtaining graft), each finger
> *CPT Changes: An Insider's View* 2002

26432   Closed treatment of distal extensor tendon insertion, with or without percutaneous pinning (eg, mallet finger)
> *CPT Assistant* Nov 98:8

26433   Repair of extensor tendon, distal insertion, primary or secondary; without graft (eg, mallet finger)
> *CPT Assistant* Nov 98:8

26434   with free graft (includes obtaining graft)

(For tenovaginotomy for trigger finger, use 26055)

26437   Realignment of extensor tendon, hand, each tendon
> *CPT Assistant* Nov 98:8

26440   Tenolysis, flexor tendon; palm OR finger, each tendon
> *CPT Assistant* Apr 02:18; *CPT Changes: An Insider's View* 2003

26442   palm AND finger, each tendon

26445   Tenolysis, extensor tendon, hand OR finger, each tendon
> *CPT Assistant* Nov 98:8, Dec 02:11, Mar 03:20; *CPT Changes: An Insider's View* 2002

26449   Tenolysis, complex, extensor tendon, finger, including forearm, each tendon
> *CPT Assistant* Nov 98:8

26450   Tenotomy, flexor, palm, open, each tendon
> *CPT Assistant* Nov 98:8

26455   Tenotomy, flexor, finger, open, each tendon
> *CPT Assistant* Nov 98:8

26460   Tenotomy, extensor, hand or finger, open, each tendon
> *CPT Assistant* Nov 98:8

26471   Tenodesis; of proximal interphalangeal joint, each joint
> *CPT Assistant* Nov 98:8

26474   of distal joint, each joint
> *CPT Assistant* Nov 98:8

26476   Lengthening of tendon, extensor, hand or finger, each tendon
> *CPT Assistant* Nov 98:8

26477   Shortening of tendon, extensor, hand or finger, each tendon
> *CPT Assistant* Nov 98:8

26478   Lengthening of tendon, flexor, hand or finger, each tendon
> *CPT Assistant* Nov 98:8

26479   Shortening of tendon, flexor, hand or finger, each tendon
> *CPT Assistant* Nov 98:8

26480   Transfer or transplant of tendon, carpometacarpal area or dorsum of hand; without free graft, each tendon
> *CPT Assistant* Nov 98:8

26483   with free tendon graft (includes obtaining graft), each tendon

26485   Transfer or transplant of tendon, palmar; without free tendon graft, each tendon
> *CPT Assistant* Nov 98:8

26489   with free tendon graft (includes obtaining graft), each tendon

26490   Opponensplasty; superficialis tendon transfer type, each tendon

26492   tendon transfer with graft (includes obtaining graft), each tendon

26494   hypothenar muscle transfer

26496   other methods

(For thumb fusion in opposition, use 26820)

26497   Transfer of tendon to restore intrinsic function; ring and small finger
> *CPT Assistant* Nov 98:8

26498   all 4 fingers

26499   Correction claw finger, other methods

26500   Reconstruction of tendon pulley, each tendon; with local tissues (separate procedure)
> *CPT Assistant* Nov 98:8

26502   with tendon or fascial graft (includes obtaining graft) (separate procedure)

26508   Release of thenar muscle(s) (eg, thumb contracture)
> *CPT Assistant* Nov 98:8

26510   Cross intrinsic transfer, each tendon
> *CPT Changes: An Insider's View* 2002

26516   Capsulodesis, metacarpophalangeal joint; single digit
> *CPT Assistant* Nov 98:8

26517   2 digits

26518   3 or 4 digits

26520   Capsulectomy or capsulotomy; metacarpophalangeal joint, each joint
> *CPT Assistant* Nov 98:8

26525   interphalangeal joint, each joint
> *CPT Assistant* Nov 98:8, Apr 02:18, Mar 03:20

(To report carpometacarpal joint arthroplasty, use 25447)

26530   Arthroplasty, metacarpophalangeal joint; each joint
   ➔ *CPT Assistant* Nov 98:8

26531   with prosthetic implant, each joint
   ➔ *CPT Assistant* Nov 98:8

26535   Arthroplasty, interphalangeal joint; each joint
   ➔ *CPT Assistant* Nov 98:8

26536   with prosthetic implant, each joint
   ➔ *CPT Assistant* Nov 98:8

26540   Repair of collateral ligament, metacarpophalangeal or interphalangeal joint
   ➔ *CPT Assistant* Nov 96:6

26541   Reconstruction, collateral ligament, metacarpophalangeal joint, single; with tendon or fascial graft (includes obtaining graft)
   ➔ *CPT Assistant* Jan 97:3

26542   with local tissue (eg, adductor advancement)
   ➔ *CPT Assistant* Jan 97:3

26545   Reconstruction, collateral ligament, interphalangeal joint, single, including graft, each joint

26546   Repair non-union, metacarpal or phalanx (includes obtaining bone graft with or without external or internal fixation)
   ➔ *CPT Assistant* Nov 96:6

26548   Repair and reconstruction, finger, volar plate, interphalangeal joint

26550   Pollicization of a digit

26551   Transfer, toe-to-hand with microvascular anastomosis; great toe wrap-around with bone graft
   ➔ *CPT Assistant* Nov 96:6, Apr 97:7, Jun 97:9, Nov 98:8, 10-11

   (For great toe with web space, use 20973)

26553   other than great toe, single
   ➔ *CPT Assistant* Nov 96:6, Apr 97:7, Jun 97:9, Nov 98:8, 10-11

26554   other than great toe, double
   ➔ *CPT Assistant* Nov 96:6, Apr 97:7, Jun 97:9, Nov 98:8, 10-11

   (Do not report code 69990 in addition to codes 26551-26554)

26555   Transfer, finger to another position without microvascular anastomosis
   ➔ *CPT Assistant* Nov 98:8, 10-11

26556   Transfer, free toe joint, with microvascular anastomosis
   ➔ *CPT Assistant* Nov 96:6, Apr 97:7, Jun 97:9, Nov 98:8

   (Do not report code 69990 in addition to code 26556)

   (To report great toe-to-hand transfer, use 20973)

26560   Repair of syndactyly (web finger) each web space; with skin flaps

26561   with skin flaps and grafts

26562   complex (eg, involving bone, nails)

26565   Osteotomy; metacarpal, each
   ➔ *CPT Assistant* Nov 98:9

26567   phalanx of finger, each

26568   Osteoplasty, lengthening, metacarpal or phalanx

26580   Repair cleft hand

26587   Reconstruction of polydactylous digit, soft tissue and bone
   ➔ *CPT Assistant* Oct 01:10, Aug 03:14, May 04:16; *CPT Changes: An Insider's View* 2002

   (For excision of polydactylous digit, soft tissue only, use 11200)

26590   Repair macrodactylia, each digit
   ➔ *CPT Assistant* Oct 01:10, Aug 03:14, May 04:16; *CPT Changes: An Insider's View* 2002

26591   Repair, intrinsic muscles of hand, each muscle
   ➔ *CPT Assistant* May 98:11, Jul 98:11, Nov 98:8, 11

26593   Release, intrinsic muscles of hand, each muscle
   ➔ *CPT Assistant* Nov 98:8, 11

26596   Excision of constricting ring of finger, with multiple Z-plasties

   (To report release of scar contracture or graft repairs see 11041-11042, 14040-14041, or 15120, 15240)

Fracture and/or Dislocation

26600   Closed treatment of metacarpal fracture, single; without manipulation, each bone

26605   with manipulation, each bone

26607   Closed treatment of metacarpal fracture, with manipulation, with external fixation, each bone
   ➔ *CPT Changes: An Insider's View* 2002

26608   Percutaneous skeletal fixation of metacarpal fracture, each bone

26615   Open treatment of metacarpal fracture, single, includes internal fixation, when performed, each bone
   ➔ *CPT Changes: An Insider's View* 2008

26641   Closed treatment of carpometacarpal dislocation, thumb, with manipulation

26645   Closed treatment of carpometacarpal fracture dislocation, thumb (Bennett fracture), with manipulation

26650   Percutaneous skeletal fixation of carpometacarpal fracture dislocation, thumb (Bennett fracture), with manipulation
   ➔ *CPT Changes: An Insider's View* 2008

26665   Open treatment of carpometacarpal fracture dislocation, thumb (Bennett fracture), includes internal fixation, when performed
   ➔ *CPT Changes: An Insider's View* 2008

26670   Closed treatment of carpometacarpal dislocation, other than thumb, with manipulation, each joint; without anesthesia
   ➔ *CPT Changes: An Insider's View* 2002

26675   requiring anesthesia

26676   Percutaneous skeletal fixation of carpometacarpal dislocation, other than thumb, with manipulation, each joint
➜ *CPT Changes: An Insider's View 2002*

26685   Open treatment of carpometacarpal dislocation, other than thumb; includes internal fixation, when performed, each joint
➜ *CPT Changes: An Insider's View 2002, 2008*

26686   complex, multiple, or delayed reduction

26700   Closed treatment of metacarpophalangeal dislocation, single, with manipulation; without anesthesia

26705   requiring anesthesia

26706   Percutaneous skeletal fixation of metacarpophalangeal dislocation, single, with manipulation

26715   Open treatment of metacarpophalangeal dislocation, single, includes internal fixation, when performed
➜ *CPT Changes: An Insider's View 2008*

26720   Closed treatment of phalangeal shaft fracture, proximal or middle phalanx, finger or thumb; without manipulation, each

26725   with manipulation, with or without skin or skeletal traction, each

26727   Percutaneous skeletal fixation of unstable phalangeal shaft fracture, proximal or middle phalanx, finger or thumb, with manipulation, each

26735   Open treatment of phalangeal shaft fracture, proximal or middle phalanx, finger or thumb, includes internal fixation, when performed, each
➜ *CPT Changes: An Insider's View 2008*

26740   Closed treatment of articular fracture, involving metacarpophalangeal or interphalangeal joint; without manipulation, each

26742   with manipulation, each

26746   Open treatment of articular fracture, involving metacarpophalangeal or interphalangeal joint, includes internal fixation, when performed, each
➜ *CPT Changes: An Insider's View 2008*

26750   Closed treatment of distal phalangeal fracture, finger or thumb; without manipulation, each

26755   with manipulation, each

26756   Percutaneous skeletal fixation of distal phalangeal fracture, finger or thumb, each

26765   Open treatment of distal phalangeal fracture, finger or thumb, includes internal fixation, when performed, each
➜ *CPT Changes: An Insider's View 2008*

26770   Closed treatment of interphalangeal joint dislocation, single, with manipulation; without anesthesia

26775   requiring anesthesia

26776   Percutaneous skeletal fixation of interphalangeal joint dislocation, single, with manipulation

26785   Open treatment of interphalangeal joint dislocation, includes internal fixation, when performed, single
➜ *CPT Changes: An Insider's View 2008*

Arthrodesis

26820   Fusion in opposition, thumb, with autogenous graft (includes obtaining graft)

26841   Arthrodesis, carpometacarpal joint, thumb, with or without internal fixation;

26842   with autograft (includes obtaining graft)

26843   Arthrodesis, carpometacarpal joint, digit, other than thumb, each;
➜ *CPT Changes: An Insider's View 2002*

26844   with autograft (includes obtaining graft)

26850   Arthrodesis, metacarpophalangeal joint, with or without internal fixation;

26852   with autograft (includes obtaining graft)

26860   Arthrodesis, interphalangeal joint, with or without internal fixation;

+ 26861   each additional interphalangeal joint (List separately in addition to code for primary procedure)

(Use 26861 in conjunction with 26860)

26862   with autograft (includes obtaining graft)

+ 26863   with autograft (includes obtaining graft), each additional joint (List separately in addition to code for primary procedure)

(Use 26863 in conjunction with 26862)

Amputation

(For hand through metacarpal bones, use 25927)

26910   Amputation, metacarpal, with finger or thumb (ray amputation), single, with or without interosseous transfer

(For repositioning, see 26550, 26555)

26951   Amputation, finger or thumb, primary or secondary, any joint or phalanx, single, including neurectomies; with direct closure

26952   with local advancement flaps (V-Y, hood)

(For repair of soft tissue defect requiring split or full thickness graft or other pedicle flaps, see 15050-15758)

Other Procedures

26989   Unlisted procedure, hands or fingers

Pelvis and Hip Joint

Including head and neck of femur.

Incision

(For incision and drainage procedures, superficial, see 10040-10160)

26990 Incision and drainage, pelvis or hip joint area; deep abscess or hematoma

26991 infected bursa

26992 Incision, bone cortex, pelvis and/or hip joint (eg, osteomyelitis or bone abscess)
➔ *CPT Assistant* Jan 02:10

27000 Tenotomy, adductor of hip, percutaneous (separate procedure)

27001 Tenotomy, adductor of hip, open

(To report bilateral procedure, report 27001 with modifier 50)

27003 Tenotomy, adductor, subcutaneous, open, with obturator neurectomy

(To report bilateral procedure, report 27003 with modifier 50)

27005 Tenotomy, hip flexor(s), open (separate procedure)

27006 Tenotomy, abductors and/or extensor(s) of hip, open (separate procedure)

27025 Fasciotomy, hip or thigh, any type

(To report bilateral procedure, report 27025 with modifier 50)

27027 Decompression fasciotomy(ies), pelvic (buttock) compartment(s) (eg, gluteus medius-minimus, gluteus maximus, iliopsoas, and/or tensor fascia lata muscle), unilateral
➔ *CPT Changes: An Insider's View* 2009

(To report bilateral procedure, report 27027 with modifier 50)

27030 Arthrotomy, hip, with drainage (eg, infection)
➔ *CPT Assistant* Nov 98:8

27033 Arthrotomy, hip, including exploration or removal of loose or foreign body
➔ *CPT Assistant* Spring 92:11

27035 Denervation, hip joint, intrapelvic or extrapelvic intra-articular branches of sciatic, femoral, or obturator nerves
➔ *CPT Assistant* Nov 98:8

(For obturator neurectomy, see 64763, 64766)

27036 Capsulectomy or capsulotomy, hip, with or without excision of heterotopic bone, with release of hip flexor muscles (ie, gluteus medius, gluteus minimus, tensor fascia latae, rectus femoris, sartorius, iliopsoas)
➔ *CPT Assistant* Jan 05:8

Excision

27040 Biopsy, soft tissue of pelvis and hip area; superficial

27041 deep, subfascial or intramuscular
➔ *CPT Assistant* Nov 98:8

(For needle biopsy of soft tissue, use 20206)

27043 ►Code is out of numerical sequence. See 27040-27080◄

27045 ►Code is out of numerical sequence. See 27040-27080◄

▲ **27047** Excision, tumor, soft tissue of pelvis and hip area, subcutaneous; less than 3 cm
➔ *CPT Assistant* Nov 98:8; *CPT Changes: An Insider's View* 2010

#● **27043** 3 cm or greater
➔ *CPT Changes: An Insider's View* 2010

▲ **27048** Excision, tumor, soft tissue of pelvis and hip area, subfascial (eg, intramuscular); less than 5 cm
➔ *CPT Changes: An Insider's View* 2010

#● **27045** 5 cm or greater
➔ *CPT Changes: An Insider's View* 2010

▲ **27049** Radical resection of tumor (eg, malignant neoplasm), soft tissue of pelvis and hip area; less than 5 cm
➔ *CPT Assistant* Nov 98:8; *CPT Changes: An Insider's View* 2010

#● **27059** 5 cm or greater
➔ *CPT Changes: An Insider's View* 2010

27050 Arthrotomy, with biopsy; sacroiliac joint

27052 hip joint

27054 Arthrotomy with synovectomy, hip joint

27057 Decompression fasciotomy(ies), pelvic (buttock) compartment(s) (eg, gluteus medius-minimus, gluteus maximus, iliopsoas, and/or tensor fascia lata muscle) with debridement of nonviable muscle, unilateral
➔ *CPT Changes: An Insider's View* 2009

(To report bilateral procedure, report 27057 with modifier 50)

27059 ►Code is out of numerical sequence. See 27040-27080◄

27060 Excision; ischial bursa

27062 trochanteric bursa or calcification

(For arthrocentesis or needling of bursa, use 20610)

27065 Excision of bone cyst or benign tumor; superficial (wing of ilium, symphysis pubis, or greater trochanter of femur) with or without autograft

27066 deep, with or without autograft

27067 with autograft requiring separate incision

27070 Partial excision (craterization, saucerization) (eg, osteomyelitis or bone abscess); superficial (eg, wing of ilium, symphysis pubis, or greater trochanter of femur)

27071 deep (subfascial or intramuscular)

▲ **27075**   Radical resection of tumor; wing of ilium, 1 pubic or ischial ramus or symphysis pubis
⊙ *CPT Changes: An Insider's View* 2010

▲ **27076**   ilium, including acetabulum, both pubic rami, or ischium and acetabulum
⊙ *CPT Changes: An Insider's View* 2010

▲ **27077**   innominate bone, total
⊙ *CPT Changes: An Insider's View* 2010

▲ **27078**   ischial tuberosity and greater trochanter of femur
⊙ *CPT Changes: An Insider's View* 2010

▶(27079 has been deleted)◀

27080   Coccygectomy, primary

(For pressure (decubitus) ulcer, see 15920, 15922 and 15931-15958)

Introduction or Removal

27086   Removal of foreign body, pelvis or hip; subcutaneous tissue
⊙ *CPT Assistant* Jul 98:8

27087   deep (subfascial or intramuscular)
⊙ *CPT Assistant* Nov 98:8

27090   Removal of hip prosthesis; (separate procedure)

27091   complicated, including total hip prosthesis, methylmethacrylate with or without insertion of spacer

27093   Injection procedure for hip arthrography; without anesthesia
⊙ *Clinical Examples in Radiology* Fall 07:7

(For radiological supervision and interpretation, use 73525. Do not report 77002 in conjunction with 73525)

27095   with anesthesia
⊙ *Clinical Examples in Radiology* Fall 07:7

(For radiological supervision and interpretation, use 73525. Do not report 77002 in conjunction with 73525)

27096   Injection procedure for sacroiliac joint, arthrography and/or anesthetic/steroid
⊙ *CPT Assistant* Nov 99:12, Apr 03:8, Apr 04:15, Jul 08:9; *CPT Changes: An Insider's View* 2000

(27096 is to be used only with imaging confirmation of intra-articular needle positioning)

(For radiological supervision and interpretation of sacroiliac joint arthrography, use 73542)

(For fluoroscopic guidance without formal arthrography, use 77003)

(Code 27096 is a unilateral procedure. For bilateral procedure, use modifier 50)

Repair, Revision, and/or Reconstruction

27097   Release or recession, hamstring, proximal
⊙ *CPT Assistant* Nov 98:8

27098   Transfer, adductor to ischium
⊙ *CPT Assistant* Nov 98:8

27100   Transfer external oblique muscle to greater trochanter including fascial or tendon extension (graft)

27105   Transfer paraspinal muscle to hip (includes fascial or tendon extension graft)

27110   Transfer iliopsoas; to greater trochanter of femur
⊙ *CPT Changes: An Insider's View* 2002

27111   to femoral neck

27120   Acetabuloplasty; (eg, Whitman, Colonna, Haygroves, or cup type)

27122   resection, femoral head (eg, Girdlestone procedure)

27125   Hemiarthroplasty, hip, partial (eg, femoral stem prosthesis, bipolar arthroplasty)
⊙ *CPT Assistant* Spring 92:8, Feb 98:11, Nov 98:8

(For prosthetic replacement following fracture of the hip, use 27236)

Partial Hip Replacement With or Without Bipolar Prosthesis
27125

The femoral neck is excised so the physician can measure and then replace the femoral stem.

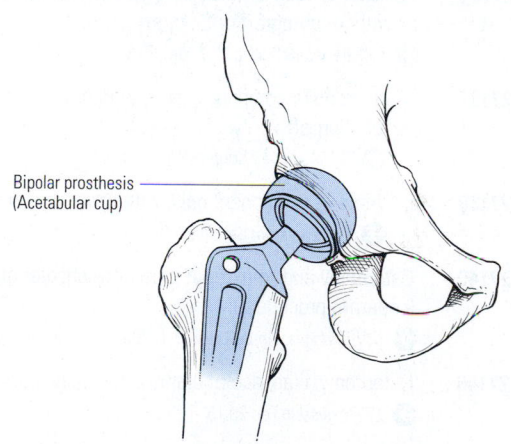

Bipolar prosthesis
(Acetabular cup)

27130   Arthroplasty, acetabular and proximal femoral prosthetic replacement (total hip arthroplasty), with or without autograft or allograft
⊙ *CPT Assistant* Spring 92:8, Jan 07:1; *CPT Changes: An Insider's View* 2002

Total Hip Replacement
27130

The femoral head is excised, osteophytes are removed, and acetabulum is reamed out before replacement is inserted in the femoral shaft.

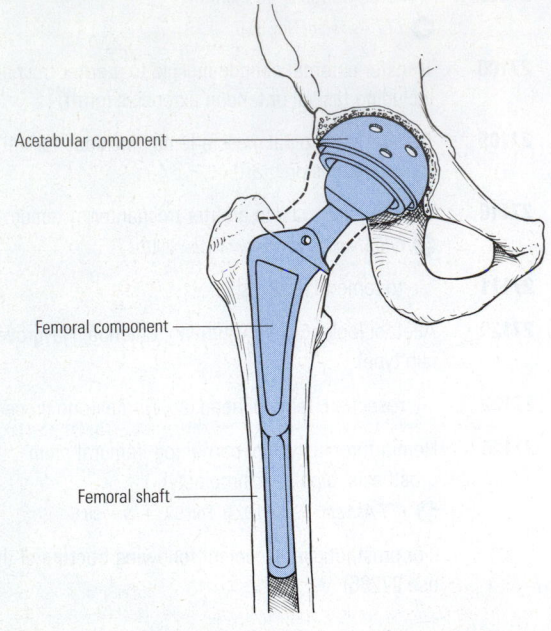

Acetabular component

Femoral component

Femoral shaft

27132   Conversion of previous hip surgery to total hip arthroplasty, with or without autograft or allograft
> *CPT Assistant* Spring 92:11, Dec 08:3; *CPT Changes: An Insider's View* 2002

27134   Revision of total hip arthroplasty; both components, with or without autograft or allograft
> *CPT Assistant* Spring 92:7, Dec 08:3

27137   acetabular component only, with or without autograft or allograft
> *CPT Assistant* Spring 92:7

27138   femoral component only, with or without allograft
> *CPT Assistant* Spring 92:7

27140   Osteotomy and transfer of greater trochanter of femur (separate procedure)
> *CPT Changes: An Insider's View* 2002

27146   Osteotomy, iliac, acetabular or innominate bone;
> *CPT Assistant* Feb 99:10

27147   with open reduction of hip

27151   with femoral osteotomy

27156   with femoral osteotomy and with open reduction of hip

27158   Osteotomy, pelvis, bilateral (eg, congenital malformation)

27161   Osteotomy, femoral neck (separate procedure)

27165   Osteotomy, intertrochanteric or subtrochanteric including internal or external fixation and/or cast
> *CPT Assistant* Spring 92:11

27170   Bone graft, femoral head, neck, intertrochanteric or subtrochanteric area (includes obtaining bone graft)
> *CPT Assistant* Spring 92:11

27175   Treatment of slipped femoral epiphysis; by traction, without reduction

27176   by single or multiple pinning, in situ

27177   Open treatment of slipped femoral epiphysis; single or multiple pinning or bone graft (includes obtaining graft)

27178   closed manipulation with single or multiple pinning

27179   osteoplasty of femoral neck (Heyman type procedure)

27181   osteotomy and internal fixation

27185   Epiphyseal arrest by epiphysiodesis or stapling, greater trochanter of femur
> *CPT Changes: An Insider's View* 2002

27187   Prophylactic treatment (nailing, pinning, plating or wiring) with or without methylmethacrylate, femoral neck and proximal femur

Fracture and/or Dislocation

27193   Closed treatment of pelvic ring fracture, dislocation, diastasis or subluxation; without manipulation

27194   with manipulation, requiring more than local anesthesia

27200   Closed treatment of coccygeal fracture

27202   Open treatment of coccygeal fracture

27215   Open treatment of iliac spine(s), tuberosity avulsion, or iliac wing fracture(s), unilateral, for pelvic bone fracture patterns that do not disrupt the pelvic ring, includes internal fixation, when performed
> *CPT Changes: An Insider's View* 2009

(To report bilateral procedure, report 27215 with modifier 50)

27216   Percutaneous skeletal fixation of posterior pelvic bone fracture and/or dislocation, for fracture patterns that disrupt the pelvic ring, unilateral (includes ipsilateral ilium, sacroiliac joint and/or sacrum)
> *CPT Changes: An Insider's View* 2009

(To report bilateral procedure, report 27216 with modifier 50)

27217   Open treatment of anterior pelvic bone fracture and/or dislocation for fracture patterns that disrupt the pelvic ring, unilateral, includes internal fixation, when performed (includes pubic symphysis and/or ipsilateral superior/inferior rami)
> *CPT Changes: An Insider's View* 2009

(To report bilateral procedure, report 27217 with modifier 50)

27218   Open treatment of posterior pelvic bone fracture and/or dislocation, for fracture patterns that disrupt the pelvic ring, unilateral, includes internal fixation, when performed (includes ipsilateral ilium, sacroiliac joint and/or sacrum)

➜ *CPT Changes: An Insider's View* 2009

(To report bilateral procedure, report 27218 with modifier 50)

27220   Closed treatment of acetabulum (hip socket) fracture(s); without manipulation

27222   with manipulation, with or without skeletal traction

27226   Open treatment of posterior or anterior acetabular wall fracture, with internal fixation

27227   Open treatment of acetabular fracture(s) involving anterior or posterior (one) column, or a fracture running transversely across the acetabulum, with internal fixation

27228   Open treatment of acetabular fracture(s) involving anterior and posterior (two) columns, includes T-fracture and both column fracture with complete articular detachment, or single column or transverse fracture with associated acetabular wall fracture, with internal fixation

27230   Closed treatment of femoral fracture, proximal end, neck; without manipulation

27232   with manipulation, with or without skeletal traction

27235   Percutaneous skeletal fixation of femoral fracture, proximal end, neck

➜ *CPT Changes: An Insider's View* 2003

Percutaneous Treatment of Femoral Fracture
27235

Femoral fracture treatment without fracture exposure

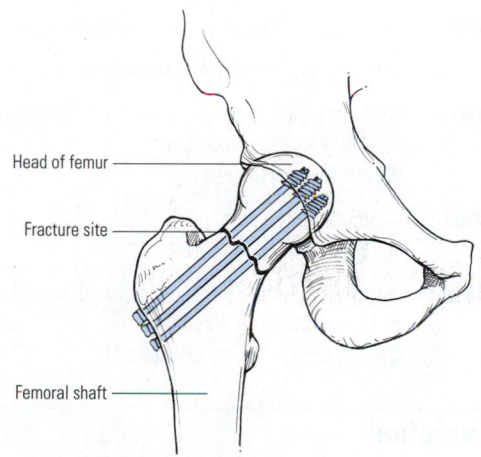

Head of femur

Fracture site

Femoral shaft

27236   Open treatment of femoral fracture, proximal end, neck, internal fixation or prosthetic replacement

➜ *CPT Assistant* Spring 92:10, Feb 98:11, Jan 07:1; *CPT Changes: An Insider's View* 2000

Open Treatment of Femoral Fracture
27236

A. Femoral fracture treatment by internal fixation device (with fracture exposure)

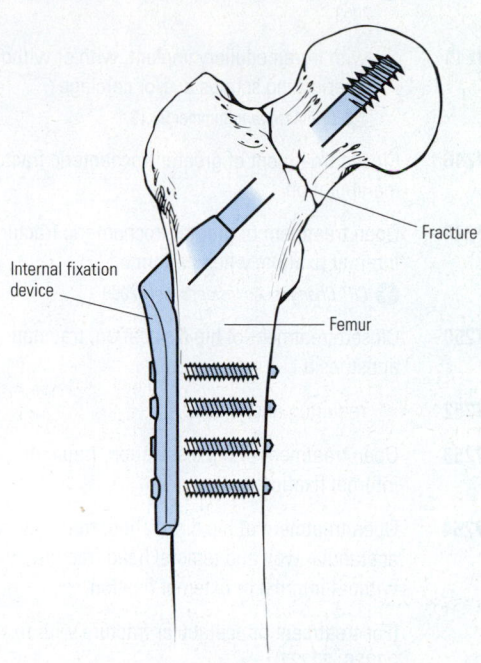

Fracture

Internal fixation device

Femur

B. Femoral fracture treatment by prosthetic replacement

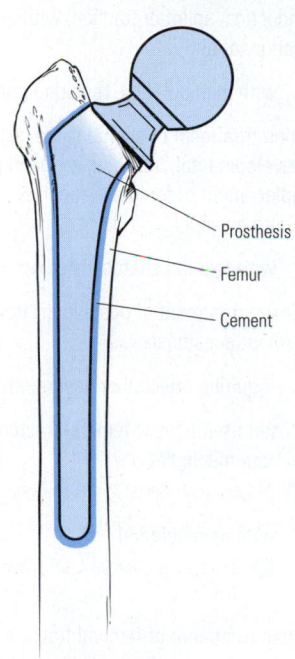

Prosthesis

Femur

Cement

27238   Closed treatment of intertrochanteric, peritrochanteric, or subtrochanteric femoral fracture; without manipulation

➜ *CPT Assistant* Summer 93:12

27240   with manipulation, with or without skin or skeletal traction

➜ *CPT Assistant* Summer 93:12

▲ =Revised code   ● =New code   ► ◄ =Contains new or revised text   ⊘ =Modifier 51 exempt

27244   Treatment of intertrochanteric, peritrochanteric, or subtrochanteric femoral fracture; with plate/screw type implant, with or without cerclage
> *CPT Assistant* Summer 93:12; *CPT Changes: An Insider's View* 2003

27245   with intramedullary implant, with or without interlocking screws and/or cerclage
> *CPT Assistant* Summer 93:12

27246   Closed treatment of greater trochanteric fracture, without manipulation

27248   Open treatment of greater trochanteric fracture, includes internal fixation, when performed
> *CPT Changes: An Insider's View* 2008

27250   Closed treatment of hip dislocation, traumatic; without anesthesia

27252   requiring anesthesia

27253   Open treatment of hip dislocation, traumatic, without internal fixation

27254   Open treatment of hip dislocation, traumatic, with acetabular wall and femoral head fracture, with or without internal or external fixation

(For treatment of acetabular fracture with fixation, see 27226, 27227)

27256   Treatment of spontaneous hip dislocation (developmental, including congenital or pathological), by abduction, splint or traction; without anesthesia, without manipulation

27257   with manipulation, requiring anesthesia

27258   Open treatment of spontaneous hip dislocation (developmental, including congenital or pathological), replacement of femoral head in acetabulum (including tenotomy, etc);

27259   with femoral shaft shortening

27265   Closed treatment of post hip arthroplasty dislocation; without anesthesia

27266   requiring regional or general anesthesia

27267   Closed treatment of femoral fracture, proximal end, head; without manipulation
> *CPT Assistant* Jan 08:4; *CPT Changes: An Insider's View* 2008

27268   with manipulation
> *CPT Assistant* Jan 08:4; *CPT Changes: An Insider's View* 2008

27269   Open treatment of femoral fracture, proximal end, head, includes internal fixation, when performed
> *CPT Assistant* Jan 08:4, Dec 08:3; *CPT Changes: An Insider's View* 2008

(Do not report 27269 in conjunction with 27033, 27253)

Manipulation

27275   Manipulation, hip joint, requiring general anesthesia

Arthrodesis

27280   Arthrodesis, sacroiliac joint (including obtaining graft)

(To report bilateral procedure, report 27280 with modifier 50)

27282   Arthrodesis, symphysis pubis (including obtaining graft)

27284   Arthrodesis, hip joint (including obtaining graft);

27286   with subtrochanteric osteotomy

Amputation

27290   Interpelviabdominal amputation (hindquarter amputation)

27295   Disarticulation of hip

Other Procedures

27299   Unlisted procedure, pelvis or hip joint
> *CPT Assistant* Jan 02:10, Dec 05:9, Dec 08:3

Femur (Thigh Region) and Knee Joint

Including tibial plateaus.

Incision

(For incision and drainage of abscess or hematoma, superficial, see 10040-10160)

27301   Incision and drainage, deep abscess, bursa, or hematoma, thigh or knee region
> *CPT Assistant* Nov 98:9, Dec 08:3

27303   Incision, deep, with opening of bone cortex, femur or knee (eg, osteomyelitis or bone abscess)
> *CPT Assistant* Nov 98:8

27305   Fasciotomy, iliotibial (tenotomy), open

(For combined Ober-Yount fasciotomy, use 27025)

27306   Tenotomy, percutaneous, adductor or hamstring; single tendon (separate procedure)
> *CPT Assistant* Nov 98:8

27307   multiple tendons
> *CPT Assistant* Nov 98:8

27310   Arthrotomy, knee, with exploration, drainage, or removal of foreign body (eg, infection)
> *CPT Assistant* Nov 98:8, Dec 08:3

Excision

27323   Biopsy, soft tissue of thigh or knee area; superficial
> *CPT Assistant* Jun 97:12

27324   deep (subfascial or intramuscular)
> *CPT Assistant* Mar 97:4, Nov 98:8

(For needle biopsy of soft tissue, use 20206)

27325   Neurectomy, hamstring muscle
> *CPT Changes: An Insider's View* 2007

27326   Neurectomy, popliteal (gastrocnemius)
➔ *CPT Changes: An Insider's View* 2007

▲ **27327**   Excision, tumor, soft tissue of thigh or knee area, subcutaneous; less than 3 cm
➔ *CPT Changes: An Insider's View* 2010

\# ● **27337**   3 cm or greater
➔ *CPT Changes: An Insider's View* 2010

▲ **27328**   Excision, tumor, soft tissue of thigh or knee area, subfascial (eg, intramuscular); less than 5 cm
➔ *CPT Changes: An Insider's View* 2010

\# ● **27339**   5 cm or greater
➔ *CPT Changes: An Insider's View* 2010

27329   ►Code is out of numerical sequence. See 27323-27365◄

27330   Arthrotomy, knee; with synovial biopsy only

27331   including joint exploration, biopsy, or removal of loose or foreign bodies
➔ *CPT Assistant* May 96:6, Nov 98:8

27332   Arthrotomy, with excision of semilunar cartilage (meniscectomy) knee; medial OR lateral
➔ *CPT Assistant* Nov 98:8

27333   medial AND lateral

27334   Arthrotomy, with synovectomy, knee; anterior OR posterior
➔ *CPT Assistant* Nov 98:8

27335   anterior AND posterior including popliteal area

27337   ►Code is out of numerical sequence. See 27323-27365◄

27339   ►Code is out of numerical sequence. See 27323-27365◄

27340   Excision, prepatellar bursa

27345   Excision of synovial cyst of popliteal space (eg, Baker's cyst)

27347   Excision of lesion of meniscus or capsule (eg, cyst, ganglion), knee
➔ *CPT Assistant* Nov 98:11

27350   Patellectomy or hemipatellectomy

27355   Excision or curettage of bone cyst or benign tumor of femur;

27356   with allograft

27357   with autograft (includes obtaining graft)
➔ *CPT Assistant* Dec 02:11

\+ **27358**   with internal fixation (List in addition to code for primary procedure)

(Use 27358 in conjunction with 27355, 27356, or 27357)

27360   Partial excision (craterization, saucerization, or diaphysectomy) bone, femur, proximal tibia and/or fibula (eg, osteomyelitis or bone abscess)
➔ *CPT Assistant* Nov 98:8

\# ▲ **27329**   Radical resection of tumor (eg, malignant neoplasm), soft tissue of thigh or knee area; less than 5 cm
➔ *CPT Changes: An Insider's View* 2010

● **27364**   5 cm or greater
➔ *CPT Changes: An Insider's View* 2010

▲ **27365**   Radical resection of tumor, femur or knee
➔ *CPT Changes: An Insider's View* 2010

►(For radical resection of tumor, soft tissue of thigh or knee area, see 27329, 27364)◄

Introduction or Removal

27370   Injection procedure for knee arthrography

(For radiological supervision and interpretation, use 73580. Do not report 77002 in conjunction with 73580)

27372   Removal of foreign body, deep, thigh region or knee area

(For removal of knee prosthesis including "total knee," use 27488)

(For surgical arthroscopic knee procedures, see 29870-29887)

Repair, Revision, and/or Reconstruction

27380   Suture of infrapatellar tendon; primary

27381   secondary reconstruction, including fascial or tendon graft

27385   Suture of quadriceps or hamstring muscle rupture; primary

27386   secondary reconstruction, including fascial or tendon graft

27390   Tenotomy, open, hamstring, knee to hip; single tendon
➔ *CPT Assistant* Nov 98:8

27391   multiple tendons, 1 leg
➔ *CPT Assistant* Nov 98:8

27392   multiple tendons, bilateral
➔ *CPT Assistant* Nov 98:8

27393   Lengthening of hamstring tendon; single tendon
➔ *CPT Assistant* Nov 98:8

27394   multiple tendons, 1 leg
➔ *CPT Assistant* Nov 98:8

27395   multiple tendons, bilateral
➔ *CPT Assistant* Nov 98:8

27396   Transplant or transfer (with muscle redirection or rerouting), thigh (eg, extensor to flexor); single tendon
→ *CPT Assistant* Nov 98:8; *CPT Changes: An Insider's View* 2009

27397   multiple tendons
→ *CPT Assistant* Nov 98:8; *CPT Changes: An Insider's View* 2009

27400   Transfer, tendon or muscle, hamstrings to femur (eg, Egger's type procedure)
→ *CPT Assistant* Nov 98:8

27403   Arthrotomy with meniscus repair, knee
→ *CPT Assistant* Nov 98:8

(For arthroscopic repair, use 29882)

27405   Repair, primary, torn ligament and/or capsule, knee; collateral

27407   cruciate

(For cruciate ligament reconstruction, use 27427)

27409   collateral and cruciate ligaments

(For ligament reconstruction, see 27427-27429)

27412   Autologous chondrocyte implantation, knee
→ *CPT Changes: An Insider's View* 2005

(Do not report 27412 in conjunction with 20926, 27331, 27570)

(For harvesting of chondrocytes, use 29870)

27415   Osteochondral allograft, knee, open
→ *CPT Changes: An Insider's View* 2005

(For arthroscopic implant of osteochondral allograft, use 29867)

(Do not report 27415 in conjunction with 27416)

27416   Osteochondral autograft(s), knee, open (eg, mosaicplasty) (includes harvesting of autograft[s])
→ *CPT Assistant* Jan 08:4; *CPT Changes: An Insider's View* 2008

(Do not report 27416 in conjunction with 27415, 29870, 29871, 29875, 29884 when performed at the same session and/or 29874, 29877, 29879, 29885-29887 when performed in the same compartment)

(For arthroscopic osteochondral autograft of knee, use 29866)

27418   Anterior tibial tubercleplasty (eg, Maquet type procedure)

27420   Reconstruction of dislocating patella; (eg, Hauser type procedure)

27422   with extensor realignment and/or muscle advancement or release (eg, Campbell, Goldwaite type procedure)

27424   with patellectomy

27425   Lateral retinacular release, open
→ *CPT Assistant* Nov 00:11; *CPT Changes: An Insider's View* 2002, 2003

(For arthroscopic lateral release, use 29873)

27427   Ligamentous reconstruction (augmentation), knee; extra-articular
→ *CPT Assistant* Nov 99:13; *CPT Changes: An Insider's View* 2000

27428   intra-articular (open)
→ *CPT Assistant* Nov 99:13, Apr 09:8; *CPT Changes: An Insider's View* 2000

27429   intra-articular (open) and extra-articular
→ *CPT Assistant* Nov 99:13, Apr 09:8; *CPT Changes: An Insider's View* 2000

(For primary repair of ligament(s) performed in conjunction with reconstruction, report 27405, 27407 or 27409 in conjunction with 27427, 27428 or 27429)

27430   Quadricepsplasty (eg, Bennett or Thompson type)

27435   Capsulotomy, posterior capsular release, knee
→ *CPT Assistant* Nov 98:8

27437   Arthroplasty, patella; without prosthesis

27438   with prosthesis

27440   Arthroplasty, knee, tibial plateau;

27441   with debridement and partial synovectomy

27442   Arthroplasty, femoral condyles or tibial plateau(s), knee;
→ *CPT Assistant* Nov 99:13

27443   with debridement and partial synovectomy

27445   Arthroplasty, knee, hinge prosthesis (eg, Walldius type)
→ *CPT Assistant* Nov 98:8

27446   Arthroplasty, knee, condyle and plateau; medial OR lateral compartment

27447   medial AND lateral compartments with or without patella resurfacing (total knee arthroplasty)
→ *CPT Assistant* Jan 07:1; *CPT Changes: An Insider's View* 2002

(For revision of total knee arthroplasty, use 27487)

(For removal of total knee prosthesis, use 27488)

27448   Osteotomy, femur, shaft or supracondylar; without fixation

(To report bilateral procedure, report 27448 with modifier 50)

27450   with fixation

(To report bilateral procedure, report 27450 with modifier 50)

27454   Osteotomy, multiple, with realignment on intramedullary rod, femoral shaft (eg, Sofield type procedure)
→ *CPT Assistant* Nov 98:8

27455   Osteotomy, proximal tibia, including fibular excision or osteotomy (includes correction of genu varus [bowleg] or genu valgus [knock-knee]); before epiphyseal closure

(To report bilateral procedure, report 27455 with modifier 50)

27457   after epiphyseal closure

(To report bilateral procedure, report 27457 with modifier 50)

27465   Osteoplasty, femur; shortening (excluding 64876)

27466   lengthening

27468   combined, lengthening and shortening with femoral segment transfer

27470   Repair, nonunion or malunion, femur, distal to head and neck; without graft (eg, compression technique)

27472   with iliac or other autogenous bone graft (includes obtaining graft)

27475   Arrest, epiphyseal, any method (eg, epiphysiodesis); distal femur
➔ *CPT Assistant* Nov 98:8

27477   tibia and fibula, proximal

27479   combined distal femur, proximal tibia and fibula

27485   Arrest, hemiepiphyseal, distal femur or proximal tibia or fibula (eg, genu varus or valgus)
➔ *CPT Assistant* Nov 98:8

27486   Revision of total knee arthroplasty, with or without allograft; 1 component

27487   femoral and entire tibial component
➔ *CPT Assistant* Nov 98:8

27488   Removal of prosthesis, including total knee prosthesis, methylmethacrylate with or without insertion of spacer, knee
➔ *CPT Assistant* Nov 98:8

27495   Prophylactic treatment (nailing, pinning, plating, or wiring) with or without methylmethacrylate, femur

27496   Decompression fasciotomy, thigh and/or knee, 1 compartment (flexor or extensor or adductor);

27497   with debridement of nonviable muscle and/or nerve

27498   Decompression fasciotomy, thigh and/or knee, multiple compartments;

27499   with debridement of nonviable muscle and/or nerve

Fracture and/or Dislocation

(For arthroscopic treatment of intercondylar spine[s] and tuberosity fracture[s] of the knee, see 29850, 29851)

(For arthroscopic treatment of tibial fracture, see 29855, 29856)

27500   Closed treatment of femoral shaft fracture, without manipulation

27501   Closed treatment of supracondylar or transcondylar femoral fracture with or without intercondylar extension, without manipulation

27502   Closed treatment of femoral shaft fracture, with manipulation, with or without skin or skeletal traction
➔ *CPT Assistant* Fall 93:22, Oct 99:5

27503   Closed treatment of supracondylar or transcondylar femoral fracture with or without intercondylar extension, with manipulation, with or without skin or skeletal traction

27506   Open treatment of femoral shaft fracture, with or without external fixation, with insertion of intramedullary implant, with or without cerclage and/or locking screws
➔ *CPT Assistant* Winter 92:10

27507   Open treatment of femoral shaft fracture with plate/screws, with or without cerclage

27508   Closed treatment of femoral fracture, distal end, medial or lateral condyle, without manipulation

27509   Percutaneous skeletal fixation of femoral fracture, distal end, medial or lateral condyle, or supracondylar or transcondylar, with or without intercondylar extension, or distal femoral epiphyseal separation

27510   Closed treatment of femoral fracture, distal end, medial or lateral condyle, with manipulation

27511   Open treatment of femoral supracondylar or transcondylar fracture without intercondylar extension, includes internal fixation, when performed
➔ *CPT Assistant* May 96:6; *CPT Changes: An Insider's View* 2008

27513   Open treatment of femoral supracondylar or transcondylar fracture with intercondylar extension, includes internal fixation, when performed
➔ *CPT Changes: An Insider's View* 2008

27514   Open treatment of femoral fracture, distal end, medial or lateral condyle, includes internal fixation, when performed
➔ *CPT Changes: An Insider's View* 2008

27516   Closed treatment of distal femoral epiphyseal separation; without manipulation

27517   with manipulation, with or without skin or skeletal traction

27519   Open treatment of distal femoral epiphyseal separation, includes internal fixation, when performed
➔ *CPT Changes: An Insider's View* 2008

27520   Closed treatment of patellar fracture, without manipulation

27524   Open treatment of patellar fracture, with internal fixation and/or partial or complete patellectomy and soft tissue repair

27530   Closed treatment of tibial fracture, proximal (plateau); without manipulation

27532   with or without manipulation, with skeletal traction

(For arthroscopic treatment, see 29855, 29856)

27535   Open treatment of tibial fracture, proximal (plateau); unicondylar, includes internal fixation, when performed
➔ *CPT Changes: An Insider's View* 2008

27536   bicondylar, with or without internal fixation

(For arthroscopic treatment, see 29855, 29856)

27538   Closed treatment of intercondylar spine(s) and/or tuberosity fracture(s) of knee, with or without manipulation

(For arthroscopic treatment, see 29850, 29851)

27540 Open treatment of intercondylar spine(s) and/or tuberosity fracture(s) of the knee, includes internal fixation, when performed
➔ *CPT Changes: An Insider's View* 2008

27550 Closed treatment of knee dislocation; without anesthesia

27552   requiring anesthesia

27556 Open treatment of knee dislocation, includes internal fixation, when performed; without primary ligamentous repair or augmentation/reconstruction
➔ *CPT Changes: An Insider's View* 2008

27557   with primary ligamentous repair
➔ *CPT Changes: An Insider's View* 2008

27558   with primary ligamentous repair, with augmentation/reconstruction
➔ *CPT Changes: An Insider's View* 2008

27560 Closed treatment of patellar dislocation; without anesthesia
➔ *CPT Assistant* Apr 02:15

(For recurrent dislocation, see 27420-27424)

27562   requiring anesthesia

27566 Open treatment of patellar dislocation, with or without partial or total patellectomy

Manipulation

27570 Manipulation of knee joint under general anesthesia (includes application of traction or other fixation devices)

Arthrodesis

27580 Arthrodesis, knee, any technique

Amputation

27590 Amputation, thigh, through femur, any level;

27591   immediate fitting technique including first cast

27592   open, circular (guillotine)

27594   secondary closure or scar revision

27596   re-amputation

27598 Disarticulation at knee

Other Procedures

27599 Unlisted procedure, femur or knee
➔ *CPT Assistant* Mar 08:14

Leg (Tibia and Fibula) and Ankle Joint

Incision

27600 Decompression fasciotomy, leg; anterior and/or lateral compartments only

27601   posterior compartment(s) only

27602   anterior and/or lateral, and posterior compartment(s)

(For incision and drainage procedures, superficial, see 10040-10160)

(For decompression fasciotomy with debridement, see 27892-27894)

27603 Incision and drainage, leg or ankle; deep abscess or hematoma

27604   infected bursa

27605 Tenotomy, percutaneous, Achilles tendon (separate procedure); local anesthesia

27606   general anesthesia

27607 Incision (eg, osteomyelitis or bone abscess), leg or ankle

27610 Arthrotomy, ankle, including exploration, drainage, or removal of foreign body
➔ *CPT Assistant* Nov 98:9

27612 Arthrotomy, posterior capsular release, ankle, with or without Achilles tendon lengthening
➔ *CPT Assistant* Nov 98:8

(See also 27685)

Excision

27613 Biopsy, soft tissue of leg or ankle area; superficial

27614   deep (subfascial or intramuscular)
➔ *CPT Assistant* Nov 98:8

(For needle biopsy of soft tissue, use 20206)

▲ **27615** Radical resection of tumor (eg, malignant neoplasm), soft tissue of leg or ankle area; less than 5 cm
➔ *CPT Changes: An Insider's View* 2010

● **27616**   5 cm or greater
➔ *CPT Changes: An Insider's View* 2010

▲ **27618** Excision, tumor, soft tissue of leg or ankle area, subcutaneous; less than 3 cm
➔ *CPT Changes: An Insider's View* 2010

#● **27632**   3 cm or greater
➔ *CPT Changes: An Insider's View* 2010

▲ **27619** Excision, tumor, soft tissue of leg or ankle area, subfascial (eg, intramuscular); less than 5 cm
➔ *CPT Changes: An Insider's View* 2010

#● **27634**   5 cm or greater
➔ *CPT Changes: An Insider's View* 2010

27620 Arthrotomy, ankle, with joint exploration, with or without biopsy, with or without removal of loose or foreign body

27625 Arthrotomy, with synovectomy, ankle;
➔ *CPT Assistant* Nov 98:8

27626   including tenosynovectomy

27630 Excision of lesion of tendon sheath or capsule (eg, cyst or ganglion), leg and/or ankle

27632   ►Code is out of numerical sequence. See 27613-27647◄

27634   ►Code is out of numerical sequence. See 27613-27647◄

27635   Excision or curettage of bone cyst or benign tumor, tibia or fibula;

27637   with autograft (includes obtaining graft)

27638   with allograft

▲ **27640**   Partial excision (craterization, saucerization, or diaphysectomy), bone (eg, osteomyelitis); tibia
➜ *CPT Changes: An Insider's View* 2010

►(For exostosis excision, use 27635)◄

▲ **27641**   fibula
➜ *CPT Changes: An Insider's View* 2010

►(For exostosis excision, use 27635)◄

▲ **27645**   Radical resection of tumor; tibia
➜ *CPT Changes: An Insider's View* 2010

▲ **27646**   fibula
➜ *CPT Changes: An Insider's View* 2010

▲ **27647**   talus or calcaneus
➜ *CPT Changes: An Insider's View* 2010

Introduction or Removal

27648   Injection procedure for ankle arthrography

(For radiological supervision and interpretation, use 73615. Do not report 77002 in conjunction with 73615)

(For ankle arthroscopy, see 29894-29898)

Repair, Revision, and/or Reconstruction

27650   Repair, primary, open or percutaneous, ruptured Achilles tendon;

27652   with graft (includes obtaining graft)

27654   Repair, secondary, Achilles tendon, with or without graft

27656   Repair, fascial defect of leg

27658   Repair, flexor tendon, leg; primary, without graft, each tendon
➜ *CPT Assistant* Nov 98:8

27659   secondary, with or without graft, each tendon

27664   Repair, extensor tendon, leg; primary, without graft, each tendon
➜ *CPT Assistant* Nov 98:8

27665   secondary, with or without graft, each tendon
➜ *CPT Assistant* Nov 98:8

27675   Repair, dislocating peroneal tendons; without fibular osteotomy

27676   with fibular osteotomy

27680   Tenolysis, flexor or extensor tendon, leg and/or ankle; single, each tendon
➜ *CPT Assistant* Nov 98:8

27681   multiple tendons (through separate incision(s))
➜ *CPT Assistant* Nov 98:8

27685   Lengthening or shortening of tendon, leg or ankle; single tendon (separate procedure)
➜ *CPT Assistant* Nov 98:8

27686   multiple tendons (through same incision), each
➜ *CPT Assistant* Nov 98:8

27687   Gastrocnemius recession (eg, Strayer procedure)

(Toe extensors are considered as a group to be a single tendon when transplanted into midfoot)

27690   Transfer or transplant of single tendon (with muscle redirection or rerouting); superficial (eg, anterior tibial extensors into midfoot)

27691   deep (eg, anterior tibial or posterior tibial through interosseous space, flexor digitorum longus, flexor hallucis longus, or peroneal tendon to midfoot or hindfoot)

+ **27692**   each additional tendon (List separately in addition to code for primary procedure)

(Use 27692 in conjunction with 27690, 27691)

27695   Repair, primary, disrupted ligament, ankle; collateral

27696   both collateral ligaments

27698   Repair, secondary, disrupted ligament, ankle, collateral (eg, Watson-Jones procedure)

27700   Arthroplasty, ankle;

27702   with implant (total ankle)

27703   revision, total ankle

27704   Removal of ankle implant

27705   Osteotomy; tibia

27707   fibula

27709   tibia and fibula

27712   multiple, with realignment on intramedullary rod (eg, Sofield type procedure)

(For osteotomy to correct genu varus [bowleg] or genu valgus [knock-knee], see 27455-27457)

27715   Osteoplasty, tibia and fibula, lengthening or shortening

27720   Repair of nonunion or malunion, tibia; without graft, (eg, compression technique)

27722   with sliding graft

27724   with iliac or other autograft (includes obtaining graft)

27725   by synostosis, with fibula, any method

27726   Repair of fibula nonunion and/or malunion with internal fixation
→ *CPT Assistant* Jan 08:4, Apr 09:9; *CPT Changes: An Insider's View* 2008

(Do not report 27726 in conjunction with 27707)

27727   Repair of congenital pseudarthrosis, tibia

27730   Arrest, epiphyseal (epiphysiodesis), open; distal tibia
→ *CPT Assistant* Nov 98:8; *CPT Changes: An Insider's View* 2003

27732   distal fibula

27734   distal tibia and fibula

27740   Arrest, epiphyseal (epiphysiodesis), any method, combined, proximal and distal tibia and fibula;
→ *CPT Assistant* Nov 98:8

27742   and distal femur

(For epiphyseal arrest of proximal tibia and fibula, use 27477)

27745   Prophylactic treatment (nailing, pinning, plating or wiring) with or without methylmethacrylate, tibia

Fracture and/or Dislocation

27750   Closed treatment of tibial shaft fracture (with or without fibular fracture); without manipulation
→ *CPT Assistant* Winter 92:10, Fall 93:21, Mar 96:10

27752   with manipulation, with or without skeletal traction
→ *CPT Assistant* Winter 92:10, Fall 93:21, Feb 96:3, Mar 96:10

27756   Percutaneous skeletal fixation of tibial shaft fracture (with or without fibular fracture) (eg, pins or screws)
→ *CPT Assistant* Winter 92:10

27758   Open treatment of tibial shaft fracture (with or without fibular fracture), with plate/screws, with or without cerclage
→ *CPT Assistant* Winter 92:10, Mar 00:11

27759   Treatment of tibial shaft fracture (with or without fibular fracture) by intramedullary implant, with or without interlocking screws and/or cerclage
→ *CPT Assistant* Winter 92:10; *CPT Changes: An Insider's View* 2003

27760   Closed treatment of medial malleolus fracture; without manipulation

27762   with manipulation, with or without skin or skeletal traction

27766   Open treatment of medial malleolus fracture, includes internal fixation, when performed
→ *CPT Changes: An Insider's View* 2008

27767   Closed treatment of posterior malleolus fracture; without manipulation
→ *CPT Changes: An Insider's View* 2008

27768   with manipulation
→ *CPT Changes: An Insider's View* 2008

27769   Open treatment of posterior malleolus fracture, includes internal fixation, when performed
→ *CPT Changes: An Insider's View* 2008

(Do not report 27767-27769 in conjunction with 27808-27823)

27780   Closed treatment of proximal fibula or shaft fracture; without manipulation
→ *CPT Assistant* Winter 92:11

27781   with manipulation

27784   Open treatment of proximal fibula or shaft fracture, includes internal fixation, when performed
→ *CPT Assistant* Mar 00:11; *CPT Changes: An Insider's View* 2008

27786   Closed treatment of distal fibular fracture (lateral malleolus); without manipulation

27788   with manipulation

27792   Open treatment of distal fibular fracture (lateral malleolus), includes internal fixation, when performed
→ *CPT Changes: An Insider's View* 2008

(For treatment of tibia and fibula shaft fractures, see 27750-27759)

27808   Closed treatment of bimalleolar ankle fracture (eg, lateral and medial malleoli, or lateral and posterior malleoli or medial and posterior malleoli); without manipulation
→ *CPT Changes: An Insider's View* 2008

27810   with manipulation
→ *CPT Changes: An Insider's View* 2008

27814   Open treatment of bimalleolar ankle fracture (eg, lateral and medial malleoli, or lateral and posterior malleoli, or medial and posterior malleoli), includes internal fixation, when performed
→ *CPT Changes: An Insider's View* 2008

27816   Closed treatment of trimalleolar ankle fracture; without manipulation

27818   with manipulation

27822   Open treatment of trimalleolar ankle fracture, includes internal fixation, when performed, medial and/or lateral malleolus; without fixation of posterior lip
→ *CPT Changes: An Insider's View* 2008

27823   with fixation of posterior lip
→ *CPT Changes: An Insider's View* 2008

27824   Closed treatment of fracture of weight bearing articular portion of distal tibia (eg, pilon or tibial plafond), with or without anesthesia; without manipulation

27825   with skeletal traction and/or requiring manipulation

27826   Open treatment of fracture of weight bearing articular surface/portion of distal tibia (eg, pilon or tibial plafond), with internal fixation, when performed; of fibula only
→ *CPT Changes: An Insider's View* 2008

27827   of tibia only
→ *CPT Changes: An Insider's View* 2008

27828   of both tibia and fibula

> *CPT Changes: An Insider's View* 2008

27829   Open treatment of distal tibiofibular joint (syndesmosis) disruption, includes internal fixation, when performed

> *CPT Assistant* Winter 92:11, Mar 09:10; *CPT Changes: An Insider's View* 2008

27830   Closed treatment of proximal tibiofibular joint dislocation; without anesthesia

27831   requiring anesthesia

27832   Open treatment of proximal tibiofibular joint dislocation, includes internal fixation, when performed, or with excision of proximal fibula

> *CPT Changes: An Insider's View* 2008

27840   Closed treatment of ankle dislocation; without anesthesia

27842   requiring anesthesia, with or without percutaneous skeletal fixation

27846   Open treatment of ankle dislocation, with or without percutaneous skeletal fixation; without repair or internal fixation

27848   with repair or internal or external fixation

(For surgical or diagnostic arthroscopic procedures, see 29894-29898)

Manipulation

27860   Manipulation of ankle under general anesthesia (includes application of traction or other fixation apparatus)

Arthrodesis

27870   Arthrodesis, ankle, open

> *CPT Changes: An Insider's View* 2003

(For arthroscopic ankle arthrodesis, use 29899)

27871   Arthrodesis, tibiofibular joint, proximal or distal

Amputation

27880   Amputation, leg, through tibia and fibula;

27881   with immediate fitting technique including application of first cast

27882   open, circular (guillotine)

27884   secondary closure or scar revision

27886   re-amputation

27888   Amputation, ankle, through malleoli of tibia and fibula (eg, Syme, Pirogoff type procedures), with plastic closure and resection of nerves

27889   Ankle disarticulation

Other Procedures

27892   Decompression fasciotomy, leg; anterior and/or lateral compartments only, with debridement of nonviable muscle and/or nerve

(For decompression fasciotomy of the leg without debridement, use 27600)

27893   posterior compartment(s) only, with debridement of nonviable muscle and/or nerve

(For decompression fasciotomy of the leg without debridement, use 27601)

27894   anterior and/or lateral, and posterior compartment(s), with debridement of nonviable muscle and/or nerve

(For decompression fasciotomy of the leg without debridement, use 27602)

27899   Unlisted procedure, leg or ankle

> *CPT Assistant* Aug 00:11

Foot and Toes

Incision

(For incision and drainage procedures, superficial, see 10040-10160)

28001   Incision and drainage, bursa, foot

> *CPT Assistant* Nov 98:9

28002   Incision and drainage below fascia, with or without tendon sheath involvement, foot; single bursal space

> *CPT Assistant* Nov 98:8

28003   multiple areas

> *CPT Assistant* Nov 98:9

28005   Incision, bone cortex (eg, osteomyelitis or bone abscess), foot

> *CPT Assistant* Nov 98:9

28008   Fasciotomy, foot and/or toe

(See also 28060, 28062, 28250)

28010   Tenotomy, percutaneous, toe; single tendon

> *CPT Assistant* Nov 98:8

28011   multiple tendons

> *CPT Assistant* Nov 98:8

(For open tenotomy, see 28230-28234)

28020   Arthrotomy, including exploration, drainage, or removal of loose or foreign body; intertarsal or tarsometatarsal joint

28022   metatarsophalangeal joint

28024   interphalangeal joint

28035   Release, tarsal tunnel (posterior tibial nerve decompression)

> *CPT Assistant* Nov 98:8

(For other nerve entrapments, see 64704, 64722)

Excision

28039 ▶Code is out of numerical sequence. See 28043-28175◀

28041 ▶Code is out of numerical sequence. See 28043-28175◀

▲ **28043** Excision, tumor, soft tissue of foot or toe, subcutaneous; less than 1.5 cm
➡ *CPT Changes: An Insider's View* 2010

\# ● **28039**   1.5 cm or greater
➡ *CPT Changes: An Insider's View* 2010

▲ **28045** Excision, tumor, soft tissue of foot or toe, subfascial (eg, intramuscular); less than 1.5 cm
➡ *CPT Changes: An Insider's View* 2010

\# ● **28041**   1.5 cm or greater
➡ *CPT Changes: An Insider's View* 2010

▲ **28046** Radical resection of tumor (eg, malignant neoplasm), soft tissue of foot or toe; less than 3 cm
➡ *CPT Changes: An Insider's View* 2010

● **28047**   3 cm or greater
➡ *CPT Changes: An Insider's View* 2010

28050 Arthrotomy with biopsy; intertarsal or tarsometatarsal joint

28052   metatarsophalangeal joint

28054   interphalangeal joint

28055 Neurectomy, intrinsic musculature of foot
➡ *CPT Changes: An Insider's View* 2007

28060 Fasciectomy, plantar fascia; partial (separate procedure)
➡ *CPT Assistant* Mar 08:14

28062   radical (separate procedure)

(For plantar fasciotomy, see 28008, 28250)

28070 Synovectomy; intertarsal or tarsometatarsal joint, each

28072   metatarsophalangeal joint, each

28080 Excision, interdigital (Morton) neuroma, single, each

28086 Synovectomy, tendon sheath, foot; flexor

28088   extensor

28090 Excision of lesion, tendon, tendon sheath, or capsule (including synovectomy) (eg, cyst or ganglion); foot
➡ *CPT Assistant* Nov 98:8

28092   toe(s), each

28100 Excision or curettage of bone cyst or benign tumor, talus or calcaneus;

28102   with iliac or other autograft (includes obtaining graft)

28103   with allograft

28104 Excision or curettage of bone cyst or benign tumor, tarsal or metatarsal, except talus or calcaneus;
➡ *CPT Changes: An Insider's View* 2002

28106   with iliac or other autograft (includes obtaining graft)

28107   with allograft

28108 Excision or curettage of bone cyst or benign tumor, phalanges of foot

(For ostectomy, partial (eg, hallux valgus, Silver type procedure), use 28290)

28110 Ostectomy, partial excision, fifth metatarsal head (bunionette) (separate procedure)
➡ *CPT Assistant* Oct 98:10, Sep 00:9

28111 Ostectomy, complete excision; first metatarsal head

28112   other metatarsal head (second, third or fourth)

28113   fifth metatarsal head

28114   all metatarsal heads, with partial proximal phalangectomy, excluding first metatarsal (eg, Clayton type procedure)

28116 Ostectomy, excision of tarsal coalition

28118 Ostectomy, calcaneus;

28119   for spur, with or without plantar fascial release

28120 Partial excision (craterization, saucerization, sequestrectomy, or diaphysectomy) bone (eg, osteomyelitis or bossing); talus or calcaneus

28122   tarsal or metatarsal bone, except talus or calcaneus
➡ *CPT Assistant* Nov 98:11

(For partial excision of talus or calcaneus, use 28120)

(For cheilectomy for hallux rigidus, use 28289)

28124   phalanx of toe

28126 Resection, partial or complete, phalangeal base, each toe
➡ *CPT Assistant* Nov 98:8

28130 Talectomy (astragalectomy)

(For calcanectomy, use 28118)

28140 Metatarsectomy

28150 Phalangectomy, toe, each toe
➡ *CPT Assistant* Nov 98:8

28153 Resection, condyle(s), distal end of phalanx, each toe
➡ *CPT Assistant* Nov 98:8

28160 Hemiphalangectomy or interphalangeal joint excision, toe, proximal end of phalanx, each
➡ *CPT Assistant* Nov 98:8

▲ **28171** Radical resection of tumor; tarsal (except talus or calcaneus)
➡ *CPT Changes: An Insider's View* 2010

▲ **28173**   metatarsal
➡ *CPT Changes: An Insider's View* 2010

▲ **28175**   phalanx of toe
➡ *CPT Changes: An Insider's View* 2010

(For talus or calcaneus, use 27647)

Introduction or Removal

28190   Removal of foreign body, foot; subcutaneous

28192   deep

28193   complicated

Repair, Revision, and/or Reconstruction

28200   Repair, tendon, flexor, foot; primary or secondary, without free graft, each tendon
      ➔ *CPT Assistant* Nov 98:8

28202   secondary with free graft, each tendon (includes obtaining graft)

28208   Repair, tendon, extensor, foot; primary or secondary, each tendon
      ➔ *CPT Assistant* Nov 98:8

28210   secondary with free graft, each tendon (includes obtaining graft)

28220   Tenolysis, flexor, foot; single tendon
      ➔ *CPT Assistant* Nov 98:8

28222   multiple tendons
      ➔ *CPT Assistant* Nov 98:8

28225   Tenolysis, extensor, foot; single tendon
      ➔ *CPT Assistant* Nov 98:8

28226   multiple tendons
      ➔ *CPT Assistant* Nov 98:8

28230   Tenotomy, open, tendon flexor; foot, single or multiple tendon(s) (separate procedure)
      ➔ *CPT Assistant* Nov 98:8

28232   toe, single tendon (separate procedure)
      ➔ *CPT Assistant* Nov 98:8

28234   Tenotomy, open, extensor, foot or toe, each tendon
      ➔ *CPT Assistant* Nov 98:8

    (For tendon transfer to midfoot or hindfoot, see 27690, 27691)

28238   Reconstruction (advancement), posterior tibial tendon with excision of accessory tarsal navicular bone (eg, Kidner type procedure)
      ➔ *CPT Changes: An Insider's View* 2002

    (For subcutaneous tenotomy, see 28010, 28011)

    (For transfer or transplant of tendon with muscle redirection or rerouting, see 27690-27692)

    (For extensor hallucis longus transfer with great toe IP fusion (Jones procedure), use 28760)

28240   Tenotomy, lengthening, or release, abductor hallucis muscle

28250   Division of plantar fascia and muscle (eg, Steindler stripping) (separate procedure)

28260   Capsulotomy, midfoot; medial release only (separate procedure)

28261   with tendon lengthening

28262   extensive, including posterior talotibial capsulotomy and tendon(s) lengthening (eg, resistant clubfoot deformity)

28264   Capsulotomy, midtarsal (eg, Heyman type procedure)

28270   Capsulotomy; metatarsophalangeal joint, with or without tenorrhaphy, each joint (separate procedure)

28272   interphalangeal joint, each joint (separate procedure)
      ➔ *CPT Assistant* Dec 02:11

28280   Syndactylization, toes (eg, webbing or Kelikian type procedure)
      ➔ *CPT Assistant* Nov 98:8

28285   Correction, hammertoe (eg, interphalangeal fusion, partial or total phalangectomy)
      ➔ *CPT Assistant* Nov 98:8, May 06:18

28286   Correction, cock-up fifth toe, with plastic skin closure (eg, Ruiz-Mora type procedure)
      ➔ *CPT Assistant* Nov 98:8

28288   Ostectomy, partial, exostectomy or condylectomy, metatarsal head, each metatarsal head

28289   Hallux rigidus correction with cheilectomy, debridement and capsular release of the first metatarsophalangeal joint
      ➔ *CPT Assistant* Nov 98:11

28290   Correction, hallux valgus (bunion), with or without sesamoidectomy; simple exostectomy (eg, Silver type procedure)
      ➔ *CPT Assistant* Dec 96:5, Nov 98:8, Jan 07:31

Hallux Valgus Correction
28290

Simple resection of the medial eminence (Silver-type procedure)

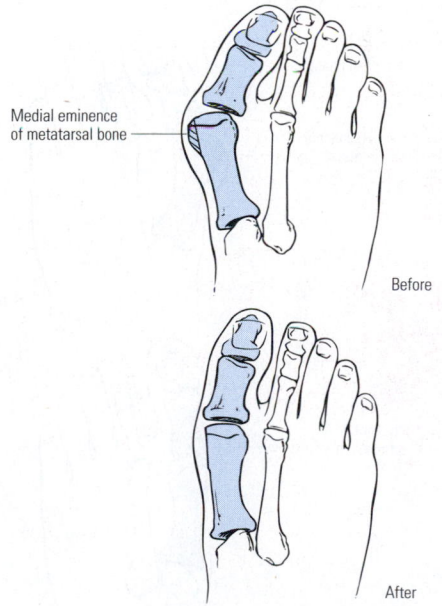

Medial eminence of metatarsal bone

Before

After

28292   Keller, McBride, or Mayo type procedure
➔ *CPT Assistant* Dec 96:5, Sep 00:9, Jan 07:31

Keller-Type Procedure
28292

Simple resection of the base of the proximal phalanx is accompanied by removal of the medial eminence. A hemi implant is optional.

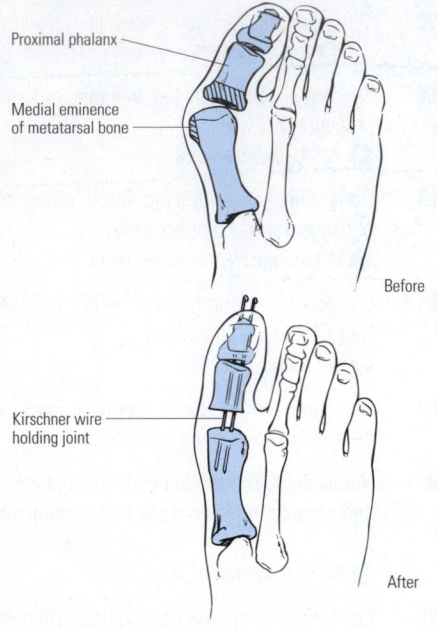

Proximal phalanx

Medial eminence
of metatarsal bone

Before

Kirschner wire
holding joint

After

28293   resection of joint with implant
➔ *CPT Assistant* Dec 96:6, Jan 07:31

Keller-Mayo Procedure With Implant
28293

A total double stem implant is usually used.

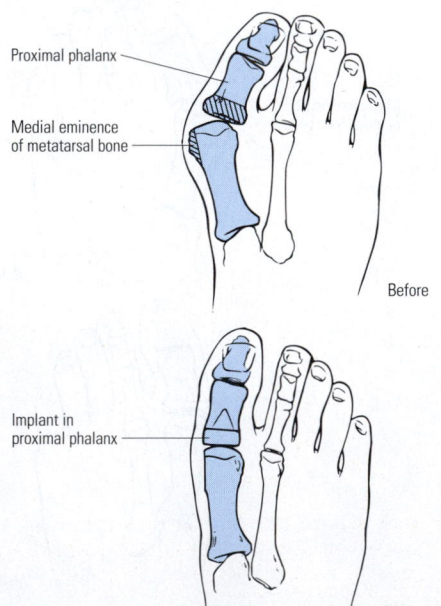

Proximal phalanx

Medial eminence
of metatarsal bone

Before

Implant in
proximal phalanx

After

28294   with tendon transplants (eg, Joplin type procedure)
➔ *CPT Assistant* Dec 96:6, Jan 07:31

Joplin Procedure
28294

A tendon transplant is an important part of the procedure.

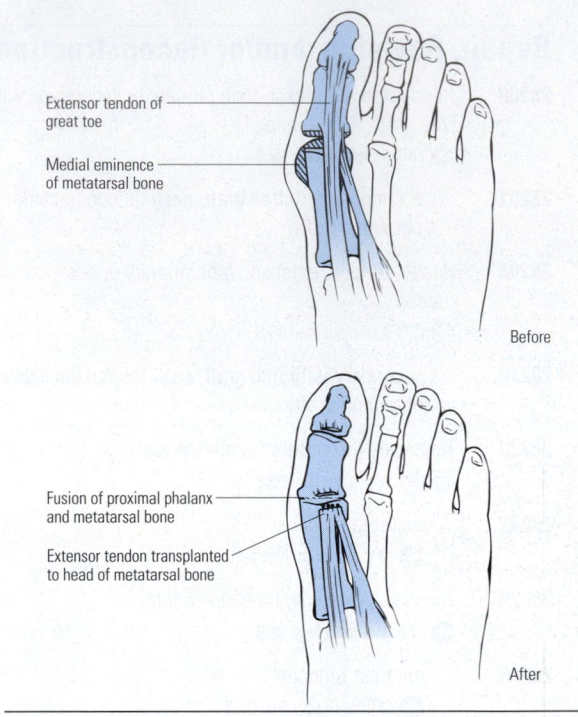

Extensor tendon of
great toe

Medial eminence
of metatarsal bone

Before

Fusion of proximal phalanx
and metatarsal bone

Extensor tendon transplanted
to head of metatarsal bone

After

28296   with metatarsal osteotomy (eg, Mitchell, Chevron, or
concentric type procedures)
➔ *CPT Assistant* Dec 96:6, Jan 97:10, Jan 07:31

Mitchell Procedure
28296

A complex, biplanar, double step-cut osteotomy through the neck of the first metatarsal is also known as the Mitchell Chevron (Austin) procedure.

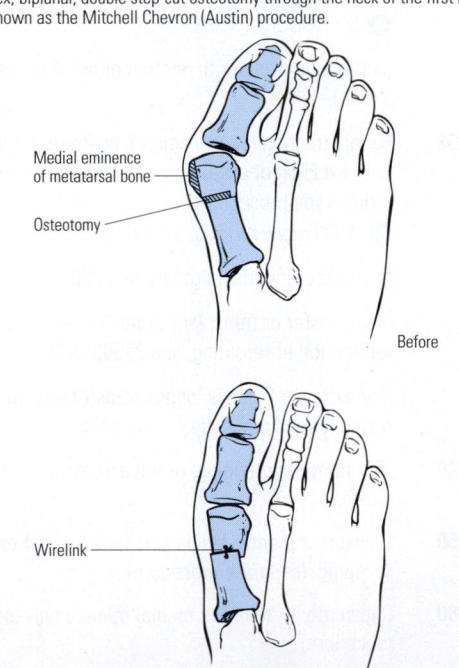

Medial eminence
of metatarsal bone

Osteotomy

Before

Wirelink

After

28297   Lapidus-type procedure
➔ *CPT Assistant* Dec 96:6, Jan 07:31

Lapidus-Type Procedure
28297

A metatarsocuneiform fusion of bones and a distal bunion repair to correct valgus deformity

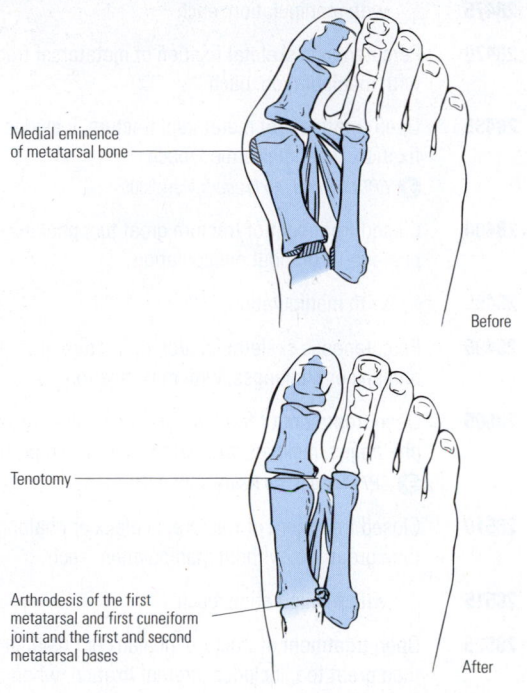

Medial eminence of metatarsal bone

Before

Tenotomy

Arthrodesis of the first metatarsal and first cuneiform joint and the first and second metatarsal bases

After

28298   by phalanx osteotomy
➔ *CPT Assistant* Dec 96:7, Jan 07:31

Phalanx Osteotomy
28298

The Akin procedure involves removal of a bony wedge from the base of the proximal phalanx to reorient the axis.

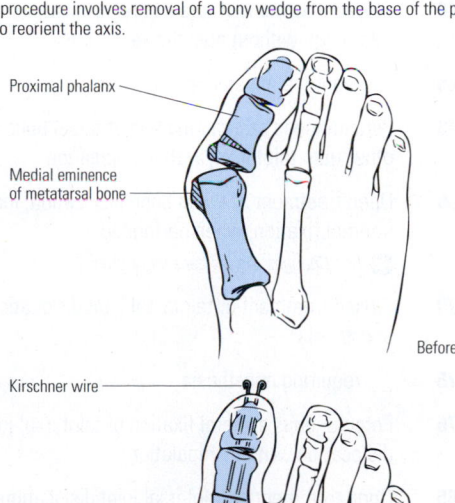

Proximal phalanx

Medial eminence of metatarsal bone

Before

Kirschner wire

After

28299   by double osteotomy
➔ *CPT Assistant* Dec 96:7, Jan 07:31; *CPT Changes: An Insider's View* 2002

Double Osteotomy
28299

A. This technique depicts a medial resection of the first metatarsal, osteotomy of the distal first metatarsal with correction of the hallux valgus, followed by an osteotomy of the proximal phalanx to correct additional angular deformity, with placement of appropriate internal fixation (eg, wire[s], pin[s], screw[s]).

PREOP

Angular deformity of proximal phalanx

Medial eminence of metatarsal bone

POSTOP

Osteotomy proximal phalanx

Osteotomy distal first metatarsal

Note: Internal fixation is not depicted, but would include screw(s), pin(s), wire(s), as needed.

B. This technique depicts hallux valgus correction (without the medial resection of the base of the proximal phalanx) with double osteotomy of the first metatarsal and placement of appropriate internal fixation (eg, wire[s], pin[s], screw[s]).

PREOP

Medial eminence of metatarsal bone

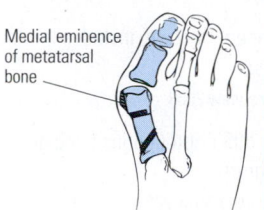

POSTOP

Double osteotomy of the metatarsal with internal fixation (eg, wire[s], pin[s], screw[s])

Note: Internal fixation depicted is for illustrative purpose only and does not suggest to limit choice of fixation options required.

28300   Osteotomy; calcaneus (eg, Dwyer or Chambers type procedure), with or without internal fixation

28302   talus

28304   Osteotomy, tarsal bones, other than calcaneus or talus;
➔ *CPT Assistant* Nov 98:8

28305   with autograft (includes obtaining graft) (eg, Fowler type)

28306   Osteotomy, with or without lengthening, shortening or angular correction, metatarsal; first metatarsal
➔ *CPT Assistant* Nov 98:8, Dec 99:7

28307   first metatarsal with autograft (other than first toe)
➔ *CPT Assistant* Nov 98:9

28308   other than first metatarsal, each

28309   multiple (eg, Swanson type cavus foot procedure)
➔ *CPT Assistant* Nov 98:8, Dec 99:7

28310   Osteotomy, shortening, angular or rotational correction; proximal phalanx, first toe (separate procedure)

28312   other phalanges, any toe

28313   Reconstruction, angular deformity of toe, soft tissue procedures only (eg, overlapping second toe, fifth toe, curly toes)
➲ *CPT Assistant* Nov 98:8

28315   Sesamoidectomy, first toe (separate procedure)

28320   Repair, nonunion or malunion; tarsal bones
➲ *CPT Assistant* Nov 98:9

28322   metatarsal, with or without bone graft (includes obtaining graft)

28340   Reconstruction, toe, macrodactyly; soft tissue resection

28341   requiring bone resection

28344   Reconstruction, toe(s); polydactyly

28345   syndactyly, with or without skin graft(s), each web

28360   Reconstruction, cleft foot

Fracture and/or Dislocation

28400   Closed treatment of calcaneal fracture; without manipulation

28405   with manipulation

28406   Percutaneous skeletal fixation of calcaneal fracture, with manipulation

28415   Open treatment of calcaneal fracture, includes internal fixation, when performed;
➲ *CPT Changes: An Insider's View* 2008

28420   with primary iliac or other autogenous bone graft (includes obtaining graft)
➲ *CPT Changes: An Insider's View* 2008

28430   Closed treatment of talus fracture; without manipulation

28435   with manipulation

28436   Percutaneous skeletal fixation of talus fracture, with manipulation

28445   Open treatment of talus fracture, includes internal fixation, when performed
➲ *CPT Changes: An Insider's View* 2008

28446   Open osteochondral autograft, talus (includes obtaining graft[s])
➲ *CPT Assistant* Jan 08:4, Dec 08:6; *CPT Changes: An Insider's View* 2008

(Do not report 28446 in conjunction with 27705, 27707)

(For arthroscopic osteochondral talus graft, use 29892)

(For open osteochondral allograft or repairs with industrial grafts, use 28899)

28450   Treatment of tarsal bone fracture (except talus and calcaneus); without manipulation, each
➲ *CPT Assistant* Dec 01:7

28455   with manipulation, each

28456   Percutaneous skeletal fixation of tarsal bone fracture (except talus and calcaneus), with manipulation, each

28465   Open treatment of tarsal bone fracture (except talus and calcaneus), includes internal fixation, when performed, each
➲ *CPT Changes: An Insider's View* 2008

28470   Closed treatment of metatarsal fracture; without manipulation, each

28475   with manipulation, each

28476   Percutaneous skeletal fixation of metatarsal fracture, with manipulation, each

28485   Open treatment of metatarsal fracture, includes internal fixation, when performed, each
➲ *CPT Changes: An Insider's View* 2008

28490   Closed treatment of fracture great toe, phalanx or phalanges; without manipulation

28495   with manipulation

28496   Percutaneous skeletal fixation of fracture great toe, phalanx or phalanges, with manipulation

28505   Open treatment of fracture, great toe, phalanx or phalanges, includes internal fixation, when performed
➲ *CPT Changes: An Insider's View* 2008

28510   Closed treatment of fracture, phalanx or phalanges, other than great toe; without manipulation, each

28515   with manipulation, each

28525   Open treatment of fracture, phalanx or phalanges, other than great toe, includes internal fixation, when performed, each
➲ *CPT Changes: An Insider's View* 2008

28530   Closed treatment of sesamoid fracture

28531   Open treatment of sesamoid fracture, with or without internal fixation

28540   Closed treatment of tarsal bone dislocation, other than talotarsal; without anesthesia

28545   requiring anesthesia

28546   Percutaneous skeletal fixation of tarsal bone dislocation, other than talotarsal, with manipulation

28555   Open treatment of tarsal bone dislocation, includes internal fixation, when performed
➲ *CPT Changes: An Insider's View* 2008

28570   Closed treatment of talotarsal joint dislocation; without anesthesia

28575   requiring anesthesia

28576   Percutaneous skeletal fixation of talotarsal joint dislocation, with manipulation

28585   Open treatment of talotarsal joint dislocation, includes internal fixation, when performed
➲ *CPT Changes: An Insider's View* 2008

28600   Closed treatment of tarsometatarsal joint dislocation; without anesthesia

28605   requiring anesthesia

 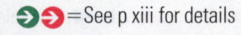

28606 Percutaneous skeletal fixation of tarsometatarsal joint dislocation, with manipulation

28615 Open treatment of tarsometatarsal joint dislocation, includes internal fixation, when performed
> *CPT Changes: An Insider's View* 2008

28630 Closed treatment of metatarsophalangeal joint dislocation; without anesthesia

28635 requiring anesthesia

28636 Percutaneous skeletal fixation of metatarsophalangeal joint dislocation, with manipulation

28645 Open treatment of metatarsophalangeal joint dislocation, includes internal fixation, when performed
> *CPT Changes: An Insider's View* 2008

28660 Closed treatment of interphalangeal joint dislocation; without anesthesia

28665 requiring anesthesia

28666 Percutaneous skeletal fixation of interphalangeal joint dislocation, with manipulation

28675 Open treatment of interphalangeal joint dislocation, includes internal fixation, when performed
> *CPT Changes: An Insider's View* 2008

Arthrodesis

28705 Arthrodesis; pantalar

28715 triple

28725 subtalar

28730 Arthrodesis, midtarsal or tarsometatarsal, multiple or transverse;

28735 with osteotomy (eg, flatfoot correction)

28737 Arthrodesis, with tendon lengthening and advancement, midtarsal, tarsal navicular-cuneiform (eg, Miller type procedure)
> *CPT Changes: An Insider's View* 2002

28740 Arthrodesis, midtarsal or tarsometatarsal, single joint

28750 Arthrodesis, great toe; metatarsophalangeal joint
> *CPT Assistant* Dec 96:7

28755 interphalangeal joint

28760 Arthrodesis, with extensor hallucis longus transfer to first metatarsal neck, great toe, interphalangeal joint (eg, Jones type procedure)
> *CPT Assistant* Nov 98:8

(For hammertoe operation or interphalangeal fusion, use 28285)

Amputation

28800 Amputation, foot; midtarsal (eg, Chopart type procedure)

28805 transmetatarsal
> *CPT Assistant* May 97:8

28810 Amputation, metatarsal, with toe, single

28820 Amputation, toe; metatarsophalangeal joint
> *CPT Assistant* May 97:8

28825 interphalangeal joint

(For amputation of tuft of distal phalanx, use 11752)

Other Procedures

28890 Extracorporeal shock wave, high energy, performed by a physician, requiring anesthesia other than local, including ultrasound guidance, involving the plantar fascia
> *CPT Assistant* Dec 05:10, Mar 06:1; *CPT Changes: An Insider's View* 2006

(For extracorporeal shock wave therapy involving musculoskeletal system not otherwise specified, see Category III codes 0019T, 0101T, 0102T)

28899 Unlisted procedure, foot or toes

Application of Casts and Strapping

The listed procedures apply when the cast application or strapping is a replacement procedure used during or after the period of follow-up care, or when the cast application or strapping is an initial service performed without a restorative treatment or procedure(s) to stabilize or protect a fracture, injury, or dislocation and/or to afford comfort to a patient. Restorative treatment or procedure(s) rendered by another physician following the application of the initial cast/splint/strap may be reported with a treatment of fracture and/or dislocation code.

A physician who applies the initial cast, strap or splint and also assumes all of the subsequent fracture, dislocation, or injury care cannot use the application of casts and strapping codes as an initial service, since the first cast/splint or strap application is included in the treatment of fracture and/or dislocation codes. (See notes under Musculoskeletal System, page 75.) A temporary cast/splint/strap is not considered to be part of the preoperative care, and the use of the modifier 56 is not applicable. Additional evaluation and management services are reportable only if significant identifiable further services are provided at the time of the cast application or strapping.

If cast application or strapping is provided as an initial service (eg, casting of a sprained ankle or knee) in which no other procedure or treatment (eg, surgical repair, reduction of a fracture, or joint dislocation) is performed or is expected to be performed by a physician rendering the initial care only, use the casting, strapping and/or supply code (99070) in addition to an evaluation and management code as appropriate.

Listed procedures include removal of cast or strapping.

(For orthotics management and training, see 97760-97762)

Body and Upper Extremity

Casts

29000   Application of halo type body cast (see 20661-20663 for insertion)
➜ *CPT Assistant* Feb 96:3, 5, Apr 02:13

29010   Application of Risser jacket, localizer, body; only
➜ *CPT Assistant* Feb 96:3, Apr 02:13

29015   including head
➜ *CPT Assistant* Feb 96:3, Apr 02:13

29020   Application of turnbuckle jacket, body; only
➜ *CPT Assistant* Feb 96:3, Apr 02:13

29025   including head
➜ *CPT Assistant* Feb 96:3, Apr 02:13

29035   Application of body cast, shoulder to hips;
➜ *CPT Assistant* Feb 96:3, Apr 02:13

29040   including head, Minerva type
➜ *CPT Assistant* Feb 96:3, Apr 02:13

29044   including 1 thigh
➜ *CPT Assistant* Feb 96:3, Apr 02:13

29046   including both thighs
➜ *CPT Assistant* Feb 96:3, Apr 02:13

29049   Application, cast; figure-of-eight
➜ *CPT Assistant* Feb 96:3, Apr 02:13; *CPT Changes: An Insider's View* 2002

29055   shoulder spica
➜ *CPT Assistant* Feb 96:3, Apr 02:13

29058   plaster Velpeau
➜ *CPT Assistant* Feb 96:3, Apr 02:13

29065   shoulder to hand (long arm)
➜ *CPT Assistant* Feb 96:3, Apr 02:13

29075   elbow to finger (short arm)
➜ *CPT Assistant* Feb 96:3-4, Apr 02:13

29085   hand and lower forearm (gauntlet)
➜ *CPT Assistant* Feb 96:3, Apr 02:13, Dec 02:11

29086   finger (eg, contracture)
➜ *CPT Assistant* Apr 02:13; *CPT Changes: An Insider's View* 2002

Splints

29105   Application of long arm splint (shoulder to hand)
➜ *CPT Assistant* Feb 96:3, Apr 02:13

29125   Application of short arm splint (forearm to hand); static
➜ *CPT Assistant* Feb 96:3-4, Apr 02:13

29126   dynamic
➜ *CPT Assistant* Feb 96:3, Apr 02:13

29130   Application of finger splint; static
➜ *CPT Assistant* Feb 96:3, Apr 02:13

29131   dynamic
➜ *CPT Assistant* Feb 96:3, Apr 02:13

Strapping—Any Age

29200   Strapping; thorax
➜ *CPT Assistant* Feb 96:3, Apr 02:13

▶(29220 has been deleted)◀

▶(To report low back strapping, use 29799)◀

29240   shoulder (eg, Velpeau)
➜ *CPT Assistant* Feb 96:3, Apr 02:13

29260   elbow or wrist
➜ *CPT Assistant* Feb 96:3, Apr 02:13

29280   hand or finger
➜ *CPT Assistant* Feb 96:3, Apr 02:13

Lower Extremity

Casts

29305   Application of hip spica cast; 1 leg
➜ *CPT Assistant* Feb 96:3, Apr 02:13

29325   1 and one-half spica or both legs
➜ *CPT Assistant* Feb 96:3, Apr 02:13

(For hip spica (body) cast, including thighs only, use 29046)

29345   Application of long leg cast (thigh to toes);
➜ *CPT Assistant* Feb 96:3, Apr 02:13

29355   walker or ambulatory type
➜ *CPT Assistant* Feb 96:3, Apr 02:13

29358   Application of long leg cast brace
➜ *CPT Assistant* Feb 96:3, Apr 02:13

29365   Application of cylinder cast (thigh to ankle)
➜ *CPT Assistant* Feb 96:3, Apr 02:13

29405   Application of short leg cast (below knee to toes);
➜ *CPT Assistant* Feb 96:3, Apr 02:13, Mar 03:17

29425   walking or ambulatory type
➜ *CPT Assistant* Feb 96:3, Apr 02:13

29435   Application of patellar tendon bearing (PTB) cast
➜ *CPT Assistant* Feb 96:3, Apr 02:13

29440   Adding walker to previously applied cast
➜ *CPT Assistant* Feb 96:3, Apr 02:13

29445   Application of rigid total contact leg cast
➜ *CPT Assistant* Feb 96:3, Apr 02:13

29450   Application of clubfoot cast with molding or manipulation, long or short leg
➔ *CPT Assistant* Feb 96:3, Apr 02:13

(To report bilateral procedure, use 29450 with modifier 50)

Splints

29505   Application of long leg splint (thigh to ankle or toes)
➔ *CPT Assistant* Feb 96:3, Apr 02:13

29515   Application of short leg splint (calf to foot)
➔ *CPT Assistant* Feb 96:3, Apr 02:13, Mar 03:18

Strapping—Any Age

29520   Strapping; hip
➔ *CPT Assistant* Feb 96:3, Apr 02:13

29530   knee
➔ *CPT Assistant* Feb 96:3, Apr 02:13

29540   ankle and/or foot
➔ *CPT Assistant* Feb 96:3, Apr 02:13, Mar 03:17; *CPT Changes: An Insider's View* 2003

▶(Do not report 29540 in conjunction with 29581)◀

29550   toes
➔ *CPT Assistant* Feb 96:3, Apr 02:13

29580   Unna boot
➔ *CPT Assistant* Feb 96:3, Jul 99:10, Apr 02:13

▶(Do not report 29580 in conjunction with 29581)◀

● **29581**   Application of multi-layer venous wound compression system, below knee
➔ *CPT Changes: An Insider's View* 2010

▶(Do not report 29581 in conjunction with 29540, 29580)◀

29590   Denis-Browne splint strapping
➔ *CPT Assistant* Feb 96:3, Apr 02:13

Removal or Repair

Codes for cast removals should be employed only for casts applied by another physician.

29700   Removal or bivalving; gauntlet, boot or body cast
➔ *CPT Assistant* Apr 02:13

29705   full arm or full leg cast
➔ *CPT Assistant* Apr 02:13

29710   shoulder or hip spica, Minerva, or Risser jacket, etc.
➔ *CPT Assistant* Apr 02:13

29715   turnbuckle jacket
➔ *CPT Assistant* Apr 02:13

29720   Repair of spica, body cast or jacket
➔ *CPT Assistant* Apr 02:13

29730   Windowing of cast
➔ *CPT Assistant* Apr 02:13

29740   Wedging of cast (except clubfoot casts)
➔ *CPT Assistant* Apr 02:13

29750   Wedging of clubfoot cast
➔ *CPT Assistant* Apr 02:13

(To report bilateral procedure, use 29750 with modifier 50)

Other Procedures

29799   Unlisted procedure, casting or strapping

Endoscopy/Arthroscopy

Surgical endoscopy/arthroscopy always includes a diagnostic endoscopy/arthroscopy.

When arthroscopy is performed in conjunction with arthrotomy, add modifier 51.

29800   Arthroscopy, temporomandibular joint, diagnostic, with or without synovial biopsy (separate procedure)

29804   Arthroscopy, temporomandibular joint, surgical

(For open procedure, use 21010)

29805   Arthroscopy, shoulder, diagnostic, with or without synovial biopsy (separate procedure)
➔ *CPT Changes: An Insider's View* 2002

(For open procedure, see 23065-23066, 23100-23101)

29806   Arthroscopy, shoulder, surgical; capsulorrhaphy
➔ *CPT Changes: An Insider's View* 2002

(For open procedure, see 23450-23466)

(To report thermal capsulorrhaphy, use 29999)

29807   repair of SLAP lesion
➔ *CPT Changes: An Insider's View* 2002

29819   with removal of loose body or foreign body
➔ *CPT Changes: An Insider's View* 2002

(For open procedure, see 23040-23044, 23107)

29820   synovectomy, partial

(For open procedure, see 23105)

29821   synovectomy, complete

(For open procedure, see 23105)

29822   debridement, limited
➔ *CPT Assistant* May 01:9

(For open procedure, see specific open shoulder procedure performed)

29823   debridement, extensive

(For open procedure, see specific open shoulder procedure performed)

29824   distal claviculectomy including distal articular surface (Mumford procedure)

➔ *CPT Changes: An Insider's View 2002*

Arthroscopy, Shoulder, Distal Claviculectomy (Mumford Procedure)
29824

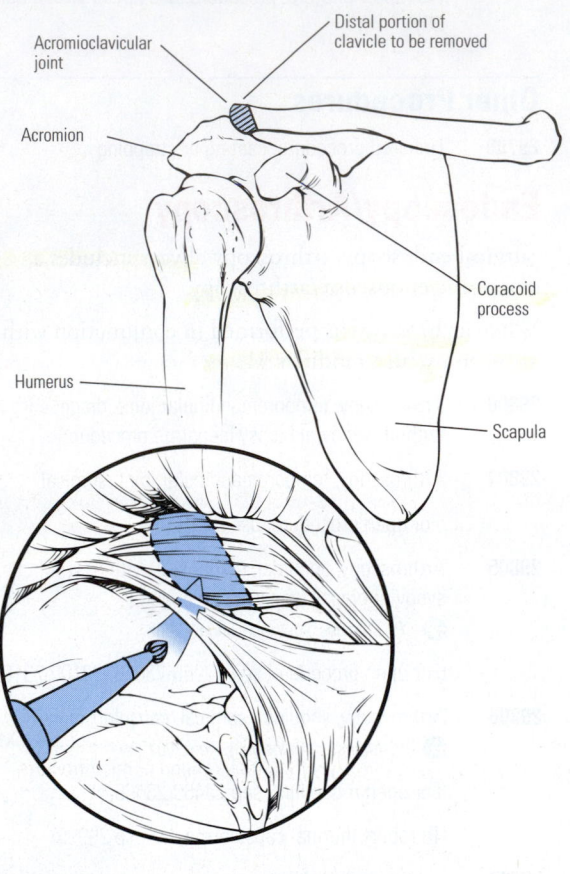

Acromioclavicular joint

Distal portion of clavicle to be removed

Acromion

Coracoid process

Humerus

Scapula

(For open procedure, use 23120)

29825   with lysis and resection of adhesions, with or without manipulation

(For open procedure, see specific open shoulder procedure performed)

29826   decompression of subacromial space with partial acromioplasty, with or without coracoacromial release

➔ *CPT Assistant* May 01:9, Aug 02:10

(For open procedure, use 23130 or 23415)

29827   with rotator cuff repair

➔ *CPT Assistant* Mar 08:14; *CPT Changes: An Insider's View* 2003

(For open or mini-open rotator cuff repair, use 23412)

(When arthroscopic subacromial decompression is performed at the same setting, use 29826 and append modifier 51)

(When arthroscopic distal clavicle resection is performed at the same setting, use 29824 and append modifier 51)

29828   biceps tenodesis

➔ *CPT Assistant* Feb 08:9; *CPT Changes: An Insider's View* 2008

(Do not report 29828 in conjunction with 29805, 29820, 29822)

(For open biceps tenodesis, use 23430)

29830   Arthroscopy, elbow, diagnostic, with or without synovial biopsy (separate procedure)

29834   Arthroscopy, elbow, surgical; with removal of loose body or foreign body

29835   synovectomy, partial

29836   synovectomy, complete

29837   debridement, limited

29838   debridement, extensive

29840   Arthroscopy, wrist, diagnostic, with or without synovial biopsy (separate procedure)

29843   Arthroscopy, wrist, surgical; for infection, lavage and drainage

29844   synovectomy, partial

29845   synovectomy, complete

➔ *CPT Assistant* Dec 03:11

29846   excision and/or repair of triangular fibrocartilage and/or joint debridement

➔ *CPT Assistant* Dec 03:11

29847   internal fixation for fracture or instability

29848   Endoscopy, wrist, surgical, with release of transverse carpal ligament

➔ *CPT Assistant* Dec 99:7

(For open procedure, use 64721)

29850   Arthroscopically aided treatment of intercondylar spine(s) and/or tuberosity fracture(s) of the knee, with or without manipulation; without internal or external fixation (includes arthroscopy)

29851   with internal or external fixation (includes arthroscopy)

(For bone graft, use 20900, 20902)

29855   Arthroscopically aided treatment of tibial fracture, proximal (plateau); unicondylar, includes internal fixation, when performed (includes arthroscopy)

➔ *CPT Changes: An Insider's View* 2008

29856   bicondylar, includes internal fixation, when performed (includes arthroscopy)

➔ *CPT Changes: An Insider's View* 2008

(For bone graft, use 20900, 20902)

29860   Arthroscopy, hip, diagnostic with or without synovial biopsy (separate procedure)

➔ *CPT Assistant* Nov 97:15, Jul 98:8

29861   Arthroscopy, hip, surgical; with removal of loose body or foreign body
➜ *CPT Assistant* Nov 97:15, Jul 98:8

29862   with debridement/shaving of articular cartilage (chondroplasty), abrasion arthroplasty, and/or resection of labrum
➜ *CPT Assistant* Nov 97:15, Jul 98:8

29863   with synovectomy
➜ *CPT Assistant* Nov 97:15, Jul 98:8

Arthroscopy of the Knee
29866-29887

Portal incisions are made on either side of the patellar tendon and compartments of the knee are examined using the arthroscope and a probe. Additional treatment is performed as needed.

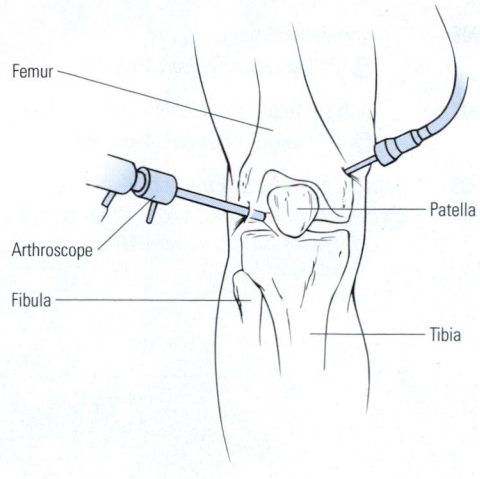

29866   Arthroscopy, knee, surgical; osteochondral autograft(s) (eg, mosaicplasty) (includes harvesting of the autograft[s])
➜ *CPT Changes: An Insider's View* 2005, 2008

(Do not report 29866 in conjunction with 29870, 29871, 29875, 29884 when performed at the same session and/or 29874, 29877, 29879, 29885-29887 when performed in the same compartment)

(For open osteochondral autograft of knee, use 27416)

29867   osteochondral allograft (eg, mosaicplasty)
➜ *CPT Changes: An Insider's View* 2005

(Do not report 29867 in conjunction with 27570, 29870, 29871, 29875, 29884 when performed at the same session and/or 29874, 29877, 29879, 29885-29887 when performed in the same compartment)

(Do not report 29867 in conjunction with 27415)

29868   meniscal transplantation (includes arthrotomy for meniscal insertion), medial or lateral
➜ *CPT Changes: An Insider's View* 2005

(Do not report 29868 in conjunction with 29870, 29871, 29875, 29880, 29883, 29884 when performed at the same session or 29874, 29877, 29881, 29882 when performed in the same compartment)

29870   Arthroscopy, knee, diagnostic, with or without synovial biopsy (separate procedure)
➜ *CPT Assistant* Dec 07:10

(For open autologous chondrocyte implantation of the knee, use 27412)

29871   Arthroscopy, knee, surgical; for infection, lavage and drainage
➜ *CPT Assistant* Aug 01:6

(For implantation of osteochondral graft for treatment of articular surface defect, see 27412, 27415, 29866, 29867)

29873   with lateral release
➜ *CPT Assistant* Dec 07:10; *CPT Changes: An Insider's View* 2003

(For open lateral release, use 27425)

29874   for removal of loose body or foreign body (eg, osteochondritis dissecans fragmentation, chondral fragmentation)
➜ *CPT Assistant* Aug 01:6, Apr 03:12

29875   synovectomy, limited (eg, plica or shelf resection) (separate procedure)
➜ *CPT Assistant* Aug 01:6

29876   synovectomy, major, 2 or more compartments (eg, medial or lateral)
➜ *CPT Assistant* Aug 01:6

29877   debridement/shaving of articular cartilage (chondroplasty)
➜ *CPT Assistant* Feb 96:9, Jun 99:11, Aug 01:7, Apr 03:7, Apr 05:14, Dec 07:10

29879   abrasion arthroplasty (includes chondroplasty where necessary) or multiple drilling or microfracture
➜ *CPT Assistant* Nov 99:13, Aug 01:7; *CPT Changes: An Insider's View* 2000

29880   with meniscectomy (medial AND lateral, including any meniscal shaving)
➜ *CPT Assistant* Jun 99:11, Aug 01:7

29881   with meniscectomy (medial OR lateral, including any meniscal shaving)
➜ *CPT Assistant* Feb 96:9, Jun 99:11, Aug 01:7, Oct 03:11, Apr 05:14, Dec 07:10

29882   with meniscus repair (medial OR lateral)
➜ *CPT Assistant* Aug 01:7, Sep 04:12, Dec 07:10

29883   with meniscus repair (medial AND lateral)
➜ *CPT Assistant* Aug 01:7, Sep 04:12, Dec 07:10

(For meniscal transplantation, medial or lateral, knee, use 29868)

29884   with lysis of adhesions, with or without manipulation (separate procedure)
➜ *CPT Assistant* Aug 01:7

29885   drilling for osteochondritis dissecans with bone grafting, with or without internal fixation (including debridement of base of lesion)
➜ *CPT Assistant* Aug 01:7

29886 drilling for intact osteochondritis dissecans lesion

➔ *CPT Assistant* Aug 01:12

29887 drilling for intact osteochondritis dissecans lesion with internal fixation

➔ *CPT Assistant* Aug 01:12

29888 Arthroscopically aided anterior cruciate ligament repair/augmentation or reconstruction

➔ *CPT Assistant* Oct 03:11, Dec 07:10

29889 Arthroscopically aided posterior cruciate ligament repair/augmentation or reconstruction

➔ *CPT Assistant* Sep 96:9, Oct 98:11, Aug 01:8, Dec 07:10

(Procedures 29888 and 29889 should not be used with reconstruction procedures 27427-27429)

29891 Arthroscopy, ankle, surgical, excision of osteochondral defect of talus and/or tibia, including drilling of the defect

➔ *CPT Assistant* Nov 97:15

29892 Arthroscopically aided repair of large osteochondritis dissecans lesion, talar dome fracture, or tibial plafond fracture, with or without internal fixation (includes arthroscopy)

➔ *CPT Assistant* Nov 97:15, Dec 08:6

29893 Endoscopic plantar fasciotomy

➔ *CPT Assistant* Nov 97:15

29894 Arthroscopy, ankle (tibiotalar and fibulotalar joints), surgical; with removal of loose body or foreign body

---

Arthroscopy of the Ankle
29894-29899

Incisions are made allowing the ankle to be examined using the arthroscope and a probe. Additional treatment is performed as needed.

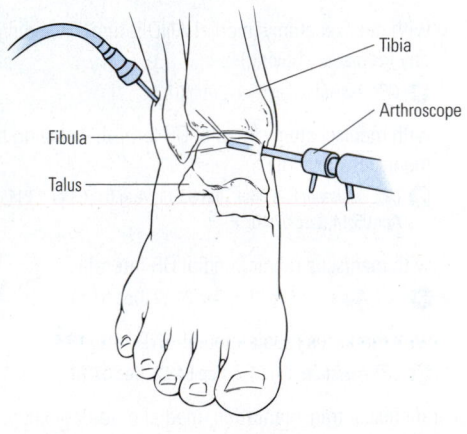

Tibia

Arthroscope

Fibula

Talus

29895 synovectomy, partial

29897 debridement, limited

29898 debridement, extensive

29899 with ankle arthrodesis

➔ *CPT Changes: An Insider's View* 2003

(For open ankle arthrodesis, use 27870)

29900 Arthroscopy, metacarpophalangeal joint, diagnostic, includes synovial biopsy

➔ *CPT Changes: An Insider's View* 2002

(Do not report 29900 with 29901, 29902)

29901 Arthroscopy, metacarpophalangeal joint, surgical; with debridement

➔ *CPT Changes: An Insider's View* 2002

29902 with reduction of displaced ulnar collateral ligament (eg, Stener lesion)

➔ *CPT Changes: An Insider's View* 2002

29904 Arthroscopy, subtalar joint, surgical; with removal of loose body or foreign body

➔ *CPT Changes: An Insider's View* 2008

29905 with synovectomy

➔ *CPT Changes: An Insider's View* 2008

29906 with debridement

➔ *CPT Changes: An Insider's View* 2008

29907 with subtalar arthrodesis

➔ *CPT Changes: An Insider's View* 2008

29999 Unlisted procedure, arthroscopy

➔ *CPT Assistant* Aug 02:10, Sep 04:12, Nov 08:10, Mar 09:10; *CPT Changes: An Insider's View* 2002

Surgery

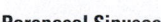

Frontal
Ethnoid
Sphenoid
Maxillary

Paranasal Sinuses

Resp
30000

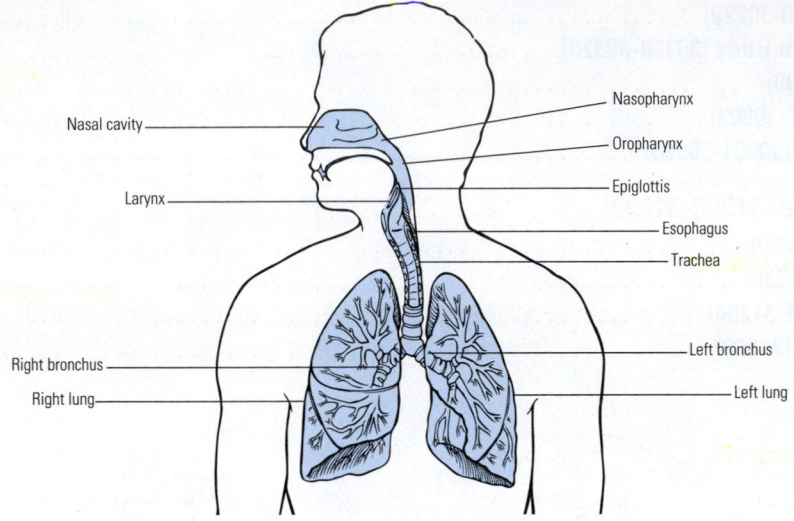

Respiratory System

Nose

Incision

30000   Drainage abscess or hematoma, nasal, internal approach

(For external approach, see 10060, 10140)

30020   Drainage abscess or hematoma, nasal septum

(For lateral rhinotomy, see specific application (eg, 30118, 30320))

Excision

30100   Biopsy, intranasal

(For biopsy skin of nose, see 11100, 11101)

30110   Excision, nasal polyp(s), simple

(30110 would normally be completed in an office setting)

(To report bilateral procedure, use 30110 with modifier 50)

30115   Excision, nasal polyp(s), extensive

(30115 would normally require the facilities available in a hospital setting)

(To report bilateral procedure, use 30115 with modifier 50)

30117   Excision or destruction (eg, laser), intranasal lesion; internal approach
   ➲ *CPT Changes: An Insider's View* 2002

30118   external approach (lateral rhinotomy)
   ➲ *CPT Changes: An Insider's View* 2002

30120   Excision or surgical planing of skin of nose for rhinophyma
   ➲ *CPT Assistant* May 07:9

30124   Excision dermoid cyst, nose; simple, skin, subcutaneous

30125   complex, under bone or cartilage

30130   Excision inferior turbinate, partial or complete, any method
   ➲ *CPT Assistant* Feb 98:11, Nov 98:11, Sep 01:10, May 03:5; *CPT Changes: An Insider's View* 2006

(For excision of superior or middle turbinate, use 30999)

30140   Submucous resection inferior turbinate, partial or complete, any method
   ➲ *CPT Assistant* Nov 98:11, Dec 02:10, Apr 03:26, May 03:5, Dec 04:18, Mar 08:14; *CPT Changes: An Insider's View* 2006

(Do not report 30130 or 30140 in conjunction with 30801, 30802, 30930)

(For submucous resection of superior or middle turbinate, use 30999)

(For endoscopic resection of concha bullosa of middle turbinate, use 31240)

(For submucous resection of nasal septum, use 30520)

30150   Rhinectomy; partial

30160   total

▶(For closure and/or reconstruction, primary or delayed, see **Integumentary System,** 13150-13160, 14060-14302, 15120, 15121, 15260, 15261, 15760, 20900-20912)◀

Introduction

30200   Injection into turbinate(s), therapeutic
   ➲ *CPT Assistant* Dec 04:19

30210   Displacement therapy (Proetz type)

30220   Insertion, nasal septal prosthesis (button)

Removal of Foreign Body

30300   Removal foreign body, intranasal; office type procedure

30310   requiring general anesthesia

30320   by lateral rhinotomy

Repair

(For obtaining tissues for graft, see 20900-20926, 21210)

30400   Rhinoplasty, primary; lateral and alar cartilages and/or elevation of nasal tip

(For columellar reconstruction, see 13150 et seq)

30410   complete, external parts including bony pyramid, lateral and alar cartilages, and/or elevation of nasal tip

30420   including major septal repair

30430   Rhinoplasty, secondary; minor revision (small amount of nasal tip work)

30435   intermediate revision (bony work with osteotomies)

30450   major revision (nasal tip work and osteotomies)

30460   Rhinoplasty for nasal deformity secondary to congenital cleft lip and/or palate, including columellar lengthening; tip only

30462   tip, septum, osteotomies

30465   Repair of nasal vestibular stenosis (eg, spreader grafting, lateral nasal wall reconstruction)
   ➲ *CPT Changes: An Insider's View* 2001

(30465 excludes obtaining graft. For graft procedure, see 20900-20926, 21210)

(30465 is used to report a bilateral procedure. For unilateral procedure, use modifier 52)

Surgical Repair of Vestibular Stenosis
30465

An incision is made in the upper lateral cartilage and continued as an osteotomy of the medial aspect of the nasal bones. The spreader graft is placed to widen the nasal vestibule.

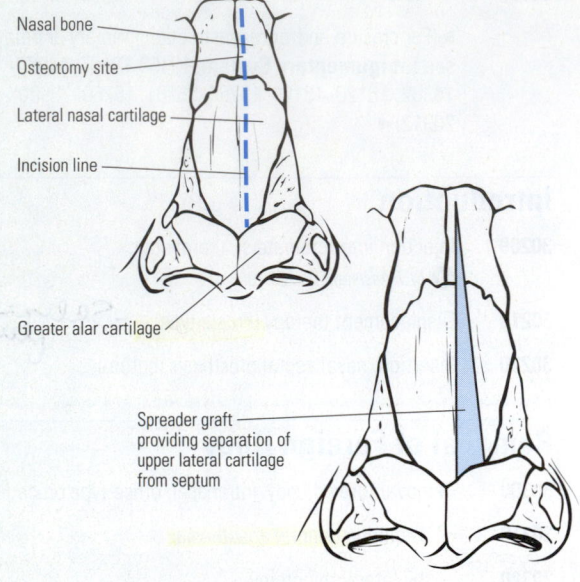

Nasal bone
Osteotomy site
Lateral nasal cartilage
Incision line
Greater alar cartilage
Spreader graft providing separation of upper lateral cartilage from septum

30520   Septoplasty or submucous resection, with or without cartilage scoring, contouring or replacement with graft
→ *CPT Assistant* Oct 97:11, Dec 02:10

(For submucous resection of turbinates, use 30140)

30540   Repair choanal atresia; intranasal

30545   transpalatine

(Do not report modifier 63 in conjunction with 30540, 30545)

30560   Lysis intranasal synechia

30580   Repair fistula; oromaxillary (combine with 31030 if antrotomy is included)

30600   oronasal

30620   Septal or other intranasal dermatoplasty (does not include obtaining graft)

30630   Repair nasal septal perforations

Destruction

▲ **30801**   Ablation, soft tissue of inferior turbinates, unilateral or bilateral, any method (eg, electrocautery, radiofrequency ablation, or tissue volume reduction); superficial
→ *CPT Changes: An Insider's View* 2002, 2006, 2010

►(For ablation of superior or middle turbinates, use 30999)◄

▲ **30802**   intramural (ie, submucosal)
→ *CPT Assistant* Mar 08:14; *CPT Changes: An Insider's View* 2010

►(Do not report 30801 in conjunction with 30802)◄

(Do not report 30801, 30802, 30930 in conjunction with 30130 or 30140)

(For cautery performed for control of nasal hemorrhage, see 30901-30906)

Other Procedures

30901   Control nasal hemorrhage, anterior, simple (limited cautery and/or packing) any method

(To report bilateral procedure, use 30901 with modifier 50)

30903   Control nasal hemorrhage, anterior, complex (extensive cautery and/or packing) any method

(To report bilateral procedure, use 30903 with modifier 50)

30905   Control nasal hemorrhage, posterior, with posterior nasal packs and/or cautery, any method; initial
→ *CPT Changes: An Insider's View* 2002

30906   subsequent

30915   Ligation arteries; ethmoidal

30920   internal maxillary artery, transantral

(For ligation external carotid artery, use 37600)

30930   Fracture nasal inferior turbinate(s), therapeutic
→ *CPT Assistant* Jul 01:11, Dec 02:10, Jul 03:15, Aug 03:14, Dec 04:18; *CPT Changes: An Insider's View* 2006

(Do not report 30801, 30802, 30930 in conjunction with 30130 or 30140)

(For fracture of superior or middle turbinate(s), use 30999)

30999   Unlisted procedure, nose

Accessory Sinuses

Incision

31000   Lavage by cannulation; maxillary sinus (antrum puncture or natural ostium)

(To report bilateral procedure, use 31000 with modifier 50)

31002   sphenoid sinus

31020   Sinusotomy, maxillary (antrotomy); intranasal

(To report bilateral procedure, use 31020 with modifier 50)

31030   radical (Caldwell-Luc) without removal of antrochoanal polyps

(To report bilateral procedure, use 31030 with modifier 50)

31032   radical (Caldwell-Luc) with removal of antrochoanal polyps

(To report bilateral procedure, use 31032 with modifier 50)

31040   Pterygomaxillary fossa surgery, any approach

(For transantral ligation of internal maxillary artery, use 30920)

31050   Sinusotomy, sphenoid, with or without biopsy;

31051   with mucosal stripping or removal of polyp(s)

31070   Sinusotomy frontal; external, simple (trephine operation)

(For frontal intranasal sinusotomy, use 31276)

Sinusotomy, Frontal
31070

A trephine is used to access the frontal sinus.

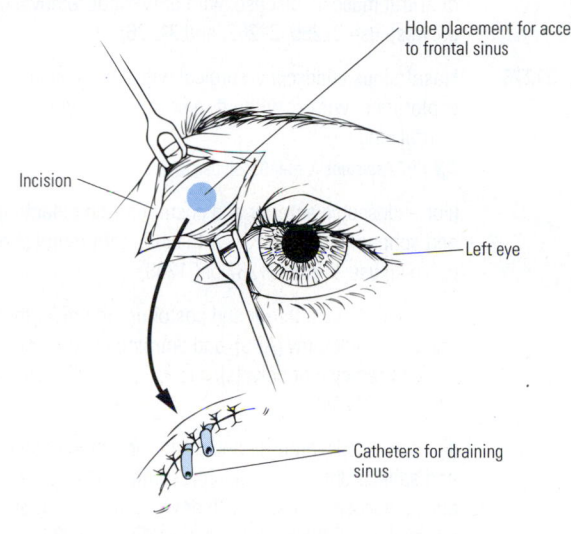

31075   transorbital, unilateral (for mucocele or osteoma, Lynch type)

31080   obliterative without osteoplastic flap, brow incision (includes ablation)

31081   obliterative, without osteoplastic flap, coronal incision (includes ablation)

31084   obliterative, with osteoplastic flap, brow incision

31085   obliterative, with osteoplastic flap, coronal incision

31086   nonobliterative, with osteoplastic flap, brow incision

31087   nonobliterative, with osteoplastic flap, coronal incision

31090   Sinusotomy, unilateral, 3 or more paranasal sinuses (frontal, maxillary, ethmoid, sphenoid)
➔ *CPT Assistant* Nov 97:15, Nov 98:11

Excision

31200   Ethmoidectomy; intranasal, anterior

31201   intranasal, total

31205   extranasal, total

31225   Maxillectomy; without orbital exenteration

31230   with orbital exenteration (en bloc)

(For orbital exenteration only, see 65110 et seq)

(For skin grafts, see 15120 et seq)

Endoscopy

A surgical sinus endoscopy includes a sinusotomy (when appropriate) and diagnostic endoscopy.

Codes 31231-31294 are used to report unilateral procedures unless otherwise specified.

The codes 31231-31235 for diagnostic evaluation refer to employing a nasal/sinus endoscope to inspect the interior of the nasal cavity and the middle and superior meatus, the turbinates, and the spheno-ethmoid recess. Any time a diagnostic evaluation is performed all these areas would be inspected and a separate code is not reported for each area.

Sinus Endoscopy
31231-31294

The physician uses an endoscope for visualizing and magnifying the internal structure of the sinuses.

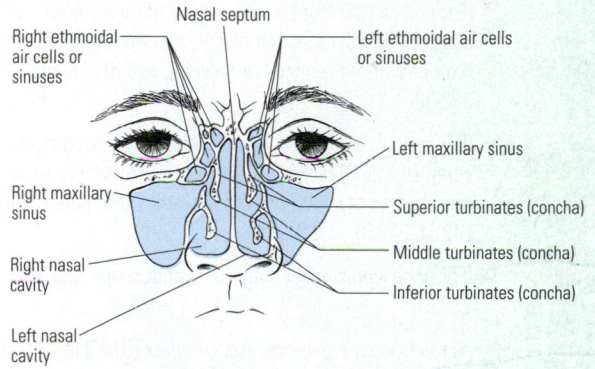

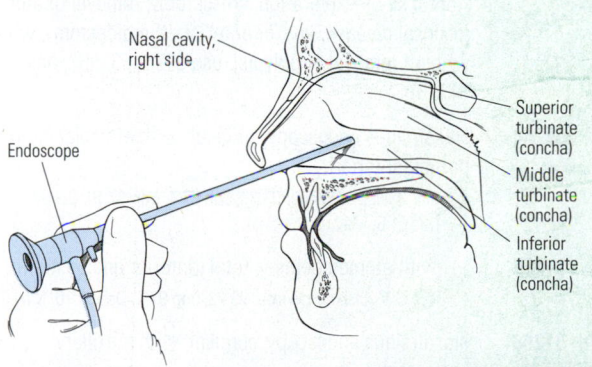

31231   Nasal endoscopy, diagnostic, unilateral or bilateral (separate procedure)
➔ *CPT Assistant* Winter 93:22, Jan 97:4

31233 Nasal/sinus endoscopy, diagnostic with maxillary sinusoscopy (via inferior meatus or canine fossa puncture)
➔ *CPT Assistant* Winter 93:22, Jan 97:4

31235 Nasal/sinus endoscopy, diagnostic with sphenoid sinusoscopy (via puncture of sphenoidal face or cannulation of ostium)
➔ *CPT Assistant* Winter 93:22, Jan 97:4

31237 Nasal/sinus endoscopy, surgical; with biopsy, polypectomy or debridement (separate procedure)
➔ *CPT Assistant* Winter 93:23, Jan 97:4, Dec 01:6, May 03:5

31238 with control of nasal hemorrhage
➔ *CPT Assistant* Winter 93:23, Jan 97:4; *CPT Changes: An Insider's View* 2002

31239 with dacryocystorhinostomy
➔ *CPT Assistant* Winter 93:23, Jan 97:4

31240 with concha bullosa resection
➔ *CPT Assistant* Winter 93:23, Jan 97:4, May 03:5

(For endoscopic osteomeatal complex [OMC] resection with antrostomy and/or anterior ethmoidectomy, with or without removal of polyp[s], use 31254 and 31256)

(For endoscopic osteomeatal complex [OMC] resection with antrostomy, removal of antral mucosal disease, and/or anterior ethmoidectomy, with or without removal of polyp[s], use 31254 and 31267)

(For endoscopic frontal sinus exploration, osteomeatal complex [OMC] resection and/or anterior ethmoidectomy, with or without removal of polyp[s], use 31254 and 31276)

(For endoscopic frontal sinus exploration, osteomeatal complex [OMC] resection, antrostomy, and/or anterior ethmoidectomy, with or without removal of polyp[s], use 31254, 31256, and 31276)

(For endoscopic nasal diagnostic endoscopy, see 31231-31235)

(For endoscopic osteomeatal complex [OMC] resection, frontal sinus exploration, antrostomy, removal of antral mucosal disease, and/or anterior ethmoidectomy, with or without removal of polyp[s], use 31254, 31267, and 31276)

31254 Nasal/sinus endoscopy, surgical; with ethmoidectomy, partial (anterior)
➔ *CPT Assistant* Winter 93:23, Jan 97:4, Sep 97:10, Oct 97:5, Dec 01:6, May 03:5

31255 with ethmoidectomy, total (anterior and posterior)
➔ *CPT Assistant* Winter 93:23, Jan 97:4, Dec 02:10, May 03:5

31256 Nasal/sinus endoscopy, surgical, with maxillary antrostomy;
➔ *CPT Assistant* Winter 93:23, Jan 97:4

(For endoscopic anterior and posterior ethmoidectomy [APE] and antrostomy, with or without removal of polyp[s], use 31255 and 31256)

(For endoscopic anterior and posterior ethmoidectomy [APE], antrostomy and removal of antral mucosal disease, with or without removal of polyp[s], use 31255 and 31267)

(For endoscopic anterior and posterior ethmoidectomy [APE], and frontal sinus exploration, with or without removal of polyp[s], use 31255 and 31276)

31267 with removal of tissue from maxillary sinus
➔ *CPT Assistant* Jan 97:4, Dec 01:6

(For endoscopic anterior and posterior ethmoidectomy [APE], and frontal sinus exploration and antrostomy, with or without removal of polyp[s], use 31255, 31256, and 31276)

(For endoscopic anterior and posterior ethmoidectomy [APE], frontal sinus exploration, antrostomy, and removal of antral mucosal disease, with or without removal of polyp[s], use 31255, 31267, and 31276)

31276 Nasal/sinus endoscopy, surgical with frontal sinus exploration, with or without removal of tissue from frontal sinus
➔ *CPT Assistant* Winter 93:24, Jan 97:4

(For endoscopic anterior and posterior ethmoidectomy and sphenoidotomy [APS], with or without removal of polyp[s], use 31255, 31287 or 31288)

(For endoscopic anterior and posterior ethmoidectomy and sphenoidotomy [APS], and antrostomy, with or without removal of polyp[s], use 31255, 31256, and 31287 or 31288)

(For endoscopic anterior and posterior ethmoidectomy and sphenoidotomy [APS], antrostomy and removal of antral mucosal disease, with or without removal of polyp[s], use 31255, 31267, and 31287 or 31288)

(For endoscopic anterior and posterior ethmoidectomy and sphenoidotomy [APS], and frontal sinus exploration with or without removal of polyp[s], use 31255, 31287 or 31288, and 31276)

(For endoscopic anterior and posterior ethmoidectomy and sphenoidotomy [APS], with or without removal of polyp[s], with frontal sinus exploration and antrostomy, use 31255, 31256, 31287 or 31288, and 31276)

(For unilateral endoscopy of 2 or more sinuses, see 31231-31235)

(For endoscopic anterior and posterior ethmoidectomy and sphenoidotomy [APS], frontal sinus exploration, antrostomy and removal of antral mucosal disease, with or without removal of polyp[s], see 31255, 31267, 31287 or 31288 and 31276)

31287 Nasal/sinus endoscopy, surgical, with sphenoidotomy;
➔ *CPT Assistant* Winter 93:24, Jan 97:4

31288 with removal of tissue from the sphenoid sinus
➔ *CPT Assistant* Winter 93:24, Jan 97:4

31290 Nasal/sinus endoscopy, surgical, with repair of cerebrospinal fluid leak; ethmoid region
➔ *CPT Assistant* Winter 93:24, Jan 97:4

31291 sphenoid region
➔ *CPT Assistant* Winter 93:24, Jan 97:4

31292 Nasal/sinus endoscopy, surgical; with medial or inferior orbital wall decompression
➔ *CPT Assistant* Winter 93:24, Jan 97:4

31293 with medial orbital wall and inferior orbital wall decompression
➔ *CPT Assistant* Winter 93:24, Jan 97:4

31294 with optic nerve decompression
➔ *CPT Assistant* Winter 93:24, Jan 97:4

Other Procedures

(For hypophysectomy, transantral or transeptal approach, use 61548)

(For transcranial hypophysectomy, use 61546)

31299 Unlisted procedure, accessory sinuses

Larynx

Excision

31300 Laryngotomy (thyrotomy, laryngofissure); with removal of tumor or laryngocele, cordectomy

31320 diagnostic

31360 Laryngectomy; total, without radical neck dissection

31365 total, with radical neck dissection
➔ *CPT Assistant* Oct 01:10

31367 subtotal supraglottic, without radical neck dissection

31368 subtotal supraglottic, with radical neck dissection

31370 Partial laryngectomy (hemilaryngectomy); horizontal

31375 laterovertical

31380 anterovertical

31382 antero-latero-vertical

31390 Pharyngolaryngectomy, with radical neck dissection; without reconstruction

31395 with reconstruction

31400 Arytenoidectomy or arytenoidopexy, external approach

(For endoscopic arytenoidectomy, use 31560)

31420 Epiglottidectomy

Introduction

⊘ **31500** Intubation, endotracheal, emergency procedure
➔ *CPT Assistant* Nov 99:32-33, Oct 03:2, Aug 04:8, Jul 06:4, Jul 07:1

(For injection procedure for segmental bronchography, use 31656)

31502 Tracheotomy tube change prior to establishment of fistula tract
➔ *CPT Assistant* Winter 90:6

Endoscopy

For endoscopic procedures, code appropriate endoscopy of each anatomic site examined. If using operating microscope, telescope, or both, use the applicable code only once per operative session.

31505 Laryngoscopy, indirect; diagnostic (separate procedure)
➔ *CPT Assistant* Nov 99:13; *CPT Changes: An Insider's View* 2000

31510 with biopsy
➔ *CPT Assistant* Nov 99:13

31511 with removal of foreign body
➔ *CPT Assistant* Nov 99:13

31512 with removal of lesion
➔ *CPT Assistant* Nov 99:13

31513 with vocal cord injection
➔ *CPT Assistant* Nov 99:13

31515 Laryngoscopy direct, with or without tracheoscopy; for aspiration

31520 diagnostic, newborn

(Do not report modifier 63 in conjunction with 31520)

31525 diagnostic, except newborn

31526 diagnostic, with operating microscope or telescope
➔ *CPT Assistant* Nov 98:11-12; *CPT Changes: An Insider's View* 2006

(Do not report code 69990 in addition to code 31526)

31527 with insertion of obturator

31528 with dilation, initial
➔ *CPT Changes: An Insider's View* 2002

31529 with dilation, subsequent
➔ *CPT Changes: An Insider's View* 2002

31530 Laryngoscopy, direct, operative, with foreign body removal;

31531 with operating microscope or telescope
➔ *CPT Assistant* Nov 98:11-12; *CPT Changes: An Insider's View* 2006

(Do not report code 69990 in addition to code 31531)

31535 Laryngoscopy, direct, operative, with biopsy;

31536 with operating microscope or telescope
➔ *CPT Assistant* Nov 98:11-12; *CPT Changes: An Insider's View* 2006

(Do not report code 69990 in addition to code 31536)

31540 Laryngoscopy, direct, operative, with excision of tumor and/or stripping of vocal cords or epiglottis;

31541   with operating microscope or telescope

➔ *CPT Assistant* Nov 98:11-12; *CPT Changes: An Insider's View* 2006

(Do not report code 69990 in addition to code 31541)

31545   Laryngoscopy, direct, operative, with operating microscope or telescope, with submucosal removal of non-neoplastic lesion(s) of vocal cord; reconstruction with local tissue flap(s)

➔ *CPT Changes: An Insider's View* 2005

31546   reconstruction with graft(s) (includes obtaining autograft)

➔ *CPT Changes: An Insider's View* 2005

(Do not report 31546 in addition to 20926 for graft harvest)

(For reconstruction of vocal cord with allograft, use 31599)

(Do not report 31545 or 31546 in conjunction with 31540, 31541, 69990)

31560   Laryngoscopy, direct, operative, with arytenoidectomy;

31561   with operating microscope or telescope

➔ *CPT Assistant* Nov 98:11-12; *CPT Changes: An Insider's View* 2006

(Do not report code 69990 in addition to code 31561)

31570   Laryngoscopy, direct, with injection into vocal cord(s), therapeutic;

31571   with operating microscope or telescope

➔ *CPT Assistant* Nov 98:11-12; *CPT Changes: An Insider's View* 2006

(Do not report code 69990 in addition to code 31571)

31575   Laryngoscopy, flexible fiberoptic; diagnostic

31576   with biopsy

31577   with removal of foreign body

31578   with removal of lesion

(To report flexible fiberoptic endoscopic evaluation of swallowing, see 92612-92613)

(To report flexible fiberoptic endoscopic evaluation with sensory testing, see 92614-92615)

(To report flexible fiberoptic endoscopic evaluation of swallowing with sensory testing, see 92616-92617)

(For flexible fiberoptic laryngoscopy as part of flexible fiberoptic endoscopic evaluation of swallowing and/or laryngeal sensory testing by cine or video recording, see 92612-92617)

31579   Laryngoscopy, flexible or rigid fiberoptic, with stroboscopy

Repair

31580   Laryngoplasty; for laryngeal web, 2-stage, with keel insertion and removal

31582   for laryngeal stenosis, with graft or core mold, including tracheotomy

31584   with open reduction of fracture

31587   Laryngoplasty, cricoid split

31588   Laryngoplasty, not otherwise specified (eg, for burns, reconstruction after partial laryngectomy)

➔ *CPT Assistant* Aug 04:11

31590   Laryngeal reinnervation by neuromuscular pedicle

Destruction

31595   Section recurrent laryngeal nerve, therapeutic (separate procedure), unilateral

Other Procedures

31599   Unlisted procedure, larynx

Trachea and Bronchi

Incision

31600   Tracheostomy, planned (separate procedure);

31601   younger than 2 years

31603   Tracheostomy, emergency procedure; transtracheal

31605   cricothyroid membrane

31610   Tracheostomy, fenestration procedure with skin flaps

(For endotracheal intubation, use 31500)

(For tracheal aspiration under direct vision, use 31515)

31611   Construction of tracheoesophageal fistula and subsequent insertion of an alaryngeal speech prosthesis (eg, voice button, Blom-Singer prosthesis)

31612   Tracheal puncture, percutaneous with transtracheal aspiration and/or injection

31613   Tracheostoma revision; simple, without flap rotation

31614   complex, with flap rotation

Endoscopy

For endoscopy procedures, code appropriate endoscopy of each anatomic site examined. Surgical bronchoscopy always includes diagnostic bronchoscopy when performed by the same physician. Codes 31622-31646 include fluoroscopic guidance, when performed.

(For tracheoscopy, see laryngoscopy codes 31515-31578)

⊙ **31615**   Tracheobronchoscopy through established tracheostomy incision

⊙+ **31620**   Endobronchial ultrasound (EBUS) during bronchoscopic diagnostic or therapeutic intervention(s) (List separately in addition to code for primary procedure[s])

➔ *CPT Assistant* Aug 05:4; *CPT Changes: An Insider's View* 2005

(Use 31620 in conjunction with 31622-31646)

⊙▲ **31622**   Bronchoscopy, rigid or flexible, including fluoroscopic guidance, when performed; diagnostic, with cell washing, when performed (separate procedure)
➔ *CPT Assistant* Jul 96:11, Nov 98:12, Dec 98:8, Mar 99:3, Apr 00:10, Jun 01:10, Jan 02:10, Sep 04:8, 12, Aug 05:4; *CPT Changes: An Insider's View* 2004, 2010

⊙ **31623**   with brushing or protected brushings
➔ *CPT Assistant* Nov 98:12, Mar 99:3, Nov 99:13, Jan 02:10, Sep 04:8, Aug 05:4, May 08:15

⊙ **31624**   with bronchial alveolar lavage
➔ *CPT Assistant* Nov 98:12, Feb 99:9, Mar 99:3, 11, Jan 02:10, Sep 04:8, Aug 05:4, May 08:15

⊙ **31625**   with bronchial or endobronchial biopsy(s), single or multiple sites
➔ *CPT Assistant* Spring 91:2, Jan 02:10, Jun 02:10, Sep 03:15, Sep 04:9, Aug 05:4; *CPT Changes: An Insider's View* 2004

Bronchoscopy
31622-31656

A rigid or flexible bronchoscope is inserted through the oropharynx and vocal cords and beyond the trachea into the right or left bronchi.

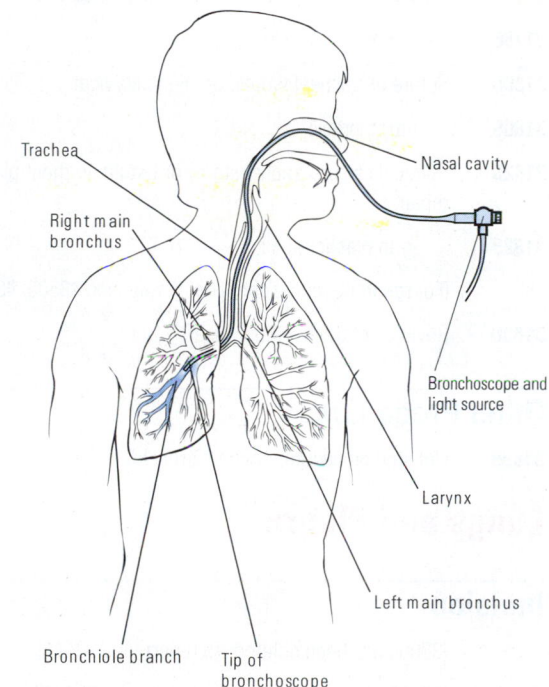

Trachea
Nasal cavity
Right main bronchus
Bronchoscope and light source
Larynx
Left main bronchus
Bronchiole branch   Tip of bronchoscope

⊙● **31626**   with placement of fiducial markers, single or multiple
➔ *CPT Changes: An Insider's View* 2010

►(Report supply of device separately)◄

⊙+● **31627**   with computer-assisted, image-guided navigation (List separately in addition to code for primary procedure[s])
➔ *CPT Changes: An Insider's View* 2010

►(31627 includes 3D reconstruction. Do not report 31627 in conjunction with 76376, 76377)◄

►(Use 31627 in conjunction with 31615, 31622-31631, 31635, 31636, 31638-31643)◄

⊙ **31628**   with transbronchial lung biopsy(s), single lobe
➔ *CPT Assistant* Jun 01:10, Jan 02:10, Sep 04:9, Aug 05:4, May 08:15; *CPT Changes: An Insider's View* 2004

(31628 should be reported only once regardless of how many transbronchial lung biopsies are performed in a lobe)

(To report transbronchial lung biopsies performed on additional lobe, use 31632)

⊙ **31629**   with transbronchial needle aspiration biopsy(s), trachea, main stem and/or lobar bronchus(i)
➔ *CPT Assistant* Apr 00:10, Jan 02:10, Sep 03:15, May 04:15, Jul 04:13, Aug 05:4; *CPT Changes: An Insider's View* 2004

(31629 should be reported only once for upper airway biopsies regardless of how many transbronchial needle aspiration biopsies are performed in the upper airway or in a lobe)

(To report transbronchial needle aspiration biopsies performed on additional lobe(s), use 31633)

31630   with tracheal/bronchial dilation or closed reduction of fracture
➔ *CPT Assistant* Jan 02:10, Aug 05:4; *CPT Changes: An Insider's View* 2005

31631   with placement of tracheal stent(s) (includes tracheal/bronchial dilation as required)
➔ *CPT Assistant* Jan 02:10, Aug 05:4; *CPT Changes: An Insider's View* 2005

(For placement of bronchial stent, see 31636, 31637)

(For revision of tracheal/bronchial stent, use 31638)

+ **31632**   with transbronchial lung biopsy(s), each additional lobe (List separately in addition to code for primary procedure)
➔ *CPT Assistant* Jan 02:10, Sep 04:9, Aug 05:4; *CPT Changes: An Insider's View* 2004

(Use 31632 in conjunction with 31628)

(31632 should be reported only once regardless of how many transbronchial lung biopsies are performed in a lobe)

+ **31633**   with transbronchial needle aspiration biopsy(s), each additional lobe (List separately in addition to code for primary procedure)
➔ *CPT Assistant* Jan 02:10, May 04:15, Jul 04:13, Sep 04:10, Aug 05:4; *CPT Changes: An Insider's View* 2004

(Use 31633 in conjunction with 31629)

(31633 should be reported only once regardless of how many transbronchial needle aspiration biopsies are performed in the trachea or the additional lobe)

⊙ **31635**   with removal of foreign body
➔ *CPT Assistant* Jan 02:10, Jun 02:10

31636   with placement of bronchial stent(s) (includes tracheal/bronchial dilation as required), initial bronchus
➔ *CPT Assistant* Aug 05:4; *CPT Changes: An Insider's View* 2005

▲=Revised code   ●=New code   ►◄=Contains new or revised text   ⊘=Modifier 51 exempt

+ **31637**   each additional major bronchus stented (List separately in addition to code for primary procedure)

→ *CPT Assistant* Aug 05:4; *CPT Changes: An Insider's View* 2005

(Use 31637 in conjunction with 31636)

31638   with revision of tracheal or bronchial stent inserted at previous session (includes tracheal/bronchial dilation as required)

→ *CPT Assistant* Aug 05:4; *CPT Changes: An Insider's View* 2005

31640   with excision of tumor

→ *CPT Assistant* Jan 02:10, Aug 05:4

▲ **31641**   with destruction of tumor or relief of stenosis by any method other than excision (eg, laser therapy, cryotherapy)

→ *CPT Assistant* Nov 99:13, Sep 00:5, Jan 02:10, Aug 05:4; *CPT Changes: An Insider's View* 2002, 2010

(For bronchoscopic photodynamic therapy, report 31641 in addition to 96570, 96571 as appropriate)

▲ **31643**   with placement of catheter(s) for intracavitary radioelement application

→ *CPT Assistant* Nov 98:12, Mar 99:3, Jan 02:10, Aug 05:4, Apr 09:3; *CPT Changes: An Insider's View* 2010

(For intracavitary radioelement application, see 77761-77763, 77785-77787)

⊙▲ **31645**   with therapeutic aspiration of tracheobronchial tree, initial (eg, drainage of lung abscess)

→ *CPT Assistant* Jan 02:10, Aug 05:4; *CPT Changes: An Insider's View* 2010

⊙▲ **31646**   with therapeutic aspiration of tracheobronchial tree, subsequent

→ *CPT Assistant* Jan 02:10, Aug 05:4; *CPT Changes: An Insider's View* 2010

(For catheter aspiration of tracheobronchial tree at bedside, use 31725)

⊙▲ **31656**   with injection of contrast material for segmental bronchography (fiberscope only)

→ *CPT Assistant* Jan 02:10; *CPT Changes: An Insider's View* 2010

(For radiological supervision and interpretation, see 71040, 71060)

Introduction

(For endotracheal intubation, use 31500)

(For tracheal aspiration under direct vision, see 31515)

31715   Transtracheal injection for bronchography

(For radiological supervision and interpretation, see 71040, 71060)

(For prolonged services, see 99354-99360)

31717   Catheterization with bronchial brush biopsy

→ *CPT Assistant* Feb 01:11

31720   Catheter aspiration (separate procedure); nasotracheal

⊙ **31725**   tracheobronchial with fiberscope, bedside

31730   Transtracheal (percutaneous) introduction of needle wire dilator/stent or indwelling tube for oxygen therapy

Excision, Repair

31750   Tracheoplasty; cervical

31755   tracheopharyngeal fistulization, each stage

31760   intrathoracic

31766   Carinal reconstruction

31770   Bronchoplasty; graft repair

31775   excision stenosis and anastomosis

(For lobectomy and bronchoplasty, use 32501)

31780   Excision tracheal stenosis and anastomosis; cervical

31781   cervicothoracic

31785   Excision of tracheal tumor or carcinoma; cervical

31786   thoracic

31800   Suture of tracheal wound or injury; cervical

31805   intrathoracic

31820   Surgical closure tracheostomy or fistula; without plastic repair

31825   with plastic repair

(For repair tracheoesophageal fistula, see 43305, 43312)

31830   Revision of tracheostomy scar

Other Procedures

31899   Unlisted procedure, trachea, bronchi

Lungs and Pleura

Incision

(32000 has been deleted. To report, use 32421)

(32002 has been deleted. To report, use 32422)

(32005 has been deleted. To report, use 32560)

(32019 has been deleted. To report, use 32550)

(32020 has been deleted. To report, use 32551)

32035   Thoracostomy; with rib resection for empyema

32036   with open flap drainage for empyema

32095   Thoracotomy, limited, for biopsy of lung or pleura

(To report wound exploration due to penetrating trauma without thoractomy, use 20102)

32100   Thoracotomy, major; with exploration and biopsy

→ *CPT Assistant* Mar 07:1

32100 ↓

(Do not report 32100 in conjunction with 19260, 19271, 19272, 32503, 32504)

32110   with control of traumatic hemorrhage and/or repair of lung tear

32120   for postoperative complications

32124   with open intrapleural pneumonolysis

32140   with cyst(s) removal, with or without a pleural procedure

32141   with excision-plication of bullae, with or without any pleural procedure

(For lung volume reduction, use 32491)

32150   with removal of intrapleural foreign body or fibrin deposit

32151   with removal of intrapulmonary foreign body

32160   with cardiac massage

(For segmental or other resections of lung, see 32480-32504)

32200   Pneumonostomy; with open drainage of abscess or cyst
➔ *CPT Assistant* Nov 97:15

⊙ **32201**   with percutaneous drainage of abscess or cyst
➔ *CPT Assistant* Nov 97:15-16, Mar 98:8

(For radiological supervision and interpretation, use 75989)

32215   Pleural scarification for repeat pneumothorax

32220   Decortication, pulmonary (separate procedure); total

32225   partial

Excision

Total Pneumonectomy = 1 lung (handwritten)

32310   Pleurectomy, parietal (separate procedure)

32320   Decortication and parietal pleurectomy

32400   Biopsy, pleura; percutaneous needle
➔ *CPT Assistant* Fall 94:1-2
➔ *Clinical Examples in Radiology* Summer 08:5, 6

(If imaging guidance is performed, see 76942, 77002, 77012, 77021)

(For fine needle aspiration, use 10021 or 10022)

(For evaluation of fine needle aspirate, see 88172, 88173)

32402   open
➔ *CPT Assistant* Fall 94:1-2

32405   Biopsy, lung or mediastinum, percutaneous needle
➔ *CPT Assistant* Fall 94:1-2, Mar 97:4, Aug 02:10
➔ *Clinical Examples in Radiology* Summer 08:5, 6

(For radiological supervision and interpretation, see 76942, 77002, 77012, 77021)

(For fine needle aspiration, use 10022)

(For evaluation of fine needle aspirate, see 88172, 88173)

Removal

32420   Pneumocentesis, puncture of lung for aspiration
➔ *CPT Assistant* Fall 94:1-2; *CPT Changes: An Insider's View* 2002

32421   Thoracentesis, puncture of pleural cavity for aspiration, initial or subsequent
➔ *CPT Changes: An Insider's View* 2008

(If imaging guidance is performed, see 76942, 77002, 77012)

(For total lung lavage, use 32997)

32422   Thoracentesis with insertion of tube, includes water seal (eg, for pneumothorax), when performed (separate procedure)
➔ *CPT Changes: An Insider's View* 2008

(Do not report 32422 in conjunction with 19260, 19271, 19272, 32503, 32504)

(If imaging guidance is performed, see 76942, 77002, 77012)

Thoracentesis
32421-32422

Accumulated fluid or air is removed from the pleural space by puncturing space between the ribs. In 32422, a tube is inserted and a syringe attached to the catheter for the removal of fluid and/or air.

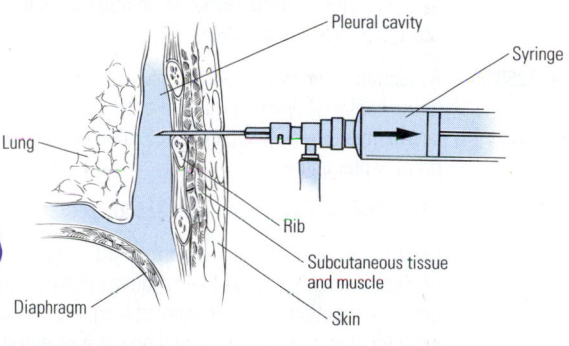

32440   Removal of lung, total pneumonectomy;
➔ *CPT Assistant* Fall 94:1

32442   with resection of segment of trachea followed by broncho-tracheal anastomosis (sleeve pneumonectomy)
➔ *CPT Assistant* Fall 94:1, 3

32445   extrapleural
➔ *CPT Assistant* Fall 94:1, 3

(For extrapleural pneumonectomy, with empyemectomy, use 32445 and 32540)

(If lung resection is performed with chest wall tumor resection, report the appropriate chest wall tumor resection code, 19260-19272, in addition to lung resection code 32440-32445)

32480   Removal of lung, other than total pneumonectomy; single lobe (lobectomy)
➔ *CPT Assistant* Spring 91:5, Fall 94:1, 4

32482 2 lobes (bilobectomy)

→ *CPT Assistant* Fall 94:1, 4, Jan 07:31

32484 single segment (segmentectomy)

→ *CPT Assistant* Fall 94:1, 4

(For removal of lung with bronchoplasty, use 32501)

32486 with circumferential resection of segment of bronchus followed by broncho-bronchial anastomosis (sleeve lobectomy)

→ *CPT Assistant* Fall 94:1, 4

32488 all remaining lung following previous removal of a portion of lung (completion pneumonectomy)

→ *CPT Assistant* Fall 94:1, 4

(For total or segmental lobectomy, with concomitant decortication, use 32320 and the appropriate removal of lung code)

32491 excision-plication of emphysematous lung(s) (bullous or non-bullous) for lung volume reduction, sternal split or transthoracic approach, with or without any pleural procedure

→ *CPT Assistant* Nov 96:7

32500 wedge resection, single or multiple

→ *CPT Assistant* Fall 94:1, 5, Mar 97:4

(If lung resection is performed with chest wall tumor resection, report the appropriate chest wall tumor resection code, 19260-19272, in addition to lung resection code 32480-32500)

+ 32501 Resection and repair of portion of bronchus (bronchoplasty) when performed at time of lobectomy or segmentectomy (List separately in addition to code for primary procedure)

(Use 32501 in conjunction with 32480, 32482, 32484)

(32501 is to be used when a portion of the bronchus to preserved lung is removed and requires plastic closure to preserve function of that preserved lung. It is not to be used for closure for the proximal end of a resected bronchus)

32503 Resection of apical lung tumor (eg, Pancoast tumor), including chest wall resection, rib(s) resection(s), neurovascular dissection, when performed; without chest wall reconstruction(s)

→ *CPT Changes: An Insider's View* 2006

32504 with chest wall reconstruction

→ *CPT Changes: An Insider's View* 2006

(Do not report 32503, 32504 in conjunction with 19260, 19271, 19272, 32100, 32422, 32551)

(For performance of lung resection in conjunction with chest wall resection, see 19260, 19271, 19272 and 32480-32500, 32503, 32504)

32540 Extrapleural enucleation of empyema (empyemectomy)

(For extrapleural enucleation of empyema (empyemectomy) with lobectomy, use 32540 and the appropriate removal of lung code)

►Introduction and Removal◄

⊙ **32550** Insertion of indwelling tunneled pleural catheter with cuff

→ *CPT Changes: An Insider's View* 2008

(Do not report 32550 in conjunction with 32421, 32422)

(If imaging guidance is performed, use 75989)

⊙ **32551** Tube thoracostomy, includes water seal (eg, for abscess, hemothorax, empyema), when performed (separate procedure)

→ *CPT Changes: An Insider's View* 2008

(Do not report 32551 in conjunction with 19260, 19271, 19272, 32503, 32504)

(If imaging guidance is performed, use 75989)

Insertion of Chest Tube
32551

A trocar is used to puncture through the space between the ribs into the pleural cavity for the insertion of a chest tube via a thoracic drainage system to drain air and/or fluid from the pleural space, promoting lung re-expansion.

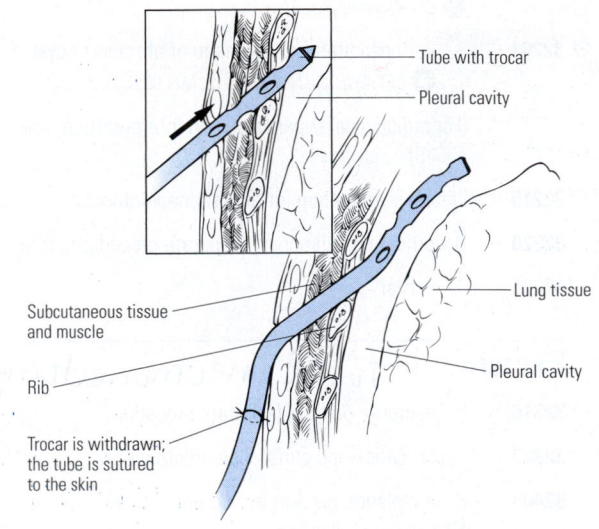

Tube with trocar

Pleural cavity

Lung tissue

Pleural cavity

Subcutaneous tissue and muscle

Rib

Trocar is withdrawn; the tube is sutured to the skin

● **32552** Removal of indwelling tunneled pleural catheter with cuff

→ *CPT Changes: An Insider's View* 2010

⊙● **32553** Placement of interstitial device(s) for radiation therapy guidance (eg, fiducial markers, dosimeter), percutaneous, intra-thoracic, single or multiple

→ *CPT Changes: An Insider's View* 2010

►(Report supply of device separately)◄

►(For imaging guidance, see 76942, 77002, 77012, 77021)◄

►(For percutaneous placement of interstitial device[s] for intra-abdominal, intrapelvic, and/or retroperitoneal radiation therapy guidance, use 49411)◄

Destruction

▶The instillation of a fibrinolytic agent may be performed multiple times per day over the course of several days. Code 32561 should be reported only once on the initial day treatment. Code 32562 should be reported only once on each subsequent day of treatment.◀

▲ **32560**   Instillation, via chest tube/catheter, agent for pleurodesis (eg, talc for recurrent or persistent pneumothorax)
➲ *CPT Changes: An Insider's View* 2008, 2010

▶(For chest tube insertion, use 32551)◀

● **32561**   Instillation(s), via chest tube/catheter, agent for fibrinolysis (eg, fibrinolytic agent for break up of multiloculated effusion); initial day
➲ *CPT Changes: An Insider's View* 2010

▶(For chest tube insertion, use 32551)◀

● **32562**   subsequent day
➲ *CPT Changes: An Insider's View* 2010

▶(For chest tube insertion, use 32551)◀

Endoscopy

Surgical thoracoscopy always includes diagnostic thoracoscopy.

For endoscopic procedures, code appropriate endoscopy of each anatomic site examined.

Thoracoscopy
32601-32665

The inside of the chest cavity is examined through a fiberoptic endoscope.

Placement of endoscope

Endoscope

Pleural cavity

Lung

Heart

Schematic transverse section of thoracic region

32601   Thoracoscopy, diagnostic (separate procedure); lungs and pleural space, without biopsy
➲ *CPT Assistant* Fall 94:1, 4

32602   lungs and pleural space, with biopsy
➲ *CPT Assistant* Fall 94:1, 4, Jun 97:5

32603   pericardial sac, without biopsy
➲ *CPT Assistant* Fall 94:1, 4

32604   pericardial sac, with biopsy
➲ *CPT Assistant* Fall 94:1, 4

32605   mediastinal space, without biopsy
➲ *CPT Assistant* Fall 94:1, 4

32606   mediastinal space, with biopsy
➲ *CPT Assistant* Fall 94:1, 5

(Surgical thoracoscopy always includes diagnostic thoracoscopy)

32650   Thoracoscopy, surgical; with pleurodesis (eg, mechanical or chemical)
➲ *CPT Assistant* Fall 94:1, 6; *CPT Changes: An Insider's View* 2002

32651   with partial pulmonary decortication
➲ *CPT Assistant* Fall 94:1, 6

32652   with total pulmonary decortication, including intrapleural pneumonolysis
➲ *CPT Assistant* Fall 94:1, 6

32653   with removal of intrapleural foreign body or fibrin deposit
➲ *CPT Assistant* Fall 94:1, 6

32654   with control of traumatic hemorrhage
➲ *CPT Assistant* Fall 94:1, 6

32655   with excision-plication of bullae, including any pleural procedure
➲ *CPT Assistant* Fall 94:1, 6, Aug 05:15

32656   with parietal pleurectomy
➲ *CPT Assistant* Fall 94:1, 6

32657   with wedge resection of lung, single or multiple
➲ *CPT Assistant* Fall 94:1, 6

32658   with removal of clot or foreign body from pericardial sac
➲ *CPT Assistant* Fall 94:1, 6

32659   with creation of pericardial window or partial resection of pericardial sac for drainage
➲ *CPT Assistant* Fall 94:1, 6

32660   with total pericardiectomy
➲ *CPT Assistant* Fall 94:1, 6

32661   with excision of pericardial cyst, tumor, or mass
➲ *CPT Assistant* Fall 94:1, 6

32662   with excision of mediastinal cyst, tumor, or mass
➲ *CPT Assistant* Fall 94:1, 6

32663   with lobectomy, total or segmental
➲ *CPT Assistant* Fall 94:1, 6

32664   with thoracic sympathectomy
> *CPT Assistant* Fall 94:1, Oct 99:10

32665   with esophagomyotomy (Heller type)
> *CPT Assistant* Fall 94:1, 6

(For exploratory thoracoscopy, and exploratory thoracoscopy with biopsy, see 32601-32606)

Repair

32800   Repair lung hernia through chest wall

32810   Closure of chest wall following open flap drainage for empyema (Clagett type procedure)

32815   Open closure of major bronchial fistula

32820   Major reconstruction, chest wall (posttraumatic)

Lung Transplantation

Lung allotransplantation involves three distinct components of physician work:

1. *Cadaver donor pneumonectomy(s)*, which include(s) harvesting the allograft and cold preservation of the allograft (perfusing with cold preservation solution and cold maintenance) (use 32850).

2. *Backbench work*:

   Preparation of a cadaver donor single lung allograft prior to transplantation, including dissection of the allograft from surrounding soft tissues to prepare the pulmonary venous/atrial cuff, pulmonary artery, and bronchus unilaterally (use 32855).

   Preparation of a cadaver donor double lung allograft prior to transplantation, including dissection of the allograft from surrounding soft tissues to prepare the pulmonary venous/atrial cuff, pulmonary artery, and bronchus bilaterally (use 32856).

3. *Recipient lung allotransplantation*, which includes transplantation of a single or double lung allograft and care of the recipient (see 32851-32854).

32850   Donor pneumonectomy(s) (including cold preservation), from cadaver donor
> *CPT Changes: An Insider's View* 2005

32851   Lung transplant, single; without cardiopulmonary bypass

32852   with cardiopulmonary bypass

32853   Lung transplant, double (bilateral sequential or en bloc); without cardiopulmonary bypass

32854   with cardiopulmonary bypass

32855   Backbench standard preparation of cadaver donor lung allograft prior to transplantation, including dissection of allograft from surrounding soft tissues to prepare pulmonary venous/atrial cuff, pulmonary artery, and bronchus; unilateral
> *CPT Changes: An Insider's View* 2005

32856   bilateral
> *CPT Changes: An Insider's View* 2005

(For repair or resection procedures on the donor lung, see 32491, 32500, 35216, or 35276)

Surgical Collapse Therapy; Thoracoplasty

(See also 32503, 32504)

32900   Resection of ribs, extrapleural, all stages

32905   Thoracoplasty, Schede type or extrapleural (all stages);

32906   with closure of bronchopleural fistula

(For open closure of major bronchial fistula, use 32815)

(For resection of first rib for thoracic outlet compression, see 21615, 21616)

32940   Pneumonolysis, extraperiosteal, including filling or packing procedures

32960   Pneumothorax, therapeutic, intrapleural injection of air

Other Procedures

32997   Total lung lavage (unilateral)
> *CPT Assistant* Nov 98:13, Nov 99:14; *CPT Changes: An Insider's View* 2000, 2002

(For bronchoscopic bronchial alveolar lavage, use 31624)

32998   Ablation therapy for reduction or eradication of 1 or more pulmonary tumor(s) including pleura or chest wall when involved by tumor extension, percutaneous, radiofrequency, unilateral
> *CPT Changes: An Insider's View* 2007

(For imaging guidance and monitoring, see 76940, 77013, 77022)

32999   Unlisted procedure, lungs and pleura
> *CPT Assistant* Jan 02:11, Feb 02:11, Jul 08:10
> *Clinical Examples in Radiology* Spring 06:8-9

Surgery

Cardiovascular System* (33010-37799) 164

The following is a listing of headings and subheadings that appear within the Cardiovascular section of the CPT Codebook. The subheadings or subsections denoted with asterisks (*) below have special instructions unique to that section. Where these are indicated, special "notes" or guidelines will be presented preceding those procedural terminology listings, referring to that subsection specifically.

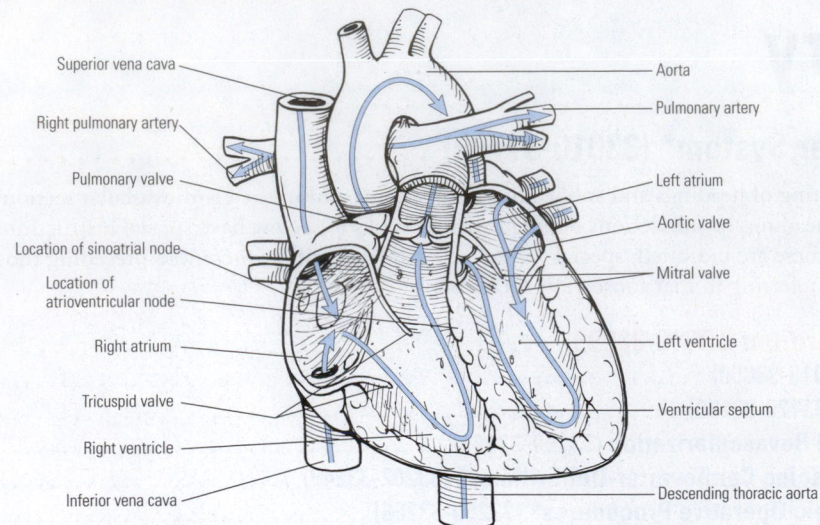

Superior vena cava
Right pulmonary artery
Pulmonary valve
Location of sinoatrial node
Location of atrioventricular node
Right atrium
Tricuspid valve
Right ventricle
Inferior vena cava
Aorta
Pulmonary artery
Left atrium
Aortic valve
Mitral valve
Left ventricle
Ventricular septum
Descending thoracic aorta

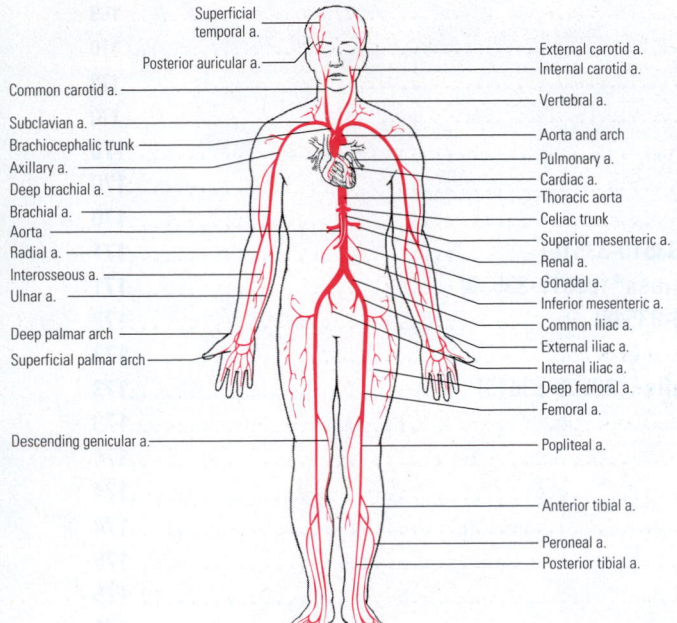

Superficial temporal a.
Posterior auricular a.
Common carotid a.
Subclavian a.
Brachiocephalic trunk
Axillary a.
Deep brachial a.
Brachial a.
Aorta
Radial a.
Interosseous a.
Ulnar a.
Deep palmar arch
Superficial palmar arch
Descending genicular a.
External carotid a.
Internal carotid a.
Vertebral a.
Aorta and arch
Pulmonary a.
Cardiac a.
Thoracic aorta
Celiac trunk
Superior mesenteric a.
Renal a.
Gonadal a.
Inferior mesenteric a.
Common iliac a.
External iliac a.
Internal iliac a.
Deep femoral a.
Femoral a.
Popliteal a.
Anterior tibial a.
Peroneal a.
Posterior tibial a.

Arteries

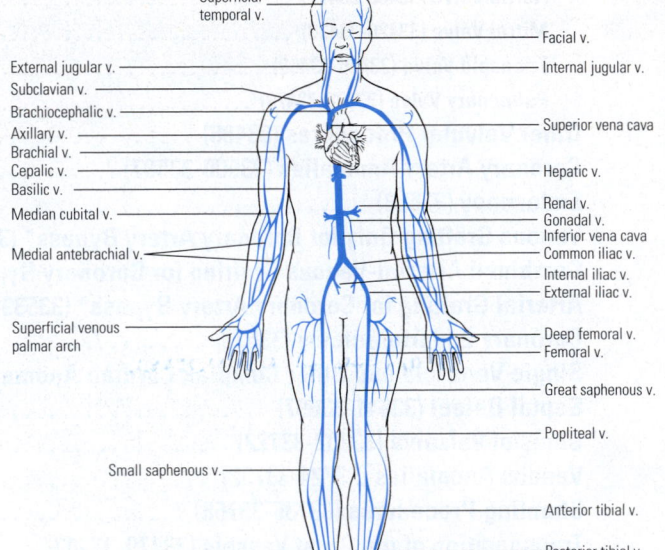

Superficial temporal v.
External jugular v.
Subclavian v.
Brachiocephalic v.
Axillary v.
Brachial v.
Cepalic v.
Basilic v.
Median cubital v.
Medial antebrachial v.
Superficial venous palmar arch
Small saphenous v.
Facial v.
Internal jugular v.
Superior vena cava
Hepatic v.
Renal v.
Gonadal v.
Inferior vena cava
Common iliac v.
Internal iliac v.
External iliac v.
Deep femoral v.
Femoral v.
Great saphenous v.
Popliteal v.
Anterior tibial v.
Posterior tibial v.
Dorsal venous arch

Veins

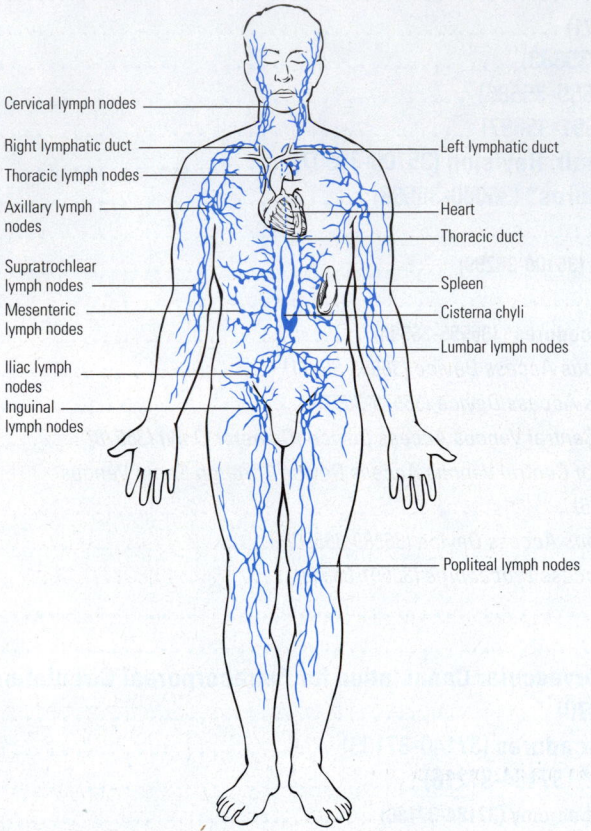

Cervical lymph nodes

Right lymphatic duct

Thoracic lymph nodes

Axillary lymph nodes

Supratrochlear lymph nodes

Mesenteric lymph nodes

Iliac lymph nodes

Inguinal lymph nodes

Left lymphatic duct

Heart

Thoracic duct

Spleen

Cisterna chyli

Lumbar lymph nodes

Popliteal lymph nodes

Cardiovascular System

Selective vascular catheterizations should be coded to include introduction and all lesser order selective catheterizations used in the approach (eg, the description for a selective right middle cerebral artery catheterization includes the introduction and placement catheterization of the right common and internal carotid arteries).

Additional second and/or third order arterial catheterizations within the same family of arteries supplied by a single first order artery should be expressed by 36218 or 36248. Additional first order or higher catheterizations in vascular families supplied by a first order vessel different from a previously selected and coded family should be separately coded using the conventions described above.

(For monitoring, operation of pump and other nonsurgical services, see 99190-99192, 99291, 99292, 99354-99360)

(For other medical or laboratory related services, see appropriate section)

(For radiological supervision and interpretation, see 75600-75978)

Heart and Pericardium

Pericardium

⊙ **33010** Pericardiocentesis; initial

(For radiological supervision and interpretation, use 76930)

⊙ **33011** subsequent

(For radiological supervision and interpretation, use 76930)

33015 Tube pericardiostomy

33020 Pericardiotomy for removal of clot or foreign body (primary procedure)

33025 Creation of pericardial window or partial resection for drainage

33030 Pericardiectomy, subtotal or complete; without cardiopulmonary bypass

33031 with cardiopulmonary bypass

33050 Excision of pericardial cyst or tumor

Cardiac Tumor

33120 Excision of intracardiac tumor, resection with cardiopulmonary bypass

➔ *CPT Assistant* Mar 07:1

33130 Resection of external cardiac tumor

➔ *CPT Assistant* Mar 07:1

Transmyocardial Revascularization

33140 Transmyocardial laser revascularization, by thoracotomy; (separate procedure)

➔ *CPT Assistant* Nov 99:14, Nov 00:5, Apr 01:7; *CPT Changes: An Insider's View* 2000, 2001, 2002

+ 33141 performed at the time of other open cardiac procedure(s) (List separately in addition to code for primary procedure)

➔ *CPT Assistant* Apr 01:7; *CPT Changes: An Insider's View* 2001

(Use 33141 in conjunction with 33400-33496, 33510-33536, 33542)

Pacemaker or Pacing Cardioverter-Defibrillator

A pacemaker system includes a pulse generator containing electronics, a battery, and one or more electrodes (leads). Pulse generators are placed in a subcutaneous "pocket" created in either a subclavicular site or underneath the abdominal muscles just below the ribcage. Electrodes may be inserted through a vein (transvenous) or they may be placed on the surface of the heart (epicardial). The epicardial location of electrodes requires a thoracotomy for electrode insertion.

A single chamber pacemaker system includes a pulse generator and one electrode inserted in either the atrium or ventricle. A dual chamber pacemaker system includes a pulse generator and one electrode inserted in the right atrium and one electrode inserted in the right ventricle. In certain circumstances, an additional electrode may be required to achieve pacing of the left ventricle (bi-ventricular pacing). In this event, transvenous (cardiac vein) placement of the electrode should be separately reported using code 33224 or 33225. Epicardial placement of the electrode should be separately reported using 33202-33203.

Like a pacemaker system, a pacing cardioverter-defibrillator system includes a pulse generator and electrodes, although pacing cardioverter-defibrillators may require multiple leads, even when only a single chamber is being paced. A pacing cardioverter-defibrillator system may be inserted in a single chamber (pacing in the ventricle) or in dual chambers (pacing in atrium and ventricle). These devices use a combination of antitachycardia pacing, low-energy cardioversion or defibrillating shocks to treat ventricular tachycardia or ventricular fibrillation.

Pacing cardioverter-defibrillator pulse generators may be implanted in a subcutaneous infraclavicular pocket or in an abdominal pocket. Removal of a pacing cardioverter-defibrillator pulse generator requires opening of the existing subcutaneous pocket and disconnection of the pulse generator from its electrode(s). A thoracotomy (or laparotomy in the case of abdominally placed pulse generators) is not required to remove the pulse generator.

The electrodes (leads) of a pacing cardioverter-defibrillator system are positioned in the heart via the venous system (transvenously), in most circumstances. In certain circumstances, an additional electrode may be required to achieve pacing of the left ventricle (bi-ventricular pacing). In this event, transvenous (cardiac vein) placement of the electrode should be separately reported using code 33224 or 33225. Epicardial placement of the electrode should be separately reported using 33202-33203.

Electrode positioning on the epicardial surface of the heart requires thoracotomy, or thoracoscopic placement of the leads. Removal of electrode(s) may first be attempted by transvenous extraction (code 33244). However, if transvenous extraction is unsuccessful, a thoracotomy may be required to remove the electrodes (code 33243). Use codes 33212, 33213, 33240 as appropriate in addition to the thoracotomy or endoscopic epicardial lead placement codes to report the insertion of the generator if done by the same physician during the same session.

When the "battery" of a pacemaker or pacing cardioverter-defibrillator is changed, it is actually the pulse generator that is changed. Replacement of a pulse generator should be reported with a code for removal of the pulse generator and another code for insertion of a pulse generator.

Repositioning of a pacemaker electrode, pacing cardioverter-defibrillator electrode(s), or a left ventricular pacing electrode is reported using 33215 or 33226, as appropriate. Replacement of a pacemaker electrode, pacing cardioverter-defibrillator electrode(s), or a left ventricular pacing electrode is reported using 33206-33208, 33210-33213, or 33224, as appropriate.

(For electronic, telephonic analysis of internal pacemaker system, see 93279, 93280, 93288, 93293, 93294)

(For radiological supervision and interpretation with insertion of pacemaker, use 71090)

33202 Insertion of epicardial electrode(s); open incision (eg, thoracotomy, median sternotomy, subxiphoid approach)
→ *CPT Changes: An Insider's View* 2007

33203 endoscopic approach (eg, thoracoscopy, pericardioscopy)
→ *CPT Changes: An Insider's View* 2007

(When epicardial lead placement is performed by the same physician at the same session as insertion of the generator, report 33202, 33203 in conjunction with 33212, 33213, as appropriate)

⊙ **33206** Insertion or replacement of permanent pacemaker with transvenous electrode(s); atrial
→ *CPT Assistant* Summer 94:10, 17, Oct 96:9, Nov 99:15, Jun 08:14

⊙ **33207** ventricular
→ *CPT Assistant* Summer 94:10, 17, Oct 96:9, Nov 99:15, Jun 08:14

⊙ **33208** atrial and ventricular
→ *CPT Assistant* Summer 94:10, 17, Jul 96:10, Nov 99:15, Jun 08:14

(Codes 33206-33208 include subcutaneous insertion of the pulse generator and transvenous placement of electrode[s])

⊙ **33210** Insertion or replacement of temporary transvenous single chamber cardiac electrode or pacemaker catheter (separate procedure)
→ *CPT Assistant* Summer 94:10, 17, Mar 07:1

Temporary Pacemaker
33210

The pacemaker pulse generator with the electrodes transvenously placed

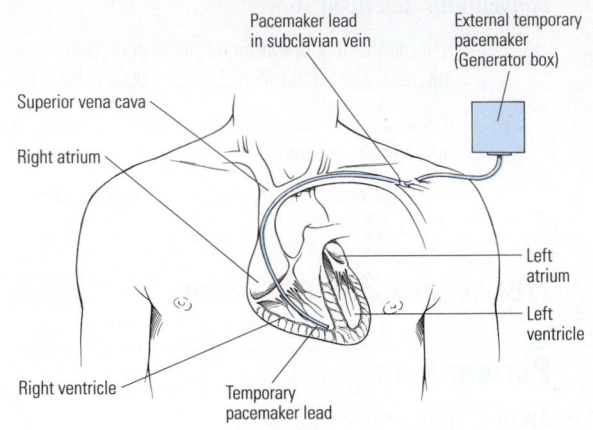

⊙ **33211** Insertion or replacement of temporary transvenous dual chamber pacing electrodes (separate procedure)
→ *CPT Assistant* Summer 94:10, 17, Mar 07:1

⊙ **33212** Insertion or replacement of pacemaker pulse generator only; single chamber, atrial or ventricular
→ *CPT Assistant* Summer 94:10, 18, Fall 94:24, May 04:15, Jun 08:14

⊙ **33213** dual chamber
→ *CPT Assistant* Summer 94:10, 18, Oct 96:10, Feb 98:11

(Use 33212, 33213, as appropriate, in conjunction with the epicardial lead placement codes 33202, 33203 to report the insertion of the generator when done by the same physician during the same session)

Implanted Pacemaker
33212-33214

A. In 33212, a pacemaker pulse generator is inserted or replaced in a single chamber.

A

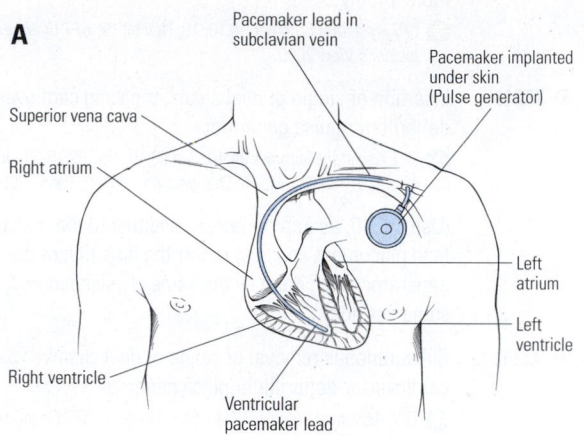

B. In 33213, a pacemaker pulse generator is inserted or replaced in two chambers. In 33214, an upgrade to an existing pacemaker system is done.

B

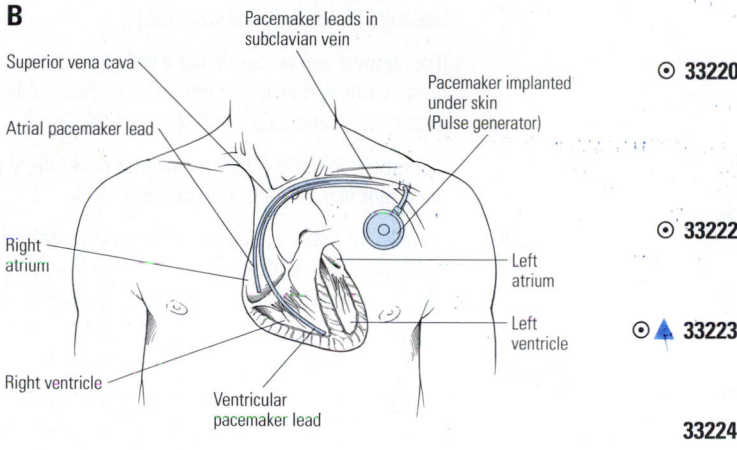

⊙ **33214**   Upgrade of implanted pacemaker system, conversion of single chamber system to dual chamber system (includes removal of previously placed pulse generator, testing of existing lead, insertion of new lead, insertion of new pulse generator)
➔ *CPT Assistant* Summer 94:10, 18, Fall 94:24, Jun 08:14

(When epicardial electrode placement is performed, report 33214 in conjunction with 33202, 33203)

33215   Repositioning of previously implanted transvenous pacemaker or pacing cardioverter-defibrillator (right atrial or right ventricular) electrode
➔ *CPT Changes: An Insider's View* 2003

⊙ ▲ **33216**   Insertion of a single transvenous electrode, permanent pacemaker or cardioverter-defibrillator
➔ *CPT Assistant* Summer 94:10, 18, Jul 96:10, Nov 99:15-16; *CPT Changes: An Insider's View* 2000, 2003, 2010

⊙ ▲ **33217**   Insertion of 2 transvenous electrodes, permanent pacemaker or cardioverter-defibrillator
➔ *CPT Assistant* Summer 94:10, 18, Jul 96:10, Nov 99:15-16, Jul 00:5, Apr 09:8; *CPT Changes: An Insider's View* 2000, 2010

(Do not report 33216-33217 in conjunction with 33214)

►(For insertion or replacement of a cardiac venous system lead, see 33224, 33225)◄

⊙ **33218**   Repair of single transvenous electrode for a single chamber, permanent pacemaker or single chamber pacing cardioverter-defibrillator
➔ *CPT Assistant* Summer 94:10, 19, Oct 96:9, Nov 99:15-16; *CPT Changes: An Insider's View* 2000

(For atrial or ventricular single chamber repair of pacemaker electrode[s] with replacement of pulse generator, see 33212 or 33213 and 33218 or 33220)

⊙ **33220**   Repair of 2 transvenous electrodes for a dual chamber permanent pacemaker or dual chamber pacing cardioverter-defibrillator
➔ *CPT Assistant* Summer 94:10, 19, Oct 96:9, Nov 99:15-16, Jun 08:14; *CPT Changes: An Insider's View* 2000

⊙ **33222**   Revision or relocation of skin pocket for pacemaker
➔ *CPT Assistant* Spring 94:30, Summer 94:10, Nov 99:15-16, Jun 08:14; *CPT Changes: An Insider's View* 2000

⊙ ▲ **33223**   Revision of skin pocket for cardioverter-defibrillator
➔ *CPT Assistant* Summer 94:10, 19, Nov 99:15-16, Jun 08:14; *CPT Changes: An Insider's View* 2000, 2010

33224   Insertion of pacing electrode, cardiac venous system, for left ventricular pacing, with attachment to previously placed pacemaker or pacing cardioverter-defibrillator pulse generator (including revision of pocket, removal, insertion, and/or replacement of generator)
➔ *CPT Assistant* Dec 07:16; *CPT Changes: An Insider's View* 2003

(When epicardial electrode placement is performed, report 33224 in conjunction with 33202, 33203)

Biventricular Pacing
33224-33226

Insertion or repositioning of venous pacing electrode

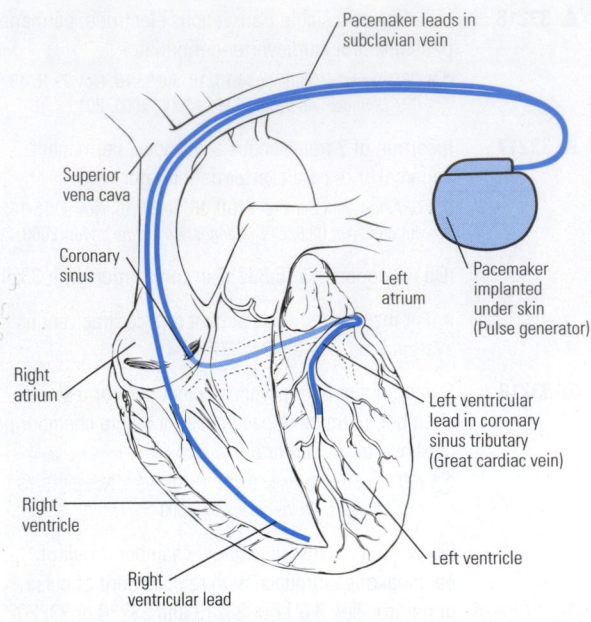

Pacemaker leads in subclavian vein

Superior vena cava

Coronary sinus

Right atrium

Right ventricle

Right ventricular lead

Left atrium

Pacemaker implanted under skin (Pulse generator)

Left ventricular lead in coronary sinus tributary (Great cardiac vein)

Left ventricle

+ 33225 Insertion of pacing electrode, cardiac venous system, for left ventricular pacing, at time of insertion of pacing cardioverter-defibrillator or pacemaker pulse generator (including upgrade to dual chamber system) (List separately in addition to code for primary procedure)

➔ CPT Assistant Dec 07:16; CPT Changes: An Insider's View 2003

(Use 33225 in conjunction with 33206, 33207, 33208, 33212, 33213, 33214, 33216, 33217, 33222, 33233, 33234, 33235, 33240, 33249)

33226 Repositioning of previously implanted cardiac venous system (left ventricular) electrode (including removal, insertion and/or replacement of generator)

➔ CPT Changes: An Insider's View 2003

⊙ **33233** Removal of permanent pacemaker pulse generator

➔ CPT Assistant Summer 94:10, 19, Fall 94:24, Oct 96:10; CPT Changes: An Insider's View 2000

⊙ **33234** Removal of transvenous pacemaker electrode(s); single lead system, atrial or ventricular

➔ CPT Assistant Summer 94:10, 19, Nov 99:16; CPT Changes: An Insider's View 2000

⊙ **33235** dual lead system

➔ CPT Assistant Summer 94:10, 19, Nov 99:16; CPT Changes: An Insider's View 2000

33236 Removal of permanent epicardial pacemaker and electrodes by thoracotomy; single lead system, atrial or ventricular

➔ CPT Assistant Summer 94:10, 19, Nov 99:16; CPT Changes: An Insider's View 2000

33237 dual lead system

➔ CPT Assistant Summer 94:10, 19, Nov 99:16; CPT Changes: An Insider's View 2000

33238 Removal of permanent transvenous electrode(s) by thoracotomy

➔ CPT Assistant Summer 94:10, 19, Nov 99:16; CPT Changes: An Insider's View 2000

⊙ **33240** Insertion of single or dual chamber pacing cardioverter-defibrillator pulse generator

➔ CPT Assistant Summer 94:40, Jun 96:10, Nov 99:16-17, Jul 00:5, Apr 04:6, Jun 08:14; CPT Changes: An Insider's View 2000

(Use 33240, as appropriate, in addition to the epicardial lead placement codes to report the insertion of the generator when done by the same physician during the same session)

⊙ **33241** Subcutaneous removal of single or dual chamber pacing cardioverter-defibrillator pulse generator

➔ CPT Assistant Summer 94:40, Nov 99:16-17; CPT Changes: An Insider's View 2000

(For removal of electrode[s] by thoracotomy, use 33243 in conjunction with 33241)

(For removal of electrode[s] by transvenous extraction, use 33244 in conjunction with 33241)

(For removal and reinsertion of a pacing cardioverter-defibrillator system (pulse generator and electrodes), report 33241 and 33243 or 33244 and 33249)

(For repair of implantable cardioverter-defibrillator pulse generator and/or leads, see 33218, 33220)

33243 Removal of single or dual chamber pacing cardioverter-defibrillator electrode(s); by thoracotomy

➔ CPT Assistant Summer 94:40, Nov 99:16-17; CPT Changes: An Insider's View 2000

⊙ **33244** by transvenous extraction

➔ CPT Assistant Summer 94:40, Nov 99:16-17, Jul 00:5; CPT Changes: An Insider's View 2000

(For subcutaneous removal of the pulse generator, use 33241 in conjunction with 33243 or 33244)

⊙ **33249** Insertion or repositioning of electrode lead(s) for single or dual chamber pacing cardioverter-defibrillator and insertion of pulse generator

➔ CPT Assistant Summer 94:21, Nov 99:16-17, Apr 04:6, May 08:14, Jun 08:14; CPT Changes: An Insider's View 2000

(For removal and reinsertion of a pacing cardioverter-defibrillator system (pulse generator and electrodes), report 33241 and 33243 or 33244 and 33249)

(For insertion of implantable cardioverter-defibrillator lead(s), without thoracotomy, use 33216)

Electrophysiologic Operative Procedures

This family of codes describes the surgical treatment of supraventricular dysrhythmias. Tissue ablation, disruption, and reconstruction can be accomplished by many methods including surgical incision or through the use of a variety of energy sources (eg, radiofrequency, cryotherapy, microwave, ultrasound, laser). If excision or isolation of the left atrial appendage by any method, including stapling, oversewing, ligation, or plication, is performed in conjunction with any of the atrial tissue ablation and reconstruction (maze) procedures (33254-33259, 33265-33266), it is considered part of the procedure. Codes 33254-33256 are only to be reported when there is no concurrently performed procedure that requires median sternotomy or cardiopulmonary bypass. The appropriate atrial tissue ablation add-on code, 33257, 33258, 33259 should be reported in addition to an open cardiac procedure requiring sternotomy or cardiopulmonary bypass if performed concurrently.

Definitions

Limited operative ablation and reconstruction includes:

Surgical isolation of triggers of supraventricular dysrhythmias by operative ablation that isolates the pulmonary veins or other anatomically defined triggers in the left or right atrium.

Extensive operative ablation and reconstruction includes:

1. The services included in "*limited*"

2. Additional ablation of atrial tissue to eliminate sustained supraventricular dysrhythmias. This must include operative ablation that involves either the right atrium, the atrial septum, or left atrium in continuity with the atrioventricular annulus.

Incision

33250   Operative ablation of supraventricular arrhythmogenic focus or pathway (eg, Wolff-Parkinson-White, atrioventricular node re-entry), tract(s) and/or focus (foci); without cardiopulmonary bypass

➔ *CPT Assistant* Summer 94:16, Nov 99:17-18; *CPT Changes: An Insider's View* 2000, 2002

(For intraoperative pacing and mapping by a separate provider, use 93631)

33251   with cardiopulmonary bypass

➔ *CPT Assistant* Summer 94:16, Nov 99:17-18; *CPT Changes: An Insider's View* 2000

33254   Operative tissue ablation and reconstruction of atria, limited (eg, modified maze procedure)

➔ *CPT Assistant* Mar 07:1; *CPT Changes: An Insider's View* 2007

33255   Operative tissue ablation and reconstruction of atria, extensive (eg, maze procedure); without cardiopulmonary bypass

➔ *CPT Assistant* Mar 07:1; *CPT Changes: An Insider's View* 2007

33256   with cardiopulmonary bypass

➔ *CPT Assistant* Mar 07:1; *CPT Changes: An Insider's View* 2007

(Do not report 33254-33256 in conjunction with 32100, 32551, 33120, 33130, 33210, 33211, 33400-33507, 33510-33523, 33533-33548, 33600-33853, 33860-33864, 33910-33920)

+ 33257   Operative tissue ablation and reconstruction of atria, performed at the time of other cardiac procedure(s), limited (eg, modified maze procedure) (List separately in addition to code for primary procedure)

➔ *CPT Changes: An Insider's View* 2008

(Use 33257 in conjunction with 33120-33130, 33250-33251, 33261, 33300-33335, 33400-33496, 33500-33507, 33510-33516, 33533-33548, 33600-33619, 33641-33697, 33702-33732, 33735-33767, 33770-33814, 33840-33877, 33910-33922, 33925-33926, 33935, 33945, 33975-33980)

+ 33258   Operative tissue ablation and reconstruction of atria, performed at the time of other cardiac procedure(s), extensive (eg, maze procedure), without cardiopulmonary bypass (List separately in addition to code for primary procedure)

➔ *CPT Changes: An Insider's View* 2008

(Use 33258 in conjunction with 33130, 33250, 33300, 33310, 33320, 33321, 33330, 33332, 33401, 33414-33417, 33420, 33470-33472, 33501-33503, 33510-33516, 33533-33536, 33690, 33735, 33737, 33800-33813, 33840-33852, 33915, 33925 when the procedure is performed without cardiopulmonary bypass)

+ 33259   Operative tissue ablation and reconstruction of atria, performed at the time of other cardiac procedure(s), extensive (eg, maze procedure), with cardiopulmonary bypass (List separately in addition to code for primary procedure)

➔ *CPT Changes: An Insider's View* 2008

(Use 33259 in conjunction with 33120, 33251, 33261, 33305, 33315, 33322, 33335, 33400, 33403-33413, 33422-33468, 33474-33478, 33496, 33500, 33504-33507, 33510-33516, 33533-33548, 33600-33688, 33692-33722, 33730, 33732, 33736, 33750-33767, 33770-33781, 33786-33788, 33814, 33853, 33860-33877, 33910, 33916-33922, 33926, 33935, 33945, 33975-33980 when the procedure is performed with cardiopulmonary bypass)

(Do not report 33257, 33258 and 33259 in conjunction with 32551, 33210, 33211, 33254-33256, 33265, 33266)

33261   Operative ablation of ventricular arrhythmogenic focus with cardiopulmonary bypass

➔ *CPT Assistant* Summer 94:16

Endoscopy

33265   Endoscopy, surgical; operative tissue ablation and reconstruction of atria, limited (eg, modified maze procedure), without cardiopulmonary bypass

➔ *CPT Assistant* Mar 07:1; *CPT Changes: An Insider's View* 2007

33266 operative tissue ablation and reconstruction of atria, extensive (eg, maze procedure), without cardiopulmonary bypass

➡ *CPT Assistant Mar 07:1; CPT Changes: An Insider's View 2007*

(Do not report 33265-33266 in conjunction with 32551, 33210, 33211)

Patient-Activated Event Recorder

33282 Implantation of patient-activated cardiac event recorder

➡ *CPT Assistant Nov 99:17-18, Jul 00:5, Jun 08:14; CPT Changes: An Insider's View 2000*

(Initial implantation includes programming. For subsequent electronic analysis and/or reprogramming, use 93285, 93291, 93298)

33284 Removal of an implantable, patient-activated cardiac event recorder

➡ *CPT Assistant Nov 99:17-18, Jul 00:5; CPT Changes: An Insider's View 2000*

Wounds of the Heart and Great Vessels

33300 Repair of cardiac wound; without bypass

33305 with cardiopulmonary bypass

33310 Cardiotomy, exploratory (includes removal of foreign body, atrial or ventricular thrombus); without bypass

➡ *CPT Changes: An Insider's View 2004*

33315 with cardiopulmonary bypass

(Do not report removal of thrombus [33310-33315] in conjunction with other cardiac procedures unless a separate incision in the heart is required to remove the atrial or ventricular thrombus)

(If removal of thrombus with cardiopulmonary bypass [33315] is reported in conjunction with 33120, 33130, 33420-33430, 33460-33468, 33496, 33542, 33545, 33641-33647, 33670, 33681, 33975-33980 which requires a separate heart incision, report 33315 with modifier 59)

33320 Suture repair of aorta or great vessels; without shunt or cardiopulmonary bypass

➡ *CPT Assistant Fall 91:7*

33321 with shunt bypass

➡ *CPT Assistant Fall 91:7*

33322 with cardiopulmonary bypass

➡ *CPT Assistant Fall 91:7*

33330 Insertion of graft, aorta or great vessels; without shunt, or cardiopulmonary bypass

33332 with shunt bypass

33335 with cardiopulmonary bypass

Cardiac Valves

(For multiple valve procedures, see 33400-33478 and add modifier 51 to the secondary valve procedure code)

Aortic Valve

33400 Valvuloplasty, aortic valve; open, with cardiopulmonary bypass

➡ *CPT Assistant Feb 05:14, Mar 07:1*

33401 open, with inflow occlusion

➡ *CPT Assistant Feb 05:14*

33403 using transventricular dilation, with cardiopulmonary bypass

➡ *CPT Assistant Feb 05:14*

(Do not report modifier 63 in conjunction with 33401, 33403)

33404 Construction of apical-aortic conduit

➡ *CPT Assistant Jan 04:28, Feb 05:14*

33405 Replacement, aortic valve, with cardiopulmonary bypass; with prosthetic valve other than homograft or stentless valve

➡ *CPT Assistant Nov 99:18, Feb 05:14; CPT Changes: An Insider's View 2000*

33406 with allograft valve (freehand)

➡ *CPT Assistant Nov 99:18, Feb 05:14; CPT Changes: An Insider's View 2002*

(For aortic valve valvotomy, [commissurotomy] with inflow occlusion, use 33401)

(For aortic valve valvotomy, [commissurotomy] with cardiopulmonary bypass, use 33403)

33410 with stentless tissue valve

➡ *CPT Assistant Nov 99:18, Feb 05:14; CPT Changes: An Insider's View 2000*

33411 Replacement, aortic valve; with aortic annulus enlargement, noncoronary cusp

➡ *CPT Assistant Feb 05:14*

33412 with transventricular aortic annulus enlargement (Konno procedure)

➡ *CPT Assistant Feb 05:14*

33413 by translocation of autologous pulmonary valve with allograft replacement of pulmonary valve (Ross procedure)

➡ *CPT Assistant Feb 05:14; CPT Changes: An Insider's View 2002*

33414 Repair of left ventricular outflow tract obstruction by patch enlargement of the outflow tract

➡ *CPT Assistant Feb 05:14*

33415 Resection or incision of subvalvular tissue for discrete subvalvular aortic stenosis

➡ *CPT Assistant Feb 05:14*

33416 Ventriculomyotomy (-myectomy) for idiopathic hypertrophic subaortic stenosis (eg, asymmetric septal hypertrophy)

➡ *CPT Assistant Feb 05:14*

33417 Aortoplasty (gusset) for supravalvular stenosis

➡ *CPT Assistant Feb 05:14*

Mitral Valve

33420   Valvotomy, mitral valve; closed heart
➔ *CPT Assistant* Feb 05:14

33422   open heart, with cardiopulmonary bypass
➔ *CPT Assistant* Feb 05:14

33425   Valvuloplasty, mitral valve, with cardiopulmonary bypass;
➔ *CPT Assistant* May 03:19, Feb 05:14

33426   with prosthetic ring
➔ *CPT Assistant* Feb 05:14

33427   radical reconstruction, with or without ring
➔ *CPT Assistant* Feb 05:14

33430   Replacement, mitral valve, with cardiopulmonary bypass
➔ *CPT Assistant* Feb 05:14

Tricuspid Valve

33460   Valvectomy, tricuspid valve, with cardiopulmonary bypass
➔ *CPT Assistant* Feb 05:14

33463   Valvuloplasty, tricuspid valve; without ring insertion
➔ *CPT Assistant* Feb 05:14

33464   with ring insertion
➔ *CPT Assistant* Feb 05:14

33465   Replacement, tricuspid valve, with cardiopulmonary bypass
➔ *CPT Assistant* Feb 05:14

33468   Tricuspid valve repositioning and plication for Ebstein anomaly
➔ *CPT Assistant* Feb 05:14

Pulmonary Valve

33470   Valvotomy, pulmonary valve, closed heart; transventricular
➔ *CPT Assistant* Feb 05:14

(Do not report modifier 63 in conjunction with 33470)

33471   via pulmonary artery
➔ *CPT Assistant* Feb 05:14

(To report percutaneous valvuloplasty of pulmonary valve, use 92990)

33472   Valvotomy, pulmonary valve, open heart; with inflow occlusion
➔ *CPT Assistant* Feb 05:14

(Do not report modifier 63 in conjunction with 33472)

33474   with cardiopulmonary bypass
➔ *CPT Assistant* Feb 05:14

33475   Replacement, pulmonary valve
➔ *CPT Assistant* Feb 05:14

33476   Right ventricular resection for infundibular stenosis, with or without commissurotomy
➔ *CPT Assistant* Feb 05:14

33478   Outflow tract augmentation (gusset), with or without commissurotomy or infundibular resection
➔ *CPT Assistant* Feb 05:14

(Use 33478 in conjunction with 33768 when a cavopulmonary anastomosis to a second superior vena cava is performed)

Other Valvular Procedures

33496   Repair of non-structural prosthetic valve dysfunction with cardiopulmonary bypass (separate procedure)
➔ *CPT Assistant* Nov 97:16, Feb 05:14

(For reoperation, use 33530 in addition to 33496)

Coronary Artery Anomalies

Basic procedures include endarterectomy or angioplasty.

33500   Repair of coronary arteriovenous or arteriocardiac chamber fistula; with cardiopulmonary bypass

33501   without cardiopulmonary bypass

33502   Repair of anomalous coronary artery from pulmonary artery origin; by ligation
➔ *CPT Changes: An Insider's View* 2006

33503   by graft, without cardiopulmonary bypass

(Do not report modifier 63 in conjunction with 33502, 33503)

33504   by graft, with cardiopulmonary bypass

33505   with construction of intrapulmonary artery tunnel (Takeuchi procedure)

33506   by translocation from pulmonary artery to aorta

(Do not report modifier 63 in conjunction with 33505, 33506)

33507   Repair of anomalous (eg, intramural) aortic origin of coronary artery by unroofing or translocation
➔ *CPT Assistant* Mar 07:1; *CPT Changes: An Insider's View* 2006

Endoscopy

Surgical vascular endoscopy always includes diagnostic endoscopy.

+ 33508   Endoscopy, surgical, including video-assisted harvest of vein(s) for coronary artery bypass procedure (List separately in addition to code for primary procedure)
➔ *CPT Changes: An Insider's View* 2003

(Use 33508 in conjunction with 33510-33523)

(For open harvest of upper extremity vein procedure, use 35500)

Do not use modifier -51 (using add on codes) [handwritten note]

Venous Grafting Only for Coronary Artery Bypass

The following codes are used to report coronary artery bypass procedures using venous grafts only. These codes should NOT be used to report the performance of coronary artery bypass procedures using arterial grafts and venous grafts during the same procedure. See 33517-33523 and 33533-33536 for reporting combined arterial-venous grafts.

Procurement of the saphenous vein graft is included in the description of the work for 33510-33516 and should not be reported as a separate service or co-surgery. To report harvesting of an upper extremity vein, use 35500 in addition to the bypass procedure. To report harvesting of a femoropopliteal vein segment, report 35572 in addition to the bypass procedure. When surgical assistant performs graft procurement, add modifier 80 to 33510-33516.

Coronary Artery Bypass—Venous Grafting Only
33510-33516

A. Use 33510 to report a single coronary venous graft.

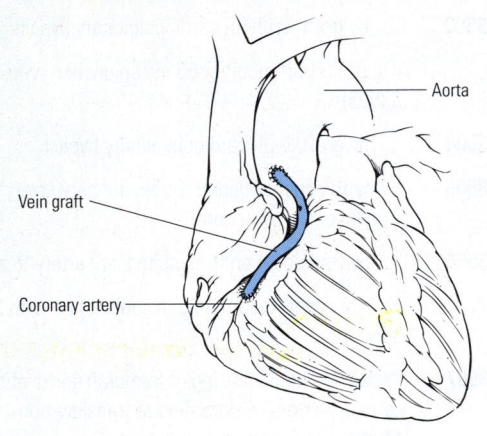

B. Report 33512 when 3 coronary venous grafts are performed.

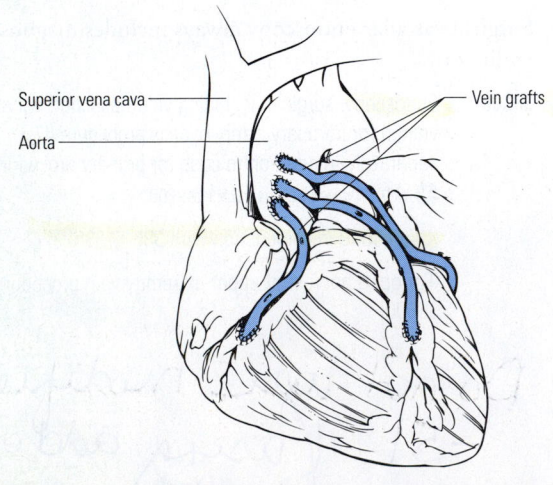

33510   Coronary artery bypass, vein only; single coronary venous graft
➔ *CPT Assistant* Fall 91:5, Winter 92:12, Jul 99:11, Apr 01:7, Feb 05:14, Jan 07:7, Mar 07:1

33511   2 coronary venous grafts
➔ *CPT Assistant* Fall 91:5, Winter 92:12, Jul 99:11, Apr 01:7, Feb 05:14, Jan 07:7, Mar 07:1

33512   3 coronary venous grafts
➔ *CPT Assistant* Fall 91:5, Winter 92:12, Apr 01:7, Feb 05:14, Jan 07:7, Mar 07:1

33513   4 coronary venous grafts
➔ *CPT Assistant* Fall 91:5, Winter 92:12, Apr 01:7, Feb 05:14, Jan 07:7, Mar 07:1

33514   5 coronary venous grafts
➔ *CPT Assistant* Fall 91:5, Winter 92:12, Apr 01:7, Feb 05:14, Jan 07:7, Mar 07:1

33516   6 or more coronary venous grafts
➔ *CPT Assistant* Fall 91:5, Winter 92:12, Jul 99:11, Apr 01:7, Feb 05:14, Jan 07:7, Mar 07:1

Combined Arterial-Venous Grafting for Coronary Bypass

The following codes are used to report coronary artery bypass procedures using venous grafts and arterial grafts during the same procedure. These codes may NOT be used alone.

To report combined arterial-venous grafts it is necessary to report two codes: (1) the appropriate combined arterial-venous graft code (33517-33523); and (2) the appropriate arterial graft code (33533-33536).

Procurement of the saphenous vein graft is included in the description of the work for 33517-33523 and should not be reported as a separate service or co-surgery. Procurement of the artery for grafting is included in the description of the work for 33533-33536 and should not be reported as a separate service or co-surgery, except when an upper extremity artery (eg, radial artery) is procured. To report harvesting of an upper extremity artery, use 35600 in addition to the bypass procedure. To report harvesting of an upper extremity vein, use 35500 in addition to the bypass procedure. To report harvesting of a femoropopliteal vein segment, report 35572 in addition to the bypass procedure. When surgical assistant performs arterial and/or venous graft procurement, add modifier 80 to 33517-33523, 33533-33536, as appropriate.

Coronary Artery Bypass—Combined Arterial-Venous Grafting
33517-33530

Both venous and arterial grafts are used in these bypass procedures. The appropriate arterial graft codes (33533-33536) must also be reported in conjunction with codes 33517-33530.

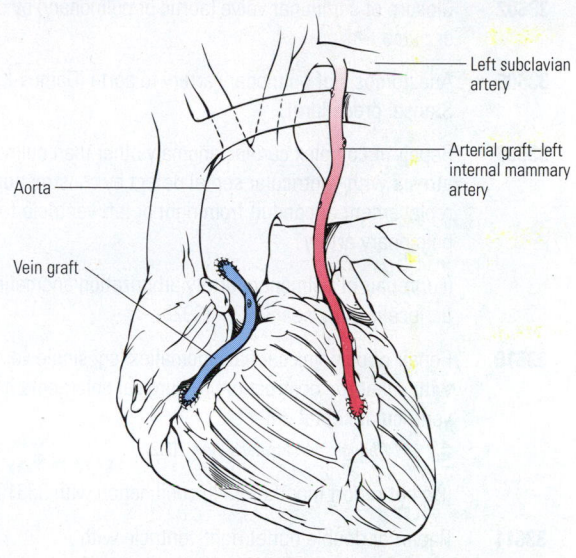

Left subclavian artery

Arterial graft—left internal mammary artery

Aorta

Vein graft

Coronary Artery Bypass—Sequential Combined Arterial-Venous Grafting
33517-33530

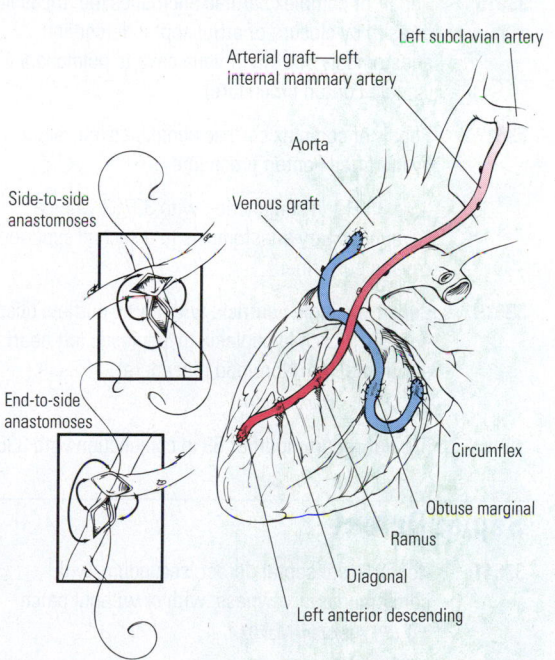

Left subclavian artery

Arterial graft—left internal mammary artery

Aorta

Side-to-side anastomoses

Venous graft

End-to-side anastomoses

Circumflex

Obtuse marginal

Ramus

Diagonal

Left anterior descending

Note: To determine the number of bypass grafts in a coronary artery bypass (CABG), count the number of distal anastomoses (contact point[s]) where the bypass graft artery or vein is sutured to the diseased coronary artery(s).

+ **33517** Coronary artery bypass, using venous graft(s) and arterial graft(s); single vein graft (List separately in addition to code for primary procedure)
> *CPT Assistant* Fall 91:5, Winter 92:13, Nov 99:18, Apr 01:7, Feb 05:14; *CPT Changes: An Insider's View* 2000, 2008

(Use 33517 in conjunction with 33533-33536)

+ **33518** 2 venous grafts (List separately in addition to code for primary procedure)
> *CPT Assistant* Fall 91:5, Winter 92:13, Apr 01:7, Feb 05:14, Jan 07:7, Mar 07:1; *CPT Changes: An Insider's View* 2008

(Use 33518 in conjunction with 33533-33536)

+ **33519** 3 venous grafts (List separately in addition to code for primary procedure)
> *CPT Assistant* Fall 91:5, Winter 92:13, Apr 01:7, Feb 05:14, Jan 07:7, Mar 07:1; *CPT Changes: An Insider's View* 2008

(Use 33519 in conjunction with 33533-33536)

+ **33521** 4 venous grafts (List separately in addition to code for primary procedure)
> *CPT Assistant* Fall 91:5, Winter 92:13, Apr 01:7, Feb 05:14, Jan 07:7, Mar 07:1; *CPT Changes: An Insider's View* 2008

(Use 33521 in conjunction with 33533-33536)

+ **33522** 5 venous grafts (List separately in addition to code for primary procedure)
> *CPT Assistant* Fall 91:5, Winter 92:13, Apr 01:7, Feb 05:14, Jan 07:7, Mar 07:1; *CPT Changes: An Insider's View* 2008

(Use 33522 in conjunction with 33533-33536)

+ **33523** 6 or more venous grafts (List separately in addition to code for primary procedure)
> *CPT Assistant* Fall 91:5, Winter 92:13, Apr 01:7, Feb 05:14, Jan 07:7, Mar 07:1; *CPT Changes: An Insider's View* 2008

(Use 33523 in conjunction with 33533-33536)

+ **33530** Reoperation, coronary artery bypass procedure or valve procedure, more than 1 month after original operation (List separately in addition to code for primary procedure)
> *CPT Assistant* Winter 90:6, Fall 91:5, Winter 92:13, Apr 01:7, Jul 01:11, Feb 05:13-14, Jan 07:7

(Use 33530 in conjunction with 33400-33496; 33510-33536, 33863)

Arterial Grafting for Coronary Artery Bypass

The following codes are used to report coronary artery bypass procedures using either arterial grafts only or a combination of arterial-venous grafts. The codes include the use of the internal mammary artery, gastroepiploic artery, epigastric artery, radial artery, and arterial conduits procured from other sites.

To report combined arterial-venous grafts it is necessary to report two codes: (1) the appropriate arterial graft code (33533-33536); and (2) the appropriate combined arterial-venous graft code (33517-33523).

Procurement of the artery for grafting is included in the description of the work for 33533-33536 and should not be reported as a separate service or co-surgery, except when an upper extremity artery (eg, radial artery) is procured. To report harvesting of an upper extremity artery, use 35600 in addition to the bypass procedure. To report harvesting of an upper extremity vein, use 35500 in addition to the bypass procedure. To report harvesting of a femoropopliteal vein segment, report 35572 in addition to the bypass procedure. When surgical assistant performs arterial and/or venous graft procurement, add modifier 80 to 33517-33523, 33533-33536, as appropriate.

33533 Coronary artery bypass, using arterial graft(s); single arterial graft

➜ *CPT Assistant* Winter 92:12, Nov 99:18, Apr 01:7, Feb 05:14, Jan 07:7, Mar 07:1; *CPT Changes: An Insider's View* 2000

33534 2 coronary arterial grafts

➜ *CPT Assistant* Winter 92:12, Apr 01:7, Feb 05:14, Jan 07:7, Mar 07:1

33535 3 coronary arterial grafts

➜ *CPT Assistant* Winter 92:12, Apr 01:7, Feb 05:14, Jan 07:7, Mar 07:1

33536 4 or more coronary arterial grafts

➜ *CPT Assistant* Winter 92:12, Apr 01:7, Feb 05:14, Jan 07:7, Mar 07:1

33542 Myocardial resection (eg, ventricular aneurysmectomy)

➜ *CPT Assistant* Winter 92:12, Mar 07:1

33545 Repair of postinfarction ventricular septal defect, with or without myocardial resection

➜ *CPT Assistant* Winter 92:12, Mar 07:1

33548 Surgical ventricular restoration procedure, includes prosthetic patch, when performed (eg, ventricular remodeling, SVR, SAVER, Dor procedures)

➜ *CPT Assistant* Nov 06:21, Dec 06:10, Mar 07:1; *CPT Changes: An Insider's View* 2006

(Do not report 33548 in conjunction with 32551, 33210, 33211, 33310, 33315)

(For Batista procedure or pachopexy, use 33999)

Coronary Endarterectomy

+ 33572 Coronary endarterectomy, open, any method, of left anterior descending, circumflex, or right coronary artery performed in conjunction with coronary artery bypass graft procedure, each vessel (List separately in addition to primary procedure)

(Use 33572 in conjunction with 33510-33516, 33533-33536)

Single Ventricle and Other Complex Cardiac Anomalies

33600 Closure of atrioventricular valve (mitral or tricuspid) by suture or patch

➜ *CPT Assistant* Mar 07:1

33602 Closure of semilunar valve (aortic or pulmonary) by suture or patch

33606 Anastomosis of pulmonary artery to aorta (Damus-Kaye-Stansel procedure)

33608 Repair of complex cardiac anomaly other than pulmonary atresia with ventricular septal defect by construction or replacement of conduit from right or left ventricle to pulmonary artery

(For repair of pulmonary artery arborization anomalies by unifocalization, see 33925-33926)

33610 Repair of complex cardiac anomalies (eg, single ventricle with subaortic obstruction) by surgical enlargement of ventricular septal defect

➜ *CPT Changes: An Insider's View* 2002

(Do not report modifier 63 in conjunction with 33610)

33611 Repair of double outlet right ventricle with intraventricular tunnel repair;

(Do not report modifier 63 in conjunction with 33611)

33612 with repair of right ventricular outflow tract obstruction

33615 Repair of complex cardiac anomalies (eg, tricuspid atresia) by closure of atrial septal defect and anastomosis of atria or vena cava to pulmonary artery (simple Fontan procedure)

33617 Repair of complex cardiac anomalies (eg, single ventricle) by modified Fontan procedure

(Use 33617 in conjunction with 33768 when a cavopulmonary anastomosis to a second superior vena cava is performed)

33619 Repair of single ventricle with aortic outflow obstruction and aortic arch hypoplasia (hypoplastic left heart syndrome) (eg, Norwood procedure)

➜ *CPT Assistant* Mar 07:1

(Do not report modifier 63 in conjunction with 33619)

Septal Defect

33641 Repair atrial septal defect, secundum, with cardiopulmonary bypass, with or without patch

➜ *CPT Assistant* Mar 07:1

33645 Direct or patch closure, sinus venosus, with or without anomalous pulmonary venous drainage

(Do not report 33645 in conjunction with 33724, 33726)

33647   Repair of atrial septal defect and ventricular septal defect, with direct or patch closure

(Do not report modifier 63 in conjunction with 33647)

(For repair of tricuspid atresia (eg, Fontan, Gago procedures), use 33615)

33660   Repair of incomplete or partial atrioventricular canal (ostium primum atrial septal defect), with or without atrioventricular valve repair

33665   Repair of intermediate or transitional atrioventricular canal, with or without atrioventricular valve repair

33670   Repair of complete atrioventricular canal, with or without prosthetic valve

(Do not report modifier 63 in conjunction with 33670)

33675   Closure of multiple ventricular septal defects;
➲ *CPT Assistant* Mar 07:1; *CPT Changes: An Insider's View* 2007

33676   with pulmonary valvotomy or infundibular resection (acyanotic)
➲ *CPT Assistant* Mar 07:1; *CPT Changes: An Insider's View* 2007

33677   with removal of pulmonary artery band, with or without gusset
➲ *CPT Assistant* Mar 07:1; *CPT Changes: An Insider's View* 2007

(Do not report 33675-33677 in conjunction with 32100, 32422, 32551, 33210, 33681, 33684, 33688)

(For transmyocardial closure, see Category III codes 0166T and 0167T)

(For percutaneous closure, use 93581)

33681   Closure of single ventricular septal defect, with or without patch;
➲ *CPT Assistant* Mar 07:1; *CPT Changes: An Insider's View* 2007

33684   with pulmonary valvotomy or infundibular resection (acyanotic)

33688   with removal of pulmonary artery band, with or without gusset

(For pulmonary vein repair requiring creation of atrial septal defect, use 33724)

33690   Banding of pulmonary artery

(Do not report modifier 63 in conjunction with 33690)

33692   Complete repair tetralogy of Fallot without pulmonary atresia;

33694   with transannular patch

(Do not report modifier 63 in conjunction with 33694)

(For ligation and takedown of a systemic-to-pulmonary artery shunt, performed in conjunction with a congenital heart procedure; see 33924)

33697   Complete repair tetralogy of Fallot with pulmonary atresia including construction of conduit from right ventricle to pulmonary artery and closure of ventricular septal defect
➲ *CPT Assistant* Mar 07:1

(For ligation and takedown of a systemic-to-pulmonary artery shunt, performed in conjunction with a congenital heart procedure; see 33924)

Sinus of Valsalva

33702   Repair sinus of Valsalva fistula, with cardiopulmonary bypass;
➲ *CPT Assistant* Mar 07:1

33710   with repair of ventricular septal defect

33720   Repair sinus of Valsalva aneurysm, with cardiopulmonary bypass

33722   Closure of aortico-left ventricular tunnel
➲ *CPT Assistant* Mar 07:1

Venous Anomalies

33724   Repair of isolated partial anomalous pulmonary venous return (eg, Scimitar Syndrome)
➲ *CPT Assistant* Mar 07:1; *CPT Changes: An Insider's View* 2007

(Do not report 33724 in conjunction with 32551, 33210, 33211)

33726   Repair of pulmonary venous stenosis
➲ *CPT Assistant* Mar 07:1; *CPT Changes: An Insider's View* 2007

(Do not report 33726 in conjunction with 32551, 33210, 33211)

33730   Complete repair of anomalous pulmonary venous return (supracardiac, intracardiac, or infracardiac types)
➲ *CPT Assistant* Mar 07:1

(Do not report modifier 63 in conjunction with 33730)

(For partial anomalous pulmonary venous return, use 33724; for repair of pulmonary venous stenosis, use 33726)

33732   Repair of cor triatriatum or supravalvular mitral ring by resection of left atrial membrane
➲ *CPT Assistant* Mar 07:1

(Do not report modifier 63 in conjunction with 33732)

Shunting Procedures

33735   Atrial septectomy or septostomy; closed heart (Blalock-Hanlon type operation)
➲ *CPT Assistant* Mar 07:1

33736   open heart with cardiopulmonary bypass

(Do not report modifier 63 in conjunction with 33735, 33736)

33737   open heart, with inflow occlusion

 ▲=Revised code   ●=New code   ▶◀=Contains new or revised text   ⊘=Modifier 51 exempt

(For transvenous method cardiac catheterization balloon atrial septectomy or septostomy (Rashkind type), use 92992)

(For blade method cardiac catheterization atrial septectomy or septostomy (Sang-Park septostomy), use 92993)

33750 Shunt; subclavian to pulmonary artery (Blalock-Taussig type operation)

33755 ascending aorta to pulmonary artery (Waterston type operation)

33762 descending aorta to pulmonary artery (Potts-Smith type operation)

(Do not report modifier 63 in conjunction with 33750, 33755, 33762)

33764 central, with prosthetic graft

33766 superior vena cava to pulmonary artery for flow to 1 lung (classical Glenn procedure)

33767 superior vena cava to pulmonary artery for flow to both lungs (bidirectional Glenn procedure)

+ 33768 Anastomosis, cavopulmonary, second superior vena cava (List separately in addition to primary procedure)

→ *CPT Assistant* Mar 07:1; *CPT Changes: An Insider's View* 2006

(Use 33768 in conjunction with 33478, 33617, 33767)

(Do not report 33768 in conjunction with 32551, 33210, 33211)

Transposition of the Great Vessels

33770 Repair of transposition of the great arteries with ventricular septal defect and subpulmonary stenosis; without surgical enlargement of ventricular septal defect

→ *CPT Assistant* Mar 07:1

33771 with surgical enlargement of ventricular septal defect

33774 Repair of transposition of the great arteries, atrial baffle procedure (eg, Mustard or Senning type) with cardiopulmonary bypass;

33775 with removal of pulmonary band

33776 with closure of ventricular septal defect

33777 with repair of subpulmonic obstruction

33778 Repair of transposition of the great arteries, aortic pulmonary artery reconstruction (eg, Jatene type);

(Do not report modifier 63 in conjunction with 33778)

33779 with removal of pulmonary band

33780 with closure of ventricular septal defect

33781 with repair of subpulmonic obstruction

→ *CPT Assistant* Mar 07:1

● **33782** Aortic root translocation with ventricular septal defect and pulmonary stenosis repair (ie, Nikaidoh procedure); without coronary ostium reimplantation

→ *CPT Changes: An Insider's View* 2010

▶(Do not report 33782 in conjunction with 33412, 33413, 33608, 33681, 33770, 33771, 33778, 33780, 33920)◀

● **33783** with reimplantation of 1 or both coronary ostia

→ *CPT Changes: An Insider's View* 2010

Truncus Arteriosus

33786 Total repair, truncus arteriosus (Rastelli type operation)

→ *CPT Assistant* Mar 07:1

(Do not report modifier 63 in conjunction with 33786)

33788 Reimplantation of an anomalous pulmonary artery

→ *CPT Assistant* Mar 07:1

(For pulmonary artery band, use 33690)

Aortic Anomalies

33800 Aortic suspension (aortopexy) for tracheal decompression (eg, for tracheomalacia) (separate procedure)

→ *CPT Assistant* Mar 07:1

33802 Division of aberrant vessel (vascular ring);

33803 with reanastomosis

33813 Obliteration of aortopulmonary septal defect; without cardiopulmonary bypass

33814 with cardiopulmonary bypass

33820 Repair of patent ductus arteriosus; by ligation

→ *CPT Assistant* Mar 07:1

Patent Ductus Arteriosus
33820

The tissues surrounding the ductus are dissected away and then several heavy ligatures are passed around the ductus and tied off on both ends.

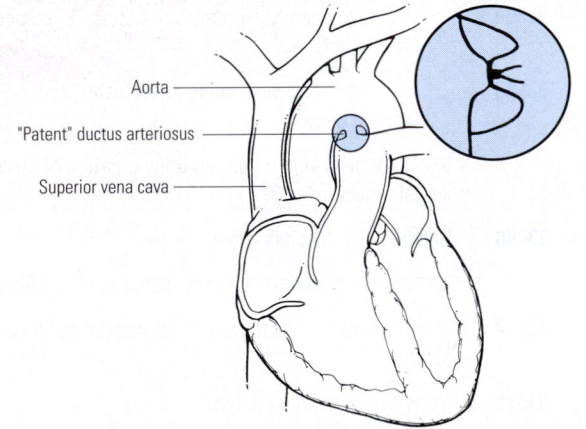

Aorta

"Patent" ductus arteriosus

Superior vena cava

33822 by division, younger than 18 years

→ *CPT Assistant* Mar 07:1

33824 by division, 18 years and older

33840 Excision of coarctation of aorta, with or without associated patent ductus arteriosus; with direct anastomosis

33845   with graft

33851   repair using either left subclavian artery or prosthetic material as gusset for enlargement

33852   Repair of hypoplastic or interrupted aortic arch using autogenous or prosthetic material; without cardiopulmonary bypass

33853   with cardiopulmonary bypass
➲ *CPT Assistant* Mar 07:1

(For repair of hypoplastic left heart syndrome (eg, Norwood type), via excision of coarctation of aorta, use 33619)

Thoracic Aortic Aneurysm

33860   Ascending aorta graft, with cardiopulmonary bypass, with or without valve suspension;
➲ *CPT Assistant* Mar 07:1

33861   with coronary reconstruction
➲ *CPT Assistant* Mar 07:1

33863   with aortic root replacement using composite prosthesis and coronary reconstruction
➲ *CPT Assistant* Feb 05:14, Mar 07:1

(For graft of ascending aorta, with cardiopulmonary bypass and valve replacement, with or without coronary implant or valve suspension; use 33860 or 33861 and 33405 or 33406)

33864   Ascending aorta graft, with cardiopulmonary bypass with valve suspension, with coronary reconstruction and valve-sparing aortic annulus remodeling (eg, David Procedure, Yacoub Procedure)
➲ *CPT Changes: An Insider's View* 2008

(Do not report 33864 in conjunction with 32551, 33210, 33211, 33400, 33860-33863)

33870   Transverse arch graft, with cardiopulmonary bypass

33875   Descending thoracic aorta graft, with or without bypass

33877   Repair of thoracoabdominal aortic aneurysm with graft, with or without cardiopulmonary bypass

Endovascular Repair of Descending Thoracic Aorta

Codes 33880-33891 represent a family of procedures to report placement of an endovascular graft for repair of the descending thoracic aorta. These codes include all device introduction, manipulation, positioning, and deployment. All balloon angioplasty and/or stent deployment within the target treatment zone for the endoprosthesis, either before or after endograft deployment, are not separately reportable. Open arterial exposure and associated closure of the arteriotomy sites (eg, 34812, 34820, 34833, 34834), introduction of guidewires and catheters (eg, 36140, 36200-36218), and extensive repair or replacement of an artery (eg, 35226, 35286) should be additionally reported. Transposition of

subclavian artery to carotid, and carotid-carotid bypass performed in conjunction with endovascular repair of the descending thoracic aorta (eg, 33889, 33891) should be separately reported. The primary codes, 33880 and 33881, include placement of all distal extensions, if required, in the distal thoracic aorta, while proximal extensions, if needed, are reported separately.

For fluoroscopic guidance in conjunction with endovascular repair of the thoracic aorta, see codes 75956-75959 as appropriate. Codes 75956 and 75957 include all angiography of the thoracic aorta and its branches for diagnostic imaging prior to deployment of the primary endovascular devices (including all routine components of modular devices), fluoroscopic guidance in the delivery of the endovascular components, and intraprocedural arterial angiography (eg, confirm position, detect endoleak, evaluate runoff). Code 75958 includes the analogous services for placement of each proximal thoracic endovascular extension. Code 75959 includes the analogous services for placement of a distal thoracic endovascular extension(s) placed during a procedure after the primary repair.

Other interventional procedures performed at the time of endovascular repair of the descending thoracic aorta should be additionally reported (eg, innominate, carotid, subclavian, visceral, or iliac artery transluminal angioplasty or stenting, arterial embolization, intravascular ultrasound) when performed before or after deployment of the aortic prostheses.

(For transcatheter placement of wireless physiologic sensor in aneurysmal sac, use 34806)

(For analysis, interpretation, and report of implanted wireless pressure sensor in aneurysmal sac, use 93982)

33880   Endovascular repair of descending thoracic aorta (eg, aneurysm, pseudoaneurysm, dissection, penetrating ulcer, intramural hematoma, or traumatic disruption); involving coverage of left subclavian artery origin, initial endoprosthesis plus descending thoracic aortic extension(s), if required, to level of celiac artery origin
➲ *CPT Changes: An Insider's View* 2006
➲ *Clinical Examples in Radiology* Winter 06:14

(For radiological supervision and interpretation, use 75956 in conjunction with 33880)

33881   not involving coverage of left subclavian artery origin, initial endoprosthesis plus descending thoracic aortic extension(s), if required, to level of celiac artery origin
➲ *CPT Changes: An Insider's View* 2006
➲ *Clinical Examples in Radiology* Winter 06:14

(For radiological supervision and interpretation, use 75957 in conjunction with 33881)

33883   Placement of proximal extension prosthesis for endovascular repair of descending thoracic aorta (eg, aneurysm, pseudoaneurysm, dissection, penetrating ulcer, intramural hematoma, or traumatic disruption); initial extension

➡ *CPT Changes: An Insider's View* 2006

➡ *Clinical Examples in Radiology* Winter 06:14

(For radiological supervision and interpretation, use 75958 in conjunction with 33883)

(Do not report 33881, 33883 when extension placement converts repair to cover left subclavian origin. Use only 33880)

+ 33884   each additional proximal extension (List separately in addition to code for primary procedure)

➡ *CPT Changes: An Insider's View* 2006

➡ *Clinical Examples in Radiology* Winter 06:14

(Use 33884 in conjunction with 33883)

(For radiological supervision and interpretation, use 75958 in conjunction with 33884)

33886   Placement of distal extension prosthesis(s) delayed after endovascular repair of descending thoracic aorta

➡ *CPT Changes: An Insider's View* 2006

➡ *Clinical Examples in Radiology* Winter 06:14

(Do not report 33886 in conjunction with 33880, 33881)

(Report 33886 once, regardless of number of modules deployed)

(For radiological supervision and interpretation, use 75959 in conjunction with 33886)

33889   Open subclavian to carotid artery transposition performed in conjunction with endovascular repair of descending thoracic aorta, by neck incision, unilateral

➡ *CPT Changes: An Insider's View* 2006

➡ *Clinical Examples in Radiology* Winter 06:15

(Do not report 33889 in conjunction with 35694)

33891   Bypass graft, with other than vein, transcervical retropharyngeal carotid-carotid, performed in conjunction with endovascular repair of descending thoracic aorta, by neck incision

➡ *CPT Changes: An Insider's View* 2006

➡ *Clinical Examples in Radiology* Winter 06:15

(Do not report 33891 in conjunction with 35509, 35601)

Pulmonary Artery

33910   Pulmonary artery embolectomy; with cardiopulmonary bypass

➡ *CPT Assistant* Mar 07:1

33915   without cardiopulmonary bypass

➡ *CPT Assistant* Mar 07:1

33916   Pulmonary endarterectomy, with or without embolectomy, with cardiopulmonary bypass

➡ *CPT Assistant* Mar 07:1

33917   Repair of pulmonary artery stenosis by reconstruction with patch or graft

➡ *CPT Assistant* Mar 07:1

33920   Repair of pulmonary atresia with ventricular septal defect, by construction or replacement of conduit from right or left ventricle to pulmonary artery

➡ *CPT Assistant* Mar 07:1

(For repair of other complex cardiac anomalies by construction or replacement of right or left ventricle to pulmonary artery conduit, use 33608)

33922   Transection of pulmonary artery with cardiopulmonary bypass

(Do not report modifier 63 in conjunction with 33922)

+ 33924   Ligation and takedown of a systemic-to-pulmonary artery shunt, performed in conjunction with a congenital heart procedure (List separately in addition to code for primary procedure)

(Use 33924 in conjunction with 33470-33475, 33600-33619, 33684-33688, 33692-33697, 33735-33767, 33770-33781, 33786, 33920-33922)

33925   Repair of pulmonary artery arborization anomalies by unifocalization; without cardiopulmonary bypass

➡ *CPT Changes: An Insider's View* 2006

33926   with cardiopulmonary bypass

➡ *CPT Changes: An Insider's View* 2006

Heart/Lung Transplantation

Heart with or without lung allotransplantation involves three distinct components of physician work:

1. *Cadaver donor cardiectomy with or without pneumonectomy*, which includes harvesting the allograft and cold preservation of the allograft (perfusing with cold preservation solution and cold maintenance) (see 33930, 33940).

2. *Backbench work*:

Preparation of a cadaver donor heart and lung allograft prior to transplantation, including dissection of the allograft from surrounding soft tissues to prepare the aorta, superior vena cava, inferior vena cava, and trachea for implantation (use 33933).

Preparation of a cadaver donor heart allograft prior to transplantation, including dissection of the allograft from surrounding soft tissues to prepare aorta, superior vena cava, inferior vena cava, pulmonary artery, and left atrium for implantation (use 33944).

3. ***Recipient heart with or without lung allotransplantation***, which includes transplantation of allograft and care of the recipient (see 33935, 33945).

(For implantation of a total replacement heart system (artificial heart) with recipient cardiectomy or heart replacement system components, see Category III codes 0051T-0053T)

33930 Donor cardiectomy-pneumonectomy (including cold preservation)
➲ *CPT Changes: An Insider's View* 2005

33933 Backbench standard preparation of cadaver donor heart/lung allograft prior to transplantation, including dissection of allograft from surrounding soft tissues to prepare aorta, superior vena cava, inferior vena cava, and trachea for implantation
➲ *CPT Changes: An Insider's View* 2005

33935 Heart-lung transplant with recipient cardiectomy-pneumonectomy

33940 Donor cardiectomy (including cold preservation)
➲ *CPT Assistant* Apr 05:10-11; *CPT Changes: An Insider's View* 2005

33944 Backbench standard preparation of cadaver donor heart allograft prior to transplantation, including dissection of allograft from surrounding soft tissues to prepare aorta, superior vena cava, inferior vena cava, pulmonary artery, and left atrium for implantation
➲ *CPT Changes: An Insider's View* 2005

(For repair or resection procedures on the donor heart, see 33300, 33310, 33320, 33400, 33463, 33464, 33510, 33641, 35216, 35276 or 35685)

33945 Heart transplant, with or without recipient cardiectomy
➲ *CPT Assistant* Fall 92:20

Cardiac Assist

▶The insertion of a ventricular assist device (VAD) can be performed via percutaneous (0048T) or transthoracic (33975, 33976, 33979) approach. The location of the ventricular assist device may be intracorporeal or extracorporeal.

Removal of a ventricular assist device (33977, 33978, 33980, 0050T) includes removal of the entire device, including the cannulas.

Replacement of a ventricular assist device pump includes the removal of the pump and insertion of a new pump, connection, de-airing, and initiation of the new pump.

Replacement of the entire ventricular assist device system, ie, pump(s) and cannulas, is reported using the insertion codes. Removal of the ventricular assist device system being replaced is not separately reported.◀

▶(For implantation or removal of ventricular assist device, extracorporeal, percutaneous transseptal access, see 0048T, 0050T. For replacement of a ventricular assist device, extracorporeal, percutaneous transseptal access, use 33999)◀

33960 Prolonged extracorporeal circulation for cardiopulmonary insufficiency; initial 24 hours

+ 33961 each additional 24 hours (List separately in addition to code for primary procedure)

(Do not report modifier 63 in conjunction with 33960, 33961)

(Use 33961 in conjunction with 33960)

(For insertion of cannula for prolonged extracorporeal circulation, use 36822)

33967 Insertion of intra-aortic balloon assist device, percutaneous
➲ *CPT Assistant* Feb 02:2; *CPT Changes: An Insider's View* 2002

33968 Removal of intra-aortic balloon assist device, percutaneous
➲ *CPT Assistant* Nov 99:19, Jan 00:10; *CPT Changes: An Insider's View* 2000

33970 Insertion of intra-aortic balloon assist device through the femoral artery, open approach
➲ *CPT Assistant* Nov 99:19; *CPT Changes: An Insider's View* 2000

33971 Removal of intra-aortic balloon assist device including repair of femoral artery, with or without graft

33973 Insertion of intra-aortic balloon assist device through the ascending aorta

33974 Removal of intra-aortic balloon assist device from the ascending aorta, including repair of the ascending aorta, with or without graft

33975 Insertion of ventricular assist device; extracorporeal, single ventricle
➲ *CPT Assistant* Feb 92:2, Jan 04:28; *CPT Changes: An Insider's View* 2002

33976 extracorporeal, biventricular
➲ *CPT Assistant* Feb 02:2; *CPT Changes: An Insider's View* 2002

33977 Removal of ventricular assist device; extracorporeal, single ventricle
➲ *CPT Assistant* Feb 02:2; *CPT Changes: An Insider's View* 2002

33978 extracorporeal, biventricular
➲ *CPT Assistant* Feb 02:2; *CPT Changes: An Insider's View* 2002

33979 Insertion of ventricular assist device, implantable intracorporeal, single ventricle
➲ *CPT Assistant* Feb 02:3, Jan 04:28; *CPT Changes: An Insider's View* 2002

Insertion of Implantable Single Ventricle Assist Device
33979

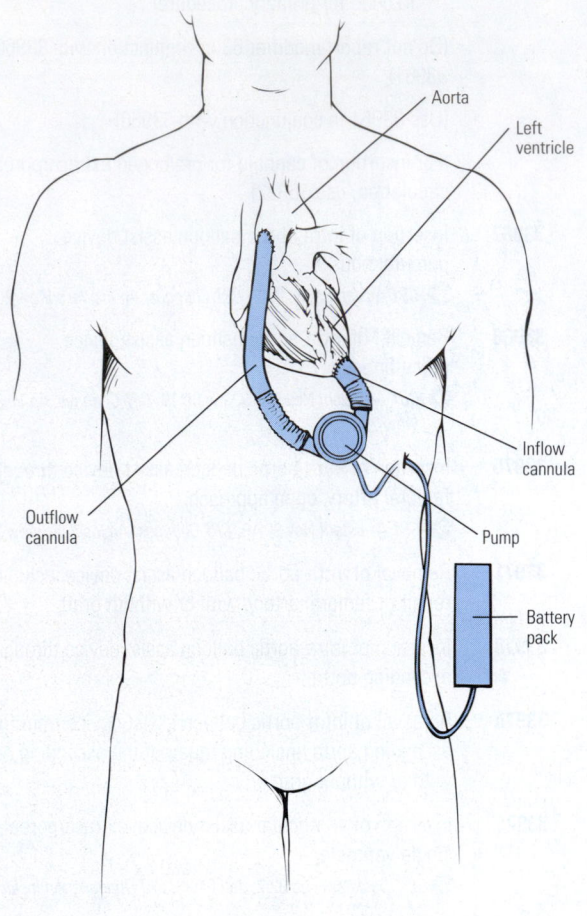

Aorta

Left ventricle

Inflow cannula

Outflow cannula

Pump

Battery pack

33980 Removal of ventricular assist device, implantable intracorporeal, single ventricle
➜ *CPT Assistant* Feb 02:3; *CPT Changes: An Insider's View* 2002

● **33981** Replacement of extracorporeal ventricular assist device, single or biventricular, pump(s), single or each pump
➜ *CPT Changes: An Insider's View* 2010

● **33982** Replacement of ventricular assist device pump(s); implantable intracorporeal, single ventricle, without cardiopulmonary bypass
➜ *CPT Changes: An Insider's View* 2010

● **33983** implantable intracorporeal, single ventricle, with cardiopulmonary bypass
➜ *CPT Changes: An Insider's View* 2010

Other Procedures

33999 Unlisted procedure, cardiac surgery
➜ *CPT Assistant* Oct 99:11, Jan 04:7, Mar 07:1

Arteries and Veins

Primary vascular procedure listings include establishing both inflow and outflow by whatever procedures necessary. Also included is that portion of the operative arteriogram performed by the surgeon, as indicated. Sympathectomy, when done, is included in the listed aortic procedures. For unlisted vascular procedure, use 37799.

Embolectomy/Thrombectomy

Arterial, With or Without Catheter

34001 Embolectomy or thrombectomy, with or without catheter; carotid, subclavian or innominate artery, by neck incision

34051 innominate, subclavian artery, by thoracic incision

34101 axillary, brachial, innominate, subclavian artery, by arm incision

34111 radial or ulnar artery, by arm incision

34151 renal, celiac, mesentery, aortoiliac artery, by abdominal incision

34201 femoropopliteal, aortoiliac artery, by leg incision

34203 popliteal-tibio-peroneal artery, by leg incision

Venous, Direct or With Catheter

34401 Thrombectomy, direct or with catheter; vena cava, iliac vein, by abdominal incision

34421 vena cava, iliac, femoropopliteal vein, by leg incision
➜ *CPT Assistant* Spring 94:30

34451 vena cava, iliac, femoropopliteal vein, by abdominal and leg incision

34471 subclavian vein, by neck incision

34490 axillary and subclavian vein, by arm incision

Venous Reconstruction

34501 Valvuloplasty, femoral vein

34502 Reconstruction of vena cava, any method

34510 Venous valve transposition, any vein donor

34520 Cross-over vein graft to venous system

34530 Saphenopopliteal vein anastomosis

plasty = repair

Endovascular Repair of Abdominal Aortic Aneurysm

Codes 34800-34826 represent a family of component procedures to report placement of an endovascular graft for abdominal aortic aneurysm repair. These codes describe open femoral or iliac artery exposure, device manipulation and deployment, and closure of the arteriotomy sites. Balloon angioplasty and/or stent deployment within the target treatment zone for the endoprosthesis, either before or after endograft deployment, are not separately reportable. Introduction of guidewires and catheters should be reported separately (eg, 36200, 36245-36248, 36140). Extensive repair or replacement of an artery should be additionally reported (eg, 35226 or 35286).

For fluoroscopic guidance in conjunction with endovascular aneurysm repair, see code 75952 or 75953, as appropriate. Code 75952 includes angiography of the aorta and its branches for diagnostic imaging prior to deployment of the endovascular device (including all routine components of modular devices), fluoroscopic guidance in the delivery of the endovascular components, and intraprocedural arterial angiography (eg, confirm position, detect endoleak, evaluate runoff). Code 75953 includes the analogous services for placement of additional extension prostheses (not for routine components of modular devices).

Other interventional procedures performed at the time of endovascular abdominal aortic aneurysm repair should be additionally reported (eg, renal transluminal angioplasty, arterial embolization, intravascular ultrasound, balloon angioplasty or stenting of native artery[s] outside the endoprosthesis target zone, when done before or after deployment of graft).

(For transcatheter placement of wireless physiologic sensor in aneurysmal sac, use 34806)

(For analysis, interpretation and report of implanted wireless pressure sensor in aneurysmal sac, use 93982)

34800 Endovascular repair of infrarenal abdominal aortic aneurysm or dissection; using aorto-aortic tube prosthesis
➔ *CPT Assistant* Dec 00:1, 4, Sep 02:3, Feb 03:2, Nov 03:5, Dec 04:18; *CPT Changes: An Insider's View* 2001

34802 using modular bifurcated prosthesis (1 docking limb)
➔ *CPT Assistant* Dec 00:1, 4, Sep 02:3, Feb 03:2, Dec 04:18; *CPT Changes: An Insider's View* 2001

Endovascular Repair of Abdominal Aortic Aneurysm
34802

[handwritten: A A A]

Using fluoroscopic guidance, a "compressed" prosthesis is introduced through arteries in the groin and advanced into position with the aneurysm. Once in the aorta, the prosthesis is expanded.

[handwritten: Triple]

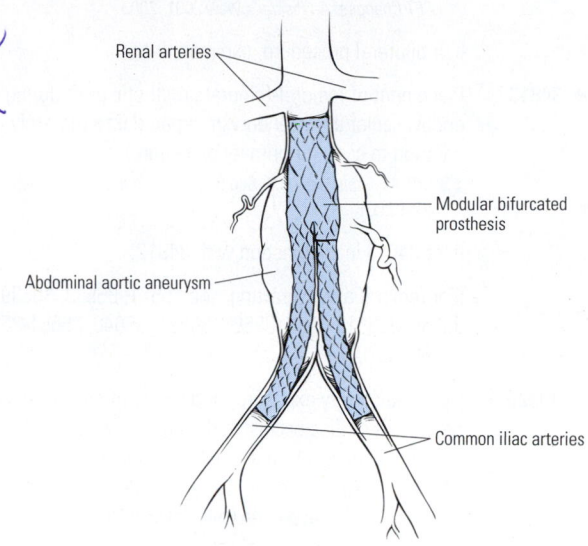

Renal arteries

Modular bifurcated prosthesis

Abdominal aortic aneurysm

Common iliac arteries

34803 using modular bifurcated prosthesis (2 docking limbs)
➔ *CPT Changes: An Insider's View* 2005

(For endovascular repair of abdominal aortic aneurysm or dissection involving visceral vessels using a fenestrated modular bifurcated prosthesis (2 docking limbs), use Category III codes 0078T, 0079T)

34804 using unibody bifurcated prosthesis
➔ *CPT Assistant* Dec 00:5, Sep 02:3, Feb 03:2; *CPT Changes: An Insider's View* 2001

34805 using aorto-uniiliac or aorto-unifemoral prosthesis
➔ *CPT Assistant* Jun 04:9, Dec 04:18; *CPT Changes: An Insider's View* 2004

+ 34806 Transcatheter placement of wireless physiologic sensor in aneurysmal sac during endovascular repair, including radiological supervision and interpretation, instrument calibration, and collection of pressure data (List separately in addition to code for primary procedure)
➔ *CPT Changes: An Insider's View* 2008, 2009

(Use 34806 in conjunction with 33880, 33881, 33886, 34800-34805, 34825, 34900)

(Do not report 34806 in conjunction with 93982)

+ 34808 Endovascular placement of iliac artery occlusion device (List separately in addition to code for primary procedure)
➔ *CPT Assistant* Dec 00:6, Sep 02:3; *CPT Changes: An Insider's View* 2001

(Use 34808 in conjunction with 34800, 34805, 34813, 34825, 34826)

(For radiological supervision and interpretation, use 75952 in conjunction with 34800-34808)

(For open arterial exposure, report 34812, 34820, 34833, 34834 as appropriate, in addition to 34800-34808)

34812   Open femoral artery exposure for delivery of endovascular prosthesis, by groin incision, unilateral

➔ *CPT Assistant* Dec 00:6, Sep 02:3, Feb 03:2, Mar 04:10, Jul 06:7; *CPT Changes: An Insider's View* 2001, 2003

(For bilateral procedure, use modifier 50)

+ 34813   Placement of femoral-femoral prosthetic graft during endovascular aortic aneurysm repair (List separately in addition to code for primary procedure)

➔ *CPT Assistant* Dec 00:6, Sep 02:3; *CPT Changes: An Insider's View* 2001

(Use 34813 in conjunction with 34812)

(For femoral artery grafting, see 35521, 35533, 35539, 35540, 35551-35558, 35566, 35621, 35646, 35651-35661, 35666, 35700)

34820   Open iliac artery exposure for delivery of endovascular prosthesis or iliac occlusion during endovascular therapy, by abdominal or retroperitoneal incision, unilateral

➔ *CPT Assistant* Dec 00:7-8, Sep 02:3, Feb 03:4, Aug 04:10, Jul 06:7; *CPT Changes: An Insider's View* 2001

(For bilateral procedure, use modifier 50)

34825   Placement of proximal or distal extension prosthesis for endovascular repair of infrarenal abdominal aortic or iliac aneurysm, false aneurysm, or dissection; initial vessel

➔ *CPT Assistant* Dec 00:5, Sep 02:3, Feb 03:3; *CPT Changes: An Insider's View* 2001, 2003

+ 34826   each additional vessel (List separately in addition to code for primary procedure)

➔ *CPT Assistant* Dec 00:6, Sep 02:3, Feb 03:3; *CPT Changes: An Insider's View* 2001

(Use 34826 in conjunction with 34825)

(Use 34825, 34826 in addition to 34800-34808, 34900 as appropriate)

(For staged procedure, use modifier 58)

(For radiological supervision and interpretation, use 75953)

34830   Open repair of infrarenal aortic aneurysm or dissection, plus repair of associated arterial trauma, following unsuccessful endovascular repair; tube prosthesis

➔ *CPT Assistant* Dec 00:6, Sep 02:3, Oct 08:10; *CPT Changes: An Insider's View* 2001

34831   aorto-bi-iliac prosthesis

➔ *CPT Assistant* Dec 00:6, Sep 02:3, Oct 08:10; *CPT Changes: An Insider's View* 2001

34832   aorto-bifemoral prosthesis

➔ *CPT Assistant* Dec 00:6, Sep 02:3, Oct 08:10; *CPT Changes: An Insider's View* 2001

34833   Open iliac artery exposure with creation of conduit for delivery of aortic or iliac endovascular prosthesis, by abdominal or retroperitoneal incision, unilateral

➔ *CPT Assistant* Aug 04:10, Feb 03:4, Jul 06:7; *CPT Changes: An Insider's View* 2003, 2006

➔ *Clinical Examples in Radiology* Winter 06:19

(For bilateral procedure, use modifier 50)

(Do not report 34833 in addition to 34820)

34834   Open brachial artery exposure to assist in the deployment of aortic or iliac endovascular prosthesis by arm incision, unilateral

➔ *CPT Assistant* Feb 03:4, Jul 06:7; *CPT Changes: An Insider's View* 2003, 2006

➔ *Clinical Examples in Radiology* Winter 06:19

(For bilateral procedure, use modifier 50)

Endovascular Repair of Iliac Aneurysm

Code 34900 represents a procedure to report introduction, positioning, and deployment of an endovascular graft for treatment of aneurysm, pseudoaneurysm, or arteriovenous malformation or trauma of the iliac artery (common, hypogastric, external). All balloon angioplasty and/or stent deployments within the target treatment zone for the endoprosthesis, either before or after endograft deployment, are included in the work of 34900 and are not separately reportable. Open femoral or iliac artery exposure (eg, 34812, 34820), introduction of guidewires and catheters (eg, 36200, 36215-36218), and extensive repair or replacement of an artery (eg, 35206-35286) should be additionally reported.

For fluoroscopic guidance in conjunction with endovascular iliac aneurysm repair, see code 75954. Code 75954 includes angiography of the aorta and iliac arteries for diagnostic imaging prior to deployment of the endovascular device (including all routine components), fluoroscopic guidance in the delivery of the endovascular components, and intraprocedural arterial angiography to confirm appropriate position of the graft, detect endoleaks, and evaluate the status of the runoff vessels (eg, evaluation for dissection, stenosis, thrombosis, distal embolization, or iatrogenic injury).

Other interventional procedures performed at the time of endovascular iliac aneurysm repair should be additionally reported (eg, transluminal angioplasty outside the aneurysm target zone, arterial embolization, intravascular ultrasound).

34900   Endovascular graft placement for repair of iliac artery (eg, aneurysm, pseudoaneurysm, arteriovenous malformation, trauma)

➔ *CPT Assistant* Feb 93:2; *CPT Changes: An Insider's View* 2003

(For radiological supervision and interpretation, use 75954)

(For placement of extension prosthesis during endovascular iliac artery repair, use 34825)

(For bilateral procedure, use modifier 50)

Direct Repair of Aneurysm or Excision (Partial or Total) and Graft Insertion for Aneurysm, Pseudoaneurysm, Ruptured Aneurysm, and Associated Occlusive Disease

Procedures 35001-35152 include preparation of artery for anastomosis including endarterectomy.

(For direct repairs associated with occlusive disease only, see 35201-35286)

(For intracranial aneurysm, see 61700 et seq)

(For endovascular repair of abdominal aortic aneurysm, see 34800-34826)

(For endovascular repair of iliac artery aneurysm, see 34900)

(For thoracic aortic aneurysm, see 33860-33875)

(For endovascular repair of descending thoracic aorta, involving coverage of left subclavian artery origin, use 33880)

35001   Direct repair of aneurysm, pseudoaneurysm, or excision (partial or total) and graft insertion, with or without patch graft; for aneurysm and associated occlusive disease, carotid, subclavian artery, by neck incision

➔ *CPT Changes: An Insider's View* 2002

35002   for ruptured aneurysm, carotid, subclavian artery, by neck incision

35005   for aneurysm, pseudoaneurysm, and associated occlusive disease, vertebral artery

➔ *CPT Changes: An Insider's View* 2002

35011   for aneurysm and associated occlusive disease, axillary-brachial artery, by arm incision

35013   for ruptured aneurysm, axillary-brachial artery, by arm incision

35021   for aneurysm, pseudoaneurysm, and associated occlusive disease, innominate, subclavian artery, by thoracic incision

➔ *CPT Changes: An Insider's View* 2002

35022   for ruptured aneurysm, innominate, subclavian artery, by thoracic incision

35045   for aneurysm, pseudoaneurysm, and associated occlusive disease, radial or ulnar artery

➔ *CPT Changes: An Insider's View* 2002

35081   for aneurysm, pseudoaneurysm, and associated occlusive disease, abdominal aorta

➔ *CPT Assistant* Dec 00:2, Dec 01:7; *CPT Changes: An Insider's View* 2002

35082   for ruptured aneurysm, abdominal aorta

35091   for aneurysm, pseudoaneurysm, and associated occlusive disease, abdominal aorta involving visceral vessels (mesenteric, celiac, renal)

➔ *CPT Assistant* Dec 00:2; *CPT Changes: An Insider's View* 2002

35092   for ruptured aneurysm, abdominal aorta involving visceral vessels (mesenteric, celiac, renal)

35102   for aneurysm, pseudoaneurysm, and associated occlusive disease, abdominal aorta involving iliac vessels (common, hypogastric, external)

➔ *CPT Changes: An Insider's View* 2002

35103   for ruptured aneurysm, abdominal aorta involving iliac vessels (common, hypogastric, external)

35111   for aneurysm, pseudoaneurysm, and associated occlusive disease, splenic artery

➔ *CPT Changes: An Insider's View* 2002

35112   for ruptured aneurysm, splenic artery

35121   for aneurysm, pseudoaneurysm, and associated occlusive disease, hepatic, celiac, renal, or mesenteric artery

➔ *CPT Changes: An Insider's View* 2002

35122   for ruptured aneurysm, hepatic, celiac, renal, or mesenteric artery

35131   for aneurysm, pseudoaneurysm, and associated occlusive disease, iliac artery (common, hypogastric, external)

➔ *CPT Assistant* Feb 03:2; *CPT Changes: An Insider's View* 2002

35132   for ruptured aneurysm, iliac artery (common, hypogastric, external)

35141   for aneurysm, pseudoaneurysm, and associated occlusive disease, common femoral artery (profunda femoris, superficial femoral)

➔ *CPT Changes: An Insider's View* 2002

35142   for ruptured aneurysm, common femoral artery (profunda femoris, superficial femoral)

35151   for aneurysm, pseudoaneurysm, and associated occlusive disease, popliteal artery

➔ *CPT Changes: An Insider's View* 2002

35152   for ruptured aneurysm, popliteal artery

Repair Arteriovenous Fistula

35180   Repair, congenital arteriovenous fistula; head and neck

35182   thorax and abdomen

35184   extremities

35188   Repair, acquired or traumatic arteriovenous fistula; head and neck

35189   thorax and abdomen

35190   extremities

Repair Blood Vessel Other Than for Fistula, With or Without Patch Angioplasty

(For AV fistula repair, see 35180-35190)

35201   Repair blood vessel, direct; neck

35206   upper extremity
➔ *CPT Assistant* Oct 00:3, Nov 03:5

35207   hand, finger

35211   intrathoracic, with bypass

35216   intrathoracic, without bypass
➔ *CPT Assistant* Apr 05:10-11

35221   intra-abdominal

35226   lower extremity

35231   Repair blood vessel with vein graft; neck

35236   upper extremity
➔ *CPT Assistant* Oct 04:8

35241   intrathoracic, with bypass

35246   intrathoracic, without bypass

35251   intra-abdominal

35256   lower extremity

35261   Repair blood vessel with graft other than vein; neck

35266   upper extremity

35271   intrathoracic, with bypass

35276   intrathoracic, without bypass

35281   intra-abdominal

35286   lower extremity

Thromboendarterectomy

(For coronary artery, see 33510-33536 and 33572)

(35301-35372 include harvest of saphenous or upper extremity vein when performed)

35301   Thromboendarterectomy, including patch graft, if performed; carotid, vertebral, subclavian, by neck incision
➔ *CPT Assistant* Jan 07:7; *CPT Changes: An Insider's View* 2007

35302   superficial femoral artery
➔ *CPT Assistant* Jan 07:7, May 07:9; *CPT Changes: An Insider's View* 2007

35303   popliteal artery
➔ *CPT Assistant* Jan 07:7, May 07:9; *CPT Changes: An Insider's View* 2007

(Do not report 35302, 35303 in conjunction with 35483, 35500)

35304   tibioperoneal trunk artery
➔ *CPT Assistant* Jan 07:7, May 07:9; *CPT Changes: An Insider's View* 2007

35305   tibial or peroneal artery, initial vessel
➔ *CPT Assistant* May 07:9; *CPT Changes: An Insider's View* 2007

+ 35306   each additional tibial or peroneal artery (List separately in addition to code for primary procedure)
➔ *CPT Assistant* Jan 07:7, May 07:9; *CPT Changes: An Insider's View* 2007

(Use 35306 in conjunction with 35305)

(Do not report 35304, 35305, 35306 in conjunction with 35485, 35500)

35311   subclavian, innominate, by thoracic incision

35321   axillary-brachial

35331   abdominal aorta

35341   mesenteric, celiac, or renal

35351   iliac

35355   iliofemoral

35361   combined aortoiliac

35363   combined aortoiliofemoral

35371   common femoral
➔ *CPT Assistant* Jan 07:7

35372   deep (profunda) femoral
➔ *CPT Assistant* Jan 07:7

Thromboendarterectomy
35371-35372

The common femoral artery (35371) or the deep (profunda) femoral artery (35372) is incised and the plaque and lining are removed, enlarging the diameter of the artery.

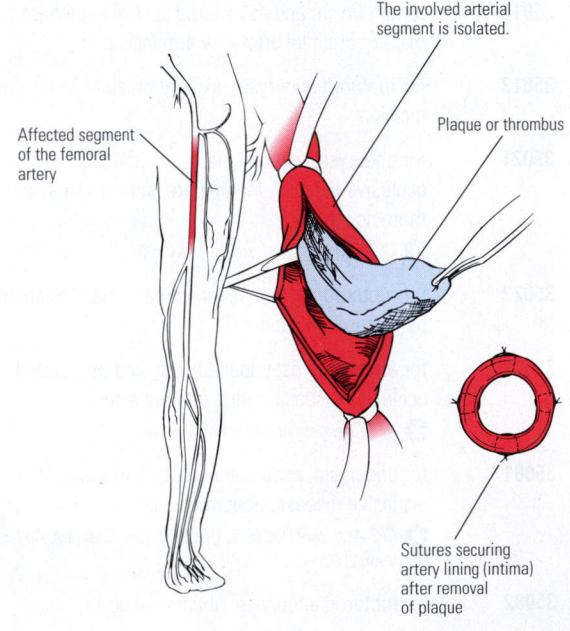

The involved arterial segment is isolated.

Affected segment of the femoral artery

Plaque or thrombus

Sutures securing artery lining (intima) after removal of plaque

+ 35390 Reoperation, carotid, thromboendarterectomy, more than 1 month after original operation (List separately in addition to code for primary procedure)
→ *CPT Assistant* Nov 97:16

(Use 35390 in conjunction with 35301)

Angioscopy

+ 35400 Angioscopy (non-coronary vessels or grafts) during therapeutic intervention (List separately in addition to code for primary procedure)
→ *CPT Assistant* Nov 97:16

Transluminal Angioplasty

If done as part of another operation, use modifier 51 or use modifier 52.

(For radiological supervision and interpretation, see 75962-75968 and 75978)

Open

35450 Transluminal balloon angioplasty, open; renal or other visceral artery
→ *CPT Assistant* Feb 97:2-3

35452 aortic
→ *CPT Assistant* Feb 97:2-3

35454 iliac
→ *CPT Assistant* Feb 97:2-3, Dec 00:1, 4, Feb 03:3

35456 femoral-popliteal
→ *CPT Assistant* Feb 97:2-3

35458 brachiocephalic trunk or branches, each vessel
→ *CPT Assistant* Feb 97:2-3, May 01:11

35459 tibioperoneal trunk and branches
→ *CPT Assistant* Feb 97:2-3

35460 venous
→ *CPT Assistant* Feb 97:2-3

Percutaneous

Codes for catheter placement and the radiologic supervision and interpretation should also be reported, in addition to the code(s) for the therapeutic aspect of the procedure.

⊙ 35470 Transluminal balloon angioplasty, percutaneous; tibioperoneal trunk or branches, each vessel
→ *CPT Assistant* Aug 96:3, Feb 97:2-3

⊙ 35471 renal or visceral artery
→ *CPT Assistant* Aug 96:3, Feb 97:2-3

⊙ 35472 aortic
→ *CPT Assistant* Aug 96:3, Feb 97:2-3

⊙ 35473 iliac
→ *CPT Assistant* Fall 93:11, Aug 96:3, Feb 97:2-3, May 01:4, Feb 03:3

Transluminal Balloon Angioplasty
35473

A balloon catheter is passed into the iliac artery and inflated to stretch the blood vessel to a larger diameter.

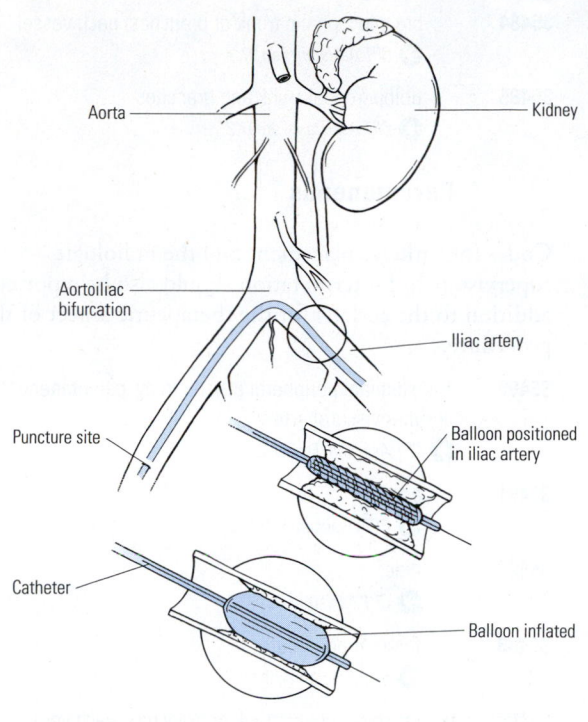

⊙ 35474 femoral-popliteal
→ *CPT Assistant* Aug 96:3, Feb 97:2-3, May 01:4, Aug 06:10, Dec 07:10
→ *Clinical Examples in Radiology* Winter 08:1,2,4,5

⊙ 35475 brachiocephalic trunk or branches, each vessel
→ *CPT Assistant* Aug 96:3, Feb 97:2-3, May 01:4, Sep 08:10

⊙ 35476 venous
→ *CPT Assistant* Aug 96:3, Feb 97:2-3, May 01:4, Dec 03:2
→ *Clinical Examples in Radiology* Spring 05:8-10, Spring 07:1-3

(For radiological supervision and interpretation, use 75978)

Transluminal Atherectomy

If done as part of another operation, use modifier 51 or use modifier 52.

(For radiological supervision and interpretation, see 75992-75996)

Open

35480 Transluminal peripheral atherectomy, open; renal or other visceral artery
→ *CPT Assistant* Feb 97:2-3

35481 aortic
→ *CPT Assistant* Feb 97:2

35482 iliac
➥ *CPT Assistant* Feb 97:2

35483 femoral-popliteal
➥ *CPT Assistant* Feb 97:2

35484 brachiocephalic trunk or branches, each vessel
➥ *CPT Assistant* Feb 97:2

35485 tibioperoneal trunk and branches
➥ *CPT Assistant* Feb 97:2

Percutaneous

Codes for catheter placement and the radiologic supervision and interpretation should also be reported, in addition to the code(s) for the therapeutic aspect of the procedure.

35490 Transluminal peripheral atherectomy, percutaneous; renal or other visceral artery
➥ *CPT Assistant* Feb 97:2

35491 aortic
➥ *CPT Assistant* Feb 97:2

35492 iliac
➥ *CPT Assistant* Feb 97:2

35493 femoral-popliteal
➥ *CPT Assistant* Feb 97:2

35494 brachiocephalic trunk or branches, each vessel
➥ *CPT Assistant* Feb 97:2

35495 tibioperoneal trunk and branches
➥ *CPT Assistant* Feb 97:2

Bypass Graft

Vein

Procurement of the saphenous vein graft is included in the description of the work for 35501-35587 and should not be reported as a separate service or co-surgery. To report harvesting of an upper extremity vein, use 35500 in addition to the bypass procedure. To report harvesting of a femoropopliteal vein segment, use 35572 in addition to the bypass procedure. To report harvesting and construction of an autogenous composite graft of two segments from two distant locations, report 35682 in addition to the bypass procedure, for autogenous composite of three or more segments from distant sites, report 35683.

+ 35500 Harvest of upper extremity vein, 1 segment, for lower extremity or coronary artery bypass procedure (List separately in addition to code for primary procedure)
➥ *CPT Assistant* Nov 98:13, Mar 99:6, Nov 99:19, Jan 07:7; *CPT Changes: An Insider's View* 2000

(Use 35500 in conjunction with 33510-33536, 35556, 35566, 35571, 35583-35587)

(For harvest of more than one vein segment, see 35682, 35683)

(For endoscopic procedure, use 33508)

35501 Bypass graft, with vein; common carotid-ipsilateral internal carotid
➥ *CPT Assistant* Apr 99:11; *CPT Changes: An Insider's View* 2007

35506 carotid-subclavian or subclavian-carotid
➥ *CPT Assistant* Oct 04:6, Jan 07:7; *CPT Changes: An Insider's View* 2007

35508 carotid-vertebral

35509 carotid-contralateral carotid
➥ *CPT Assistant* Jan 07:7, May 07:9; *CPT Changes: An Insider's View* 2007

35510 carotid-brachial
➥ *CPT Assistant* Oct 04:6, Nov 07:8; *CPT Changes: An Insider's View* 2004

35511 subclavian-subclavian

35512 subclavian-brachial
➥ *CPT Assistant* Oct 04:7; *CPT Changes: An Insider's View* 2004

35515 subclavian-vertebral

35516 subclavian-axillary

35518 axillary-axillary
➥ *CPT Assistant* Oct 04:9

35521 axillary-femoral

(For bypass graft performed with synthetic graft, use 35621)

35522 axillary-brachial
➥ *CPT Assistant* Oct 04:9; *CPT Changes: An Insider's View* 2004

35523 brachial-ulnar or -radial
➥ *CPT Changes: An Insider's View* 2008

(Do not report 35523 in conjunction with 35206, 35500, 35525, 36838)

(For bypass graft performed with synthetic conduit, use 37799)

35525 brachial-brachial
➥ *CPT Assistant* Oct 04:10; *CPT Changes: An Insider's View* 2004

35526 aortosubclavian or carotid

(For bypass graft performed with synthetic graft, use 35626)

35531 aortoceliac or aortomesenteric

35533 axillary-femoral-femoral

(For bypass graft performed with synthetic graft, use 35654)

35535 hepatorenal
➥ *CPT Changes: An Insider's View* 2009

(Do not report 35535 in conjunction with 35221, 35251, 35281, 35500, 35536, 35560, 35631, 35636)

35536   splenorenal
→ *CPT Assistant* Jun 99:10

35537   aortoiliac
→ *CPT Assistant* Jan 07:7; *CPT Changes: An Insider's View* 2007

(For bypass graft performed with synthetic graft, use 35637)

(Do not report 35537 in conjunction with 35538)

35538   aortobi-iliac
→ *CPT Assistant* Jan 07:7; *CPT Changes: An Insider's View* 2007

(For bypass graft performed with synthetic graft, use 35638)

(Do not report 35538 in conjunction with 35537)

35539   aortofemoral
→ *CPT Assistant* Jan 07:7; *CPT Changes: An Insider's View* 2007

(For bypass graft performed with synthetic graft, use 35647)

(Do not report 35539 in conjunction with 35540)

35540   aortobifemoral
→ *CPT Assistant* Jan 07:7; *CPT Changes: An Insider's View* 2007

(For bypass graft performed with synthetic graft, use 35646)

(Do not report 35540 in conjunction with 35539)

35548   aortoiliofemoral, unilateral

(For bypass graft performed with synthetic graft, use 37799)

35549   aortoiliofemoral, bilateral

(For bypass graft performed with synthetic graft, use 37799)

35551   aortofemoral-popliteal

35556   femoral-popliteal
→ *CPT Assistant* Fall 92:20, May 97:10, Jan 07:7, Nov 07:8

35558   femoral-femoral

35560   aortorenal
→ *CPT Assistant* Jun 99:10

35563   ilioiliac

35565   iliofemoral
→ *CPT Assistant* Oct 04:8

35566   femoral-anterior tibial, posterior tibial, peroneal artery or other distal vessels
→ *CPT Assistant* Jan 07:7, Nov 07:8

35570   tibial-tibial, peroneal-tibial, or tibial/peroneal trunk-tibial
→ *CPT Changes: An Insider's View* 2009

(Do not report 35570 in conjunction with 35256, 35286)

35571   popliteal-tibial, -peroneal artery or other distal vessels
→ *CPT Assistant* Jan 07:7, Nov 07:8

Bypass Graft, Vein
35571

The physician creates a bypass around the popliteal artery, using a harvested vein that is sutured to the tibial artery.

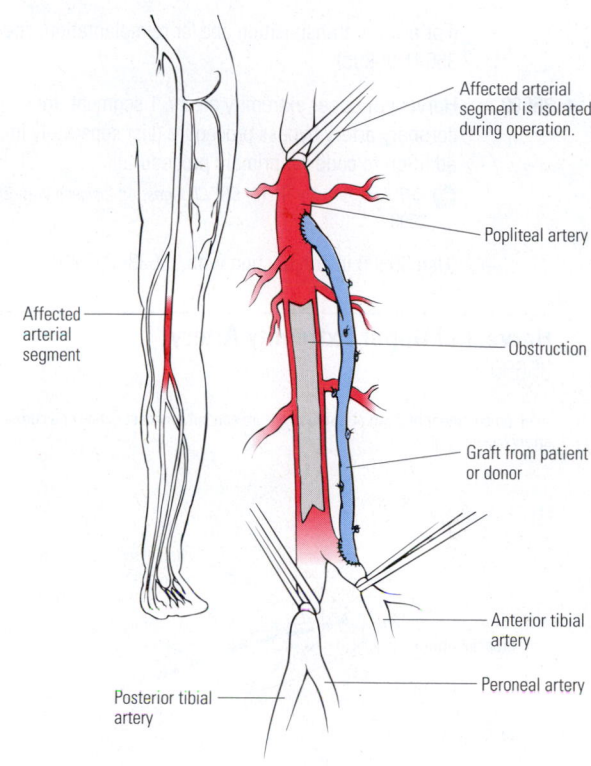

Affected arterial segment is isolated during operation.

Popliteal artery

Affected arterial segment

Obstruction

Graft from patient or donor

Anterior tibial artery

Peroneal artery

Posterior tibial artery

+ 35572   Harvest of femoropopliteal vein, 1 segment, for vascular reconstruction procedure (eg, aortic, vena caval, coronary, peripheral artery) (List separately in addition to code for primary procedure)
→ *CPT Assistant* Jan 07:28; *CPT Changes: An Insider's View* 2003

(Use 35572 in conjunction with 33510-33516, 33517-33523, 33533-33536, 34502, 34520, 35001, 35002, 35011-35022, 35102, 35103, 35121-35152, 35231-35256, 35501-35587, 35879-35907)

(For bilateral procedure, use modifier 50)

In-Situ Vein

(To report aortobifemoral bypass using synthetic conduit, and femoral-popliteal bypass with vein conduit in-situ, use 35646 and 35583. To report aorto[uni]femoral bypass with synthetic conduit, and femoral-popliteal bypass with vein conduit in-situ, use 35647 and 35583. To report aortofemoral bypass using vein conduit, and femoral-popliteal bypass with vein conduit in-situ, use 35539 and 35583)

35583   In-situ vein bypass; femoral-popliteal
➲ *CPT Assistant* Jan 07:7, Nov 07:8

35585   femoral-anterior tibial, posterior tibial, or peroneal
artery
➲ *CPT Assistant* Jan 07:7, Nov 07:8

35587   popliteal-tibial, peroneal
➲ *CPT Assistant* Apr 99:11, Jan 07:7, Nov 07:8

Other Than Vein

(For arterial transposition and/or reimplantation, see 35691-35695)

+ 35600   Harvest of upper extremity artery, 1 segment, for coronary artery bypass procedure (List separately in addition to code for primary procedure)
➲ *CPT Assistant* Apr 07:12; *CPT Changes: An Insider's View* 2001, 2008

(Use 35600 in conjunction with 33533—33536)

Harvest of Upper Extremity Artery
35600

Open procurement of a radial artery to secure conduit for construction of a coronary artery bypass graft

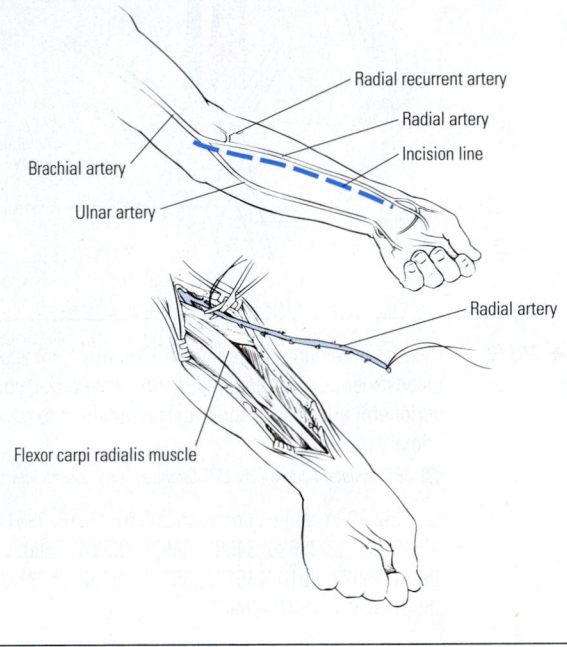

Radial recurrent artery
Radial artery
Incision line
Brachial artery
Ulnar artery
Radial artery
Flexor carpi radialis muscle

35601   Bypass graft, with other than vein; common carotid-ipsilateral internal carotid
➲ *CPT Assistant* Jul 06:7, Jan 07:7; *CPT Changes: An Insider's View* 2007

35606   carotid-subclavian

(For open transcervical common carotid-common carotid bypass performed in conjunction with endovascular repair of descending thoracic aorta, use 33891)

(For open subclavian to carotid artery transposition performed in conjunction with endovascular thoracic aneurysm repair by neck incision, use 33889)

35612   subclavian-subclavian

35616   subclavian-axillary

35621   axillary-femoral
➲ *CPT Assistant* Jan 07:7

35623   axillary-popliteal or -tibial

35626   aortosubclavian or carotid

35631   aortoceliac, aortomesenteric, aortorenal

35632   ilio-celiac
➲ *CPT Changes: An Insider's View* 2009

(Do not report 35632 in conjunction with 35221, 35251, 35281, 35531, 35631)

35633   ilio-mesenteric
➲ *CPT Changes: An Insider's View* 2009

(Do not report 35633 in conjunction with 35221, 35251, 35281, 35531, 35631)

35634   iliorenal
➲ *CPT Changes: An Insider's View* 2009

(Do not report 35634 in conjunction with 35221, 35251, 35281, 35560, 35536, 35631)

35636   splenorenal (splenic to renal arterial anastomosis)

35637   aortoiliac
➲ *CPT Assistant* Jan 07:7; *CPT Changes: An Insider's View* 2007

(Do not report 35637 in conjunction with 35638, 35646)

35638   aortobi-iliac
➲ *CPT Assistant* Jan 07:7; *CPT Changes: An Insider's View* 2007

(Do not report 35638 in conjunction with 35637, 35646)

(For open placement of aortobi-iliac prosthesis following unsuccessful endovascular repair, use 34831)

35642   carotid-vertebral

35645   subclavian-vertebral

35646   aortobifemoral
➲ *CPT Assistant* Jan 07:7; *CPT Changes: An Insider's View* 2002

(For bypass graft performed with vein graft, use 35540)

(For open placement of aortobifemoral prosthesis following unsuccessful endovascular repair, use 34832)

35647   aortofemoral
➲ *CPT Assistant* Jan 07:7; *CPT Changes: An Insider's View* 2002

(For bypass graft performed with vein graft, use 35539)

35650   axillary-axillary

35651   aortofemoral-popliteal

35654   axillary-femoral-femoral
➲ *CPT Assistant* Jan 07:7

35656   femoral-popliteal
➲ *CPT Assistant* Nov 07:8

35661	femoral-femoral

➔ *CPT Assistant* Dec 04:6, Jan 07:7

35663	ilioiliac

35665	iliofemoral

➔ *CPT Assistant* Jan 07:7

35666	femoral-anterior tibial, posterior tibial, or peroneal artery

➔ *CPT Assistant* Nov 07:8

35671	popliteal-tibial or -peroneal artery

Composite Grafts

Codes 35682-35683 are used to report harvest and anastomosis of multiple vein segments from distant sites for use as arterial bypass graft conduits. These codes are intended for use when the two or more vein segments are harvested from a limb other than that undergoing bypass. Add-on codes 35682 and 35683 may be reported in addition to codes 35556, 35566, 35571, 35583-35587, as appropriate.

+ **35681** Bypass graft; composite, prosthetic and vein (List separately in addition to code for primary procedure)

➔ *CPT Assistant* Nov 98:13-14, Mar 99:6, Apr 99:11

(Do not report 35681 in addition to 35682, 35683)

+ **35682** autogenous composite, 2 segments of veins from 2 locations (List separately in addition to code for primary procedure)

➔ *CPT Assistant* Nov 98:13-14, Mar 99:6, Apr 99:11, Sep 02:4

(Do not report 35682 in addition to 35681, 35683)

+ **35683** autogenous composite, 3 or more segments of vein from 2 or more locations (List separately in addition to code for primary procedure)

➔ *CPT Assistant* Nov 98:13-14, Mar 99:6, Apr 99:11, Sep 02:4

(Do not report 35683 in addition to 35681, 35682)

Adjuvant Techniques

Adjuvant (additional) technique(s) may be required at the time a bypass graft is created to improve patency of the lower extremity autogenous or synthetic bypass graft (eg, femoral-popliteal, femoral-tibial, or popliteal-tibial arteries). Code 35685 should be reported in addition to the primary synthetic bypass graft procedure, when an interposition of venous tissue (vein patch or cuff) is placed at the anastomosis between the synthetic bypass conduit and the involved artery (includes harvest).

Code 35686 should be reported in addition to the primary bypass graft procedure, when autogenous vein is used to create a fistula between the tibial or peroneal artery and vein at or beyond the distal bypass anastomosis site of the involved artery.

(For composite graft(s), see 35681-35683)

+ **35685** Placement of vein patch or cuff at distal anastomosis of bypass graft, synthetic conduit (List separately in addition to code for primary procedure)

➔ *CPT Assistant* Sep 02:3; *CPT Changes: An Insider's View* 2002

(Use 35685 in conjunction with 35656, 35666, or 35671)

+ **35686** Creation of distal arteriovenous fistula during lower extremity bypass surgery (non-hemodialysis) (List separately in addition to code for primary procedure)

➔ *CPT Assistant* Sep 02:3; *CPT Changes: An Insider's View* 2002

(Use 35686 in conjunction with 35556, 35566, 35571, 35583-35587, 35623, 35656, 35666, 35671)

Arterial Transposition

35691	Transposition and/or reimplantation; vertebral to carotid artery

35693	vertebral to subclavian artery

35694	subclavian to carotid artery

(For open subclavian to carotid artery transposition performed in conjunction with endovascular repair of descending thoracic aorta, use 33889)

35695	carotid to subclavian artery

+ **35697** Reimplantation, visceral artery to infrarenal aortic prosthesis, each artery (List separately in addition to code for primary procedure)

➔ *CPT Changes: An Insider's View* 2004

(Do not report 35697 in conjunction with 33877)

Excision, Exploration, Repair, Revision

+ **35700** Reoperation, femoral-popliteal or femoral (popliteal)-anterior tibial, posterior tibial, peroneal artery, or other distal vessels, more than 1 month after original operation (List separately in addition to code for primary procedure)

(Use 35700 in conjunction with 35556, 35566, 35571, 35583, 35585, 35587, 35656, 35666, 35671)

35701	Exploration (not followed by surgical repair), with or without lysis of artery; carotid artery

35721	femoral artery

➔ *CPT Assistant* Jun 96:8

35741	popliteal artery

35761	other vessels

35800	Exploration for postoperative hemorrhage, thrombosis or infection; neck

35820	chest

35840	abdomen

➔ *CPT Assistant* May 97:8

35860	extremity

➔ *CPT Assistant* Fall 92:21

35870 Repair of graft-enteric fistula

35875 Thrombectomy of arterial or venous graft (other than hemodialysis graft or fistula);

➔ *CPT Assistant* Nov 98:14, Feb 99:6, Mar 99:6, Apr 00:10

35876 with revision of arterial or venous graft

➔ *CPT Assistant* Nov 98:14

(For thrombectomy of hemodialysis graft or fistula, see 36831, 36833)

Codes 35879 and 35881 describe open revision of graft-threatening stenoses of lower extremity arterial bypass graft(s) (previously constructed with autogenous vein conduit) using vein patch angioplasty or segmental vein interposition techniques. For thrombectomy with revision of any non-coronary arterial or venous graft, including those of the lower extremity, (other than hemodialysis graft or fistula), use 35876. For direct repair (other than for fistula) of a lower extremity blood vessel (with or without patch angioplasty), use 35226. For repair (other than for fistula) of a lower extremity blood vessel using a vein graft, use 35256.

35879 Revision, lower extremity arterial bypass, without thrombectomy, open; with vein patch angioplasty

➔ *CPT Assistant* Nov 99:19; *CPT Changes: An Insider's View* 2000

35881 with segmental vein interposition

➔ *CPT Assistant* Nov 99:19; *CPT Changes: An Insider's View* 2000

(For revision of femoral anastomosis of synthetic arterial bypass graft, see 35883, 35884)

(For excision of infected graft, see 35901-35907 and appropriate revascularization code)

35883 Revision, femoral anastomosis of synthetic arterial bypass graft in groin, open; with nonautogenous patch graft (eg, Dacron, ePTFE, bovine pericardium)

➔ *CPT Assistant* Jan 07:7; *CPT Changes: An Insider's View* 2007

(For bilateral procedure, use modifier 50)

(Do not report 35883 in conjunction with 35700, 35875, 35876, 35884)

35884 with autogenous vein patch graft

➔ *CPT Assistant* Jan 07:7; *CPT Changes: An Insider's View* 2007

(For bilateral procedure, use modifier 50)

(Do not report 35884 in conjunction with 35700, 35875, 35876, 35883)

35901 Excision of infected graft; neck

35903 extremity

35905 thorax

35907 abdomen

Vascular Injection Procedures

Listed services for injection procedures include necessary local anesthesia, introduction of needles or catheter, injection of contrast media with or without automatic power injection, and/or necessary pre- and postinjection care specifically related to the injection procedure.

Catheters, drugs, and contrast media are not included in the listed service for the injection procedures.

Selective vascular catheterization should be coded to include introduction and all lesser order selective catheterization used in the approach (eg, the description for a selective right middle cerebral artery catheterization includes the introduction and placement catheterization of the right common and internal carotid arteries).

Additional second and/or third order arterial catheterization within the same family of arteries or veins supplied by a single first order vessel should be expressed by 36012, 36218, or 36248.

Additional first order or higher catheterization in vascular families supplied by a first order vessel different from a previously selected and coded family should be separately coded using the conventions described above.

(For radiological supervision and interpretation, see **Radiology**)

(For injection procedures in conjunction with cardiac catheterization, see 93541-93545)

(For chemotherapy of malignant disease, see 96401-96549)

Intravenous

An intracatheter is a sheathed combination of needle and short catheter.

36000 Introduction of needle or intracatheter, vein

➔ *CPT Assistant* Summer 95:2, Apr 98:1, 3, 7, Jul 98:1, Apr 03:26, Oct 03:2, Jul 06:4, Feb 07:10, Jul 07:1, Dec 08:7

36002 Injection procedures (eg, thrombin) for percutaneous treatment of extremity pseudoaneurysm

➔ *CPT Changes: An Insider's View* 2002

(For imaging guidance, see 76942, 77002, 77012, 77021)

(For ultrasound guided compression repair of pseudoaneurysms, use 76936)

(Do not report 36002 for vascular sealant of an arteriotomy site)

Injection Procedure (eg, Thrombin) for Percutaneous Treatment of Extremity Pseudoaneurysm
36002

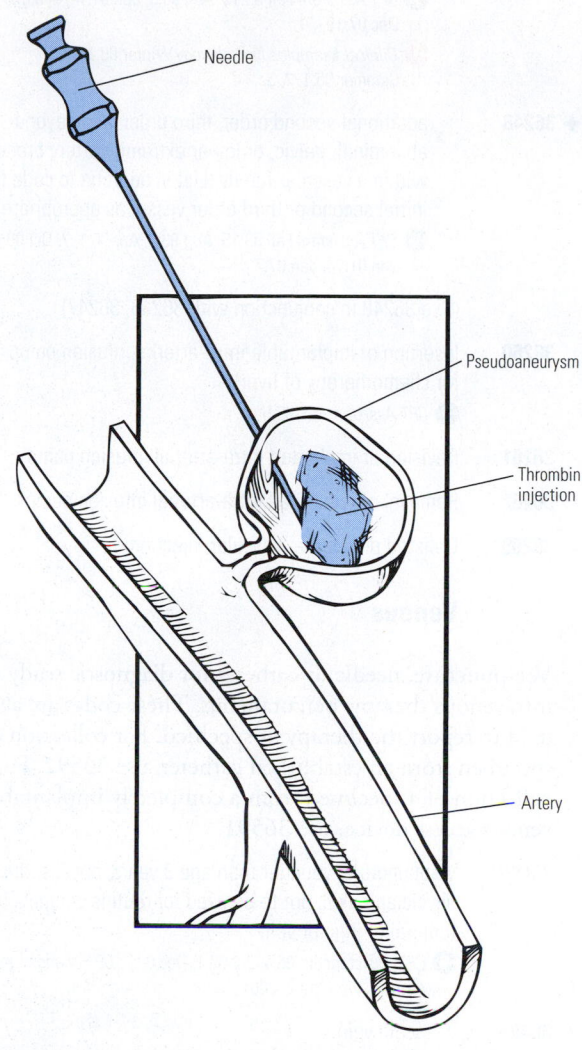

Needle

Pseudoaneurysm

Thrombin injection

Artery

36005   Injection procedure for extremity venography (including introduction of needle or intracatheter)
> *CPT Changes: An Insider's View* 2002

(For radiological supervision and interpretation, see 75820, 75822)

36010   Introduction of catheter, superior or inferior vena cava
> *CPT Assistant* Aug 96:2, Apr 98:7, Sep 00:11, May 01:10, Jul 03:12, Oct 08:11, Jan 09:7
> *Clinical Examples in Radiology* Winter 05:5-6, Spring 08:7-8

36011   Selective catheter placement, venous system; first order branch (eg, renal vein, jugular vein)
> *CPT Assistant* Aug 96:11, Apr 98:7, Jul 03:12, Dec 03:2

36012   second order, or more selective, branch (eg, left adrenal vein, petrosal sinus)
> *CPT Assistant* Aug 96:11, Sep 98:7, Jul 03:12

36013   Introduction of catheter, right heart or main pulmonary artery
> *CPT Assistant* Aug 96:11, Oct 08:11, Jan 09:7

36014   Selective catheter placement, left or right pulmonary artery
> *CPT Assistant* Aug 96:11, Apr 98:7

36015   Selective catheter placement, segmental or subsegmental pulmonary artery
> *CPT Assistant* Aug 96:11, Sep 00:11

(For insertion of flow directed catheter (eg, Swan-Ganz), use 93503)

(For venous catheterization for selective organ blood sampling, use 36500)

Intra-Arterial—Intra-Aortic

(For radiological supervision and interpretation, see **Radiology**)

36100   Introduction of needle or intracatheter, carotid or vertebral artery
> *CPT Assistant* Aug 96:11

(For bilateral procedure, report 36100 with modifier 50)

36120   Introduction of needle or intracatheter; retrograde brachial artery
> *CPT Assistant* Fall 93:16, Aug 96:3

36140   extremity artery
> *CPT Assistant* Fall 93:16, Aug 96:3, Nov 99:32-33, Oct 03:2, Jul 06:4,7, Jul 07:1, Dec 07:11, Dec 07:10

(For insertion of arteriovenous cannula, see 36810-36821)

►(36145 has been deleted. To report see 36147, 36148)◄

⊙● **36147**   Introduction of needle and/or catheter, arteriovenous shunt created for dialysis (graft/fistula); initial access with complete radiological evaluation of dialysis access, including fluoroscopy, image documentation and report (includes access of shunt, injection[s] of contrast, and all necessary imaging from the arterial anastomosis and adjacent artery through entire venous outflow including the inferior or superior vena cava)
> *CPT Changes: An Insider's View* 2010

►(If 36147 indicates the need for a therapeutic intervention requiring a second catheterization of the shunt, use 36148)◄

►(Do not report 36147 in conjunction with 75791)◄

⊙+● **36148**   additional access for therapeutic intervention (List separately in addition to code for primary procedure)
> *CPT Changes: An Insider's View* 2010

►(Use 36148 in conjunction with 36147)◄

36160   Introduction of needle or intracatheter, aortic, translumbar
> *CPT Assistant* Aug 96:3

36200   Introduction of catheter, aorta
> *CPT Assistant* Fall 93:16, Aug 96:3, Jul 06:7, Dec 07:10,
> Dec 07:14, Apr 08:11

36215   Selective catheter placement, arterial system; each first order thoracic or brachiocephalic branch, within a vascular family
> *CPT Assistant* Fall 93:15, Aug 96:3, Nov 97:16, Apr 98:9,
> Sep 00:11, Oct 00:4, Feb 03:3

(For catheter placement for coronary angiography, use 93508)

36216   initial second order thoracic or brachiocephalic branch, within a vascular family
> *CPT Assistant* Fall 93:15, Aug 96:3, Oct 00:4, Dec 07:10

36217   initial third order or more selective thoracic or brachiocephalic branch, within a vascular family
> *CPT Assistant* Fall 93:15, Aug 96:3, Oct 00:4, Dec 07:10
> *Clinical Examples in Radiology* Summer 07:1,2

+ 36218   additional second order, third order, and beyond, thoracic or brachiocephalic branch, within a vascular family (List in addition to code for initial second or third order vessel as appropriate)
> *CPT Assistant* Fall 93:15, Aug 96:3, Oct 00:4, Jul 06:7,
> Dec 07:10

(Use 36218 in conjunction with 36216, 36217)

▶(For angiography, see 36147, 75600-75774, 75791)◀

(For angioplasty, see 35470-35475)

(For transcatheter therapies, see 37200-37208, 61624, 61626)

(When coronary artery, arterial conduit (eg, internal mammary, inferior epigastric or free radical artery) or venous bypass graft angiography is performed in conjunction with cardiac catheterization, see the appropriate cardiac catheterization, injection procedure, and imaging supervision code(s) (93501-93556) in the **Medicine** section of the CPT codebook. When coronary artery, arterial coronary conduit or venous bypass graft angiography is performed without concomitant left heart cardiac catheterization, use 93508. When internal mammary artery angiography only is performed without a concomitant left heart cardiac catheterization, use 36216 or 36217 as appropriate.)

36245   Selective catheter placement, arterial system; each first order abdominal, pelvic, or lower extremity artery branch, within a vascular family
> *CPT Assistant* Fall 93:15, Aug 96:3, Jan 01:14, Jan 07:7,
> Dec 07:10
> *Clinical Examples in Radiology* Summer 08:3

36246   initial second order abdominal, pelvic, or lower extremity artery branch, within a vascular family
> *CPT Assistant* Fall 93:15, Aug 96:3, Jan 01:14, Jan 07:7,
> Dec 07:11, Dec 07:10

36247   initial third order or more selective abdominal, pelvic, or lower extremity artery branch, within a vascular family
> *CPT Assistant* Fall 93:15, Aug 96:3, Jan 01:14, Jan 07:7,
> Dec 07:10
> *Clinical Examples in Radiology* Winter 08:1,2,4,5,
> Summer 08:1, 2, 3

+ 36248   additional second order, third order, and beyond, abdominal, pelvic, or lower extremity artery branch, within a vascular family (List in addition to code for initial second or third order vessel as appropriate)
> *CPT Assistant* Fall 93:15, Aug 96:3, Apr 98:1, 7, Oct 00:4,
> Jan 01:14, Jan 07:7

(Use 36248 in conjunction with 36246, 36247)

36260   Insertion of implantable intra-arterial infusion pump (eg, for chemotherapy of liver)
> *CPT Assistant* Fall 95:5

36261   Revision of implanted intra-arterial infusion pump

36262   Removal of implanted intra-arterial infusion pump

36299   Unlisted procedure, vascular injection

Venous

Venipuncture, needle or catheter for diagnostic study or intravenous therapy, percutaneous. These codes are also used to report the therapy as specified. For collection of a specimen from an established catheter, use 36592. For collection of a specimen from a completely implantable venous access device, use 36591.

36400   Venipuncture, younger than age 3 years, necessitating physician's skill, not to be used for routine venipuncture; femoral or jugular vein
> *CPT Assistant* Jul 06:4, Jul 07:1, Dec 08:7; *CPT Changes: An
> Insider's View* 2002, 2004

36405   scalp vein
> *CPT Assistant* Jul 06:4, Jul 07:1, Dec 08:7

36406   other vein
> *CPT Assistant* Jul 06:4, Jul 07:1

36410   Venipuncture, age 3 years or older, necessitating physician's skill (separate procedure), for diagnostic or therapeutic purposes (not to be used for routine venipuncture)
> *CPT Assistant* Jun 96:10, May 01:11, Aug 02:2, Oct 03:10,
> Feb 07:10, Jul 07:1, Dec 08:7; *CPT Changes: An Insider's View*
> 2004
> *Clinical Examples in Radiology* Spring 09:8

36415   Collection of venous blood by venipuncture
> *CPT Assistant* Jun 96:10, Mar 98:10, Oct 99:11, Aug 00:2,
> Feb 07:10, Jul 07:1, Dec 08:7; *CPT Changes: An Insider's View*
> 2003

(Do not report modifier 63 in conjunction with 36415)

36416   Collection of capillary blood specimen (eg, finger, heel, ear stick)
> *CPT Changes: An Insider's View* 2003

36420   Venipuncture, cutdown; younger than age 1 year
> *CPT Assistant* Nov 99:32-33, Aug 00:2, Oct 03:2, Jul 06:4

(Do not report modifier 63 in conjunction with 36420)

36425   age 1 or over
> *Clinical Examples in Radiology* Summer 08:1, 2

36430   Transfusion, blood or blood components
> *CPT Assistant* Aug 97:18, Nov 99:32-33, Aug 00:2, Mar 01:10, Oct 03:2, Jul 06:4, Jul 07:1

36440   Push transfusion, blood, 2 years or younger
> *CPT Assistant* Aug 00:2, Oct 03:2, Jul 06:4, Jul 07:1

36450   Exchange transfusion, blood; newborn

(Do not report modifier 63 in conjunction with 36450)

36455   other than newborn

36460   Transfusion, intrauterine, fetal

(Do not report modifier 63 in conjunction with 36460)

(For radiological supervision and interpretation, use 76941)

36468   Single or multiple injections of sclerosing solutions, spider veins (telangiectasia); limb or trunk

36469   face

36470   Injection of sclerosing solution; single vein

36471   multiple veins, same leg

36475   Endovenous ablation therapy of incompetent vein, extremity, inclusive of all imaging guidance and monitoring, percutaneous, radiofrequency; first vein treated
> *CPT Changes: An Insider's View* 2005
> *Clinical Examples in Radiology* Fall 08:10

+ 36476   second and subsequent veins treated in a single extremity, each through separate access sites (List separately in addition to code for primary procedure)
> *CPT Changes: An Insider's View* 2005

(Use 36476 in conjunction with 36475)

(Do not report 36475, 36476 in conjunction with 36000-36005, 36410, 36425, 36478, 36479, 37204, 75894, 76000, 76001, 76937, 76942, 76998, 77022, 93970, 93971)

36478   Endovenous ablation therapy of incompetent vein, extremity, inclusive of all imaging guidance and monitoring, percutaneous, laser; first vein treated
> *CPT Changes: An Insider's View* 2005

+ 36479   second and subsequent veins treated in a single extremity, each through separate access sites (List separately in addition to code for primary procedure)
> *CPT Changes: An Insider's View* 2005

(Use 36479 in conjunction with 36478)

(Do not report 36478, 36479 in conjunction with 36000-36005, 36410, 36425, 36475, 36476, 37204, 75894, 76000, 76001, 76937, 76942, 76998, 77022, 93970, 93971)

⊙▲ **36481**   Percutaneous portal vein catheterization by any method
> *CPT Assistant* Oct 96:1, Mar 02:10, Dec 03:2; *CPT Changes: An Insider's View* 2010

(For radiological supervision and interpretation, see 75885, 75887)

36500   Venous catheterization for selective organ blood sampling

(For catheterization in superior or inferior vena cava, use 36010)

(For radiological supervision and interpretation, use 75893)

36510   Catheterization of umbilical vein for diagnosis or therapy, newborn
> *CPT Assistant* Nov 99:5-6, Aug 00:2, Oct 03:2, Jul 06:4, Jul 07:1

(Do not report modifier 63 in conjunction with 36510)

36511   Therapeutic apheresis; for white blood cells
> *CPT Changes: An Insider's View* 2003

36512   for red blood cells
> *CPT Changes: An Insider's View* 2003

36513   for platelets
> *CPT Changes: An Insider's View* 2003

36514   for plasma pheresis
> *CPT Changes: An Insider's View* 2003

36515   with extracorporeal immunoadsorption and plasma reinfusion
> *CPT Changes: An Insider's View* 2003

36516   with extracorporeal selective adsorption or selective filtration and plasma reinfusion
> *CPT Changes: An Insider's View* 2003

(For physician evaluation, use modifier 26)

36522   Photopheresis, extracorporeal
> *CPT Assistant* Fall 93:25

(36540 has been deleted. To report, use 36591)

(36550 has been deleted. To report, use 36593)

The Central Venous Access Procedures Table

	Non-tunneled	Tunneled Without Port or Pump	Central Tunneled	Tunneled With Port	Tunneled With Pump	Peripheral	<5 years	>5 years
Insertion								
Catheter	36555						36555	
	36556							36556
		36557	36557				36557	
		36558	36558					36558
	36568					36568	36568	
	36569					36569		36569
Device			36560	36560			36560	
			36561	36561				36561
			36563		36563			36563
		36565	36565					36565
			36566	36566				
	36570 (w port)			36570 (w port)		36570 (w port)	36570 (w port)	
				36571 (w port)		36571 (w port)		36571 (w port)
Repair								
Catheter	36575	36575	36575			36575		
Device			36576	36576	36576	36576		
Partial Replacement- Central Venous Access Device (Catheter only)								
			36578	36578	36578	36578	36578	36578
Central Replacement								
Catheter	36580							
		36581	36581					
	36854 (w/o port or pump)			36585 (w port)		36584 (w/o port or pump)		
Device			36582	36582				
			36583		36583			
						36585 (w port)		
Removal								
Catheter		36589						
Device			36590	36590	36590	36590		
Removal of Obstructive Material from Device								
	36595 (pericatheter) 36596 (intraluminal)	36595 (pericatheter) 36596 (intraluminal)	36595 (pericatheter) 36596 (intraluminal)	36595 (pericatheter) 36596 (intraluminal)	36595 (pericatheter) 36596 (intraluminal)	36595 (pericatheter) 36596 (intraluminal)		
Repositioning of Catheter								
36597	36597	36597	36597	36597	36597	36597	36597	36597

Central Venous Access Procedures

To qualify as a central venous access catheter or device, the tip of the catheter/device must terminate in the subclavian, brachiocephalic (innominate) or iliac veins, the superior or inferior vena cava, or the right atrium. The venous access device may be either centrally inserted (jugular, subclavian, femoral vein or inferior vena cava catheter entry site) or peripherally inserted (eg, basilic or cephalic vein). The device may be accessed for use either via exposed catheter (external to the skin), via a subcutaneous port or via a subcutaneous pump.

The procedures involving these types of devices fall into five categories:

1. **Insertion** (placement of catheter through a newly established venous access)

2. **Repair** (fixing device without replacement of either catheter or port/pump, other than pharmacologic or mechanical correction of intracatheter or pericatheter occlusion [see 36595 or 36596])

3. **Partial replacement** of only the catheter component associated with a port/pump device, but not entire device

4. **Complete replacement** of entire device via same venous access site (complete exchange)

5. **Removal** of entire device.

There is no coding distinction between venous access achieved percutaneously versus by cutdown or based on catheter size.

For the repair, partial (catheter only) replacement, complete replacement, or removal of both catheters (placed from separate venous access sites) of a multi-catheter device, with or without subcutaneous ports/pumps, use the appropriate code describing the service with a frequency of two.

If an existing central venous access device is removed and a new one placed via a separate venous access site, appropriate codes for both procedures (removal of old, if code exists, and insertion of new device) should be reported.

When imaging is used for these procedures, either for gaining access to the venous entry site or for manipulating the catheter into final central position, use 76937, 77001.

(For refilling and maintenance of an implantable pump or reservoir for intravenous or intra-arterial drug delivery, use 96522)

Insertion of Central Venous Access Device

⊙ **36555**   Insertion of non-tunneled centrally inserted central venous catheter; younger than 5 years of age

➲ *CPT Assistant* Dec 04:7, Jul 06:4, Jul 07:1, Jun 08:8; *CPT Changes: An Insider's View* 2004

➡ *Clinical Examples in Radiology* Summer 06:8-9, Spring 09:10, Winter 09:9

(For peripherally inserted non-tunneled central venous catheter, younger than 5 years of age, use 36568)

Insertion of Non-Tunneled Centrally Inserted Central Venous Catheter
36555

During placement of a central venous catheter, a short tract is developed as the catheter is advanced from the skin entry site to the point of venous cannulation. The catheter tip must reside in the subclavian, innominate or iliac veins, the inferior or superior vena cava, or right atrium to be considered a "central venous" catheter.

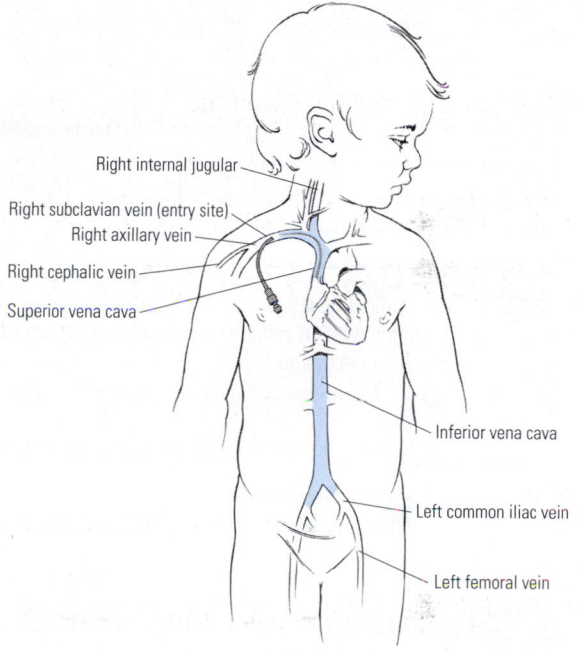

Right internal jugular
Right subclavian vein (entry site)
Right axillary vein
Right cephalic vein
Superior vena cava
Inferior vena cava
Left common iliac vein
Left femoral vein

36556   age 5 years or older

➲ *CPT Assistant* Dec 04:7, Jun 08:8; *CPT Changes: An Insider's View* 2004

➡ *Clinical Examples in Radiology* Summer 06:8-9, Spring 08:7,8, Spring 09:10, Winter 09:8, 9

(For peripherally inserted non-tunneled central venous catheter, age 5 years or older, use 36569)

Insertion of Non-Tunneled Centrally Inserted Central Venous Catheter
36556

During placement of a central venous catheter, a short tract is developed as the catheter is advanced from the skin entry site to the point of venous cannulation. The catheter tip must reside in the subclavian, innominate or iliac veins, the inferior or superior vena cava, or right atrium, to be considered a "central venous" catheter.

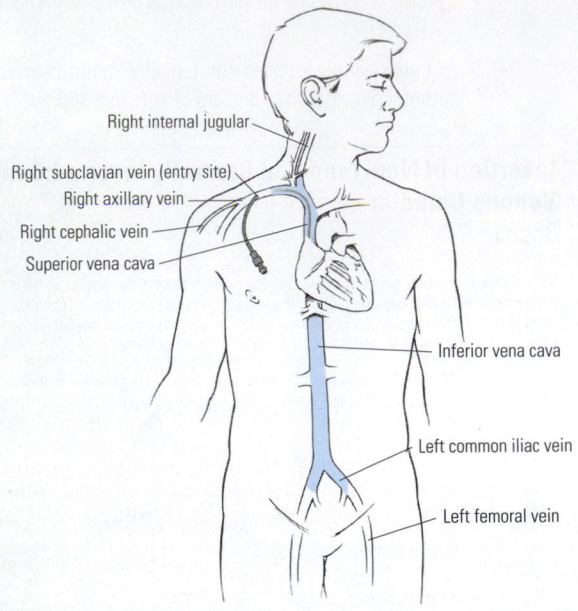

Insertion of Tunneled Central Venous Catheter
36557-36558

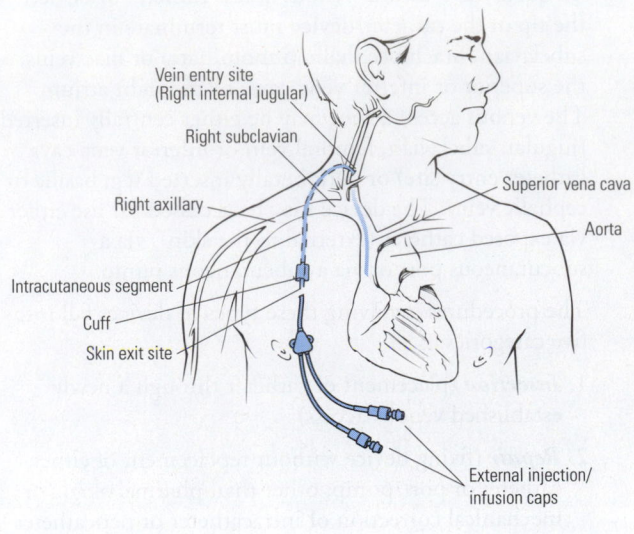

⊙ **36557** Insertion of tunneled centrally inserted central venous catheter, without subcutaneous port or pump; younger than 5 years of age

➤ *CPT Assistant* Dec 04:7, Jun 08:8; *CPT Changes: An Insider's View* 2004

➤ *Clinical Examples in Radiology* Spring 09:10, Winter 09:9

⊙ **36558** age 5 years or older

➤ *CPT Assistant* Dec 04:7, Jun 08:8; *CPT Changes: An Insider's View* 2004

➤ *Clinical Examples in Radiology* Spring 09:10, Winter 09:9

(For peripherally inserted central venous catheter with port, 5 years or older, use 36571)

⊙ **36560** Insertion of tunneled centrally inserted central venous access device, with subcutaneous port; younger than 5 years of age

➤ *CPT Assistant* Dec 04:7, Jun 08:8; *CPT Changes: An Insider's View* 2004

➤ *Clinical Examples in Radiology* Spring 09:10, Winter 09:9

(For peripherally inserted central venous access device with subcutaneous port, younger than 5 years of age, use 36570)

⊙ **36561** age 5 years or older

➤ *CPT Assistant* Dec 04:7, Jun 08:8; *CPT Changes: An Insider's View* 2004

➤ *Clinical Examples in Radiology* Spring 09:10, Winter 09:9

(For peripherally inserted central venous catheter with subcutaneous port, 5 years or older, use 36571)

⊙ **36563** Insertion of tunneled centrally inserted central venous access device with subcutaneous pump

➤ *CPT Assistant* Dec 04:8, Jun 08:8; *CPT Changes: An Insider's View* 2004

➤ *Clinical Examples in Radiology* Spring 09:10, Winter 09:9

⊙ **36565** Insertion of tunneled centrally inserted central venous access device, requiring 2 catheters via 2 separate venous access sites; without subcutaneous port or pump (eg, Tesio type catheter)

➤ *CPT Assistant* Dec 04:8, Jun 08:8; *CPT Changes: An Insider's View* 2004

➤ *Clinical Examples in Radiology* Spring 09:10, Winter 09:9

⊙ **36566** with subcutaneous port(s)

➤ *CPT Assistant* Dec 04:8, Jun 08:8; *CPT Changes: An Insider's View* 2004

➤ *Clinical Examples in Radiology* Spring 09:10, Winter 09:9

⊙ **36568** Insertion of peripherally inserted central venous catheter (PICC), without subcutaneous port or pump; younger than 5 years of age
➔ *CPT Assistant* Oct 04:14, Dec 04:8, May 05:13, Jun 08:8; *CPT Changes: An Insider's View* 2004
➔ *Clinical Examples in Radiology* Spring 09:10, Winter 09:9

(For placement of centrally inserted non-tunneled central venous catheter, without subcutaneous port or pump, younger than 5 years of age, use 36555)

36569 age 5 years or older
➔ *CPT Assistant* Oct 04:14, Dec 04:8, May 05:13, Jun 08:8; *CPT Changes: An Insider's View* 2004
➔ *Clinical Examples in Radiology* Inaugural 04:1-2, Spring 08:7,8, Fall 08:5, 6, Spring 09:10, Winter 09:9

(For placement of centrally inserted non-tunneled central venous catheter, without subcutaneous port or pump, age 5 years or older, use 36556)

⊙ **36570** Insertion of peripherally inserted central venous access device, with subcutaneous port; younger than 5 years of age
➔ *CPT Assistant* Dec 04:8, Jun 08:8; *CPT Changes: An Insider's View* 2004
➔ *Clinical Examples in Radiology* Spring 09:10, Winter 09:9

(For insertion of tunneled centrally inserted central venous access device with subcutaneous port, younger than 5 years of age, use 36560)

⊙ **36571** age 5 years or older
➔ *CPT Assistant* Dec 04:9, Jun 08:8; *CPT Changes: An Insider's View* 2004
➔ *Clinical Examples in Radiology* Spring 09:10, Winter 09:9

(For insertion of tunneled centrally inserted central venous access device with subcutaneous port, age 5 years or older, use 36561)

Implantable Venous Access Port
36570-36571, 36576, 36578

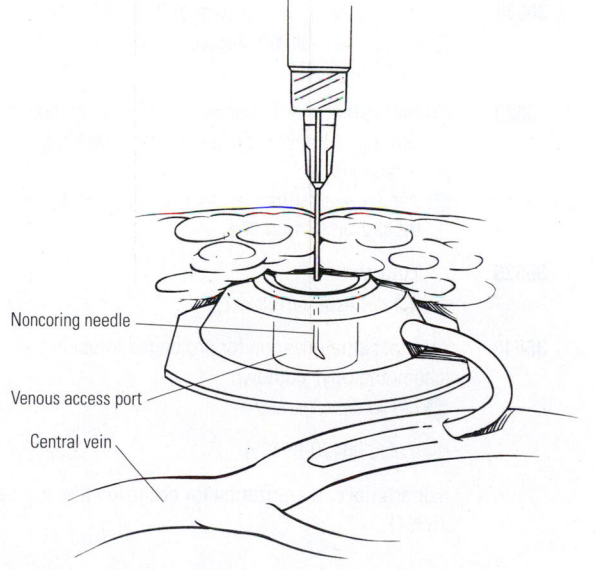

Noncoring needle
Venous access port
Central vein

Repair of Central Venous Access Device

(For mechanical removal of pericatheter obstructive material, use 36595)

(For mechanical removal of intracatheter obstructive material, use 36596)

36575 Repair of tunneled or non-tunneled central venous access catheter, without subcutaneous port or pump, central or peripheral insertion site
➔ *CPT Changes: An Insider's View* 2004
➔ *Clinical Examples in Radiology* Spring 09:10

⊙ **36576** Repair of central venous access device, with subcutaneous port or pump, central or peripheral insertion site
➔ *CPT Assistant* Dec 04:9, Jun 08:8; *CPT Changes: An Insider's View* 2004
➔ *Clinical Examples in Radiology* Spring 09:10

Partial Replacement of Central Venous Access Device (Catheter Only)

⊙ **36578** Replacement, catheter only, of central venous access device, with subcutaneous port or pump, central or peripheral insertion site
➔ *CPT Assistant* Dec 04:10, Jun 08:8; *CPT Changes: An Insider's View* 2004
➔ *Clinical Examples in Radiology* Spring 09:10, Winter 09:9

(For complete replacement of entire device through same venous access, use 36582 or 36583)

Complete Replacement of Central Venous Access Device Through Same Venous Access Site

36580 Replacement, complete, of a non-tunneled centrally inserted central venous catheter, without subcutaneous port or pump, through same venous access
➔ *CPT Assistant* Dec 04:10, Jun 08:8; *CPT Changes: An Insider's View* 2004
➔ *Clinical Examples in Radiology* Spring 09:10, Winter 09:9

⊙ **36581** Replacement, complete, of a tunneled centrally inserted central venous catheter, without subcutaneous port or pump, through same venous access
➔ *CPT Assistant* Dec 04:10, Jun 08:8; *CPT Changes: An Insider's View* 2004
➔ *Clinical Examples in Radiology* Spring 09:10, Winter 09:9

⊙ **36582** Replacement, complete, of a tunneled centrally inserted central venous access device, with subcutaneous port, through same venous access
➔ *CPT Assistant* Dec 04:10, Jun 08:8; *CPT Changes: An Insider's View* 2004
➔ *Clinical Examples in Radiology* Spring 09:10, Winter 09:9

⊙ **36583** Replacement, complete, of a tunneled centrally inserted central venous access device, with subcutaneous pump, through same venous access
➜ *CPT Assistant* Dec 04:10-11, Jun 08:8; *CPT Changes: An Insider's View* 2004
➜ *Clinical Examples in Radiology* Spring 09:10, Winter 09:9

36584 Replacement, complete, of a peripherally inserted central venous catheter (PICC), without subcutaneous port or pump, through same venous access
➜ *CPT Assistant* Dec 04:11, Jun 08:8; *CPT Changes: An Insider's View* 2004
➜ *Clinical Examples in Radiology* Spring 09:10, Winter 09:9

⊙ **36585** Replacement, complete, of a peripherally inserted central venous access device, with subcutaneous port, through same venous access
➜ *CPT Assistant* Dec 04:11, Jun 08:8; *CPT Changes: An Insider's View* 2004
➜ *Clinical Examples in Radiology* Spring 09:10, Winter 09:9

Removal of Central Venous Access Device

36589 Removal of tunneled central venous catheter, without subcutaneous port or pump
➜ *CPT Assistant* Dec 04:11, Jun 08:8; *CPT Changes: An Insider's View* 2004

⊙ **36590** Removal of tunneled central venous access device, with subcutaneous port or pump, central or peripheral insertion
➜ *CPT Assistant* Dec 04:11, Jun 08:8; *CPT Changes: An Insider's View* 2004
➜ *Clinical Examples in Radiology* Spring 08:7,8

(Do not report 36589 or 36590 for removal of non-tunneled central venous catheters)

Other Central Venous Access Procedures

36591 Collection of blood specimen from a completely implantable venous access device
➜ *CPT Assistant* Apr 08:9; *CPT Changes: An Insider's View* 2008

(Do not report 36591 in conjunction with any other service)

(For collection of venous blood specimen by venipuncture, use 36415)

(For collection of capillary blood specimen, use 36416)

36592 Collection of blood specimen using established central or peripheral catheter, venous, not otherwise specified
➜ *CPT Assistant* Apr 08:9; *CPT Changes: An Insider's View* 2008

(For blood collection from an established arterial catheter, use 37799)

(Do not report 36592 in conjunction with any other service)

36593 Declotting by thrombolytic agent of implanted vascular access device or catheter
➜ *CPT Assistant* Apr 08:9; *CPT Changes: An Insider's View* 2008

36595 Mechanical removal of pericatheter obstructive material (eg, fibrin sheath) from central venous device via separate venous access
➜ *CPT Assistant* Dec 04:9, 12; *CPT Changes: An Insider's View* 2004

(Do not report 36595 in conjunction with 36593)

(For venous catheterization, see 36010-36012)

(For radiological supervision and interpretation, use 75901)

36596 Mechanical removal of intraluminal (intracatheter) obstructive material from central venous device through device lumen
➜ *CPT Assistant* Dec 04:9, 12; *CPT Changes: An Insider's View* 2004

(Do not report 36596 in conjunction with 36593)

(For venous catheterization, see 36010-36012)

(For radiological supervision and interpretation, use 75902)

36597 Repositioning of previously placed central venous catheter under fluoroscopic guidance
➜ *CPT Assistant* Dec 04:12; *CPT Changes: An Insider's View* 2004

(For fluoroscopic guidance, use 76000)

36598 Contrast injection(s) for radiologic evaluation of existing central venous access device, including fluoroscopy, image documentation and report
➜ *CPT Changes: An Insider's View* 2006
➜ *Clinical Examples in Radiology* Winter 06:15, Spring 08:7,8

(Do not report 36598 in conjunction with 76000)

(Do not report 36598 in conjunction with 36595, 36596)

(For complete diagnostic studies, see 75820, 75825, 75827)

Arterial

36600 Arterial puncture, withdrawal of blood for diagnosis
➜ *CPT Assistant* Fall 95:7, Aug 00:2, Oct 03:2, Jul 05:11, Jul 06:4, Feb 07:10, Jul 07:1

⊘ **36620** Arterial catheterization or cannulation for sampling, monitoring or transfusion (separate procedure); percutaneous
➜ *CPT Assistant* Fall 95:7, Apr 98:3, Nov 99:32-33, Aug 00:2, Oct 03:2, Jul 06:4, Jul 07:1

36625 cutdown
➜ *CPT Assistant* Fall 95:7

36640 Arterial catheterization for prolonged infusion therapy (chemotherapy), cutdown
➜ *CPT Assistant* Fall 95:7

(See also 96420-96425)

(For arterial catheterization for occlusion therapy, see 75894)

⊙=Moderate sedation ✚=Add-on code ✗=FDA approval pending #=Resequenced code ➜➜=See p xiii for details

36660   Catheterization, umbilical artery, newborn, for diagnosis or therapy

➔ *CPT Assistant* Fall 95:8, Oct 03:2, Jul 06:4, Jul 07:1; *CPT Changes: An Insider's View* 2008

(Do not report modifier 63 in conjunction with 36660)

Intraosseous

36680   Placement of needle for intraosseous infusion

Hemodialysis Access, Intervascular Cannulation for Extracorporeal Circulation, or Shunt Insertion

36800   Insertion of cannula for hemodialysis, other purpose (separate procedure); vein to vein

➔ *CPT Assistant* Fall 93:3

36810   arteriovenous, external (Scribner type)

➔ *CPT Assistant* Fall 93:3, May 97:10

36815   arteriovenous, external revision, or closure

➔ *CPT Assistant* Fall 93:3

36818   Arteriovenous anastomosis, open; by upper arm cephalic vein transposition

➔ *CPT Assistant* Jul 05:9; *CPT Changes: An Insider's View* 2005

(Do not report 36818 in conjunction with 36819, 36820, 36821, 36830 during a unilateral upper extremity procedure. For bilateral upper extremity open arteriovenous anastomoses performed at the same operative session, use modifier 50 or 59 as appropriate)

36819   by upper arm basilic vein transposition

➔ *CPT Assistant* Nov 99:20, Jul 05:9; *CPT Changes: An Insider's View* 2000, 2002

(Do not report 36819 in conjunction with 36818, 36820, 36821, 36830 during a unilateral upper extremity procedure. For bilateral upper extremity open arteriovenous anastomoses performed at the same operative session, use modifier 50 or 59 as appropriate)

36820   by forearm vein transposition

➔ *CPT Assistant* Fall 93:4, Jul 05:9; *CPT Changes: An Insider's View* 2002

36821   direct, any site (eg, Cimino type) (separate procedure)

➔ *CPT Assistant* Fall 93:3, Feb 97:2, Nov 99:20, Jul 05:9; *CPT Changes: An Insider's View* 2000

Arteriovenous Anastomosis, Direct
36821

A section of artery and a neighboring vein are joined, allowing blood to flow down the artery and into the vein for the purpose of increasing blood flow, usually in hemodialysis.

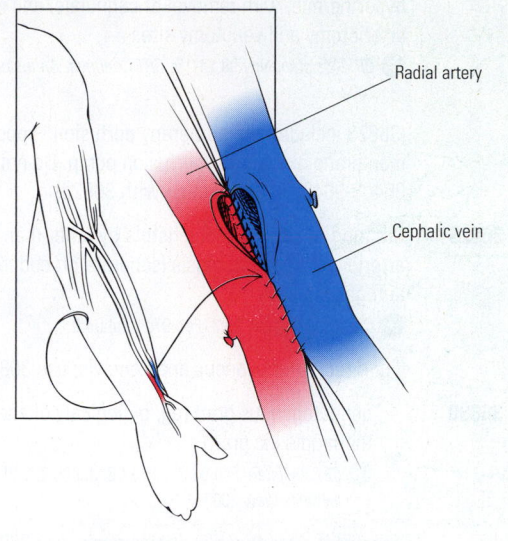

Radial artery

Cephalic vein

36822   Insertion of cannula(s) for prolonged extracorporeal circulation for cardiopulmonary insufficiency (ECMO) (separate procedure)

➔ *CPT Assistant* Feb 97:11

Insertion of Cannulas for Prolonged Extracorporeal Circulation Membrane Oxygenation (ECMO)
36822

The patient's venous blood is shunted and oxygenated outside of the body, bypassing the lungs. The treated blood is returned to body tissues through the femoral artery.

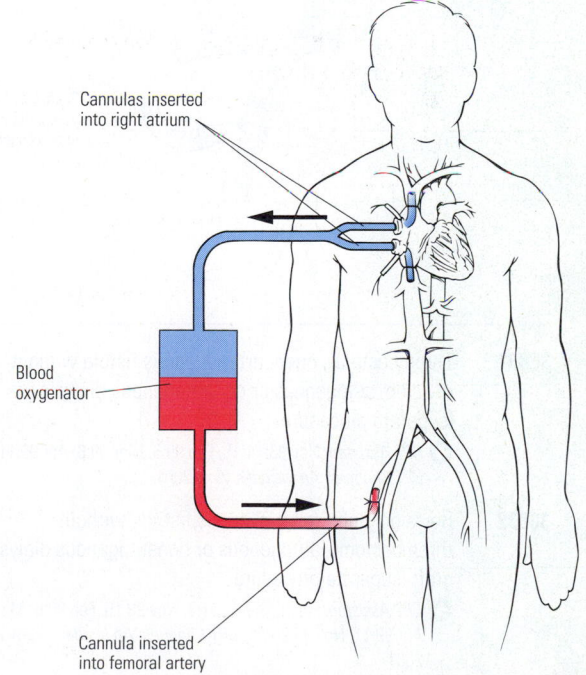

Cannulas inserted into right atrium

Blood oxygenator

Cannula inserted into femoral artery

(For maintenance of prolonged extracorporeal circulation, see 33960, 33961)

36823 Insertion of arterial and venous cannula(s) for isolated extracorporeal circulation including regional chemotherapy perfusion to an extremity, with or without hyperthermia, with removal of cannula(s) and repair of arteriotomy and venotomy sites

➔ *CPT Assistant* Nov 98:14-15; *CPT Changes: An Insider's View* 2002

(36823 includes chemotherapy perfusion supported by a membrane oxygenator/perfusion pump. Do not report 96409-96425 in conjunction with 36823)

36825 Creation of arteriovenous fistula by other than direct arteriovenous anastomosis (separate procedure); autogenous graft

➔ *CPT Assistant* Fall 93:3, Feb 97:2, Jul 05:9

(For direct arteriovenous anastomosis, use 36821)

36830 nonautogenous graft (eg, biological collagen, thermoplastic graft)

➔ *CPT Assistant* Fall 93:3, Feb 97:2, Jul 05:9; *CPT Changes: An Insider's View* 2003

(For direct arteriovenous anastomosis, use 36821)

Arteriovenous Fistula
36825-36830

A donor's vein (36825) or a synthetic vein (36830) is used to connect an artery and vein.

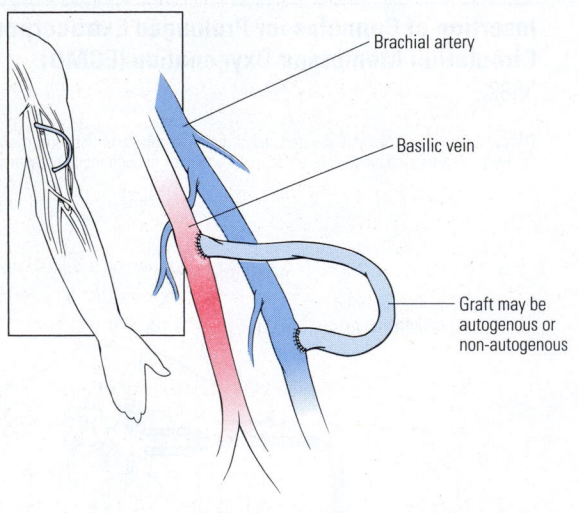

Brachial artery

Basilic vein

Graft may be autogenous or non-autogenous

36831 Thrombectomy, open, arteriovenous fistula without revision, autogenous or nonautogenous dialysis graft (separate procedure)

➔ *CPT Assistant* Nov 98:14-15, Feb 99:6, Mar 99:6, Apr 99:11; *CPT Changes: An Insider's View* 2001

36832 Revision, open, arteriovenous fistula; without thrombectomy, autogenous or nonautogenous dialysis graft (separate procedure)

➔ *CPT Assistant* Fall 93:3, Feb 97:2, Nov 98:15, Feb 99:6, Mar 99:6, Apr 99:11, Nov 99:20-21; *CPT Changes: An Insider's View* 2000, 2001

36833 with thrombectomy, autogenous or nonautogenous dialysis graft (separate procedure)

➔ *CPT Assistant* Nov 98:15, Feb 99:6, Apr 99:11

▶(36834 has been deleted. To report an arteriovenous access fistula or graft revision, use 36832)◀

36835 Insertion of Thomas shunt (separate procedure)

36838 Distal revascularization and interval ligation (DRIL), upper extremity hemodialysis access (steal syndrome)

➔ *CPT Changes: An Insider's View* 2004

(Do not report 36838 in conjunction with 35512, 35522, 35523, 36832, 37607, 37618)

36860 External cannula declotting (separate procedure); without balloon catheter

➔ *CPT Assistant* Fall 93:3, Feb 97:2, Nov 98:15, Feb 99:6, May 01:3

36861 with balloon catheter

➔ *CPT Assistant* Fall 93:3, Feb 97:2, May 01:3

(If imaging guidance is performed, use 76000)

⊙ **36870** Thrombectomy, percutaneous, arteriovenous fistula, autogenous or nonautogenous graft (includes mechanical thrombus extraction and intra-graft thrombolysis)

➔ *CPT Assistant* May 01:3; *CPT Changes: An Insider's View* 2001

➔ *Clinical Examples in Radiology* Spring 05:8-10, Summer 06:7, 12

(Do not report 36870 in conjunction with 36593)

▶(For catheterization, see 36147, 36148)◀

▶(For radiological supervision and interpretation, see 36147, 75791)◀

Portal Decompression Procedures

37140 Venous anastomosis, open; portocaval

➔ *CPT Changes: An Insider's View* 2003

(For peritoneal-venous shunt, use 49425)

37145 renoportal

37160 caval-mesenteric

37180 splenorenal, proximal

37181 splenorenal, distal (selective decompression of esophagogastric varices, any technique)

(For percutaneous procedure, use 37182)

37182 Insertion of transvenous intrahepatic portosystemic shunt(s) (TIPS) (includes venous access, hepatic and portal vein catheterization, portography with hemodynamic evaluation, intrahepatic tract formation/dilatation, stent placement and all associated imaging guidance and documentation)

➔ *CPT Assistant* Dec 03:2; *CPT Changes: An Insider's View* 2003

(Do not report 75885 or 75887 in conjunction with 37182)

(For open procedure, use 37140)

⊙▲ **37183** Revision of transvenous intrahepatic portosystemic shunt(s) (TIPS) (includes venous access, hepatic and portal vein catheterization, portography with hemodynamic evaluation, intrahepatic tract recanulization/dilatation, stent placement and all associated imaging guidance and documentation)

➲ *CPT Assistant* Dec 03:2; *CPT Changes: An Insider's View* 2003, 2010

(Do not report 75885 or 75887 in conjunction with 37183)

►(For repair of arteriovenous aneurysm, use 36832)◄

Transcatheter Procedures

Codes for catheter placement and the radiologic supervision and interpretation should also be reported, in addition to the code(s) for the therapeutic aspect of the procedure.

Mechanical Thrombectomy

Code(s) for catheter placement(s), diagnostic studies, and other percutaneous interventions (eg, transluminal balloon angioplasty, stent placement) provided are separately reportable.

Codes 37184-37188 specifically include intraprocedural fluoroscopic radiological supervision and interpretation services for guidance of the procedure.

Intraprocedural injection(s) of a thrombolytic agent is an included service and not separately reportable in conjunction with mechanical thrombectomy. However, subsequent or prior continuous infusion of a thrombolytic is not an included service and is separately reportable (see 37201, 75896, 75898).

For coronary mechanical thrombectomy, use 92973.

For mechanical thrombectomy for dialysis fistula, use 36870.

Arterial Mechanical Thrombectomy

Arterial mechanical thrombectomy may be performed as a "primary" transcatheter procedure with pretreatment planning, performance of the procedure, and postprocedure evaluation focused on providing this service. Typically, the diagnosis of thrombus has been made prior to the procedure, and a mechanical thrombectomy is planned preoperatively. Primary mechanical thrombectomy is reported per vascular family using 37184 for the initial vessel treated and 37185 for second or all subsequent vessel(s) within the same vascular family. To report mechanical thrombectomy of an additional vascular family treated through a separate access site, use modifier 51 in conjunction with 37184-37185.

Primary mechanical thrombectomy may precede or follow another percutaneous intervention. Most commonly primary mechanical thrombectomy will precede another percutaneous intervention with the decision regarding the need for other services not made until after mechanical thrombectomy has been performed. Occasionally, the performance of primary mechanical thrombectomy may follow another percutaneous intervention.

Do **NOT** report 37184-37185 for mechanical thrombectomy performed for the retrieval of short segments of thrombus or embolus evident during other percutaneous interventional procedures. See 37186 for these procedures.

Arterial mechanical thrombectomy is considered a "secondary" transcatheter procedure for removal or retrieval of short segments of thrombus or embolus when performed either before or after another percutaneous intervention (eg, percutaneous transluminal balloon angioplasty, stent placement). Secondary mechanical thrombectomy is reported using 37186. Do **NOT** report 37186 in conjunction with 37184-37185.

Venous Mechanical Thrombectomy

Use 37187 to report the initial application of venous mechanical thrombectomy. To report bilateral venous mechanical thrombectomy performed through a separate access site(s), use modifier 50 in conjunction with 37187. For repeat treatment on a subsequent day during a course of thrombolytic therapy, use 37188.

Arterial Mechanical Thrombectomy

⊙ **37184** Primary percutaneous transluminal mechanical thrombectomy, noncoronary, arterial or arterial bypass graft, including fluoroscopic guidance and intraprocedural pharmacological thrombolytic injection(s); initial vessel

➲ *CPT Changes: An Insider's View* 2006
➲ *Clinical Examples in Radiology* Winter 06:15

(Do not report 37184 in conjunction with 76000, 76001, 96374, 99143-99150)

⊙✚ **37185** second and all subsequent vessel(s) within the same vascular family (List separately in addition to code for primary mechanical thrombectomy procedure)

➲ *CPT Changes: An Insider's View* 2006
➲ *Clinical Examples in Radiology* Winter 06:15

(Do not report 37185 in conjunction with 76000, 76001, 96375)

⊙✚ **37186** Secondary percutaneous transluminal thrombectomy (eg, nonprimary mechanical, snare basket, suction technique), noncoronary, arterial or arterial bypass graft, including fluoroscopic guidance and intraprocedural pharmacological thrombolytic injections, provided in conjunction with another percutaneous intervention other than primary mechanical thrombectomy (List separately in addition to code for primary procedure)

➲ *CPT Changes: An Insider's View* 2006
➲ *Clinical Examples in Radiology* Winter 06:15

(Do not report 37186 in conjunction with 76000, 76001, 96375)

Venous Mechanical Thrombectomy

⊙ **37187** Percutaneous transluminal mechanical thrombectomy, vein(s), including intraprocedural pharmacological thrombolytic injections and fluoroscopic guidance
➲ *CPT Changes: An Insider's View* 2006
➲ *Clinical Examples in Radiology* Winter 06:15

(Do not report 37187 in conjunction with 76000, 76001, 96375)

⊙ **37188** Percutaneous transluminal mechanical thrombectomy, vein(s), including intraprocedural pharmacological thrombolytic injections and fluoroscopic guidance, repeat treatment on subsequent day during course of thrombolytic therapy
➲ *CPT Changes: An Insider's View* 2006
➲ *Clinical Examples in Radiology* Winter 06:15

(Do not report 37188 in conjunction with 76000, 76001, 96375)

Other Procedures

37195 Thrombolysis, cerebral, by intravenous infusion
➲ *CPT Assistant* Nov 97:16

37200 Transcatheter biopsy

(For radiological supervision and interpretation, use 75970)

37201 Transcatheter therapy, infusion for thrombolysis other than coronary
➲ *CPT Assistant* Feb 97:2, Feb 01:10, May 01:4
➲ *Clinical Examples in Radiology* Spring 08:7,8

(For radiological supervision and interpretation, use 75896)

37202 Transcatheter therapy, infusion other than for thrombolysis, any type (eg, spasmolytic, vasoconstrictive)
➲ *CPT Assistant* Oct 96:11, Jan 98:11, Apr 98:3, 9

(For thrombolysis of coronary vessels, see 92975, 92977)

(For radiological supervision and interpretation, use 75896)

⊙ **37203** Transcatheter retrieval, percutaneous, of intravascular foreign body (eg, fractured venous or arterial catheter)

(For radiological supervision and interpretation, use 75961)

37204 Transcatheter occlusion or embolization (eg, for tumor destruction, to achieve hemostasis, to occlude a vascular malformation), percutaneous, any method, non-central nervous system, non-head or neck
➲ *CPT Assistant* Sep 98:2, Oct 98:10, Feb 08:5, Apr 09:8
➲ *Clinical Examples in Radiology* Winter 07:1-3, Winter 08:4,5, Summer 08:1, 2, 3

(See also 61624, 61626)

(For radiological supervision and interpretation, use 75894)

(For uterine fibroid embolization [uterine artery embolization performed to treat uterine fibroids], use 37210)

(For obstetrical and gynecologic embolization procedures other than uterine fibroid embolization [eg, embolization to treat obstetrical or postpartum hemorrhage], use 37204)

37205 Transcatheter placement of an intravascular stent(s) (except coronary, carotid, and vertebral vessel), percutaneous; initial vessel
➲ *CPT Assistant* Fall 93:18, Feb 97:2, May 01:4, Feb 03:3, Dec 03:2; *CPT Changes: An Insider's View* 2005
➲ *Clinical Examples in Radiology* Winter 06:19

(For radiological supervision and interpretation, use 75960)

(For coronary stent placement, see 92980, 92981; intracranial, use 61635)

+ **37206** each additional vessel (List separately in addition to code for primary procedure)
➲ *CPT Assistant* Fall 93:18, Feb 97:2, Feb 03:3

(Use 37206 in conjunction with 37205)

(For transcatheter placement of intravascular cervical carotid artery stent(s), see 37215, 37216)

(For transcatheter placement of extracranial vertebral or intrathoracic carotid artery stent(s), see Category III codes 0075T, 0076T)

(For radiological supervision and interpretation, use 75960)

37207 Transcatheter placement of an intravascular stent(s) (non-coronary vessel), open; initial vessel
➲ *CPT Assistant* Feb 97:2, Feb 03:3

+ **37208** each additional vessel (List separately in addition to code for primary procedure)
➲ *CPT Assistant* Feb 97:2, Feb 03:3

(Use 37208 in conjunction with 37207)

(For radiological supervision and interpretation, use 75960)

(For catheterizations, see 36215-36248)

(For transcatheter placement of intracoronary stent(s), see 92980, 92981)

37209 Exchange of a previously placed intravascular catheter during thrombolytic therapy
➲ *CPT Changes: An Insider's View* 2006
➲ *Clinical Examples in Radiology* Winter 06:19

(For radiological supervision and interpretation, use 75900)

⊙ **37210**   Uterine fibroid embolization (UFE, embolization of the uterine arteries to treat uterine fibroids, leiomyomata), percutaneous approach inclusive of vascular access, vessel selection, embolization, and all radiological supervision and interpretation, intraprocedural roadmapping, and imaging guidance necessary to complete the procedure

➲ *CPT Assistant* Jan 07:7, Feb 08:5; *CPT Changes: An Insider's View* 2007

➲ *Clinical Examples in Radiology* Winter 07:2, Winter 08:4,5

(37210 includes all catheterizations and intraprocedural imaging required for a UFE procedure to confirm the presence of previously known fibroids and to roadmap vascular anatomy to enable appropriate therapy)

(Do not report 37210 in conjunction with 36200, 36245-36248, 37204, 75894, 75898)

(For all other non-central nervous system (CNS) embolization procedures, use 37204)

⊙ **37215**   Transcatheter placement of intravascular stent(s), cervical carotid artery, percutaneous; with distal embolic protection

➲ *CPT Assistant* May 05:7; *CPT Changes: An Insider's View* 2005

⊙ **37216**   without distal embolic protection

➲ *CPT Assistant* May 05:7; *CPT Changes: An Insider's View* 2005

(37215 and 37216 include all ipsilateral selective carotid catheterization, all diagnostic imaging for ipsilateral, cervical and cerebral carotid arteriography, and all related radiological supervision and interpretation. When ipsilateral carotid arteriogram (including imaging and selective catheterization) confirms the need for carotid stenting, 37215 and 37216 are inclusive of these services. If carotid stenting is not indicated, then the appropriate codes for carotid catheterization and imaging should be reported in lieu of 37215 and 37216)

(Do not report 37215, 37216 in conjunction with 75671, 75680)

(For transcatheter placement of extracranial vertebral or intrathoracic carotid artery stent(s), see Category III codes 0075T, 0076T)

(For percutaneous transcatheter placement of intravascular stents other than coronary, carotid, or vertebral, see 37205, 37206)

Intravascular Ultrasound Services

Intravascular ultrasound services include all transducer manipulations and repositioning within the specific vessel being examined, both before and after therapeutic intervention (eg, stent placement).

Vascular access for intravascular ultrasound performed during a therapeutic intervention is not reported separately.

+ **37250**   Intravascular ultrasound (non-coronary vessel) during diagnostic evaluation and/or therapeutic intervention; initial vessel (List separately in addition to code for primary procedure)

➲ *CPT Assistant* Nov 96:7, Nov 97:17, Nov 99:20; *CPT Changes: An Insider's View* 2000

+ **37251**   each additional vessel (List separately in addition to code for primary procedure)

➲ *CPT Assistant* Nov 96:7, Nov 97:17, Nov 99:20; *CPT Changes: An Insider's View* 2000

(Use 37251 in conjunction with 37250)

(For catheterizations, see 36215-36248)

(For transcatheter therapies, see 37200-37208, 61624, 61626)

(For radiological supervision and interpretation see 75945, 75946)

Endoscopy

Surgical vascular endoscopy always includes diagnostic endoscopy.

37500   Vascular endoscopy, surgical, with ligation of perforator veins, subfascial (SEPS)

➲ *CPT Changes: An Insider's View* 2003

(For open procedure, use 37760)

37501   Unlisted vascular endoscopy procedure

➲ *CPT Changes: An Insider's View* 2003

Ligation

(For phleborrhaphy and arteriorrhaphy, see 35201-35286)

37565   Ligation, internal jugular vein

37600   Ligation; external carotid artery

37605   internal or common carotid artery

37606   internal or common carotid artery, with gradual occlusion, as with Selverstone or Crutchfield clamp

(For transcatheter permanent arterial occlusion or embolization, see 61624-61626)

(For endovascular temporary arterial balloon occlusion, use 61623)

(For ligation treatment of intracranial aneurysm, use 61703)

37607   Ligation or banding of angioaccess arteriovenous fistula

37609   Ligation or biopsy, temporal artery

37615   Ligation, major artery (eg, post-traumatic, rupture); neck

37616   chest

37617   abdomen

37618   extremity

37620 Interruption, partial or complete, of inferior vena cava by suture, ligation, plication, clip, extravascular, intravascular (umbrella device)

➔ *CPT Assistant* Nov 00:10, May 01:10, Oct 08:11

➔ *Clinical Examples in Radiology* Winter 05:5-6

(For radiological supervision and interpretation, use 75940)

37650 Ligation of femoral vein

(For bilateral procedure, report 37650 with modifier 50)

37660 Ligation of common iliac vein

37700 Ligation and division of long saphenous vein at saphenofemoral junction, or distal interruptions

➔ *CPT Assistant* Aug 96:10

(Do not report 37700 in conjunction with 37718, 37722)

(For bilateral procedure, report 37700 with modifier 50)

Ligation and Division of Long Saphenous Vein
37700

The physician ligates sections of the saphenous vein along the leg.

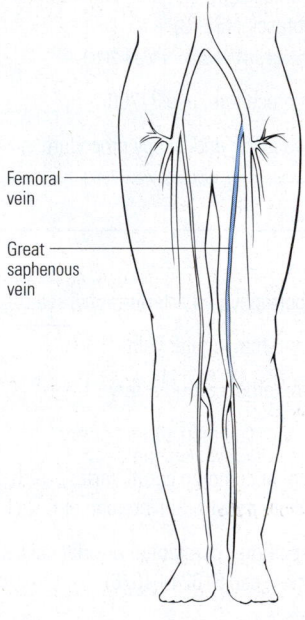

Femoral vein

Great saphenous vein

37718 Ligation, division, and stripping, short saphenous vein

➔ *CPT Changes: An Insider's View* 2006

(For bilateral procedure, use modifier 50)

(Do not report 37718 in conjunction with 37735, 37780)

37722 Ligation, division, and stripping, long (greater) saphenous veins from saphenofemoral junction to knee or below

➔ *CPT Changes: An Insider's View* 2006

(For ligation and stripping of the short saphenous vein, use 37718)

(For bilateral procedure, report 37722 with modifier 50)

(Do not report 37722 in conjunction with 37700, 37735)

(For ligation, division, and stripping of the greater saphenous vein, use 37722. For ligation, division, and stripping of the short saphenous vein, use 37718)

37735 Ligation and division and complete stripping of long or short saphenous veins with radical excision of ulcer and skin graft and/or interruption of communicating veins of lower leg, with excision of deep fascia

(Do not report 37735 in conjunction with 37700, 37718, 37722, 37780)

(For bilateral procedure, report 37735 with modifier 50)

▲ **37760** Ligation of perforator veins, subfascial, radical (Linton type), including skin graft, when performed, open, 1 leg

➔ *CPT Changes: An Insider's View* 2003, 2010

(For endoscopic procedure, use 37500)

● **37761** Ligation of perforator vein(s), subfascial, open, including ultrasound guidance, when performed, 1 leg

➔ *CPT Changes: An Insider's View* 2010

▶(For bilateral procedure, report 37761 with modifier 50)◀

▶(Do not report 37760, 37761 in conjunction with 76937, 76942, 76998, 93971)◀

▶(For endoscopic ligation of subfascial perforator veins, use 37500)◀

37765 Stab phlebectomy of varicose veins, 1 extremity; 10-20 stab incisions

➔ *CPT Assistant* Aug 04:6; *CPT Changes: An Insider's View* 2004

(For less than 10 incisions, use 37799)

(For more than 20 incisions, use 37766)

37766 more than 20 incisions

➔ *CPT Assistant* Aug 04:6; *CPT Changes: An Insider's View* 2004

37780 Ligation and division of short saphenous vein at saphenopopliteal junction (separate procedure)

➔ *CPT Assistant* Aug 96:10

(For bilateral procedure, report 37780 with modifier 50)

37785 Ligation, division, and/or excision of varicose vein cluster(s), 1 leg

➔ *CPT Assistant* Aug 04:5; *CPT Changes: An Insider's View* 2004

(For bilateral procedure, report 37785 with modifier 50)

Other Procedures

37788 Penile revascularization, artery, with or without vein graft

37790 Penile venous occlusive procedure

37799 Unlisted procedure, vascular surgery

➔ *CPT Assistant* Spring 93:12, Fall 93:3, Feb 97:10, Sep 97:10, May 01:11, Oct 04:16

Hemic and Lymphatic Systems

Spleen

Excision

38100   Splenectomy; total (separate procedure)
→ *CPT Assistant* Jul 93:9, Summer 93:10

38101   partial (separate procedure)
→ *CPT Assistant* Summer 93:10

+ 38102   total, en bloc for extensive disease, in conjunction with other procedure (List in addition to code for primary procedure)
→ *CPT Assistant* Summer 93:10

Repair

38115   Repair of ruptured spleen (splenorrhaphy) with or without partial splenectomy
→ *CPT Assistant* Summer 93:10

Laparoscopy

Surgical laparoscopy always includes diagnostic laparoscopy. To report a diagnostic laparoscopy (peritoneoscopy) (separate procedure), use 49320.

38120   Laparoscopy, surgical, splenectomy
→ *CPT Assistant* Nov 99:20-21, Mar 00:8; *CPT Changes: An Insider's View* 2000

38129   Unlisted laparoscopy procedure, spleen
→ *CPT Assistant* Nov 99:20-21, Mar 00:8; *CPT Changes: An Insider's View* 2000

Introduction

38200   Injection procedure for splenoportography

(For radiological supervision and interpretation, use 75810)

General

Bone Marrow or Stem Cell Services/Procedures

Codes 38207-38215 describe various steps used to preserve, prepare and purify bone marrow/stem cells prior to transplantation or reinfusion. Each code may be reported only once per day regardless of the quantity of bone marrow/stem cells manipulated.

38204   Management of recipient hematopoietic progenitor cell donor search and cell acquisition
→ *CPT Changes: An Insider's View* 2003

38205   Blood-derived hematopoietic progenitor cell harvesting for transplantation, per collection; allogenic
→ *CPT Changes: An Insider's View* 2003

38206   autologous
→ *CPT Changes: An Insider's View* 2003

38207   Transplant preparation of hematopoietic progenitor cells; cryopreservation and storage
→ *CPT Assistant* Jul 03:9; *CPT Changes: An Insider's View* 2003

(For diagnostic cryopreservation and storage, see 88240)

38208   thawing of previously frozen harvest, without washing
→ *CPT Assistant* Jul 03:9; *CPT Changes: An Insider's View* 2003, 2004

(For diagnostic thawing and expansion of frozen cells, see 88241)

38209   thawing of previously frozen harvest, with washing
→ *CPT Changes: An Insider's View* 2003, 2004

38210   specific cell depletion within harvest, T-cell depletion
→ *CPT Changes: An Insider's View* 2003

38211   tumor cell depletion
→ *CPT Changes: An Insider's View* 2003

38212   red blood cell removal
→ *CPT Changes: An Insider's View* 2003

38213   platelet depletion
→ *CPT Changes: An Insider's View* 2003

38214   plasma (volume) depletion
→ *CPT Changes: An Insider's View* 2003

38215   cell concentration in plasma, mononuclear, or buffy coat layer
→ *CPT Changes: An Insider's View* 2003

(Do not report 38207-38215 in conjunction with 88182, 88184-88189)

38220   Bone marrow; aspiration only
→ *CPT Assistant* Jan 04:26, Jun 07:10; *CPT Changes: An Insider's View* 2002, 2003

38221   biopsy, needle or trocar
→ *CPT Changes: An Insider's View* 2002, 2003

(For bone marrow biopsy interpretation, use 88305)

38230   Bone marrow harvesting for transplantation
→ *CPT Assistant* Apr 96:1

(For autologous and allogenic blood-derived peripheral stem cell harvesting for transplantation, see 38205-38206)

Bone Marrow Harvesting for Transplantation
38230

A biopsy needle is inserted into the marrow cavity of the iliac crest and bone marrow is removed from the donor.

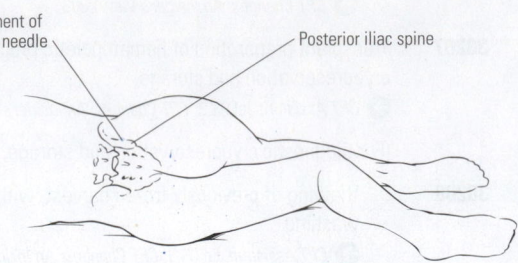

Placement of biopsy needle
Posterior iliac spine

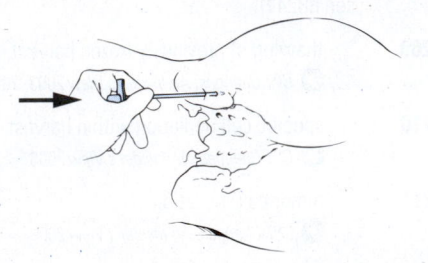

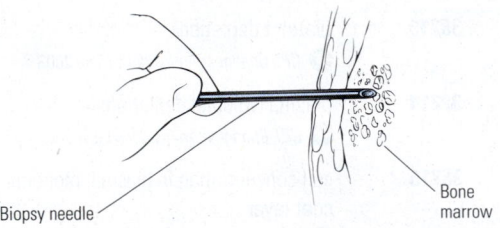

Biopsy needle

Bone marrow

38240	Bone marrow or blood-derived peripheral stem cell transplantation; allogenic — *Close relative*

➔ *CPT Assistant* Apr 96:2, Nov 98:15; Nov 99:21; *CPT Changes: An Insider's View* 2000

38241   autologous — *Patient's own*

➔ *CPT Assistant* Apr 96:2, Nov 98:15, Nov 99:21; *CPT Changes: An Insider's View* 2000

38242   allogeneic donor lymphocyte infusions

➔ *CPT Changes: An Insider's View* 2003

(For bone marrow aspiration, use 38220)

(For modification, treatment, and processing of bone marrow or blood-derived stem cell specimens for transplantation, use 38210-38213)

▶(For cryopreservation, freezing, and storage of blood-derived stem cells for transplantation, use 38207)◀

▶(For thawing and expansion of blood-derived stem cells for transplantation, see 38208, 38209)◀

(For compatibility studies, see 86812-86822)

Lymph Nodes and Lymphatic Channels

Incision

38300	Drainage of lymph node abscess or lymphadenitis; simple
38305	extensive
38308	Lymphangiotomy or other operations on lymphatic channels
38380	Suture and/or ligation of thoracic duct; cervical approach
38381	thoracic approach
38382	abdominal approach

Excision

(For injection for sentinel node identification, use 38792)

38500   Biopsy or excision of lymph node(s); open, superficial

➔ *CPT Assistant* Jun 97:5, Jul 99:7, Oct 05:23, Dec 07:8, Sep 08:5, Jan 09:7; *CPT Changes: An Insider's View* 2001

(Do not report 38500 with 38700-38780)

38505   by needle, superficial (eg, cervical, inguinal, axillary)

➔ *CPT Assistant* Jul 99:6, Jan 09:7

(If imaging guidance is performed, see 76942, 77012, 77021)

(For fine needle aspiration, use 10021 or 10022)

(For evaluation of fine needle aspirate, see 88172, 88173)

38510   open, deep cervical node(s)

➔ *CPT Assistant* May 98:10, Jul 99:6; *CPT Changes: An Insider's View* 2001

38520   open, deep cervical node(s) with excision scalene fat pad

➔ *CPT Assistant* May 98:10, Jul 99:6; *CPT Changes: An Insider's View* 2001

38525   open, deep axillary node(s)

➔ *CPT Assistant* May 98:10, Jul 99:7, Oct 05:23, Dec 07:8, Sep 08:5; *CPT Changes: An Insider's View* 2001

38530   open, internal mammary node(s)

➔ *CPT Assistant* May 98:10, Jul 99:6; *CPT Changes: An Insider's View* 2001

(Do not report 38530 with 38720-38746)

(For percutaneous needle biopsy, retroperitoneal lymph node or mass, use 49180. For fine needle aspiration, use 10022)

38542   Dissection, deep jugular node(s)

➔ *CPT Assistant* Jul 99:7

(For radical cervical neck dissection, use 38720)

38550   Excision of cystic hygroma, axillary or cervical; without deep neurovascular dissection

38555   with deep neurovascular dissection

Limited Lymphadenectomy for Staging

38562   Limited lymphadenectomy for staging (separate procedure); pelvic and para-aortic

➲ *CPT Assistant* Mar 01:10

(When combined with prostatectomy, use 55812 or 55842)

(When combined with insertion of radioactive substance into prostate, use 55862)

38564   retroperitoneal (aortic and/or splenic)

Laparoscopy

Surgical laparoscopy always includes diagnostic laparoscopy. To report a diagnostic laparoscopy (peritoneoscopy) (separate procedure), use 49320.

38570   Laparoscopy, surgical; with retroperitoneal lymph node sampling (biopsy), single or multiple

➲ *CPT Assistant* Nov 99:21, Mar 00:8; *CPT Changes: An Insider's View* 2000

38571   with bilateral total pelvic lymphadenectomy

➲ *CPT Assistant* Nov 99:21, Mar 00:8; *CPT Changes: An Insider's View* 2000

38572   with bilateral total pelvic lymphadenectomy and peri-aortic lymph node sampling (biopsy), single or multiple

➲ *CPT Assistant* Nov 99:21; *CPT Changes: An Insider's View* 2000

(For drainage of lymphocele to peritoneal cavity, use 49323)

38589   Unlisted laparoscopy procedure, lymphatic system

➲ *CPT Assistant* Nov 99:21, Mar 00:8; *CPT Changes: An Insider's View* 2000

Radical Lymphadenectomy (Radical Resection of Lymph Nodes)

(For limited pelvic and retroperitoneal lymphadenectomies, see 38562, 38564)

38700   Suprahyoid lymphadenectomy

➲ *CPT Assistant* Aug 02:8

(For bilateral procedure, report 38700 with modifier 50)

38720   Cervical lymphadenectomy (complete)

➲ *CPT Assistant* Oct 01:10, Aug 02:8

(For bilateral procedure, report 38720 with modifier 50)

38724   Cervical lymphadenectomy (modified radical neck dissection)

➲ *CPT Assistant* Jan 01:13, Aug 02:8

38740   Axillary lymphadenectomy; superficial

38745   complete

+ **38746**   Thoracic lymphadenectomy, regional, including mediastinal and peritracheal nodes (List separately in addition to code for primary procedure)

+ **38747**   Abdominal lymphadenectomy, regional, including celiac, gastric, portal, peripancreatic, with or without para-aortic and vena caval nodes (List separately in addition to code for primary procedure)

➲ *CPT Assistant* Nov 98:15

38760   Inguinofemoral lymphadenectomy, superficial, including Cloquets node (separate procedure)

(For bilateral procedure, report 38760 with modifier 50)

38765   Inguinofemoral lymphadenectomy, superficial, in continuity with pelvic lymphadenectomy, including external iliac, hypogastric, and obturator nodes (separate procedure)

(For bilateral procedure, report 38765 with modifier 50)

38770   Pelvic lymphadenectomy, including external iliac, hypogastric, and obturator nodes (separate procedure)

(For bilateral procedure, report 38770 with modifier 50)

38780   Retroperitoneal transabdominal lymphadenectomy, extensive, including pelvic, aortic, and renal nodes (separate procedure)

(For excision and repair of lymphedematous skin and subcutaneous tissue, see 15004-15005, 15570-15650)

Introduction

38790   Injection procedure; lymphangiography

➲ *CPT Assistant* Jul 99:6

(For bilateral procedure, report 38790 with modifier 50)

(For radiological supervision and interpretation, see 75801-75807)

38792   for identification of sentinel node

➲ *CPT Assistant* Nov 98:15, Jul 99:6, Dec 99:8, Sep 08:5; *CPT Changes: An Insider's View* 2008

(For excision of sentinel node, see 38500-38542)

(For nuclear medicine lymphatics and lymph gland imaging, use 78195)

38794   Cannulation, thoracic duct

Other Procedures

38999   Unlisted procedure, hemic or lymphatic system

➲ *CPT Assistant* May 98:10

Mediastinum and Diaphragm

Mediastinum

Incision

39000   Mediastinotomy with exploration, drainage, removal of foreign body, or biopsy; cervical approach

---

39010   transthoracic approach, including either transthoracic or median sternotomy

Excision

39200   Excision of mediastinal cyst

39220   Excision of mediastinal tumor

     (For substernal thyroidectomy, use 60270)

     (For thymectomy, use 60520)

Endoscopy

39400   Mediastinoscopy, with or without biopsy

Other Procedures

39499   Unlisted procedure, mediastinum

Diaphragm

Repair

     (For transabdominal repair of diaphragmatic [esophageal hiatal] hernia, see 43324, 43325)

39501   Repair, laceration of diaphragm, any approach

➲ *CPT Assistant* Nov 00:3

39502   Repair, paraesophageal hiatus hernia, transabdominal, with or without fundoplasty, vagotomy, and/or pyloroplasty, except neonatal

▶(For laparoscopic paraesophageal hernia repair, see 43281, 43282)◀

39503   Repair, neonatal diaphragmatic hernia, with or without chest tube insertion and with or without creation of ventral hernia

     (Do not report modifier 63 in conjunction with 39503)

39520   Repair, diaphragmatic hernia (esophageal hiatal); transthoracic

▶(For laparoscopic paraesophageal hernia repair, see 43281, 43282)◀

39530   combined, thoracoabdominal

39531   combined, thoracoabdominal, with dilation of stricture (with or without gastroplasty)

39540   Repair, diaphragmatic hernia (other than neonatal), traumatic; acute

➲ *CPT Assistant* Nov 00:9, Nov 03, Jun 08:3

39541   chronic

39545   Imbrication of diaphragm for eventration, transthoracic or transabdominal, paralytic or nonparalytic

➲ *CPT Assistant* Nov 00:3

39560   Resection, diaphragm; with simple repair (eg, primary suture)

➲ *CPT Assistant* Nov 99:21, Nov 00:3; *CPT Changes: An Insider's View* 2000

39561   with complex repair (eg, prosthetic material, local muscle flap)

➲ *CPT Assistant* Nov 99:21, Nov 00:3; *CPT Changes: An Insider's View* 2000

Other Procedures

39599   Unlisted procedure, diaphragm

Surgery

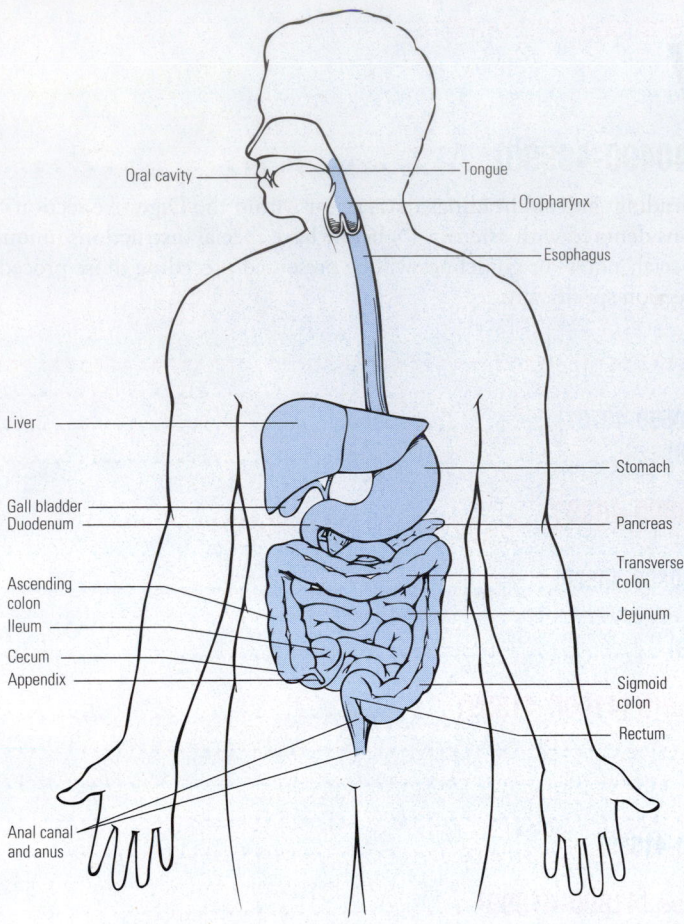

Oral cavity

Tongue

Oropharynx

Esophagus

Liver

Stomach

Gall bladder

Duodenum

Pancreas

Transverse colon

Ascending colon

Jejunum

Ileum

Cecum

Appendix

Sigmoid colon

Rectum

Anal canal and anus

Digestive System

Lips

(For procedures on skin of lips, see 10040 et seq)

Excision

40490   Biopsy of lip

40500   Vermilionectomy (lip shave), with mucosal advancement

40510   Excision of lip; transverse wedge excision with primary closure

40520   V-excision with primary direct linear closure

(For excision of mucous lesions, see 40810-40816)

40525   full thickness, reconstruction with local flap (eg, Estlander or fan)

40527   full thickness, reconstruction with cross lip flap (Abbe-Estlander)

40530   Resection of lip, more than one-fourth, without reconstruction

(For reconstruction, see 13131 et seq)

Repair (Cheiloplasty)

40650   Repair lip, full thickness; vermilion only
     ➲ *CPT Assistant* Jul 00:10

40652   up to half vertical height
     ➲ *CPT Assistant* Jul 00:10

40654   over one-half vertical height, or complex

40700   Plastic repair of cleft lip/nasal deformity; primary, partial or complete, unilateral

40701   primary bilateral, 1-stage procedure

40702   primary bilateral, 1 of 2 stages

40720   secondary, by recreation of defect and reclosure

(For bilateral procedure, report 40720 with modifier 50)

(To report rhinoplasty only for nasal deformity secondary to congenital cleft lip, see 30460, 30462)

(For repair of cleft lip, with cross lip pedicle flap (Abbe-Estlander type), use 40527)

40761   with cross lip pedicle flap (Abbe-Estlander type), including sectioning and inserting of pedicle

(For repair cleft palate, see 42200 et seq)

(For other reconstructive procedures, see 14060, 14061, 15120-15261, 15574, 15576, 15630)

Other Procedures

40799   Unlisted procedure, lips

Vestibule of Mouth

The vestibule is the part of the oral cavity outside the dentoalveolar structures; it includes the mucosal and submucosal tissue of lips and cheeks.

Incision

40800   Drainage of abscess, cyst, hematoma, vestibule of mouth; simple

40801   complicated

40804   Removal of embedded foreign body, vestibule of mouth; simple

40805   complicated

40806   Incision of labial frenum (frenotomy)

Excision, Destruction

40808   Biopsy, vestibule of mouth

40810   Excision of lesion of mucosa and submucosa, vestibule of mouth; without repair

40812   with simple repair

40814   with complex repair

40816   complex, with excision of underlying muscle

40818   Excision of mucosa of vestibule of mouth as donor graft

40819   Excision of frenum, labial or buccal (frenumectomy, frenulectomy, frenectomy)

40820   Destruction of lesion or scar of vestibule of mouth by physical methods (eg, laser, thermal, cryo, chemical)

Repair

40830   Closure of laceration, vestibule of mouth; 2.5 cm or less

40831   over 2.5 cm or complex

40840   Vestibuloplasty; anterior

40842   posterior, unilateral

40843   posterior, bilateral

40844   entire arch

40845   complex (including ridge extension, muscle repositioning)

(For skin grafts, see 15002 et seq)

Other Procedures

40899   Unlisted procedure, vestibule of mouth

Tongue and Floor of Mouth

Incision

41000   Intraoral incision and drainage of abscess, cyst, or hematoma of tongue or floor of mouth; lingual

41005   sublingual, superficial

41006   sublingual, deep, supramylohyoid

41007   submental space

41008   submandibular space

41009   masticator space

41010   Incision of lingual frenum (frenotomy)

41015   Extraoral incision and drainage of abscess, cyst, or hematoma of floor of mouth; sublingual

41016   submental

41017   submandibular

41018   masticator space

(For frenoplasty, use 41520)

41019   Placement of needles, catheters, or other device(s) into the head and/or neck region (percutaneous, transoral, or transnasal) for subsequent interstitial radioelement application
➜ *CPT Changes: An Insider's View* 2008

(For imaging guidance, see 76942, 77002, 77012, 77021)

(For stereotactic insertion of intracranial brachytherapy radiation sources, use 61770)

(For interstitial radioelement application, see 77776-77787)

Excision

41100   Biopsy of tongue; anterior two-thirds

41105   posterior one-third

41108   Biopsy of floor of mouth

41110   Excision of lesion of tongue without closure

41112   Excision of lesion of tongue with closure; anterior two-thirds

41113   posterior one-third

41114   with local tongue flap

(List 41114 in addition to code 41112 or 41113)

41115   Excision of lingual frenum (frenectomy)

41116   Excision, lesion of floor of mouth

41120   Glossectomy; less than one-half tongue

41130   hemiglossectomy

41135   partial, with unilateral radical neck dissection

41140   complete or total, with or without tracheostomy, without radical neck dissection

41145   complete or total, with or without tracheostomy, with unilateral radical neck dissection

41150   composite procedure with resection floor of mouth and mandibular resection, without radical neck dissection

41153   composite procedure with resection floor of mouth, with suprahyoid neck dissection

41155   composite procedure with resection floor of mouth, mandibular resection, and radical neck dissection (Commando type)
➜ *CPT Assistant* Jan 01:13

Repair

41250   Repair of laceration 2.5 cm or less; floor of mouth and/or anterior two-thirds of tongue

41251   posterior one-third of tongue

41252   Repair of laceration of tongue, floor of mouth, over 2.6 cm or complex

Other Procedures

41500   Fixation of tongue, mechanical, other than suture (eg, K-wire)

41510   Suture of tongue to lip for micrognathia (Douglas type procedure)

41512   Tongue base suspension, permanent suture technique
➜ *CPT Changes: An Insider's View* 2009

(For fixation of tongue, mechanical, other than suture, use 41500)

(For suture of tongue to lip for micrognathia, use 41510)

41520   Frenoplasty (surgical revision of frenum, eg, with Z-plasty)

(For frenotomy, see 40806, 41010)

41530   Submucosal ablation of the tongue base, radiofrequency, 1 or more sites, per session
➜ *CPT Changes: An Insider's View* 2009

41599   Unlisted procedure, tongue, floor of mouth
➜ *CPT Assistant* Dec 00:14

Dentoalveolar Structures

Incision

41800   Drainage of abscess, cyst, hematoma from dentoalveolar structures

41805   Removal of embedded foreign body from dentoalveolar structures; soft tissues

41806   bone

Excision, Destruction

41820   Gingivectomy, excision gingiva, each quadrant

41821   Operculectomy, excision pericoronal tissues

41822   Excision of fibrous tuberosities, dentoalveolar structures

41823   Excision of osseous tuberosities, dentoalveolar structures

41825   Excision of lesion or tumor (except listed above), dentoalveolar structures; without repair

41826   with simple repair

41827   with complex repair

             (For nonexcisional destruction, use 41850)

41828   Excision of hyperplastic alveolar mucosa, each quadrant (specify)

41830   Alveolectomy, including curettage of osteitis or sequestrectomy

41850   Destruction of lesion (except excision), dentoalveolar structures

Other Procedures

41870   Periodontal mucosal grafting

41872   Gingivoplasty, each quadrant (specify)

41874   Alveoloplasty, each quadrant (specify)

             (For closure of lacerations, see 40830, 40831)

             (For segmental osteotomy, use 21206)

             (For reduction of fractures, see 21421-21490)

41899   Unlisted procedure, dentoalveolar structures

Palate and Uvula

Incision

42000   Drainage of abscess of palate, uvula

Excision, Destruction

42100   Biopsy of palate, uvula

42104   Excision, lesion of palate, uvula; without closure

42106   with simple primary closure

42107   with local flap closure

             ▶(For skin graft, see 14040-14302)◀

             (For mucosal graft, use 40818)

42120   Resection of palate or extensive resection of lesion

             ▶(For reconstruction of palate with extraoral tissue, see 14040-14302, 15050, 15120, 15240, 15576)◀

42140   Uvulectomy, excision of uvula

42145   Palatopharyngoplasty (eg, uvulopalatopharyngoplasty, uvulopharyngoplasty)

             → *CPT Assistant* Dec 04:19

             (For removal of exostosis of the bony palate, see 21031, 21032)

42160   Destruction of lesion, palate or uvula (thermal, cryo or chemical)

Repair

42180   Repair, laceration of palate; up to 2 cm

42182   over 2 cm or complex

42200   Palatoplasty for cleft palate, soft and/or hard palate only

42205   Palatoplasty for cleft palate, with closure of alveolar ridge; soft tissue only

42210   with bone graft to alveolar ridge (includes obtaining graft)

42215   Palatoplasty for cleft palate; major revision

42220   secondary lengthening procedure

42225   attachment pharyngeal flap

42226   Lengthening of palate, and pharyngeal flap

42227   Lengthening of palate, with island flap

42235   Repair of anterior palate, including vomer flap

             (For repair of oronasal fistula, use 30600)

42260   Repair of nasolabial fistula

             (For repair of cleft lip, see 40700 et seq)

42280   Maxillary impression for palatal prosthesis

42281   Insertion of pin-retained palatal prosthesis

Other Procedures

42299   Unlisted procedure, palate, uvula

             → *CPT Assistant* Dec 04:19

Salivary Gland and Ducts

[handwritten: Salivary glands — Parotid, Submandibular, Sublingual]

Incision

42300   Drainage of abscess; parotid, simple

42305   parotid, complicated

42310   Drainage of abscess; submaxillary or sublingual, intraoral

             → *CPT Changes: An Insider's View* 2003

42320   submaxillary, external

42330   Sialolithotomy; submandibular (submaxillary), sublingual or parotid, uncomplicated, intraoral

42335   submandibular (submaxillary), complicated, intraoral

42340   parotid, extraoral or complicated intraoral

Excision

42400   Biopsy of salivary gland; needle

(For fine needle aspiration, see 10021, 10022)

(For evaluation of fine needle aspirate, see 88172, 88173)

(If imaging guidance is performed, see 76942, 77002, 77012, 77021)

42405   incisional

(If imaging guidance is performed, see 76942, 77002, 77012, 77021)

42408   Excision of sublingual salivary cyst (ranula)

42409   Marsupialization of sublingual salivary cyst (ranula)

42410   Excision of parotid tumor or parotid gland; lateral lobe, without nerve dissection

42415   lateral lobe, with dissection and preservation of facial nerve

42420   total, with dissection and preservation of facial nerve

42425   total, en bloc removal with sacrifice of facial nerve

42426   total, with unilateral radical neck dissection

(For suture or grafting of facial nerve, see 64864, 64865, 69740, 69745)

42440   Excision of submandibular (submaxillary) gland

42450   Excision of sublingual gland

Repair

42500   Plastic repair of salivary duct, sialodochoplasty; primary or simple

42505   secondary or complicated

42507   Parotid duct diversion, bilateral (Wilke type procedure);

42508   with excision of 1 submandibular gland

42509   with excision of both submandibular glands

42510   with ligation of both submandibular (Wharton's) ducts

Other Procedures

42550   Injection procedure for sialography

(For radiological supervision and interpretation, use 70390)

42600   Closure salivary fistula

42650   Dilation salivary duct

42660   Dilation and catheterization of salivary duct, with or without injection

42665   Ligation salivary duct, intraoral

42699   Unlisted procedure, salivary glands or ducts

Pharynx, Adenoids, and Tonsils

Incision

42700   Incision and drainage abscess; peritonsillar

42720   retropharyngeal or parapharyngeal, intraoral approach

42725   retropharyngeal or parapharyngeal, external approach

Excision, Destruction

42800   Biopsy; oropharynx

42802   hypopharynx

42804   nasopharynx, visible lesion, simple

42806   nasopharynx, survey for unknown primary lesion

(For laryngoscopic biopsy, see 31510, 31535, 31536)

42808   Excision or destruction of lesion of pharynx, any method

42809   Removal of foreign body from pharynx

42810   Excision branchial cleft cyst or vestige, confined to skin and subcutaneous tissues

42815   Excision branchial cleft cyst, vestige, or fistula, extending beneath subcutaneous tissues and/or into pharynx

42820   Tonsillectomy and adenoidectomy; younger than age 12
➲ *CPT Assistant* Feb 98:11, Mar 08:15, May 08:14

42821   age 12 or over
➲ *CPT Assistant* Aug 97:18, Feb 98:11, Mar 08:15, May 08:14

42825   Tonsillectomy, primary or secondary; younger than age 12
➲ *CPT Assistant* Aug 97:18, Feb 98:11, Mar 08:15

42826   age 12 or over
➲ *CPT Assistant* Aug 97:18, Feb 98:11, Mar 08:15

42830   Adenoidectomy, primary; younger than age 12

42831   age 12 or over

42835   Adenoidectomy, secondary; younger than age 12

42836   age 12 or over
➲ *CPT Assistant* Feb 98:11

42842   Radical resection of tonsil, tonsillar pillars, and/or retromolar trigone; without closure

42844   closure with local flap (eg, tongue, buccal)

42845   closure with other flap

(For closure with other flap(s), use appropriate number for flap(s))

(When combined with radical neck dissection, use also 38720)

42860   Excision of tonsil tags

42870   Excision or destruction lingual tonsil, any method
(separate procedure)

(For resection of the nasopharynx [eg, juvenile
angiofibroma] by bicoronal and/or transzygomatic
approach, see 61586 and 61600)

42890   Limited pharyngectomy

42892   Resection of lateral pharyngeal wall or pyriform sinus,
direct closure by advancement of lateral and posterior
pharyngeal walls

(When combined with radical neck dissection, use also
38720)

▲ **42894**   Resection of pharyngeal wall requiring closure with
myocutaneous or fasciocutaneous flap or free muscle,
skin, or fascial flap with microvascular anastamosis
➜ *CPT Assistant* Nov 07:8; *CPT Changes: An Insider's View* 2010

(When combined with radical neck dissection, use also
38720)

(For limited pharyngectomy with radical neck dissection,
use 38720 with 42890)

▶(For flap used for reconstruction, see 15732, 15734,
15756, 15757, 15758)◀

Repair

42900   Suture pharynx for wound or injury

42950   Pharyngoplasty (plastic or reconstructive operation on
pharynx)

(For pharyngeal flap, use 42225)

42953   Pharyngoesophageal repair

(For closure with myocutaneous or other flap, use
appropriate number in addition)

Other Procedures

42955   Pharyngostomy (fistulization of pharynx, external for
feeding)

42960   Control oropharyngeal hemorrhage, primary or secondary
(eg, post-tonsillectomy); simple

42961   complicated, requiring hospitalization

42962   with secondary surgical intervention

42970   Control of nasopharyngeal hemorrhage, primary or
secondary (eg, postadenoidectomy); simple, with
posterior nasal packs, with or without anterior packs
and/or cautery
➜ *CPT Changes: An Insider's View* 2002

42971   complicated, requiring hospitalization

42972   with secondary surgical intervention

42999   Unlisted procedure, pharynx, adenoids, or tonsils

Esophagus

Incision

(For esophageal intubation with laparotomy, use 43510)

43020   Esophagotomy, cervical approach, with removal of
foreign body

43030   Cricopharyngeal myotomy

43045   Esophagotomy, thoracic approach, with removal of
foreign body

Excision

(For gastrointestinal reconstruction for previous
esophagectomy, see 43360, 43361)

43100   Excision of lesion, esophagus, with primary repair;
cervical approach

43101   thoracic or abdominal approach

(For wide excision of malignant lesion of cervical
esophagus, with total laryngectomy without radical neck
dissection, see 43107, 43116, 43124, and 31360)

(For wide excision of malignant lesion of cervical
esophagus, with total laryngectomy with radical neck
dissection, see 43107, 43116, 43124, and 31365)

43107   Total or near total esophagectomy, without thoracotomy;
with pharyngogastrostomy or cervical
esophagogastrostomy, with or without pyloroplasty
(transhiatal)

43108   with colon interposition or small intestine
reconstruction, including intestine mobilization,
preparation and anastomosis(es)
➜ *CPT Changes: An Insider's View* 2002

43112   Total or near total esophagectomy, with thoracotomy;
with pharyngogastrostomy or cervical
esophagogastrostomy, with or without pyloroplasty

43113   with colon interposition or small intestine
reconstruction, including intestine mobilization,
preparation, and anastomosis(es)
➜ *CPT Changes: An Insider's View* 2002

43116   Partial esophagectomy, cervical, with free intestinal
graft, including microvascular anastomosis, obtaining the
graft and intestinal reconstruction
➜ *CPT Assistant* Nov 97:17, Nov 98:16

(Do not report 43116 in conjunction with 69990)

(Report 43116 with the modifier 52 appended if intestinal
or free jejunal graft with microvascular anastomosis is
performed by another physician)

(For free jejunal graft with microvascular anastomosis
performed by another physician, use 43496)

43117   Partial esophagectomy, distal two-thirds, with thoracotomy and separate abdominal incision, with or without proximal gastrectomy; with thoracic esophagogastrostomy, with or without pyloroplasty (Ivor Lewis)

43118   with colon interposition or small intestine reconstruction, including intestine mobilization, preparation, and anastomosis(es)
➔ *CPT Changes: An Insider's View* 2002

(For total esophagectomy with gastropharyngostomy, see 43107, 43124)

(For esophagogastrectomy (lower third) and vagotomy, use 43122)

43121   Partial esophagectomy, distal two-thirds, with thoracotomy only, with or without proximal gastrectomy, with thoracic esophagogastrostomy, with or without pyloroplasty

43122   Partial esophagectomy, thoracoabdominal or abdominal approach, with or without proximal gastrectomy; with esophagogastrostomy, with or without pyloroplasty

43123   with colon interposition or small intestine reconstruction, including intestine mobilization, preparation, and anastomosis(es)
➔ *CPT Changes: An Insider's View* 2002

43124   Total or partial esophagectomy, without reconstruction (any approach), with cervical esophagostomy

43130   Diverticulectomy of hypopharynx or esophagus, with or without myotomy; cervical approach

43135   thoracic approach

Endoscopy

For endoscopic procedures, code appropriate endoscopy of each anatomic site examined.

Surgical endoscopy always includes diagnostic endoscopy.

⊙ **43200**   Esophagoscopy, rigid or flexible; diagnostic, with or without collection of specimen(s) by brushing or washing (separate procedure)
➔ *CPT Assistant* Spring 91:7, Spring 94:1, Jun 98:10, Nov 99:21, Sep 03:3, Oct 08:6; *CPT Changes: An Insider's View* 2000

⊙ **43201**   with directed submucosal injection(s), any substance
➔ *CPT Changes: An Insider's View* 2003

(For injection sclerosis of esophageal varices, use 43204)

⊙ **43202**   with biopsy, single or multiple
➔ *CPT Assistant* Spring 94:1, Oct 08:6

⊙ **43204**   with injection sclerosis of esophageal varices
➔ *CPT Assistant* Spring 94:1, Oct 08:6

⊙ **43205**   with band ligation of esophageal varices
➔ *CPT Assistant* Spring 94:1, Oct 08:6

⊙ **43215**   with removal of foreign body
➔ *CPT Assistant* Spring 94:1, Oct 08:6

(For radiological supervision and interpretation, use 74235)

⊙ **43216**   with removal of tumor(s), polyp(s), or other lesion(s) by hot biopsy forceps or bipolar cautery
➔ *CPT Assistant* Spring 94:1, Oct 08:6

⊙ **43217**   with removal of tumor(s), polyp(s), or other lesion(s) by snare technique
➔ *CPT Assistant* Spring 94:1, Oct 08:6

⊙ **43219**   with insertion of plastic tube or stent
➔ *CPT Assistant* Spring 94:2, Oct 08:6

⊙ **43220**   with balloon dilation (less than 30 mm diameter)
➔ *CPT Assistant* Spring 94:2, Jan 97:10, May 05:3, Oct 08:6

(If imaging guidance is performed, use 74360)

(For endoscopic dilation with balloon 30 mm diameter or larger, use 43458)

(For dilation without visualization, use 43450-43453)

(For diagnostic fiberoptic esophagogastroscopy, use 43200, 43235)

(For fiberoptic esophagogastroscopy with biopsy or collection of specimen, use 43200, 43202, 43235, 43239)

(For fiberoptic esophagogastroscopy with removal of foreign body, use 43215, 43247)

(For fiberoptic esophagogastroscopy with removal of polyp(s), use 43217, 43251)

⊙ **43226**   with insertion of guide wire followed by dilation over guide wire
➔ *CPT Assistant* Spring 94:2

(For radiological supervision and interpretation, use 74360)

⊙ **43227**   with control of bleeding (eg, injection, bipolar cautery, unipolar cautery, laser, heater probe, stapler, plasma coagulator)
➔ *CPT Assistant* Spring 94:2, Oct 08:6; *CPT Changes: An Insider's View* 2002

⊙ **43228**   with ablation of tumor(s), polyp(s), or other lesion(s), not amenable to removal by hot biopsy forceps, bipolar cautery or snare technique
➔ *CPT Assistant* Spring 94:2, Nov 98:21, Oct 08:6

(For esophagoscopic photodynamic therapy, report 43228 in addition to 96570, 96571 as appropriate)

⊙ **43231**   with endoscopic ultrasound examination
➔ *CPT Assistant* Oct 01:4, May 04:6, Oct 08:6, Mar 09:8; *CPT Changes: An Insider's View* 2001

(Do not report 43231 in conjunction with 76975)

⊙ **43232**   with transendoscopic ultrasound-guided intramural or transmural fine needle aspiration/biopsy(s)

➔ *CPT Assistant* Oct 01:4, Mar 04:11, May 04:6, Oct 08:6, Mar 09:8; *CPT Changes: An Insider's View* 2001

(Do not report 43232 in conjunction with 76942, 76975)

(For interpretation of specimen, see 88172-88173)

⊙ **43234**   Upper gastrointestinal endoscopy, simple primary examination (eg, with small diameter flexible endoscope) (separate procedure)

➔ *CPT Assistant* May 07:10

⊙ **43235**   Upper gastrointestinal endoscopy including esophagus, stomach, and either the duodenum and/or jejunum as appropriate; diagnostic, with or without collection of specimen(s) by brushing or washing (separate procedure)

➔ *CPT Assistant* Spring 94:4, Dec 97:11, Jun 03:11, Sep 03:3, Oct 08:6

Upper Gastrointestinal Endoscopy
43235

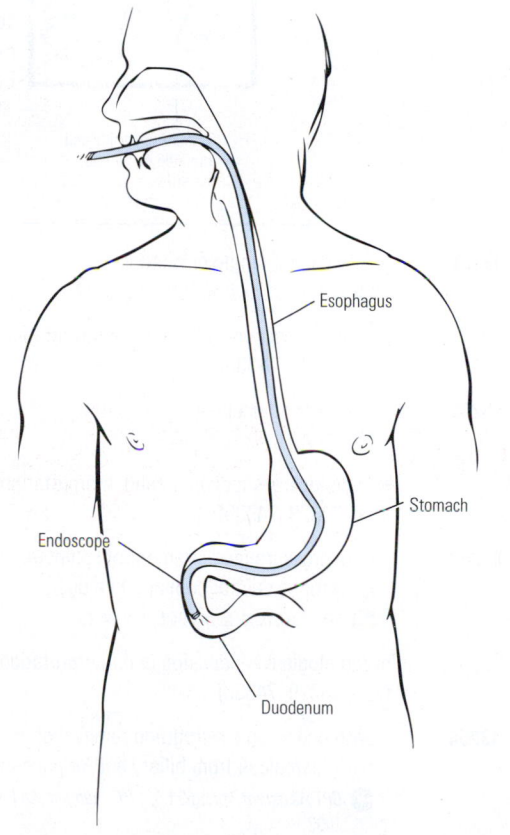

Esophagus

Stomach

Endoscope

Duodenum

⊙ **43236**   with directed submucosal injection(s), any substance

➔ *CPT Changes: An Insider's View* 2003

(For injection sclerosis of esophageal and/or gastric varices, use 43243)

⊙ **43237**   with endoscopic ultrasound examination limited to the esophagus

➔ *CPT Changes: An Insider's View* 2004

(Do not report 43237 in conjunction with 76942, 76975)

⊙ **43238**   with transendoscopic ultrasound-guided intramural or transmural fine needle aspiration/biopsy(s), esophagus (includes endoscopic ultrasound examination limited to the esophagus)

➔ *CPT Changes: An Insider's View* 2004

(Do not report 43238 in conjunction with 76942 or 76975)

⊙ **43239**   with biopsy, single or multiple

➔ *CPT Assistant* Spring 94:4, Apr 98:14, Feb 99:11, Oct 01:4, Nov 07:9

⊙ **43240**   with transmural drainage of pseudocyst

➔ *CPT Assistant* Oct 01:4; *CPT Changes: An Insider's View* 2001

⊙ **43241**   with transendoscopic intraluminal tube or catheter placement

➔ *CPT Assistant* Spring 94:4, Nov 01:7, Apr 09:3; *CPT Changes: An Insider's View* 2001

⊙ **43242**   with transendoscopic ultrasound-guided intramural or transmural fine needle aspiration/biopsy(s) (includes endoscopic ultrasound examination of the esophagus, stomach, and either the duodenum and/or jejunum as appropriate)

➔ *CPT Assistant* Oct 01:4, Mar 09:8; *CPT Changes: An Insider's View* 2001, 2004

(Do not report 43242 in conjunction with 76942, 76975)

(For transendoscopic fine needle aspiration/biopsy limited to esophagus, use 43238)

(For interpretation of specimen, see 88172-88173)

⊙ **43243**   with injection sclerosis of esophageal and/or gastric varices

➔ *CPT Assistant* Spring 94:4

⊙ **43244**   with band ligation of esophageal and/or gastric varices

➔ *CPT Assistant* Spring 94:4

⊙ **43245**   with dilation of gastric outlet for obstruction (eg, balloon, guide wire, bougie)

➔ *CPT Assistant* Spring 94:4, Oct 01:4, Jan 04:26; *CPT Changes: An Insider's View* 2002, 2003

(Do not report 43245 in conjunction with 43256)

⊙ **43246**   with directed placement of percutaneous gastrostomy tube

➔ *CPT Assistant* Spring 94:4, Feb 97:10

(For nonendoscopic percutaneous placement of gastrostomy tube, see 49440)

⊙ **43247**   with removal of foreign body

➔ *CPT Assistant* Spring 94:4

(For radiological supervision and interpretation, use 74235)

⊙ **43248**   with insertion of guide wire followed by dilation of esophagus over guide wire
→ *CPT Assistant* Spring 94:4, Dec 97:11, Oct 08:6

⊙ **43249**   with balloon dilation of esophagus (less than 30 mm diameter)
→ *CPT Assistant* May 05:3

⊙ **43250**   with removal of tumor(s), polyp(s), or other lesion(s) by hot biopsy forceps or bipolar cautery
→ *CPT Assistant* Spring 94:4, Feb 99:11, Nov 07:9

⊙ **43251**   with removal of tumor(s), polyp(s), or other lesion(s) by snare technique
→ *CPT Assistant* Spring 94:4, Oct 04:12, Nov 07:9

⊙ **43255**   with control of bleeding, any method
→ *CPT Assistant* Spring 94:4

⊙ **43256**   with transendoscopic stent placement (includes predilation)
→ *CPT Changes: An Insider's View* 2001

⊙ **43257**   with delivery of thermal energy to the muscle of lower esophageal sphincter and/or gastric cardia, for treatment of gastroesophageal reflux disease
→ *CPT Assistant* May 05:3; *CPT Changes: An Insider's View* 2005

⊙ **43258**   with ablation of tumor(s), polyp(s), or other lesion(s) not amenable to removal by hot biopsy forceps, bipolar cautery or snare technique
→ *CPT Assistant* Spring 94:4

(For injection sclerosis of esophageal varices, use 43204, 43243)

⊙ **43259**   with endoscopic ultrasound examination, including the esophagus, stomach, and either the duodenum and/or jejunum as appropriate
→ *CPT Assistant* Spring 94:4, May 04:7, Mar 09:8; *CPT Changes: An Insider's View* 2004

(Do not report 43259 in conjunction with 76975)

⊙ **43260**   Endoscopic retrograde cholangiopancreatography (ERCP); diagnostic, with or without collection of specimen(s) by brushing or washing (separate procedure)
→ *CPT Assistant* Spring 94:5, Oct 04:13, May 08:14, Aug 08:12

(For radiological supervision and interpretation, see 74328, 74329, 74330)

Endoscopic Retrograde Cholangiopancreatography (ERCP)
43260

Examination of the hepatobiliary system (pancreatic ducts, hepatic ducts, common bile ducts, duodenal papilla [ampulla of Vater] and gallbladder [if present]) is performed through a side-viewing flexible fiberoptic endoscope.

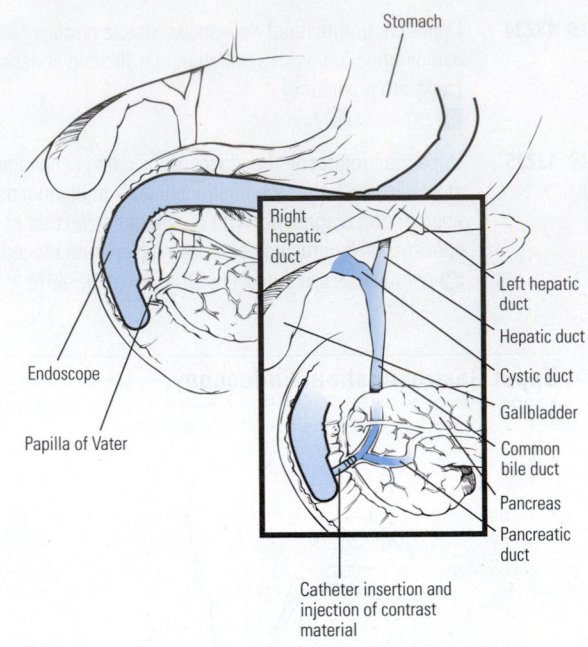

⊙ **43261**   with biopsy, single or multiple
→ *CPT Assistant* Spring 94:5, Aug 08:12

(For radiological supervision and interpretation, see 74328, 74329, 74330)

⊙ **43262**   with sphincterotomy/papillotomy
→ *CPT Assistant* Spring 94:5, Oct 04:13

(For radiological supervision and interpretation, see 74328, 74329, 74330)

⊙ **43263**   with pressure measurement of sphincter of Oddi (pancreatic duct or common bile duct)
→ *CPT Assistant* Spring 94:5, Oct 04:13

(For radiological supervision and interpretation, see 74328, 74329, 74330)

⊙ **43264**   with endoscopic retrograde removal of calculus/calculi from biliary and/or pancreatic ducts
→ *CPT Assistant* Spring 94:5; *CPT Changes: An Insider's View* 2002

(When done with sphincterotomy, also use 43262)

(For radiological supervision and interpretation, see 74328, 74329, 74330)

⊙ **43265**   with endoscopic retrograde destruction, lithotripsy of calculus/calculi, any method
→ *CPT Assistant* Spring 94:5; *CPT Changes: An Insider's View* 2002

(When done with sphincterotomy, also use 43262)

(For radiological supervision and interpretation, see 74328, 74329, 74330)

⊙ **43267**   with endoscopic retrograde insertion of nasobiliary or nasopancreatic drainage tube
➔ *CPT Assistant* Spring 94:6

(When done with sphincterotomy, also use 43262)

(For radiological supervision and interpretation, see 74328, 74329, 74330)

⊙ **43268**   with endoscopic retrograde insertion of tube or stent into bile or pancreatic duct
➔ *CPT Assistant* Spring 94:6, Sep 04:13, Oct 04:12

(When done with sphincterotomy, also use 43262)

(For radiological supervision and interpretation, see 74328, 74329, 74330)

⊙ **43269**   with endoscopic retrograde removal of foreign body and/or change of tube or stent
➔ *CPT Assistant* Spring 94:6

(When done with sphincterotomy, also use 43262)

(For radiological supervision and interpretation, see 74328, 74329, 74330)

⊙ **43271**   with endoscopic retrograde balloon dilation of ampulla, biliary and/or pancreatic duct(s)
➔ *CPT Assistant* Spring 94:6

(When done with sphincterotomy, also use 43262)

(For radiological supervision and interpretation, see 74328, 74329, 74330)

⊙ **43272**   with ablation of tumor(s), polyp(s), or other lesion(s) not amenable to removal by hot biopsy forceps, bipolar cautery or snare technique

(For radiological supervision and interpretation, see 74328, 74329, 74330)

⊙+ **43273**   Endoscopic cannulation of papilla with direct visualization of common bile duct(s) and/or pancreatic duct(s) (List separately in addition to code(s) for primary procedure)
➔ *CPT Changes: An Insider's View* 2009

▶(Use 43273 in conjunction with 43260-43265, 43267-43272)◀

Laparoscopy

Surgical laparoscopy always includes diagnostic laparoscopy. To report a diagnostic laparoscopy (peritoneoscopy) (separate procedure), use 49320.

43279   Laparoscopy, surgical, esophagomyotomy (Heller type), with fundoplasty, when performed
➔ *CPT Changes: An Insider's View* 2009

(For open approach, see 43330, 43331)

(Do not report 43279 in conjunction with 43280)

43280   Laparoscopy, surgical, esophagogastric fundoplasty (eg, Nissen, Toupet procedures)
➔ *CPT Assistant* Nov 99:22, Mar 00:8, Dec 02:2; *CPT Changes: An Insider's View* 2000

(Do not report 43280 in conjunction with 43279)

(For open approach, use 43324)

Laparoscopic Fundoplasty
43280

With the esophagus and fundus held aside, sutures are placed in both crus diaphragmatis muscles below the esophagus to bring them together to close the hiatal hernia, and the anterior and posterior walls of the fundus are wrapped and stitched around the esophagus to complete the laparoscopic fundoplasty.

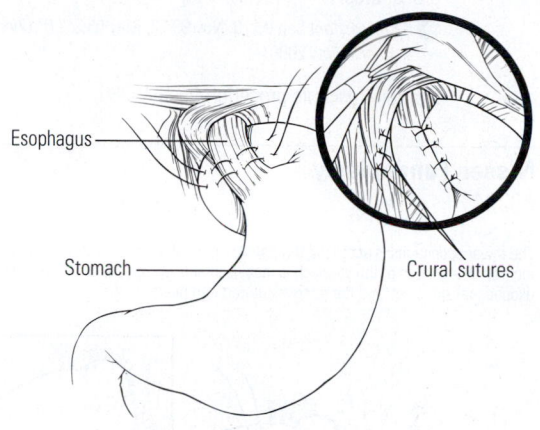

Esophagus
Stomach
Crural sutures

● **43281**   Laparoscopy, surgical, repair of paraesophageal hernia, includes fundoplasty, when performed; without implantation of mesh
➔ *CPT Changes: An Insider's View* 2010

● **43282**   with implantation of mesh
➔ *CPT Changes: An Insider's View* 2010

▶(For transthoracic paraesophageal hernia repair, use 39520. For transabdominal paraesophageal hernia repair, use 39502)◀

▶(Do not report 43281, 43282 in conjunction with 43280, 43450, 43453, 43456, 43458, 49568)◀

43289   Unlisted laparoscopy procedure, esophagus
➔ *CPT Assistant* Nov 99:22, Mar 00:8; *CPT Changes: An Insider's View* 2000

Repair

43300   Esophagoplasty (plastic repair or reconstruction), cervical approach; without repair of tracheoesophageal fistula

43305   with repair of tracheoesophageal fistula

43310   Esophagoplasty (plastic repair or reconstruction), thoracic approach; without repair of tracheoesophageal fistula

43312   with repair of tracheoesophageal fistula

43313   Esophagoplasty for congenital defect (plastic repair or reconstruction), thoracic approach; without repair of congenital tracheoesophageal fistula
➔ *CPT Changes: An Insider's View* 2002

43314   with repair of congenital tracheoesophageal fistula
➔ *CPT Changes: An Insider's View* 2002

(Do not report modifier 63 in conjunction with 43313, 43314)

43320   Esophagogastrostomy (cardioplasty), with or without vagotomy and pyloroplasty, transabdominal or transthoracic approach

43324   Esophagogastric fundoplasty (eg, Nissen, Belsey IV, Hill procedures)
➔ *CPT Assistant* Sep 96:10, Nov 99:22, May 05:3; *CPT Changes: An Insider's View* 2000

(For laparoscopic procedure, use 43280)

Nissen Fundoplasty
43324

The lower esophagus is accessed through an upper abdominal or lower thoracic incision. The fundus of the stomach is mobilized and wrapped around the lower esophageal sphincter, and the wrap is sutured into place.

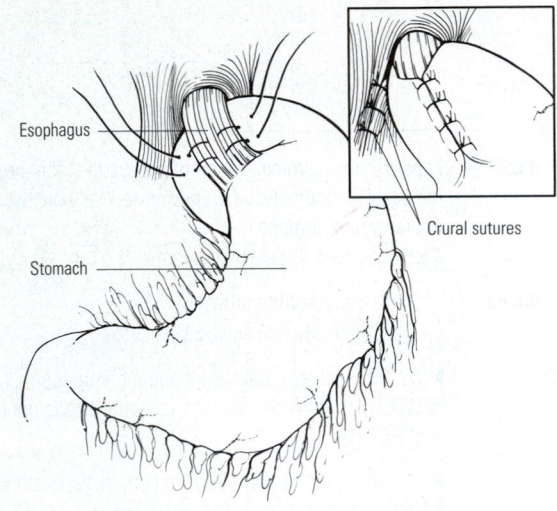

Esophagus

Crural sutures

Stomach

43325   Esophagogastric fundoplasty; with fundic patch (Thal-Nissen procedure)
➔ *CPT Assistant* Winter 90:6

(For cricopharyngeal myotomy, use 43030)

43326   with gastroplasty (eg, Collis)
➔ *CPT Assistant* Winter 90:6

43330   Esophagomyotomy (Heller type); abdominal approach
➔ *CPT Assistant* Nov 99:22; *CPT Changes: An Insider's View* 2000

(For laparoscopic esophagomyotomy procedure, use 43279)

43331   thoracic approach
➔ *CPT Assistant* Nov 99:22; *CPT Changes: An Insider's View* 2000

(For thoracoscopic esophagomyotomy, use 32665)

43340   Esophagojejunostomy (without total gastrectomy); abdominal approach

43341   thoracic approach

43350   Esophagostomy, fistulization of esophagus, external; abdominal approach

43351   thoracic approach

43352   cervical approach

43360   Gastrointestinal reconstruction for previous esophagectomy, for obstructing esophageal lesion or fistula, or for previous esophageal exclusion; with stomach, with or without pyloroplasty

43361   with colon interposition or small intestine reconstruction, including intestine mobilization, preparation, and anastomosis(es)
➔ *CPT Changes: An Insider's View* 2002

43400   Ligation, direct, esophageal varices

43401   Transection of esophagus with repair, for esophageal varices

43405   Ligation or stapling at gastroesophageal junction for pre-existing esophageal perforation

43410   Suture of esophageal wound or injury; cervical approach
➔ *CPT Assistant* Jun 96:7

43415   transthoracic or transabdominal approach

43420   Closure of esophagostomy or fistula; cervical approach

43425   transthoracic or transabdominal approach

(For repair of esophageal hiatal hernia, see 39520 et seq)

Manipulation

(For associated esophagogram, use 74220)

43450   Dilation of esophagus, by unguided sound or bougie, single or multiple passes
➔ *CPT Assistant* Spring 94:1, Jan 97:10, Apr 98:14, Jun 98:10

(For radiological supervision and interpretation, use 74360)

⊙ **43453**   Dilation of esophagus, over guide wire
➔ *CPT Assistant* Spring 94:1, Jan 97:10, Dec 97:11

(For dilation with direct visualization, use 43220)

(For dilation of esophagus, by balloon or dilator, see 43220, 43458, and 74360)

(For radiological supervision and interpretation, use 74360)

⊙ **43456**   Dilation of esophagus, by balloon or dilator, retrograde
➔ *CPT Assistant* Spring 94:3, Jan 97:10, May 05:3

(For radiological supervision and interpretation, use 74360)

⊙ **43458** Dilation of esophagus with balloon (30 mm diameter or larger) for achalasia
➔ *CPT Assistant* Spring 94:3, Jan 97:10, May 05:3

(For dilation with balloon less than 30 mm diameter, use 43220)

(For radiological supervision and interpretation, use 74360)

43460 Esophagogastric tamponade, with balloon (Sengstaken type)
➔ *CPT Changes: An Insider's View* 2009

(For removal of esophageal foreign body by balloon catheter, see 43215, 43247, 74235)

Other Procedures

43496 Free jejunum transfer with microvascular anastomosis
➔ *CPT Assistant* Nov 96:8, Apr 97:4, Jun 97:10, Nov 97:17, Nov 98:16

(Do not report code 69990 in addition to code 43496)

43499 Unlisted procedure, esophagus
➔ *CPT Assistant* May 07:10

Stomach

Incision

43500 Gastrotomy; with exploration or foreign body removal

43501   with suture repair of bleeding ulcer

43502   with suture repair of pre-existing esophagogastric laceration (eg, Mallory-Weiss)

43510   with esophageal dilation and insertion of permanent intraluminal tube (eg, Celestin or Mousseaux-Barbin)

43520 Pyloromyotomy, cutting of pyloric muscle (Fredet-Ramstedt type operation)

(Do not report modifier 63 in conjunction with 43520)

Excision

43600 Biopsy of stomach; by capsule, tube, peroral (1 or more specimens)

43605   by laparotomy

43610 Excision, local; ulcer or benign tumor of stomach

43611   malignant tumor of stomach

43620 Gastrectomy, total; with esophagoenterostomy

43621   with Roux-en-Y reconstruction

43622   with formation of intestinal pouch, any type

43631 Gastrectomy, partial, distal; with gastroduodenostomy

43632   with gastrojejunostomy

43633   with Roux-en-Y reconstruction

43634   with formation of intestinal pouch

✛ **43635** Vagotomy when performed with partial distal gastrectomy (List separately in addition to code[s] for primary procedure)
➔ *CPT Assistant* Nov 97:17

(Use 43635 in conjunction with 43631, 43632, 43633, 43634)

43640 Vagotomy including pyloroplasty, with or without gastrostomy; truncal or selective

(For pyloroplasty, use 43800)

(For vagotomy, see 64752-64760)

43641   parietal cell (highly selective)

(For upper gastrointestinal endoscopy, see 43234-43259)

Laparoscopy

Surgical laparoscopy always includes diagnostic laparoscopy. To report a diagnostic laparoscopy (peritoneoscopy) (separate procedure), use 49320.

(For upper gastrointestinal endoscopy including esophagus, stomach, and either the duodenum and/or jejunum, see 43235-43259)

43644 Laparoscopy, surgical, gastric restrictive procedure; with gastric bypass and Roux-en-Y gastroenterostomy (roux limb 150 cm or less)
➔ *CPT Assistant* May 05:3; *CPT Changes: An Insider's View* 2005

(Do not report 43644 in conjunction with 43846, 49320)

(Esophagogastroduodenoscopy [EGD] performed for a separate condition should be reported with modifier 59)

(For greater than 150 cm, use 43645)

(For open procedure, use 43846)

43645   with gastric bypass and small intestine reconstruction to limit absorption
➔ *CPT Assistant* May 05:3; *CPT Changes: An Insider's View* 2005

(Do not report 43645 in conjunction with 49320, 43847)

43647 Laparoscopy, surgical; implantation or replacement of gastric neurostimulator electrodes, antrum
➔ *CPT Assistant* Mar 07:4; *CPT Changes: An Insider's View* 2007

43648   revision or removal of gastric neurostimulator electrodes, antrum
➔ *CPT Assistant* Mar 07:4; *CPT Changes: An Insider's View* 2007

(For open approach, see 43881, 43882)

(For insertion of gastric neurostimulator pulse generator, use 64590)

(For revision or removal of gastric neurostimulator pulse generator, use 64595)

(For electronic analysis and programming of gastric neurostimulator pulse generator, see 95980-95982)

(For laparoscopic implantation, revision, or removal of gastric neurostimulator electrodes, lesser curvature [morbid obesity], see Category III codes 0155T, 0156T)

▶(For electronic analysis and programming of gastric neurostimulator, see 95980-95982)◀

43651   Laparoscopy, surgical; transection of vagus nerves, truncal

➔ *CPT Assistant* Nov 99:22, Mar 00:8; *CPT Changes: An Insider's View* 2000

43652   transection of vagus nerves, selective or highly selective

➔ *CPT Assistant* Nov 99:22, Mar 00:8; *CPT Changes: An Insider's View* 2000

43653   gastrostomy, without construction of gastric tube (eg, Stamm procedure) (separate procedure)

➔ *CPT Assistant* Nov 99:22, Mar 00:8; *CPT Changes: An Insider's View* 2000

43659   Unlisted laparoscopy procedure, stomach

➔ *CPT Assistant* Nov 99:22, Mar 00:8, Apr 06:19, Jun 06:16, Dec 07:12; *CPT Changes: An Insider's View* 2000

Introduction

(43750 has been deleted. To report percutaneous gastrostomy tube insertion, use 43246)

43752   Naso- or oro-gastric tube placement, requiring physician's skill and fluoroscopic guidance (includes fluoroscopy, image documentation and report)

➔ *CPT Assistant* Jan 02:11, Apr 03:7, Oct 03:2, Jul 06:4, Feb 07:10, Jul 07:1, Aug 08:7; *CPT Changes: An Insider's View* 2001, 2004

(For percutaneous placement of gastrostomy tube, use 49440)

(For enteric tube placement, see 44500, 74340)

(Do not report 43752 in conjunction with critical care codes 99291-99292, neonatal critical care codes 99468, 99469, pediatric critical care codes 99471, 99472 or low birth weight intensive care service codes 99478, 99479)

43760   Change of gastrostomy tube, percutaneous, without imaging or endoscopic guidance

➔ *CPT Assistant* Apr 08:11, Aug 08:7; *CPT Changes: An Insider's View* 2008

▶(To report fluoroscopically guided replacement of gastrostomy tube, use 49450)◀

(For endoscopic placement of gastrostomy tube, use 43246)

▲ **43761**   Repositioning of a naso- or oro-gastric feeding tube, through the duodenum for enteric nutrition

➔ *CPT Assistant* Oct 96:9, Nov 99:22, Jun 08:8, Aug 08:7; *CPT Changes: An Insider's View* 2000, 2008, 2010

(If imaging guidance is performed, use 76000)

(For endoscopic conversion of a gastrostomy tube to jejunostomy tube, use 44373)

(For placement of a long gastrointestinal tube into the duodenum, use 44500)

(Do not report 43761 in conjunction with 44500, 49446)

Bariatric Surgery

Bariatric surgical procedures may involve the stomach, duodenum, jejunum, and/or the ileum.

Laparoscopy

Surgical laparoscopy always includes diagnostic laparoscopy. To report a diagnostic laparoscopy (separate procedure), use 49320.

Typical postoperative follow-up care (see Surgery Guidelines, CPT Surgical Package Definition) after gastric restriction using the adjustable gastric restrictive device includes subsequent restrictive device adjustment(s) through the postoperative period for the typical patient. Adjustment consists of changing the gastric restrictive device component diameter by injection or aspiration of fluid through the subcutaneous port component.

43770   Laparoscopy, surgical, gastric restrictive procedure; placement of adjustable gastric restrictive device (eg, gastric band and subcutaneous port components)

➔ *CPT Changes: An Insider's View* 2006, 2008

(For individual component placement, report 43770 with modifier 52)

43771   revision of adjustable gastric restrictive device component only

➔ *CPT Changes: An Insider's View* 2006, 2008

43772   removal of adjustable gastric restrictive device component only

➔ *CPT Changes: An Insider's View* 2006, 2008

43773   removal and replacement of adjustable gastric restrictive device component only

➔ *CPT Changes: An Insider's View* 2006, 2008

(Do not report 43773 in conjunction with 43772)

43774   removal of adjustable gastric restrictive device and subcutaneous port components

➔ *CPT Changes: An Insider's View* 2006, 2008

(For removal and replacement of both gastric band and subcutaneous port components, use 43659)

● **43775**   longitudinal gastrectomy (ie, sleeve gastrectomy)

➔ *CPT Changes: An Insider's View* 2010

▶(For open gastric restrictive procedure, without gastric bypass, for morbid obesity, other than vertical-banded gastroplasty, use 43843)◀

Other Procedures

43800   Pyloroplasty

(For pyloroplasty and vagotomy, use 43640)

43810   Gastroduodenostomy

43820   Gastrojejunostomy; without vagotomy

43825   with vagotomy, any type

43830   Gastrostomy, open; without construction of gastric tube (eg, Stamm procedure) (separate procedure)
→ *CPT Assistant* Nov 99:22; *CPT Changes: An Insider's View* 2000

43831   neonatal, for feeding
→ *CPT Assistant* Nov 99:22; *CPT Changes: An Insider's View* 2000

(For change of gastrostomy tube, use 43760)

(Do not report modifier 63 in conjunction with 43831)

43832   with construction of gastric tube (eg, Janeway procedure)
→ *CPT Assistant* Nov 99:22; *CPT Changes: An Insider's View* 2000

(For percutaneous endoscopic gastrostomy, use 43246)

43840   Gastrorrhaphy, suture of perforated duodenal or gastric ulcer, wound, or injury

43842   Gastric restrictive procedure, without gastric bypass, for morbid obesity; vertical-banded gastroplasty
→ *CPT Assistant* May 98:5

43843   other than vertical-banded gastroplasty
→ *CPT Assistant* May 98:5

►(For laparoscopic longitudinal gastrectomy [ie, sleeve gastrectomy], use 43775)◄

43845   Gastric restrictive procedure with partial gastrectomy, pylorus-preserving duodenoileostomy and ileoileostomy (50 to 100 cm common channel) to limit absorption (biliopancreatic diversion with duodenal switch)
→ *CPT Assistant* May 05:3; *CPT Changes: An Insider's View* 2005

(Do not report 43845 in conjunction with 43633, 43847, 44130, 49000)

43846   Gastric restrictive procedure, with gastric bypass for morbid obesity; with short limb (150 cm or less) Roux-en-Y gastroenterostomy
→ *CPT Assistant* May 98:5, May 05:3; *CPT Changes: An Insider's View* 2005

(For greater than 150 cm, use 43847)

(For laparoscopic procedure, use 43644)

Gastric Bypass for Morbid Obesity
43846

The stomach is partitioned with a staple line on the lesser curvature (no band, no gastric transection). A short limb of small bowel (less than 100 cm) is divided and anastomosed to the small upper stomach pouch.

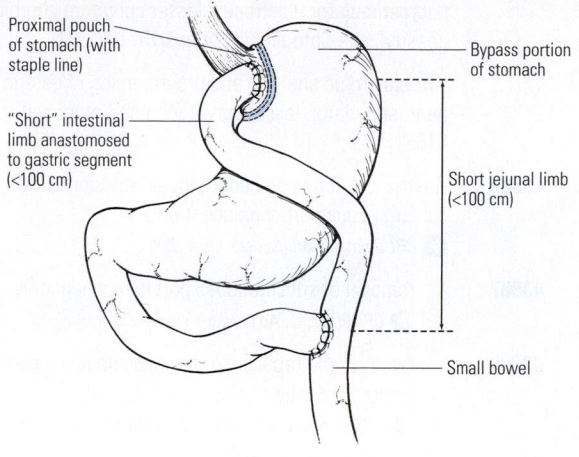

Proximal pouch of stomach (with staple line)

"Short" intestinal limb anastomosed to gastric segment (<100 cm)

Bypass portion of stomach

Short jejunal limb (<100 cm)

Small bowel

43847   with small intestine reconstruction to limit absorption
→ *CPT Assistant* May 98:5, May 02:7; *CPT Changes: An Insider's View* 2002

43848   Revision, open, of gastric restrictive procedure for morbid obesity, other than adjustable gastric restrictive device (separate procedure)
→ *CPT Assistant* May 98:5, Apr 06:1; *CPT Changes: An Insider's View* 2006, 2008

(For laparoscopic adjustable gastric restrictive procedures, see 43770-43774)

(For gastric restrictive port procedures, see 43886-43888)

43850   Revision of gastroduodenal anastomosis (gastroduodenostomy) with reconstruction; without vagotomy

43855   with vagotomy

43860   Revision of gastrojejunal anastomosis (gastrojejunostomy) with reconstruction, with or without partial gastrectomy or intestine resection; without vagotomy
→ *CPT Changes: An Insider's View* 2002

43865   with vagotomy

43870   Closure of gastrostomy, surgical

43880   Closure of gastrocolic fistula

43881   Implantation or replacement of gastric neurostimulator electrodes, antrum, open
→ *CPT Assistant* Mar 07:4; *CPT Changes: An Insider's View* 2007

43882   Revision or removal of gastric neurostimulator electrodes, antrum, open
→ *CPT Assistant* Mar 07:4; *CPT Changes: An Insider's View* 2007

(For laparoscopic approach, see 43647, 43648)

(For insertion of gastric neurostimulator pulse generator, use 64590)

(For revision or removal of gastric neurostimulator pulse generator, use 64595)

(For electronic analysis and programming of gastric neurostimulator pulse generator, see 95980-95982)

(For open implantation, revision, or removal of gastric neurostimulator electrodes, lesser curvature [morbid obesity], see Category III codes 0157T, 0158T)

(For electronic analysis and programming of gastric neurostimulator, lesser curvature, use Category III code 0162T)

43886   Gastric restrictive procedure, open; revision of subcutaneous port component only
➤ *CPT Changes: An Insider's View* 2006

43887   removal of subcutaneous port component only
➤ *CPT Changes: An Insider's View* 2006

43888   removal and replacement of subcutaneous port component only
➤ *CPT Changes: An Insider's View* 2006

(Do not report 43888 in conjunction with 43774, 43887)

(For laparoscopic removal of both gastric restrictive device and subcutaneous port components, use 43774)

(For removal and replacement of both gastric restrictive device and subcutaneous port components, use 43659)

43999   Unlisted procedure, stomach

Intestines (Except Rectum)

Incision

44005   Enterolysis (freeing of intestinal adhesion) (separate procedure)
➤ *CPT Assistant* Winter 90:6, Nov 97:17, Nov 99:23, Jan 00:11, Apr 00:10; *CPT Changes: An Insider's View* 2000

(Do not report 44005 in addition to 45136)

(For laparoscopic approach, use 44180)

44010   Duodenotomy, for exploration, biopsy(s), or foreign body removal

+ 44015 Tube or needle catheter jejunostomy for enteral alimentation, intraoperative, any method (List separately in addition to primary procedure)
➤ *CPT Assistant* Mar 02:10

44020   Enterotomy, small intestine, other than duodenum; for exploration, biopsy(s), or foreign body removal
➤ *CPT Changes: An Insider's View* 2002

44021   for decompression (eg, Baker tube)

44025   Colotomy, for exploration, biopsy(s), or foreign body removal

(For exteriorization of intestine (Mikulicz resection with crushing of spur), see 44602-44605)

44050   Reduction of volvulus, intussusception, internal hernia, by laparotomy

44055   Correction of malrotation by lysis of duodenal bands and/or reduction of midgut volvulus (eg, Ladd procedure)

(Do not report modifier 63 in conjunction with 44055)

Excision

Intestinal allotransplantation involves three distinct components of physician work:

1. ***Cadaver donor enterectomy***, which includes harvesting the intestine graft and cold preservation of the graft (perfusing with cold preservation solution and cold maintenance) (use 44132). ***Living donor enterectomy***, which includes harvesting the intestine graft, cold preservation of the graft (perfusing with cold preservation solution and cold maintenance), and care of the donor (use 44133).

2. ***Backbench work***:

    Standard preparation of an intestine allograft prior to transplantation includes mobilization and fashioning of the superior mesenteric artery and vein (see 44715).

    Additional reconstruction of an intestine allograft prior to transplantation may include venous and/or arterial anastomosis(es) (see 44720-44721).

3. ***Recipient intestinal allotransplantation with or without recipient enterectomy***, which includes transplantation of allograft and care of the recipient (see 44135, 44136).

44100   Biopsy of intestine by capsule, tube, peroral (1 or more specimens)

44110   Excision of 1 or more lesions of small or large intestine not requiring anastomosis, exteriorization, or fistulization; single enterotomy
➤ *CPT Changes: An Insider's View* 2002

44111   multiple enterotomies

44120   Enterectomy, resection of small intestine; single resection and anastomosis
➤ *CPT Assistant* Mar 04:3, Aug 08:7

(Do not report 44120 in addition to 45136)

+ 44121   each additional resection and anastomosis (List separately in addition to code for primary procedure)

(Use 44121 in conjunction with 44120)

44125   with enterostomy

44126   Enterectomy, resection of small intestine for congenital atresia, single resection and anastomosis of proximal segment of intestine; without tapering
➤ *CPT Changes: An Insider's View* 2002

44127   with tapering

➔ *CPT Changes: An Insider's View* 2002

Enterectomy, Resection for Congenital Atresia
44127

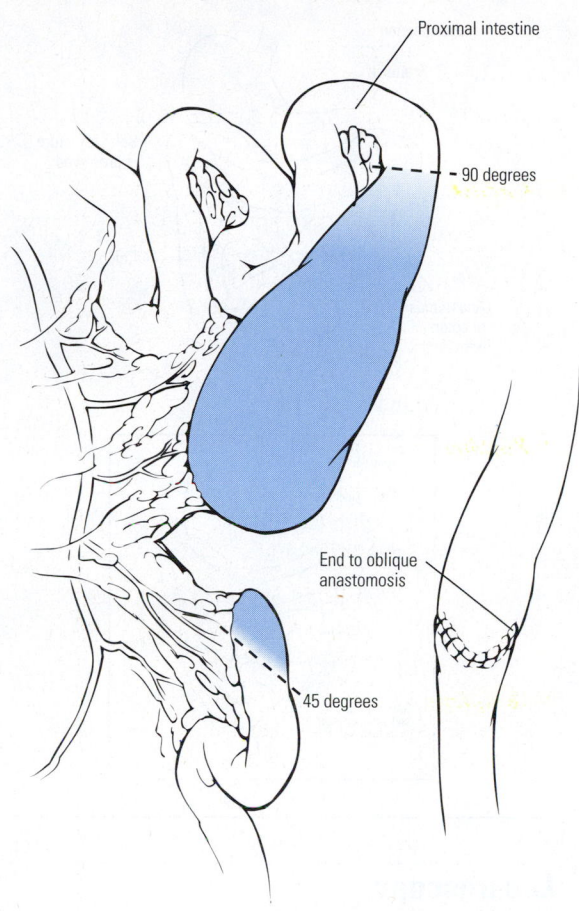

Proximal intestine

90 degrees

End to oblique anastomosis

45 degrees

+ 44128   each additional resection and anastomosis (List separately in addition to code for primary procedure)

➔ *CPT Changes: An Insider's View* 2002

(Use 44128 in conjunction with 44126, 44127)

(Do not report modifier 63 in conjunction with 44126, 44127, 44128)

44130   Enteroenterostomy, anastomosis of intestine, with or without cutaneous enterostomy (separate procedure)

44132   Donor enterectomy (including cold preservation), open; from cadaver donor

➔ *CPT Changes: An Insider's View* 2001, 2005

44133   partial, from living donor

➔ *CPT Changes: An Insider's View* 2001

(For backbench intestinal graft preparation or reconstruction, see 44715, 44720, 44721)

44135   Intestinal allotransplantation; from cadaver donor

➔ *CPT Changes: An Insider's View* 2001

44136   from living donor

➔ *CPT Changes: An Insider's View* 2001

44137   Removal of transplanted intestinal allograft, complete

➔ *CPT Changes: An Insider's View* 2005

(For partial removal of transplant allograft, see 44120, 44121, 44140)

+ 44139   Mobilization (take-down) of splenic flexure performed in conjunction with partial colectomy (List separately in addition to primary procedure)

(Use 44139 in conjunction with 44140-44147)

44140   Colectomy, partial; with anastomosis

➔ *CPT Assistant* Fall 92:23, Aug 08:7, Nov 08:7

(For laparoscopic procedure, use 44204)

Colectomy, Partial
44140

A segment of the colon is resected and an anastomosis is performed between the remaining ends of the colon.

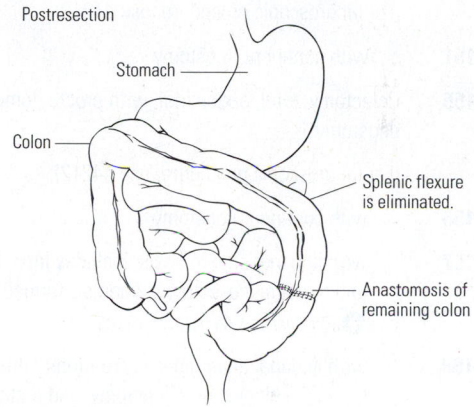

Postresection

Stomach

Colon

Splenic flexure is eliminated.

Anastomosis of remaining colon

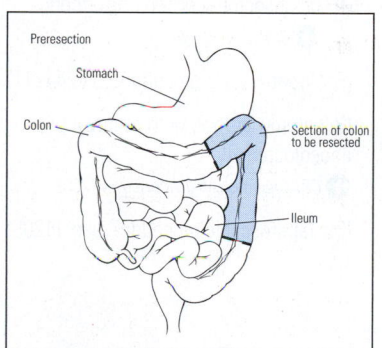

Preresection

Stomach

Colon

Section of colon to be resected

Ileum

44141   with skin level cecostomy or colostomy
➔ *CPT Assistant* Fall 92:24, Nov 08:7

44143   with end colostomy and closure of distal segment
(Hartmann type procedure)
➔ *CPT Assistant* Fall 92:24, Nov 08:7

(For laparoscopic procedure, use 44206)

44144   with resection, with colostomy or ileostomy and
creation of mucofistula
➔ *CPT Assistant* Fall 92:24, Nov 08:7

44145   with coloproctostomy (low pelvic anastomosis)
➔ *CPT Assistant* Fall 92:24

(For laparoscopic procedure, use 44207)

44146   with coloproctostomy (low pelvic anastomosis), with
colostomy
➔ *CPT Assistant* Fall 92:24, Nov 08:7

(For laparoscopic procedure, use 44208)

44147   abdominal and transanal approach
➔ *CPT Assistant* Fall 92:24, Nov 08:7

44150   Colectomy, total, abdominal, without proctectomy; with
ileostomy or ileoproctostomy

(For laparoscopic procedure, use 44210)

44151   with continent ileostomy

44155   Colectomy, total, abdominal, with proctectomy; with
ileostomy

(For laparoscopic procedure, use 44212)

44156   with continent ileostomy

44157   with ileoanal anastomosis, includes loop ileostomy,
and rectal mucosectomy, when performed
➔ *CPT Changes: An Insider's View* 2007

44158   with ileoanal anastomosis, creation of ileal reservoir
(S or J), includes loop ileostomy, and rectal
mucosectomy, when performed
➔ *CPT Changes: An Insider's View* 2007

(For laparoscopic procedure, use 44211)

44160   Colectomy, partial, with removal of terminal ileum with
ileocolostomy
➔ *CPT Changes: An Insider's View* 2002

(For laparoscopic procedure, use 44205)

Colectomy With Removal of Terminal Ileum and Ileocolostomy
44160

A segment of the colon and terminal ileum is removed and an anastomosis is performed between the remaining ileum and colon.

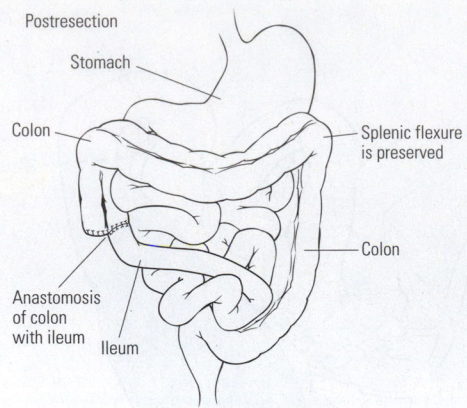

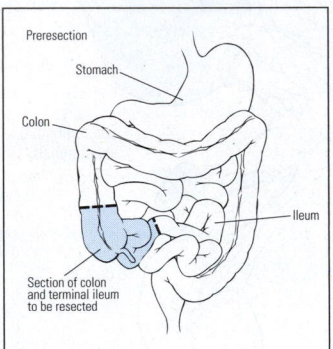

Laparoscopy

Surgical laparoscopy always includes diagnostic laparoscopy. To report a diagnostic laparoscopy (peritoneoscopy) (separate procedure), use 49320.

Incision

44180   Laparoscopy, surgical, enterolysis (freeing of intestinal
adhesion) (separate procedure)
➔ *CPT Changes: An Insider's View* 2006

(For laparoscopy with salpingolysis, ovariolysis, use 58660)

Enterostomy—External Fistulization of Intestines

44186   Laparoscopy, surgical; jejunostomy (eg, for
decompression or feeding)
➔ *CPT Changes: An Insider's View* 2006

44187   ileostomy or jejunostomy, non-tube
➔ *CPT Changes: An Insider's View* 2006

(For open procedure, use 44310)

44188   Laparoscopy, surgical, colostomy or skin level cecostomy
   ➔ *CPT Changes: An Insider's View* 2006

(For open procedure, use 44320)

(Do not report 44188 in conjunction with 44970)

Excision

44202   Laparoscopy, surgical; enterectomy, resection of small intestine, single resection and anastomosis
   ➔ *CPT Assistant* Nov 99:23, Mar 00:9, May 03:2, Apr 06:1; *CPT Changes: An Insider's View* 2000, 2002, 2006

+ 44203   each additional small intestine resection and anastomosis (List separately in addition to code for primary procedure)
   ➔ *CPT Assistant* May 03:2; *CPT Changes: An Insider's View* 2002

(Use 44203 in conjunction with 44202)

(For open procedure, see 44120, 44121)

44204   colectomy, partial, with anastomosis
   ➔ *CPT Assistant* May 03:3, Apr 06:1,19; *CPT Changes: An Insider's View* 2002

(For open procedure, use 44140)

44205   colectomy, partial, with removal of terminal ileum with ileocolostomy
   ➔ *CPT Assistant* May 03:3, Apr 06:1; *CPT Changes: An Insider's View* 2002

(For open procedure, use 44160)

44206   colectomy, partial, with end colostomy and closure of distal segment (Hartmann type procedure)
   ➔ *CPT Assistant* May 03:3, Apr 06:1; *CPT Changes: An Insider's View* 2003

(For open procedure, use 44143)

44207   colectomy, partial, with anastomosis, with coloproctostomy (low pelvic anastomosis)
   ➔ *CPT Assistant* May 03:3, Apr 06:1; *CPT Changes: An Insider's View* 2003

(For open procedure, use 44145)

44208   colectomy, partial, with anastomosis, with coloproctostomy (low pelvic anastomosis) with colostomy
   ➔ *CPT Assistant* May 03:3, Apr 06:1; *CPT Changes: An Insider's View* 2003

(For open procedure, use 44146)

44210   colectomy, total, abdominal, without proctectomy, with ileostomy or ileoproctostomy
   ➔ *CPT Assistant* May 03:3; *CPT Changes: An Insider's View* 2003

(For open procedure, use 44150)

44211   colectomy, total, abdominal, with proctectomy, with ileoanal anastomosis, creation of ileal reservoir (S or J), with loop ileostomy, includes rectal mucosectomy, when performed
   ➔ *CPT Assistant* May 03:3; *CPT Changes: An Insider's View* 2003, 2007

(For open procedure, see 44157, 44158)

44212   colectomy, total, abdominal, with proctectomy, with ileostomy
   ➔ *CPT Assistant* May 03:3; *CPT Changes: An Insider's View* 2003

(For open procedure, use 44155)

+ 44213   Laparoscopy, surgical, mobilization (take-down) of splenic flexure performed in conjunction with partial colectomy (List separately in addition to primary procedure)
   ➔ *CPT Changes: An Insider's View* 2006

(Use 44213 in conjunction with 44204-44208)

(For open procedure, use 44139)

Repair

44227   Laparoscopy, surgical, closure of enterostomy, large or small intestine, with resection and anastomosis
   ➔ *CPT Changes: An Insider's View* 2006

(For open procedure, see 44625, 44626)

Other Procedures

44238   Unlisted laparoscopy procedure, intestine (except rectum)
   ➔ *CPT Assistant* May 03:4; *CPT Changes: An Insider's View* 2003

Enterostomy—External Fistulization of Intestines

44300   Placement, enterostomy or cecostomy, tube open (eg, for feeding or decompression) (separate procedure)
   ➔ *CPT Assistant* Mar 02:10, Aug 08:7; *CPT Changes: An Insider's View* 2008

(For percutaneous placement of duodenostomy, jejunostomy, gastro-jejunostomy or cecostomy [or other colonic] tube including fluoroscopic imaging guidance, see 49441-49442)

44310   Ileostomy or jejunostomy, non-tube
   ➔ *CPT Assistant* Mar 02:10, Apr 06:1; *CPT Changes: An Insider's View* 2006

(For laparoscopic procedure, use 44187)

(Do not report 44310 in conjunction with 44144, 44150-44151, 44155, 44156, 45113, 45119, 45136)

44312   Revision of ileostomy; simple (release of superficial scar) (separate procedure)
   ➔ *CPT Assistant* Spring 93:35

44314   complicated (reconstruction in-depth) (separate procedure)

44316 Continent ileostomy (Kock procedure) (separate procedure)

(For fiberoptic evaluation, use 44385)

44320 Colostomy or skin level cecostomy;
→ *CPT Changes: An Insider's View* 2006

(For laparoscopic procedure, use 44188)

(Do not report 44320 in conjunction with 44141, 44144, 44146, 44605, 45110, 45119, 45126, 45563, 45805, 45825, 50810, 51597, 57307, or 58240)

44322 with multiple biopsies (eg, for congenital megacolon) (separate procedure)
→ *CPT Changes: An Insider's View* 2002

44340 Revision of colostomy; simple (release of superficial scar) (separate procedure)

44345 complicated (reconstruction in-depth) (separate procedure)

44346 with repair of paracolostomy hernia (separate procedure)

Endoscopy, Small Intestine and Stomal

Surgical endoscopy always includes diagnostic endoscopy.

(For upper gastrointestinal endoscopy, see 43234-43258)

⊙ **44360** Small intestinal endoscopy, enteroscopy beyond second portion of duodenum, not including ileum; diagnostic, with or without collection of specimen(s) by brushing or washing (separate procedure)
→ *CPT Assistant* Spring 94:7

⊙ **44361** with biopsy, single or multiple

⊙ **44363** with removal of foreign body

⊙ **44364** with removal of tumor(s), polyp(s), or other lesion(s) by snare technique

⊙ **44365** with removal of tumor(s), polyp(s), or other lesion(s) by hot biopsy forceps or bipolar cautery

⊙ **44366** with control of bleeding (eg, injection, bipolar cautery, unipolar cautery, laser, heater probe, stapler, plasma coagulator)
→ *CPT Changes: An Insider's View* 2002

⊙ **44369** with ablation of tumor(s), polyp(s), or other lesion(s) not amenable to removal by hot biopsy forceps, bipolar cautery or snare technique

⊙ **44370** with transendoscopic stent placement (includes predilation)
→ *CPT Assistant* Nov 01:7; *CPT Changes: An Insider's View* 2001

⊙ **44372** with placement of percutaneous jejunostomy tube
→ *CPT Assistant* Spring 94:7

⊙ **44373** with conversion of percutaneous gastrostomy tube to percutaneous jejunostomy tube
→ *CPT Assistant* Spring 94:7

(For fiberoptic jejunostomy through stoma, use 43235)

⊙ **44376** Small intestinal endoscopy, enteroscopy beyond second portion of duodenum, including ileum; diagnostic, with or without collection of specimen(s) by brushing or washing (separate procedure)
→ *CPT Assistant* Spring 94:7

⊙ **44377** with biopsy, single or multiple
→ *CPT Assistant* Spring 94:7

⊙ **44378** with control of bleeding (eg, injection, bipolar cautery, unipolar cautery, laser, heater probe, stapler, plasma coagulator)
→ *CPT Assistant* Spring 94:7; *CPT Changes: An Insider's View* 2002

⊙ **44379** with transendoscopic stent placement (includes predilation)
→ *CPT Assistant* Nov 01:7; *CPT Changes: An Insider's View* 2001

⊙ **44380** Ileoscopy, through stoma; diagnostic, with or without collection of specimen(s) by brushing or washing (separate procedure)

⊙ **44382** with biopsy, single or multiple

⊙ **44383** with transendoscopic stent placement (includes predilation)
→ *CPT Assistant* Nov 01:7; *CPT Changes: An Insider's View* 2001

⊙ **44385** Endoscopic evaluation of small intestinal (abdominal or pelvic) pouch; diagnostic, with or without collection of specimen(s) by brushing or washing (separate procedure)

⊙ **44386** with biopsy, single or multiple

⊙ **44388** Colonoscopy through stoma; diagnostic, with or without collection of specimen(s) by brushing or washing (separate procedure)
→ *CPT Assistant* Nov 07:8

⊙ **44389** with biopsy, single or multiple

⊙ **44390** with removal of foreign body

⊙ **44391** with control of bleeding (eg, injection, bipolar cautery, unipolar cautery, laser, heater probe, stapler, plasma coagulator)
→ *CPT Changes: An Insider's View* 2002

⊙ **44392** with removal of tumor(s), polyp(s), or other lesion(s) by hot biopsy forceps or bipolar cautery

⊙ **44393** with ablation of tumor(s), polyp(s), or other lesion(s) not amenable to removal by hot biopsy forceps, bipolar cautery or snare technique

⊙ **44394** with removal of tumor(s), polyp(s), or other lesion(s) by snare technique

(For colonoscopy per rectum, see 45330-45385)

⊙ **44397** with transendoscopic stent placement (includes predilation)
→ *CPT Assistant* Nov 01:7; *CPT Changes: An Insider's View* 2001

Introduction

⊙⊘ **44500**   Introduction of long gastrointestinal tube (eg, Miller-Abbott) (separate procedure)

(For radiological supervision and interpretation, use 74340)

(For naso- or oro-gastric tube placement, use 43752)

Repair

44602   Suture of small intestine (enterorrhaphy) for perforated ulcer, diverticulum, wound, injury or rupture; single perforation

44603   multiple perforations

44604   Suture of large intestine (colorrhaphy) for perforated ulcer, diverticulum, wound, injury or rupture (single or multiple perforations); without colostomy

44605   with colostomy

44615   Intestinal stricturoplasty (enterotomy and enterorrhaphy) with or without dilation, for intestinal obstruction

44620   Closure of enterostomy, large or small intestine;
➔ *CPT Assistant* Nov 97:17, May 02:7

44625   with resection and anastomosis other than colorectal
➔ *CPT Assistant* Nov 97:17

44626   with resection and colorectal anastomosis (eg, closure of Hartmann type procedure)
➔ *CPT Assistant* Nov 97:17

(For laparoscopic procedure, use 44227)

44640   Closure of intestinal cutaneous fistula

44650   Closure of enteroenteric or enterocolic fistula

44660   Closure of enterovesical fistula; without intestinal or bladder resection

44661   with intestine and/or bladder resection
➔ *CPT Changes: An Insider's View* 2002

(For closure of renocolic fistula, see 50525, 50526)

(For closure of gastrocolic fistula, use 43880)

(For closure of rectovesical fistula, see 45800, 45805)

44680   Intestinal plication (separate procedure)

Other Procedures

44700   Exclusion of small intestine from pelvis by mesh or other prosthesis, or native tissue (eg, bladder or omentum)
➔ *CPT Assistant* Nov 97:18; *CPT Changes: An Insider's View* 2002

(For therapeutic radiation clinical treatment, see **Radiation Oncology** section)

+ **44701**   Intraoperative colonic lavage (List separately in addition to code for primary procedure)
➔ *CPT Changes: An Insider's View* 2003

(Use 44701 in conjunction with 44140, 44145, 44150, or 44604 as appropriate)

(Do not report 44701 in conjunction with 44300, 44950-44960)

44715   Backbench standard preparation of cadaver or living donor intestine allograft prior to transplantation, including mobilization and fashioning of the superior mesenteric artery and vein
➔ *CPT Changes: An Insider's View* 2005

44720   Backbench reconstruction of cadaver or living donor intestine allograft prior to transplantation; venous anastomosis, each
➔ *CPT Changes: An Insider's View* 2005

44721   arterial anastomosis, each
➔ *CPT Assistant* Apr 05:10-11; *CPT Changes: An Insider's View* 2005

44799   Unlisted procedure, intestine
➔ *CPT Assistant* Dec 00:14, May 08:15, Nov 08:11

(For unlisted laparoscopic procedure, intestine except rectum, use 44238)

Meckel's Diverticulum and the Mesentery

Excision

44800   Excision of Meckel's diverticulum (diverticulectomy) or omphalomesenteric duct

44820   Excision of lesion of mesentery (separate procedure)

(With intestine resection, see 44120 or 44140 et seq)

Suture

44850   Suture of mesentery (separate procedure)

(For reduction and repair of internal hernia, use 44050)

Other Procedures

44899   Unlisted procedure, Meckel's diverticulum and the mesentery

Appendix

Incision

44900   Incision and drainage of appendiceal abscess; open
➔ *CPT Assistant* Nov 97:18

⊙ **44901**   percutaneous
➔ *CPT Assistant* Nov 97:18, Mar 98:8

(For radiological supervision and interpretation, use 75989)

Excision

44950 Appendectomy;
➜ *CPT Assistant* Feb 92:22, Sep 96:4, Aug 02:2, Nov 08:7

(Incidental appendectomy during intra-abdominal surgery does not usually warrant a separate identification. If necessary to report, add modifier 52)

+ 44955 when done for indicated purpose at time of other major procedure (not as separate procedure) (List separately in addition to code for primary procedure)
➜ *CPT Assistant* Fall 92:22, Sep 96:4, Apr 97:3, Nov 08:7

44960 for ruptured appendix with abscess or generalized peritonitis
➜ *CPT Assistant* Fall 92:22, Nov 08:7

Laparoscopy

Surgical laparoscopy always includes diagnostic laparoscopy. To report a diagnostic laparoscopy (peritoneoscopy) (separate procedure), use 49320.

44970 Laparoscopy, surgical, appendectomy
➜ *CPT Assistant* Nov 99:23, Mar 00:9, Apr 06:1,20; *CPT Changes: An Insider's View* 2000

44979 Unlisted laparoscopy procedure, appendix
➜ *CPT Assistant* Nov 99:23, Mar 00:9; *CPT Changes: An Insider's View* 2000

Rectum

Incision

45000 Transrectal drainage of pelvic abscess

45005 Incision and drainage of submucosal abscess, rectum

45020 Incision and drainage of deep supralevator, pelvirectal, or retrorectal abscess

(See also 46050, 46060)

Excision

45100 Biopsy of anorectal wall, anal approach (eg, congenital megacolon)

(For endoscopic biopsy, use 45305)

45108 Anorectal myomectomy

45110 Proctectomy; complete, combined abdominoperineal, with colostomy

(For laparoscopic procedure, use 45395)

45111 partial resection of rectum, transabdominal approach

45112 Proctectomy, combined abdominoperineal, pull-through procedure (eg, colo-anal anastomosis)
➜ *CPT Assistant* Nov 97:18

(For colo-anal anastomosis with colonic reservoir or pouch, use 45119)

45113 Proctectomy, partial, with rectal mucosectomy, ileoanal anastomosis, creation of ileal reservoir (S or J), with or without loop ileostomy

45114 Proctectomy, partial, with anastomosis; abdominal and transsacral approach

45116 transsacral approach only (Kraske type)

45119 Proctectomy, combined abdominoperineal pull-through procedure (eg, colo-anal anastomosis), with creation of colonic reservoir (eg, J-pouch), with diverting enterostomy when performed
➜ *CPT Assistant* Nov 97:18, Apr 06:1; *CPT Changes: An Insider's View* 2006

(For laparoscopic procedure, use 45397)

45120 Proctectomy, complete (for congenital megacolon), abdominal and perineal approach; with pull-through procedure and anastomosis (eg, Swenson, Duhamel, or Soave type operation)

45121 with subtotal or total colectomy, with multiple biopsies

45123 Proctectomy, partial, without anastomosis, perineal approach

45126 Pelvic exenteration for colorectal malignancy, with proctectomy (with or without colostomy), with removal of bladder and ureteral transplantations, and/or hysterectomy, or cervicectomy, with or without removal of tube(s), with or without removal of ovary(s), or any combination thereof
➜ *CPT Assistant* Nov 98:16

45130 Excision of rectal procidentia, with anastomosis; perineal approach

45135 abdominal and perineal approach

45136 Excision of ileoanal reservoir with ileostomy
➜ *CPT Changes: An Insider's View* 2002

(Do not report 45136 in addition to 44005, 44120, 44310)

45150 Division of stricture of rectum

45160 Excision of rectal tumor by proctotomy, transsacral or transcoccygeal approach

▶(45170 has been deleted. To report excision of rectal tumor, transanal approach, see 45171, 45172)◀

(For transanal endoscopic microsurgical [ie, TEMS] excision of rectal tumor, use 0184T)

● **45171** Excision of rectal tumor, transanal approach; not including muscularis propria (ie, partial thickness)
➜ *CPT Changes: An Insider's View* 2010

● **45172** including muscularis propria (ie, full thickness)
➜ *CPT Changes: An Insider's View* 2010

▶(For destruction of rectal tumor, transanal approach, use 45190)◀

Destruction

45190   Destruction of rectal tumor (eg, electrodesiccation, electrosurgery, laser ablation, laser resection, cryosurgery) transanal approach

→ *CPT Changes: An Insider's View* 2002

►(For excision of rectal tumor, transanal approach, see 45171, 45172)◄

Endoscopy

Definitions

Proctosigmoidoscopy is the examination of the rectum and sigmoid colon.

Sigmoidoscopy is the examination of the entire rectum, sigmoid colon and may include examination of a portion of the descending colon.

Colonoscopy is the examination of the entire colon, from the rectum to the cecum, and may include the examination of the terminal ileum.

For an incomplete colonoscopy, with full preparation for a colonoscopy, use a colonoscopy code with the modifier 52 and provide documentation.

Surgical endoscopy always includes diagnostic endoscopy.

►For computed tomographic colonography, see 74261-74263.◄

45300   Proctosigmoidoscopy, rigid; diagnostic, with or without collection of specimen(s) by brushing or washing (separate procedure)

→ *CPT Assistant* Spring 94:8, Oct 97:6, Apr 06:1

⊙ **45303**   with dilation (eg, balloon, guide wire, bougie)

→ *CPT Assistant* Spring 94:8, Oct 97:6, Apr 06:1; *CPT Changes: An Insider's View* 2002

(For radiological supervision and interpretation, use 74360)

⊙ **45305**   with biopsy, single or multiple

→ *CPT Assistant* Spring 94:8, Oct 97:6, Apr 06:1

⊙ **45307**   with removal of foreign body

→ *CPT Assistant* Spring 94:8, Oct 97:6, Apr 06:1

⊙ **45308**   with removal of single tumor, polyp, or other lesion by hot biopsy forceps or bipolar cautery

→ *CPT Assistant* Spring 94:8, Oct 97:6, Apr 06:1

⊙ **45309**   with removal of single tumor, polyp, or other lesion by snare technique

→ *CPT Assistant* Spring 94:8, Oct 97:6, Apr 06:1

⊙ **45315**   with removal of multiple tumors, polyps, or other lesions by hot biopsy forceps, bipolar cautery or snare technique

→ *CPT Assistant* Spring 94:8, Oct 97:6, Apr 06:1

⊙ **45317**   with control of bleeding (eg, injection, bipolar cautery, unipolar cautery, laser, heater probe, stapler, plasma coagulator)

→ *CPT Assistant* Spring 94:8, Oct 97:6, Apr 06:1; *CPT Changes: An Insider's View* 2002

⊙ **45320**   with ablation of tumor(s), polyp(s), or other lesion(s) not amenable to removal by hot biopsy forceps, bipolar cautery or snare technique (eg, laser)

→ *CPT Assistant* Spring 94:8, Oct 97:6, Apr 06:1

⊙ **45321**   with decompression of volvulus

→ *CPT Assistant* Spring 94:8, Oct 97:6, Apr 06:1

⊙ **45327**   with transendoscopic stent placement (includes predilation)

→ *CPT Assistant* Nov 01:7, Apr 06:1; *CPT Changes: An Insider's View* 2001

45330   Sigmoidoscopy, flexible; diagnostic, with or without collection of specimen(s) by brushing or washing (separate procedure)

→ *CPT Assistant* Spring 94:9, May 05:3, May 07:10, Nov 07:8

45331   with biopsy, single or multiple

→ *CPT Assistant* Spring 94:9, Sep 96:6, Jan 07:28

⊙ **45332**   with removal of foreign body

→ *CPT Assistant* Winter 90:3, Spring 94:9

⊙ **45333**   with removal of tumor(s), polyp(s), or other lesion(s) by hot biopsy forceps or bipolar cautery

→ *CPT Assistant* Winter 90:3, Spring 94:9

⊙ **45334**   with control of bleeding (eg, injection, bipolar cautery, unipolar cautery, laser, heater probe, stapler, plasma coagulator)

→ *CPT Assistant* Spring 94:9, Sep 96:6, Jan 07:28; *CPT Changes: An Insider's View* 2002

⊙ **45335**   with directed submucosal injection(s), any substance

→ *CPT Assistant* Mar 03:22; *CPT Changes: An Insider's View* 2003

⊙ **45337**   with decompression of volvulus, any method

→ *CPT Assistant* Spring 94:9

⊙ **45338**   with removal of tumor(s), polyp(s), or other lesion(s) by snare technique

→ *CPT Assistant* Spring 94:9

⊙ **45339**   with ablation of tumor(s), polyp(s), or other lesion(s) not amenable to removal by hot biopsy forceps, bipolar cautery or snare technique

→ *CPT Assistant* Spring 94:9

⊙ **45340**   with dilation by balloon, 1 or more strictures

→ *CPT Changes: An Insider's View* 2003

(Do not report 45340 in conjunction with 45345)

⊙ **45341**   with endoscopic ultrasound examination

→ *CPT Assistant* Oct 01:4, May 05:3; *CPT Changes: An Insider's View* 2001

⊙ **45342**   with transendoscopic ultrasound guided intramural or transmural fine needle aspiration/biopsy(s)

→ *CPT Assistant* Oct 01:4, May 05:3; *CPT Changes: An Insider's View* 2001

(Do not report 45341, 45342 in conjunction with 76942, 76975)

▲=Revised code   ●=New code   ►◄=Contains new or revised text   ⊘=Modifier 51 exempt

(For interpretation of specimen, see 88172-88173)

(For transrectal ultrasound utilizing rigid probe device, use 76872)

⊙ **45345** with transendoscopic stent placement (includes predilation)

➔ *CPT Assistant* Nov 01:7; *CPT Changes: An Insider's View* 2001

⊙ **45355** Colonoscopy, rigid or flexible, transabdominal via colotomy, single or multiple

(For fiberoptic colonoscopy beyond 25cm to splenic flexure, see 45330-45345)

⊙ **45378** Colonoscopy, flexible, proximal to splenic flexure; diagnostic, with or without collection of specimen(s) by brushing or washing, with or without colon decompression (separate procedure)

➔ *CPT Assistant* Spring 94:9, Aug 99:3, Jan 02:12, Jan 04:4, May 05:3

Colonoscopy
45378

A colonoscope is inserted in the anus and moved through the colon past the splenic flexure in order to visualize the lumen of the rectum and colon.

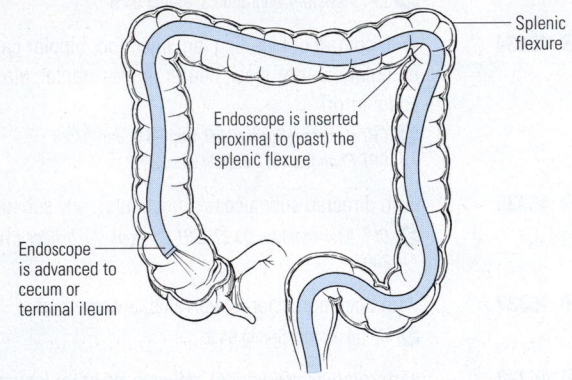

⊙ **45379** with removal of foreign body

➔ *CPT Assistant* Spring 94:9, Aug 99:3

⊙ **45380** with biopsy, single or multiple

➔ *CPT Assistant* Spring 94:9, Jan 96:7, Feb 99:11, Aug 99:3, Jan 04:7, Jul 04:15

⊙ **45381** with directed submucosal injection(s), any substance

➔ *CPT Assistant* Mar 03:22, Jan 04:7; *CPT Changes: An Insider's View* 2003

⊙ **45382** with control of bleeding (eg, injection, bipolar cautery, unipolar cautery, laser, heater probe, stapler, plasma coagulator)

➔ *CPT Assistant* Spring 94:9, Aug 99:3; *CPT Changes: An Insider's View* 2002

⊙ **45383** with ablation of tumor(s), polyp(s), or other lesion(s) not amenable to removal by hot biopsy forceps, bipolar cautery or snare technique

➔ *CPT Assistant* Spring 94:9, Aug 99:3, Jan 04:4

Colonoscopy With Lesion Ablation or Removal
45383, 45385

Insertion and advancement of a colonoscope through the colon and past the splenic flexure for ablation (45383) or removal (45385) of tumors, polyps, or other lesions

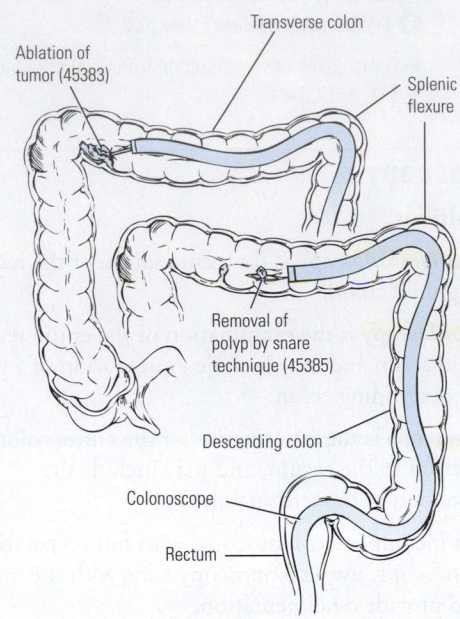

⊙ **45384** with removal of tumor(s), polyp(s), or other lesion(s) by hot biopsy forceps or bipolar cautery

➔ *CPT Assistant* Spring 94:9, Jul 98:10, Feb 99:11, Aug 99:3, Jan 04:6, Jul 04:15

⊙ **45385** with removal of tumor(s), polyp(s), or other lesion(s) by snare technique

➔ *CPT Assistant* Spring 94:9, Jan 96:7, Jul 98:10, Aug 99:3, Jan 04:5, Jul 04:15

(For small intestine and stomal endoscopy, see 44360-44393)

⊙ **45386** with dilation by balloon, 1 or more strictures

➔ *CPT Changes: An Insider's View* 2003

(Do not report 45386 in conjunction with 45387)

⊙ **45387** with transendoscopic stent placement (includes predilation)

➔ *CPT Assistant* Nov 01:7; *CPT Changes: An Insider's View* 2001

⊙ **45391** with endoscopic ultrasound examination

➔ *CPT Assistant* May 05:3; *CPT Changes: An Insider's View* 2005

(Do not report 45391 in conjunction with 45330, 45341, 45342, 45378, 76872)

⊙ **45392**   with transendoscopic ultrasound guided intramural or transmural fine needle aspiration/biopsy(s)
↪ *CPT Assistant* May 05:3; *CPT Changes: An Insider's View* 2005

(Do not report 45392 in conjunction with 45330, 45341, 45342, 45378, 76872)

Laparoscopy

Surgical laparoscopy always includes diagnostic laparoscopy. To report a diagnostic laparoscopy (peritoneoscopy) (separate procedure), use 49320.

Excision

45395   Laparoscopy, surgical; proctectomy, complete, combined abdominoperineal, with colostomy
↪ *CPT Changes: An Insider's View* 2006

(For open procedure, use 45110)

45397   proctectomy, combined abdominoperineal pull-through procedure (eg, colo-anal anastomosis), with creation of colonic reservoir (eg, J-pouch), with diverting enterostomy, when performed
↪ *CPT Changes: An Insider's View* 2006

(For open procedure, use 45119)

Repair

45400   Laparoscopy, surgical; proctopexy (for prolapse)
↪ *CPT Changes: An Insider's View* 2006

(For open procedure, use 45540, 45541)

45402   proctopexy (for prolapse), with sigmoid resection
↪ *CPT Changes: An Insider's View* 2006

(For open procedure, use 45550)

45499   Unlisted laparoscopy procedure, rectum
↪ *CPT Changes: An Insider's View* 2006

Repair

45500   Proctoplasty; for stenosis

45505   for prolapse of mucous membrane

45520   Perirectal injection of sclerosing solution for prolapse
↪ *CPT Assistant* Jul 01:11, Aug 01:10

45540   Proctopexy (eg, for prolapse); abdominal approach
↪ *CPT Changes: An Insider's View* 2006

(For laparoscopic procedure, use 45400)

45541   perineal approach

45550   with sigmoid resection, abdominal approach
↪ *CPT Changes: An Insider's View* 2006

(For laparoscopic procedure, use 45402)

45560   Repair of rectocele (separate procedure)

(For repair of rectocele with posterior colporrhaphy, use 57250)

45562   Exploration, repair, and presacral drainage for rectal injury;

45563   with colostomy

45800   Closure of rectovesical fistula;

45805   with colostomy

45820   Closure of rectourethral fistula;

45825   with colostomy

(For rectovaginal fistula closure, see 57300-57308)

Manipulation

45900   Reduction of procidentia (separate procedure) under anesthesia

45905   Dilation of anal sphincter (separate procedure) under anesthesia other than local

45910   Dilation of rectal stricture (separate procedure) under anesthesia other than local

45915   Removal of fecal impaction or foreign body (separate procedure) under anesthesia
↪ *CPT Changes: An Insider's View* 2003

Other Procedures

Surgical diagnostic anorectal exam (45990) includes the following elements: external perineal exam, digital rectal exam, pelvic exam (when performed), diagnostic anoscopy, and diagnostic rigid proctoscopy.

45990   Anorectal exam, surgical, requiring anesthesia (general, spinal, or epidural), diagnostic
↪ *CPT Changes: An Insider's View* 2006

(Do not report 45990 in conjunction with 45300-45327, 46600, 57410, 99170)

45999   Unlisted procedure, rectum

(For unlisted laparoscopic procedure, rectum, use 45499)

Anus

▶For incision of thrombosed external hemorrhoid, use 46083. For ligation of internal hemorrhoid(s), see 46221, 46945, 46946. For excision of internal and/or external hemorrhoid(s), see 46250-46262, 46320. For injection of hemorrhoid(s), use 46500. For destruction of internal hemorrhoid(s) by thermal energy, use 46930. For destruction of hemorrhoid(s) by cryosurgery, use 46999. For hemorrhoidopexy, use 46947.◄

Incision

(For subcutaneous fistulotomy, use 46270)

46020   Placement of seton

➔ *CPT Changes: An Insider's View* 2002

(Do not report 46020 in addition to 46060, 46280, 46600)

Placement of Seton
46020

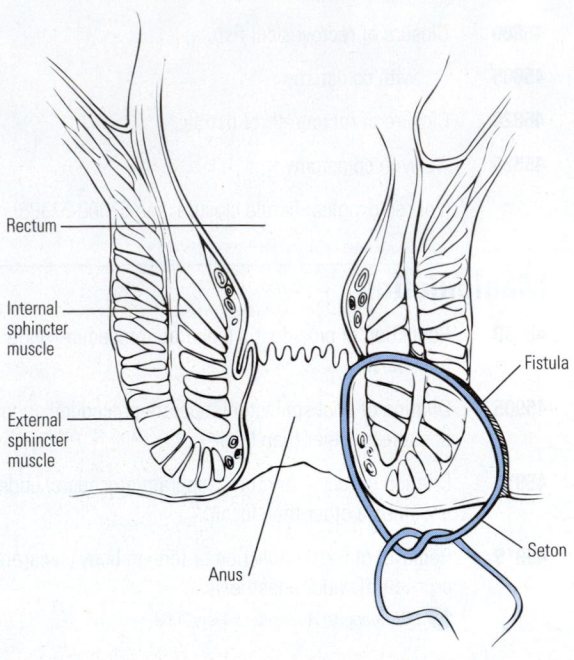

Rectum

Internal
sphincter
muscle

External
sphincter
muscle

Anus

Fistula

Seton

46030   Removal of anal seton, other marker

46040   Incision and drainage of ischiorectal and/or perirectal abscess (separate procedure)

46045   Incision and drainage of intramural, intramuscular, or submucosal abscess, transanal, under anesthesia

46050   Incision and drainage, perianal abscess, superficial

(See also 45020, 46060)

46060   Incision and drainage of ischiorectal or intramural abscess, with fistulectomy or fistulotomy, submuscular, with or without placement of seton

(Do not report 46060 in addition to 46020)

(See also 45020)

46070   Incision, anal septum (infant)

(For anoplasty, see 46700-46705)

(Do not report modifier 63 in conjunction with 46070)

46080   Sphincterotomy, anal, division of sphincter (separate procedure)

46083   Incision of thrombosed hemorrhoid, external

➔ *CPT Assistant* Jun 97:10

Excision

▲ **46200**   Fissurectomy, including sphincterotomy, when performed

➔ *CPT Changes: An Insider's View* 2010

▶(46210, 46211 have been deleted. To report, use 46999)◀

46220   ▶Code is out of numerical sequence. See 46200-46288◀

▲ **46221**   Hemorrhoidectomy, internal, by rubber band ligation(s)

➔ *CPT Assistant* Oct 97:8; *CPT Changes: An Insider's View* 2010

▲ **46945**   Hemorrhoidectomy, internal, by ligation other than rubber band; single hemorrhoid column/group

➔ *CPT Changes: An Insider's View* 2010

▲ **46946**   2 or more hemorrhoid columns/groups

➔ *CPT Changes: An Insider's View* 2010

▲ **46220**   Excision of single external papilla or tag, anus

➔ *CPT Changes: An Insider's View* 2010

▲ **46230**   Excision of multiple external papillae or tags, anus

➔ *CPT Changes: An Insider's View* 2010

▲ **46320**   Excision of thrombosed hemorrhoid, external

➔ *CPT Changes: An Insider's View* 2010

Hemorrhoidectomy Procedure

Hemorrhoidectomy of Internal Prolapsed Hemorrhoid Columns 46250-46262

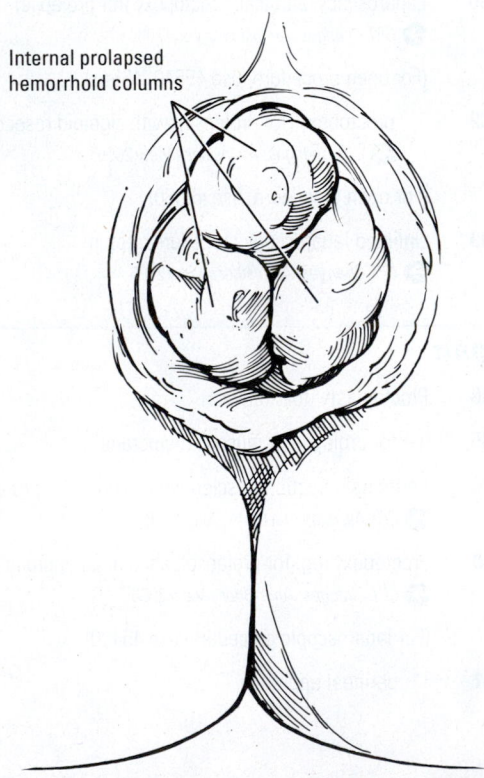

Internal prolapsed
hemorrhoid columns

Anal column is considered to be an internal hemorrhoid with 3 major areas in the anal canal: right posterior (1 o'clock), right anterior (5 o'clock), and left lateral (9 o'clock) positions of the anus

▲ **46250**   Hemorrhoidectomy, external, 2 or more columns/groups
  ➔ *CPT Changes: An Insider's View* 2010

  ►(For hemorrhoidectomy, external, single column/group, use 46999)◄

▲ **46255**   Hemorrhoidectomy, internal and external, single column/group;
  ➔ *CPT Changes: An Insider's View* 2010

46257   with fissurectomy

▲ **46258**   with fistulectomy, including fissurectomy, when performed
  ➔ *CPT Changes: An Insider's View* 2010

▲ **46260**   Hemorrhoidectomy, internal and external, 2 or more columns/groups;
  ➔ *CPT Changes: An Insider's View* 2010

46261   with fissurectomy

▲ **46262**   with fistulectomy, including fissurectomy, when performed
  ➔ *CPT Assistant* May 05:3; *CPT Changes: An Insider's View* 2010

46270   Surgical treatment of anal fistula (fistulectomy/fistulotomy); subcutaneous

▲ **46275**   intersphincteric
  ➔ *CPT Changes: An Insider's View* 2010

▲ **46280**   transsphincteric, suprasphincteric, extrasphincteric or multiple, including placement of seton, when performed
  ➔ *CPT Changes: An Insider's View* 2010

  (Do not report 46280 in conjunction with 46020)

46285   second stage

46288   Closure of anal fistula with rectal advancement flap

46320   ►Code is out of numerical sequence. See 46200-46288◄

Introduction

46500   Injection of sclerosing solution, hemorrhoids
  ➔ *CPT Assistant* May 05:3

46505   Chemodenervation of internal anal sphincter
  ➔ *CPT Changes: An Insider's View* 2006

  (For chemodenervation of other muscles, see 64612-64614, 64640)

  (Report the specific service in conjunction with the specific substance(s) or drug(s) provided)

Endoscopy

Surgical endoscopy always includes diagnostic endoscopy.

46600   Anoscopy; diagnostic, with or without collection of specimen(s) by brushing or washing (separate procedure)
  ➔ *CPT Assistant* Spring 94:9, Oct 97:6, Apr 06:1

  (Do not report 46600 in addition to 46020)

46604   with dilation (eg, balloon, guide wire, bougie)
  ➔ *CPT Assistant* Spring 94:9, Oct 97:6; *CPT Changes: An Insider's View* 2002

46606   with biopsy, single or multiple
  ➔ *CPT Assistant* Spring 94:9, Oct 97:6

46608   with removal of foreign body
  ➔ *CPT Assistant* Spring 94:9, Oct 97:6

46610   with removal of single tumor, polyp, or other lesion by hot biopsy forceps or bipolar cautery
  ➔ *CPT Assistant* Spring 94:10, Oct 97:6

46611   with removal of single tumor, polyp, or other lesion by snare technique
  ➔ *CPT Assistant* Spring 94:10, Oct 97:6

46612   with removal of multiple tumors, polyps, or other lesions by hot biopsy forceps, bipolar cautery or snare technique
  ➔ *CPT Assistant* Spring 94:10, Oct 97:6

46614   with control of bleeding (eg, injection, bipolar cautery, unipolar cautery, laser, heater probe, stapler, plasma coagulator)
  ➔ *CPT Assistant* Spring 94:10, Oct 97:6; *CPT Changes: An Insider's View* 2002

46615   with ablation of tumor(s), polyp(s), or other lesion(s) not amenable to removal by hot biopsy forceps, bipolar cautery or snare technique
  ➔ *CPT Assistant* Spring 94:10, Oct 97:6

Repair

46700   Anoplasty, plastic operation for stricture; adult

46705   infant

  (For simple incision of anal septum, use 46070)

  (Do not report modifier 63 in conjunction with 46705)

46706   Repair of anal fistula with fibrin glue
  ➔ *CPT Changes: An Insider's View* 2003

● **46707**   Repair of anorectal fistula with plug (eg, porcine small intestine submucosa [SIS])
  ➔ *CPT Changes: An Insider's View* 2010

46710   Repair of ileoanal pouch fistula/sinus (eg, perineal or vaginal), pouch advancement; transperineal approach
  ➔ *CPT Changes: An Insider's View* 2006

46712   combined transperineal and transabdominal approach
  ➔ *CPT Changes: An Insider's View* 2006

46715   Repair of low imperforate anus; with anoperineal fistula (cut-back procedure)

46716   with transposition of anoperineal or anovestibular fistula

  (Do not report modifier 63 in conjunction with 46715, 46716)

46730   Repair of high imperforate anus without fistula; perineal or sacroperineal approach

---

▲=Revised code   ●=New code   ►◄=Contains new or revised text   ⊘=Modifier 51 exempt

46735   combined transabdominal and sacroperineal
approaches

(Do not report modifier 63 in conjunction with 46730,
46735)

46740   Repair of high imperforate anus with rectourethral or
rectovaginal fistula; perineal or sacroperineal approach

46742   combined transabdominal and sacroperineal
approaches

(Do not report modifier 63 in conjunction with 46740,
46742)

46744   Repair of cloacal anomaly by anorectovaginoplasty and
urethroplasty, sacroperineal approach

(Do not report modifier 63 in conjunction with 46744)

46746   Repair of cloacal anomaly by anorectovaginoplasty and
urethroplasty, combined abdominal and sacroperineal
approach;

46748   with vaginal lengthening by intestinal graft or pedicle
flaps

46750   Sphincteroplasty, anal, for incontinence or prolapse; adult

46751   child

46753   Graft (Thiersch operation) for rectal incontinence and/or
prolapse

46754   Removal of Thiersch wire or suture, anal canal

46760   Sphincteroplasty, anal, for incontinence, adult; muscle
transplant

46761   levator muscle imbrication (Park posterior anal repair)

46762   implantation artificial sphincter

 # 46947   Hemorrhoidopexy (eg, for prolapsing internal
hemorrhoids) by stapling
➜ *CPT Assistant* May 05:3, 14; *CPT Changes: An Insider's View*
2005

Destruction

46900   Destruction of lesion(s), anus (eg, condyloma, papilloma,
molluscum contagiosum, herpetic vesicle), simple;
chemical

46910   electrodesiccation

46916   cryosurgery

46917   laser surgery

46922   surgical excision

46924   Destruction of lesion(s), anus (eg, condyloma, papilloma,
molluscum contagiosum, herpetic vesicle), extensive (eg,
laser surgery, electrosurgery, cryosurgery, chemosurgery)
➜ *CPT Changes: An Insider's View* 2002

46930   Destruction of internal hemorrhoid(s) by thermal energy
(eg, infrared coagulation, cautery, radiofrequency)
➜ *CPT Changes: An Insider's View* 2009

►(46934-46936 have been deleted)◄

►(46937, 46938 have been deleted. To report, use
45190)◄

46940   Curettage or cautery of anal fissure, including dilation of
anal sphincter (separate procedure); initial
➜ *CPT Changes: An Insider's View* 2002

46942   subsequent

46945   ►Code is out of numerical sequence. See 46200-
46288◄

46946   ►Code is out of numerical sequence. See 46200-
46288◄

46947   ►Code is out of numerical sequence. See 46700-
46947◄

Other Procedures

46999   Unlisted procedure, anus
➜ *CPT Assistant* Oct 97:8

Liver

Incision

47000   Biopsy of liver, needle; percutaneous
➜ *CPT Assistant* Fall 93:12

(If imaging guidance is performed, see 76942, 77002,
77012, 77021)

+ 47001   when done for indicated purpose at time of other
major procedure (List separately in addition to code
for primary procedure)
➜ *CPT Assistant* Jun 07:10

(If imaging guidance is performed, see 76942, 77002)

(For fine needle aspiration in conjunction with 47000,
47001, see 10021, 10022)

(For evaluation of fine needle aspirate in conjunction with
47000, 47001, see 88172, 88173)

47010   Hepatotomy; for open drainage of abscess or cyst, 1 or 2
stages
➜ *CPT Assistant* Nov 97:18

⊙ **47011**   for percutaneous drainage of abscess or cyst, 1 or 2
stages
➜ *CPT Assistant* Nov 97:18, Mar 98:8

(For radiological supervision and interpretation, use
75989)

47015   Laparotomy, with aspiration and/or injection of hepatic
parasitic (eg, amoebic or echinococcal) cyst(s) or
abscess(es)

Excision

47100   Biopsy of liver, wedge

47120   Hepatectomy, resection of liver; partial lobectomy
➜ *CPT Assistant* May 98:10

47122	trisegmentectomy
47125	total left lobectomy
47130	total right lobectomy

Liver Transplantation

Liver allotransplantation involves three distinct components of physician work:

1. ***Cadaver donor hepatectomy***, which includes harvesting the graft and cold preservation of the graft (perfusing with cold preservation solution and cold maintenance) (use 47133). ***Living donor hepatectomy***, which includes harvesting the graft, cold preservation of the graft (perfusing with cold preservation solution and cold maintenance), and care of the donor (see 47140-47142).

2. ***Backbench work***:

   Standard preparation of the whole liver graft will include one of the following:

   Preparation of whole liver graft (including cholecystectomy, if necessary, and dissection and removal of surrounding soft tissues to prepare vena cava, portal vein, hepatic artery, and common bile duct for implantation) (use 47143).

   Preparation as described for whole liver graft, plus trisegment split into two partial grafts (use 47144).

   Preparation as described for whole liver graft, plus lobe split into two partial grafts (use 47145).

   Additional reconstruction of the liver graft may include venous and/or arterial anastomosis(es) (see 47146, 47147).

3. ***Recipient liver allotransplantation***, which includes recipient hepatectomy (partial or whole), transplantation of the allograft (partial or whole), and care of the recipient (see 47135, 47136).

47133	Donor hepatectomy (including cold preservation), from cadaver donor

➔ *CPT Changes: An Insider's View* 2005

47135	Liver allotransplantation; orthotopic, partial or whole, from cadaver or living donor, any age
47136	heterotopic, partial or whole, from cadaver or living donor, any age

47140	Donor hepatectomy (including cold preservation), from living donor; left lateral segment only (segments II and III)

➔ *CPT Changes: An Insider's View* 2004, 2005

47141	total left lobectomy (segments II, III and IV)

➔ *CPT Changes: An Insider's View* 2004

47142	total right lobectomy (segments V, VI, VII and VIII)

➔ *CPT Changes: An Insider's View* 2004

47143	Backbench standard preparation of cadaver donor whole liver graft prior to allotransplantation, including cholecystectomy, if necessary, and dissection and removal of surrounding soft tissues to prepare the vena cava, portal vein, hepatic artery, and common bile duct for implantation; without trisegment or lobe split

➔ *CPT Assistant* Apr 05:10, 12; *CPT Changes: An Insider's View* 2005

47144	with trisegment split of whole liver graft into 2 partial liver grafts (ie, left lateral segment [segments II and III] and right trisegment [segments I and IV through VIII])

➔ *CPT Changes: An Insider's View* 2005, 2009

47145	with lobe split of whole liver graft into 2 partial liver grafts (ie, left lobe [segments II, III, and IV] and right lobe [segments I and V through VIII])

➔ *CPT Changes: An Insider's View* 2005

47146	Backbench reconstruction of cadaver or living donor liver graft prior to allotransplantation; venous anastomosis, each

➔ *CPT Changes: An Insider's View* 2005

47147	arterial anastomosis, each

➔ *CPT Changes: An Insider's View* 2005

(Do not report 47143-47147 in conjunction with 47120-47125, 47600, 47610)

Repair

47300	Marsupialization of cyst or abscess of liver
47350	Management of liver hemorrhage; simple suture of liver wound or injury
47360	complex suture of liver wound or injury, with or without hepatic artery ligation
47361	exploration of hepatic wound, extensive debridement, coagulation and/or suture, with or without packing of liver
47362	re-exploration of hepatic wound for removal of packing

Laparoscopy

Surgical laparoscopy always includes diagnostic laparoscopy. To report a diagnostic laparoscopy (peritoneoscopy) (separate procedure), use 49320.

47370	Laparoscopy, surgical, ablation of 1 or more liver tumor(s); radiofrequency

➔ *CPT Assistant* Oct 02:2; *CPT Changes: An Insider's View* 2002

(For imaging guidance, use 76940)

47371	cryosurgical

➔ *CPT Changes: An Insider's View* 2002

(For imaging guidance, use 76940)

47379	Unlisted laparoscopic procedure, liver

➔ *CPT Assistant* Aug 06:10, Dec 07:12; *CPT Changes: An Insider's View* 2001

Other Procedures

47380 Ablation, open, of 1 or more liver tumor(s); radiofrequency
→ *CPT Assistant* Oct 02:1; *CPT Changes: An Insider's View* 2002
→ *Clinical Examples in Radiology* Summer 08:3

(For imaging guidance, use 76940)

47381 cryosurgical
→ *CPT Changes: An Insider's View* 2002

(For imaging guidance, use 76940)

⊙▲ **47382** Ablation, 1 or more liver tumor(s), percutaneous, radiofrequency
→ *CPT Assistant* Oct 02:1; *CPT Changes: An Insider's View* 2002, 2010
→ *Clinical Examples in Radiology* Spring 08:1,2, Summer 08:3

(For imaging guidance and monitoring, see 76940, 77013, 77022)

47399 Unlisted procedure, liver

Biliary Tract

Incision

47400 Hepaticotomy or hepaticostomy with exploration, drainage, or removal of calculus

47420 Choledochotomy or choledochostomy with exploration, drainage, or removal of calculus, with or without cholecystotomy; without transduodenal sphincterotomy or sphincteroplasty

47425 with transduodenal sphincterotomy or sphincteroplasty

47460 Transduodenal sphincterotomy or sphincteroplasty, with or without transduodenal extraction of calculus (separate procedure)

47480 Cholecystotomy or cholecystostomy with exploration, drainage, or removal of calculus (separate procedure)

47490 Percutaneous cholecystostomy

(For radiological supervision and interpretation, use 75989)

Introduction

47500 Injection procedure for percutaneous transhepatic cholangiography

(For radiological supervision and interpretation, use 74320)

47505 Injection procedure for cholangiography through an existing catheter (eg, percutaneous transhepatic or T-tube)

(For radiological supervision and interpretation, use 74305)

47510 Introduction of percutaneous transhepatic catheter for biliary drainage

(For radiological supervision and interpretation, use 75980)

47511 Introduction of percutaneous transhepatic stent for internal and external biliary drainage

(For radiological supervision and interpretation, use 75982)

⊙▲ **47525** Change of percutaneous biliary drainage catheter
→ *CPT Changes: An Insider's View* 2010

(For radiological supervision and interpretation, use 75984)

47530 Revision and/or reinsertion of transhepatic tube

(For radiological supervision and interpretation, use 75984)

Endoscopy

Surgical endoscopy always includes diagnostic endoscopy.

+ **47550** Biliary endoscopy, intraoperative (choledochoscopy) (List separately in addition to code for primary procedure)

47552 Biliary endoscopy, percutaneous via T-tube or other tract; diagnostic, with or without collection of specimen(s) by brushing and/or washing (separate procedure)

47553 with biopsy, single or multiple

47554 with removal of calculus/calculi
→ *CPT Changes: An Insider's View* 2002

47555 with dilation of biliary duct stricture(s) without stent

47556 with dilation of biliary duct stricture(s) with stent

(For ERCP, see 43260-43272, 74363)

(If imaging guidance is performed, see 74363, 75982)

Laparoscopy

Surgical laparoscopy always includes diagnostic laparoscopy. To report a diagnostic laparoscopy (peritoneoscopy) (separate procedure), use 49320.

47560 Laparoscopy, surgical; with guided transhepatic cholangiography, without biopsy
→ *CPT Assistant* Nov 99:23, Mar 00:9; *CPT Changes: An Insider's View* 2000

47561 with guided transhepatic cholangiography with biopsy
→ *CPT Assistant* Nov 99:23, Mar 00:9; *CPT Changes: An Insider's View* 2000

47562 cholecystectomy
→ *CPT Assistant* Nov 99:23, Mar 00:9, Sep 03:3, Dec 07:12; *CPT Changes: An Insider's View* 2000

Laparoscopic Cholecystectomy
47562

The gallbladder is dissected and removed from the liver bed under laparoscopic guidance.

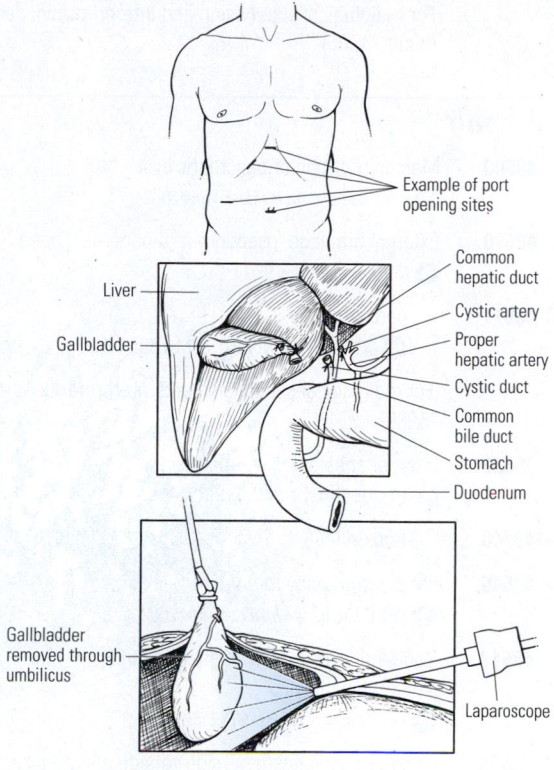

Liver
Gallbladder
Example of port opening sites
Common hepatic duct
Cystic artery
Proper hepatic artery
Cystic duct
Common bile duct
Stomach
Duodenum
Gallbladder removed through umbilicus
Laparoscope

47563   cholecystectomy with cholangiography
> *CPT Assistant* Nov 99:23, Mar 00:9, Dec 00:14, Dec 07:12; *CPT Changes: An Insider's View* 2000

47564   cholecystectomy with exploration of common duct
> *CPT Assistant* Nov 99:23, Mar 00:9; *CPT Changes: An Insider's View* 2000

47570   cholecystoenterostomy
> *CPT Assistant* Nov 99:23, Mar 00:9; *CPT Changes: An Insider's View* 2000

47579   Unlisted laparoscopy procedure, biliary tract
> *CPT Assistant* Nov 99:23, Mar 00:9; *CPT Changes: An Insider's View* 2000

Excision

47600   Cholecystectomy;
> *CPT Assistant* Fall 92:19, Nov 99:24; *CPT Changes: An Insider's View* 2000

47605   with cholangiography
> *CPT Assistant* Nov 99:24, Apr 02:19; *CPT Changes: An Insider's View* 2000

(For laparoscopic approach, see 47562-47564)

47610   Cholecystectomy with exploration of common duct;
> *CPT Assistant* Apr 02:19

(For cholecystectomy with exploration of common duct with biliary endoscopy, use 47610 with 47550)

47612   with choledochoenterostomy

47620   with transduodenal sphincterotomy or sphincteroplasty, with or without cholangiography

47630   Biliary duct stone extraction, percutaneous via T-tube tract, basket, or snare (eg, Burhenne technique)
> *CPT Assistant* Jun 98:10

(For radiological supervision and interpretation, use 74327)

47700   Exploration for congenital atresia of bile ducts, without repair, with or without liver biopsy, with or without cholangiography

(Do not report modifier 63 in conjunction with 47700)

47701   Portoenterostomy (eg, Kasai procedure)

(Do not report modifier 63 in conjunction with 47701)

47711   Excision of bile duct tumor, with or without primary repair of bile duct; extrahepatic

47712   intrahepatic

(For anastomosis, see 47760-47800)

47715   Excision of choledochal cyst

Repair

(47719 has been deleted)

47720   Cholecystoenterostomy; direct
> *CPT Assistant* Nov 99:24; *CPT Changes: An Insider's View* 2000

(For laparoscopic approach, use 47570)

47721   with gastroenterostomy

47740   Roux-en-Y

47741   Roux-en-Y with gastroenterostomy

47760   Anastomosis, of extrahepatic biliary ducts and gastrointestinal tract

47765   Anastomosis, of intrahepatic ducts and gastrointestinal tract

47780   Anastomosis, Roux-en-Y, of extrahepatic biliary ducts and gastrointestinal tract

47785   Anastomosis, Roux-en-Y, of intrahepatic biliary ducts and gastrointestinal tract

47800   Reconstruction, plastic, of extrahepatic biliary ducts with end-to-end anastomosis

47801   Placement of choledochal stent

47802   U-tube hepaticoenterostomy

47900   Suture of extrahepatic biliary duct for pre-existing injury (separate procedure)

Other Procedures

47999   Unlisted procedure, biliary tract

Pancreas

(For peroral pancreatic endoscopic procedures, see 43260-43272)

Incision

48000   Placement of drains, peripancreatic, for acute pancreatitis;

48001   with cholecystostomy, gastrostomy, and jejunostomy

48020   Removal of pancreatic calculus
    → *CPT Assistant* Spring 91:7

Excision

48100   Biopsy of pancreas, open (eg, fine needle aspiration, needle core biopsy, wedge biopsy)
    → *CPT Changes: An Insider's View* 2002

48102   Biopsy of pancreas, percutaneous needle

(For radiological supervision and interpretation, see 76942, 77002, 77012, 77021)

(For fine needle aspiration, use 10022)

(For evaluation of fine needle aspirate, see 88172, 88173)

48105   Resection or debridement of pancreas and peripancreatic tissue for acute necrotizing pancreatitis
    → *CPT Changes: An Insider's View* 2007

48120   Excision of lesion of pancreas (eg, cyst, adenoma)

48140   Pancreatectomy, distal subtotal, with or without splenectomy; without pancreaticojejunostomy

48145   with pancreaticojejunostomy

48146   Pancreatectomy, distal, near-total with preservation of duodenum (Child-type procedure)

48148   Excision of ampulla of Vater

48150   Pancreatectomy, proximal subtotal with total duodenectomy, partial gastrectomy, choledochoenterostomy and gastrojejunostomy (Whipple-type procedure); with pancreatojejunostomy

48152   without pancreatojejunostomy

48153   Pancreatectomy, proximal subtotal with near-total duodenectomy, choledochoenterostomy and duodenojejunostomy (pylorus-sparing, Whipple-type procedure); with pancreatojejunostomy

48154   without pancreatojejunostomy

48155   Pancreatectomy, total

48160   Pancreatectomy, total or subtotal, with autologous transplantation of pancreas or pancreatic islet cells
    → *CPT Changes: An Insider's View* 2002

Introduction

+ 48400   Injection procedure for intraoperative pancreatography (List separately in addition to code for primary procedure)
    → *CPT Assistant* Dec 07:12

(For radiological supervision and interpretation, see 74300-74305)

Repair

48500   Marsupialization of pancreatic cyst
    → *CPT Changes: An Insider's View* 2002

48510   External drainage, pseudocyst of pancreas; open
    → *CPT Assistant* Nov 97:18

⊙ **48511**   percutaneous
    → *CPT Assistant* Nov 97:18, Mar 98:8

(For radiological supervision and interpretation, use 75989)

48520   Internal anastomosis of pancreatic cyst to gastrointestinal tract; direct

48540   Roux-en-Y

48545   Pancreatorrhaphy for injury
    → *CPT Changes: An Insider's View* 2002

48547   Duodenal exclusion with gastrojejunostomy for pancreatic injury
    → *CPT Changes: An Insider's View* 2002

48548   Pancreaticojejunostomy, side-to-side anastomosis (Puestow-type operation)
    → *CPT Changes: An Insider's View* 2007

Pancreas Transplantation

Pancreas allotransplantation involves three distinct components of physician work:

1. ***Cadaver donor pancreatectomy***, which includes harvesting the pancreas graft, with or without duodenal segment, and cold preservation of the graft (perfusing with cold preservation solution and cold maintenance) (use 48550).

2. ***Backbench work***:

    Standard preparation of a cadaver donor pancreas allograft prior to transplantation includes dissection of the allograft from surrounding soft tissues, splenectomy, duodenotomy, ligation of bile duct, ligation of mesenteric vessels, and Y-graft arterial anastomoses from the iliac artery to the superior mesenteric artery and to the splenic artery (use 48551).

    Additional reconstruction of a cadaver donor pancreas allograft prior to transplantation may include venous anastomosis(es) (use 48552).

3. *Recipient pancreas allotransplantation*, which includes transplantation of allograft, and care of the recipient (use 48554).

48550 Donor pancreatectomy (including cold preservation), with or without duodenal segment for transplantation
➔ *CPT Assistant* Apr 05:10, 12; *CPT Changes: An Insider's View* 2005

48551 Backbench standard preparation of cadaver donor pancreas allograft prior to transplantation, including dissection of allograft from surrounding soft tissues, splenectomy, duodenotomy, ligation of bile duct, ligation of mesenteric vessels, and Y-graft arterial anastomoses from iliac artery to superior mesenteric artery and to splenic artery
➔ *CPT Changes: An Insider's View* 2005

48552 Backbench reconstruction of cadaver donor pancreas allograft prior to transplantation, venous anastomosis, each
➔ *CPT Changes: An Insider's View* 2005

(Do not report 48551 and 48552 in conjunction with 35531, 35563, 35685, 38100-38102, 44010, 44820, 44850, 47460, 47505-47525, 47550-47556, 48100-48120, 48545)

48554 Transplantation of pancreatic allograft

48556 Removal of transplanted pancreatic allograft

Other Procedures

48999 Unlisted procedure, pancreas
➔ *CPT Assistant* Dec 07:12

Abdomen, Peritoneum, and Omentum

Incision

49000 Exploratory laparotomy, exploratory celiotomy with or without biopsy(s) (separate procedure)
➔ *CPT Assistant* Fall 92:23, Mar 01:10, Nov 08:7

(To report wound exploration due to penetrating trauma without laparotomy, use 20102)

49002 Reopening of recent laparotomy
➔ *CPT Assistant* Fall 92:23, Nov 08:7

(To report re-exploration of hepatic wound for removal of packing, use 47362)

49010 Exploration, retroperitoneal area with or without biopsy(s) (separate procedure)

(To report wound exploration due to penetrating trauma without laparotomy, use 20102)

49020 Drainage of peritoneal abscess or localized peritonitis, exclusive of appendiceal abscess; open

(For appendiceal abscess, use 44900)

⊙ **49021** percutaneous

(For radiological supervision and interpretation, use 75989)

49040 Drainage of subdiaphragmatic or subphrenic abscess; open
➔ *CPT Assistant* Nov 97:18

⊙ **49041** percutaneous
➔ *CPT Assistant* Nov 97:18, Mar 98:8

(For radiological supervision and interpretation, use 75989)

49060 Drainage of retroperitoneal abscess; open
➔ *CPT Assistant* Nov 97:18, Nov 99:24, Jul 01:11, Aug 01:10; *CPT Changes: An Insider's View* 2000

⊙ **49061** percutaneous
➔ *CPT Assistant* Nov 97:18, Mar 98:8, Nov 99:24, Jul 01:11, Aug 01:10; *CPT Changes: An Insider's View* 2000

(For laparoscopic drainage, use 49323)

(For radiological supervision and interpretation, use 75989)

49062 Drainage of extraperitoneal lymphocele to peritoneal cavity, open
➔ *CPT Assistant* Nov 97:19, Jul 01:11, Aug 01:10

49080 Peritoneocentesis, abdominal paracentesis, or peritoneal lavage (diagnostic or therapeutic); initial

49081 subsequent

(If imaging guidance is performed, see 76942, 77012)

Excision, Destruction

(For lysis of intestinal adhesions, use 44005)

49180 Biopsy, abdominal or retroperitoneal mass, percutaneous needle
➔ *CPT Assistant* Fall 93:11

(If imaging guidance is performed, see 76942, 77002, 77012, 77021)

(For fine needle aspiration, use 10021 or 10022)

(For evaluation of fine needle aspirate, see 88172, 88173)

(49200, 49201 have been deleted. To report, see 49203-49205, 58957, 58958)

49203 Excision or destruction, open, intra-abdominal tumors, cysts or endometriomas, 1 or more peritoneal, mesenteric, or retroperitoneal primary or secondary tumors; largest tumor 5 cm diameter or less
➔ *CPT Changes: An Insider's View* 2008

49204 largest tumor 5.1-10.0 cm diameter
➔ *CPT Changes: An Insider's View* 2008

49205   largest tumor greater than 10.0 cm diameter

➔ *CPT Changes: An Insider's View* 2008

(Do not report 49203-49205 in conjunction with 38770, 38780, 49000, 49010, 49215, 50010, 50205, 50225, 50236, 50250, 50290, 58900-58960)

(For partial or total nephrectomy, use 50220 or 50240 in conjunction with 49203-49205)

(For colectomy, use 44140 in conjunction with 49203-49205)

(For small bowel resection, use 44120 in conjunction with 49203-49205)

(For vena caval resection with reconstruction, use 49203-49205 in conjunction with 37799)

(For resection of recurrent ovarian, tubal, primary peritoneal, or uterine malignancy, see 58957, 58958)

(For cryoablation of renal tumors, see 50250, 50593)

49215   Excision of presacral or sacrococcygeal tumor

(Do not report modifier 63 in conjunction with 49215)

49220   Staging laparotomy for Hodgkins disease or lymphoma (includes splenectomy, needle or open biopsies of both liver lobes, possibly also removal of abdominal nodes, abdominal node and/or bone marrow biopsies, ovarian repositioning)

➔ *CPT Changes: An Insider's View* 2002

49250   Umbilectomy, omphalectomy, excision of umbilicus (separate procedure)

49255   Omentectomy, epiploectomy, resection of omentum (separate procedure)

➔ *CPT Assistant* Nov 99:24; *CPT Changes: An Insider's View* 2000

Laparoscopy

Surgical laparoscopy always includes diagnostic laparoscopy. To report a diagnostic laparoscopy (peritoneoscopy), (separate procedure), use 49320.

For laparoscopic fulguration or excision of lesions of the ovary, pelvic viscera, or peritoneal surface use 58662.

49320   Laparoscopy, abdomen, peritoneum, and omentum, diagnostic, with or without collection of specimen(s) by brushing or washing (separate procedure)

➔ *CPT Assistant* Nov 99:24, Mar 00:9, Apr 06:19, Mar 07:4, Nov 07:1, Dec 08:7; *CPT Changes: An Insider's View* 2000, 2001

Laparoscopy
49320

The physician inserts a fiberoptic laparoscope to observe the necessary organs in these procedures.

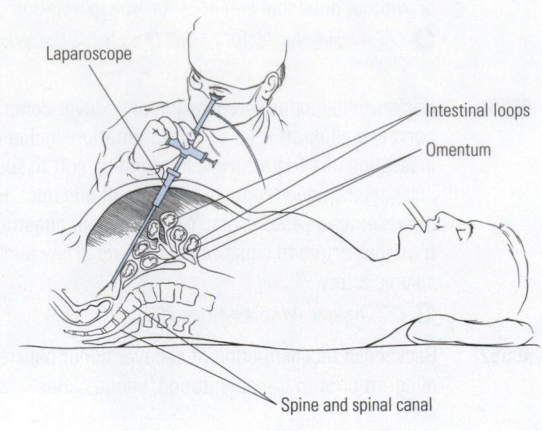

Laparoscope / Intestinal loops / Omentum / Spine and spinal canal

49321   Laparoscopy, surgical; with biopsy (single or multiple)

➔ *CPT Assistant* Nov 99:24, Mar 00:9; *CPT Changes: An Insider's View* 2000, 2001

49322   with aspiration of cavity or cyst (eg, ovarian cyst) (single or multiple)

➔ *CPT Assistant* Nov 99:24, Mar 00:9; *CPT Changes: An Insider's View* 2000

49323   with drainage of lymphocele to peritoneal cavity

➔ *CPT Assistant* Nov 99:24, Mar 00:9, May 00:4, Jul 01:11, Aug 01:10; *CPT Changes: An Insider's View* 2000

(For percutaneous or open drainage, see 49060, 49061)

49324   with insertion of intraperitoneal cannula or catheter, permanent

➔ *CPT Changes: An Insider's View* 2007

(For subcutaneous extension of intraperitoneal catheter with remote chest exit site, use 49435 in conjunction with 49324)

(For open insertion of permanent intraperitoneal cannula or catheter, use 49421)

49325   with revision of previously placed intraperitoneal cannula or catheter, with removal of intraluminal obstructive material if performed

➔ *CPT Changes: An Insider's View* 2007

+ 49326   with omentopexy (omental tacking procedure) (List separately in addition to code for primary procedure)

➔ *CPT Changes: An Insider's View* 2007

(Use 49326 in conjunction with 49324, 49325)

49329   Unlisted laparoscopy procedure, abdomen, peritoneum and omentum

➔ *CPT Assistant* Nov 99:24, Mar 00:9, Feb 06:16; *CPT Changes: An Insider's View* 2000

Introduction, Revision, Removal

49400   Injection of air or contrast into peritoneal cavity (separate procedure)

➡ *Clinical Examples in Radiology* Fall 07:1,2

(For radiological supervision and interpretation, use 74190)

49402   Removal of peritoneal foreign body from peritoneal cavity

➡ *CPT Changes: An Insider's View* 2007

(For lysis of intestinal adhesions, use 44005)

⊙● **49411**   Placement of interstitial device(s) for radiation therapy guidance (eg, fiducial markers, dosimeter), percutaneous, intra-abdominal, intra-pelvic (except prostate), and/or retroperitoneum, single or multiple

➡ *CPT Changes: An Insider's View* 2010

►(Report supply of device separately)◄

►(For imaging guidance, see 76942, 77002, 77012, 77021)◄

►(For percutaneous placement of interstitial device[s] for intra-thoracic radiation therapy guidance, use 32553)◄

49419   Insertion of intraperitoneal cannula or catheter, with subcutaneous reservoir, permanent (ie, totally implantable)

➡ *CPT Changes: An Insider's View* 2003

(For removal, use 49422)

49420   Insertion of intraperitoneal cannula or catheter for drainage or dialysis; temporary

➡ *CPT Assistant* Fall 93:2

49421   permanent

➡ *CPT Assistant* Fall 93:2, Jul 06:19

(For laparoscopic insertion of permanent intraperitoneal cannula or catheter, use 49324)

(For subcutaneous extension of intraperitoneal catheter with remote chest exit site, use 49435 in conjunction with 49421)

49422   Removal of permanent intraperitoneal cannula or catheter

(For removal of a temporary catheter/cannula, use appropriate E/M code)

49423   Exchange of previously placed abscess or cyst drainage catheter under radiological guidance (separate procedure)

➡ *CPT Assistant* Nov 97:19, Mar 98:8

(For radiological supervision and interpretation, use 75984)

49424   Contrast injection for assessment of abscess or cyst via previously placed drainage catheter or tube (separate procedure)

➡ *CPT Assistant* Nov 97:19, Mar 98:8, Nov 03:14; *CPT Changes: An Insider's View* 2002

(For radiological supervision and interpretation, use 76080)

49425   Insertion of peritoneal-venous shunt

49426   Revision of peritoneal-venous shunt

(For shunt patency test, use 78291)

49427   Injection procedure (eg, contrast media) for evaluation of previously placed peritoneal-venous shunt

(For radiological supervision and interpretation, see 75809, 78291)

49428   Ligation of peritoneal-venous shunt

49429   Removal of peritoneal-venous shunt

＋ **49435**   Insertion of subcutaneous extension to intraperitoneal cannula or catheter with remote chest exit site (List separately in addition to code for primary procedure)

➡ *CPT Changes: An Insider's View* 2007

(Use 49435 in conjunction with 49324, 49421)

49436   Delayed creation of exit site from embedded subcutaneous segment of intraperitoneal cannula or catheter

➡ *CPT Changes: An Insider's View* 2007

Initial Placement

Do not additionally report 43752 for placement of a nasogastric (NG) or orogastric (OG) tube to insufflate the stomach prior to percutaneous gastrointestinal tube placement. NG or OG tube placement is considered part of the procedure in this family of codes.

⊙ **49440**   Insertion of gastrostomy tube, percutaneous, under fluoroscopic guidance including contrast injection(s), image documentation and report

➡ *CPT Assistant* Jan 08:8, Jun 08:8, Aug 08:7; *CPT Changes: An Insider's View* 2008

(For conversion to a gastro-jejunostomy tube at the time of initial gastrostomy tube placement, use 49440 in conjunction with 49446)

⊙ **49441**   Insertion of duodenostomy or jejunostomy tube, percutaneous, under fluoroscopic guidance including contrast injection(s), image documentation and report

➡ *CPT Assistant* Jan 08:8, Jun 08:8, Aug 08:7; *CPT Changes: An Insider's View* 2008

(For conversion of gastrostomy tube to gastro-jejunostomy tube, use 49446)

⊙ **49442**   Insertion of cecostomy or other colonic tube, percutaneous, under fluoroscopic guidance including contrast injection(s), image documentation and report

➡ *CPT Assistant* Jan 08:8, Jun 08:8, Aug 08:7; *CPT Changes: An Insider's View* 2008

Conversion

⊙ **49446**   Conversion of gastrostomy tube to gastro-jejunostomy tube, percutaneous, under fluoroscopic guidance including contrast injection(s), image documentation and report

➔ *CPT Changes: An Insider's View* 2008

(For conversion to a gastro-jejunostomy tube at the time of initial gastrostomy tube placement, use 49446 in conjunction with 49440)

Replacement

If an existing gastrostomy, duodenostomy, jejunostomy, gastro-jejunostomy, or cecostomy (or other colonic) tube is removed and a new tube is placed via a separate percutaneous access site, the placement of the new tube is not considered a replacement and would be reported using the appropriate initial placement codes 49440-49442.

49450   Replacement of gastrostomy or cecostomy (or other colonic) tube, percutaneous, under fluoroscopic guidance including contrast injection(s), image documentation and report

➔ *CPT Changes: An Insider's View* 2008

▶(To report a percutaneous change of a gastrostomy tube without imaging or endoscopic guidance, use 43760)◀

49451   Replacement of duodenostomy or jejunostomy tube, percutaneous, under fluoroscopic guidance including contrast injection(s), image documentation and report

➔ *CPT Assistant* Jan 08:8, Jun 08:8, Aug 08:7; *CPT Changes: An Insider's View* 2008

49452   Replacement of gastro-jejunostomy tube, percutaneous, under fluoroscopic guidance including contrast injection(s), image documentation and report

➔ *CPT Changes: An Insider's View* 2008

Mechanical Removal of Obstructive Material

49460   Mechanical removal of obstructive material from gastrostomy, duodenostomy, jejunostomy, gastro-jejunostomy, or cecostomy (or other colonic) tube, any method, under fluoroscopic guidance including contrast injection(s), if performed, image documentation and report

➔ *CPT Changes: An Insider's View* 2008

(Do not report 49460 in conjunction with 49450-49452, 49465)

Other

49465   Contrast injection(s) for radiological evaluation of existing gastrostomy, duodenostomy, jejunostomy, gastro-jejunostomy, or cecostomy (or other colonic) tube, from a percutaneous approach including image documentation and report

➔ *CPT Changes: An Insider's View* 2008

(Do not report 49465 in conjunction with 49450-49460)

Repair

Hernioplasty, Herniorrhaphy, Herniotomy

The hernia repair codes in this section are categorized primarily by the type of hernia (inguinal, femoral, incisional, etc).

Some types of hernias are further categorized as "initial" or "recurrent" based on whether or not the hernia has required previous repair(s).

Additional variables accounted for by some of the codes include patient age and clinical presentation (reducible vs. incarcerated or strangulated).

With the exception of the incisional hernia repairs (see 49560-49566) the use of mesh or other prostheses is not separately reported.

The excision/repair of strangulated organs or structures such as testicle(s), intestine, ovaries are reported by using the appropriate code for the excision/repair (eg, 44120, 54520, and 58940) in addition to the appropriate code for the repair of the strangulated hernia.

(For reduction and repair of intra-abdominal hernia, use 44050)

(For debridement of abdominal wall, see 11042, 11043)

(Codes 49491-49651 are unilateral procedures. To report bilateral procedure, report modifier 50 with the appropriate procedure code)

49491   Repair, initial inguinal hernia, preterm infant (younger than 37 weeks gestation at birth), performed from birth up to 50 weeks postconception age, with or without hydrocelectomy; reducible

➔ *CPT Assistant* Mar 04:2, Jun 08:3; *CPT Changes: An Insider's View* 2002

49492   incarcerated or strangulated

➔ *CPT Assistant* Mar 04:2, Jun 08:3; *CPT Changes: An Insider's View* 2002

(Do not report modifier 63 in conjunction with 49491, 49492)

(Postconception age equals gestational age at birth plus age of infant in weeks at the time of the hernia repair. Initial inguinal hernia repairs that are performed on preterm infants who are older than 50 weeks postconception age and younger than age 6 months at the time of surgery, should be reported using codes 49495, 49496)

49495   Repair, initial inguinal hernia, full term infant younger than age 6 months, or preterm infant older than 50 weeks postconception age and younger than age 6 months at the time of surgery, with or without hydrocelectomy; reducible

➲ *CPT Assistant* Winter 93:6, Winter 94:13, Jan 04:27, Mar 04:10, May 04:14, Nov 07:9, Jun 08:3; *CPT Changes: An Insider's View* 2002

49496   incarcerated or strangulated

➲ *CPT Assistant* Winter 93:6, Winter 94:13, Jan 04:27, Mar 04:10, May 04:14, Jun 08:3

(Do not report modifier 63 in conjunction with 49495, 49496)

(Postconception age equals gestational age at birth plus age in weeks at the time of the hernia repair. Initial inguinal hernia repairs that are performed on preterm infants who are younger than or up to 50 weeks postconception age but younger than 6 months of age since birth, should be reported using codes 49491, 49492. Inguinal hernia repairs on infants age 6 months to younger than 5 years should be reported using codes 49500-49501)

49500   Repair initial inguinal hernia, age 6 months to younger than 5 years, with or without hydrocelectomy; reducible

➲ *CPT Assistant* Winter 94:13, Jan 04:27, Mar 04:10, Nov 07:9, Jun 08:3; *CPT Changes: An Insider's View* 2002

49501   incarcerated or strangulated

➲ *CPT Assistant* Winter 94:13, Jan 04:27, Mar 04:12, Jun 08:3; *CPT Changes: An Insider's View* 2002

49505   Repair initial inguinal hernia, age 5 years or older; reducible

➲ *CPT Assistant* Winter 94:13, Sep 00:10, Jan 04:27, Mar 04:12, Jun 08:3

49507   incarcerated or strangulated

➲ *CPT Assistant* Winter 94:13, Jan 04:27, Mar 04:10, Jun 08:3

(For inguinal hernia repair, with simple orchiectomy, see 49505 or 49507 and 54520)

(For inguinal hernia repair, with excision of hydrocele or spermatocele, see 49505 or 49507 and 54840 or 55040)

49520   Repair recurrent inguinal hernia, any age; reducible

➲ *CPT Assistant* Winter 94:13, Sep 03:3, Jan 04:27, Mar 04:3, Jun 08:3

49521   incarcerated or strangulated

➲ *CPT Assistant* Winter 94:13, Jan 04:27, Mar 04:10, Jun 08:3

49525   Repair inguinal hernia, sliding, any age

➲ *CPT Assistant* Winter 94:14, Jan 04:27, Mar 04:10, Nov 07:9, Jun 08:3

(For incarcerated or strangulated inguinal hernia repair, see 49496, 49501, 49507, 49521)

49540   Repair lumbar hernia

➲ *CPT Assistant* Winter 94:14, Jun 08:3

49550   Repair initial femoral hernia, any age; reducible

➲ *CPT Assistant* Winter 94:14, Jun 08:3

49553   incarcerated or strangulated

➲ *CPT Assistant* Winter 94:14, Jun 08:3

49555   Repair recurrent femoral hernia; reducible

➲ *CPT Assistant* Winter 94:14, Jun 08:3

49557   incarcerated or strangulated

➲ *CPT Assistant* Winter 94:14, Jun 08:3

49560   Repair initial incisional or ventral hernia; reducible

➲ *CPT Assistant* Winter 93:6, Winter 94:14, Nov 97:19, Jun 08:3

49561   incarcerated or strangulated

➲ *CPT Assistant* Winter 94:14, Jun 08:3

49565   Repair recurrent incisional or ventral hernia; reducible

➲ *CPT Assistant* Winter 94:14, Nov 97:19, Jun 08:3

49566   incarcerated or strangulated

➲ *CPT Assistant* Winter 94:14, Jun 08:3

+ 49568   Implantation of mesh or other prosthesis for open incisional or ventral hernia repair or mesh for closure of debridement for necrotizing soft tissue infection (List separately in addition to code for the incisional or ventral hernia repair)

➲ *CPT Assistant* Winter 94:14, Nov 97:19, Sep 01:11, Nov 05:15, Nov 07:9, Jun 08:3; *CPT Changes: An Insider's View* 2008, 2009

(Use 49568 in conjunction with 11004-11006, 49560-49566)

49570   Repair epigastric hernia (eg, preperitoneal fat); reducible (separate procedure)

➲ *CPT Assistant* Winter 94:15, Jun 08:3

49572   incarcerated or strangulated

➲ *CPT Assistant* Winter 94:15, Jun 08:3

49580   Repair umbilical hernia, younger than age 5 years; reducible

➲ *CPT Assistant* Winter 94:15, Jun 08:3

49582   incarcerated or strangulated

➲ *CPT Assistant* Winter 94:15, Jun 08:3

49585   Repair umbilical hernia, age 5 years or older; reducible

➲ *CPT Assistant* Winter 94:15

49587   incarcerated or strangulated

➲ *CPT Assistant* Winter 94:15

49590   Repair spigelian hernia

➲ *CPT Assistant* Winter 94:15

49600 Repair of small omphalocele, with primary closure
➜ *CPT Assistant* Winter 94:15

(Do not report modifier 63 in conjunction with 49600)

49605 Repair of large omphalocele or gastroschisis; with or without prosthesis
➜ *CPT Assistant* Winter 94:15

49606 with removal of prosthesis, final reduction and closure, in operating room
➜ *CPT Assistant* Winter 94:15

(Do not report modifier 63 in conjunction with 49605, 49606)

49610 Repair of omphalocele (Gross type operation); first stage
➜ *CPT Assistant* Winter 94:15

49611 second stage
➜ *CPT Assistant* Winter 94:15

(Do not report modifier 63 in conjunction with 49610, 49611)

(For diaphragmatic or hiatal hernia repair, see 39502-39541)

(For surgical repair of omentum, use 49999)

Laparoscopy

Surgical laparoscopy always includes diagnostic laparoscopy. To report a diagnostic laparoscopy (peritoneoscopy) (separate procedure), use 49320.

49650 Laparoscopy, surgical; repair initial inguinal hernia
➜ *CPT Assistant* Nov 99:24, Mar 00:9; *CPT Changes: An Insider's View* 2000

49651 repair recurrent inguinal hernia
➜ *CPT Assistant* Nov 99:24, Mar 00:9; *CPT Changes: An Insider's View* 2000

49652 Laparoscopy, surgical, repair, ventral, umbilical, spigelian or epigastric hernia (includes mesh insertion, when performed); reducible
➜ *CPT Changes: An Insider's View* 2009

(Do not report 49652 in conjunction with 44180, 49568)

49653 incarcerated or strangulated
➜ *CPT Changes: An Insider's View* 2009

(Do not report 49653 in conjunction with 44180, 49568)

49654 Laparoscopy, surgical, repair, incisional hernia (includes mesh insertion, when performed); reducible
➜ *CPT Changes: An Insider's View* 2009

(Do not report 49654 in conjunction with 44180, 49568)

49655 incarcerated or strangulated
➜ *CPT Changes: An Insider's View* 2009

(Do not report 49655 in conjunction with 44180, 49568)

49656 Laparoscopy, surgical, repair, recurrent incisional hernia (includes mesh insertion, when performed); reducible
➜ *CPT Changes: An Insider's View* 2009

(Do not report 49656 in conjunction with 44180, 49568)

49657 incarcerated or strangulated
➜ *CPT Changes: An Insider's View* 2009

(Do not report 49657 in conjunction with 44180, 49568)

49659 Unlisted laparoscopy procedure, hernioplasty, herniorrhaphy, herniotomy
➜ *CPT Assistant* Nov 99:25, Mar 00:9, Sep 01:11, Nov 05:15, Feb 06:16, Jan 09:7; *CPT Changes: An Insider's View* 2000

Suture

49900 Suture, secondary, of abdominal wall for evisceration or dehiscence

(For suture of ruptured diaphragm, see 39540, 39541)

(For debridement of abdominal wall, see 11042, 11043)

Other Procedures

49904 Omental flap, extra-abdominal (eg, for reconstruction of sternal and chest wall defects)
➜ *CPT Changes: An Insider's View* 2003

(Code 49904 includes harvest and transfer. If a second surgeon harvests the omental flap, then the 2 surgeons should code 49904 as co-surgeons, using modifier 62)

+ 49905 Omental flap, intra-abdominal (List separately in addition to code for primary procedure)
➜ *CPT Assistant* Nov 00:11; *CPT Changes: An Insider's View* 2003

(Do not report 49905 in conjunction with 44700)

49906 Free omental flap with microvascular anastomosis
➜ *CPT Assistant* Nov 96:8, Apr 97:8, Nov 98:16

(Do not report code 69990 in addition to 49906)

49999 Unlisted procedure, abdomen, peritoneum and omentum
➜ *CPT Assistant* Jul 06:19, Sep 07:10, Nov 07:9, Aug 08:7
➜ *Clinical Examples in Radiology* Fall 07:1,2

Urinary System (50010-53899) 249

The following is a listing of headings and subheadings that appear within the Urinary System section of the CPT codebook. The subheadings or subsections denoted with asterisks (*) below have special instructions unique to that section. Where these are indicated, special "notes" or guidelines will be presented preceding those procedural terminology listings referring to that subsection specifically.

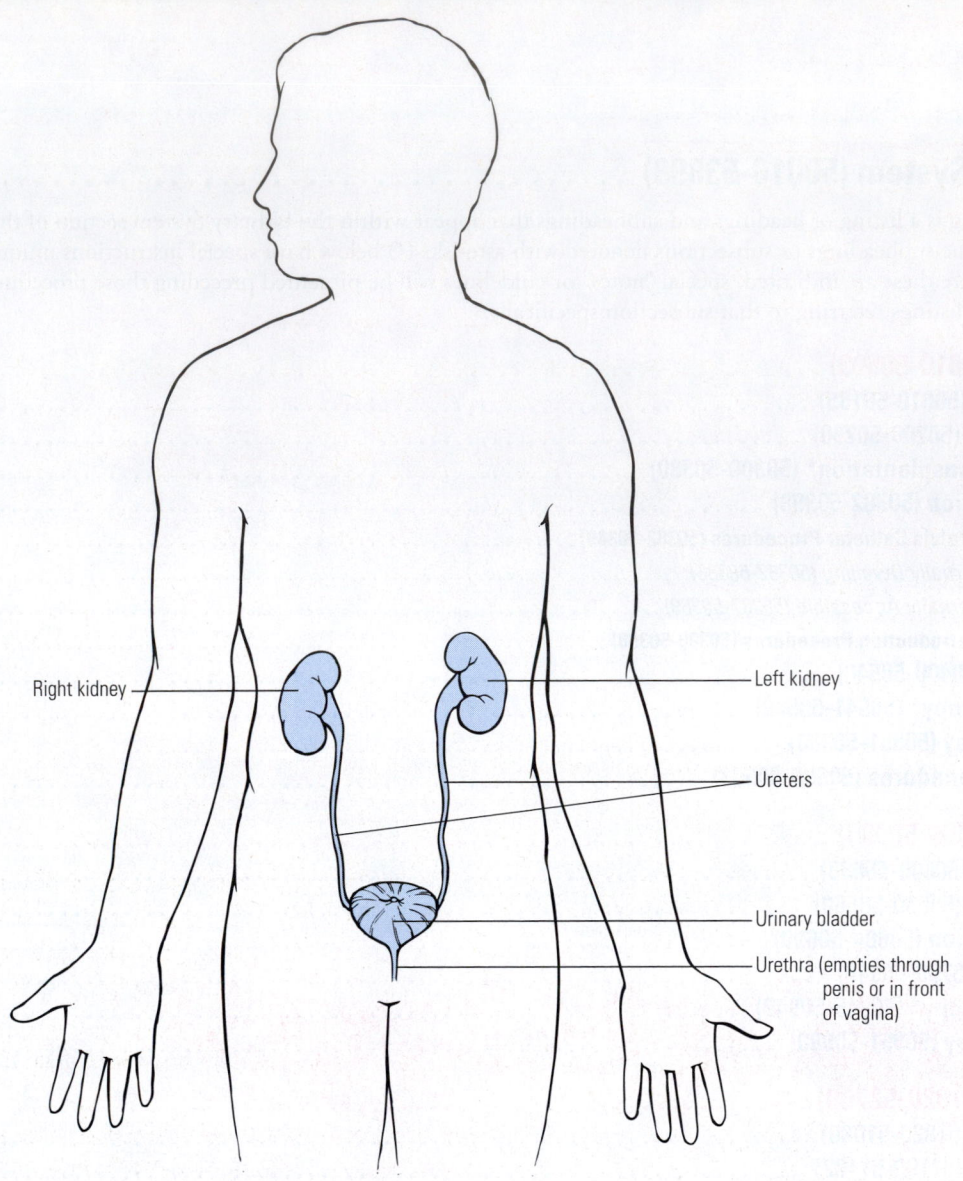

Right kidney

Left kidney

Ureters

Urinary bladder

Urethra (empties through
penis or in front
of vagina)

Urinary System

(For provision of chemotherapeutic agents, report both the specific service in addition to code(s) for the specific substance(s) or drug(s) provided)

Kidney

Incision

(For retroperitoneal exploration, abscess, tumor, or cyst, see 49010, 49060, 49203-49205)

50010   Renal exploration, not necessitating other specific procedures

(For laparoscopic ablation of renal mass lesion(s), use 50542)

50020   Drainage of perirenal or renal abscess; open
➜ *CPT Assistant* Nov 97:19, Oct 01:8

Drainage of Renal Abscess
50020

An incision is made to the abscess cavity and the site is irrigated and drained.

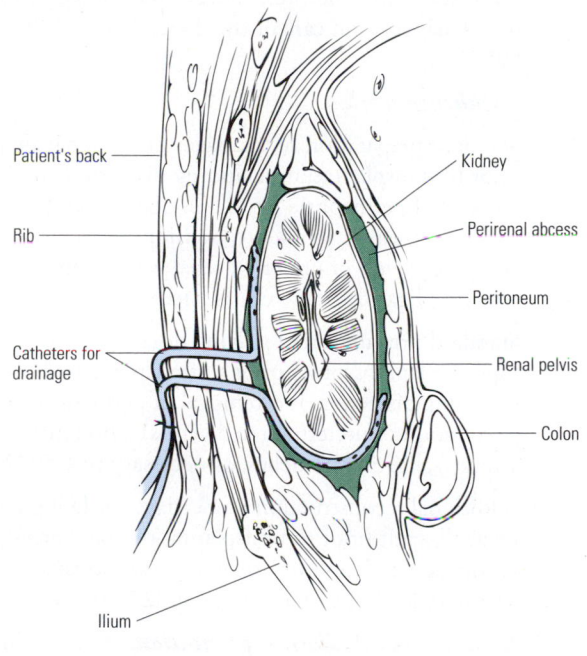

Patient's back
Rib
Catheters for drainage
Ilium
Kidney
Perirenal abcess
Peritoneum
Renal pelvis
Colon

⊙ **50021**   percutaneous
➜ *CPT Assistant* Nov 97:19, Mar 98:8, Oct 01:8

(For radiological supervision and interpretation, use 75989)

50040   Nephrostomy, nephrotomy with drainage
➜ *CPT Assistant* Spring 93:35, Oct 01:8

50045   Nephrotomy, with exploration
➜ *CPT Assistant* Oct 01:8

(For renal endoscopy performed in conjunction with this procedure, see 50570-50580)

50060   Nephrolithotomy; removal of calculus
➜ *CPT Assistant* Oct 01:8

Nephrolithotomy With Calculus Removal
50060-50075

A kidney stone (calculus) is removed by an incision in the kidney. Use 50070 if complicated by a congenital kidney abnormality.

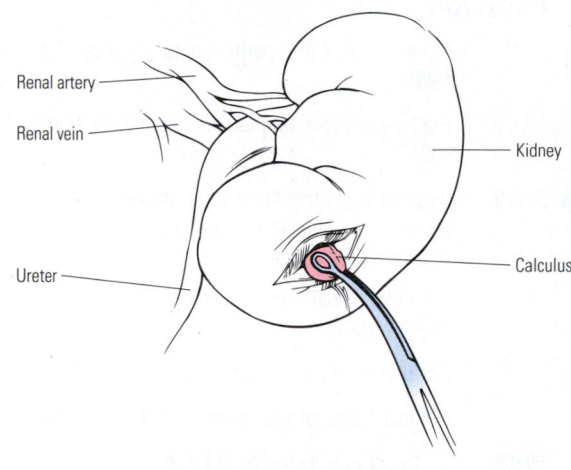

Renal artery
Renal vein
Ureter
Kidney
Calculus

50065   secondary surgical operation for calculus
➜ *CPT Assistant* Oct 01:8

50070   complicated by congenital kidney abnormality
➜ *CPT Assistant* Oct 01:8

50075   removal of large staghorn calculus filling renal pelvis and calyces (including anatrophic pyelolithotomy)
➜ *CPT Assistant* Oct 01:8

50080   Percutaneous nephrostolithotomy or pyelostolithotomy, with or without dilation, endoscopy, lithotripsy, stenting, or basket extraction; up to 2 cm
➜ *CPT Assistant* Oct 01:8, Dec 08:7

50081   over 2 cm
➜ *CPT Assistant* Oct 01:8, Dec 08:7

(For establishment of nephrostomy without nephrostolithotomy, see 50040, 50395, 52334)

(For fluoroscopic guidance, see 76000, 76001)

50100   Transection or repositioning of aberrant renal vessels (separate procedure)
➜ *CPT Assistant* Oct 01:8

50120   Pyelotomy; with exploration
➜ *CPT Assistant* Oct 01:8

(For renal endoscopy performed in conjunction with this procedure, see 50570-50580)

50125   with drainage, pyelostomy
➜ *CPT Assistant* Oct 01:8

50130   with removal of calculus (pyelolithotomy, pelviolithotomy, including coagulum pyelolithotomy)
→ *CPT Assistant* Oct 01:8

50135   complicated (eg, secondary operation, congenital kidney abnormality)
→ *CPT Assistant* Oct 01:8

(For supply of anticarcinogenic agents, use 99070 in addition to code for primary procedure)

Excision

(For excision of retroperitoneal tumor or cyst, see 49203-49205)

(For laparoscopic ablation of renal mass lesion(s), use 50542)

⊙▲ **50200**   Renal biopsy; percutaneous, by trocar or needle
→ *CPT Assistant* Fall 93:13, Oct 01:8; *CPT Changes: An Insider's View* 2010

(For radiological supervision and interpretation, see 76942, 77002, 77012, 77021)

(For fine needle aspiration, use 10022)

(For evaluation of fine needle aspirate, see 88172, 88173)

50205   by surgical exposure of kidney
→ *CPT Assistant* Oct 01:8

50220   Nephrectomy, including partial ureterectomy, any open approach including rib resection;
→ *CPT Assistant* Oct 01:8, Nov 02:3, Aug 08:7; *CPT Changes: An Insider's View* 2002

50225   complicated because of previous surgery on same kidney
→ *CPT Assistant* Oct 01:8, Nov 02:3

50230   radical, with regional lymphadenectomy and/or vena caval thrombectomy
→ *CPT Assistant* Oct 01:8, Nov 02:3

(When vena caval resection with reconstruction is necessary, use 37799)

50234   Nephrectomy with total ureterectomy and bladder cuff; through same incision
→ *CPT Assistant* Oct 01:8, Nov 02:3

50236   through separate incision
→ *CPT Assistant* Oct 01:8, Nov 02:3

50240   Nephrectomy, partial
→ *CPT Assistant* Oct 01:8, Nov 02:3, Jan 03:20, Apr 05:10, 12, Aug 08:7

(For laparoscopic partial nephrectomy, use 50543)

50250   Ablation, open, 1 or more renal mass lesion(s), cryosurgical, including intraoperative ultrasound, if performed
→ *CPT Changes: An Insider's View* 2006

(For laparoscopic ablation of renal mass lesions, use 50542)

(For cryoablation of renal tumors, use 50593)

50280   Excision or unroofing of cyst(s) of kidney
→ *CPT Assistant* Nov 99:25, Oct 01:8; *CPT Changes: An Insider's View* 2000

(For laparoscopic ablation of renal cysts, use 50541)

50290   Excision of perinephric cyst
→ *CPT Assistant* Oct 01:8

Renal Transplantation

Renal *auto*transplantation includes reimplantation of the autograft as the primary procedure, along with secondary extra-corporeal procedure(s) (eg, partial nephrectomy, nephrolithotomy) reported with modifier 51 (see 50380 and applicable secondary procedure(s)).

Renal *allo*transplantation involves three distinct components of physician work:

1. *Cadaver donor nephrectomy, unilateral or bilateral*, which includes harvesting the graft(s) and cold preservation of the graft(s) (perfusing with cold preservation solution and cold maintenance) (use 50300). *Living donor nephrectomy*, which includes harvesting the graft, cold preservation of the graft (perfusing with cold preservation solution and cold maintenance), and care of the donor (see 50320, 50547).

2. *Backbench work*:

   Standard preparation of a cadaver donor renal allograft prior to transplantation including dissection and removal of perinephric fat, diaphragmatic and retroperitoneal attachments; excision of adrenal gland; and preparation of ureter(s), renal vein(s), and renal artery(s), ligating branches, as necessary (use 50323).

   Standard preparation of a living donor renal allograft (open or laparoscopic) prior to transplantation including dissection and removal of perinephric fat and preparation of ureter(s), renal vein(s), and renal artery(s), ligating branches, as necessary (use 50325).

   Additional reconstruction of a cadaver or living donor renal allograft prior to transplantation may include venous, arterial, and/or ureteral anastomosis(es) necessary for implantation (see 50327-50329).

3. *Recipient renal allotransplantation*, which includes transplantation of the allograft (with or without recipient nephrectomy) and care of the recipient (see 50360, 50365).

(For dialysis, see 90935-90999)

(For laparoscopic donor nephrectomy, use 50547)

(For laparoscopic drainage of lymphocele to peritoneal cavity, use 49323)

⊙=Moderate sedation   ✛=Add-on code   ✗=FDA approval pending   #=Resequenced code   ⊙➡=See p xiii for details

50300   Donor nephrectomy (including cold preservation); from cadaver donor, unilateral or bilateral

➔ *CPT Assistant* Nov 99:25, Apr 05:10-12; *CPT Changes: An Insider's View* 2000, 2005

50320   open, from living donor

➔ *CPT Assistant* Nov 99:25, May 00:4; *CPT Changes: An Insider's View* 2000, 2005

50323   Backbench standard preparation of cadaver donor renal allograft prior to transplantation, including dissection and removal of perinephric fat, diaphragmatic and retroperitoneal attachments, excision of adrenal gland, and preparation of ureter(s), renal vein(s), and renal artery(s), ligating branches, as necessary

➔ *CPT Assistant* Apr 05:10-11; *CPT Changes: An Insider's View* 2005

(Do not report 50323 in conjunction with 60540, 60545)

50325   Backbench standard preparation of living donor renal allograft (open or laparoscopic) prior to transplantation, including dissection and removal of perinephric fat and preparation of ureter(s), renal vein(s), and renal artery(s), ligating branches, as necessary

➔ *CPT Changes: An Insider's View* 2005

50327   Backbench reconstruction of cadaver or living donor renal allograft prior to transplantation; venous anastomosis, each

➔ *CPT Changes: An Insider's View* 2005

50328   arterial anastomosis, each

➔ *CPT Changes: An Insider's View* 2005

50329   ureteral anastomosis, each

➔ *CPT Changes: An Insider's View* 2005

50340   Recipient nephrectomy (separate procedure)

(For bilateral procedure, report 50340 with modifier 50)

50360   Renal allotransplantation, implantation of graft; without recipient nephrectomy

➔ *CPT Changes: An Insider's View* 2005

50365   with recipient nephrectomy

➔ *CPT Assistant* Apr 05:10-11

(For bilateral procedure, report 50365 with modifier 50)

50370   Removal of transplanted renal allograft

50380   Renal autotransplantation, reimplantation of kidney

➔ *CPT Assistant* Apr 05:10, 12

(For renal autotransplantation extra-corporeal [bench] surgery, use autotransplantation as the primary procedure and report secondary procedure[s] [eg, partial nephrectomy, nephrolithotomy] with modifier 51)

Introduction

Renal Pelvis Catheter Procedures

Internally Dwelling

⊙ **50382**   Removal (via snare/capture) and replacement of internally dwelling ureteral stent via percutaneous approach, including radiological supervision and interpretation

➔ *CPT Changes: An Insider's View* 2006

➔ *Clinical Examples in Radiology* Winter 06:15, Spring 08:5

(For bilateral procedure, use modifier 50)

(For removal and replacement of an internally dwelling ureteral stent via a transurethral approach, use 50385)

⊙ **50384**   Removal (via snare/capture) of internally dwelling ureteral stent via percutaneous approach, including radiological supervision and interpretation

➔ *CPT Changes: An Insider's View* 2006

➔ *Clinical Examples in Radiology* Winter 06:16, Spring 08:5

(For bilateral procedure, use modifier 50)

(Do not report 50382, 50384 in conjunction with 50395)

(For removal of an internally dwelling ureteral stent via a transurethral approach, use 50386)

⊙ **50385**   Removal (via snare/capture) and replacement of internally dwelling ureteral stent via transurethral approach, without use of cystoscopy, including radiological supervision and interpretation

➔ *CPT Changes: An Insider's View* 2008

➔ *Clinical Examples in Radiology* Spring 08:5

⊙ **50386**   Removal (via snare/capture) of internally dwelling ureteral stent via transurethral approach, without use of cystoscopy, including radiological supervision and interpretation

➔ *CPT Changes: An Insider's View* 2008

➔ *Clinical Examples in Radiology* Spring 08:4

Externally Accessible

⊙ **50387**   Removal and replacement of externally accessible transnephric ureteral stent (eg, external/internal stent) requiring fluoroscopic guidance, including radiological supervision and interpretation

➔ *CPT Changes: An Insider's View* 2006

➔ *Clinical Examples in Radiology* Winter 06:16, Spring 08:5

(For bilateral procedure, use modifier 50)

(For removal and replacement of externally accessible ureteral stent via ureterostomy or ilieal conduit, use 50688)

(For removal without replacement of an externally accessible ureteral stent not requiring fluoroscopic guidance, see **Evaluation and Management** services codes)

50389   Removal of nephrostomy tube, requiring fluoroscopic guidance (eg, with concurrent indwelling ureteral stent)

→ *CPT Changes: An Insider's View* 2006

→ *Clinical Examples in Radiology* Winter 06:16

(Removal of nephrostomy tube not requiring fluoroscopic guidance is considered inherent to E/M services. Report the appropriate level of E/M service provided)

Other Introduction Procedures

50390   Aspiration and/or injection of renal cyst or pelvis by needle, percutaneous

→ *CPT Assistant* Fall 93:14, Dec 97:7, Oct 01:8, Oct 05:18, Oct 08:8

(For radiological supervision and interpretation, see 74425, 74470, 76942, 77002, 77012, 77021)

(For evaluation of fine needle aspirate, see 88172, 88173)

50391   Instillation(s) of therapeutic agent into renal pelvis and/or ureter through established nephrostomy, pyelostomy or ureterostomy tube (eg, anticarcinogenic or antifungal agent)

→ *CPT Assistant* Oct 05:18; *CPT Changes: An Insider's View* 2005

50392   Introduction of intracatheter or catheter into renal pelvis for drainage and/or injection, percutaneous

→ *CPT Assistant* Dec 97:7, Oct 01:8, Oct 05:18, Oct 08:8

(For radiological supervision and interpretation, see 74475, 76942, 77012)

Introduction of Catheter Into Renal Pelvis
50392

The physician inserts a catheter into the renal pelvis in order to drain urine and/or give an injection.

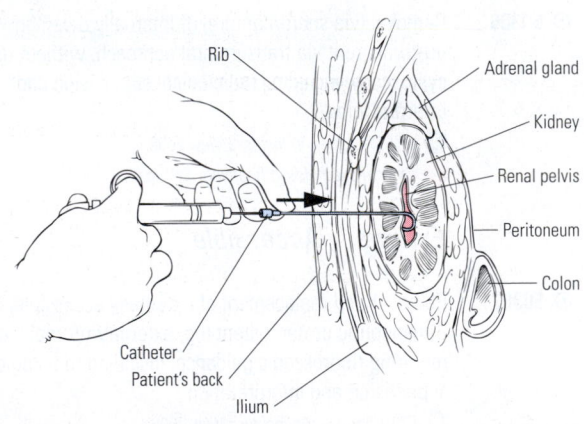

50393   Introduction of ureteral catheter or stent into ureter through renal pelvis for drainage and/or injection, percutaneous

→ *CPT Assistant* Fall 93:14, Oct 01:8, Oct 05:18

→ *Clinical Examples in Radiology* Summer 06:1-3

(For radiological supervision and interpretation, see 74480, 76942, 77002, 77012)

50394   Injection procedure for pyelography (as nephrostogram, pyelostogram, antegrade pyeloureterograms) through nephrostomy or pyelostomy tube, or indwelling ureteral catheter

→ *CPT Assistant* Fall 93:15, Dec 97:7, Oct 01:8, Oct 05:18

→ *Clinical Examples in Radiology* Summer 06:1-3

(For radiological supervision and interpretation, use 74425)

50395   Introduction of guide into renal pelvis and/or ureter with dilation to establish nephrostomy tract, percutaneous

→ *CPT Assistant* Oct 01:8, Oct 05:18, Sep 06:1, Dec 08:7, Jan 09:7

(For radiological supervision and interpretation, see 74475, 74480, 74485)

(For nephrostolithotomy, see 50080, 50081)

(For retrograde percutaneous nephrostomy, use 52334)

(For endoscopic surgery, see 50551-50561)

50396   Manometric studies through nephrostomy or pyelostomy tube, or indwelling ureteral catheter

→ *CPT Assistant* Fall 93:16, Dec 97:7, Oct 01:8

(For radiological supervision and interpretation, see 74425, 74475, 74480)

50398   Change of nephrostomy or pyelostomy tube

→ *CPT Assistant* Oct 01:8

(For radiological supervision and interpretation, use 75984)

Repair

50400   Pyeloplasty (Foley Y-pyeloplasty), plastic operation on renal pelvis, with or without plastic operation on ureter, nephropexy, nephrostomy, pyelostomy, or ureteral splinting; simple

→ *CPT Assistant* Nov 99:25, May 00:4, Oct 01:8; *CPT Changes: An Insider's View* 2000

50405   complicated (congenital kidney abnormality, secondary pyeloplasty, solitary kidney, calycoplasty)

→ *CPT Assistant* Nov 99:25, May 00:4, Oct 01:8; *CPT Changes: An Insider's View* 2000

(For laparoscopic approach, use 50544)

50500   Nephrorrhaphy, suture of kidney wound or injury

50520   Closure of nephrocutaneous or pyelocutaneous fistula

50525   Closure of nephrovisceral fistula (eg, renocolic), including visceral repair; abdominal approach

50526   thoracic approach

50540   Symphysiotomy for horseshoe kidney with or without pyeloplasty and/or other plastic procedure, unilateral or bilateral (1 operation)

Laparoscopy

Surgical laparoscopy always includes diagnostic laparoscopy. To report a diagnostic laparoscopy (peritoneoscopy) (separate procedure), use 49320.

50541   Laparoscopy, surgical; ablation of renal cysts

➔ *CPT Assistant* Nov 99:25, May 00:4, Oct 01:8, Nov 02:3, Jan 03:20; *CPT Changes: An Insider's View* 2000

50542   ablation of renal mass lesion(s)

➔ *CPT Assistant* Nov 02:3, Jan 03:21, Aug 04:12; *CPT Changes: An Insider's View* 2003

(For open procedure, see 50220-50240)

(For cryosurgical ablation, see 50250, 50593)

50543   partial nephrectomy

➔ *CPT Assistant* Nov 02:3, Jan 03:21; *CPT Changes: An Insider's View* 2003

(For open procedure, use 50240)

50544   pyeloplasty

➔ *CPT Assistant* Nov 99:25, May 00:4, Oct 01:8; *CPT Changes: An Insider's View* 2000

50545   radical nephrectomy (includes removal of Gerota's fascia and surrounding fatty tissue, removal of regional lymph nodes, and adrenalectomy)

➔ *CPT Assistant* Oct 01:8; *CPT Changes: An Insider's View* 2001

(For open procedure, use 50230)

Laparoscopic Radical Nephrectomy
50545

Radical nephrectomy (includes removal of Gerota's fascia and surrounding fatty tissue, removal of regional lymph nodes, and adrenalectomy)

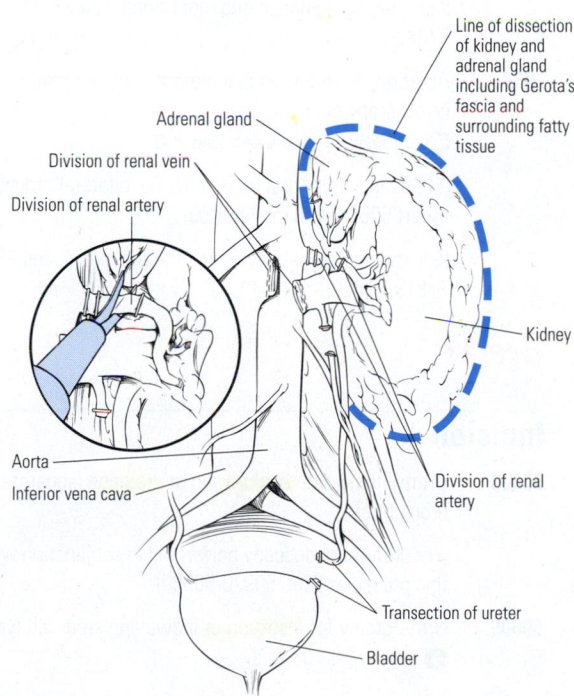

50546   nephrectomy, including partial ureterectomy

➔ *CPT Assistant* Nov 99:25, May 00:4, Oct 01:8; *CPT Changes: An Insider's View* 2000, 2001

Laparoscopic Nephrectomy
50546

A kidney is dissected and removed under laparoscopic guidance.

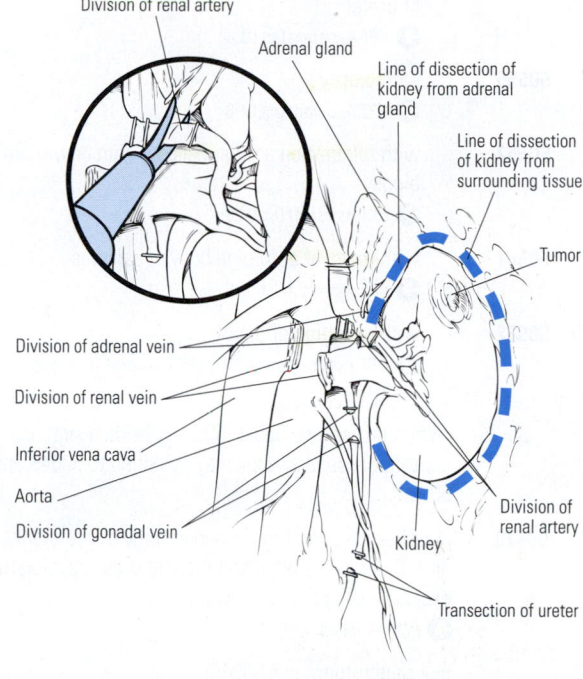

50547   donor nephrectomy (including cold preservation), from living donor

➔ *CPT Assistant* Nov 99:25, May 00:4, Oct 01:8; *CPT Changes: An Insider's View* 2000, 2005

(For open procedure, use 50320)

(For backbench renal allograft standard preparation prior to transplantation, use 50325)

(For backbench renal allograft reconstruction prior to transplantation, see 50327-50329)

50548   nephrectomy with total ureterectomy

➔ *CPT Assistant* Nov 99:25, May 00:4, Oct 01:8; *CPT Changes: An Insider's View* 2000, 2001

(For open procedure, see 50234, 50236)

50549   Unlisted laparoscopy procedure, renal

➔ *CPT Assistant* Nov 99:25, Mar 00:9, May 00:4, Feb 06:16; *CPT Changes: An Insider's View* 2000

(For laparoscopic drainage of lymphocele to peritoneal cavity, use 49323)

Endoscopy

(For supplies and materials, use 99070)

50551   Renal endoscopy through established nephrostomy or pyelostomy, with or without irrigation, instillation, or ureteropyelography, exclusive of radiologic service;
➲ *CPT Assistant* Oct 01:8, Jan 03:21

50553   with ureteral catheterization, with or without dilation of ureter .
➲ *CPT Assistant* Oct 01:8

50555   with biopsy
➲ *CPT Assistant* Oct 01:8

50557   with fulguration and/or incision, with or without biopsy
➲ *CPT Assistant* Oct 01:8

50561   with removal of foreign body or calculus
➲ *CPT Assistant* Oct 01:8, Jan 03:21

50562   with resection of tumor
➲ *CPT Assistant* Jan 03:21; *CPT Changes: An Insider's View* 2003

(When procedures 50570-50580 provide a significant identifiable service, they may be added to 50045 and 50120)

50570   Renal endoscopy through nephrotomy or pyelotomy, with or without irrigation, instillation, or ureteropyelography, exclusive of radiologic service;
➲ *CPT Assistant* Oct 01:8

(For nephrotomy, use 50045)

(For pyelotomy, use 50120)

50572   with ureteral catheterization, with or without dilation of ureter
➲ *CPT Assistant* Oct 01:8

50574   with biopsy
➲ *CPT Assistant* Oct 01:8

50575   with endopyelotomy (includes cystoscopy, ureteroscopy, dilation of ureter and ureteral pelvic junction, incision of ureteral pelvic junction and insertion of endopyelotomy stent)
➲ *CPT Assistant* Oct 01:8, Aug 02:11

50576   with fulguration and/or incision, with or without biopsy
➲ *CPT Assistant* Oct 01:8

50580   with removal of foreign body or calculus
➲ *CPT Assistant* Oct 01:8

Other Procedures

50590   Lithotripsy, extracorporeal shock wave
➲ *CPT Assistant* Jul 01:11, Aug 01:10, Oct 01:8, Jul 03:16, Aug 03:14

Lithotripsy
50590

The physician breaks up a kidney stone (calculus) by directing shock waves through a liquid surrounding the patient.

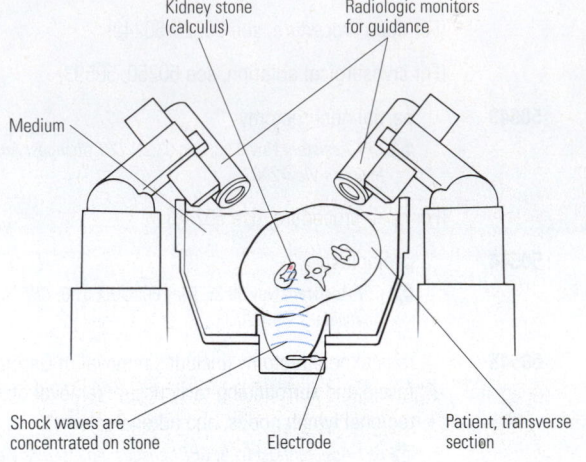

Kidney stone (calculus)
Radiologic monitors for guidance
Medium
Shock waves are concentrated on stone
Electrode
Patient, transverse section

⊙ **50592**   Ablation, 1 or more renal tumor(s), percutaneous, unilateral, radiofrequency
➲ *CPT Changes: An Insider's View* 2006
➲ *Clinical Examples in Radiology* Winter 06:16

(50592 is a unilateral procedure. For bilateral procedure, report 50592 with modifier 50)

(For imaging guidance and monitoring, see 76940, 77013, 77022)

⊙ **50593**   Ablation, renal tumor(s), unilateral, percutaneous, cryotherapy
➲ *CPT Changes: An Insider's View* 2008

(50593 is a unilateral procedure. For bilateral procedure, report 50593 with modifier 50)

(For imaging guidance and monitoring, see codes 76940, 77013, 77022)

Ureter

Incision

50600   Ureterotomy with exploration or drainage (separate procedure)

(For ureteral endoscopy performed in conjunction with this procedure, see 50970-50980)

50605   Ureterotomy for insertion of indwelling stent, all types
➲ *CPT Assistant* Oct 01:8

Indwelling Ureteral Stent
50605

The physician makes an incision in the ureter (ureterotomy) and inserts a stent. For placement using cystourethroscopic technique, use 52332.

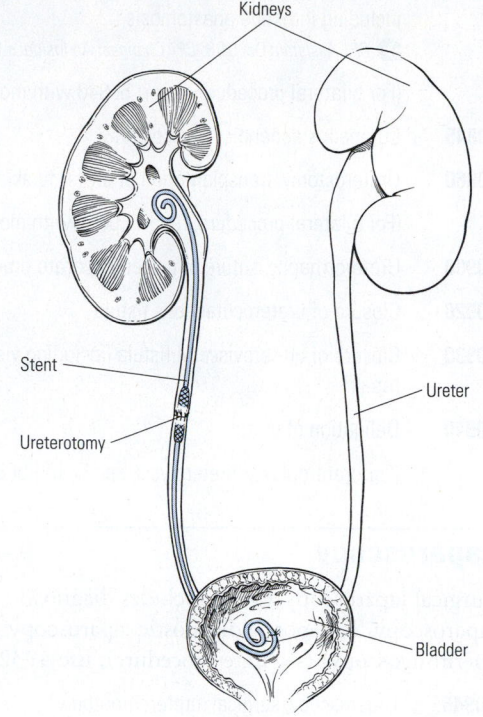

Kidneys

Stent

Ureterotomy

Ureter

Bladder

50610	Ureterolithotomy; upper one-third of ureter
	➔ *CPT Assistant* Nov 99:26, Oct 01:8; *CPT Changes: An Insider's View* 2000
50620	middle one-third of ureter
	➔ *CPT Assistant* Nov 99:26, Oct 01:8; *CPT Changes: An Insider's View* 2000
50630	lower one-third of ureter
	➔ *CPT Assistant* Nov 99:26, Oct 01:8; *CPT Changes: An Insider's View* 2000

(For laparoscopic approach, use 50945)

(For transvesical ureterolithotomy, use 51060)

(For cystotomy with stone basket extraction of ureteral calculus, use 51065)

(For endoscopic extraction or manipulation of ureteral calculus, see 50080, 50081, 50561, 50961, 50980, 52320-52330, 52352, 52353)

Excision

(For ureterocele, see 51535, 52300)

50650   Ureterectomy, with bladder cuff (separate procedure)

50660   Ureterectomy, total, ectopic ureter, combination abdominal, vaginal and/or perineal approach

Introduction

50684   Injection procedure for ureterography or ureteropyelography through ureterostomy or indwelling ureteral catheter

(For radiological supervision and interpretation, use 74425)

50686   Manometric studies through ureterostomy or indwelling ureteral catheter

50688   Change of ureterostomy tube or externally accessible ureteral stent via ileal conduit
➔ *CPT Changes: An Insider's View* 2006
➤ *Clinical Examples in Radiology* Winter 06:20

(If imaging guidance is performed, use 75984)

50690   Injection procedure for visualization of ileal conduit and/or ureteropyelography, exclusive of radiologic service

(For radiological supervision and interpretation, use 74425)

Repair

50700   Ureteroplasty, plastic operation on ureter (eg, stricture)

50715   Ureterolysis, with or without repositioning of ureter for retroperitoneal fibrosis

(For bilateral procedure, report 50715 with modifier 50)

50722   Ureterolysis for ovarian vein syndrome

50725   Ureterolysis for retrocaval ureter, with reanastomosis of upper urinary tract or vena cava

50727   Revision of urinary-cutaneous anastomosis (any type urostomy);

50728   with repair of fascial defect and hernia

50740   Ureteropyelostomy, anastomosis of ureter and renal pelvis
➔ *CPT Assistant* Oct 01:8

50750   Ureterocalycostomy, anastomosis of ureter to renal calyx
➔ *CPT Assistant* Oct 01:8

50760   Ureteroureterostomy
➔ *CPT Assistant* Oct 01:8

50770   Transureteroureterostomy, anastomosis of ureter to contralateral ureter

(Codes 50780-50785 include minor procedures to prevent vesicoureteral reflux)

50780   Ureteroneocystostomy; anastomosis of single ureter to bladder
➔ *CPT Assistant* Oct 01:8

(For bilateral procedure, report 50780 with modifier 50)

(When combined with cystourethroplasty or vesical neck revision, use 51820)

50782   anastomosis of duplicated ureter to bladder
➔ *CPT Assistant* Oct 01:8

50783 with extensive ureteral tailoring
→ *CPT Assistant* Oct 01:8

50785 with vesico-psoas hitch or bladder flap
→ *CPT Assistant* Oct 01:8

(For bilateral procedure, report 50785 with modifier 50)

50800 Ureteroenterostomy, direct anastomosis of ureter to intestine
→ *CPT Assistant* Oct 01:8

(For bilateral procedure, report 50800 with modifier 50)

50810 Ureterosigmoidostomy, with creation of sigmoid bladder and establishment of abdominal or perineal colostomy, including intestine anastomosis
→ *CPT Assistant* Oct 01:8; *CPT Changes: An Insider's View* 2002

50815 Ureterocolon conduit, including intestine anastomosis
→ *CPT Assistant* Oct 01:8

(For bilateral procedure, report 50815 with modifier 50)

50820 Ureteroileal conduit (ileal bladder), including intestine anastomosis (Bricker operation)
→ *CPT Assistant* Oct 01:8; *CPT Changes: An Insider's View* 2002

(For bilateral procedure, report 50820 with modifier 50)

(For combination of 50800-50820 with cystectomy, see 51580-51595)

Ureteroileal Conduit
50820

The ureters are connected to a segment of intestine to divert urine flow through an opening in the skin.

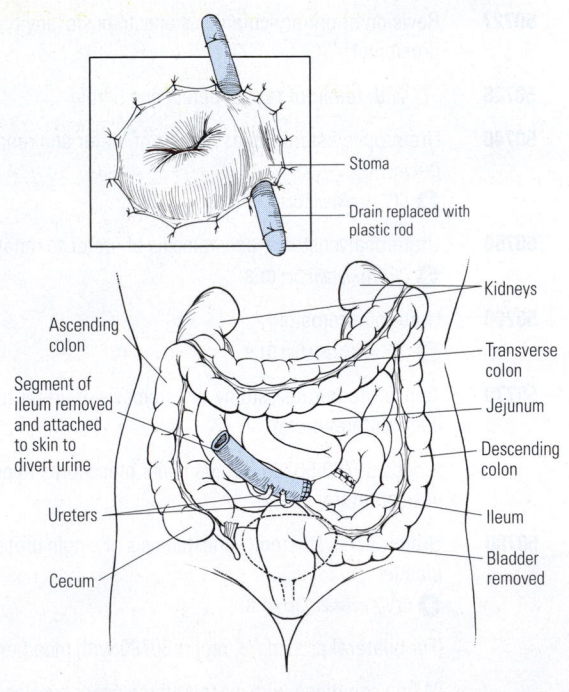

50825 Continent diversion, including intestine anastomosis using any segment of small and/or large intestine (Kock pouch or Camey enterocystoplasty)
→ *CPT Assistant* Oct 01:8; *CPT Changes: An Insider's View* 2002

50830 Urinary undiversion (eg, taking down of ureteroileal conduit, ureterosigmoidostomy or ureteroenterostomy with ureteroureterostomy or ureteroneocystostomy)
→ *CPT Assistant* Oct 01:8

50840 Replacement of all or part of ureter by intestine segment, including intestine anastomosis
→ *CPT Assistant* Oct 01:8; *CPT Changes: An Insider's View* 2002

(For bilateral procedure, report 50840 with modifier 50)

50845 Cutaneous appendico-vesicostomy

50860 Ureterostomy, transplantation of ureter to skin

(For bilateral procedure, report 50860 with modifier 50)

50900 Ureterorrhaphy, suture of ureter (separate procedure)

50920 Closure of ureterocutaneous fistula

50930 Closure of ureterovisceral fistula (including visceral repair)

50940 Deligation of ureter

(For ureteroplasty, ureterolysis, see 50700-50860)

Laparoscopy

Surgical laparoscopy always includes diagnostic laparoscopy. To report a diagnostic laparoscopy (peritoneoscopy) (separate procedure), use 49320.

50945 Laparoscopy, surgical; ureterolithotomy
→ *CPT Assistant* Nov 99:26, May 00:4, Oct 01:8, Sep 06:13; *CPT Changes: An Insider's View* 2000

50947 ureteroneocystostomy with cystoscopy and ureteral stent placement
→ *CPT Assistant* Oct 01:8; *CPT Changes: An Insider's View* 2001

Laparoscopic Ureteroneocystostomy
50947

Ureteroneocystostomy with cystoscopy and ureteral stent placement

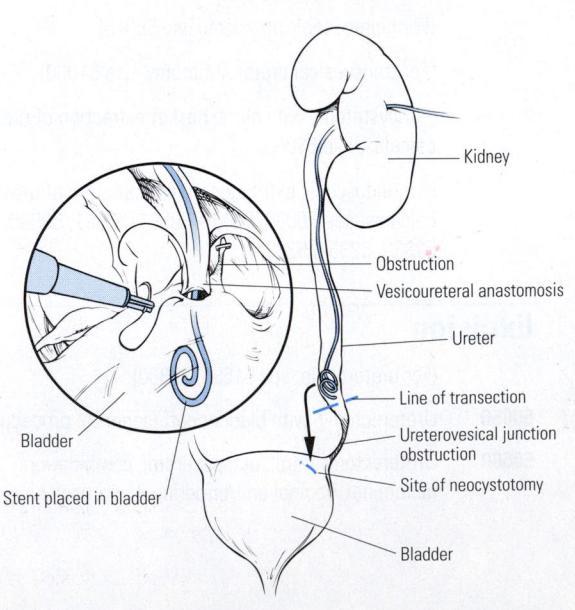

50948   ureteroneocystostomy without cystoscopy and
ureteral stent placement
➔ *CPT Assistant* Oct 01:8; *CPT Changes: An Insider's View*
2001

(For open ureteroneocystostomy, see 50780-50785)

50949   Unlisted laparoscopy procedure, ureter
➔ *CPT Assistant* Oct 01:8; *CPT Changes: An Insider's View* 2001

Endoscopy

50951   Ureteral endoscopy through established ureterostomy,
with or without irrigation, instillation, or
ureteropyelography, exclusive of radiologic service;
➔ *CPT Assistant* Oct 01:8

50953   with ureteral catheterization, with or without dilation
of ureter
➔ *CPT Assistant* Oct 01:8

50955   with biopsy
➔ *CPT Assistant* Oct 01:8

50957   with fulguration and/or incision, with or without
biopsy
➔ *CPT Assistant* Oct 01:8

50961   with removal of foreign body or calculus
➔ *CPT Assistant* Oct 01:8, Mar 07:10, Apr 07:12

(When procedures 50970-50980 provide a significant
identifiable service, they may be added to 50600)

50970   Ureteral endoscopy through ureterotomy, with or without
irrigation, instillation, or ureteropyelography, exclusive of
radiologic service;
➔ *CPT Assistant* Oct 01:8

(For ureterotomy, use 50600)

50972   with ureteral catheterization, with or without dilation
of ureter
➔ *CPT Assistant* Oct 01:8

50974   with biopsy
➔ *CPT Assistant* Oct 01:8

50976   with fulguration and/or incision, with or without
biopsy
➔ *CPT Assistant* Oct 01:8

50980   with removal of foreign body or calculus
➔ *CPT Assistant* Oct 01:8

Bladder

Incision

(51000 has been deleted. To report, use 51100)

(51005 has been deleted. To report, use 51101)

(51010 has been deleted. To report, use 51102)

51020   Cystotomy or cystostomy; with fulguration and/or
insertion of radioactive material

51030   with cryosurgical destruction of intravesical lesion

51040   Cystostomy, cystotomy with drainage

51045   Cystotomy, with insertion of ureteral catheter or stent
(separate procedure)

51050   Cystolithotomy, cystotomy with removal of calculus,
without vesical neck resection

51060   Transvesical ureterolithotomy

51065   Cystotomy, with calculus basket extraction and/or
ultrasonic or electrohydraulic fragmentation of ureteral
calculus
➔ *CPT Changes: An Insider's View* 2002

51080   Drainage of perivesical or prevesical space abscess

Removal

51100   Aspiration of bladder; by needle
➔ *CPT Changes: An Insider's View* 2008

51101   by trocar or intracatheter
➔ *CPT Changes: An Insider's View* 2008

51102   with insertion of suprapubic catheter
➔ *CPT Changes: An Insider's View* 2008

(For imaging guidance, see 76942, 77002, 77012)

Excision

51500   Excision of urachal cyst or sinus, with or without
umbilical hernia repair

51520   Cystotomy; for simple excision of vesical neck (separate
procedure)

51525   for excision of bladder diverticulum, single or multiple
(separate procedure)

51530   for excision of bladder tumor

(For transurethral resection, see 52234-52240, 52305)

51535   Cystotomy for excision, incision, or repair of ureterocele

(For bilateral procedure, report 51535 with modifier 50)

(For transurethral excision, use 52300)

51550   Cystectomy, partial; simple

51555   complicated (eg, postradiation, previous surgery,
difficult location)

51565   Cystectomy, partial, with reimplantation of ureter(s) into
bladder (ureteroneocystostomy)

51570   Cystectomy, complete; (separate procedure)
➔ *CPT Assistant* Spring 93:35

51575   with bilateral pelvic lymphadenectomy, including
external iliac, hypogastric, and obturator nodes
➔ *CPT Assistant* Spring 93:35

51580   Cystectomy, complete, with ureterosigmoidostomy or
ureterocutaneous transplantations;

51585   with bilateral pelvic lymphadenectomy, including
external iliac, hypogastric, and obturator nodes

▲=Revised code   ●=New code   ►◄=Contains new or revised text   ⊘=Modifier 51 exempt

51590   Cystectomy, complete, with ureteroileal conduit or sigmoid bladder, including intestine anastomosis;
➔ *CPT Changes: An Insider's View* 2002

51595   with bilateral pelvic lymphadenectomy, including external iliac, hypogastric, and obturator nodes

51596   Cystectomy, complete, with continent diversion, any open technique, using any segment of small and/or large intestine to construct neobladder
➔ *CPT Changes: An Insider's View* 2002

51597   Pelvic exenteration, complete, for vesical, prostatic or urethral malignancy, with removal of bladder and ureteral transplantations, with or without hysterectomy and/or abdominoperineal resection of rectum and colon and colostomy, or any combination thereof

(For pelvic exenteration for gynecologic malignancy, use 58240)

Introduction

51600   Injection procedure for cystography or voiding urethrocystography

(For radiological supervision and interpretation, see 74430, 74455)

51605   Injection procedure and placement of chain for contrast and/or chain urethrocystography

(For radiological supervision and interpretation, use 74430)

51610   Injection procedure for retrograde urethrocystography

(For radiological supervision and interpretation, use 74450)

51700   Bladder irrigation, simple, lavage and/or instillation

(Codes 51701-51702 are reported only when performed independently. Do not report 51701-51702 when catheter insertion is an inclusive component of another procedure.)

51701   Insertion of non-indwelling bladder catheter (eg, straight catheterization for residual urine)
➔ *CPT Assistant* Jul 06:4, Jan 07:31, Jul 07:1; *CPT Changes: An Insider's View* 2003

51702   Insertion of temporary indwelling bladder catheter; simple (eg, Foley)
➔ *CPT Assistant* Oct 03:10, Jul 06:4, Jan 07:31, Jul 07:1; *CPT Changes: An Insider's View* 2003

51703   complicated (eg, altered anatomy, fractured catheter/balloon)
➔ *CPT Assistant* Jan 07:31; *CPT Changes: An Insider's View* 2003

51705   Change of cystostomy tube; simple
➔ *CPT Assistant* Dec 07:13

51710   complicated
➔ *CPT Assistant* Dec 07:13

(If imaging guidance is performed, use 75984)

51715   Endoscopic injection of implant material into the submucosal tissues of the urethra and/or bladder neck

51720   Bladder instillation of anticarcinogenic agent (including retention time)
➔ *CPT Assistant* Nov 02:11; *CPT Changes: An Insider's View* 2007

Urodynamics

▶The following section (51725-51792) lists procedures that may be used separately or in many and varied combinations.◀

When multiple procedures are performed in the same investigative session, modifier 51 should be employed.

All procedures in this section imply that these services are performed by, or are under the direct supervision of, a physician and that all instruments, equipment, fluids, gases, probes, catheters, technician's fees, medications, gloves, trays, tubing and other sterile supplies be provided by the physician. When the physician only interprets the results and/or operates the equipment, a professional component, modifier 26, should be used to identify physicians' services.

51725   Simple cystometrogram (CMG) (eg, spinal manometer)
➔ *CPT Assistant* Sep 02:6

▲ **51726**   Complex cystometrogram (ie, calibrated electronic equipment);
➔ *CPT Assistant* Sep 02:6; *CPT Changes: An Insider's View* 2010

● **51727**   with urethral pressure profile studies (ie, urethral closure pressure profile), any technique
➔ *CPT Changes: An Insider's View* 2010

● **51728**   with voiding pressure studies (ie, bladder voiding pressure), any technique
➔ *CPT Changes: An Insider's View* 2010

● **51729**   with voiding pressure studies (ie, bladder voiding pressure) and urethral pressure profile studies (ie, urethral closure pressure profile), any technique
➔ *CPT Changes: An Insider's View* 2010

\# ✚ ▲ **51797**   Voiding pressure studies, intra-abdominal (ie, rectal, gastric, intraperitoneal) (List separately in addition to code for primary procedure)
➔ *CPT Assistant* Dec 01:7, Sep 02:6; *CPT Changes: An Insider's View* 2008, 2010

▶(Use 51797 in conjunction with 51728, 51729)◀

51736   Simple uroflowmetry (UFR) (eg, stop-watch flow rate, mechanical uroflowmeter)
➔ *CPT Assistant* Sep 02:6

51741   Complex uroflowmetry (eg, calibrated electronic equipment)
➔ *CPT Assistant* Sep 02:6

▶(51772 has been deleted. To report urethral pressure profile studies, see 51727, 51729)◀

51784 Electromyography studies (EMG) of anal or urethral sphincter, other than needle, any technique
→ *CPT Assistant* Sep 02:6

51785 Needle electromyography studies (EMG) of anal or urethral sphincter, any technique
→ *CPT Assistant* Apr 02:6, Sep 02:6, Jul 04:13

51792 Stimulus evoked response (eg, measurement of bulbocavernosus reflex latency time)
→ *CPT Assistant* Apr 02:6, Sep 02:6

►(51795 has been deleted. To report bladder voiding pressure studies, see 51728, 51729)◄

51797 ►Code is out of numerical sequence. See 51725-51798◄

51798 Measurement of post-voiding residual urine and/or bladder capacity by ultrasound, non-imaging
→ *CPT Assistant* Dec 05:3; *CPT Changes: An Insider's View* 2003

Measurement of Postvoiding
51798

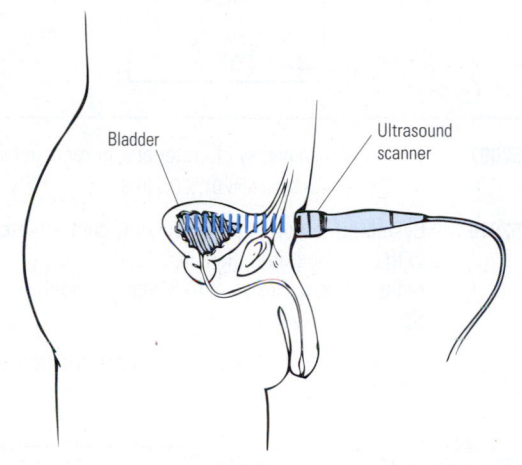

Bladder

Ultrasound scanner

Repair

51800 Cystoplasty or cystourethroplasty, plastic operation on bladder and/or vesical neck (anterior Y-plasty, vesical fundus resection), any procedure, with or without wedge resection of posterior vesical neck

51820 Cystourethroplasty with unilateral or bilateral ureteroneocystostomy

51840 Anterior vesicourethropexy, or urethropexy (eg, Marshall-Marchetti-Krantz, Burch); simple
→ *CPT Assistant* Jan 97:1, Nov 97:19, Apr 98:15, Jun 02:7, May 06:17

51841 complicated (eg, secondary repair)
→ *CPT Assistant* Jan 97:1, Jun 02:7

(For urethropexy (Pereyra type), use 57289)

51845 Abdomino-vaginal vesical neck suspension, with or without endoscopic control (eg, Stamey, Raz, modified Pereyra)
→ *CPT Assistant* Jan 97:3

51860 Cystorrhaphy, suture of bladder wound, injury or rupture; simple

51865 complicated

51880 Closure of cystostomy (separate procedure)

51900 Closure of vesicovaginal fistula, abdominal approach

(For vaginal approach, see 57320-57330)

51920 Closure of vesicouterine fistula;

51925 with hysterectomy

(For closure of vesicoenteric fistula, see 44660, 44661)

(For closure of rectovesical fistula, see 45800-45805)

51940 Closure, exstrophy of bladder
→ *CPT Changes: An Insider's View* 2002

(See also 54390)

51960 Enterocystoplasty, including intestinal anastomosis
→ *CPT Changes: An Insider's View* 2002

51980 Cutaneous vesicostomy

Laparoscopy

Surgical laparoscopy always includes diagnostic laparoscopy. To report a diagnostic laparoscopy (peritoneoscopy) (separate procedure), use 49320.

51990 Laparoscopy, surgical; urethral suspension for stress incontinence
→ *CPT Assistant* Nov 99:26, May 00:4; *CPT Changes: An Insider's View* 2000

51992 sling operation for stress incontinence (eg, fascia or synthetic)
→ *CPT Assistant* Nov 99:26, May 00:4; *CPT Changes: An Insider's View* 2000

(For open sling operation for stress incontinence, use 57288)

(For reversal or removal of sling operation for stress incontinence, use 57287)

Laparoscopic Sling Suspension Urinary Incontinence

51990

Nonabsorbable sutures are placed laparoscopically into the endopelvic fascia at the bladder neck region on each side and secured to the ipsilateral pectineal ligament. The sutures are tied using extra vaginal-urethral knots so as to create a hammock type suspension of the bladder neck, without urethral occlusion.

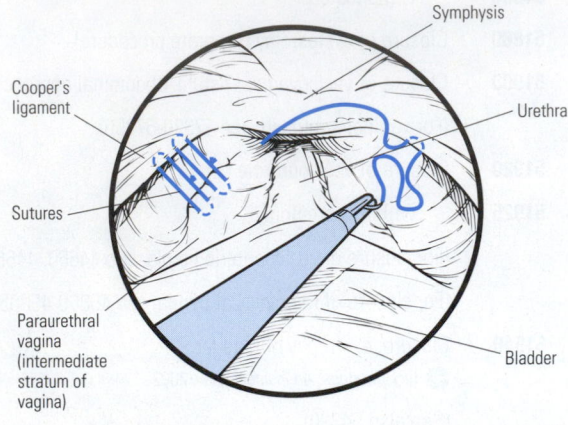

51999   Unlisted laparoscopy procedure, bladder
⊙ *CPT Changes: An Insider's View* 2006

Endoscopy—Cystoscopy, Urethroscopy, Cystourethroscopy

Endoscopic descriptions are listed so that the main procedure can be identified without having to list all the minor related functions performed at the same time. For example: meatotomy, urethral calibration and/or dilation, urethroscopy, and cystoscopy prior to a transurethral resection of prostate; ureteral catheterization following extraction of ureteral calculus; internal urethrotomy and bladder neck fulguration when performing a cystourethroscopy for the female urethral syndrome. When the secondary procedure requires significant additional time and effort, it may be identified by the addition of modifier 22.

For example: urethrotomy performed for a documented pre-existing stricture or bladder neck contracture.

52000   Cystourethroscopy (separate procedure)
⊙ *CPT Assistant* Oct 00:7, May 01:5, Sep 04:11, Oct 05:23, Nov 07:9

52001   Cystourethroscopy with irrigation and evacuation of multiple obstructing clots
⊙ *CPT Changes: An Insider's View* 2002, 2003

(Do not report 52001 in conjunction with 52000)

52005   Cystourethroscopy, with ureteral catheterization, with or without irrigation, instillation, or ureteropyelography, exclusive of radiologic service;
⊙ *CPT Assistant* Sep 00:11, Jan 01:13, May 01:5, Oct 01:8

Cystourethroscopy With Ureteral Catheterization

52005

A cystourethroscope is passed through the urethra and bladder in order to view the urinary collecting system.

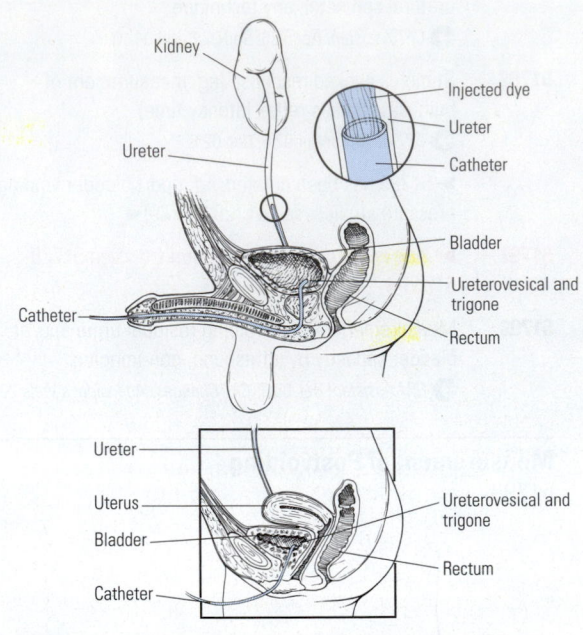

52007   with brush biopsy of ureter and/or renal pelvis
⊙ *CPT Assistant* May 01:5, Oct 01:8

52010   Cystourethroscopy, with ejaculatory duct catheterization, with or without irrigation, instillation, or duct radiography, exclusive of radiologic service
⊙ *CPT Assistant* May 01:5

(For radiological supervision and interpretation, use 74440)

Transurethral Surgery

Urethra and Bladder

52204   Cystourethroscopy, with biopsy(s)
⊙ *CPT Assistant* May 01:5, Sep 01:1, Sep 03:16; *CPT Changes: An Insider's View* 2007

52214   Cystourethroscopy, with fulguration (including cryosurgery or laser surgery) of trigone, bladder neck, prostatic fossa, urethra, or periurethral glands
⊙ *CPT Assistant* May 01:5, Sep 01:1

(For transurethral fulguration of prostate tissue performed within the postoperative period of 52601 or 52630 performed by the same physician, append modifier 78)

(For transurethral fulguration of prostate tissue performed within the postoperative period of a related procedure performed by the same physician, append modifier 78)

(For transurethral fulguration of prostate for postoperative bleeding performed by the same physician, append modifier 78)

52224   Cystourethroscopy, with fulguration (including cryosurgery or laser surgery) or treatment of MINOR (less than 0.5 cm) lesion(s) with or without biopsy
➔ *CPT Assistant* May 01:5, Sep 01:1, Dec 07:7

52234   Cystourethroscopy, with fulguration (including cryosurgery or laser surgery) and/or resection of; SMALL bladder tumor(s) (0.5 up to 2.0 cm)
➔ *CPT Assistant* May 01:5, Sep 01:1, Oct 02:12, Jan 03:21; *CPT Changes: An Insider's View* 2005

52235   MEDIUM bladder tumor(s) (2.0 to 5.0 cm)
➔ *CPT Assistant* May 01:5, Sep 01:1, Oct 02:12, Jan 03:21

52240   LARGE bladder tumor(s)
➔ *CPT Assistant* May 01:5, Sep 01:1

52250   Cystourethroscopy with insertion of radioactive substance, with or without biopsy or fulguration
➔ *CPT Assistant* May 01:5, Sep 01:1

52260   Cystourethroscopy, with dilation of bladder for interstitial cystitis; general or conduction (spinal) anesthesia
➔ *CPT Assistant* May 01:5, Sep 01:1, Oct 05:23

52265   local anesthesia
➔ *CPT Assistant* May 01:5, Sep 01:1

52270   Cystourethroscopy, with internal urethrotomy; female
➔ *CPT Assistant* May 01:5, Sep 01:1

52275   male
➔ *CPT Assistant* May 01:5, Sep 01:1

52276   Cystourethroscopy with direct vision internal urethrotomy
➔ *CPT Assistant* May 01:5, Sep 01:1

52277   Cystourethroscopy, with resection of external sphincter (sphincterotomy)
➔ *CPT Assistant* May 01:5, Sep 01:1

52281   Cystourethroscopy, with calibration and/or dilation of urethral stricture or stenosis, with or without meatotomy, with or without injection procedure for cystography, male or female
➔ *CPT Assistant* Nov 97:20, May 01:5, Sep 01:1, Jun 07:10

▲ **52282**   Cystourethroscopy, with insertion of permanent urethral stent
➔ *CPT Assistant* Nov 97:20, May 01:5, Sep 01:1; *CPT Changes: An Insider's View* 2010

►(For placement of temporary prostatic urethral stent, use 53855)◄

52283   Cystourethroscopy, with steroid injection into stricture
➔ *CPT Assistant* May 01:5, Sep 01:1

52285   Cystourethroscopy for treatment of the female urethral syndrome with any or all of the following: urethral meatotomy, urethral dilation, internal urethrotomy, lysis of urethrovaginal septal fibrosis, lateral incisions of the bladder neck, and fulguration of polyp(s) of urethra, bladder neck, and/or trigone
➔ *CPT Assistant* May 01:5, Sep 01:1

52290   Cystourethroscopy; with ureteral meatotomy, unilateral or bilateral
➔ *CPT Assistant* May 01:5, Sep 01:1

52300   with resection or fulguration of orthotopic ureterocele(s), unilateral or bilateral
➔ *CPT Assistant* May 01:5, Sep 01:1

52301   with resection or fulguration of ectopic ureterocele(s), unilateral or bilateral
➔ *CPT Assistant* May 01:5, Sep 01:1

52305   with incision or resection of orifice of bladder diverticulum, single or multiple
➔ *CPT Assistant* May 01:5, Sep 01:1

52310   Cystourethroscopy, with removal of foreign body, calculus, or ureteral stent from urethra or bladder (separate procedure); simple
➔ *CPT Assistant* May 01:5, Sep 01:1

52315   complicated
➔ *CPT Assistant* May 01:5, Sep 01:1

52317   Litholapaxy: crushing or fragmentation of calculus by any means in bladder and removal of fragments; simple or small (less than 2.5 cm)
➔ *CPT Assistant* May 01:5, Sep 01:1

52318   complicated or large (over 2.5 cm)
➔ *CPT Assistant* May 01:5, Sep 01:1

Ureter and Pelvis

Therapeutic cystourethroscopy always includes diagnostic cystourethroscopy. To report a diagnostic cystourethroscopy, use 52000. Therapeutic cystourethroscopy with ureteroscopy and/or pyeloscopy always includes diagnostic cystourethroscopy with ureteroscopy and/or pyeloscopy. To report a diagnostic cystourethroscopy with ureteroscopy and/or pyeloscopy, use 52351.

Do not report 52000 in conjunction with 52320-52343.

Do not report 52351 in conjunction with 52344-52346, 52352-52355.

The insertion and removal of a temporary ureteral catheter (52005) during diagnostic or therapeutic cystourethroscopic with ureteroscopy and/or pyeloscopy is included in 52320-52355 and should not be reported separately.

To report insertion of a self-retaining, indwelling stent performed during diagnostic or therapeutic cystourethroscopy with ureteroscopy and/or pyeloscopy, report 52332, in addition to primary procedure(s) performed (52320-52355), and append modifier 51. 52332 is used to report a unilateral procedure unless otherwise specified.

For bilateral insertion of self-retaining, indwelling ureteral stents, use code 52332, and append modifier 50.

To report cystourethroscopic removal of a self-retaining, indwelling ureteral stent, see 52310, 52315, and append modifier 58, if appropriate.

52320 Cystourethroscopy (including ureteral catheterization); with removal of ureteral calculus

➔ *CPT Assistant* Mar 96:1, May 96:11, Jan 01:13, May 01:5, Sep 01:1, Oct 01:8

52325 with fragmentation of ureteral calculus (eg, ultrasonic or electro-hydraulic technique)

➔ *CPT Assistant* Mar 96:1, May 96:11, May 01:5, Sep 01:1, Oct 01:8, Dec 07:13

52327 with subureteric injection of implant material

➔ *CPT Assistant* Mar 96:1, May 96:11, May 01:5, Sep 01:1, Oct 01:8

52330 with manipulation, without removal of ureteral calculus

➔ *CPT Assistant* Mar 96:1, May 96:11, Sep 00:11, May 01:5, Sep 01:1, Oct 01:8

52332 Cystourethroscopy, with insertion of indwelling ureteral stent (eg, Gibbons or double-J type)

➔ *CPT Assistant* Mar 96:1, May 96:11, Nov 96:8, Jan 01:13, May 01:5, Sep 01:1, Oct 01:8, Oct 05:18

52334 Cystourethroscopy with insertion of ureteral guide wire through kidney to establish a percutaneous nephrostomy, retrograde

➔ *CPT Assistant* Mar 96:11, May 96:11, May 01:5, Sep 01:1, Oct 01:8

(For percutaneous nephrostolithotomy, see 50080, 50081; for establishment of nephrostomy tract only, use 50395)

(For cystourethroscopy, with ureteroscopy and/or pyeloscopy, see 52351-52355)

(For cystourethroscopy with incision, fulguration, or resection of congenital posterior urethral valves or obstructive hypertrophic mucosal folds, use 52400)

52341 Cystourethroscopy; with treatment of ureteral stricture (eg, balloon dilation, laser, electrocautery, and incision)

➔ *CPT Assistant* Nov 96:9, Apr 01:4, May 01:5, Sep 01:1, Oct 01:8; *CPT Changes: An Insider's View* 2001

52342 with treatment of ureteropelvic junction stricture (eg, balloon dilation, laser, electrocautery, and incision)

➔ *CPT Assistant* Apr 01:4, May 01:5, Sep 01:1, Oct 01:8, Aug 02:11; *CPT Changes: An Insider's View* 2001

52343 with treatment of intra-renal stricture (eg, balloon dilation, laser, electrocautery, and incision)

➔ *CPT Assistant* Apr 01:4, May 01:5, Sep 01:1, Oct 01:8; *CPT Changes: An Insider's View* 2001

52344 Cystourethroscopy with ureteroscopy; with treatment of ureteral stricture (eg, balloon dilation, laser, electrocautery, and incision)

➔ *CPT Assistant* Apr 01:4, May 01:5, Sep 01:1, Oct 01:8; *CPT Changes: An Insider's View* 2001

52345 with treatment of ureteropelvic junction stricture (eg, balloon dilation, laser, electrocautery, and incision)

➔ *CPT Assistant* Apr 01:4, May 01:5, Sep 01:1, Oct 01:8; *CPT Changes: An Insider's View* 2001

52346 with treatment of intra-renal stricture (eg, balloon dilation, laser, electrocautery, and incision)

➔ *CPT Assistant* Apr 01:4, May 01:5, Sep 01:1, Oct 01:8; *CPT Changes: An Insider's View* 2001

(For transurethral resection or incision of ejaculatory ducts, use 52402)

52351 Cystourethroscopy, with ureteroscopy and/or pyeloscopy; diagnostic

➔ *CPT Assistant* Apr 01:4, May 01:5, Sep 01:1, Oct 01:8; *CPT Changes: An Insider's View* 2001

(For radiological supervision and interpretation, use 74485)

(Do not report 52351 in conjunction with 52341-52346, 52352-52355)

52352 with removal or manipulation of calculus (ureteral catheterization is included)

➔ *CPT Assistant* Apr 01:4, May 01:5, Sep 01:1, Oct 01:8, Jun 07:10; *CPT Changes: An Insider's View* 2001

52353 with lithotripsy (ureteral catheterization is included)

➔ *CPT Assistant* Apr 01:4, May 01:5, Sep 01:1, Oct 01:8, Dec 07:13, Apr 09:8; *CPT Changes: An Insider's View* 2001

52354 with biopsy and/or fulguration of ureteral or renal pelvic lesion

➔ *CPT Assistant* Apr 01:4, May 01:5, Sep 01:1, Oct 01:8; *CPT Changes: An Insider's View* 2001, 2003

52355 with resection of ureteral or renal pelvic tumor

➔ *CPT Assistant* Apr 01:4, May 01:5, Sep 01:1, Oct 01:8, Jan 03:21; *CPT Changes: An Insider's View* 2001, 2003

Vesical Neck and Prostate

52400 Cystourethroscopy with incision, fulguration, or resection of congenital posterior urethral valves, or congenital obstructive hypertrophic mucosal folds

➔ *CPT Assistant* Apr 01:4; *CPT Changes: An Insider's View* 2001

52402 Cystourethroscopy with transurethral resection or incision of ejaculatory ducts

➔ *CPT Changes: An Insider's View* 2005

52450 Transurethral incision of prostate

➔ *CPT Assistant* Apr 01:4, Jul 05:15

52500 Transurethral resection of bladder neck (separate procedure)

➔ *CPT Assistant* Apr 01:4, Jan 04:27, Jul 05:15

(52510 has been deleted) TURP

52601 Transurethral electrosurgical resection of prostate, including control of postoperative bleeding, complete (vasectomy, meatotomy, cystourethroscopy, urethral calibration and/or dilation, and internal urethrotomy are included)

➔ *CPT Assistant* Nov 97:20, Apr 01:4, Jun 03:6

(For other approaches, see 55801-55845)

Transurethral Resection of Prostate, Complete
52601

The physician removes the prostate gland using an electrocautery knife.

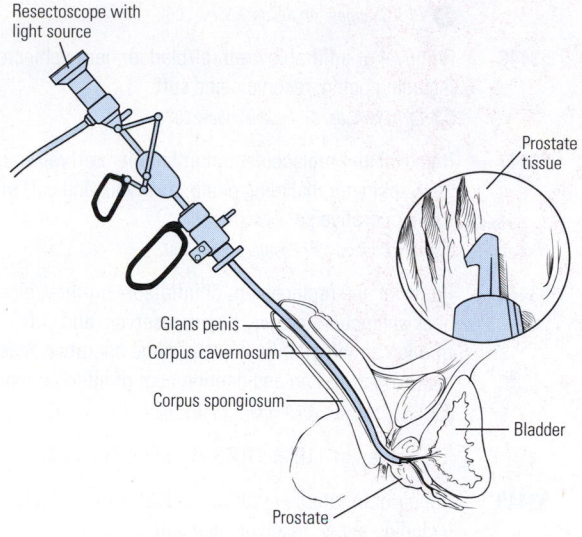

Resectoscope with light source

Prostate tissue

Glans penis

Corpus cavernosum

Corpus spongiosum

Bladder

Prostate

Contact Laser Vaporization of Prostate
52648

A laser is used to vaporize the prostate.

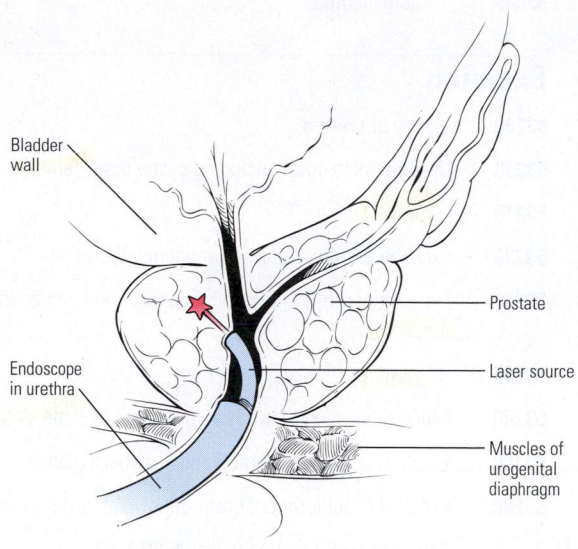

Bladder wall

Endoscope in urethra

Prostate

Laser source

Muscles of urogenital diaphragm

(52606 has been deleted. For transurethral fulguration of prostate, use 52214)

(52612, 52614, 52620 have been deleted. For first stage transurethral partial resection of prostate, use 52601. For second stage partial resection of prostate, use 52601 with modifier 58. For transurethral resection of residual or regrowth of obstructive prostate tissue, use 52630)

52630 Transurethral resection; residual or regrowth of obstructive prostate tissue including control of postoperative bleeding, complete (vasectomy, meatotomy, cystourethroscopy, urethral calibration and/or dilation, and internal urethrotomy are included)
➲ *CPT Assistant* Apr 01:4; *CPT Changes: An Insider's View* 2009

(For resection of residual prostate tissue performed within the postoperative period of a related procedure performed by the same physician, append modifier 78)

52640   of postoperative bladder neck contracture
➲ *CPT Assistant* Apr 01:4

52647 Laser coagulation of prostate, including control of postoperative bleeding, complete (vasectomy, meatotomy, cystourethroscopy, urethral calibration and/or dilation, and internal urethrotomy are included if performed)
➲ *CPT Assistant* Nov 97:20, Mar 98:11, Apr 01:4, Nov 06:21; *CPT Changes: An Insider's View* 2006

52648 Laser vaporization of prostate, including control of postoperative bleeding, complete (vasectomy, meatotomy, cystourethroscopy, urethral calibration and/or dilation, internal urethrotomy and transurethral resection of prostate are included if performed)
➲ *CPT Assistant* Mar 98:11, Apr 01:5, Jul 05:15, Nov 06:21; *CPT Changes: An Insider's View* 2006

52649 Laser enucleation of the prostate with morcellation, including control of postoperative bleeding, complete (vasectomy, meatotomy, cystourethroscopy, urethral calibration and/or dilation, internal urethrotomy and transurethral resection of prostate are included if performed)
➲ *CPT Changes: An Insider's View* 2008

(Do not report 52649 in conjunction with 52000, 52276, 52281, 52601, 52647, 52648, 53020, 55250)

52700 Transurethral drainage of prostatic abscess
➲ *CPT Assistant* Apr 01:4

(For litholapaxy, use 52317, 52318)

Urethra

(For endoscopy, see cystoscopy, urethroscopy, cystourethroscopy, 52000-52700)

(For injection procedure for urethrocystography, see 51600-51610)

Incision

53000 Urethrotomy or urethrostomy, external (separate procedure); pendulous urethra

53010   perineal urethra, external

53020 Meatotomy, cutting of meatus (separate procedure); except infant

53025   infant

(Do not report modifier 63 in conjunction with 53025)

53040 Drainage of deep periurethral abscess

(For subcutaneous abscess, see 10060, 10061)

53060	Drainage of Skene's gland abscess or cyst
53080	Drainage of perineal urinary extravasation; uncomplicated (separate procedure)
53085	complicated

Excision

53200	Biopsy of urethra
53210	Urethrectomy, total, including cystostomy; female
53215	male
53220	Excision or fulguration of carcinoma of urethra
53230	Excision of urethral diverticulum (separate procedure); female
53235	male
53240	Marsupialization of urethral diverticulum, male or female
53250	Excision of bulbourethral gland (Cowper's gland)
53260	Excision or fulguration; urethral polyp(s), distal urethra
	(For endoscopic approach, see 52214, 52224)
53265	urethral caruncle
53270	Skene's glands
53275	urethral prolapse

Repair

	(For hypospadias, see 54300-54352)
53400	Urethroplasty; first stage, for fistula, diverticulum, or stricture (eg, Johannsen type)
53405	second stage (formation of urethra), including urinary diversion
53410	Urethroplasty, 1-stage reconstruction of male anterior urethra
53415	Urethroplasty, transpubic or perineal, 1-stage, for reconstruction or repair of prostatic or membranous urethra
53420	Urethroplasty, 2-stage reconstruction or repair of prostatic or membranous urethra; first stage
53425	second stage
53430	Urethroplasty, reconstruction of female urethra
53431	Urethroplasty with tubularization of posterior urethra and/or lower bladder for incontinence (eg, Tenago, Leadbetter procedure)
	➲ CPT Changes: An Insider's View 2002
53440	Sling operation for correction of male urinary incontinence (eg, fascia or synthetic)
	➲ CPT Changes: An Insider's View 2003
53442	Removal or revision of sling for male urinary incontinence (eg, fascia or synthetic)
	➲ CPT Changes: An Insider's View 2003

53444	Insertion of tandem cuff (dual cuff)
	➲ CPT Changes: An Insider's View 2002
53445	Insertion of inflatable urethral/bladder neck sphincter, including placement of pump, reservoir, and cuff
	➲ CPT Changes: An Insider's View 2002
53446	Removal of inflatable urethral/bladder neck sphincter, including pump, reservoir, and cuff
	➲ CPT Changes: An Insider's View 2002
53447	Removal and replacement of inflatable urethral/bladder neck sphincter including pump, reservoir, and cuff at the same operative session
	➲ CPT Changes: An Insider's View 2002
53448	Removal and replacement of inflatable urethral/bladder neck sphincter including pump, reservoir, and cuff through an infected field at the same operative session including irrigation and debridement of infected tissue
	➲ CPT Changes: An Insider's View 2002
	(Do not report 11040-11043 in addition to 53448)
53449	Repair of inflatable urethral/bladder neck sphincter, including pump, reservoir, and cuff
	➲ CPT Changes: An Insider's View 2002
53450	Urethromeatoplasty, with mucosal advancement
	(For meatotomy, see 53020, 53025)
53460	Urethromeatoplasty, with partial excision of distal urethral segment (Richardson type procedure)
53500	Urethrolysis, transvaginal, secondary, open, including cystourethroscopy (eg, postsurgical obstruction, scarring)
	➲ CPT Assistant Sep 04:11; CPT Changes: An Insider's View 2004
	(For urethrolysis by retropubic approach, use 53899)
	(Do not report 53500 in conjunction with 52000)
53502	Urethrorrhaphy, suture of urethral wound or injury, female
53505	Urethrorrhaphy, suture of urethral wound or injury; penile
53510	perineal
53515	prostatomembranous
53520	Closure of urethrostomy or urethrocutaneous fistula, male (separate procedure)
	(For closure of urethrovaginal fistula, use 57310)
	(For closure of urethrorectal fistula, see 45820, 45825)

Manipulation

	(For radiological supervision and interpretation, use 74485)
53600	Dilation of urethral stricture by passage of sound or urethral dilator, male; initial
53601	subsequent
53605	Dilation of urethral stricture or vesical neck by passage of sound or urethral dilator, male, general or conduction (spinal) anesthesia

(For dilation of urethral stricture, male, performed under local anesthesia, see 53600, 53601, 53620, 53621)

53620 Dilation of urethral stricture by passage of filiform and follower, male; initial

53621   subsequent

53660 Dilation of female urethra including suppository and/or instillation; initial

53661   subsequent

53665 Dilation of female urethra, general or conduction (spinal) anesthesia

(For urethral catheterization, see 51701-51703)

(For dilation of urethra performed under local anesthesia, female, see 53660, 53661)

Other Procedures

(For 2 or 3 glass urinalysis, use 81020)

53850 Transurethral destruction of prostate tissue; by microwave thermotherapy
➜ *CPT Assistant* Nov 97:20, Apr 01:6

53852   by radiofrequency thermotherapy
➜ *CPT Assistant* Nov 97:20, Apr 01:6

(53853 has been deleted. To report, use 55899)

● **53855** Insertion of a temporary prostatic urethral stent, including urethral measurement
➜ *CPT Changes: An Insider's View* 2010

▶(For insertion of permanent urethral stent, use 52282)◀

53899 Unlisted procedure, urinary system
➜ *CPT Assistant* Aug 04:12, Sep 04:11, Oct 05:18, 23-24, Feb 06:14
➜ *Clinical Examples in Radiology* Summer 06:1-3

Notes

⊙=Moderate sedation ✚=Add-on code ✗=FDA approval pending #=Resequenced code ➡➡=See p xiii for details

Male Genital System (54000-55899) 269

The following is a listing of headings and subheadings that appear within the Male Genital System section of the CPT codebook. The subheadings or subsections denoted with asterisks (*) below have special instructions unique to that section. Where these are indicated, special "notes" or guidelines will be presented preceding those procedural terminology listings, referring to that subsection specifically.

M/F
54000

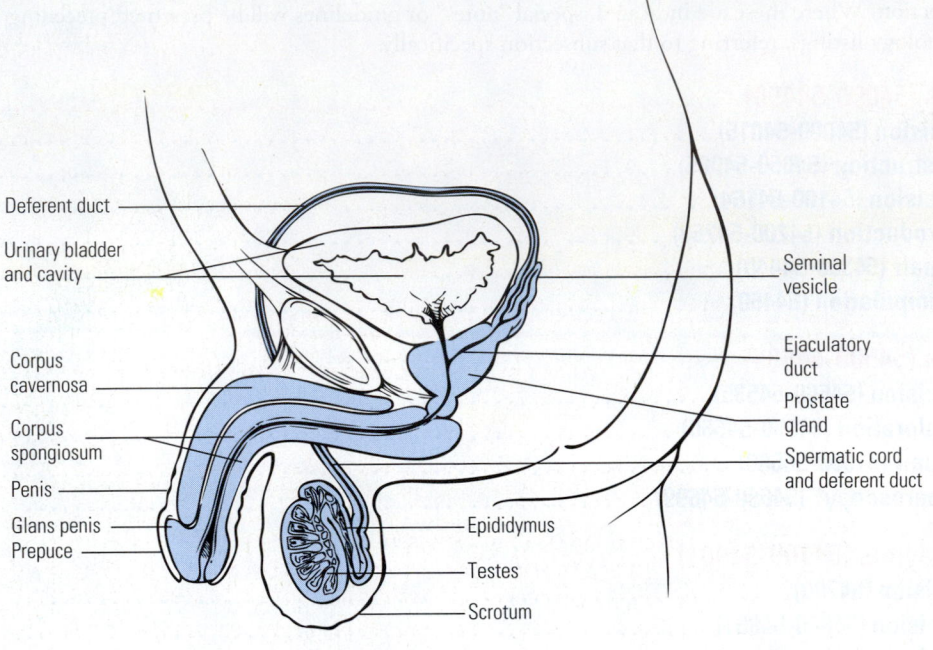

Male Genital System

Penis

Incision

(For abdominal perineal gangrene debridement, see 11004-11006)

54000   Slitting of prepuce, dorsal or lateral (separate procedure); newborn

(Do not report modifier 63 in conjunction with 54000)

54001   except newborn

54015   Incision and drainage of penis, deep

(For skin and subcutaneous abscess, see 10060-10160)

Destruction

54050   Destruction of lesion(s), penis (eg, condyloma, papilloma, molluscum contagiosum, herpetic vesicle), simple; chemical

54055   electrodesiccation

54056   cryosurgery

54057   laser surgery

54060   surgical excision

54065   Destruction of lesion(s), penis (eg, condyloma, papilloma, molluscum contagiosum, herpetic vesicle), extensive (eg, laser surgery, electrosurgery, cryosurgery, chemosurgery)
➔ *CPT Changes: An Insider's View* 2002

(For destruction or excision of other lesions, see **Integumentary System**)

Excision

54100   Biopsy of penis; (separate procedure)   (simple)
➔ *CPT Assistant* Nov 99:26; *CPT Changes: An Insider's View* 2000

54105   deep structures   (complex)

54110   Excision of penile plaque (Peyronie disease);

54111   with graft to 5 cm in length
➔ *CPT Assistant* Aug 99:5

54112   with graft greater than 5 cm in length

54115   Removal foreign body from deep penile tissue (eg, plastic implant)

54120   Amputation of penis; partial

54125   complete

54130   Amputation of penis, radical; with bilateral inguinofemoral lymphadenectomy

54135   in continuity with bilateral pelvic lymphadenectomy, including external iliac, hypogastric and obturator nodes

(For lymphadenectomy (separate procedure), see 38760-38770)

54150   Circumcision, using clamp or other device with regional dorsal penile or ring block
➔ *CPT Assistant* Sep 96:11, May 98:11, Apr 03:27, Aug 03:6, May 07:10, Jul 07:5; *CPT Changes: An Insider's View* 2007

(Do not report modifier 63 in conjunction with 54150)

(Report 54150 with modifier 52 when performed without dorsal penile or ring block)

54160   Circumcision, surgical excision other than clamp, device, or dorsal slit; neonate (28 days of age or less)
➔ *CPT Assistant* Sep 96:11, May 98:11, May 07:10, Jul 07:5; *CPT Changes: An Insider's View* 2007

(Do not report modifier 63 in conjunction with 54160)

54161   older than 28 days of age
➔ *CPT Assistant* Sep 96:11, Dec 96:10, May 98:11, Jul 07:5; *CPT Changes: An Insider's View* 2007

54162   Lysis or excision of penile post-circumcision adhesions
➔ *CPT Changes: An Insider's View* 2002

54163   Repair incomplete circumcision
➔ *CPT Changes: An Insider's View* 2002

54164   Frenulotomy of penis
➔ *CPT Changes: An Insider's View* 2002

(Do not report 54164 with circumcision codes 54150-54161, 54162, 54163)

Introduction

54200   Injection procedure for Peyronie disease;

54205   with surgical exposure of plaque

54220   Irrigation of corpora cavernosa for priapism

54230   Injection procedure for corpora cavernosography

(For radiological supervision and interpretation, use 74445)

54231   Dynamic cavernosometry, including intracavernosal injection of vasoactive drugs (eg, papaverine, phentolamine)

54235   Injection of corpora cavernosa with pharmacologic agent(s) (eg, papaverine, phentolamine)
➔ *CPT Assistant* Sep 96:10

54240   Penile plethysmography

54250   Nocturnal penile tumescence and/or rigidity test

Repair

(For other urethroplasties, see 53400-53430)

(For penile revascularization, use 37788)

54300   Plastic operation of penis for straightening of chordee (eg, hypospadias), with or without mobilization of urethra

---

 ▲=Revised code   ●=New code   ►◄=Contains new or revised text   ⊘=Modifier 51 exempt

54304 Plastic operation on penis for correction of chordee or for first stage hypospadias repair with or without transplantation of prepuce and/or skin flaps

54308 Urethroplasty for second stage hypospadias repair (including urinary diversion); less than 3 cm

54312 greater than 3 cm

54316 Urethroplasty for second stage hypospadias repair (including urinary diversion) with free skin graft obtained from site other than genitalia

54318 Urethroplasty for third stage hypospadias repair to release penis from scrotum (eg, third stage Cecil repair)

54322 1-stage distal hypospadias repair (with or without chordee or circumcision); with simple meatal advancement (eg, Magpi, V-flap)

54324 with urethroplasty by local skin flaps (eg, flip-flap, prepucial flap)

54326 with urethroplasty by local skin flaps and mobilization of urethra

54328 with extensive dissection to correct chordee and urethroplasty with local skin flaps, skin graft patch, and/or island flap
➲ CPT Assistant Oct 04:15

(For urethroplasty and straightening of chordee, use 54308)

54332 1-stage proximal penile or penoscrotal hypospadias repair requiring extensive dissection to correct chordee and urethroplasty by use of skin graft tube and/or island flap
➲ CPT Assistant Mar 04:11, Sep 04:12

54336 1-stage perineal hypospadias repair requiring extensive dissection to correct chordee and urethroplasty by use of skin graft tube and/or island flap
➲ CPT Assistant Oct 04:15

54340 Repair of hypospadias complications (ie, fistula, stricture, diverticula); by closure, incision, or excision, simple

54344 requiring mobilization of skin flaps and urethroplasty with flap or patch graft

54348 requiring extensive dissection and urethroplasty with flap, patch or tubed graft (includes urinary diversion)

54352 Repair of hypospadias cripple requiring extensive dissection and excision of previously constructed structures including re-release of chordee and reconstruction of urethra and penis by use of local skin as grafts and island flaps and skin brought in as flaps or grafts

54360 Plastic operation on penis to correct angulation

54380 Plastic operation on penis for epispadias distal to external sphincter;

54385 with incontinence

54390 with exstrophy of bladder

54400 Insertion of penile prosthesis; non-inflatable (semi-rigid)

54401 inflatable (self-contained)

(For removal or replacement of penile prosthesis, see 54415, 54416)

54405 Insertion of multi-component, inflatable penile prosthesis, including placement of pump, cylinders, and reservoir
➲ CPT Changes: An Insider's View 2002

(For reduced services, report 54405 with modifier 52)

54406 Removal of all components of a multi-component, inflatable penile prosthesis without replacement of prosthesis
➲ CPT Changes: An Insider's View 2002

(For reduced services, report 54406 with modifier 52)

54408 Repair of component(s) of a multi-component, inflatable penile prosthesis
➲ CPT Changes: An Insider's View 2002

54410 Removal and replacement of all component(s) of a multi-component, inflatable penile prosthesis at the same operative session
➲ CPT Changes: An Insider's View 2002

54411 Removal and replacement of all components of a multi-component inflatable penile prosthesis through an infected field at the same operative session, including irrigation and debridement of infected tissue
➲ CPT Changes: An Insider's View 2002

(For reduced services, report 54411 with modifier 52)

(Do not report 11040-11043 in addition to 54411)

54415 Removal of non-inflatable (semi-rigid) or inflatable (self-contained) penile prosthesis, without replacement of prosthesis
➲ CPT Changes: An Insider's View 2002

54416 Removal and replacement of non-inflatable (semi-rigid) or inflatable (self-contained) penile prosthesis at the same operative session
➲ CPT Changes: An Insider's View 2002

54417 Removal and replacement of non-inflatable (semi-rigid) or inflatable (self-contained) penile prosthesis through an infected field at the same operative session, including irrigation and debridement of infected tissue
➲ CPT Changes: An Insider's View 2002

(Do not report 11040-11043 in addition to 54417)

54420 Corpora cavernosa-saphenous vein shunt (priapism operation), unilateral or bilateral

54430 Corpora cavernosa-corpus spongiosum shunt (priapism operation), unilateral or bilateral

54435 Corpora cavernosa-glans penis fistulization (eg, biopsy needle, Winter procedure, rongeur, or punch) for priapism

54440 Plastic operation of penis for injury

Manipulation

54450   Foreskin manipulation including lysis of preputial adhesions and stretching

Testis

Excision

(For abdominal perineal gangrene debridement, see 11004-11006)

54500   Biopsy of testis, needle (separate procedure)

(For fine needle aspiration, see 10021, 10022)

(For evaluation of fine needle aspirate, see 88172, 88173)

54505   Biopsy of testis, incisional (separate procedure)
➔ *CPT Assistant* Oct 01:8

(For bilateral procedure, report 54505 with modifier 50)

(When combined with vasogram, seminal vesiculogram, or epididymogram, use 55300)

54512   Excision of extraparenchymal lesion of testis
➔ *CPT Assistant* Oct 01:8, Aug 05:13; *CPT Changes: An Insider's View* 2001

54520   Orchiectomy, simple (including subcapsular), with or without testicular prosthesis, scrotal or inguinal approach
➔ *CPT Assistant* Winter 94:13, Oct 01:8, Mar 04:3

(For bilateral procedure, report 54520 with modifier 50)

54522   Orchiectomy, partial
➔ *CPT Assistant* Oct 01:8; *CPT Changes: An Insider's View* 2001

54530   Orchiectomy, radical, for tumor; inguinal approach
➔ *CPT Assistant* Oct 01:8

54535   with abdominal exploration
➔ *CPT Assistant* Oct 01:8

Radical
> 80%

(For orchiectomy with repair of hernia, see 49505 or 49507 and 54520)

(For radical retroperitoneal lymphadenectomy, use 38780)

Exploration

54550   Exploration for undescended testis (inguinal or scrotal area)
➔ *CPT Assistant* Oct 01:8

(For bilateral procedure, report 54550 with modifier 50)

54560   Exploration for undescended testis with abdominal exploration
➔ *CPT Assistant* Oct 01:8

(For bilateral procedure, report 54560 with modifier 50)

Repair

54600   Reduction of torsion of testis, surgical, with or without fixation of contralateral testis
➔ *CPT Assistant* Aug 05:13

54620   Fixation of contralateral testis (separate procedure)

54640   Orchiopexy, inguinal approach, with or without hernia repair
➔ *CPT Assistant* Oct 01:8, Jan 04:27, Mar 04:10

(For bilateral procedure, report 54640 with modifier 50)

(For inguinal hernia repair performed in conjunction with inguinal orchiopexy, see 49495-49525)

54650   Orchiopexy, abdominal approach, for intra-abdominal testis (eg, Fowler-Stephens)
➔ *CPT Assistant* Nov 99:26, May 00:4, Oct 01:8; *CPT Changes: An Insider's View* 2000

(For laparoscopic approach, use 54692)

54660   Insertion of testicular prosthesis (separate procedure)
➔ *CPT Assistant* Oct 01:8

(For bilateral procedure, report 54660 with modifier 50)

54670   Suture or repair of testicular injury
➔ *CPT Assistant* Oct 01:8

54680   Transplantation of testis(es) to thigh (because of scrotal destruction)
➔ *CPT Assistant* Oct 01:8

Laparoscopy

Surgical laparoscopy always includes diagnostic laparoscopy. To report a diagnostic laparoscopy (peritoneoscopy) (separate procedure), use 49320.

54690   Laparoscopy, surgical; orchiectomy
➔ *CPT Assistant* Nov 99:26, Mar 00:5, Oct 01:8; *CPT Changes: An Insider's View* 2000

54692   orchiopexy for intra-abdominal testis
➔ *CPT Assistant* Nov 99:27, May 00:4, Oct 01:8; *CPT Changes: An Insider's View* 2000

Laparoscopic Orchiopexy
54692

Surgical fixation of an undescended testis in the scrotum under laparoscopic guidance

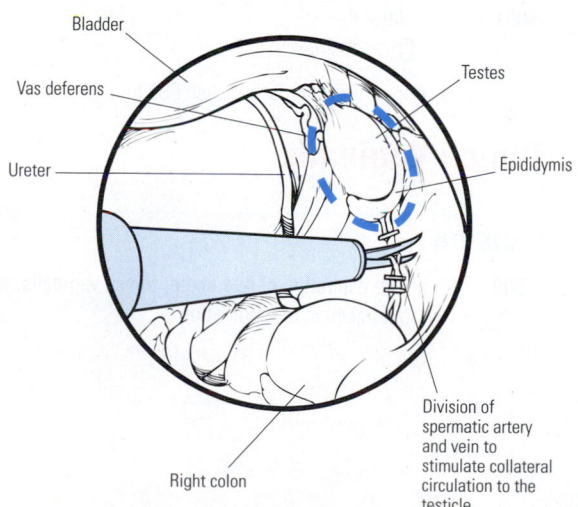

Bladder

Vas deferens

Ureter

Testes

Epididymis

Right colon

Division of spermatic artery and vein to stimulate collateral circulation to the testicle

54699   Unlisted laparoscopy procedure, testis

➔ *CPT Assistant* Nov 99:27, Mar 00:9; *CPT Changes: An Insider's View* 2000

Epididymis

Incision

54700   Incision and drainage of epididymis, testis and/or scrotal space (eg, abscess or hematoma)

➔ *CPT Assistant* Oct 01:8

(For debridement of necrotizing soft tissue infection of external genitalia, see 11004-11006)

Excision

54800   Biopsy of epididymis, needle

➔ *CPT Assistant* Oct 01:8

(For fine needle aspiration, see 10021, 10022)

(For evaluation of fine needle aspirate, see 88172, 88173)

54830   Excision of local lesion of epididymis

➔ *CPT Assistant* Oct 01:8

54840   Excision of spermatocele, with or without epididymectomy

➔ *CPT Assistant* Oct 01:8

54860   Epididymectomy; unilateral

54861   bilateral

Exploration

54865   Exploration of epididymis, with or without biopsy

➔ *CPT Changes: An Insider's View* 2007

Repair

54900   Epididymovasostomy, anastomosis of epididymis to vas deferens; unilateral

➔ *CPT Assistant* Nov 98:16

54901   bilateral

➔ *CPT Assistant* Nov 98:16

(For operating microscope, use 69990)

Tunica Vaginalis

Incision

55000   Puncture aspiration of hydrocele, tunica vaginalis, with or without injection of medication

Excision

55040   Excision of hydrocele; unilateral

55041   bilateral

(With hernia repair, see 49495-49501)

Repair

55060   Repair of tunica vaginalis hydrocele (Bottle type)

Scrotum

Incision

55100   Drainage of scrotal wall abscess

(See also 54700)

(For debridement of necrotizing soft tissue infection of external genitalia, see 11004-11006)

55110   Scrotal exploration

55120   Removal of foreign body in scrotum

Excision

(For excision of local lesion of skin of scrotum, see **Integumentary System**)

55150   Resection of scrotum

Repair

55175   Scrotoplasty; simple

55180   complicated

Vas Deferens

Incision

55200   Vasotomy, cannulization with or without incision of vas, unilateral or bilateral (separate procedure)

Excision

55250   Vasectomy, unilateral or bilateral (separate procedure), including postoperative semen examination(s)

➔ *CPT Assistant* Jun 98:10, Jul 98:10

Introduction

55300   Vasotomy for vasograms, seminal vesiculograms, or epididymograms, unilateral or bilateral

(For radiological supervision and interpretation, use 74440)

(When combined with biopsy of testis, see 54505 and use modifier 51)

Repair

55400   Vasovasostomy, vasovasorrhaphy
➲ *CPT Assistant* Nov 98:16, Oct 01:8

(For bilateral procedure, report 55400 with modifier 50)

(For operating microscope, use 69990)

Suture

55450   Ligation (percutaneous) of vas deferens, unilateral or bilateral (separate procedure)

Spermatic Cord

Excision

55500   Excision of hydrocele of spermatic cord, unilateral (separate procedure)
➲ *CPT Assistant* Oct 01:8

55520   Excision of lesion of spermatic cord (separate procedure)
➲ *CPT Assistant* Sep 00:10, Oct 01:8

55530   Excision of varicocele or ligation of spermatic veins for varicocele; (separate procedure)
➲ *CPT Assistant* Oct 01:8

55535   abdominal approach
➲ *CPT Assistant* Oct 01:8

55540   with hernia repair
➲ *CPT Assistant* Oct 01:8

Laparoscopy

Surgical laparoscopy always includes diagnostic laparoscopy. To report a diagnostic laparoscopy (peritoneoscopy) (separate procedure), use 49320.

55550   Laparoscopy, surgical, with ligation of spermatic veins for varicocele
➲ *CPT Assistant* Nov 99:27, Mar 00:9, Oct 01:8; *CPT Changes: An Insider's View* 2000

55559   Unlisted laparoscopy procedure, spermatic cord
➲ *CPT Assistant* Nov 99:27, Mar 00:9; *CPT Changes: An Insider's View* 2000

Seminal Vesicles

Incision

55600   Vesiculotomy;

(For bilateral procedure, report 55600 with modifier 50)

55605   complicated

Excision

55650   Vesiculectomy, any approach

(For bilateral procedure, report 55650 with modifier 50)

55680   Excision of Mullerian duct cyst

(For injection procedure, see 52010, 55300)

Prostate

Incision

55700   Biopsy, prostate; needle or punch, single or multiple, any approach
➲ *CPT Assistant* May 96:3

(If imaging guidance is performed, use 76942)

(For fine needle aspiration, see 10021, 10022)

(For evaluation of fine needle aspirate, see 88172, 88173)

(For transperineal stereotactic template guided saturation prostate biopsies, use 55706)

55705   incisional, any approach

55706   Biopsies, prostate, needle, transperineal, stereotactic template guided saturation sampling, including imaging guidance
➲ *CPT Changes: An Insider's View* 2009

(Do not report 55706 in conjunction with 55700)

55720   Prostatotomy, external drainage of prostatic abscess, any approach; simple

55725   complicated

(For transurethral drainage, use 52700)

Excision

(For transurethral removal of prostate, see 52601-52640)

(For transurethral destruction of prostate, see 53850-53852)

(For limited pelvic lymphadenectomy for staging (separate procedure), use 38562)

(For independent node dissection, see 38770-38780)

55801   Prostatectomy, perineal, subtotal (including control of postoperative bleeding, vasectomy, meatotomy, urethral calibration and/or dilation, and internal urethrotomy)
➲ *CPT Assistant* Jun 03:6-7

55810   Prostatectomy, perineal radical;

55812   with lymph node biopsy(s) (limited pelvic lymphadenectomy)

55815 with bilateral pelvic lymphadenectomy, including external iliac, hypogastric and obturator nodes

(If 55815 is carried out on separate days, use 38770 with modifier 50 and 55810)

55821 Prostatectomy (including control of postoperative bleeding, vasectomy, meatotomy, urethral calibration and/or dilation, and internal urethrotomy); suprapubic, subtotal, 1 or 2 stages
➔ *CPT Assistant* Jun 03:6

55831 retropubic, subtotal
➔ *CPT Assistant* Jun 03:7

55840 Prostatectomy, retropubic radical, with or without nerve sparing;
➔ *CPT Assistant* Jun 03:8

55842 with lymph node biopsy(s) (limited pelvic lymphadenectomy)
➔ *CPT Assistant* Jun 03:8

55845 with bilateral pelvic lymphadenectomy, including external iliac, hypogastric, and obturator nodes
➔ *CPT Assistant* Jun 03:8

(If 55845 is carried out on separate days, use 38770 with modifier 50 and 55840)

(For laparoscopic retropubic radical prostatectomy, use 55866)

55860 Exposure of prostate, any approach, for insertion of radioactive substance;

(For application of interstitial radioelement, see 77776-77778)

55862 with lymph node biopsy(s) (limited pelvic lymphadenectomy)

55865 with bilateral pelvic lymphadenectomy, including external iliac, hypogastric and obturator nodes

Laparoscopy

Surgical laparoscopy always includes diagnostic laparoscopy. To report a diagnostic laparoscopy (peritoneoscopy) (separate procedure), use 49320.

55866 Laparoscopy, surgical prostatectomy, retropubic radical, including nerve sparing
➔ *CPT Assistant* Jun 03:8; *CPT Changes: An Insider's View* 2003

(For open procedure, use 55840)

Other Procedures

(For artificial insemination, see 58321, 58322)

55870 Electroejaculation

▲ **55873** Cryosurgical ablation of the prostate (includes ultrasonic guidance and monitoring)
➔ *CPT Assistant* Apr 01:4, Sep 02:9, Jun 03:8; *CPT Changes: An Insider's View* 2001, 2010

55875 Transperineal placement of needles or catheters into prostate for interstitial radioelement application, with or without cystoscopy
➔ *CPT Assistant* May 07:1, Apr 09:3; *CPT Changes: An Insider's View* 2007

(For placement of needles or catheters into pelvic organs and/or genitalia [except prostate] for interstitial radioelement application, use 55920)

(For interstitial radioelement application, see 77776-77787)

(For ultrasonic guidance for interstitial radioelement application, use 76965)

▲ **55876** Placement of interstitial device(s) for radiation therapy guidance (eg, fiducial markers, dosimeter), percutaneous, prostate, single or multiple
➔ *CPT Assistant* May 07:1, Oct 07:1; *CPT Changes: An Insider's View* 2007, 2010

(Report supply of device separately)

(For imaging guidance, see 76942, 77002, 77012, 77021)

55899 Unlisted procedure, male genital system
➔ *CPT Assistant* Jun 03:8
➔ *Clinical Examples in Radiology* Spring 06:8-9

Reproductive System Procedures

55920 Placement of needles or catheters into pelvic organs and/or genitalia (except prostate) for subsequent interstitial radioelement application
➔ *CPT Changes: An Insider's View* 2008

(For placement of needles or catheters into prostate, use 55875)

(For insertion of uterine tandems and/or vaginal ovoids for clinical brachytherapy, use 57155)

(For insertion of Heyman capsules for clinical brachytherapy, use 58346)

Intersex Surgery

55970 Intersex surgery; male to female

55980 female to male

Female Genital System (56405-58999) 277

The following is a listing of headings and subheadings that appear within the Female Genital System section of the CPT codebook. The subheadings or subsections denoted with asterisks (*) below have special instructions unique to that section. Where these are indicated, special "notes" or guidelines will be presented preceding those procedural terminology listings, referring to that subsection specifically.

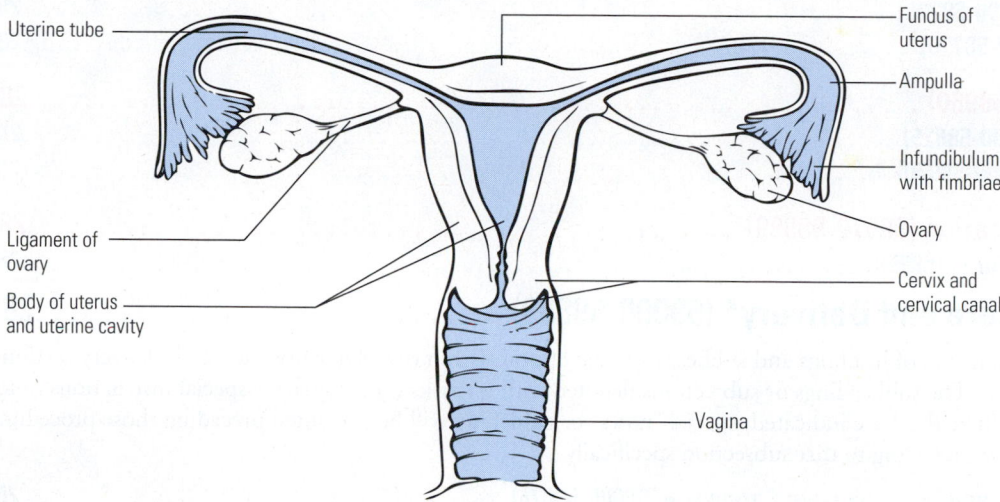

Maternity Care and Delivery* (59000-59899) 286

The following is a listing of headings and subheadings that appear within the Maternity Care and Delivery section of the CPT codebook. The subheadings or subsections denoted with asterisks (*) below have special instructions unique to that section. Where these are indicated, special "notes" or guidelines will be presented preceding those procedural terminology listings, referring to that subsection specifically.

Endocrine System (60000-60699) 290

The following is a listing of headings and subheadings that appear within the Endocrine System section of the CPT codebook. The subheadings or subsections denoted with asterisks (*) below have special instructions unique to that section. Where these are indicated, special "notes" or guidelines will be presented preceding those procedural terminology listings, referring to that subsection specifically.

Female Genital System

(For pelvic laparotomy, use 49000)

(For excision or destruction of endometriomas, open method, see 49203-49205, 58957, 58958)

(For paracentesis, see 49080, 49081)

(For secondary closure of abdominal wall evisceration or disruption, use 49900)

(For fulguration or excision of lesions, laparoscopic approach, use 58662)

(For chemotherapy, see 96401-96549)

Vulva, Perineum, and Introitus

Definitions

The following definitions apply to the vulvectomy codes (56620-56640):

A *simple* procedure is the removal of skin and superficial subcutaneous tissues.

A *radical* procedure is the removal of skin and deep subcutaneous tissue.

A *partial* procedure is the removal of less than 80% of the vulvar area.

A *complete* procedure is the removal of greater than 80% of the vulvar area.

Incision

(For incision and drainage of sebaceous cyst, furuncle, or abscess, see 10040, 10060, 10061)

56405	Incision and drainage of vulva or perineal abscess
56420	Incision and drainage of Bartholin's gland abscess

(For incision and drainage of Skene's gland abscess or cyst, use 53060)

56440	Marsupialization of Bartholin's gland cyst
56441	Lysis of labial adhesions

> CPT Assistant Winter 90:7

56442	Hymenotomy, simple incision

> CPT Changes: An Insider's View 2007

(handwritten note: Cyst is incised, drained & edges sutured to sides to keep cyst open)

Destruction

56501	Destruction of lesion(s), vulva; simple (eg, laser surgery, electrosurgery, cryosurgery, chemosurgery)

> CPT Changes: An Insider's View 2002

56515	extensive (eg, laser surgery, electrosurgery, cryosurgery, chemosurgery)

> CPT Changes: An Insider's View 2002

(For destruction of Skene's gland cyst or abscess, use 53270)

(For cautery destruction of urethral caruncle, use 53265)

(handwritten note: Destruction = Eradication (not excision); excision = removal)

Excision

56605	Biopsy of vulva or perineum (separate procedure); 1 lesion

> CPT Assistant Sep 00:9

+ 56606	each separate additional lesion (List separately in addition to code for primary procedure)

(Use 56606 in conjunction with 56605)

(For excision of local lesion, see 11420-11426, 11620-11626)

56620	Vulvectomy simple; partial
56625	complete

(For skin graft, see 15002 et seq)

56630	Vulvectomy, radical, partial;

(For skin graft, if used, see 15004-15005, 15120, 15121, 15240, 15241)

56631	with unilateral inguinofemoral lymphadenectomy
56632	with bilateral inguinofemoral lymphadenectomy
56633	Vulvectomy, radical, complete;
56634	with unilateral inguinofemoral lymphadenectomy
56637	with bilateral inguinofemoral lymphadenectomy
56640	Vulvectomy, radical, complete, with inguinofemoral, iliac, and pelvic lymphadenectomy

(For bilateral procedure, report 56640 with modifier 50)

(For lymphadenectomy, see 38760-38780)

56700	Partial hymenectomy or revision of hymenal ring
56740	Excision of Bartholin's gland or cyst

(For excision of Skene's gland, use 53270)

(For excision of urethral caruncle, use 53265)

(For excision or fulguration of urethral carcinoma, use 53220)

(For excision or marsupialization of urethral diverticulum, see 53230, 53240)

Repair

(For repair of urethra for mucosal prolapse, use 53275)

56800	Plastic repair of introitus
56805	Clitoroplasty for intersex state

56810 Perineoplasty, repair of perineum, nonobstetrical (separate procedure)

(See also 56800)

(For repair of wounds to genitalia, see 12001-12007, 12041-12047, 13131-13133)

(For repair of recent injury of vagina and perineum, nonobstetrical, use 57210)

(For anal sphincteroplasty, see 46750, 46751)

(For episiorrhaphy, episioperineorrhaphy for recent injury of vulva and/or perineum, nonobstetrical, use 57210)

Endoscopy

56820 Colposcopy of the vulva;
➜ *CPT Assistant* Feb 03:5; *CPT Changes: An Insider's View* 2003

56821 with biopsy(s)
➜ *CPT Assistant* Feb 03:5, Jun 03:11; *CPT Changes: An Insider's View* 2003

(For colposcopic examinations/procedures involving the vagina, see 57420, 57421; cervix, see 57452-57461)

Vagina

Incision

57000 Colpotomy; with exploration
➜ *CPT Assistant* Nov 07:1

57010 with drainage of pelvic abscess

57020 Colpocentesis (separate procedure)

57022 Incision and drainage of vaginal hematoma; obstetrical/postpartum
➜ *CPT Changes: An Insider's View* 2001, 2002

57023 non-obstetrical (eg, post-trauma, spontaneous bleeding)
➜ *CPT Changes: An Insider's View* 2001

Destruction

57061 Destruction of vaginal lesion(s); simple (eg, laser surgery, electrosurgery, cryosurgery, chemosurgery)
➜ *CPT Assistant* Apr 96:11; *CPT Changes: An Insider's View* 2002

57065 extensive (eg, laser surgery, electrosurgery, cryosurgery, chemosurgery)
➜ *CPT Assistant* Apr 96:11; *CPT Changes: An Insider's View* 2002

Excision

57100 Biopsy of vaginal mucosa; simple (separate procedure)

57105 extensive, requiring suture (including cysts)

57106 Vaginectomy, partial removal of vaginal wall;
➜ *CPT Assistant* Nov 98:17, Oct 99:5

Vaginectomy, Partial Removal of Vaginal Wall
57106

A specific portion of the upper or lower vaginal wall is excised.

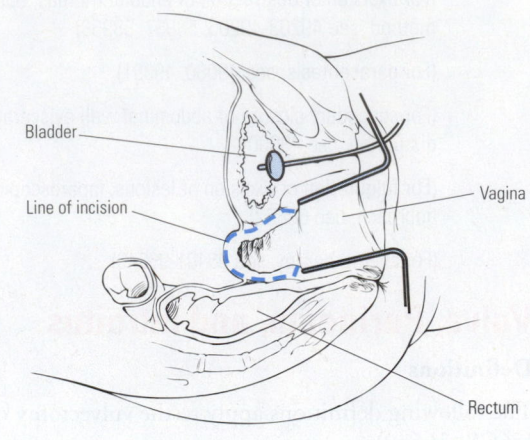

57107 with removal of paravaginal tissue (radical vaginectomy)
➜ *CPT Assistant* Nov 98:17, Oct 99:5

57109 with removal of paravaginal tissue (radical vaginectomy) with bilateral total pelvic lymphadenectomy and para-aortic lymph node sampling (biopsy)
➜ *CPT Assistant* Nov 98:17, Oct 99:5

57110 Vaginectomy, complete removal of vaginal wall;
➜ *CPT Assistant* Nov 98:17, Oct 99:5

57111 with removal of paravaginal tissue (radical vaginectomy)
➜ *CPT Assistant* Nov 98:17, Oct 99:5

Vaginectomy, Complete Removal of Vaginal Wall (Radical Vaginectomy)
57111

Removal of all of the vaginal wall and removal of paravaginal tissue (the highly vascular supporting connective tissue next to the vagina)

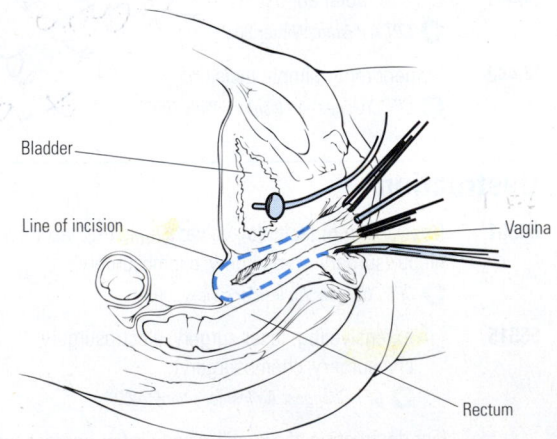

57112   with removal of paravaginal tissue (radical vaginectomy) with bilateral total pelvic lymphadenectomy and para-aortic lymph node sampling (biopsy)

> *CPT Assistant* Nov 98:17, Oct 99:5

57120   Colpocleisis (Le Fort type)

57130   Excision of vaginal septum

57135   Excision of vaginal cyst or tumor

Introduction

57150   Irrigation of vagina and/or application of medicament for treatment of bacterial, parasitic, or fungoid disease

57155   Insertion of uterine tandems and/or vaginal ovoids for clinical brachytherapy

> *CPT Assistant* Feb 02:8, Apr 09:3; *CPT Changes: An Insider's View* 2002

(For placement of needles or catheters into pelvic organs and/or genitalia [except prostate] for interstitial radioelement application, use 55920)

(For insertion of radioelement sources or ribbons, see 77761-77763, 77785-77787)

57160   Fitting and insertion of pessary or other intravaginal support device

> *CPT Assistant* Nov 96:9, Oct 98:11, Jun 00:11

57170   Diaphragm or cervical cap fitting with instructions

57180   Introduction of any hemostatic agent or pack for spontaneous or traumatic nonobstetrical vaginal hemorrhage (separate procedure)

> *CPT Assistant* Nov 07:1

Repair

(For urethral suspension, Marshall-Marchetti-Krantz type, abdominal approach, see 51840, 51841)

(For laparoscopic suspension, use 51990)

57200   Colporrhaphy, suture of injury of vagina (nonobstetrical)

57210   Colpoperineorrhaphy, suture of injury of vagina and/or perineum (nonobstetrical)

57220   Plastic operation on urethral sphincter, vaginal approach (eg, Kelly urethral plication)

> *CPT Assistant* Winter 90:7

57230   Plastic repair of urethrocele

> *CPT Assistant* Winter 90:7

57240   Anterior colporrhaphy, repair of cystocele with or without repair of urethrocele

> *CPT Assistant* Winter 90:7, Jan 97:3, Jun 02:5

57250   Posterior colporrhaphy, repair of rectocele with or without perineorrhaphy

> *CPT Assistant* Winter 90:7, Jun 02:4

(For repair of rectocele (separate procedure) without posterior colporrhaphy, use 45560)

57260   Combined anteroposterior colporrhaphy;

> *CPT Assistant* Jun 02:5

57265   with enterocele repair

> *CPT Assistant* Jun 02:6

+ 57267   Insertion of mesh or other prosthesis for repair of pelvic floor defect, each site (anterior, posterior compartment), vaginal approach (List separately in addition to code for primary procedure)

> *CPT Assistant* Jul 05:16; *CPT Changes: An Insider's View* 2005

(Use 57267 in conjunction with 45560, 57240-57265, 57285)

57268   Repair of enterocele, vaginal approach (separate procedure)

> *CPT Assistant* Jun 02:6

57270   Repair of enterocele, abdominal approach (separate procedure)

> *CPT Assistant* Jun 02:6

57280   Colpopexy, abdominal approach

> *CPT Assistant* Jan 97:3, Jun 02:6

57282   Colpopexy, vaginal; extra-peritoneal approach (sacrospinous, iliococcygeus)

> *CPT Assistant* Jan 97:3, Jun 02:6; *CPT Changes: An Insider's View* 2005

57283   intra-peritoneal approach (uterosacral, levator myorrhaphy)

> *CPT Changes: An Insider's View* 2005

57284   Paravaginal defect repair (including repair of cystocele, if performed); open abdominal approach

> *CPT Assistant* Jan 97:1, Jun 02:7, Jul 05:16; *CPT Changes: An Insider's View* 2008

(Do not report 57284 in conjunction with 51840, 51841, 51990, 57240, 57260, 57265, 58152, 58267)

57285   vaginal approach

> *CPT Changes: An Insider's View* 2008

(Do not report 57285 in conjunction with 51990, 57240, 57260, 57265, 58267)

57287   Removal or revision of sling for stress incontinence (eg, fascia or synthetic)

> *CPT Assistant* Jun 02:7; *CPT Changes: An Insider's View* 2001

57288   Sling operation for stress incontinence (eg, fascia or synthetic)

> *CPT Assistant* Nov 99:28, May 00:4, Oct 00:7, Apr 02:18, Jun 02:7; *CPT Changes: An Insider's View* 2000

(For laparoscopic approach, use 51992)

57289   Pereyra procedure, including anterior colporrhaphy

> *CPT Assistant* Jan 97:3, Jun 02:7

57291   Construction of artificial vagina; without graft

57292   with graft

57295   Revision (including removal) of prosthetic vaginal graft; vaginal approach
→ *CPT Changes: An Insider's View* 2006

57296   open abdominal approach
→ *CPT Changes: An Insider's View* 2007

►(For laparoscopic approach, use 57426)◄

57300   Closure of rectovaginal fistula; vaginal or transanal approach
→ *CPT Assistant* Nov 97:21

57305   abdominal approach
→ *CPT Assistant* Nov 97:21

57307   abdominal approach, with concomitant colostomy
→ *CPT Assistant* Nov 97:21

57308   transperineal approach, with perineal body reconstruction, with or without levator plication
→ *CPT Assistant* Nov 97:21

57310   Closure of urethrovaginal fistula;

57311   with bulbocavernosus transplant

57320   Closure of vesicovaginal fistula; vaginal approach

(For concomitant cystostomy, see 51020-51040, 51101, 51102)

57330   transvesical and vaginal approach

(For abdominal approach, use 51900)

57335   Vaginoplasty for intersex state

Manipulation

57400   Dilation of vagina under anesthesia (other than local)
→ *CPT Changes: An Insider's View* 2009

57410   Pelvic examination under anesthesia (other than local)
→ *CPT Assistant* Spring 93:34, Apr 06:1, Nov 07:1; *CPT Changes: An Insider's View* 2009

57415   Removal of impacted vaginal foreign body (separate procedure) under anesthesia (other than local)
→ *CPT Changes: An Insider's View* 2009

(For removal without anesthesia of an impacted vaginal foreign body, use the appropriate E/M code)

►Endoscopy/Laparoscopy◄

57420   Colposcopy of the entire vagina, with cervix if present;
→ *CPT Assistant* Feb 03:5; *CPT Changes: An Insider's View* 2003

57421   with biopsy(s) of vagina/cervix
→ *CPT Assistant* Feb 03:5, Jun 03:11, Jun 06:16; *CPT Changes: An Insider's View* 2003, 2006

(For colposcopic visualization of cervix and adjacent upper vagina, use 57452)

(When reporting colposcopies of multiple sites, use modifier 51 as appropriate. For colposcopic examinations/procedures involving the vulva, see 56820, 56821; cervix, see 57452-57461)

(For endometrial sampling (biopsy) performed in conjunction with colposcopy, use 58110)

57423   Paravaginal defect repair (including repair of cystocele, if performed), laparoscopic approach
→ *CPT Changes: An Insider's View* 2008

(Do not report 57423 in conjunction with 49320, 51840, 51841, 51990, 57240, 57260, 58152, 58267)

57425   Laparoscopy, surgical, colpopexy (suspension of vaginal apex)
→ *CPT Changes: An Insider's View* 2004

● **57426**   Revision (including removal) of prosthetic vaginal graft, laparoscopic approach
→ *CPT Changes: An Insider's View* 2010

►(For vaginal approach, see 57295. For open abdominal approach, see 57296)◄

Cervix Uteri

(For cervicography, see Category III code 0003T)

Contains temporary codes for emerging technology [handwritten]

Endoscopy

(For colposcopic examinations/procedures involving the vulva, see 56820, 56821; vagina, see 57420, 57421)

57452   Colposcopy of the cervix including upper/adjacent vagina;
→ *CPT Assistant* Apr 00:5, Feb 03:5, Jun 03:10; *CPT Changes: An Insider's View* 2003

(Do not report 57452 in addition to 57454-57461)

57454   with biopsy(s) of the cervix and endocervical curettage
→ *CPT Assistant* Apr 00:5, Feb 03:5, Jun 03:10; *CPT Changes: An Insider's View* 2003

57455   with biopsy(s) of the cervix
→ *CPT Assistant* Apr 00:5, Feb 03:5, Jun 03:10; *CPT Changes: An Insider's View* 2003

57456   with endocervical curettage
→ *CPT Assistant* Apr 00:5, Jan 03:23, Feb 03:5, Jun 03:10; *CPT Changes: An Insider's View* 2003

57460   with loop electrode biopsy(s) of the cervix   *LEEP* [handwritten]
→ *CPT Assistant* Apr 00:5, Jan 03:23, Feb 03:5, Jun 03:10, Jul 05:15; *CPT Changes: An Insider's View* 2003

57461   with loop electrode conization of the cervix
→ *CPT Assistant* Jan 03:23, Feb 03:5, Jun 03:10, Dec 06:15; *CPT Changes: An Insider's View* 2003

(Do not report 57456 in addition to 57461)

(For endometrial sampling [biopsy] performed in conjunction with colposcopy, use 58110)

Excision

(For radical surgical procedures, see 58200-58240)

57500   Biopsy of cervix, single or multiple, or local excision of lesion, with or without fulguration (separate procedure)
➔ *CPT Changes: An Insider's View* 2008

57505   Endocervical curettage (not done as part of a dilation and curettage)
➔ *CPT Assistant* Jul 05:15

57510   Cautery of cervix; electro or thermal
➔ *CPT Changes: An Insider's View* 2002

57511   cryocautery, initial or repeat

57513   laser ablation

57520   Conization of cervix, with or without fulguration, with or without dilation and curettage, with or without repair; cold knife or laser
➔ *CPT Assistant* Apr 00:5

(See also 58120)

57522   loop electrode excision
➔ *CPT Assistant* Apr 00:5, Mar 03:22, Jul 03:15

57530   Trachelectomy (cervicectomy), amputation of cervix (separate procedure)

57531   Radical trachelectomy, with bilateral total pelvic lymphadenectomy and para-aortic lymph node sampling biopsy, with or without removal of tube(s), with or without removal of ovary(s)
➔ *CPT Assistant* Nov 97:21

(For radical abdominal hysterectomy, use 58210)

57540   Excision of cervical stump, abdominal approach;

57545   with pelvic floor repair

57550   Excision of cervical stump, vaginal approach;

57555   with anterior and/or posterior repair

57556   with repair of enterocele

(For insertion of intrauterine device, use 58300)

(For insertion of any hemostatic agent or pack for control of spontaneous non-obstetrical hemorrhage, see 57180)

57558   Dilation and curettage of cervical stump
➔ *CPT Changes: An Insider's View* 2007

Repair

57700   Cerclage of uterine cervix, nonobstetrical

57720   Trachelorrhaphy, plastic repair of uterine cervix, vaginal approach

Manipulation

57800   Dilation of cervical canal, instrumental (separate procedure)

Corpus Uteri

Excision

58100   Endometrial sampling (biopsy) with or without endocervical sampling (biopsy), without cervical dilation, any method (separate procedure)

(For endocervical curettage only, use 57505)

(For endometrial sampling (biopsy) performed in conjunction with colposcopy (57420, 57421, 57452-57461), use 58110)

+ 58110   Endometrial sampling (biopsy) performed in conjunction with colposcopy (List separately in addition to code for primary procedure)
➔ *CPT Changes: An Insider's View* 2006

(Use 58110 in conjunction with 57420, 57421, 57452-57461)

58120   Dilation and curettage, diagnostic and/or therapeutic (nonobstetrical)   *D+C*
➔ *CPT Assistant* Fall 95:16, Nov 97:21, May 03:19

(For postpartum hemorrhage, use 59160)

58140   Myomectomy, excision of fibroid tumor(s) of uterus, 1 to 4 intramural myoma(s) with total weight of 250 g or less and/or removal of surface myomas; abdominal approach
➔ *CPT Assistant* Feb 03:15, Jun 03:5; *CPT Changes: An Insider's View* 2002, 2003

58145   vaginal approach

58146   Myomectomy, excision of fibroid tumor(s) of uterus, 5 or more intramural myomas and/or intramural myomas with total weight greater than 250 g, abdominal approach
➔ *CPT Assistant* Feb 03:15, Jun 03:5; *CPT Changes: An Insider's View* 2003

(Do not report 58146 in addition to 58140-58145, 58150-58240)

Hysterectomy Procedures

58150   Total abdominal hysterectomy (corpus and cervix), with or without removal of tube(s), with or without removal of ovary(s);
➔ *CPT Assistant* Dec 96:10, Apr 97:3, Nov 97:21, Sep 00:9, Aug 01:11

58152   with colpo-urethrocystopexy (eg, Marshall-Marchetti-Krantz, Burch)
➔ *CPT Assistant* Jan 97:1, Nov 97:22

(For urethrocystopexy without hysterectomy, see 51840, 51841)

58180   Supracervical abdominal hysterectomy (subtotal hysterectomy), with or without removal of tube(s), with or without removal of ovary(s)

58200   Total abdominal hysterectomy, including partial vaginectomy, with para-aortic and pelvic lymph node sampling, with or without removal of tube(s), with or without removal of ovary(s)

58210   Radical abdominal hysterectomy, with bilateral total pelvic lymphadenectomy and para-aortic lymph node sampling (biopsy), with or without removal of tube(s), with or without removal of ovary(s)
  ➔ *CPT Assistant* Fall 92:21

   (For radical hysterectomy with ovarian transposition, use also 58825)

58240   Pelvic exenteration for gynecologic malignancy, with total abdominal hysterectomy or cervicectomy, with or without removal of tube(s), with or without removal of ovary(s), with removal of bladder and ureteral transplantations, and/or abdominoperineal resection of rectum and colon and colostomy, or any combination thereof

   (For pelvic exenteration for lower urinary tract or male genital malignancy, use 51597)

58260   Vaginal hysterectomy, for uterus 250 g or less;
  ➔ *CPT Changes: An Insider's View* 2003

58262   with removal of tube(s), and/or ovary(s)

58263   with removal of tube(s), and/or ovary(s), with repair of enterocele

   (Do not report 58263 in addition to 57283)

58267   with colpo-urethrocystopexy (Marshall-Marchetti-Krantz type, Pereyra type) with or without endoscopic control

58270   with repair of enterocele

   (For repair of enterocele with removal of tubes and/or ovaries, use 58263)

58275   Vaginal hysterectomy, with total or partial vaginectomy;
  ➔ *CPT Changes: An Insider's View* 2002

58280   with repair of enterocele

58285   Vaginal hysterectomy, radical (Schauta type operation)
  ➔ *CPT Assistant* Nov 07:1

58290   Vaginal hysterectomy, for uterus greater than 250 g;
  ➔ *CPT Changes: An Insider's View* 2003

58291   with removal of tube(s) and/or ovary(s)
  ➔ *CPT Changes: An Insider's View* 2003

58292   with removal of tube(s) and/or ovary(s), with repair of enterocele
  ➔ *CPT Changes: An Insider's View* 2003

58293   with colpo-urethrocystopexy (Marshall-Marchetti-Krantz type, Pereyra type) with or without endoscopic control
  ➔ *CPT Changes: An Insider's View* 2003

58294   with repair of enterocele
  ➔ *CPT Changes: An Insider's View* 2003

Introduction

   (For insertion/removal of implantable contraceptive capsules, see 11975, 11976, 11977)

58300   Insertion of intrauterine device (IUD)
  ➔ *CPT Assistant* Apr 98:14

58301   Removal of intrauterine device (IUD)
  ➔ *CPT Assistant* Apr 98:14

58321   Artificial insemination; intra-cervical

58322   intra-uterine

58323   Sperm washing for artificial insemination
  ➔ *CPT Assistant* Jan 98:6

58340   Catheterization and introduction of saline or contrast material for saline infusion sonohysterography (SIS) or hysterosalpingography
  ➔ *CPT Assistant* Nov 97:22, Jul 99:8, Mar 09:11; *CPT Changes: An Insider's View* 2004

   (For radiological supervision and interpretation of saline infusion sonohysterography, use 76831)

   (For radiological supervision and interpretation of hysterosalpingography, use 74740)

58345   Transcervical introduction of fallopian tube catheter for diagnosis and/or re-establishing patency (any method), with or without hysterosalpingography
  ➔ *CPT Assistant* Nov 97:22, Mar 09:11

   (For radiological supervision and interpretation, use 74742)

58346   Insertion of Heyman capsules for clinical brachytherapy
  ➔ *CPT Assistant* Feb 02:8, Apr 09:3; *CPT Changes: An Insider's View* 2002

   (For placement of needles or catheters into pelvic organs and/or genitalia [except prostate] for interstitial radioelement application, use 55920)

   (For insertion of radioelement sources or ribbons, see 77761-77763, 77785-77787)

58350   Chromotubation of oviduct, including materials
  ➔ *CPT Assistant* May 02:19, Dec 08:7

   (For materials supplied by physician, use 99070)

58353   Endometrial ablation, thermal, without hysteroscopic guidance
  ➔ *CPT Assistant* Mar 02:11, Apr 02:19; *CPT Changes: An Insider's View* 2001

   (For hysteroscopic procedure, use 58563)

58356   Endometrial cryoablation with ultrasonic guidance, including endometrial curettage, when performed
  ➔ *CPT Changes: An Insider's View* 2005

   (Do not report 58356 in conjunction with 58100, 58120, 58340, 76700, 76856)

Repair

58400 Uterine suspension, with or without shortening of round ligaments, with or without shortening of sacrouterine ligaments; (separate procedure)

58410   with presacral sympathectomy
→ *CPT Assistant* Mar 07:9

(For anastomosis of tubes to uterus, use 58752)

58520 Hysterorrhaphy, repair of ruptured uterus (nonobstetrical)

58540 Hysteroplasty, repair of uterine anomaly (Strassman type)

(For closure of vesicouterine fistula, use 51920)

Laparoscopy/Hysteroscopy

Surgical laparoscopy always includes diagnostic laparoscopy. To report a diagnostic laparoscopy (peritoneoscopy) (separate procedure), use 49320. To report a diagnostic hysteroscopy (separate procedure), use 58555.

58541 Laparoscopy, surgical, supracervical hysterectomy, for uterus 250 g or less;
→ *CPT Assistant* Nov 07:1; *CPT Changes: An Insider's View* 2007

58542   with removal of tube(s) and/or ovary(s)
→ *CPT Assistant* Nov 07:1; *CPT Changes: An Insider's View* 2007

(Do not report 58541, 58542 in conjunction with 49320, 57000, 57180, 57410, 58140-58146, 58545, 58546, 58561, 58661, 58670, 58671)

58543 Laparoscopy, surgical, supracervical hysterectomy, for uterus greater than 250 g;
→ *CPT Assistant* Nov 07:1; *CPT Changes: An Insider's View* 2007

58544   with removal of tube(s) and/or ovary(s)
→ *CPT Assistant* Nov 07:1; *CPT Changes: An Insider's View* 2007

(Do not report 58543-58544 in conjunction with 49320, 57000, 57180, 57410, 58140-58146, 58545, 58546, 58561, 58661, 58670, 58671)

58545 Laparoscopy, surgical, myomectomy, excision; 1 to 4 intramural myomas with total weight of 250 g or less and/or removal of surface myomas
→ *CPT Assistant* Jun 03:5, 12; *CPT Changes: An Insider's View* 2003

58546   5 or more intramural myomas and/or intramural myomas with total weight greater than 250 g
→ *CPT Assistant* Jun 03:12, Jan 04:26; *CPT Changes: An Insider's View* 2003

58548 Laparoscopy, surgical, with radical hysterectomy, with bilateral total pelvic lymphadenectomy and para-aortic lymph node sampling (biopsy), with removal of tube(s) and ovary(s), if performed
→ *CPT Assistant* Nov 07:1; *CPT Changes: An Insider's View* 2007

(Do not report 58548 in conjunction with 38570-38572, 58210, 58285, 58550-58554)

58550 Laparoscopy, surgical, with vaginal hysterectomy, for uterus 250 g or less;
→ *CPT Assistant* Nov 99:28, Mar 00:9; *CPT Changes: An Insider's View* 2000, 2003

58552   with removal of tube(s) and/or ovary(s)
→ *CPT Assistant* Nov 07:1; *CPT Changes: An Insider's View* 2003

(Do not report 58550-58552 in conjunction with 49320, 57000, 57180, 57410, 58140-58146, 58545, 58546, 58561, 58661, 58670, 58671)

58553 Laparoscopy, surgical, with vaginal hysterectomy, for uterus greater than 250 g;
→ *CPT Changes: An Insider's View* 2003

58554   with removal of tube(s) and/or ovary(s)
→ *CPT Changes: An Insider's View* 2003

(Do not report 58553-58554 in conjunction with 49320, 57000, 57180, 57410, 58140-58146, 58545, 58546, 58561, 58661, 58670, 58671)

58555 Hysteroscopy, diagnostic (separate procedure)
→ *CPT Assistant* Nov 99:28, Mar 00:10; *CPT Changes: An Insider's View* 2000

58558 Hysteroscopy, surgical; with sampling (biopsy) of endometrium and/or polypectomy, with or without D & C
→ *CPT Assistant* Nov 99:28, Mar 00:10, Sep 02:10, Jan 03:7, May 03:19; *CPT Changes: An Insider's View* 2000

58559   with lysis of intrauterine adhesions (any method)
→ *CPT Assistant* Nov 99:28, Mar 00:10; *CPT Changes: An Insider's View* 2000

58560   with division or resection of intrauterine septum (any method)
→ *CPT Assistant* Nov 99:28, Mar 00:10; *CPT Changes: An Insider's View* 2000

58561   with removal of leiomyomata
→ *CPT Assistant* Nov 99:28, Mar 00:10, Jan 03:7; *CPT Changes: An Insider's View* 2000

58562   with removal of impacted foreign body
→ *CPT Assistant* Nov 99:28, Mar 00:10; *CPT Changes: An Insider's View* 2000

58563   with endometrial ablation (eg, endometrial resection, electrosurgical ablation, thermoablation)
→ *CPT Assistant* Nov 99:28, Mar 00:10, Mar 02:11, Apr 02:19, Jan 03:7; *CPT Changes: An Insider's View* 2000, 2002

Hysteroscopy
58563

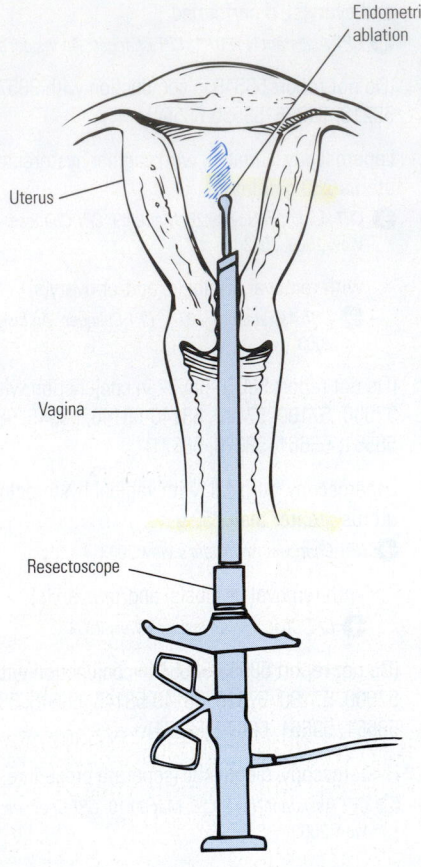

Endometrial ablation

Uterus

Vagina

Resectoscope

58565   with bilateral fallopian tube cannulation to induce occlusion by placement of permanent implants

→ *CPT Changes: An Insider's View* 2005

(Do not report 58565 in conjunction with 58555 or 57800)

(For unilateral procedure, use modifier 52)

58570   Laparoscopy, surgical, with total hysterectomy, for uterus 250 g or less;

→ *CPT Changes: An Insider's View* 2008

58571   with removal of tube(s) and/or ovary(s)

→ *CPT Changes: An Insider's View* 2008

58572   Laparoscopy, surgical, with total hysterectomy, for uterus greater than 250 g;

→ *CPT Changes: An Insider's View* 2008

58573   with removal of tube(s) and/or ovary(s)

→ *CPT Changes: An Insider's View* 2008

(Do not report 58570-58573 in conjunction with 49320, 57000, 57180, 57410, 58140-58146, 58150, 58545, 58546, 58561, 58661, 58670, 58671)

58578   Unlisted laparoscopy procedure, uterus

→ *CPT Assistant* Nov 99:28, Mar 00:10, Mar 07:9; *CPT Changes: An Insider's View* 2000

58579   Unlisted hysteroscopy procedure, uterus

→ *CPT Assistant* Nov 99:28, Mar 00:10; *CPT Changes: An Insider's View* 2000

Oviduct/Ovary

Incision

58600   Ligation or transection of fallopian tube(s), abdominal or vaginal approach, unilateral or bilateral

→ *CPT Assistant* Nov 99:28; *CPT Changes: An Insider's View* 2000

58605   Ligation or transection of fallopian tube(s), abdominal or vaginal approach, postpartum, unilateral or bilateral, during same hospitalization (separate procedure)

→ *CPT Assistant* Nov 99:28; *CPT Changes: An Insider's View* 2000

(For laparoscopic procedures, use 58670, 58671)

+ 58611   Ligation or transection of fallopian tube(s) when done at the time of cesarean delivery or intra-abdominal surgery (not a separate procedure) (List separately in addition to code for primary procedure)

→ *CPT Changes: An Insider's View* 2002

58615   Occlusion of fallopian tube(s) by device (eg, band, clip, Falope ring) vaginal or suprapubic approach

→ *CPT Assistant* Nov 99:28; *CPT Changes: An Insider's View* 2000

(For laparoscopic approach, use 58671)

(For lysis of adnexal adhesions, use 58740)

Laparoscopy

Surgical laparoscopy always includes diagnostic laparoscopy. To report a diagnostic laparoscopy (peritoneoscopy) (separate procedure), use 49320.

58660   Laparoscopy, surgical; with lysis of adhesions (salpingolysis, ovariolysis) (separate procedure)

→ *CPT Assistant* Nov 99:28, Mar 00:10, Mar 03:22; *CPT Changes: An Insider's View* 2000

58661   with removal of adnexal structures (partial or total oophorectomy and/or salpingectomy)

→ *CPT Assistant* Nov 99:28, Mar 00:10, Jan 02:11, Nov 07:1; *CPT Changes: An Insider's View* 2000

58662   with fulguration or excision of lesions of the ovary, pelvic viscera, or peritoneal surface by any method

→ *CPT Assistant* Nov 99:28, Mar 00:10; *CPT Changes: An Insider's View* 2000

58670   with fulguration of oviducts (with or without transection)

→ *CPT Assistant* Nov 99:29, Mar 00:10; *CPT Changes: An Insider's View* 2000

58671   with occlusion of oviducts by device (eg, band, clip, or Falope ring)

→ *CPT Assistant* Nov 99:29, Mar 00:10; *CPT Changes: An Insider's View* 2000

58672   with fimbrioplasty

→ *CPT Assistant* Nov 99:29, Mar 00:10; *CPT Changes: An Insider's View* 2000

58673   with salpingostomy (salpingoneostomy)
→ *CPT Assistant* Nov 99:29, Mar 00:10, May 02:19; *CPT Changes: An Insider's View* 2000

(Codes 58672 and 58673 are used to report unilateral procedures. For bilateral procedure, use modifier 50)

58679   Unlisted laparoscopy procedure, oviduct, ovary
→ *CPT Assistant* Nov 99:29, Mar 00:10; *CPT Changes: An Insider's View* 2000

(For laparoscopic aspiration of ovarian cyst, use 49322)

(For laparoscopic biopsy of the ovary or fallopian tube, use 49321)

Excision

58700   Salpingectomy, complete or partial, unilateral or bilateral (separate procedure)

58720   Salpingo-oophorectomy, complete or partial, unilateral or bilateral (separate procedure)
→ *CPT Assistant* Sep 00:9, Jul 06:19

Repair

58740   Lysis of adhesions (salpingolysis, ovariolysis)
→ *CPT Assistant* Sep 96:9, Nov 99:29; *CPT Changes: An Insider's View* 2000

(For laparoscopic approach, use 58660)

(For excision or destruction of endometriomas, open method, see 49203-49205, 58957, 58958)

(For fulguration or excision of lesions, laparoscopic approach, use 58662)

58750   Tubotubal anastomosis

58752   Tubouterine implantation

58760   Fimbrioplasty
→ *CPT Assistant* Nov 99:29; *CPT Changes: An Insider's View* 2000

(For laparoscopic approach, use 58672)

58770   Salpingostomy (salpingoneostomy)
→ *CPT Assistant* Nov 99:29; *CPT Changes: An Insider's View* 2000

(For laparoscopic approach, use 58673)

Ovary

Incision

58800   Drainage of ovarian cyst(s), unilateral or bilateral (separate procedure); vaginal approach

58805   abdominal approach

58820   Drainage of ovarian abscess; vaginal approach, open
→ *CPT Assistant* Nov 97:22

58822   abdominal approach
→ *CPT Assistant* Nov 97:22

⊙ 58823   Drainage of pelvic abscess, transvaginal or transrectal approach, percutaneous (eg, ovarian, pericolic)
→ *CPT Assistant* Nov 97:22, Mar 98:8

(For radiological supervision and interpretation, use 75989)

58825   Transposition, ovary(s)

Excision

58900   Biopsy of ovary, unilateral or bilateral (separate procedure)
→ *CPT Assistant* Nov 99:29; *CPT Changes: An Insider's View* 2000

(For laparoscopic biopsy of the ovary or fallopian tube, use 49321)

58920   Wedge resection or bisection of ovary, unilateral or bilateral

58925   Ovarian cystectomy, unilateral or bilateral

58940   Oophorectomy, partial or total, unilateral or bilateral;
→ *CPT Assistant* Mar 04:3

(For oophorectomy with concomitant debulking for ovarian malignancy, use 58952)

58943   for ovarian, tubal or primary peritoneal malignancy, with para-aortic and pelvic lymph node biopsies, peritoneal washings, peritoneal biopsies, diaphragmatic assessments, with or without salpingectomy(s), with or without omentectomy
→ *CPT Changes: An Insider's View* 2001

58950   Resection (initial) of ovarian, tubal or primary peritoneal malignancy with bilateral salpingo-oophorectomy and omentectomy;
→ *CPT Changes: An Insider's View* 2001, 2007

58951   with total abdominal hysterectomy, pelvic and limited para-aortic lymphadenectomy
→ *CPT Assistant* Aug 01:11

58952   with radical dissection for debulking (ie, radical excision or destruction, intra-abdominal or retroperitoneal tumors)
→ *CPT Assistant* Dec 96:10, Aug 01:11; *CPT Changes: An Insider's View* 2001

(For resection of recurrent ovarian, tubal, primary peritoneal, or uterine malignancy, see 58957, 58958)

58953   Bilateral salpingo-oophorectomy with omentectomy, total abdominal hysterectomy and radical dissection for debulking;
→ *CPT Assistant* Feb 02:8; *CPT Changes: An Insider's View* 2002

58954   with pelvic lymphadenectomy and limited para-aortic lymphadenectomy
→ *CPT Assistant* Feb 02:9; *CPT Changes: An Insider's View* 2002

58956   Bilateral salpingo-oophorectomy with total omentectomy, total abdominal hysterectomy for malignancy
→ *CPT Changes: An Insider's View* 2005

(Do not report 58956 in conjunction with 49255, 58150, 58180, 58262, 58263, 58550, 58661, 58700, 58720, 58900, 58925, 58940, 58957, 58958)

58957   Resection (tumor debulking) of recurrent ovarian, tubal, primary peritoneal, uterine malignancy (intra-abdominal, retroperitoneal tumors), with omentectomy, if performed;

➔ *CPT Changes: An Insider's View* 2007

58958   with pelvic lymphadenectomy and limited para-aortic lymphadenectomy

➔ *CPT Changes: An Insider's View* 2007

(Do not report 58957, 58958 in conjunction with 38770, 38780, 44005, 49000, 49203-49215, 49255, 58900-58960)

58960   Laparotomy, for staging or restaging of ovarian, tubal, or primary peritoneal malignancy (second look), with or without omentectomy, peritoneal washing, biopsy of abdominal and pelvic peritoneum, diaphragmatic assessment with pelvic and limited para-aortic lymphadenectomy

➔ *CPT Changes: An Insider's View* 2001

(Do not report 58960 in conjunction with 58957, 58958)

In Vitro Fertilization

58970   Follicle puncture for oocyte retrieval, any method

(For radiological supervision and interpretation, use 76948)

58974   Embryo transfer, intrauterine

58976   Gamete, zygote, or embryo intrafallopian transfer, any method

➔ *CPT Assistant* Nov 99:29; *CPT Changes: An Insider's View* 2000

(For laparoscopic adnexal procedures, see 58660-58673)

Other Procedures

58999   Unlisted procedure, female genital system (nonobstetrical)

Maternity Care and Delivery

The services normally provided in uncomplicated maternity cases include antepartum care, delivery, and postpartum care.

Antepartum care includes the initial and subsequent history, physical examinations, recording of weight, blood pressures, fetal heart tones, routine chemical urinalysis, and monthly visits up to 28 weeks gestation, biweekly visits to 36 weeks gestation, and weekly visits until delivery. Any other visits or services within this time period should be coded separately.

Delivery services include admission to the hospital, the admission history and physical examination, management of uncomplicated labor, vaginal delivery (with or without episiotomy, with or without forceps), or cesarean delivery. Medical problems complicating labor and delivery management may require additional resources and should be identified by utilizing the codes in the **Medicine** and **Evaluation and Management Services** section in addition to codes for maternity care.

Postpartum care includes hospital and office visits following vaginal or cesarean section delivery.

For medical complications of pregnancy (eg, cardiac problems, neurological problems, diabetes, hypertension, toxemia, hyperemesis, pre-term labor, premature rupture of membranes), see services in the **Medicine** and **Evaluation and Management Services** section.

For surgical complications of pregnancy (eg, appendectomy, hernia, ovarian cyst, Bartholin cyst), see services in the **Surgery** section.

If a physician provides all or part of the antepartum and/or postpartum patient care but does not perform delivery due to termination of pregnancy by abortion or referral to another physician for delivery, see the antepartum and postpartum care codes 59425-59426 and 59430.

(For circumcision of newborn, see 54150, 54160)

▶Antepartum and Fetal Invasive Services◀

▶(For fetal intrauterine transfusion, use 36460)◀

▶(For unlisted fetal invasive procedure, use 59897)◀

59000   Amniocentesis; diagnostic

➔ *CPT Assistant* Apr 97:2, Feb 02:7, Aug 02:2, May 04:2; *CPT Changes: An Insider's View* 2002

(For radiological supervision and interpretation, use 76946)

59001   therapeutic amniotic fluid reduction (includes ultrasound guidance)

➔ *CPT Assistant* Feb 02:7, Aug 02:2; *CPT Changes: An Insider's View* 2002

Amniocentesis, Therapeutic Amniotic Fluid Reduction
59001

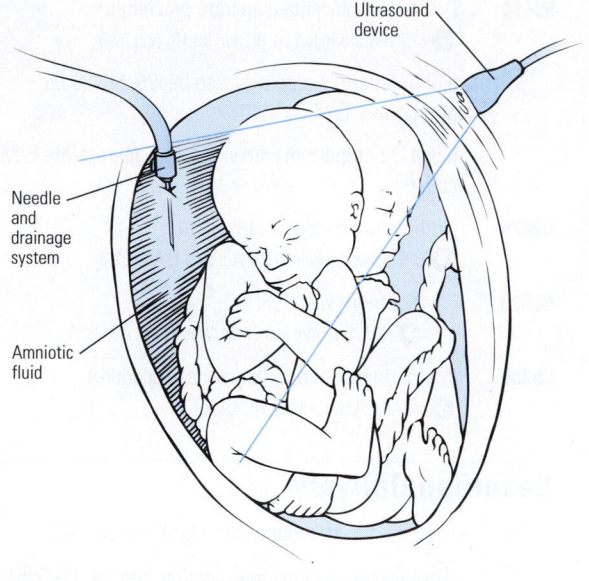

Ultrasound device

Needle and drainage system

Amniotic fluid

59012　Cordocentesis (intrauterine), any method
> *CPT Assistant* Aug 02:2

(For radiological supervision and interpretation, use 76941)

59015　Chorionic villus sampling, any method
> *CPT Assistant* Apr 97:2, Aug 02:2

(For radiological supervision and interpretation, use 76945)

59020　Fetal contraction stress test
> *CPT Assistant* Apr 97:2, Aug 02:2

59025　Fetal non-stress test
> *CPT Assistant* Apr 97:2, May 98:10, Oct 04:10, Dec 08:8

59030　Fetal scalp blood sampling
> *CPT Assistant* Aug 02:3

(For repeat fetal scalp blood sampling, use 59030 and see modifiers 76 and 77)

59050　Fetal monitoring during labor by consulting physician (ie, non-attending physician) with written report; supervision and interpretation
> *CPT Assistant* Nov 97:22

59051　interpretation only
> *CPT Assistant* Nov 97:22

59070　Transabdominal amnioinfusion, including ultrasound guidance
> *CPT Assistant* May 04:2; *CPT Changes: An Insider's View* 2004

59072　Fetal umbilical cord occlusion, including ultrasound guidance
> *CPT Assistant* May 04:2; *CPT Changes: An Insider's View* 2004

59074　Fetal fluid drainage (eg, vesicocentesis, thoracocentesis, paracentesis), including ultrasound guidance
> *CPT Assistant* May 04:2, 4, Dec 04:19; *CPT Changes: An Insider's View* 2004

59076　Fetal shunt placement, including ultrasound guidance
> *CPT Assistant* May 04:2, 4, Dec 04:19; *CPT Changes: An Insider's View* 2004

Excision

59100　Hysterotomy, abdominal (eg, for hydatidiform mole, abortion)

(When tubal ligation is performed at the same time as hysterotomy, use 58611 in addition to 59100)

59120　Surgical treatment of ectopic pregnancy; tubal or ovarian, requiring salpingectomy and/or oophorectomy, abdominal or vaginal approach

59121　tubal or ovarian, without salpingectomy and/or oophorectomy

59130　abdominal pregnancy

59135　interstitial, uterine pregnancy requiring total hysterectomy

59136　interstitial, uterine pregnancy with partial resection of uterus

59140　cervical, with evacuation

59150　Laparoscopic treatment of ectopic pregnancy; without salpingectomy and/or oophorectomy
> *CPT Assistant* Sep 96:9

Laparoscopic Treatment of Ectopic Pregnancy
59150

The site of gestation is located with a laparoscope and a small incision is made above the site. The ectopic pregnancy is then removed.

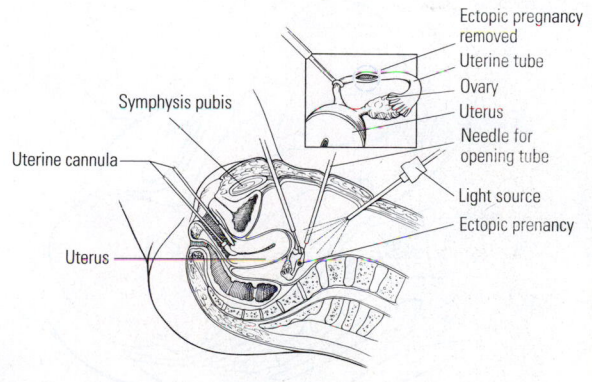

Ectopic pregnancy removed
Uterine tube
Ovary
Uterus
Needle for opening tube
Light source
Ectopic prenancy
Symphysis pubis
Uterine cannula
Uterus

59151　with salpingectomy and/or oophorectomy

59160　Curettage, postpartum
> *CPT Assistant* Nov 97:22, Sep 02:11

Introduction

(For intrauterine fetal transfusion, use 36460)

(For introduction of hypertonic solution and/or prostaglandins to initiate labor, see 59850-59857)

59200 Insertion of cervical dilator (eg, laminaria, prostaglandin) (separate procedure)
> *CPT Assistant* Fall 93:9, Apr 97:3

Repair

(For tracheloplasty, use 57700)

59300 Episiotomy or vaginal repair, by other than attending physician

59320 Cerclage of cervix, during pregnancy; vaginal
> *CPT Assistant* Aug 02:2, Nov 06:21, Feb 07:10

59325 abdominal
> *CPT Assistant* Aug 02:2, Nov 06:21, Feb 07:10

59350 Hysterorrhaphy of ruptured uterus
> *CPT Assistant* Aug 02:2

Vaginal Delivery, Antepartum and Postpartum Care

59400 Routine obstetric care including antepartum care, vaginal delivery (with or without episiotomy, and/or forceps) and postpartum care
> *CPT Assistant* Feb 96:1, Mar 96:11, Feb 97:11, Apr 97:3, Apr 98:15, Jun 98:10, Aug 02:3, Feb 03:15

Vaginal Delivery
59400-59410

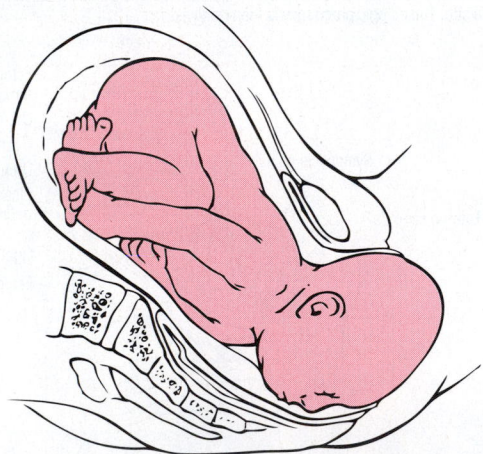

59409 Vaginal delivery only (with or without episiotomy and/or forceps);
> *CPT Assistant* Feb 96:1, Mar 96:11, Jul 96:11, Sep 96:4, Feb 97:11, Apr 97:1, Aug 02:3

59410 including postpartum care

59412 External cephalic version, with or without tocolysis
> *CPT Assistant* Fall 94:21, Feb 96:1, Aug 02:2-3

(Use 59412 in addition to code[s] for delivery)

59414 Delivery of placenta (separate procedure)
> *CPT Assistant* Jun 96:10, Jun 98:10, Aug 02:3

(For antepartum care only, see 59425, 59426 or appropriate E/M code(s))

(For 1-3 antepartum care visits, see appropriate E/M code(s))

59425 Antepartum care only; 4-6 visits
> *CPT Assistant* Fall 94:21, Apr 97:11, Aug 02:3

59426 7 or more visits
> *CPT Assistant* Fall 94:21, Apr 97:11, Aug 02:3

59430 Postpartum care only (separate procedure)
> *CPT Assistant* Jun 96:10, Aug 02:3

Cesarean Delivery

(For standby attendance for infant, use 99360)

(For low cervical cesarean section, see 59510, 59515, 59525)

Cesarean Delivery
59510-59515

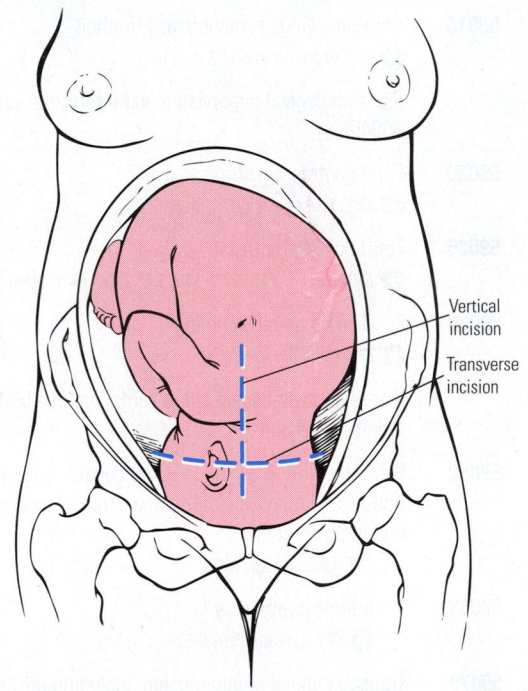

Vertical incision

Transverse incision

59510 Routine obstetric care including antepartum care, cesarean delivery, and postpartum care
> *CPT Assistant* Jul 96:11, Sep 96:4, Oct 96:10, Feb 97:11, Apr 97:2, Aug 02:3

59514   Cesarean delivery only;

→ *CPT Assistant* Oct 96:10, Feb 97:11

59515   including postpartum care

(For classic cesarean section, see 59510, 59515, 59525)

+ 59525   Subtotal or total hysterectomy after cesarean delivery (List separately in addition to code for primary procedure)

(Use 59525 in conjunction with 59510, 59514, 59515, 59618, 59620, 59622)

(For extraperitoneal cesarean section, or cesarean section with subtotal or total hysterectomy, see 59510, 59515, 59525)

Delivery After Previous Cesarean Delivery

Patients who have had a previous cesarean delivery and now present with the expectation of a vaginal delivery are coded using codes 59610-59622. If the patient has a successful vaginal delivery after a previous cesarean delivery (VBAC), use codes 59610-59614. If the attempt is unsuccessful and another cesarean delivery is carried out, use codes 59618-59622. To report elective cesarean deliveries use code 59510, 59514 or 59515.

59610   Routine obstetric care including antepartum care, vaginal delivery (with or without episiotomy, and/or forceps) and postpartum care, after previous cesarean delivery

→ *CPT Assistant* Feb 96:2, Apr 97:3, Aug 02:3

59612   Vaginal delivery only, after previous cesarean delivery (with or without episiotomy and/or forceps);

→ *CPT Assistant* Feb 96:2, Aug 02:3

59614   including postpartum care

→ *CPT Assistant* Feb 96:2

59618   Routine obstetric care including antepartum care, cesarean delivery, and postpartum care, following attempted vaginal delivery after previous cesarean delivery

→ *CPT Assistant* Feb 96:2, Aug 02:4

59620   Cesarean delivery only, following attempted vaginal delivery after previous cesarean delivery;

→ *CPT Assistant* Feb 96:2

59622   including postpartum care

→ *CPT Assistant* Feb 96:2

Abortion

(For medical treatment of spontaneous complete abortion, any trimester, use E/M codes 99201-99233)

(For surgical treatment of spontaneous abortion, use 59812)

59812   Treatment of incomplete abortion, any trimester, completed surgically

→ *CPT Assistant* Fall 93:9, Fall 95:16

59820   Treatment of missed abortion, completed surgically; first trimester

→ *CPT Assistant* Fall 93:9, Fall 95:16, Feb 99:10

59821   second trimester

→ *CPT Assistant* Fall 93:9, Fall 95:16

59830   Treatment of septic abortion, completed surgically

→ *CPT Assistant* Fall 93:9

59840   Induced abortion, by dilation and curettage

→ *CPT Assistant* Fall 93:9, Sep 03:16

59841   Induced abortion, by dilation and evacuation

→ *CPT Assistant* Fall 93:9

59850   Induced abortion, by 1 or more intra-amniotic injections (amniocentesis-injections), including hospital admission and visits, delivery of fetus and secundines;

→ *CPT Assistant* Fall 93:10

59851   with dilation and curettage and/or evacuation

→ *CPT Assistant* Fall 93:10

59852   with hysterotomy (failed intra-amniotic injection)

→ *CPT Assistant* Fall 93:10

(For insertion of cervical dilator, use 59200)

59855   Induced abortion, by 1 or more vaginal suppositories (eg, prostaglandin) with or without cervical dilation (eg, laminaria), including hospital admission and visits, delivery of fetus and secundines;

59856   with dilation and curettage and/or evacuation

59857   with hysterotomy (failed medical evacuation)

Other Procedures

59866   Multifetal pregnancy reduction(s) (MPR)

59870   Uterine evacuation and curettage for hydatidiform mole

→ *CPT Assistant* Feb 99:10

59871   Removal of cerclage suture under anesthesia (other than local)

→ *CPT Assistant* Nov 97:22, Nov 06:21, Feb 07:10

▲ 59897   Unlisted fetal invasive procedure, including ultrasound
           guidance, when performed
           ➜ *CPT Assistant* May 04:5; *CPT Changes: An Insider's View* 2004,
             2010

  59898   Unlisted laparoscopy procedure, maternity care and
           delivery
           ➜ *CPT Assistant* Nov 99:29, Mar 00:10; *CPT Changes: An Insider's
             View* 2000

  59899   Unlisted procedure, maternity care and delivery
           ➜ *CPT Assistant* Jun 97:10

Endocrine System

(For pituitary and pineal surgery, see **Nervous System**)

Thyroid Gland

Incision

  60000   Incision and drainage of thyroglossal duct cyst, infected
           ➜ *CPT Changes: An Insider's View* 2002

Excision

           (60001 has been deleted. To report, use 60300)

  60100   Biopsy thyroid, percutaneous core needle
           ➜ *CPT Assistant* Jun 97:5, Jun 07:10

           (If imaging guidance is performed, see 76942, 77002,
           77012, 77021)

           (For fine needle aspiration, use 10021 or 10022)

           (For evaluation of fine needle aspirate, see 88172, 88173)

  60200   Excision of cyst or adenoma of thyroid, or transection of
           isthmus

  60210   Partial thyroid lobectomy, unilateral; with or without
           isthmusectomy

  60212   with contralateral subtotal lobectomy, including
               isthmusectomy

  60220   Total thyroid lobectomy, unilateral; with or without
           isthmusectomy

Thyroid Lobectomy
60220

The thyroid is exposed via a transverse cervical incision. The superior and inferior thyroid vessels serving the lobe are ligated, the isthmus is severed, and the entire thyroid lobe is resected.

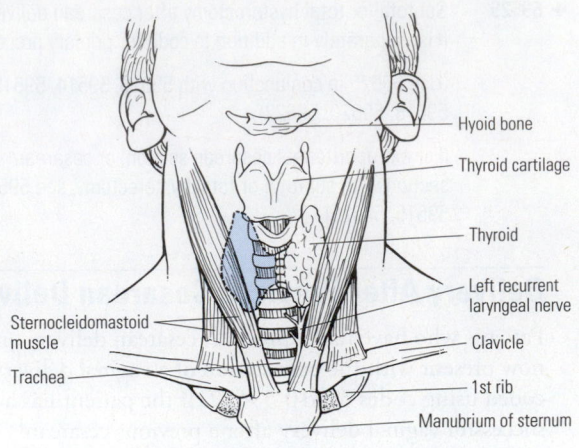

Hyoid bone
Thyroid cartilage
Thyroid
Left recurrent laryngeal nerve
Sternocleidomastoid muscle
Clavicle
Trachea
1st rib
Manubrium of sternum

  60225   with contralateral subtotal lobectomy, including
               isthmusectomy

  60240   Thyroidectomy, total or complete

           (For thyroidectomy, subtotal or partial, use 60271)

  60252   Thyroidectomy, total or subtotal for malignancy; with
           limited neck dissection
           ➜ *CPT Assistant* Nov 00:10

  60254   with radical neck dissection
           ➜ *CPT Assistant* Nov 00:10

  60260   Thyroidectomy, removal of all remaining thyroid tissue
           following previous removal of a portion of thyroid

           (For bilateral procedure, report 60260 with modifier 50)

  60270   Thyroidectomy, including substernal thyroid; sternal split
           or transthoracic approach
           ➜ *CPT Changes: An Insider's View* 2002

  60271   cervical approach

  60280   Excision of thyroglossal duct cyst or sinus;

  60281   recurrent

           (For thyroid ultrasonography, use 76536)

Removal

60300 Aspiration and/or injection, thyroid cyst
➲ *CPT Changes: An Insider's View* 2008

(For fine needle aspiration, see 10021, 10022)

(If imaging guidance is performed, see 76942, 77012)

Parathyroid, Thymus, Adrenal Glands, Pancreas, and Carotid Body

Excision

(For pituitary and pineal surgery, see **Nervous System**)

60500 Parathyroidectomy or exploration of parathyroid(s);

60502 re-exploration

60505 with mediastinal exploration, sternal split or transthoracic approach

✛ **60512** Parathyroid autotransplantation (List separately in addition to code for primary procedure)

(Use 60512 in conjunction with 60500, 60502, 60505, 60212, 60225, 60240, 60252, 60254, 60260, 60270, 60271)

Posterior View of the Pharynx
60512

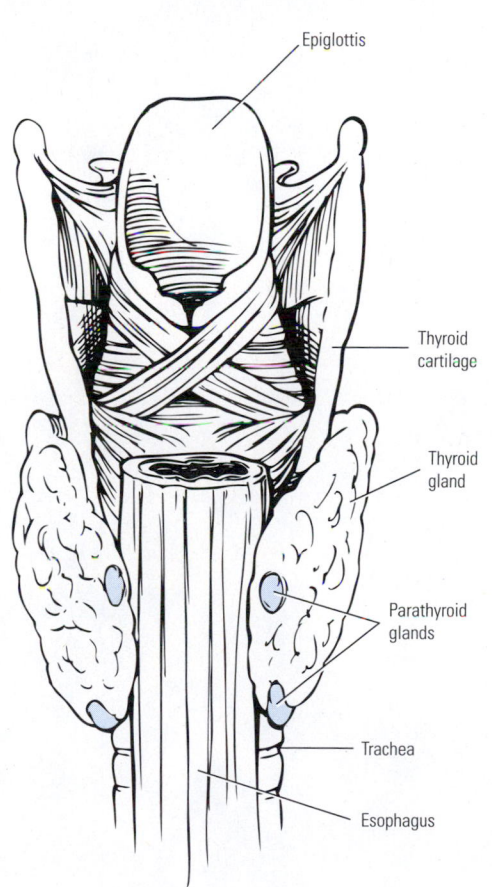

- Epiglottis
- Thyroid cartilage
- Thyroid gland
- Parathyroid glands
- Trachea
- Esophagus

60520 Thymectomy, partial or total; transcervical approach (separate procedure)

60521 sternal split or transthoracic approach, without radical mediastinal dissection (separate procedure)
➲ *CPT Assistant* Dec 07:12

60522 sternal split or transthoracic approach, with radical mediastinal dissection (separate procedure)

60540 Adrenalectomy, partial or complete, or exploration of adrenal gland with or without biopsy, transabdominal, lumbar or dorsal (separate procedure);
➲ *CPT Assistant* Nov 98:17

60545 with excision of adjacent retroperitoneal tumor
➲ *CPT Assistant* Nov 98:17

(Do not report 60540, 60545 in conjunction with 50323)

(For bilateral procedure, report 60540 with modifier 50)

(For excision of remote or disseminated pheochromocytoma, see 49203-49205)

(For laparoscopic approach, use 60650)

60600 Excision of carotid body tumor; without excision of carotid artery

60605 with excision of carotid artery

Laparoscopy

Surgical laparoscopy always includes diagnostic laparoscopy. To report a diagnostic laparoscopy (peritoneoscopy) (separate procedure), use 49320.

60650 Laparoscopy, surgical, with adrenalectomy, partial or complete, or exploration of adrenal gland with or without biopsy, transabdominal, lumbar or dorsal
➲ *CPT Assistant* Nov 99:30, Mar 00:10, Nov 01:8; *CPT Changes: An Insider's View* 2000

Laparoscopic Adrenalectomy
60650

An adrenal gland is dissected and removed under laparoscopic guidance. Multiple small blood vessels from the vena cava and the aorta do not follow standard anatomic pattern, requiring intricate dissection.

Left

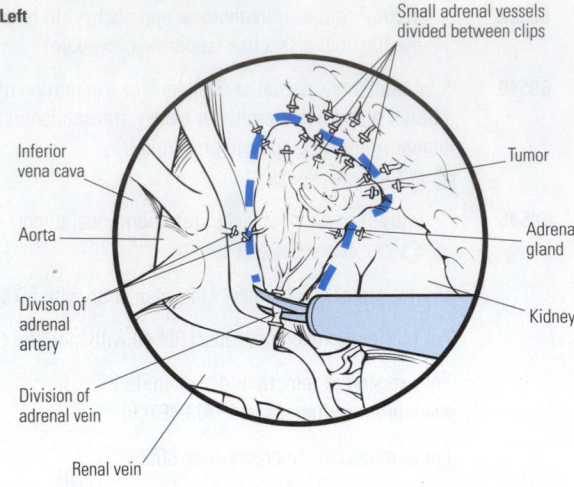

- Inferior vena cava
- Aorta
- Divison of adrenal artery
- Division of adrenal vein
- Renal vein
- Small adrenal vessels divided between clips
- Tumor
- Adrenal gland
- Kidney

Right

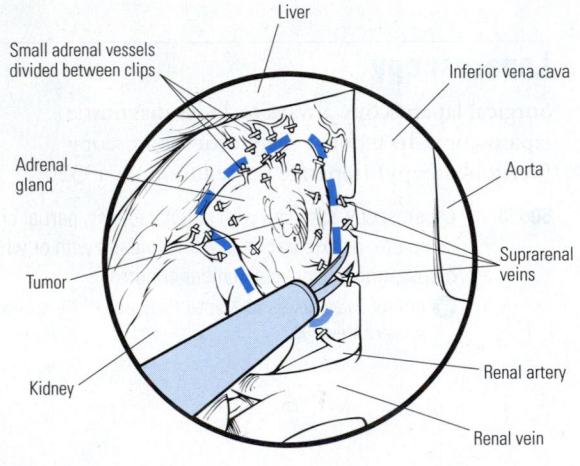

- Small adrenal vessels divided between clips
- Adrenal gland
- Tumor
- Kidney
- Liver
- Inferior vena cava
- Aorta
- Suprarenal veins
- Renal artery
- Renal vein

60659   Unlisted laparoscopy procedure, endocrine system
➜ *CPT Assistant* Nov 99:30, Mar 00:10; *CPT Changes: An Insider's View* 2000

Other Procedures

60699   Unlisted procedure, endocrine system
➜ *CPT Assistant* Feb 06:16, Dec 07:12

Nervous System (61000-64999) 296

The following is a listing of headings and subheadings that appear within the Nervous System section of the CPT codebook. The subheadings or subsections denoted with asterisks (*) below have special instructions unique to that section. Where these are indicated, special "notes" or guidelines will be presented preceding those procedural terminology listings, referring to that subsection specifically.

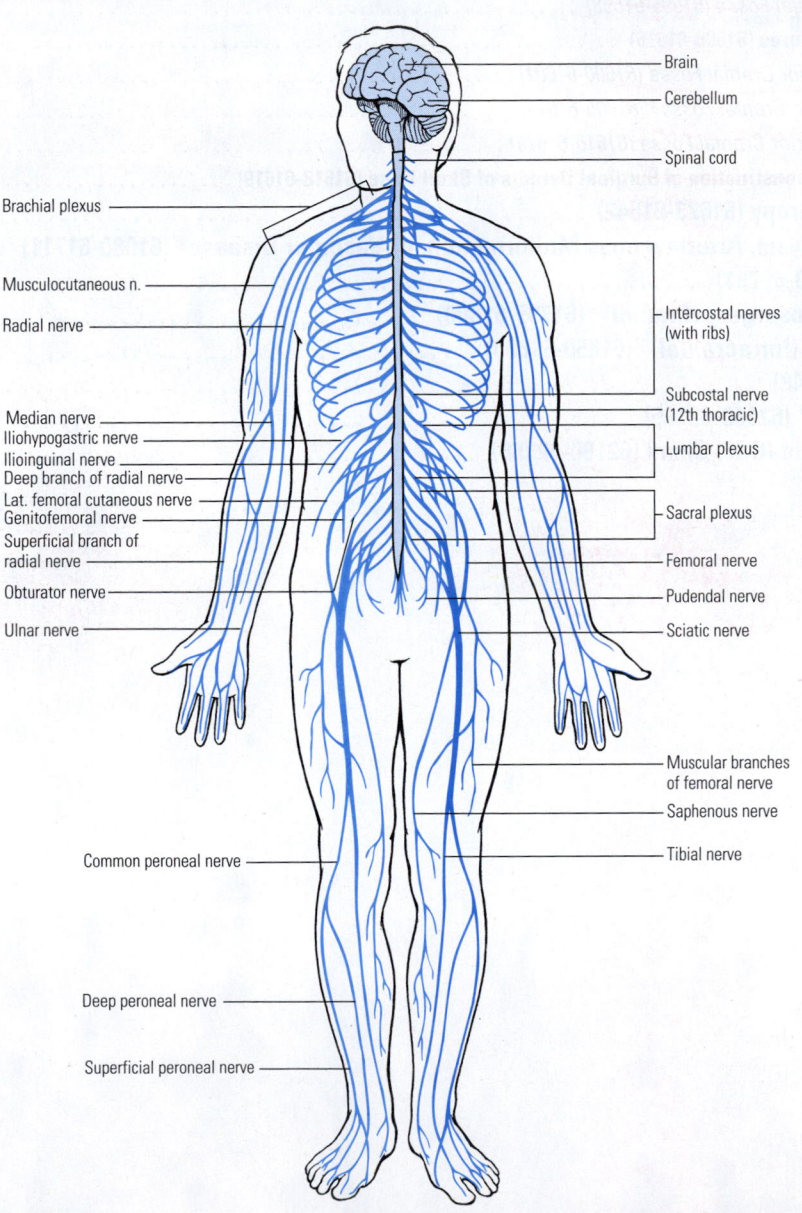

Brain

Cerebellum

Spinal cord

Brachial plexus

Musculocutaneous n.

Radial nerve

Intercostal nerves (with ribs)

Subcostal nerve (12th thoracic)

Median nerve
Iliohypogastric nerve
Ilioinguinal nerve
Deep branch of radial nerve
Lat. femoral cutaneous nerve
Genitofemoral nerve
Superficial branch of radial nerve

Obturator nerve

Ulnar nerve

Lumbar plexus

Sacral plexus

Femoral nerve

Pudendal nerve

Sciatic nerve

Muscular branches of femoral nerve

Saphenous nerve

Common peroneal nerve

Tibial nerve

Deep peroneal nerve

Superficial peroneal nerve

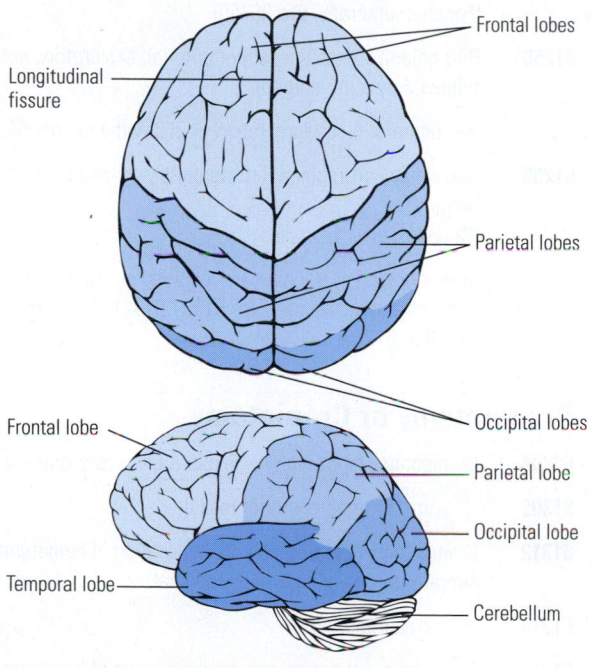

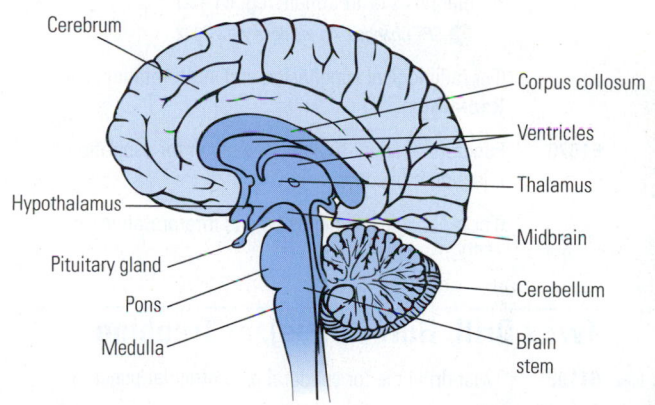

Nervous System

Skull, Meninges, and Brain

(For injection procedure for cerebral angiography, see 36100-36218)

(For injection procedure for ventriculography, see 61026, 61120)

(For injection procedure for pneumoencephalography, use 61055)

Injection, Drainage, or Aspiration

61000 Subdural tap through fontanelle, or suture, infant, unilateral or bilateral; initial

61001 subsequent taps

61020 Ventricular puncture through previous burr hole, fontanelle, suture, or implanted ventricular catheter/reservoir; without injection

61026 with injection of medication or other substance for diagnosis or treatment
➜ *CPT Changes: An Insider's View* 2002

61050 Cisternal or lateral cervical (C1-C2) puncture; without injection (separate procedure)

61055 with injection of medication or other substance for diagnosis or treatment (eg, C1-C2)
➜ *CPT Changes: An Insider's View* 2002

(For radiological supervision and interpretation, see **Radiology**)

61070 Puncture of shunt tubing or reservoir for aspiration or injection procedure

(For radiological supervision and interpretation, use 75809)

Twist Drill, Burr Hole(s), or Trephine

61105 Twist drill hole for subdural or ventricular puncture

⊘ **61107** Twist drill hole(s) for subdural, intracerebral, or ventricular puncture; for implanting ventricular catheter, pressure recording device, or other intracerebral monitoring device
➜ *CPT Changes: An Insider's View* 2007

(For intracranial neuroendoscopic ventricular catheter placement, use 62160)

(For twist drill or burr hole performed to place thermal perfusion probe, use Category III code 0077T)

61108 for evacuation and/or drainage of subdural hematoma

61120 Burr hole(s) for ventricular puncture (including injection of gas, contrast media, dye, or radioactive material)

61140 Burr hole(s) or trephine; with biopsy of brain or intracranial lesion

61150 with drainage of brain abscess or cyst

61151 with subsequent tapping (aspiration) of intracranial abscess or cyst

61154 Burr hole(s) with evacuation and/or drainage of hematoma, extradural or subdural

(For bilateral procedure, report 61154 with modifier 50)

61156 Burr hole(s); with aspiration of hematoma or cyst, intracerebral

61210 for implanting ventricular catheter, reservoir, EEG electrode(s), pressure recording device, or other cerebral monitoring device (separate procedure)
➜ *CPT Changes: An Insider's View* 2007, 2008

(For intracranial neuroendoscopic ventricular catheter placement, use 62160)

61215 Insertion of subcutaneous reservoir, pump or continuous infusion system for connection to ventricular catheter
➜ *CPT Assistant* Spring 93:13

(For refilling and maintenance of an implantable infusion pump for spinal or brain drug therapy, use 95990)

(For chemotherapy, use 96450)

61250 Burr hole(s) or trephine, supratentorial, exploratory, not followed by other surgery

(For bilateral procedure, report 61250 with modifier 50)

61253 Burr hole(s) or trephine, infratentorial, unilateral or bilateral
➜ *CPT Assistant* Sep 02:10

(If burr hole[s] or trephine are followed by craniotomy at same operative session, use 61304-61321; do not use 61250 or 61253)

Craniectomy or Craniotomy

61304 Craniectomy or craniotomy, exploratory; supratentorial

61305 infratentorial (posterior fossa)

61312 Craniectomy or craniotomy for evacuation of hematoma, supratentorial; extradural or subdural

61313 intracerebral

61314 Craniectomy or craniotomy for evacuation of hematoma, infratentorial; extradural or subdural

61315 intracerebellar

+ **61316** Incision and subcutaneous placement of cranial bone graft (List separately in addition to code for primary procedure)
➜ *CPT Changes: An Insider's View* 2003

(Use 61316 in conjunction with 61304, 61312, 61313, 61322, 61323, 61340, 61570, 61571, 61680-61705)

61320   Craniectomy or craniotomy, drainage of intracranial abscess; supratentorial

61321   infratentorial

61322   Craniectomy or craniotomy, decompressive, with or without duraplasty, for treatment of intracranial hypertension, without evacuation of associated intraparenchymal hematoma; without lobectomy
➲ *CPT Changes: An Insider's View* 2003

(Do not report 61313 in addition to 61322)

(For subtemporal decompression, use 61340)

61323   with lobectomy
➲ *CPT Changes: An Insider's View* 2003

(Do not report 61313 in addition to 61323)

(For subtemporal decompression, use 61340)

61330   Decompression of orbit only, transcranial approach

(For bilateral procedure, report 61330 with modifier 50)

61332   Exploration of orbit (transcranial approach); with biopsy

61333   with removal of lesion

61334   with removal of foreign body

61340   Subtemporal cranial decompression (pseudotumor cerebri, slit ventricle syndrome)
➲ *CPT Changes: An Insider's View* 2003

(For bilateral procedure, report 61340 with modifier 50)

(For decompressive craniotomy or craniectomy for intracranial hypertension, without hematoma evacuation, see 61322, 61323)

61343   Craniectomy, suboccipital with cervical laminectomy for decompression of medulla and spinal cord, with or without dural graft (eg, Arnold-Chiari malformation)

61345   Other cranial decompression, posterior fossa

(For orbital decompression by lateral wall approach, Kroenlein type, use 67445)

61440   Craniotomy for section of tentorium cerebelli (separate procedure)

61450   Craniectomy, subtemporal, for section, compression, or decompression of sensory root of gasserian ganglion

61458   Craniectomy, suboccipital; for exploration or decompression of cranial nerves

61460   for section of 1 or more cranial nerves

61470   for medullary tractotomy

61480   for mesencephalic tractotomy or pedunculotomy

61490   Craniotomy for lobotomy, including cingulotomy

(For bilateral procedure, report 61490 with modifier 50)

61500   Craniectomy; with excision of tumor or other bone lesion of skull

61501   for osteomyelitis

61510   Craniectomy, trephination, bone flap craniotomy; for excision of brain tumor, supratentorial, except meningioma

61512   for excision of meningioma, supratentorial

61514   for excision of brain abscess, supratentorial

61516   for excision or fenestration of cyst, supratentorial

(For excision of pituitary tumor or craniopharyngioma, see 61545, 61546, 61548)

+ 61517   Implantation of brain intracavitary chemotherapy agent (List separately in addition to code for primary procedure)
➲ *CPT Changes: An Insider's View* 2003

(Use 61517 only in conjunction with 61510 or 61518)

(Do not report 61517 for brachytherapy insertion. For intracavitary insertion of radioelement sources or ribbons, see 77785-77787)

61518   Craniectomy for excision of brain tumor, infratentorial or posterior fossa; except meningioma, cerebellopontine angle tumor, or midline tumor at base of skull

61519   meningioma

61520   cerebellopontine angle tumor

61521   midline tumor at base of skull

61522   Craniectomy, infratentorial or posterior fossa; for excision of brain abscess

61524   for excision or fenestration of cyst

61526   Craniectomy, bone flap craniotomy, transtemporal (mastoid) for excision of cerebellopontine angle tumor;
➲ *CPT Assistant* Summer 91:8

61530   combined with middle/posterior fossa craniotomy/craniectomy

61531   Subdural implantation of strip electrodes through 1 or more burr or trephine hole(s) for long-term seizure monitoring

(For stereotactic implantation of electrodes, use 61760)

(For craniotomy for excision of intracranial arteriovenous malformation, see 61680-61692)

61533   Craniotomy with elevation of bone flap; for subdural implantation of an electrode array, for long-term seizure monitoring

(For continuous EEG monitoring, see 95950-95954)

61534   for excision of epileptogenic focus without electrocorticography during surgery

61535   for removal of epidural or subdural electrode array, without excision of cerebral tissue (separate procedure)

61536   for excision of cerebral epileptogenic focus, with electrocorticography during surgery (includes removal of electrode array)

61537   for lobectomy, temporal lobe, without electrocorticography during surgery
➜ *CPT Changes: An Insider's View* 2004

61538   for lobectomy, temporal lobe, with electrocorticography during surgery
➜ *CPT Changes: An Insider's View* 2004

61539   for lobectomy, other than temporal lobe, partial or total, with electrocorticography during surgery
➜ *CPT Changes: An Insider's View* 2004

61540   for lobectomy, other than temporal lobe, partial or total, without electrocorticography during surgery
➜ *CPT Changes: An Insider's View* 2004

61541   for transection of corpus callosum

61542   for total hemispherectomy

61543   for partial or subtotal (functional) hemispherectomy
➜ *CPT Changes: An Insider's View* 2004

61544   for excision or coagulation of choroid plexus

61545   for excision of craniopharyngioma

(For craniotomy for selective amygdalohippocampectomy, use 61566)

(For craniotomy for multiple subpial transections during surgery, use 61567)

61546   Craniotomy for hypophysectomy or excision of pituitary tumor, intracranial approach

61548   Hypophysectomy or excision of pituitary tumor, transnasal or transseptal approach, nonstereotactic
➜ *CPT Assistant* Nov 98:17

(Do not report code 69990 in addition to code 61548)

61550   Craniectomy for craniosynostosis; single cranial suture

61552   multiple cranial sutures

(For cranial reconstruction for orbital hypertelorism, see 21260-21263)

(For reconstruction, see 21172-21180)

61556   Craniotomy for craniosynostosis; frontal or parietal bone flap

61557   bifrontal bone flap

61558   Extensive craniectomy for multiple cranial suture craniosynostosis (eg, cloverleaf skull); not requiring bone grafts

61559   recontouring with multiple osteotomies and bone autografts (eg, barrel-stave procedure) (includes obtaining grafts)

(For reconstruction, see 21172-21180)

61563   Excision, intra and extracranial, benign tumor of cranial bone (eg, fibrous dysplasia); without optic nerve decompression

61564   with optic nerve decompression

(For reconstruction, see 21181-21183)

61566   Craniotomy with elevation of bone flap; for selective amygdalohippocampectomy
➜ *CPT Changes: An Insider's View* 2004

61567   for multiple subpial transections, with electrocorticography during surgery
➜ *CPT Changes: An Insider's View* 2004

61570   Craniectomy or craniotomy; with excision of foreign body from brain

61571   with treatment of penetrating wound of brain

(For sequestrectomy for osteomyelitis, use 61501)

61575   Transoral approach to skull base, brain stem or upper spinal cord for biopsy, decompression or excision of lesion;

61576   requiring splitting of tongue and/or mandible (including tracheostomy)

(For arthrodesis, use 22548)

Surgery of Skull Base

The surgical management of lesions involving the skull base (base of anterior, middle, and posterior cranial fossae) often requires the skills of several surgeons of different surgical specialties working together or in tandem during the operative session. These operations are usually not staged because of the need for definitive closure of dura, subcutaneous tissues, and skin to avoid serious infections such as osteomyelitis and/or meningitis.

The procedures are categorized according to (1) *approach procedure* necessary to obtain adequate exposure to the lesion (pathologic entity), (2) *definitive procedure(s)* necessary to biopsy, excise or otherwise treat the lesion, and (3) *repair/reconstruction* of the defect present following the definitive procedure(s).

The *approach procedure* is described according to anatomical area involved, ie, anterior cranial fossa, middle cranial fossa, posterior cranial fossa, and brain stem or upper spinal cord.

The *definitive procedure(s)* describes the repair, biopsy, resection, or excision of various lesions of the skull base and, when appropriate, primary closure of the dura, mucous membranes, and skin.

The *repair/reconstruction procedure(s)* is reported separately if extensive dural grafting, cranioplasty, local or regional myocutaneous pedicle flaps, or extensive skin grafts are required.

For primary closure, see the appropriate codes (ie, 15732, 15756-15758).

When one surgeon performs the approach procedure, another surgeon performs the definitive procedure, and another surgeon performs the repair/reconstruction procedure, each surgeon reports only the code for the specific procedure performed.

If one surgeon performs more than one procedure (ie, approach procedure and definitive procedure), then both codes are reported, adding modifier 51 to the secondary, additional procedure(s).

Approach Procedures

Anterior Cranial Fossa

61580   Craniofacial approach to anterior cranial fossa; extradural, including lateral rhinotomy, ethmoidectomy, sphenoidectomy, without maxillectomy or orbital exenteration
➔ *CPT Assistant* Winter 93:17, Spring 94:11

61581   extradural, including lateral rhinotomy, orbital exenteration, ethmoidectomy, sphenoidectomy and/or maxillectomy
➔ *CPT Assistant* Winter 93:17, Spring 94:11

61582   extradural, including unilateral or bifrontal craniotomy, elevation of frontal lobe(s), osteotomy of base of anterior cranial fossa
➔ *CPT Assistant* Winter 93:17, Spring 94:11

61583   intradural, including unilateral or bifrontal craniotomy, elevation or resection of frontal lobe, osteotomy of base of anterior cranial fossa
➔ *CPT Assistant* Winter 93:17, Spring 94:11

61584   Orbitocranial approach to anterior cranial fossa, extradural, including supraorbital ridge osteotomy and elevation of frontal and/or temporal lobe(s); without orbital exenteration
➔ *CPT Assistant* Winter 93:18

61585   with orbital exenteration
➔ *CPT Assistant* Winter 93:18

61586   Bicoronal, transzygomatic and/or LeFort I osteotomy approach to anterior cranial fossa with or without internal fixation, without bone graft
➔ *CPT Assistant* Winter 93:18, Nov 96:12

Middle Cranial Fossa

61590   Infratemporal pre-auricular approach to middle cranial fossa (parapharyngeal space, infratemporal and midline skull base, nasopharynx), with or without disarticulation of the mandible, including parotidectomy, craniotomy, decompression and/or mobilization of the facial nerve and/or petrous carotid artery
➔ *CPT Assistant* Winter 93:18

61591   Infratemporal post-auricular approach to middle cranial fossa (internal auditory meatus, petrous apex, tentorium, cavernous sinus, parasellar area, infratemporal fossa) including mastoidectomy, resection of sigmoid sinus, with or without decompression and/or mobilization of contents of auditory canal or petrous carotid artery
➔ *CPT Assistant* Winter 93:18

61592   Orbitocranial zygomatic approach to middle cranial fossa (cavernous sinus and carotid artery, clivus, basilar artery or petrous apex) including osteotomy of zygoma, craniotomy, extra- or intradural elevation of temporal lobe
➔ *CPT Assistant* Winter 93:18

Posterior Cranial Fossa

61595   Transtemporal approach to posterior cranial fossa, jugular foramen or midline skull base, including mastoidectomy, decompression of sigmoid sinus and/or facial nerve, with or without mobilization
➔ *CPT Assistant* Winter 93:18

61596   Transcochlear approach to posterior cranial fossa, jugular foramen or midline skull base, including labyrinthectomy, decompression, with or without mobilization of facial nerve and/or petrous carotid artery
➔ *CPT Assistant* Winter 93:18

61597   Transcondylar (far lateral) approach to posterior cranial fossa, jugular foramen or midline skull base, including occipital condylectomy, mastoidectomy, resection of C1-C3 vertebral body(s), decompression of vertebral artery, with or without mobilization
➔ *CPT Assistant* Winter 93:18

61598   Transpetrosal approach to posterior cranial fossa, clivus or foramen magnum, including ligation of superior petrosal sinus and/or sigmoid sinus
➔ *CPT Assistant* Winter 93:18

Definitive Procedures

Base of Anterior Cranial Fossa

61600   Resection or excision of neoplastic, vascular or infectious lesion of base of anterior cranial fossa; extradural
➔ *CPT Assistant* Winter 93:19, Spring 94:12, Nov 96:12

61601   intradural, including dural repair, with or without graft
➔ *CPT Assistant* Winter 93:19, Spring 94:12

Base of Middle Cranial Fossa

61605   Resection or excision of neoplastic, vascular or infectious lesion of infratemporal fossa, parapharyngeal space, petrous apex; extradural
➔ *CPT Assistant* Winter 93:19

61606   intradural, including dural repair, with or without graft
➔ *CPT Assistant* Winter 93:20

61607 Resection or excision of neoplastic, vascular or infectious lesion of parasellar area, cavernous sinus, clivus or midline skull base; extradural
> *CPT Assistant* Winter 93:20

61608 intradural, including dural repair, with or without graft
> *CPT Assistant* Winter 93:20

Codes 61609-61612 are reported in addition to code(s) for primary procedure(s) 61605-61608. Report only one transection or ligation of carotid artery code per operative session.

+ 61609 Transection or ligation, carotid artery in cavernous sinus; without repair (List separately in addition to code for primary procedure)
> *CPT Assistant* Winter 93:20

+ 61610 with repair by anastomosis or graft (List separately in addition to code for primary procedure)
> *CPT Assistant* Winter 93:20

+ 61611 Transection or ligation, carotid artery in petrous canal; without repair (List separately in addition to code for primary procedure)
> *CPT Assistant* Winter 93:20

+ 61612 with repair by anastomosis or graft (List separately in addition to code for primary procedure)
> *CPT Assistant* Winter 93:20

61613 Obliteration of carotid aneurysm, arteriovenous malformation, or carotid-cavernous fistula by dissection within cavernous sinus
> *CPT Assistant* Winter 93:20

Base of Posterior Cranial Fossa

61615 Resection or excision of neoplastic, vascular or infectious lesion of base of posterior cranial fossa, jugular foramen, foramen magnum, or C1-C3 vertebral bodies; extradural
> *CPT Assistant* Winter 93:20

61616 intradural, including dural repair, with or without graft

Repair and/or Reconstruction of Surgical Defects of Skull Base

61618 Secondary repair of dura for cerebrospinal fluid leak, anterior, middle or posterior cranial fossa following surgery of the skull base; by free tissue graft (eg, pericranium, fascia, tensor fascia lata, adipose tissue, homologous or synthetic grafts)
> *CPT Assistant* Winter 93:20, Spring 94:19, Mar 00:11

61619 by local or regionalized vascularized pedicle flap or myocutaneous flap (including galea, temporalis, frontalis or occipitalis muscle)
> *CPT Assistant* Winter 93:20, Spring 94:19, Mar 00:11

Endovascular Therapy

61623 Endovascular temporary balloon arterial occlusion, head or neck (extracranial/intracranial) including selective catheterization of vessel to be occluded, positioning and inflation of occlusion balloon, concomitant neurological monitoring, and radiologic supervision and interpretation of all angiography required for balloon occlusion and to exclude vascular injury post occlusion
> *CPT Changes: An Insider's View* 2003

(If selective catheterization and angiography of arteries other than artery to be occluded is performed, use appropriate catheterization and radiologic supervision and interpretation codes)

(If complete diagnostic angiography of the artery to be occluded is performed immediately prior to temporary occlusion, use appropriate radiologic supervision and interpretation codes only)

61624 Transcatheter permanent occlusion or embolization (eg, for tumor destruction, to achieve hemostasis, to occlude a vascular malformation), percutaneous, any method; central nervous system (intracranial, spinal cord)
> *CPT Assistant* Jun 99:10, Nov 06:8; *CPT Changes: An Insider's View* 2003
> *Clinical Examples in Radiology* Summer 07:2

(See also 37204)

(For radiological supervision and interpretation, use 75894)

61626 non-central nervous system, head or neck (extracranial, brachiocephalic branch)

(See also 37204)

(For radiological supervision and interpretation, use 75894)

61630 Balloon angioplasty, intracranial (eg, atherosclerotic stenosis), percutaneous
> *CPT Changes: An Insider's View* 2006
> *Clinical Examples in Radiology* Winter 06:16

61635 Transcatheter placement of intravascular stent(s), intracranial (eg, atherosclerotic stenosis), including balloon angioplasty, if performed
> *CPT Changes: An Insider's View* 2006
> *Clinical Examples in Radiology* Winter 06:16

(61630 and 61635 include all selective vascular catheterization of the target vascular family, all diagnostic imaging for arteriography of the target vascular family, and all related radiological supervision and interpretation. When diagnostic arteriogram (including imaging and selective catheterization) confirms the need for angioplasty or stent placement, 61630 and 61635 are inclusive of these services. If angioplasty or stenting are not indicated, then the appropriate codes for selective catheterization and imaging should be reported in lieu of 61630 and 61635)

61640   Balloon dilatation of intracranial vasospasm, percutaneous; initial vessel
➔ *CPT Changes: An Insider's View* 2006
➔ *Clinical Examples in Radiology* Winter 06:16

+ 61641   each additional vessel in same vascular family (List separately in addition to code for primary procedure)
➔ *CPT Changes: An Insider's View* 2006
➔ *Clinical Examples in Radiology* Winter 06:16

+ 61642   each additional vessel in different vascular family (List separately in addition to code for primary procedure)
➔ *CPT Changes: An Insider's View* 2006
➔ *Clinical Examples in Radiology* Winter 06:16

(Use 61641 and 61642 in conjunction with 61640)

(61640, 61641, 61642 include all selective vascular catheterization of the target vessel, contrast injection(s), vessel measurement, roadmapping, postdilatation angiography, and fluoroscopic guidance for the balloon dilatation)

Surgery for Aneurysm, Arteriovenous Malformation, or Vascular Disease

Includes craniotomy when appropriate for procedure.

61680   Surgery of intracranial arteriovenous malformation; supratentorial, simple

61682   supratentorial, complex

61684   infratentorial, simple

61686   infratentorial, complex

61690   dural, simple

61692   dural, complex

61697   Surgery of complex intracranial aneurysm, intracranial approach; carotid circulation
➔ *CPT Changes: An Insider's View* 2001

61698   vertebrobasilar circulation
➔ *CPT Changes: An Insider's View* 2001

(61697, 61698 involve aneurysms that are larger than 15 mm or with calcification of the aneurysm neck, or with incorporation of normal vessels into the aneurysm neck, or a procedure requiring temporary vessel occlusion, trapping or cardiopulmonary bypass to successfully treat the aneurysm)

61700   Surgery of simple intracranial aneurysm, intracranial approach; carotid circulation
➔ *CPT Assistant* Jun 99:11, Jul 99:10; *CPT Changes: An Insider's View* 2001

Intracranial Aneurysm, Intracranial Approach
61700

Placement of ligating clip across the neck of an intracranial aneurysm

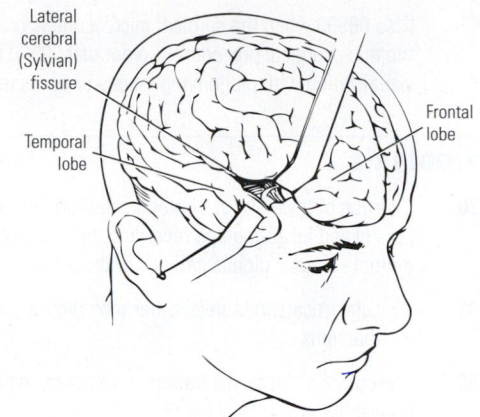

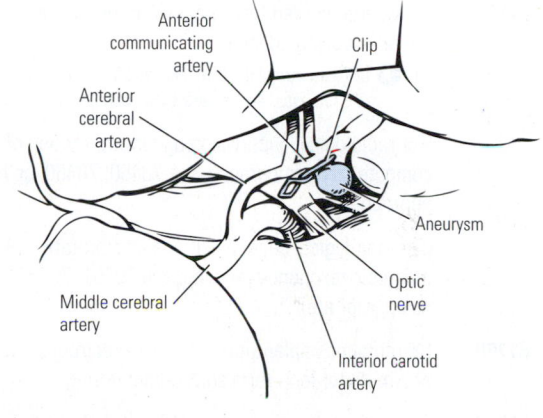

61702   vertebrobasilar circulation
➔ *CPT Changes: An Insider's View* 2001

61703   Surgery of intracranial aneurysm, cervical approach by application of occluding clamp to cervical carotid artery (Selverstone-Crutchfield type)

(For cervical approach for direct ligation of carotid artery, see 37600-37606)

61705   Surgery of aneurysm, vascular malformation or carotid-cavernous fistula; by intracranial and cervical occlusion of carotid artery

61708   by intracranial electrothrombosis

(For ligation or gradual occlusion of internal/common carotid artery, see 37605, 37606)

61710   by intra-arterial embolization, injection procedure, or balloon catheter

61711 Anastomosis, arterial, extracranial-intracranial (eg, middle cerebral/cortical) arteries

(For carotid or vertebral thromboendarterectomy, use 35301)

(Use 69990 when the surgical microscope is employed for the microsurgical procedure. Do not use 69990 for visualization with magnifying loupes or corrected vision)

Stereotaxis

61720 Creation of lesion by stereotactic method, including burr hole(s) and localizing and recording techniques, single or multiple stages; globus pallidus or thalamus

61735 subcortical structure(s) other than globus pallidus or thalamus

61750 Stereotactic biopsy, aspiration, or excision, including burr hole(s), for intracranial lesion;
➲ *CPT Assistant* Nov 99:30; *CPT Changes: An Insider's View* 2000

61751 with computed tomography and/or magnetic resonance guidance
➲ *CPT Assistant* Jun 96:10, Nov 99:30, Dec 04:20; *CPT Changes: An Insider's View* 2000, 2003

(For radiological supervision and interpretation of computerized tomography, see 70450, 70460, or 70470 as appropriate)

(For radiological supervision and interpretation of magnetic resonance imaging, see 70551, 70552, or 70553 as appropriate)

61760 Stereotactic implantation of depth electrodes into the cerebrum for long-term seizure monitoring

61770 Stereotactic localization, including burr hole(s), with insertion of catheter(s) or probe(s) for placement of radiation source
➲ *CPT Changes: An Insider's View* 2001

61790 Creation of lesion by stereotactic method, percutaneous, by neurolytic agent (eg, alcohol, thermal, electrical, radiofrequency); gasserian ganglion

61791 trigeminal medullary tract

(61793 has been deleted. To report, see 61796-61800, 63620-63621)

Stereotactic Radiosurgery (Cranial)

Cranial stereotactic radiosurgery is a distinct procedure that utilizes externally generated ionizing radiation to inactivate or eradicate defined target(s) in the head without the need to make an incision. The target is defined by and the treatment is delivered using high-resolution stereotactic imaging. Stereotactic radiosurgery codes and headframe application procedures are reported by the neurosurgeon. The radiation oncologist reports the appropriate code(s) for clinical treatment planning, physics and dosimetry, treatment delivery, and management from the **Radiation Oncology** section

(77261-77790). Any necessary planning, dosimetry, targeting, positioning, or blocking by the neurosurgeon is included in the stereotactic radiation surgery services. The same physician should not report stereotactic radiosurgery services with radiation treatment management codes (77427-77435).

Cranial stereotactic radiosurgery is typically performed in a single planning and treatment session, using a rigidly attached stereotactic guiding device, other immobilization technology and/or a stereotactic image-guidance system, but can be performed with more than one planning session and in a limited number of treatment sessions, up to a maximum of five sessions. Do not report stereotactic radiosurgery more than once per lesion per course of treatment when the treatment requires more than one session.

Codes 61796 and 61797 involve stereotactic radiosurgery for simple cranial lesions. Simple cranial lesions are lesions less than 3.5 cm in maximum dimension that do not meet the definition of a complex lesion provided below. Report code 61796 when all lesions are simple.

Codes 61798 and 61799 involve stereotactic radiosurgery for complex cranial lesions and procedures that create therapeutic lesions (eg, thalamotomy or pallidotomy). All lesions 3.5 cm in maximum dimension or greater are complex. When performing therapeutic lesion creation procedures, report code 61798 only once regardless of the number of lesions created. Schwannomas, arterio-venous malformations, pituitary tumors, glomus tumors, pineal region tumors and cavernous sinus/parasellar/petroclival tumors are complex. Any lesion that is adjacent (5mm or less) to the optic nerve/optic chasm/optic tract or within the brainstem is complex. If treating multiple lesions, and any single lesion treated is complex, use 61798.

Do not report codes 61796-61800 in conjunction with code 20660.

Codes 61796-61799 include computer-assisted planning. Do not report codes 61796-61799 in conjunction with 61795.

▶(For intensity modulated beam delivery plan and treatment, see 77301, 77418. For stereotactic body radiation therapy, see 77373, 77435)◀

+ 61795 Stereotactic computer-assisted volumetric (navigational) procedure, intracranial, extracranial, or spinal (List separately in addition to code for primary procedure)
➲ *CPT Assistant* Nov 99:30, Oct 01:10, Jan 06:46, May 08:15, Jul 08:10, Oct 08:10; *CPT Changes: An Insider's View* 2000

61796 Stereotactic radiosurgery (particle beam, gamma ray, or linear accelerator); 1 simple cranial lesion
➲ *CPT Changes: An Insider's View* 2009

(Do not report 61796 more than once per course of treatment)

(Do not report 61796 in conjunction with 61798)

+ 61797   each additional cranial lesion, simple (List separately in addition to code for primary procedure)

➔ *CPT Changes: An Insider's View* 2009

(Use 61797 in conjunction with 61796, 61798)

(For each course of treatment, 61797 and 61799 may be reported no more than once per lesion. Do not report any combination of 61797 and 61799 more than 4 times for entire course of treatment regardless of number of lesions treated)

61798   1 complex cranial lesion

➔ *CPT Changes: An Insider's View* 2009

(Do not report 61798 more than once per course of treatment)

(Do not report 61798 in conjunction with 61796)

+ 61799   each additional cranial lesion, complex (List separately in addition to code for primary procedure)

➔ *CPT Changes: An Insider's View* 2009

(Use 61799 in conjunction with 61798)

(For each course of treatment, 61797 and 61799 may be reported no more than once per lesion. Do not report any combination of 61797 and 61799 more than 4 times for entire course of treatment regardless of number of lesions treated)

+ 61800   Application of stereotactic headframe for stereotactic radiosurgery (List separately in addition to code for primary procedure)

➔ *CPT Changes: An Insider's View* 2009

(Use 61800 in conjunction with 61796, 61798)

Neurostimulators (Intracranial)

Codes 61850-61888 apply to both simple and complex neurostimulators. For initial or subsequent electronic analysis and programming of neurostimulator pulse generators, see codes 95970-95975.

Microelectrode recording, when performed by the operating surgeon in association with implantation of neurostimulator electrode arrays, is an inclusive service and should not be reported separately. If another physician participates in neurophysiological mapping during a deep brain stimulator implantation procedure, this service may be reported by the other physician with codes 95961-95962.

61850   Twist drill or burr hole(s) for implantation of neurostimulator electrodes, cortical

➔ *CPT Assistant* Sep 99:5, Nov 99:30; *CPT Changes: An Insider's View* 2000

61860   Craniectomy or craniotomy for implantation of neurostimulator electrodes, cerebral, cortical

➔ *CPT Assistant* Sep 99:5, Nov 99:30; *CPT Changes: An Insider's View* 2000

61863   Twist drill, burr hole, craniotomy, or craniectomy with stereotactic implantation of neurostimulator electrode array in subcortical site (eg, thalamus, globus pallidus, subthalamic nucleus, periventricular, periaqueductal gray), without use of intraoperative microelectrode recording; first array

➔ *CPT Assistant* Sep 99:5; *CPT Changes: An Insider's View* 2004

+ 61864   each additional array (List separately in addition to primary procedure)

➔ *CPT Assistant* Sep 99:5; *CPT Changes: An Insider's View* 2004

(Use 61864 in conjunction with 61863)

61867   Twist drill, burr hole, craniotomy, or craniectomy with stereotactic implantation of neurostimulator electrode array in subcortical site (eg, thalamus, globus pallidus, subthalamic nucleus, periventricular, periaqueductal gray), with use of intraoperative microelectrode recording; first array

➔ *CPT Changes: An Insider's View* 2004

+ 61868   each additional array (List separately in addition to primary procedure)

➔ *CPT Changes: An Insider's View* 2004

(Use 61868 in conjunction with 61867)

Placement of Cranial Neurostimulator
61867-61868, 61885

Placement of subcortical (eg, thalamic) neurostimulator electrode via burr hole (61867-61868) with connection of the electrode to an implanted programmable pulse generator (61885) in the infraclavicular area

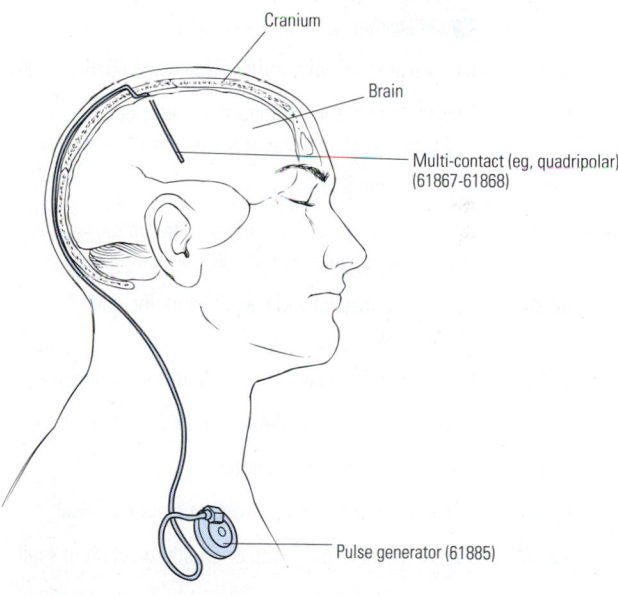

Cranium

Brain

Multi-contact (eg, quadripolar) (61867-61868)

Pulse generator (61885)

61870   Craniectomy for implantation of neurostimulator electrodes, cerebellar; cortical

61875   subcortical

61880 Revision or removal of intracranial neurostimulator electrodes

61885 Insertion or replacement of cranial neurostimulator pulse generator or receiver, direct or inductive coupling; with connection to a single electrode array
→ *CPT Assistant* Sep 99:5, Nov 99:30, Jun 00:3, Apr 01:8, Sep 03:3; *CPT Changes: An Insider's View* 2000, 2005

61886 with connection to 2 or more electrode arrays
→ *CPT Assistant* Nov 99:30, Jun 00:3, Apr 01:8; *CPT Changes: An Insider's View* 2000

(For open placement of cranial nerve (eg, vagal, trigeminal) neurostimulator electrode(s), use 64573)

(For percutaneous placement of cranial nerve (eg, vagal, trigeminal) neurostimulator electrode(s), use 64553)

(For revision or removal of cranial nerve (eg, vagal, trigeminal) neurostimulator electrode(s), use 64585)

61888 Revision or removal of cranial neurostimulator pulse generator or receiver

(Do not report 61888 in conjunction with 61885 or 61886 for the same pulse generator)

Repair

62000 Elevation of depressed skull fracture; simple, extradural

62005 compound or comminuted, extradural

62010 with repair of dura and/or debridement of brain

62100 Craniotomy for repair of dural/cerebrospinal fluid leak, including surgery for rhinorrhea/otorrhea
→ *CPT Changes: An Insider's View* 2002

(For repair of spinal dural/CSF leak, see 63707, 63709)

62115 Reduction of craniomegalic skull (eg, treated hydrocephalus); not requiring bone grafts or cranioplasty

62116 with simple cranioplasty

62117 requiring craniotomy and reconstruction with or without bone graft (includes obtaining grafts)

62120 Repair of encephalocele, skull vault, including cranioplasty

62121 Craniotomy for repair of encephalocele, skull base

62140 Cranioplasty for skull defect; up to 5 cm diameter

62141 larger than 5 cm diameter

62142 Removal of bone flap or prosthetic plate of skull

62143 Replacement of bone flap or prosthetic plate of skull

62145 Cranioplasty for skull defect with reparative brain surgery

62146 Cranioplasty with autograft (includes obtaining bone grafts); up to 5 cm diameter

62147 larger than 5 cm diameter

+ 62148 Incision and retrieval of subcutaneous cranial bone graft for cranioplasty (List separately in addition to code for primary procedure)
→ *CPT Changes: An Insider's View* 2003

(Use 62148 in conjunction with 62140-62147)

Neuroendoscopy

Surgical endoscopy always includes diagnostic endoscopy.

+ 62160 Neuroendoscopy, intracranial, for placement or replacement of ventricular catheter and attachment to shunt system or external drainage (List separately in addition to code for primary procedure)
→ *CPT Assistant* Jun 07:11; *CPT Changes: An Insider's View* 2003

(Use 62160 only in conjunction with 61107, 61210, 62220-62230, 62258)

62161 Neuroendoscopy, intracranial; with dissection of adhesions, fenestration of septum pellucidum or intraventricular cysts (including placement, replacement, or removal of ventricular catheter)
→ *CPT Changes: An Insider's View* 2003

62162 with fenestration or excision of colloid cyst, including placement of external ventricular catheter for drainage
→ *CPT Changes: An Insider's View* 2003

62163 with retrieval of foreign body
→ *CPT Changes: An Insider's View* 2003

62164 with excision of brain tumor, including placement of external ventricular catheter for drainage
→ *CPT Changes: An Insider's View* 2003

62165 with excision of pituitary tumor, transnasal or trans-sphenoidal approach
→ *CPT Changes: An Insider's View* 2003

Cerebrospinal Fluid (CSF) Shunt

62180 Ventriculocisternostomy (Torkildsen type operation)

62190 Creation of shunt; subarachnoid/subdural-atrial, -jugular, -auricular

62192 subarachnoid/subdural-peritoneal, -pleural, other terminus

62194 Replacement or irrigation, subarachnoid/subdural catheter

62200 Ventriculocisternostomy, third ventricle;

62201 stereotactic, neuroendoscopic method
→ *CPT Assistant* Aug 07:15; *CPT Changes: An Insider's View* 2003

(For intracranial neuroendoscopic procedures, see 62161-62165)

62220 Creation of shunt; ventriculo-atrial, -jugular, -auricular

(For intracranial neuroendoscopic ventricular catheter placement, use 62160)

62223   ventriculo-peritoneal, -pleural, other terminus

(For intracranial neuroendoscopic ventricular catheter placement, use 62160)

Cerebrospinal Fluid (CSF) Shunt (Ventricular Peritoneal)
62223

A ventriculostomy is performed to drain CSF into the peritoneal cavity.

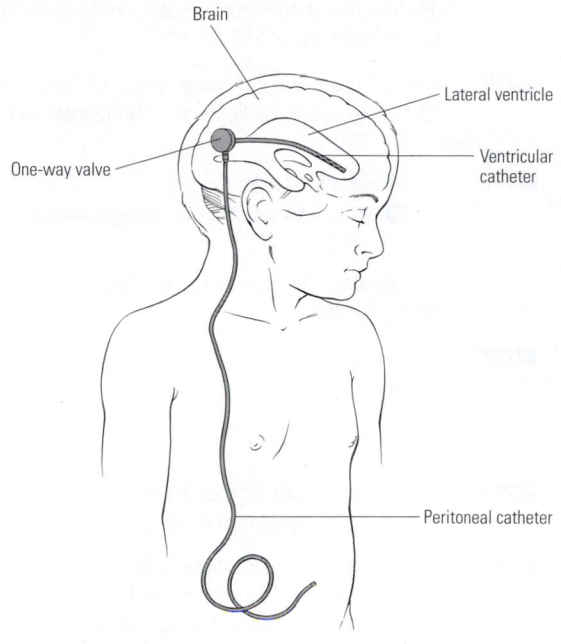

Brain

Lateral ventricle

One-way valve

Ventricular catheter

Peritoneal catheter

62225   Replacement or irrigation, ventricular catheter

(For intracranial neuroendoscopic ventricular catheter placement, use 62160)

62230   Replacement or revision of cerebrospinal fluid shunt, obstructed valve, or distal catheter in shunt system
➲ *CPT Changes: An Insider's View* 2002

(For intracranial neuroendoscopic ventricular catheter placement, use 62160)

62252   Reprogramming of programmable cerebrospinal shunt
➲ *CPT Changes: An Insider's View* 2001, 2002

62256   Removal of complete cerebrospinal fluid shunt system; without replacement
➲ *CPT Changes: An Insider's View* 2002

62258   with replacement by similar or other shunt at same operation

(For percutaneous irrigation or aspiration of shunt reservoir, use 61070)

(For reprogramming of programmable CSF shunt, use 62252)

(For intracranial neuroendoscopic ventricular catheter placement, use 62160)

Spine and Spinal Cord

(For application of caliper or tongs, use 20660)

(For treatment of fracture or dislocation of spine, see 22305-22327)

Injection, Drainage, or Aspiration

Injection of contrast during fluoroscopic guidance and localization is an inclusive component of 62263, 62264, 62267, 62270-62273, 62280-62282, 62310-62319. Fluoroscopic guidance and localization is reported with 77003, unless a formal contrast study (myelography, epidurography, or arthrography) is performed, in which case the use of fluoroscopy is included in the supervision and interpretation codes.

For radiologic supervision and interpretation of epidurography, use 72275. Code 72275 is only to be used when an epidurogram is performed, images documented, and a formal radiologic report is issued.

Code 62263 describes a catheter-based treatment involving targeted injection of various substances (eg, hypertonic saline, steroid, anesthetic) via an indwelling epidural catheter. Code 62263 includes percutaneous insertion and removal of an epidural catheter (remaining in place over a several-day period), for the administration of multiple injections of a neurolytic agent(s) performed during serial treatment sessions (ie, spanning two or more treatment days). If required, adhesions or scarring may also be lysed by mechanical means. Code 62263 is **not** reported for each adhesiolysis treatment, but should be reported **once** to describe the entire series of injections/infusions spanning two or more treatment days.

Code 62264 describes multiple adhesiolysis treatment sessions performed on the same day. Adhesions or scarring may be lysed by injections of neurolytic agent(s). If required, adhesions or scarring may also be lysed mechanically using a percutaneously-deployed catheter.

Codes 62263 and 62264 include the procedure of injections of contrast for epidurography (72275) and fluoroscopic guidance and localization (77003) during initial or subsequent sessions.

(Report 01996 for daily hospital management of continuous epidural or subarachnoid drug administration performed in conjunction with 62318-62319)

62263   Percutaneous lysis of epidural adhesions using solution injection (eg, hypertonic saline, enzyme) or mechanical means (eg, catheter) including radiologic localization (includes contrast when administered), multiple adhesiolysis sessions; 2 or more days
➲ *CPT Assistant* Nov 99:33, Dec 99:11, Mar 02:11, Dec 02:10, Nov 05:14, Jul 08:9; *CPT Changes: An Insider's View* 2000, 2003

(62263 includes codes 72275 and 77003)

62264   1 day
➔ *CPT Assistant* Nov 05:14, Jul 08:9; *CPT Changes: An Insider's View* 2003

(Do not report 62264 with 62263)

(62264 includes codes 72275 and 77003)

62267   Percutaneous aspiration within the nucleus pulposus, intervertebral disc, or paravertebral tissue for diagnostic purposes
➔ *CPT Changes: An Insider's View* 2009

▶(For imaging, use 77003)◀

(Do not report 62267 in conjunction with 10022, 20225, 62287, 62290, 62291)

62268   Percutaneous aspiration, spinal cord cyst or syrinx

(For radiological supervision and interpretation, see 76942, 77002, 77012)

62269   Biopsy of spinal cord, percutaneous needle

(For radiological supervision and interpretation, see 76942, 77002, 77012)

(For fine needle aspiration, see 10021, 10022)

(For evaluation of fine needle aspirate, see 88172, 88173)

62270   Spinal puncture, lumbar, diagnostic
➔ *CPT Assistant* Nov 99:32-33, Oct 03:2, Jul 06:4, Jul 07:1; *CPT Changes: An Insider's View* 2000, 2002

62272   Spinal puncture, therapeutic, for drainage of cerebrospinal fluid (by needle or catheter)
➔ *CPT Assistant* Nov 99:32-33; *CPT Changes: An Insider's View* 2000

62273   Injection, epidural, of blood or clot patch
➔ *CPT Assistant* Nov 99:32-34; *CPT Changes: An Insider's View* 2000

(For injection of diagnostic or therapeutic substance(s), see 62310, 62311, 62318, 62319)

62280   Injection/infusion of neurolytic substance (eg, alcohol, phenol, iced saline solutions), with or without other therapeutic substance; subarachnoid
➔ *CPT Assistant* Nov 99:32-34, Jan 00:2, Jul 08:9; *CPT Changes: An Insider's View* 2000

62281   epidural, cervical or thoracic
➔ *CPT Assistant* Apr 96:11, Nov 99:32-34, Jan 00:2, Jul 08:9; *CPT Changes: An Insider's View* 2000

62282   epidural, lumbar, sacral (caudal)
➔ *CPT Assistant* Apr 96:11, Nov 99:32-34, Jan 00:2, Jul 08:9; *CPT Changes: An Insider's View* 2000

62284   Injection procedure for myelography and/or computed tomography, spinal (other than C1-C2 and posterior fossa)
➔ *CPT Assistant* Fall 93:13, Sep 04:13; *CPT Changes: An Insider's View* 2003, 2008
➔ *Clinical Examples in Radiology* Fall 06:5-6, 11-12

(For injection procedure at C1-C2, use 61055)

(For radiological supervision and interpretation, see **Radiology**)

62287   Decompression procedure, percutaneous, of nucleus pulposus of intervertebral disc, any method, single or multiple levels, lumbar (eg, manual or automated percutaneous discectomy, percutaneous laser discectomy)
➔ *CPT Assistant* Nov 99:34, Mar 02:11; *CPT Changes: An Insider's View* 2000, 2009

(For fluoroscopic guidance, use 77003)

(Do not report 62287 in conjunction with 62267)

(For injection of non-neurolytic diagnostic or therapeutic substance(s), see 62310, 62311)

62290   Injection procedure for discography, each level; lumbar
➔ *CPT Assistant* Nov 99:35, Apr 03:27; *CPT Changes: An Insider's View* 2000

62291   cervical or thoracic
➔ *CPT Assistant* Nov 99:35; *CPT Changes: An Insider's View* 2000

(For radiological supervision and interpretation, see 72285, 72295)

62292   Injection procedure for chemonucleolysis, including discography, intervertebral disc, single or multiple levels, lumbar
➔ *CPT Assistant* Oct 99:10

62294   Injection procedure, arterial, for occlusion of arteriovenous malformation, spinal

62310   Injection, single (not via indwelling catheter), not including neurolytic substances, with or without contrast (for either localization or epidurography), of diagnostic or therapeutic substance(s) (including anesthetic, antispasmodic, opioid, steroid, other solution), epidural or subarachnoid; cervical or thoracic
➔ *CPT Assistant* Nov 99:32-35, Jan 00:2, Dec 00:15, Sep 04:5, Jul 08:9, Nov 08:11; *CPT Changes: An Insider's View* 2000

62311   lumbar, sacral (caudal)
➔ *CPT Assistant* Nov 99:32-35, Jan 00:1, Dec 00:15, Sep 04:5, Jul 08:9, Nov 08:11; *CPT Changes: An Insider's View* 2000

62318   Injection, including catheter placement, continuous infusion or intermittent bolus, not including neurolytic substances, with or without contrast (for either localization or epidurography), of diagnostic or therapeutic substance(s) (including anesthetic, antispasmodic, opioid, steroid, other solution), epidural or subarachnoid; cervical or thoracic
➔ *CPT Assistant* Nov 99:32-35, Jan 00:2, Dec 00:15, Oct 01:9, Jul 08:9, Nov 08:11; *CPT Changes: An Insider's View* 2000

62319   lumbar, sacral (caudal)
➔ *CPT Assistant* Nov 99:32-35, Jan 00:2, Dec 00:15, Oct 01:9, Jul 08:9, Nov 08:11; *CPT Changes: An Insider's View* 2000

(For transforaminal epidural injection, see 64479-64484)

(Report 01996 for daily hospital management of continuous epidural or subarachnoid drug administration performed in conjunction with 62318-62319)

Catheter Implantation

(For percutaneous placement of intrathecal or epidural catheter, see codes 62270-62273, 62280-62284, 62310-62319)

62350 Implantation, revision or repositioning of tunneled intrathecal or epidural catheter, for long-term medication administration via an external pump or implantable reservoir/infusion pump; without laminectomy

➔ *CPT Assistant* Nov 99:36; *CPT Changes: An Insider's View* 2000, 2001

62351 with laminectomy

➔ *CPT Assistant* Nov 99:36; *CPT Changes: An Insider's View* 2000

(For refilling and maintenance of an implantable infusion pump for spinal or brain drug therapy, see 95990, 95991)

62355 Removal of previously implanted intrathecal or epidural catheter

Reservoir/Pump Implantation

62360 Implantation or replacement of device for intrathecal or epidural drug infusion; subcutaneous reservoir

62361 nonprogrammable pump

62362 programmable pump, including preparation of pump, with or without programming

➔ *CPT Assistant* Mar 97:11

Intrathecal or Epidural Drug Infusion Pump Implantation
62362

The reservoir is placed in the subcutaneous tissues and attached to a previously placed catheter for intrathecal or epidural drug infusion.

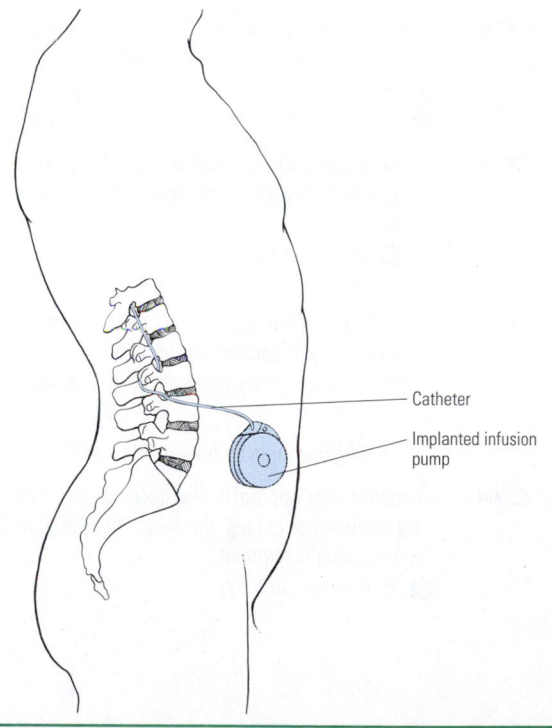

Catheter

Implanted infusion pump

62365 Removal of subcutaneous reservoir or pump, previously implanted for intrathecal or epidural infusion

62367 Electronic analysis of programmable, implanted pump for intrathecal or epidural drug infusion (includes evaluation of reservoir status, alarm status, drug prescription status); without reprogramming

62368 with reprogramming

➔ *CPT Assistant* Nov 02:10, Jul 06:1

(For refilling and maintenance of an implantable infusion pump for spinal or brain drug therapy, use 95990-95991)

Posterior Extradural Laminotomy or Laminectomy for Exploration/ Decompression of Neural Elements or Excision of Herniated Intervertebral Discs

(When 63001-63048 are followed by arthrodesis, see 22590-22614)

63001 Laminectomy with exploration and/or decompression of spinal cord and/or cauda equina, without facetectomy, foraminotomy or discectomy (eg, spinal stenosis), 1 or 2 vertebral segments; cervical

➔ *CPT Assistant* Jan 01:12, Jun 07:1

63003 thoracic

➔ *CPT Assistant* Jan 01:12

63005 lumbar, except for spondylolisthesis

➔ *CPT Assistant* Jan 01:12

Lumbar Laminectomy
63005

With the patient prone and under general anesthesia, the laminae and underlying ligamentum flavum are removed.

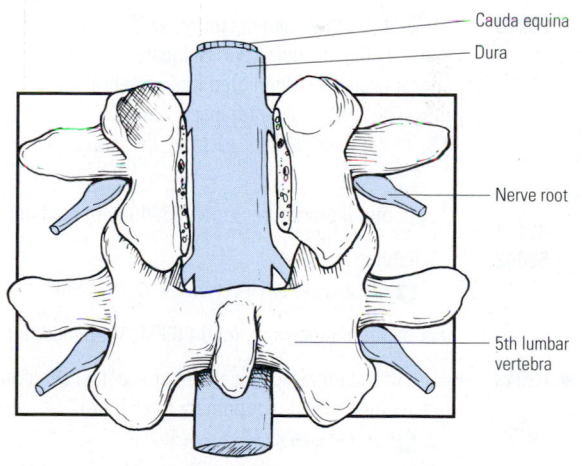

Cauda equina

Dura

Nerve root

5th lumbar vertebra

63011 sacral

➔ *CPT Assistant* Jan 01:12

63012   Laminectomy with removal of abnormal facets and/or pars inter-articularis with decompression of cauda equina and nerve roots for spondylolisthesis, lumbar (Gill type procedure)
➔ *CPT Assistant* Jan 01:12

63015   Laminectomy with exploration and/or decompression of spinal cord and/or cauda equina, without facetectomy, foraminotomy or discectomy (eg, spinal stenosis), more than 2 vertebral segments; cervical
➔ *CPT Assistant* Jan 01:12

63016   thoracic
➔ *CPT Assistant* Jan 01:12

63017   lumbar
➔ *CPT Assistant* Jan 01:12

63020   Laminotomy (hemilaminectomy), with decompression of nerve root(s), including partial facetectomy, foraminotomy and/or excision of herniated intervertebral disc, including open and endoscopically-assisted approaches; 1 interspace, cervical
➔ *CPT Assistant* Nov 99:36, Jan 01:12; *CPT Changes: An Insider's View* 2000, 2009

(For bilateral procedure, report 63020 with modifier 50)

63030   1 interspace, lumbar
➔ *CPT Assistant* Mar 96:7, Nov 99:36, Jan 01:12, Feb 01:10, Sep 02:10, Oct 04:12, Oct 08:10; *CPT Changes: An Insider's View* 2000, 2009

(For bilateral procedure, report 63030 with modifier 50)

+ 63035   each additional interspace, cervical or lumbar (List separately in addition to code for primary procedure)
➔ *CPT Assistant* Fall 91:8, Mar 96:7, Nov 99:36, Jan 01:12, Feb 01:10; *CPT Changes: An Insider's View* 2000, 2009

(Use 63035 in conjunction with 63020-63030)

(For bilateral procedure, report 63035 with modifier 50)

63040   Laminotomy (hemilaminectomy), with decompression of nerve root(s), including partial facetectomy, foraminotomy and/or excision of herniated intervertebral disc, reexploration, single interspace; cervical
➔ *CPT Assistant* Jan 99:11, Jan 01:12; *CPT Changes: An Insider's View* 2001

(For bilateral procedure, report 63040 with modifier 50)

63042   lumbar
➔ *CPT Assistant* Jan 99:11, Jan 01:12, Oct 08:10

(For bilateral procedure, report 63042 with modifier 50)

+ 63043   each additional cervical interspace (List separately in addition to code for primary procedure)
➔ *CPT Changes: An Insider's View* 2001

(Use 63043 in conjunction with 63040)

(For bilateral procedure, report 63043 with modifier 50)

+ 63044   each additional lumbar interspace (List separately in addition to code for primary procedure)
➔ *CPT Changes: An Insider's View* 2001

(Use 63044 in conjunction with 63042)

(For bilateral procedure, report 63044 with modifier 50)

63045   Laminectomy, facetectomy and foraminotomy (unilateral or bilateral with decompression of spinal cord, cauda equina and/or nerve root[s], [eg, spinal or lateral recess stenosis]), single vertebral segment; cervical
➔ *CPT Assistant* Jan 01:12

63046   thoracic
➔ *CPT Assistant* Jan 99:11, Jan 01:12

63047   lumbar
➔ *CPT Assistant* Jan 99:11, Jan 01:12, Feb 01:10, Nov 02:11, Apr 08:11, Jul 08:7, Oct 08:10

+ 63048   each additional segment, cervical, thoracic, or lumbar (List separately in addition to code for primary procedure)
➔ *CPT Assistant* Fall 91:8, Jan 99:11, Jan 01:12

(Use 63048 in conjunction with 63045-63047)

63050   Laminoplasty, cervical, with decompression of the spinal cord, 2 or more vertebral segments;
➔ *CPT Changes: An Insider's View* 2005

63051   with reconstruction of the posterior bony elements (including the application of bridging bone graft and non-segmental fixation devices (eg, wire, suture, mini-plates), when performed)
➔ *CPT Changes: An Insider's View* 2005

(Do not report 63050 or 63051 in conjunction with 22600, 22614, 22840-22842, 63001, 63015, 63045, 63048, 63295 for the same vertebral segment(s))

Transpedicular or Costovertebral Approach for Posterolateral Extradural Exploration/Decompression

63055   Transpedicular approach with decompression of spinal cord, equina and/or nerve root(s) (eg, herniated intervertebral disc), single segment; thoracic
➔ *CPT Assistant* Nov 99:36; *CPT Changes: An Insider's View* 2000

63056   lumbar (including transfacet, or lateral extraforaminal approach) (eg, far lateral herniated intervertebral disc)
➔ *CPT Assistant* Nov 99:36; *CPT Changes: An Insider's View* 2000

+ 63057   each additional segment, thoracic or lumbar (List separately in addition to code for primary procedure)
➔ *CPT Assistant* Nov 99:36; *CPT Changes: An Insider's View* 2000

(Use 63057 in conjunction with 63055, 63056)

63064   Costovertebral approach with decompression of spinal cord or nerve root(s) (eg, herniated intervertebral disc), thoracic; single segment
➔ *CPT Assistant* Fall 92:19

+ 63066   each additional segment (List separately in addition to code for primary procedure)

(Use 63066 in conjunction with 63064)

(For excision of thoracic intraspinal lesions by laminectomy, see 63266, 63271, 63276, 63281, 63286)

Anterior or Anterolateral Approach for Extradural Exploration/Decompression

For the following codes, when two surgeons work together as primary surgeons performing distinct part(s) of spinal cord exploration/decompression operation, each surgeon should report his/her distinct operative work by appending modifier 62 to the procedure code (and any associated add-on codes for that procedure code as long as both surgeons continue to work together as primary surgeons). In this situation, modifier 62 may be appended to the definitive procedure code(s) 63075, 63077, 63081, 63085, 63087, 63090 and, as appropriate, to associated additional interspace add-on code(s) 63076, 63078 or additional segment add-on code(s) 63082, 63086, 63088, 63091 as long as both surgeons continue to work together as primary surgeons.

63075   Discectomy, anterior, with decompression of spinal cord and/or nerve root(s), including osteophytectomy; cervical, single interspace

➲ CPT Assistant Nov 98:18, Jan 01:12, Feb 02:4; CPT Changes: An Insider's View 2002

+ 63076   cervical, each additional interspace (List separately in addition to code for primary procedure)

➲ CPT Assistant Nov 98:18, Jan 01:12, Feb 02:4; CPT Changes: An Insider's View 2002

(Use 63076 in conjunction with 63075)

63077   thoracic, single interspace

➲ CPT Assistant Nov 98:18, Jan 01:12, Feb 02:4; CPT Changes: An Insider's View 2002

+ 63078   thoracic, each additional interspace (List separately in addition to code for primary procedure)

➲ CPT Assistant Nov 98:18, Jan 01:12, Feb 02:4; CPT Changes: An Insider's View 2002

(Use 63078 in conjunction with 63077)

(Do not report code 69990 in addition to codes 63075-63078)

63081   Vertebral corpectomy (vertebral body resection), partial or complete, anterior approach with decompression of spinal cord and/or nerve root(s); cervical, single segment

➲ CPT Assistant Spring 93:37, Feb 02:4; CPT Changes: An Insider's View 2002

+ 63082   cervical, each additional segment (List separately in addition to code for primary procedure)

➲ CPT Assistant Spring 93:37, Feb 02:4; CPT Changes: An Insider's View 2002

(Use 63082 in conjunction with 63081)

(For transoral approach, see 61575, 61576)

63085   Vertebral corpectomy (vertebral body resection), partial or complete, transthoracic approach with decompression of spinal cord and/or nerve root(s); thoracic, single segment

➲ CPT Assistant Spring 93:37, Feb 02:4; CPT Changes: An Insider's View 2002

+ 63086   thoracic, each additional segment (List separately in addition to code for primary procedure)

➲ CPT Assistant Spring 93:37, Feb 02:4; CPT Changes: An Insider's View 2002

(Use 63086 in conjunction with 63085)

63087   Vertebral corpectomy (vertebral body resection), partial or complete, combined thoracolumbar approach with decompression of spinal cord, cauda equina or nerve root(s), lower thoracic or lumbar; single segment

➲ CPT Assistant Spring 93:37, Feb 02:4; CPT Changes: An Insider's View 2002

+ 63088   each additional segment (List separately in addition to code for primary procedure)

➲ CPT Assistant Spring 93:37, Feb 02:4; CPT Changes: An Insider's View 2002

(Use 63088 in conjunction with 63087)

63090   Vertebral corpectomy (vertebral body resection), partial or complete, transperitoneal or retroperitoneal approach with decompression of spinal cord, cauda equina or nerve root(s), lower thoracic, lumbar, or sacral; single segment

➲ CPT Assistant Spring 93:37, Mar 96:6, Feb 02:4; CPT Changes: An Insider's View 2002

+ 63091   each additional segment (List separately in addition to code for primary procedure)

➲ CPT Assistant Spring 93:37, Mar 96:6, Feb 02:4; CPT Changes: An Insider's View 2002

(Use 63091 in conjunction with 63090)

(Procedures 63081-63091 include discectomy above and/or below vertebral segment)

(If followed by arthrodesis, see 22548-22812)

(For reconstruction of spine, use appropriate vertebral corpectomy codes 63081-63091, bone graft codes 20930-20938, arthrodesis codes 22548-22812, and spinal instrumentation codes 22840-22855)

Lateral Extracavitary Approach for Extradural Exploration/Decompression

63101   Vertebral corpectomy (vertebral body resection), partial or complete, lateral extracavitary approach with decompression of spinal cord and/or nerve root(s) (eg, for tumor or retropulsed bone fragments); thoracic, single segment

➲ CPT Changes: An Insider's View 2004

63102   lumbar, single segment

➲ CPT Changes: An Insider's View 2004

+ **63103**   thoracic or lumbar, each additional segment (List separately in addition to code for primary procedure)

➲ *CPT Changes: An Insider's View* 2004

(Use 63103 in conjunction with 63101 and 63102)

Incision

63170   Laminectomy with myelotomy (eg, Bischof or DREZ type), cervical, thoracic, or thoracolumbar

63172   Laminectomy with drainage of intramedullary cyst/syrinx; to subarachnoid space

63173   to peritoneal or pleural space

➲ *CPT Changes: An Insider's View* 2004

63180   Laminectomy and section of dentate ligaments, with or without dural graft, cervical; 1 or 2 segments

63182   more than 2 segments

63185   Laminectomy with rhizotomy; 1 or 2 segments

63190   more than 2 segments

63191   Laminectomy with section of spinal accessory nerve

(For bilateral procedure, report 63191 with modifier 50)

(For resection of sternocleidomastoid muscle, use 21720)

63194   Laminectomy with cordotomy, with section of 1 spinothalamic tract, 1 stage; cervical

63195   thoracic

63196   Laminectomy with cordotomy, with section of both spinothalamic tracts, 1 stage; cervical

63197   thoracic

63198   Laminectomy with cordotomy with section of both spinothalamic tracts, 2 stages within 14 days; cervical

63199   thoracic

63200   Laminectomy, with release of tethered spinal cord, lumbar

Excision by Laminectomy of Lesion Other Than Herniated Disc

63250   Laminectomy for excision or occlusion of arteriovenous malformation of spinal cord; cervical

63251   thoracic

63252   thoracolumbar

63265   Laminectomy for excision or evacuation of intraspinal lesion other than neoplasm, extradural; cervical

63266   thoracic

63267   lumbar

63268   sacral

63270   Laminectomy for excision of intraspinal lesion other than neoplasm, intradural; cervical

63271   thoracic

63272   lumbar

63273   sacral

63275   Laminectomy for biopsy/excision of intraspinal neoplasm; extradural, cervical

63276   extradural, thoracic

63277   extradural, lumbar

63278   extradural, sacral

63280   intradural, extramedullary, cervical

63281   intradural, extramedullary, thoracic

63282   intradural, extramedullary, lumbar

63283   intradural, sacral

63285   intradural, intramedullary, cervical

63286   intradural, intramedullary, thoracic

63287   intradural, intramedullary, thoracolumbar

63290   combined extradural-intradural lesion, any level

(For drainage of intramedullary cyst/syrinx, use 63172, 63173)

+ **63295**   Osteoplastic reconstruction of dorsal spinal elements, following primary intraspinal procedure (List separately in addition to code for primary procedure)

➲ *CPT Changes: An Insider's View* 2005

(Use 63295 in conjunction with 63172, 63173, 63185, 63190, 63200-63290)

(Do not report 63295 in conjunction with 22590-22614, 22840-22844, 63050, 63051 for the same vertebral segment(s))

Excision, Anterior or Anterolateral Approach, Intraspinal Lesion

For the following codes, when two surgeons work together as primary surgeons performing distinct part(s) of an anterior approach for an intraspinal excision, each surgeon should report his/her distinct operative work by appending modifier 62 to the single definitive procedure code. In this situation, modifier 62 may be appended to the definitive procedure code(s) 63300-63307 and, as appropriate, to the associated additional segment add-on code 63308 as long as both surgeons continue to work together as primary surgeons.

(For arthrodesis, see 22548-22585)

(For reconstruction of spine, see 20930-20938)

63300   Vertebral corpectomy (vertebral body resection), partial or complete, for excision of intraspinal lesion, single segment; extradural, cervical

➲ *CPT Assistant* Feb 02:4

63301   extradural, thoracic by transthoracic approach

➲ *CPT Assistant* Feb 02:4

63302   extradural, thoracic by thoracolumbar approach
>   *CPT Assistant* Feb 02:4

63303   extradural, lumbar or sacral by transperitoneal or retroperitoneal approach
>   *CPT Assistant* Feb 02:4

63304   intradural, cervical
>   *CPT Assistant* Feb 02:4

63305   intradural, thoracic by transthoracic approach
>   *CPT Assistant* Feb 02:4

63306   intradural, thoracic by thoracolumbar approach
>   *CPT Assistant* Feb 02:4

63307   intradural, lumbar or sacral by transperitoneal or retroperitoneal approach
>   *CPT Assistant* Feb 02:4

+ 63308   each additional segment (List separately in addition to codes for single segment)
>   *CPT Assistant* Feb 02:4

(Use 63308 in conjunction with 63300-63307)

Stereotaxis

63600   Creation of lesion of spinal cord by stereotactic method, percutaneous, any modality (including stimulation and/or recording)

63610   Stereotactic stimulation of spinal cord, percutaneous, separate procedure not followed by other surgery

63615   Stereotactic biopsy, aspiration, or excision of lesion, spinal cord

Stereotactic Radiosurgery (Spinal)

Spinal stereotactic radiosurgery is a distinct procedure that utilizes externally generated ionizing radiation to inactivate or eradicate defined target(s) in the spine without the need to make an incision. The target is defined by and the treatment is delivered using high-resolution stereotactic imaging. These codes are reported by the surgeon. The radiation oncologist reports the appropriate code(s) for clinical treatment planning, physics and dosimetry, treatment delivery and management from the **Radiation Oncology** section (77261-77790). Any necessary planning, dosimetry, targeting, positioning, or blocking by the neurosurgeon is included in the stereotactic radiation surgery services. The same physician should not report stereotactic radiosurgery services with radiation treatment management codes (77427-77432).

Spinal stereotactic radiosurgery is typically performed in a single planning and treatment session using a stereotactic image-guidance system, but can be performed with a planning session and in a limited number of treatment sessions, up to a maximum of five sessions. Do not report stereotactic radiosurgery more than once per lesion per course of treatment when the treatment requires greater than one session.

Stereotactic spinal surgery is only used when the tumor being treated affects spinal neural tissue or abuts the dura mater. Arteriovenous malformations must be subdural. For other radiation services of the spine, see **Radiation Oncology** services.

Codes 63620, 63621 include computer-assisted planning. Do not report 63620, 63621 in conjunction with 61795.

▶(For intensity modulated beam delivery plan and treatment, see 77301, 77418. For stereotactic body radiation therapy, see 77373, 77435)◀

63620   Stereotactic radiosurgery (particle beam, gamma ray, or linear accelerator); 1 spinal lesion
>   *CPT Changes: An Insider's View* 2009

(Do not report 63620 more than once per course of treatment)

+ 63621   each additional spinal lesion (List separately in addition to code for primary procedure)
>   *CPT Changes: An Insider's View* 2009

(Report 63621 in conjunction with 63620)

(For each course of treatment, 63621 may be reported no more than once per lesion. Do not report 63621 more than 2 times for entire course of treatment regardless of number of lesions treated)

Neurostimulators (Spinal)

Codes 63650-63688 apply to both simple and complex neurostimulators. For initial or subsequent electronic analysis and programming of neurostimulator pulse generators, see codes 95970-95975.

▶Codes 63650, 63655, and 63661-63664 describe the operative placement, revision, replacement, or removal of the spinal neurostimulator system components to provide spinal electrical stimulation. A neurostimulator system includes an implanted neurostimulator, external controller, extension, and collection of contacts. Multiple contacts or electrodes (4 or more) provide the actual electrical stimulation in the epidural space.

For percutaneously placed neurostimulator systems (63650, 63661, 63663), the contacts are on a catheter-like lead. An array defines the collection of contacts that are on one catheter.

For systems placed via an open surgical exposure (63655, 63662, 63664), the contacts are on a plate or paddle-shaped surface.

Do not report 63661 or 63663 when removing or replacing a temporary percutaneously placed array for an external generator.◀

63650   Percutaneous implantation of neurostimulator electrode array, epidural
>   *CPT Assistant* Jun 98:3-4, Nov 98:18, Mar 99:11, Apr 99:10, Sep 99:3, Dec 08:8

Percutaneous Implantation of Neurostimulator Electrodes
63650

Single catheter electrode array is inserted percutaneously into the epidural space. A simple or complex receiver is subcutaneously implanted.

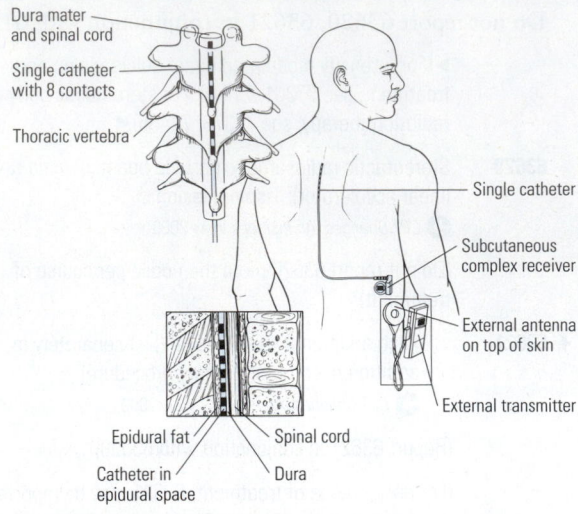

63655

Laminectomy for implantation of neurostimulator electrodes, plate/paddle, epidural

➜ *CPT Assistant* Jun 98:3-4, Nov 98:18, Sep 99:3-4, Dec 08:8

Placement of Neurostimulator Electrodes Through Laminectomy
63655

The electrode plate or paddle is placed in the epidural space via open exposure through large laminotomy or small laminectomy. The simple or complex receiver is subcutaneously implanted.

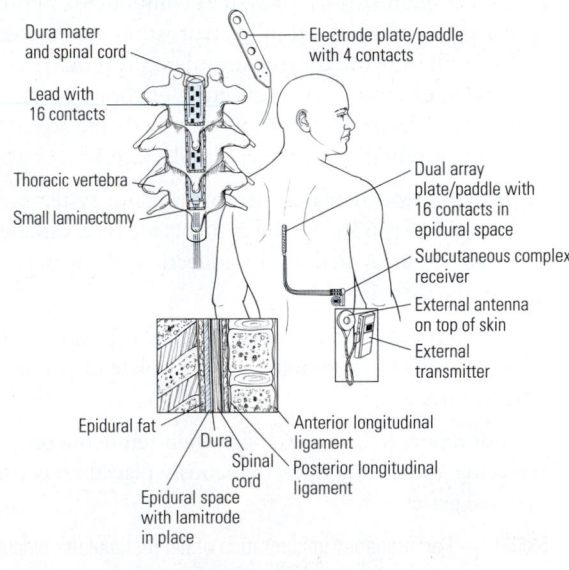

▶(63660 has been deleted. To report, see 63661-63664)◀

● **63661** Removal of spinal neurostimulator electrode percutaneous array(s), including fluoroscopy, when performed

➜ *CPT Changes: An Insider's View* 2010

● **63662** Removal of spinal neurostimulator electrode plate/paddle(s) placed via laminotomy or laminectomy, including fluoroscopy, when performed

➜ *CPT Changes: An Insider's View* 2010

● **63663** Revision including replacement, when performed, of spinal neurostimulator electrode percutaneous array(s), including fluoroscopy, when performed

➜ *CPT Changes: An Insider's View* 2010

▶(Do not report 63663 in conjunction with 63661, 63662 for the same spinal level)◀

● **63664** Revision including replacement, when performed, of spinal neurostimulator electrode plate/paddle(s) placed via laminotomy or laminectomy, including fluoroscopy, when performed

➜ *CPT Changes: An Insider's View* 2010

▶(Do not report 63664 in conjunction with 63661, 63662 for the same spinal level)◀

63685 Insertion or replacement of spinal neurostimulator pulse generator or receiver, direct or inductive coupling

➜ *CPT Assistant* Jun 98:3-4, Sep 99:5; *CPT Changes: An Insider's View* 2005

(Do not report 63685 in conjunction with 63688 for the same pulse generator or receiver)

63688 Revision or removal of implanted spinal neurostimulator pulse generator or receiver

➜ *CPT Assistant* Jun 98:3-4, Sep 99:5

(For electronic analysis of implanted neurostimulator pulse generator system, see 95970-95975)

Repair

63700 Repair of meningocele; less than 5 cm diameter

63702   larger than 5 cm diameter

(Do not use modifier 63 in conjunction with 63700, 63702)

63704 Repair of myelomeningocele; less than 5 cm diameter

63706   larger than 5 cm diameter

(Do not use modifier 63 in conjunction with 63704, 63706)

(For complex skin closure, see **Integumentary System**)

63707 Repair of dural/cerebrospinal fluid leak, not requiring laminectomy

➜ *CPT Changes: An Insider's View* 2002

63709 Repair of dural/cerebrospinal fluid leak or pseudomeningocele, with laminectomy

➜ *CPT Changes: An Insider's View* 2002

63710   Dural graft, spinal

(For laminectomy and section of dentate ligaments, with or without dural graft, cervical, see 63180, 63182)

Shunt, Spinal CSF

63740   Creation of shunt, lumbar, subarachnoid-peritoneal, -pleural, or other; including laminectomy
➡ *CPT Assistant* Winter 90:8

63741   percutaneous, not requiring laminectomy
➡ *CPT Assistant* Winter 90:8

63744   Replacement, irrigation or revision of lumbosubarachnoid shunt

63746   Removal of entire lumbosubarachnoid shunt system without replacement

(For insertion of subarachnoid catheter with reservoir and/or pump for intermittent or continuous infusion of drug including laminectomy, see 62351 and 62360, 62361 or 62362)

(For insertion or replacement of subarachnoid or epidural catheter, with reservoir and/or pump for drug infusion without laminectomy, see 62350 and 62360, 62361 or 62362)

Extracranial Nerves, Peripheral Nerves, and Autonomic Nervous System

(For intracranial surgery on cranial nerves, see 61450, 61460, 61790)

Introduction/Injection of Anesthetic Agent (Nerve Block), Diagnostic or Therapeutic

▶(For destruction by neurolytic agent or chemodenervation, see 62280-62282, 64600-64681)◀

▶(For epidural or subarachnoid injection, see 62310-62319)◀

▶(Codes 64479-64495 are unilateral procedures. For bilateral procedures, use modifier 50)◀

▶(For fluoroscopic guidance and localization for needle placement and injection in conjunction with 64479-64484, use 77003)◀

Somatic Nerves

64400   Injection, anesthetic agent; trigeminal nerve, any division or branch
➡ *CPT Assistant* Jul 98:10, May 99:8, Nov 99:36, Apr 05:13; *CPT Changes: An Insider's View* 2000

64402   facial nerve
➡ *CPT Assistant* Jul 98:10, Apr 05:13

64405   greater occipital nerve
➡ *CPT Assistant* Jul 98:10, Apr 05:13

64408   vagus nerve
➡ *CPT Assistant* Jul 98:10, Apr 05:13

64410   phrenic nerve
➡ *CPT Assistant* Jul 98:10, Apr 05:13

64412   spinal accessory nerve
➡ *CPT Assistant* Jul 98:10, Apr 05:13, Aug 07:15

64413   cervical plexus
➡ *CPT Assistant* Jul 98:10, Apr 05:13

64415   brachial plexus, single
➡ *CPT Assistant* Fall 92:17, Jul 98:10, May 99:8, Oct 01:9, Feb 04:7, Apr 05:13, Nov 06:23; *CPT Changes: An Insider's View* 2003

64416   brachial plexus, continuous infusion by catheter (including catheter placement)
➡ *CPT Assistant* Feb 04:7, Apr 05:13; *CPT Changes: An Insider's View* 2003, 2009

(Do not report 64416 in conjunction with 01996)

64417   axillary nerve
➡ *CPT Assistant* Jul 98:10, Apr 05:13

64418   suprascapular nerve
➡ *CPT Assistant* Jul 98:10, Apr 05:13, Aug 07:15

64420   intercostal nerve, single
➡ *CPT Assistant* Jul 98:10, Apr 05:13

64421   intercostal nerves, multiple, regional block
➡ *CPT Assistant* Jul 98:10, Apr 05:13

64425   ilioinguinal, iliohypogastric nerves
➡ *CPT Assistant* Jul 98:10, Apr 05:13

64430   pudendal nerve
➡ *CPT Assistant* Jul 98:10, Apr 05:13

64435   paracervical (uterine) nerve
➡ *CPT Assistant* Jul 98:10, Mar 03:22, Jul 03:15, Apr 05:13

64445   sciatic nerve, single
➡ *CPT Assistant* Jul 98:10, May 99:8, Feb 04:8, Apr 05:13; *CPT Changes: An Insider's View* 2003

64446   sciatic nerve, continuous infusion by catheter (including catheter placement)
➡ *CPT Assistant* Feb 04:9, Apr 05:13; *CPT Changes: An Insider's View* 2003, 2009

(Do not report 64446 in conjunction with 01996)

64447   femoral nerve, single
➡ *CPT Assistant* Feb 04:9, Apr 05:13; *CPT Changes: An Insider's View* 2003

(Do not report 64447 in conjunction with 01996)

64448   femoral nerve, continuous infusion by catheter (including catheter placement)
➡ *CPT Assistant* Feb 04:10, Apr 05:13; *CPT Changes: An Insider's View* 2003, 2009

(Do not report 64448 in conjunction with 01996)

64449   lumbar plexus, posterior approach, continuous infusion by catheter (including catheter placement)
> *CPT Assistant* Apr 05:13; *CPT Changes: An Insider's View* 2004, 2009

(Do not report 64449 in conjunction with 01996)

64450   other peripheral nerve or branch
> *CPT Assistant* Jul 98:10, Nov 99:37, Dec 99:7, Oct 01:9, Aug 03:6, Apr 05:13, Jan 09:6; *CPT Changes: An Insider's View* 2000

64455   Injection(s), anesthetic agent and/or steroid, plantar common digital nerve(s) (eg, Morton's neuroma)
> *CPT Changes: An Insider's View* 2009

(Do not report 64455 in conjunction with 64632)

►(Codes 64470-64476 have been deleted. To report, see 64490-64495)◄

64479   Injection, anesthetic agent and/or steroid, transforaminal epidural; cervical or thoracic, single level
> *CPT Assistant* Nov 99:33, 37, Feb 00:4, Jul 08:9, Nov 08:11; *CPT Changes: An Insider's View* 2000
> *Clinical Examples in Radiology* Summer 08:9

+ 64480   cervical or thoracic, each additional level (List separately in addition to code for primary procedure)
> *CPT Assistant* Nov 99:33, 37, Feb 00:4, Feb 05:14, Jul 08:9; *CPT Changes: An Insider's View* 2000
> *Clinical Examples in Radiology* Summer 08:9

(Use 64480 in conjunction with 64479)

64483   lumbar or sacral, single level
> *CPT Assistant* Nov 99:33, 37, Feb 00:4, Jul 08:9; *CPT Changes: An Insider's View* 2000

+ 64484   lumbar or sacral, each additional level (List separately in addition to code for primary procedure)
> *CPT Assistant* Nov 99:33, 37, Feb 00:4, Feb 05:14, Jul 08:9, Nov 08:11; *CPT Changes: An Insider's View* 2000

(Use 64484 in conjunction with 64483)

►Paravertebral Spinal Nerves and Branches◄

►(Image guidance [fluoroscopy or CT] and any injection of contrast are inclusive components of 64490-64495. Imaging guidance and localization are required for the performance of paravertebral facet joint injections described by codes 64490-64495. If imaging is not used, report 20550-20553. If ultrasound guidance is used, report 64999)◄

►(For bilateral procedures, use modifier 50)◄

►(For injection of the T12-L1 joint, or nerves innervating that joint, use 64493)◄

● **64490**   Injection(s), diagnostic or therapeutic agent, paravertebral facet (zygapophyseal) joint (or nerves innervating that joint) with image guidance (fluoroscopy or CT), cervical or thoracic; single level
> *CPT Changes: An Insider's View* 2010

+● 64491   second level (List separately in addition to code for primary procedure)
> *CPT Changes: An Insider's View* 2010

+● 64492   third and any additional level(s) (List separately in addition to code for primary procedure)
> *CPT Changes: An Insider's View* 2010

►(Do not report 64492 more than once per day)◄

►(Use 64491, 64492 in conjunction with 64490)◄

● **64493**   Injection(s), diagnostic or therapeutic agent, paravertebral facet (zygapophyseal) joint (or nerves innervating that joint) with image guidance (fluoroscopy or CT), lumbar or sacral; single level
> *CPT Changes: An Insider's View* 2010

+● 64494   second level (List separately in addition to code for primary procedure)
> *CPT Changes: An Insider's View* 2010

+● 64495   third and any additional level(s) (List separately in addition to code for primary procedure)
> *CPT Changes: An Insider's View* 2010

►(Do not report 64495 more than once per day)◄

►(Use 64494, 64495 in conjunction with 64493)◄

►Autonomic Nerves◄

64505   Injection, anesthetic agent; sphenopalatine ganglion
> *CPT Assistant* Jul 98:10, Apr 05:13

64508   carotid sinus (separate procedure)
> *CPT Assistant* Jul 98:10, Apr 05:13

64510   stellate ganglion (cervical sympathetic)
> *CPT Assistant* Jul 98:10, Apr 05:13

64517   superior hypogastric plexus
> *CPT Assistant* Oct 04:11, Apr 05:13; *CPT Changes: An Insider's View* 2004

64520   lumbar or thoracic (paravertebral sympathetic)
> *CPT Assistant* Jul 98:10, Apr 05:13

64530   celiac plexus, with or without radiologic monitoring
> *CPT Assistant* Jul 98:10, Apr 05:13

Neurostimulators (Peripheral Nerve)

Codes 64553-64595 apply to both simple and complex neurostimulators. For initial or subsequent electronic analysis and programming of neurostimulator pulse generators, see codes 95970-95975.

64550   Application of surface (transcutaneous) neurostimulator
> *CPT Assistant* Jan 02:11, Apr 02:18

64553   Percutaneous implantation of neurostimulator electrodes; cranial nerve

➲ *CPT Assistant* Nov 99:38, Apr 01:9; *CPT Changes: An Insider's View* 2000

(For open placement of cranial nerve (eg, vagal, trigeminal) neurostimulator pulse generator or receiver, see 61885, 61886, as appropriate)

64555   peripheral nerve (excludes sacral nerve)

➲ *CPT Changes: An Insider's View* 2002

64560   autonomic nerve

64561   sacral nerve (transforaminal placement)

➲ *CPT Changes: An Insider's View* 2002

64565   neuromuscular

➲ *CPT Assistant* Jul 00:11, Dec 08:8

64573   Incision for implantation of neurostimulator electrodes; cranial nerve

➲ *CPT Assistant* Sep 99:4, Nov 99:38, Apr 01:8; *CPT Changes: An Insider's View* 2000

(For open placement of cranial nerve (eg, vagal, trigeminal) neurostimulator pulse generator or receiver, see 61885, 61886, as appropriate)

(For revision or removal of cranial nerve (eg, vagal, trigeminal) neurostimulator pulse generator or receiver, use 61888)

Implantation Neurostimulator Electrodes, Cranial Nerve (Vagal Nerve Stimulation)
61885, 64573

Open incision for implantation of a neurostimulator electrode (64573) on the vagus nerve (a cranial nerve) with connection of the electrode to an implanted programmable pulse generator (61885) in the infraclavicular area

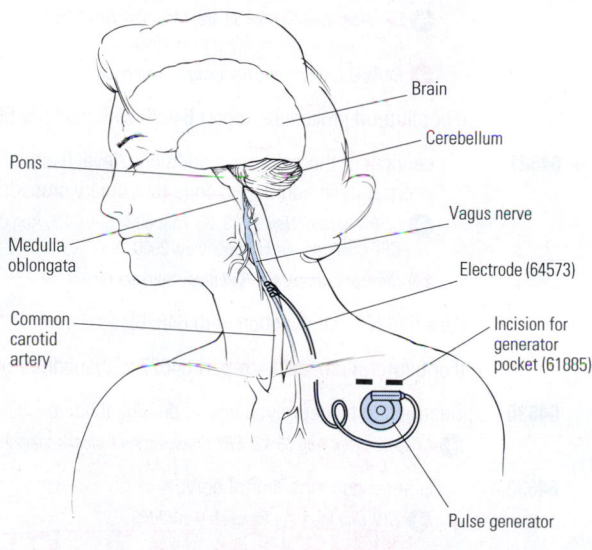

64575   peripheral nerve (excludes sacral nerve)

➲ *CPT Changes: An Insider's View* 2002

64577   autonomic nerve

64580   neuromuscular

64581   sacral nerve (transforaminal placement)

➲ *CPT Changes: An Insider's View* 2002

Incisional Implantation of Sacral Nerve Neurostimulator
64581

Posterior View

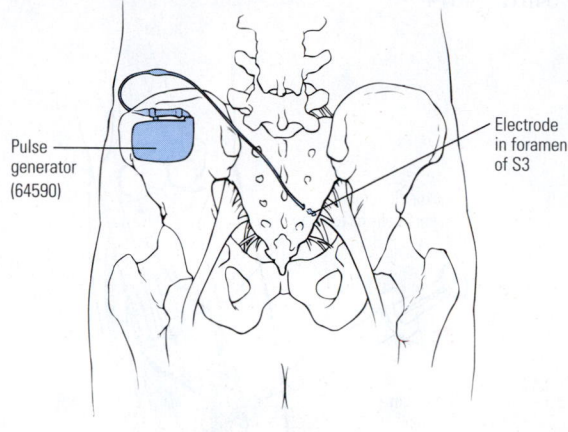

64585   Revision or removal of peripheral neurostimulator electrodes

64590   Insertion or replacement of peripheral or gastric neurostimulator pulse generator or receiver, direct or inductive coupling

➲ *CPT Assistant* Sep 99:4, Apr 01:8, Mar 07:4, Apr 07:7; *CPT Changes: An Insider's View* 2002, 2005, 2007

(Do not report 64590 in conjunction with 64595)

64595   Revision or removal of peripheral or gastric neurostimulator pulse generator or receiver

➲ *CPT Assistant* Sep 99:3, Mar 07:4, Jan 08:8; *CPT Changes: An Insider's View* 2007

Destruction by Neurolytic Agent (eg, Chemical, Thermal, Electrical or Radiofrequency)

Codes 64600-64681 include the injection of other therapeutic agents (eg, corticosteroids). (For therapies that are not destructive of the target nerve [eg, pulsed radiofrequency]), use 64999)

Somatic Nerves

64600   Destruction by neurolytic agent, trigeminal nerve; supraorbital, infraorbital, mental, or inferior alveolar branch

➲ *CPT Assistant* Aug 05:13

64605   second and third division branches at foramen ovale

➲ *CPT Assistant* Aug 05:13

64610   second and third division branches at foramen ovale under radiologic monitoring

➔ *CPT Assistant* Aug 05:13

64612   Chemodenervation of muscle(s); muscle(s) innervated by facial nerve (eg, for blepharospasm, hemifacial spasm)

➔ *CPT Assistant* Oct 98:10, Apr 01:2, Aug 05:13, Sep 06:5, Dec 08:9, Jan 09:8; *CPT Changes: An Insider's View* 2000, 2001

Chemodenervation of Extremity
64612-64614

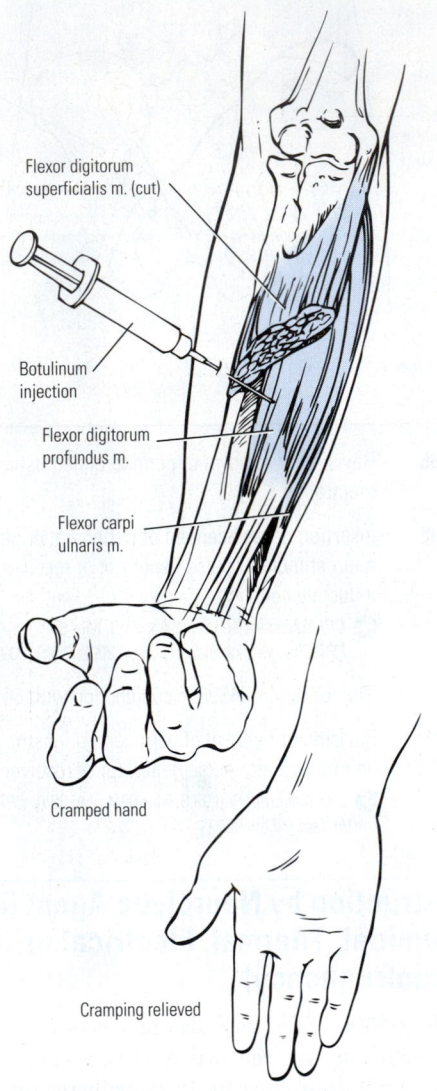

Flexor digitorum superficialis m. (cut)

Botulinum injection

Flexor digitorum profundus m.

Flexor carpi ulnaris m.

Cramped hand

Cramping relieved

64613   neck muscle(s) (eg, for spasmodic torticollis, spasmodic dysphonia)

➔ *CPT Assistant* Sep 00:10, Apr 01:2, Aug 05:13, Sep 06:5, Dec 08:9, Jan 09:8; *CPT Changes: An Insider's View* 2001, 2006

64614   extremity(s) and/or trunk muscle(s) (eg, for dystonia, cerebral palsy, multiple sclerosis)

➔ *CPT Assistant* Apr 01:2, Feb 05:14, Aug 05:13, Sep 06:5, Dec 08:9; *CPT Changes: An Insider's View* 2001

(For chemodenervation guided by needle electromyography or muscle electrical stimulation, see 95873, 95874)

(For chemodenervation for strabismus involving the extraocular muscles, use 67345)

(For chemodenervation of internal anal sphincter, use 46505)

64620   Destruction by neurolytic agent, intercostal nerve

➔ *CPT Assistant* Nov 99:38, Aug 05:13; *CPT Changes: An Insider's View* 2000

(For fluoroscopic guidance and localization for needle placement and neurolysis in conjunction with 64622-64627, use 77003)

64622   Destruction by neurolytic agent, paravertebral facet joint nerve; lumbar or sacral, single level

➔ *CPT Assistant* Nov 99:33, 39, Dec 99:7, Mar 00:4, Sep 04:5, Aug 05:13; *CPT Changes: An Insider's View* 2000

➔ *Clinical Examples in Radiology* Summer 08:9, 13

(For bilateral procedure, report 64622 with modifier 50)

+ 64623   lumbar or sacral, each additional level (List separately in addition to code for primary procedure)

➔ *CPT Assistant* Nov 99:33, 39, Mar 00:4, Sep 04:5, Aug 05:13; *CPT Changes: An Insider's View* 2000

➔ *Clinical Examples in Radiology* Summer 08:9

(Use 64623 in conjunction with 64622)

(For bilateral procedure, report 64623 with modifier 50)

64626   cervical or thoracic, single level

➔ *CPT Assistant* Nov 99:33, 39, Mar 00:4, Sep 04:5, Aug 05:13; *CPT Changes: An Insider's View* 2000

➔ *Clinical Examples in Radiology* Summer 08:9

(For bilateral procedure, report 64626 with modifier 50)

+ 64627   cervical or thoracic, each additional level (List separately in addition to code for primary procedure)

➔ *CPT Assistant* Nov 99:33, 39, Mar 00:4, Sep 04:5, Aug 05:13; *CPT Changes: An Insider's View* 2000

➔ *Clinical Examples in Radiology* Summer 08:9

(Use 64627 in conjunction with 64626)

(For bilateral procedure, report 64627 with modifier 50)

64630   Destruction by neurolytic agent; pudendal nerve

➔ *CPT Assistant* Aug 05:13; *CPT Changes: An Insider's View* 2001

64632   plantar common digital nerve

➔ *CPT Changes: An Insider's View* 2009

(Do not report 64632 in conjunction with 64455)

64640   other peripheral nerve or branch

➔ *CPT Assistant* Aug 05:13

Sympathetic Nerves

64650 Chemodenervation of eccrine glands; both axillae
➲ *CPT Changes: An Insider's View* 2006

64653   other area(s) (eg, scalp, face, neck), per day
➲ *CPT Changes: An Insider's View* 2006

(Report the specific service in conjunction with code(s) for the specific substance(s) or drug(s) provided)

(For chemodenervation of extremities (eg, hands or feet), use 64999)

64680 Destruction by neurolytic agent, with or without radiologic monitoring; celiac plexus
➲ *CPT Assistant* Feb 99:10, Aug 05:13; *CPT Changes: An Insider's View* 2004

64681   superior hypogastric plexus
➲ *CPT Assistant* Aug 05:13, Dec 07:13; *CPT Changes: An Insider's View* 2004

Neuroplasty (Exploration, Neurolysis or Nerve Decompression)

Neuroplasty is the decompression or freeing of intact nerve from scar tissue, including external neurolysis and/or transposition.

(For internal neurolysis requiring use of operating microscope, use 64727)

(For facial nerve decompression, use 69720)

(For neuroplasty with nerve wrapping, see 64702-64727, 64999)

64702 Neuroplasty; digital, 1 or both, same digit
➲ *CPT Assistant* Jun 01:11

64704   nerve of hand or foot
➲ *CPT Assistant* Jun 01:11

64708 Neuroplasty, major peripheral nerve, arm or leg; other than specified
➲ *CPT Assistant* Jun 01:11

64712   sciatic nerve
➲ *CPT Assistant* Jun 01:11

64713   brachial plexus
➲ *CPT Assistant* Jun 01:11

64714   lumbar plexus
➲ *CPT Assistant* Jun 97:11, Sep 98:16, Jun 01:11

64716 Neuroplasty and/or transposition; cranial nerve (specify)
➲ *CPT Assistant* Jun 01:11

64718   ulnar nerve at elbow
➲ *CPT Assistant* Jun 01:11, Mar 09:10

64719   ulnar nerve at wrist
➲ *CPT Assistant* Jun 01:11, Mar 09:10

64721 median nerve at carpal tunnel
➲ *CPT Assistant* Fall 92:17, Sep 97:10, Jun 01:11, Nov 06:23

(For arthroscopic procedure, use 29848)

64722 Decompression; unspecified nerve(s) (specify)
➲ *CPT Assistant* Sep 98:16, May 99:11, Jun 01:11, Oct 04:12

64726   plantar digital nerve
➲ *CPT Assistant* Jun 01:11

+ 64727 Internal neurolysis, requiring use of operating microscope (List separately in addition to code for neuroplasty) (Neuroplasty includes external neurolysis)
➲ *CPT Assistant* Nov 98:19, Jun 01:11

(Do not report code 69990 in addition to code 64727)

Transection or Avulsion

(For stereotactic lesion of gasserian ganglion, use 61790)

64732 Transection or avulsion of; supraorbital nerve
➲ *CPT Assistant* Nov 99:39; *CPT Changes: An Insider's View* 2000

64734   infraorbital nerve

64736   mental nerve

64738   inferior alveolar nerve by osteotomy

64740   lingual nerve

64742   facial nerve, differential or complete

64744   greater occipital nerve

64746   phrenic nerve

(For section of recurrent laryngeal nerve, use 31595)

64752   vagus nerve (vagotomy), transthoracic

64755   vagus nerves limited to proximal stomach (selective proximal vagotomy, proximal gastric vagotomy, parietal cell vagotomy, supra- or highly selective vagotomy)
➲ *CPT Assistant* Nov 99:39; *CPT Changes: An Insider's View* 2000, 2002

(For laparoscopic approach, use 43652)

64760   vagus nerve (vagotomy), abdominal
➲ *CPT Assistant* Nov 99:39; *CPT Changes: An Insider's View* 2000

(For laparoscopic approach, use 43651)

64761   pudendal nerve

(For bilateral procedure, report 64761 with modifier 50)

64763 Transection or avulsion of obturator nerve, extrapelvic, with or without adductor tenotomy

(For bilateral procedure, report 64763 with modifier 50)

64766 Transection or avulsion of obturator nerve, intrapelvic, with or without adductor tenotomy

(For bilateral procedure, report 64766 with modifier 50)

64771 Transection or avulsion of other cranial nerve, extradural

64772 Transection or avulsion of other spinal nerve, extradural

(For excision of tender scar, skin and subcutaneous tissue, with or without tiny neuroma, see 11400-11446, 13100-13153)

Excision

Somatic Nerves

(For Morton neurectomy, use 28080)

64774 Excision of neuroma; cutaneous nerve, surgically identifiable

64776   digital nerve, 1 or both, same digit

+ 64778   digital nerve, each additional digit (List separately in addition to code for primary procedure)

(Use 64778 in conjunction with 64776)

64782   hand or foot, except digital nerve

+ 64783   hand or foot, each additional nerve, except same digit (List separately in addition to code for primary procedure)

(Use 64783 in conjunction with 64782)

64784   major peripheral nerve, except sciatic

64786   sciatic nerve

+ 64787 Implantation of nerve end into bone or muscle (List separately in addition to neuroma excision)

(Use 64787 in conjunction with 64774-64786)

64788 Excision of neurofibroma or neurolemmoma; cutaneous nerve

64790   major peripheral nerve

64792   extensive (including malignant type)

64795 Biopsy of nerve

Sympathetic Nerves

64802 Sympathectomy, cervical

(For bilateral procedure, report 64802 with modifier 50)

64804 Sympathectomy, cervicothoracic

(For bilateral procedure, report 64804 with modifier 50)

64809 Sympathectomy, thoracolumbar

(For bilateral procedure, report 64809 with modifier 50)

64818 Sympathectomy, lumbar

(For bilateral procedure, report 64818 with modifier 50)

64820 Sympathectomy; digital arteries, each digit
    ➲ CPT Assistant Jan 04:27; CPT Changes: An Insider's View 2002

(Do not report 69990 in addition to code 64820)

64821   radial artery
    ➲ CPT Changes: An Insider's View 2002

(Do not report 69990 in addition to code 64821)

64822   ulnar artery
    ➲ CPT Changes: An Insider's View 2002

(Do not report 69990 in addition to code 64822)

64823   superficial palmar arch
    ➲ CPT Changes: An Insider's View 2002

(Do not report 69990 in addition to code 64823)

Neurorrhaphy

64831 Suture of digital nerve, hand or foot; 1 nerve
    ➲ CPT Assistant Apr 00:5

+ 64832   each additional digital nerve (List separately in addition to code for primary procedure)
    ➲ CPT Assistant Apr 00:5

(Use 64832 in conjunction with 64831)

64834 Suture of 1 nerve; hand or foot, common sensory nerve
    ➲ CPT Changes: An Insider's View 2008

64835   median motor thenar
    ➲ CPT Changes: An Insider's View 2008

64836   ulnar motor
    ➲ CPT Changes: An Insider's View 2008

+ 64837 Suture of each additional nerve, hand or foot (List separately in addition to code for primary procedure)

(Use 64837 in conjunction with 64834-64836)

64840 Suture of posterior tibial nerve

64856 Suture of major peripheral nerve, arm or leg, except sciatic; including transposition

64857   without transposition

64858 Suture of sciatic nerve

+ 64859 Suture of each additional major peripheral nerve (List separately in addition to code for primary procedure)

(Use 64859 in conjunction with 64856, 64857)

64861 Suture of; brachial plexus

64862   lumbar plexus

64864 Suture of facial nerve; extracranial

64865   infratemporal, with or without grafting

64866 Anastomosis; facial-spinal accessory

64868   facial-hypoglossal

64870   facial-phrenic

+ 64872 Suture of nerve; requiring secondary or delayed suture (List separately in addition to code for primary neurorrhaphy)

(Use 64872 in conjunction with 64831-64865)

+ 64874   requiring extensive mobilization, or transposition of nerve (List separately in addition to code for nerve suture)

(Use 64874 in conjunction with 64831-64865)

+ 64876   requiring shortening of bone of extremity (List separately in addition to code for nerve suture)

(Use 64876 in conjunction with 64831-64865)

Neurorrhaphy With Nerve Graft, Vein Graft, or Conduit

64885 Nerve graft (includes obtaining graft), head or neck; up to 4 cm in length
➡️ *CPT Assistant* Nov 00:11

64886 more than 4 cm length
➡️ *CPT Assistant* Nov 00:11

64890 Nerve graft (includes obtaining graft), single strand, hand or foot; up to 4 cm length

64891 more than 4 cm length

64892 Nerve graft (includes obtaining graft), single strand, arm or leg; up to 4 cm length

64893 more than 4 cm length

64895 Nerve graft (includes obtaining graft), multiple strands (cable), hand or foot; up to 4 cm length
➡️ *CPT Assistant* Nov 00:11

64896 more than 4 cm length
➡️ *CPT Assistant* Nov 00:11

64897 Nerve graft (includes obtaining graft), multiple strands (cable), arm or leg; up to 4 cm length
➡️ *CPT Assistant* Nov 00:11

64898 more than 4 cm length
➡️ *CPT Assistant* Nov 00:11

+ 64901 Nerve graft, each additional nerve; single strand (List separately in addition to code for primary procedure)
➡️ *CPT Assistant* Nov 00:11

(Use 64901 in conjunction with 64885-64893)

+ 64902 multiple strands (cable) (List separately in addition to code for primary procedure)
➡️ *CPT Assistant* Nov 00:11

(Use 64902 in conjunction with 64885, 64886, 64895-64898)

64905 Nerve pedicle transfer; first stage

64907 second stage

64910 Nerve repair; with synthetic conduit or vein allograft (eg, nerve tube), each nerve
➡️ *CPT Assistant* Nov 07:4; *CPT Changes: An Insider's View* 2007

64911 with autogenous vein graft (includes harvest of vein graft), each nerve
➡️ *CPT Assistant* Nov 07:4; *CPT Changes: An Insider's View* 2007

(Do not report 69990 in addition to 64910, 64911)

Other Procedures

64999 Unlisted procedure, nervous system
➡️ *CPT Assistant* Apr 96:11, Sep 98:16, Oct 98:10, Jan 00:10, Aug 00:7, Sep 00:10, Feb 02:10, Nov 03:5, Oct 04:11, Apr 05:13, Aug 05:13, Sep 05:9, Sep 07:10, Nov 07:4, Dec 07:8, Jul 08:9, Sep 08:11

Notes

⊙=Moderate sedation   ✚=Add-on code   ✗=FDA approval pending   #=Resequenced code   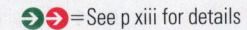=See p xiii for details

Eye and Ocular Adnexa (65091-68899) 323

The following is a listing of headings and subheadings that appear within the Eye and Ocular Adnexa section of the CPT codebook. The subheadings or subsections denoted with asterisks (*) below have special instructions unique to that section. Where these are indicated, special "notes" or guidelines will be presented preceding those procedural terminology listings, referring to that subsection specifically.

Oc/Au
65091

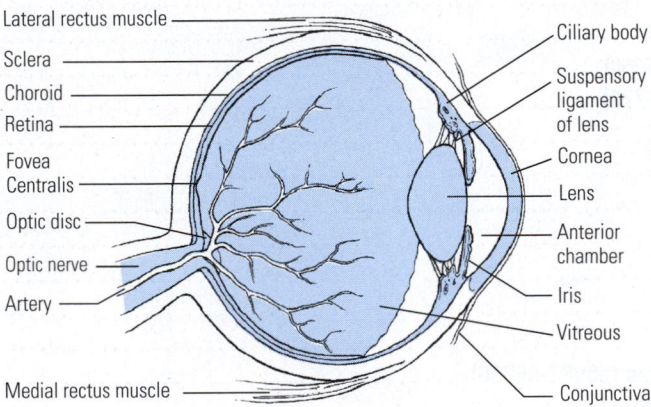

Eye anatomy

Lateral rectus muscle
Sclera
Choroid
Retina
Fovea Centralis
Optic disc
Optic nerve
Artery
Medial rectus muscle
Ciliary body
Suspensory ligament of lens
Cornea
Lens
Anterior chamber
Iris
Vitreous
Conjunctiva

Eye and Ocular Adnexa

(For diagnostic and treatment ophthalmological services, see **Medicine, Ophthalmology,** and 92002 et seq)

(Do not report code 69990 in addition to codes 65091-68850)

Eyeball

Removal of Eye

65091 Evisceration of ocular contents; without implant

65093   with implant

65101 Enucleation of eye; without implant

65103   with implant, muscles not attached to implant

65105   with implant, muscles attached to implant

(For conjunctivoplasty after enucleation, see 68320 et seq)

65110 Exenteration of orbit (does not include skin graft), removal of orbital contents; only

65112   with therapeutic removal of bone

65114   with muscle or myocutaneous flap

(For skin graft to orbit (split skin), see 15120, 15121; free, full thickness, see 15260, 15261)

(For eyelid repair involving more than skin, see 67930 et seq)

Secondary Implant(s) Procedures

An ocular implant is an implant inside muscular cone; an orbital implant is an implant outside muscular cone.

65125 Modification of ocular implant with placement or replacement of pegs (eg, drilling receptacle for prosthesis appendage) (separate procedure)

65130 Insertion of ocular implant secondary; after evisceration, in scleral shell

65135   after enucleation, muscles not attached to implant

65140   after enucleation, muscles attached to implant

65150 Reinsertion of ocular implant; with or without conjunctival graft

65155   with use of foreign material for reinforcement and/or attachment of muscles to implant

65175 Removal of ocular implant

(For orbital implant (implant outside muscle cone) insertion, use 67550; removal, use 67560)

Removal of Foreign Body

(For removal of implanted material: ocular implant, use 65175; anterior segment implant, use 65920; posterior segment implant, use 67120; orbital implant, use 67560)

(For diagnostic x-ray for foreign body, use 70030)

(For diagnostic echography for foreign body, use 76529)

(For removal of foreign body from orbit: frontal approach, use 67413; lateral approach, use 67430; transcranial approach, use 61334)

(For removal of foreign body from eyelid, embedded, use 67938)

(For removal of foreign body from lacrimal system, use 68530)

65205 Removal of foreign body, external eye; conjunctival superficial

➔ *CPT Assistant* Mar 05:17

65210   conjunctival embedded (includes concretions), subconjunctival, or scleral nonperforating

65220   corneal, without slit lamp

65222   corneal, with slit lamp

(For repair of corneal laceration with foreign body, use 65275)

65235 Removal of foreign body, intraocular; from anterior chamber of eye or lens

➔ *CPT Changes: An Insider's View* 2002

(For removal of implanted material from anterior segment, use 65920)

65260   from posterior segment, magnetic extraction, anterior or posterior route

65265   from posterior segment, nonmagnetic extraction

(For removal of implanted material from posterior segment, use 67120)

Repair of Laceration

(For fracture of orbit, see 21385 et seq)

(For repair of wound of eyelid, skin, linear, simple, see 12011-12018; intermediate, layered closure, see 12051-12057; linear, complex, see 13150-13160; other, see 67930, 67935)

(For repair of wound of lacrimal system, use 68700)

(For repair of operative wound, use 66250)

65270 Repair of laceration; conjunctiva, with or without nonperforating laceration sclera, direct closure

65272   conjunctiva, by mobilization and rearrangement, without hospitalization

65273   conjunctiva, by mobilization and rearrangement, with hospitalization

---

65275	cornea, nonperforating, with or without removal foreign body
65280	cornea and/or sclera, perforating, not involving uveal tissue
65285	cornea and/or sclera, perforating, with reposition or resection of uveal tissue
65286	application of tissue glue, wounds of cornea and/or sclera

➲ *CPT Assistant* May 99:11, Apr 09:5

(Repair of laceration includes use of conjunctival flap and restoration of anterior chamber, by air or saline injection when indicated)

(For repair of iris or ciliary body, use 66680)

● **65290**   Repair of wound, extraocular muscle, tendon and/or Tenon's capsule

Anterior Segment

Cornea

Excision

65400	Excision of lesion, cornea (keratectomy, lamellar, partial), except pterygium
65410	Biopsy of cornea
65420	Excision or transposition of pterygium; without graft

➲ *CPT Assistant* Dec 07:13

65426	with graft

Removal or Destruction

65430	Scraping of cornea, diagnostic, for smear and/or culture
65435	Removal of corneal epithelium; with or without chemocauterization (abrasion, curettage)
65436	with application of chelating agent (eg, EDTA)
65450	Destruction of lesion of cornea by cryotherapy, photocoagulation or thermocauterization

Cryotherapy of Lesion on Cornea
65450

A freezing probe is applied directly to the corneal defect to destroy it.

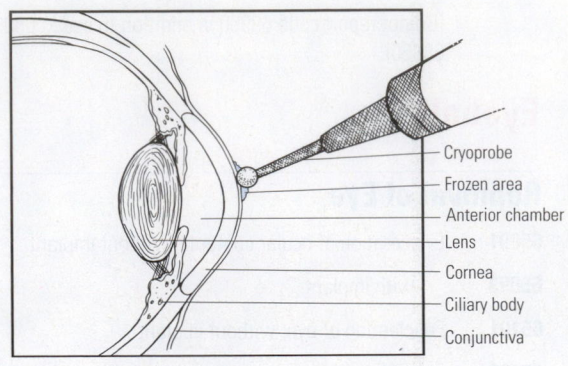

Cryoprobe
Frozen area
Anterior chamber
Lens
Cornea
Ciliary body
Conjunctiva

65600	Multiple punctures of anterior cornea (eg, for corneal erosion, tattoo)

Keratoplasty

Corneal transplant includes use of fresh or preserved grafts. The preparation of donor material is included for penetrating or anterior lamellar keratoplasty, but reported separately for endothelial keratoplasty. Do not report 65710-65757 in conjunction with 92025.

(Keratoplasty excludes refractive keratoplasty procedures, 65760, 65765, and 65767)

65710	Keratoplasty (corneal transplant); anterior lamellar

➲ *CPT Assistant* Oct 02:8, Apr 09:5; *CPT Changes: An Insider's View* 2009

65730	penetrating (except in aphakia or pseudophakia)

➲ *CPT Assistant* Oct 02:8, Feb 06:1, Apr 09:5; *CPT Changes: An Insider's View* 2009

65750	penetrating (in aphakia)

➲ *CPT Assistant* Oct 02:8, Apr 09:5

65755	penetrating (in pseudophakia)

➲ *CPT Assistant* Winter 90:8, Oct 02:9, Apr 09:5

65756	endothelial

➲ *CPT Changes: An Insider's View* 2009

+ 65757	Backbench preparation of corneal endothelial allograft prior to transplantation (List separately in addition to code for primary procedure)

➲ *CPT Changes: An Insider's View* 2009

(Use 65757 in conjunction with 65756)

Other Procedures

Do not report 65760-65771 in conjunction with 92025.

65760	Keratomileusis

➲ *CPT Assistant* Oct 02:9

65765	Keratophakia

➲ *CPT Assistant* Oct 02:10

65767   Epikeratoplasty

➔ *CPT Assistant* Winter 90:8, Oct 02:10

65770   Keratoprosthesis

➔ *CPT Assistant* Oct 02:10

65771   Radial keratotomy

➔ *CPT Assistant* Winter 90:8, Oct 02:10

65772   Corneal relaxing incision for correction of surgically induced astigmatism

➔ *CPT Assistant* Oct 02:10, 12

65775   Corneal wedge resection for correction of surgically induced astigmatism

➔ *CPT Assistant* Oct 02:10, 12

(For fitting of contact lens for treatment of disease, use 92070)

(For unlisted procedures on cornea, use 66999)

65780   Ocular surface reconstruction; amniotic membrane transplantation

➔ *CPT Assistant* May 04:10; *CPT Changes: An Insider's View* 2004

65781   limbal stem cell allograft (eg, cadaveric or living donor)

➔ *CPT Assistant* May 04:10; *CPT Changes: An Insider's View* 2004

65782   limbal conjunctival autograft (includes obtaining graft)

➔ *CPT Assistant* Feb 04:11, May 04:10, Feb 05:15-16; *CPT Changes: An Insider's View* 2004

(For harvesting conjunctival allograft, living donor, use 68371)

Anterior Chamber

Incision

65800   Paracentesis of anterior chamber of eye (separate procedure); with diagnostic aspiration of aqueous

65805   with therapeutic release of aqueous

65810   with removal of vitreous and/or discission of anterior hyaloid membrane, with or without air injection

65815   with removal of blood, with or without irrigation and/or air injection

(For injection, see 66020-66030)

(For removal of blood clot, use 65930)

65820   Goniotomy

➔ *CPT Assistant* Sep 05:12

(Do not report modifier 63 in conjunction with 65820)

(For use of ophthalmic endoscope with 65820, use 66990)

65850   Trabeculotomy ab externo

65855   Trabeculoplasty by laser surgery, 1 or more sessions (defined treatment series)

➔ *CPT Assistant* Mar 98:7, Mar 03:23

(If re-treatment is necessary after several months because of disease progression, a new treatment or treatment series should be reported with a modifier, if necessary, to indicate lesser or greater complexity)

(For trabeculectomy, use 66170)

65860   Severing adhesions of anterior segment, laser technique (separate procedure)

65865   Severing adhesions of anterior segment of eye, incisional technique (with or without injection of air or liquid) (separate procedure); goniosynechiae

(For trabeculoplasty by laser surgery, use 65855)

65870   anterior synechiae, except goniosynechiae

65875   posterior synechiae

➔ *CPT Assistant* Sep 05:12

(For use of ophthalmic endoscope with 65875, use 66990)

65880   corneovitreal adhesions

(For laser surgery, use 66821)

Removal

65900   Removal of epithelial downgrowth, anterior chamber of eye

➔ *CPT Changes: An Insider's View* 2002

65920   Removal of implanted material, anterior segment of eye

➔ *CPT Assistant* Sep 05:12; *CPT Changes: An Insider's View* 2002

(For use of ophthalmic endoscope with 65920, use 66990)

65930   Removal of blood clot, anterior segment of eye

➔ *CPT Changes: An Insider's View* 2002

Introduction

66020   Injection, anterior chamber of eye (separate procedure); air or liquid

➔ *CPT Changes: An Insider's View* 2002

66030   medication

(For unlisted procedures on anterior segment, use 66999)

Anterior Sclera

Excision

(For removal of intraocular foreign body, use 65235)

(For operations on posterior sclera, use 67250, 67255)

66130   Excision of lesion, sclera

66150   Fistulization of sclera for glaucoma; trephination with iridectomy

66155   thermocauterization with iridectomy

66160   sclerectomy with punch or scissors, with iridectomy

66165   iridencleisis or iridotasis

66170   trabeculectomy ab externo in absence of previous surgery
> *CPT Assistant* Jul 03:4, Nov 03:10

(For trabeculotomy ab externo, use 65850)

(For repair of operative wound, use 66250)

(For dilation of Schlemm's Canal with or without retention of device, see 0176T, 0177T)

66172   trabeculectomy ab externo with scarring from previous ocular surgery or trauma (includes injection of antifibrotic agents)
> *CPT Assistant* Jul 03:4, Nov 03:10

(For transciliary body sclera fistulization, use Category III code 0123T)

Aqueous Shunt

66180   Aqueous shunt to extraocular reservoir (eg, Molteno, Schocket, Denver-Krupin)
> *CPT Assistant* Winter 90:8, Aug 03:9, Sep 03:2

66185   Revision of aqueous shunt to extraocular reservoir
> *CPT Assistant* Winter 90:8

(For removal of implanted shunt, use 67120)

Repair or Revision

(For scleral procedures in retinal surgery, see 67101 et seq)

66220   Repair of scleral staphyloma; without graft

66225   with graft

(For scleral reinforcement, see 67250, 67255)

66250   Revision or repair of operative wound of anterior segment, any type, early or late, major or minor procedure

(For unlisted procedures on anterior sclera, use 66999)

Iris, Ciliary Body

Incision

66500   Iridotomy by stab incision (separate procedure); except transfixion

66505   with transfixion as for iris bombe

(For iridotomy by photocoagulation, use 66761)

Excision

66600   Iridectomy, with corneoscleral or corneal section; for removal of lesion

66605   with cyclectomy

66625   peripheral for glaucoma (separate procedure)

66630   sector for glaucoma (separate procedure)

66635   optical (separate procedure)

(For coreoplasty by photocoagulation, use 66762)

Repair

66680   Repair of iris, ciliary body (as for iridodialysis)

(For reposition or resection of uveal tissue with perforating wound of cornea or sclera, use 65285)

66682   Suture of iris, ciliary body (separate procedure) with retrieval of suture through small incision (eg, McCannel suture)

Destruction

66700   Ciliary body destruction; diathermy

66710   cyclophotocoagulation, transscleral
> *CPT Assistant* Mar 05:20, Sep 05:5; *CPT Changes: An Insider's View* 2005

66711   cyclophotocoagulation, endoscopic
> *CPT Assistant* Mar 05:20, Sep 05:5, 12; *CPT Changes: An Insider's View* 2005

(Do not report 66711 in conjunction with 66990)

⊙ **66720**   cryotherapy

66740   cyclodialysis

66761   Iridotomy/iridectomy by laser surgery (eg, for glaucoma) (1 or more sessions)
> *CPT Assistant* Mar 98:7

66762   Iridoplasty by photocoagulation (1 or more sessions) (eg, for improvement of vision, for widening of anterior chamber angle)
> *CPT Assistant* Mar 98:7

66770   Destruction of cyst or lesion iris or ciliary body (nonexcisional procedure)

(For excision lesion iris, ciliary body, see 66600, 66605; for removal of epithelial downgrowth, use 65900)

(For unlisted procedures on iris, ciliary body, use 66999)

Lens

Incision

66820   Discission of secondary membranous cataract (opacified posterior lens capsule and/or anterior hyaloid); stab incision technique (Ziegler or Wheeler knife)

66821   laser surgery (eg, YAG laser) (1 or more stages)

66825   Repositioning of intraocular lens prosthesis, requiring an incision (separate procedure)

Removal

Lateral canthotomy, iridectomy, iridotomy, anterior capsulotomy, posterior capsulotomy, the use of viscoelastic agents, enzymatic zonulysis, use of other pharmacologic agents, and subconjunctival or sub-tenon injections are included as part of the code for the extraction of lens.

66830   Removal of secondary membranous cataract (opacified posterior lens capsule and/or anterior hyaloid) with corneo-scleral section, with or without iridectomy (iridocapsulotomy, iridocapsulectomy)

66840   Removal of lens material; aspiration technique, 1 or more stages
➜ *CPT Assistant* Fall 92:4, Jan 09:7, Apr 09:9

66850   phacofragmentation technique (mechanical or ultrasonic) (eg, phacoemulsification), with aspiration
➜ *CPT Assistant* Fall 92:6, Jan 09:7, Apr 09:9

66852   pars plana approach, with or without vitrectomy
➜ *CPT Assistant* Fall 92:8, Jan 09:7, Apr 09:9

66920   intracapsular
➜ *CPT Assistant* Fall 92:8

66930   intracapsular, for dislocated lens
➜ *CPT Assistant* Fall 92:8

66940   extracapsular (other than 66840, 66850, 66852)
➜ *CPT Assistant* Fall 92:4, Jan 09:7, Apr 09:9

(For removal of intralenticular foreign body without lens extraction, use 65235)

(For repair of operative wound, use 66250)

Intraocular Lens Procedures

66982   Extracapsular cataract removal with insertion of intraocular lens prosthesis (1-stage procedure), manual or mechanical technique (eg, irrigation and aspiration or phacoemulsification), complex, requiring devices or techniques not generally used in routine cataract surgery (eg, iris expansion device, suture support for intraocular lens, or primary posterior capsulorrhexis) or performed on patients in the amblyogenic developmental stage
➜ *CPT Assistant* Feb 01:7, Nov 03:10; *CPT Changes: An Insider's View* 2001, 2002

66983   Intracapsular cataract extraction with insertion of intraocular lens prosthesis (1 stage procedure)
➜ *CPT Assistant* Fall 92:5, 8, Nov 03:10

66984   Extracapsular cataract removal with insertion of intraocular lens prosthesis (1 stage procedure), manual or mechanical technique (eg, irrigation and aspiration or phacoemulsification)
➜ *CPT Assistant* Fall 92:5, 8, Feb 01:7, Nov 03:10, Mar 05:11

(For complex extracapsular cataract removal, use 66982)

66985   Insertion of intraocular lens prosthesis (secondary implant), not associated with concurrent cataract removal
➜ *CPT Assistant* Sep 05:12

(To code implant at time of concurrent cataract surgery, see 66982, 66983, 66984)

(For intraocular lens prosthesis supplied by physician, use 99070)

(For ultrasonic determination of intraocular lens power, use 76519)

(For removal of implanted material from anterior segment, use 65920)

(For secondary fixation (separate procedure), use 66682)

(For use of ophthalmic endoscope with 66985, use 66990)

66986   Exchange of intraocular lens
➜ *CPT Assistant* Sep 05:12

(For use of ophthalmic endoscope with 66986, use 66990)

Other Procedures

+ **66990**   Use of ophthalmic endoscope (List separately in addition to code for primary procedure)
➜ *CPT Assistant* Sep 05:12, Oct 08:3; *CPT Changes: An Insider's View* 2003

▶(66990 may be used only with codes 65820, 65875, 65920, 66985, 66986, 67036, 67039, 67040, 67041, 67042, 67043, 67112, 67113)◀

66999   Unlisted procedure, anterior segment of eye

Posterior Segment

Vitreous

67005   Removal of vitreous, anterior approach (open sky technique or limbal incision); partial removal
➜ *CPT Assistant* Fall 92:4

67010   subtotal removal with mechanical vitrectomy
➜ *CPT Assistant* Fall 92:4

(For removal of vitreous by paracentesis of anterior chamber, use 65810)

(For removal of corneovitreal adhesions, use 65880)

67015   Aspiration or release of vitreous, subretinal or choroidal fluid, pars plana approach (posterior sclerotomy)

67025   Injection of vitreous substitute, pars plana or limbal approach (fluid-gas exchange), with or without aspiration (separate procedure)

67027   Implantation of intravitreal drug delivery system (eg, ganciclovir implant), includes concomitant removal of vitreous
➜ *CPT Assistant* Nov 97:23, Nov 98:1

Intravitreal Drug Delivery System
67027

A drug delivery system that releases medication into the vitreous is implanted into the vitreous by pars plana incision.

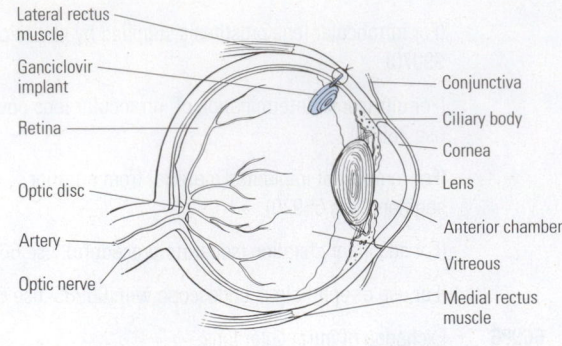

(For removal, use 67121)

67028 Intravitreal injection of a pharmacologic agent (separate procedure)

→ *CPT Assistant* Winter 90:9

67030 Discission of vitreous strands (without removal), pars plana approach

67031 Severing of vitreous strands, vitreous face adhesions, sheets, membranes or opacities, laser surgery (1 or more stages)

67036 Vitrectomy, mechanical, pars plana approach;

→ *CPT Assistant* Fall 92:6, Oct 08:3

(For application of intraocular epiretinal radiation with 67036, use 0190T)

(67038 has been deleted. To report, see 67041, 67042, 67043)

67039 with focal endolaser photocoagulation

→ *CPT Assistant* Winter 90:9, Sep 05:12

67040 with endolaser panretinal photocoagulation

→ *CPT Assistant* Winter 90:9, Sep 05:12, Jul 07:12

67041 with removal of preretinal cellular membrane (eg, macular pucker)

→ *CPT Changes: An Insider's View* 2008

67042 with removal of internal limiting membrane of retina (eg, for repair of macular hole, diabetic macular edema), includes, if performed, intraocular tamponade (ie, air, gas or silicone oil)

→ *CPT Changes: An Insider's View* 2008

67043 with removal of subretinal membrane (eg, choroidal neovascularization), includes, if performed, intraocular tamponade (ie, air, gas or silicone oil) and laser photocoagulation

→ *CPT Changes: An Insider's View* 2008

(For use of ophthalmic endoscope with 67036, 67039, 67040-67043, use 66990)

(For associated lensectomy, use 66850)

(For use of vitrectomy in retinal detachment surgery, see 67108, 67113)

(For associated removal of foreign body, see 65260, 65265)

(For unlisted procedures on vitreous, use 67299)

Retina or Choroid

Repair

(If diathermy, cryotherapy and/or photocoagulation are combined, report under principal modality used)

67101 Repair of retinal detachment, 1 or more sessions; cryotherapy or diathermy, with or without drainage of subretinal fluid

→ *CPT Assistant* Mar 98:7

67105 photocoagulation, with or without drainage of subretinal fluid

→ *CPT Assistant* Mar 98:7

67107 Repair of retinal detachment; scleral buckling (such as lamellar scleral dissection, imbrication or encircling procedure), with or without implant, with or without cryotherapy, photocoagulation, and drainage of subretinal fluid

Repair of Retinal Detachment
67107

The retinal tear is treated externally by placing a hot or cold probe over the sclera and then depressing it. The burn seals the choroid to the retina at the site of the tear. The healing scar is supported by the encircling band, which buckles the eye.

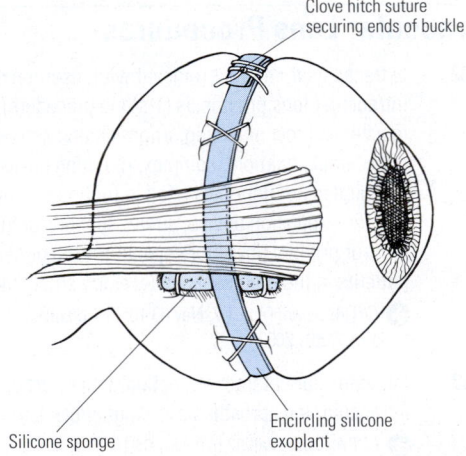

67108 with vitrectomy, any method, with or without air or gas tamponade, focal endolaser photocoagulation, cryotherapy, drainage of subretinal fluid, scleral buckling, and/or removal of lens by same technique

→ *CPT Assistant* Winter 90:9

67110 by injection of air or other gas (eg, pneumatic retinopexy)

→ *CPT Assistant* Winter 90:9

67112   by scleral buckling or vitrectomy, on patient having previous ipsilateral retinal detachment repair(s) using scleral buckling or vitrectomy techniques

(For aspiration or drainage of subretinal or subchoroidal fluid, use 67015)

(For use of ophthalmic endoscope with 67112, use 66990)

67113   Repair of complex retinal detachment (eg, proliferative vitreoretinopathy, stage C-1 or greater, diabetic traction retinal detachment, retinopathy of prematurity, retinal tear of greater than 90 degrees), with vitrectomy and membrane peeling, may include air, gas, or silicone oil tamponade, cryotherapy, endolaser photocoagulation, drainage of subretinal fluid, scleral buckling, and/or removal of lens

➔ *CPT Changes: An Insider's View* 2008

(To report vitrectomy, pars plana approach, other than in retinal detachment surgery, see 67036-67043)

►(For use of ophthalmic endoscope with 67113, use 66990)◄

67115   Release of encircling material (posterior segment)

67120   Removal of implanted material, posterior segment; extraocular

67121   intraocular

➔ *CPT Assistant* Nov 97:23, Nov 98:19

(For removal from anterior segment, use 65920)

(For removal of foreign body, see 65260, 65265)

Prophylaxis

►Codes 67141, 67145 include treatment at one or more sessions that may occur at different encounters. These codes should be reported once during a defined treatment period.◄

Repetitive services. The services listed below are often performed in multiple sessions or groups of sessions. The methods of reporting vary.

The following descriptors are intended to include all sessions in a defined treatment period.

67141   Prophylaxis of retinal detachment (eg, retinal break, lattice degeneration) without drainage, 1 or more sessions; cryotherapy, diathermy

➔ *CPT Assistant* Mar 98:7, Oct 08:3

67145   photocoagulation (laser or xenon arc)

➔ *CPT Assistant* Fall 92:4, Mar 98:7

Destruction

►Codes 67208, 67210, 67218, 67220, 67227, 67228, 67229 include treatment at one or more sessions that may occur at different encounters. These codes should be reported once during a defined treatment period.◄

67208   Destruction of localized lesion of retina (eg, macular edema, tumors), 1 or more sessions; cryotherapy, diathermy

➔ *CPT Assistant* Mar 98:7, Nov 98:19, Oct 08:3

67210   photocoagulation

➔ *CPT Assistant* Mar 98:7, Nov 98:19, Oct 08:3

67218   radiation by implantation of source (includes removal of source)

➔ *CPT Assistant* Mar 98:7, Oct 08:3

67220   Destruction of localized lesion of choroid (eg, choroidal neovascularization); photocoagulation (eg, laser), 1 or more sessions

➔ *CPT Assistant* Nov 98:19, Nov 99:39, Feb 01:8, Oct 08:3; *CPT Changes: An Insider's View* 2000, 2001

(For destruction of macular drusen, photocoagulation, use Category III code 0017T)

(For destruction of localized lesion of choroid by transpupillary thermotherapy, use Category III code 0016T)

67221   photodynamic therapy (includes intravenous infusion)

➔ *CPT Assistant* Feb 01:8, Sep 01:10, Jun 02:10; *CPT Changes: An Insider's View* 2001

+ 67225   photodynamic therapy, second eye, at single session (List separately in addition to code for primary eye treatment)

➔ *CPT Assistant* Jun 02:10; *CPT Changes: An Insider's View* 2002

(Use 67225 in conjunction with 67221)

67227   Destruction of extensive or progressive retinopathy (eg, diabetic retinopathy), 1 or more sessions, cryotherapy, diathermy

➔ *CPT Assistant* Mar 98:7, Oct 08:3; *CPT Changes: An Insider's View* 2008

67228   Treatment of extensive or progressive retinopathy, 1 or more sessions; (eg, diabetic retinopathy), photocoagulation

➔ *CPT Assistant* Mar 98:7, Oct 08:3; *CPT Changes: An Insider's View* 2008

67229   preterm infant (less than 37 weeks gestation at birth), performed from birth up to 1 year of age (eg, retinopathy of prematurity), photocoagulation or cryotherapy

➔ *CPT Changes: An Insider's View* 2008

(For bilateral procedure, use modifier 50)

(For unlisted procedures on retina, use 67299)

Posterior Sclera

Repair

(For excision lesion sclera, use 66130)

67250   Scleral reinforcement (separate procedure); without graft

---

67255 with graft

(For repair scleral staphyloma, see 66220, 66225)

Other Procedures

67299 Unlisted procedure, posterior segment

Ocular Adnexa

Extraocular Muscles of Right Eye

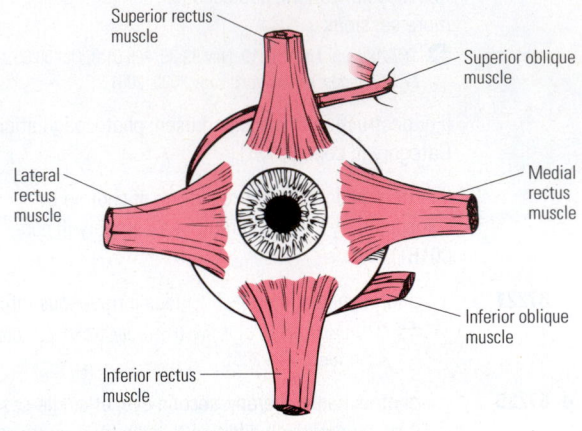

Extraocular Muscles

67311 Strabismus surgery, recession or resection procedure; 1 horizontal muscle

➔ *CPT Assistant* Summer 93:20, Mar 97:5, Nov 98:19, Sep 02:10

Strabismus Surgery—Horizontal Muscles
67311-67312

In Figure A, the medial or lateral rectus muscle is made weaker by recession (retroplacement of the muscle attachment). In Figure B, it is made stronger by resection (removal of a segment). Use 67311 for one horizontal muscle and 67312 for two muscles of the same eye.

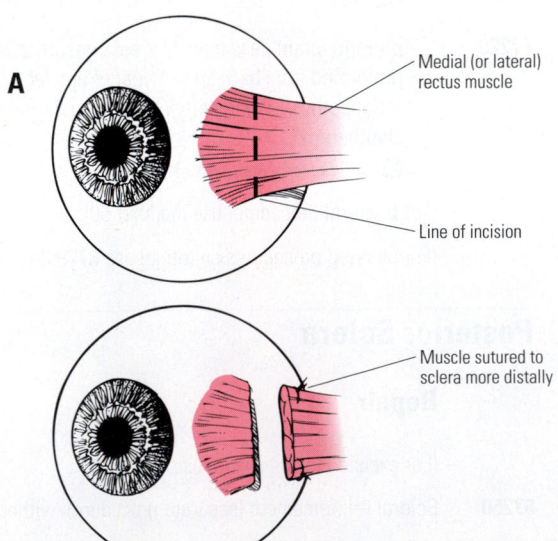

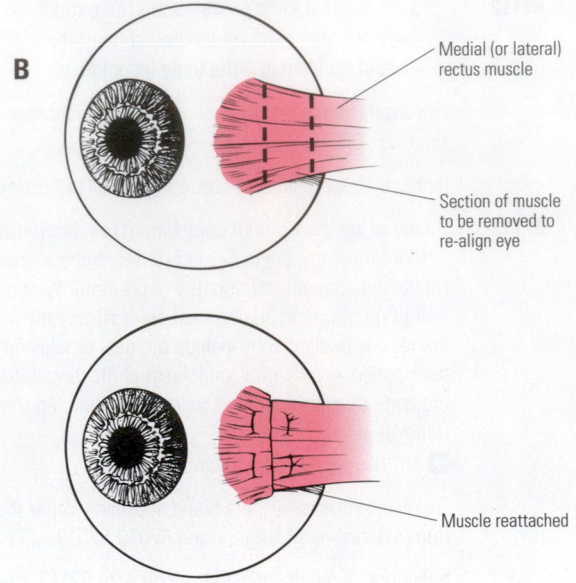

67312 2 horizontal muscles

➔ *CPT Assistant* Summer 93:20, Mar 97:5

67314 1 vertical muscle (excluding superior oblique)

➔ *CPT Assistant* Summer 93:20, Mar 97:5

67316 2 or more vertical muscles (excluding superior oblique)

➔ *CPT Assistant* Summer 93:20, Mar 97:5

(For adjustable sutures, use 67335 in addition to codes 67311-67334 for primary procedure reflecting number of muscles operated on)

Strabismus Surgery—Vertical Muscles
67314-67316

Either the superior or inferior rectus muscle is strengthened or weakened. Use 67316 for two muscles of the same eye.

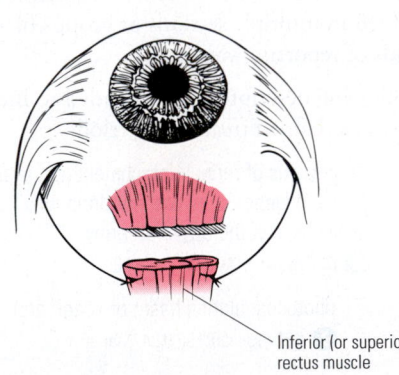

67318 Strabismus surgery, any procedure, superior oblique muscle

➔ *CPT Assistant* Summer 93:20, Mar 97:5, Nov 98:19

+ 67320   Transposition procedure (eg, for paretic extraocular muscle), any extraocular muscle (specify) (List separately in addition to code for primary procedure)

→ *CPT Assistant* Summer 93:20, Mar 97:5

(Use 67320 in conjunction with 67311-67318)

Transposition Procedure
67320

The extraocular muscles are transposed.

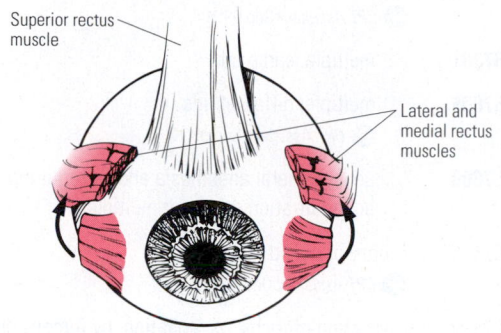

Superior rectus muscle

Lateral and medial rectus muscles

+ 67331   Strabismus surgery on patient with previous eye surgery or injury that did not involve the extraocular muscles (List separately in addition to code for primary procedure)

→ *CPT Assistant* Summer 93:20, Mar 97:5

(Use 67331 in conjunction with 67311-67318)

+ 67332   Strabismus surgery on patient with scarring of extraocular muscles (eg, prior ocular injury, strabismus or retinal detachment surgery) or restrictive myopathy (eg, dysthyroid ophthalmopathy) (List separately in addition to code for primary procedure)

→ *CPT Assistant* Summer 93:20, Mar 97:5

(Use 67332 in conjunction with 67311-67318)

+ 67334   Strabismus surgery by posterior fixation suture technique, with or without muscle recession (List separately in addition to code for primary procedure)

→ *CPT Assistant* Summer 93:20, Mar 97:5

(Use 67334 in conjunction with 67311-67318)

+ 67335   Placement of adjustable suture(s) during strabismus surgery, including postoperative adjustment(s) of suture(s) (List separately in addition to code for specific strabismus surgery)

→ *CPT Assistant* Summer 93:20, Mar 97:5

(Use 67335 in conjunction with 67311-67334)

Strabismus Surgery—Adjustable Sutures
67335

Sutures are tied in such a way as to allow the tension on the muscle to be adjusted after the anesthetic is not affecting the position of the globe.

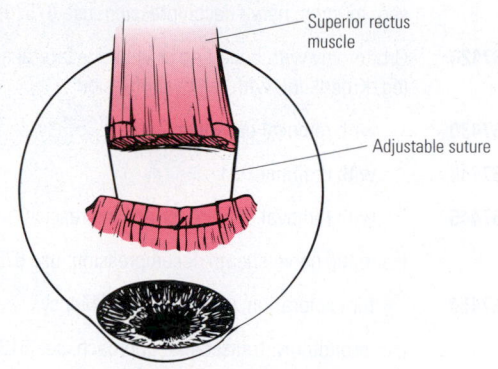

Superior rectus muscle

Adjustable suture

+ 67340   Strabismus surgery involving exploration and/or repair of detached extraocular muscle(s) (List separately in addition to code for primary procedure)

→ *CPT Assistant* Summer 93:20, Mar 97:5

(Use 67340 in conjunction with 67311-67334)

67343   Release of extensive scar tissue without detaching extraocular muscle (separate procedure)

→ *CPT Assistant* Summer 93:20, Mar 97:5

(Use 67343 in conjunction with 67311-67340, when such procedures are performed other than on the affected muscle)

67345   Chemodenervation of extraocular muscle

→ *CPT Assistant* Summer 93:20, Mar 97:5, Apr 00:2

(For chemodenervation for blepharospasm and other neurological disorders, see 64612 and 64613)

67346   Biopsy of extraocular muscle

→ *CPT Changes: An Insider's View* 2007

(For repair of wound, extraocular muscle, tendon or Tenon's capsule, use 65290)

Other Procedures

67399   Unlisted procedure, ocular muscle

Orbit

Exploration, Excision, Decompression

67400   Orbitotomy without bone flap (frontal or transconjunctival approach); for exploration, with or without biopsy

67405   with drainage only

67412   with removal of lesion

67413   with removal of foreign body

67414   with removal of bone for decompression
→ *CPT Assistant* Jul 99:10

67415   Fine needle aspiration of orbital contents

(For exenteration, enucleation, and repair, see 65101 et seq; for optic nerve decompression, use 67570)

67420   Orbitotomy with bone flap or window, lateral approach (eg, Kroenlein); with removal of lesion

67430   with removal of foreign body

67440   with drainage

67445   with removal of bone for decompression

(For optic nerve sheath decompression, use 67570)

67450   for exploration, with or without biopsy

(For orbitotomy, transcranial approach, see 61330-61334)

(For orbital implant, see 67550, 67560)

(For removal of eyeball or for repair after removal, see 65091-65175)

Other Procedures

67500   Retrobulbar injection; medication (separate procedure, does not include supply of medication)

67505   alcohol

67515   Injection of medication or other substance into Tenon's capsule
→ *CPT Changes: An Insider's View* 2002

(For subconjunctival injection, use 68200)

67550   Orbital implant (implant outside muscle cone); insertion

67560   removal or revision

(For ocular implant (implant inside muscle cone), see 65093-65105, 65130-65175)

(For treatment of fractures of malar area, orbit, see 21355 et seq)

67570   Optic nerve decompression (eg, incision or fenestration of optic nerve sheath)

67599   Unlisted procedure, orbit

Eyelids

Incision

67700   Blepharotomy, drainage of abscess, eyelid

67710   Severing of tarsorrhaphy

67715   Canthotomy (separate procedure)

(For canthoplasty, use 67950)

(For division of symblepharon, use 68340)

Excision, Destruction

Codes for removal of lesion include more than skin (ie, involving lid margin, tarsus, and/or palpebral conjunctiva).

(For removal of lesion, involving mainly skin of eyelid, see 11310-11313; 11440-11446; 11640-11646; 17000-17004)

(For repair of wounds, blepharoplasty, grafts, reconstructive surgery, see 67930-67975)

67800   Excision of chalazion; single
→ *CPT Assistant* Sep 99:10

67801   multiple, same lid

67805   multiple, different lids
→ *CPT Assistant* Sep 99:10

67808   under general anesthesia and/or requiring hospitalization, single or multiple

67810   Biopsy of eyelid
→ *CPT Assistant* Dec 04:19

67820   Correction of trichiasis; epilation, by forceps only
→ *CPT Assistant* Jul 98:10

Trichiasis
67820-67825

When the eyelashes are ingrown or misdirected (trichiasis), the physician uses a biomicroscope and forceps to remove the offending eyelashes. Report 67825 when cryosurgery or electrosurgery is used to destroy the follicles.

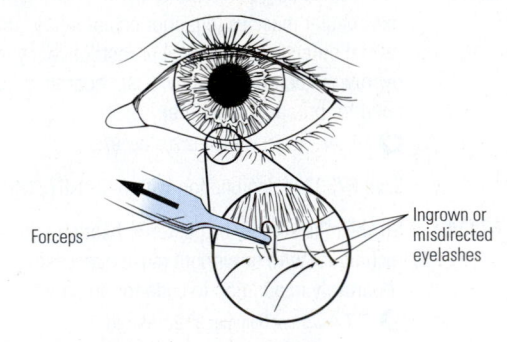

Forceps   Ingrown or misdirected eyelashes

67825   epilation by other than forceps (eg, by electrosurgery, cryotherapy, laser surgery)
→ *CPT Assistant* Jul 98:10

67830   incision of lid margin

67835   incision of lid margin, with free mucous membrane graft

67840   Excision of lesion of eyelid (except chalazion) without closure or with simple direct closure

(For excision and repair of eyelid by reconstructive surgery, see 67961, 67966)

67850   Destruction of lesion of lid margin (up to 1 cm)

(For Mohs micrographic surgery, see 17311-17315)

(For initiation or follow-up care of topical chemotherapy (eg, 5-FU or similar agents), see appropriate office visits)

Tarsorrhaphy

67875   Temporary closure of eyelids by suture (eg, Frost suture)
➔ *CPT Assistant* Winter 90:9

67880   Construction of intermarginal adhesions, median tarsorrhaphy, or canthorrhaphy;

67882   with transposition of tarsal plate

(For severing of tarsorrhaphy, use 67710)

(For canthoplasty, reconstruction canthus, use 67950)

(For canthotomy, use 67715)

Repair (Brow Ptosis, Blepharoptosis, Lid Retraction, Ectropion, Entropion)

67900   Repair of brow ptosis (supraciliary, mid-forehead or coronal approach)

(For forehead rhytidectomy, use 15824)

67901   Repair of blepharoptosis; frontalis muscle technique with suture or other material (eg, banked fascia)
➔ *CPT Assistant* Sep 00:7, Oct 06:11; *CPT Changes: An Insider's View* 2006

67902   frontalis muscle technique with autologous fascial sling (includes obtaining fascia)
➔ *CPT Assistant* Sep 00:7, Oct 06:11; *CPT Changes: An Insider's View* 2006

67903   (tarso) levator resection or advancement, internal approach
➔ *CPT Assistant* Sep 00:7, Oct 06:11

67904   (tarso) levator resection or advancement, external approach
➔ *CPT Assistant* Sep 00:7, Oct 06:11

67906   superior rectus technique with fascial sling (includes obtaining fascia)
➔ *CPT Assistant* Sep 00:7, Oct 06:11

67908   conjunctivo-tarso-Muller's muscle-levator resection (eg, Fasanella-Servat type)
➔ *CPT Assistant* Sep 00:7, Oct 06:11

67909   Reduction of overcorrection of ptosis

67911   Correction of lid retraction

(For obtaining autogenous graft materials, see 20920, 20922 or 20926)

(For correction of trichiasis by mucous membrane graft, use 67835)

67912   Correction of lagophthalmos, with implantation of upper eyelid lid load (eg, gold weight)
➔ *CPT Assistant* May 04:12, Aug 04:10, Oct 06:11; *CPT Changes: An Insider's View* 2004

67914   Repair of ectropion; suture

67915   thermocauterization

67916   excision tarsal wedge
➔ *CPT Assistant* Feb 04:11, May 04:12, Feb 05:16, Oct 06:11; *CPT Changes: An Insider's View* 2004

67917   extensive (eg, tarsal strip operations)
➔ *CPT Assistant* Feb 04:11, May 04:12, Oct 06:11; *CPT Changes: An Insider's View* 2004

(For correction of everted punctum, use 68705)

67921   Repair of entropion; suture

67922   thermocauterization

67923   excision tarsal wedge
➔ *CPT Assistant* May 04:12, Oct 06:11; *CPT Changes: An Insider's View* 2004

67924   extensive (eg, tarsal strip or capsulopalpebral fascia repairs operation)
➔ *CPT Assistant* May 04:12, Oct 06:11; *CPT Changes: An Insider's View* 2004

(For repair of cicatricial ectropion or entropion requiring scar excision or skin graft, see also 67961 et seq)

Reconstruction

Codes for blepharoplasty involve more than skin (ie, involving lid margin, tarsus, and/or palpebral conjunctiva).

67930   Suture of recent wound, eyelid, involving lid margin, tarsus, and/or palpebral conjunctiva direct closure; partial thickness

67935   full thickness

67938   Removal of embedded foreign body, eyelid

(For repair of skin of eyelid, see 12011-12018; 12051-12057; 13150-13153)

(For tarsorrhaphy, canthorrhaphy, see 67880, 67882)

(For repair of blepharoptosis and lid retraction, see 67901-67911)

(For blepharoplasty for entropion, ectropion, see 67916, 67917, 67923, 67924)

(For correction of blepharochalasis (blepharorhytidectomy), see 15820-15823)

(For repair of skin of eyelid, adjacent tissue transfer, see 14060, 14061; preparation for graft, use 15004; free graft, see 15120, 15121, 15260, 15261)

(For excision of lesion of eyelid, use 67800 et seq)

(For repair of lacrimal canaliculi, use 68700)

67950   Canthoplasty (reconstruction of canthus)

67961   Excision and repair of eyelid, involving lid margin, tarsus, conjunctiva, canthus, or full thickness, may include preparation for skin graft or pedicle flap with adjacent tissue transfer or rearrangement; up to one-fourth of lid margin

67966   over one-fourth of lid margin

(For canthoplasty, use 67950)

(For free skin grafts, see 15120, 15121, 15260, 15261)

(For tubed pedicle flap preparation, use 15576; for delay, use 15630; for attachment, use 15650)

67971 Reconstruction of eyelid, full thickness by transfer of tarsoconjunctival flap from opposing eyelid; up to two-thirds of eyelid, 1 stage or first stage

67973   total eyelid, lower, 1 stage or first stage

67974   total eyelid, upper, 1 stage or first stage

67975   second stage

Other Procedures

67999 Unlisted procedure, eyelids

Conjunctiva

(For removal of foreign body, see 65205 et seq)

Incision and Drainage

68020 Incision of conjunctiva, drainage of cyst

68040 Expression of conjunctival follicles (eg, for trachoma)

Excision and/or Destruction

68100 Biopsy of conjunctiva

68110 Excision of lesion, conjunctiva; up to 1 cm

68115   over 1 cm

68130   with adjacent sclera

68135 Destruction of lesion, conjunctiva

Injection

(For injection into Tenon's capsule or retrobulbar injection, see 67500-67515)

68200 Subconjunctival injection
➔ *CPT Assistant* Aug 03:15

Conjunctivoplasty

(For wound repair, see 65270-65273)

68320 Conjunctivoplasty; with conjunctival graft or extensive rearrangement
➔ *CPT Assistant* Feb 04:11

68325   with buccal mucous membrane graft (includes obtaining graft)

68326 Conjunctivoplasty, reconstruction cul-de-sac; with conjunctival graft or extensive rearrangement

68328   with buccal mucous membrane graft (includes obtaining graft)

68330 Repair of symblepharon; conjunctivoplasty, without graft

68335   with free graft conjunctiva or buccal mucous membrane (includes obtaining graft)

68340   division of symblepharon, with or without insertion of conformer or contact lens

Other Procedures

68360 Conjunctival flap; bridge or partial (separate procedure)

68362   total (such as Gunderson thin flap or purse string flap)

(For conjunctival flap for perforating injury, see 65280, 65285)

(For repair of operative wound, use 66250)

(For removal of conjunctival foreign body, see 65205, 65210)

68371 Harvesting conjunctival allograft, living donor
➔ *CPT Assistant* May 04:10; *CPT Changes: An Insider's View* 2004

68399 Unlisted procedure, conjunctiva

Lacrimal System

Incision

68400 Incision, drainage of lacrimal gland

68420 Incision, drainage of lacrimal sac (dacryocystotomy or dacryocystostomy)

68440 Snip incision of lacrimal punctum

Excision

68500 Excision of lacrimal gland (dacryoadenectomy), except for tumor; total

68505   partial

68510 Biopsy of lacrimal gland

68520 Excision of lacrimal sac (dacryocystectomy)

68525 Biopsy of lacrimal sac

68530 Removal of foreign body or dacryolith, lacrimal passages

68540 Excision of lacrimal gland tumor; frontal approach

68550   involving osteotomy

Repair

68700 Plastic repair of canaliculi

68705 Correction of everted punctum, cautery

68720 Dacryocystorhinostomy (fistulization of lacrimal sac to nasal cavity)
➔ *CPT Assistant* Sep 01:10, Jul 03:15, Aug 03:14

68745 Conjunctivorhinostomy (fistulization of conjunctiva to nasal cavity); without tube

68750   with insertion of tube or stent

68760   Closure of the lacrimal punctum; by thermocauterization, ligation, or laser surgery

68761   by plug, each
> *CPT Assistant* Jun 96:10, Jan 07:28

Closure of Lacrimal Punctum by Plug
68761

The physician inserts a lacrimal duct implant into a lacrimal punctum.

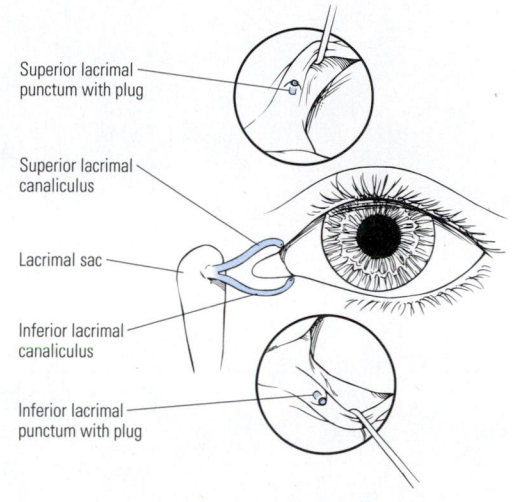

68770   Closure of lacrimal fistula (separate procedure)

Probing and/or Related Procedures

68801   Dilation of lacrimal punctum, with or without irrigation

(To report a bilateral procedure, use 68801 with modifier 50)

68810   Probing of nasolacrimal duct, with or without irrigation;
> *CPT Assistant* Nov 02:11, Oct 08:3

(For bilateral procedure, report 68810 with modifier 50)

68811   requiring general anesthesia
> *CPT Assistant* Nov 02:11, Oct 08:3

(For bilateral procedure, report 68811 with modifier 50)

68815   with insertion of tube or stent
> *CPT Assistant* Nov 02:11, Oct 08:3

(See also 92018)

(For bilateral procedure, report 68815 with modifier 50)

68816   with transluminal balloon catheter dilation
> *CPT Changes: An Insider's View* 2008

Probing of Nasolacrimal Duct
68816

A balloon catheter is in the nasolacrimal duct.

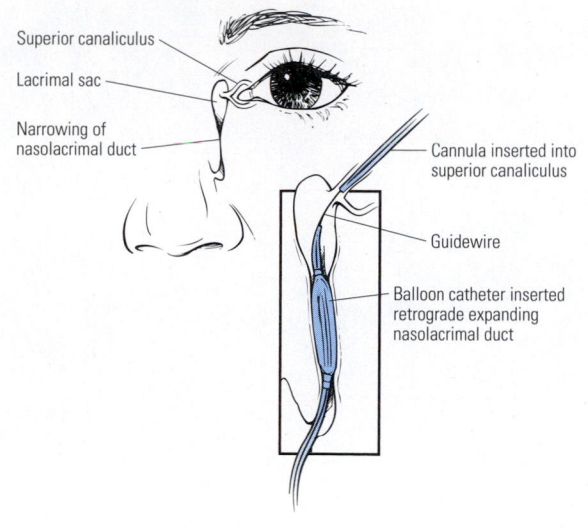

(Do not report 68816 in conjunction with 68810, 68811, 68815)

(For bilateral procedure, report 68816 with modifier 50)

68840   Probing of lacrimal canaliculi, with or without irrigation

68850   Injection of contrast medium for dacryocystography
> *CPT Assistant* Feb 01:9

(For radiological supervision and interpretation, see 70170, 78660)

Other Procedures

68899   Unlisted procedure, lacrimal system

Notes

⊙=Moderate sedation ✚=Add-on code ✗=FDA approval pending #=Resequenced code 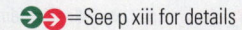=See p xiii for details

Auditory System (69000-69979) **338**

The following is a listing of headings and subheadings that appear within the Auditory System and Operating Microscope sections of the CPT codebook. The subheadings or subsections denoted with asterisks (*) below have special instructions unique to that section. Where these are indicated, special "notes" or guidelines will be presented preceding those procedural terminology listings, referring to that subsection specifically.

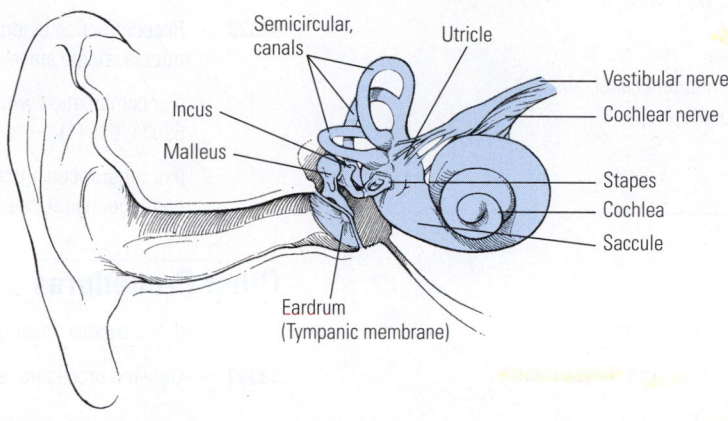

Auditory System

(For diagnostic services (eg, audiometry, vestibular tests), see 92502 et seq)

External Ear

Incision

69000 Drainage external ear, abscess or hematoma; simple
→ *CPT Assistant* Oct 97:11, Oct 99:10

69005   complicated

69020 Drainage external auditory canal, abscess
→ *CPT Assistant* Oct 97:11

69090 Ear piercing

Excision

69100 Biopsy external ear

69105 Biopsy external auditory canal

69110 Excision external ear; partial, simple repair

69120   complete amputation

(For reconstruction of ear, see 15120 et seq)

69140 Excision exostosis(es), external auditory canal

69145 Excision soft tissue lesion, external auditory canal

69150 Radical excision external auditory canal lesion; without neck dissection

69155   with neck dissection

(For resection of temporal bone, use 69535)

(For skin grafting, see 15004-15261)

Removal

69200 Removal foreign body from external auditory canal; without general anesthesia

69205   with general anesthesia

69210 Removal impacted cerumen (separate procedure), 1 or both ears
→ *CPT Assistant* Apr 03:9, Jul 05:14

69220 Debridement, mastoidectomy cavity, simple (eg, routine cleaning)

(For bilateral procedure, report 69220 with modifier 50)

69222 Debridement, mastoidectomy cavity, complex (eg, with anesthesia or more than routine cleaning)

(For bilateral procedure, report 69222 with modifier 50)

Repair

▶(For suture of wound or injury of external ear, see 12011-14302)◀

⊙ **69300** Otoplasty, protruding ear, with or without size reduction

(For bilateral procedure, report 69300 with modifier 50)

69310 Reconstruction of external auditory canal (meatoplasty) (eg, for stenosis due to injury, infection) (separate procedure)
→ *CPT Changes: An Insider's View* 2002

69320 Reconstruction external auditory canal for congenital atresia, single stage

(For combination with middle ear reconstruction, see 69631, 69641)

(For other reconstructive procedures with grafts (eg, skin, cartilage, bone), see 13150-15760, 21230-21235)

Other Procedures

(For otoscopy under general anesthesia, use 92502)

69399 Unlisted procedure, external ear

Middle Ear

Introduction

69400 Eustachian tube inflation, transnasal; with catheterization

69401   without catheterization

69405 Eustachian tube catheterization, transtympanic

Incision

69420 Myringotomy including aspiration and/or eustachian tube inflation

69421 Myringotomy including aspiration and/or eustachian tube inflation requiring general anesthesia

69424 Ventilating tube removal requiring general anesthesia
→ *CPT Assistant* Mar 05:17; *CPT Changes: An Insider's View* 2003

(For bilateral procedure, report 69424 with modifier 50)

(Do not report code 69424 in conjunction with 69205, 69210, 69420, 69421, 69433-69676, 69710-69745, 69801-69930)

69433 Tympanostomy (requiring insertion of ventilating tube), local or topical anesthesia

(For bilateral procedure, report 69433 with modifier 50)

Tympanostomy
69433-69436

A ventilating tube is inserted into the opening of the tympanum.

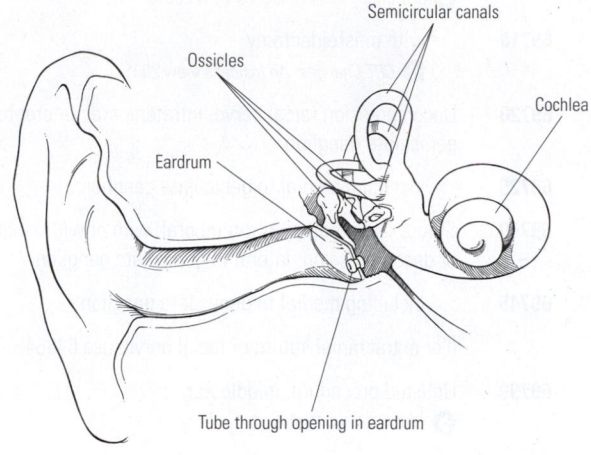

69436   Tympanostomy (requiring insertion of ventilating tube), general anesthesia

(For bilateral procedure, report 69436 with modifier 50)

69440   Middle ear exploration through postauricular or ear canal incision

(For atticotomy, see 69601 et seq)

69450   Tympanolysis, transcanal

Excision

69501   Transmastoid antrotomy (simple mastoidectomy)

69502   Mastoidectomy; complete

69505   modified radical

69511   radical

(For skin graft, see 15004 et seq)

(For mastoidectomy cavity debridement, see 69220, 69222)

69530   Petrous apicectomy including radical mastoidectomy

69535   Resection temporal bone, external approach

(For middle fossa approach, see 69950-69970)

69540   Excision aural polyp

69550   Excision aural glomus tumor; transcanal

69552   transmastoid

69554   extended (extratemporal)

Repair

69601   Revision mastoidectomy; resulting in complete mastoidectomy

69602   resulting in modified radical mastoidectomy

69603   resulting in radical mastoidectomy

69604   resulting in tympanoplasty

(For planned secondary tympanoplasty after mastoidectomy, see 69631, 69632)

69605   with apicectomy

(For skin graft, see 15120, 15121, 15260, 15261)

69610   Tympanic membrane repair, with or without site preparation of perforation for closure, with or without patch
➜ *CPT Assistant* Mar 01:10, Mar 03:21, Aug 08:4

69620   Myringoplasty (surgery confined to drumhead and donor area)
➜ *CPT Assistant* Mar 01:10, Aug 08:4

69631   Tympanoplasty without mastoidectomy (including canalplasty, atticotomy and/or middle ear surgery), initial or revision; without ossicular chain reconstruction
➜ *CPT Assistant* Jul 98:11, Mar 01:10, Mar 07:9, Aug 08:4

69632   with ossicular chain reconstruction (eg, postfenestration)

69633   with ossicular chain reconstruction and synthetic prosthesis (eg, partial ossicular replacement prosthesis [PORP], total ossicular replacement prosthesis [TORP])

69635   Tympanoplasty with antrotomy or mastoidotomy (including canalplasty, atticotomy, middle ear surgery, and/or tympanic membrane repair); without ossicular chain reconstruction

69636   with ossicular chain reconstruction

Tympanoplasty
69635-69646

A graft is used to repair the tympanic membrane perforation.

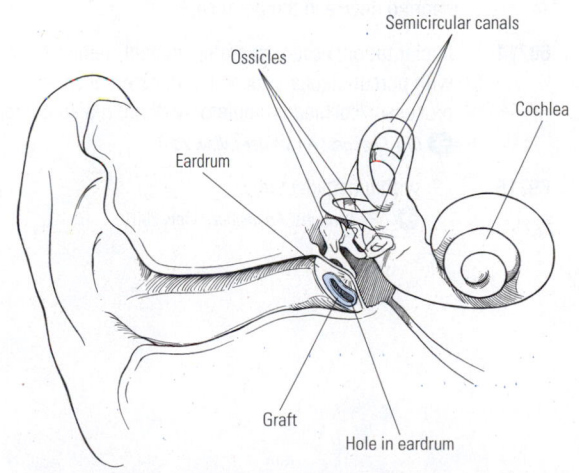

69637 with ossicular chain reconstruction and synthetic prosthesis (eg, partial ossicular replacement prosthesis [PORP], total ossicular replacement prosthesis [TORP])

69641 Tympanoplasty with mastoidectomy (including canalplasty, middle ear surgery, tympanic membrane repair); without ossicular chain reconstruction

69642 with ossicular chain reconstruction

69643 with intact or reconstructed wall, without ossicular chain reconstruction

69644 with intact or reconstructed canal wall, with ossicular chain reconstruction

69645 radical or complete, without ossicular chain reconstruction

69646 radical or complete, with ossicular chain reconstruction

69650 Stapes mobilization

69660 Stapedectomy or stapedotomy with reestablishment of ossicular continuity, with or without use of foreign material;

69661 with footplate drill out

69662 Revision of stapedectomy or stapedotomy

69666 Repair oval window fistula

69667 Repair round window fistula

69670 Mastoid obliteration (separate procedure)

69676 Tympanic neurectomy

(For bilateral procedure, report 69676 with modifier 50)

Other Procedures

69700 Closure postauricular fistula, mastoid (separate procedure)

69710 Implantation or replacement of electromagnetic bone conduction hearing device in temporal bone

(Replacement procedure includes removal of old device)

69711 Removal or repair of electromagnetic bone conduction hearing device in temporal bone

69714 Implantation, osseointegrated implant, temporal bone, with percutaneous attachment to external speech processor/cochlear stimulator; without mastoidectomy
➜ *CPT Changes: An Insider's View* 2001

69715 with mastoidectomy
➜ *CPT Changes: An Insider's View* 2001

69717 Replacement (including removal of existing device), osseointegrated implant, temporal bone, with percutaneous attachment to external speech processor/cochlear stimulator; without mastoidectomy
➜ *CPT Changes: An Insider's View* 2001

69718 with mastoidectomy
➜ *CPT Changes: An Insider's View* 2001

69720 Decompression facial nerve, intratemporal; lateral to geniculate ganglion

69725 including medial to geniculate ganglion

69740 Suture facial nerve, intratemporal, with or without graft or decompression; lateral to geniculate ganglion

69745 including medial to geniculate ganglion

(For extracranial suture of facial nerve, use 64864)

69799 Unlisted procedure, middle ear
➜ *CPT Assistant* Oct 99:10

Inner Ear

Incision and/or Destruction

69801 Labyrinthotomy, with or without cryosurgery including other nonexcisional destructive procedures or perfusion of vestibuloactive drugs (single or multiple perfusions); transcanal
➜ *CPT Assistant* Nov 96:12

(69801 includes all required infusions performed on initial and subsequent days of treatment)

69802 with mastoidectomy

69805 Endolymphatic sac operation; without shunt

69806 with shunt
➜ *CPT Assistant* Nov 96:12

69820 Fenestration semicircular canal

69840 Revision fenestration operation

Excision

69905 Labyrinthectomy; transcanal

69910 with mastoidectomy

69915 Vestibular nerve section, translabyrinthine approach

(For transcranial approach, use 69950)

Introduction

69930 Cochlear device implantation, with or without mastoidectomy

Cochlear Device Implantation
69930

An internal coil is attached to the temporal bone and the ground wire attached to the internal coil is connected to the temporalis muscle.

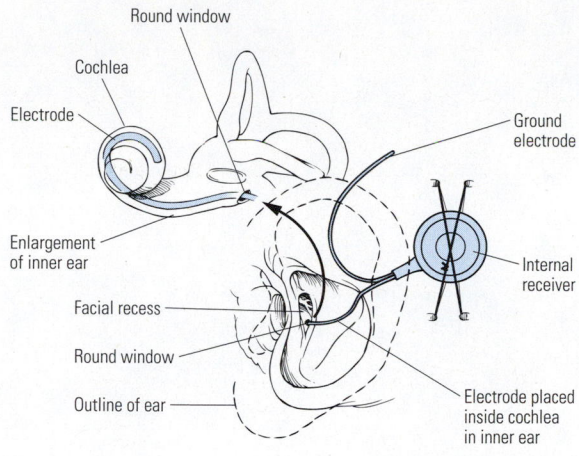

Operating Microscope

The surgical microscope is employed when the surgical services are performed using the techniques of microsurgery. Code 69990 should be reported (without modifier 51 appended) in addition to the code for the primary procedure performed. Do not use 69990 for visualization with magnifying loupes or corrected vision. Do not report 69990 in addition to procedures where use of the operating microscope is an inclusive component (15756-15758, 15842, 19364, 19368, 20955-20962, 20969-20973, 22856-22861, 26551-26554, 26556, 31526, 31531, 31536, 31541, 31545, 31546, 31561, 31571, 43116, 43496, 49906, 61548, 63075-63078, 64727, 64820-64823, 65091-68850, 0184T).

+ 69990 Microsurgical techniques, requiring use of operating microscope (List separately in addition to code for primary procedure)

> *CPT Assistant* Nov 98:20, Apr 99:11, Jun 99:11, Jul 99:11, Oct 99:10, Oct 00:3, Oct 02:8, Jan 04:28, Mar 05:11, Jul 05:14, Aug 05:1, Nov 07:4, Sep 08:10, Mar 09:10; *CPT Changes: An Insider's View* 2002

Other Procedures

69949 Unlisted procedure, inner ear

Temporal Bone, Middle Fossa Approach

(For external approach, use 69535)

69950 Vestibular nerve section, transcranial approach

69955 Total facial nerve decompression and/or repair (may include graft)

69960 Decompression internal auditory canal

69970 Removal of tumor, temporal bone

Other Procedures

69979 Unlisted procedure, temporal bone, middle fossa approach

> *CPT Assistant* Jan 07:30

Operating Microscope
69990

A surgical operating microscope is used to obtain good visualization of the fine structures in the operating field. The lens system may be operated by hand or foot controls to adjust to working distance, with interchangeable oculars providing magnification as needed.

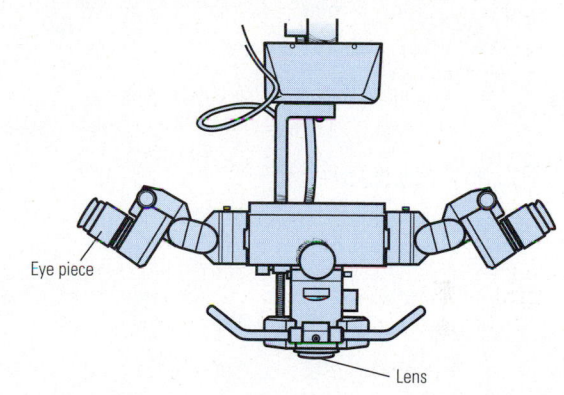

Notes

 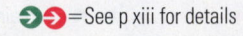

Radiology Guidelines (Including Nuclear Medicine and Diagnostic Ultrasound)

Radiology

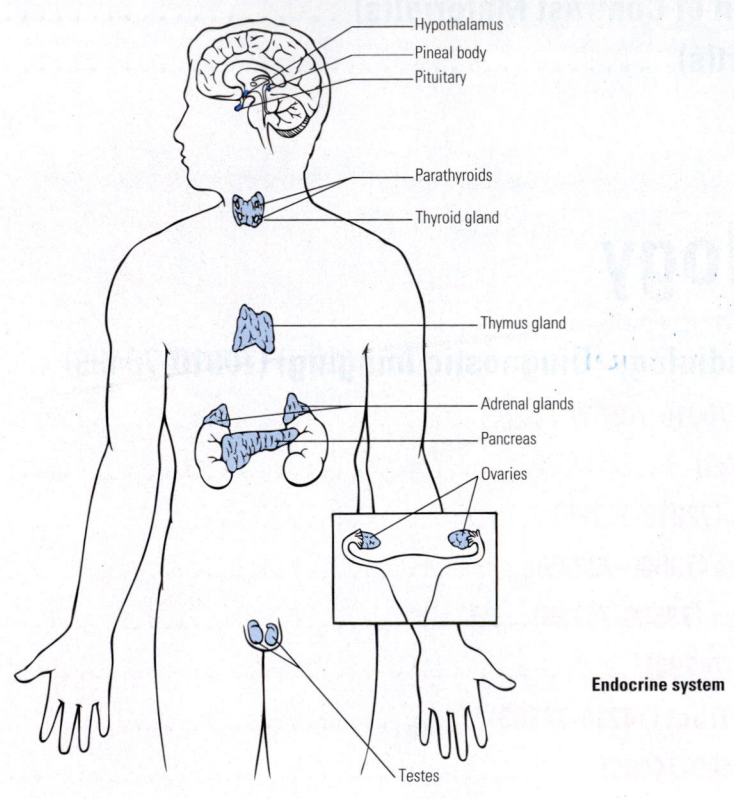

Endocrine system

Radiology Guidelines (Including Nuclear Medicine and Diagnostic Ultrasound)

Items used by all physicians in reporting their services are presented in the **Introduction.** Some of the commonalities are repeated here for the convenience of those physicians referring to this section on **Radiology (Including Nuclear Medicine and Diagnostic Ultrasound).** Other definitions and items unique to Radiology are also listed.

Subject Listings

Subject listings apply when radiological services are performed by or under the responsible supervision of a physician.

Separate Procedures

Some of the procedures or services listed in the CPT codebook that are commonly carried out as an integral component of a total service or procedure have been identified by the inclusion of the term "separate procedure." The codes designated as "separate procedure" should not be reported in addition to the code for the total procedure or service of which it is considered an integral component.

However, when a procedure or service that is designated as a "separate procedure" is carried out independently or considered to be unrelated or distinct from other procedures/services provided at that time, it may be reported by itself, or in addition to other procedures/services by appending modifier 59 to the specific "separate procedure" code to indicate that the procedure is not considered to be a component of another procedure, but is a distinct, independent procedure. This may represent a different session or patient encounter, different procedure or surgery, different site or organ system, separate incision/excision, separate lesion, separate injury, or area of injury in extensive injuries.

Unlisted Service or Procedure

A service or procedure may be provided that is not listed in this edition of the CPT codebook. When reporting such a service, the appropriate "Unlisted Procedure" code may be used to indicate the service, identifying it by "Special Report" as discussed below. The "Unlisted Procedures" and accompanying codes for **Radiology (Including Nuclear Medicine and Diagnostic Ultrasound)** are as follows:

76496	Unlisted fluoroscopic procedure (eg, diagnostic, interventional)
76497	Unlisted computed tomography procedure (eg, diagnostic, interventional)
76498	Unlisted magnetic resonance procedure (eg, diagnostic, interventional)
76499	Unlisted diagnostic radiographic procedure
76999	Unlisted ultrasound procedure (eg, diagnostic, interventional)
77299	Unlisted procedure, therapeutic radiology clinical treatment planning
77399	Unlisted procedure, medical radiation physics, dosimetry and treatment devices, and special services
77499	Unlisted procedure, therapeutic radiology treatment management
77799	Unlisted procedure, clinical brachytherapy
78099	Unlisted endocrine procedure, diagnostic nuclear medicine
78199	Unlisted hematopoietic, reticuloendothelial and lymphatic procedure, diagnostic nuclear medicine
78299	Unlisted gastrointestinal procedure, diagnostic nuclear medicine
78399	Unlisted musculoskeletal procedure, diagnostic nuclear medicine
78499	Unlisted cardiovascular procedure, diagnostic nuclear medicine

⊙=Moderate sedation   ✚=Add-on code   ✔=FDA approval pending   #=Resequenced code   ➔➔=See p xiii for details

78599	Unlisted respiratory procedure, diagnostic nuclear medicine
78699	Unlisted nervous system procedure, diagnostic nuclear medicine
78799	Unlisted genitourinary procedure, diagnostic nuclear medicine
78999	Unlisted miscellaneous procedure, diagnostic nuclear medicine
79999	Radiopharmaceutical therapy, unlisted procedure

Special Report

►A service that is rarely provided, unusual, variable, or new may require a special report. Pertinent information should include an adequate definition or description of the nature, extent, and need for the procedure; and the time, effort, and equipment necessary to provide the service.◄

Supervision and Interpretation

When a procedure is performed by two physicians, the radiologic portion of the procedure is designated as "radiological supervision and interpretation." When a physician performs both the procedure and provides imaging supervision and interpretation, a combination of procedure codes outside the 70000 series and imaging supervision and interpretation codes are to be used.

(The Radiological Supervision and Interpretation codes are not applicable to the Radiation Oncology subsection.)

Administration of Contrast Material(s)

The phrase "with contrast" used in the codes for procedures performed using contrast for imaging enhancement represents contrast material administered intravascularly, intra-articularly or intrathecally.

For intra-articular injection, use the appropriate joint injection code. If radiographic arthrography is performed, also use the arthrography supervision and interpretation code for the appropriate joint (which includes fluoroscopy). If computed tomography (CT) or magnetic resonance (MR) arthrography are performed without radiographic arthrography, use the appropriate joint injection code, the appropriate CT or MR code ("with contrast" or "without followed by contrast"), and the appropriate imaging guidance code for needle placement for contrast injection.

For spine examinations using computed tomography, magnetic resonance imaging, magnetic resonance angiography, "with contrast" includes intrathecal or intravascular injection. For intrathecal injection, use also 61055 or 62284.

Injection of intravascular contrast material is part of the "with contrast" CT, computed tomographic angiography (CTA), magnetic resonance imaging (MRI), and magnetic resonance angiography (MRA) procedures.

Oral and/or rectal contrast administration alone does not qualify as a study "with contrast."

Written Report(s)

A written report signed by the interpreting physician should be considered an integral part of a radiologic procedure or interpretation.

Radiology

[handwritten: MRI = yellow MRA = CT =   CTA = Ultrasound =]

Diagnostic Radiology (Diagnostic Imaging)

Head and Neck

70010 Myelography, posterior fossa, radiological supervision and interpretation
➡ *CPT Assistant* Mar 05:11, Dec 07:16

70015 Cisternography, positive contrast, radiological supervision and interpretation

70030 Radiologic examination, eye, for detection of foreign body

70100 Radiologic examination, mandible; partial, less than 4 views

70110 complete, minimum of 4 views

70120 Radiologic examination, mastoids; less than 3 views per side

70130 complete, minimum of 3 views per side

70134 Radiologic examination, internal auditory meati, complete

70140 Radiologic examination, facial bones; less than 3 views

70150 complete, minimum of 3 views

70160 Radiologic examination, nasal bones, complete, minimum of 3 views

70170 Dacryocystography, nasolacrimal duct, radiological supervision and interpretation

70190 Radiologic examination; optic foramina

70200 orbits, complete, minimum of 4 views

70210 Radiologic examination, sinuses, paranasal, less than 3 views

70220 Radiologic examination, sinuses, paranasal, complete, minimum of 3 views

70240 Radiologic examination, sella turcica

70250 Radiologic examination, skull; less than 4 views
➡ *CPT Changes: An Insider's View* 2004

70260 complete, minimum of 4 views
➡ *CPT Changes: An Insider's View* 2004

70300 Radiologic examination, teeth; single view

70310 partial examination, less than full mouth

70320 complete, full mouth

70328 Radiologic examination, temporomandibular joint, open and closed mouth; unilateral

70330 bilateral

70332 Temporomandibular joint arthrography, radiological supervision and interpretation
➡ *CPT Assistant* Feb 07:11

(Do not report 70332 in conjunction with 77002)

70336 Magnetic resonance (eg, proton) imaging, temporomandibular joint(s) *[handwritten: MRI]*
➡ *CPT Assistant* Jul 99:11, Jul 01:7; *CPT Changes: An Insider's View* 2001

70350 Cephalogram, orthodontic

70355 Orthopantogram

70360 Radiologic examination; neck, soft tissue

70370 pharynx or larynx, including fluoroscopy and/or magnification technique

70371 Complex dynamic pharyngeal and speech evaluation by cine or video recording
➡ *CPT Assistant* Dec 04:17

70373 Laryngography, contrast, radiological supervision and interpretation

70380 Radiologic examination, salivary gland for calculus

70390 Sialography, radiological supervision and interpretation

70450 Computed tomography, head or brain; without contrast material *[handwritten: CT]*
➡ *CPT Assistant* Apr 96:11; *CPT Changes: An Insider's View* 2003
➡ *Clinical Examples in Radiology* Winter 08:6

70460 with contrast material(s)
➡ *CPT Assistant* Apr 96:11

70470 without contrast material, followed by contrast material(s) and further sections
➡ *CPT Assistant* Apr 96:11

(To report 3D rendering, see 76376, 76377)

70480 Computed tomography, orbit, sella, or posterior fossa or outer, middle, or inner ear; without contrast material
➡ *CPT Changes: An Insider's View* 2003 *[handwritten: CT]*

70481 with contrast material(s)
➡ *CPT Assistant* Apr 08:11

70482 without contrast material, followed by contrast material(s) and further sections

(To report 3D rendering, see 76376, 76377)

70486 Computed tomography, maxillofacial area; without contrast material *[handwritten: CT]*
➡ *CPT Assistant* Mar 02:11; *CPT Changes: An Insider's View* 2003
➡ *Clinical Examples in Radiology* Winter 07:4-5, Spring 07:4

70487 with contrast material(s)

70488 without contrast material, followed by contrast material(s) and further sections

(To report 3D rendering, see 76376, 76377)

70490 Computed tomography, soft tissue neck; without contrast material   *CT*
> CPT Changes: An Insider's View 2003

70491   with contrast material(s)

70492   without contrast material followed by contrast material(s) and further sections

(To report 3D rendering, see 76376, 76377)

(For cervical spine, see 72125, 72126)

70496 Computed tomographic angiography, head, with contrast material(s), including noncontrast images, if performed, and image postprocessing   *CTA*
> CPT Assistant Jul 01:4, Dec 05:7, Jan 07:31; CPT Changes: An Insider's View 2001, 2008

70498 Computed tomographic angiography, neck, with contrast material(s), including noncontrast images, if performed, and image postprocessing   *CTA*
> CPT Assistant Jul 01:4, Dec 05:7, Jan 07:31; CPT Changes: An Insider's View 2001, 2008
> Clinical Examples in Radiology Winter 09:2

70540 Magnetic resonance (eg, proton) imaging, orbit, face, *MRI* and/or neck; without contrast material(s)
> CPT Assistant Jul 01:6, Mar 07:7; CPT Changes: An Insider's View 2001, 2007
> Clinical Examples in Radiology Spring 05:3, Summer 07:7

(For head or neck magnetic resonance angiography studies, see 70544-70546, 70547-70549)

70542   with contrast material(s)
> CPT Assistant Jul 01:6; CPT Changes: An Insider's View 2001
> Clinical Examples in Radiology Spring 05:3, Summer 07:7

70543   without contrast material(s), followed by contrast material(s) and further sequences
> CPT Assistant Jul 01:6; CPT Changes: An Insider's View 2001
> Clinical Examples in Radiology Spring 05:2-3, Winter 07:7, 11, Summer 07:7

(Report 70540-70543 once per imaging session)

70544 Magnetic resonance angiography, head; without contrast material(s)   *MRA*
> CPT Assistant Sep 01:5, Dec 05:7, Jan 07:31; CPT Changes: An Insider's View 2001

70545   with contrast material(s)
> CPT Assistant Jul 01:5, Dec 05:7; CPT Changes: An Insider's View 2001

70546   without contrast material(s), followed by contrast material(s) and further sequences
> CPT Assistant Jul 01:5, Dec 05:7, Jan 07:31; CPT Changes: An Insider's View 2001

70547 Magnetic resonance angiography, neck; without contrast material(s)   *MRA*
> CPT Assistant Sep 01:5, Dec 05:7, Jan 07:31; CPT Changes: An Insider's View 2001
> Clinical Examples in Radiology Winter 09:2

70548   with contrast material(s)
> CPT Assistant Sep 01:6, Dec 05:7, Jan 07:31; CPT Changes: An Insider's View 2001
> Clinical Examples in Radiology Winter 09:2

70549   without contrast material(s), followed by contrast material(s) and further sequences
> CPT Assistant Sep 01:6, Dec 05:7, Jan 07:31; CPT Changes: An Insider's View 2001
> Clinical Examples in Radiology Winter 09:2

70551 Magnetic resonance (eg, proton) imaging, brain (including brain stem); without contrast material   *MRI*
> CPT Assistant May 98:10, Mar 05:20, Feb 07:6

70552   with contrast material(s)
> CPT Assistant Jul 01:6, Mar 05:20, Feb 07:6

70553   without contrast material, followed by contrast material(s) and further sequences
> CPT Assistant Nov 97:24, Jul 01:6, Mar 05:20, Feb 07:6
> Clinical Examples in Radiology Spring 05:2, Spring 06:4-5

(For magnetic spectroscopy, use 76390)

Functional MRI involves identification and mapping of stimulation of brain function. When neurofunctional tests are administered by a technologist or other non-physician or non-psychologist, use 70554. When neurofunctional tests are entirely administered by a physician or psychologist, use 70555.

70554 Magnetic resonance imaging, brain, functional MRI; including test selection and administration of repetitive body part movement and/or visual stimulation, not requiring physician or psychologist administration
> CPT Assistant Feb 07:6, Mar 07:7, Aug 08:13; CPT Changes: An Insider's View 2007   *MRI*

(Do not report 70554 in conjunction with 96020)

70555   requiring physician or psychologist administration of entire neurofunctional testing
> CPT Assistant Feb 07:6, Mar 07:7; CPT Changes: An Insider's View 2007

(Do not report 70555 unless 96020 is performed)

(Do not report 70554, 70555 in conjunction with 70551-70553 unless a separate diagnostic MRI is performed)

70557 Magnetic resonance (eg, proton) imaging, brain (including brain stem and skull base), during open intracranial procedure (eg, to assess for residual tumor or residual vascular malformation); without contrast material
> CPT Changes: An Insider's View 2004   *MRI*

70558   with contrast material(s)
> CPT Changes: An Insider's View 2004

70559   without contrast material(s), followed by contrast material(s) and further sequences
> CPT Changes: An Insider's View 2004

(For stereotactic biopsy of intracranial lesion with magnetic resonance guidance, use 61751. 70557, 70558 or 70559 may be reported only if a separate report is generated. Report only 1 of the above codes once per operative session. Do not use these codes in conjunction with 61751, 77021, 77022)

Chest

(For fluoroscopic or ultrasonic guidance for needle placement procedures (eg, biopsy, aspiration, injection, localization device) of the thorax, see 76942, 77002)

71010   Radiologic examination, chest; single view, frontal
➔ *CPT Assistant* Aug 00:1, Feb 07:10, Jul 07:1, Jul 07:6

71015   stereo, frontal
➔ *CPT Assistant* Feb 07:10, Jul 07:1

71020   Radiologic examination, chest, 2 views, frontal and lateral;
➔ *CPT Assistant* Sep 03:3, Mar 05:11, Feb 07:10, Jul 07:1, Jul 07:6

71021   with apical lordotic procedure

71022   with oblique projections
➔ *CPT Assistant* Jul 07:6

71023   with fluoroscopy
➔ *CPT Assistant* Aug 03:14, Dec 08:7

71030   Radiologic examination, chest, complete, minimum of 4 views;
➔ *CPT Assistant* Jul 07:6

(For concurrent computer-aided detection [CAD] performed in addition to codes 71010, 71020, 71021, 71022, and 71030, use 0174T. Do not report 71010, 71020, 71021, 71022, and 71030 in conjunction with 0175T for CAD performed remotely from the primary interpretation)

71034   with fluoroscopy
➔ *CPT Assistant* Aug 03:14, Dec 08:7

(For separate chest fluoroscopy, use 76000)

71035   Radiologic examination, chest, special views (eg, lateral decubitus, Bucky studies)

71040   Bronchography, unilateral, radiological supervision and interpretation

71060   Bronchography, bilateral, radiological supervision and interpretation

71090   Insertion pacemaker, fluoroscopy and radiography, radiological supervision and interpretation
➔ *CPT Assistant* Aug 02:11, May 08:14

(For procedure, see appropriate organ or site)

71100   Radiologic examination, ribs, unilateral; 2 views

71101   including posteroanterior chest, minimum of 3 views

71110   Radiologic examination, ribs, bilateral; 3 views

71111   including posteroanterior chest, minimum of 4 views

71120   Radiologic examination; sternum, minimum of 2 views

71130   sternoclavicular joint or joints, minimum of 3 views

71250   Computed tomography, thorax; without contrast material
➔ *CPT Assistant* Jul 07:13; *CPT Changes: An Insider's View* 2003
➔ *Clinical Examples in Radiology* Fall 08:7   CT

71260   with contrast material(s)
➔ *CPT Assistant* Jul 01:4
➔ *Clinical Examples in Radiology* Summer 05:4, Fall 08:7, 11, 12

71270   without contrast material, followed by contrast material(s) and further sections
➔ *CPT Assistant* Jun 01:10, Jul 07:13
➔ *Clinical Examples in Radiology* Fall 08:7

►(For cardiac computed tomography of the heart, see 75571-75574)◄

(To report 3D rendering, see 76376, 76377)

71275   Computed tomographic angiography, chest (noncoronary), with contrast material(s), including noncontrast images, if performed, and image postprocessing
➔ *CPT Assistant* Jul 01:4, Jun 05:11, Dec 05:7, Jan 07:31, Mar 07:7; *CPT Changes: An Insider's View* 2001, 2007, 2008
➔ *Clinical Examples in Radiology* Spring 05:7, Fall 08:11, 12, Spring 09:11

►(For coronary artery computed tomographic angiography including calcification score and/or cardiac morphology, use 75574)◄

71550   Magnetic resonance (eg, proton) imaging, chest (eg, for evaluation of hilar and mediastinal lymphadenopathy); without contrast material(s)
➔ *CPT Assistant* Jul 01:7; *CPT Changes: An Insider's View* 2001

71551   with contrast material(s)
➔ *CPT Assistant* Jul 01:7; *CPT Changes: An Insider's View* 2001

71552   without contrast material(s), followed by contrast material(s) and further sequences
➔ *CPT Assistant* Jul 01:7; *CPT Changes: An Insider's View* 2001

(For breast MRI, see 77058, 77059)

71555   Magnetic resonance angiography, chest (excluding myocardium), with or without contrast material(s)
➔ *CPT Assistant* Fall 95:2, Dec 05:7, Jan 07:31
MRA

Spine and Pelvis

72010   Radiologic examination, spine, entire, survey study, anteroposterior and lateral
➔ *CPT Assistant* May 02:18, Jan 07:29

72020   Radiologic examination, spine, single view, specify level

72040   Radiologic examination, spine, cervical; 2 or 3 views
➔ *CPT Assistant* Sep 01:7; *CPT Changes: An Insider's View* 2001

72050   minimum of 4 views

72052   complete, including oblique and flexion and/or extension studies

---

72069   Radiologic examination, spine, thoracolumbar, standing (scoliosis)
➔ *CPT Assistant* Winter 90:9

72070   Radiologic examination, spine; thoracic, 2 views
➔ *CPT Assistant* Sep 01:7; *CPT Changes: An Insider's View* 2001

72072   thoracic, 3 views
➔ *CPT Assistant* Sep 01:7; *CPT Changes: An Insider's View* 2001

72074   thoracic, minimum of 4 views
➔ *CPT Assistant* Sep 01:7; *CPT Changes: An Insider's View* 2001

72080   thoracolumbar, 2 views
➔ *CPT Assistant* Sep 01:7; *CPT Changes: An Insider's View* 2001

72090   scoliosis study, including supine and erect studies

72100   Radiologic examination, spine, lumbosacral; 2 or 3 views
➔ *CPT Assistant* Sep 01:7; *CPT Changes: An Insider's View* 2001

72110   minimum of 4 views
➔ *CPT Assistant* Sep 01:7; *CPT Changes: An Insider's View* 2001

72114   complete, including bending views

72120   Radiologic examination, spine, lumbosacral, bending views only, minimum of 4 views

(Contrast material in CT of spine is either by intrathecal or intravenous injection. For intrathecal injection, use also 61055 or 62284. IV injection of contrast material is part of the CT procedure)

72125   Computed tomography, cervical spine; without contrast material   *CT*
➔ *CPT Changes: An Insider's View* 2003

72126   with contrast material

72127   without contrast material, followed by contrast material(s) and further sections

(For intrathecal injection procedure, see 61055, 62284)

72128   Computed tomography, thoracic spine; without contrast material   *CT*
➔ *CPT Changes: An Insider's View* 2003

72129   with contrast material

(For intrathecal injection procedure, see 61055, 62284)

72130   without contrast material, followed by contrast material(s) and further sections

(For intrathecal injection procedure, see 61055, 62284)

72131   Computed tomography, lumbar spine; without contrast material   *CT*
➔ *CPT Changes: An Insider's View* 2003
➔ *Clinical Examples in Radiology* Summer 07:11

72132   with contrast material
➔ *CPT Assistant* Fall 93:13
➔ *Clinical Examples in Radiology* Fall 06:5-6, 11-12

72133   without contrast material, followed by contrast material(s) and further sections

(For intrathecal injection procedure, see 61055, 62284)

(To report 3D rendering, see 76376, 76377)

72141   Magnetic resonance (eg, proton) imaging, spinal canal and contents, cervical; without contrast material   *MRI*

72142   with contrast material(s)

(For cervical spinal canal imaging without contrast material followed by contrast material, use 72156)

72146   Magnetic resonance (eg, proton) imaging, spinal canal and contents, thoracic; without contrast material   *MRI*
➔ *CPT Assistant* May 99:10

72147   with contrast material(s)
➔ *CPT Assistant* May 99:10

(For thoracic spinal canal imaging without contrast material followed by contrast material, use 72157)

72148   Magnetic resonance (eg, proton) imaging, spinal canal and contents, lumbar; without contrast material   *MRI*
➔ *CPT Assistant* Nov 05:15
➔ *Clinical Examples in Radiology* Spring 06:6,11

72149   with contrast material(s)

(For lumbar spinal canal imaging without contrast material followed by contrast material, use 72158)

72156   Magnetic resonance (eg, proton) imaging, spinal canal and contents, without contrast material, followed by contrast material(s) and further sequences; cervical   *MRI*

72157   thoracic

72158   lumbar

72159   Magnetic resonance angiography, spinal canal and contents, with or without contrast material(s)   *MRA*
➔ *CPT Assistant* Dec 05:7, Jan 07:31

72170   Radiologic examination, pelvis; 1 or 2 views
➔ *CPT Assistant* Sep 01:7, Mar 03:23; *CPT Changes: An Insider's View* 2001
➔ *Clinical Examples in Radiology* Spring 05:12

72190   complete, minimum of 3 views

(For pelvimetry, use 74710)

72191   Computed tomographic angiography, pelvis, with contrast material(s), including noncontrast images, if performed, and image postprocessing   *CTA*
➔ *CPT Assistant* Jul 01:4, 6, Dec 05:7, Jan 07:31; *CPT Changes: An Insider's View* 2001, 2008
➔ *Clinical Examples in Radiology* Summer 08:8

(For CTA aorto-iliofemoral runoff, use 75635)

72192   Computed tomography, pelvis; without contrast material
➔ *CPT Assistant* Mar 05:1, 4, Mar 07:10; *CPT Changes: An Insider's View* 2003
➔ *Clinical Examples in Radiology* Winter 06:11, Spring 07:3, 11, Summer 07:11   *CT*

72193   with contrast material(s)

→ *CPT Assistant* Mar 05:1, 4, Mar 07:10

→ *Clinical Examples in Radiology* Winter 05:1, 7, Spring 07:3, 11

72194   without contrast material, followed by contrast material(s) and further sections

→ *CPT Assistant* Mar 05:1, 4, Mar 07:10

→ *Clinical Examples in Radiology* Spring 07:3, 11

(To report 3D rendering, see 76376, 76377)

▶(For computed tomographic colonography, diagnostic, see 74261-74262. For computed tomographic colonography, screening, use 74263)◀

▶(Do not report 72192-72194 in conjunction with 74261-74263)◀

72195   Magnetic resonance (eg, proton) imaging, pelvis; without contrast material(s)   *MRI*

→ *CPT Assistant* Jul 01:7, Jun 06:17; *CPT Changes: An Insider's View* 2001

→ *Clinical Examples in Radiology* Spring 06:8-9, Fall 06:7-8, Summer 07:4,5

72196   with contrast material(s)

→ *CPT Assistant* Jul 01:7, Jun 06:17; *CPT Changes: An Insider's View* 2001

→ *Clinical Examples in Radiology* Spring 06:8-9, Fall 06:7-8

72197   without contrast material(s), followed by contrast material(s) and further sequences

→ *CPT Assistant* Jul 01:7; *CPT Changes: An Insider's View* 2001

→ *Clinical Examples in Radiology* Spring 06:8-9, Fall 06:2-3, 7-8

72198   Magnetic resonance angiography, pelvis, with or without contrast material(s)   *MRA*

→ *CPT Assistant* Dec 05:7, Jan 07:31

72200   Radiologic examination, sacroiliac joints; less than 3 views

72202   3 or more views

72220   Radiologic examination, sacrum and coccyx, minimum of 2 views

72240   Myelography, cervical, radiological supervision and interpretation

→ *CPT Assistant* Fall 93:13

→ *Clinical Examples in Radiology* Fall 06:5-6, 11-12

(For complete cervical myelography, see 61055, 62284, 72240)

72255   Myelography, thoracic, radiological supervision and interpretation

(For complete thoracic myelography, see 61055, 62284, 72255)

72265   Myelography, lumbosacral, radiological supervision and interpretation

→ *CPT Assistant* Fall 93:13, Aug 00:7

(For complete lumbosacral myelography, see 61055, 62284, 72265)

72270   Myelography, 2 or more regions (eg, lumbar/thoracic, cervical/thoracic, lumbar/cervical, lumbar/thoracic/cervical), radiological supervision and interpretation

→ *CPT Changes: An Insider's View* 2004

(For complete myelography of entire spinal canal, see 61055, 62284, 72270)

72275   Epidurography, radiological supervision and interpretation

→ *CPT Assistant* Nov 99:40, Jan 00:2, Aug 00:7, Jul 08:9; *CPT Changes: An Insider's View* 2000

(72275 includes 77003)

(For injection procedure, see 62280-62282, 62310-62319, 64479-64484)

(Use 72275 only when an epidurogram is performed, images documented, and a formal radiologic report is issued)

Epidurography
72275

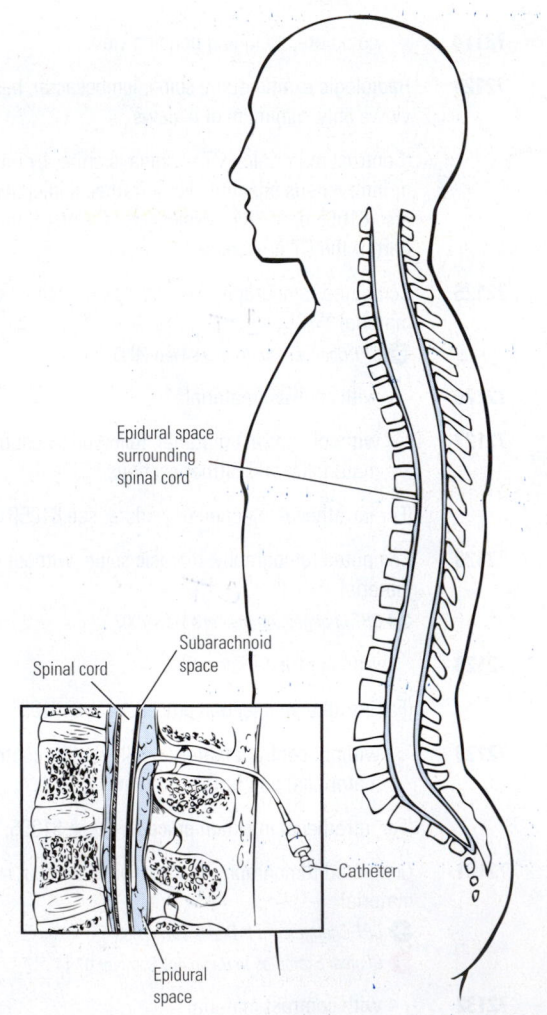

Epidural space surrounding spinal cord

Subarachnoid space

Spinal cord

Catheter

Epidural space

72285   Discography, cervical or thoracic, radiological supervision and interpretation
> *CPT Assistant* Nov 99:35, 40; *CPT Changes: An Insider's View* 2000

▲ **72291**   Radiological supervision and interpretation, percutaneous vertebroplasty, vertebral augmentation, or sacral augmentation (sacroplasty), including cavity creation, per vertebral body or sacrum; under fluoroscopic guidance
> *CPT Assistant* Mar 07:7; *CPT Changes: An Insider's View* 2007, 2010

▲ **72292**   under CT guidance
> *CPT Assistant* Mar 07:7; *CPT Changes: An Insider's View* 2007, 2010

►(For procedure, see 22520-22525, 0200T, 0201T)◄

72295   Discography, lumbar, radiological supervision and interpretation
> *CPT Assistant* Apr 03:27

Upper Extremities

(For stress views, any joint, use 77071)

73000   Radiologic examination; clavicle, complete

73010   scapula, complete

73020   Radiologic examination, shoulder; 1 view

73030   complete, minimum of 2 views

73040   Radiologic examination, shoulder, arthrography, radiological supervision and interpretation
> *CPT Assistant* Jul 01:7, Feb 07:11
> *Clinical Examples in Radiology* Spring 05:6, Spring 09:6, 7

(Do not report 77002 in conjunction with 73040)

73050   Radiologic examination; acromioclavicular joints, bilateral, with or without weighted distraction

73060   humerus, minimum of 2 views

73070   Radiologic examination, elbow; 2 views
> *CPT Assistant* Winter 90:9, Sep 01:8; *CPT Changes: An Insider's View* 2001

73080   complete, minimum of 3 views

73085   Radiologic examination, elbow, arthrography, radiological supervision and interpretation
> *CPT Assistant* Feb 07:11
> *Clinical Examples in Radiology* Spring 05:6

(Do not report 77002 in conjunction with 73085)

73090   Radiologic examination; forearm, 2 views
> *CPT Assistant* Sep 01:8, Apr 02:14; *CPT Changes: An Insider's View* 2001

73092   upper extremity, infant, minimum of 2 views

73100   Radiologic examination, wrist; 2 views
> *CPT Assistant* Winter 90:9, Sep 01:8; *CPT Changes: An Insider's View* 2001

73110   complete, minimum of 3 views
> *CPT Assistant* Mar 97:10, Nov 06:22

73115   Radiologic examination, wrist, arthrography, radiological supervision and interpretation
> *CPT Assistant* Feb 07:11
> *Clinical Examples in Radiology* Spring 05:6

(Do not report 77002 in conjunction with 73115)

73120   Radiologic examination, hand; 2 views
> *CPT Assistant* Winter 90:9

73130   minimum of 3 views
> *Clinical Examples in Radiology* Winter 05:9

73140   Radiologic examination, finger(s), minimum of 2 views
> *CPT Assistant* Jan 07:29

73200   Computed tomography, upper extremity; without contrast material
> *CPT Changes: An Insider's View* 2003

73201   with contrast material(s)
> *Clinical Examples in Radiology* Spring 09:6, 7

73202   without contrast material, followed by contrast material(s) and further sections

(To report 3D rendering, see 76376, 76377)

73206   Computed tomographic angiography, upper extremity, with contrast material(s), including noncontrast images, if performed, and image postprocessing
> *CPT Assistant* Jul 01:5, Dec 05:7, Jan 07:31; *CPT Changes: An Insider's View* 2001, 2008

73218   Magnetic resonance (eg, proton) imaging, upper extremity, other than joint; without contrast material(s)
> *CPT Assistant* Jul 01:7; *CPT Changes: An Insider's View* 2001

73219   with contrast material(s)
> *CPT Assistant* Jul 01:7; *CPT Changes: An Insider's View* 2001

73220   without contrast material(s), followed by contrast material(s) and further sequences
> *CPT Assistant* Jul 01:7; *CPT Changes: An Insider's View* 2001

73221   Magnetic resonance (eg, proton) imaging, any joint of upper extremity; without contrast material(s)
> *CPT Assistant* Jul 01:7; *CPT Changes: An Insider's View* 2001

73222   with contrast material(s)
> *CPT Assistant* Jul 01:7; *CPT Changes: An Insider's View* 2001
> *Clinical Examples in Radiology* Spring 05:5

73223   without contrast material(s), followed by contrast material(s) and further sequences
> *CPT Assistant* Jul 01:7; *CPT Changes: An Insider's View* 2001
> *Clinical Examples in Radiology* Spring 09:6

73225   Magnetic resonance angiography, upper extremity, with or without contrast material(s)
> *CPT Assistant* Dec 05:7, Jan 07:31

Lower Extremities

(For stress views, any joint, use 77071)

73500 Radiologic examination, hip, unilateral; 1 view
→ *Clinical Examples in Radiology* Spring 05:12

73510 complete, minimum of 2 views
→ *CPT Assistant* Spring 92:9, May 99:10, Apr 02:19, Mar 03:23
→ *Clinical Examples in Radiology* Spring 05:12

73520 Radiologic examination, hips, bilateral, minimum of 2 views of each hip, including anteroposterior view of pelvis
→ *CPT Assistant* Apr 02:19
→ *Clinical Examples in Radiology* Spring 05:12

73525 Radiologic examination, hip, arthrography, radiological supervision and interpretation
→ *CPT Assistant* Feb 07:11
→ *Clinical Examples in Radiology* Spring 05:6

(Do not report 73525 in conjunction with 77002)

73530 Radiologic examination, hip, during operative procedure

73540 Radiologic examination, pelvis and hips, infant or child, minimum of 2 views

73542 Radiological examination, sacroiliac joint arthrography, radiological supervision and interpretation
→ *CPT Assistant* Nov 99:40-41, Jul 08:9; *CPT Changes: An Insider's View* 2000
→ *Clinical Examples in Radiology* Spring 05:6

(Do not report 73542 in conjunction with 77002)

(For procedure, use 27096. If formal arthrography is not performed, recorded, and a formal radiologic report is not issued, use 77003 for fluoroscopic guidance for sacroiliac joint injections)

73550 Radiologic examination, femur, 2 views
→ *CPT Assistant* Sep 01:8; *CPT Changes: An Insider's View* 2001

73560 Radiologic examination, knee; 1 or 2 views

73562 3 views
→ *CPT Assistant* Apr 02:15
→ *Clinical Examples in Radiology* Fall 06:4

73564 complete, 4 or more views
→ *CPT Assistant* Jun 98:11, Nov 98:21
→ *Clinical Examples in Radiology* Fall 06:4

73565 both knees, standing, anteroposterior
→ *CPT Assistant* Winter 90:9
→ *Clinical Examples in Radiology* Fall 06:4

73580 Radiologic examination, knee, arthrography, radiological supervision and interpretation
→ *CPT Assistant* Feb 07:11
→ *Clinical Examples in Radiology* Spring 05:6

(Do not report 73580 in conjunction with 77002)

73590 Radiologic examination; tibia and fibula, 2 views
→ *CPT Assistant* Sep 01:8; *CPT Changes: An Insider's View* 2001

73592 lower extremity, infant, minimum of 2 views

73600 Radiologic examination, ankle; 2 views
→ *CPT Assistant* Sep 01:8, Apr 02:15, Mar 03:9; *CPT Changes: An Insider's View* 2001

73610 complete, minimum of 3 views
→ *CPT Assistant* Apr 02:15, Mar 03:9

73615 Radiologic examination, ankle, arthrography, radiological supervision and interpretation
→ *CPT Assistant* Feb 07:11

(Do not report 73615 in conjunction with 77002)

73620 Radiologic examination, foot; 2 views
→ *CPT Assistant* Sep 01:8, Apr 02:15, Mar 03:9; *CPT Changes: An Insider's View* 2001

73630 complete, minimum of 3 views
→ *Clinical Examples in Radiology* Summer 07:12

73650 Radiologic examination; calcaneus, minimum of 2 views

73660 toe(s), minimum of 2 views

73700 Computed tomography, lower extremity; without contrast material
→ *CPT Assistant* Mar 07:10; *CPT Changes: An Insider's View* 2003
→ *Clinical Examples in Radiology* Fall 08:10

73701 with contrast material(s)
→ *CPT Assistant* Mar 07:10

73702 without contrast material, followed by contrast material(s) and further sections
→ *CPT Assistant* Mar 07:10

(To report 3D rendering, see 76376, 76377)

73706 Computed tomographic angiography, lower extremity, with contrast material(s), including noncontrast images, if performed, and image postprocessing
→ *CPT Assistant* Jul 01:5-6, Dec 05:7, Jan 07:31, Apr 08:11; *CPT Changes: An Insider's View* 2001, 2008
→ *Clinical Examples in Radiology* Summer 08:8

(For CTA aorto-iliofemoral runoff, use 75635)

73718 Magnetic resonance (eg, proton) imaging, lower extremity other than joint; without contrast material(s)
→ *CPT Assistant* Jul 01:3; *CPT Changes: An Insider's View* 2001
→ *Clinical Examples in Radiology* Spring 07:7-9, 12, Summer 07:4,5

73719 with contrast material(s)
→ *CPT Assistant* Jul 01:3; *CPT Changes: An Insider's View* 2001
→ *Clinical Examples in Radiology* Spring 07:7-9, 12, Summer 07:4,5

73720 without contrast material(s), followed by contrast material(s) and further sequences
→ *CPT Assistant* Jul 01:3; *CPT Changes: An Insider's View* 2001
→ *Clinical Examples in Radiology* Spring 07:7-9, 12, Summer 07:4,5

73721   Magnetic resonance (eg, proton) imaging, any joint of lower extremity; without contrast material

→ *CPT Assistant* Jul 01:3, Jun 06:17; *CPT Changes: An Insider's View* 2001

→ *Clinical Examples in Radiology* Spring 07:7-9, 12, Summer 07:4,5

73722   with contrast material(s)

→ *CPT Assistant* Jul 01:3, Jun 06:17; *CPT Changes: An Insider's View* 2001

→ *Clinical Examples in Radiology* Spring 07:7-9, 12, Summer 07:4,5

73723   without contrast material(s), followed by contrast material(s) and further sequences

→ *CPT Assistant* Jul 01:3; *CPT Changes: An Insider's View* 2001

→ *Clinical Examples in Radiology* Spring 07:7-9, 12, Summer 07:4,5

73725   Magnetic resonance angiography, lower extremity, with or without contrast material(s)

→ *CPT Assistant* Dec 05:7, Jan 07:31

→ *Clinical Examples in Radiology* Spring 06:1-3

Abdomen

74000   Radiologic examination, abdomen; single anteroposterior view

→ *CPT Assistant* Nov 98:21

→ *Clinical Examples in Radiology* Spring 07:4

74010   anteroposterior and additional oblique and cone views

→ *CPT Assistant* Jan 07:29

→ *Clinical Examples in Radiology* Spring 07:4,8

74020   complete, including decubitus and/or erect views

74022   complete acute abdomen series, including supine, erect, and/or decubitus views, single view chest

→ *CPT Changes: An Insider's View* 2003

74150   Computed tomography, abdomen; without contrast material

→ *CPT Assistant* Oct 02:12, Mar 05:1, 4; *CPT Changes: An Insider's View* 2003

→ *Clinical Examples in Radiology* Spring 07:3, 11, Fall 08:7

74160   with contrast material(s)

→ *CPT Assistant* Mar 05:1, 4

→ *Clinical Examples in Radiology* Spring 07:3, 11, Fall 08:7

74170   without contrast material, followed by contrast material(s) and further sections

→ *CPT Assistant* Mar 05:4

→ *Clinical Examples in Radiology* Winter 05:1, 7-8, 12, Spring 07:3, 11, Fall 08:7

(To report 3D rendering, see 76376, 76377)

►(For computed tomographic colonography, diagnostic, see 74261-74262. For computed tomographic colonography, screening, use 74263)◄

►(Do not report 74150-74170 in conjunction with 74261-74263)◄

74175   Computed tomographic angiography, abdomen, with contrast material(s), including noncontrast images, if performed, and image postprocessing

→ *CPT Assistant* Jul 01:6, Dec 05:7, Jan 07:31; *CPT Changes: An Insider's View* 2001, 2008

→ *Clinical Examples in Radiology* Summer 08:8

(For CTA aorto-iliofemoral runoff, use 75635)

74181   Magnetic resonance (eg, proton) imaging, abdomen; without contrast material(s)

→ *CPT Assistant* Jul 01:3, Nov 07:9; *CPT Changes: An Insider's View* 2001

→ *Clinical Examples in Radiology* Fall 07:3, Spring 09:4

74182   with contrast material(s)

→ *CPT Assistant* Jul 01:3; *CPT Changes: An Insider's View* 2001

74183   without contrast material(s), followed by with contrast material(s) and further sequences

→ *CPT Assistant* Jul 01:3; *CPT Changes: An Insider's View* 2001

74185   Magnetic resonance angiography, abdomen, with or without contrast material(s)

→ *CPT Assistant* Dec 05:7, Jan 07:31

→ *Clinical Examples in Radiology* Spring 06:1-3

74190   Peritoneogram (eg, after injection of air or contrast), radiological supervision and interpretation

→ *Clinical Examples in Radiology* Fall 07:1,2

(For procedure, use 49400)

(For computed tomography, see 72192 or 74150)

Gastrointestinal Tract

(For percutaneous placement of gastrostomy tube, use 43246)

74210   Radiologic examination; pharynx and/or cervical esophagus

74220   esophagus

74230   Swallowing function, with cineradiography/videoradiography

→ *CPT Assistant* Dec 04:17; *CPT Changes: An Insider's View* 2002

→ *Clinical Examples in Radiology* Summer 06:4-5

74235   Removal of foreign body(s), esophageal, with use of balloon catheter, radiological supervision and interpretation

(For procedure, see 43215, 43247)

74240   Radiologic examination, gastrointestinal tract, upper; with or without delayed films, without KUB

74241   with or without delayed films, with KUB

74245   with small intestine, includes multiple serial films

→ *CPT Changes: An Insider's View* 2002

74246   Radiological examination, gastrointestinal tract, upper, air contrast, with specific high density barium, effervescent agent, with or without glucagon; with or without delayed films, without KUB

74247   with or without delayed films, with KUB

74249   with small intestine follow-through
➲ *CPT Changes: An Insider's View* 2002

74250   Radiologic examination, small intestine, includes multiple serial films;
➲ *CPT Changes: An Insider's View* 2002

74251   via enteroclysis tube

74260   Duodenography, hypotonic

● **74261**   Computed tomographic (CT) colonography, diagnostic, including image postprocessing; without contrast material
➲ *CPT Changes: An Insider's View* 2010

● **74262**   with contrast material(s) including non-contrast images, if performed
➲ *CPT Changes: An Insider's View* 2010

▶(Do not report 74261, 74262 in conjunction with 72192-72194, 74150-74170, 74263, 76376, 76377)◀

● **74263**   Computed tomographic (CT) colonography, screening, including image postprocessing
➲ *CPT Changes: An Insider's View* 2010

▶(Do not report 74263 in conjunction with 72192-72194, 74150-74170, 74261, 74262, 76376, 76377)◀

74270   Radiologic examination, colon; contrast (eg, barium) enema, with or without KUB
➲ *CPT Assistant* May 03:19; *CPT Changes: An Insider's View* 2009

74280   air contrast with specific high density barium, with or without glucagon

74283   Therapeutic enema, contrast or air, for reduction of intussusception or other intraluminal obstruction (eg, meconium ileus)
➲ *CPT Assistant* Nov 97:24

74290   Cholecystography, oral contrast;

74291   additional or repeat examination or multiple day examination

74300   Cholangiography and/or pancreatography; intraoperative, radiological supervision and interpretation
➲ *CPT Assistant* Nov 99:41, Dec 00:14; *CPT Changes: An Insider's View* 2000

✚ **74301**   additional set intraoperative, radiological supervision and interpretation (List separately in addition to code for primary procedure)

(Use 74301 in conjunction with 74300)

74305   through existing catheter, radiological supervision and interpretation
➲ *CPT Assistant* Nov 99:41; *CPT Changes: An Insider's View* 2000, 2002

(For procedure, see 47505, 48400, 47560-47561, 47563)

(For biliary duct stone extraction, percutaneous, see 47630, 74327)

74320   Cholangiography, percutaneous, transhepatic, radiological supervision and interpretation
➲ *CPT Assistant* Feb 07:11

74327   Postoperative biliary duct calculus removal, percutaneous via T-tube tract, basket, or snare (eg, Burhenne technique), radiological supervision and interpretation
➲ *CPT Changes: An Insider's View* 2002

(For procedure, use 47630)

74328   Endoscopic catheterization of the biliary ductal system, radiological supervision and interpretation

(For procedure, see 43260-43272 as appropriate)

74329   Endoscopic catheterization of the pancreatic ductal system, radiological supervision and interpretation

(For procedure, see 43260-43272 as appropriate)

74330   Combined endoscopic catheterization of the biliary and pancreatic ductal systems, radiological supervision and interpretation

(For procedure, see 43260-43272 as appropriate)

74340   Introduction of long gastrointestinal tube (eg, Miller-Abbott), including multiple fluoroscopies and films, radiological supervision and interpretation

(For tube placement, use 44500)

(74350 has been deleted. To report gastrostomy tube placement, use 49440)

74355   Percutaneous placement of enteroclysis tube, radiological supervision and interpretation
➲ *CPT Assistant* Feb 07:11

74360   Intraluminal dilation of strictures and/or obstructions (eg, esophagus), radiological supervision and interpretation
➲ *CPT Assistant* Spring 94:3, Oct 08:6

74363   Percutaneous transhepatic dilation of biliary duct stricture with or without placement of stent, radiological supervision and interpretation
➲ *CPT Changes: An Insider's View* 2002

(For procedure, see 47510, 47511, 47555, 47556)

Urinary Tract

74400   Urography (pyelography), intravenous, with or without KUB, with or without tomography

74410   Urography, infusion, drip technique and/or bolus technique;

74415   with nephrotomography

74420   Urography, retrograde, with or without KUB
➲ *CPT Assistant* Sep 00:11

74425   Urography, antegrade (pyelostogram, nephrostogram, loopogram), radiological supervision and interpretation
➲ *CPT Assistant* Fall 93:14, Dec 97:7, Oct 05:18
➲ *Clinical Examples in Radiology* Summer 06:1-3

74430 Cystography, minimum of 3 views, radiological supervision and interpretation

74440 Vasography, vesiculography, or epididymography, radiological supervision and interpretation

74445 Corpora cavernosography, radiological supervision and interpretation
➔ *CPT Assistant* Feb 07:11

74450 Urethrocystography, retrograde, radiological supervision and interpretation

74455 Urethrocystography, voiding, radiological supervision and interpretation

74470 Radiologic examination, renal cyst study, translumbar, contrast visualization, radiological supervision and interpretation
➔ *CPT Assistant* Oct 05:18, Feb 07:11

74475 Introduction of intracatheter or catheter into renal pelvis for drainage and/or injection, percutaneous, radiological supervision and interpretation
➔ *CPT Assistant* Dec 97:7, Oct 05:18, Feb 07:11

74480 Introduction of ureteral catheter or stent into ureter through renal pelvis for drainage and/or injection, percutaneous, radiological supervision and interpretation
➔ *CPT Assistant* Fall 93:14, Oct 05:18
➔ *Clinical Examples in Radiology* Summer 06:1-3, Summer 08:12

(For transurethral surgery [ureter and pelvis], see 52320-52355)

74485 Dilation of nephrostomy, ureters, or urethra, radiological supervision and interpretation
➔ *CPT Assistant* Oct 05:18, Dec 08:7, Jan 09:7
➔ *Clinical Examples in Radiology* Summer 06:1-3

(For dilation of ureter without radiologic guidance, use 52341, 52344)

(For change of nephrostomy or pyelostomy tube, use 50398)

Gynecological and Obstetrical

(For abdomen and pelvis, see 72170-72190, 74000-74170)

74710 Pelvimetry, with or without placental localization

74740 Hysterosalpingography, radiological supervision and interpretation
➔ *CPT Assistant* Nov 97:24, Jul 99:8, Mar 09:11

(For introduction of saline or contrast for hysterosalpingography, see 58340)

74742 Transcervical catheterization of fallopian tube, radiological supervision and interpretation

(For procedure, use 58345)

74775 Perineogram (eg, vaginogram, for sex determination or extent of anomalies)

Heart

▶Cardiac magnetic imaging differs from traditional magnetic resonance imaging (MRI) in its ability to provide a physiologic evaluation of cardiac function. Traditional MRI relies on static images to obtain clinical diagnoses based upon anatomic information. Improvement in spatial and temporal resolution has expanded the application from an anatomic test and includes physiologic evaluation of cardiac function. Flow and velocity assessment for valves and intracardiac shunts is performed in addition to a function and morphologic evaluation. Use 75559 with 75565 to report flow with pharmacologic wall motion stress evaluation without contrast. Use 75563 with 75565 to report flow with pharmacologic perfusion stress with contrast.

Cardiac MRI for velocity flow mapping can be reported in conjunction with 75557, 75559, 75561, or 75563.

Listed procedures may be performed independently or in the course of overall medical care. If the physician providing these services is also responsible for diagnostic workup and/or follow-up care of the patient, see appropriate sections also. Only one procedure in the series 75557-75563 is appropriately reported per session. Only one add-on code for flow velocity can be reported per session.

▶Cardiac MRI studies may be performed at rest and/or during pharmacologic stress. Therefore, the appropriate stress testing code from the 93015-93018 series should be reported in addition to 75559 or 75563.◀

Cardiac computed tomography (CT) and coronary computed tomographic angiography (CTA) include the axial source images of the pre-contrast, arterial phase sequence, and venous phase sequence (if performed), as well as the two-dimensional and three-dimensional reformatted images resulting from the study, including cine review. Contrast enhanced cardiac CT and coronary CTA codes 75571-75574 include any quantitative assessment when performed as part of the same encounter. Report only one computed tomography heart service per encounter.◀

(For separate injection procedures for vascular radiology, see **Surgery** section, 36000-36299)

(For cardiac catheterization procedures, see 93501-93556)

▶(75552-75556 have been deleted. To report, see 75557, 75559, 75561, 75563, 75565)◀

75557 Cardiac magnetic resonance imaging for morphology and function without contrast material;
➔ *CPT Changes: An Insider's View* 2008
➔ *Clinical Examples in Radiology* Spring 09:2

75559 with stress imaging
➔ *CPT Changes: An Insider's View* 2008
➔ *Clinical Examples in Radiology* Spring 09:2

75561   Cardiac magnetic resonance imaging for morphology and function without contrast material(s), followed by contrast material(s) and further sequences;
> *CPT Changes: An Insider's View* 2008
> *Clinical Examples in Radiology* Spring 09:2

75563   with stress imaging
> *CPT Changes: An Insider's View* 2008
> *Clinical Examples in Radiology* Spring 09:2

▶(75558, 75560, 75562, 75564 have been deleted. To report flow velocity, use 75565)◀

+ ● 75565   Cardiac magnetic resonance imaging for velocity flow mapping (List separately in addition to code for primary procedure)
> *CPT Changes: An Insider's View* 2010

▶(Use 75565 in conjunction with 75557, 75559, 75561, 75563)◀

▶(Do not report 75557, 75559, 75561, 75563, 75565 in conjunction with 76376, 76377)◀

● 75571   Computed tomography, heart, without contrast material, with quantitative evaluation of coronary calcium
> *CPT Changes: An Insider's View* 2010

● 75572   Computed tomography, heart, with contrast material, for evaluation of cardiac structure and morphology (including 3D image postprocessing, assessment of cardiac function, and evaluation of venous structures, if performed)
> *CPT Changes: An Insider's View* 2010

● 75573   Computed tomography, heart, with contrast material, for evaluation of cardiac structure and morphology in the setting of congenital heart disease (including 3D image postprocessing, assessment of LV cardiac function, RV structure and function and evaluation of venous structures, if performed)
> *CPT Changes: An Insider's View* 2010

● 75574   Computed tomographic angiography, heart, coronary arteries and bypass grafts (when present), with contrast material, including 3D image postprocessing (including evaluation of cardiac structure and morphology, assessment of cardiac function, and evaluation of venous structures, if performed)
> *CPT Changes: An Insider's View* 2010

Vascular Procedures

Aorta and Arteries

Selective vascular catheterizations should be coded to include introduction and all lesser order selective catheterizations used in the approach (eg, the description for a selective right middle cerebral artery catheterization includes the introduction and placement catheterization of the right common and internal carotid arteries).

Additional second and/or third order arterial catheterizations within the same family of arteries supplied by a single first order artery should be expressed by 36218 or 36248. Additional first order or higher catheterizations in vascular families supplied by a first order vessel different from a previously selected and coded family should be separately coded using the conventions described above.

For angiography performed in conjunction with therapeutic transcatheter radiological supervision and interpretation services, see the **Radiology Transcatheter Procedures** guidelines.

Diagnostic angiography (radiological supervision and interpretation) codes should NOT be used with interventional procedures for:

1. Contrast injections, angiography, roadmapping, and/or fluoroscopic guidance for the intervention,

2. Vessel measurement, and

3. Post-angioplasty/stent angiography,

as this work is captured in the radiological supervision and interpretation code(s).

Diagnostic angiography performed at the time of an interventional procedure is separately reportable if:

1. No prior catheter-based angiographic study is available and a full diagnostic study is performed, and the decision to intervene is based on the diagnostic study, OR

2. A prior study is available, but as documented in the medical record:

   a. The patient's condition with respect to the clinical indication has changed since the prior study, OR

   b. There is inadequate visualization of the anatomy and/or pathology, OR

   c. There is a clinical change during the procedure that requires new evaluation outside the target area of intervention.

Diagnostic angiography performed at a separate setting from an interventional procedure is separately reported.

Diagnostic angiography performed at the time of an interventional procedure is NOT separately reportable if it is specifically included in the interventional code descriptor.

(For intravenous procedure, see 36000-36013, 36400-36425 and 36100-36248 for intra-arterial procedure)

(For radiological supervision and interpretation, see 75600-75978)

75600   Aortography, thoracic, without serialography, radiological supervision and interpretation

(For injection procedure, use 93544)

Aortography
75600-75630

A radiographic contrast study is performed on the abdominal or thoracic aorta.

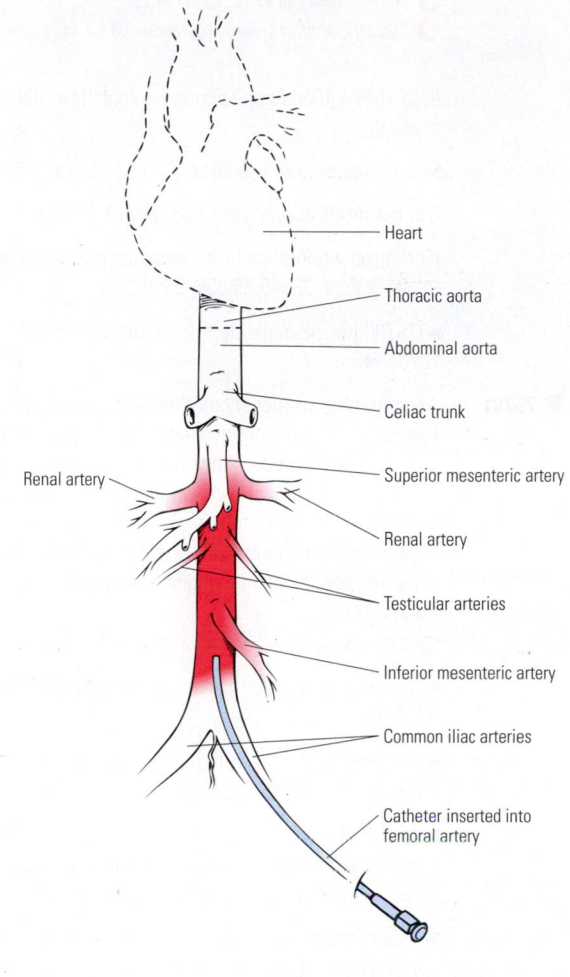

Heart

Thoracic aorta

Abdominal aorta

Celiac trunk

Superior mesenteric artery

Renal artery

Renal artery

Testicular arteries

Inferior mesenteric artery

Common iliac arteries

Catheter inserted into femoral artery

75605   Aortography, thoracic, by serialography, radiological supervision and interpretation

➲ *CPT Assistant* Spring 94:29, Dec 98:9

(For injection procedure, use 93544)

75625   Aortography, abdominal, by serialography, radiological supervision and interpretation

➲ *CPT Assistant* Fall 93:16, Jan 01:14, Dec 07:14, Apr 08:11

➲ *Clinical Examples in Radiology* Winter 08:1,2,4,5,9

(For injection procedure, use 93544)

75630   Aortography, abdominal plus bilateral iliofemoral lower extremity, catheter, by serialography, radiological supervision and interpretation

➲ *CPT Assistant* Fall 93:16, Jan 01:14, Apr 08:11

75635   Computed tomographic angiography, abdominal aorta and bilateral iliofemoral lower extremity runoff, with contrast material(s), including noncontrast images, if performed, and image postprocessing

➲ *CPT Assistant* Jul 01:4-5, Dec 05:7, Jan 07:31; *CPT Changes: An Insider's View* 2001, 2008

➲ *Clinical Examples in Radiology* Spring 06:1-3, Summer 08:7, 8

75650   Angiography, cervicocerebral, catheter, including vessel origin, radiological supervision and interpretation

➲ *CPT Assistant* Spring 94:29, Apr 98:9, Oct 00:6

75658   Angiography, brachial, retrograde, radiological supervision and interpretation

75660   Angiography, external carotid, unilateral, selective, radiological supervision and interpretation

➲ *Clinical Examples in Radiology* Winter 09:2

Angiography, Carotid Artery
75660-75680

A radiographic contrast study is performed on the carotid artery vascular family.

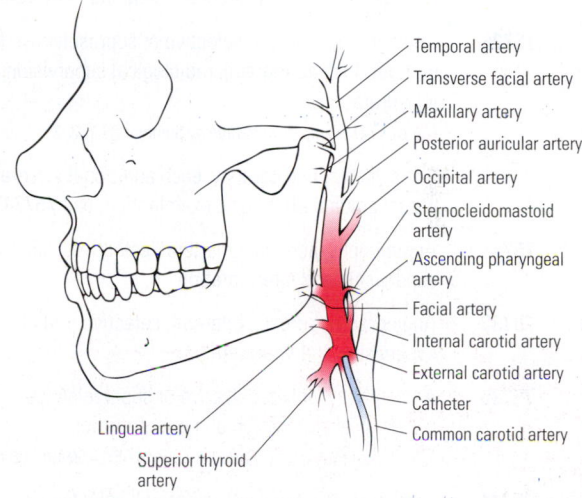

Temporal artery

Transverse facial artery

Maxillary artery

Posterior auricular artery

Occipital artery

Sternocleidomastoid artery

Ascending pharyngeal artery

Facial artery

Internal carotid artery

External carotid artery

Catheter

Common carotid artery

Lingual artery

Superior thyroid artery

75662   Angiography, external carotid, bilateral, selective, radiological supervision and interpretation

➲ *Clinical Examples in Radiology* Spring 09:2, Winter 09:2

75665   Angiography, carotid, cerebral, unilateral, radiological supervision and interpretation

➲ *Clinical Examples in Radiology* Winter 09:2

75671   Angiography, carotid, cerebral, bilateral, radiological supervision and interpretation

➲ *CPT Assistant* Oct 00:6

➲ *Clinical Examples in Radiology* Summer 07:1,2, Winter 09:2

75676   Angiography, carotid, cervical, unilateral, radiological supervision and interpretation

➲ *Clinical Examples in Radiology* Winter 09:2

75680 Angiography, carotid, cervical, bilateral, radiological supervision and interpretation
> *CPT Assistant* Oct 00:6
> *Clinical Examples in Radiology* Summer 07:1,2, Winter 09:2

75685 Angiography, vertebral, cervical, and/or intracranial, radiological supervision and interpretation
> *CPT Assistant* Oct 00:6

75705 Angiography, spinal, selective, radiological supervision and interpretation

75710 Angiography, extremity, unilateral, radiological supervision and interpretation
> *CPT Assistant* Apr 99:11, Jan 01:14

75716 Angiography, extremity, bilateral, radiological supervision and interpretation
> *CPT Assistant* Fall 93:16, Jan 01:14, Dec 07:14, Apr 08:11
> *Clinical Examples in Radiology* Winter 08:1,2,4,5,9

75722 Angiography, renal, unilateral, selective (including flush aortogram), radiological supervision and interpretation

75724 Angiography, renal, bilateral, selective (including flush aortogram), radiological supervision and interpretation

75726 Angiography, visceral, selective or supraselective (with or without flush aortogram), radiological supervision and interpretation
> *Clinical Examples in Radiology* Summer 08:1, 2, 3

(For selective angiography, each additional visceral vessel studied after basic examination, use 75774)

75731 Angiography, adrenal, unilateral, selective, radiological supervision and interpretation

75733 Angiography, adrenal, bilateral, selective, radiological supervision and interpretation

75736 Angiography, pelvic, selective or supraselective, radiological supervision and interpretation
> *Clinical Examples in Radiology* Spring 05:14, Winter 08:4,5

75741 Angiography, pulmonary, unilateral, selective, radiological supervision and interpretation

(For injection procedure, use 93541)

75743 Angiography, pulmonary, bilateral, selective, radiological supervision and interpretation
> *CPT Assistant* Spring 94:29, Apr 98:7

(For injection procedure, use 93541)

75746 Angiography, pulmonary, by nonselective catheter or venous injection, radiological supervision and interpretation

(For injection procedure, use 93541)

(For introduction of catheter, injection procedure, see 93501-93533, 93539, 93540, 93545, 93556)

75756 Angiography, internal mammary, radiological supervision and interpretation

(For introduction of catheter, injection procedure, see 93501-93533, 93545, 93556)

+ 75774 Angiography, selective, each additional vessel studied after basic examination, radiological supervision and interpretation (List separately in addition to code for primary procedure)
> *CPT Assistant* Fall 93:17, Spring 94:29
> *Clinical Examples in Radiology* Winter 08:1,2,4,5, Summer 08:1, 2, 3

(Use 75774 in addition to code for specific initial vessel studied)

▶(For angiography, see 36147, 75600-75774, 75791)◀

(For catheterizations, see codes 36215-36248)

(For introduction of catheter, injection procedure, see 93501-93533, 93545, 93555, 93556)

▶(75790 has been deleted. To report, see 36147, 75791)◀

● **75791** Angiography, arteriovenous shunt (eg, dialysis patient fistula/graft), complete evaluation of dialysis access, including fluoroscopy, image documentation and report (includes injections of contrast and all necessary imaging from the arterial anastomosis and adjacent artery through entire venous outflow including the inferior or superior vena cava), radiological supervision and interpretation
> *CPT Changes: An Insider's View* 2010

▶(Do not report 75791 in conjunction with 36147, 36148)◀

▶(For introduction of catheter, if necessary, see 36140, 36215-36217, 36245-36247)◀

▶(Use 75791 only if radiological evaluation is performed through an already existing access into the shunt or from an access that is not a direct puncture of the shunt)◀

▶(For radiological evaluation with needle/catheter introduction, AV dialysis shunt, complete procedure, use 36147)◀

Veins and Lymphatics

For venography performed in conjunction with therapeutic transcatheter radiological supervision and interpretation services, see the **Radiology Transcatheter Procedures** guidelines.

Diagnostic venography (radiological supervision and interpretation) codes should NOT be used with interventional procedures for:

1. Contrast injections, venography, roadmapping, and/or fluoroscopic guidance for the intervention,

2. Vessel measurement, and

3. Post-angioplasty/stent venography,

as this work is captured in the radiological supervision and interpretation code(s).

Diagnostic venography performed at the time of an interventional procedure is separately reportable if:

1. No prior catheter-based venographic study is available and a full diagnostic study is performed, and decision to intervene is based on the diagnostic study, OR

2. A prior study is available, but as documented in the medical record:

   a. The patient's condition with respect to the clinical indication has changed since the prior study, OR

   b. There is inadequate visualization of the anatomy and/or pathology, OR

   c. There is a clinical change during the procedure that requires new evaluation outside the target area of intervention.

Diagnostic venography performed at a separate setting from an interventional procedure is separately reported.

Diagnostic venography performed at the time of an interventional procedure is NOT separately reportable if it is specifically included in the interventional code descriptor.

(For injection procedure for venous system, see 36000-36015, 36400-36510)

(For injection procedure for lymphatic system, use 38790)

75801 Lymphangiography, extremity only, unilateral, radiological supervision and interpretation

75803 Lymphangiography, extremity only, bilateral, radiological supervision and interpretation

75805 Lymphangiography, pelvic/abdominal, unilateral, radiological supervision and interpretation

75807 Lymphangiography, pelvic/abdominal, bilateral, radiological supervision and interpretation

75809 Shuntogram for investigation of previously placed indwelling nonvascular shunt (eg, LeVeen shunt, ventriculoperitoneal shunt, indwelling infusion pump), radiological supervision and interpretation
> *CPT Assistant* Feb 07:11, Jul 08:13, Aug 08:13, Sep 08:10; *CPT Changes: An Insider's View* 2001

(For procedure, see 49427 or 61070)

75810 Splenoportography, radiological supervision and interpretation
> *CPT Assistant* Feb 07:11

75820 Venography, extremity, unilateral, radiological supervision and interpretation
> *CPT Assistant* Oct 97:10, May 08:14
> *Clinical Examples in Radiology* Summer 06:8-9, Spring 08:12

Venography
75820-75822

A radiographic contrast study is performed on the veins of the lower extremities.

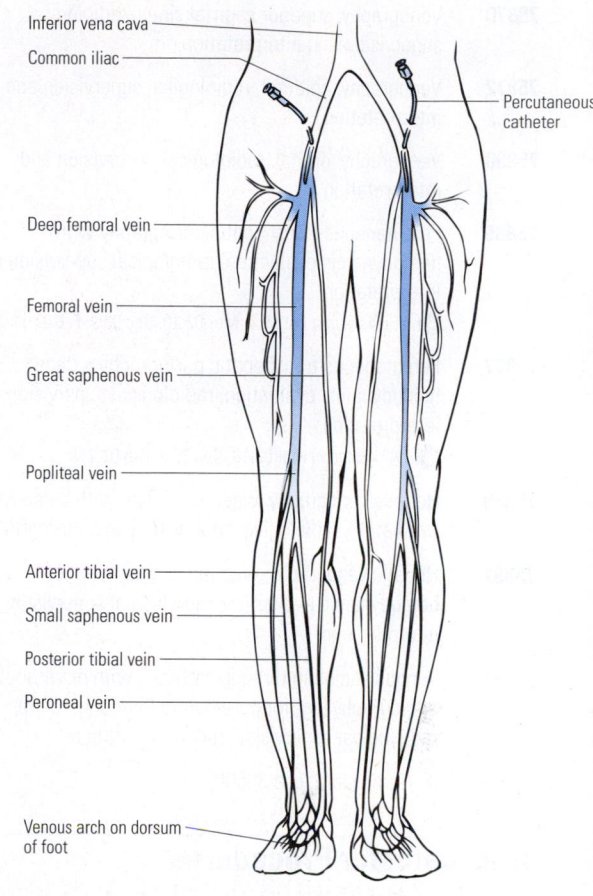

Inferior vena cava
Common iliac
Percutaneous catheter
Deep femoral vein
Femoral vein
Great saphenous vein
Popliteal vein
Anterior tibial vein
Small saphenous vein
Posterior tibial vein
Peroneal vein
Venous arch on dorsum of foot

75822 Venography, extremity, bilateral, radiological supervision and interpretation

75825 Venography, caval, inferior, with serialography, radiological supervision and interpretation
> *Clinical Examples in Radiology* Winter 05:5-6

75827 Venography, caval, superior, with serialography, radiological supervision and interpretation
> *CPT Assistant* Apr 98:12

75831 Venography, renal, unilateral, selective, radiological supervision and interpretation
> *CPT Assistant* Sep 98:7

75833 Venography, renal, bilateral, selective, radiological supervision and interpretation
> *CPT Assistant* Sep 98:7

75840 Venography, adrenal, unilateral, selective, radiological supervision and interpretation

75842 Venography, adrenal, bilateral, selective, radiological supervision and interpretation

75860 Venography, venous sinus (eg, petrosal and inferior sagittal) or jugular, catheter, radiological supervision and interpretation
➔ *CPT Changes: An Insider's View* 2004

75870 Venography, superior sagittal sinus, radiological supervision and interpretation

75872 Venography, epidural, radiological supervision and interpretation

75880 Venography, orbital, radiological supervision and interpretation

75885 Percutaneous transhepatic portography with hemodynamic evaluation, radiological supervision and interpretation
➔ *CPT Assistant* Oct 96:4, Mar 02:10, Dec 03:2, Feb 07:11

75887 Percutaneous transhepatic portography without hemodynamic evaluation, radiological supervision and interpretation
➔ *CPT Assistant* Mar 02:10, Dec 03:2, Feb 07:11

75889 Hepatic venography, wedged or free, with hemodynamic evaluation, radiological supervision and interpretation

75891 Hepatic venography, wedged or free, without hemodynamic evaluation, radiological supervision and interpretation

75893 Venous sampling through catheter, with or without angiography (eg, for parathyroid hormone, renin), radiological supervision and interpretation

(For procedure, use 36500)

Transcatheter Procedures

Therapeutic transcatheter radiological supervision and interpretation code(s) include the following services associated with that intervention:

1. Contrast injections, angiography/venography, roadmapping, and fluoroscopic guidance for the intervention,

2. Vessel measurement, and

3. Completion angiography/venography (except for those uses permitted by 75898).

Unless specifically included in the code descriptor, diagnostic angiography/venography performed at the time of transcatheter therapeutic radiological and interpretation service(s) is separately reportable (eg, no prior catheter-based diagnostic angiography/venography study of the target vessel is available, prior diagnostic study is inadequate, patient's condition with respect to the clinical indication has changed since the prior study or during the intervention). See 75600-75893.

Codes 75956 and 75957 include all angiography of the thoracic aorta and its branches for diagnostic imaging prior to deployment of the primary endovascular devices (including all routine components of modular devices), fluoroscopic guidance in the delivery of the endovascular components, and intraprocedural arterial angiography (eg, confirm position, detect endoleak, evaluate runoff).

Code 75958 includes the analogous services for placement of each proximal thoracic endovascular extension. Code 75959 includes the analogous services for placement of a distal thoracic endovascular extension(s) placed during a procedure after the primary repair.

75894 Transcatheter therapy, embolization, any method, radiological supervision and interpretation
➔ *CPT Assistant* Sep 98:7, Feb 08:5
➔ *Clinical Examples in Radiology* Winter 07:1-3, Summer 07:2, Winter 08:4,5, Summer 08:1, 2, 3

(For uterine fibroid embolization [uterine artery embolization performed to treat uterine fibroids], use 37210)

(For obstetrical and gynecologic embolization procedures other than uterine fibroid embolization [eg, embolization to treat obstetrical or postpartum hemorrhage], use 37204)

75896 Transcatheter therapy, infusion, any method (eg, thrombolysis other than coronary), radiological supervision and interpretation
➔ *CPT Assistant* May 01:4
➔ *Clinical Examples in Radiology* Spring 08:7,8

(For infusion for coronary disease, see 92975, 92977)

75898 Angiography through existing catheter for follow-up study for transcatheter therapy, embolization or infusion
➔ *CPT Assistant* Dec 07:11; *CPT Changes: An Insider's View* 2002
➔ *Clinical Examples in Radiology* Summer 07:2, Winter 08:4,5, Summer 08:1, 2, 3

75900 Exchange of a previously placed intravascular catheter during thrombolytic therapy with contrast monitoring, radiological supervision and interpretation
➔ *CPT Changes: An Insider's View* 2006
➔ *Clinical Examples in Radiology* Winter 06:20

(For procedure, use 37209)

75901 Mechanical removal of pericatheter obstructive material (eg, fibrin sheath) from central venous device via separate venous access, radiologic supervision and interpretation
➔ *CPT Assistant* Jul 03:13, Dec 04:12; *CPT Changes: An Insider's View* 2003

(For procedure, use 36595)

(For venous catheterization, see 36010-36012)

75902 Mechanical removal of intraluminal (intracatheter) obstructive material from central venous device through device lumen, radiologic supervision and interpretation

→ *CPT Assistant* Jul 03:13, Dec 04:12; *CPT Changes: An Insider's View* 2003

(For procedure, use 36596)

(For venous catheterization, see 36010-36012)

75940 Percutaneous placement of IVC filter, radiological supervision and interpretation

→ *CPT Assistant* Nov 00:11, Oct 08:11

→ *Clinical Examples in Radiology* Winter 05:5-6

75945 Intravascular ultrasound (non-coronary vessel), radiological supervision and interpretation; initial vessel

+ 75946 each additional non-coronary vessel (List separately in addition to code for primary procedure)

(Use 75946 in conjunction with 75945)

(For catheterizations, see codes 36215-36248)

(For transcatheter therapies, see codes 37200-37208, 61624, 61626)

(For procedure, see 37250, 37251)

75952 Endovascular repair of infrarenal abdominal aortic aneurysm or dissection, radiological supervision and interpretation

→ *CPT Changes: An Insider's View* 2001

(For implantation of endovascular grafts, see 34800-34808)

(For radiologic supervision and interpretation of endovascular repair of abdominal aortic aneurysm involving visceral vessels, see Category III codes 0078T-0081T)

75953 Placement of proximal or distal extension prosthesis for endovascular repair of infrarenal aortic or iliac artery aneurysm, pseudoaneurysm, or dissection, radiological supervision and interpretation

→ *CPT Assistant* Feb 03:3; *CPT Changes: An Insider's View* 2001, 2003

(For implantation of endovascular extension prostheses, see 34825, 34826)

75954 Endovascular repair of iliac artery aneurysm, pseudoaneurysm, arteriovenous malformation, or trauma, radiological supervision and interpretation

→ *CPT Assistant* Feb 03:3; *CPT Changes: An Insider's View* 2003

(For implantation of endovascular graft, see 34900)

75956 Endovascular repair of descending thoracic aorta (eg, aneurysm, pseudoaneurysm, dissection, penetrating ulcer, intramural hematoma, or traumatic disruption); involving coverage of left subclavian artery origin, initial endoprosthesis plus descending thoracic aortic extension(s), if required, to level of celiac artery origin, radiological supervision and interpretation

→ *CPT Changes: An Insider's View* 2006

→ *Clinical Examples in Radiology* Winter 06:17

(For implantation of endovascular graft, use 33880)

75957 not involving coverage of left subclavian artery origin, initial endoprosthesis plus descending thoracic aortic extension(s), if required, to level of celiac artery origin, radiological supervision and interpretation

→ *CPT Changes: An Insider's View* 2006

→ *Clinical Examples in Radiology* Winter 06:17

(For implantation of endovascular graft, use 33881)

75958 Placement of proximal extension prosthesis for endovascular repair of descending thoracic aorta (eg, aneurysm, pseudoaneurysm, dissection, penetrating ulcer, intramural hematoma, or traumatic disruption), radiological supervision and interpretation

→ *CPT Changes: An Insider's View* 2006

→ *Clinical Examples in Radiology* Winter 06:17

(Report 75958 for each proximal extension)

(For implantation of proximal endovascular extension, see 33883, 33884)

75959 Placement of distal extension prosthesis(s) (delayed) after endovascular repair of descending thoracic aorta, as needed, to level of celiac origin, radiological supervision and interpretation

→ *CPT Changes: An Insider's View* 2006

→ *Clinical Examples in Radiology* Winter 06:17

(Do not report 75959 in conjunction with 75956, 75957)

(Report 75959 once, regardless of number of modules deployed)

(For implantation of distal endovascular extension, use 33886)

75960 Transcatheter introduction of intravascular stent(s) (except coronary, carotid, and vertebral vessel), percutaneous and/or open, radiological supervision and interpretation, each vessel

→ *CPT Assistant* Fall 93:18, Oct 96:2, May 01:4, Dec 03:2; *CPT Changes: An Insider's View* 2005

(For procedure, see 37205-37208)

(For radiologic supervision and interpretation for transcatheter placement of extracranial vertebral or intrathoracic carotid artery stent(s), see Category III codes 0075T, 0076T)

75961 Transcatheter retrieval, percutaneous, of intravascular foreign body (eg, fractured venous or arterial catheter), radiological supervision and interpretation

(For procedure, use 37203)

75962 Transluminal balloon angioplasty, peripheral artery, radiological supervision and interpretation

→ *CPT Assistant* Fall 93:18, May 01:4

→ *Clinical Examples in Radiology* Spring 07:1-3, Winter 08:1,2,4,5

+ 75964 Transluminal balloon angioplasty, each additional peripheral artery, radiological supervision and interpretation (List separately in addition to code for primary procedure)

→ *CPT Assistant* Dec 07:10

(Use 75964 in conjunction with 75962)

75966 Transluminal balloon angioplasty, renal or other visceral artery, radiological supervision and interpretation

+ 75968 Transluminal balloon angioplasty, each additional visceral artery, radiological supervision and interpretation (List separately in addition to code for primary procedure)

(Use 75968 in conjunction with 75966)

(For percutaneous transluminal coronary angioplasty, see 92982-92984)

75970 Transcatheter biopsy, radiological supervision and interpretation

(For injection procedure only for transcatheter therapy or biopsy, see 36100-36299)

(For transcatheter renal and ureteral biopsy, use 52007)

(For percutaneous needle biopsy of pancreas, use 48102; of retroperitoneal lymph node or mass, use 49180)

75978 Transluminal balloon angioplasty, venous (eg, subclavian stenosis), radiological supervision and interpretation
➔ *CPT Assistant* Oct 96:4, Feb 97:2, May 01:4, Dec 03:2
➔ *Clinical Examples in Radiology* Spring 05:8-10, Spring 07:1-3

75980 Percutaneous transhepatic biliary drainage with contrast monitoring, radiological supervision and interpretation
➔ *CPT Assistant* Feb 07:11

75982 Percutaneous placement of drainage catheter for combined internal and external biliary drainage or of a drainage stent for internal biliary drainage in patients with an inoperable mechanical biliary obstruction, radiological supervision and interpretation
➔ *CPT Assistant* Feb 07:11

75984 Change of percutaneous tube or drainage catheter with contrast monitoring (eg, genitourinary system, abscess), radiological supervision and interpretation
➔ *CPT Assistant* Nov 97:24; *CPT Changes: An Insider's View* 2008

(For percutaneous replacement of gastrostomy, duodenostomy, jejunostomy, gastro-jejunostomy, or cecostomy [or other colonic] tube including fluoroscopic imaging guidance, see 49450-49452)

(For change of nephrostomy or pyelostomy tube only, use 50398)

(For introduction procedure only for percutaneous biliary drainage, see 47510, 47511)

(For percutaneous cholecystostomy, use 47490)

(For change of percutaneous biliary drainage catheter only, use 47525)

(For percutaneous nephrostolithotomy or pyelostolithotomy, see 50080, 50081)

(For removal and/or replacement of an internally dwelling ureteral stent via a transurethral approach, see 50385-50386)

75989 Radiological guidance (ie, fluoroscopy, ultrasound, or computed tomography), for percutaneous drainage (eg, abscess, specimen collection), with placement of catheter, radiological supervision and interpretation
➔ *CPT Assistant* Nov 97:24, Mar 98:8, Feb 07:11; *CPT Changes: An Insider's View* 2001, 2002

Transluminal Atherectomy

75992 Transluminal atherectomy, peripheral artery, radiological supervision and interpretation

(For procedure, see 35481-35485, 35491-35495)

+ 75993 Transluminal atherectomy, each additional peripheral artery, radiological supervision and interpretation (List separately in addition to code for primary procedure)

(Use 75993 in conjunction with 75992)

(For procedure, see 35481-35485, 35491-35495)

75994 Transluminal atherectomy, renal, radiological supervision and interpretation

(For procedure, see 35480, 35490)

75995 Transluminal atherectomy, visceral, radiological supervision and interpretation

(For procedure, see 35480, 35490)

+ 75996 Transluminal atherectomy, each additional visceral artery, radiological supervision and interpretation (List separately in addition to code for primary procedure)

(Use 75996 in conjunction with 75995)

(For procedure, see 35480, 35490)

Other Procedures

(For computed tomography cerebral perfusion analysis, see Category III code 0042T)

(For arthrography of shoulder, use 73040; elbow, use 73085; wrist, use 73115; hip, use 73525; knee, use 73580; ankle, use 73615)

76000 Fluoroscopy (separate procedure), up to 1 hour physician time, other than 71023 or 71034 (eg, cardiac fluoroscopy)
➔ *CPT Assistant* Apr 96:11, Nov 99:32, Dec 00:14, Apr 03:7, Jul 03:16, Aug 03:14, Jul 08:9, Aug 08:7, Dec 08:7, Dec 08:9; *CPT Changes: An Insider's View* 2000

76001 Fluoroscopy, physician time more than 1 hour, assisting a nonradiologic physician (eg, nephrostolithotomy, ERCP, bronchoscopy, transbronchial biopsy)

76010 Radiologic examination from nose to rectum for foreign body, single view, child
➔ *CPT Changes: An Insider's View* 2001

76080 Radiologic examination, abscess, fistula or sinus tract study, radiological supervision and interpretation
➔ *CPT Assistant* Nov 97:24, Mar 98:8, Nov 03:14, Dec 06:10, Jan 09:8

(For contrast injection[s] and radiological assessment of gastrostomy, duodenostomy, jejunostomy, gastro-jejunostomy, or cecostomy [or other colonic] tube including fluoroscopic imaging guidance, use 49465)

76098 Radiological examination, surgical specimen

76100 Radiologic examination, single plane body section (eg, tomography), other than with urography

76101 Radiologic examination, complex motion (ie, hypercycloidal) body section (eg, mastoid polytomography), other than with urography; unilateral

76102 bilateral

(For nephrotomography, use 74415)

76120 Cineradiography/videoradiography, except where specifically included

➲ *CPT Assistant* Sep 00:4, Apr 04:15; *CPT Changes: An Insider's View* 2002

+ 76125 Cineradiography/videoradiography to complement routine examination (List separately in addition to code for primary procedure)

➲ *CPT Assistant* Oct 97:1, Sep 00:4; *CPT Changes: An Insider's View* 2002

76140 Consultation on X-ray examination made elsewhere, written report

➲ *CPT Assistant* Summer 91:13, Oct 97:1

76150 Xeroradiography

(76150 is to be used for non-mammographic studies only)

76350 Subtraction in conjunction with contrast studies

(2D reformatting is no longer separately reported. To report 3D rendering, see 76376, 76377)

(76376, 76377 require concurrent physician supervision of image postprocessing 3D manipulation of volumetric data set and image rendering)

76376 3D rendering with interpretation and reporting of computed tomography, magnetic resonance imaging, ultrasound, or other tomographic modality; not requiring image postprocessing on an independent workstation

➲ *CPT Assistant* Dec 05:1, 7, Jan 07:31, Jul 08:3; *CPT Changes: An Insider's View* 2006

➲ *Clinical Examples in Radiology* Winter 06:17, Spring 06:8-9, Fall 06:9-10, Winter 07:4-5, Summer 08:8, Fall 08:12, Spring 09:4

(Use 76376 in conjunction with code[s] for base imaging procedure[s])

►(Do not report 76376 in conjunction with 31627, 70496, 70498, 70544-70549, 71275, 71555, 72159, 72191, 72198, 73206, 73225, 73706, 73725, 74175, 74185, 74261-74263, 75557, 75559, 75561, 75563, 75565, 75571-75574, 75635, 76377, 78000-78999, 0159T)◄

76377 requiring image postprocessing on an independent workstation

➲ *CPT Assistant* Dec 05:1, Jan 07:31, Jul 08:3; *CPT Changes: An Insider's View* 2006

➲ *Clinical Examples in Radiology* Winter 06:17, Spring 06:8-9, Fall 06:9-10, Winter 07:4-5, Summer 07:1,2, Summer 08:8, Fall 08:12, Spring 09:5

(Use 76377 in conjunction with code[s] for base imaging procedure[s])

►(Do not report 76377 in conjunction with 70496, 70498, 70544-70549, 71275, 71555, 72159, 72191, 72198, 73206, 73225, 73706, 73725, 74175, 74185, 74261-74263, 75557, 75559, 75561, 75563, 75565, 75571-75574, 75635, 76376, 78000-78999, 0159T)◄

(To report computer-aided detection, including computer algorithm analysis of MRI data for lesion detection/characterization, pharmacokinetic analysis, breast MRI, use Category III code 0159T)

76380 Computed tomography, limited or localized follow-up study

➲ *CPT Assistant* Jul 07:13; *CPT Changes: An Insider's View* 2002, 2003

76390 Magnetic resonance spectroscopy

➲ *CPT Assistant* Nov 97:25

(For magnetic resonance imaging, use appropriate MRI body site code)

76496 Unlisted fluoroscopic procedure (eg, diagnostic, interventional)

➲ *CPT Changes: An Insider's View* 2003

➲ *Clinical Examples in Radiology* Fall 07:3

76497 Unlisted computed tomography procedure (eg, diagnostic, interventional)

➲ *CPT Assistant* Jun 05:11; *CPT Changes: An Insider's View* 2003

➲ *Clinical Examples in Radiology* Spring 05:1, 7

76498 Unlisted magnetic resonance procedure (eg, diagnostic, interventional)

➲ *CPT Changes: An Insider's View* 2003

➲ *Clinical Examples in Radiology* Fall 08:11, Spring 09:11

76499 Unlisted diagnostic radiographic procedure

➲ *CPT Assistant* Jul 99:10, Sep 00:4, Apr 04:15, Nov 06:22, Mar 08:15; *CPT Changes: An Insider's View* 2003

Diagnostic Ultrasound

All diagnostic ultrasound examinations require permanently recorded images with measurements, when such measurements are clinically indicated. For those codes whose sole diagnostic goal is a biometric measure (ie, 76514, 76516, and 76519), permanently recorded images are not required. A final, written report should be issued for inclusion in the patient's medical record. The prescription form for the intraocular lens satisfies the written report requirement for 76519. For those anatomic regions that have "complete" and "limited" ultrasound codes, note the elements that comprise a "complete" exam. The report should contain a description of these elements or the reason that an element could not be visualized (eg, obscured by bowel gas, surgically absent).

If less than the required elements for a "complete" exam are reported (eg, limited number of organs or limited portion of region evaluated), the "limited" code for that anatomic region should be used once per patient exam session. A "limited" exam of an anatomic region should not be reported for the same exam session as a "complete" exam of that same region.

Evaluation of vascular structures using both color and spectral Doppler is separately reportable. To report, see **Noninvasive Vascular Diagnostic Studies** (93875-93990). However, color Doppler alone, when performed for anatomic structure identification in conjunction with a real-time ultrasound examination, is not reported separately.

Ultrasound guidance procedures also require permanently recorded images of the site to be localized, as well as a documented description of the localization process, either separately or within the report of the procedure for which the guidance is utilized.

Use of ultrasound, without thorough evaluation of organ(s) or anatomic region, image documentation, and final, written report, is not separately reportable.

Definitions

A-mode implies a one-dimensional ultrasonic measurement procedure.

M-mode implies a one-dimensional ultrasonic measurement procedure with movement of the trace to record amplitude and velocity of moving echo-producing structures.

B-scan implies a two-dimensional ultrasonic scanning procedure with a two-dimensional display.

Real-time scan implies a two-dimensional ultrasonic scanning procedure with display of both two-dimensional structure and motion with time.

(To report diagnostic vascular ultrasound studies, see 93875-93990)

(For focused ultrasound ablation treatment of uterine leiomyomata, see Category III codes 0071T, 0072T)

Head and Neck

76506 Echoencephalography, real time with image documentation (gray scale) (for determination of ventricular size, delineation of cerebral contents, and detection of fluid masses or other intracranial abnormalities), including A-mode encephalography as secondary component where indicated

➔ *CPT Assistant* Mar 07:7; *CPT Changes: An Insider's View* 2007, 2008

76510 Ophthalmic ultrasound, diagnostic; B-scan and quantitative A-scan performed during the same patient encounter

➔ *CPT Assistant* Dec 05:3; *CPT Changes: An Insider's View* 2005

76511 quantitative A-scan only

➔ *CPT Assistant* Winter 93:12, Oct 96:9, Nov 99:42, Jul 04:12, Dec 05:3; *CPT Changes: An Insider's View* 2005

76512 B-scan (with or without superimposed non-quantitative A-scan)

➔ *CPT Assistant* Winter 93:12, Oct 96:9, Dec 05:3; *CPT Changes: An Insider's View* 2005

76513 anterior segment ultrasound, immersion (water bath) B-scan or high resolution biomicroscopy

➔ *CPT Assistant* Winter 93:12, Nov 99:42; *CPT Changes: An Insider's View* 2000

(For scanning computerized ophthalmic diagnostic imaging of the anterior and posterior segments using technology other than ultrasound, see 92135, 0187T)

76514 corneal pachymetry, unilateral or bilateral (determination of corneal thickness)

➔ *CPT Assistant* Jul 04:12, 15, Feb 05:13, Jun 05:11, Dec 05:3; *CPT Changes: An Insider's View* 2004

76516 Ophthalmic biometry by ultrasound echography, A-scan;

➔ *CPT Assistant* Oct 03:10, Dec 05:3

76519 with intraocular lens power calculation

➔ *CPT Assistant* Winter 93:12, Oct 03:10, Dec 05:3

(For partial coherence interferometry, use 92136)

76529 Ophthalmic ultrasonic foreign body localization

➔ *CPT Assistant* Winter 93:12

76536 Ultrasound, soft tissues of head and neck (eg, thyroid, parathyroid, parotid), real time with image documentation

➔ *CPT Assistant* Mar 07:7; *CPT Changes: An Insider's View* 2002, 2007

Chest

76604 Ultrasound, chest (includes mediastinum), real time with image documentation

➔ *CPT Changes: An Insider's View* 2002, 2007

76645 Ultrasound, breast(s) (unilateral or bilateral), real time with image documentation

➔ *CPT Changes: An Insider's View* 2002, 2007

➔ *Clinical Examples in Radiology* Fall 05:8, Fall 08:2, 3, 9

Abdomen and Retroperitoneum

A complete ultrasound examination of the abdomen (76700) consists of real time scans of the liver, gall bladder, common bile duct, pancreas, spleen, kidneys, and the upper abdominal aorta and inferior vena cava including any demonstrated abdominal abnormality.

A complete ultrasound examination of the retroperitoneum (76770) consists of real time scans of the kidneys, abdominal aorta, common iliac artery origins, and inferior vena cava, including any demonstrated retroperitoneal abnormality. Alternatively, if clinical history suggests urinary tract pathology, complete evaluation of the kidneys and urinary bladder also comprises a complete retroperitoneal ultrasound.

Use of ultrasound, without thorough evaluation of organ(s) or anatomic region, image documentation and final, written report, is not separately reportable.

76700 Ultrasound, abdominal, real time with image documentation; complete

➔ *CPT Assistant* Fall 93:13, Oct 01:3, Dec 05:3, Mar 07:7; *CPT Changes: An Insider's View* 2002, 2007

➔ *Clinical Examples in Radiology* Winter 05:9, 11, Fall 07:4, Spring 08:10

76705 limited (eg, single organ, quadrant, follow-up)

➔ *CPT Assistant* Fall 93:13, Oct 01:3, Apr 03:27, Dec 05:3, Feb 09:22

➔ *Clinical Examples in Radiology* Winter 05:9, 11, Fall 07:4

76770 Ultrasound, retroperitoneal (eg, renal, aorta, nodes), real time with image documentation; complete

➔ *CPT Assistant* May 99:10, Jun 99:10; *CPT Changes: An Insider's View* 2002, 2007

➔ *Clinical Examples in Radiology* Winter 05:9, 11, Fall 07:4, Winter 08:12

76775 limited

➔ *CPT Assistant* May 99:10, Jun 99:10, Dec 05:3, Feb 09:22

➔ *Clinical Examples in Radiology* Winter 05:9, 11, Winter 07:8-10, Spring 07:5-6, Fall 07:4

76776 Ultrasound, transplanted kidney, real time and duplex Doppler with image documentation

➔ *CPT Assistant* Mar 07:7; *CPT Changes: An Insider's View* 2007

(For ultrasound of transplanted kidney without duplex Doppler, use 76775)

(Do not report 76776 in conjunction with 93975, 93976)

Spinal Canal

76800 Ultrasound, spinal canal and contents

➔ *CPT Assistant* Apr 98:15; *CPT Changes: An Insider's View* 2002

Pelvis

Obstetrical

Codes 76801 and 76802 include determination of the number of gestational sacs and fetuses, gestational sac/fetal measurements appropriate for gestation (younger than 14 weeks 0 days), survey of visible fetal and placental anatomic structure, qualitative assessment of amniotic fluid volume/gestational sac shape and examination of the maternal uterus and adnexa.

Codes 76805 and 76810 include determination of number of fetuses and amniotic/chorionic sacs, measurements appropriate for gestational age (older than or equal to 14 weeks 0 days), survey of intracranial/spinal/abdominal anatomy, 4 chambered heart, umbilical cord insertion site, placenta location and amniotic fluid assessment and, when visible, examination of maternal adnexa.

Codes 76811 and 76812 include all elements of codes 76805 and 76810 plus detailed anatomic evaluation of the fetal brain/ventricles, face, heart/outflow tracts and chest anatomy, abdominal organ specific anatomy, number/length/architecture of limbs and detailed evaluation of the umbilical cord and placenta and other fetal anatomy as clinically indicated.

Report should document the results of the evaluation of each element described above or the reason for non-visualization.

Code 76815 represents a focused "quick look" exam limited to the assessment of one or more of the elements listed in code 76815.

Code 76816 describes an examination designed to reassess fetal size and interval growth or reevaluate one or more anatomic abnormalities of a fetus previously demonstrated on ultrasound, and should be coded once for each fetus requiring reevaluation using modifier 59 for each fetus after the first.

Code 76817 describes a transvaginal obstetric ultrasound performed separately or in addition to one of the transabdominal examinations described above. For transvaginal examinations performed for non-obstetrical purposes, use code 76830.

76801 Ultrasound, pregnant uterus, real time with image documentation, fetal and maternal evaluation, first trimester (< 14 weeks 0 days), transabdominal approach; single or first gestation

➔ *CPT Assistant* Mar 03:7, Nov 05:15; *CPT Changes: An Insider's View* 2003

➔ *Clinical Examples in Radiology* Winter 07:6-7

(To report first trimester fetal nuchal translucency measurement, use 76813)

+ 76802 each additional gestation (List separately in addition to code for primary procedure)

➔ *CPT Assistant* Mar 03:7, Nov 05:15; *CPT Changes: An Insider's View* 2003

➔ *Clinical Examples in Radiology* Winter 07:6-7

(Use 76802 in conjunction with 76801)

(To report first trimester fetal nuchal translucency measurement, use 76814)

76805 Ultrasound, pregnant uterus, real time with image documentation, fetal and maternal evaluation, after first trimester (> or = 14 weeks 0 days), transabdominal approach; single or first gestation

➔ *CPT Assistant* Apr 97:2, Nov 97:25, Oct 01:3, Aug 02:2, Mar 03:7; *CPT Changes: An Insider's View* 2002, 2003

➔ *Clinical Examples in Radiology* Winter 05:3-4

+ 76810 each additional gestation (List separately in addition to code for primary procedure)

➔ *CPT Assistant* Apr 97:2, Oct 01:3, Aug 02:2, Mar 03:7; *CPT Changes: An Insider's View* 2003

➔ *Clinical Examples in Radiology* Winter 05:4

(Use 76810 in conjunction with 76805)

76811 Ultrasound, pregnant uterus, real time with image documentation, fetal and maternal evaluation plus detailed fetal anatomic examination, transabdominal approach; single or first gestation

➡ *CPT Assistant* Mar 03:7; *CPT Changes: An Insider's View* 2003

➡ *Clinical Examples in Radiology* Winter 05:4

+ 76812 each additional gestation (List separately in addition to code for primary procedure)

➡ *CPT Assistant* Mar 03:7; *CPT Changes: An Insider's View* 2003

(Use 76812 in conjunction with 76811)

76813 Ultrasound, pregnant uterus, real time with image documentation, first trimester fetal nuchal translucency measurement, transabdominal or transvaginal approach; single or first gestation

➡ *CPT Assistant* Mar 07:7; *CPT Changes: An Insider's View* 2007

➡ *Clinical Examples in Radiology* Winter 07:6

+ 76814 each additional gestation (List separately in addition to code for primary procedure)

➡ *CPT Assistant* Mar 07:7; *CPT Changes: An Insider's View* 2007

➡ *Clinical Examples in Radiology* Winter 07:6

(Use 76814 in conjunction with 76813)

76815 Ultrasound, pregnant uterus, real time with image documentation, limited (eg, fetal heart beat, placental location, fetal position and/or qualitative amniotic fluid volume), 1 or more fetuses

➡ *CPT Assistant* Apr 97:2, Nov 97:25, Oct 01:3, Dec 01:6, Aug 02:2, Mar 03:7, Nov 03:14; *CPT Changes: An Insider's View* 2003

➡ *Clinical Examples in Radiology* Winter 07:6-7

(Use 76815 only once per exam and not per element)

(To report first trimester fetal nuchal translucency measurement, see 76813, 76814)

76816 Ultrasound, pregnant uterus, real time with image documentation, follow-up (eg, re-evaluation of fetal size by measuring standard growth parameters and amniotic fluid volume, re-evaluation of organ system(s) suspected or confirmed to be abnormal on a previous scan), transabdominal approach, per fetus

➡ *CPT Assistant* Apr 97:2, Oct 01:3, Aug 02:2, Mar 03:7; *CPT Changes: An Insider's View* 2003

(Report 76816 with modifier 59 for each additional fetus examined in a multiple pregnancy)

76817 Ultrasound, pregnant uterus, real time with image documentation, transvaginal

➡ *CPT Assistant* Mar 03:7; *CPT Changes: An Insider's View* 2003

(For non-obstetrical transvaginal ultrasound, use 76830)

(If transvaginal examination is done in addition to transabdominal obstetrical ultrasound exam, use 76817 in addition to appropriate transabdominal exam code)

76818 Fetal biophysical profile; with non-stress testing

➡ *CPT Assistant* Apr 97:2, May 98:10, Sep 01:4, Oct 01:3, Dec 01:6, Oct 04:10; *CPT Changes: An Insider's View* 2001

76819 without non-stress testing

➡ *CPT Assistant* Sep 01:8, Dec 01:6; *CPT Changes: An Insider's View* 2001, 2002

(Fetal biophysical profile assessments for the second and any additional fetuses, should be reported separately by code 76818 or 76819 with the modifier 59 appended)

(For amniotic fluid index without non-stress test, use 76815)

76820 Doppler velocimetry, fetal; umbilical artery

➡ *CPT Assistant* Dec 05:3; *CPT Changes: An Insider's View* 2005

76821 middle cerebral artery

➡ *CPT Assistant* Dec 05:3; *CPT Changes: An Insider's View* 2005

76825 Echocardiography, fetal, cardiovascular system, real time with image documentation (2D), with or without M-mode recording;

➡ *CPT Assistant* Apr 97:2, Aug 02:2

76826 follow-up or repeat study

➡ *CPT Assistant* Apr 97:2, Aug 02:2

76827 Doppler echocardiography, fetal, pulsed wave and/or continuous wave with spectral display; complete

➡ *CPT Assistant* Apr 97:2, Aug 02:2, Dec 05:3; *CPT Changes: An Insider's View* 2005

76828 follow-up or repeat study

➡ *CPT Assistant* Apr 97:2, Aug 02:2, Dec 05:3

(To report the use of color mapping, use 93325)

Nonobstetrical

Code 76856 includes the complete evaluation of the female pelvic anatomy. Elements of this examination include a description and measurements of the uterus and adnexal structures, measurement of the endometrium, measurement of the bladder (when applicable), and a description of any pelvic pathology (eg, ovarian cysts, uterine leiomyomata, free pelvic fluid).

Code 76856 is also applicable to a complete evaluation of the male pelvis. Elements of the examination include evaluation and measurement (when applicable) of the urinary bladder, evaluation of the prostate and seminal vesicles to the extent that they are visualized transabdominally, and any pelvic pathology (eg, bladder tumor, enlarged prostate, free pelvic fluid, pelvic abscess).

Code 76857 represents a focused examination limited to the assessment of one or more elements listed in code 76856 and/or the reevaluation of one or more pelvic abnormalities previously demonstrated on ultrasound. Code 76857, rather than 76770, should be utilized if the urinary bladder alone (ie, not including the kidneys) is imaged, whereas code 51798 should be utilized if a bladder volume or post-void residual measurement is obtained without imaging the bladder.

Use of ultrasound, without thorough evaluation of organ(s) or anatomic region, image documentation, and final, written report, is not separately reportable.

76830 Ultrasound, transvaginal
➔ *CPT Assistant* Aug 96:10, Jul 99:8, Aug 02:2, Mar 03:7, Dec 05:3, Feb 09:22; *CPT Changes: An Insider's View* 2002
➔ *Clinical Examples in Radiology* Inaugural 04:6-7, Spring 08:9

(For obstetrical transvaginal ultrasound, use 76817)

(If transvaginal examination is done in addition to transabdominal non-obstetrical ultrasound exam, use 76830 in addition to appropriate transabdominal exam code)

76831 Saline infusion sonohysterography (SIS), including color flow Doppler, when performed
➔ *CPT Assistant* Nov 97:25, Jul 99:8, Dec 05:3, Mar 09:11; *CPT Changes: An Insider's View* 2004

(For introduction of saline for saline infusion sonohysterography, use 58340)

76856 Ultrasound, pelvic (nonobstetric), real time with image documentation; complete
➔ *CPT Assistant* Oct 01:3, Dec 05:3, Jan 06:47, Mar 07:7, Feb 09:22; *CPT Changes: An Insider's View* 2002, 2007
➔ *Clinical Examples in Radiology* Inaugural 04:6-7, Spring 08:9

76857 limited or follow-up (eg, for follicles)
➔ *CPT Assistant* Jun 97:10, Oct 01:3, Dec 05:3, Sep 07:10
➔ *Clinical Examples in Radiology* Spring 08:9

Genitalia

76870 Ultrasound, scrotum and contents
➔ *CPT Assistant* May 05:3; *CPT Changes: An Insider's View* 2002

76872 Ultrasound, transrectal;
➔ *CPT Assistant* May 96:3, Nov 99:42; *CPT Changes: An Insider's View* 2000, 2004

76873 prostate volume study for brachytherapy treatment planning (separate procedure)
➔ *CPT Assistant* Nov 99:42; *CPT Changes: An Insider's View* 2000

Extremities

76880 Ultrasound, extremity, nonvascular, real time with image documentation
➔ *CPT Assistant* Mar 07:7; *CPT Changes: An Insider's View* 2002, 2007

76885 Ultrasound, infant hips, real time with imaging documentation; dynamic (requiring physician manipulation)
➔ *CPT Assistant* Nov 97:25; *CPT Changes: An Insider's View* 2002

76886 limited, static (not requiring physician manipulation)
➔ *CPT Assistant* Nov 97:25; *CPT Changes: An Insider's View* 2002

Ultrasonic Guidance Procedures

76930 Ultrasonic guidance for pericardiocentesis, imaging supervision and interpretation
➔ *CPT Changes: An Insider's View* 2001

76932 Ultrasonic guidance for endomyocardial biopsy, imaging supervision and interpretation
➔ *CPT Changes: An Insider's View* 2001

76936 Ultrasound guided compression repair of arterial pseudoaneurysm or arteriovenous fistulae (includes diagnostic ultrasound evaluation, compression of lesion and imaging)

+ 76937 Ultrasound guidance for vascular access requiring ultrasound evaluation of potential access sites, documentation of selected vessel patency, concurrent realtime ultrasound visualization of vascular needle entry, with permanent recording and reporting (List separately in addition to code for primary procedure)
➔ *CPT Assistant* Dec 04:13, Jan 09:7; *CPT Changes: An Insider's View* 2004
➔ *Clinical Examples in Radiology* Inaugural 04:1-2, Winter 05:5-6, Summer 06:8-9, Spring 08:7,8, Fall 08:5, 6, Spring 09:8, 10, Winter 09:8, 9

▶(Do not use 76937 in conjunction with 37760, 37761, or 76942)◀

(If extremity venous non-invasive vascular diagnostic study is performed separate from venous access guidance, use 93965, 93970 or 93971)

76940 Ultrasound guidance for, and monitoring of, parenchymal tissue ablation
➔ *CPT Assistant* Oct 02:2, Mar 07:7; *CPT Changes: An Insider's View* 2004, 2007
➔ *Clinical Examples in Radiology* Spring 08:1,2

(Do not report 76940 in conjunction with 76998)

(For ablation, see 32998, 47370-47382, 50592, 50593)

76941 Ultrasonic guidance for intrauterine fetal transfusion or cordocentesis, imaging supervision and interpretation
➔ *CPT Changes: An Insider's View* 2001

(For procedure, see 36460, 59012)

76942 Ultrasonic guidance for needle placement (eg, biopsy, aspiration, injection, localization device), imaging supervision and interpretation
➔ *CPT Assistant* Fall 93:12, Fall 94:2, May 96:3, Jun 97:5, Oct 01:2, May 04:7, Dec 04:12, Apr 05:15-16, Aug 08:7, Mar 09:8; *CPT Changes: An Insider's View* 2001
➔ *Clinical Examples in Radiology* Summer 05:1, 2, 6, Fall 05:1, Summer 08:5, 6, Fall 08:2, 3, Winter 09:9

▶(Do not report 76942 in conjunction with 37760, 37661, 43232, 43237, 43242, 45341, 45342, or 76975)◀

76945 Ultrasonic guidance for chorionic villus sampling, imaging supervision and interpretation
➔ *CPT Changes: An Insider's View* 2001

(For procedure, use 59015)

76946   Ultrasonic guidance for amniocentesis, imaging supervision and interpretation

> *CPT Changes: An Insider's View* 2001

76948   Ultrasonic guidance for aspiration of ova, imaging supervision and interpretation

> *CPT Changes: An Insider's View* 2001

76950   Ultrasonic guidance for placement of radiation therapy fields

> *CPT Changes: An Insider's View* 2001

▶(For placement of interstitial device[s] for radiation therapy guidance, see 31627, 32553, 49411, 55876)◀

76965   Ultrasonic guidance for interstitial radioelement application

Other Procedures

76970   Ultrasound study follow-up (specify)

76975   Gastrointestinal endoscopic ultrasound, supervision and interpretation

> *CPT Assistant* Spring 94:5, May 04:7, Mar 09:8; *CPT Changes: An Insider's View* 2001

(Do not report 76975 in conjunction with 43231, 43232, 43237, 43238, 43242, 43259, 45341, 45342, or 76942)

76977   Ultrasound bone density measurement and interpretation, peripheral site(s), any method

> *CPT Assistant* Nov 98:21

76998   Ultrasonic guidance, intraoperative

> *CPT Assistant* Mar 07:7; *CPT Changes: An Insider's View* 2007

▶(Do not report 76998 in conjunction with 36475-36479, 37760, 37761, 47370-47382)◀

(For ultrasound guidance for open and laparoscopic radiofrequency tissue ablation, use 76940)

76999   Unlisted ultrasound procedure (eg, diagnostic, interventional)

> *CPT Changes: An Insider's View* 2003

Radiologic Guidance

Fluoroscopic Guidance

+ 77001   Fluoroscopic guidance for central venous access device placement, replacement (catheter only or complete), or removal (includes fluoroscopic guidance for vascular access and catheter manipulation, any necessary contrast injections through access site or catheter with related venography radiologic supervision and interpretation, and radiographic documentation of final catheter position) (List separately in addition to code for primary procedure)

> *CPT Assistant* Mar 07:7, Jul 08:9; *CPT Changes: An Insider's View* 2007

> *Clinical Examples in Radiology* Spring 08:7,8, Fall 08:5, 6, Winter 09:8, 9

(Do not use 77001 in conjunction with 77002)

(If formal extremity venography is performed from separate venous access and separately interpreted, use 36005 and 75820, 75822, 75825, or 75827)

77002   Fluoroscopic guidance for needle placement (eg, biopsy, aspiration, injection, localization device)

> *CPT Assistant* Feb 07:11, Mar 07:7, May 07:1, Jun 07:10, Jul 08:9, Aug 08:7, Dec 08:9; *CPT Changes: An Insider's View* 2007

> *Clinical Examples in Radiology* Summer 08:5, 6, Spring 09:6, 7, Winter 09:9

(See appropriate surgical code for procedure and anatomic location)

(77002 includes all radiographic arthrography with the exception of supervision and interpretation for CT and MR arthrography)

(Do not report 77002 in addition to 70332, 73040, 73085, 73115, 73525, 73580, 73615)

(77002 is included in the organ/anatomic specific radiological supervision and interpretation procedures 49440, 74320, 74355, 74445, 74470, 74475, 75809, 75810, 75885, 75887, 75980, 75982, 75989)

▲ **77003**   Fluoroscopic guidance and localization of needle or catheter tip for spine or paraspinous diagnostic or therapeutic injection procedures (epidural, transforaminal epidural, subarachnoid, or sacroiliac joint), including neurolytic agent destruction

> *CPT Assistant* Mar 07:7, Jul 08:9; *CPT Changes: An Insider's View* 2007, 2010

> *Clinical Examples in Radiology* Summer 08:9, 13, Winter 09:9

(Injection of contrast during fluoroscopic guidance and localization [77003] is included in 22526, 22527, 62263, 62264, 62267, 62270-62282, 62310-62319)

(Fluoroscopic guidance for subarachnoid puncture for diagnostic radiographic myelography is included in supervision and interpretation codes 72240-72270)

(For epidural or subarachnoid needle or catheter placement and injection, see 62270-62282, 62310-62319)

(For sacroiliac joint arthrography, see 27096, 73542. If formal arthrography is not performed and recorded, and a formal radiographic report is not issued, use 77003 for fluoroscopic guidance for sacroiliac joint injections)

▶(For paravertebral facet joint injection, see 64490-64495. For transforaminal epidural needle placement and injection, see 64479-64484)◀

(For destruction by neurolytic agent, see 64600-64680)

(For percutaneous or endoscopic lysis of epidural adhesions, 62263, 62264 include fluoroscopic guidance and localization)

Computed Tomography Guidance

77011   Computed tomography guidance for stereotactic localization
→ *CPT Assistant* Mar 07:7; *CPT Changes: An Insider's View* 2007

77012   Computed tomography guidance for needle placement (eg, biopsy, aspiration, injection, localization device), radiological supervision and interpretation
→ *CPT Assistant* Mar 07:7, May 07:1, Jun 07:10, Aug 08:7; *CPT Changes: An Insider's View* 2007
→ *Clinical Examples in Radiology* Summer 08:5, 6, Fall 08:3

77013   Computed tomography guidance for, and monitoring of, parenchymal tissue ablation
→ *CPT Assistant* Mar 07:7; *CPT Changes: An Insider's View* 2007

(Do not report 77013 in conjunction with 20982)

(For percutaneous radiofrequency ablation, see 32998, 47382, 50592, 50593)

77014   Computed tomography guidance for placement of radiation therapy fields
→ *CPT Assistant* Mar 07:7; *CPT Changes: An Insider's View* 2007

►(For placement of interstitial device[s] for radiation therapy guidance, see 31627, 32553, 49411, 55876)◄

Magnetic Resonance Guidance

77021   Magnetic resonance guidance for needle placement (eg, for biopsy, needle aspiration, injection, or placement of localization device) radiological supervision and interpretation
→ *CPT Assistant* Mar 07:7, May 07:1, Jun 07:10, Aug 08:7; *CPT Changes: An Insider's View* 2007
→ *Clinical Examples in Radiology* Summer 08:5, 6, 13, Fall 08:3

(For procedure, see appropriate organ or site)

77022   Magnetic resonance guidance for, and monitoring of, parenchymal tissue ablation
→ *CPT Assistant* Mar 07:7; *CPT Changes: An Insider's View* 2007

(For percutaneous radiofrequency ablation, see 32998, 47382, 50592, 50593)

(For focused ultrasound ablation treatment of uterine leiomyomata, see Category III codes 0071T, 0072T)

Other Radiologic Guidance

77031   Stereotactic localization guidance for breast biopsy or needle placement (eg, for wire localization or for injection), each lesion, radiological supervision and interpretation
→ *CPT Assistant* Mar 07:7; *CPT Changes: An Insider's View* 2007
→ *Clinical Examples in Radiology* Fall 08:3

(For procedure, see 10022, 19000-19103, 19290, 19291)

(For injection for sentinel node localization without lymphoscintigraphy, use 38792)

77032   Mammographic guidance for needle placement, breast (eg, for wire localization or for injection), each lesion, radiological supervision and interpretation
→ *CPT Assistant* Mar 07:7; *CPT Changes: An Insider's View* 2007
→ *Clinical Examples in Radiology* Fall 08:3, 4

(For procedure, see 10022, 19000, 19102, 19103, 19290, 19291)

(For injection for sentinel node localization without lymphoscintigraphy, use 38792)

Breast, Mammography

(For mammographic guidance for needle placement of breast lesion, use 77032)

+ 77051   Computer-aided detection (computer algorithm analysis of digital image data for lesion detection) with further physician review for interpretation, with or without digitization of film radiographic images; diagnostic mammography (List separately in addition to code for primary procedure)
→ *CPT Assistant* Mar 07:7, Apr 07:1; *CPT Changes: An Insider's View* 2007
→ *Clinical Examples in Radiology* Winter 09:7

(Use 77051 in conjunction with 77055, 77056)

+ 77052   screening mammography (List separately in addition to code for primary procedure)
→ *CPT Assistant* Mar 07:7, Apr 07:1; *CPT Changes: An Insider's View* 2007
→ *Clinical Examples in Radiology* Winter 09:6, 7, 8

(Use 77052 in conjunction with 77057)

77053   Mammary ductogram or galactogram, single duct, radiological supervision and interpretation
→ *CPT Assistant* Mar 07:7; *CPT Changes: An Insider's View* 2007

(For mammary ductogram or galactogram injection, use 19030)

77054   Mammary ductogram or galactogram, multiple ducts, radiological supervision and interpretation
→ *CPT Assistant* Mar 07:7; *CPT Changes: An Insider's View* 2007

77055   Mammography; unilateral
→ *CPT Assistant* Mar 07:7; *CPT Changes: An Insider's View* 2007
→ *Clinical Examples in Radiology* Fall 08:2, 4, Winter 09:7

77056   bilateral
→ *CPT Assistant* Mar 07:7; *CPT Changes: An Insider's View* 2007
→ *Clinical Examples in Radiology* Winter 09:7

(Use 77055, 77056 in conjunction with 77051 for computer-aided detection applied to a diagnostic mammogram)

77057 Screening mammography, bilateral (2-view film study of each breast)

→ *CPT Assistant* Mar 07:7; *CPT Changes: An Insider's View* 2007
➔ *Clinical Examples in Radiology* Winter 09:6, 7

(Use 77057 in conjunction with 77052 for computer-aided detection applied to a screening mammogram)

(For electrical impedance breast scan, use 76499)

Screening Mammography
77057

Mammogram

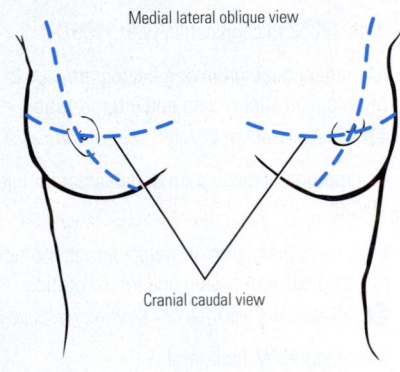

Medial lateral oblique view

Cranial caudal view

77058 Magnetic resonance imaging, breast, without and/or with contrast material(s); unilateral

→ *CPT Assistant* Mar 07:7; *CPT Changes: An Insider's View* 2007

77059 bilateral

→ *CPT Assistant* Mar 07:7, Jul 07:6; *CPT Changes: An Insider's View* 2007

Bone/Joint Studies

77071 Manual application of stress performed by physician for joint radiography, including contralateral joint if indicated

→ *CPT Assistant* Mar 07:7; *CPT Changes: An Insider's View* 2007

(For radiographic interpretation of stressed images, see appropriate anatomic site and number of views)

77072 Bone age studies

→ *CPT Assistant* Mar 07:7; *CPT Changes: An Insider's View* 2007

77073 Bone length studies (orthoroentgenogram, scanogram)

→ *CPT Assistant* Mar 07:7; *CPT Changes: An Insider's View* 2007
➔ *Clinical Examples in Radiology* Summer 07:12, Fall 08:10

77074 Radiologic examination, osseous survey; limited (eg, for metastases)

→ *CPT Assistant* Mar 07:7; *CPT Changes: An Insider's View* 2007

77075 complete (axial and appendicular skeleton)

→ *CPT Assistant* Mar 07:7; *CPT Changes: An Insider's View* 2007

77076 Radiologic examination, osseous survey, infant

→ *CPT Assistant* Mar 07:7; *CPT Changes: An Insider's View* 2007

77077 Joint survey, single view, 2 or more joints (specify)

→ *CPT Assistant* Mar 07:7; *CPT Changes: An Insider's View* 2007

77078 Computed tomography, bone mineral density study, 1 or more sites; axial skeleton (eg, hips, pelvis, spine)

→ *CPT Assistant* Mar 07:7; *CPT Changes: An Insider's View* 2007

77079 appendicular skeleton (peripheral) (eg, radius, wrist, heel)

→ *CPT Assistant* Mar 07:7; *CPT Changes: An Insider's View* 2007

77080 Dual-energy X-ray absorptiometry (DXA), bone density study, 1 or more sites; axial skeleton (eg, hips, pelvis, spine)

→ *CPT Assistant* Mar 07:7; *CPT Changes: An Insider's View* 2007
➔ *Clinical Examples in Radiology* Fall 07:11

77081 appendicular skeleton (peripheral) (eg, radius, wrist, heel)

→ *CPT Assistant* Mar 07:7; *CPT Changes: An Insider's View* 2007

77082 vertebral fracture assessment

→ *CPT Assistant* Mar 07:7; *CPT Changes: An Insider's View* 2007

(For dual energy x-ray absorptiometry [DXA] body composition study, use 76499)

77083 Radiographic absorptiometry (eg, photodensitometry, radiogrammetry), 1 or more sites

→ *CPT Assistant* Mar 07:7; *CPT Changes: An Insider's View* 2007

77084 Magnetic resonance (eg, proton) imaging, bone marrow blood supply

→ *CPT Assistant* Mar 07:7; *CPT Changes: An Insider's View* 2007

Radiation Oncology

Listings for Radiation Oncology provide for teletherapy and brachytherapy to include initial consultation, clinical treatment planning, simulation, medical radiation physics, dosimetry, treatment devices, special services, and clinical treatment management procedures. They include normal follow-up care during course of treatment and for three months following its completion.

When a service or procedure is provided that is not listed in this edition of the CPT codebook it should be identified by a Special Report (see page 304) and one of the following unlisted procedure codes:

77299 Unlisted procedure, therapeutic radiology clinical treatment planning

77399 Unlisted procedure, medical radiation physics, dosimetry and treatment devices, and special services

77499 Unlisted procedure, therapeutic radiology treatment management

77799 Unlisted procedure, clinical brachytherapy

For treatment by injectable or ingestible isotopes, see subsection **Nuclear Medicine.**

Consultation: Clinical Management

Preliminary consultation, evaluation of patient prior to decision to treat, or full medical care (in addition to treatment management) when provided by the therapeutic radiologist may be identified by the appropriate procedure codes from **Evaluation and Management, Medicine,** or **Surgery** sections.

Clinical Treatment Planning (External and Internal Sources)

The clinical treatment planning process is a complex service including interpretation of special testing, tumor localization, treatment volume determination, treatment time/dosage determination, choice of treatment modality, determination of number and size of treatment ports, selection of appropriate treatment devices, and other procedures.

Definitions

Simple planning requires a single treatment area of interest encompassed in a single port or simple parallel opposed ports with simple or no blocking.

Intermediate planning requires 3 or more converging ports, 2 separate treatment areas, multiple blocks, or special time dose constraints.

Complex planning requires highly complex blocking, custom shielding blocks, tangential ports, special wedges or compensators, three or more separate treatment areas, rotational or special beam considerations, combination of therapeutic modalities.

77261	Therapeutic radiology treatment planning; simple
	➔ *CPT Assistant* Fall 91:12, 15, Oct 97:2
77262	intermediate
	➔ *CPT Assistant* Fall 91:12, 15, Oct 97:2, Apr 09:3
77263	complex
	➔ *CPT Assistant* Fall 91:15, Oct 97:2, Apr 09:3

Definitions

Simple simulation of a single treatment area with either a single port or parallel opposed ports. Simple or no blocking.

Intermediate simulation of three or more converging ports, two separate treatment areas, multiple blocks.

Complex simulation of tangential portals, three or more treatment areas, rotation or arc therapy, complex blocking, custom shielding blocks, brachytherapy source verification, hyperthermia probe verification, any use of contrast materials.

Three-dimensional (3D) computer-generated 3D reconstruction of tumor volume and surrounding critical normal tissue structures from direct CT scans and/or MRI data in preparation for non-coplanar or coplanar therapy. The simulation uses documented 3D beam's eye view volume-dose displays of multiple or moving beams. Documentation with 3D volume reconstruction and dose distribution is required.

Simulation may be carried out on a dedicated simulator, a radiation therapy treatment unit, or diagnostic X-ray machine.

77280	Therapeutic radiology simulation-aided field setting; simple
	➔ *CPT Assistant* Fall 91:15, Oct 97:2, Nov 97:26, Apr 09:10
	➔ *Clinical Examples in Radiology* Summer 08:12
77285	intermediate
	➔ *CPT Assistant* Fall 91:15, Oct 97:3
	➔ *Clinical Examples in Radiology* Summer 08:12
77290	complex
	➔ *CPT Assistant* Fall 91:12, 15, Oct 97:3, Apr 09:3, Apr 09:10
	➔ *Clinical Examples in Radiology* Summer 08:12
77295	3-dimensional
	➔ *CPT Assistant* Fall 91:15, Oct 97:3, Nov 97:26, May 05:7, Oct 07:1
77299	Unlisted procedure, therapeutic radiology clinical treatment planning

Medical Radiation Physics, Dosimetry, Treatment Devices, and Special Services

77300 Basic radiation dosimetry calculation, central axis depth dose calculation, TDF, NSD, gap calculation, off axis factor, tissue inhomogeneity factors, calculation of non-ionizing radiation surface and depth dose, as required during course of treatment, only when prescribed by the treating physician

➜ *CPT Assistant* Fall 91:14, Oct 97:3, Dec 08:9; *CPT Changes: An Insider's View* 2002

➜ *Clinical Examples in Radiology* Summer 08:12

77301 Intensity modulated radiotherapy plan, including dose-volume histograms for target and critical structure partial tolerance specifications

➜ *CPT Assistant* Mar 05:1, 6, May 05:7, Oct 07:1; *CPT Changes: An Insider's View* 2002

(Dose plan is optimized using inverse or forward planning technique for modulated beam delivery [eg, binary, dynamic MLC] to create highly conformal dose distribution. Computer plan distribution must be verified for positional accuracy based on dosimetric verification of the intensity map with verification of treatment set-up and interpretation of verification methodology)

77305 Teletherapy, isodose plan (whether hand or computer calculated); simple (1 or 2 parallel opposed unmodified ports directed to a single area of interest)

➜ *CPT Assistant* Fall 91:15, Oct 97:3

77310 intermediate (3 or more treatment ports directed to a single area of interest)

➜ *CPT Assistant* Fall 91:15, Oct 97:3

77315 complex (mantle or inverted Y, tangential ports, the use of wedges, compensators, complex blocking, rotational beam, or special beam considerations)

➜ *CPT Assistant* Fall 91:15, Oct 97:3

(Only 1 teletherapy isodose plan may be reported for a given course of therapy to a specific treatment area)

77321 Special teletherapy port plan, particles, hemibody, total body

➜ *CPT Assistant* Fall 91:14, Oct 97:4

77326 Brachytherapy isodose plan; simple (calculation made from single plane, 1 to 4 sources/ribbon application, remote afterloading brachytherapy, 1 to 8 sources)

➜ *CPT Assistant* Winter 91:17, Apr 09:3; *CPT Changes: An Insider's View* 2003

(For definition of source/ribbon, see page 332)

77327 intermediate (multiplane dosage calculations, application involving 5 to 10 sources/ribbons, remote afterloading brachytherapy, 9 to 12 sources)

➜ *CPT Assistant* Winter 91:17, Apr 09:3

77328 complex (multiplane isodose plan, volume implant calculations, over 10 sources/ribbons used, special spatial reconstruction, remote afterloading brachytherapy, over 12 sources)

➜ *CPT Assistant* Winter 91:17, Apr 09:3

77331 Special dosimetry (eg, TLD, microdosimetry) (specify), only when prescribed by the treating physician

➜ *CPT Assistant* Fall 91:13, Oct 97:4

77332 Treatment devices, design and construction; simple (simple block, simple bolus)

➜ *CPT Assistant* Oct 97:4

➜ *Clinical Examples in Radiology* Summer 07:10, Summer 08:12

77333 intermediate (multiple blocks, stents, bite blocks, special bolus)

➜ *CPT Assistant* Oct 97:3

➜ *Clinical Examples in Radiology* Summer 07:10, Summer 08:12

77334 complex (irregular blocks, special shields, compensators, wedges, molds or casts)

➜ *CPT Assistant* Fall 91:14, Oct 97:4, Dec 08:9

➜ *Clinical Examples in Radiology* Summer 07:9,10, Summer 08:12

77336 Continuing medical physics consultation, including assessment of treatment parameters, quality assurance of dose delivery, and review of patient treatment documentation in support of the radiation oncologist, reported per week of therapy

➜ *CPT Assistant* Fall 91:15, Oct 97:4, Nov 98:21

➜ *Clinical Examples in Radiology* Summer 07:9,10, Summer 08:12

● **77338** Multi-leaf collimator (MLC) device(s) for intensity modulated radiation therapy (IMRT), design and construction per IMRT plan

➜ *CPT Changes: An Insider's View* 2010

▶(Do not report 77338 more than once per IMRT plan)◄

▶(For immobilization in IMRT treatment, see 77332-77334)◄

▶(Do not report 77338 in conjunction with 0073T, compensator based IMRT)◄

77370 Special medical radiation physics consultation

➜ *CPT Assistant* Fall 91:14, Oct 97:4

➜ *Clinical Examples in Radiology* Summer 08:12

Stereotactic Radiation Treatment Delivery

⊙▲ **77371** Radiation treatment delivery, stereotactic radiosurgery (SRS), complete course of treatment of cranial lesion(s) consisting of 1 session; multi-source Cobalt 60 based

➜ *CPT Assistant* Mar 07:7, Oct 07:1; *CPT Changes: An Insider's View* 2007, 2008, 2010

77372 linear accelerator based

➜ *CPT Assistant* Mar 07:7, Oct 07:1; *CPT Changes: An Insider's View* 2007, 2008

(For radiation treatment management, use 77432)

77373   Stereotactic body radiation therapy, treatment delivery, per fraction to 1 or more lesions, including image guidance, entire course not to exceed 5 fractions

➲ *CPT Assistant* Mar 07:7, Oct 07:1; *CPT Changes: An Insider's View* 2007

(Do not report 77373 in conjunction with 77401-77416, 77418)

(For single fraction cranial lesion[s], see 77371, 77372)

Other Procedures

77399   Unlisted procedure, medical radiation physics, dosimetry and treatment devices, and special services

➲ *CPT Assistant* Nov 98:21

Radiation Treatment Delivery

(Radiation treatment delivery [77401-77416] recognizes the technical component and the various energy levels)

▶(For intra-fraction localization and tracking of target, use 0197T)◀

77401   Radiation treatment delivery, superficial and/or ortho voltage

➲ *CPT Assistant* Apr 03:14, Aug 03:10, Oct 07:1

➲ *Clinical Examples in Radiology* Summer 08:12

77402   Radiation treatment delivery, single treatment area, single port or parallel opposed ports, simple blocks or no blocks; up to 5 MeV

➲ *CPT Assistant* Apr 03:14, Aug 03:10, Oct 07:1

➲ *Clinical Examples in Radiology* Spring 07:7-9, 12, Summer 08:12

77403   6-10 MeV

➲ *CPT Assistant* Apr 03:14

➲ *Clinical Examples in Radiology* Spring 07:7-9, 12, Summer 08:12

77404   11-19 MeV

➲ *CPT Assistant* Apr 03:14

➲ *Clinical Examples in Radiology* Spring 07:7-9, 12, Summer 08:12

77406   20 MeV or greater

➲ *CPT Assistant* Apr 03:14, Aug 03:10, Oct 07:1

➲ *Clinical Examples in Radiology* Spring 07:7-9, 12, Summer 08:12

77407   Radiation treatment delivery, 2 separate treatment areas, 3 or more ports on a single treatment area, use of multiple blocks; up to 5 MeV

➲ *CPT Assistant* Apr 03:14, Aug 03:10, Oct 07:1

➲ *Clinical Examples in Radiology* Spring 07:7-9, 12, Summer 08:12

77408   6-10 MeV

➲ *CPT Assistant* Apr 03:14

➲ *Clinical Examples in Radiology* Spring 07:7-9, 12, Summer 08:12

77409   11-19 MeV

➲ *CPT Assistant* Apr 03:14

➲ *Clinical Examples in Radiology* Spring 07:7, Summer 08:12

77411   20 MeV or greater

➲ *CPT Assistant* Apr 03:14, Aug 03:10, Oct 07:1

➲ *Clinical Examples in Radiology* Spring 07:7-9, 12, Summer 08:12

77412   Radiation treatment delivery, 3 or more separate treatment areas, custom blocking, tangential ports, wedges, rotational beam, compensators, electron beam; up to 5 MeV

➲ *CPT Assistant* Apr 03:14, Aug 03:10, Oct 07:1; *CPT Changes: An Insider's View* 2006

➲ *Clinical Examples in Radiology* Winter 06:20, Spring 07:7-9, 12, Summer 08:12

77413   6-10 MeV

➲ *CPT Assistant* Fall 91:14, Apr 03:14

➲ *Clinical Examples in Radiology* Spring 07:7-9, 12, Summer 08:12

77414   11-19 MeV

➲ *CPT Assistant* Apr 03:14

➲ *Clinical Examples in Radiology* Spring 07:7-9, 12, Summer 08:12

77416   20 MeV or greater

➲ *CPT Assistant* Aug 03:10, Oct 07:1

➲ *Clinical Examples in Radiology* Spring 07:7-9, 12, Summer 08:12

77417   Therapeutic radiology port film(s)

➲ *CPT Assistant* Fall 91:14, Dec 97:11, Feb 06:14, Oct 07:1

77418   Intensity modulated treatment delivery, single or multiple fields/arcs, via narrow spatially and temporally modulated beams, binary, dynamic MLC, per treatment session

➲ *CPT Assistant* Mar 05:1, 6, May 05:7; *CPT Changes: An Insider's View* 2002, 2005

➲ *Clinical Examples in Radiology* Summer 07:9

(For intensity modulated treatment planning, use 77301)

(For compensator-based beam modulation treatment delivery, use Category III code 0073T)

77421   Stereoscopic X-ray guidance for localization of target volume for the delivery of radiation therapy

➲ *CPT Assistant* Oct 07:1; *CPT Changes: An Insider's View* 2006

➲ *Clinical Examples in Radiology* Winter 06:18, Fall 08:10

(Do not report 77421 in conjunction with 77432, 77435)

▶(For placement of interstitial device[s] for radiation therapy guidance, see 31627, 32553, 49411, 55876)◀

Neutron Beam Treatment Delivery

77422   High energy neutron radiation treatment delivery; single treatment area using a single port or parallel-opposed ports with no blocks or simple blocking

➲ *CPT Changes: An Insider's View* 2006

➲ *Clinical Examples in Radiology* Winter 06:18

77423 1 or more isocenter(s) with coplanar or non-coplanar geometry with blocking and/or wedge, and/or compensator(s)

> *CPT Changes: An Insider's View* 2006

> *Clinical Examples in Radiology* Winter 06:18

Radiation Treatment Management

Radiation treatment management is reported in units of five fractions or treatment sessions, regardless of the actual time period in which the services are furnished. The services need not be furnished on consecutive days. Multiple fractions representing two or more treatment sessions furnished on the same day may be counted separately as long as there has been a distinct break in therapy sessions, and the fractions are of the character usually furnished on different days. Code 77427 is also reported if there are three or four fractions beyond a multiple of five at the end of a course of treatment; one or two fractions beyond a multiple of five at the end of a course of treatment are not reported separately. The professional services furnished during treatment management typically consist of:

- Review of port films;

- Review of dosimetry, dose delivery, and treatment parameters;

- Review of patient treatment set-up;

- Examination of patient for medical evaluation and management (eg, assessment of the patient's response to treatment, coordination of care and treatment, review of imaging and/or lab test results).

77427 Radiation treatment management, 5 treatments

> *CPT Assistant* Nov 99:42, Feb 00:7, Oct 07:1; *CPT Changes: An Insider's View* 2000

> *Clinical Examples in Radiology* Summer 08:12

77431 Radiation therapy management with complete course of therapy consisting of 1 or 2 fractions only

> *CPT Assistant* Winter 90:10, Oct 97:4

> *Clinical Examples in Radiology* Summer 08:12

(77431 is not to be used to fill in the last week of a long course of therapy)

77432 Stereotactic radiation treatment management of cranial lesion(s) (complete course of treatment consisting of 1 session)

> *CPT Assistant* Oct 97:4; *CPT Changes: An Insider's View* 2008

(The same physician should not report both stereotactic radiosurgery services [61796-61800] and radiation treatment management [77432 or 77435] for cranial lesions)

(For stereotactic body radiation therapy treatment, use 77435)

77435 Stereotactic body radiation therapy, treatment management, per treatment course, to 1 or more lesions, including image guidance, entire course not to exceed 5 fractions

> *CPT Assistant* Mar 07:7, Oct 07:1; *CPT Changes: An Insider's View* 2007

(Do not report 77435 in conjunction with 77427-77432)

(The same physician should not report both stereotactic radiosurgery services [63620, 63621] and radiation treatment management [77435] for extracranial lesions)

77470 Special treatment procedure (eg, total body irradiation, hemibody radiation, per oral, endocavitary or intraoperative cone irradiation)

> *CPT Assistant* Winter 91:22, Oct 97:1, Apr 09:3; *CPT Changes: An Insider's View* 2001

> *Clinical Examples in Radiology* Summer 08:12

(77470 assumes that the procedure is performed 1 or more times during the course of therapy, in addition to daily or weekly patient management)

77499 Unlisted procedure, therapeutic radiology treatment management

> *CPT Assistant* Nov 99:42, Feb 00:7; *CPT Changes: An Insider's View* 2000

Proton Beam Treatment Delivery

Definitions

Simple proton treatment delivery to a single treatment area utilizing a single non-tangential/oblique port, custom block with compensation (77522) and without compensation (77520).

Intermediate proton treatment delivery to one or more treatment areas utilizing two or more ports or one or more tangential/oblique ports, with custom blocks and compensators.

Complex proton treatment delivery to one or more treatment areas utilizing two or more ports per treatment area with matching or patching fields and/or multiple isocenters, with custom blocks and compensators.

77520 Proton treatment delivery; simple, without compensation

> *CPT Assistant* Nov 99:43; *CPT Changes: An Insider's View* 2000, 2001

77522 simple, with compensation

> *CPT Changes: An Insider's View* 2001

77523 intermediate

> *CPT Assistant* Nov 99:43; *CPT Changes: An Insider's View* 2000, 2001

77525 complex

> *CPT Changes: An Insider's View* 2001

Hyperthermia

Hyperthermia treatments as listed in this section include external (superficial and deep), interstitial, and intracavitary.

Radiation therapy when given concurrently is listed separately.

Hyperthermia is used only as an adjunct to radiation therapy or chemotherapy. It may be induced by a variety of sources (eg, microwave, ultrasound, low energy radio-frequency conduction, or by probes).

The listed treatments include management during the course of therapy and follow-up care for three months after completion.

Preliminary consultation is not included (see **Evaluation and Management** 99241-99255).

Physics planning and interstitial insertion of temperature sensors, and use of external or interstitial heat generating sources are included.

The following descriptors are included in the treatment schedule:

⊙ **77600** Hyperthermia, externally generated; superficial (ie, heating to a depth of 4 cm or less)
➜ *CPT Assistant* Winter 91:22

⊙ **77605** deep (ie, heating to depths greater than 4 cm)
➜ *CPT Assistant* Winter 91:22

⊙ **77610** Hyperthermia generated by interstitial probe(s); 5 or fewer interstitial applicators
➜ *CPT Assistant* Winter 91:22

⊙ **77615** more than 5 interstitial applicators
➜ *CPT Assistant* Winter 91:22

Clinical Intracavitary Hyperthermia

77620 Hyperthermia generated by intracavitary probe(s)
➜ *CPT Assistant* Winter 91:22

Clinical Brachytherapy

Clinical brachytherapy requires the use of either natural or man-made radioelements applied into or around a treatment field of interest. The supervision of radioelements and dose interpretation are performed solely by the therapeutic radiologist.

Services 77750-77799 include admission to the hospital and daily visits.

For insertion of ovoids and tandems, use 57155.

For insertion of Heyman capsules, use 58346.

Definitions

(Sources refer to intracavitary placement or permanent interstitial placement; ribbons refer to temporary interstitial placement)

A simple application has one to four sources/ribbons.

An intermediate application has five to 10 sources/ribbons.

A complex application has greater than 10 sources/ribbons.

(For high dose rate electronic brachytherapy, per fraction, use Category III code 0182T)

77750 Infusion or instillation of radioelement solution (includes 3-month follow-up care)
➜ *CPT Assistant* Sep 05:1; *CPT Changes: An Insider's View* 2005

(For administration of radiolabeled monoclonal antibodies, use 79403)

(For non-antibody radiopharmaceutical therapy by intravenous administration only, not including 3-month follow-up care, use 79101)

77761 Intracavitary radiation source application; simple
➜ *CPT Assistant* Winter 91:23, Jan 96:7, Mar 99:3, Feb 02:7, Sep 05:1; *CPT Changes: An Insider's View* 2001

77762 intermediate
➜ *CPT Assistant* Winter 91:23, Feb 02:7, Sep 05:1

77763 complex
➜ *CPT Assistant* Winter 91:23, Mar 99:3, Feb 02:7, Sep 05:1

(Do not report 77761-77763 in conjunction with Category III code 0182T)

77776 Interstitial radiation source application; simple
➜ *CPT Assistant* Winter 91:23, Sep 05:1, Aug 08:7; *CPT Changes: An Insider's View* 2001

77777 intermediate
➜ *CPT Assistant* Winter 91:23, Sep 05:1, May 07:1, Aug 08:7

77778 complex
➜ *CPT Assistant* Winter 91:23, Apr 04:6, Sep 05:1, May 07:1

(Do not report 77776-77778 in conjunction with Category III code 0182T)

(77781 has been deleted. To report, see 77785, 77786)

(77782-77784 have been deleted. To report, see 77785-77787)

77785 Remote afterloading high dose rate radionuclide brachytherapy; 1 channel
➜ *CPT Changes: An Insider's View* 2009

77786 2-12 channels
➜ *CPT Changes: An Insider's View* 2009

77787 over 12 channels
➜ *CPT Changes: An Insider's View* 2009

▶ (Do not report ... ◀

77789 Surface application of radiation source
➜ *CPT Assistant* Sep 05:1; *CPT Changes: An Insider's View* 2001

(Do not report 77789 in conjunction with Category III code 0182T)

77790 Supervision, handling, loading of radiation source
➜ *CPT Assistant* Sep 05:1; *CPT Changes: An Insider's View* 2001

77799 Unlisted procedure, clinical brachytherapy
➜ *CPT Assistant* Sep 05:1

Nuclear Medicine

Listed procedures may be performed independently or in the course of overall medical care. If the physician providing these services is also responsible for diagnostic work-up and/or follow-up care of patient, see appropriate sections also.

Radioimmunoassay tests are found in the **Clinical Pathology** section (codes 82000-84999). These codes can be appropriately used by any specialist performing such tests in a laboratory licensed and/or certified for radioimmunoassays. The reporting of these tests is not confined to clinical pathology laboratories alone.

The services listed do not include the radiopharmaceutical or drug. Diagnostic and therapeutic radiopharmaceuticals and drugs supplied by the physician should be reported separately using the appropriate supply code(s), in addition to the procedure code.

Diagnostic

Endocrine System

78000   Thyroid uptake; single determination
> *CPT Assistant* Dec 05:7, 9, Jan 07:31

78001   multiple determinations
> *CPT Assistant* Jan 07:31

78003   stimulation, suppression or discharge (not including initial uptake studies)
> *CPT Assistant* Jan 07:31

78006   Thyroid imaging, with uptake; single determination
> *CPT Assistant* Jan 07:31

78007   multiple determinations
> *CPT Assistant* Jan 07:31

78010   Thyroid imaging; only
> *CPT Assistant* Jan 07:31

78011   with vascular flow
> *CPT Assistant* Jan 07:31

78015   Thyroid carcinoma metastases imaging; limited area (eg, neck and chest only)
> *CPT Assistant* Nov 98:21, Jan 07:31

78016   with additional studies (eg, urinary recovery)
> *CPT Assistant* Jan 07:31

78018   whole body
> *CPT Assistant* Apr 99:4, Jan 07:31

+ 78020   Thyroid carcinoma metastases uptake (List separately in addition to code for primary procedure)
> *CPT Assistant* Nov 98:21, Apr 99:4, Jan 07:31

(Use 78020 in conjunction with 78018 only)

78070   Parathyroid imaging
> *CPT Assistant* Jan 07:31

78075   Adrenal imaging, cortex and/or medulla
> *CPT Assistant* Jan 07:31

78099   Unlisted endocrine procedure, diagnostic nuclear medicine
> *CPT Assistant* Dec 05:7, Jan 07:31

(For chemical analysis, see **Chemistry** section)

Hematopoietic, Reticuloendothelial and Lymphatic System

78102   Bone marrow imaging; limited area
> *CPT Assistant* Dec 05:7

78103   multiple areas

78104   whole body

78110   Plasma volume, radiopharmaceutical volume-dilution technique (separate procedure); single sampling

78111   multiple samplings

78120   Red cell volume determination (separate procedure); single sampling

78121   multiple samplings

78122   Whole blood volume determination, including separate measurement of plasma volume and red cell volume (radiopharmaceutical volume-dilution technique)

78130   Red cell survival study;

78135   differential organ/tissue kinetics (eg, splenic and/or hepatic sequestration)

78140   Labeled red cell sequestration, differential organ/tissue (eg, splenic and/or hepatic)

78185   Spleen imaging only, with or without vascular flow

(If combined with liver study, use procedures 78215 and 78216)

78190   Kinetics, study of platelet survival, with or without differential organ/tissue localization

78191   Platelet survival study

78195   Lymphatics and lymph nodes imaging
> *CPT Assistant* Nov 98:22, Jul 99:6, Nov 99:43, Dec 99:8, Sep 08:5; *CPT Changes: An Insider's View* 2000, 2002

(For sentinel node identification without scintigraphy imaging, use 38792)

(For sentinel node excision, see 38500-38542)

78199   Unlisted hematopoietic, reticuloendothelial and lymphatic procedure, diagnostic nuclear medicine
> *CPT Assistant* Dec 05:7

(For chemical analysis, see **Chemistry** section)

Gastrointestinal System

78201   Liver imaging; static only
> *CPT Assistant* Dec 05:7

78202   with vascular flow

         (For spleen imaging only, use 78185)

78205   Liver imaging (SPECT);
> *CPT Assistant* Nov 98:22

78206   with vascular flow
> *CPT Assistant* Nov 98:22

78215   Liver and spleen imaging; static only

78216   with vascular flow

78220   Liver function study with hepatobiliary agents, with serial images

78223   Hepatobiliary ductal system imaging, including gallbladder, with or without pharmacologic intervention, with or without quantitative measurement of gallbladder function

78230   Salivary gland imaging;

78231   with serial images

78232   Salivary gland function study

78258   Esophageal motility

78261   Gastric mucosa imaging

78262   Gastroesophageal reflux study

78264   Gastric emptying study

78267   Urea breath test, C-14 (isotopic); acquisition for analysis
> *CPT Assistant* Nov 99:43; *CPT Changes: An Insider's View* 2000, 2005
> *Clinical Examples in Radiology* Fall 07:9

78268   analysis
> *CPT Assistant* Nov 99:43; *CPT Changes: An Insider's View* 2000
> *Clinical Examples in Radiology* Fall 07:9

78270   Vitamin B-12 absorption study (eg, Schilling test); without intrinsic factor

78271   with intrinsic factor

78272   Vitamin B-12 absorption studies combined, with and without intrinsic factor

78278   Acute gastrointestinal blood loss imaging

78282   Gastrointestinal protein loss

78290   Intestine imaging (eg, ectopic gastric mucosa, Meckel's localization, volvulus)
> *CPT Changes: An Insider's View* 2002

78291   Peritoneal-venous shunt patency test (eg, for LeVeen, Denver shunt)

         (For injection procedure, use 49427)

78299   Unlisted gastrointestinal procedure, diagnostic nuclear medicine
> *CPT Assistant* Dec 05:7

Musculoskeletal System

Bone and joint imaging can be used in the diagnosis of a variety of inflammatory processes (eg, osteomyelitis), as well as for localization of primary and/or metastatic neoplasms.

78300   Bone and/or joint imaging; limited area
> *CPT Assistant* Mar 97:11, Dec 05:7
> *Clinical Examples in Radiology* Winter 09:5

78305   multiple areas
> *CPT Assistant* Mar 97:11
> *Clinical Examples in Radiology* Winter 09:5

78306   whole body
> *CPT Assistant* Mar 97:11, Jan 02:10, Jun 03:11
> *Clinical Examples in Radiology* Summer 06:7, 12, Winter 09:3, 4, 5

78315   3 phase study
> *CPT Assistant* Jan 02:10
> *Clinical Examples in Radiology* Summer 06:7, 12, Winter 09:4, 5

78320   tomographic (SPECT)
> *CPT Assistant* Mar 97:11, Jun 03:11, Jan 08:9
> *Clinical Examples in Radiology* Winter 09:4, 5

78350   Bone density (bone mineral content) study, 1 or more sites; single photon absorptiometry
> *CPT Assistant* Nov 97:26

78351   dual photon absorptiometry, 1 or more sites
> *CPT Assistant* Nov 97:26

         (For radiographic bone density [photodensitometry], use 77083)

78399   Unlisted musculoskeletal procedure, diagnostic nuclear medicine
> *CPT Assistant* Dec 05:7

Cardiovascular System

▶Myocardial perfusion and cardiac blood pool imaging studies may be performed at rest and/or during stress. When performed during exercise and/or pharmacologic stress, the appropriate stress testing code from the 93015-93018 series should be reported in addition to 78451-78454, 78472-78492.◀

78414   Determination of central c-v hemodynamics (non-imaging) (eg, ejection fraction with probe technique) with or without pharmacologic intervention or exercise, single or multiple determinations
> *CPT Assistant* Dec 05:7

78428   Cardiac shunt detection

78445   Non-cardiac vascular flow imaging (ie, angiography, venography)

● **78451**   Myocardial perfusion imaging, tomographic (SPECT) (including attenuation correction, qualitative or quantitative wall motion, ejection fraction by first pass or gated technique, additional quantification, when performed); single study, at rest or stress (exercise or pharmacologic)
➔ *CPT Changes: An Insider's View* 2010

● **78452**   multiple studies, at rest and/or stress (exercise or pharmacologic) and/or redistribution and/or rest reinjection
➔ *CPT Changes: An Insider's View* 2010

● **78453**   Myocardial perfusion imaging, planar (including qualitative or quantitative wall motion, ejection fraction by first pass or gated technique, additional quantification, when performed); single study, at rest or stress (exercise or pharmacologic)
➔ *CPT Changes: An Insider's View* 2010

● **78454**   multiple studies, at rest and/or stress (exercise or pharmacologic) and/or redistribution and/or rest reinjection
➔ *CPT Changes: An Insider's View* 2010

78456   Acute venous thrombosis imaging, peptide
➔ *CPT Assistant* Nov 99:43; *CPT Changes: An Insider's View* 2000

78457   Venous thrombosis imaging, venogram; unilateral
➔ *CPT Assistant* Nov 99:43; *CPT Changes: An Insider's View* 2000

78458   bilateral
➔ *CPT Assistant* Nov 99:43; *CPT Changes: An Insider's View* 2000

78459   Myocardial imaging, positron emission tomography (PET), metabolic evaluation
➔ *CPT Assistant* Jun 96:5, Nov 97:26

(For myocardial perfusion study, see 78491-78492)

▶(78460–78465 have been deleted. To report, see 78451–78454)◀

78466   Myocardial imaging, infarct avid, planar; qualitative or quantitative

78468   with ejection fraction by first pass technique

78469   tomographic SPECT with or without quantification

78472   Cardiac blood pool imaging, gated equilibrium; planar, single study at rest or stress (exercise and/or pharmacologic), wall motion study plus ejection fraction, with or without additional quantitative processing
➔ *CPT Assistant* Nov 98:22, Jun 99:8, Nov 99:44; *CPT Changes: An Insider's View* 2000

(For assessment of right ventricular ejection fraction by first pass technique, use 78496)

78473   multiple studies, wall motion study plus ejection fraction, at rest and stress (exercise and/or pharmacologic), with or without additional quantification
➔ *CPT Assistant* Jun 99:11

▶(Do not report 78472, 78473 in conjunction with 78451-78454, 78481, 78483, 78494)◀

▶(78478, 78480 have been deleted. To report, see 78451–78454)◀

78481   Cardiac blood pool imaging (planar), first pass technique; single study, at rest or with stress (exercise and/or pharmacologic), wall motion study plus ejection fraction, with or without quantification

78483   multiple studies, at rest and with stress (exercise and/or pharmacologic), wall motion study plus ejection fraction, with or without quantification

(For cerebral blood flow study, use 78610)

▶(Do not report 78481-78483 in conjunction with 78451–78454)◀

78491   Myocardial imaging, positron emission tomography (PET), perfusion; single study at rest or stress
➔ *CPT Assistant* Nov 97:27

78492   multiple studies at rest and/or stress
➔ *CPT Assistant* Nov 97:27

78494   Cardiac blood pool imaging, gated equilibrium, SPECT, at rest, wall motion study plus ejection fraction, with or without quantitative processing
➔ *CPT Assistant* Nov 98:22, Jun 99:3

+ **78496**   Cardiac blood pool imaging, gated equilibrium, single study, at rest, with right ventricular ejection fraction by first pass technique (List separately in addition to code for primary procedure)
➔ *CPT Assistant* Nov 98:22, Jun 99:3, 11

(Use 78496 in conjunction with 78472)

78499   Unlisted cardiovascular procedure, diagnostic nuclear medicine
➔ *CPT Assistant* Dec 05:7
➔ *Clinical Examples in Radiology* Summer 08:12

Respiratory System

78580   Pulmonary perfusion imaging, particulate
➔ *CPT Assistant* Mar 99:4, Dec 05:7

▶(Do not report 78580 in conjunction with 78451-78454)◀

78584   Pulmonary perfusion imaging, particulate, with ventilation; single breath
➔ *CPT Assistant* Mar 99:4

78585   rebreathing and washout, with or without single breath
➔ *CPT Assistant* Mar 99:4

78586   Pulmonary ventilation imaging, aerosol; single projection
➔ *CPT Assistant* Mar 99:4

78587   multiple projections (eg, anterior, posterior, lateral views)
➔ *CPT Assistant* Mar 99:4

78588   Pulmonary perfusion imaging, particulate, with ventilation imaging, aerosol, 1 or multiple projections
➔ *CPT Assistant* Nov 98:22, Mar 99:4

78591 Pulmonary ventilation imaging, gaseous, single breath, single projection
➔ *CPT Assistant* Mar 99:4

78593 Pulmonary ventilation imaging, gaseous, with rebreathing and washout with or without single breath; single projection
➔ *CPT Assistant* Mar 99:4

78594 multiple projections (eg, anterior, posterior, lateral views)

78596 Pulmonary quantitative differential function (ventilation/perfusion) study
➔ *CPT Assistant* Winter 90:10

78599 Unlisted respiratory procedure, diagnostic nuclear medicine
➔ *CPT Assistant* Dec 05:7

Nervous System

78600 Brain imaging, less than 4 static views;
➔ *CPT Assistant* Dec 05:7; *CPT Changes: An Insider's View* 2008

78601 with vascular flow
➔ *CPT Changes: An Insider's View* 2008

78605 Brain imaging, minimum 4 static views;
➔ *CPT Changes: An Insider's View* 2008

78606 with vascular flow
➔ *CPT Changes: An Insider's View* 2008

78607 Brain imaging, tomographic (SPECT)
➔ *CPT Changes: An Insider's View* 2008

78608 Brain imaging, positron emission tomography (PET); metabolic evaluation

78609 perfusion evaluation

78610 Brain imaging, vascular flow only

(78615 has been deleted. To report, use 78610)

78630 Cerebrospinal fluid flow, imaging (not including introduction of material); cisternography

(For injection procedure, see 61000-61070, 62270-62319)

78635 ventriculography

(For injection procedure, see 61000-61070, 62270-62294)

78645 shunt evaluation

(For injection procedure, see 61000-61070, 62270-62294)

78647 tomographic (SPECT)

78650 Cerebrospinal fluid leakage detection and localization
➔ *CPT Changes: An Insider's View* 2002

(For injection procedure, see 61000-61070, 62270-62294)

78660 Radiopharmaceutical dacryocystography

78699 Unlisted nervous system procedure, diagnostic nuclear medicine
➔ *CPT Assistant* Dec 05:7

Genitourinary System

78700 Kidney imaging morphology;
➔ *CPT Assistant* Dec 05:7, Mar 07:7; *CPT Changes: An Insider's View* 2007

78701 with vascular flow

78707 with vascular flow and function, single study without pharmacological intervention
➔ *CPT Assistant* Nov 97:27, Mar 07:7; *CPT Changes: An Insider's View* 2007

78708 with vascular flow and function, single study, with pharmacological intervention (eg, angiotensin converting enzyme inhibitor and/or diuretic)
➔ *CPT Assistant* Nov 97:27, Mar 07:7; *CPT Changes: An Insider's View* 2007

78709 with vascular flow and function, multiple studies, with and without pharmacological intervention (eg, angiotensin converting enzyme inhibitor and/or diuretic)
➔ *CPT Assistant* Nov 97:27, Mar 07:7; *CPT Changes: An Insider's View* 2007

(For introduction of radioactive substance in association with renal endoscopy, see 77776-77778)

78710 tomographic (SPECT)
➔ *CPT Assistant* Nov 97:27, Mar 07:7; *CPT Changes: An Insider's View* 2007

78725 Kidney function study, non-imaging radioisotopic study
➔ *CPT Assistant* Nov 98:22

+ 78730 Urinary bladder residual study (List separately in addition to code for primary procedure)
➔ *CPT Assistant* Mar 07:7; *CPT Changes: An Insider's View* 2007

(Use 78730 in conjunction with 78740)

(For measurement of postvoid residual urine and/or bladder capacity by ultrasound, nonimaging, use 51798)

(For ultrasound imaging of the bladder only, with measurement of postvoid residual urine when performed, use 76857)

78740 Ureteral reflux study (radiopharmaceutical voiding cystogram)

(Use 78740 in conjunction with 78730 for urinary bladder residual study)

(For catheterization, see 51701, 51702, 51703)

78761 Testicular imaging with vascular flow
➔ *CPT Assistant* Mar 07:7; *CPT Changes: An Insider's View* 2007

78799 Unlisted genitourinary procedure, diagnostic nuclear medicine
➔ *CPT Assistant* Dec 05:7

(For chemical analysis, see **Chemistry** section)

Other Procedures

(For specific organ, see appropriate heading)

(For radiophosphorus tumor identification, ocular, see 78800)

78800   Radiopharmaceutical localization of tumor or distribution of radiopharmaceutical agent(s); limited area
➲ *CPT Assistant* Dec 05:7; *CPT Changes: An Insider's View* 2004
➲ *Clinical Examples in Radiology* Summer 06:6, 10-11

(For specific organ, see appropriate heading)

78801   multiple areas

78802   whole body, single day imaging
➲ *CPT Assistant* Jun 03:11; *CPT Changes: An Insider's View* 2004
➲ *Clinical Examples in Radiology* Summer 06:6, 10-11

78803   tomographic (SPECT)
➲ *CPT Assistant* Jun 03:11
➲ *Clinical Examples in Radiology* Summer 06:6, 10-11

78804   whole body, requiring 2 or more days imaging
➲ *CPT Changes: An Insider's View* 2004

78805   Radiopharmaceutical localization of inflammatory process; limited area
➲ *CPT Assistant* Nov 99:44; *CPT Changes: An Insider's View* 2001

78806   whole body
➲ *CPT Assistant* Nov 99:44, Jun 03:11; *CPT Changes: An Insider's View* 2000

78807   tomographic (SPECT)
➲ *CPT Assistant* Jun 03:11

(For imaging bone infectious or inflammatory disease with a bone imaging radiopharmaceutical, see 78300, 78305, 78306)

78808   Injection procedure for radiopharmaceutical localization by non-imaging probe study, intravenous (eg, parathyroid adenoma)
➲ *CPT Changes: An Insider's View* 2009

(For sentinel lymph node identification, use 38792)

(For PET of brain, see 78608, 78609)

(For PET myocardial imaging, see 78459, 78491, 78492)

78811   Positron emission tomography (PET) imaging; limited area (eg, chest, head/neck)
➲ *CPT Assistant* Dec 05:7; *CPT Changes: An Insider's View* 2005, 2008
➲ *Clinical Examples in Radiology* Spring 05:13, 15

78812   skull base to mid-thigh
➲ *CPT Assistant* Dec 05:7; *CPT Changes: An Insider's View* 2005, 2008
➲ *Clinical Examples in Radiology* Spring 05:13, 15

78813   whole body
➲ *CPT Assistant* Dec 05:7; *CPT Changes: An Insider's View* 2005, 2008
➲ *Clinical Examples in Radiology* Spring 05:13, 15

78814   Positron emission tomography (PET) with concurrently acquired computed tomography (CT) for attenuation correction and anatomical localization imaging; limited area (eg, chest, head/neck)
➲ *CPT Assistant* Feb 05:13, Jun 05:10, Dec 05:7; *CPT Changes: An Insider's View* 2005, 2008
➲ *Clinical Examples in Radiology* Spring 05:13, 15

78815   skull base to mid-thigh
➲ *CPT Assistant* Feb 05:13, Jun 05:10, Dec 05:7; *CPT Changes: An Insider's View* 2005, 2008
➲ *Clinical Examples in Radiology* Spring 05:13, 15

78816   whole body
➲ *CPT Assistant* Feb 05:13, Jun 05:10, Dec 05:7; *CPT Changes: An Insider's View* 2005, 2008
➲ *Clinical Examples in Radiology* Spring 05:13, 15

(Report 78811-78816 only once per imaging session)

(Computed tomography [CT] performed for other than attenuation correction and anatomical localization is reported using the appropriate site specific CT code with modifier 59)

(78890, 78891 have been deleted)

78999   Unlisted miscellaneous procedure, diagnostic nuclear medicine
➲ *CPT Assistant* Dec 05:7
➲ *Clinical Examples in Radiology* Summer 08:12

Therapeutic

The oral and intravenous administration codes in this section are inclusive of the mode of administration. For intra-arterial, intra-cavitary, and intra-articular administration, also use the appropriate injection and/or procedure codes, as well as imaging guidance and radiological supervision and interpretation codes, when appropriate.

79005   Radiopharmaceutical therapy, by oral administration
➲ *CPT Assistant* Sep 05:1; *CPT Changes: An Insider's View* 2005
➲ *Clinical Examples in Radiology* Spring 05:14

(For monoclonal antibody therapy, use 79403)

79101   Radiopharmaceutical therapy, by intravenous administration
➲ *CPT Assistant* Sep 05:1; *CPT Changes: An Insider's View* 2005

►(Do not report 79101 in conjunction with 36400, 36410, 79403, 96360, 96374 or 96375, 96409)◄

(For radiolabeled monoclonal antibody by intravenous infusion, use 79403)

(For infusion or instillation of non-antibody radioelement solution that includes 3 months follow-up care, use 77750)

79200   Radiopharmaceutical therapy, by intracavitary administration
➲ *CPT Assistant* Sep 05:1; *CPT Changes: An Insider's View* 2005

79300   Radiopharmaceutical therapy, by interstitial radioactive colloid administration
➔ *CPT Assistant* Sep 05:1; *CPT Changes: An Insider's View* 2005

79403   Radiopharmaceutical therapy, radiolabeled monoclonal antibody by intravenous infusion
➔ *CPT Assistant* Sep 05:1; *CPT Changes: An Insider's View* 2004

(For pre-treatment imaging, see 78802, 78804)

(Do not report 79403 in conjunction with 79101)

79440   Radiopharmaceutical therapy, by intra-articular administration
➔ *CPT Assistant* Sep 05:1; *CPT Changes: An Insider's View* 2005

79445   Radiopharmaceutical therapy, by intra-arterial particulate administration
➔ *CPT Assistant* Sep 05:1, Dec 06:10; *CPT Changes: An Insider's View* 2005

►(Do not report 79445 in conjunction with 96373, 96420)◄

(Use appropriate procedural and radiological supervision and interpretation codes for the angiographic and interventional procedures provided prerequisite to intra-arterial radiopharmaceutical therapy)

79999   Radiopharmaceutical therapy, unlisted procedure
➔ *CPT Assistant* Mar 05:11, Sep 05:1, Jan 07:30; *CPT Changes: An Insider's View* 2005

Notes

⊙=Moderate sedation　✚=Add-on code　✗=FDA approval pending　#=Resequenced code　➡➊=See p xiii for details

Pathology and Laboratory Guidelines

Pathology and Laboratory

Table of Drugs and the Appropriate Qualitative Screening, Confirmatory, and Quantitative Codes

Drug Qualitative	Multiple Drug Class Method	Single Drug Class Method	Confirmation	Qualitative
Alcohols	80100[a]	80101[b]	80102[c]	82055 or 82075[d]
Amphetamines	80100[a]	80101[b]	80102[c]	82145
Barbiturates	80100[a]	80101[b]	80102[c]	80184 or 82205[e]
Benzodiazepines	80100[a]	80101[b]	80102[c]	80154
Cocaine and metabolites	80100[a]	80101[b]	80102[c]	82520
Methadone	80100[a]	80101[b]	80102[c]	83840
Methaqualone	80100[a]	80101[b]	80102[c]	80299 or 82491[f]
Opiates	80100[a]	80101[b]	80102[c]	83925
Phencyclidine	80100[a]	80101[b]	80102[c]	83992
Phenothiazines	80100[a]	80101[b]	80102[c]	84022
Propoxyphene	80100[a]	80101[b]	80102[c]	80299 or 82491[f]
Tetrahydrocan-nabinoids	80100[a]	80101[b]	80102[c]	80299 or 82491[f]
Tricyclic antidepressants	80100[a]	80101[b]	80102[c]	80152, 80160, 80166, 80174, 80182[g] 80299 or 82491[f]

[a] Use code **80100** for each combination of mobile phase with stationary phase.

[b] Use code **80101** for each single drug class tested and reported.

[c] Use code **80102** for each combination of mobile phase with stationary phase used for drug confirmation.

[d] Code **82055** for "Alcohol (ethanol); any specimen except breath," and code **82075** for "Alcohol (ethanol); breath."

[e] Code **80184** for "Phenobarbital," **80188** for "Primidone," and **82205** for "Barbiturates, not elsewhere specified."

[f] If there is no appropriate quantitative code for the drug listed, use code **82491** for chromatographic determination or **80299** for other methods.

[g] Code **80152** "Amitriptyline," **80160** for "Desipramine," **80166** for "Doxepin," **80174** for "Imipramine," or **80182** for "Nortriptyline."

Pathology and Laboratory Guidelines

Items used by all physicians in reporting their services are presented in the **Introduction.** Some of the commonalities are repeated here for the convenience of those physicians referring to this section on **Pathology and Laboratory.** Other definitions and items unique to Pathology and Laboratory are also listed.

Services in Pathology and Laboratory

Services in Pathology and Laboratory are provided by a physician or by technologists under responsible supervision of a physician.

Separate or Multiple Procedures

It is appropriate to designate multiple procedures that are rendered on the same date by separate entries.

Unlisted Service or Procedure

A service or procedure may be provided that is not listed in this edition of the CPT codebook. When reporting such a service, the appropriate "Unlisted Procedure" code may be used to indicate the service, identifying it by "Special Report" as discussed below. The "Unlisted Procedures" and accompanying codes for **Pathology and Laboratory** are as follows:

81099	Unlisted urinalysis procedure
84999	Unlisted chemistry procedure
85999	Unlisted hematology and coagulation procedure
86486	unlisted antigen, each
86849	Unlisted immunology procedure
86999	Unlisted transfusion medicine procedure
87999	Unlisted microbiology procedure
88099	Unlisted necropsy (autopsy) procedure
88199	Unlisted cytopathology procedure
88299	Unlisted cytogenetic study
88399	Unlisted surgical pathology procedure
89240	Unlisted miscellaneous pathology test
● **89398**	Unlisted reproductive medicine laboratory procedure

Special Report

►A service that is rarely provided, unusual, variable, or new may require a special report. Pertinent information should include an adequate definition or description of the nature, extent, and need for the procedure; and the time, effort, and equipment necessary to provide the service.◄

Notes

⊙=Moderate sedation ✚=Add-on code ✗=FDA approval pending #=Resequenced code ➡➡=See p xiii for details

Pathology and Laboratory

Organ or Disease-Oriented Panels

These panels were developed for coding purposes only and should not be interpreted as clinical parameters. The tests listed with each panel identify the defined components of that panel.

These panel components are not intended to limit the performance of other tests. If one performs tests in addition to those specifically indicated for a particular panel, those tests should be reported separately in addition to the panel code.

▶Do not report two or more panel codes that include any of the same constituent tests performed from the same patient collection. If a group of tests overlaps two or more panels, report the panel that incorporates the greater number of tests to fulfill the code definition and report the remaining tests using individual test codes (eg, do not report 80047 in conjunction with 80053).◀

80047   Basic metabolic panel (Calcium, ionized)

This panel must include the following:

Calcium, ionized (82330)

Carbon dioxide (82374)

Chloride (82435)

Creatinine (82565)

Glucose (82947)

Potassium (84132)

Sodium (84295)

Urea Nitrogen (BUN) (84520)

    ➔ *CPT Assistant* Apr 08:5; *CPT Changes: An Insider's View* 2008

[handwritten note: All test must be done to code 80047. List separately if all not done.]

80048   Basic metabolic panel (Calcium, total)

    ➔ *CPT Changes: An Insider's View* 2008

This panel must include the following:

Calcium, total (82310)

Carbon dioxide (82374)

Chloride (82435)

Creatinine (82565)

Glucose (82947)

Potassium (84132)

Sodium (84295)

Urea nitrogen (BUN) (84520)

    ➔ *CPT Assistant* Jan 98:6, Sep 99:11, Nov 99:44, Jan 00:7, Aug 05:9; *CPT Changes: An Insider's View* 2000, 2008, 2009

80050   General health panel

This panel must include the following:

Comprehensive metabolic panel (80053)

Blood count, complete (CBC), automated and automated differential WBC count (85025 or 85027 and 85004)

OR

Blood count, complete (CBC), automated (85027) and appropriate manual differential WBC count (85007 or 85009)

Thyroid stimulating hormone (TSH) (84443)

    ➔ *CPT Assistant* Winter 92:14, Summer 93:14, Jun 97:10, Nov 97:28, Jan 98:6, Sep 99:11; *CPT Changes: An Insider's View* 2001, 2004

80051   Electrolyte panel

This panel must include the following:

Carbon dioxide (82374)

Chloride (82435)

Potassium (84132)

Sodium (84295)

    ➔ *CPT Assistant* Nov 97:28, Jan 98:7, Sep 99:11

80053   Comprehensive metabolic panel

This panel must include the following:

Albumin (82040)

Bilirubin, total (82247)

Calcium, total (82310)

Carbon dioxide (bicarbonate) (82374)

Chloride (82435)

Creatinine (82565)

Glucose (82947)

Phosphatase, alkaline (84075)

Potassium (84132)

Protein, total (84155)

Sodium (84295)

Transferase, alanine amino (ALT) (SGPT) (84460)

Transferase, aspartate amino (AST) (SGOT) (84450)

Urea nitrogen (BUN) (84520)

    ➔ *CPT Assistant* Jan 98:6, Nov 98:23, Sep 99:11, Nov 99:44, May 00:11, Jan 05:46, Apr 08:5; *CPT Changes: An Insider's View* 2000, 2009

▲=Revised code   ●=New code   ▶ ◀=Contains new or revised text   ⊘=Modifier 51 exempt   American Medical Association   **389**

▲ **80055** Obstetric panel

This panel must include the following:

Blood count, complete (CBC), automated and automated differential WBC count (85025 or 85027 and 85004)

OR

Blood count, complete (CBC), automated (85027) and appropriate manual differential WBC count (85007 or 85009)

Hepatitis B surface antigen (HBsAg) (87340)

Antibody, rubella (86762)

Syphilis test, non-treponemal antibody; qualitative (eg, VDRL, RPR, ART) (86592)

➲ *CPT Changes: An Insider's View* 2010

Antibody screen, RBC, each serum technique (86850)

Blood typing, ABO (86900) AND

Blood typing, Rh (D) (86901)

➲ *CPT Assistant* Winter 92:14, Summer 93:14, Jun 97:10, Apr 99:6, Sep 99:11; *CPT Changes: An Insider's View* 2004

►(When syphilis screening is performed using a treponemal antibody approach [86780], do not use 80055. Use the individual codes for the tests performed in the obstetric panel)◄

80061 Lipid panel

This panel must include the following:

Cholesterol, serum, total (82465)

Lipoprotein, direct measurement, high density cholesterol (HDL cholesterol) (83718)

Triglycerides (84478)

➲ *CPT Assistant* Winter 92:14, Summer 93:14, Jun 97:10, Sep 99:11, Mar 00:11, Feb 05:9

80069 Renal function panel

This panel must include the following:

Albumin (82040)

Calcium, total (82310)

Carbon dioxide (bicarbonate) (82374)

Chloride (82435)

Creatinine (82565)

Glucose (82947)

Phosphorus inorganic (phosphate) (84100)

Potassium (84132)

Sodium (84295)

Urea nitrogen (BUN) (84520)

➲ *CPT Assistant* Sep 99:11, Nov 99:44; *CPT Changes: An Insider's View* 2000, 2009

80074 Acute hepatitis panel

This panel must include the following:

Hepatitis A antibody (HAAb), IgM antibody (86709)

Hepatitis B core antibody (HBcAb), IgM antibody (86705)

Hepatitis B surface antigen (HBsAg) (87340)

Hepatitis C antibody (86803)

➲ *CPT Assistant* Sep 99:11, Nov 99:45; *CPT Changes: An Insider's View* 2000

80076 Hepatic function panel

This panel must include the following:

Albumin (82040)

Bilirubin, total (82247)

Bilirubin, direct (82248)

Phosphatase, alkaline (84075)

Protein, total (84155)

Transferase, alanine amino (ALT) (SGPT) (84460)

Transferase, aspartate amino (AST) (SGOT) (84450)

➲ *CPT Assistant* Winter 92:14, Summer 93:14, Jun 97:10, Jan 98:6, Apr 99:6, Sep 99:11, Nov 99:45, Jan 00:7, Aug 05:9; *CPT Changes: An Insider's View* 2000

Drug Testing

The following list contains examples of drugs or classes of drugs that are commonly assayed by qualitative screen, followed by confirmation with a second method:

- Alcohols
- Amphetamines
- Barbiturates
- Benzodiazepines
- Cocaine and metabolites
- Methadones
- Methaqualones
- Opiates
- Phencyclidines
- Phenothiazines
- Propoxyphenes
- Tetrahydrocannabinoids
- Tricyclic antidepressants

Confirmed drugs may also be quantitated.

Use 80100 for each multiple drug class chromatographic procedure. Use 80102 for each procedure necessary for confirmation. For chromatography, each combination of stationary and mobile phase is to be counted as one procedure. For example, if detection of three drugs by chromatography requires one stationary phase with three mobile phases, use 80100 three times. However, if multiple drugs can be detected using a single analysis (eg, one stationary phase with one mobile phase), use 80100 only once.

For quantitation of drugs screened, use appropriate code in **Chemistry** section (82000-84999) or **Therapeutic Drug Assay** section (80150-80299).

80100   Drug screen, qualitative; multiple drug classes chromatographic method, each procedure
➔ *CPT Assistant* Fall 93:26, Mar 00:2, Aug 05:9; *CPT Changes: An Insider's View* 2001

80101   single drug class method (eg, immunoassay, enzyme assay), each drug class
➔ *CPT Assistant* Fall 93:26, Mar 00:2, Nov 06:22; *CPT Changes: An Insider's View* 2001

80102   Drug confirmation, each procedure
➔ *CPT Assistant* Fall 93:26, Mar 00:2; *CPT Changes: An Insider's View* 2001

80103   Tissue preparation for drug analysis
➔ *CPT Assistant* Aug 05:9

Therapeutic Drug Assays

The material for examination may be from any source. Examination is quantitative. For nonquantitative testing, see Drug Testing (80100-80103).
➔ *CPT Assistant* (80150-80299) Winter 92:14, Fall 93:26, Mar 00:1

80150   Amikacin
➔ *CPT Assistant* Aug 05:9

80152   Amitriptyline

80154   Benzodiazepines

80156   Carbamazepine; total
➔ *CPT Changes: An Insider's View* 2001

80157   free
➔ *CPT Changes: An Insider's View* 2001

80158   Cyclosporine

80160   Desipramine

80162   Digoxin

80164   Dipropylacetic acid (valproic acid)

80166   Doxepin

80168   Ethosuximide

80170   Gentamicin

80172   Gold

80173   Haloperidol
➔ *CPT Changes: An Insider's View* 2001

80174   Imipramine

80176   Lidocaine

80178   Lithium

80182   Nortriptyline

80184   Phenobarbital

80185   Phenytoin; total

80186   free

80188   Primidone

80190   Procainamide;

80192   with metabolites (eg, n-acetyl procainamide)

80194   Quinidine

80195   Sirolimus
➔ *CPT Assistant* Mar 06:6; *CPT Changes: An Insider's View* 2006

80196   Salicylate

80197   Tacrolimus

80198   Theophylline

80200   Tobramycin

80201   Topiramate
➔ *CPT Assistant* Nov 97:28

80202   Vancomycin

80299   Quantitation of drug, not elsewhere specified
➔ *CPT Assistant* Mar 00:3, Oct 04:14, Aug 05:9

Evocative/Suppression Testing

The following test panels involve the administration of evocative or suppressive agents, and the baseline and subsequent measurement of their effects on chemical constituents. These codes are to be used for the reporting of the laboratory component of the overall testing protocol. For the physician's administration of the evocative or suppressive agents, see 96360, 96361, 96372-96374, 96375; for the supplies and drugs, see 99070. To report physician attendance and monitoring during the testing, use the appropriate evaluation and management code, including the prolonged physician care codes if required. Prolonged physician care codes are not separately reported when evocative/suppression testing involves prolonged infusions reported with 96360, 96361. In the code descriptors where reference is made to a particular analyte (eg, Cortisol: 82533 x 2) the "x 2" refers to the number of times the test for that particular analyte is performed.

80400 ACTH stimulation panel; for adrenal insufficiency

This panel must include the following:

Cortisol (82533 x 2)

→ *CPT Assistant* Summer 94:1, Fall 94:10, Aug 05:9

80402 for 21 hydroxylase deficiency

This panel must include the following:

Cortisol (82533 x 2)

17 hydroxyprogesterone (83498 x 2)

→ *CPT Assistant* Summer 94:1, Fall 94:10

80406 for 3 beta-hydroxydehydrogenase deficiency

This panel must include the following:

Cortisol (82533 x 2)

17 hydroxypregnenolone (84143 x 2)

→ *CPT Assistant* Summer 94:1, Fall 94:10

80408 Aldosterone suppression evaluation panel (eg, saline infusion)

This panel must include the following:

Aldosterone (82088 x 2)

Renin (84244 x 2)

→ *CPT Assistant* Summer 94:1, Fall 94:10

80410 Calcitonin stimulation panel (eg, calcium, pentagastrin)

This panel must include the following:

Calcitonin (82308 x 3)

→ *CPT Assistant* Summer 94:1, Fall 94:11

80412 Corticotropic releasing hormone (CRH) stimulation panel

This panel must include the following:

Cortisol (82533 x 6)

Adrenocorticotropic hormone (ACTH) (82024 x 6)

→ *CPT Assistant* Summer 94:1, Fall 94:11

80414 Chorionic gonadotropin stimulation panel; testosterone response

This panel must include the following:

Testosterone (84403 x 2 on 3 pooled blood samples)

→ *CPT Assistant* Summer 94:1, Fall 94:11; *CPT Changes: An Insider's View* 2009

80415 estradiol response

This panel must include the following:

Estradiol (82670 x 2 on 3 pooled blood samples)

→ *CPT Assistant* Summer 94:1, Fall 94:11; *CPT Changes: An Insider's View* 2009

80416 Renal vein renin stimulation panel (eg, captopril)

This panel must include the following:

Renin (84244 x 6)

→ *CPT Assistant* Summer 94:1

80417 Peripheral vein renin stimulation panel (eg, captopril)

This panel must include the following:

Renin (84244 x 2)

80418 Combined rapid anterior pituitary evaluation panel

This panel must include the following:

Adrenocorticotropic hormone (ACTH) (82024 x 4)

Luteinizing hormone (LH) (83002 x 4)

Follicle stimulating hormone (FSH) (83001 x 4)

Prolactin (84146 x 4)

Human growth hormone (HGH) (83003 x 4)

Cortisol (82533 x 4)

Thyroid stimulating hormone (TSH) (84443 x 4)

→ *CPT Assistant* Summer 94:1, Fall 94:13

80420 Dexamethasone suppression panel, 48 hour

This panel must include the following:

Free cortisol, urine (82530 x 2)

Cortisol (82533 x 2)

Volume measurement for timed collection (81050 x 2)

→ *CPT Assistant* Fall 94:13

(For single dose dexamethasone, use 82533)

→ *CPT Assistant* Summer 94:1

80422 Glucagon tolerance panel; for insulinoma

This panel must include the following:

Glucose (82947 x 3)

Insulin (83525 x 3)

→ *CPT Assistant* Summer 94:1, Fall 94:13

80424 for pheochromocytoma

This panel must include the following:

Catecholamines, fractionated (82384 x 2)

→ *CPT Assistant* Summer 94:1, Fall 94:14

80426 Gonadotropin releasing hormone stimulation panel

This panel must include the following:

Follicle stimulating hormone (FSH) (83001 x 4)

Luteinizing hormone (LH) (83002 x 4)

→ *CPT Assistant* Summer 94:1, Fall 94:14

80428 Growth hormone stimulation panel (eg, arginine infusion, l-dopa administration)

This panel must include the following:

Human growth hormone (HGH) (83003 x 4)

→ *CPT Assistant* Summer 94:1, Fall 94:14

80430   Growth hormone suppression panel (glucose administration)

This panel must include the following:

Glucose (82947 x 3)

Human growth hormone (HGH) (83003 x 4)
➲ *CPT Assistant* Summer 94:1, Fall 94:14

80432   Insulin-induced C-peptide suppression panel

This panel must include the following:

Insulin (83525)

C-peptide (84681 x 5)

Glucose (82947 x 5)
➲ *CPT Assistant* Summer 94:1, Fall 94:15

80434   Insulin tolerance panel; for ACTH insufficiency

This panel must include the following:

Cortisol (82533 x 5)

Glucose (82947 x 5)
➲ *CPT Assistant* Summer 94:1, Fall 94:15

80435   for growth hormone deficiency

This panel must include the following:

Glucose (82947 x 5)

Human growth hormone (HGH) (83003 x 5)
➲ *CPT Assistant* Summer 94:1, Fall 94:15

80436   Metyrapone panel

This panel must include the following:

Cortisol (82533 x 2)

11 deoxycortisol (82634 x 2)
➲ *CPT Assistant* Summer 94:1, Fall 94:16

80438   Thyrotropin releasing hormone (TRH) stimulation panel; 1 hour

This panel must include the following:

Thyroid stimulating hormone (TSH) (84443 x 3)
➲ *CPT Assistant* Summer 94:1, Fall 94:16

80439   2 hour

This panel must include the following:

Thyroid stimulating hormone (TSH) (84443 x 4)
➲ *CPT Assistant* Summer 94:1, Fall 94:16

80440   for hyperprolactinemia

This panel must include the following:

Prolactin (84146 x 3)
➲ *CPT Assistant* Summer 94:1, Fall 94:16, Aug 05:9

Consultations (Clinical Pathology)

A clinical pathology consultation is a service, including a written report, rendered by the pathologist in response to a request from an attending physician in relation to a test result(s) requiring additional medical interpretive judgment.

Reporting of a test result(s) without medical interpretive judgment is not considered a clinical pathology consultation.

80500   Clinical pathology consultation; limited, without review of patient's history and medical records
➲ *CPT Assistant* Apr 97:9, Nov 02:9, Aug 05:9

80502   comprehensive, for a complex diagnostic problem, with review of patient's history and medical records
➲ *CPT Assistant* Apr 97:9, Nov 02:9, Aug 05:9

(These codes may also be used for pharmacokinetic consultations)

(For consultations involving the examination and evaluation of the patient, see 99241-99255)

Urinalysis

For specific analyses, see appropriate section.

81000   Urinalysis, by dip stick or tablet reagent for bilirubin, glucose, hemoglobin, ketones, leukocytes, nitrite, pH, protein, specific gravity, urobilinogen, any number of these constituents; non-automated, with microscopy
➲ *CPT Assistant* Winter 90, Winter 91:10, Fall 93:25, Aug 05:9

81001   automated, with microscopy

81002   non-automated, without microscopy
➲ *CPT Assistant* Mar 98:3, Apr 07:1

81003   automated, without microscopy
➲ *CPT Assistant* Apr 07:1

81005   Urinalysis; qualitative or semiquantitative, except immunoassays
➲ *CPT Assistant* Winter 90, Winter 91:10, Fall 93:25

(For non-immunoassay reagent strip urinalysis, see 81000, 81002)

(For immunoassay, qualitative or semiquantitative, use 83518)

(For microalbumin, see 82043, 82044)

81007   bacteriuria screen, except by culture or dipstick
➲ *CPT Changes: An Insider's View* 2001

(For culture, see 87086-87088)

(For dipstick, use 81000 or 81002)

81015   microscopic only

(For sperm evaluation for retrograde ejaculation, use 89331)

81020   2 or 3 glass test
> *CPT Assistant* Winter 90, Winter 91:10

81025   Urine pregnancy test, by visual color comparison methods
> *CPT Assistant* Mar 98:3

81050   Volume measurement for timed collection, each

81099   Unlisted urinalysis procedure
> *CPT Assistant* Aug 05:9

Chemistry

The material for examination may be from any source unless otherwise specified in the code descriptor. When an analyte is measured in multiple specimens from different sources, or in specimens that are obtained at different times, the analyte is reported separately for each source and for each specimen. The examination is quantitative unless specified. To report an organ or disease oriented panel, see codes 80048-80076.

When a code describes a method where measurement of multiple analytes may require one or several procedures, each procedure is coded separately (eg, 82491-82492, 82541-82544). For example, if two analytes are measured using column chromatography using a single stationary or mobile phase, use 82492. If the same two analytes are measured using different stationary or mobile phase conditions, 82491 would be used twice. If a total of four analytes are measured where two analytes are measured with a single stationary and mobile phase, and the other two analytes are measured using a different stationary and mobile phase, use 82492 twice. If a total of three analytes are measured where two analytes are measured using a single stationary or mobile phase condition, and the third analyte is measured separately using a different stationary or mobile phase procedure, use 82492 once for the two analytes measured under the same condition, and use 82491 once for the third analyte measured separately.

Clinical information derived from the results of laboratory data that is mathematically calculated (eg, free thyroxine index [T7]) is considered part of the test procedure and therefore is not a separately reportable service.

82000   Acetaldehyde, blood
> *CPT Assistant* Aug 05:9

82003   Acetaminophen

82009   Acetone or other ketone bodies, serum; qualitative

82010   quantitative

82013   Acetylcholinesterase

(Acid, gastric, see gastric acid, 82926, 82928)

(Acid phosphatase, see 84060-84066)

82016   Acylcarnitines; qualitative, each specimen
> *CPT Assistant* Nov 98:23

82017   quantitative, each specimen
> *CPT Assistant* Nov 98:23; *CPT Changes: An Insider's View* 2000

(For carnitine, use 82379)

82024   Adrenocorticotropic hormone (ACTH)

82030   Adenosine, 5-monophosphate, cyclic (cyclic AMP)

82040   Albumin; serum, plasma or whole blood
> *CPT Assistant* Dec 99:2; *CPT Changes: An Insider's View* 2009

82042   urine or other source, quantitative, each specimen
> *CPT Changes: An Insider's View* 2001

82043   urine, microalbumin, quantitative
> *CPT Assistant* Summer 94:2

82044   urine, microalbumin, semiquantitative (eg, reagent strip assay)
> *CPT Assistant* Summer 94:2, Mar 98:3, Sep 02:10

(For prealbumin, use 84134)

82045   ischemia modified
> *CPT Changes: An Insider's View* 2005

82055   Alcohol (ethanol); any specimen except breath

(For other volatiles, alcohol, use 84600)

82075   breath

82085   Aldolase

82088   Aldosterone

(Alkaline phosphatase, see 84075, 84080)

82101   Alkaloids, urine, quantitative
> *CPT Assistant* Aug 05:9

(Alphaketoglutarate, see 82009, 82010)

(Alpha tocopherol [Vitamin E], use 84446)

82103   Alpha-1-antitrypsin; total

82104   phenotype

82105   Alpha-fetoprotein (AFP); serum

82106   amniotic fluid

82107   AFP-L3 fraction isoform and total AFP (including ratio)
> *CPT Changes: An Insider's View* 2007

82108   Aluminum

82120   Amines, vaginal fluid, qualitative
> *CPT Assistant* Nov 99:45; *CPT Changes: An Insider's View* 2000

(For combined pH and amines test for vaginitis, use 82120 and 83986)

82127   Amino acids; single, qualitative, each specimen
> *CPT Assistant* Nov 98:24

82128   multiple, qualitative, each specimen
> *CPT Assistant* Nov 98:24

82131   single, quantitative, each specimen
> *CPT Assistant* May 98:11, Nov 98:24

82135   Aminolevulinic acid, delta (ALA)

82136   Amino acids, 2 to 5 amino acids, quantitative, each specimen
> *CPT Assistant* Nov 98:24

82139   Amino acids, 6 or more amino acids, quantitative, each specimen
> *CPT Assistant* Nov 98:24

82140   Ammonia

82143   Amniotic fluid scan (spectrophotometric)

(For L/S ratio, use 83661)

(Amobarbital, see 80100-80103 for qualitative analysis, 82205 for quantitative analysis)

82145   Amphetamine or methamphetamine

(For qualitative analysis, see 80100-80103)

82150   Amylase

82154   Androstanediol glucuronide
> *CPT Assistant* Summer 94:5

82157   Androstenedione

82160   Androsterone

82163   Angiotensin II

82164   Angiotensin I - converting enzyme (ACE)

(Antidiuretic hormone (ADH), use 84588)

(Antimony, use 83015)

(Antitrypsin, alpha-1-, see 82103, 82104)

82172   Apolipoprotein, each

82175   Arsenic

(For heavy metal screening, use 83015)

82180   Ascorbic acid (Vitamin C), blood

(Aspirin, see acetylsalicylic acid, 80196)

(Atherogenic index, blood, ultracentrifugation, quantitative, use 83701)

82190   Atomic absorption spectroscopy, each analyte

82205   Barbiturates, not elsewhere specified
> *CPT Assistant* Jul 03:7, Aug 05:9

(For qualitative analysis, see 80100-80103)

(For B-Natriuretic peptide, use 83880)

82232   Beta-2 microglobulin

(Bicarbonate, use 82374)

82239   Bile acids; total

82240   cholylglycine

(For bile pigments, urine, see 81000-81005)

82247   Bilirubin; total
> *CPT Assistant* Nov 98:24, Apr 99:6, Dec 99:1, Jan 00:7, Dec 08:5

82248   direct
> *CPT Assistant* Nov 98:24, Apr 99:6, Dec 99:1

82252   feces, qualitative

82261   Biotinidase, each specimen
> *CPT Assistant* Nov 98:24

82270   Blood, occult, by peroxidase activity (eg, guaiac), qualitative; feces, consecutive collected specimens with single determination, for colorectal neoplasm screening (ie, patient was provided 3 cards or single triple card for consecutive collection)
> *CPT Assistant* Sep 03:15, Feb 06:7, Apr 08:5; *CPT Changes: An Insider's View* 2002, 2006

82271   other sources
> *CPT Assistant* Feb 06:7; *CPT Changes: An Insider's View* 2006

82272   Blood, occult, by peroxidase activity (eg, guaiac), qualitative, feces, 1-3 simultaneous determinations, performed for other than colorectal neoplasm screening
> *CPT Assistant* Feb 06:7, Apr 08:5; *CPT Changes: An Insider's View* 2006, 2008

(Blood urea nitrogen [BUN], see 84520, 84525)

82274   Blood, occult, by fecal hemoglobin determination by immunoassay, qualitative, feces, 1-3 simultaneous determinations
> *CPT Changes: An Insider's View* 2002

82286   Bradykinin

82300   Cadmium
> *CPT Assistant* Aug 05:9

▲ **82306**   Vitamin D; 25 hydroxy, includes fraction(s), if performed
> *CPT Changes: An Insider's View* 2010

#▲ **82652**   1, 25 dihydroxy, includes fraction(s), if performed
> *CPT Changes: An Insider's View* 2010

►(82307 has been deleted. For 25 hydroxy vitamin D, use 82306)◄

82308   Calcitonin

82310   Calcium; total
> *CPT Assistant* Dec 99:2

82330   ionized

82331   after calcium infusion test

82340   urine quantitative, timed specimen

82355   Calculus; qualitative analysis
> *CPT Changes: An Insider's View* 2002

82360   quantitative analysis, chemical

82365   infrared spectroscopy

82370   X-ray diffraction
> *CPT Changes: An Insider's View* 2001

(Carbamates, see individual listings)

▲=Revised code   ●=New code   ►◄=Contains new or revised text   ⊘=Modifier 51 exempt

82373 Carbohydrate deficient transferrin
➔ *CPT Changes: An Insider's View* 2001

82374 Carbon dioxide (bicarbonate)
➔ *CPT Assistant* Dec 99:2

(See also 82803)

82375 Carboxyhemoglobin; quantitative
➔ *CPT Changes: An Insider's View* 2009

82376 qualitative
➔ *CPT Changes: An Insider's View* 2009

(For transcutaneous measurement of carboxyhemoglobin, use 88740)

82378 Carcinoembryonic antigen (CEA)
➔ *CPT Assistant* Fall 93:25, Aug 96:11

82379 Carnitine (total and free), quantitative, each specimen
➔ *CPT Assistant* Nov 98:24

(For acylcarnitine, see 82016, 82017)

82380 Carotene

82382 Catecholamines; total urine

82383 blood

82384 fractionated

(For urine metabolites, see 83835, 84585)

82387 Cathepsin-D

82390 Ceruloplasmin

82397 Chemiluminescent assay
➔ *CPT Assistant* Fall 93:25

82415 Chloramphenicol
➔ *CPT Assistant* Aug 05:9

82435 Chloride; blood
➔ *CPT Assistant* Dec 99:2

82436 urine

82438 other source
➔ *CPT Assistant* Jul 03:7

(For sweat collection by iontophoresis, use 89230)

82441 Chlorinated hydrocarbons, screen

(Chlorpromazine, use 84022)

▶(Cholecalciferol [Vitamin D], use 82306)◀

82465 Cholesterol, serum or whole blood, total
➔ *CPT Assistant* Dec 99:2, Mar 00:11, Feb 05:9; *CPT Changes: An Insider's View* 2001

(For high density lipoprotein [HDL], use 83718)

82480 Cholinesterase; serum

82482 RBC

82485 Chondroitin B sulfate, quantitative

(Chorionic gonadotropin, see gonadotropin, 84702, 84703)

82486 Chromatography, qualitative; column (eg, gas liquid or HPLC), analyte not elsewhere specified
➔ *CPT Assistant* Nov 98:24-25

82487 paper, 1-dimensional, analyte not elsewhere specified

82488 paper, 2-dimensional, analyte not elsewhere specified

82489 thin layer, analyte not elsewhere specified

82491 Chromatography, quantitative, column (eg, gas liquid or HPLC); single analyte not elsewhere specified, single stationary and mobile phase
➔ *CPT Assistant* Fall 93:25, Nov 98:24-25, Mar 00:3

82492 multiple analytes, single stationary and mobile phase
➔ *CPT Assistant* Nov 98:24-25, Mar 00:3

82495 Chromium

82507 Citrate
➔ *CPT Assistant* Aug 05:9

82520 Cocaine or metabolite

(Cocaine, qualitative analysis, see 80100-80103)

(Codeine, qualitative analysis, see 80100-80103)

(Codeine, quantitative analysis, see 82101)

(Complement, see 86160-86162)

82523 Collagen cross links, any method

82525 Copper

(Coproporphyrin, see 84119, 84120)

(Corticosteroids, use 83491)

82528 Corticosterone

82530 Cortisol; free
➔ *CPT Assistant* Summer 94:3

82533 total
➔ *CPT Assistant* Summer 94:3

(C-peptide, use 84681)

82540 Creatine

82541 Column chromatography/mass spectrometry (eg, GC/MS, or HPLC/MS), analyte not elsewhere specified; qualitative, single stationary and mobile phase
➔ *CPT Assistant* Nov 98:24-25

82542 quantitative, single stationary and mobile phase
➔ *CPT Assistant* Nov 98:24-25

82543 stable isotope dilution, single analyte, quantitative, single stationary and mobile phase
➔ *CPT Assistant* Nov 98:24-25

82544 stable isotope dilution, multiple analytes, quantitative, single stationary and mobile phase
➔ *CPT Assistant* Nov 98:24-25, Dec 99:7

82550 Creatine kinase (CK), (CPK); total
➔ *CPT Assistant* Feb 98:1, Dec 99:2

82552   isoenzymes
> *CPT Assistant* Feb 98:1

82553   MB fraction only
> *CPT Assistant* Feb 98:1

82554   isoforms
> *CPT Assistant* Feb 98:1

82565 Creatinine; blood
> *CPT Assistant* Dec 99:2

82570   other source

82575   clearance

82585 Cryofibrinogen

82595 Cryoglobulin, qualitative or semi-quantitative (eg, cryocrit)
> *CPT Changes: An Insider's View* 2001

(For quantitative, cryoglobulin, see 82784, 82785)

(Crystals, pyrophosphate vs urate, use 89060)

82600 Cyanide
> *CPT Assistant* Aug 05:9

82607 Cyanocobalamin (Vitamin B-12);

82608   unsaturated binding capacity

(Cyclic AMP, use 82030)

(Cyclic GMP, use 83008)

(Cyclosporine, use 80158)

82610 Cystatin C
> *CPT Assistant* Apr 08:5, Aug 08:13; *CPT Changes: An Insider's View* 2008

82615 Cystine and homocystine, urine, qualitative

82626 Dehydroepiandrosterone (DHEA)
> *CPT Assistant* Summer 94:4

82627 Dehydroepiandrosterone-sulfate (DHEA-S)
> *CPT Assistant* Summer 94:4

(Delta-aminolevulinic acid (ALA), use 82135)

82633 Desoxycorticosterone, 11-

82634 Deoxycortisol, 11-

(Dexamethasone suppression test, use 80420)

(Diastase, urine, use 82150)

82638 Dibucaine number

(Dichloroethane, use 84600)

(Dichloromethane, use 84600)

(Diethylether, use 84600)

82646 Dihydrocodeinone

(For qualitative analysis, see 80100-80103)

82649 Dihydromorphinone

(For qualitative analysis, see 80100-80103)

82651 Dihydrotestosterone (DHT)

82652 ▶Code is out of numerical sequence. See 82000-84999◀

82654 Dimethadione

(For qualitative analysis, see 80100-80103)

(Diphenylhydantoin, use 80185)

(Dipropylacetic acid, use 80164)

(Dopamine, see 82382-82384)

(Duodenal contents, see individual enzymes; for intubation and collection, use 89100)

82656 Elastase, pancreatic (EL-1), fecal, qualitative or semi-quantitative
> *CPT Assistant* Sep 05:9; *CPT Changes: An Insider's View* 2005

82657 Enzyme activity in blood cells, cultured cells, or tissue, not elsewhere specified; nonradioactive substrate, each specimen
> *CPT Assistant* Nov 98:25

82658   radioactive substrate, each specimen
> *CPT Assistant* Nov 98:25

82664 Electrophoretic technique, not elsewhere specified

(Endocrine receptor assays, see 84233-84235)

82666 Epiandrosterone

(Epinephrine, see 82382-82384)

82668 Erythropoietin

82670 Estradiol

82671 Estrogens; fractionated

82672   total

(Estrogen receptor assay, use 84233)

82677 Estriol

82679 Estrone

(Ethanol, see 82055 and 82075)

82690 Ethchlorvynol

(Ethyl alcohol, see 82055 and 82075)

82693 Ethylene glycol

82696 Etiocholanolone

(For fractionation of ketosteroids, use 83593)

82705 Fat or lipids, feces; qualitative
> *CPT Assistant* Aug 05:9

82710   quantitative

82715 Fat differential, feces, quantitative

82725 Fatty acids, nonesterified

82726 Very long chain fatty acids
> *CPT Assistant* Nov 98:25

(For long-chain [C20-22] omega-3 fatty acids in red blood cell [RBC] membranes, use Category III code 0111T)

▲=Revised code   ●=New code   ▶ ◀=Contains new or revised text   ⊘=Modifier 51 exempt

82728   Ferritin

(Fetal hemoglobin, see hemoglobin 83030, 83033, and 85460)

(Fetoprotein, alpha-1, see 82105, 82106)

82731   Fetal fibronectin, cervicovaginal secretions, semi-quantitative
➔ *CPT Assistant* Nov 98:25

82735   Fluoride

82742   Flurazepam

(For qualitative analysis, see 80100-80103)

(Foam stability test, use 83662)

82746   Folic acid; serum

82747   RBC

(Follicle stimulating hormone [FSH], use 83001)

82757   Fructose, semen

(Fructosamine, use 82985)

(Fructose, TLC screen, use 84375)

82759   Galactokinase, RBC

82760   Galactose

82775   Galactose-1-phosphate uridyl transferase; quantitative

82776   screen

▲ **82784**   Gammaglobulin (immunoglobulin); IgA, IgD, IgG, IgM, each
➔ *CPT Assistant* Spring 94:31, Aug 00:11; *CPT Changes: An Insider's View* 2010

▲ **82785**   IgE
➔ *CPT Assistant* Spring 94:31; *CPT Changes: An Insider's View* 2010

(For allergen specific IgE, see 86003, 86005)

▲ **82787**   immunoglobulin subclasses (eg, IgG1, 2, 3, or 4), each
➔ *CPT Changes: An Insider's View* 2001, 2010

(Gamma-glutamyltransferase [GGT], use 82977)

82800   Gases, blood, pH only
➔ *CPT Assistant* Aug 05:9

82803   Gases, blood, any combination of pH, pCO_2, pO_2, CO_2, HCO_3 (including calculated O_2 saturation);

(Use 82803 for 2 or more of the above listed analytes)

82805   with O_2 saturation, by direct measurement, except pulse oximetry

82810   Gases, blood, O_2 saturation only, by direct measurement, except pulse oximetry

(For pulse oximetry, use 94760)

82820   Hemoglobin-oxygen affinity (pO_2 for 50% hemoglobin saturation with oxygen)

82926   Gastric acid, free and total, each specimen

82928   Gastric acid, free or total, each specimen

82938   Gastrin after secretin stimulation

82941   Gastrin
➔ *CPT Assistant* Aug 05:9

(Gentamicin, use 80170)

(GGT, use 82977)

(GLC, gas liquid chromatography, use 82486)

82943   Glucagon

82945   Glucose, body fluid, other than blood
➔ *CPT Changes: An Insider's View* 2001

82946   Glucagon tolerance test

82947   Glucose; quantitative, blood (except reagent strip)
➔ *CPT Assistant* Summer 93:14, Summer 94:5, Sep 99:10, Dec 99:2, Jun 02:3, Feb 05:9; *CPT Changes: An Insider's View* 2001

82948   blood, reagent strip
➔ *CPT Assistant* Summer 94:5, Jan 99:10

82950   post glucose dose (includes glucose)
➔ *CPT Assistant* Sep 99:10, Jun 02:3, Feb 05:9

82951   tolerance test (GTT), 3 specimens (includes glucose)
➔ *CPT Assistant* Feb 01:10, Feb 05:9

82952   tolerance test, each additional beyond 3 specimens
➔ *CPT Assistant* Feb 01:10

82953   tolbutamide tolerance test

(For insulin tolerance test, see 80434, 80435)

(For leucine tolerance test, use 80428)

(For semiquantitative urine glucose, see 81000, 81002, 81005, 81099)

82955   Glucose-6-phosphate dehydrogenase (G6PD); quantitative

82960   screen

(For glucose tolerance test with medication, use 96374 in addition)

82962   Glucose, blood by glucose monitoring device(s) cleared by the FDA specifically for home use
➔ *CPT Assistant* Summer 94:4, Jan 99:10

82963   Glucosidase, beta

82965   Glutamate dehydrogenase

82975   Glutamine (glutamic acid amide)

82977   Glutamyltransferase, gamma (GGT)
➔ *CPT Assistant* Dec 99:1

82978   Glutathione

82979   Glutathione reductase, RBC

82980   Glutethimide

(Glycohemoglobin, use 83036)

82985   Glycated protein
➔ *CPT Assistant* Summer 94:2

(Gonadotropin, chorionic, see 84702, 84703)

83001 Gonadotropin; follicle stimulating hormone (FSH)
➜ *CPT Assistant* Aug 05:9

83002   luteinizing hormone (LH)

(For luteinizing releasing factor [LRH], use 83727)

83003 Growth hormone, human (HGH) (somatotropin)

(For antibody to human growth hormone, use 86277)

83008 Guanosine monophosphate (GMP), cyclic

83009 Helicobacter pylori, blood test analysis for urease activity, non-radioactive isotope (eg, C-13)
➜ *CPT Changes: An Insider's View* 2005

(For H. pylori, breath test analysis for urease activity, see 83013, 83014)

83010 Haptoglobin; quantitative

83012   phenotypes

83013 Helicobacter pylori; breath test analysis for urease activity, non-radioactive isotope (eg, C-13)
➜ *CPT Assistant* Nov 98:25, Feb 99:8, Nov 99:45; *CPT Changes: An Insider's View* 2001, 2002, 2005

83014   drug administration
➜ *CPT Assistant* Nov 98:25, Feb 99:8, Nov 99:45; *CPT Changes: An Insider's View* 2005

(For H. pylori, stool, use 87338. For H. pylori, liquid scintillation counter, see 78267, 78268. For H. pylori, enzyme immunoassay, use 87339)

(For H. pylori, blood test analysis for urease activity, use 83009)

83015 Heavy metal (eg, arsenic, barium, beryllium, bismuth, antimony, mercury); screen

83018   quantitative, each

83020 Hemoglobin fractionation and quantitation; electrophoresis (eg, A2, S, C, and/or F)
➜ *CPT Assistant* Nov 98:25

83021   chromatography (eg, A2, S, C, and/or F)
➜ *CPT Assistant* Nov 98:25, Dec 99:7

(For glycosylated [A1c] hemoglobin analysis, by chromatography, in the absence of an identified hemoglobin variant, use 83036)

83026 Hemoglobin; by copper sulfate method, non-automated

83030   F (fetal), chemical

83033   F (fetal), qualitative
➜ *CPT Changes: An Insider's View* 2001

83036   glycosylated (A1C)
➜ *CPT Assistant* Summer 94:2, Feb 06:7, Oct 06:15; *CPT Changes: An Insider's View* 2006

(For glycosylated [A1c] hemoglobin analysis, by chromatography, in the setting of an identified hemoglobin variant, use 83021)

(For fecal hemoglobin detection by immunoassay, use 82274)

83037   glycosylated (A1C) by device cleared by FDA for home use
➜ *CPT Assistant* Feb 06:7, Oct 06:15; *CPT Changes: An Insider's View* 2006

83045   methemoglobin, qualitative

83050   methemoglobin, quantitative

(For transcutaneous quantitative methemoglobin determination, use 88741)

83051   plasma

83055   sulfhemoglobin, qualitative

83060   sulfhemoglobin, quantitative

83065   thermolabile

83068   unstable, screen

83069   urine

83070 Hemosiderin; qualitative

83071   quantitative

(Heroin, see 80100-80103)

(HIAA, use 83497)

(High performance liquid chromatography [HPLC], use 82486)

83080 b-Hexosaminidase, each assay
➜ *CPT Assistant* Nov 98:25

83088 Histamine

(Hollander test, use 91052)

83090 Homocysteine
➜ *CPT Assistant* Jan 01:13; *CPT Changes: An Insider's View* 2001

83150 Homovanillic acid (HVA)
➜ *CPT Assistant* Aug 05:9

(Hormones, see individual alphabetic listings in **Chemistry** section)

(Hydrogen breath test, use 91065)

83491 Hydroxycorticosteroids, 17- (17-OHCS)
➜ *CPT Assistant* Aug 05:9

(For cortisol, see 82530, 82533. For deoxycortisol, use 82634)

83497 Hydroxyindolacetic acid, 5-(HIAA)

(For urine qualitative test, use 81005)

(5-Hydroxytryptamine, use 84260)

83498 Hydroxyprogesterone, 17-d

83499 Hydroxyprogesterone, 20-

83500 Hydroxyproline; free
➜ *CPT Assistant* Aug 05:9

83505   total

▲ **83516** Immunoassay for analyte other than infectious agent antibody or infectious agent antigen; qualitative or semiquantitative, multiple step method
→ *CPT Assistant* Nov 98:25; *CPT Changes: An Insider's View* 2010

▲ **83518** qualitative or semiquantitative, single step method (eg, reagent strip)
→ *CPT Assistant* Fall 93:26; *CPT Changes: An Insider's View* 2010

▲ **83519** quantitative, by radioimmunoassay (eg, RIA)
→ *CPT Assistant* Fall 93:26, Summer 94:2; *CPT Changes: An Insider's View* 2010

▲ **83520** quantitative, not otherwise specified
→ *CPT Assistant* Fall 93:26; *CPT Changes: An Insider's View* 2010

(For immunoassays for antibodies to infectious agent antigens, see analyte and method specific codes in the **Immunology** section)

(For immunoassay of tumor antigen not elsewhere specified, use 86316)

(Immunoglobulins, see 82784, 82785)

83525 Insulin; total

(For proinsulin, use 84206)

83527 free
→ *CPT Assistant* Summer 94:5

83528 Intrinsic factor

(For intrinsic factor antibodies, use 86340)

83540 Iron
→ *CPT Assistant* Fall 93:25

83550 Iron binding capacity

83570 Isocitric dehydrogenase (IDH)

(Isonicotinic acid hydrazide, INH, see code for specific method)

(Isopropyl alcohol, use 84600)

83582 Ketogenic steroids, fractionation

(Ketone bodies, for serum, see 82009, 82010; for urine, see 81000-81003)

83586 Ketosteroids, 17- (17-KS); total

83593 fractionation

83605 Lactate (lactic acid)
→ *CPT Assistant* Aug 05:9

83615 Lactate dehydrogenase (LD), (LDH);
→ *CPT Assistant* Fall 93:25, Feb 98:1, Dec 99:2

83625 isoenzymes, separation and quantitation
→ *CPT Assistant* Fall 93:25, Feb 98:1

83630 Lactoferrin, fecal; qualitative
→ *CPT Assistant* Feb 06:7; *CPT Changes: An Insider's View* 2005, 2006

83631 quantitative
→ *CPT Assistant* Feb 06:7, Jan 07:29; *CPT Changes: An Insider's View* 2006

83632 Lactogen, human placental (HPL) human chorionic somatomammotropin

83633 Lactose, urine; qualitative

83634 quantitative

(For tolerance, see 82951, 82952)

(For breath hydrogen test for lactase deficiency, use 91065)

83655 Lead

83661 Fetal lung maturity assessment; lecithin sphingomyelin (L/S) ratio
→ *CPT Changes: An Insider's View* 2001

83662 foam stability test

83663 fluorescence polarization
→ *CPT Changes: An Insider's View* 2001

83664 lamellar body density
→ *CPT Changes: An Insider's View* 2001

(For phosphatidylglycerol, use 84081)

83670 Leucine aminopeptidase (LAP)

83690 Lipase

83695 Lipoprotein (a)
→ *CPT Assistant* Feb 06:7; *CPT Changes: An Insider's View* 2006

83698 Lipoprotein-associated phospholipase A_2 (Lp-PLA$_2$)
→ *CPT Changes: An Insider's View* 2007

83700 Lipoprotein, blood; electrophoretic separation and quantitation
→ *CPT Assistant* Feb 06:7; *CPT Changes: An Insider's View* 2006

83701 high resolution fractionation and quantitation of lipoproteins including lipoprotein subclasses when performed (eg, electrophoresis, ultracentrifugation)
→ *CPT Assistant* Feb 06:7; *CPT Changes: An Insider's View* 2006

83704 quantitation of lipoprotein particle numbers and lipoprotein particle subclasses (eg, by nuclear magnetic resonance spectroscopy)
→ *CPT Assistant* Feb 06:7; *CPT Changes: An Insider's View* 2006

83718 Lipoprotein, direct measurement; high density cholesterol (HDL cholesterol)
→ *CPT Assistant* Oct 99:11, Mar 00:11, Feb 05:9

83719 VLDL cholesterol
→ *CPT Assistant* Oct 99:11

83721 LDL cholesterol
→ *CPT Assistant* Nov 98:25, Oct 99:11

(For fractionation by high resolution electrophoresis or ultracentrifugation, use 83701)

(For lipoprotein particle numbers and subclasses analysis by nuclear magnetic resonance spectroscopy, use 83704)

83727   Luteinizing releasing factor (LRH)

(Luteinizing hormone [LH], use 83002)

(For qualitative analysis, see 80100-80103)

(Macroglobulins, alpha-2, use 86329)

83735   Magnesium

83775   Malate dehydrogenase

(Maltose tolerance, see 82951, 82952)

(Mammotropin, use 84146)

83785   Manganese

(Marijuana, see 80100-80103)

83788   Mass spectrometry and tandem mass spectrometry (MS, MS/MS), analyte not elsewhere specified; qualitative, each specimen
> *CPT Assistant* Nov 98:26

83789   quantitative, each specimen
> *CPT Assistant* Nov 98:26

83805   Meprobamate
> *CPT Assistant* Aug 05:9

(For qualitative analysis, see 80100-80103)

83825   Mercury, quantitative

(Mercury screen, use 83015)

83835   Metanephrines

(For catecholamines, see 82382-82384)

83840   Methadone

(For methadone qualitative analysis, see 80100-80103)

(Methamphetamine, see 80100-80103, 82145)

(Methanol, use 84600)

83857   Methemalbumin

(Methemoglobin, see hemoglobin 83045, 83050)

83858   Methsuximide

(Methyl alcohol, use 84600)

(Microalbumin, see 82043 for quantitative, see 82044 for semiquantitative)

(Microglobulin, beta-2, use 82232)

83864   Mucopolysaccharides, acid; quantitative

83866   screen

83872   Mucin, synovial fluid (Ropes test)

83873   Myelin basic protein, cerebrospinal fluid
> *CPT Changes: An Insider's View* 2002

(For oligoclonal bands, use 83916)

83874   Myoglobin
> *CPT Assistant* Feb 98:1

(Nalorphine, use 83925)

83876   Myeloperoxidase (MPO)
> *CPT Changes: An Insider's View* 2009

83880   Natriuretic peptide
> *CPT Assistant* Jul 03:7; *CPT Changes: An Insider's View* 2003

83883   Nephelometry, each analyte not elsewhere specified

83885   Nickel

83887   Nicotine

Codes 83890-83914 are intended for use with molecular diagnostic techniques for analysis of nucleic acids.

Codes 83890-83914 are coded by procedure rather than analyte.

Code separately for each procedure used in an analysis. For example, a procedure requiring isolation of DNA, restriction endonuclease digestion, electrophoresis, and nucleic acid probe amplification would be coded 83890, 83892, 83894, and 83898.

When molecular diagnostic procedures are performed to test for oncology, hematology, neurology or inherited disorder, use the appropriate modifier to specify probe type or condition tested. (See **Appendix I** for a listing of appropriate modifiers to report with molecular diagnostic and cytogenetic procedures.)

Each nucleic acid preparation may include a digestate, undigested nucleic acid, or other uniquely modified nucleic acid sample (eg, newly synthesized oligonucleotide).

▶(For microbial identification, see 87149, 87150, 87152, 87153, 87470-87801)◀

(For array technology using more than 10 probes, see 88384-88386)

83890   Molecular diagnostics; molecular isolation or extraction, each nucleic acid type (ie, DNA or RNA)
> *CPT Assistant* Fall 93:26, Nov 98:26, Jul 05:1, Jan 06:5; *CPT Changes: An Insider's View* 2009

83891   isolation or extraction of highly purified nucleic acid, each nucleic acid type (ie, DNA or RNA)
> *CPT Assistant* Nov 98:26, Jul 05:1, Jan 06:5; *CPT Changes: An Insider's View* 2009

83892   enzymatic digestion, each enzyme treatment
> *CPT Assistant* Fall 93:26, Jul 05:1, Jan 06:5; *CPT Changes: An Insider's View* 2009

83893   dot/slot blot production, each nucleic acid preparation
> *CPT Assistant* Nov 98:26, Jul 05:1, Jan 06:5; *CPT Changes: An Insider's View* 2009

83894   separation by gel electrophoresis (eg, agarose, polyacrylamide), each nucleic acid preparation
> *CPT Assistant* Fall 93:25, Nov 98:26, Jul 05:1, Jan 06:5; *CPT Changes: An Insider's View* 2009

83896   nucleic acid probe, each
> *CPT Assistant* Fall 93:26, Aug 02:10, Jul 05:1, Jan 06:5

83897 nucleic acid transfer (eg, Southern, Northern), each nucleic acid preparation
➜ CPT Assistant Nov 98:26, Jul 05:1, Jan 06:5; CPT Changes: An Insider's View 2009

83898 amplification, target, each nucleic acid sequence
➜ CPT Assistant Fall 93:26, Nov 98:26, Jul 05:1, Jan 06:5, Feb 06:7, Apr 08:5; CPT Changes: An Insider's View 2001, 2006, 2008

(For multiplex target amplification, see 83900, 83901)

(For signal amplification, use 83908)

83900 amplification, target, multiplex, first 2 nucleic acid sequences
➜ CPT Assistant Jan 06:5, Feb 06:7, Apr 08:5; CPT Changes: An Insider's View 2006, 2008

+ 83901 amplification, target, multiplex, each additional nucleic acid sequence beyond 2 (List separately in addition to code for primary procedure)
➜ CPT Assistant Nov 98:26, Jul 05:1, Aug 05:9, Jan 06:5, Feb 06:7, Apr 08:5; CPT Changes: An Insider's View 2006, 2008

(Use 83901 in conjunction with 83900)

83902 reverse transcription
➜ CPT Assistant Jul 05:1, Jan 06:5; CPT Changes: An Insider's View 2001

83903 mutation scanning, by physical properties (eg, single strand conformational polymorphisms [SSCP], heteroduplex, denaturing gradient gel electrophoresis [DGGE], RNA'ase A), single segment, each
➜ CPT Assistant Nov 98:26, Jul 05:1, Jan 06:5

83904 mutation identification by sequencing, single segment, each segment
➜ CPT Assistant Nov 98:26, Jul 05:1, Jan 06:5

83905 mutation identification by allele specific transcription, single segment, each segment
➜ CPT Assistant Nov 98:26, Jul 05:1, Jan 06:5

83906 mutation identification by allele specific translation, single segment, each segment
➜ CPT Assistant Nov 98:26, Jul 05:1, Jan 06:5

83907 lysis of cells prior to nucleic acid extraction (eg, stool specimens, paraffin embedded tissue), each specimen
➜ CPT Assistant Jan 06:5, Feb 06:7; CPT Changes: An Insider's View 2006, 2009

83908 amplification, signal, each nucleic acid sequence
➜ CPT Assistant Jan 06:5, Feb 06:7, Apr 08:5; CPT Changes: An Insider's View 2006, 2008

(For target amplification, see 83898, 83900, 83901)

83909 separation and identification by high resolution technique (eg, capillary electrophoresis), each nucleic acid preparation
➜ CPT Assistant Jan 06:5, Feb 06:7; CPT Changes: An Insider's View 2006, 2009

83912 interpretation and report
➜ CPT Assistant Jul 05:1, Jan 06:5

83913 RNA stabilization
➜ CPT Changes: An Insider's View 2007

83914 Mutation identification by enzymatic ligation or primer extension, single segment, each segment (eg, oligonucleotide ligation assay [OLA], single base chain extension [SBCE], or allele-specific primer extension [ASPE])
➜ CPT Assistant Feb 06:7; CPT Changes: An Insider's View 2006

83915 Nucleotidase 5'-

83916 Oligoclonal immune (oligoclonal bands)
➜ CPT Changes: An Insider's View 2002

83918 Organic acids; total, quantitative, each specimen
➜ CPT Assistant Mar 96:11, Nov 98:26; CPT Changes: An Insider's View 2001

83919 qualitative, each specimen
➜ CPT Assistant Nov 98:26

83921 Organic acid, single, quantitative
➜ CPT Changes: An Insider's View 2001

83925 Opiate(s), drug and metabolites, each procedure
➜ CPT Changes: An Insider's View 2009

83930 Osmolality; blood

83935 urine

83937 Osteocalcin (bone g1a protein)
➜ CPT Assistant Summer 94:5

83945 Oxalate

83950 Oncoprotein; HER-2/neu
➜ CPT Changes: An Insider's View 2002, 2009

(For tissue, see 88342, 88365)

83951 des-gamma-carboxy-prothrombin (DCP)
➜ CPT Changes: An Insider's View 2009

83970 Parathormone (parathyroid hormone)

(Pesticide, quantitative, see code for specific method. For screen for chlorinated hydrocarbons, use 82441)

▲ **83986** pH; body fluid, not otherwise specified
➜ CPT Changes: An Insider's View 2010

● **83987** exhaled breath condensate
➜ CPT Changes: An Insider's View 2010

(For blood pH, see 82800, 82803)

83992 Phencyclidine (PCP)

(For qualitative analysis, see 80100-80103)

(Phenobarbital, use 80184)

83993 Calprotectin, fecal
➜ CPT Assistant Apr 08:5; CPT Changes: An Insider's View 2008

84022 Phenothiazine
➜ CPT Assistant Aug 05:9

(For qualitative analysis, see 80100, 80101)

84030 Phenylalanine (PKU), blood

(Phenylalanine-tyrosine ratio, see 84030, 84510)

84035	Phenylketones, qualitative

84060 Phosphatase, acid; total

84061   forensic examination

84066   prostatic

84075 Phosphatase, alkaline;
➔ *CPT Assistant* Dec 99:2

84078   heat stable (total not included)

84080   isoenzymes

84081 Phosphatidylglycerol

(Phosphates inorganic, use 84100)

(Phosphates, organic, see code for specific method. For cholinesterase, see 82480, 82482)

84085 Phosphogluconate, 6-, dehydrogenase, RBC

84087 Phosphohexose isomerase

84100 Phosphorus inorganic (phosphate);
➔ *CPT Assistant* Dec 99:2, Aug 05:9

84105   urine

(Pituitary gonadotropins, see 83001-83002)

(PKU, see 84030, 84035)

84106 Porphobilinogen, urine; qualitative

84110   quantitative

84119 Porphyrins, urine; qualitative

84120   quantitation and fractionation

84126 Porphyrins, feces; quantitative

84127   qualitative

(Porphyrin precursors, see 82135, 84106, 84110)

(For protoporphyrin, RBC, see 84202, 84203)

84132 Potassium; serum, plasma or whole blood
➔ *CPT Assistant* Dec 99:2, Jun 02:3; *CPT Changes: An Insider's View* 2009

84133   urine

84134 Prealbumin

(For microalbumin, see 82043, 82044)

84135 Pregnanediol

84138 Pregnanetriol

84140 Pregnenolone
➔ *CPT Assistant* Summer 94:6

84143 17-hydroxypregnenolone
➔ *CPT Assistant* Summer 94:6

84144 Progesterone

(Progesterone receptor assay, use 84234)

(For proinsulin, use 84206)

● **84145** Procalcitonin (PCT)
➔ *CPT Changes: An Insider's View* 2010

84146 Prolactin

84150 Prostaglandin, each

84152 Prostate specific antigen (PSA); complexed (direct measurement)
➔ *CPT Changes: An Insider's View* 2001

84153   total
➔ *CPT Assistant* Fall 93:26, May 96:10, Aug 96:10, Jan 97:10, Nov 98:26, Aug 99:5, Dec 99:10

84154   free
➔ *CPT Assistant* Nov 98:26, Aug 99:5, Dec 99:10

84155 Protein, total, except by refractometry; serum, plasma or whole blood
➔ *CPT Assistant* Dec 99:2, Jan 00:7; *CPT Changes: An Insider's View* 2004, 2009

84156   urine
➔ *CPT Changes: An Insider's View* 2004

84157   other source (eg, synovial fluid, cerebrospinal fluid)
➔ *CPT Changes: An Insider's View* 2004

84160 Protein, total, by refractometry, any source
➔ *CPT Changes: An Insider's View* 2004

(For urine total protein by dipstick method, use 81000-81003)

84163 Pregnancy-associated plasma protein-A (PAPP-A)
➔ *CPT Changes: An Insider's View* 2005

84165 Protein; electrophoretic fractionation and quantitation, serum
➔ *CPT Changes: An Insider's View* 2004, 2005

84166   electrophoretic fractionation and quantitation, other fluids with concentration (eg, urine, CSF)
➔ *CPT Changes: An Insider's View* 2005

84181 Western Blot, with interpretation and report, blood or other body fluid

84182 Western Blot, with interpretation and report, blood or other body fluid, immunological probe for band identification, each

(For Western Blot tissue analysis, use 88371)

84202 Protoporphyrin, RBC; quantitative
➔ *CPT Assistant* Aug 05:9

84203   screen

84206 Proinsulin

(Pseudocholinesterase, use 82480)

84207 Pyridoxal phosphate (Vitamin B-6)

84210 Pyruvate

84220 Pyruvate kinase

84228 Quinine

84233 Receptor assay; estrogen

84234   progesterone

84235	endocrine, other than estrogen or progesterone (specify hormone)
84238	non-endocrine (specify receptor)
	➲ *CPT Assistant* Nov 05:14; *CPT Changes: An Insider's View* 2006
84244	Renin
84252	Riboflavin (Vitamin B-2)
	(Salicylates, use 80196)
	(Secretin test, see 99070, 89100 and appropriate analyses)
84255	Selenium
84260	Serotonin
	(For urine metabolites (HIAA), use 83497)
84270	Sex hormone binding globulin (SHBG)
	➲ *CPT Assistant* Summer 94:4
84275	Sialic acid
	(Sickle hemoglobin, use 85660)
84285	Silica
84295	Sodium; serum, plasma or whole blood
	➲ *CPT Assistant* Dec 99:2; *CPT Changes: An Insider's View* 2009
84300	urine
	➲ *CPT Assistant* Aug 05:9
84302	other source
	➲ *CPT Assistant* Jul 03:7; *CPT Changes: An Insider's View* 2003
	(Somatomammotropin, use 83632)
	(Somatotropin, use 83003)
84305	Somatomedin
	➲ *CPT Assistant* Summer 94:4
84307	Somatostatin
	➲ *CPT Assistant* Summer 94:4
84311	Spectrophotometry, analyte not elsewhere specified
84315	Specific gravity (except urine)
	(For specific gravity, urine, see 81000-81003)
	(Stone analysis, see 82355-82370)
84375	Sugars, chromatographic, TLC or paper chromatography
84376	Sugars (mono-, di-, and oligosaccharides); single qualitative, each specimen
	➲ *CPT Assistant* Nov 98:26-27, Dec 99:7
84377	multiple qualitative, each specimen
	➲ *CPT Assistant* Nov 98:26-27, Jul 03:7
84378	single quantitative, each specimen
	➲ *CPT Assistant* Nov 98:26-27
84379	multiple quantitative, each specimen
	➲ *CPT Assistant* Nov 98:26-27, Dec 99:7, Jul 03:7

84392	Sulfate, urine
	(Sulfhemoglobin, see hemoglobin, 83055, 83060)
	(T-3, see 84479-84481)
	(T-4, see 84436-84439)
84402	Testosterone; free
	➲ *CPT Assistant* Aug 05:9
84403	total
84425	Thiamine (Vitamin B-1)
84430	Thiocyanate
● **84431**	Thromboxane metabolite(s), including thromboxane if performed, urine
	➲ *CPT Changes: An Insider's View* 2010
	▶(For concurrent urine creatinine determination, use 84431 in conjunction with 82570)◀
84432	Thyroglobulin
	➲ *CPT Assistant* Summer 94:2
	(Thyroglobulin, antibody, use 86800)
	(Thyrotropin releasing hormone [TRH] test, see 80438, 80439)
84436	Thyroxine; total
	➲ *CPT Assistant* Fall 93:25, Summer 94:3
84437	requiring elution (eg, neonatal)
84439	free
84442	Thyroxine binding globulin (TBG)
84443	Thyroid stimulating hormone (TSH)
	➲ *CPT Assistant* Summer 94:3
84445	Thyroid stimulating immune globulins (TSI)
	➲ *CPT Assistant* Summer 94:3; *CPT Changes: An Insider's View* 2002
	(Tobramycin, use 80200)
84446	Tocopherol alpha (Vitamin E)
	(Tolbutamide tolerance, use 82953)
84449	Transcortin (cortisol binding globulin)
	➲ *CPT Assistant* Summer 94:6
84450	Transferase; aspartate amino (AST) (SGOT)
	➲ *CPT Assistant* Dec 99:2
84460	alanine amino (ALT) (SGPT)
	➲ *CPT Assistant* Dec 99:2
84466	Transferrin
	➲ *CPT Assistant* Summer 94:4
	(Iron binding capacity, use 83550)
84478	Triglycerides
	➲ *CPT Assistant* Dec 99:2, Mar 00:11, Feb 05:9
84479	Thyroid hormone (T3 or T4) uptake or thyroid hormone binding ratio (THBR)
	➲ *CPT Assistant* Fall 93:25, Summer 94:3

84480 Triiodothyronine T3; total (TT-3)

84481 　free

84482 　reverse
　　➔ *CPT Assistant* Summer 94:2

84484 Troponin, quantitative
　　➔ *CPT Assistant* Nov 97:29, Jan 98:6, Feb 98:1

　　(For troponin, qualitative assay, use 84512)

84485 Trypsin; duodenal fluid

84488 　feces, qualitative

84490 　feces, quantitative, 24-hour collection

84510 Tyrosine

　　(Urate crystal identification, use 89060)

84512 Troponin, qualitative
　　➔ *CPT Assistant* Nov 97:29, Jan 98:6, Feb 98:1

　　(For troponin, quantitative assay, use 84484)

84520 Urea nitrogen; quantitative
　　➔ *CPT Assistant* Dec 99:2

84525 　semiquantitative (eg, reagent strip test)
　　➔ *CPT Assistant* Mar 98:3

84540 Urea nitrogen, urine

84545 Urea nitrogen, clearance

84550 Uric acid; blood
　　➔ *CPT Assistant* Dec 99:2

84560 　other source

84577 Urobilinogen, feces, quantitative

84578 Urobilinogen, urine; qualitative

84580 　quantitative, timed specimen

84583 　semiquantitative

　　(Uroporphyrins, use 84120)

　　(Valproic acid [dipropylacetic acid], use 80164)

84585 Vanillylmandelic acid (VMA), urine

84586 Vasoactive intestinal peptide (VIP)
　　➔ *CPT Assistant* Summer 94:6

84588 Vasopressin (antidiuretic hormone, ADH)

84590 Vitamin A
　　➔ *CPT Assistant* Aug 05:9

　　(Vitamin B-1, use 84425)

　　(Vitamin B-2, use 84252)

　　(Vitamin B-6, use 84207)

　　(Vitamin B-12, use 82607)

　　(Vitamin B-12, absorption (Schilling), see 78270, 78271)

　　(Vitamin C, use 82180)

　　►(Vitamin D, see 82306, 82652)◄

　　(Vitamin E, use 84446)

84591 Vitamin, not otherwise specified
　　➔ *CPT Changes: An Insider's View* 2001

84597 Vitamin K

　　(VMA, use 84585)

84600 Volatiles (eg, acetic anhydride, carbon tetrachloride, dichloroethane, dichloromethane, diethylether, isopropyl alcohol, methanol)
　　➔ *CPT Assistant* Aug 05:9

　　(For acetaldehyde, use 82000)

　　(Volume, blood, RISA or Cr-51, see 78110, 78111)

84620 Xylose absorption test, blood and/or urine

　　(For administration, use 99070)

84630 Zinc

84681 C-peptide

84702 Gonadotropin, chorionic (hCG); quantitative

84703 　qualitative

　　(For urine pregnancy test by visual color comparison, use 81025)

84704 　free beta chain
　　➔ *CPT Assistant* Apr 08:5, Aug 08:13; *CPT Changes: An Insider's View* 2008

84830 Ovulation tests, by visual color comparison methods for human luteinizing hormone

84999 Unlisted chemistry procedure
　　➔ *CPT Assistant* Oct 00:24, Aug 05:9

Hematology and Coagulation

　　(For blood banking procedures, see **Transfusion Medicine**)

　　(Agglutinins, see **Immunology**)

　　(Antiplasmin, use 85410)

　　(Antithrombin III, see 85300, 85301)

85002 Bleeding time
　　➔ *CPT Assistant* Aug 05:9

85004 Blood count; automated differential WBC count
　　➔ *CPT Assistant* Jan 04:26; *CPT Changes: An Insider's View* 2003

85007 　blood smear, microscopic examination with manual differential WBC count
　　➔ *CPT Assistant* Jul 03:7, Jan 04:26; *CPT Changes: An Insider's View* 2003

85008 　blood smear, microscopic examination without manual differential WBC count
　　➔ *CPT Assistant* Jul 03:8, Jan 04:26; *CPT Changes: An Insider's View* 2003

　　(For other fluids [eg, CSF], see 89050, 89051)

85009   manual differential WBC count, buffy coat
> *CPT Assistant* Jul 03:7, Jan 04:26; *CPT Changes: An Insider's View* 2003

(Eosinophils, nasal smear, use 89190)

85013   spun microhematocrit

85014   hematocrit (Hct)
> *CPT Assistant* Jul 03:7; *CPT Changes: An Insider's View* 2003

85018   hemoglobin (Hgb)
> *CPT Assistant* Jul 03:8; *CPT Changes: An Insider's View* 2003

(For other hemoglobin determination, see 83020-83069)

(For immunoassay, hemoglobin, fecal, use 82274)

▶(For transcutaneous hemoglobin measurement, use 88738)◀

85025   complete (CBC), automated (Hgb, Hct, RBC, WBC and platelet count) and automated differential WBC count
> *CPT Assistant* Jul 00:11, Jul 03:7, Jan 04:26; *CPT Changes: An Insider's View* 2003

85027   complete (CBC), automated (Hgb, Hct, RBC, WBC and platelet count)
> *CPT Assistant* Jul 03:8, Jan 04:26; *CPT Changes: An Insider's View* 2003

85032   manual cell count (erythrocyte, leukocyte, or platelet) each
> *CPT Assistant* Jul 03:8, Nov 03:15; *CPT Changes: An Insider's View* 2003

85041   red blood cell (RBC), automated
> *CPT Assistant* Jul 03:8; *CPT Changes: An Insider's View* 2003

(Do not report code 85041 in conjunction with 85025 or 85027)

85044   reticulocyte, manual
> *CPT Assistant* Jul 03:8; *CPT Changes: An Insider's View* 2003

85045   reticulocyte, automated
> *CPT Assistant* Jul 03:8; *CPT Changes: An Insider's View* 2003

85046   reticulocytes, automated, including 1 or more cellular parameters (eg, reticulocyte hemoglobin content [CHr], immature reticulocyte fraction [IRF], reticulocyte volume [MRV], RNA content), direct measurement
> *CPT Assistant* Nov 98:27; *CPT Changes: An Insider's View* 2005

85048   leukocyte (WBC), automated
> *CPT Assistant* Jul 03:8; *CPT Changes: An Insider's View* 2003

85049   platelet, automated
> *CPT Changes: An Insider's View* 2003

85055   Reticulated platelet assay
> *CPT Changes: An Insider's View* 2004

85060   Blood smear, peripheral, interpretation by physician with written report

85097   Bone marrow, smear interpretation
> *CPT Assistant* Winter 92:17, Jul 98:4, Mar 03:22; *CPT Changes: An Insider's View* 2002

(For special stains, see 88312, 88313)

(For bone biopsy, see 20220, 20225, 20240, 20245, 20250, 20251)

85130   Chromogenic substrate assay
> *CPT Assistant* Aug 05:9

(Circulating anti-coagulant screen [mixing studies], see 85611, 85732)

85170   Clot retraction

85175   Clot lysis time, whole blood dilution

(Clotting factor I [fibrinogen], see 85384, 85385)

85210   Clotting; factor II, prothrombin, specific
> *CPT Assistant* Aug 05:9

(See also 85610-85613)

85220   factor V (AcG or proaccelerin), labile factor

85230   factor VII (proconvertin, stable factor)

85240   factor VIII (AHG), 1-stage

85244   factor VIII related antigen

85245   factor VIII, VW factor, ristocetin cofactor

85246   factor VIII, VW factor antigen

85247   factor VIII, von Willebrand factor, multimetric analysis

85250   factor IX (PTC or Christmas)

85260   factor X (Stuart-Prower)

85270   factor XI (PTA)

85280   factor XII (Hageman)

85290   factor XIII (fibrin stabilizing)

85291   factor XIII (fibrin stabilizing), screen solubility

85292   prekallikrein assay (Fletcher factor assay)

85293   high molecular weight kininogen assay (Fitzgerald factor assay)

85300   Clotting inhibitors or anticoagulants; antithrombin III, activity
> *CPT Assistant* Aug 05:9

85301   antithrombin III, antigen assay

85302   protein C, antigen

85303   protein C, activity

85305   protein S, total

85306   protein S, free

85307   Activated Protein C (APC) resistance assay
> *CPT Changes: An Insider's View* 2001

85335   Factor inhibitor test

85337   Thrombomodulin

(For mixing studies for inhibitors, use 85732)

85345   Coagulation time; Lee and White

85347   activated

85348   other methods

(Differential count, see 85007 et seq)

(Duke bleeding time, use 85002)

(Eosinophils, nasal smear, use 89190)

85360   Euglobulin lysis

(Fetal hemoglobin, see 83030, 83033, 85460)

85362   Fibrin(ogen) degradation (split) products (FDP) (FSP); agglutination slide, semiquantitative

(Immunoelectrophoresis, use 86320)

85366   paracoagulation

85370   quantitative

85378   Fibrin degradation products, D-dimer; qualitative or semiquantitative
➔ *CPT Assistant* Jul 03:8; *CPT Changes: An Insider's View* 2003

85379   quantitative

(For ultrasensitive and standard sensitivity quantitative D-dimer, use 85379)

85380   ultrasensitive (eg, for evaluation for venous thromboembolism), qualitative or semiquantitative
➔ *CPT Assistant* Jul 03:8; *CPT Changes: An Insider's View* 2003

85384   Fibrinogen; activity

85385   antigen

85390   Fibrinolysins or coagulopathy screen, interpretation and report

85396   Coagulation/fibrinolysis assay, whole blood (eg, viscoelastic clot assessment), including use of any pharmacologic additive(s), as indicated, including interpretation and written report, per day
➔ *CPT Changes: An Insider's View* 2004

85397   Coagulation and fibrinolysis, functional activity, not otherwise specified (eg, ADAMTS-13), each analyte
➔ *CPT Changes: An Insider's View* 2009

85400   Fibrinolytic factors and inhibitors; plasmin
➔ *CPT Assistant* Aug 05:9

85410   alpha-2 antiplasmin

85415   plasminogen activator

85420   plasminogen, except antigenic assay

85421   plasminogen, antigenic assay

(Fragility, red blood cell, see 85547, 85555-85557)

85441   Heinz bodies; direct

85445   induced, acetyl phenylhydrazine

(Hematocrit [PCV], see 85014, 85025, 85027)

(Hemoglobin, see 83020-83068, 85018, 85025, 85027)

85460   Hemoglobin or RBCs, fetal, for fetomaternal hemorrhage; differential lysis (Kleihauer-Betke)
➔ *CPT Assistant* Fall 93:25

(See also 83030, 83033)

(Hemolysins, see 86940, 86941)

85461   rosette

85475   Hemolysin, acid

(See also 86940, 86941)

85520   Heparin assay
➔ *CPT Assistant* Aug 05:9

85525   Heparin neutralization

85530   Heparin-protamine tolerance test

85536   Iron stain, peripheral blood
➔ *CPT Changes: An Insider's View* 2001

(For iron stains on bone marrow or other tissues with physician evaluation, use 88313)

85540   Leukocyte alkaline phosphatase with count

85547   Mechanical fragility, RBC

85549   Muramidase

(Nitroblue tetrazolium dye test, use 86384)

85555   Osmotic fragility, RBC; unincubated

85557   incubated

(Packed cell volume, use 85013)

(Partial thromboplastin time, see 85730, 85732)

(Parasites, blood [eg, malaria smears], use 87207)

(Plasmin, use 85400)

(Plasminogen, use 85420)

(Plasminogen activator, use 85415)

85576   Platelet, aggregation (in vitro), each agent
➔ *CPT Assistant* Jul 96:10; *CPT Changes: An Insider's View* 2003

▶(For thromboxane metabolite[s], including thromboxane, if performed, measurement[s] in urine, use 84431)◀

85597   Platelet neutralization

85610   Prothrombin time;
➔ *CPT Assistant* Aug 05:9

85611   substitution, plasma fractions, each

85612   Russell viper venom time (includes venom); undiluted

85613   diluted

(Red blood cell count, see 85025, 85027, 85041)

85635   Reptilase test

(Reticulocyte count, see 85044, 85045)

85651   Sedimentation rate, erythrocyte; non-automated

85652   automated

85660 Sickling of RBC, reduction

(Hemoglobin electrophoresis, use 83020)

(Smears [eg, for parasites, malaria], use 87207)

85670 Thrombin time; plasma

85675   titer

85705 Thromboplastin inhibition, tissue
➔ *CPT Assistant* Aug 05:9

(For individual clotting factors, see 85245-85247)

85730 Thromboplastin time, partial (PTT); plasma or whole blood

85732   substitution, plasma fractions, each

85810 Viscosity

(von Willebrand factor assay, see 85245-85247)

(WBC count, see 85025, 85027, 85048, 89050)

85999 Unlisted hematology and coagulation procedure
➔ *CPT Assistant* Aug 05:9

Immunology

(Acetylcholine receptor antibody, see 83519, 86255, 86256)

(Actinomyces, antibodies to, use 86602)

(Adrenal cortex antibodies, see 86255, 86256)

86000 Agglutinins, febrile (eg, Brucella, Francisella, Murine typhus, Q fever, Rocky Mountain spotted fever, scrub typhus), each antigen
➔ *CPT Assistant* Aug 05:9

(For antibodies to infectious agents, see 86602-86804)

86001 Allergen specific IgG quantitative or semiquantitative, each allergen
➔ *CPT Changes: An Insider's View* 2001

(Agglutinins and autohemolysins, see 86940, 86941)

86003 Allergen specific IgE; quantitative or semiquantitative, each allergen
➔ *CPT Assistant* Spring 94:31

(For total quantitative IgE, use 82785)

86005   qualitative, multiallergen screen (dipstick, paddle, or disk)
➔ *CPT Assistant* Spring 94:31

(For total qualitative IgE, use 83518)

(Alpha-1 antitrypsin, see 82103, 82104)

(Alpha-1 feto-protein, see 82105, 82106)

(Anti-AChR [acetylcholine receptor] antibody titer, see 86255, 86256)

(Anticardiolipin antibody, use 86147)

(Anti-DNA, use 86225)

(Anti-deoxyribonuclease titer, use 86215)

86021 Antibody identification; leukocyte antibodies

86022   platelet antibodies

86023   platelet associated immunoglobulin assay

86038 Antinuclear antibodies (ANA);

86039   titer

(Antistreptococcal antibody, ie, anti-DNAse, use 86215)

(Antistreptokinase titer, use 86590)

86060 Antistreptolysin 0; titer

(For antibodies to infectious agents, see 86602-86804)

86063   screen

(For antibodies to infectious agents, see 86602-86804)

(Blastomyces, antibodies to, use 86612)

86077 Blood bank physician services; difficult cross match and/or evaluation of irregular antibody(s), interpretation and written report

86078   investigation of transfusion reaction including suspicion of transmissible disease, interpretation and written report

86079   authorization for deviation from standard blood banking procedures (eg, use of outdated blood, transfusion of Rh incompatible units), with written report

(Brucella, antibodies to, use 86622)

(Candida, antibodies to, use 86628. For skin testing, use 86485)

86140 C-reactive protein;
➔ *CPT Assistant* Aug 05:9; *CPT Changes: An Insider's View* 2002

(Candidiasis, use 86628)

86141   high sensitivity (hsCRP)
➔ *CPT Changes: An Insider's View* 2002

86146 Beta 2 Glycoprotein I antibody, each
➔ *CPT Changes: An Insider's View* 2001

86147 Cardiolipin (phospholipid) antibody, each Ig class
➔ *CPT Changes: An Insider's View* 2001

86148 Anti-phosphatidylserine (phospholipid) antibody
➔ *CPT Assistant* Nov 97:30, Jul 03:8, Nov 03:5

(To report antiprothrombin [phospholipid cofactor] antibody, use Category III code 0030T)

86155 Chemotaxis assay, specify method

(Clostridium difficile toxin, use 87230)

(Coccidioides, antibodies to, see 86635. For skin testing, use 86490)

86156 Cold agglutinin; screen

86157   titer

86160   Complement; antigen, each component

86161   functional activity, each component

86162   total hemolytic (CH50)

86171   Complement fixation tests, each antigen

(Coombs test, see 86880-86886)

86185   Counterimmunoelectrophoresis, each antigen

(Cryptococcus, antibodies to, use 86641)

86200   Cyclic citrullinated peptide (CCP), antibody
➔ *CPT Assistant* Mar 06:6; *CPT Changes: An Insider's View* 2006

86215   Deoxyribonuclease, antibody
➔ *CPT Assistant* Aug 05:9

86225   Deoxyribonucleic acid (DNA) antibody; native or double stranded

(Echinococcus, antibodies to, see code for specific method)

(For HIV antibody tests, see 86701-86703)

86226   single stranded

(Anti D.S., DNA, IFA, eg, using C.Lucilae, see 86255 and 86256)

86235   Extractable nuclear antigen, antibody to, any method (eg, nRNP, SS-A, SS-B, Sm, RNP, Sc170, J01), each antibody

86243   Fc receptor

(Filaria, antibodies to, see code for specific method)

86255   Fluorescent noninfectious agent antibody; screen, each antibody
➔ *CPT Assistant* Nov 98:27

86256   titer, each antibody

(Fluorescent technique for antigen identification in tissue, use 88346; for indirect fluorescence, use 88347)

(FTA, see 86781)

(Gel [agar] diffusion tests, use 86331)

86277   Growth hormone, human (HGH), antibody

86280   Hemagglutination inhibition test (HAI)

(For rubella, use 86762)

(For antibodies to infectious agents, see 86602-86804)

86294   Immunoassay for tumor antigen, qualitative or semiquantitative (eg, bladder tumor antigen)
➔ *CPT Changes: An Insider's View* 2001

86300   Immunoassay for tumor antigen, quantitative; CA 15-3 (27.29)
➔ *CPT Assistant* Aug 05:9; *CPT Changes: An Insider's View* 2001

86301   CA 19-9
➔ *CPT Changes: An Insider's View* 2001

86304   CA 125
➔ *CPT Changes: An Insider's View* 2001

(For measurement of serum HER-2/neu oncoprotein, see 83950)

(For hepatitis delta agent, antibody, use 86692)

● **86305**   Human epididymis protein 4 (HE4)
➔ *CPT Changes: An Insider's View* 2010

86308   Heterophile antibodies; screening

(For antibodies to infectious agents, see 86602-86804)

86309   titer

(For antibodies to infectious agents, see 86602-86804)

86310   titers after absorption with beef cells and guinea pig kidney

(Histoplasma, antibodies to, use 86698. For skin testing, use 86510)

(For antibodies to infectious agents, see 86602-86804)

(Human growth hormone antibody, use 86277)

86316   Immunoassay for tumor antigen, other antigen, quantitative (eg, CA 50, 72-4, 549), each
➔ *CPT Assistant* May 96:11, Aug 96:11, Apr 98:15, Aug 99:5, Dec 99:10; *CPT Changes: An Insider's View* 2001

86317   Immunoassay for infectious agent antibody, quantitative, not otherwise specified
➔ *CPT Assistant* Nov 97:30-31

(For immunoassay techniques for antigens, see 83516, 83518, 83519, 83520, 87301-87450, 87810-87899)

(For particle agglutination procedures, use 86403)

86318   Immunoassay for infectious agent antibody, qualitative or semiquantitative, single step method (eg, reagent strip)
➔ *CPT Assistant* Mar 07:10

86320   Immunoelectrophoresis; serum

86325   other fluids (eg, urine, cerebrospinal fluid) with concentration
➔ *CPT Changes: An Insider's View* 2002

86327   crossed (2-dimensional assay)

86329   Immunodiffusion; not elsewhere specified
➔ *CPT Assistant* Aug 00:11

86331   gel diffusion, qualitative (Ouchterlony), each antigen or antibody

86332   Immune complex assay

86334   Immunofixation electrophoresis; serum
➔ *CPT Changes: An Insider's View* 2005

86335   other fluids with concentration (eg, urine, CSF)
➔ *CPT Changes: An Insider's View* 2005

86336   Inhibin A
➔ *CPT Changes: An Insider's View* 2002

86337   Insulin antibodies

86340   Intrinsic factor antibodies

(Leptospira, antibodies to, use 86720)

(Leukoagglutinins, use 86021)

86341   Islet cell antibody
➜ *CPT Assistant* Summer 94:6

86343   Leukocyte histamine release test (LHR)

86344   Leukocyte phagocytosis

● **86352**   Cellular function assay involving stimulation (eg, mitogen or antigen) and detection of biomarker (eg, ATP)
➜ *CPT Changes: An Insider's View* 2010

86353   Lymphocyte transformation, mitogen (phytomitogen) or antigen induced blastogenesis

(Malaria antibodies, use 86750)

▶(For cellular function assay involving stimulation and detection of biomarker, use 86352)◀

86355   B cells, total count
➜ *CPT Assistant* Mar 06:6, Apr 08:5; *CPT Changes: An Insider's View* 2006

86356   Mononuclear cell antigen, quantitative (eg, flow cytometry), not otherwise specified, each antigen
➜ *CPT Assistant* Apr 08:5; *CPT Changes: An Insider's View* 2008

(Do not report 88187-88189 for interpretation of 86355, 86356, 86357, 86359, 86360, 86361, 86367)

86357   Natural killer (NK) cells, total count
➜ *CPT Assistant* Mar 06:6, Apr 08:5; *CPT Changes: An Insider's View* 2006

86359   T cells; total count
➜ *CPT Assistant* Nov 97:30, Apr 08:5

86360   absolute CD4 and CD8 count, including ratio
➜ *CPT Assistant* Nov 97:30, Jan 07:29, Apr 08:5

86361   absolute CD4 count
➜ *CPT Assistant* Nov 97:30, Apr 08:5

86367   Stem cells (ie, CD34), total count
➜ *CPT Assistant* Mar 06:6, Apr 08:5; *CPT Changes: An Insider's View* 2006

(For flow cytometric immunophenotyping for the assessment of potential hematolymphoid neoplasia, see 88184-88189)

86376   Microsomal antibodies (eg, thyroid or liver-kidney), each

86378   Migration inhibitory factor test (MIF)

(Mitochondrial antibody, liver, see 86255, 86256)

(Mononucleosis, see 86308-86310)

86382   Neutralization test, viral

86384   Nitroblue tetrazolium dye test (NTD)

(Ouchterlony diffusion, use 86331)

(Platelet antibodies, see 86022, 86023)

86403   Particle agglutination; screen, each antibody
➜ *CPT Assistant* Aug 05:9

86406   titer, each antibody

(Pregnancy test, see 84702, 84703)

(Rapid plasma reagin test (RPR), see 86592, 86593)

86430   Rheumatoid factor; qualitative

86431   quantitative

(Serologic test for syphilis, see 86592, 86593)

86480   Tuberculosis test, cell mediated immunity measurement of gamma interferon antigen response
➜ *CPT Assistant* Mar 06:6; *CPT Changes: An Insider's View* 2006

86485   Skin test; candida

(For antibody, candida, use 86628)

86486   unlisted antigen, each
➜ *CPT Changes: An Insider's View* 2008

86490   coccidioidomycosis

86510   histoplasmosis
➜ *CPT Assistant* Aug 05:9

(For histoplasma, antibody, use 86698)

86580   tuberculosis, intradermal

(For tuberculosis test, cell mediated immunity measurement of gamma interferon antigen response, use 86480)

(For skin tests for allergy, see 95010-95199)

(Smooth muscle antibody, see 86255, 86256)

(Sporothrix, antibodies to, see code for specific method)

(86586 has been deleted. For skin testing, unlisted antigen, use 86486. For flow cytometry, quantitative, not otherwise specified, use 86356)

86590   Streptokinase, antibody

(For antibodies to infectious agents, see 86602-86804)

(Streptolysin O antibody, see antistreptolysin O, 86060, 86063)

▲ **86592**   Syphilis test, non-treponemal antibody; qualitative (eg, VDRL, RPR, ART)
➜ *CPT Changes: An Insider's View* 2010

(For antibodies to infectious agents, see 86602-86804)

▲ **86593**   quantitative
➜ *CPT Changes: An Insider's View* 2010

(For antibodies to infectious agents, see 86602-86804)

(Tetanus antibody, use 86774)

(Thyroglobulin antibody, use 86800)

(Thyroglobulin, use 84432)

(Thyroid microsomal antibody, use 86376)

(For toxoplasma antibody, see 86777-86778)

The following codes (86602-86804) are qualitative or semiquantitative immunoassays performed by multiple-step methods for the detection of antibodies to infectious agents. For immunoassays by single-step method (eg, reagent strips), use code 86318. Procedures for the identification of antibodies should be coded as precisely as possible. For example, an antibody to a virus could be coded with increasing specificity for virus, family, genus, species, or type. In some cases, further precision may be added to codes by specifying the class of immunoglobulin being detected. When multiple tests are done to detect antibodies to organisms classified more precisely than the specificity allowed by available codes, it is appropriate to code each as a separate service. For example, a test for antibody to an enterovirus is coded as 86658. Coxsackie viruses are enteroviruses, but there are no codes for the individual species of enterovirus. If assays are performed for antibodies to coxsackie A and B species, each assay should be separately coded. Similarly, if multiple assays are performed for antibodies of different immuno-globulin classes, each assay should be coded separately. When a coding option exists for reporting IgM specific antibodies (eg, 86632), the corresponding nonspecific code (eg, 86631) may be reported for performance of either an antibody analysis not specific for a particular immunoglobulin class or for an IgG analysis.

> (For the detection of antibodies other than those to infectious agents, see specific antibody [eg, 86021-86023, 86376, 86800, 86850-86870] or specific method [eg, 83516, 86255, 86256]).

> (For infectious agent/antigen detection, see 87260-87899)

> ➔ CPT Assistant Fall 93:26

86602   Antibody; actinomyces
> ➔ CPT Assistant Aug 05:9

86603   adenovirus

86606   Aspergillus

86609   bacterium, not elsewhere specified

86611   Bartonella
> ➔ CPT Changes: An Insider's View 2001

86612   Blastomyces

86615   Bordetella

86617   Borrelia burgdorferi (Lyme disease) confirmatory test (eg, Western Blot or immunoblot)

86618   Borrelia burgdorferi (Lyme disease)

86619   Borrelia (relapsing fever)

86622   Brucella

86625   Campylobacter

86628   Candida

> (For skin test, candida, use 86485)

86631   Chlamydia

86632   Chlamydia, IgM
> ➔ CPT Assistant Nov 97:31

> (For chlamydia antigen, see 87270, 87320. For fluorescent antibody technique, see 86255, 86256)

86635   Coccidioides

86638   Coxiella burnetii (Q fever)

86641   Cryptococcus

86644   cytomegalovirus (CMV)

86645   cytomegalovirus (CMV), IgM
> ➔ CPT Assistant Jul 03:7

86648   Diphtheria

86651   encephalitis, California (La Crosse)

86652   encephalitis, Eastern equine

86653   encephalitis, St. Louis

86654   encephalitis, Western equine

86658   enterovirus (eg, coxsackie, echo, polio)

> (Trichinella, antibodies to, use 86784)

> (Trypanosoma, antibodies to, see code for specific method)

> (Tuberculosis, use 86580 for skin testing)

> (Viral antibodies, see code for specific method)

86663   Epstein-Barr (EB) virus, early antigen (EA)

86664   Epstein-Barr (EB) virus, nuclear antigen (EBNA)

86665   Epstein-Barr (EB) virus, viral capsid (VCA)

86666   Ehrlichia
> ➔ CPT Changes: An Insider's View 2001

86668   Francisella tularensis

86671   fungus, not elsewhere specified

86674   Giardia lamblia

86677   Helicobacter pylori
> ➔ CPT Assistant Jan 98:6

86682   helminth, not elsewhere specified

86684   Haemophilus influenza

86687   HTLV-I

86688   HTLV-II

86689   HTLV or HIV antibody, confirmatory test (eg, Western Blot)
> ➔ CPT Assistant Mar 08:3

86692   hepatitis, delta agent
> ➔ CPT Assistant Nov 97:31

> (For hepatitis delta agent, antigen, use 87380)

86694   herpes simplex, non-specific type test

86695   herpes simplex, type 1

| 86696 | herpes simplex, type 2 |
| | → *CPT Changes: An Insider's View* 2001 |

| 86698 | histoplasma |

| 86701 | HIV-1 |
| | → *CPT Assistant* Aug 05:9, Mar 08:3, Apr 08:5 |

| 86702 | HIV-2 |
| | → *CPT Assistant* Mar 08:3, Apr 08:5 |

| 86703 | HIV-1 and HIV-2, single assay |
| | → *CPT Assistant* Nov 97:31, Mar 08:3, Apr 08:5 |

(When HIV antibody immunoassay [HIV testing 86701-86703] is performed using a kit or transportable instrument that wholly or in part consists of a single use, disposable analytical chamber, the service may be identified by adding modifier 92 to the usual code)

(For HIV-1 antigen, use 87390)

(For HIV-2 antigen, use 87391)

(For confirmatory test for HIV antibody (eg, Western Blot), use 86689)

| 86704 | Hepatitis B core antibody (HBcAb); total |
| | → *CPT Assistant* Nov 97:31-32; *CPT Changes: An Insider's View* 2001 |

| 86705 | IgM antibody |
| | → *CPT Assistant* Nov 97:31-32 |

| 86706 | Hepatitis B surface antibody (HBsAb) |
| | → *CPT Assistant* Nov 97:31-32 |

| 86707 | Hepatitis Be antibody (HBeAb) |
| | → *CPT Assistant* Nov 97:31-32 |

| 86708 | Hepatitis A antibody (HAAb); total |
| | → *CPT Assistant* Nov 97:31-32, Jun 00:11; *CPT Changes: An Insider's View* 2001 |

| 86709 | IgM antibody |
| | → *CPT Assistant* Nov 97:31-32, Jun 00:11 |

| 86710 | Antibody; influenza virus |

| 86713 | Legionella |

| 86717 | Leishmania |

| 86720 | Leptospira |

| 86723 | Listeria monocytogenes |

| 86727 | lymphocytic choriomeningitis |

| 86729 | lymphogranuloma venereum |

| 86732 | mucormycosis |

| 86735 | mumps |

| 86738 | mycoplasma |

| 86741 | Neisseria meningitidis |

| 86744 | Nocardia |

| 86747 | parvovirus |

| 86750 | Plasmodium (malaria) |

| 86753 | protozoa, not elsewhere specified |

| 86756 | respiratory syncytial virus |

| 86757 | Rickettsia |
| | → *CPT Changes: An Insider's View* 2001 |

| 86759 | rotavirus |

| 86762 | rubella |

| 86765 | rubeola |

| 86768 | Salmonella |

| 86771 | Shigella |

| 86774 | tetanus |

| 86777 | Toxoplasma |

| 86778 | Toxoplasma, IgM |

● 86780	Treponema pallidum
	→ *CPT Changes: An Insider's View* 2010
	►(86781 has been deleted)◄
	►(For syphilis testing by non-treponemal antibody analysis, see 86592-86593)◄

| 86784 | Trichinella |

| 86787 | varicella-zoster |

| 86788 | West Nile virus, IgM |
| | → *CPT Changes: An Insider's View* 2007 |

| 86789 | West Nile virus |
| | → *CPT Changes: An Insider's View* 2007 |

| 86790 | virus, not elsewhere specified |

| 86793 | Yersinia |

86800	Thyroglobulin antibody
	→ *CPT Assistant* Aug 05:9
	(For thyroglobulin, use 84432)

| 86803 | Hepatitis C antibody; |
| | → *CPT Assistant* Nov 97:31-32 |

| 86804 | confirmatory test (eg, immunoblot) |
| | → *CPT Assistant* Nov 97:31-32 |

Tissue Typing

| 86805 | Lymphocytotoxicity assay, visual crossmatch; with titration |

| 86806 | without titration |

| 86807 | Serum screening for cytotoxic percent reactive antibody (PRA); standard method |
| | → *CPT Assistant* Jun 01:11 |

| 86808 | quick method |
| | → *CPT Assistant* Jun 01:11 |

| 86812 | HLA typing; A, B, or C (eg, A10, B7, B27), single antigen |
| | → *CPT Assistant* Mar 03:23, Jun 06:17 |

| 86813 | A, B, or C, multiple antigens |
| | → *CPT Assistant* Mar 03:23, Jun 06:17 |

86816   DR/DQ, single antigen
> *CPT Assistant* Mar 03:23

86817   DR/DQ, multiple antigens
> *CPT Assistant* Mar 03:23

86821   lymphocyte culture, mixed (MLC)
> *CPT Assistant* Mar 03:23

86822   lymphocyte culture, primed (PLC)
> *CPT Assistant* Mar 03:23

(For HLA typing by molecular pathology techniques, see 83890-83914 with appropriate genetic testing modifiers 4A-4G)

● **86825**   Human leukocyte antigen (HLA) crossmatch, non-cytotoxic (eg, using flow cytometry); first serum sample or dilution
> *CPT Changes: An Insider's View* 2010

+● **86826**   each additional serum sample or sample dilution (List separately in addition to primary procedure)
> *CPT Changes: An Insider's View* 2010

►(Do not report 86825, 86826 in conjunction with 86355, 86359, 88184-88189 for antibody surface markers integral to crossmatch testing)◄

►(For autologous HLA crossmatch, see 86825, 86826)◄

►(For lymphocytotoxicity visual crossmatch, see 86805, 86806)◄

86849   Unlisted immunology procedure
> *CPT Assistant* Mar 98:10

Transfusion Medicine

(For apheresis, use 36511, 36512)

(For therapeutic phlebotomy, use 99195)

86850   Antibody screen, RBC, each serum technique
> *CPT Assistant* Fall 93:25, Aug 05:9, Apr 08:5

86860   Antibody elution (RBC), each elution

86870   Antibody identification, RBC antibodies, each panel for each serum technique
> *CPT Assistant* Fall 93:25, Mar 01:10

86880   Antihuman globulin test (Coombs test); direct, each antiserum

86885   indirect, qualitative, each reagent red cell
> *CPT Assistant* Apr 08:5; *CPT Changes: An Insider's View* 2008

86886   indirect, each antibody titer
> *CPT Assistant* Apr 08:5; *CPT Changes: An Insider's View* 2008

(For indirect antihuman globulin [Coombs] test for RBC antibody screening, use 86850)

(For indirect antihuman globulin [Coombs] test for RBC antibody identification using reagent red cell panels, use 86870)

86890   Autologous blood or component, collection processing and storage; predeposited
> *CPT Assistant* Apr 96:2

86891   intra- or postoperative salvage

(For physician services to autologous donors, see 99201-99204)

86900   Blood typing; ABO
> *CPT Assistant* Aug 05:9

86901   Rh (D)
> *CPT Assistant* Fall 93:25

86903   antigen screening for compatible blood unit using reagent serum, per unit screened

86904   antigen screening for compatible unit using patient serum, per unit screened

86905   RBC antigens, other than ABO or Rh (D), each

86906   Rh phenotyping, complete

86910   Blood typing, for paternity testing, per individual; ABO, Rh and MN

86911   each additional antigen system

86920   Compatibility test each unit; immediate spin technique
> *CPT Assistant* Mar 06:6

86921   incubation technique
> *CPT Assistant* Mar 06:6

86922   antiglobulin technique
> *CPT Assistant* Mar 06:6

86923   electronic
> *CPT Assistant* Mar 06:6; *CPT Changes: An Insider's View* 2006

(Do not use 86923 in conjunction with 86920-86922 for same unit crossmatch)

86927   Fresh frozen plasma, thawing, each unit

86930   Frozen blood, each unit; freezing (includes preparation)
> *CPT Assistant* Apr 96:2, Jul 03:8; *CPT Changes: An Insider's View* 2003

86931   thawing
> *CPT Assistant* Jul 03:8; *CPT Changes: An Insider's View* 2003

86932   freezing (includes preparation) and thawing
> *CPT Assistant* Jul 03:8; *CPT Changes: An Insider's View* 2003

86940   Hemolysins and agglutinins; auto, screen, each

86941   incubated

86945   Irradiation of blood product, each unit
> *CPT Assistant* Dec 07:14

86950   Leukocyte transfusion

(For leukapheresis, use 36511)

86960   Volume reduction of blood or blood product (eg, red blood cells or platelets), each unit
> *CPT Assistant* Mar 06:6; *CPT Changes: An Insider's View* 2006

86965   Pooling of platelets or other blood products

 ▲=Revised code   ●=New code   ►◄=Contains new or revised text   ⊘=Modifier 51 exempt

86970   Pretreatment of RBCs for use in RBC antibody detection, identification, and/or compatibility testing; incubation with chemical agents or drugs, each

86971   incubation with enzymes, each

86972   by density gradient separation

86975   Pretreatment of serum for use in RBC antibody identification; incubation with drugs, each

86976   by dilution

86977   incubation with inhibitors, each

86978   by differential red cell absorption using patient RBCs or RBCs of known phenotype, each absorption

86985   Splitting of blood or blood products, each unit
→ *CPT Assistant* Apr 96:2

86999   Unlisted transfusion medicine procedure
→ *CPT Assistant* Aug 05:9, Nov 05:14, Mar 09:10, Apr 09:9

Microbiology

Includes bacteriology, mycology, parasitology, and virology.

►Presumptive identification of microorganisms is defined as identification by colony morphology, growth on selective media, Gram stains, or up to three tests (eg, catalase, oxidase, indole, urease). Definitive identification of microorganisms is defined as an identification to the genus or species level that requires additional tests (eg, biochemical panels, slide cultures). If additional studies involve molecular probes, nucleic acid sequencing, chromatography, or immunologic techniques, these should be separately coded using 87140-87158, in addition to definitive identification codes. The molecular diagnostic codes (eg, 83890-83914) are not to be used in combination with or instead of the procedures represented by 87140-87158. For multiple specimens/sites use modifier 59. For repeat laboratory tests performed on the same day, use modifier 91.◄

87001   Animal inoculation, small animal; with observation
→ *CPT Assistant* Aug 05:9

87003   with observation and dissection

87015   Concentration (any type), for infectious agents
→ *CPT Changes: An Insider's View* 2001

(Do not report 87015 in conjunction with 87177)

87040   Culture, bacterial; blood, aerobic, with isolation and presumptive identification of isolates (includes anaerobic culture, if appropriate)
→ *CPT Assistant* Aug 97:18, Jun 02:2; *CPT Changes: An Insider's View* 2001, 2004

87045   stool, aerobic, with isolation and preliminary examination (eg, KIA, LIA), Salmonella and Shigella species
→ *CPT Changes: An Insider's View* 2001, 2002, 2004

87046   stool, aerobic, additional pathogens, isolation and presumptive identification of isolates, each plate
→ *CPT Changes: An Insider's View* 2001, 2002, 2004, 2005

87070   any other source except urine, blood or stool, aerobic, with isolation and presumptive identification of isolates
→ *CPT Assistant* Aug 97:18, Nov 01:10, Oct 03:10; *CPT Changes: An Insider's View* 2001, 2004

(For urine, use 87088)

87071   quantitative, aerobic with isolation and presumptive identification of isolates, any source except urine, blood or stool
→ *CPT Assistant* Jun 02:3, Sep 03:3; *CPT Changes: An Insider's View* 2001

(For urine, use 87088)

87073   quantitative, anaerobic with isolation and presumptive identification of isolates, any source except urine, blood or stool
→ *CPT Assistant* Jun 02:3; *CPT Changes: An Insider's View* 2001

(For definitive identification of isolates, use 87076 or 87077. For typing of isolates see 87140-87158)

87075   any source, except blood, anaerobic with isolation and presumptive identification of isolates
→ *CPT Changes: An Insider's View* 2001, 2004

87076   anaerobic isolate, additional methods required for definitive identification, each isolate
→ *CPT Changes: An Insider's View* 2001

87077   aerobic isolate, additional methods required for definitive identification, each isolate
→ *CPT Assistant* Nov 01:10; *CPT Changes: An Insider's View* 2001

87081   Culture, presumptive, pathogenic organisms, screening only;
→ *CPT Assistant* Nov 01:10; *CPT Changes: An Insider's View* 2001

87084   with colony estimation from density chart

87086   Culture, bacterial; quantitative colony count, urine
→ *CPT Changes: An Insider's View* 2001

87088   with isolation and presumptive identification of each isolate, urine
→ *CPT Changes: An Insider's View* 2001, 2007

87101   Culture, fungi (mold or yeast) isolation, with presumptive identification of isolates; skin, hair, or nail
→ *CPT Assistant* Sep 99:10, Aug 05:9; *CPT Changes: An Insider's View* 2001

87102   other source (except blood)

87103   blood

87106   Culture, fungi, definitive identification, each organism; yeast
→ *CPT Changes: An Insider's View* 2001

87107   mold
→ *CPT Changes: An Insider's View* 2001

87109　Culture, mycoplasma, any source

87110　Culture, chlamydia, any source
> *CPT Changes: An Insider's View* 2001

(For immunofluorescence staining of shell vials, use 87140)

87116　Culture, tubercle or other acid-fast bacilli (eg, TB, AFB, mycobacteria) any source, with isolation and presumptive identification of isolates
> *CPT Changes: An Insider's View* 2001

(For concentration, use 87015)

87118　Culture, mycobacterial, definitive identification, each isolate
> *CPT Changes: An Insider's View* 2001

87140　Culture, typing; immunofluorescent method, each antiserum
> *CPT Assistant* Nov 01:10, Sep 03:3; *CPT Changes: An Insider's View* 2001

87143　gas liquid chromatography (GLC) or high pressure liquid chromatography (HPLC) method
> *CPT Changes: An Insider's View* 2001

87147　immunologic method, other than immunofluoresence (eg, agglutination grouping), per antiserum
> *CPT Assistant* Apr 02:18, Oct 03:10; *CPT Changes: An Insider's View* 2001

▲ **87149**　identification by nucleic acid (DNA or RNA) probe, direct probe technique, per culture or isolate, each organism probed
> *CPT Assistant* Nov 01:10; *CPT Changes: An Insider's View* 2001, 2010

►(Do not report 87149 in conjunction with 83890-83914)◄

● **87150**　identification by nucleic acid (DNA or RNA) probe, amplified probe technique, per culture or isolate, each organism probed
> *CPT Changes: An Insider's View* 2010

►(Do not report 87150 in conjunction with 83890-83914)◄

87152　identification by pulse field gel typing
> *CPT Changes: An Insider's View* 2001

►(Do not report 87152 in conjunction with 83890-83914)◄

● **87153**　identification by nucleic acid sequencing method, each isolate (eg, sequencing of the 16S rRNA gene)
> *CPT Changes: An Insider's View* 2010

87158　other methods
> *CPT Assistant* Nov 01:10, Sep 03:3

87164　Dark field examination, any source (eg, penile, vaginal, oral, skin); includes specimen collection

87166　without collection

87168　Macroscopic examination; arthropod
> *CPT Changes: An Insider's View* 2001

87169　parasite
> *CPT Changes: An Insider's View* 2001

87172　Pinworm exam (eg, cellophane tape prep)
> *CPT Changes: An Insider's View* 2001

87176　Homogenization, tissue, for culture
> *CPT Changes: An Insider's View* 2001

87177　Ova and parasites, direct smears, concentration and identification
> *CPT Assistant* Jul 03:8, Nov 03:15, Mar 06:6

(Do not report 87177 in conjunction with 87015)

(For direct smears from a primary source, use 87207)

(For coccidia or microsporidia exam, use 87207)

(For complex special stain (trichrome, iron hematoxylin), use 87209)

(For nucleic acid probes in cytologic material, use 88365)

87181　Susceptibility studies, antimicrobial agent; agar dilution method, per agent (eg, antibiotic gradient strip)
> *CPT Assistant* Nov 01:10; *CPT Changes: An Insider's View* 2001

87184　disk method, per plate (12 or fewer agents)
> *CPT Assistant* Nov 01:10; *CPT Changes: An Insider's View* 2001

87185　enzyme detection (eg, beta lactamase), per enzyme
> *CPT Assistant* Nov 01:10; *CPT Changes: An Insider's View* 2001

87186　microdilution or agar dilution (minimum inhibitory concentration [MIC] or breakpoint), each multi-antimicrobial, per plate
> *CPT Assistant* Nov 01:10; *CPT Changes: An Insider's View* 2001

+ **87187**　microdilution or agar dilution, minimum lethal concentration (MLC), each plate (List separately in addition to code for primary procedure)
> *CPT Assistant* Nov 01:10; *CPT Changes: An Insider's View* 2001

(Use 87187 in conjunction with 87186 or 87188)

87188　macrobroth dilution method, each agent
> *CPT Assistant* Nov 01:10; *CPT Changes: An Insider's View* 2001

87190　mycobacteria, proportion method, each agent
> *CPT Changes: An Insider's View* 2001

(For other mycobacterial susceptibility studies, see 87181, 87184, 87186, or 87188)

87197　Serum bactericidal titer (Schlicter test)

87205　Smear, primary source with interpretation; Gram or Giemsa stain for bacteria, fungi, or cell types
> *CPT Assistant* Aug 05:9; *CPT Changes: An Insider's View* 2001

87206　fluorescent and/or acid fast stain for bacteria, fungi, parasites, viruses or cell types
> *CPT Changes: An Insider's View* 2001

87207 special stain for inclusion bodies or parasites (eg, malaria, coccidia, microsporidia, trypanosomes, herpes viruses)

➔ *CPT Assistant* Jul 03:8, Mar 06:6; *CPT Changes: An Insider's View* 2001, 2003

(For direct smears with concentration and identification, use 87177)

(For thick smear preparation, use 87015)

(For fat, meat, fibers, nasal eosinophils, and starch, see miscellaneous section)

87209 complex special stain (eg, trichrome, iron hemotoxylin) for ova and parasites

➔ *CPT Assistant* Mar 06:6; *CPT Changes: An Insider's View* 2006

87210 wet mount for infectious agents (eg, saline, India ink, KOH preps)

➔ *CPT Changes: An Insider's View* 2001

(For KOH examination of skin, hair or nails, see 87220)

87220 Tissue examination by KOH slide of samples from skin, hair, or nails for fungi or ectoparasite ova or mites (eg, scabies)

➔ *CPT Changes: An Insider's View* 2001

87230 Toxin or antitoxin assay, tissue culture (eg, Clostridium difficile toxin)

87250 Virus isolation; inoculation of embryonated eggs, or small animal, includes observation and dissection

➔ *CPT Changes: An Insider's View* 2001

87252 tissue culture inoculation, observation, and presumptive identification by cytopathic effect

➔ *CPT Changes: An Insider's View* 2001

87253 tissue culture, additional studies or definitive identification (eg, hemabsorption, neutralization, immunofluoresence stain), each isolate

➔ *CPT Changes: An Insider's View* 2001

(Electron microscopy, use 88348)

(Inclusion bodies in tissue sections, see 88304-88309; in smears, see 87207-87210; in fluids, use 88106)

87254 centrifuge enhanced (shell vial) technique, includes identification with immunofluorescence stain, each virus

➔ *CPT Assistant* Jul 03:8; *CPT Changes: An Insider's View* 2001, 2003

(Report 87254 in addition to 87252 as appropriate)

87255 including identification by non-immunologic method, other than by cytopathic effect (eg, virus specific enzymatic activity)

➔ *CPT Assistant* Jul 03:9; *CPT Changes: An Insider's View* 2003

►These codes are intended for primary source only. For similar studies on culture material, refer to codes 87140-87158. Infectious agents by antigen detection, immunofluorescence microscopy, or nucleic acid probe techniques should be reported as precisely as possible. The molecular diagnostic codes (eg, 83890-83914) are not to be used in combination with or instead of the procedures represented by 87470-87801. The most specific code possible should be reported. If there is no specific agent code, the general methodology code (eg, 87299, 87449, 87450, 87797, 87798, 87799, 87899) should be used. For identification of antibodies to many of the listed infectious agents, see 86602-86804. When separate results are reported for different species or strain of organisms, each result should be coded separately. Use modifier 59 when separate results are reported for different species or strains that are described by the same code.◄

87260 Infectious agent antigen detection by immunofluorescent technique; adenovirus

➔ *CPT Assistant* Nov 97:32; *CPT Changes: An Insider's View* 2001

87265 Bordetella pertussis/parapertussis

➔ *CPT Assistant* Nov 97:32

87267 Enterovirus, direct fluorescent antibody (DFA)

➔ *CPT Assistant* Jul 03:8

87269 giardia

➔ *CPT Changes: An Insider's View* 2004

87270 Chlamydia trachomatis

➔ *CPT Assistant* Nov 97:32

87271 Cytomegalovirus, direct fluorescent antibody (DFA)

➔ *CPT Assistant* Jul 03:7

87272 cryptosporidium

➔ *CPT Assistant* Nov 97:32; *CPT Changes: An Insider's View* 2004

87273 Herpes simplex virus type 2

➔ *CPT Changes: An Insider's View* 2001

87274 Herpes simplex virus type 1

➔ *CPT Assistant* Nov 97:32; *CPT Changes: An Insider's View* 2001

87275 influenza B virus

➔ *CPT Changes: An Insider's View* 2001

87276 influenza A virus

➔ *CPT Assistant* Nov 97:32

87277 Legionella micdadei

➔ *CPT Changes: An Insider's View* 2001

87278 Legionella pneumophila

➔ *CPT Assistant* Nov 97:32

87279 Parainfluenza virus, each type

➔ *CPT Changes: An Insider's View* 2001

87280 respiratory syncytial virus

➔ *CPT Assistant* Nov 97:32

87281 Pneumocystis carinii

➔ *CPT Changes: An Insider's View* 2001

87283 Rubeola

➔ *CPT Changes: An Insider's View* 2001

87285 Treponema pallidum

➔ *CPT Assistant* Nov 97:32

87290   Varicella zoster virus

➔ *CPT Assistant* Nov 97:32

87299   not otherwise specified, each organism

➔ *CPT Assistant* Nov 97:32, Nov 01:10; *CPT Changes: An Insider's View* 2001

87300   Infectious agent antigen detection by immunofluorescent technique, polyvalent for multiple organisms, each polyvalent antiserum

➔ *CPT Assistant* Aug 05:9; *CPT Changes: An Insider's View* 2001

(For physician evaluation of infectious disease agents by immunofluorescence, use 88346)

87301   Infectious agent antigen detection by enzyme immunoassay technique, qualitative or semiquantitative, multiple-step method; adenovirus enteric types 40/41

➔ *CPT Assistant* Nov 97:32, Nov 99:46

87305   Aspergillus

➔ *CPT Changes: An Insider's View* 2007

87320   Chlamydia trachomatis

➔ *CPT Assistant* Nov 97:32

87324   Clostridium difficile toxin(s)

➔ *CPT Assistant* Nov 97:32; *CPT Changes: An Insider's View* 2001

87327   Cryptococcus neoformans

➔ *CPT Changes: An Insider's View* 2001

(For Cryptococcus latex agglutination, use 86403)

87328   cryptosporidium

➔ *CPT Assistant* Nov 97:32; *CPT Changes: An Insider's View* 2004

87329   giardia

➔ *CPT Changes: An Insider's View* 2004

87332   cytomegalovirus

➔ *CPT Assistant* Nov 97:32

87335   Escherichia coli 0157

➔ *CPT Assistant* Nov 97:32

(For giardia antigen, use 87329)

87336   Entamoeba histolytica dispar group

➔ *CPT Changes: An Insider's View* 2001

87337   Entamoeba histolytica group

➔ *CPT Changes: An Insider's View* 2001

87338   Helicobacter pylori, stool

➔ *CPT Assistant* Nov 99:46; *CPT Changes: An Insider's View* 2000

87339   Helicobacter pylori

➔ *CPT Changes: An Insider's View* 2001

(For H. pylori, stool, use 87338. For H. pylori, breath and blood by mass spectrometry, see 83013, 83014. For H. pylori, liquid scintillation counter, see 78267, 78268)

87340   hepatitis B surface antigen (HBsAg)

➔ *CPT Assistant* Nov 97:32, Jan 00:11

87341   hepatitis B surface antigen (HBsAg) neutralization

➔ *CPT Changes: An Insider's View* 2001

87350   hepatitis Be antigen (HBeAg)

➔ *CPT Assistant* Nov 97:32

87380   hepatitis, delta agent

➔ *CPT Assistant* Nov 97:32

87385   Histoplasma capsulatum

➔ *CPT Assistant* Nov 97:32

87390   HIV-1

➔ *CPT Assistant* Nov 97:32

87391   HIV-2

➔ *CPT Assistant* Nov 97:32

87400   Influenza, A or B, each

➔ *CPT Assistant* Jun 01:11, Dec 01:6, Aug 05:9; *CPT Changes: An Insider's View* 2001

87420   respiratory syncytial virus

➔ *CPT Assistant* Nov 97:32

87425   rotavirus

➔ *CPT Assistant* Nov 97:32

87427   Shiga-like toxin

➔ *CPT Changes: An Insider's View* 2001

87430   Streptococcus, group A

➔ *CPT Assistant* Nov 97:32

87449   Infectious agent antigen detection by enzyme immunoassay technique qualitative or semiquantitative; multiple step method, not otherwise specified, each organism

➔ *CPT Assistant* Nov 97:32, Jan 00:11, Nov 01:10; *CPT Changes: An Insider's View* 2001

87450   single step method, not otherwise specified, each organism

➔ *CPT Assistant* Nov 97:33; *CPT Changes: An Insider's View* 2001

87451   multiple step method, polyvalent for multiple organisms, each polyvalent antiserum

➔ *CPT Changes: An Insider's View* 2001

87470   Infectious agent detection by nucleic acid (DNA or RNA); Bartonella henselae and Bartonella quintana, direct probe technique

➔ *CPT Assistant* Nov 97:33-34

87471   Bartonella henselae and Bartonella quintana, amplified probe technique

87472   Bartonella henselae and Bartonella quintana, quantification

87475   Borrelia burgdorferi, direct probe technique

87476   Borrelia burgdorferi, amplified probe technique

87477   Borrelia burgdorferi, quantification

87480   Candida species, direct probe technique

87481   Candida species, amplified probe technique

87482   Candida species, quantification

87485   Chlamydia pneumoniae, direct probe technique

87486   Chlamydia pneumoniae, amplified probe technique

▲ =Revised code   ●=New code   ►◄=Contains new or revised text   ⊘=Modifier 51 exempt

87487	Chlamydia pneumoniae, quantification
87490	Chlamydia trachomatis, direct probe technique
87491	Chlamydia trachomatis, amplified probe technique
87492	Chlamydia trachomatis, quantification
● 87493	Clostridium difficile, toxin gene(s), amplified probe technique

   ➲ *CPT Changes: An Insider's View* 2010

87495	cytomegalovirus, direct probe technique
87496	cytomegalovirus, amplified probe technique
87497	cytomegalovirus, quantification
87498	enterovirus, amplified probe technique

   ➲ *CPT Changes: An Insider's View* 2007

87500	vancomycin resistance (eg, enterococcus species van A, van B), amplified probe technique

   ➲ *CPT Assistant* Apr 08:5; *CPT Changes: An Insider's View* 2008

87510	Gardnerella vaginalis, direct probe technique

   ➲ *CPT Assistant* Aug 05:9

87511	Gardnerella vaginalis, amplified probe technique
87512	Gardnerella vaginalis, quantification
87515	hepatitis B virus, direct probe technique
87516	hepatitis B virus, amplified probe technique
87517	hepatitis B virus, quantification
87520	hepatitis C, direct probe technique
87521	hepatitis C, amplified probe technique
87522	hepatitis C, quantification
87525	hepatitis G, direct probe technique
87526	hepatitis G, amplified probe technique
87527	hepatitis G, quantification
87528	Herpes simplex virus, direct probe technique
87529	Herpes simplex virus, amplified probe technique
87530	Herpes simplex virus, quantification
87531	Herpes virus-6, direct probe technique
87532	Herpes virus-6, amplified probe technique
87533	Herpes virus-6, quantification
87534	HIV-1, direct probe technique
87535	HIV-1, amplified probe technique

   ➲ *CPT Assistant* Mar 08:3

87536	HIV-1, quantification
87537	HIV-2, direct probe technique
87538	HIV-2, amplified probe technique
87539	HIV-2, quantification
87540	Legionella pneumophila, direct probe technique
87541	Legionella pneumophila, amplified probe technique
87542	Legionella pneumophila, quantification
87550	Mycobacteria species, direct probe technique
87551	Mycobacteria species, amplified probe technique
87552	Mycobacteria species, quantification
87555	Mycobacteria tuberculosis, direct probe technique
87556	Mycobacteria tuberculosis, amplified probe technique
87557	Mycobacteria tuberculosis, quantification
87560	Mycobacteria avium-intracellulare, direct probe technique
87561	Mycobacteria avium-intracellulare, amplified probe technique
87562	Mycobacteria avium-intracellulare, quantification
87580	Mycoplasma pneumoniae, direct probe technique
87581	Mycoplasma pneumoniae, amplified probe technique
87582	Mycoplasma pneumoniae, quantification
87590	Neisseria gonorrhoeae, direct probe technique
87591	Neisseria gonorrhoeae, amplified probe technique
87592	Neisseria gonorrhoeae, quantification
87620	papillomavirus, human, direct probe technique

   ➲ *CPT Assistant* Feb 02:10, Aug 05:9

87621	papillomavirus, human, amplified probe technique
87622	papillomavirus, human, quantification
87640	Staphylococcus aureus, amplified probe technique

   ➲ *CPT Assistant* Aug 07:7; *CPT Changes: An Insider's View* 2007

87641	Staphylococcus aureus, methicillin resistant, amplified probe technique

   ➲ *CPT Assistant* Aug 07:7; *CPT Changes: An Insider's View* 2007

(For assays that detect methicillin resistance and identify Staphylococcus aureus using a single nucleic acid sequence, use 87641)

87650	Streptococcus, group A, direct probe technique
87651	Streptococcus, group A, amplified probe technique
87652	Streptococcus, group A, quantification
87653	Streptococcus, group B, amplified probe technique

   ➲ *CPT Assistant* Aug 07:7; *CPT Changes: An Insider's View* 2007

87660	Trichomonas vaginalis, direct probe technique

   ➲ *CPT Changes: An Insider's View* 2004

87797	Infectious agent detection by nucleic acid (DNA or RNA), not otherwise specified; direct probe technique, each organism

   ➲ *CPT Assistant* Nov 97:34, Nov 01:10, Aug 05:9; *CPT Changes: An Insider's View* 2001

87798	amplified probe technique, each organism

   ➲ *CPT Assistant* Nov 97:34, Nov 01:10, Aug 07:7; *CPT Changes: An Insider's View* 2001

87799 quantification, each organism
➲ *CPT Assistant* Nov 97:34; *CPT Changes: An Insider's View* 2001

87800 Infectious agent detection by nucleic acid (DNA or RNA), multiple organisms; direct probe(s) technique
➲ *CPT Assistant* Aug 05:9; *CPT Changes: An Insider's View* 2001

87801 amplified probe(s) technique
➲ *CPT Changes: An Insider's View* 2001

(For each specific organism nucleic acid detection from a primary source, see 87470-87660. For detection of specific infectious agents not otherwise specified, see 87797, 87798, or 87799 1 time for each agent)

87802 Infectious agent antigen detection by immunoassay with direct optical observation; Streptococcus, group B
➲ *CPT Assistant* Jun 03:12; *CPT Changes: An Insider's View* 2002

87803 Clostridium difficile toxin A
➲ *CPT Assistant* Jun 03:12; *CPT Changes: An Insider's View* 2002

87804 Influenza
➲ *CPT Assistant* Jun 03:11-12; *CPT Changes: An Insider's View* 2002

87807 respiratory syncytial virus
➲ *CPT Changes: An Insider's View* 2005

87808 Trichomonas vaginalis
➲ *CPT Changes: An Insider's View* 2007

87809 adenovirus
➲ *CPT Assistant* Apr 08:5; *CPT Changes: An Insider's View* 2008

87810 Chlamydia trachomatis
➲ *CPT Assistant* Nov 97:34, Jan 98:6; *CPT Changes: An Insider's View* 2009

87850 Neisseria gonorrhoeae
➲ *CPT Assistant* Nov 97:34, Jan 98:6

87880 Streptococcus, group A
➲ *CPT Assistant* Nov 97:34, Jan 98:6, Dec 98:8

87899 not otherwise specified
➲ *CPT Assistant* Jan 98:6, Jun 01:11

87900 Infectious agent drug susceptibility phenotype prediction using regularly updated genotypic bioinformatics
➲ *CPT Assistant* Mar 06:6; *CPT Changes: An Insider's View* 2006

87901 Infectious agent genotype analysis by nucleic acid (DNA or RNA); HIV-1, reverse transcriptase and protease
➲ *CPT Assistant* Aug 05:9, Mar 06:6; *CPT Changes: An Insider's View* 2001, 2002

(For infectious agent drug susceptibility phenotype prediction for HIV-1, use 87900)

87902 Hepatitis C virus
➲ *CPT Changes: An Insider's View* 2002

87903 Infectious agent phenotype analysis by nucleic acid (DNA or RNA) with drug resistance tissue culture analysis, HIV 1; first through 10 drugs tested
➲ *CPT Assistant* Apr 04:15, Mar 06:6; *CPT Changes: An Insider's View* 2001, 2002

+ 87904 each additional drug tested (List separately in addition to code for primary procedure)
➲ *CPT Assistant* Apr 04:15, Mar 06:6; *CPT Changes: An Insider's View* 2001, 2002, 2006

(Use 87904 in conjunction with 87903)

87905 Infectious agent enzymatic activity other than virus (eg, sialidase activity in vaginal fluid)
➲ *CPT Changes: An Insider's View* 2009

(For virus isolation including identification by non-immunologic method, other than by cytopathic effect, use 87255)

87999 Unlisted microbiology procedure
➲ *CPT Assistant* Aug 05:9

Anatomic Pathology

Postmortem Examination

Procedures 88000 through 88099 represent physician services only. Use modifier 90 for outside laboratory services.
➲ *CPT Assistant* Fall 93:26

88000 Necropsy (autopsy), gross examination only; without CNS
➲ *CPT Assistant* Aug 05:9

88005 with brain

88007 with brain and spinal cord

88012 infant with brain

88014 stillborn or newborn with brain

88016 macerated stillborn

88020 Necropsy (autopsy), gross and microscopic; without CNS

88025 with brain

88027 with brain and spinal cord

88028 infant with brain

88029 stillborn or newborn with brain

88036 Necropsy (autopsy), limited, gross and/or microscopic; regional

88037 single organ

88040 Necropsy (autopsy); forensic examination

88045 coroner's call

88099 Unlisted necropsy (autopsy) procedure

Cytopathology

88104 Cytopathology, fluids, washings or brushings, except cervical or vaginal; smears with interpretation
➲ *CPT Assistant* Spring 91:6, Fall 94:3, Aug 05:9

88106   simple filter method with interpretation
⮕ *CPT Assistant* Fall 94:3; *CPT Changes: An Insider's View* 2007

88107   smears and simple filter preparation with interpretation
⮕ *CPT Assistant* Fall 94:3; *CPT Changes: An Insider's View* 2007

(For nongynecological selective cellular enhancement including filter transfer techniques, use 88112)

88108   Cytopathology, concentration technique, smears and interpretation (eg, Saccomanno technique)
⮕ *CPT Assistant* Fall 94:3, Nov 97:34, Jan 98:6

(For cervical or vaginal smears, see 88150-88155)

(For gastric intubation with lavage, see 89130-89141, 91055)

(For x-ray localization, use 74340)

88112   Cytopathology, selective cellular enhancement technique with interpretation (eg, liquid based slide preparation method), except cervical or vaginal
⮕ *CPT Changes: An Insider's View* 2004

(Do not report 88112 with 88108)

88125   Cytopathology, forensic (eg, sperm)

88130   Sex chromatin identification; Barr bodies

88140   peripheral blood smear, polymorphonuclear drumsticks
⮕ *CPT Assistant* Nov 98:27-28, Mar 06:6

(For Guard stain, use 88313)

Codes 88141-88155, 88164-88167, 88174-88175 are used to report cervical or vaginal screening by various methods and to report physician interpretation services. Use codes 88150-88154 to report conventional Pap smears that are examined using non-Bethesda reporting. Use codes 88164-88167 to report conventional Pap smears that are examined using the Bethesda System of reporting. Use codes 88142-88143 to report liquid-based specimens processed as thin-layer preparations that are examined using any system of reporting (Bethesda or non-Bethesda). Use codes 88174-88175 to report automated screening of liquid-based specimens that are examined using any system of reporting (Bethesda or non-Bethesda). Within each of these three code families choose the one code that describes the screening method(s) used. Codes 88141 and 88155 should be reported in addition to the screening code chosen when the additional services are provided. Manual rescreening requires a complete visual reassessment of the entire slide initially screened by either an automated or manual process. Manual review represents an assessment of selected cells or regions of a slide identified by initial automated review.

88141   Cytopathology, cervical or vaginal (any reporting system), requiring interpretation by physician
⮕ *CPT Assistant* Nov 97:35, Jan 98:6, Jan 99:11, May 99:6, Nov 99:46, Mar 04:6, Mar 05:16

(Use 88141 in conjunction with 88142-88154, 88164-88167, 88174-88175)

88142   Cytopathology, cervical or vaginal (any reporting system), collected in preservative fluid, automated thin layer preparation; manual screening under physician supervision
⮕ *CPT Assistant* Nov 97:34-35, Jan 98:6, Nov 98:28, May 99:6, Jul 03:7, Mar 04:4

88143   with manual screening and rescreening under physician supervision
⮕ *CPT Assistant* Nov 97:34-35, Nov 98:28, May 99:6, Jul 03:7, Mar 04:4, Mar 05:16

(For automated screening of automated thin layer preparation, see 88174, 88175)

88147   Cytopathology smears, cervical or vaginal; screening by automated system under physician supervision
⮕ *CPT Assistant* Nov 97:35, Nov 98:28, Jan 99:11, May 99:6, Nov 99:46, Mar 04:6

88148   screening by automated system with manual rescreening under physician supervision
⮕ *CPT Assistant* Jan 99:1, May 99:6, Nov 99:46, Mar 04:6; *CPT Changes: An Insider's View* 2000

88150   Cytopathology, slides, cervical or vaginal; manual screening under physician supervision
⮕ *CPT Assistant* Winter 91:19, Nov 97:34-35, Nov 98:28, May 99:6, Mar 04:5

88152   with manual screening and computer-assisted rescreening under physician supervision
⮕ *CPT Assistant* Nov 97:35, Jan 98:6, May 99:6, Mar 04:5

88153   with manual screening and rescreening under physician supervision
⮕ *CPT Assistant* Nov 97:34-35, Nov 98:28, May 99:6, Mar 04:5, Mar 05:16

88154   with manual screening and computer-assisted rescreening using cell selection and review under physician supervision
⮕ *CPT Assistant* Nov 97:34-35, Nov 98:28, May 99:6, Mar 04:5

+ 88155   Cytopathology, slides, cervical or vaginal, definitive hormonal evaluation (eg, maturation index, karyopyknotic index, estrogenic index) (List separately in addition to code[s] for other technical and interpretation services)
⮕ *CPT Assistant* Nov 97:35, Nov 98:28, May 99:6, Nov 99:46, Mar 04:5

(Use 88155 in conjunction with 88142-88154, 88164-88167, 88174-88175)

88160   Cytopathology, smears, any other source; screening and interpretation
⮕ *CPT Assistant* Jan 98:6

88161   preparation, screening and interpretation
⮕ *CPT Assistant* Aug 97:18, Jan 98:6

88162   extended study involving over 5 slides and/or multiple stains

(For aerosol collection of sputum, use 89220)

(For special stains, see 88312-88314)

88164   Cytopathology, slides, cervical or vaginal (the Bethesda System); manual screening under physician supervision

➲ *CPT Assistant* Nov 98:28, May 99:6, Mar 04:5

88165   with manual screening and rescreening under physician supervision

➲ *CPT Assistant* Nov 98:28, May 99:6, Mar 04:5, Mar 05:16

88166   with manual screening and computer-assisted rescreening under physician supervision

➲ *CPT Assistant* Nov 98:28, May 99:6, Mar 04:5

88167   with manual screening and computer-assisted rescreening using cell selection and review under physician supervision

➲ *CPT Assistant* Nov 98:28, May 99:6, Jul 03:7, Mar 04:5

(To report collection of specimen via fine needle aspiration, see 10021, 10022)

88172   Cytopathology, evaluation of fine needle aspirate; immediate cytohistologic study to determine adequacy of specimen(s)

➲ *CPT Assistant* Fall 93:26, Fall 94:2, Dec 98:8, Aug 07:15; *CPT Changes: An Insider's View* 2001

88173   interpretation and report

➲ *CPT Assistant* Fall 93:26, Fall 94:2, Dec 98:8

(For fine needle aspirate, see 10021, 10022)

(Do not report 88172, 88173 in conjunction with 88333 and 88334 for the same specimen)

88174   Cytopathology, cervical or vaginal (any reporting system), collected in preservative fluid, automated thin layer preparation; screening by automated system, under physician supervision

➲ *CPT Assistant* Jul 03:9, Mar 04:4; *CPT Changes: An Insider's View* 2003

88175   with screening by automated system and manual rescreening or review, under physician supervision

➲ *CPT Assistant* Jul 03:9, Mar 04:4, Mar 06:6; *CPT Changes: An Insider's View* 2003, 2006

(For manual screening, see 88142, 88143)

88182   Flow cytometry, cell cycle or DNA analysis

(For DNA ploidy analysis by morphometric technique, use 88358)

88184   Flow cytometry, cell surface, cytoplasmic, or nuclear marker, technical component only; first marker

➲ *CPT Assistant* Dec 07:14; *CPT Changes: An Insider's View* 2005

+ 88185   each additional marker (List separately in addition to code for first marker)

➲ *CPT Assistant* Dec 07:14; *CPT Changes: An Insider's View* 2005

(Report 88185 in conjunction with 88184)

88187   Flow cytometry, interpretation; 2 to 8 markers

➲ *CPT Assistant* Apr 05:14; *CPT Changes: An Insider's View* 2005

88188   9 to 15 markers

➲ *CPT Assistant* Apr 05:14; *CPT Changes: An Insider's View* 2005

88189   16 or more markers

➲ *CPT Assistant* Apr 05:14; *CPT Changes: An Insider's View* 2005

(Do not report 88187-88189 for interpretation of 86355, 86356, 86357, 86359, 86360, 86361, 86367)

88199   Unlisted cytopathology procedure

(For electron microscopy, see 88348, 88349)

Cytogenetic Studies

When molecular diagnostic procedures are performed to test for oncologic or inherited disorder, use the appropriate modifier to specify probe type or condition tested. (See **Appendix I** for a listing of appropriate modifiers to report with molecular diagnostic and cytogenetic procedures.)

(For acetylcholinesterase, use 82013)

(For alpha-fetoprotein, serum or amniotic fluid, see 82105, 82106)

(For laser microdissection of cells from tissue sample, see 88380)

88230   Tissue culture for non-neoplastic disorders; lymphocyte

➲ *CPT Assistant* Nov 98:29, Oct 99:2, Aug 05:9, May 08:5

88233   skin or other solid tissue biopsy

➲ *CPT Assistant* Nov 98:29, Oct 99:2, May 08:5

88235   amniotic fluid or chorionic villus cells

➲ *CPT Assistant* Nov 98:29, Oct 99:2, May 08:5

88237   Tissue culture for neoplastic disorders; bone marrow, blood cells

➲ *CPT Assistant* Nov 98:29, Oct 99:2, May 08:5

88239   solid tumor

➲ *CPT Assistant* Nov 98:29, Oct 99:2, May 08:5

88240   Cryopreservation, freezing and storage of cells, each cell line

➲ *CPT Assistant* Nov 98:29, Oct 99:2, Jul 03:9, May 08:5

(For therapeutic cryopreservation and storage, use 38207)

88241   Thawing and expansion of frozen cells, each aliquot

➲ *CPT Assistant* Nov 98:29, Oct 99:2, Jul 03:9, May 08:5

(For therapeutic thawing of previous harvest, use 38208)

88245   Chromosome analysis for breakage syndromes; baseline Sister Chromatid Exchange (SCE), 20-25 cells

➲ *CPT Assistant* Nov 98:29, Oct 99:2, Jul 05:1, May 08:5

88248   baseline breakage, score 50-100 cells, count 20 cells, 2 karyotypes (eg, for ataxia telangiectasia, Fanconi anemia, fragile X)

➲ *CPT Assistant* Nov 98:29, Oct 99:2, Jul 05:1, May 08:5

88249   score 100 cells, clastogen stress (eg, diepoxybutane, mitomycin C, ionizing radiation, UV radiation)

➲ *CPT Assistant* Nov 98:29, Oct 99:2, Jul 05:1, May 08:5

▲=Revised code   ●=New code   ►◄=Contains new or revised text   ⊘=Modifier 51 exempt

88261   Chromosome analysis; count 5 cells, 1 karyotype, with banding
➔ *CPT Assistant* Nov 98:29, Oct 99:2, Jul 05:1, May 08:5

88262   count 15-20 cells, 2 karyotypes, with banding
➔ *CPT Assistant* Nov 98:29, Oct 99:2, May 08:5

88263   count 45 cells for mosaicism, 2 karyotypes, with banding
➔ *CPT Assistant* Nov 98:29, Oct 99:2, Jul 05:1, May 08:5

88264   analyze 20-25 cells
➔ *CPT Assistant* Nov 98:29, Oct 99:2, Jul 05:1, May 08:5

88267   Chromosome analysis, amniotic fluid or chorionic villus, count 15 cells, 1 karyotype, with banding
➔ *CPT Assistant* Jul 05:1

88269   Chromosome analysis, in situ for amniotic fluid cells, count cells from 6-12 colonies, 1 karyotype, with banding
➔ *CPT Assistant* Jul 05:1

88271   Molecular cytogenetics; DNA probe, each (eg, FISH)
➔ *CPT Assistant* Nov 98:29, Mar 99:10, Oct 99:3, Jun 02:11, Jul 05:1, May 08:5

88272   chromosomal in situ hybridization, analyze 3-5 cells (eg, for derivatives and markers)
➔ *CPT Assistant* Nov 98:29, Mar 99:10, Oct 99:3, Jun 02:11, Jul 05:1, May 08:5

88273   chromosomal in situ hybridization, analyze 10-30 cells (eg, for microdeletions)
➔ *CPT Assistant* Nov 98:29, Mar 99:10, Oct 99:3, Jun 02:11, Jul 05:1, May 08:5

88274   interphase in situ hybridization, analyze 25-99 cells
➔ *CPT Assistant* Nov 98:29, Mar 99:10, Oct 99:3, Jun 02:11, Jul 05:1, May 08:5

88275   interphase in situ hybridization, analyze 100-300 cells
➔ *CPT Assistant* Nov 98:29, Mar 99:10, Oct 99:3, Jun 02:11, Jul 05:1, May 08:5

88280   Chromosome analysis; additional karyotypes, each study
➔ *CPT Assistant* Jul 05:1, May 08:5

88283   additional specialized banding technique (eg, NOR, C-banding)
➔ *CPT Assistant* Jul 05:1, May 08:5

88285   additional cells counted, each study
➔ *CPT Assistant* Jul 05:1, Dec 07:14, May 08:5

88289   additional high resolution study
➔ *CPT Assistant* Oct 99:3, Jul 05:1

88291   Cytogenetics and molecular cytogenetics, interpretation and report
➔ *CPT Assistant* Nov 98:29, Oct 99:3, Jul 05:1, May 08:5

88299   Unlisted cytogenetic study
➔ *CPT Assistant* Oct 99:3

Surgical Pathology

Services 88300 through 88309 include accession, examination, and reporting. They do not include the services designated in codes 88311 through 88365 and 88399, which are coded in addition when provided.

The unit of service for codes 88300 through 88309 is the specimen.

A specimen is defined as tissue or tissues that is (are) submitted for individual and separate attention, requiring individual examination and pathologic diagnosis. Two or more such specimens from the same patient (eg, separately identified endoscopic biopsies, skin lesions) are each appropriately assigned an individual code reflective of its proper level of service.

Service code 88300 is used for any specimen that in the opinion of the examining pathologist can be accurately diagnosed without microscopic examination. Service code 88302 is used when gross and microscopic examination is performed on a specimen to confirm identification and the absence of disease. Service codes 88304 through 88309 describe all other specimens requiring gross and microscopic examination, and represent additional ascending levels of physician work. Levels 88302 through 88309 are specifically defined by the assigned specimens.

Any unlisted specimen should be assigned to the code which most closely reflects the physician work involved when compared to other specimens assigned to that code.

(Do not report 88302-88309 on the same specimen as part of Mohs surgery)

88300   **Level I** - Surgical pathology, gross examination only
➔ *CPT Assistant* Winter 91:18, Sep 00:10, Aug 05:9

88302   **Level II** - Surgical pathology, gross and microscopic examination

   Appendix, incidental

   Fallopian tube, sterilization

   Fingers/toes, amputation, traumatic

   Foreskin, newborn

   Hernia sac, any location

   Hydrocele sac

   Nerve

   Skin, plastic repair

   Sympathetic ganglion

   Testis, castration

   Vaginal mucosa, incidental

   Vas deferens, sterilization
➔ *CPT Assistant* Winter 91:18, Sep 00:10, Nov 06:1, Jan 07:29

88304   **Level III** - Surgical pathology, gross and microscopic examination

   Abortion, induced

 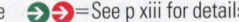

Abscess

Aneurysm - arterial/ventricular

Anus, tag

Appendix, other than incidental

Artery, atheromatous plaque

Bartholin's gland cyst

Bone fragment(s), other than pathologic fracture

Bursa/synovial cyst

Carpal tunnel tissue

Cartilage, shavings

Cholesteatoma

Colon, colostomy stoma

Conjunctiva - biopsy/pterygium

Cornea

Diverticulum - esophagus/small intestine

Dupuytren's contracture tissue

Femoral head, other than fracture

Fissure/fistula

Foreskin, other than newborn

Gallbladder

Ganglion cyst

Hematoma

Hemorrhoids

Hydatid of Morgagni

Intervertebral disc

Joint, loose body

Meniscus

Mucocele, salivary

Neuroma - Morton's/traumatic

Pilonidal cyst/sinus

Polyps, inflammatory - nasal/sinusoidal

Skin - cyst/tag/debridement

Soft tissue, debridement

Soft tissue, lipoma

Spermatocele

Tendon/tendon sheath

Testicular appendage

Thrombus or embolus

Tonsil and/or adenoids

Varicocele

Vas deferens, other than sterilization

Vein, varicosity

→ *CPT Assistant* Winter 91:18, Spring 91:2, Aug 97:18, Sep 00:10, Jan 07:29; *CPT Changes: An Insider's View* 2002

88305   **Level IV** - Surgical pathology, gross and microscopic examination

Abortion - spontaneous/missed

Artery, biopsy

Bone marrow, biopsy

Bone exostosis

Brain/meninges, other than for tumor resection

Breast, biopsy, not requiring microscopic evaluation of surgical margins

Breast, reduction mammoplasty

Bronchus, biopsy

Cell block, any source

Cervix, biopsy

Colon, biopsy

Duodenum, biopsy

Endocervix, curettings/biopsy

Endometrium, curettings/biopsy

Esophagus, biopsy

Extremity, amputation, traumatic

Fallopian tube, biopsy

Fallopian tube, ectopic pregnancy

Femoral head, fracture

Fingers/toes, amputation, non-traumatic

Gingiva/oral mucosa, biopsy

Heart valve

Joint, resection

Kidney, biopsy

Larynx, biopsy

Leiomyoma(s), uterine myomectomy - without uterus

Lip, biopsy/wedge resection

Lung, transbronchial biopsy

Lymph node, biopsy

Muscle, biopsy

Nasal mucosa, biopsy

Nasopharynx/oropharynx, biopsy

Nerve, biopsy

Odontogenic/dental cyst

Omentum, biopsy

Ovary with or without tube, non-neoplastic

Ovary, biopsy/wedge resection

Parathyroid gland

Peritoneum, biopsy

Pituitary tumor

Placenta, other than third trimester

Pleura/pericardium - biopsy/tissue

Polyp, cervical/endometrial

Polyp, colorectal

Polyp, stomach/small intestine

Prostate, needle biopsy

Prostate, TUR

Salivary gland, biopsy

Sinus, paranasal biopsy

Skin, other than cyst/tag/debridement/plastic repair

Small intestine, biopsy

Soft tissue, other than tumor/mass/lipoma/debridement

Spleen

Stomach, biopsy

Synovium

Testis, other than tumor/biopsy/castration

Thyroglossal duct/brachial cleft cyst

Tongue, biopsy

Tonsil, biopsy

Trachea, biopsy

Ureter, biopsy

Urethra, biopsy

Urinary bladder, biopsy

Uterus, with or without tubes and ovaries, for prolapse

Vagina, biopsy

Vulva/labia, biopsy

➔ *CPT Assistant* Winter 90:2, Winter 91:18, Spring 91:6, Winter 92:17, Aug 97:18, Jul 98:4, Nov 98:29-30, Jul 00:4, Sep 00:10, Dec 00:15, Jul 05:13, Nov 06:1, Jan 07:29; *CPT Changes: An Insider's View* 2002

88307 **Level V** - Surgical pathology, gross and microscopic examination

Adrenal, resection

Bone - biopsy/curettings

Bone fragment(s), pathologic fracture

Brain, biopsy

Brain/meninges, tumor resection

Breast, excision of lesion, requiring microscopic evaluation of surgical margins

Breast, mastectomy - partial/simple

Cervix, conization

Colon, segmental resection, other than for tumor

Extremity, amputation, non-traumatic

Eye, enucleation

Kidney, partial/total nephrectomy

Larynx, partial/total resection

Liver, biopsy - needle/wedge

Liver, partial resection

Lung, wedge biopsy

Lymph nodes, regional resection

Mediastinum, mass

Myocardium, biopsy

Odontogenic tumor

Ovary with or without tube, neoplastic

Pancreas, biopsy

Placenta, third trimester

Prostate, except radical resection

Salivary gland

Sentinel lymph node

Small intestine, resection, other than for tumor

Soft tissue mass (except lipoma) - biopsy/simple excision

Stomach - subtotal/total resection, other than for tumor

Testis, biopsy

Thymus, tumor

Thyroid, total/lobe

Ureter, resection

Urinary bladder, TUR

Uterus, with or without tubes and ovaries, other than neoplastic/prolapse

➔ *CPT Assistant* Winter 91:18, Winter 92:18, Jul 98:4, Nov 98:29-30, Jul 99:10, Jul 00:4, Sep 00:10, Dec 00:15, Dec 03:11, Nov 06:1, Jan 07:29; *CPT Changes: An Insider's View* 2001

88309 **Level VI** - Surgical pathology, gross and microscopic examination

Bone resection

Breast, mastectomy - with regional lymph nodes

Colon, segmental resection for tumor

Colon, total resection

Esophagus, partial/total resection

Extremity, disarticulation

Fetus, with dissection

Larynx, partial/total resection - with regional lymph nodes

Lung - total/lobe/segment resection

Pancreas, total/subtotal resection

Prostate, radical resection

Small intestine, resection for tumor

Soft tissue tumor, extensive resection

Stomach - subtotal/total resection for tumor

Testis, tumor

Tongue/tonsil -resection for tumor

Urinary bladder, partial/total resection

Uterus, with or without tubes and ovaries, neoplastic

Vulva, total/subtotal resection

➔ *CPT Assistant* Winter 91:18, Spring 91:2, Fall 93:2, 26, Jul 00:4, Sep 00:10, Dec 03:11, Nov 06:1, Jan 07:29

(For fine needle aspiration, see 10021, 10022)

(For evaluation of fine needle aspirate, see 88172-88173)

(Do not report 88302-88309 on the same specimen as part of Mohs surgery)

+ 88311   Decalcification procedure (List separately in addition to code for surgical pathology examination)

➔ *CPT Assistant* Winter 92:18, Jul 98:4, Jun 02:11, Nov 02:7, Nov 06:1

▲ 88312   Special stains; Group I for microorganisms (eg, Gridley, acid fast, methenamine silver), including interpretation and report, each

➔ *CPT Assistant* Winter 91:19, Jun 02:11, Nov 02:7, Nov 06:1; *CPT Changes: An Insider's View* 2004, 2010

▲ 88313   Group II, all other (eg, iron, trichrome), except immunocytochemistry and immunoperoxidase stains, including interpretation and report, each

➔ *CPT Assistant* Jun 02:11, Nov 02:7, Mar 03:22, Nov 03:15, Jun 06:17, Nov 06:1; *CPT Changes: An Insider's View* 2010

(For immunocytochemistry and immunoperoxidase tissue studies, use 88342)

+▲ 88314   histochemical staining with frozen section(s), including interpretation and report (List separately in addition to code for primary procedure)

➔ *CPT Assistant* Nov 02:7, Nov 06:1; *CPT Changes: An Insider's View* 2010

▶(Use 88314 in conjunction with 88302-88309)◀

(Do not report 88314 with 17311-17315 for routine frozen section stain [eg, hematoxylin and eosin, toluidine blue], performed during Mohs surgery. When a nonroutine histochemical stain on frozen tissue is utilized, report 88314 with modifier 59)

88318   Determinative histochemistry to identify chemical components (eg, copper, zinc)

88319   Determinative histochemistry or cytochemistry to identify enzyme constituents, each

88321   Consultation and report on referred slides prepared elsewhere

➔ *CPT Assistant* Winter 91:19, Apr 97:9, Oct 00:7, Dec 02:10

88323   Consultation and report on referred material requiring preparation of slides

➔ *CPT Assistant* Winter 91:19, Apr 97:9, Oct 00:7, Dec 02:10

88325   Consultation, comprehensive, with review of records and specimens, with report on referred material

➔ *CPT Assistant* Winter 91:19, Apr 97:9, Dec 02:10

88329   Pathology consultation during surgery;

➔ *CPT Assistant* Winter 91:19, Apr 97:12, Aug 97:18, Jan 07:29

88331   first tissue block, with frozen section(s), single specimen

➔ *CPT Assistant* Winter 91:19, Spring 91:2, Apr 97:12, Aug 97:18, Jul 00:4, Nov 02:7, Mar 06:6, Nov 06:1, Jan 07:29; *CPT Changes: An Insider's View* 2001

88332   each additional tissue block with frozen section(s)

➔ *CPT Assistant* Winter 91:19, Apr 97:12, Aug 97:18, Jul 00:4, Mar 06:6, Jan 07:29

88333   cytologic examination (eg, touch prep, squash prep), initial site

➔ *CPT Assistant* Mar 06:6, Jan 07:29, Jun 08:15; *CPT Changes: An Insider's View* 2006

88334   cytologic examination (eg, touch prep, squash prep), each additional site

➔ *CPT Assistant* Mar 06:6, Jan 07:29; *CPT Changes: An Insider's View* 2006

(For intraoperative consultation on a specimen requiring both frozen section and cytologic evaluation, use 88331 and 88334)

(For percutaneous needle biopsy requiring intraprocedural cytologic examination, use 88333)

(Do not report 88333 and 88334 for non-intraoperative cytologic examination, see 88160-88162)

(Do not report 88333 and 88334 for intraprocedural cytologic evaluation of fine needle aspirate, see 88172)

88342   Immunohistochemistry (including tissue immunoperoxidase), each antibody

➔ *CPT Assistant* Winter 91:17, Jul 00:10, Nov 02:6-7, Nov 06:1; *CPT Changes: An Insider's View* 2004

(Do not report 88342 in conjunction with 88360 or 88361 for the same antibody)

(For quantitative or semiquantitative immunohistochemistry, see 88360, 88361)

88346   Immunofluorescent study, each antibody; direct method

88347   indirect method

88348   Electron microscopy; diagnostic

88349   scanning

88355 Morphometric analysis; skeletal muscle

88356 nerve

88358 tumor (eg, DNA ploidy)
> *CPT Assistant* Jul 98:4, Jul 99:11, Jun 02:11, Jun 06:17; *CPT Changes: An Insider's View* 2004

(Do not report 88358 with 88313 unless each procedure is for a different special stain)

88360 Morphometric analysis, tumor immunohistochemistry (eg, Her-2/neu, estrogen receptor/progesterone receptor), quantitative or semiquantitative, each antibody; manual
> *CPT Changes: An Insider's View* 2005

88361 using computer-assisted technology
> *CPT Changes: An Insider's View* 2004, 2005

(Do not report 88360, 88361 with 88342 unless each procedure is for a different antibody)

(For morphometric analysis using in situ hybridization techniques, see 88367, 88368)

(When semi-thin plastic-embedded sections are performed in conjunction with morphometric analysis, only the morphometric analysis should be reported; if performed as an independent procedure, see codes 88300-88309 for surgical pathology.)

88362 Nerve teasing preparations

88365 In situ hybridization (eg, FISH), each probe
> *CPT Assistant* Jun 02:11, Mar 05:16; *CPT Changes: An Insider's View* 2005

(Do not report 88365 in conjunction with 88367, 88368 for the same probe)

88367 Morphometric analysis, in situ hybridization (quantitative or semi-quantitative) each probe; using computer-assisted technology
> *CPT Assistant* Mar 05:16; *CPT Changes: An Insider's View* 2005

88368 manual
> *CPT Assistant* Mar 05:16; *CPT Changes: An Insider's View* 2005

88371 Protein analysis of tissue by Western Blot, with interpretation and report;

88372 immunological probe for band identification, each

88380 Microdissection (ie, sample preparation of microscopically identified target); laser capture
> *CPT Assistant* Apr 02:17, Apr 08:5; *CPT Changes: An Insider's View* 2002, 2008

88381 manual
> *CPT Assistant* Apr 08:5; *CPT Changes: An Insider's View* 2008

(Do not report 88380 in conjunction with 88381)

88384 Array-based evaluation of multiple molecular probes; 11 through 50 probes
> *CPT Assistant* Jan 06:5, Mar 06:6; *CPT Changes: An Insider's View* 2006

88385 51 through 250 probes
> *CPT Assistant* Jan 06:5, Mar 06:6, May 08:5; *CPT Changes: An Insider's View* 2006

88386 251 through 500 probes
> *CPT Assistant* Jan 06:5, Mar 06:6, May 08:5, May 08:14; *CPT Changes: An Insider's View* 2006

(For preparation of array-based evaluation, see 83890-83892, 83898-83901)

(For preparation and analyses of less than 11 probes, see 83890-83914)

● **88387** Macroscopic examination, dissection, and preparation of tissue for non-microscopic analytical studies (eg, nucleic acid-based molecular studies); each tissue preparation (eg, a single lymph node)
> *CPT Changes: An Insider's View* 2010

►(Do not report 88387 for tissue preparation for microbiologic cultures or flow cytometric studies)◄

►(Do not report 88387 in conjunction with 88388, 88329-88334)◄

✚● **88388** in conjunction with a touch imprint, intraoperative consultation, or frozen section, each tissue preparation (eg, a single lymph node) (List separately in addition to code for primary procedure)
> *CPT Changes: An Insider's View* 2010

►(Use 88388 in conjunction with 88329-88334)◄

►(Do not report 88387 or 88388 for tissue preparation for microbiologic cultures or flow cytometric studies)◄

88399 Unlisted surgical pathology procedure

(88400 has been deleted. To report, use 88720)

In Vivo (eg, Transcutaneous) Laboratory Procedures

88720 Bilirubin, total, transcutaneous
> *CPT Changes: An Insider's View* 2009

(For transdermal oxygen saturation, see 94760-94762)

● **88738** Hemoglobin (Hgb), quantitative, transcutaneous
> *CPT Changes: An Insider's View* 2010

►(For in vitro hemoglobin measurement, use 85018)◄

88740 Hemoglobin, quantitative, transcutaneous, per day; carboxyhemoglobin
> *CPT Changes: An Insider's View* 2009

(For in vitro carboxyhemoglobin measurement, use 82375)

88741 methemoglobin
> *CPT Changes: An Insider's View* 2009

(For in vitro quantitative methemoglobin determination, use 83050)

Other Procedures

89049 Caffeine halothane contracture test (CHCT) for malignant hyperthermia susceptibility, including interpretation and report

➔ *CPT Assistant* Mar 06:6, May 06:19; *CPT Changes: An Insider's View* 2006

89050 Cell count, miscellaneous body fluids (eg, cerebrospinal fluid, joint fluid), except blood;

➔ *CPT Assistant* Aug 05:9; *CPT Changes: An Insider's View* 2002

89051 with differential count

89055 Leukocyte assessment, fecal, qualitative or semiquantitative

➔ *CPT Assistant* Jul 03:9; *CPT Changes: An Insider's View* 2003, 2004

89060 Crystal identification by light microscopy with or without polarizing lens analysis, tissue or any body fluid (except urine)

➔ *CPT Changes: An Insider's View* 2007

(Do not report 89060 for crystal identification on paraffin-embedded tissue)

89100 Duodenal intubation and aspiration; single specimen (eg, simple bile study or afferent loop culture) plus appropriate test procedure

89105 collection of multiple fractional specimens with pancreatic or gallbladder stimulation, single or double lumen tube

➔ *CPT Assistant* Aug 05:9

(For radiological localization, use 74340)

(For chemical analyses, see **Chemistry,** this section)

(Electrocardiogram, see 93000-93268)

(Esophagus acid perfusion test [Bernstein], see 91030)

89125 Fat stain, feces, urine, or respiratory secretions

➔ *CPT Changes: An Insider's View* 2001

89130 Gastric intubation and aspiration, diagnostic, each specimen, for chemical analyses or cytopathology;

89132 after stimulation

89135 Gastric intubation, aspiration, and fractional collections (eg, gastric secretory study); 1 hour

89136 2 hours

89140 2 hours including gastric stimulation (eg, histalog, pentagastrin)

89141 3 hours, including gastric stimulation

(For gastric lavage, therapeutic, use 91105)

(For radiologic localization of gastric tube, use 74340)

(For chemical analyses, see 82926, 82928)

(Joint fluid chemistry, see **Chemistry,** this section)

89160 Meat fibers, feces

89190 Nasal smear for eosinophils

(Occult blood, feces, use 82270)

(Paternity tests, use 86910)

89220 Sputum, obtaining specimen, aerosol induced technique (separate procedure)

➔ *CPT Assistant* Aug 05:9; *CPT Changes: An Insider's View* 2004

89225 Starch granules, feces

➔ *CPT Changes: An Insider's View* 2004

89230 Sweat collection by iontophoresis

➔ *CPT Changes: An Insider's View* 2004

89235 Water load test

➔ *CPT Changes: An Insider's View* 2004

89240 Unlisted miscellaneous pathology test

➔ *CPT Assistant* Nov 05:14, Jan 07:30; *CPT Changes: An Insider's View* 2004

Reproductive Medicine Procedures

89250 Culture of oocyte(s)/embryo(s), less than 4 days;

➔ *CPT Assistant* Nov 97:35-36, Jan 98:6, Oct 98:1, Apr 04:2, May 04:16, Jun 04:9; *CPT Changes: An Insider's View* 2004

89251 with co-culture of oocyte(s)/embryos

➔ *CPT Assistant* Nov 97:35-36, Jan 98:6, Oct 98:1, Apr 04:2; *CPT Changes: An Insider's View* 2004

(For extended culture of oocyte[s]/embryo[s], see 89272)

89253 Assisted embryo hatching, microtechniques (any method)

➔ *CPT Assistant* Nov 97:35-36, Jan 98:6, Oct 98:1, Apr 04:2, May 04:16, Jun 04:9

89254 Oocyte identification from follicular fluid

➔ *CPT Assistant* Nov 97:35-36, Jan 98:6, Oct 98:1, Apr 04:2, May 04:16, Jun 04:9

89255 Preparation of embryo for transfer (any method)

➔ *CPT Assistant* Nov 97:35-36, Jan 98:6, Oct 98:1, Apr 04:2, May 04:16, Jun 04:9

89257 Sperm identification from aspiration (other than seminal fluid)

➔ *CPT Assistant* Nov 97:35-36, Jan 98:6, Oct 98:1, Nov 98:30, Apr 04:2

(For semen analysis, see 89300-89320)

(For sperm identification from testis tissue, use 89264)

89258 Cryopreservation; embryo(s)

➔ *CPT Assistant* Nov 97:36, Jan 98:6, Oct 98:1, Apr 04:2, 4; *CPT Changes: An Insider's View* 2004

89259 sperm

➔ *CPT Assistant* Nov 97:36, Jan 98:6, Oct 98:1, Apr 04:2, 4

(For cryopreservation of reproductive tissue, testicular, use 89335)

89260 Sperm isolation; simple prep (eg, sperm wash and swim-up) for insemination or diagnosis with semen analysis

➲ *CPT Assistant* Nov 97:36, Jan 98:6, Oct 98:1, Apr 04:3-4

89261 complex prep (eg, Percoll gradient, albumin gradient) for insemination or diagnosis with semen analysis

➲ *CPT Assistant* Nov 97:36, Jan 98:6, Oct 98:1, Apr 04:3-4

(For semen analysis without sperm wash or swim-up, use 89320)

89264 Sperm identification from testis tissue, fresh or cryopreserved

➲ *CPT Assistant* Nov 98:30, Apr 04:3-4

(For biopsy of testis, see 54500, 54505)

(For sperm identification from aspiration, use 89257)

(For semen analysis, see 89300-89320)

89268 Insemination of oocytes

➲ *CPT Assistant* Apr 04:3-4; *CPT Changes: An Insider's View* 2004

89272 Extended culture of oocyte(s)/embryo(s), 4-7 days

➲ *CPT Assistant* Apr 04:3-4; *CPT Changes: An Insider's View* 2004

89280 Assisted oocyte fertilization, microtechnique; less than or equal to 10 oocytes

➲ *CPT Assistant* Apr 04:3-4; *CPT Changes: An Insider's View* 2004

89281 greater than 10 oocytes

➲ *CPT Assistant* Apr 04:3-4; *CPT Changes: An Insider's View* 2004

89290 Biopsy, oocyte polar body or embryo blastomere, microtechnique (for pre-implantation genetic diagnosis); less than or equal to 5 embryos

➲ *CPT Assistant* Apr 04:5; *CPT Changes: An Insider's View* 2004

89291 greater than 5 embryos

➲ *CPT Assistant* Apr 04:3, 5; *CPT Changes: An Insider's View* 2004

89300 Semen analysis; presence and/or motility of sperm including Huhner test (post coital)

➲ *CPT Assistant* Nov 97:36, Jul 98:10, Oct 98:4, Apr 04:3, Aug 05:9

89310 motility and count (not including Huhner test)

➲ *CPT Assistant* Jul 03:9, Apr 04:3; *CPT Changes: An Insider's View* 2003

89320 volume, count, motility, and differential

➲ *CPT Assistant* Apr 04:3, Apr 08:5; *CPT Changes: An Insider's View* 2008

(Skin tests, see 86485-86580 and 95010-95199)

89321 sperm presence and motility of sperm, if performed

➲ *CPT Changes: An Insider's View* 2001, 2008

▶(To report Hyaluronan binding assay [HBA], use 89398)◀

89322 volume, count, motility, and differential using strict morphologic criteria (eg, Kruger)

➲ *CPT Assistant* Apr 08:5; *CPT Changes: An Insider's View* 2008

89325 Sperm antibodies

(For medicolegal identification of sperm, use 88125)

89329 Sperm evaluation; hamster penetration test

89330 cervical mucus penetration test, with or without spinnbarkeit test

➲ *CPT Assistant* Nov 05:14

89331 Sperm evaluation, for retrograde ejaculation, urine (sperm concentration, motility, and morphology, as indicated)

➲ *CPT Assistant* Apr 08:5; *CPT Changes: An Insider's View* 2008

(For semen analysis on concurrent semen specimen, see 89300-89322 in conjunction with 89331)

(For detection of sperm in urine, use 81015)

89335 Cryopreservation, reproductive tissue, testicular

➲ *CPT Assistant* Apr 04:5; *CPT Changes: An Insider's View* 2004

(For cryopreservation of embryo[s], use 89258. For cryopreservation of sperm, use 89259)

▶(For cryopreservation, ovarian reproductive tissue, oocytes, use 89240)◀

89342 Storage (per year); embryo(s)

➲ *CPT Assistant* Apr 04:5; *CPT Changes: An Insider's View* 2004

89343 sperm/semen

➲ *CPT Assistant* Apr 04:5; *CPT Changes: An Insider's View* 2004

89344 reproductive tissue, testicular/ovarian

➲ *CPT Assistant* Apr 04:5; *CPT Changes: An Insider's View* 2004

89346 oocyte(s)

➲ *CPT Assistant* Apr 04:5; *CPT Changes: An Insider's View* 2004, 2005

89352 Thawing of cryopreserved; embryo(s)

➲ *CPT Assistant* Apr 04:5; *CPT Changes: An Insider's View* 2004

89353 sperm/semen, each aliquot

➲ *CPT Assistant* Apr 04:5; *CPT Changes: An Insider's View* 2004

89354 reproductive tissue, testicular/ovarian

➲ *CPT Assistant* Apr 04:5; *CPT Changes: An Insider's View* 2004

89356 oocytes, each aliquot

➲ *CPT Assistant* Apr 04:5, Aug 05:9; *CPT Changes: An Insider's View* 2004

● **89398** Unlisted reproductive medicine laboratory procedure

➲ *CPT Changes: An Insider's View* 2010

Medicine Guidelines

Medicine

Medicine Guidelines

In addition to the definitions and commonly used terms presented in the **Introduction**, several other items unique to this section on **Medicine** are defined or identified here.

Multiple Procedures

It is appropriate to designate multiple procedures that are rendered on the same date by separate entries. For example: If individual medical psychotherapy (90829) is rendered in addition to subsequent hospital care (eg, 99231), the psychotherapy would be reported separately from the hospital visit. In this instance, both 99231 and 90829 would be reported.

Add-on Codes

Some of the listed procedures are commonly carried out in addition to the primary procedure performed. All add-on codes found in the CPT codebook are exempt from the multiple procedure concept. They are exempt from the use of modifier 51, as these procedures are not reported as stand-alone codes. These additional or supplemental procedures are designated as "add-on" codes. Add-on codes in the CPT codebook can be readily identified by specific descriptor nomenclature which includes phrases such as "each additional" or "(List separately in addition to primary procedure)."

Separate Procedures

Some of the procedures or services listed in the CPT codebook that are commonly carried out as an integral component of a total service or procedure have been identified by the inclusion of the term "separate procedure." The codes designated as "separate procedure" should not be reported in addition to the code for the total procedure or service of which it is considered an integral component.

However, when a procedure or service that is designated as a "separate procedure" is carried out independently or considered to be unrelated or distinct from other procedures/services provided at that time, it may be reported by itself, or in addition to other procedures/services by appending modifier 59 to the specific "separate procedure" code to indicate that the procedure is not considered to be a component of

another procedure, but is a distinct, independent procedure. This may represent a different session or patient encounter, different procedure or surgery, different site or organ system, separate incision/excision, separate lesion, or separate injury (or area of injury in extensive injuries).

Unlisted Service or Procedure

A service or procedure may be provided that is not listed in this edition of the CPT codebook. When reporting such a service, the appropriate "Unlisted Procedure" code may be used to indicate the service, identifying it by "Special Report" as discussed on this page. The "Unlisted Procedures" and accompanying codes for **Medicine** are as follows:

90399	Unlisted immune globulin
90749	Unlisted vaccine/toxoid
90899	Unlisted psychiatric service or procedure
90999	Unlisted dialysis procedure, inpatient or outpatient
91299	Unlisted diagnostic gastroenterology procedure
92499	Unlisted ophthalmological service or procedure
92700	Unlisted otorhinolaryngological service or procedure
93799	Unlisted cardiovascular service or procedure
94799	Unlisted pulmonary service or procedure
95199	Unlisted allergy/clinical immunologic service or procedure
95999	Unlisted neurological or neuromuscular diagnostic procedure
96379	Unlisted therapeutic, prophylactic, or diagnostic intravenous or intra-arterial injection or infusion
96549	Unlisted chemotherapy procedure
96999	Unlisted special dermatological service or procedure
97039	Unlisted modality (specify type and time if constant attendance)
97139	Unlisted therapeutic procedure (specify)
97799	Unlisted physical medicine/rehabilitation service or procedure
99199	Unlisted special service, procedure or report
99600	Unlisted home visit service or procedure

Special Report

▶A service that is rarely provided, unusual, variable, or new may require a special report. Pertinent information should include an adequate definition or description of the nature, extent, and need for the procedure; and the time, effort, and equipment necessary to provide the service.◀

Materials Supplied by Physician

Supplies and materials provided by the physician (eg, sterile trays/drugs), over and above those usually included with the procedure(s) rendered are reported separately. List drugs, trays, supplies, and materials provided. Identify as 99070 or specific supply code.

Medicine

►Immune Globulins, Serum or Recombinant Products◄

►Codes 90281-90399 identify the serum globulins, extracted from human blood; or recombinant immune globulin products created in a laboratory through genetic modification of human and/or animal proteins. Both are reported in addition to the administration codes 96365-96368, 96372, 96374, 96375 as appropriate. Modifier 51 should not be reported with this section of products codes when performed with another procedure. The serum or recombinant globulin products listed here include broad-spectrum anti-infective immune globulins, antitoxins, various isoantibodies, and monoclonal antibodies.◄

90281   Immune globulin (Ig), human, for intramuscular use
> *CPT Assistant* Nov 98:30, Jan 99:3, Sep 99:10; *CPT Changes: An Insider's View* 2008

90283   Immune globulin (IgIV), human, for intravenous use
> *CPT Assistant* Nov 98:30, Jan 99:3; *CPT Changes: An Insider's View* 2008

90284   Immune globulin (SCIg), human, for use in subcutaneous infusions, 100 mg, each
> *CPT Changes: An Insider's View* 2008

90287   Botulinum antitoxin, equine, any route
> *CPT Assistant* Nov 98:30, Jan 99:3; *CPT Changes: An Insider's View* 2008

90288   Botulism immune globulin, human, for intravenous use
> *CPT Assistant* Nov 98:30, Jan 99:3; *CPT Changes: An Insider's View* 2008

90291   Cytomegalovirus immune globulin (CMV-IgIV), human, for intravenous use
> *CPT Assistant* Nov 98:30, Jan 99:3; *CPT Changes: An Insider's View* 2008

90296   Diphtheria antitoxin, equine, any route
> *CPT Assistant* Nov 98:30, Jan 99:3; *CPT Changes: An Insider's View* 2008

90371   Hepatitis B immune globulin (HBIg), human, for intramuscular use
> *CPT Assistant* Nov 98:30, Jan 99:3; *CPT Changes: An Insider's View* 2008

90375   Rabies immune globulin (RIg), human, for intramuscular and/or subcutaneous use
> *CPT Assistant* Nov 98:30, Jan 99:3; *CPT Changes: An Insider's View* 2008

90376   Rabies immune globulin, heat-treated (RIg-HT), human, for intramuscular and/or subcutaneous use
> *CPT Assistant* Nov 98:30, Jan 99:3; *CPT Changes: An Insider's View* 2008

▲ **90378**   Respiratory syncytial virus, monoclonal antibody, recombinant, for intramuscular use, 50 mg, each
> *CPT Assistant* Jan 99:3, Nov 99:47, Jun 00:10; *CPT Changes: An Insider's View* 2000, 2001, 2008, 2010

►(90379 has been deleted)◄

90384   Rho(D) immune globulin (RhIg), human, full-dose, for intramuscular use
> *CPT Assistant* Nov 98:30, Jan 99:3; *CPT Changes: An Insider's View* 2008

90385   Rho(D) immune globulin (RhIg), human, mini-dose, for intramuscular use
> *CPT Assistant* Nov 98:30, Jan 99:3; *CPT Changes: An Insider's View* 2008

90386   Rho(D) immune globulin (RhIgIV), human, for intravenous use
> *CPT Assistant* Nov 98:30, Jan 99:3; *CPT Changes: An Insider's View* 2008

90389   Tetanus immune globulin (TIg), human, for intramuscular use
> *CPT Assistant* Nov 98:30, Jan 99:3; *CPT Changes: An Insider's View* 2008

90393   Vaccinia immune globulin, human, for intramuscular use
> *CPT Assistant* Nov 98:30, Jan 99:3; *CPT Changes: An Insider's View* 2008

90396   Varicella-zoster immune globulin, human, for intramuscular use
> *CPT Assistant* Nov 98:30, Jan 99:3; *CPT Changes: An Insider's View* 2008

90399   Unlisted immune globulin
> *CPT Assistant* Nov 98:30, Jan 99:3, Feb 99:11, Sep 99:10; *CPT Changes: An Insider's View* 2008

Immunization Administration for Vaccines/Toxoids

Codes 90465-90474 must be reported in addition to the vaccine and toxoid code(s) 90476-90749.

Report codes 90465-90468 only when the physician provides face-to-face counseling of the patient and family during the administration of a vaccine. For immunization administration of any vaccine that is not accompanied by face-to-face physician counseling to the patient/family, report codes 90471-90474.

If a significant separately identifiable Evaluation and Management service (eg, office or other outpatient services, preventive medicine services) is performed, the appropriate E/M service code should be reported in addition to the vaccine and toxoid administration codes.

(For allergy testing, see 95004 et seq)

▲=Revised code   ●=New code   ►◄=Contains new or revised text   ⊘=Modifier 51 exempt

(For skin testing of bacterial, viral, fungal extracts, see 86485-86580)

(For therapeutic or diagnostic injections, see 96372-96379)

90465   Immunization administration younger than 8 years of age (includes percutaneous, intradermal, subcutaneous, or intramuscular injections) when the physician counsels the patient/family; first injection (single or combination vaccine/toxoid), per day

> *CPT Assistant* Apr 05:1-3, Aug 05:15, Nov 05:1, Jan 09:3, Jan 09:8; *CPT Changes: An Insider's View* 2005

(Do not report 90465 in conjunction with 90467)

+ 90466   each additional injection (single or combination vaccine/toxoid), per day (List separately in addition to code for primary procedure)

> *CPT Assistant* Apr 05:1-3, Aug 05:15, Nov 05:1, Jan 09:3, Jan 09:8; *CPT Changes: An Insider's View* 2005

(Use 90466 in conjunction with 90465 or 90467)

90467   Immunization administration younger than age 8 years (includes intranasal or oral routes of administration) when the physician counsels the patient/family; first administration (single or combination vaccine/toxoid), per day

> *CPT Assistant* Apr 05:1-3, Aug 05:15, Jan 09:3, Jan 09:8; *CPT Changes: An Insider's View* 2005

(Do not report 90467 in conjunction with 90465)

+ 90468   each additional administration (single or combination vaccine/toxoid), per day (List separately in addition to code for primary procedure)

> *CPT Assistant* Apr 05:1-3, Aug 05:15, Jan 09:3, Jan 09:8; *CPT Changes: An Insider's View* 2005

(Use 90468 in conjunction with 90465 or 90467)

90471   Immunization administration (includes percutaneous, intradermal, subcutaneous, or intramuscular injections); 1 vaccine (single or combination vaccine/toxoid)

> *CPT Assistant* Nov 98:31, Jan 99:2, Apr 99:10, Oct 99:9, Nov 99:47-48, Nov 00:10, Feb 01:5, Jul 01:2, Nov 02:11, Mar 04:11, Apr 04:14, Apr 05:1-3, 5, Nov 05:1, Jan 09:8; *CPT Changes: An Insider's View* 2002, 2005

(Do not report 90471 in conjunction with 90473)

+ 90472   each additional vaccine (single or combination vaccine/toxoid) (List separately in addition to code for primary procedure)

> *CPT Assistant* Nov 98:31, Jan 99:2, Apr 99:10, Oct 99:9, Nov 99:47-48, Nov 00:10, Feb 01:5, Jul 01:2, Nov 02:11, Mar 04:11, Apr 04:14, Apr 05:1-3, Nov 05:1, Jan 09:3, Jan 09:8; *CPT Changes: An Insider's View* 2000

(Use 90472 in conjunction with 90471 or 90473)

(For administration of immune globulins, see 90281-90399, 96360, 96361, 96365-96368, 96374)

(For intravesical administration of BCG vaccine, see 51720, 90586)

90473   Immunization administration by intranasal or oral route; 1 vaccine (single or combination vaccine/toxoid)

> *CPT Assistant* Feb 01:5, Nov 02:11, Apr 04:14, Apr 05:1-3, Jan 09:3, Jan 09:8; *CPT Changes: An Insider's View* 2002

(Do not report 90473 in conjunction with 90471)

+ 90474   each additional vaccine (single or combination vaccine/toxoid) (List separately in addition to code for primary procedure)

> *CPT Assistant* Feb 01:5, Nov 02:11, Apr 04:14, Apr 05:1-3, Jan 09:3, Jan 09:8; *CPT Changes: An Insider's View* 2002

(Use 90474 in conjunction with 90471 or 90473)

Vaccines, Toxoids

To assist users to report the most recent new or revised vaccine product codes, the American Medical Association (AMA) currently uses the CPT Website, which features updates of CPT Editorial Panel actions regarding these products. Once approved by the CPT Editorial Panel, these codes will be made available for release on a semi-annual (twice a year: July 1 and January 1) basis. As part of the electronic distribution, there is a six-month implementation period from the initial release date (ie, codes released on January 1 are eligible for use on July 1 and codes released on July 1 are eligible for use January 1).

The CPT Editorial Panel, in recognition of the public health interest in vaccine products, has chosen to publish new vaccine product codes prior to approval by the U. S. Food and Drug Administration (FDA). These codes are indicated with the ✂ symbol and will be tracked by the AMA to monitor FDA approval status. Once the FDA status changes to approval, the ✂ symbol will be removed. CPT users should refer to the AMA Internet site (www.ama-assn.org/ama/pub/category/10902.html) for the most up-to-date information on codes with the ✂ symbol.

Codes 90476-90748 identify the vaccine product **only.** To report the administration of a vaccine/toxoid, the vaccine/toxoid product codes 90476-90749 must be used in addition to an immunization administration code(s) 90465-90474. Modifier 51 should not be reported for the vaccines, toxoids when performed with these administration procedures.

If a significantly separately identifiable Evaluation and Management (E/M) service (eg, office or other outpatient services, preventive medicine services) is performed, the appropriate E/M service code should be reported in addition to the vaccine and toxoid administration codes.

To meet the reporting requirements of immunization registries, vaccine distribution programs, and reporting systems (eg, Vaccine Adverse Event Reporting System) the exact vaccine product administered needs to be reported. Multiple codes for a particular vaccine are provided in the CPT codebook when the schedule (number of doses or timing) differs for two or more products of the same vaccine type (eg, hepatitis A, Hib) or the vaccine product is available in more than one chemical formulation, dosage, or route of administration.

▶The "when administered to" age descriptions included in CPT vaccine codes are not intended to identify a product's licensed age indication. The term "preservative free" includes use for vaccines that contain no preservative and vaccines that contain trace amounts of preservative agents that are not present in a sufficient concentration for the purpose of preserving the final vaccine formulation. The absence of a designation regarding a preservative does not necessarily indicate the presence or absence of preservative in the vaccine. Refer to the product's prescribing information (PI) for the licensed age indication before administering vaccine to a patient.◀

Separate codes are available for combination vaccines (eg, DTP-Hib, DtaP-Hib, HepB-Hib). It is inappropriate to code each component of a combination vaccine separately. If a specific vaccine code is not available, the unlisted procedure code should be reported, until a new code becomes available.

(For immune globulins, see codes 90281-90399, 96365-96368, 96372-96375 for administration of immune globulins)

➔ *CPT Assistant* Nov 99:48

90476   Adenovirus vaccine, type 4, live, for oral use
➔ *CPT Assistant* Nov 98:31-33, Jan 99:2, Sep 99:10, Oct 99:9; *CPT Changes: An Insider's View* 2008

90477   Adenovirus vaccine, type 7, live, for oral use
➔ *CPT Assistant* Nov 98:31-33, Jan 99:2, Oct 99:9; *CPT Changes: An Insider's View* 2008

90581   Anthrax vaccine, for subcutaneous use
➔ *CPT Assistant* Nov 98:31-33, Jan 99:2, Oct 99:9; *CPT Changes: An Insider's View* 2008

90585   Bacillus Calmette-Guerin vaccine (BCG) for tuberculosis, live, for percutaneous use
➔ *CPT Assistant* Nov 98:31-33, Jan 99:2, Oct 99:9; *CPT Changes: An Insider's View* 2008

90586   Bacillus Calmette-Guerin vaccine (BCG) for bladder cancer, live, for intravesical use
➔ *CPT Assistant* Nov 98:31-33, Jan 99:2, Oct 99:9, Nov 02:11; *CPT Changes: An Insider's View* 2008

90632   Hepatitis A vaccine, adult dosage, for intramuscular use
➔ *CPT Assistant* Nov 98:31-33, Jan 99:2, Oct 99:9; *CPT Changes: An Insider's View* 2008

90633   Hepatitis A vaccine, pediatric/adolescent dosage-2 dose schedule, for intramuscular use
➔ *CPT Assistant* Nov 98:31-33, Jan 99:2, Oct 99:9; *CPT Changes: An Insider's View* 2008

90634   Hepatitis A vaccine, pediatric/adolescent dosage-3 dose schedule, for intramuscular use
➔ *CPT Assistant* Nov 98:31-33, Jan 99:2, Oct 99:9; *CPT Changes: An Insider's View* 2008

90636   Hepatitis A and hepatitis B vaccine (HepA-HepB), adult dosage, for intramuscular use
➔ *CPT Assistant* Nov 98:31-33, Jan 99:2, Oct 99:9; *CPT Changes: An Insider's View* 2008

90645   Hemophilus influenza b vaccine (Hib), HbOC conjugate (4 dose schedule), for intramuscular use
➔ *CPT Assistant* Nov 98:31-33, Jan 99:2, Oct 99:9; *CPT Changes: An Insider's View* 2008

90646   Hemophilus influenza b vaccine (Hib), PRP-D conjugate, for booster use only, intramuscular use
➔ *CPT Assistant* Nov 98:31-33, Jan 99:2, Oct 99:9; *CPT Changes: An Insider's View* 2008

90647   Hemophilus influenza b vaccine (Hib), PRP-OMP conjugate (3 dose schedule), for intramuscular use
➔ *CPT Assistant* Nov 98:31-33, Jan 99:2, Oct 99:9; *CPT Changes: An Insider's View* 2008

90648   Hemophilus influenza b vaccine (Hib), PRP-T conjugate (4 dose schedule), for intramuscular use
➔ *CPT Assistant* Nov 98:31-33, Jan 99:2, Oct 99:9; *CPT Changes: An Insider's View* 2008

90649   Human Papilloma virus (HPV) vaccine, types 6, 11, 16, 18 (quadrivalent), 3 dose schedule, for intramuscular use
➔ *CPT Assistant* Dec 05:9, Jun 06:8, Sep 06:14, Jul 07:13; *CPT Changes: An Insider's View* 2006, 2008

✗ **90650**   Human Papilloma virus (HPV) vaccine, types 16, 18, bivalent, 3 dose schedule, for intramuscular use
➔ *CPT Changes: An Insider's View* 2009

90655   Influenza virus vaccine, split virus, preservative free, when administered to children 6-35 months of age, for intramuscular use
➔ *CPT Assistant* Oct 99:9, Feb 04:2, Apr 07:12, Apr 08:8; *CPT Changes: An Insider's View* 2004, 2007, 2008

90656   Influenza virus vaccine, split virus, preservative free, when administered to individuals 3 years and older, for intramuscular use
➔ *CPT Assistant* Apr 08:8; *CPT Changes: An Insider's View* 2005, 2007, 2008

90657   Influenza virus vaccine, split virus, when administered to children 6-35 months of age, for intramuscular use
➔ *CPT Assistant* Nov 98:31-33, Jan 99:2, Oct 99:9, Feb 02:10, Feb 04:2, Apr 05:5, Apr 08:8; *CPT Changes: An Insider's View* 2004, 2007, 2008

90658   Influenza virus vaccine, split virus, when administered to individuals 3 years of age and older, for intramuscular use
➔ *CPT Assistant* Nov 98:31-33, Jan 99:2, Oct 99:9, Feb 04:2, Apr 07:12, Apr 08:8; *CPT Changes: An Insider's View* 2004, 2007, 2008

90660   Influenza virus vaccine, live, for intranasal use
➔ *CPT Assistant* Nov 98:31-33, Jan 99:2, Oct 99:9, Mar 04:11, Apr 04:14; *CPT Changes: An Insider's View* 2008

✗ **90661**   Influenza virus vaccine, derived from cell cultures, subunit, preservative and antibiotic free, for intramuscular use
➔ *CPT Assistant* Apr 08:8; *CPT Changes: An Insider's View* 2008

/ **90662**   Influenza virus vaccine, split virus, preservative free, enhanced immunogenicity via increased antigen content, for intramuscular use

➔ *CPT Assistant* Apr 08:8; *CPT Changes: An Insider's View* 2008

/ **90663**   Influenza virus vaccine, pandemic formulation

➔ *CPT Assistant* Apr 08:8; *CPT Changes: An Insider's View* 2008

90665   Lyme disease vaccine, adult dosage, for intramuscular use

➔ *CPT Assistant* Nov 98:31-33, Jan 99:2, Oct 99:9; *CPT Changes: An Insider's View* 2008

▲ **90669**   Pneumococcal conjugate vaccine, 7 valent, for intramuscular use

➔ *CPT Assistant* Nov 98:31-33, Jan 99:2, Oct 99:9, Jun 00:10; *CPT Changes: An Insider's View* 2001, 2007, 2008, 2010

/ ● **90670**   Pneumococcal conjugate vaccine, 13 valent, for intramuscular use

➔ *CPT Changes: An Insider's View* 2010

90675   Rabies vaccine, for intramuscular use

➔ *CPT Assistant* Nov 98:31-33, Jan 99:2, Oct 99:9; *CPT Changes: An Insider's View* 2008

90676   Rabies vaccine, for intradermal use

➔ *CPT Assistant* Nov 98:31-33, Jan 99:2, Oct 99:9; *CPT Changes: An Insider's View* 2008

90680   Rotavirus vaccine, pentavalent, 3 dose schedule, live, for oral use

➔ *CPT Assistant* Nov 98:31-33, Jan 99:2, Oct 99:9, Jun 05:6, Dec 05:9, Jun 06:8; *CPT Changes: An Insider's View* 2006, 2008

90681   Rotavirus vaccine, human, attenuated, 2 dose schedule, live, for oral use

➔ *CPT Changes: An Insider's View* 2009

90690   Typhoid vaccine, live, oral

➔ *CPT Assistant* Nov 98:31-33, Jan 99:2, Oct 99:9; *CPT Changes: An Insider's View* 2008

90691   Typhoid vaccine, Vi capsular polysaccharide (ViCPs), for intramuscular use

➔ *CPT Assistant* Nov 98:31-33, Jan 99:2, Oct 99:9; *CPT Changes: An Insider's View* 2008

90692   Typhoid vaccine, heat- and phenol-inactivated (H-P), for subcutaneous or intradermal use

➔ *CPT Assistant* Nov 98:31-33, Jan 99:2, Oct 99:9, Jan 08:4; *CPT Changes: An Insider's View* 2008

90693   Typhoid vaccine, acetone-killed, dried (AKD), for subcutaneous use (U.S. military)

➔ *CPT Assistant* Nov 98:31-33, Jan 99:2, Oct 99:9; *CPT Changes: An Insider's View* 2004, 2008

90696   Diphtheria, tetanus toxoids, acellular pertussis vaccine and poliovirus vaccine, inactivated (DTaP-IPV), when administered to children 4 through 6 years of age, for intramuscular use

➔ *CPT Changes: An Insider's View* 2009

90698   Diphtheria, tetanus toxoids, acellular pertussis vaccine, haemophilus influenza Type B, and poliovirus vaccine, inactivated (DTaP - Hib - IPV), for intramuscular use

➔ *CPT Assistant* Oct 99:9, Dec 05:9, Jun 06:8; *CPT Changes: An Insider's View* 2008, 2009

90700   Diphtheria, tetanus toxoids, and acellular pertussis vaccine (DTaP), when administered to individuals younger than 7 years, for intramuscular use

➔ *CPT Assistant* Jan 96:5, Apr 97:10, Nov 98:31-33, Jan 99:2, Oct 99:9, Nov 03:13; *CPT Changes: An Insider's View* 2005, 2007, 2008

90701   Diphtheria, tetanus toxoids, and whole cell pertussis vaccine (DTP), for intramuscular use

➔ *CPT Assistant* Jan 96:6, Apr 97:10, Nov 98:31-33, Jan 99:2, Oct 99:9; *CPT Changes: An Insider's View* 2008

90702   Diphtheria and tetanus toxoids (DT) adsorbed when administered to individuals younger than 7 years, for intramuscular use

➔ *CPT Assistant* Jan 96:6, Aug 96:10, Apr 97:10, Nov 98:31-33, Jan 99:2, Sep 99:10, Oct 99:9, Jun 00:10, Feb 07:11; *CPT Changes: An Insider's View* 2001, 2007, 2008

90703   Tetanus toxoid adsorbed, for intramuscular use

➔ *CPT Assistant* Jan 96:6, Apr 97:10, Nov 98:31-33, Jan 99:2, Sep 99:10, Oct 99:9; *CPT Changes: An Insider's View* 2004, 2008

90704   Mumps virus vaccine, live, for subcutaneous use

➔ *CPT Assistant* Apr 97:10, Nov 98:31-33, Jan 99:2, Oct 99:9; *CPT Changes: An Insider's View* 2004, 2008

90705   Measles virus vaccine, live, for subcutaneous use

➔ *CPT Assistant* Apr 97:10, Nov 98:31-33, Jan 99:2, Oct 99:9; *CPT Changes: An Insider's View* 2004, 2008

90706   Rubella virus vaccine, live, for subcutaneous use

➔ *CPT Assistant* Apr 97:10, Nov 98:31-33, Jan 99:2, Oct 99:9; *CPT Changes: An Insider's View* 2004, 2008

90707   Measles, mumps and rubella virus vaccine (MMR), live, for subcutaneous use

➔ *CPT Assistant* Jan 96:6, May 96:10, Apr 97:10, Nov 98:31-33, Jan 99:2, Oct 99:9, Apr 05:1, 5; *CPT Changes: An Insider's View* 2004, 2008

90708   Measles and rubella virus vaccine, live, for subcutaneous use

➔ *CPT Assistant* Apr 97:10, Nov 98:31-33, Jan 99:2, Oct 99:9; *CPT Changes: An Insider's View* 2004, 2008

90710   Measles, mumps, rubella, and varicella vaccine (MMRV), live, for subcutaneous use

➔ *CPT Assistant* May 96:10, Apr 97:10, Nov 98:31-33, Jan 99:2, Oct 99:9, Dec 05:9, Jun 06:8; *CPT Changes: An Insider's View* 2008

90712   Poliovirus vaccine, (any type[s]) (OPV), live, for oral use

➔ *CPT Assistant* Jan 96:6, Apr 97:10, Nov 98:31-33, Jan 99:2, Oct 99:9; *CPT Changes: An Insider's View* 2008

90713   Poliovirus vaccine, inactivated (IPV), for subcutaneous or intramuscular use

➔ *CPT Assistant* Apr 97:10, Nov 98:31-33, Jan 99:2, Oct 99:9, Jun 05:6; *CPT Changes: An Insider's View* 2006, 2008

90714   Tetanus and diphtheria toxoids (Td) adsorbed, preservative free, when administered to individuals 7 years or older, for intramuscular use

➔ *CPT Assistant* Jun 05:6; *CPT Changes: An Insider's View* 2006, 2007, 2008

90715   Tetanus, diphtheria toxoids and acellular pertussis vaccine (Tdap), when administered to individuals 7 years or older, for intramuscular use

➲ *CPT Assistant* Oct 99:9, Jun 05:6, Dec 05:9, Jun 06:8; *CPT Changes: An Insider's View* 2006, 2007, 2008

90716   Varicella virus vaccine, live, for subcutaneous use

➲ *CPT Assistant* Jan 96:6, May 96:10, Apr 97:10, Nov 98:31-33, Jan 99:2, Oct 99:9; *CPT Changes: An Insider's View* 2008

90717   Yellow fever vaccine, live, for subcutaneous use

➲ *CPT Assistant* Apr 97:10, Nov 98:31-33, Jan 99:2, Oct 99:9; *CPT Changes: An Insider's View* 2008

90718   Tetanus and diphtheria toxoids (Td) adsorbed when administered to individuals 7 years or older, for intramuscular use

➲ *CPT Assistant* Aug 96:10, Apr 97:10, Nov 98:31-33, Jan 99:2, Oct 99:9, Jun 00:10, Feb 07:11; *CPT Changes: An Insider's View* 2001, 2004, 2007, 2008

90719   Diphtheria toxoid, for intramuscular use

➲ *CPT Assistant* Apr 97:10, Nov 98:31-33, Jan 99:2, Sep 99:10, Oct 99:9; *CPT Changes: An Insider's View* 2008

90720   Diphtheria, tetanus toxoids, and whole cell pertussis vaccine and Hemophilus influenza B vaccine (DTP-Hib), for intramuscular use

➲ *CPT Assistant* Jan 96:5, Apr 97:10, Nov 98:31-33, Jan 99:2, Oct 99:9; *CPT Changes: An Insider's View* 2008

90721   Diphtheria, tetanus toxoids, and acellular pertussis vaccine and Hemophilus influenza B vaccine (DtaP-Hib), for intramuscular use

➲ *CPT Assistant* Jan 96:5, Apr 97:10, Nov 98:31-33, Jan 99:2, Oct 99:9; *CPT Changes: An Insider's View* 2000, 2008

90723   Diphtheria, tetanus toxoids, acellular pertussis vaccine, Hepatitis B, and poliovirus vaccine, inactivated (DtaP-HepB-IPV), for intramuscular use

➲ *CPT Assistant* Apr 97:10, Oct 99:9; *CPT Changes: An Insider's View* 2001, 2008

90725   Cholera vaccine for injectable use

➲ *CPT Assistant* Apr 97:10, Nov 98:31-33, Jan 99:2, Oct 99:9; *CPT Changes: An Insider's View* 2008

90727   Plague vaccine, for intramuscular use

➲ *CPT Assistant* Apr 97:10, Nov 98:31-33, Jan 99:2, Oct 99:9; *CPT Changes: An Insider's View* 2004, 2008

90732   Pneumococcal polysaccharide vaccine, 23-valent, adult or immunosuppressed patient dosage, when administered to individuals 2 years or older, for subcutaneous or intramuscular use

➲ *CPT Assistant* Apr 97:10, Nov 98:31-33, Jan 99:2, Oct 99:9; *CPT Changes: An Insider's View* 2002, 2007, 2008

90733   Meningococcal polysaccharide vaccine (any group(s)), for subcutaneous use

➲ *CPT Assistant* Apr 97:10, Nov 98:31-33, Jan 99:2, Oct 99:9, Dec 99:7; *CPT Changes: An Insider's View* 2001, 2004, 2008

90734   Meningococcal conjugate vaccine, serogroups A, C, Y and W-135 (tetravalent), for intramuscular use

➲ *CPT Assistant* Oct 99:9; *CPT Changes: An Insider's View* 2008

90735   Japanese encephalitis virus vaccine, for subcutaneous use

➲ *CPT Assistant* Apr 97:10, Nov 98:31-33, Jan 99:2, Oct 99:9; *CPT Changes: An Insider's View* 2008

90736   Zoster (shingles) vaccine, live, for subcutaneous injection

➲ *CPT Assistant* Dec 05:9, Jun 06:8, Jul 07:13; *CPT Changes: An Insider's View* 2006, 2008

▲ **90738**   Japanese encephalitis virus vaccine, inactivated, for intramuscular use

➲ *CPT Changes: An Insider's View* 2009, 2010

90740   Hepatitis B vaccine, dialysis or immunosuppressed patient dosage (3 dose schedule), for intramuscular use

➲ *CPT Assistant* Apr 97:10, Oct 99:9, Apr 01:10; *CPT Changes: An Insider's View* 2001, 2008

90743   Hepatitis B vaccine, adolescent (2 dose schedule), for intramuscular use

➲ *CPT Assistant* Apr 97:10, Oct 99:9; *CPT Changes: An Insider's View* 2001, 2008

90744   Hepatitis B vaccine, pediatric/adolescent dosage (3 dose schedule), for intramuscular use

➲ *CPT Assistant* Jan 96:5, Apr 97:10, Jun 97:10, Nov 98:31-33, Jan 99:2, Oct 99:9, Nov 99:48-49, Jun 00:10; *CPT Changes: An Insider's View* 2000, 2001, 2008

90746   Hepatitis B vaccine, adult dosage, for intramuscular use

➲ *CPT Assistant* Jan 96:5, Apr 97:10, Nov 98:31-33, Jan 99:2, Oct 99:9; *CPT Changes: An Insider's View* 2008

90747   Hepatitis B vaccine, dialysis or immunosuppressed patient dosage (4 dose schedule), for intramuscular use

➲ *CPT Assistant* Jan 96:5, Apr 97:10, Jun 97:10, Nov 98:31-33, Jan 99:2, Oct 99:9, Jun 00:10, Apr 01:10; *CPT Changes: An Insider's View* 2001, 2008

90748   Hepatitis B and Hemophilus influenza b vaccine (HepB-Hib), for intramuscular use

➲ *CPT Assistant* Apr 97:10, Nov 97:37, Nov 98:31-33, Jan 99:2, Sep 99:10, Oct 99:9; *CPT Changes: An Insider's View* 2008

90749   Unlisted vaccine/toxoid

➲ *CPT Assistant* Jan 96:6, Apr 97:10, Jun 97:10, Nov 98:31-33, Jan 99:2, Oct 99:9, Nov 02:11; *CPT Changes: An Insider's View* 2008

(90760 has been deleted. To report, use 96360)

(90761 has been deleted. To report, use 96361)

(90765 has been deleted. To report, use 96365)

(90766 has been deleted. To report, use 96366)

(90767 has been deleted. To report, use 96367)

(90768 has been deleted. To report, use 96368)

(90769 has been deleted. To report, use 96369)

(90770 has been deleted. To report, use 96370)

(90771 has been deleted. To report, use 96371)

(90772 has been deleted. To report, use 96372)

(90773 has been deleted. To report, use 96373)

(90774 has been deleted. To report, use 96374)

(90775 has been deleted. To report, use 96375)

(90776 has been deleted. To report, use 96376)

(90779 has been deleted. To report, use 96379)

Psychiatry

Hospital care by the attending physician in treating a psychiatric inpatient or partial hospitalization may be initial or subsequent in nature (see 99221-99233) and may include exchanges with nursing and ancillary personnel. Hospital care services involve a variety of responsibilities unique to the medical management of inpatients, such as physician hospital orders, interpretation of laboratory or other medical diagnostic studies and observations.

Some patients receive hospital evaluation and management services only and others receive evaluation and management services and other procedures. If other procedures such as electroconvulsive therapy or psychotherapy are rendered in addition to hospital evaluation and management services, these should be listed separately (ie, hospital care service plus electroconvulsive therapy or when psychotherapy is done, an appropriate code defining psychotherapy with medical evaluation and management services). Modifier 22 may be used to indicate a more extensive service. Modifier 52 may be used to signify a service that is reduced or less extensive than the usual procedure.

Other evaluation and management services, such as office medical service or other patient encounters, may be described as listed in the section on **Evaluation and Management,** if appropriate.

The evaluation and management services should not be reported separately, when reporting codes 90805, 90807, 90809, 90811, 90813, 90815, 90817, 90819, 90822, 90824, 90827, 90829.

Consultation for psychiatric evaluation of a patient includes examination of a patient and exchange of information with the primary physician and other informants such as nurses or family members, and preparation of a report. These consultation services (99241-99255) are limited to initial or follow-up evaluation and do not involve psychiatric treatment.

➲ *CPT Assistant* Nov 97:37

Psychiatric Diagnostic or Evaluative Interview Procedures

Psychiatric diagnostic interview examination includes a history, mental status, and a disposition, and may include communication with family or other sources, ordering and medical interpretation of laboratory or other medical diagnostic studies. In certain circumstances other informants will be seen in lieu of the patient.

Interactive psychiatric diagnostic interview examination is typically furnished to children. It involves the use of physical aids and non-verbal communication to overcome barriers to therapeutic interaction between the clinician and a patient who has not yet developed, or has lost, either the expressive language communication skills to explain his/her symptoms and response to treatment, or the receptive communication skills to understand the clinician if he/she were to use ordinary adult language for communication.

➲ *CPT Assistant* Nov 97:37-38

90801   Psychiatric diagnostic interview examination
➲ *CPT Assistant* Summer 92:12, Nov 97:39-40, Mar 01:5, Mar 02:4, May 05:1

90802   Interactive psychiatric diagnostic interview examination using play equipment, physical devices, language interpreter, or other mechanisms of communication
➲ *CPT Assistant* Nov 97:39-40, Mar 01:5, Mar 02:4, May 05:1

Psychiatric Therapeutic Procedures

Psychotherapy is the treatment for mental illness and behavioral disturbances in which the clinician establishes a professional contract with the patient and, through definitive therapeutic communication, attempts to alleviate the emotional disturbances, reverse or change maladaptive patterns of behavior, and encourage personality growth and development. The codes for reporting psychotherapy are divided into two broad categories: Interactive Psychotherapy; and Insight Oriented, Behavior Modifying and/or Supportive Psychotherapy.

Interactive psychotherapy is typically furnished to children. It involves the use of physical aids and non-verbal communication to overcome barriers to therapeutic interaction between the clinician and a patient who has not yet developed, or has lost, either the expressive language communication skills to explain his/her symptoms and response to treatment, or the receptive communication skills to understand the clinician if he/she were to use ordinary adult language for communication.

Insight oriented, behavior modifying and/or supportive psychotherapy refers to the development of insight or affective understanding, the use of behavior modification techniques, the use of supportive interactions, the use of cognitive discussion of reality, or any combination of the above to provide therapeutic change.

Some patients receive psychotherapy only and others receive psychotherapy and medical evaluation and management services. These evaluation and management services involve a variety of responsibilities unique to the medical management of psychiatric patients, such as medical diagnostic evaluation (eg, evaluation of comorbid medical conditions, drug interactions, and physical examinations), drug management when indicated, physician orders, interpretation of laboratory or other medical diagnostic studies and observations.

In reporting psychotherapy, the appropriate code is chosen on the basis of the type of psychotherapy (interactive using non-verbal techniques versus insight oriented, behavior modifying and/or supportive using verbal techniques), the place of service (office versus inpatient), the face-to-face time spent with the patient during psychotherapy, and whether evaluation and management services are furnished on the same date of service as psychotherapy.

To report medical evaluation and management services furnished on a day when psychotherapy is not provided, select the appropriate code from the **Evaluation and Management Services Guidelines.**

➔ *CPT Assistant* Nov 97:38

Office or Other Outpatient Facility

Insight Oriented, Behavior Modifying and/or Supportive Psychotherapy

90804   Individual psychotherapy, insight oriented, behavior modifying and/or supportive, in an office or outpatient facility, approximately 20 to 30 minutes face-to-face with the patient;
➔ *CPT Assistant* Nov 97:39, Jul 99:10, Mar 01:5, Mar 02:4, Oct 02:11, May 05:1

90805   with medical evaluation and management services
➔ *CPT Assistant* Nov 97:39, Jul 99:10, Mar 01:5, Mar 02:4, May 05:1

90806   Individual psychotherapy, insight oriented, behavior modifying and/or supportive, in an office or outpatient facility, approximately 45 to 50 minutes face-to-face with the patient;
➔ *CPT Assistant* Nov 97:39, Jul 99:10, Mar 01:6, Mar 02:4, Sep 03:3, Sep 04:13, Mar 05:16, May 05:1

90807   with medical evaluation and management services
➔ *CPT Assistant* Nov 97:39, Jul 99:10, Mar 01:6, May 05:1

90808   Individual psychotherapy, insight oriented, behavior modifying and/or supportive, in an office or outpatient facility, approximately 75 to 80 minutes face-to-face with the patient;
➔ *CPT Assistant* Nov 97:39, Jul 99:10, Mar 01:5, Mar 02:4, May 05:1

90809   with medical evaluation and management services
➔ *CPT Assistant* Nov 97:39, Jul 99:10, Mar 01:5, May 05:1

Interactive Psychotherapy

90810   Individual psychotherapy, interactive, using play equipment, physical devices, language interpreter, or other mechanisms of non-verbal communication, in an office or outpatient facility, approximately 20 to 30 minutes face-to-face with the patient;
➔ *CPT Assistant* Nov 97:39, Mar 01:5, Mar 02:4, May 05:1

90811   with medical evaluation and management services
➔ *CPT Assistant* Nov 97:39, Mar 01:5, May 05:1

90812   Individual psychotherapy, interactive, using play equipment, physical devices, language interpreter, or other mechanisms of non-verbal communication, in an office or outpatient facility, approximately 45 to 50 minutes face-to-face with the patient;
➔ *CPT Assistant* Nov 97:39, Mar 01:5, Mar 02:4, May 05:1

90813   with medical evaluation and management services
➔ *CPT Assistant* Nov 97:39, Mar 01:5, Mar 02:4, May 05:1

90814   Individual psychotherapy, interactive, using play equipment, physical devices, language interpreter, or other mechanisms of non-verbal communication, in an office or outpatient facility, approximately 75 to 80 minutes face-to-face with the patient;
➔ *CPT Assistant* Nov 97:39, Mar 01:5, Mar 02:4, May 05:1

90815   with medical evaluation and management services
➔ *CPT Assistant* Nov 97:39, Mar 01:5, Mar 02:4, May 05:1

Inpatient Hospital, Partial Hospital or Residential Care Facility

Insight Oriented, Behavior Modifying and/or Supportive Psychotherapy

90816   Individual psychotherapy, insight oriented, behavior modifying and/or supportive, in an inpatient hospital, partial hospital or residential care setting, approximately 20 to 30 minutes face-to-face with the patient;
➔ *CPT Assistant* Nov 97:39-40, Mar 01:6-7, Mar 02:4, May 05:1

90817   with medical evaluation and management services
➔ *CPT Assistant* Nov 97:39-40, Mar 01:6-7, Mar 02:4, May 05:1

90818   Individual psychotherapy, insight oriented, behavior modifying and/or supportive, in an inpatient hospital, partial hospital or residential care setting, approximately 45 to 50 minutes face-to-face with the patient;
➔ *CPT Assistant* Nov 97:39-40, Mar 01:6-7, Mar 02:4, May 05:1

90819   with medical evaluation and management services
➔ *CPT Assistant* Summer 92:24, Nov 97:39-40, Mar 01:6-7, Mar 02:4, May 05:1

90821   Individual psychotherapy, insight oriented, behavior modifying and/or supportive, in an inpatient hospital, partial hospital or residential care setting, approximately 75 to 80 minutes face-to-face with the patient;
➔ *CPT Assistant* Nov 97:39-40, Mar 01:6-7, Mar 02:4, May 05:1

90822   with medical evaluation and management services
➔ *CPT Assistant* Nov 97:39-40, Mar 01:6-7, Mar 02:4, May 05:1

Interactive Psychotherapy

90823   Individual psychotherapy, interactive, using play equipment, physical devices, language interpreter, or other mechanisms of non-verbal communication, in an inpatient hospital, partial hospital or residential care setting, approximately 20 to 30 minutes face-to-face with the patient;
➜ *CPT Assistant* Nov 97:40, Mar 01:6-7, Mar 02:4, May 05:1

90824   with medical evaluation and management services
➜ *CPT Assistant* Nov 97:40, Mar 01:6-7, Mar 02:4, May 05:1

90826   Individual psychotherapy, interactive, using play equipment, physical devices, language interpreter, or other mechanisms of non-verbal communication, in an inpatient hospital, partial hospital or residential care setting, approximately 45 to 50 minutes face-to-face with the patient;
➜ *CPT Assistant* Nov 97:40, Mar 01:6-7, Mar 02:4, May 05:1

90827   with medical evaluation and management services
➜ *CPT Assistant* Nov 97:40, Mar 01:6-7, Mar 02:4, May 05:1

90828   Individual psychotherapy, interactive, using play equipment, physical devices, language interpreter, or other mechanisms of non-verbal communication, in an inpatient hospital, partial hospital or residential care setting, approximately 75 to 80 minutes face-to-face with the patient;
➜ *CPT Assistant* Nov 97:40, Mar 01:6-7, Mar 02:4, May 05:1

90829   with medical evaluation and management services
➜ *CPT Assistant* Summer 92:13, Nov 97:40, Mar 01:6-7, Mar 02:4, May 05:1

Other Psychotherapy

90845   Psychoanalysis
➜ *CPT Assistant* Summer 92:15, Nov 97:40-41, Mar 01:8, Mar 02:4, May 05:1, Feb 06:15

90846   Family psychotherapy (without the patient present)
➜ *CPT Assistant* Summer 92:15, Nov 97:40-41, Mar 01:8, Mar 02:4, May 05:1

90847   Family psychotherapy (conjoint psychotherapy) (with patient present)
➜ *CPT Assistant* Summer 92:15, Nov 97:40-41, Mar 01:5, Mar 02:4, May 05:1

90849   Multiple-family group psychotherapy
➜ *CPT Assistant* Summer 92:15, Nov 97:40-41, Mar 01:5, Mar 02:4, May 05:1

90853   Group psychotherapy (other than of a multiple-family group)
➜ *CPT Assistant* Summer 92:15, Nov 97:40-41, Mar 01:8, Mar 02:4, May 05:1

90857   Interactive group psychotherapy
➜ *CPT Assistant* Summer 92:15, Nov 97:40-41, Mar 01:8, Mar 02:4, May 05:1

Other Psychiatric Services or Procedures

(For repetitive transcranial magnetic stimulation for treatment of clinical depression, see Category III codes 0160T, 0161T)

(For analysis/programming of neurostimulators used for vagus nerve stimulation therapy, see 95970, 95974, 95975)

90862   Pharmacologic management, including prescription, use, and review of medication with no more than minimal medical psychotherapy
➜ *CPT Assistant* Summer 92:16, Nov 97:40-41, Mar 01:5, Mar 02:4, May 05:1, Dec 06:10

90865   Narcosynthesis for psychiatric diagnostic and therapeutic purposes (eg, sodium amobarbital (Amytal) interview)
➜ *CPT Assistant* Nov 97:41, Mar 01:5, Mar 02:4, May 05:1

90870   Electroconvulsive therapy (includes necessary monitoring)
➜ *CPT Assistant* Summer 92:16, Mar 01:5, Mar 02:4, May 05:1; *CPT Changes: An Insider's View* 2006

90875   Individual psychophysiological therapy incorporating biofeedback training by any modality (face-to-face with the patient), with psychotherapy (eg, insight oriented, behavior modifying or supportive psychotherapy); approximately 20-30 minutes
➜ *CPT Assistant* Nov 96:15, Sep 97:11, Nov 97:41, Apr 98:14, Jun 99:5, Mar 01:5, Mar 02:4, Mar 05:16, May 05:1

90876   approximately 45-50 minutes
➜ *CPT Assistant* Nov 96:15, Sep 97:11, Nov 97:41, Jun 99:5, Mar 01:5, Mar 05:16, May 05:1

90880   Hypnotherapy
➜ *CPT Assistant* Summer 92:16, Nov 97:41, Mar 01:5, Mar 02:4, May 05:1

90882   Environmental intervention for medical management purposes on a psychiatric patient's behalf with agencies, employers, or institutions
➜ *CPT Assistant* Summer 92:16, Mar 01:5, Mar 02:4, May 05:1

90885   Psychiatric evaluation of hospital records, other psychiatric reports, psychometric and/or projective tests, and other accumulated data for medical diagnostic purposes
➜ *CPT Assistant* Nov 97:41, Mar 01:5, Mar 02:4, Oct 04:10, May 05:1

90887   Interpretation or explanation of results of psychiatric, other medical examinations and procedures, or other accumulated data to family or other responsible persons, or advising them how to assist patient
➜ *CPT Assistant* Summer 92:17, Mar 01:5, Mar 02:4, Oct 02:11, May 05:1

90889   Preparation of report of patient's psychiatric status, history, treatment, or progress (other than for legal or consultative purposes) for other physicians, agencies, or insurance carriers
➜ *CPT Assistant* Summer 92:17, Mar 01:5, Mar 02:4, May 05:1

90899   Unlisted psychiatric service or procedure
➜ *CPT Assistant* Mar 01:5, Mar 02:4, May 05:1

Biofeedback

(For psychophysiological therapy incorporating biofeedback training, see 90875, 90876)

90901 Biofeedback training by any modality
➜ *CPT Assistant* Sep 97:11, Apr 98:14, Jun 98:10, Jun 99:5, May 02:18, Sep 04:13, Mar 05:16

90911 Biofeedback training, perineal muscles, anorectal or urethral sphincter, including EMG and/or manometry
➜ *CPT Assistant* Sep 97:11, Nov 97:41, Jun 98:10, Jun 99:5

(For testing of rectal sensation, tone and compliance, use 91120)

(For incontinence treatment by pulsed magnetic neuromodulation, use 53899)

Dialysis

(90918, 90922 have been deleted. To report ESRD-related services for patients younger than 2 years of age, see 90951-90953, 90963, 90967)

(90919, 90923 have been deleted. To report ESRD-related services for patients between 2 and 11 years of age, see 90954-90956, 90964, 90968)

(90920, 90924 have been deleted. To report ESRD-related services for patients between 12 and 19 years of age, see 90957-90959, 90965, 90969)

(90921, 90925 have been deleted. To report ESRD-related services for patients 20 years of age and older, see 90960-90962, 90966, 90970)

Hemodialysis

Codes 90935, 90937 are reported to describe the hemodialysis procedure with all evaluation and management services related to the patient's renal disease on the day of the hemodialysis procedure. These codes are used for inpatient ESRD and non-ESRD procedures or for outpatient non-ESRD dialysis services. Code 90935 is reported if only one evaluation of the patient is required related to that hemodialysis procedure. Code 90937 is reported when patient re-evaluation(s) is required during a hemodialysis procedure. Use modifier 25 with Evaluation and Management codes for separately identifiable services unrelated to the dialysis procedure or renal failure which cannot be rendered during the dialysis session.

(For home visit hemodialysis services performed by a non-physician health care professional, use 99512)

(For cannula declotting, see 36831, 36833, 36860, 36861)

(For declotting of implanted vascular access device or catheter by thrombolytic agent, use 36593)
➜ *CPT Assistant* Nov 99:49

(For collection of blood specimen from a partially or completely implantable venous access device, use 36591)

(For prolonged physician attendance, see 99354-99360)

90935 Hemodialysis procedure with single physician evaluation
➜ *CPT Assistant* Fall 93:2, May 02:17, Jan 03:22

90937 Hemodialysis procedure requiring repeated evaluation(s) with or without substantial revision of dialysis prescription
➜ *CPT Assistant* Fall 93:2, May 02:17, Jan 03:22

90940 Hemodialysis access flow study to determine blood flow in grafts and arteriovenous fistulae by an indicator method
➜ *CPT Assistant* Jan 03:22, May 06:18; *CPT Changes: An Insider's View* 2001, 2006
➜ *Clinical Examples in Radiology* Summer 06:7, 12

(For duplex scan of hemodialysis access, use 93990)

Miscellaneous Dialysis Procedures

Codes 90945, 90947 describe dialysis procedures other than hemodialysis (eg, peritoneal dialysis, hemofiltration or continuous renal replacement therapies), and all evaluation and management services related to the patient's renal disease on the day of the procedure. Code 90945 is reported if only one evaluation of the patient is required related to that procedure. Code 90947 is reported when patient re-evaluation(s) is required during a procedure. Utilize modifier 25 with Evaluation and Management codes for separately identifiable services unrelated to the procedure or the renal failure which cannot be rendered during the dialysis session.

(For insertion of intraperitoneal cannula or catheter, see 49420, 49421)

(For prolonged physician attendance, see 99354-99360)

90945 Dialysis procedure other than hemodialysis (eg, peritoneal dialysis, hemofiltration, or other continuous renal replacement therapies), with single physician evaluation
➜ *CPT Assistant* Fall 93:2, Nov 97:41, Jul 98:10, Oct 01:11, Jan 03:22; *CPT Changes: An Insider's View* 2001

(For home infusion of peritoneal dialysis, use 99601, 99602)

90947 Dialysis procedure other than hemodialysis (eg, peritoneal dialysis, hemofiltration, or other continuous renal replacement therapies) requiring repeated physician evaluations, with or without substantial revision of dialysis prescription
➜ *CPT Assistant* Fall 93:2, Nov 97:41, Jul 98:10, Oct 01:11, Jan 03:22; *CPT Changes: An Insider's View* 2001

End-Stage Renal Disease Services

Codes 90951-90962 are reported **once** per month to distinguish age-specific services related to the patient's end-stage renal disease (ESRD) performed in an outpatient setting with three levels of service based on the number of face-to-face visits. ESRD-related physician services include establishment of a dialyzing cycle, outpatient evaluation and management of the dialysis visits, telephone calls, and patient management during the dialysis provided during a full month. In the circumstances where the patient has had a complete assessment visit during the month and services are provided over a period of less than a month, 90951-90962 may be used according to the number of visits performed.

Codes 90963-90966 are reported once per month for a full month of service to distinguish age-specific services for end-stage renal disease (ESRD) services for home dialysis patients.

For ESRD and non-ESRD dialysis services performed in an inpatient setting, and for non-ESRD dialysis services performed in an outpatient setting, see 90935-90937 and 90945-90947.

Evaluation and Management services unrelated to ESRD services that cannot be performed during the dialysis session may be reported separately.

Codes 90967-90970 are reported to distinguish age-specific services for end-stage renal disease (ESRD) services for less than a full month of service, per day, for services provided under the following circumstances: home dialysis patients less than a full month, transient patients, partial month where there was one or more face-to-face visits without the complete assessment, the patient was hospitalized before a complete assessment was furnished, dialysis was stopped due to recovery or death, or the patient received a kidney transplant. For reporting purposes, each month is considered 30 days.

Examples:

ESRD-related services:

ESRD-related services are initiated on July 1 for a 57-year-old male. On July 11, he is admitted to the hospital as an inpatient and is discharged on July 27. He has had a complete assessment and the physician has performed two face-to-face visits prior to admission. Another face-to-face visit occurs after discharge during the month.

In this example, 90961 is reported for the three face-to-face outpatient visits. Report inpatient E/M services as appropriate. Dialysis procedures rendered during the hospitalization (July 11-27) should be reported as appropriate (90935-90937, 90945-90947).

If the patient did not have a complete assessment during the month or was a transient or dialysis was stopped due to recovery or death, 90970 would be used to report each day outside the inpatient hospitalization as described in the home dialysis example below.

ESRD-related services for the home dialysis patient:

Home ESRD-related services are initiated on July 1 for a 57-year-old male. On July 11, he is admitted to the hospital as an inpatient and is discharged on July 27.

In this example, 90970 should be reported for each day outside of the inpatient hospitalization (30 days/month less 17 days/hospitalization = 13 days). Report inpatient E/M services as appropriate. Dialysis procedures rendered during the hospitalization (July 11-27) should be reported as appropriate (90935-90937, 90945-90947).

90951 End-stage renal disease (ESRD) related services monthly, for patients younger than 2 years of age to include monitoring for the adequacy of nutrition, assessment of growth and development, and counseling of parents; with 4 or more face-to-face physician visits per month
➔ *CPT Changes: An Insider's View* 2009

90952 with 2-3 face-to-face physician visits per month
➔ *CPT Changes: An Insider's View* 2009

90953 with 1 face-to-face physician visit per month
➔ *CPT Changes: An Insider's View* 2009

90954 End-stage renal disease (ESRD) related services monthly, for patients 2-11 years of age to include monitoring for the adequacy of nutrition, assessment of growth and development, and counseling of parents; with 4 or more face-to-face physician visits per month
➔ *CPT Changes: An Insider's View* 2009

90955 with 2-3 face-to-face physician visits per month
➔ *CPT Changes: An Insider's View* 2009

90956 with 1 face-to-face physician visit per month
➔ *CPT Changes: An Insider's View* 2009

90957 End-stage renal disease (ESRD) related services monthly, for patients 12-19 years of age to include monitoring for the adequacy of nutrition, assessment of growth and development, and counseling of parents; with 4 or more face-to-face physician visits per month
➔ *CPT Changes: An Insider's View* 2009

90958 with 2-3 face-to-face physician visits per month
➔ *CPT Changes: An Insider's View* 2009

90959 with 1 face-to-face physician visit per month
➔ *CPT Changes: An Insider's View* 2009

90960 End-stage renal disease (ESRD) related services monthly, for patients 20 years of age and older; with 4 or more face-to-face physician visits per month
➔ *CPT Changes: An Insider's View* 2009

90961 with 2-3 face-to-face physician visits per month
➔ *CPT Changes: An Insider's View* 2009

90962   with 1 face-to-face physician visit per month
➔ *CPT Changes: An Insider's View* 2009

90963   End-stage renal disease (ESRD) related services for home dialysis per full month, for patients younger than 2 years of age to include monitoring for the adequacy of nutrition, assessment of growth and development, and counseling of parents
➔ *CPT Changes: An Insider's View* 2009

90964   End-stage renal disease (ESRD) related services for home dialysis per full month, for patients 2-11 years of age to include monitoring for the adequacy of nutrition, assessment of growth and development, and counseling of parents
➔ *CPT Changes: An Insider's View* 2009

90965   End-stage renal disease (ESRD) related services for home dialysis per full month, for patients 12-19 years of age to include monitoring for the adequacy of nutrition, assessment of growth and development, and counseling of parents
➔ *CPT Changes: An Insider's View* 2009

90966   End-stage renal disease (ESRD) related services for home dialysis per full month, for patients 20 years of age and older
➔ *CPT Changes: An Insider's View* 2009

90967   End-stage renal disease (ESRD) related services for dialysis less than a full month of service, per day; for patients younger than 2 years of age
➔ *CPT Changes: An Insider's View* 2009

90968   for patients 2-11 years of age
➔ *CPT Changes: An Insider's View* 2009

90969   for patients 12-19 years of age
➔ *CPT Changes: An Insider's View* 2009

90970   for patients 20 years of age and older
➔ *CPT Changes: An Insider's View* 2009

Other Dialysis Procedures

90989   Dialysis training, patient, including helper where applicable, any mode, completed course
➔ *CPT Assistant* Fall 93:5, Jun 01:10

90993   Dialysis training, patient, including helper where applicable, any mode, course not completed, per training session
➔ *CPT Assistant* Winter 90:11, Fall 93:5, Jun 01:10

90997   Hemoperfusion (eg, with activated charcoal or resin)

90999   Unlisted dialysis procedure, inpatient or outpatient

Gastroenterology

(For duodenal intubation and aspiration, see 89100-89105)

(For gastrointestinal radiologic procedures, see 74210-74363)

(For esophagoscopy procedures, see 43200-43228; upper GI endoscopy 43234-43259; endoscopy, small intestine and stomal 44360-44393; proctosigmoidoscopy 45300-45321; sigmoidoscopy 45330-45339; colonoscopy 45355-45385; anoscopy 46600-46615)

91000   Esophageal intubation and collection of washings for cytology, including preparation of specimens (separate procedure)

91010   Esophageal motility (manometric study of the esophagus and/or gastroesophageal junction) study;
➔ *CPT Assistant* Nov 97:42

91011   with mecholyl or similar stimulant

91012   with acid perfusion studies

91020   Gastric motility (manometric) studies
➔ *CPT Assistant* Nov 97:42

91022   Duodenal motility (manometric) study
➔ *CPT Changes: An Insider's View* 2006

(If gastrointestinal endoscopy is performed, use 43235)

(If fluoroscopy is performed, use 76000)

(If gastric motility study is performed, use 91020)

91030   Esophagus, acid perfusion (Bernstein) test for esophagitis

91034   Esophagus, gastroesophageal reflux test; with nasal catheter pH electrode(s) placement, recording, analysis and interpretation
➔ *CPT Assistant* May 05:3; *CPT Changes: An Insider's View* 2005

Esophageal Acid Reflux Test
91034

A catheter with a pH electrode is placed into the esophagus, either through the nares or swallowed, to measure intraesophageal pH (an indicator of gastric reflux).

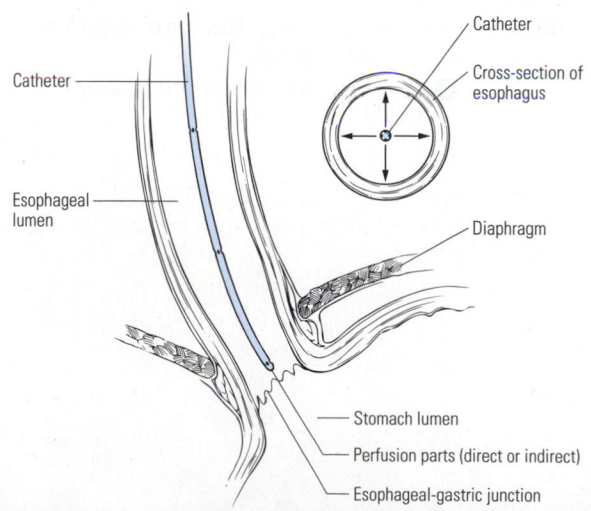

91035 with mucosal attached telemetry pH electrode placement, recording, analysis and interpretation
➔ *CPT Assistant* May 05:3; *CPT Changes: An Insider's View* 2005

91037 Esophageal function test, gastroesophageal reflux test with nasal catheter intraluminal impedance electrode(s) placement, recording, analysis and interpretation;
➔ *CPT Assistant* May 05:3; *CPT Changes: An Insider's View* 2005

91038 prolonged (greater than 1 hour, up to 24 hours)
➔ *CPT Assistant* May 05:3; *CPT Changes: An Insider's View* 2005

91040 Esophageal balloon distension provocation study
➔ *CPT Assistant* May 05:3; *CPT Changes: An Insider's View* 2005

(For balloon dilatation with endoscopy, see 43220, 43249, 43456, or 43458)

91052 Gastric analysis test with injection of stimulant of gastric secretion (eg, histamine, insulin, pentagastrin, calcium and secretin)

(For gastric biopsy by capsule, peroral, via tube, 1 or more specimens, use 43600)

(For gastric laboratory procedures, see also 89130-89141)

91055 Gastric intubation, washings, and preparing slides for cytology (separate procedure)

(For gastric lavage, therapeutic, use 91105)

(For biopsy by capsule, small intestine, per oral, via tube [1 or more specimens], use 44100)

91065 Breath hydrogen test (eg, for detection of lactase deficiency, fructose intolerance, bacterial overgrowth, or oro-cecal gastrointestinal transit)
➔ *CPT Assistant* May 05:3; *CPT Changes: An Insider's View* 2005

(For H. pylori breath test analysis, use 83013 for non-radioactive (C-13) isotope or 78268 for radioactive (C-14) isotope)

(91100 has been deleted)

(To report placement of an esophageal tamponade tube for management of variceal bleeding, use 43460. To report placement of a long intestinal Miller-Abbott tube, use 44500)

91105 Gastric intubation, and aspiration or lavage for treatment (eg, for ingested poisons)
➔ *CPT Assistant* Winter 91:7, Spring 93:34, Sep 96:10, Nov 99:49, Aug 00:2, Feb 07:10, Jul 07:1

Gastric Intubation
91105

A large-bore gastric lavage tube is inserted orally through the esophagus into the stomach for expedient lavage and evacuation of stomach contents (eg, poisonings, hemorrhage).

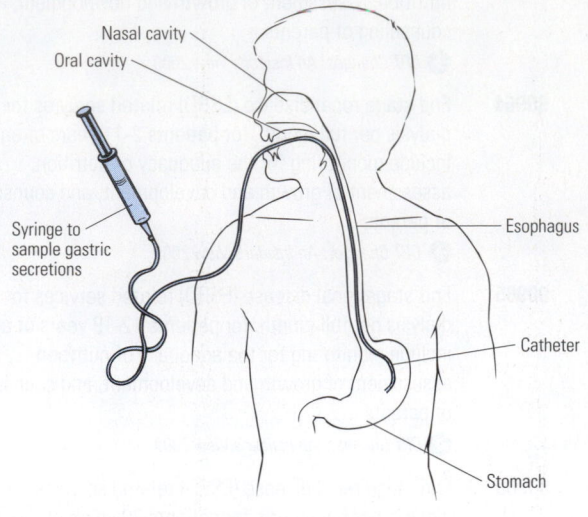

Nasal cavity
Oral cavity
Syringe to sample gastric secretions
Esophagus
Catheter
Stomach

(For cholangiography, see 47500, 74320)

(For abdominal paracentesis, see 49080, 49081; with instillation of medication, see 96440, 96445)

(For peritoneoscopy, use 49320; with biopsy, use 49321)

(For peritoneoscopy and guided transhepatic cholangiography, use 47560; with biopsy, use 47561)

(For splenoportography, see 38200, 75810)

91110 Gastrointestinal tract imaging, intraluminal (eg, capsule endoscopy), esophagus through ileum, with physician interpretation and report
➔ *CPT Assistant* Oct 04:15, Aug 05:14; *CPT Changes: An Insider's View* 2004

(Visualization of the colon is not reported separately)

(Append modifier 52 if the ileum is not visualized)

91111 Gastrointestinal tract imaging, intraluminal (eg, capsule endoscopy), esophagus with physician interpretation and report
➔ *CPT Changes: An Insider's View* 2007

(Do not report 91111 in conjunction with 91110)

91120 Rectal sensation, tone, and compliance test (ie, response to graded balloon distention)
➔ *CPT Assistant* May 05:3; *CPT Changes: An Insider's View* 2005

(For biofeedback training, use 90911)

(For anorectal manometry, use 91122)

91122 Anorectal manometry

91123 Pulsed irrigation of fecal impaction
➔ *CPT Changes: An Insider's View* 2002

Gastric Physiology

91132   Electrogastrography, diagnostic, transcutaneous;
    ➔ *CPT Changes: An Insider's View* 2001

91133   with provocative testing
    ➔ *CPT Changes: An Insider's View* 2001

Other Procedures

91299   Unlisted diagnostic gastroenterology procedure
    ➔ *CPT Assistant* Aug 05:14

Ophthalmology

(For surgical procedures, see **Surgery,** Eye and Ocular Adnexa, 65091 et seq)

Definitions

Intermediate ophthalmological services describes an evaluation of a new or existing condition complicated with a new diagnostic or management problem not necessarily relating to the primary diagnosis, including history, general medical observation, external ocular and adnexal examination and other diagnostic procedures as indicated; may include the use of mydriasis for ophthalmoscopy.

For example:

a. Review of history, external examination, ophthalmoscopy, biomicroscopy for an acute complicated condition (eg, iritis) not requiring comprehensive ophthalmological services.

b. Review of interval history, external examination, ophthalmoscopy, biomicroscopy and tonometry in established patient with known cataract not requiring comprehensive ophthalmological services.

Comprehensive ophthalmological services describes a general evaluation of the complete visual system. The comprehensive services constitute a single service entity but need not be performed at one session. The service includes history, general medical observation, external and ophthalmoscopic examinations, gross visual fields and basic sensorimotor examination. It often includes, as indicated: biomicroscopy, examination with cycloplegia or mydriasis and tonometry. It always includes initiation of diagnostic and treatment programs.

Intermediate and comprehensive ophthalmological services constitute integrated services in which medical decision making cannot be separated from the examining techniques used. Itemization of service components, such as slit lamp examination, keratometry, routine ophthalmoscopy, retinoscopy, tonometry, or motor evaluation is not applicable.

For example:

The comprehensive services required for diagnosis and treatment of a patient with symptoms indicating possible disease of the visual system, such as glaucoma, cataract or retinal disease, or to rule out disease of the visual system, new or established patient.

Initiation of diagnostic and treatment program includes the prescription of medication, and arranging for special ophthalmological diagnostic or treatment services, consultations, laboratory procedures and radiological services.

Special ophthalmological services describes services in which a special evaluation of part of the visual system is made, which goes beyond the services included under general ophthalmological services, or in which special treatment is given. Special ophthalmological services may be reported in addition to the general ophthalmological services or evaluation and management services.

For example:

Fluorescein angioscopy, quantitative visual field examination, refraction or extended color vision examination (such as Nagel's anomaloscope) should be separately reported.

Prescription of lenses, when required, is included in 92015. It includes specification of lens type (monofocal, bifocal, other), lens power, axis, prism, absorptive factor, impact resistance, and other factors.

Interpretation and report by the physician is an integral part of special ophthalmological services where indicated. Technical procedures (which may or may not be performed by the physician personally) are often part of the service, but should not be mistaken to constitute the service itself.
    ➔ *CPT Assistant* Nov 97:42-43

General Ophthalmological Services

New Patient

Solely for the purposes of distinguishing between new and established patients, **professional services** are those face-to-face services rendered by a physician and reported by a specific code(s). A new patient is one who has not received any professional services from the physician or another physician of the same specialty who belongs to the same group practice within the past three years.

92002   Ophthalmological services: medical examination and evaluation with initiation of diagnostic and treatment program; intermediate, new patient
    ➔ *CPT Assistant* Feb 97:6, Aug 98:3, Jun 05:11, Dec 05:10, Jan 07:30, Jan 08:1, Sep 08:7

92004   comprehensive, new patient, 1 or more visits
    ➔ *CPT Assistant* Feb 97:6, Aug 98:3, Jun 05:11, Dec 05:10, Jan 07:30, Jan 08:1, Sep 08:7

Established Patient

Solely for the purposes of distinguishing between new and established patients, **professional services** are those face-to-face services rendered by a physician and reported by a specific code(s). An established patient is one who has received professional services from the physician or another physician of the same specialty who belongs to the same group practice within the past three years.

92012   Ophthalmological services: medical examination and evaluation, with initiation or continuation of diagnostic and treatment program; intermediate, established patient
> *CPT Assistant* Feb 97:6, Aug 98:3, Jun 05:11, Dec 05:10, Jan 07:30, Jan 08:1, Sep 08:7

92014   comprehensive, established patient, 1 or more visits
> *CPT Assistant* Feb 97:6, Aug 98:3, Dec 99:10, Jun 05:11, Dec 05:10, Jan 07:30, Jan 08:1, Sep 08:7

(For surgical procedures, see **Surgery,** Eye and Ocular Adnexa, 65091 et seq)

Special Ophthalmological Services

92015   Determination of refractive state
> *CPT Assistant* Mar 96:11, Feb 97:6, Aug 98:3, Aug 06:11

92018   Ophthalmological examination and evaluation, under general anesthesia, with or without manipulation of globe for passive range of motion or other manipulation to facilitate diagnostic examination; complete
> *CPT Assistant* Feb 97:6, Aug 98:3

92019   limited
> *CPT Assistant* Feb 97:6, Aug 98:3

92020   Gonioscopy (separate procedure)
> *CPT Assistant* Feb 97:6, Aug 98:3

(For gonioscopy under general anesthesia, use 92018)

92025   Computerized corneal topography, unilateral or bilateral, with interpretation and report
> *CPT Changes: An Insider's View* 2007

(Do not report 92025 in conjunction with 65710-65771)

(92025 is not used for manual keratoscopy, which is part of a single system Evaluation and Management or ophthalmological service)

92060   Sensorimotor examination with multiple measurements of ocular deviation (eg, restrictive or paretic muscle with diplopia) with interpretation and report (separate procedure)
> *CPT Assistant* Feb 97:6, Aug 98:3

92065   Orthoptic and/or pleoptic training, with continuing medical direction and evaluation
> *CPT Assistant* Feb 97:6, Jun 98:10, Aug 98:3

92070   Fitting of contact lens for treatment of disease, including supply of lens
> *CPT Assistant* Feb 97:6, Aug 98:3

92081   Visual field examination, unilateral or bilateral, with interpretation and report; limited examination (eg, tangent screen, Autoplot, arc perimeter, or single stimulus level automated test, such as Octopus 3 or 7 equivalent)
> *CPT Assistant* Feb 97:6, Aug 98:3

92082   intermediate examination (eg, at least 2 isopters on Goldmann perimeter, or semiquantitative, automated suprathreshold screening program, Humphrey suprathreshold automatic diagnostic test, Octopus program 33)
> *CPT Assistant* Feb 97:6, Aug 98:3

92083   extended examination (eg, Goldmann visual fields with at least 3 isopters plotted and static determination within the central 30°, or quantitative, automated threshold perimetry, Octopus program G-1, 32 or 42, Humphrey visual field analyzer full threshold programs 30-2, 24-2, or 30/60-2)
> *CPT Assistant* Feb 97:6, Aug 98:3

(Gross visual field testing (eg, confrontation testing) is a part of general ophthalmological services and is not reported separately)

92100   Serial tonometry (separate procedure) with multiple measurements of intraocular pressure over an extended time period with interpretation and report, same day (eg, diurnal curve or medical treatment of acute elevation of intraocular pressure)
> *CPT Assistant* Feb 97:6, Jun 98:10, Aug 98:3

92120   Tonography with interpretation and report, recording indentation tonometer method or perilimbal suction method
> *CPT Assistant* Feb 97:6, Aug 98:3

▶(For measurement of ocular blood flow, use Category III code 0198T)◀

92130   Tonography with water provocation
> *CPT Assistant* Feb 97:6, Aug 98:3

92135   Scanning computerized ophthalmic diagnostic imaging, posterior segment, (eg, scanning laser) with interpretation and report, unilateral
> *CPT Assistant* Aug 98:3, Nov 98:33, Mar 99:10, Apr 99:10; *CPT Changes: An Insider's View* 2008

92136   Ophthalmic biometry by partial coherence interferometry with intraocular lens power calculation
> *CPT Assistant* Aug 98:3, Apr 02:18; *CPT Changes: An Insider's View* 2002

92140   Provocative tests for glaucoma, with interpretation and report, without tonography
> *CPT Assistant* Feb 97:6, Aug 98:3

Ophthalmoscopy

Routine ophthalmoscopy is part of general and special ophthalmologic services whenever indicated. It is a non-itemized service and is not reported separately.

92225   Ophthalmoscopy, extended, with retinal drawing (eg, for retinal detachment, melanoma), with interpretation and report; initial

➲ *CPT Assistant* Feb 97:6, Aug 98:2, Dec 99:10

Extended Ophthalmoscopy
92225, 92226

Illustration of retinal structures to document for comparison with future examinations

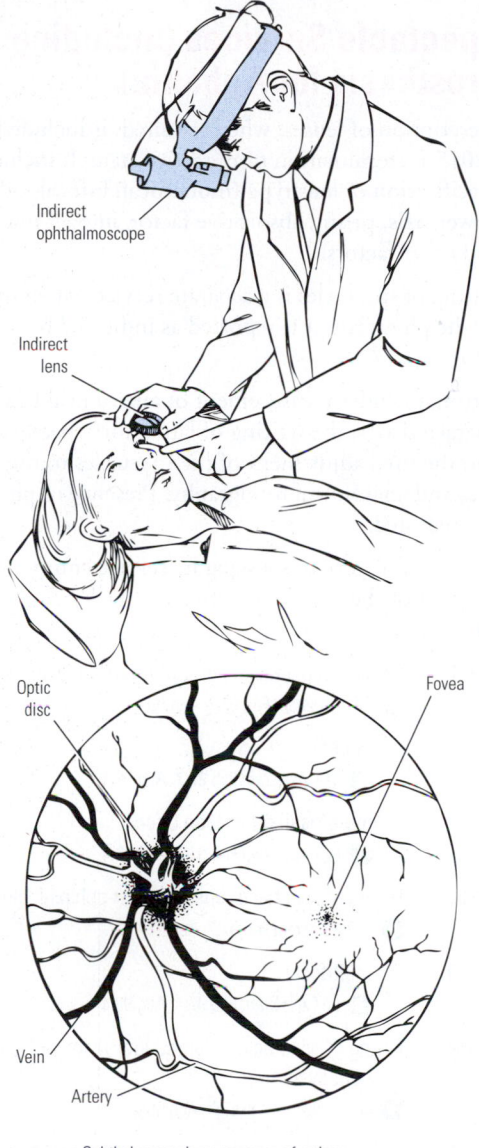

Indirect ophthalmoscope

Indirect lens

Optic disc

Fovea

Vein

Artery

Ophthalmoscopic appearance of retina

92226   subsequent

➲ *CPT Assistant* Feb 97:6, Aug 98:2

92230   Fluorescein angioscopy with interpretation and report

➲ *CPT Assistant* Feb 97:6

92235   Fluorescein angiography (includes multiframe imaging) with interpretation and report

➲ *CPT Assistant* Feb 97:6

Fluorescein Angiography
92235

Fluorescein dye is injected in a peripheral vein to enhance imaging. Serial multiframe angiography is performed to evaluate choroidal and retinal circulation. In this illustration, arteries display an even fluorescence, while veins appear striped from the laminar dye flow.

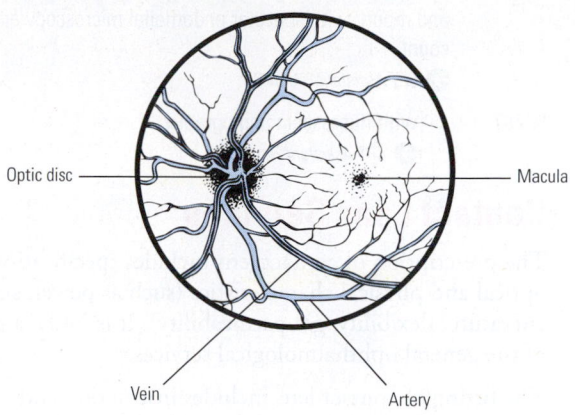

Optic disc

Macula

Vein

Artery

92240   Indocyanine-green angiography (includes multiframe imaging) with interpretation and report

92250   Fundus photography with interpretation and report

➲ *CPT Assistant* Feb 97:6, Apr 99:10

92260   Ophthalmodynamometry

➲ *CPT Assistant* Feb 97:6

(For ophthalmoscopy under general anesthesia, use 92018)

Other Specialized Services

92265   Needle oculoelectromyography, 1 or more extraocular muscles, 1 or both eyes, with interpretation and report

➲ *CPT Assistant* Feb 97:6

92270   Electro-oculography with interpretation and report

➲ *CPT Assistant* Feb 97:6, Aug 08:12

92275   Electroretinography with interpretation and report

➲ *CPT Assistant* Feb 97:6

(For electronystagmography for vestibular function studies, see 92541 et seq)

(For ophthalmic echography (diagnostic ultrasound), see 76511-76529)

92283   Color vision examination, extended, eg, anomaloscope or equivalent

➲ *CPT Assistant* Feb 97:6

(Color vision testing with pseudoisochromatic plates [such as HRR or Ishihara] is not reported separately. It is included in the appropriate general or ophthalmological service, or 99172)

92284   Dark adaptation examination with interpretation and report

➲ *CPT Assistant* Feb 97:6

92285 External ocular photography with interpretation and report for documentation of medical progress (eg, close-up photography, slit lamp photography, goniophotography, stereo-photography)
➔ *CPT Assistant* Feb 97:6, Sep 97:10

92286 Special anterior segment photography with interpretation and report; with specular endothelial microscopy and cell count
➔ *CPT Assistant* Feb 97:6

92287 with fluorescein angiography
➔ *CPT Assistant* Feb 97:6

Contact Lens Services

The prescription of contact lens includes specification of optical and physical characteristics (such as power, size, curvature, flexibility, gas-permeability). It is NOT a part of the general ophthalmological services.

The fitting of contact lens includes instruction and training of the wearer and incidental revision of the lens during the training period.

Follow-up of successfully fitted extended wear lenses is reported as part of a general ophthalmological service (92012 et seq).

The supply of contact lenses may be reported as part of the service of fitting. It may also be reported separately by using the appropriate supply codes.

(For therapeutic or surgical use of contact lens, see 68340, 92070)

92310 Prescription of optical and physical characteristics of and fitting of contact lens, with medical supervision of adaptation; corneal lens, both eyes, except for aphakia
➔ *CPT Assistant* Feb 97:6

(For prescription and fitting of 1 eye, add modifier 52)

92311 corneal lens for aphakia, 1 eye
➔ *CPT Assistant* Feb 97:6

92312 corneal lens for aphakia, both eyes
➔ *CPT Assistant* Feb 97:6

92313 corneoscleral lens
➔ *CPT Assistant* Feb 97:7, Mar 03:1

92314 Prescription of optical and physical characteristics of contact lens, with medical supervision of adaptation and direction of fitting by independent technician; corneal lens, both eyes except for aphakia
➔ *CPT Assistant* Feb 97:7

(For prescription and fitting of 1 eye, add modifier 52)

92315 corneal lens for aphakia, 1 eye
➔ *CPT Assistant* Feb 97:7

92316 corneal lens for aphakia, both eyes
➔ *CPT Assistant* Feb 97:7

92317 corneoscleral lens
➔ *CPT Assistant* Feb 97:7

92325 Modification of contact lens (separate procedure), with medical supervision of adaptation
➔ *CPT Assistant* Feb 97:7

92326 Replacement of contact lens
➔ *CPT Assistant* Feb 97:7

(For prescription, fitting, and/or medical supervision of ocular prosthetic adaptation by a physician, see Evaluation and Management services or General Ophthalmological service codes 92002-92014)

Spectacle Services (Including Prosthesis for Aphakia)

Prescription of lenses, when required, is included in 92015 Determination of refractive state. It includes specification of lens type (monofocal, bifocal, other), lens power, axis, prism, absorptive factor, impact resistance, and other factors.

Fitting of spectacles is a separate service; when provided by the physician, it is reported as indicated by 92340-92371.

Fitting includes measurement of anatomical facial characteristics, the writing of laboratory specifications, and the final adjustment of the spectacles to the visual axes and anatomical topography. Presence of physician is not required.

Supply of materials is a separate service component; it is not part of the service of fitting spectacles.
➔ *CPT Assistant* Nov 97:43

92340 Fitting of spectacles, except for aphakia; monofocal
➔ *CPT Assistant* Feb 97:7, Aug 98:4

92341 bifocal
➔ *CPT Assistant* Feb 97:7, Aug 98:4

92342 multifocal, other than bifocal
➔ *CPT Assistant* Feb 97:7, Aug 98:4

92352 Fitting of spectacle prosthesis for aphakia; monofocal
➔ *CPT Assistant* Feb 97:7, Aug 98:4

92353 multifocal
➔ *CPT Assistant* Feb 97:7, Aug 98:4

92354 Fitting of spectacle mounted low vision aid; single element system
➔ *CPT Assistant* Feb 97:7, Aug 98:4

92355 telescopic or other compound lens system
➔ *CPT Assistant* Feb 97:7, Aug 98:4

92358 Prosthesis service for aphakia, temporary (disposable or loan, including materials)
➔ *CPT Assistant* Feb 97:7, Aug 98:4

92370 Repair and refitting spectacles; except for aphakia
➔ *CPT Assistant* Feb 97:7

92371 spectacle prosthesis for aphakia
➔ *CPT Assistant* Feb 97:7, Aug 98:4

Other Procedures

92499   Unlisted ophthalmological service or procedure
➔ *CPT Assistant* Feb 97:7

Special Otorhinolaryngologic Services

Diagnostic or treatment procedures that are reported as evaluation and management services (eg, otoscopy, anterior rhinoscopy, tuning fork test, removal of non-impacted cerumen) are not reported separately.

Special otorhinolaryngologic services are those diagnostic and treatment services not included in an Evaluation and Management service. These services are reported separately, using codes 92502-92700.

Code 92506 is used to report evaluation of speech production, receptive language, and expressive language abilities. Tests may examine speech sound production, articulatory movements of oral musculature, the patient's ability to understand the meaning and intent of written and verbal expressions, and the appropriate formulation and utterance of expressive thought. In contrast, 92626 and 92627 are reported for an evaluation of auditory rehabilitation status determining the patient's ability to use residual hearing in order to identify the acoustic characteristics of sounds associated with speech communication.

(For laryngoscopy with stroboscopy, use 31579)

92502   Otolaryngologic examination under general anesthesia

92504   Binocular microscopy (separate diagnostic procedure)
➔ *CPT Assistant* Jul 05:14

92506   Evaluation of speech, language, voice, communication, and/or auditory processing
➔ *CPT Assistant* Sep 04:13, Dec 04:14, Mar 05:7, Jan 06:7, Mar 09:11; *CPT Changes: An Insider's View* 2006

92507   Treatment of speech, language, voice, communication, and/or auditory processing disorder; individual
➔ *CPT Assistant* Dec 04:14, Jan 06:7; *CPT Changes: An Insider's View* 2006

92508   group, 2 or more individuals
➔ *CPT Assistant* Dec 04:14

(For auditory rehabilitation, prelingual hearing loss, use 92630)

(For auditory rehabilitation, postlingual hearing loss, use 92633)

(For cochlear implant programming, see 92601-92604)

92511   Nasopharyngoscopy with endoscope (separate procedure)

92512   Nasal function studies (eg, rhinomanometry)

92516   Facial nerve function studies (eg, electroneuronography)

92520   Laryngeal function studies (ie, aerodynamic testing and acoustic testing)
➔ *CPT Assistant* Dec 04:17, Jan 06:7; *CPT Changes: An Insider's View* 2006

(For performance of a single test, use modifier 52)

(To report flexible fiberoptic laryngeal evaluation of swallowing and laryngeal sensory testing, see 92611-92617)

(To report other testing of laryngeal function (eg, electroglottography), use 92700)

92526   Treatment of swallowing dysfunction and/or oral function for feeding

Vestibular Function Tests, Without Electrical Recording

92531   Spontaneous nystagmus, including gaze

92532   Positional nystagmus test
➔ *CPT Changes: An Insider's View* 2002

(Do not report 92531, 92532 with evaluation and management services)

92533   Caloric vestibular test, each irrigation (binaural, bithermal stimulation constitutes 4 tests)
➔ *CPT Assistant* May 96:5

92534   Optokinetic nystagmus test
➔ *CPT Changes: An Insider's View* 2002

Vestibular Function Tests, With Recording (eg, ENG)

● **92540**   Basic vestibular evaluation, includes spontaneous nystagmus test with eccentric gaze fixation nystagmus, with recording, positional nystagmus test, minimum of 4 positions, with recording, optokinetic nystagmus test, bidirectional foveal and peripheral stimulation, with recording, and oscillating tracking test, with recording
➔ *CPT Changes: An Insider's View* 2010

►(Do not report 92540 in conjunction with 92541, 92542, 92544, or 92545)◄

92541   Spontaneous nystagmus test, including gaze and fixation nystagmus, with recording
➔ *CPT Assistant* Feb 05:13, Aug 08:12

►(Do not report 92541 in conjunction with 92542, 92544, 92545)◄

92542   Positional nystagmus test, minimum of 4 positions, with recording
➔ *CPT Assistant* Feb 05:13, Aug 08:12

►(Do not report 92542 in conjunction with 92541, 92544, 92545)◄

92543   Caloric vestibular test, each irrigation (binaural, bithermal stimulation constitutes 4 tests), with recording
➔ *CPT Assistant* May 96:5, Oct 04:10, Feb 05:13, Sep 06:13, Aug 08:12

92544 Optokinetic nystagmus test, bidirectional, foveal or peripheral stimulation, with recording

➲ *CPT Assistant* Feb 05:13, Aug 08:12

►(Do not report 92544 in conjunction with 92541, 92542, 92545)◄

92545 Oscillating tracking test, with recording

➲ *CPT Assistant* Feb 05:13, Aug 08:12

92546 Sinusoidal vertical axis rotational testing

➲ *CPT Assistant* Sep 04:13, Feb 05:13, Aug 08:12

+ 92547 Use of vertical electrodes (List separately in addition to code for primary procedure)

➲ *CPT Assistant* May 04:14, Feb 05:13, Aug 08:12

(Use 92547 in conjunction with 92541-92546)

(For unlisted vestibular tests, use 92700)

92548 Computerized dynamic posturography

Audiologic Function Tests

The audiometric tests listed below require the use of calibrated electronic equipment, recording of results and a report with interpretation. Hearing tests (such as whispered voice, tuning fork) that are otorhinolaryngologic Evaluation and Management services are not reported separately. All services include testing of both ears. Use modifier 52 if a test is applied to one ear instead of two ears. All codes (except 92559) apply to testing of individuals. For testing of groups, use 92559 and specify test(s) used.

(For evaluation of speech, language and/or hearing problems through observation and assessment of performance, use 92506)

● **92550** Tympanometry and reflex threshold measurements

➲ *CPT Changes: An Insider's View* 2010

►(Do not report 92550 in conjunction with 92567, 92568)◄

92551 Screening test, pure tone, air only

92552 Pure tone audiometry (threshold); air only

92553 air and bone

92555 Speech audiometry threshold;

92556 with speech recognition

92557 Comprehensive audiometry threshold evaluation and speech recognition (92553 and 92556 combined)

➲ *CPT Assistant* Sep 07:11

(For hearing aid evaluation and selection, see 92590-92595)

92559 Audiometric testing of groups

92560 Bekesy audiometry; screening

92561 diagnostic

92562 Loudness balance test, alternate binaural or monaural

➲ *CPT Assistant* Mar 05:7, 9

92563 Tone decay test

92564 Short increment sensitivity index (SISI)

➲ *CPT Assistant* Oct 96:9

92565 Stenger test, pure tone

92567 Tympanometry (impedance testing)

➲ *CPT Assistant* Winter 90:11

92568 Acoustic reflex testing, threshold

➲ *CPT Assistant* Jan 06:7, Sep 07:11; *CPT Changes: An Insider's View* 2006, 2010

►(92569 has been deleted. For acoustic reflex decay testing performed in conjunction with tympanometry, use 92570)◄

● **92570** Acoustic immittance testing, includes tympanometry (impedance testing), acoustic reflex threshold testing, and acoustic reflex decay testing

➲ *CPT Changes: An Insider's View* 2010

►(Do not report 92570 in conjunction with 92567, 92568)◄

92571 Filtered speech test

➲ *CPT Assistant* Mar 05:7

92572 Staggered spondaic word test

➲ *CPT Assistant* Mar 05:7

92575 Sensorineural acuity level test

92576 Synthetic sentence identification test

➲ *CPT Assistant* Mar 05:7

92577 Stenger test, speech

92579 Visual reinforcement audiometry (VRA)

92582 Conditioning play audiometry

92583 Select picture audiometry

92584 Electrocochleography

92585 Auditory evoked potentials for evoked response audiometry and/or testing of the central nervous system; comprehensive

➲ *CPT Assistant* Winter 90:11; *CPT Changes: An Insider's View* 2001

92586 limited

➲ *CPT Changes: An Insider's View* 2001

92587 Evoked otoacoustic emissions; limited (single stimulus level, either transient or distortion products)

➲ *CPT Assistant* Sep 07:11

92588 comprehensive or diagnostic evaluation (comparison of transient and/or distortion product otoacoustic emissions at multiple levels and frequencies)

(For central auditory function evaluation, see 92620, 92621)

92590   Hearing aid examination and selection; monaural

92591   binaural

92592   Hearing aid check; monaural

92593   binaural

92594   Electroacoustic evaluation for hearing aid; monaural

92595   binaural

92596   Ear protector attenuation measurements

92597   Evaluation for use and/or fitting of voice prosthetic device to supplement oral speech

(To report augmentative and alternative communication device services, see 92605, 92607, 92608)

Evaluative and Therapeutic Services

Codes 92601 and 92603 describe post-operative analysis and fitting of previously placed external devices, connection to the cochlear implant, and programming of the stimulator. Codes 92602 and 92604 describe subsequent sessions for measurements and adjustment of the external transmitter and re-programming of the internal stimulator.

(For placement of cochlear implant, use 69930)

92601   Diagnostic analysis of cochlear implant, patient younger than 7 years of age; with programming
        ➜ CPT Assistant Mar 03:1, Jan 06:7; CPT Changes: An Insider's View 2003

92602   subsequent reprogramming
        ➜ CPT Assistant Mar 03:1, 21, Jan 06:7; CPT Changes: An Insider's View 2003

(Do not report 92602 in addition to 92601)

(For aural rehabilitation services following cochlear implant, including evaluation of rehabilitation status, see 92626-92627, 92630-92633)

92603   Diagnostic analysis of cochlear implant, age 7 years or older; with programming
        ➜ CPT Assistant Mar 03:2, 4, Jan 06:7; CPT Changes: An Insider's View 2003

92604   subsequent reprogramming
        ➜ CPT Assistant Mar 03:2, 21, Jan 06:7; CPT Changes: An Insider's View 2003

(Do not report 92604 in addition to 92603)

A View of the Outer Cochlear Implant
92601-92604

An example of the elements that are addressed in the diagnostic analysis and reprogramming of the cochlear implant

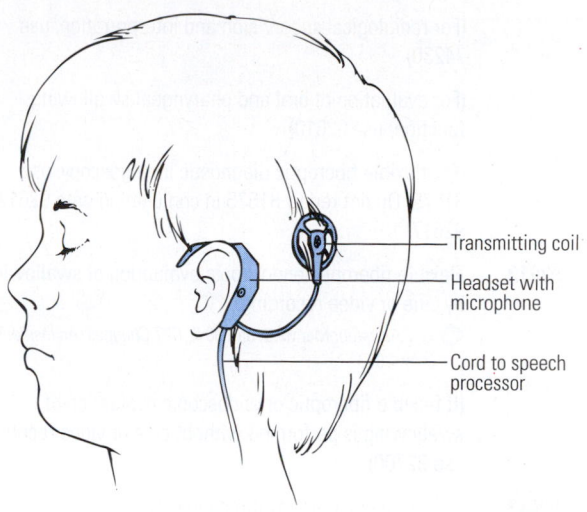

— Transmitting coil

— Headset with microphone

— Cord to speech processor

92605   Evaluation for prescription of non-speech-generating augmentative and alternative communication device
        ➜ CPT Assistant Mar 03:2, 4; CPT Changes: An Insider's View 2003

92606   Therapeutic service(s) for the use of non-speech-generating device, including programming and modification
        ➜ CPT Assistant Mar 03:2, 4; CPT Changes: An Insider's View 2003

92607   Evaluation for prescription for speech-generating augmentative and alternative communication device, face-to-face with the patient; first hour
        ➜ CPT Assistant Mar 03:2, 4, Dec 04:16; CPT Changes: An Insider's View 2003

(For evaluation for prescription of a non-speech-generating device, use 92605)

+ 92608   each additional 30 minutes (List separately in addition to code for primary procedure)
        ➜ CPT Assistant Mar 03:2, 5, Dec 04:16; CPT Changes: An Insider's View 2003

(Use 92608 in conjunction with 92607)

92609   Therapeutic services for the use of speech-generating device, including programming and modification
        ➜ CPT Assistant Mar 03:2, 4, Dec 04:16; CPT Changes: An Insider's View 2003

(For therapeutic service(s) for the use of a non-speech-generating device, use 92606)

92610   Evaluation of oral and pharyngeal swallowing function
        ➜ CPT Assistant Mar 03:2, 5, Dec 04:17; CPT Changes: An Insider's View 2003

(For motion fluoroscopic evaluation of swallowing function, use 92611)

(For flexible endoscopic examination, use 92612-92617)

92611 Motion fluoroscopic evaluation of swallowing function by cine or video recording
➜ *CPT Assistant* Mar 03:2, 5, Dec 04:17, Jan 06:7; *CPT Changes: An Insider's View* 2003
➜ *Clinical Examples in Radiology* Summer 06:4-5

(For radiological supervision and interpretation, use 74230)

(For evaluation of oral and pharyngeal swallowing function, use 92610)

(For flexible fiberoptic diagnostic laryngoscopy, use 31575. Do not report 31575 in conjunction with 92612-92617)

92612 Flexible fiberoptic endoscopic evaluation of swallowing by cine or video recording;
➜ *CPT Assistant* Mar 03:6, Jan 06:7; *CPT Changes: An Insider's View* 2003

(If flexible fiberoptic or endoscopic evaluation of swallowing is performed without cine or video recording, use 92700)

92613 physician interpretation and report only
➜ *CPT Assistant* Jan 06:7; *CPT Changes: An Insider's View* 2003

(To report an evaluation of oral and pharyngeal swallowing function, use 92610)

(To report motion fluoroscopic evaluation of swallowing function, use 92611)

92614 Flexible fiberoptic endoscopic evaluation, laryngeal sensory testing by cine or video recording;
➜ *CPT Assistant* Mar 03:6, Jan 06:7; *CPT Changes: An Insider's View* 2003

(If flexible fiberoptic or endoscopic evaluation of swallowing is performed without cine or video recording, use 92700)

92615 physician interpretation and report only
➜ *CPT Assistant* Mar 03:6, Jan 06:7; *CPT Changes: An Insider's View* 2003

92616 Flexible fiberoptic endoscopic evaluation of swallowing and laryngeal sensory testing by cine or video recording;
➜ *CPT Assistant* Mar 03:6, Jan 06:7; *CPT Changes: An Insider's View* 2003

(If flexible fiberoptic or endoscopic evaluation of swallowing is performed without cine or video recording, use 92700)

92617 physician interpretation and report only
➜ *CPT Assistant* Mar 03:6, Jan 06:7; *CPT Changes: An Insider's View* 2003

92620 Evaluation of central auditory function, with report; initial 60 minutes
➜ *CPT Assistant* Mar 05:7-8; *CPT Changes: An Insider's View* 2005

92621 each additional 15 minutes
➜ *CPT Assistant* Mar 05:7; *CPT Changes: An Insider's View* 2005

(Do not report 92620, 92621 in conjunction with 92506)

92625 Assessment of tinnitus (includes pitch, loudness matching, and masking)
➜ *CPT Assistant* Mar 05:7-10; *CPT Changes: An Insider's View* 2005

(Do not report 92625 in conjunction with 92562)

(For unilateral assessment, use modifier 52)

92626 Evaluation of auditory rehabilitation status; first hour
➜ *CPT Assistant* Jan 06:7; *CPT Changes: An Insider's View* 2006

+ 92627 each additional 15 minutes (List separately in addition to code for primary procedure)
➜ *CPT Assistant* Jan 06:7; *CPT Changes: An Insider's View* 2006

(Use 92627 in conjunction with 92626)

(When reporting 92626, 92627, use the face-to-face time with the patient or family)

92630 Auditory rehabilitation; prelingual hearing loss
➜ *CPT Assistant* Jan 06:7; *CPT Changes: An Insider's View* 2006

92633 postlingual hearing loss
➜ *CPT Assistant* Jan 06:7; *CPT Changes: An Insider's View* 2006

Special Diagnostic Procedures

92640 Diagnostic analysis with programming of auditory brainstem implant, per hour
➜ *CPT Changes: An Insider's View* 2007

(Report nonprogramming services separately [eg, cardiac monitoring])

Other Procedures

92700 Unlisted otorhinolaryngological service or procedure
➜ *CPT Assistant* Sep 04:14, Oct 04:10, Jan 06:7, Sep 06:13, Sep 07:11; *CPT Changes: An Insider's View* 2003

Cardiovascular

Therapeutic Services and Procedures

(For nonsurgical septal reduction therapy [eg, alcohol ablation], use 93799)

92950 Cardiopulmonary resuscitation (eg, in cardiac arrest)
➜ *CPT Assistant* Jan 96:7, Oct 04:14, Nov 07:5

(See also critical care services, 99291, 99292)

⊙ **92953** Temporary transcutaneous pacing
➜ *CPT Assistant* Nov 99:49, Feb 07:10, Jul 07:1

(For physician direction of ambulance or rescue personnel outside the hospital, use 99288)

⊙ **92960**   Cardioversion, elective, electrical conversion of
arrhythmia; external
➔ *CPT Assistant* Summer 93:13, Nov 99:49, Jun 00:5, Nov 00:9,
Jul 01:11; *CPT Changes: An Insider's View* 2000

⊙ **92961**   internal (separate procedure)
➔ *CPT Assistant* Summer 93:13, Nov 99:49, Jun 00:5, Jul 00:5,
Nov 00:9; *CPT Changes: An Insider's View* 2000

►(Do not report 92961 in conjunction with 93282-93284,
93287, 93289, 93295, 93296, 93618-93624, 93631,
93640-93642, 93650-93652, 93662)◄

92970   Cardioassist-method of circulatory assist; internal

92971   external

(For balloon atrial-septostomy, use 92992)

(For placement of catheters for use in circulatory assist
devices such as intra-aortic balloon pump, use 33970)

⊙✚ **92973**   Percutaneous transluminal coronary thrombectomy (List
separately in addition to code for primary procedure)
➔ *CPT Assistant* Mar 02:2, 10, Mar 04:10; *CPT Changes: An
Insider's View* 2002

(Use 92973 in conjunction with 92980, 92982)

⊙✚ **92974**   Transcatheter placement of radiation delivery device for
subsequent coronary intravascular brachytherapy (List
separately in addition to code for primary procedure)
➔ *CPT Assistant* Mar 02:2; *CPT Changes: An Insider's View* 2002

(Use 92974 in conjunction with 92980, 92982, 92995,
93508)

►(For intravascular radioelement application, see 77785-
77787)◄

⊙ **92975**   Thrombolysis, coronary; by intracoronary infusion,
including selective coronary angiography

92977   by intravenous infusion

(For thrombolysis of vessels other than coronary, see
37201, 75896)

(For cerebral thrombolysis, use 37195)

⊙✚ **92978**   Intravascular ultrasound (coronary vessel or graft) during
diagnostic evaluation and/or therapeutic intervention
including imaging supervision, interpretation and report;
initial vessel (List separately in addition to code for
primary procedure)
➔ *CPT Assistant* Nov 97:43-44, Nov 99:49, Mar 02:2, Jan 07:28;
CPT Changes: An Insider's View 2000

Intravascular Ultrasound (Coronary Vessel or Graft)
92978

A catheter with a transducer at its tip is inserted and threaded through a selected
coronary artery(s) or coronary bypass graft(s).

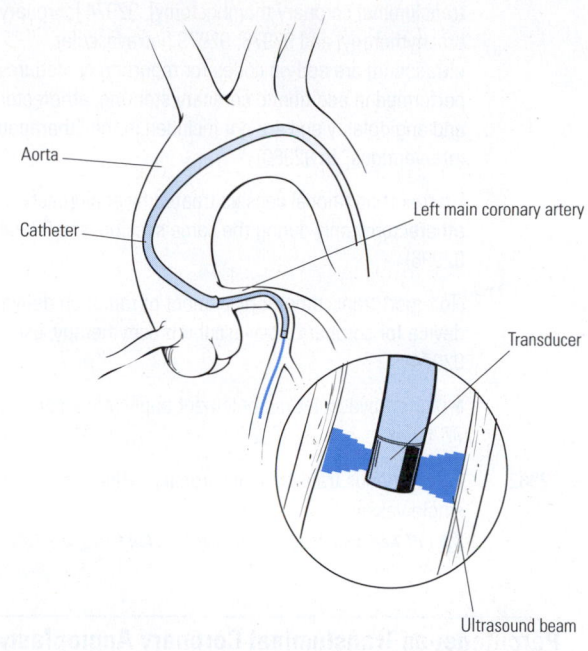

⊙✚ **92979**   each additional vessel (List separately in addition to
code for primary procedure)
➔ *CPT Assistant* Nov 97:43-44, Nov 99:49; *CPT Changes: An
Insider's View* 2000

(Use 92979 in conjunction with 92978)

(Intravascular ultrasound services include all transducer
manipulations and repositioning within the specific
vessel being examined, both before and after therapeutic
intervention [eg, stent placement])

►(For intravascular spectroscopy, use 0205T)◄

⊙ **92980**   Transcatheter placement of an intracoronary stent(s),
percutaneous, with or without other therapeutic
intervention, any method; single vessel
➔ *CPT Assistant* Aug 96:2, Dec 96:11, Apr 98:9, Aug 98:3,
Aug 00:11, Mar 01:11, Apr 01:10, Mar 02:2, Aug 03:10, Apr 05:14

⊙✚ **92981**   each additional vessel (List separately in addition to
code for primary procedure)
➔ *CPT Assistant* Mar 01:11, Apr 01:10, Aug 03:10

(Use 92981 in conjunction with 92980)

(Codes 92980, 92981 are used to report coronary artery stenting. Coronary angioplasty [92982, 92984] or atherectomy [92995, 92996], in the same artery, is considered part of the stenting procedure and is not reported separately. Codes 92973 [percutaneous transluminal coronary thombectomy], 92974 [coronary brachytherapy] and 92978, 92979 [intravascular ultrasound] are add-on codes for reporting procedures performed in addition to coronary stenting, atherectomy, and angioplasty and are not included in the "therapeutic interventions" in 92980)

(To report additional vessels treated by angioplasty or atherectomy only during the same session, see 92984, 92996)

(To report transcatheter placement of radiation delivery device for coronary intravascular brachytherapy, use 92974)

▶(For intravascular radioelement application, see 77785-77787)◀

⊙ **92982**   Percutaneous transluminal coronary balloon angioplasty; single vessel

➔ *CPT Assistant* Winter 92:15, Aug 96:2, Apr 97:10, Mar 02:2, Apr 05:14

Percutaneous Transluminal Coronary Angioplasty (PTCA)
92982

PTCA of a single coronary vessel

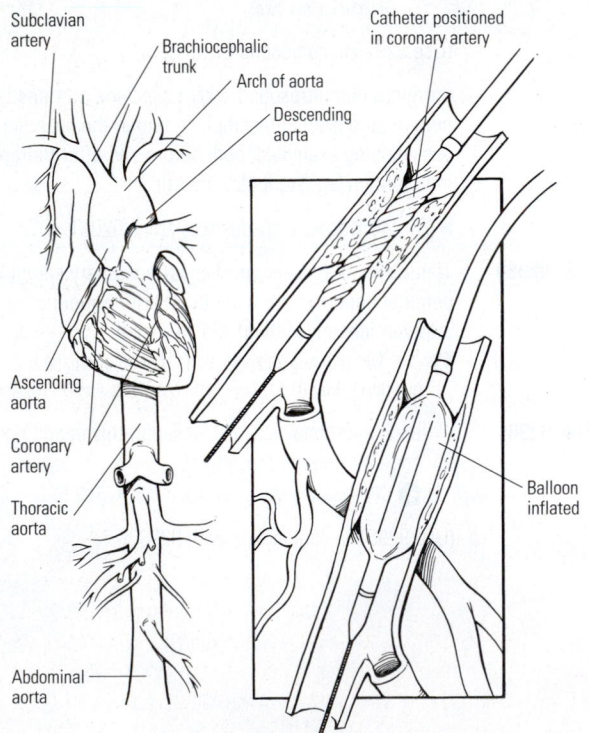

⊙+ **92984**   each additional vessel (List separately in addition to code for primary procedure)

➔ *CPT Assistant* Winter 92:15, Aug 96:2, Dec 96:11, Apr 97:10, Apr 05:14

(Use 92984 in conjunction with 92980, 92982, 92995)

(For stent placement following completion of angioplasty or atherectomy, see 92980, 92981)

(To report transcatheter placement of radiation delivery device for coronary intravascular brachytherapy, use 92974)

▶(For intravascular radioelement application, see 77785-77787)◀

⊙ **92986**   Percutaneous balloon valvuloplasty; aortic valve

⊙ **92987**   mitral valve

92990   pulmonary valve

➔ *CPT Assistant* Winter 91:3

92992   Atrial septectomy or septostomy; transvenous method, balloon (eg, Rashkind type) (includes cardiac catheterization)

➔ *CPT Assistant* Nov 97:44, Apr 98:3, 10, Nov 07:9

92993   blade method (Park septostomy) (includes cardiac catheterization)

➔ *CPT Assistant* Apr 98:10

⊙ **92995**   Percutaneous transluminal coronary atherectomy, by mechanical or other method, with or without balloon angioplasty; single vessel

➔ *CPT Assistant* Winter 92:15

⊙+ **92996**   each additional vessel (List separately in addition to code for primary procedure)

➔ *CPT Assistant* Winter 92:15, Apr 98:3

(Use 92996 in conjunction with 92980, 92982, 92995)

(For stent placement following completion of angioplasty or atherectomy, see 92980, 92981)

(To report additional vessels treated by angioplasty only during the same session, use 92984)

92997   Percutaneous transluminal pulmonary artery balloon angioplasty; single vessel

➔ *CPT Assistant* Nov 97:44

+ **92998**   each additional vessel (List separately in addition to code for primary procedure)

➔ *CPT Assistant* Nov 97:44

(Use 92998 in conjunction with 92997)

Cardiography

Codes 93040-93042 are appropriate when an order for the test is triggered by an event, the rhythm strip is used to help diagnose the presence or absence of an arrhythmia, and a report is generated. There must be a specific order for an electrocardiogram or rhythm strip followed by a separate, signed, written, and retrievable report. It is not appropriate to use these codes for reviewing the telemetry monitor strips taken from a monitoring system. The need for an electrocardiogram or rhythm strip should be supported by documentation in the patient medical record.

Cardiovascular monitoring services are diagnostic medical procedures using in-person and remote technology to assess cardiovascular rhythm (ECG) data.

Attended surveillance: is the immediate availability of a remote technician to respond to rhythm or device alert transmissions from a patient, either from an implanted or wearable monitoring or therapy device, as they are generated and transmitted to the remote surveillance location or center.

►***Electrocardiographic rhythm derived elements:*** elements derived from recordings of the electrical activation of the heart including, but not limited to heart rhythm, rate, ST analysis, heart rate variability, T-wave alternans.◄

Mobile cardiovascular telemetry (MCT): continuously records the electrocardiographic rhythm from external electrodes placed on the patient's body. Segments of the ECG data are automatically (without patient intervention) transmitted to a remote surveillance location by cellular or landline telephone signal. The segments of the rhythm, selected for transmission, are triggered automatically (MCT device algorithm) by rapid and slow heart rates or by the patient during a symptomatic episode. There is continuous real time data analysis by preprogrammed algorithms in the device and attended surveillance of the transmitted rhythm segments by a surveillance center technician to evaluate any arrhythmias and to determine signal quality. The surveillance center technician reviews the data and notifies the physician depending on the prescribed criteria.

ECG rhythm derived elements are distinct from physiologic data, even when the same device is capable of producing both. Implantable cardiovascular monitor (ICM) device services are always separately reported from Implantable cardioverter-defibrillator (ICD) service.

For other services related to a wearable defibrillator, see 93745.

(For echocardiography, see 93303-93350)

(For electrocardiogram, 64 leads or greater, with graphic presentation and analysis, see 0178T-0180T)

93000   Electrocardiogram, routine ECG with at least 12 leads; with interpretation and report
→ *CPT Assistant* Aug 97:9, Feb 05:9, Mar 05:1, 11, Jul 08:3

93005   tracing only, without interpretation and report
→ *CPT Assistant* Aug 97:9, Mar 05:1

93010   interpretation and report only
→ *CPT Assistant* Aug 97:9, Mar 05:1, Apr 07:1

(For ECG monitoring, see 99354-99360)

93012   Telephonic transmission of post-symptom electrocardiogram rhythm strip(s), 24-hour attended monitoring, per 30 day period of time; tracing only
→ *CPT Assistant* Jun 96:2, Oct 05:14; *CPT Changes: An Insider's View* 2003

93014   physician review with interpretation and report only
→ *CPT Assistant* Jun 96:2, Oct 05:14, Mar 09:5, Apr 09:7

(Do not report 93014 in conjunction with 93228, 93229)

93015   Cardiovascular stress test using maximal or submaximal treadmill or bicycle exercise, continuous electrocardiographic monitoring, and/or pharmacological stress; with physician supervision, with interpretation and report
→ *CPT Assistant* Apr 96:11, Jun 96:10, Aug 02:10, Jul 08:3

93016   physician supervision only, without interpretation and report
→ *CPT Assistant* Apr 96:11, Aug 02:10, Jul 08:3

93017   tracing only, without interpretation and report
→ *CPT Assistant* Aug 02:10, Jul 08:3

93018   interpretation and report only
→ *CPT Assistant* Apr 96:11, Jun 96:10, Jul 08:3

(For inert gas rebreathing measurement, see Category III codes 0104T, 0105T)

93024   Ergonovine provocation test

93025   Microvolt T-wave alternans for assessment of ventricular arrhythmias
→ *CPT Assistant* Mar 02:3; *CPT Changes: An Insider's View* 2002

93040   Rhythm ECG, 1-3 leads; with interpretation and report
→ *CPT Assistant* Apr 04:8

93041   tracing only without interpretation and report
→ *CPT Assistant* Apr 04:8

93042   interpretation and report only
→ *CPT Assistant* Apr 04:8

93224   Wearable electrocardiographic rhythm derived monitoring for 24 hours by continuous original waveform recording and storage, with visual superimposition scanning; includes recording, scanning analysis with report, physician review and interpretation
→ *CPT Assistant* Oct 05:14, Apr 07:3, Mar 08:4, Mar 09:5; *CPT Changes: An Insider's View* 2009

93225   recording (includes connection, recording, and disconnection)
→ *CPT Assistant* Oct 05:14, Apr 07:3, Mar 09:5; *CPT Changes: An Insider's View* 2009

93226 scanning analysis with report
→ *CPT Assistant* Oct 05:14, Apr 07:3, Mar 09:5; *CPT Changes: An Insider's View* 2009

93227 physician review and interpretation
→ *CPT Assistant* Apr 07:3, Mar 09:5, Apr 09:7; *CPT Changes: An Insider's View* 2009

93228 Wearable mobile cardiovascular telemetry with electrocardiographic recording, concurrent computerized real time data analysis and greater than 24 hours of accessible ECG data storage (retrievable with query) with ECG triggered and patient selected events transmitted to a remote attended surveillance center for up to 30 days; physician review and interpretation with report
→ *CPT Changes: An Insider's View* 2009

(Report 93228 only once per 30 days)

(Do not report 93228 in conjunction with 93014)

93229 technical support for connection and patient instructions for use, attended surveillance, analysis and physician prescribed transmission of daily and emergent data reports
→ *CPT Changes: An Insider's View* 2009

(Report 93229 only once per 30 days)

(Do not report 93229 in conjunction with 93014)

(For wearable cardiovascular monitors that do not perform automatic ECG triggered transmissions to an attended surveillance center, see 93224-93227, 93230-93272)

93230 Wearable electrocardiographic rhythm derived monitoring for 24 hours by continuous original waveform recording and storage without superimposition scanning utilizing a device capable of producing a full miniaturized printout; includes recording, microprocessor-based analysis with report, physician review and interpretation
→ *CPT Assistant* Oct 05:14, Apr 07:3, Mar 09:5; *CPT Changes: An Insider's View* 2009

93231 recording (includes connection, recording, and disconnection)
→ *CPT Assistant* Oct 05:14, Apr 07:3, Mar 09:5; *CPT Changes: An Insider's View* 2009

93232 microprocessor-based analysis with report
→ *CPT Assistant* Oct 05:14, Apr 07:3, Mar 09:5; *CPT Changes: An Insider's View* 2009

93233 physician review and interpretation
→ *CPT Assistant* Oct 05:14, Apr 07:3, Mar 09:5, Apr 09:7; *CPT Changes: An Insider's View* 2009

93235 Wearable electrocardiographic rhythm derived monitoring for 24 hours by continuous computerized monitoring and non-continuous recording, and real-time data analysis utilizing a device capable of producing intermittent full-sized waveform tracings, possibly patient activated; includes monitoring and real-time data analysis with report, physician review and interpretation
→ *CPT Assistant* Oct 05:14, Apr 07:3, Mar 09:5; *CPT Changes: An Insider's View* 2009

93236 monitoring and real-time data analysis with report
→ *CPT Assistant* Oct 05:14, Apr 07:3, Mar 09:5; *CPT Changes: An Insider's View* 2009

93237 physician review and interpretation
→ *CPT Assistant* Oct 05:14, Apr 07:3, Mar 09:5; *CPT Changes: An Insider's View* 2009

(For wearable mobile telemetry with ECG triggered transmissions to an attended surveillance center, see 93228, 93229)

93268 Wearable patient activated electrocardiographic rhythm derived event recording with presymptom memory loop, 24-hour attended monitoring, per 30 day period of time; includes transmission, physician review and interpretation
→ *CPT Assistant* Jun 96:2, Nov 99:49-50, Oct 05:14, Apr 07:3, Mar 08:4, Mar 09:5; *CPT Changes: An Insider's View* 2003, 2009

93270 recording (includes connection, recording, and disconnection)
→ *CPT Assistant* Jun 96:2, Oct 05:14, Apr 07:3, Mar 09:5; *CPT Changes: An Insider's View* 2009

93271 monitoring, receipt of transmissions, and analysis
→ *CPT Assistant* Jun 96:2, Oct 05:14, Apr 07:3, Mar 09:5; *CPT Changes: An Insider's View* 2009

93272 physician review and interpretation
→ *CPT Assistant* Jun 96:2, Apr 98:14, Nov 99:49-50, Oct 05:14, Apr 07:3, Mar 09:5, Apr 09:7; *CPT Changes: An Insider's View* 2009

(For postsymptom recording, see 93012, 93014)

(For implanted patient activated cardiac event recording, see 33282, 93285, 93291, 93298)

93278 Signal-averaged electrocardiography (SAECG), with or without ECG

(For interpretation and report only, use 93278 with modifier 26)

(For unlisted cardiographic procedure, use 93799)

▶Implantable and Wearable Cardiac Device Evaluations◄

▶Cardiac device evaluation services are diagnostic medical procedures using in-person and remote technology to assess device therapy and cardiovascular physiologic data. Codes 93279-93299 describe this technology and technical/professional physician and service center practice. Codes 93279-93292 are reported per procedure. Codes 93293-93296 are reported no more than **once** every 90 days. Do not report 93293-93296 if the monitoring period is less than 30 days. Codes 93297, 93298 are reported no more than **once** up to every 30 days. Do not report 93297-93299 if the monitoring period is less than 10 days.

A service center may report 93296 or 93299 during a period in which a physician performs an in-person interrogation device evaluation. A physician may not report an in-person and remote interrogation of the same device during the same period. Report only remote services when an in-person interrogation device evaluation is performed during a period of remote interrogation device evaluation. A period is established by the initiation of the remote monitoring or the 91st day of a pacemaker or implantable cardioverter-defibrillator (ICD) monitoring or the 31st day of an implantable loop recorder (ILR) or implantable cardiovascular monitor (ICM) monitoring and extends for the subsequent 90 or 30 days, respectively, for which remote monitoring is occurring. Programming device evaluations and in-person interrogation device evaluations may not be reported on the same date by the same physician. Programming device evaluations and remote interrogation device evaluations may both be reported during the remote interrogation device evaluation period.

For monitoring by wearable devices, see 93224-93272. ◄

ECG rhythm derived elements are distinct from physiologic data, even when the same device is capable of producing both. ICM device services are always separately reported from ICD services. When ILR data is derived from an ICD or pacemaker, do not report ILR services with pacemaker or ICD services.

For other services related to a wearable defibrillator, use 93745.

Do not report 93012, 93014 when performing 93279-93289, 93291-93296 or 93298-93299. Do not report 93040-93042 when performing 93279-93289, 93291-93296, or 93298-93299.

The pacemaker and ICD interrogation device evaluations, peri-procedural device evaluations and programming, and programming device evaluations may not be reported in conjunction with pacemaker or ICD device and/or lead insertion or revision services by the same physician.

The following definitions and instructions apply to codes 93279-93299:

Attended surveillance: the immediate availability of a remote technician to respond to rhythm or device alert transmissions from a patient, either from an implanted or wearable monitoring or therapy device, as they are generated and transmitted to the remote surveillance location or center.

Device, single lead: a pacemaker or implantable cardioverter-defibrillator with pacing and sensing function in only one chamber of the heart.

Device, dual lead: a pacemaker or implantable cardioverter-defibrillator with pacing and sensing function in only two chambers of the heart.

Device, multiple lead: a pacemaker or implantable cardioverter-defibrillator with pacing and sensing function in three or more chambers of the heart.

►*Electrocardiographic rhythm derived elements:* elements derived from recordings of the electrical activation of the heart including, but not limited to heart rhythm, rate, ST analysis, heart rate variability, T-wave alternans.◄

Implantable cardiovascular monitor (ICM): an implantable cardiovascular device used to assist the physician in the management of non-rhythm related cardiac conditions such as heart failure. The device collects longitudinal physiologic cardiovascular data elements from one or more internal sensors (such as right ventricular pressure, left atrial pressure or an index of lung water) and/or external sensors (such as blood pressure or body weight) for patient assessment and management. The data are stored and transmitted to the physician by either local telemetry or remotely to an Internet based file server or surveillance technician. The function of the ICM may be an additional function of an implantable cardiac device (eg, implantable cardioverter-defibrillator) or a function of a stand-alone device. When ICM functionality is included in an ICD device, the ICM data and the ICD heart rhythm data such as sensing, pacing and tachycardia detection therapy are distinct and therefore, the monitoring processes are distinct.

Implantable cardioverter-defibrillator (ICD): an implantable device that provides high-energy and low-energy stimulation to one or more chambers of the heart to terminate rapid heart rhythms called tachycardia or fibrillation. ICDs also have pacemaker functions to treat slow heart rhythms called bradycardia. In addition to the tachycardia and bradycardia functions, the ICD may or may not include the functionality of an implantable cardiovascular monitor or an implantable loop recorder.

Implantable loop recorder (ILR): an implantable device that continuously records the electrocardiographic rhythm triggered automatically by rapid and slow heart rates or by the patient during a symptomatic episode. The ILR function may be the only function of the device or it may be part of a pacemaker or implantable cardioverter-defibrillator device. The data are stored and transmitted to the physician by either local telemetry or remotely to an Internet based file server or surveillance technician.

►*Interrogation device evaluation:* an evaluation of an implantable device such as a cardiac pacemaker, implantable cardioverter-defibrillator, implantable cardiovascular monitor, or implantable loop recorder. Using an office, hospital, or emergency room instrument or via a remote interrogation system, stored and measured information about the lead(s) when present, sensor(s) when present, battery and the implanted device function, as well as data collected about the patient's heart rhythm and heart rate is retrieved. The retrieved information is evaluated to determine the current programming of the device and to evaluate certain aspects of the device function such as battery voltage, lead impedance, tachycardia detection settings, and rhythm treatment settings.◄

The components that must be evaluated for the various types of implantable cardiac devices are listed below. (The required components for both remote and in-person interrogations are the same.)

Pacemaker: Programmed parameters, lead(s), battery, capture and sensing function and heart rhythm.

Implantable cardioverter-defibrillator: Programmed parameters, lead(s), battery, capture and sensing function, presence or absence of therapy for ventricular tachyarrhythmias and underlying heart rhythm.

Implantable cardiovascular monitor: Programmed parameters and analysis of at least one recorded physiologic cardiovascular data element from either internal or external sensors.

Implantable loop recorder: Programmed parameters and the heart rate and rhythm during recorded episodes from both patient initiated and device algorithm detected events, when present.

Interrogation device evaluation (remote): a procedure performed for patients with pacemakers, implantable cardioverter-defibrillators or implantable loop recorders using data obtained remotely. All device functions, including the programmed parameters, lead(s), battery, capture and sensing function, presence or absence of therapy for ventricular tachyarrhythmias (for ICDs) and underlying heart rhythm are evaluated.

The components that must be evaluated for the various types of implantable cardiac devices are listed below. (The required components for both remote and in person interrogations are the same.)

Pacemaker: Programmed parameters, lead(s), battery, capture and sensing function, and heart rhythm.

Implantable cardioverter-defibrillator: Programmed parameters, lead(s), battery, capture and sensing function, presence or absence of therapy for ventricular tachyarrhythmias, and underlying heart rhythm.

Implantable cardiovascular monitor: Programmed parameters and analysis of at least one recorded physiologic cardiovascular data element from either internal or external sensors.

Implantable loop recorder: Programmed parameters and the heart rate and rhythm during recorded episodes from both patient-initiated and device algorithm detected events, when present.

Pacemaker: an implantable device that provides low energy localized stimulation to one or more chambers of the heart to initiate contraction in that chamber.

Peri-procedural device evaluation and programming: an evaluation of an implantable device system (either a pacemaker or implantable cardioverter defibrillator) to adjust the device to settings appropriate for the patient prior to a surgery, procedure, or test. The device system data are interrogated to evaluate the lead(s), sensor(s), and battery in addition to review of stored information,

including patient and system measurements. The device is programmed to settings appropriate for the surgery, procedure, or test, as required. A second evaluation and programming are performed after the surgery, procedure, or test to provide settings appropriate to the post procedural situation, as required. If one provider performs both the pre- and post-evaluation and programming service, the appropriate code, either 93286 or 93287, would be reported two times. If one provider performs the pre-surgical service and a separate provider performs the post-surgical service, each reports either 93286 or 93287 only one time.

Physiologic cardiovascular data elements: data elements from one or more internal sensors (such as right ventricular pressure, left atrial pressure or an index of lung water) and/or external sensors (such as blood pressure or body weight) for patient assessment and management. It does not include ECG rhythm derived data elements.

▶*Programming device evaluation (in person):* a procedure performed for patients with a pacemaker, implantable cardioverter-defibrillator, or implantable loop recorder. All device functions, including the battery, programmable settings and lead(s), when present, are evaluated. To assess capture thresholds, iterative adjustments (eg, progressive changes in pacing output of a pacing lead) of the programmable parameters are conducted. The iterative adjustments provide information that permits the operator to assess and select the most appropriate final program parameters to provide for consistent delivery of the appropriate therapy and to verify the function of the device. The final program parameters may or may not change after evaluation.◀

The programming device evaluation includes all of the components of the interrogation device evaluation (remote) or the interrogation device evaluation (in person), and it includes the selection of patient specific programmed parameters depending on the type of device.

The components that must be evaluated for the various types of programming device evaluations are listed below. (See also required interrogation device evaluation [remote and in person] components above.)

Pacemaker: Programmed parameters, lead(s), battery, capture and sensing function, and heart rhythm. Often, but not always, the sensor rate response, lower and upper heart rates, AV intervals, pacing voltage and pulse duration, sensing value, and diagnostics will be adjusted during a programming evaluation.

Implantable cardioverter-defibrillator: Programmed parameters, lead(s), battery, capture and sensing function, presence or absence of therapy for ventricular tachyarrhythmias and underlying heart rhythm. Often, but not always, the sensor rate response, lower and upper heart rates, AV intervals, pacing voltage and pulse duration, sensing value, and diagnostics will be adjusted during a programming evaluation. In addition, ventricular tachycardia detection and therapies are sometimes altered depending on the interrogated data, patient's rhythm, symptoms, and condition.

Implantable loop recorder: Programmed parameters and the heart rhythm during recorded episodes from both patient initiated and device algorithm detected events. Often, but not always, the tachycardia and bradycardia detection criteria will be adjusted during a programming evaluation.

Transtelephonic rhythm strip pacemaker evaluation: service of transmission of an electrocardiographic rhythm strip over the telephone by the patient using a transmitter and recorded by a receiving location using a receiver/recorder (also commonly known as transtelephonic pacemaker monitoring). The electrocardiographic rhythm strip is recorded both with and without a magnet applied over the pacemaker. The rhythm strip is evaluated for heart rate and rhythm, atrial and ventricular capture (if observed) and atrial and ventricular sensing (if observed). In addition, the battery status of the pacemaker is determined by measurement of the paced rate on the electrocardiographic rhythm strip recorded with the magnet applied.

▲ **93279** Programming device evaluation (in person) with iterative adjustment of the implantable device to test the function of the device and select optimal permanent programmed values with physician analysis, review and report; single lead pacemaker system

➔ *CPT Changes: An Insider's View* 2009, 2010

(Do not report 93279 in conjunction with 93286, 93288)

▲ **93280** dual lead pacemaker system

➔ *CPT Changes: An Insider's View* 2009, 2010

(Do not report 93280 in conjunction with 93286, 93288)

▲ **93281** multiple lead pacemaker system

➔ *CPT Changes: An Insider's View* 2009, 2010

(Do not report 93281 in conjunction with 93286, 93288)

▲ **93282** single lead implantable cardioverter-defibrillator system

➔ *CPT Changes: An Insider's View* 2009, 2010

(Do not report 93282 in conjunction with 93287, 93289, 93745)

▲ **93283** dual lead implantable cardioverter-defibrillator system

➔ *CPT Changes: An Insider's View* 2009, 2010

(Do not report 93283 in conjunction with 93287, 93289)

▲ **93284** multiple lead implantable cardioverter-defibrillator system

➔ *CPT Changes: An Insider's View* 2009, 2010

(Do not report 93284 in conjunction with 93287, 93289)

▲ **93285** implantable loop recorder system

➔ *CPT Changes: An Insider's View* 2009, 2010

►(Do not report 93285 in conjunction with 33282, 93279-93284, 93291)◄

▲ **93286** Peri-procedural device evaluation (in person) and programming of device system parameters before or after a surgery, procedure, or test with physician analysis, review and report; single, dual, or multiple lead pacemaker system

➔ *CPT Changes: An Insider's View* 2009, 2010

(Report 93286 once before and once after surgery, procedure, or test, when device evaluation and programming is performed before and after surgery, procedure, or test)

(Do not report 93286 in conjunction with 93279-93281, 93288)

▲ **93287** single, dual, or multiple lead implantable cardioverter-defibrillator system

➔ *CPT Changes: An Insider's View* 2009, 2010

(Report 93287 once before and once after surgery, procedure, or test, when device evaluation and programming is performed before and after surgery, procedure, or test)

(Do not report 93287 in conjunction with 93282-93284, 93289)

93288 Interrogation device evaluation (in person) with physician analysis, review and report, includes connection, recording and disconnection per patient encounter; single, dual, or multiple lead pacemaker system

➔ *CPT Changes: An Insider's View* 2009

(Do not report 93288 in conjunction with 93279-93281, 93286, 93294, 93296)

93289 single, dual, or multiple lead implantable cardioverter-defibrillator system, including analysis of heart rhythm derived data elements

➔ *CPT Changes: An Insider's View* 2009

(For monitoring physiologic cardiovascular data elements derived from an ICD, use 93290)

(Do not report 93289 in conjunction with 93282-93284, 93287, 93295, 93296)

93290 implantable cardiovascular monitor system, including analysis of 1 or more recorded physiologic cardiovascular data elements from all internal and external sensors

➔ *CPT Changes: An Insider's View* 2009

(For heart rhythm derived data elements, use 93289)

(Do not report 93290 in conjunction with 93297, 93299)

93291 implantable loop recorder system, including heart rhythm derived data analysis

➔ *CPT Changes: An Insider's View* 2009

(Do not report 93291 in conjunction with 33282, 93288-93290, 93298, 93299)

93292 wearable defibrillator system

→ *CPT Changes: An Insider's View* 2009

(Do not report 93292 in conjunction with 93745)

93293 Transtelephonic rhythm strip pacemaker evaluation(s) single, dual, or multiple lead pacemaker system, includes recording with and without magnet application with physician analysis, review and report(s), up to 90 days

→ *CPT Changes: An Insider's View* 2009

(Do not report 93293 in conjunction with 93294)

(For in person evaluation, see 93040, 93041, 93042)

(Report 93293 only once per 90 days)

93294 Interrogation device evaluation(s) (remote), up to 90 days; single, dual, or multiple lead pacemaker system with interim physician analysis, review(s) and report(s)

→ *CPT Changes: An Insider's View* 2009

(Do not report 93294 in conjunction with 93288, 93293)

(Report 93294 only once per 90 days)

93295 single, dual, or multiple lead implantable cardioverter-defibrillator system with interim physician analysis, review(s) and report(s)

→ *CPT Changes: An Insider's View* 2009

(For remote monitoring of physiologic cardiovascular data elements derived from an ICD, use 93297)

(Do not report 93295 in conjunction with 93289)

(Report 93295 only once per 90 days)

93296 single, dual, or multiple lead pacemaker system or implantable cardioverter-defibrillator system, remote data acquisition(s), receipt of transmissions and technician review, technical support and distribution of results

→ *CPT Changes: An Insider's View* 2009

(Do not report 93296 in conjunction with 93288, 93289, 93299)

(Report 93296 only once per 90 days)

93297 Interrogation device evaluation(s), (remote) up to 30 days; implantable cardiovascular monitor system, including analysis of 1 or more recorded physiologic cardiovascular data elements from all internal and external sensors, physician analysis, review(s) and report(s)

→ *CPT Changes: An Insider's View* 2009

(For heart rhythm derived data elements, use 93295)

(Do not report 93297 in conjunction with 93290, 93298)

(Report 93297 only once per 30 days)

93298 implantable loop recorder system, including analysis of recorded heart rhythm data, physician analysis, review(s) and report(s)

→ *CPT Changes: An Insider's View* 2009

▶(Do not report 93298 in conjunction with 33282, 93291, 93297)◀

(Report 93298 only once per 30 days)

93299 implantable cardiovascular monitor system or implantable loop recorder system, remote data acquisition(s), receipt of transmissions and technician review, technical support and distribution of results

→ *CPT Changes: An Insider's View* 2009

(Do not report 93299 in conjunction with 93290, 93291, 93296)

(Report 93299 only once per 30 days)

Echocardiography

Echocardiography includes obtaining ultrasonic signals from the heart and great vessels, with real time image and/or Doppler ultrasonic signal documentation, with interpretation and report. When interpretation is performed separately, use modifier 26.

▶A complete transthoracic echocardiogram without spectral or color flow Doppler (93307) is a comprehensive procedure that includes 2-dimensional and, when performed, selected M-mode examination of the left and right atria, left and right ventricles, the aortic, mitral, and tricuspid valves, the pericardium, and adjacent portions of the aorta. Multiple views are required to obtain a complete functional and anatomic evaluation, and appropriate measurements are obtained and recorded. Despite significant effort, identification and measurement of some structures may not always be possible. In such instances, the reason that an element could not be visualized must be documented. Additional structures that may be visualized (eg, pulmonary veins, pulmonary artery, pulmonic valve, inferior vena cava) would be included as part of the service.

A complete transthoracic echocardiogram with spectral and color flow Doppler (93306) is a comprehensive procedure that includes spectral Doppler and color flow Doppler in addition to the 2-dimensional and selected M-mode examinations, when performed. Spectral Doppler (93320, 93321) and color flow Doppler (93325) provide information regarding intracardiac blood flow and hemodynamics.◀

A follow-up or limited echocardiographic study (93308) is an examination that does not evaluate or document the attempt to evaluate all the structures that comprise the complete echocardiographic exam. This is typically limited to, or performed in follow-up of a focused clinical concern.

In stress echocardiography, echocardiographic images are recorded from multiple cardiac windows before, after, and in some protocols, during stress. The stress is achieved by (1) walking on a treadmill; (2) using a bicycle (supine or upright); or (3) the administration of pharmacological agents that either simulate exercise (by increasing heart rate, blood pressure, or myocardial contractility) or alter coronary flow (vasodilation). The patient's ECG, heart rate, and blood pressure are monitored at baseline, throughout the procedure and during recovery. Reports are prepared to evaluate (1) the duration of stress, the reason for stopping, and the hemodynamic response to stress; (2) the electrocardiographic response to stress; and (3) the echocardiographic response to stress.

►When a stress echocardiogram is performed with a complete cardiovascular stress test (93015) (continuous electrocardiographic monitoring, physician supervision, interpretation and report), use 93351. Code 93350 is used to report the performance and interpretation of a stress echocardiogram only, with the components of the cardiovascular stress test reported separately using the appropriate codes (93016–93018).◄

When left ventricular endocardial borders cannot be adequately identified by standard echocardiographic imaging, echocardiographic contrast may be infused intravenously both at rest and with stress to achieve that purpose. Code 93352 is used to report the administration of echocardiographic contrast agent in conjunction with the stress echocardiography codes (93350 or 93351). Supply of contrast agent and/or drugs used for pharmacological stress is reported separately in addition to the procedure code.

Report of an echocardiographic study, whether complete or limited, includes an interpretation of all obtained information, documentation of all clinically relevant findings including quantitative measurements obtained, plus a description of any recognized abnormalities. Pertinent images, videotape, and/or digital data are archived for permanent storage and are available for subsequent review. Use of echocardiography not meeting these criteria is not separately reportable.

Use of ultrasound, without thorough evaluation of organ(s) or anatomic region, image documentation and final, written report, is not separately reportable.

(For fetal echocardiography, see 76825-76828)

93303   Transthoracic echocardiography for congenital cardiac anomalies; complete
➔ *CPT Assistant* Nov 97:44, Dec 97:5, Sep 05:10-11, Mar 08:4
➔ *Clinical Examples in Radiology* Fall 06:9-10

93304   follow-up or limited study
➔ *CPT Assistant* Nov 97:44, Dec 97:5
➔ *Clinical Examples in Radiology* Fall 06:9-10

93306   Echocardiography, transthoracic, real-time with image documentation (2D), includes M-mode recording, when performed, complete, with spectral Doppler echocardiography, and with color flow Doppler echocardiography
➔ *CPT Changes: An Insider's View* 2009

(For transthoracic echocardiography without spectral and color Doppler, use 93307)

93307   Echocardiography, transthoracic, real-time with image documentation (2D), includes M-mode recording, when performed, complete, without spectral or color Doppler echocardiography
➔ *CPT Assistant* Dec 97:5, Sep 05:11; *CPT Changes: An Insider's View* 2009
➔ *Clinical Examples in Radiology* Fall 06:9-10

(Do not report 93307 in conjunction with 93320, 93321, 93325)

93308   Echocardiography, transthoracic, real-time with image documentation (2D), includes M-mode recording, when performed, follow-up or limited study
➔ *CPT Assistant* Dec 97:5, Sep 05:11; *CPT Changes: An Insider's View* 2009
➔ *Clinical Examples in Radiology* Fall 06:9-10

⊙ **93312**   Echocardiography, transesophageal, real-time with image documentation (2D) (with or without M-mode recording); including probe placement, image acquisition, interpretation and report
➔ *CPT Assistant* Dec 97:5, Jan 00:10

Transesophageal Echocardiography (TEE)
93312-93318

An endoscopic ultrasound transducer is passed through the mouth into the esophagus and 2-dimensional images are obtained from the posterior aspect of the heart.

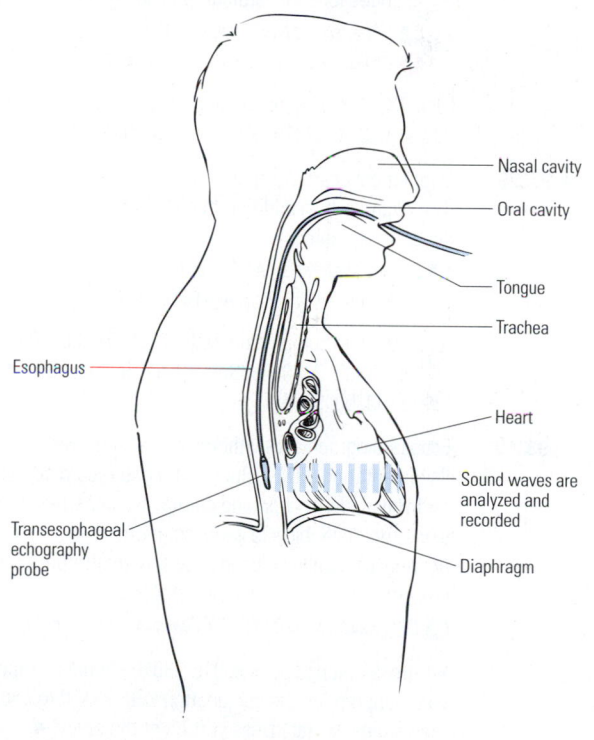

Nasal cavity

Oral cavity

Tongue

Trachea

Esophagus

Heart

Transesophageal echography probe

Sound waves are analyzed and recorded

Diaphragm

⊙ **93313**   placement of transesophageal probe only
➔ *CPT Assistant* Dec 97:5, Mar 08:4

⊙ **93314**   image acquisition, interpretation and report only
➔ *CPT Assistant* Dec 97:5, Jan 00:10

⊙ **93315** Transesophageal echocardiography for congenital cardiac anomalies; including probe placement, image acquisition, interpretation and report

➔ *CPT Assistant* Nov 97:44, Dec 97:5

⊙ **93316** placement of transesophageal probe only

➔ *CPT Assistant* Nov 97:44, Dec 97:5

⊙ **93317** image acquisition, interpretation and report only

➔ *CPT Assistant* Nov 97:44, Dec 97:5

⊙ **93318** Echocardiography, transesophageal (TEE) for monitoring purposes, including probe placement, real time 2-dimensional image acquisition and interpretation leading to ongoing (continuous) assessment of (dynamically changing) cardiac pumping function and to therapeutic measures on an immediate time basis

➔ *CPT Assistant* Mar 08:4; *CPT Changes: An Insider's View* 2001

+ **93320** Doppler echocardiography, pulsed wave and/or continuous wave with spectral display (List separately in addition to codes for echocardiographic imaging); complete

➔ *CPT Assistant* Nov 97:44, Dec 97:5, Mar 08:4

➔ *Clinical Examples in Radiology* Fall 06:9-10

(Use 93320 in conjunction with 93303, 93304, 93312, 93314, 93315, 93317, 93350, 93351)

+ **93321** follow-up or limited study (List separately in addition to codes for echocardiographic imaging)

➔ *CPT Assistant* Nov 97:44, Dec 97:5

➔ *Clinical Examples in Radiology* Fall 06:9-10

(Use 93321 in conjunction with 93303, 93304, 93308, 93312, 93314, 93315, 93317, 93350, 93351)

+ **93325** Doppler echocardiography color flow velocity mapping (List separately in addition to codes for echocardiography)

➔ *CPT Assistant* Nov 97:44, Dec 97:5

➔ *Clinical Examples in Radiology* Fall 06:9-10

(Use 93325 in conjunction with 76825, 76826, 76827, 76828, 93303, 93304, 93308, 93312, 93314, 93315, 93317, 93350, 93351)

93350 Echocardiography, transthoracic, real-time with image documentation (2D), includes M-mode recording, when performed, during rest and cardiovascular stress test using treadmill, bicycle exercise and/or pharmacologically induced stress, with interpretation and report;

➔ *CPT Assistant* Aug 02:11; *CPT Changes: An Insider's View* 2009

►(Stress testing codes 93016-93018 should be reported, when appropriate, in conjunction with 93350 to capture the cardiovascular stress portion of the study)◄

►(Do not report 93350 in conjunction with 93015)◄

93351 including performance of continuous electrocardiographic monitoring, with physician supervision

➔ *CPT Changes: An Insider's View* 2009

(Do not report 93351 in conjunction with 93015-93018, 93350)

+ **93352** Use of echocardiographic contrast agent during stress echocardiography (List separately in addition to code for primary procedure)

➔ *CPT Changes: An Insider's View* 2009

(Do not report 93352 more than once per stress echocardiogram)

(Use 93352 in conjunction with 93350, 93351)

Cardiac Catheterization

Cardiac catheterization is a diagnostic medical procedure which includes introduction, positioning and repositioning of catheter(s), when necessary, recording of intracardiac and intravascular pressure, obtaining blood samples for measurement of blood gases or dilution curves and cardiac output measurements (Fick or other method, with or without rest and exercise and/or studies) with or without electrode catheter placement, final evaluation and report of procedure. When selective injection procedures are performed without a preceding cardiac catheterization, these services should be reported using codes in the Vascular Injection Procedures section, 36011-36015 and 36215-36218.

When coronary artery, arterial coronary conduit or venous bypass graft angiography is performed without concomitant left heart cardiac catheterization, use 93508. Injection procedures 93539, 93540, 93544, and 93545 represent separate identifiable services and may be reported in conjunction with one another in addition to 93508, as appropriate. To report imaging supervision, interpretation and report in conjunction with 93508, use 93556.

Modifier 51 should not be appended to 93503, 93539, 93540, 93544-93556.

➔ *CPT Assistant* Nov 98:33

⊙ **93501** Right heart catheterization

➔ *CPT Assistant* Spring 94:24, Jan 98:11, Apr 98:2, Apr 00:10, Mar 08:4; *CPT Changes: An Insider's View* 2008

Right Heart Catheterization
93501

The physician introduces a cardiac catheter into the venous system. The catheter is directed into the right atrium, right ventricle, and pulmonary artery.

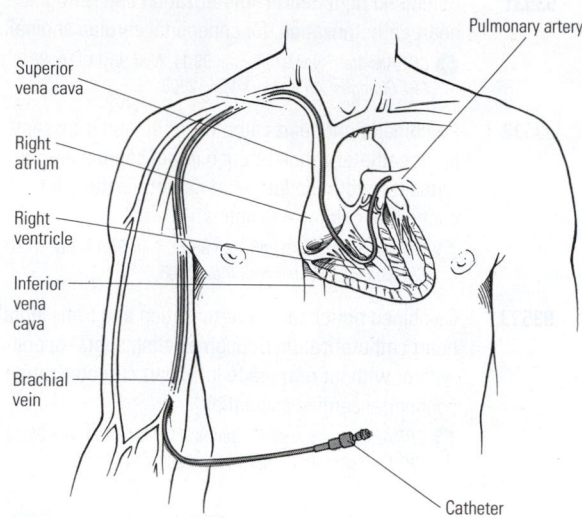

Catheter is advanced retrograde through the arterial system to the ascending aorta; pressures are measured in the aortic root; the catheter is manipulated using fluoroscopic guidance into the ostium of a coronary artery, arterial bypass conduit, or venous coronary bypass graft.

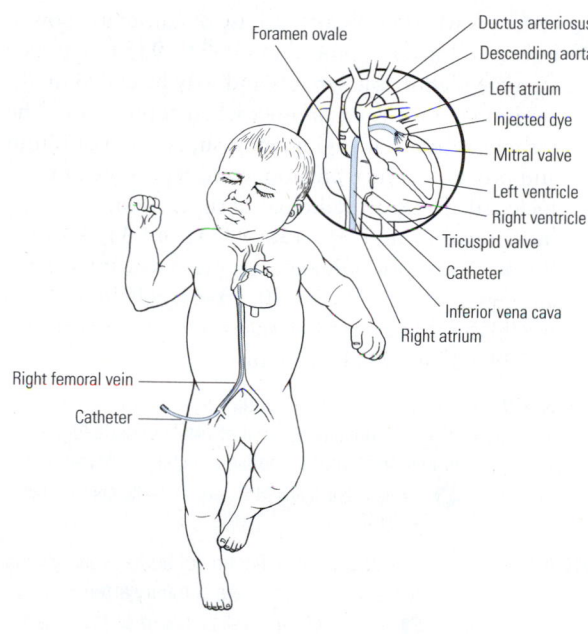

(For bundle of His recording, use 93600)

⊘ **93503**   Insertion and placement of flow directed catheter (eg, Swan-Ganz) for monitoring purposes

➜ *CPT Assistant* Winter 91:3, Fall 95:8, Feb 97:5, Apr 98:2, Mar 08:4

(For subsequent monitoring, see 99356-99357)

⊙ **93505**   Endomyocardial biopsy

➜ *CPT Assistant* Apr 98:2, Apr 00:10; *CPT Changes: An Insider's View* 2008

⊙ **93508**   Catheter placement in coronary artery(s), arterial coronary conduit(s), and/or venous coronary bypass graft(s) for coronary angiography without concomitant left heart catheterization

➜ *CPT Assistant* Nov 97:44-45, Jan 98:11, Apr 98:2, Apr 00:10, Aug 00:11, Dec 07:15; *CPT Changes: An Insider's View* 2008

(93508 is to be used only when left heart catheterization 93510, 93511, 93524, 93526 is not performed)

(93508 is to be used only once per procedure)

Coronary Angiography Without Concomitant Left Heart Catheterization
93508

Cardiac catheterization procedure performed wherein the catheter does not cross the aortic valve into the left ventricle (left heart catheterization).

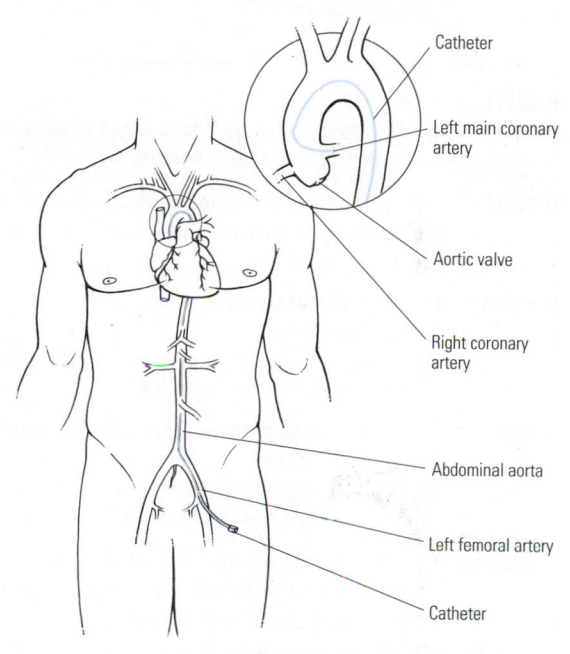

(To report transcatheter placement of radiation delivery device for coronary intravascular brachytherapy, use 92974)

►(For intravascular radioelement application, see 77785-77787)◄

⊙ **93510**   Left heart catheterization, retrograde, from the brachial artery, axillary artery or femoral artery; percutaneous

➜ *CPT Assistant* Spring 94:26, Nov 97:44-45, Jan 98:11, Apr 98:2; *CPT Changes: An Insider's View* 2008

Left Heart Catheterization
93510

A catheter is inserted into the arterial system and then into the left ventricle.

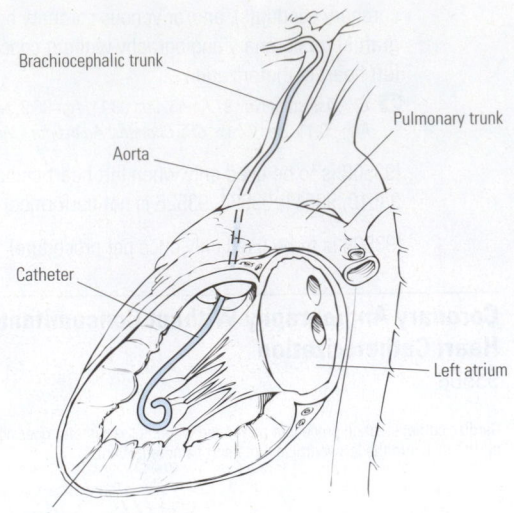

⊙ **93511**　　by cutdown
> *CPT Assistant* Spring 94:24, Nov 97:44-45, Jan 98:11, Apr 98:2; *CPT Changes: An Insider's View* 2008

⊙ **93514**　　Left heart catheterization by left ventricular puncture
> *CPT Assistant* Spring 94:24, Jan 98:11, Apr 98:2; *CPT Changes: An Insider's View* 2008

⊙ **93524**　　Combined transseptal and retrograde left heart catheterization
> *CPT Assistant* Spring 94:24, Nov 97:44-45, Jan 98:11, Apr 98:2; *CPT Changes: An Insider's View* 2008

⊙ **93526**　　Combined right heart catheterization and retrograde left heart catheterization
> *CPT Assistant* Spring 94:28, Nov 97:44-45, Jan 98:11, Apr 98:2; *CPT Changes: An Insider's View* 2008

⊙ **93527**　　Combined right heart catheterization and transseptal left heart catheterization through intact septum (with or without retrograde left heart catheterization)
> *CPT Assistant* Jan 98:11, Apr 98:2; *CPT Changes: An Insider's View* 2008

⊙ **93528**　　Combined right heart catheterization with left ventricular puncture (with or without retrograde left heart catheterization)
> *CPT Assistant* Jan 98:11, Apr 98:2, Mar 08:4; *CPT Changes: An Insider's View* 2008

⊙ **93529**　　Combined right heart catheterization and left heart catheterization through existing septal opening (with or without retrograde left heart catheterization)
> *CPT Assistant* Jan 98:11, Apr 98:2, Mar 08:4; *CPT Changes: An Insider's View* 2008

⊙ **93530**　　Right heart catheterization, for congenital cardiac anomalies
> *CPT Assistant* Nov 97:45, Jan 98:11, Mar 98:11, Apr 98:3, 6-7; *CPT Changes: An Insider's View* 2008

93531　　Combined right heart catheterization and retrograde left heart catheterization, for congenital cardiac anomalies
> *CPT Assistant* Nov 97:45, Jan 98:11, Mar 98:11, Apr 98:8, 10-11; *CPT Changes: An Insider's View* 2008

93532　　Combined right heart catheterization and transseptal left heart catheterization through intact septum with or without retrograde left heart catheterization, for congenital cardiac anomalies
> *CPT Assistant* Nov 97:45, Jan 98:11, Mar 98:11, Apr 98:10-11; *CPT Changes: An Insider's View* 2008

93533　　Combined right heart catheterization and transseptal left heart catheterization through existing septal opening, with or without retrograde left heart catheterization, for congenital cardiac anomalies
> *CPT Assistant* Nov 97:45, Jan 98:11, Mar 98:11, Apr 98:12-13; *CPT Changes: An Insider's View* 2008

Injection Procedures

When injection procedures are performed in conjunction with cardiac catheterization, these services do not include introduction of catheters but do include repositioning of catheters when necessary and use of automatic power injectors. Injection procedures 93539-93545 represent separate identifiable services and may be coded in conjunction with one another when appropriate. The technical details of angiography, supervision of filming and processing, interpretation, and report are not included. To report radiological supervision, interpretation, and report for 93542 or 93543, use 93555. To report radiological supervision, interpretation, and report for 93539, 93540, 93541, 93544, or 93545, use 93556. Modifier 51 should not be appended to 93539, 93540, 93544-93556.

⊙⊘ **93539**　　Injection procedure during cardiac catheterization; for selective opacification of arterial conduits (eg, internal mammary), whether native or used for bypass
> *CPT Assistant* Spring 94:27, Nov 97:44-45, Apr 98:1, Oct 01:11, Dec 07:15

⊙⊘ **93540**　　for selective opacification of aortocoronary venous bypass grafts, 1 or more coronary arteries
> *CPT Assistant* Spring 94:27, Nov 97:44-45, Apr 98:3

⊙ **93541**　　for pulmonary angiography
> *CPT Assistant* Spring 94:28, Nov 97:44-45, Apr 98:3, Jan 01:16; *CPT Changes: An Insider's View* 2008

⊙ **93542**   for selective right ventricular or right atrial
                angiography
                → *CPT Assistant* Spring 94:24, Nov 97:44-45, Apr 98:3,
                   Jan 01:16; *CPT Changes: An Insider's View* 2008

⊙ **93543**   for selective left ventricular or left atrial angiography
                → *CPT Assistant* Spring 94:28, Nov 97:44-45, Apr 98:3,
                   Jan 01:16; *CPT Changes: An Insider's View* 2008

⊙⊘ **93544**   for aortography
                → *CPT Assistant* Spring 94:28, Nov 97:44-45, Apr 98:3,
                   Jan 01:16

⊙⊘ **93545**   for selective coronary angiography (injection of
                radiopaque material may be by hand)
                → *CPT Assistant* Spring 94:28, Nov 97:44-45, Apr 98:3,
                   Jan 01:16, Nov 02:10, Dec 07:15

⊙⊘ **93555**   Imaging supervision, interpretation and report for
                injection procedure(s) during cardiac catheterization;
                ventricular and/or atrial angiography
                → *CPT Assistant* Spring 94:28, Oct 97:10, Nov 97:44-45, Apr 98:3,
                   11-12

⊙⊘ **93556**   pulmonary angiography, aortography, and/or selective
                coronary angiography including venous bypass grafts
                and arterial conduits (whether native or used in
                bypass)
                → *CPT Assistant* Spring 94:28, Oct 97:10, Nov 97:44-45,
                   Apr 98:3, 11-12

⊙ **93561**   Indicator dilution studies such as dye or thermal dilution,
                including arterial and/or venous catheterization; with
                cardiac output measurement (separate procedure)
                → *CPT Assistant* Winter 91:25, Summer 95:2, Aug 00:2, Feb 07:10,
                   Jul 07:1

⊙ **93562**   subsequent measurement of cardiac output
                → *CPT Assistant* Winter 91:25, Summer 95:2, Aug 00:2,
                   Feb 07:10, Jul 07:1

                (93561, 93562 are not to be used with cardiac
                catheterization codes)

                (For radioisotope method of cardiac output, see 78472,
                78473, or 78481)

⊙+ **93571**   Intravascular Doppler velocity and/or pressure derived
                coronary flow reserve measurement (coronary vessel or
                graft) during coronary angiography including
                pharmacologically induced stress; initial vessel (List
                separately in addition to code for primary procedure)
                → *CPT Assistant* Nov 98:33, Apr 00:2, Mar 08:4

Intravascular Distal Blood Flow Velocity
93571

A Doppler guidewire is positioned in a proximal coronary artery with the transducer
beam parallel to blood flow to measure blood flow velocity.

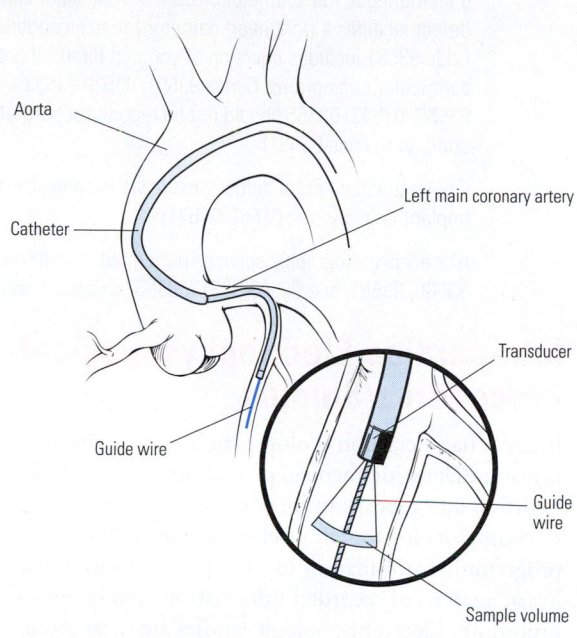

⊙+ **93572**   each additional vessel (List separately in addition to
                code for primary procedure)
                → *CPT Assistant* Nov 98:34, Apr 00:2

                (Intravascular distal coronary blood flow velocity
                measurements include all Doppler transducer
                manipulations and repositioning within the specific
                vessel being examined, during coronary angiography or
                therapeutic intervention [eg, angioplasty])

                (For unlisted cardiac catheterization procedure, use
                93799)

Repair of Septal Defect

93580   Percutaneous transcatheter closure of congenital
                interatrial communication (ie, Fontan fenestration, atrial
                septal defect) with implant
                → *CPT Assistant* Mar 03:23; *CPT Changes: An Insider's View* 2003

                (Percutaneous transcatheter closure of atrial septal
                defect includes a right heart catheterization procedure.
                Code 93580 includes injection of contrast for atrial and
                ventricular angiograms. Codes 93501, 93529-93533,
                93539, 93543, 93555 should not be reported separately in
                addition to code 93580)

93581   Percutaneous transcatheter closure of a congenital ventricular septal defect with implant

➜ *CPT Assistant* Mar 03:23, Mar 08:4; *CPT Changes: An Insider's View* 2003

(Percutaneous transcatheter closure of ventricular septal defect includes a right heart catheterization procedure. Code 93581 includes injection of contrast for atrial and ventricular angiograms. Codes 93501, 93529-93533, 93539, 93543, 93555 should not be reported separately in addition to code 93581)

(For ventricular septal defect closure via transmyocardial implant delivery, see 0166T, 0167T)

(For echocardiographic services performed in addition to 93580, 93581, see 93303-93317, 93662 as appropriate)

Intracardiac Electrophysiological Procedures/Studies

Intracardiac electrophysiologic studies (EPS) are an invasive diagnostic medical procedure which include the insertion and repositioning of electrode catheters, recording of electrograms before and during pacing or programmed stimulation of multiple locations in the heart, analysis of recorded information, and report of the procedure. Electrophysiologic studies are most often performed with two or more electrode catheters. In many circumstances, patients with arrhythmias are evaluated and treated at the same encounter. In this situation, a diagnostic *electrophysiologic study* is performed, induced tachycardia(s) are *mapped*, and on the basis of the diagnostic and mapping information, the tissue is *ablated*. Electrophysiologic study(ies), mapping, and ablation represent distinctly different procedures, requiring individual reporting whether performed on the same or subsequent dates.

Definitions

Arrhythmia Induction: In most electrophysiologic studies, an attempt is made to induce arrhythmia(s) from single or multiple sites within the heart. Arrhythmia induction is achieved by performing pacing at different rates, programmed stimulation (introduction of critically timed electrical impulses), and other techniques. Because arrhythmia induction occurs via the same catheter(s) inserted for the electrophysiologic study(ies), catheter insertion and temporary pacemaker codes are not additionally reported. Codes 93600-93603, 93610-93612 and 93618 are used to describe unusual situations where there may be recording, pacing or an attempt at arrhythmia induction from only one site in the heart. Code 93619 describes only evaluation of the sinus node, atrioventricular node and His-Purkinje conduction system, without arrhythmia induction. Codes 93620-93624 and 93640-93642 all include recording, pacing and attempted arrhythmia induction from one or more site(s) in the heart.

Mapping: Mapping is a distinct procedure performed in addition to a diagnostic electrophysiologic procedure and should be separately reported using 93609 or 93613. Do not report standard mapping (93609) in addition to 3D mapping (93613). When a tachycardia is induced, the site of tachycardia origination or its electrical path through the heart is often defined by mapping. Mapping creates a multidimensional depiction of a tachycardia by recording multiple electrograms obtained sequentially or simultaneously from multiple catheter sites in the heart. Depending upon the technique, certain types of mapping catheters may be repositioned from point-to-point within the heart, allowing sequential recording from the various sites to construct maps. Other types of mapping catheters allow mapping without a point-to-point technique by allowing simultaneous recording from many electrodes on the same catheter and computer-assisted three dimensional reconstruction of the tachycardia activation sequence.

Ablation: Once the part of the heart involved in the tachycardia is localized, the tachycardia may be treated by ablation (the delivery of a radiofrequency energy to the area to selectively destroy cardiac tissue). Ablation procedures (93651-93652) may be performed: independently on a date subsequent to a diagnostic electrophysiologic study and mapping; or, at the time a diagnostic electrophysiologic study, tachycardia(s) induction and mapping is performed. When an electrophysiologic study, mapping, and ablation are performed on the same date, each procedure should be separately reported. In reporting catheter ablation, 93651 and/or 93652 should be reported once to describe ablation of cardiac arrhythmias, regardless of the number of arrhythmias ablated.

Modifier 51 should not be appended to 93600-93603, 93610, 93612, 93615-93618, 93631.

⊘ **93600**   Bundle of His recording

➜ *CPT Assistant* Summer 94:12, Aug 97:9, Apr 04:9, Jul 04:13, Aug 05:13, Dec 07:16, Mar 08:4

⊘ **93602**   Intra-atrial recording

➜ *CPT Assistant* Summer 94:12, Aug 97:9, Apr 04:9, Jul 04:13, Aug 05:13

⊘ **93603**   Right ventricular recording

➜ *CPT Assistant* Summer 94:12, Aug 97:9, Apr 04:9, Jul 04:13, Aug 05:13

⊙+ **93609**   Intraventricular and/or intra-atrial mapping of tachycardia site(s) with catheter manipulation to record from multiple sites to identify origin of tachycardia (List separately in addition to code for primary procedure)

➜ *CPT Assistant* Summer 94:12, Aug 97:9, Apr 04:9, Aug 05:13; *CPT Changes: An Insider's View* 2002

(Use 93609 in conjunction with 93620, 93651, 93652)

(Do not report 93609 in addition to 93613)

⊘ **93610**   Intra-atrial pacing

➜ *CPT Assistant* Summer 94:12, Aug 97:9, Apr 04:9, Jul 04:13

⊘ **93612** Intraventricular pacing
→ *CPT Assistant* Summer 94:12, Aug 97:9, Apr 04:9, Jul 04:13

(Do not report 93612 in conjunction with 93620-93622)

⊙+ **93613** Intracardiac electrophysiologic 3-dimensional mapping (List separately in addition to code for primary procedure)
→ *CPT Assistant* Apr 04:8, Aug 05:13; *CPT Changes: An Insider's View* 2002

(Use 93613 in conjunction with 93620, 93651, 93652)

(Do not report 93613 in addition to 93609)

⊙⊘ **93615** Esophageal recording of atrial electrogram with or without ventricular electrogram(s);
→ *CPT Assistant* Summer 94:12, Aug 97:9, Apr 04:9, Aug 05:13

⊙⊘ **93616**   with pacing
→ *CPT Assistant* Summer 94:12, Aug 97:9, Apr 04:9, Aug 05:13

⊙⊘ **93618** Induction of arrhythmia by electrical pacing
→ *CPT Assistant* Summer 94:12, Aug 97:9, Oct 97:10, Apr 99:10, Jun 00:5, Nov 00:9, Apr 04:9, Jul 04:13, Aug 05:13, Dec 07:16

(For intracardiac phonocardiogram, use 93799)

⊙ **93619** Comprehensive electrophysiologic evaluation with right atrial pacing and recording, right ventricular pacing and recording, His bundle recording, including insertion and repositioning of multiple electrode catheters, without induction or attempted induction of arrhythmia
→ *CPT Assistant* Aug 97:9, Oct 97:10, Nov 00:9, Apr 04:9, Jul 04:13, Aug 05:13, Dec 07:16; *CPT Changes: An Insider's View* 2002, 2008

(Do not report 93619 in conjunction with 93600, 93602, 93610, 93612, 93618, or 93620-93622)

⊙ **93620** Comprehensive electrophysiologic evaluation including insertion and repositioning of multiple electrode catheters with induction or attempted induction of arrhythmia; with right atrial pacing and recording, right ventricular pacing and recording, His bundle recording
→ *CPT Assistant* Summer 94:12, Aug 97:9, Oct 97:10, Jul 98:10, Aug 98:7, Nov 00:9, Apr 04:9, Jul 04:13, Aug 05:13, Dec 07:16, Oct 08:10; *CPT Changes: An Insider's View* 2002, 2003, 2008

(Do not report 93620 in conjunction with 93600, 93602, 93610, 93612, 93618 or 93619)

⊙+ **93621**   with left atrial pacing and recording from coronary sinus or left atrium (List separately in addition to code for primary procedure)
→ *CPT Assistant* Summer 94:12, Aug 97:9, Oct 97:10, Jul 98:10, Aug 98:7, Nov 98:34, Nov 00:9, Apr 04:9, Jul 04:13, Aug 05:13, Dec 07:16, Oct 08:10; *CPT Changes: An Insider's View* 2002

(Use 93621 in conjunction with 93620)

⊙+ **93622**   with left ventricular pacing and recording (List separately in addition to code for primary procedure)
→ *CPT Assistant* Summer 94:14, Aug 97:9, Oct 97:10, Jul 98:10, Aug 98:7, Nov 98:34, Nov 00:9, Apr 04:9, Jul 04:13, Aug 05:13, Dec 07:16, Mar 08:4; *CPT Changes: An Insider's View* 2002

(Use 93622 in conjunction with 93620)

+ **93623** Programmed stimulation and pacing after intravenous drug infusion (List separately in addition to code for primary procedure)
→ *CPT Assistant* Summer 94:14, Aug 97:9, Nov 00:9, Aug 05:13, Dec 07:16, Oct 08:10

(Use 93623 in conjunction with 93619, 93620)

⊙ **93624** Electrophysiologic follow-up study with pacing and recording to test effectiveness of therapy, including induction or attempted induction of arrhythmia
→ *CPT Assistant* Summer 94:14, Aug 97:9, Nov 00:9, Aug 05:13, Dec 07:16; *CPT Changes: An Insider's View* 2008

⊘ **93631** Intra-operative epicardial and endocardial pacing and mapping to localize the site of tachycardia or zone of slow conduction for surgical correction
→ *CPT Assistant* Summer 94:14, Aug 97:9, Nov 00:9, Aug 05:13, Dec 07:16

(For operative ablation of an arrhythmogenic focus or pathway by a separate provider, see 33250-33261)

⊙ **93640** Electrophysiologic evaluation of single or dual chamber pacing cardioverter-defibrillator leads including defibrillation threshold evaluation (induction of arrhythmia, evaluation of sensing and pacing for arrhythmia termination) at time of initial implantation or replacement;
→ *CPT Assistant* Summer 94:14, Aug 97:9, Apr 99:10, Nov 99:50, Nov 00:9, Aug 05:13; *CPT Changes: An Insider's View* 2000, 2008

⊙ **93641**   with testing of single or dual chamber pacing cardioverter-defibrillator pulse generator
→ *CPT Assistant* Summer 94:14, Aug 97:9, Apr 99:10, Nov 99:50, Jun 00:5, Jul 00:5, Nov 00:9, Aug 05:13; *CPT Changes: An Insider's View* 2000, 2008

►(For subsequent or periodic electronic analysis and/or reprogramming of single or dual chamber pacing cardioverter-defibrillators, see 93282, 93283, 93289, 93292, 93295, 93642)◄

⊙ **93642** Electrophysiologic evaluation of single or dual chamber pacing cardioverter-defibrillator (includes defibrillation threshold evaluation, induction of arrhythmia, evaluation of sensing and pacing for arrhythmia termination, and programming or reprogramming of sensing or therapeutic parameters)
→ *CPT Assistant* Summer 94:14, Aug 97:9, Nov 99:50, Jun 00:5, Nov 00:9, Aug 05:13; *CPT Changes: An Insider's View* 2000, 2008

⊙ **93650** Intracardiac catheter ablation of atrioventricular node function, atrioventricular conduction for creation of complete heart block, with or without temporary pacemaker placement
→ *CPT Assistant* Summer 94:15, Aug 97:9, Nov 00:9, Aug 05:13; *CPT Changes: An Insider's View* 2008

⊙ **93651** Intracardiac catheter ablation of arrhythmogenic focus; for treatment of supraventricular tachycardia by ablation of fast or slow atrioventricular pathways, accessory atrioventricular connections or other atrial foci, singly or in combination
→ *CPT Assistant* Summer 94:15, Aug 97:9, Nov 00:9, Aug 05:13, Dec 07:16; *CPT Changes: An Insider's View* 2008

⊙ **93652**   for treatment of ventricular tachycardia

➔ *CPT Assistant* Summer 94:15, Aug 97:9, Nov 00:9,
Aug 05:13, Mar 08:4; *CPT Changes: An Insider's View* 2008

93660   Evaluation of cardiovascular function with tilt table
evaluation, with continuous ECG monitoring and
intermittent blood pressure monitoring, with or without
pharmacological intervention

➔ *CPT Changes: An Insider's View* 2008

(For testing of autonomic nervous system function, see
95921-95923)

+ **93662**   Intracardiac echocardiography during
therapeutic/diagnostic intervention, including imaging
supervision and interpretation (List separately in addition
to code for primary procedure)

➔ *CPT Assistant* Mar 03:23; *CPT Changes: An Insider's View* 2001

(Use 93662 in conjunction with 92987, 93527, 93532,
93580, 93581, 93621, 93622, 93651, or 93652, as
appropriate)

(Do not report 92961 in addition to 93662)

Peripheral Arterial Disease Rehabilitation

Peripheral arterial disease (PAD) rehabilitative physical
exercise consists of a series of sessions, lasting 45-60
minutes per session, involving use of either a motorized
treadmill or a track to permit each patient to achieve
symptom-limited claudication. Each session is supervised
by an exercise physiologist or nurse. The supervising
provider monitors the individual patient's claudication
threshold and other cardiovascular limitations for
adjustment of workload. During this supervised
rehabilitation program, the development of new
arrhythmias, symptoms that might suggest angina or the
continued inability of the patient to progress to an
adequate level of exercise may require physician review
and examination of the patient. These physician services
would be separately reported with an appropriate level
E/M service code.

93668   Peripheral arterial disease (PAD) rehabilitation, per
session

➔ *CPT Changes: An Insider's View* 2001

Noninvasive Physiologic Studies and Procedures

(For arterial cannulization and recording of direct arterial
pressure, use 36620)

(For radiographic injection procedures, see 36000-36299)

(For vascular cannulization for hemodialysis, see 36800-
36821)

(For chemotherapy for malignant disease, see 96409-
96549)

(For penile plethysmography, use 54240)

▲ **93701**   Bioimpedance-derived physiologic cardiovascular
analysis

➔ *CPT Assistant* Mar 02:3, Mar 08:4; *CPT Changes: An Insider's
View* 2002, 2010

►(For left ventricular filling pressure indirect
measurement by computerized calibration of the arterial
waveform response to Valsalva, use 93799)◄

93720   Plethysmography, total body; with interpretation and
report

➔ *CPT Assistant* Mar 99:10, Sep 03:15

93721   tracing only, without interpretation and report

➔ *CPT Assistant* Mar 99:10

93722   interpretation and report only

➔ *CPT Assistant* Mar 99:10

(For regional plethysmography, see 93875-93931)

93724   Electronic analysis of antitachycardia pacemaker system
(includes electrocardiographic recording, programming of
device, induction and termination of tachycardia via
implanted pacemaker, and interpretation of recordings)

➔ *CPT Assistant* Summer 94:23

(93727 has been deleted. For programming of
implantable loop recorder, use 93285. For interrogation of
implantable loop recorder, see 93291, 93298)

(93731, 93732 have been deleted. For interrogation of
dual lead pacemaker, see 93288, 93294. For programming
of dual chamber pacemaker, use 93280)

(93733 has been deleted. For transtelephonic rhythm strip
pacemaker, single and dual, or multiple lead pacemaker
evaluation, use 93293)

(93734, 93735 have been deleted. For interrogation of
single lead pacemaker, see 93288, 93294. For
programming of single lead pacemaker, use 93279)

(93736 has been deleted. For transtelephonic rhythm strip
pacemaker, single and dual, or multiple lead pacemaker
evaluation, use 93293)

93740   Temperature gradient studies

(93741, 93742 have been deleted. For interrogation of
single implantable cardioverter-defibrillator [ICD], see
93289, 93295. For programming of single ICD, use 93282.
For interrogation of wearable cardioverter-defibrillator,
use 93292)

(93743, 93744 have been deleted. For interrogation of
dual implantable cardioverter-defibrillator [ICD], see
93289, 93295. For programming of dual ICD, use 93283)

93745   Initial set-up and programming by a physician of
wearable cardioverter-defibrillator includes initial
programming of system, establishing baseline electronic
ECG, transmission of data to data repository, patient
instruction in wearing system and patient reporting of
problems or events

➔ *CPT Changes: An Insider's View* 2005

(Do not report 93745 in conjunction with 93282, 93292)

● **93750**   Interrogation of ventricular assist device (VAD), in person, with physician analysis of device parameters (eg, drivelines, alarms, power surges), review of device function (eg, flow and volume status, septum status, recovery), with programming, if performed, and report
➲ *CPT Changes: An Insider's View* 2010

►(Do not report 93750 in conjunction with 33975, 33976, 33979, 33981-33983)◄

(93760, 93762 have been deleted)

93770   Determination of venous pressure

(For central venous cannulization see 36555-36556, 36500)

93784   Ambulatory blood pressure monitoring, utilizing a system such as magnetic tape and/or computer disk, for 24 hours or longer; including recording, scanning analysis, interpretation and report

93786   recording only

93788   scanning analysis with report

93790   physician review with interpretation and report

Other Procedures

93797   Physician services for outpatient cardiac rehabilitation; without continuous ECG monitoring (per session)

93798   with continuous ECG monitoring (per session)

93799   Unlisted cardiovascular service or procedure
➲ *CPT Assistant* Mar 98:11, Mar 02:10, Nov 05:15, Apr 09:9

Noninvasive Vascular Diagnostic Studies

Vascular studies include patient care required to perform the studies, supervision of the studies and interpretation of study results with copies for patient records of hard copy output with analysis of all data, including bidirectional vascular flow or imaging when provided.

The use of a simple hand-held or other Doppler device that does not produce hard copy output, or that produces a record that does not permit analysis of bidirectional vascular flow, is considered to be part of the physical examination of the vascular system and is not separately reported.

Duplex scan (eg, 93880, 93882) describes an ultrasonic scanning procedure for characterizing the pattern and direction of blood flow in arteries or veins with the production of real-time images integrating B-mode two-dimensional vascular structure, Doppler spectral analysis, and color flow Doppler imaging.

Noninvasive physiologic studies are performed using equipment separate and distinct from the duplex scanner. Codes 93875, 93965, 93922, 93923, and 93924 describe the evaluation of non-imaging physiologic recordings of pressures, Doppler analysis of bi-directional blood flow, plethysmography, and/or oxygen tension measurements appropriate for the anatomic area studied.

Cerebrovascular Arterial Studies

A complete transcranial Doppler (TCD) study (93886) includes ultrasound evaluation of the right and left anterior circulation territories and the posterior circulation territory (to include vertebral arteries and basilar artery). In a limited TCD study (93888) there is ultrasound evaluation of two or fewer of these territories. For TCD, ultrasound evaluation is a reasonable and concerted attempt to identify arterial signals through an acoustic window.

93875   Noninvasive physiologic studies of extracranial arteries, complete bilateral study (eg, periorbital flow direction with arterial compression, ocular pneumoplethysmography, Doppler ultrasound spectral analysis)
➲ *CPT Assistant* Jun 96:9, Dec 97:10, Dec 05:3
➲ *Clinical Examples in Radiology* Spring 07:5-6

93880   Duplex scan of extracranial arteries; complete bilateral study
➲ *CPT Assistant* Jun 96:9, Dec 05:3
➲ *Clinical Examples in Radiology* Fall 07:6, Winter 09:2

93882   unilateral or limited study
➲ *CPT Assistant* Jun 96:9, Dec 05:3
➲ *Clinical Examples in Radiology* Fall 07:6, Winter 09:2

(To report common carotid intima-media thickness (IMT) study for evaluation of atherosclerotic burden or coronary heart disease risk factor assessment, use Category III code 0126T)

93886   Transcranial Doppler study of the intracranial arteries; complete study
➲ *CPT Assistant* Jun 96:9, Dec 05:3

93888   limited study
➲ *CPT Assistant* Jun 96:9, Dec 05:3

93890   vasoreactivity study
➲ *CPT Assistant* Dec 05:3; *CPT Changes: An Insider's View* 2005

93892   emboli detection without intravenous microbubble injection
➲ *CPT Assistant* Dec 05:3; *CPT Changes: An Insider's View* 2005

93893   emboli detection with intravenous microbubble injection
➲ *CPT Assistant* Dec 05:3; *CPT Changes: An Insider's View* 2005

(Do not report 93890-93893 in conjunction with 93888)

Extremity Arterial Studies (Including Digits)

93922 Noninvasive physiologic studies of upper or lower extremity arteries, single level, bilateral (eg, ankle/brachial indices, Doppler waveform analysis, volume plethysmography, transcutaneous oxygen tension measurement)
➔ *CPT Assistant* Jun 96:9, Dec 05:3

93923 Noninvasive physiologic studies of upper or lower extremity arteries, multiple levels or with provocative functional maneuvers, complete bilateral study (eg, segmental blood pressure measurements, segmental Doppler waveform analysis, segmental volume plethysmography, segmental transcutaneous oxygen tension measurements, measurements with postural provocative tests, measurements with reactive hyperemia)
➔ *CPT Assistant* Jun 96:9, Jun 01:10, Dec 05:3

93924 Noninvasive physiologic studies of lower extremity arteries, at rest and following treadmill stress testing, complete bilateral study
➔ *CPT Assistant* Jun 96:9, Dec 05:3

93925 Duplex scan of lower extremity arteries or arterial bypass grafts; complete bilateral study
➔ *CPT Assistant* Jun 96:9, Dec 05:3

93926 unilateral or limited study
➔ *CPT Assistant* Jun 96:9, Oct 01:2, Dec 05:3

93930 Duplex scan of upper extremity arteries or arterial bypass grafts; complete bilateral study
➔ *CPT Assistant* Jun 96:9, Dec 05:3

93931 unilateral or limited study
➔ *CPT Assistant* Jun 96:9, Oct 01:2, Dec 05:3

Extremity Venous Studies (Including Digits)

93965 Noninvasive physiologic studies of extremity veins, complete bilateral study (eg, Doppler waveform analysis with responses to compression and other maneuvers, phleborheography, impedance plethysmography)
➔ *CPT Assistant* Jun 96:9, Dec 05:3; *CPT Changes: An Insider's View* 2007

93970 Duplex scan of extremity veins including responses to compression and other maneuvers; complete bilateral study
➔ *CPT Assistant* Jun 96:9, Dec 05:3

93971 unilateral or limited study
➔ *CPT Assistant* Jun 96:9, Oct 01:2, Mar 03:21, Dec 05:3
➔ *Clinical Examples in Radiology* Winter 08:11

Visceral and Penile Vascular Studies

93975 Duplex scan of arterial inflow and venous outflow of abdominal, pelvic, scrotal contents and/or retroperitoneal organs; complete study
➔ *CPT Assistant* Apr 96:11, Jun 96:9, Dec 05:3
➔ *Clinical Examples in Radiology* Winter 08:10, Spring 08:9

93976 limited study
➔ *CPT Assistant* Apr 96:11, Jun 96:9, Dec 05:3
➔ *Clinical Examples in Radiology* Spring 08:10

93978 Duplex scan of aorta, inferior vena cava, iliac vasculature, or bypass grafts; complete study
➔ *CPT Assistant* Jun 96:9, Dec 05:3
➔ *Clinical Examples in Radiology* Spring 07:5-6

93979 unilateral or limited study
➔ *CPT Assistant* Jun 96:9, Dec 05:3

93980 Duplex scan of arterial inflow and venous outflow of penile vessels; complete study
➔ *CPT Assistant* Jun 96:9, Dec 05:3

93981 follow-up or limited study
➔ *CPT Assistant* Jun 96:9, Dec 05:3

93982 Noninvasive physiologic study of implanted wireless pressure sensor in aneurysmal sac following endovascular repair, complete study including recording, analysis of pressure and waveform tracings, interpretation and report
➔ *CPT Changes: An Insider's View* 2008

(Do not report 93982 in conjunction with 34806)

Extremity Arterial-Venous Studies

93990 Duplex scan of hemodialysis access (including arterial inflow, body of access and venous outflow)
➔ *CPT Assistant* Jun 96:9, Dec 05:3
➔ *Clinical Examples in Radiology* Spring 07:5-6

(For measurement of hemodialysis access flow using indicator dilution methods, use 90940)

Pulmonary

Ventilator Management

94002 Ventilation assist and management, initiation of pressure or volume preset ventilators for assisted or controlled breathing; hospital inpatient/observation, initial day
➔ *CPT Assistant* Feb 07:10, Mar 07:10, Apr 07:3, Jul 07:1, Nov 08:5; *CPT Changes: An Insider's View* 2007

94003 hospital inpatient/observation, each subsequent day
➔ *CPT Assistant* Feb 07:10, Apr 07:3, Jul 07:1, Nov 08:5; *CPT Changes: An Insider's View* 2007

94004 nursing facility, per day

➲ *CPT Assistant* Feb 07:10, Apr 07:3, Jul 07:1, Nov 08:5; *CPT Changes: An Insider's View* 2007

(Do not report 94002-94004 in conjunction with Evaluation and Management services 99201-99499)

94005 Home ventilator management care plan oversight of a patient (patient not present) in home, domiciliary or rest home (eg, assisted living) requiring review of status, review of laboratories and other studies and revision of orders and respiratory care plan (as appropriate), within a calendar month, 30 minutes or more

➲ *CPT Assistant* Mar 07:11, Apr 07:3, Nov 08:5; *CPT Changes: An Insider's View* 2007

(Do not report 94005 in conjunction with 99339, 99340, 99374-99378)

(Ventilator management care plan oversight is reported separately from home or domiciliary, rest home [eg, assisted living] services. A physician may report 94005, when performed, including when a different physician reports 99339, 99340, 99374-99378 for the same 30 days)

Other Procedures

Codes 94010-94799 include laboratory procedure(s) and interpretation of test results. If a separate identifiable Evaluation and Management service is performed, the appropriate E/M service code should be reported in addition to 94010-94799.

➲ *CPT Assistant* Summer 95:4, Feb 96:9, Mar 96:10, Jan 99:8, Feb 99:9

94010 Spirometry, including graphic record, total and timed vital capacity, expiratory flow rate measurement(s), with or without maximal voluntary ventilation

➲ *CPT Assistant* Summer 91:16, Summer 95:4, Feb 96:9, Nov 97:45, Nov 98:35, Feb 99:9, Aug 03:15, Jul 05:11, Nov 08:5

⊙● **94011** Measurement of spirometric forced expiratory flows in an infant or child through 2 years of age

➲ *CPT Changes: An Insider's View* 2010

⊙● **94012** Measurement of spirometric forced expiratory flows, before and after bronchodilator, in an infant or child through 2 years of age

➲ *CPT Changes: An Insider's View* 2010

⊙● **94013** Measurement of lung volumes (ie, functional residual capacity [FRC], forced vital capacity [FVC], and expiratory reserve volume [ERV]) in an infant or child through 2 years of age

➲ *CPT Changes: An Insider's View* 2010

94014 Patient-initiated spirometric recording per 30-day period of time; includes reinforced education, transmission of spirometric tracing, data capture, analysis of transmitted data, periodic recalibration and physician review and interpretation

➲ *CPT Assistant* Summer 95:4, Nov 98:34, Jan 99:8, Jul 05:11, Nov 08:5; *CPT Changes: An Insider's View* 2000

94015 recording (includes hook-up, reinforced education, data transmission, data capture, trend analysis, and periodic recalibration)

➲ *CPT Assistant* Summer 95:4, Nov 98:34, Jan 99:8, Jul 05:11, Nov 08:5

94016 physician review and interpretation only

➲ *CPT Assistant* Summer 95:4, Nov 98:34, Jan 99:8, Jul 05:11, Nov 08:5

94060 Bronchodilation responsiveness, spirometry as in 94010, pre- and post-bronchodilator administration

➲ *CPT Assistant* Summer 95:4, Feb 96:9, Feb 97:10, Nov 98:34, Jan 99:8, Feb 99:9, Jul 05:11, Nov 08:5; *CPT Changes: An Insider's View* 2005

(Report bronchodilator supply separately with 99070 or appropriate supply code)

(For prolonged exercise test for bronchospasm with pre- and post-spirometry, use 94620)

94070 Bronchospasm provocation evaluation, multiple spirometric determinations as in 94010, with administered agents (eg, antigen[s], cold air, methacholine)

➲ *CPT Assistant* Summer 91:16, Summer 95:4, Feb 96:9, Nov 97:45, Jan 99:8, Jul 05:11, Nov 08:5; *CPT Changes: An Insider's View* 2005

(Report antigen[s] administration separately with 99070 or appropriate supply code)

94150 Vital capacity, total (separate procedure)

➲ *CPT Assistant* Summer 95:4, Feb 96:9, Jul 05:11, Nov 08:5

94200 Maximum breathing capacity, maximal voluntary ventilation

➲ *CPT Assistant* Summer 95:4, Feb 96:9, Aug 03:15, Jul 05:11, Nov 08:5

94240 Functional residual capacity or residual volume: helium method, nitrogen open circuit method, or other method

➲ *CPT Assistant* Summer 95:4, Feb 96:9, Jul 05:11, Nov 08:5

94250 Expired gas collection, quantitative, single procedure (separate procedure)

➲ *CPT Assistant* Summer 95:4, Feb 96:9, Jul 05:11, Nov 08:5

94260 Thoracic gas volume

➲ *CPT Assistant* Summer 95:4, Feb 96:9, Jul 05:11, Nov 08:5

(For plethysmography, see 93720-93722)

94350 Determination of maldistribution of inspired gas: multiple breath nitrogen washout curve including alveolar nitrogen or helium equilibration time

➲ *CPT Assistant* Summer 95:4, Feb 96:9, Jul 05:11, Nov 08:5

94360 Determination of resistance to airflow, oscillatory or plethysmographic methods

➲ *CPT Assistant* Summer 95:4, Feb 96:9, Jul 05:11, Nov 08:5

94370 Determination of airway closing volume, single breath tests

➲ *CPT Assistant* Summer 95:4, Feb 96:9, Jul 05:11, Nov 08:5

94375 Respiratory flow volume loop

➲ *CPT Assistant* Summer 95:4, Feb 96:9, Oct 03:2, Jul 05:11, Jul 06:4, Jul 07:1, Nov 08:5

94400 Breathing response to CO_2 (CO_2 response curve)
→ *CPT Assistant* Summer 95:4, Feb 96:9, Jul 05:11, Nov 08:5

94450 Breathing response to hypoxia (hypoxia response curve)
→ *CPT Assistant* Summer 95:4, Feb 96:9, Jul 05:11, Nov 08:5

(For high altitude simulation test [HAST], see 94452, 94453)

94452 High altitude simulation test (HAST), with physician interpretation and report;
→ *CPT Assistant* Jul 05:11, Nov 08:5; *CPT Changes: An Insider's View* 2005

(For obtaining arterial blood gases, use 36600)

(Do not report 94452 in conjunction with 94453, 94760, 94761)

94453 with supplemental oxygen titration
→ *CPT Assistant* Jul 05:11, Nov 08:5; *CPT Changes: An Insider's View* 2005

(For obtaining arterial blood gases, use 36600)

(Do not report 94453 in conjunction with 94452, 94760, 94761)

⊘ **94610** Intrapulmonary surfactant administration by a physician through endotracheal tube
→ *CPT Assistant* Apr 07:3, Jul 08:7, Nov 08:5; *CPT Changes: An Insider's View* 2007

►(Do not report 94610 in conjunction with 99468-99472)◄

(For endotracheal intubation, use 31500)

(Report 94610 once per dosing episode)

94620 Pulmonary stress testing; simple (eg, 6-minute walk test, prolonged exercise test for bronchospasm with pre- and post-spirometry and oximetry)
→ *CPT Assistant* Summer 95:4, Feb 96:9, Nov 98:35, Jan 99:8, Mar 04:10, Jul 05:11, 13, Apr 07:3, Jun 07:11, Nov 08:5; *CPT Changes: An Insider's View* 2007

94621 complex (including measurements of CO_2 production, O_2 uptake, and electrocardiographic recordings)
→ *CPT Assistant* Summer 95:4, Nov 98:35, Jan 99:8, Aug 02:10, Jul 05:11, Nov 08:5

94640 Pressurized or nonpressurized inhalation treatment for acute airway obstruction or for sputum induction for diagnostic purposes (eg, with an aerosol generator, nebulizer, metered dose inhaler or intermittent positive pressure breathing [IPPB] device)
→ *CPT Assistant* Summer 95:4, Feb 96:9, May 98:10, Apr 00:11, Jul 05:11, Apr 07:3, Nov 08:5; *CPT Changes: An Insider's View* 2003

(For more than 1 inhalation treatment performed on the same date, append modifier 76)

(For continuous inhalation treatment of 1 hour or more, see 94644, 94645)

94642 Aerosol inhalation of pentamidine for pneumocystis carinii pneumonia treatment or prophylaxis
→ *CPT Assistant* Summer 95:4, Feb 96:9, Jul 05:11, Nov 08:5

94644 Continuous inhalation treatment with aerosol medication for acute airway obstruction; first hour
→ *CPT Assistant* Apr 07:3, Nov 08:5; *CPT Changes: An Insider's View* 2007

(For services of less than 1 hour, use 94640)

+ **94645** each additional hour (List separately in addition to code for primary procedure)
→ *CPT Assistant* Apr 07:3, Nov 08:5; *CPT Changes: An Insider's View* 2007

(Use 94645 in conjunction with 94644)

94660 Continuous positive airway pressure ventilation (CPAP), initiation and management
→ *CPT Assistant* Fall 92:30, Spring 95:4, Summer 95:4, Feb 96:9, Jan 99:10, Aug 00:2, Oct 03:2, Jul 05:11, Jul 06:4, Feb 07:10, Jul 07:1, Nov 08:5

94662 Continuous negative pressure ventilation (CNP), initiation and management
→ *CPT Assistant* Fall 92:30, Spring 94:4, Summer 95:4, Feb 96:9, Aug 00:2, Jul 05:11, Feb 07:10, Jul 07:1, Nov 08:5

94664 Demonstration and/or evaluation of patient utilization of an aerosol generator, nebulizer, metered dose inhaler or IPPB device
→ *CPT Assistant* Summer 95:4, Feb 96:9, May 98:10, Apr 00:11, Jul 05:11, Nov 08:5; *CPT Changes: An Insider's View* 2003

(94664 can be reported 1 time only per day of service)

94667 Manipulation chest wall, such as cupping, percussing, and vibration to facilitate lung function; initial demonstration and/or evaluation
→ *CPT Assistant* Summer 95:4, Feb 96:9, Jul 05:11, Nov 08:5

94668 subsequent
→ *CPT Assistant* Summer 95:4, Feb 96:9, Jul 05:11

94680 Oxygen uptake, expired gas analysis; rest and exercise, direct, simple
→ *CPT Assistant* Summer 95:4, Feb 96:9, Jul 05:11

94681 including CO_2 output, percentage oxygen extracted
→ *CPT Assistant* Summer 95:4, Feb 96:9, Jul 05:11

94690 rest, indirect (separate procedure)
→ *CPT Assistant* Summer 95:4, Feb 96:9, Jul 05:11

(For single arterial puncture, use 36600)

94720 Carbon monoxide diffusing capacity (eg, single breath, steady state)
→ *CPT Assistant* Summer 95:4, Feb 96:9, Jul 05:11; *CPT Changes: An Insider's View* 2002

94725 Membrane diffusion capacity
→ *CPT Assistant* Summer 95:4, Feb 96:9, Jul 05:11

94750 Pulmonary compliance study (eg, plethysmography, volume and pressure measurements)
→ *CPT Assistant* Summer 95:4, Feb 96:9, Jul 05:11; *CPT Changes: An Insider's View* 2002

94760 Noninvasive ear or pulse oximetry for oxygen saturation; single determination

> *CPT Assistant* Summer 95:4, Feb 96:9, Feb 97:10, Jul 98:2, Oct 03:2, Jul 05:11, Feb 06:9, Jul 06:4, Feb 07:10, Apr 07:1, Jul 07:1

(For blood gases, see 82803-82810)

94761 multiple determinations (eg, during exercise)

> *CPT Assistant* Summer 95:4, Feb 96:9, Jul 98:2, Jun 99:10, Jul 05:11, Feb 06:9, Jul 06:4, Feb 07:10, Apr 07:1, Jun 07:11, Jul 07:1, Dec 08:5

94762 by continuous overnight monitoring (separate procedure)

> *CPT Assistant* Summer 95:4, Feb 96:9, Jul 98:2, Oct 03:2, Jul 05:11, Feb 06:9, Jul 06:4, Feb 07:10, Apr 07:1, Jul 07:1, Dec 08:5

(For other in vivo laboratory procedures, see 88720-88741)

94770 Carbon dioxide, expired gas determination by infrared analyzer

> *CPT Assistant* Summer 95:4, Feb 96:9, Jul 05:11

(For bronchoscopy, see 31622-31656)

(For placement of flow directed catheter, use 93503)

(For venipuncture, use 36410)

(For central venous catheter placement, see 36555-36556)

(For arterial puncture, use 36600)

(For arterial catheterization, use 36620)

(For thoracentesis, use 32421)

(For phlebotomy, therapeutic, use 99195)

(For lung biopsy, needle, use 32405)

(For intubation, orotracheal or nasotracheal, use 31500)

94772 Circadian respiratory pattern recording (pediatric pneumogram), 12-24 hour continuous recording, infant

> *CPT Assistant* Summer 95:4, Feb 96:9, Jul 05:11

(Separate procedure codes for electromyograms, EEG, ECG, and recordings of respiration are excluded when 94772 is reported)

94774 Pediatric home apnea monitoring event recording including respiratory rate, pattern and heart rate per 30-day period of time; includes monitor attachment, download of data, physician review, interpretation, and preparation of a report

> *CPT Assistant* Apr 07:3, Mar 08:4; *CPT Changes: An Insider's View* 2007

(Do not report 94774 in conjunction with 94775-94777 during the same reporting period)

94775 monitor attachment only (includes hook-up, initiation of recording and disconnection)

> *CPT Assistant* Apr 07:3, Mar 08:4; *CPT Changes: An Insider's View* 2007

94776 monitoring, download of information, receipt of transmission(s) and analyses by computer only

> *CPT Assistant* Apr 07:3, Mar 08:4; *CPT Changes: An Insider's View* 2007

94777 physician review, interpretation and preparation of report only

> *CPT Assistant* Apr 07:3, Mar 08:4; *CPT Changes: An Insider's View* 2007

(When oxygen saturation monitoring is used in addition to heart rate and respiratory monitoring, it is not reported separately)

(Do not report 94774-94777 in conjunction with 93224-93272)

(Do not report apnea recording device separately)

(For sleep study, see 95805-95811)

94799 Unlisted pulmonary service or procedure

> *CPT Assistant* Summer 95:4, Feb 96:9, Mar 96:10, Jul 05:11

Allergy and Clinical Immunology

Definitions

Immunotherapy (desensitization, hyposensitization) is the parenteral administration of allergenic extracts as antigens at periodic intervals, usually on an increasing dosage scale to a dosage which is maintained as maintenance therapy. Indications for immunotherapy are determined by appropriate diagnostic procedures coordinated with clinical judgment and knowledge of the natural history of allergic diseases.

Other therapy: for medical conferences on the use of mechanical and electronic devices (precipitators, air conditioners, air filters, humidifiers, dehumidifiers), climatotherapy, physical therapy, occupational and recreational therapy, see **Evaluation and Management** section.

Do not report Evaluation and Management (E/M) services for test interpretation and report. If a significant separately identifiable E/M service is performed, the appropriate E/M service code should be reported using modifier 25.

Allergy Testing

(For allergy laboratory tests, see 86000-86999)

(For therapy for severe or intractable allergic disease, see 96365-96368, 96372, 96374, 96375)

95004 Percutaneous tests (scratch, puncture, prick) with allergenic extracts, immediate type reaction, including test interpretation and report by a physician, specify number of tests

> *CPT Assistant* Summer 91:15; *CPT Changes: An Insider's View* 2007, 2008

95010 Percutaneous tests (scratch, puncture, prick) sequential and incremental, with drugs, biologicals or venoms, immediate type reaction, including test interpretation and report by a physician, specify number of tests

➔ CPT Assistant Summer 91:15; CPT Changes: An Insider's View 2009

95012 Nitric oxide expired gas determination

➔ CPT Assistant Mar 07:11, Apr 07:6; CPT Changes: An Insider's View 2007

(For nitric oxide determination by spectroscopy, use Category III code 0064T)

95015 Intracutaneous (intradermal) tests, sequential and incremental, with drugs, biologicals, or venoms, immediate type reaction, including test interpretation and report by a physician, specify number of tests

➔ CPT Assistant Summer 91:15; CPT Changes: An Insider's View 2003, 2009

95024 Intracutaneous (intradermal) tests with allergenic extracts, immediate type reaction, including test interpretation and report by a physician, specify number of tests

➔ CPT Assistant Summer 91:15; CPT Changes: An Insider's View 2003, 2008

95027 Intracutaneous (intradermal) tests, sequential and incremental, with allergenic extracts for airborne allergens, immediate type reaction, including test interpretation and report by a physician, specify number of tests

➔ CPT Assistant Summer 91:15, Jun 97:10, Dec 07:9; CPT Changes: An Insider's View 2003, 2008

95028 Intracutaneous (intradermal) tests with allergenic extracts, delayed type reaction, including reading, specify number of tests

➔ CPT Assistant Summer 91:14; CPT Changes: An Insider's View 2003

95044 Patch or application test(s) (specify number of tests)

➔ CPT Assistant Summer 91:15, Spring 94:31

95052 Photo patch test(s) (specify number of tests)

➔ CPT Assistant Spring 94:31

95056 Photo tests

➔ CPT Assistant Summer 91:16

95060 Ophthalmic mucous membrane tests

➔ CPT Assistant Summer 91:16

95065 Direct nasal mucous membrane test

➔ CPT Assistant Summer 91:15

95070 Inhalation bronchial challenge testing (not including necessary pulmonary function tests); with histamine, methacholine, or similar compounds

➔ CPT Assistant Summer 91:16

95071 with antigens or gases, specify

➔ CPT Assistant Summer 91:16

(For pulmonary function tests, see 94060, 94070)

95075 Ingestion challenge test (sequential and incremental ingestion of test items, eg, food, drug or other substance such as metabisulfite)

➔ CPT Assistant Summer 91:16, Sep 01:10, Oct 02:11

Allergen Immunotherapy

Codes 95115-95199 include the professional services necessary for allergen immunotherapy. Office visit codes may be used in addition to allergen immunotherapy if other identifiable services are provided at that time.

95115 Professional services for allergen immunotherapy not including provision of allergenic extracts; single injection

➔ CPT Assistant Fall 91:19, Spring 94:30, Summer 95:4, May 96:1, Nov 98:35, Apr 00:4, Feb 05:10-12, Nov 05:1, Nov 06:23, Dec 07:9

95117 2 or more injections

➔ CPT Assistant Fall 91:19, Spring 94:30, Summer 95:4, May 96:1, Aug 96:10, Nov 98:35, Apr 00:4, Feb 05:10-12, Nov 05:1, Nov 06:23, Dec 07:9

95120 Professional services for allergen immunotherapy in prescribing physicians office or institution, including provision of allergenic extract; single injection

➔ CPT Assistant Fall 91:19, Spring 94:30, Summer 95:4, May 96:2, Nov 98:35, Feb 05:10-12

95125 2 or more injections

➔ CPT Assistant Fall 91:19, Spring 94:30, Summer 95:4, May 96:2, Aug 96:10, Nov 98:35, Feb 05:10, 12

95130 single stinging insect venom

➔ CPT Assistant Fall 91:19, Summer 95:4, May 96:2, Jun 96:10, Nov 98:35, Sep 99:10, Feb 05:10, 12

95131 2 stinging insect venoms

➔ CPT Assistant Fall 91:19, Summer 95:4, May 96:2, Jun 96:10, Nov 98:35, Sep 99:10, Feb 05:10, 12

95132 3 stinging insect venoms

➔ CPT Assistant Fall 91:19, Summer 95:4, May 96:2, Nov 98:35, Sep 99:11, Feb 05:10, 12

95133 4 stinging insect venoms

➔ CPT Assistant Fall 91:19, Summer 95:4, May 96:2, Nov 98:35, Sep 99:11, Feb 05:10, 12

95134 5 stinging insect venoms

➔ CPT Assistant Fall 91:19, Summer 95:4, May 96:2, Nov 98:35, Sep 99:11, Feb 05:10, 12

95144 Professional services for the supervision of preparation and provision of antigens for allergen immunotherapy, single dose vial(s) (specify number of vials)

➔ CPT Assistant Fall 91:19, Spring 94:30, Summer 95:4, May 96:11, Nov 98:35, Feb 05:10-11; CPT Changes: An Insider's View 2002

(A single dose vial contains a single dose of antigen administered in 1 injection)

95145 Professional services for the supervision of preparation and provision of antigens for allergen immunotherapy (specify number of doses); single stinging insect venom

➔ CPT Assistant Fall 91:19, Summer 95:4, May 96:11, Nov 98:35, Feb 05:10-12; CPT Changes: An Insider's View 2002

95146   2 single stinging insect venoms
➲ *CPT Assistant* Fall 91:19, Summer 95:4, May 96:11, Nov 98:35, Feb 05:10-12

95147   3 single stinging insect venoms
➲ *CPT Assistant* Fall 91:19, Summer 95:4, May 96:11, Nov 98:35, Feb 05:10-12

95148   4 single stinging insect venoms
➲ *CPT Assistant* Fall 91:19, Summer 95:4, May 96:11, Nov 98:35, Feb 05:10-12

95149   5 single stinging insect venoms
➲ *CPT Assistant* Fall 91:19, Summer 95:4, May 96:11, Nov 98:35, Feb 05:10-12

95165   Professional services for the supervision of preparation and provision of antigens for allergen immunotherapy; single or multiple antigens (specify number of doses)
➲ *CPT Assistant* Fall 91:19, Spring 94:30, Summer 95:4, May 96:11, Nov 98:35, Apr 00:4, Apr 01:11, Feb 05:10-12, Jun 05:9; *CPT Changes: An Insider's View* 2002

95170   whole body extract of biting insect or other arthropod (specify number of doses)
➲ *CPT Assistant* Fall 91:19, Spring 94:30, Summer 95:4, May 96:12, Apr 01:11, Feb 05:10-12, Jun 05:9

(For allergy immunotherapy reporting, a dose is the amount of antigen[s] administered in a single injection from a multiple dose vial)

95180   Rapid desensitization procedure, each hour (eg, insulin, penicillin, equine serum)
➲ *CPT Assistant* Summer 95:4; *CPT Changes: An Insider's View* 2002

95199   Unlisted allergy/clinical immunologic service or procedure
➲ *CPT Assistant* Summer 95:4, Nov 98:35

(For skin testing of bacterial, viral, fungal extracts, see 86485-86580, 95028)

(For special reports on allergy patients, use 99080)

(For testing procedures such as radioallergosorbent testing [RAST], rat mast cell technique [RMCT], mast cell degranulation test [MCDT], lymphocytic transformation test [LTT], leukocyte histamine release [LHR], migration inhibitory factor test [MIF], transfer factor test [TFT], nitroblue tetrazolium dye test [NTD], see Immunology section in **Pathology** or use 95199)

Endocrinology

95250   Ambulatory continuous glucose monitoring of interstitial tissue fluid via a subcutaneous sensor for a minimum of 72 hours; sensor placement, hook-up, calibration of monitor, patient training, removal of sensor, and printout of recording
➲ *CPT Changes: An Insider's View* 2002, 2006, 2009

(Do not report 95250 more than once per month)

(Do not report 95250 in conjunction with 99091)

95251   interpretation and report
➲ *CPT Changes: An Insider's View* 2006, 2009

(Do not report 95251 more than once per month)

(Do not report 95251 in conjunction with 99091)

Neurology and Neuromuscular Procedures

Neurologic services are typically consultative, and any of the levels of consultation (99241-99255) may be appropriate.

In addition, services and skills outlined under **Evaluation and Management** levels of service appropriate to neurologic illnesses should be reported similarly.

The EEG, autonomic function, evoked potential, reflex tests, EMG, NCV, and MEG services (95812-95829 and 95860-95967) include recording, interpretation by a physician, and report. For interpretation only, use modifier 26. For EMG guidance, see 95873, 95874.

(For repetitive transcranial magnetic stimulation for treatment of clinical depression, see Category III codes 0160T, 0161T)

(Do not report codes 95860-95875 in addition to 96000-96004)

Sleep Testing

Sleep studies and polysomnography refer to the continuous and simultaneous monitoring and recording of various physiological and pathophysiological parameters of sleep for 6 or more hours with physician review, interpretation and report. The studies are performed to diagnose a variety of sleep disorders and to evaluate a patient's response to therapies such as nasal continuous positive airway pressure (NCPAP). Polysomnography is distinguished from sleep studies by the inclusion of sleep staging which is defined to include a 1-4 lead electroencephalogram (EEG), an electro-oculogram (EOG), and a submental electromyogram (EMG). Additional parameters of sleep include (1) ECG; (2) airflow; (3) ventilation and respiratory effort; (4) gas exchange by oximetry, transcutaneous monitoring, or end tidal gas analysis; (5) extremity muscle activity, motor activity-movement; (6) extended EEG monitoring; (7) penile tumescence; (8) gastroesophageal reflux; (9) continuous blood pressure monitoring; (10) snoring; (11) body positions; etc.

The sleep services (95805-95811) include recording, interpretation and report. For interpretation only, use modifier 26.

For a study to be reported as polysomnography, sleep must be recorded and staged.

▲=Revised code   ●=New code   ▶◀=Contains new or revised text   ⊘=Modifier 51 exempt

(Report with modifier 52 if less than 6 hours of recording or in other cases of reduced services as appropriate)

(For unattended sleep study, use 95806)

95803   Actigraphy testing, recording, analysis, interpretation, and report (minimum of 72 hours to 14 consecutive days of recording)

➔ *CPT Changes: An Insider's View* 2009

(Do not report 95803 more than once in any 14 day period)

(Do not report 95803 in conjunction with 95806-95811)

95805   Multiple sleep latency or maintenance of wakefulness testing, recording, analysis and interpretation of physiological measurements of sleep during multiple trials to assess sleepiness

➔ *CPT Assistant* Nov 97:45-46, Nov 98:35, Dec 01:3, Sep 02:2-3, Mar 08:4

▲ **95806**   Sleep study, unattended, simultaneous recording of, heart rate, oxygen saturation, respiratory airflow, and respiratory effort (eg, thoracoabdominal movement)

(Do not report 95806 in conjunction with 93012, 93014, 93041-93227, 93228, 93229, 93230-93272, 0203T, 0204T)

(For unattended sleep study that measures heart rate, oxygen saturation, respiratory analysis, and sleep time, use 0203T)

(For unattended sleep study that measures heart rate, oxygen saturation, and respiratory analysis, use 0204T)

➔ *CPT Assistant* Nov 97:45-46, Aug 98:10, Nov 98:35; *CPT Changes: An Insider's View* 2010

95807   Sleep study, simultaneous recording of ventilation, respiratory effort, ECG or heart rate, and oxygen saturation, attended by a technologist

➔ *CPT Assistant* Nov 97:46, Nov 98:35, Mar 08:4

95808   Polysomnography; sleep staging with 1-3 additional parameters of sleep, attended by a technologist

➔ *CPT Assistant* Sep 96:11, Nov 97:46, Feb 98:6, Nov 98:35, Sep 02:2-3, Mar 08:4

95810   sleep staging with 4 or more additional parameters of sleep, attended by a technologist

➔ *CPT Assistant* Feb 98:6, Nov 98:35, Sep 02:2-3

95811   sleep staging with 4 or more additional parameters of sleep, with initiation of continuous positive airway pressure therapy or bilevel ventilation, attended by a technologist

➔ *CPT Assistant* Nov 97:46, Feb 98:6, Nov 98:35, Sep 02:2-3, Mar 08:4

Routine Electroencephalography (EEG)

EEG codes 95812-95822 include hyperventilation and/or photic stimulation when appropriate. Routine EEG codes 95816-95822 include 20 to 40 minutes of recording. Extended EEG codes 95812-95813 include reporting times longer than 40 minutes.

95812   Electroencephalogram (EEG) extended monitoring; 41-60 minutes

➔ *CPT Assistant* Winter 94:18, Nov 98:35; *CPT Changes: An Insider's View* 2003

95813   greater than 1 hour

➔ *CPT Assistant* Winter 94:18, Nov 98:35

95816   Electroencephalogram (EEG); including recording awake and drowsy

➔ *CPT Assistant* Sep 96:11, Nov 98:35, Nov 99:51, Jul 00:1; *CPT Changes: An Insider's View* 2000, 2003

95819   including recording awake and asleep

➔ *CPT Assistant* Nov 98:35, Nov 99:51, Jul 00:1; *CPT Changes: An Insider's View* 2000, 2003

95822   recording in coma or sleep only

➔ *CPT Assistant* Nov 98:35; *CPT Changes: An Insider's View* 2003

95824   cerebral death evaluation only

➔ *CPT Assistant* Nov 98:35

95827   all night recording

➔ *CPT Assistant* Nov 98:35; *CPT Changes: An Insider's View* 2003

(For 24-hour EEG monitoring, see 95950-95953 or 95956)

(For EEG during nonintracranial surgery, use 95955)

(For Wada test, use 95958)

(For digital analysis of EEG, use 95957)

95829   Electrocorticogram at surgery (separate procedure)

➔ *CPT Assistant* Nov 98:35

95830   Insertion by physician of sphenoidal electrodes for electroencephalographic (EEG) recording

Muscle and Range of Motion Testing

95831   Muscle testing, manual (separate procedure) with report; extremity (excluding hand) or trunk

➔ *CPT Assistant* Nov 99:51, Dec 99:10, Mar 00:11, Jul 00:2, Nov 01:5, Apr 03:28, Dec 03:7, Feb 04:5, May 08:9; *CPT Changes: An Insider's View* 2000

95832   hand, with or without comparison with normal side

➔ *CPT Assistant* Nov 99:51, Dec 99:10, Mar 00:11, Jul 00:2, Nov 01:5, Apr 03:28, Dec 03:7, Feb 04:5, May 08:9

95833   total evaluation of body, excluding hands

➔ *CPT Assistant* Nov 99:51, Dec 99:10, Jul 00:2, Nov 01:5, Jul 02:2, Apr 03:28, Dec 03:7, Feb 04:5, May 08:9

95834   total evaluation of body, including hands

➔ *CPT Assistant* Nov 99:51, Dec 99:10, Jul 00:2, Nov 01:5, Apr 03:28, Dec 03:7, Feb 04:5, May 08:9

95851   Range of motion measurements and report (separate procedure); each extremity (excluding hand) or each trunk section (spine)
> *CPT Assistant* Sep 99:10, Nov 01:5, Apr 03:28, Dec 03:7, Feb 04:5, Dec 07:16, May 08:9

95852   hand, with or without comparison with normal side
> *CPT Assistant* Nov 01:5, Apr 03:28, Dec 03:7, May 08:9

95857   Tensilon test for myasthenia gravis

Electromyography   —muscle test

Needle electromyographic procedures include the interpretation of electrical waveforms measured by equipment that produces both visible and audible components of electrical signals recorded from the muscle(s) studied by the needle electrode.

95860   Needle electromyography; 1 extremity with or without related paraspinal areas
> *CPT Assistant* Nov 97:46, Jul 00:2, Apr 02:2, May 03:20, Jun 03:3, Feb 04:4, Jul 04:6, Oct 04:15, Jun 06:8, Sep 06:5, Aug 08:12, Jan 09:8; *CPT Changes: An Insider's View* 2003

95861   2 extremities with or without related paraspinal areas
> *CPT Assistant* Nov 97:46, Jul 00:2, Apr 02:2, May 03:20, Jun 03:3, Feb 04:4, Jul 04:6, Oct 04:15, Jun 05:9, Jun 06:8, Sep 06:5, Aug 08:12, Jan 09:8; *CPT Changes: An Insider's View* 2003

(For dynamic electromyography performed during motion analysis studies, see 96002-96003)

95863   3 extremities with or without related paraspinal areas
> *CPT Assistant* Nov 97:46, Jul 00:2, Apr 02:2, May 03:20, Jun 03:3, Feb 04:4, Jul 04:6, Oct 04:15, Jun 06:8, Sep 06:5; *CPT Changes: An Insider's View* 2003

95864   4 extremities with or without related paraspinal areas
> *CPT Assistant* Nov 97:46, Jul 00:2, Jan 02:11, Apr 02:2, May 03:20, Jun 03:3, Feb 04:4, Jul 04:6, Oct 04:15, Jun 06:8, Sep 06:5, Aug 08:12, Jan 09:8; *CPT Changes: An Insider's View* 2003

95865   larynx
> *CPT Assistant* Sep 06:5, Dec 07:16, Jan 09:8; *CPT Changes: An Insider's View* 2006

(Do not report modifier 50 in conjunction with 95865)

(For unilateral procedure, report modifier 52 in conjunction with 95865)

95866   hemidiaphragm
> *CPT Changes: An Insider's View* 2006

95867   cranial nerve supplied muscle(s), unilateral
> *CPT Assistant* Apr 02:2, May 03:20, Jun 03:3, Jun 06:8, Sep 06:5, Dec 07:16, Aug 08:12, Jan 09:8; *CPT Changes: An Insider's View* 2003

95868   cranial nerve supplied muscles, bilateral
> *CPT Assistant* Apr 02:2, May 03:20, Jun 03:3, Jun 06:8, Sep 06:5, Dec 07:16, Jan 09:8; *CPT Changes: An Insider's View* 2003

95869   thoracic paraspinal muscles (excluding T1 or T12)
> *CPT Assistant* Nov 97:46, Apr 02:2, May 03:20, Jun 03:3, Feb 04:4, Jun 06:8, Sep 06:5, Jan 09:8; *CPT Changes: An Insider's View* 2003

95870   limited study of muscles in 1 extremity or non-limb (axial) muscles (unilateral or bilateral), other than thoracic paraspinal, cranial nerve supplied muscles, or sphincters
> *CPT Assistant* Nov 97:46, Nov 99:51, Jul 00:2, Apr 02:2, May 03:20, Jun 03:3, Feb 04:4, Jul 04:6, Jun 05:9, Jun 06:8, Sep 06:5, Jan 09:8; *CPT Changes: An Insider's View* 2000

(To report a complete study of the extremities, see 95860-95864)

(For anal or urethral sphincter, detrusor, urethra, perineum musculature, see 51785-51792)

(For eye muscles, use 92265)

95872   Needle electromyography using single fiber electrode, with quantitative measurement of jitter, blocking and/or fiber density, any/all sites of each muscle studied
> *CPT Assistant* Apr 02:2, May 03:20, Jun 03:3, Sep 06:5, Jan 09:8

Guidance for Chemodenervation and Ischemic Muscle Testing

+ 95873   Electrical stimulation for guidance in conjunction with chemodenervation (List separately in addition to code for primary procedure)
> *CPT Changes: An Insider's View* 2006

+ 95874   Needle electromyography for guidance in conjunction with chemodenervation (List separately in addition to code for primary procedure)
> *CPT Changes: An Insider's View* 2006

(Use 95873, 95874 in conjunction with 64612-64614)

(Do not report 95874 in conjunction with 95873)

(Do not report 95873, 95874 in conjunction with 95860-95870)

95875   Ischemic limb exercise test with serial specimen(s) acquisition for muscle(s) metabolite(s)
> *CPT Assistant* Jun 03:3; *CPT Changes: An Insider's View* 2002, 2003

(For listing of nerves considered for separate study, see **Appendix J**)

Nerve Conduction Tests

▶The following applies to nerve conduction tests (95900-95904): Codes 95900-95904 describe nerve conduction tests when performed with individually placed stimulating, recording, and ground electrodes. The stimulating, recording, and ground electrode placement and the test design must be individualized to the patient's unique anatomy. Nerves tested must be limited to the specific nerves and conduction studies needed for the particular clinical question being investigated. The stimulating electrode must be placed directly over the nerve to be tested, and stimulation parameters properly adjusted to avoid stimulating other nerves or nerve branches. In most motor nerve conduction studies, and in some sensory and mixed nerve conduction studies,

---

both proximal and distal stimulation will be used. Motor nerve conduction study recordings must be made from electrodes placed directly over the motor point of the specific muscle to be tested. Sensory nerve conduction study recordings must be made from electrodes placed directly over the specific nerve to be tested. Waveforms must be reviewed on site in real time, and the technique (stimulus site, recording site, ground site, filter settings) must be adjusted, as appropriate, as the test proceeds in order to minimize artifact, and to minimize the chances of unintended stimulation of adjacent nerves and the unintended recording from adjacent muscles or nerves. Reports must be prepared on site by the examiner, and consist of the work product of the interpretation of numerous test results, using well-established techniques to assess the amplitude, latency, and configuration of waveforms elicited by stimulation at each site of each nerve tested. This includes the calculation of nerve conduction velocities, sometimes including specialized F-wave indices, along with comparison to normal values, summarization of clinical and electrodiagnostic data, and physician or other qualified health care professional interpretation.

Code 95905 describes nerve conduction tests when performed with preconfigured electrodes customized to a specific anatomic site.◄

⊘ **95900** Nerve conduction, amplitude and latency/velocity study, each nerve; motor, without F-wave study

➡ *CPT Assistant* Jan 96:2, Nov 99:51-52, Jan 00:10, Jul 00:3, Apr 02:2, Apr 03:4, May 03:20, Jul 04:13, Mar 05:17, Dec 05:9, Jun 06:8, Feb 08:2; *CPT Changes: An Insider's View* 2000

⊘ **95903** motor, with F-wave study

➡ *CPT Assistant* Jan 96:2, Nov 99:51-52, Jan 00:10, Jul 00:3,12, Apr 02:2, Apr 03:4, May 03:20, Mar 05:17, Dec 05:9, Jun 06:8, Feb 08:2

⊘ **95904** sensory

➡ *CPT Assistant* Jan 96:2, Sep 99:11, Nov 99:51-52, Jul 00:12, Apr 02:2, Apr 03:4, May 03:20, Mar 05:17, Dec 05:9, Jun 06:8, Jul 07:15, Feb 08:2; *CPT Changes: An Insider's View* 2002

(Report 95900, 95903, and/or 95904 only once when multiple sites on the same nerve are stimulated or recorded)

⊘● **95905** Motor and/or sensory nerve conduction, using preconfigured electrode array(s), amplitude and latency/velocity study, each limb, includes F-wave study when performed, with interpretation and report

➡ *CPT Changes: An Insider's View* 2010

►(Report 95905 only once per limb studied)◄

►(Do not report 95905 in conjunction with 95900-95904, 95934-95936)◄

Intraoperative Neurophysiology

✚ **95920** Intraoperative neurophysiology testing, per hour (List separately in addition to code for primary procedure)

➡ *CPT Assistant* Winter 90:14, Nov 98:35-36, Nov 99:52, Jun 05:9

(Use 95920 in conjunction with the study performed, 92585, 95822, 95860, 95861, 95867, 95868, 95870, 95900, 95904, 95925-95937)

(Code 95920 describes ongoing electrophysiologic testing and monitoring performed during surgical procedures. Code 95920 is reported per hour of service, and includes only the ongoing electrophysiologic monitoring time distinct from performance of specific type(s) of baseline electrophysiologic study(s) (95860, 95861, 95867, 95868, 95870, 95900, 95904, 95928, 95929, 95933-95937) or interpretation of specific type(s) of baseline electrophysiologic study(s) (92585, 95822, 95870, 95925-95928, 95929, 95930). The time spent performing or interpreting the baseline electrophysiologic study(s) should not be counted as intraoperative monitoring, but represents separately reportable procedures. Code 95920 should be used once per hour even if multiple electrophysiologic studies are performed. The baseline electrophysiologic study(s) should be used once per operative session.)

(For electrocorticography, use 95829)

(For intraoperative EEG during nonintracranial surgery, use 95955)

(For intraoperative functional cortical or subcortical mapping, see 95961-95962)

(For intraoperative neurostimulator programming and analysis, see 95970-95975)

Autonomic Function Tests

95921 Testing of autonomic nervous system function; cardiovagal innervation (parasympathetic function), including 2 or more of the following: heart rate response to deep breathing with recorded R-R interval, Valsalva ratio, and 30:15 ratio

➡ *CPT Assistant* Nov 98:35-36, Apr 02:2, Oct 03:11, Feb 06:15

95922 vasomotor adrenergic innervation (sympathetic adrenergic function), including beat-to-beat blood pressure and R-R interval changes during Valsalva maneuver and at least 5 minutes of passive tilt

➡ *CPT Assistant* Nov 98:35-36, Apr 02:2, Jun 03:11, Feb 06:15, Nov 06:23, Dec 08:4

95923 sudomotor, including 1 or more of the following: quantitative sudomotor axon reflex test (QSART), silastic sweat imprint, thermoregulatory sweat test, and changes in sympathetic skin potential

➡ *CPT Assistant* Nov 98:35-36, Apr 02:2, Feb 06:15

Evoked Potentials and Reflex Tests

95925   Short-latency somatosensory evoked potential study, stimulation of any/all peripheral nerves or skin sites, recording from the central nervous system; in upper limbs
➔ *CPT Assistant* Nov 98:35-36, Apr 02:2

95926   in lower limbs
➔ *CPT Assistant* May 01:11, Apr 02:2

95927   in the trunk or head
➔ *CPT Assistant* Apr 02:2

(To report a unilateral study, use modifier 52)

(For auditory evoked potentials, use 92585)

95928   Central motor evoked potential study (transcranial motor stimulation); upper limbs
➔ *CPT Changes: An Insider's View* 2005

95929   lower limbs
➔ *CPT Changes: An Insider's View* 2005

95930   Visual evoked potential (VEP) testing central nervous system, checkerboard or flash

95933   Orbicularis oculi (blink) reflex, by electrodiagnostic testing
➔ *CPT Assistant* Nov 98:35-36

95934   H-reflex, amplitude and latency study; record gastrocnemius/soleus muscle
➔ *CPT Assistant* Jan 96:3, Nov 98:35-36, Jul 01:11, Apr 02:2, Jun 06:8

95936   record muscle other than gastrocnemius/soleus muscle
➔ *CPT Assistant* Jan 96:3, Apr 02:2, Jun 06:8

(To report a bilateral study, use modifier 50)

95937   Neuromuscular junction testing (repetitive stimulation, paired stimuli), each nerve, any 1 method
➔ *CPT Assistant* Nov 98:35-36, Apr 02:2, Jun 06:8

Special EEG Tests

95950   Monitoring for identification and lateralization of cerebral seizure focus, electroencephalographic (eg, 8 channel EEG) recording and interpretation, each 24 hours
➔ *CPT Assistant* Nov 98:35

95951   Monitoring for localization of cerebral seizure focus by cable or radio, 16 or more channel telemetry, combined electroencephalographic (EEG) and video recording and interpretation (eg, for presurgical localization), each 24 hours
➔ *CPT Assistant* Nov 98:35, Mar 03:21, Dec 04:18

Electroencephalographic (EEG) Monitoring and Video Recording
95951

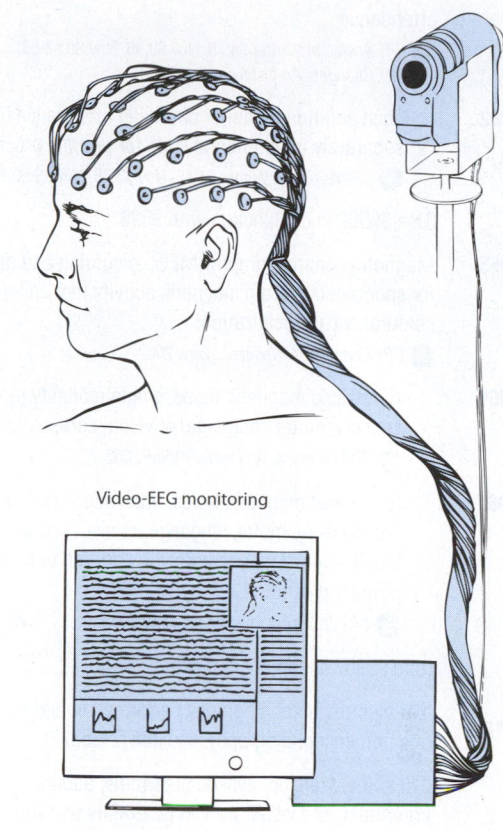

Video-EEG monitoring

95953   Monitoring for localization of cerebral seizure focus by computerized portable 16 or more channel EEG, electroencephalographic (EEG) recording and interpretation, each 24 hours
➔ *CPT Assistant* Nov 98:35

95954   Pharmacological or physical activation requiring physician attendance during EEG recording of activation phase (eg, thiopental activation test)
➔ *CPT Assistant* Winter 94:18, Nov 98:35

95955   Electroencephalogram (EEG) during nonintracranial surgery (eg, carotid surgery)
➔ *CPT Assistant* Nov 98:35

95956   Monitoring for localization of cerebral seizure focus by cable or radio, 16 or more channel telemetry, electroencephalographic (EEG) recording and interpretation, each 24 hours
➔ *CPT Assistant* Nov 98:35

95957   Digital analysis of electroencephalogram (EEG) (eg, for epileptic spike analysis)
➔ *CPT Assistant* Winter 94:18, Nov 98:35

95958   Wada activation test for hemispheric function, including electroencephalographic (EEG) monitoring
➔ *CPT Assistant* Nov 98:35

▲=Revised code   ●=New code   ▶◀=Contains new or revised text   ⊘=Modifier 51 exempt   American Medical Association   **481**

95961   Functional cortical and subcortical mapping by stimulation and/or recording of electrodes on brain surface, or of depth electrodes, to provoke seizures or identify vital brain structures; initial hour of physician attendance

➜ *CPT Assistant* Winter 94:18, Nov 98:35, Nov 99:52-53; *CPT Changes: An Insider's View* 2000

+ 95962   each additional hour of physician attendance (List separately in addition to code for primary procedure)

➜ *CPT Assistant* Winter 94:18, Nov 98:35, Nov 99:52-53

(Use 95962 in conjunction with 95961)

95965   Magnetoencephalography (MEG), recording and analysis; for spontaneous brain magnetic activity (eg, epileptic cerebral cortex localization)

➜ *CPT Changes: An Insider's View* 2002

95966   for evoked magnetic fields, single modality (eg, sensory, motor, language, or visual cortex localization)

➜ *CPT Changes: An Insider's View* 2002

+ 95967   for evoked magnetic fields, each additional modality (eg, sensory, motor, language, or visual cortex localization) (List separately in addition to code for primary procedure)

➜ *CPT Changes: An Insider's View* 2002

(Use 95967 in conjunction with 95966)

(For electroencephalography performed in addition to magnetoencephalography, see 95812-95827)

(For somatosensory evoked potentials, auditory evoked potentials, and visual evoked potentials performed in addition to magnetic evoked field responses, see 92585, 95925, 95926, and/or 95930)

(For computerized tomography performed in addition to magnetoencephalography, see 70450-70470, 70496)

(For magnetic resonance imaging performed in addition to magnetoencephalography, see 70551-70553)

Neurostimulators, Analysis-Programming

A simple neurostimulator pulse generator/transmitter (95970, 95971) is one capable of affecting three or fewer of the following: pulse amplitude, pulse duration, pulse frequency, eight or more electrode contacts, cycling, stimulation train duration, train spacing, number of programs, number of channels, alternating electrode polarities, dose time (stimulation parameters changing in time periods of minutes including dose lockout times), more than one clinical feature (eg, rigidity, dyskinesia, tremor). A complex neurostimulator pulse generator/ transmitter (95970, 95972- 95975) is one capable of affecting more than three of the above.

Code 95970 describes subsequent electronic analysis of a previously-implanted simple or complex brain, spinal cord, or peripheral neurostimulator pulse generator system, without reprogramming. Code 95971 describes intraoperative or subsequent electronic analysis of an implanted simple spinal cord, or peripheral (ie, peripheral nerve, autonomic nerve, neuromuscular) neurostimulator pulse generator system, with programming. Codes 95972 and 95973 describe intraoperative (at initial insertion/revision) or subsequent electronic analysis of an implanted complex spinal cord or peripheral (except cranial nerve) neurostimulator pulse generator system, with programming. Codes 95974 and 95975 describe intraoperative (at initial insertion/revision) or subsequent electronic analysis of an implanted complex cranial nerve neurostimulator pulse generator system, with programming. Codes 95978 and 95979 describe initial or subsequent electronic analysis of an implanted brain neurostimulator pulse generator system, with programming.

Code 95980 describes intraoperative electronic analysis of an implanted gastric neurostimulator pulse generator system, with programming; code 95981 describes subsequent analysis of the device; code 95982 describes subsequent analysis and reprogramming. For electronic analysis and reprogramming of gastric neurostimulator, lesser curvature, see 95980-95982.

(For insertion of neurostimulator pulse generator, see 61885, 63685, 64590)

(For revision or removal of neurostimulator pulse generator or receiver, see 61888, 63688, 64595)

▶(For implantation of neurostimulator electrodes, see 43647, 43881, 61850-61875, 63650-63655, 64553-64580, 0155T, 0157T. For revision or removal of neurostimulator electrodes, see 43648, 43882, 61880, 63661-63664, 64585, 0156T, 0158T)◀

95970   Electronic analysis of implanted neurostimulator pulse generator system (eg, rate, pulse amplitude and duration, configuration of wave form, battery status, electrode selectability, output modulation, cycling, impedance and patient compliance measurements); simple or complex brain, spinal cord, or peripheral (ie, cranial nerve, peripheral nerve, autonomic nerve, neuromuscular) neurostimulator pulse generator/transmitter, without reprogramming

➜ *CPT Assistant* Nov 98:36-37, Sep 99:1, Nov 99:53-54, Aug 05:7, Sep 05:10; *CPT Changes: An Insider's View* 2000

95971   simple spinal cord, or peripheral (ie, peripheral nerve, autonomic nerve, neuromuscular) neurostimulator pulse generator/transmitter, with intraoperative or subsequent programming

➜ *CPT Assistant* Nov 98:36-37, Sep 99:1, Nov 99:53-54, Aug 05:7; *CPT Changes: An Insider's View* 2000, 2005

95972   complex spinal cord, or peripheral (except cranial nerve) neurostimulator pulse generator/transmitter, with intraoperative or subsequent programming, first hour

➜ *CPT Assistant* Nov 98:36-37, Sep 99:1, Nov 99:53-54, Aug 05:7; *CPT Changes: An Insider's View* 2000, 2005

+ 95973   complex spinal cord, or peripheral (except cranial nerve) neurostimulator pulse generator/transmitter, with intraoperative or subsequent programming, each additional 30 minutes after first hour (List separately in addition to code for primary procedure)

➔ *CPT Assistant* Nov 98:36-37, Sep 99:1, Nov 99:53-54, Aug 05:7; *CPT Changes: An Insider's View* 2000, 2005

(Use 95973 in conjunction with 95972)

95974   complex cranial nerve neurostimulator pulse generator/transmitter, with intraoperative or subsequent programming, with or without nerve interface testing, first hour

➔ *CPT Assistant* Nov 98:36-37, Sep 99:1, Nov 99:53-54, Sep 05:10

+ 95975   complex cranial nerve neurostimulator pulse generator/transmitter, with intraoperative or subsequent programming, each additional 30 minutes after first hour (List separately in addition to code for primary procedure)

➔ *CPT Assistant* Nov 98:36-37, Sep 99:1, Nov 99:53-54, Sep 05:10

(Use 95975 in conjunction with 95974)

(For electronic analysis programming of gastric neurostimulator, lesser curvature, use Category III code 0162T)

95978   Electronic analysis of implanted neurostimulator pulse generator system (eg, rate, pulse amplitude and duration, battery status, electrode selectability and polarity, impedance and patient compliance measurements), complex deep brain neurostimulator pulse generator/transmitter, with initial or subsequent programming; first hour

➔ *CPT Assistant* Aug 05:7; *CPT Changes: An Insider's View* 2005

+ 95979   each additional 30 minutes after first hour (List separately in addition to code for primary procedure)

➔ *CPT Assistant* Aug 05:7; *CPT Changes: An Insider's View* 2005

(Use 95979 in conjunction with 95978)

95980   Electronic analysis of implanted neurostimulator pulse generator system (eg, rate, pulse amplitude and duration, configuration of wave form, battery status, electrode selectability, output modulation, cycling, impedance and patient measurements) gastric neurostimulator pulse generator/transmitter; intraoperative, with programming

➔ *CPT Assistant* Jan 08:8; *CPT Changes: An Insider's View* 2008

95981   subsequent, without reprogramming

➔ *CPT Assistant* Jan 08:8; *CPT Changes: An Insider's View* 2008

95982   subsequent, with reprogramming

➔ *CPT Assistant* Jan 08:8; *CPT Changes: An Insider's View* 2008

Other Procedures

95990   Refilling and maintenance of implantable pump or reservoir for drug delivery, spinal (intrathecal, epidural) or brain (intraventricular);

➔ *CPT Assistant* Nov 02:4, Nov 05:1, Jul 06:1; *CPT Changes: An Insider's View* 2003

(For analysis and/or reprogramming of implantable infusion pump, see 62367-62368)

(For refill and maintenance of implanted infusion pump or reservoir for systemic drug therapy [eg, chemotherapy or insulin], use 96522)

95991   administered by physician

➔ *CPT Assistant* Nov 05:1, Jul 06:1; *CPT Changes: An Insider's View* 2004

⊘ **95992**   Canalith repositioning procedure(s) (eg, Epley maneuver, Semont maneuver), per day

➔ *CPT Changes: An Insider's View* 2009

(Do not report 95992 in conjunction with 92531, 92532)

95999   Unlisted neurological or neuromuscular diagnostic procedure

➔ *CPT Assistant* Feb 99:11, Jan 02:11, Mar 07:4, Apr 07:7, Dec 08:10

Motion Analysis

Codes 96000-96004 describe services performed as part of a major therapeutic or diagnostic decision making process. Motion analysis is performed in a dedicated motion analysis laboratory (ie, a facility capable of performing videotaping from the front, back and both sides, computerized 3D kinematics, 3D kinetics, and dynamic electromyography). Code 96000 may include 3D kinetics and stride characteristics. Codes 96002-96003 describe dynamic electromyography.

Code 96004 should only be reported once regardless of the number of study(ies) reviewed/interpreted.

(For performance of needle electromyography procedures, see 95860-95875)

(For gait training, use 97116)

96000   Comprehensive computer-based motion analysis by video-taping and 3D kinematics;

➔ *CPT Assistant* Aug 02:5, Jun 03:2; *CPT Changes: An Insider's View* 2002

96001   with dynamic plantar pressure measurements during walking

➔ *CPT Assistant* Aug 02:5, Jun 03:2; *CPT Changes: An Insider's View* 2002

96002   Dynamic surface electromyography, during walking or other functional activities, 1-12 muscles

➔ *CPT Assistant* Aug 02:5, Jun 03:3; *CPT Changes: An Insider's View* 2002

96003   Dynamic fine wire electromyography, during walking or other functional activities, 1 muscle

➔ *CPT Assistant* Aug 02:5, Jun 03:3; *CPT Changes: An Insider's View* 2002

(Do not report 96002, 96003 in conjunction with 95860-95864, 95869-95872)

96004   Physician review and interpretation of comprehensive computer-based motion analysis, dynamic plantar pressure measurements, dynamic surface electromyography during walking or other functional activities, and dynamic fine wire electromyography, with written report

➔ *CPT Assistant* Aug 02:5, Jun 03:3; *CPT Changes: An Insider's View* 2002

Functional Brain Mapping

Code 96020 includes selection and administration of testing of language, memory, cognition, movement, sensation, and other neurological functions when conducted in association with functional neuroimaging, monitoring of performance of this testing, and determination of validity of neurofunctional testing relative to separately interpreted functional magnetic resonance images.

96020   Neurofunctional testing selection and administration during noninvasive imaging functional brain mapping, with test administered entirely by a physician or psychologist, with review of test results and report

➔ *CPT Assistant* Feb 07:6; *CPT Changes: An Insider's View* 2007

(For functional magnetic resonance imaging [fMRI], brain, use 70555)

(Do not report 96020 in conjunction with 96101-96103, 96116-96120)

(Do not report 96020 in conjunction with 70554)

(Evaluation and Management services codes should not be reported on the same day as 96020)

Medical Genetics and Genetic Counseling Services

These services are provided by trained genetic counselors and may include obtaining a structured family genetic history, pedigree construction, analysis for genetic risk assessment, and counseling of the patient and family. These activities may be provided during one or more sessions and may include review of medical data and family information, face-to-face interviews, and counseling services.

96040   Medical genetics and genetic counseling services, each 30 minutes face-to-face with patient/family

➔ *CPT Assistant* Aug 07:9; *CPT Changes: An Insider's View* 2007

(For genetic counseling and education provided by a physician to an individual, see the appropriate Evaluation and Management codes)

(For genetic counseling and education provided by a physician to a group, use 99078)

(For education regarding genetic risks by a nonphysician to a group, see 98961, 98962)

(For genetic counseling and/or risk factor reduction intervention provided by a physician to patient(s) without symptoms or established disease, see 99401-99412)

Central Nervous System Assessments/Tests (eg, Neuro-Cognitive, Mental Status, Speech Testing)

The following codes are used to report the services provided during testing of the cognitive function of the central nervous system. The testing of cognitive processes, visual motor responses, and abstractive abilities is accomplished by the combination of several types of testing procedures. It is expected that the administration of these tests will generate material that will be formulated into a report.

(For development of cognitive skills, see 97532, 97533)

(For mini-mental status examination performed by a physician, see **Evaluation and Management** services codes)

96101   Psychological testing (includes psychodiagnostic assessment of emotionality, intellectual abilities, personality and psychopathology, eg, MMPI, Rorschach, WAIS), per hour of the psychologist's or physician's time, both face-to-face time administering tests to the patient and time interpreting these test results and preparing the report

➔ *CPT Changes: An Insider's View* 2006, 2008

(96101 is also used in those circumstances when additional time is necessary to integrate other sources of clinical data, including previously completed and reported technician- and computer-administered tests)

(Do not report 96101 for the interpretation and report of 96102, 96103)

96102   Psychological testing (includes psychodiagnostic assessment of emotionality, intellectual abilities, personality and psychopathology, eg, MMPI and WAIS), with qualified health care professional interpretation and report, administered by technician, per hour of technician time, face-to-face

➔ *CPT Changes: An Insider's View* 2006

96103   Psychological testing (includes psychodiagnostic assessment of emotionality, intellectual abilities, personality and psychopathology, eg, MMPI), administered by a computer, with qualified health care professional interpretation and report

➔ *CPT Changes: An Insider's View* 2006

96105   Assessment of aphasia (includes assessment of expressive and receptive speech and language function, language comprehension, speech production ability, reading, spelling, writing, eg, by Boston Diagnostic Aphasia Examination) with interpretation and report, per hour

➔ *CPT Assistant* Jul 96:8, May 05:1

96110   Developmental testing; limited (eg, Developmental Screening Test II, Early Language Milestone Screen), with interpretation and report

➔ *CPT Assistant* Jul 96:9, May 05:1

96111   extended (includes assessment of motor, language, social, adaptive and/or cognitive functioning by standardized developmental instruments) with interpretation and report

➔ *CPT Assistant* Jul 96:9, May 05:1; *CPT Changes: An Insider's View* 2005

96116   Neurobehavioral status exam (clinical assessment of thinking, reasoning and judgment, eg, acquired knowledge, attention, language, memory, planning and problem solving, and visual spatial abilities), per hour of the psychologist's or physician's time, both face-to-face time with the patient and time interpreting test results and preparing the report

➔ *CPT Changes: An Insider's View* 2006

96118   Neuropsychological testing (eg, Halstead-Reitan Neuropsychological Battery, Wechsler Memory Scales and Wisconsin Card Sorting Test), per hour of the psychologist's or physician's time, both face-to-face time administering tests to the patient and time interpreting these test results and preparing the report

➔ *CPT Changes: An Insider's View* 2006, 2008

(96118 is also used in those circumstances when additional time is necessary to integrate other sources of clinical data, including previously completed and reported technician- and computer-administered tests)

(Do not report 96118 for the interpretation and report of 96119 or 96120)

96119   Neuropsychological testing (eg, Halstead-Reitan Neuropsychological Battery, Wechsler Memory Scales and Wisconsin Card Sorting Test), with qualified health care professional interpretation and report, administered by technician, per hour of technician time, face-to-face

➔ *CPT Changes: An Insider's View* 2006

96120   Neuropsychological testing (eg, Wisconsin Card Sorting Test), administered by a computer, with qualified health care professional interpretation and report

➔ *CPT Changes: An Insider's View* 2006

96125   Standardized cognitive performance testing (eg, Ross Information Processing Assessment) per hour of a qualified health care professional's time, both face-to-face time administering tests to the patient and time interpreting these test results and preparing the report

➔ *CPT Changes: An Insider's View* 2008

(For psychological and neuropsychological testing by a physician or psychologist, see 96101-96103, 96118-96120)

Health and Behavior Assessment/Intervention

Health and behavior assessment procedures are used to identify the psychological, behavioral, emotional, cognitive, and social factors important to the prevention, treatment, or management of physical health problems.

The focus of the assessment is not on mental health but on the biopsychosocial factors important to physical health problems and treatments. The focus of the intervention is to improve the patient's health and well-being utilizing cognitive, behavioral, social, and/or psychophysiological procedures designed to ameliorate specific disease-related problems.

Codes 96150-96155 describe services offered to patients who present with primary physical illnesses, diagnoses, or symptoms and may benefit from assessments and interventions that focus on the biopsychosocial factors related to the patient's health status. These services do not represent preventive medicine counseling and risk factor reduction interventions.

For patients that require psychiatric services (90801-90899) as well as health and behavior assessment/intervention (96150-96155), report the predominant service performed. Do not report 96150-96155 in conjunction with 90801-90899 on the same date.

Evaluation and Management services codes (including Counseling Risk Factor Reduction and Behavior Change Intervention [99401-99412]), should not be reported on the same day.

(For health and behavior assessment and/or intervention performed by a physician, see **Evaluation and Management** or **Preventive Medicine** services codes)

96150   Health and behavior assessment (eg, health-focused clinical interview, behavioral observations, psychophysiological monitoring, health-oriented questionnaires), each 15 minutes face-to-face with the patient; initial assessment

➔ *CPT Assistant* Mar 02:4, Feb 04:11, Mar 04:10, May 05:1, Jun 05:10; *CPT Changes: An Insider's View* 2002

96151   re-assessment

➔ *CPT Assistant* Mar 02:4, Feb 04:11, Mar 04:10, May 05:1, Jun 05:10; *CPT Changes: An Insider's View* 2002

96152   Health and behavior intervention, each 15 minutes, face-to-face; individual

➔ *CPT Assistant* Mar 02:4, Feb 04:11, Mar 04:10, May 05:1, Jun 05:10; *CPT Changes: An Insider's View* 2002

96153   group (2 or more patients)

➔ *CPT Assistant* Mar 02:4, Feb 04:11, Mar 04:10, May 05:1, Jun 05:10; *CPT Changes: An Insider's View* 2002

96154   family (with the patient present)

➔ *CPT Assistant* Mar 02:4, Feb 04:11, Mar 04:10, May 05:1, Jun 05:10; *CPT Changes: An Insider's View* 2002

96155 family (without the patient present)
➔ *CPT Assistant* Mar 02:4, 12, Feb 04:11, Mar 04:10, May 05:1, Jun 05:10; *CPT Changes: An Insider's View* 2002

Hydration, Therapeutic, Prophylactic, Diagnostic Injections and Infusions, and Chemotherapy and Other Highly Complex Drug or Highly Complex Biologic Agent Administration

Physician work related to hydration, injection, and infusion services predominantly involves affirmation of treatment plan and direct supervision of staff.

If a significant, separately identifiable Evaluation and Management service is performed, the appropriate E/M service code should be reported using modifier 25 in addition to 96360-96549. For same day E/M service, a different diagnosis is not required.

If performed to facilitate the infusion or injection, the following services are included and are not reported separately:

a. Use of local anesthesia

b. IV start

c. Access to indwelling IV, subcutaneous catheter or port

d. Flush at conclusion of infusion

e. Standard tubing, syringes, and supplies

(For declotting a catheter or port, use 36593)

When multiple drugs are administered, report the service(s) and the specific materials or drugs for each.

When administering multiple infusions, injections or combinations, only one "initial" service code should be reported, unless protocol requires that two separate IV sites must be used. If an injection or infusion is of a subsequent or concurrent nature, even if it is the first such service within that group of services, then a subsequent or concurrent code from the appropriate section should be reported (eg, the first IV push given subsequent to an initial one-hour infusion is reported using a subsequent IV push code).

▶In order to determine which service should be reported as the initial service when there is more than one type of service, hierarchies have been created. These vary by whether the physician or a facility is reporting. The order of selection for physicians is based upon the physician knowledge of the clinical condition(s) and treatment(s). The hierarchy that facilities are to use is based upon a structural algorithm. When these codes are reported by

the physician, the "initial" code that best describes the key or primary reason for the encounter should always be reported irrespective of the order in which the infusions or injections occur.◀

▶When these codes are reported *by the facility*, the following instructions apply. The initial code should be selected using a hierarchy whereby chemotherapy services are primary to therapeutic, prophylactic, and diagnostic services which are primary to hydration services. Infusions are primary to pushes, which are primary to injections. This hierarchy is to be followed by facilities and supersedes parenthetical instructions for add-on codes that suggest an add-on of a higher hierarchical position may be reported in conjunction with a base code of a lower position. (For example, the hierarchy would not permit reporting 96376 with 96360, as 96376 is a higher order code. IV push is primary to hydration.)◀

When reporting codes for which infusion time is a factor, use the actual time over which the infusion is administered. Intravenous or intra-arterial push is defined as: (a) an injection in which the health care professional who administers the substance/drug is continuously present to administer the injection and observe the patient, or (b) an infusion of 15 minutes or less.

Hydration

Codes 96360-96361 are intended to report a hydration IV infusion to consist of a pre-packaged fluid and electrolytes (eg, normal saline, D5-1/2 normal saline+30mEq KCl/liter), but are not used to report infusion of drugs or other substances. Hydration IV infusions typically require direct physician supervision for purposes of consent, safety oversight, or intraservice supervision of staff. Typically such infusions require little special handling to prepare or dispose of, and staff that administer these do not typically require advanced practice training. After initial set-up, infusion typically entails little patient risk and thus little monitoring. These codes are not intended to be reported by the physician in the facility setting.

96360 Intravenous infusion, hydration; initial, 31 minutes to 1 hour
➔ *CPT Changes: An Insider's View* 2009

(Do not report 96360 if performed as a concurrent infusion service)

(Do not report intravenous infusion for hydration of 30 minutes or less)

+ **96361** each additional hour (List separately in addition to code for primary procedure)
➔ *CPT Changes: An Insider's View* 2009

(Use 96361 in conjunction with 96360)

(Report 96361 for hydration infusion intervals of greater than 30 minutes beyond 1 hour increments)

(Report 96361 to identify hydration if provided as a secondary or subsequent service after a different initial service [96360, 96365, 96374, 96409, 96413] is administered through the same IV access)

Therapeutic, Prophylactic, and Diagnostic Injections and Infusions (Excludes Chemotherapy and Other Highly Complex Drug or Highly Complex Biologic Agent Administration)

A therapeutic, prophylactic, or diagnostic IV infusion or injection (other than hydration) is for the administration of substances/drugs. When fluids are used to administer the drug(s), the administration of the fluid is considered incidental hydration and is not separately reportable. These services typically require direct physician supervision for any or all purposes of patient assessment, provision of consent, safety oversight, and intra-service supervision of staff. Typically, such infusions require special consideration to prepare, dose or dispose of, require practice training and competency for staff who administer the infusions, and require periodic patient assessment with vital sign monitoring during the infusion. These codes are not intended to be reported by the physician in the facility setting.

See codes 96401-96549 for the administration of chemotherapy or other highly complex drug or highly complex biologic agent services. These highly complex services require advanced practice training and competency for staff who provide these services; special considerations for preparation, dosage or disposal; and commonly, these services entail significant patient risk and frequent monitoring. Examples are frequent changes in the infusion rate, prolonged presence of nurse administering the solution for patient monitoring and infusion adjustments, and frequent conferring with the physician about these issues.

(Do not report 96365-96379 with codes for which IV push or infusion is an inherent part of the procedure [eg, administration of contrast material for a diagnostic imaging study])

96365   Intravenous infusion, for therapy, prophylaxis, or diagnosis (specify substance or drug); initial, up to 1 hour
→ *CPT Changes: An Insider's View* 2009

+ 96366   each additional hour (List separately in addition to code for primary procedure)
→ *CPT Changes: An Insider's View* 2009

(Report 96366 in conjunction with 96365, 96367)

(Report 96366 for additional hour[s] of sequential infusion)

(Report 96366 for infusion intervals of greater than 30 minutes beyond 1 hour increments)

+ 96367   additional sequential infusion, up to 1 hour (List separately in addition to code for primary procedure)
→ *CPT Changes: An Insider's View* 2009

(Report 96367 in conjunction with 96365, 96374, 96409, 96413 if provided as a secondary or subsequent service after a different initial service is administered through the same IV access. Report 96367 only once per sequential infusion of same infusate mix)

+ 96368   concurrent infusion (List separately in addition to code for primary procedure)
→ *CPT Changes: An Insider's View* 2009

(Report 96368 only once per encounter)

(Report 96368 in conjunction with 96365, 96366, 96413, 96415, 96416)

96369   Subcutaneous infusion for therapy or prophylaxis (specify substance or drug); initial, up to 1 hour, including pump set-up and establishment of subcutaneous infusion site(s)
→ *CPT Changes: An Insider's View* 2009

(For infusions of 15 minutes or less, use 96372)

+ 96370   each additional hour (List separately in addition to code for primary procedure)
→ *CPT Changes: An Insider's View* 2009

(Use 96370 in conjunction with 96369)

(Use 96370 for infusion intervals of greater than 30 minutes beyond 1 hour increments)

+ 96371   additional pump set-up with establishment of new subcutaneous infusion site(s) (List separately in addition to code for primary procedure)
→ *CPT Changes: An Insider's View* 2009

(Use 96371 in conjunction with 96369)

(Use 96369, 96371 only once per encounter)

96372   Therapeutic, prophylactic, or diagnostic injection (specify substance or drug); subcutaneous or intramuscular
→ *CPT Changes: An Insider's View* 2009

(For administration of vaccines/toxoids, see 96365, 96366, 90471, 90472)

(Report 96372 for non-antineoplastic hormonal therapy injections)

(Report 96401 for anti-neoplastic nonhormonal injection therapy)

(Report 96402 for anti-neoplastic hormonal injection therapy)

(Physicians do not report 96372 for injections given without direct physician supervision. To report, use 99211. Hospitals may report 96372 when the physician is not present)

(96372 does not include injections for allergen immunotherapy. For allergen immunotherapy injections, see 95115-95117)

96373   intra-arterial
→ *CPT Changes: An Insider's View* 2009

▲ = Revised code   ● = New code   ▶ ◀ = Contains new or revised text   ⊘ = Modifier 51 exempt

96374   intravenous push, single or initial substance/drug
> *CPT Changes: An Insider's View* 2009

+ 96375   each additional sequential intravenous push of a new substance/drug (List separately in addition to code for primary procedure)
> *CPT Changes: An Insider's View* 2009

(Use 96375 in conjunction with 96365, 96374, 96409, 96413)

(Report 96375 to identify intravenous push of a new substance/drug if provided as a secondary or subsequent service after a different initial service is administered through the same IV access)

+ 96376   each additional sequential intravenous push of the same substance/drug provided in a facility (List separately in addition to code for primary procedure)
> *CPT Changes: An Insider's View* 2009

(Do not report 96376 for a push performed within 30 minutes of a reported push of the same substance or drug)

(96376 may be reported by facilities only)

96379   Unlisted therapeutic, prophylactic, or diagnostic intravenous or intra-arterial injection or infusion
> *CPT Changes: An Insider's View* 2009

(For allergy immunology, see 95004 et seq)

Chemotherapy and Other Highly Complex Drug or Highly Complex Biologic Agent Administration

Chemotherapy administration codes 96401-96549 apply to parenteral administration of non-radionuclide anti-neoplastic drugs; and also to anti-neoplastic agents provided for treatment of noncancer diagnoses (eg, cyclophosphamide for auto-immune conditions) or to substances such as certain monoclonal antibody agents, and other biologic response modifiers. The highly complex infusion of chemotherapy or other drug or biologic agents requires physician work and/or clinical staff monitoring well beyond that of therapeutic drug agents (96360-96379) because the incidence of severe adverse patient reactions are typically greater. These services can be provided by any physician. Chemotherapy services are typically highly complex and require direct physician supervision for any or all purposes of patient assessment, provision of consent, safety oversight, and intraservice supervision of staff. Typically, such chemotherapy services require advanced practice training and competency for staff who provide these services; special considerations for preparation, dosage, or disposal; and commonly, these services entail significant patient risk and frequent monitoring. Examples are frequent changes in the infusion rate, prolonged presence of the nurse administering the solution for patient monitoring and infusion adjustments, and frequent conferring with the physician about these issues. When performed to

facilitate the infusion of injection, preparation of chemotherapy agent(s), highly complex agent(s), or other highly complex drugs is included and is not reported separately. To report infusions that do not require this level of complexity, see 96360-96379. Codes 96401-96402, 96409-96425, 96521-96523 are not intended to be reported by the physician in the facility setting.

The term "chemotherapy" in 96401-96549 includes other highly complex drugs or highly complex biologic agents.

Report separate codes for each parenteral method of administration employed when chemotherapy is administered by different techniques. The administration of medications (eg, antibiotics, steroidal agents, antiemetics, narcotics, analgesics) administered independently or sequentially as supportive management of chemotherapy administration, should be separately reported using 96360, 96361, 96365, 96379 as appropriate.

Report both the specific service as well as code(s) for the specific substance(s) or drug(s) provided. The fluid used to administer the drug(s) is considered incidental hydration and is not separately reportable.

Regional (isolation) chemotherapy perfusion should be reported using the codes for arterial infusion (96420-96425). Placement of the intra-arterial catheter should be reported using the appropriate code from the **Cardiovascular Surgery** section. Placement of arterial and venous cannula(s) for extracorporeal circulation via a membrane oxygenator perfusion pump should be reported using 36823. Code 36823 includes dose calculation and administration of the chemotherapy agent by injection into the perfusate. Do not report 96409-96425 in conjunction with 36823.

(For home infusion services, see 99601-99602)

Injection and Intravenous Infusion Chemotherapy and Other Highly Complex Drug or Highly Complex Biologic Agent Administration

Intravenous or intra-arterial push is defined as: (a) an injection in which the healthcare professional who administers the substance/drug is continuously present to administer the injection and observe the patient, or (b) an infusion of 15 minutes or less.

96401   Chemotherapy administration, subcutaneous or intramuscular; non-hormonal anti-neoplastic
> *CPT Assistant* Nov 05:1, Jan 06:47, Jan 07:30, May 07:3, Jun 07:4, Feb 09:17; *CPT Changes: An Insider's View* 2006

96402   hormonal anti-neoplastic
> *CPT Assistant* Nov 05:1, Jan 07:30, May 07:3, Feb 09:17; *CPT Changes: An Insider's View* 2006

96405   Chemotherapy administration; intralesional, up to and including 7 lesions

➔ *CPT Assistant* Sep 96:5, Aug 97:19, Feb 01:10, Jul 01:2, Nov 05:1, Jan 07:30, May 07:3, Feb 09:17; *CPT Changes: An Insider's View* 2006

96406   intralesional, more than 7 lesions

➔ *CPT Assistant* Sep 96:5, Aug 97:19, Feb 01:10, Jul 01:2, Nov 05:1, Jan 07:30, May 07:3, Feb 09:17; *CPT Changes: An Insider's View* 2006

96409   intravenous, push technique, single or initial substance/drug

➔ *CPT Assistant* Nov 05:1, Jan 07:30, May 07:3, Feb 09:17; *CPT Changes: An Insider's View* 2006

+ 96411   intravenous, push technique, each additional substance/drug (List separately in addition to code for primary procedure)

➔ *CPT Assistant* Nov 05:1, Jan 07:30, May 07:3, Feb 09:17; *CPT Changes: An Insider's View* 2006

(Use 96411 in conjunction with 96409, 96413)

96413   Chemotherapy administration, intravenous infusion technique; up to 1 hour, single or initial substance/drug

➔ *CPT Assistant* Nov 05:1, Jan 07:30, May 07:3, Sep 07:3, Dec 07:15, Feb 09:17; *CPT Changes: An Insider's View* 2006

(Report 96361 to identify hydration if administered as a secondary or subsequent service in association with 96413 through the same IV access)

(Report 96366, 96367, 96375 to identify therapeutic, prophylactic, or diagnostic drug infusion or injection, if administered as a secondary or subsequent service in association with 96413 through the same IV access)

+ 96415   each additional hour (List separately in addition to code for primary procedure)   *> 30 minutes*

➔ *CPT Assistant* Nov 05:1, Jan 07:30, May 07:3, Sep 07:3, Dec 07:15, Feb 09:17; *CPT Changes: An Insider's View* 2006, 2007

(Use 96415 in conjunction with 96413)

(Report 96415 for infusion intervals of greater than 30 minutes beyond 1-hour increments)

96416   initiation of prolonged chemotherapy infusion (more than 8 hours), requiring use of a portable or implantable pump

➔ *CPT Assistant* Nov 05:1, Jan 07:30, May 07:3, Sep 07:3, Dec 07:15, Feb 09:17; *CPT Changes: An Insider's View* 2006

(For refilling and maintenance of a portable or an implantable infusion pump or reservoir for drug delivery, see 96521-96523)

+ 96417   each additional sequential infusion (different substance/drug), up to 1 hour (List separately in addition to code for primary procedure)

➔ *CPT Assistant* Nov 05:1, Jan 07:30, May 07:3, Jun 07:4, Feb 09:17; *CPT Changes: An Insider's View* 2006

(Use 96417 in conjunction with 96413)

(Report only once per sequential infusion. Report 96415 for additional hour(s) of sequential infusion)

Intra-Arterial Chemotherapy and Other Highly Complex Drug or Highly Complex Biologic Agent Administration

96420   Chemotherapy administration, intra-arterial; push technique

➔ *CPT Assistant* Aug 97:19, Nov 98:37, Nov 99:54, Feb 01:10, Jul 01:2, Nov 05:1, Jan 07:30, May 07:3, Jun 07:4, Feb 09:17

⬤ *Clinical Examples in Radiology* Summer 08:1, 2, 4

96422   infusion technique, up to 1 hour

➔ *CPT Assistant* Dec 96:10, Aug 97:19, Nov 98:37, Feb 01:10, Jul 01:2, Nov 05:1, Jan 07:30, May 07:3, Dec 07:15, Feb 09:17

+ 96423   infusion technique, each additional hour (List separately in addition to code for primary procedure)

➔ *CPT Assistant* Dec 96:10, Nov 98:37, Feb 01:10, Jul 01:2, Nov 05:1, Jan 07:30, May 07:3, Dec 07:15, Feb 09:17; *CPT Changes: An Insider's View* 2006, 2007

(Use 96423 in conjunction with 96422)

(Report 96423 for infusion intervals of greater than 30 minutes beyond 1-hour increments)

(For regional chemotherapy perfusion via membrane oxygenator perfusion pump to an extremity, use 36823)

96425   infusion technique, initiation of prolonged infusion (more than 8 hours), requiring the use of a portable or implantable pump

➔ *CPT Assistant* Nov 99:54, Feb 01:10, Jul 01:2, Nov 05:1, Jan 07:30, May 07:3, Jun 07:4, Feb 09:17

(For refilling and maintenance of a portable pump or an implantable infusion pump or reservoir for drug delivery, see 96521-96523)

Other Injection and Infusion Services

Code 96523 does not require direct physician supervision. Codes 96521-96523 may be reported when these devices are used for therapeutic drugs other than chemotherapy.

(For collection of blood specimen from a completely implantable venous access device, use 36591)

96440   Chemotherapy administration into pleural cavity, requiring and including thoracentesis

➔ *CPT Assistant* Feb 01:10, Jul 01:2, Nov 05:1, Jan 07:30, May 07:3, Jun 07:4, Feb 09:17

96445   Chemotherapy administration into peritoneal cavity, requiring and including peritoneocentesis

➔ *CPT Assistant* Feb 01:10, Jul 01:2, Nov 05:1, Jan 07:30, May 07:3,10, Feb 09:17

96450   Chemotherapy administration, into CNS (eg, intrathecal), requiring and including spinal puncture

➔ *CPT Assistant* Feb 01:10, Jul 01:2, Nov 05:1, Jan 07:30, May 07:3, Feb 09:17; *CPT Changes: An Insider's View* 2002

(For intravesical (bladder) chemotherapy administration, use 51720)

(For insertion of subarachnoid catheter and reservoir for infusion of drug, see 62350, 62351, 62360-62362; for insertion of intraventricular catheter and reservoir, see 61210, 61215)

96521   Refilling and maintenance of portable pump

→ *CPT Assistant* Nov 05:1, Jan 07:30, May 07:3, Feb 09:17; *CPT Changes: An Insider's View* 2006

96522   Refilling and maintenance of implantable pump or reservoir for drug delivery, systemic (eg, intravenous, intra-arterial)

→ *CPT Assistant* Jul 06:1, Jan 07:30, May 07:3, Feb 09:17; *CPT Changes: An Insider's View* 2006

(For refilling and maintenance of an implantable infusion pump for spinal or brain drug infusion, use 95990-95991)

96523   Irrigation of implanted venous access device for drug delivery systems

→ *CPT Assistant* Jan 07:30, May 07:3, Feb 09:17; *CPT Changes: An Insider's View* 2006

(Do not report 96523 if any other services are provided on the same day)

96542   Chemotherapy injection, subarachnoid or intraventricular via subcutaneous reservoir, single or multiple agents

→ *CPT Assistant* Aug 97:19, Jul 01:2, Nov 05:1, Jan 07:30, May 07:3, Feb 09:17

(For radioactive isotope therapy, use 79005)

96549   Unlisted chemotherapy procedure

→ *CPT Assistant* Aug 97:19, Jul 01:2, Nov 05:1, Jan 07:30, May 07:3, Jun 07:4

Photodynamic Therapy

(To report ocular photodynamic therapy, use 67221)

96567   Photodynamic therapy by external application of light to destroy premalignant and/or malignant lesions of the skin and adjacent mucosa (eg, lip) by activation of photosensitive drug(s), each phototherapy exposure session

→ *CPT Assistant* Aug 03:15; *CPT Changes: An Insider's View* 2002

+▲ 96570   Photodynamic therapy by endoscopic application of light to ablate abnormal tissue via activation of photosensitive drug(s); first 30 minutes (List separately in addition to code for endoscopy or bronchoscopy procedures of lung and gastrointestinal tract)

→ *CPT Assistant* Nov 99:54, Sep 00:5; *CPT Changes: An Insider's View* 2000, 2010

+▲ 96571   each additional 15 minutes (List separately in addition to code for endoscopy or bronchoscopy procedures of lung and gastrointestinal tract)

→ *CPT Assistant* Nov 99:54, Sep 00:5; *CPT Changes: An Insider's View* 2000, 2010

(96570, 96571 are to be used in addition to bronchoscopy, endoscopy codes)

(Use 96570, 96571 in conjunction with 31641, 43228 as appropriate)

Special Dermatological Procedures

Dermatologic services are typically consultative, and any of the five levels of consultation (99241-99255) may be appropriate.

In addition, services and skills outlined under **Evaluation and Management** levels of service appropriate to dermatologic illnesses should be coded similarly.

(For intralesional injections, see 11900, 11901)

(For Tzanck smear, see 88160-88161)

96900   Actinotherapy (ultraviolet light)

96902   Microscopic examination of hairs plucked or clipped by the examiner (excluding hair collected by the patient) to determine telogen and anagen counts, or structural hair shaft abnormality

→ *CPT Assistant* Nov 97:46-47

96904   Whole body integumentary photography, for monitoring of high risk patients with dysplastic nevus syndrome or a history of dysplastic nevi, or patients with a personal or familial history of melanoma

→ *CPT Changes: An Insider's View* 2007

96910   Photochemotherapy; tar and ultraviolet B (Goeckerman treatment) or petrolatum and ultraviolet B

96912   psoralens and ultraviolet A (PUVA)

96913   Photochemotherapy (Goeckerman and/or PUVA) for severe photoresponsive dermatoses requiring at least 4-8 hours of care under direct supervision of the physician (includes application of medication and dressings)

96920   Laser treatment for inflammatory skin disease (psoriasis); total area less than 250 sq cm

→ *CPT Changes: An Insider's View* 2003

96921   250 sq cm to 500 sq cm

→ *CPT Changes: An Insider's View* 2003

96922   over 500 sq cm

→ *CPT Changes: An Insider's View* 2003

►(For laser destruction of premalignant lesions, see 17000-17004)◄

►(For laser destruction of cutaneous vascular proliferative lesions, see 17106-17108)◄

►(For laser destruction of benign lesions, see 17110-17111)◄

►(For laser destruction of malignant lesions, see 17260-17286)◄

96999   Unlisted special dermatological service or procedure

Physical Medicine and Rehabilitation

Codes 97001-97755 should be used to report each distinct procedure performed. Do not append modifier 51 to 97001-97755.

(For muscle testing, range of joint motion, electromyography, see 95831 et seq)

(For biofeedback training by EMG, use 90901)

(For transcutaneous nerve stimulation (TNS), use 64550)

97001   Physical therapy evaluation
➔ *CPT Assistant* Nov 97:47, Feb 00:11, Sep 01:10, Oct 02:11, Dec 03:4, Feb 04:5, Apr 05:13, Aug 06:11, May 08:9

97002   Physical therapy re-evaluation
➔ *CPT Assistant* Nov 97:47, Feb 00:11, Sep 01:10, Oct 02:11, Dec 03:4, Feb 04:5, May 08:9

97003   Occupational therapy evaluation
➔ *CPT Assistant* Nov 97:47, Oct 02:11, Feb 04:5, Aug 06:11, May 08:9

97004   Occupational therapy re-evaluation
➔ *CPT Assistant* Nov 97:47, Oct 02:11, Feb 04:5, May 08:9

97005   Athletic training evaluation
➔ *CPT Assistant* Jun 02:9, Feb 04:5; *CPT Changes: An Insider's View* 2002

97006   Athletic training re-evaluation
➔ *CPT Assistant* Jun 02:9, Feb 04:5; *CPT Changes: An Insider's View* 2002

Modalities

Any physical agent applied to produce therapeutic changes to biologic tissue; includes but not limited to thermal, acoustic, light, mechanical, or electric energy.

Supervised

The application of a modality that does not require direct (one-on-one) patient contact by the provider.

97010   Application of a modality to 1 or more areas; hot or cold packs
➔ *CPT Assistant* Summer 95:5, Apr 96:11, Nov 97:47, Dec 98:1, Nov 01:5, Aug 02:11, Aug 06:11

97012   traction, mechanical
➔ *CPT Assistant* Summer 95:5, Apr 96:11, Nov 97:47, Dec 98:1, May 99:11, Nov 01:5, Aug 02:11, Dec 03:4, Oct 04:9

97014   electrical stimulation (unattended)
➔ *CPT Assistant* Summer 95:5, Apr 96:11, Nov 97:47, May 98:10, Nov 01:5, Jan 02:11, Apr 02:18, Aug 02:11, Dec 03:4

(For acupuncture with electrical stimulation, see 97813, 97814)

97016   vasopneumatic devices
➔ *CPT Assistant* Summer 95:6, Apr 96:11, Dec 98:1, Nov 01:5, Aug 02:11, May 05:14

97018   paraffin bath
➔ *CPT Assistant* Summer 95:6, Apr 96:11, Dec 98:1, Nov 01:5, Aug 02:11

97022   whirlpool
➔ *CPT Assistant* Summer 95:6, Apr 96:11, May 98:10, Dec 98:1, Nov 01:5, Aug 02:11

97024   diathermy (eg, microwave)
➔ *CPT Assistant* Summer 95:6, Apr 96:11, Dec 98:1, Nov 01:5, Aug 02:11; *CPT Changes: An Insider's View* 2006

97026   infrared
➔ *CPT Assistant* Summer 95:6, Apr 96:11, Dec 98:1, Nov 01:5, Aug 02:11

97028   ultraviolet
➔ *CPT Assistant* Summer 95:6, Apr 96:11, Dec 98:1, Nov 01:5, Aug 02:11

Constant Attendance

The application of a modality that requires direct (one-on-one) patient contact by the provider.

97032   Application of a modality to 1 or more areas; electrical stimulation (manual), each 15 minutes
➔ *CPT Assistant* Summer 95:6, Dec 98:1, Nov 01:5, Apr 02:18, Jul 04:14

97033   iontophoresis, each 15 minutes
➔ *CPT Assistant* Summer 95:7, Dec 98:1, Nov 01:5

97034   contrast baths, each 15 minutes
➔ *CPT Assistant* Summer 95:7, Dec 98:1, Nov 01:5

97035   ultrasound, each 15 minutes
➔ *CPT Assistant* Summer 95:7, Sep 96:10, Dec 98:1, Nov 01:5

97036   Hubbard tank, each 15 minutes
➔ *CPT Assistant* Summer 95:7, Dec 98:1, Nov 01:5

97039   Unlisted modality (specify type and time if constant attendance)
➔ *CPT Assistant* Summer 95:7, May 98:10, Dec 98:1, Jan 00:10, Nov 01:5, May 05:14

Therapeutic Procedures

A manner of effecting change through the application of clinical skills and/or services that attempt to improve function.

Physician or therapist required to have direct (one-on-one) patient contact.

97110   Therapeutic procedure, 1 or more areas, each 15 minutes; therapeutic exercises to develop strength and endurance, range of motion and flexibility
➔ *CPT Assistant* Summer 95:7, Feb 97:10, Nov 98:37, Dec 99:11, Mar 05:11, Apr 05:14, Aug 05:11, Dec 05:8, Mar 06:15, Aug 06:11, May 08:13

97112   neuromuscular reeducation of movement, balance, coordination, kinesthetic sense, posture, and/or proprioception for sitting and/or standing activities
➔ *CPT Assistant* Summer 95:7, Feb 97:10, Apr 05:14, Aug 05:11, Mar 06:15, Aug 06:11, May 08:13; *CPT Changes: An Insider's View* 2002

▲=Revised code   ●=New code   ►◄=Contains new or revised text   ⊘=Modifier 51 exempt   American Medical Association   **491**

97113 aquatic therapy with therapeutic exercises
> CPT Assistant Summer 95:7, Feb 97:10, Apr 05:14, Mar 06:15, Aug 06:11

97116 gait training (includes stair climbing)
> CPT Assistant Summer 95:8, Sep 96:7, Feb 97:10, Jun 03:3, Apr 05:14, Mar 06:15, Aug 06:11

(Use 96000-96003 to report comprehensive gait and motion analysis procedures)

97124 massage, including effleurage, petrissage and/or tapotement (stroking, compression, percussion)
> CPT Assistant Summer 95:8, May 96:10, Feb 97:10, Dec 99:7, Apr 05:14, May 05:14, Mar 06:15, Aug 06:11

(For myofascial release, use 97140)

97139 Unlisted therapeutic procedure (specify)
> CPT Assistant Summer 95:8, Feb 97:10, Apr 05:14, Aug 06:11

97140 Manual therapy techniques (eg, mobilization/manipulation, manual lymphatic drainage, manual traction), 1 or more regions, each 15 minutes
> CPT Assistant Nov 98:37, Feb 99:10, Mar 99:1, Jul 99:11, Aug 01:10, Dec 03:5

97150 Therapeutic procedure(s), group (2 or more individuals)
> CPT Assistant Summer 95:8, Dec 96:10, Feb 97:10, Oct 99:10, Nov 99:54-55, Dec 99:11, Apr 05:14, Aug 06:11

(Report 97150 for each member of group)

(Group therapy procedures involve constant attendance of the physician or therapist, but by definition do not require one-on-one patient contact by the physician or therapist)

(For manipulation under general anesthesia, see appropriate anatomic section in **Musculoskeletal System**)

(For osteopathic manipulative treatment [OMT], see 98925-98929)

97530 Therapeutic activities, direct (one-on-one) patient contact by the provider (use of dynamic activities to improve functional performance), each 15 minutes
> CPT Assistant Summer 95:9, Dec 01:6, Apr 03:26, Jul 03:15, Aug 05:11, May 08:13

97532 Development of cognitive skills to improve attention, memory, problem solving (includes compensatory training), direct (one-on-one) patient contact by the provider, each 15 minutes
> CPT Assistant Dec 01:1; CPT Changes: An Insider's View 2001

97533 Sensory integrative techniques to enhance sensory processing and promote adaptive responses to environmental demands, direct (one-on-one) patient contact by the provider, each 15 minutes
> CPT Assistant Dec 01:1; CPT Changes: An Insider's View 2001

97535 Self-care/home management training (eg, activities of daily living (ADL) and compensatory training, meal preparation, safety procedures, and instructions in use of assistive technology devices/adaptive equipment) direct one-on-one contact by provider, each 15 minutes
> CPT Assistant Sep 96:7, Apr 00:11, Dec 03:6; CPT Changes: An Insider's View 2002

97537 Community/work reintegration training (eg, shopping, transportation, money management, avocational activities and/or work environment/modification analysis, work task analysis, use of assistive technology device/adaptive equipment), direct one-on-one contact by provider, each 15 minutes
> CPT Assistant Sep 96:7, Dec 03:6; CPT Changes: An Insider's View 2004

(For wheelchair management/propulsion training, use 97542)

97542 Wheelchair management (eg, assessment, fitting, training), each 15 minutes
> CPT Assistant Sep 96:8; CPT Changes: An Insider's View 2006

97545 Work hardening/conditioning; initial 2 hours
> CPT Assistant Apr 03:26, Jul 03:15, May 08:13

+ 97546 each additional hour (List separately in addition to code for primary procedure)

(Use 97546 in conjunction with 97545)

Active Wound Care Management

Active wound care procedures are performed to remove devitalized and/or necrotic tissue and promote healing. Provider is required to have direct (one-on-one) patient contact.

(Do not report 97597-97602 in conjunction with 11040-11044)

97597 Removal of devitalized tissue from wound(s), selective debridement, without anesthesia (eg, high pressure waterjet with/without suction, sharp selective debridement with scissors, scalpel and forceps), with or without topical application(s), wound assessment, and instruction(s) for ongoing care, may include use of a whirlpool, per session; total wound(s) surface area less than or equal to 20 square centimeters
> CPT Assistant Jun 05:1, 10; CPT Changes: An Insider's View 2005

97598 total wound(s) surface area greater than 20 square centimeters
> CPT Assistant Jun 05:1, 10; CPT Changes: An Insider's View 2005

97602 Removal of devitalized tissue from wound(s), non-selective debridement, without anesthesia (eg, wet-to-moist dressings, enzymatic, abrasion), including topical application(s), wound assessment, and instruction(s) for ongoing care, per session
> CPT Assistant May 02:5, Jun 05:1, 10, Sep 08:11; CPT Changes: An Insider's View 2001

97605 Negative pressure wound therapy (eg, vacuum assisted drainage collection), including topical application(s), wound assessment, and instruction(s) for ongoing care, per session; total wound(s) surface area less than or equal to 50 square centimeters
> CPT Assistant Apr 05:13, Jun 05:1, 10; CPT Changes: An Insider's View 2005

97606　　total wound(s) surface area greater than 50 square centimeters

➡ *CPT Assistant* Apr 05:13, Jun 05:1, 10; *CPT Changes: An Insider's View* 2005

Tests and Measurements

Requires direct one-on-one patient contact.

(For muscle testing, manual or electrical, joint range of motion, electromyography or nerve velocity determination, see 95831-95904)

97750　　Physical performance test or measurement (eg, musculoskeletal, functional capacity), with written report, each 15 minutes

➡ *CPT Assistant* Summer 95:5, Feb 97:10, Aug 98:11, Mar 00:11, Nov 01:5, May 02:18, Apr 03:28, Dec 03:7, Feb 04:5, Feb 07:12, May 08:9

97755　　Assistive technology assessment (eg, to restore, augment or compensate for existing function, optimize functional tasks and/or maximize environmental accessibility), direct one-on-one contact by provider, with written report, each 15 minutes

➡ *CPT Changes: An Insider's View* 2004

(To report augmentative and alternative communication devices, see 92605, 92607)

Orthotic Management and Prosthetic Management

97760　　Orthotic(s) management and training (including assessment and fitting when not otherwise reported), upper extremity(s), lower extremity(s) and/or trunk, each 15 minutes

➡ *CPT Assistant* Dec 05:8, 11, Feb 07:8; *CPT Changes: An Insider's View* 2006

(Code 97760 should not be reported with 97116 for the same extremity)

97761　　Prosthetic training, upper and/or lower extremity(s), each 15 minutes

➡ *CPT Assistant* Dec 05:8, 11, Feb 07:8; *CPT Changes: An Insider's View* 2006

97762　　Checkout for orthotic/prosthetic use, established patient, each 15 minutes

➡ *CPT Assistant* Dec 05:8, 11, Feb 07:8; *CPT Changes: An Insider's View* 2006

Other Procedures

(For extracorporeal shock wave musculoskeletal therapy, see Category III codes 0019T, 0101T, 0102T)

97799　　Unlisted physical medicine/rehabilitation service or procedure

➡ *CPT Assistant* Summer 95:5, Oct 99:10

Medical Nutrition Therapy

97802　　Medical nutrition therapy; initial assessment and intervention, individual, face-to-face with the patient, each 15 minutes

➡ *CPT Assistant* Apr 03:10, Nov 03:1, Feb 09:13; *CPT Changes: An Insider's View* 2001

97803　　re-assessment and intervention, individual, face-to-face with the patient, each 15 minutes

➡ *CPT Assistant* Apr 03:10, Nov 03:1, Feb 09:13; *CPT Changes: An Insider's View* 2001

97804　　group (2 or more individual(s)), each 30 minutes

➡ *CPT Assistant* Apr 03:10, Nov 03:1, Feb 09:13; *CPT Changes: An Insider's View* 2001

(For medical nutrition therapy assessment and/or intervention performed by a physician, see **Evaluation and Management** or **Preventive Medicine** service codes)

Acupuncture

Acupuncture is reported based on 15-minute increments of personal (face-to-face) contact with the patient, not the duration of acupuncture needle(s) placement.

If no electrical stimulation is used during a 15-minute increment, use 97810, 97811. If electrical stimulation of any needle is used during a 15-minute increment, use 97813, 97814.

Only one code may be reported for each 15-minute increment. Use either 97810 or 97813 for the initial 15-minute increment. Only one initial code is reported per day.

Evaluation and Management services may be reported separately, using modifier 25, if the patient's condition requires a significant separately identifiable E/M service, above and beyond the usual preservice and postservice work associated with the acupuncture services. The time of the E/M service is not included in the time of the acupuncture service.

97810　　Acupuncture, 1 or more needles; without electrical stimulation, initial 15 minutes of personal one-on-one contact with the patient

➡ *CPT Assistant* Jan 05:16-17, Jun 05:5, Jun 06:20, Aug 06:4; *CPT Changes: An Insider's View* 2005

(Do not report 97810 in conjunction with 97813)

+ 97811　　without electrical stimulation, each additional 15 minutes of personal one-on-one contact with the patient, with re-insertion of needle(s) (List separately in addition to code for primary procedure)

➡ *CPT Assistant* Jan 05:16, Jun 05:5, Aug 06:4; *CPT Changes: An Insider's View* 2005, 2006

(Use 97811 in conjunction with 97810, 97813)

Acupuncture, Needle
97810-97811

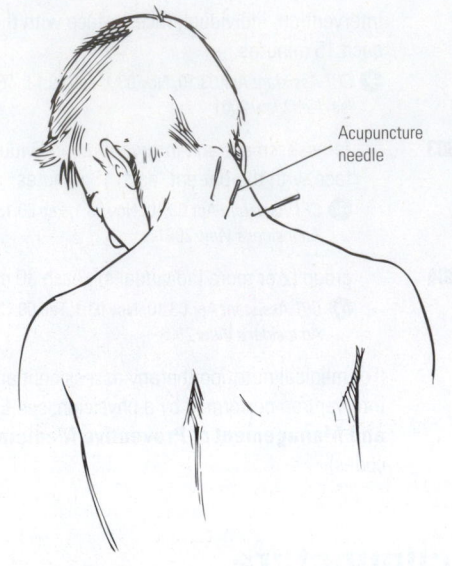

Acupuncture needle

97813   with electrical stimulation, initial 15 minutes of personal one-on-one contact with the patient
> *CPT Assistant* Jan 05:16-18, Jun 05:5, Jun 06:20, Aug 06:4; *CPT Changes: An Insider's View* 2005, 2006

(Do not report 97813 in conjunction with 97810)

+ 97814   with electrical stimulation, each additional 15 minutes of personal one-on-one contact with the patient, with re-insertion of needle(s) (List separately in addition to code for primary procedure)
> *CPT Assistant* Jan 05:16, Jun 05:5, Aug 06:4; *CPT Changes: An Insider's View* 2005, 2006

(Use 97814 in conjunction with 97810, 97813)

Osteopathic Manipulative Treatment

Osteopathic manipulative treatment (OMT) is a form of manual treatment applied by a physician to eliminate or alleviate somatic dysfunction and related disorders. This treatment may be accomplished by a variety of techniques.

Evaluation and Management services may be reported separately if, using modifier 25, the patient's condition requires a significant separately identifiable E/M service, above and beyond the usual preservice and postservice work associated with the procedure. The E/M service may be caused or prompted by the same symptoms or condition for which the OMT service was provided. As such, different diagnoses are not required for the reporting of the OMT and E/M service on the same date.

Body regions referred to are: head region; cervical region; thoracic region; lumbar region; sacral region; pelvic region; lower extremities; upper extremities; rib cage region; abdomen and viscera region.
> *CPT Assistant* Nov 98:37-38

98925   Osteopathic manipulative treatment (OMT); 1-2 body regions involved
> *CPT Assistant* May 96:10, Jan 97:8, 10, Jul 98:10, Aug 00:11, Dec 00:15

98926   3-4 body regions involved
> *CPT Assistant* May 96:10, Jan 97:8, Aug 00:11, Dec 00:15

98927   5-6 body regions involved
> *CPT Assistant* May 96:10, Jan 97:8, Aug 00:11, Dec 00:15

98928   7-8 body regions involved
> *CPT Assistant* May 96:10, Jan 97:8, Aug 00:11, Dec 00:15

98929   9-10 body regions involved
> *CPT Assistant* May 96:10, Jan 97:8, 10, Aug 00:11

Chiropractic Manipulative Treatment

Chiropractic manipulative treatment (CMT) is a form of manual treatment to influence joint and neurophysiological function. This treatment may be accomplished using a variety of techniques.

The chiropractic manipulative treatment codes include a pre-manipulation patient assessment. Additional Evaluation and Management services may be reported separately using modifier 25, if the patient's condition requires a significant separately identifiable E/M service, above and beyond the usual preservice and postservice work associated with the procedure. The E/M service may be caused or prompted by the same symptoms or condition for which the CMT service was provided. As such, different diagnoses are not required for the reporting of the CMT and E/M service on the same date.

For purposes of CMT, the five spinal regions referred to are: cervical region (includes atlanto-occipital joint); thoracic region (includes costovertebral and costotransverse joints); lumbar region; sacral region; and pelvic (sacro-iliac joint) region. The five extraspinal regions referred to are: head (including temporomandibular joint, excluding atlanto-occipital) region; lower extremities; upper extremities; rib cage (excluding costotransverse and costovertebral joints) and abdomen.
> *CPT Assistant* Nov 98:38

98940   Chiropractic manipulative treatment (CMT); spinal, 1-2 regions
> *CPT Assistant* Jan 97:7, 11, Feb 99:10, Dec 00:15, Mar 06:15, Dec 07:16, 17

98941   spinal, 3-4 regions
> *CPT Assistant* Jan 97:7, 11, Mar 97:10, Feb 99:10, Dec 00:15, Mar 06:15, Dec 07:16, 17

98942   spinal, 5 regions
→ *CPT Assistant* Jan 97:7, 11, Feb 99:10, Dec 00:15,
Mar 06:15, Dec 07:16, 17

98943   extraspinal, 1 or more regions
→ *CPT Assistant* Jan 97:7, 11, Mar 97:10, Feb 99:10,
Dec 00:15, Mar 06:15, Dec 07:16, 17

Education and Training for Patient Self-Management

The following codes are used to report educational and training services prescribed by a physician and provided by a qualified, nonphysician healthcare professional using a standardized curriculum to an individual or a group of patients for the treatment of established illness(s)/disease(s) or to delay comorbidity(s). Education and training for patient self-management may be reported with these codes only when using a standardized curriculum as described below. This curriculum may be modified as necessary for the clinical needs, cultural norms and health literacy of the individual patient(s).

The purpose of the educational and training services is to teach the patient (may include caregiver[s]) how to effectively self-manage the patient's illness(s)/disease(s) or delay disease comorbidity(s) in conjunction with the patient's professional healthcare team. Education and training related to subsequent reinforcement or due to changes in the patient's condition or treatment plan are reported in the same manner as the original education and training. The type of education and training provided for the patient's clinical condition will be identified by the appropriate diagnosis code(s) reported.

The qualifications of the nonphysician healthcare professionals and the content of the educational and training program must be consistent with guidelines or standards established or recognized by a physician society, nonphysician healthcare professional society/association, or other appropriate source.

> (For counseling and education provided by a physician to an individual, see the appropriate Evaluation and Management codes)
>
> (For counseling and education provided by a physician to a group, use 99078)
>
> (For counseling and/or risk factor reduction intervention provided by a physician to patient(s) without symptoms or established disease, see 99401-99412)
>
> (For medical nutrition therapy, see 97802-97804)
>
> (For health and behavior assessment/intervention that is not part of a standardized curriculum, see 96150-96155)
>
> (For education provided as genetic counseling services, use 96040. For education to a group regarding genetic risks, see 98961, 98962)

98960   Education and training for patient self-management by a qualified, nonphysician health care professional using a standardized curriculum, face-to-face with the patient (could include caregiver/family) each 30 minutes; individual patient
→ *CPT Changes: An Insider's View* 2006

98961   2-4 patients
→ *CPT Assistant* Aug 07:9, Aug 08:3, Feb 09:13; *CPT Changes: An Insider's View* 2006

98962   5-8 patients
→ *CPT Assistant* Aug 07:9, Aug 08:3, Feb 09:13; *CPT Changes: An Insider's View* 2006

Non-Face-to-Face Nonphysician Services

Telephone Services

Telephone services are non-face-to-face assessment and management services provided by a qualified health care professional to a patient using the telephone. These codes are used to report episodes of care by the qualified health care professional initiated by an established patient or guardian of an established patient. If the telephone service ends with a decision to see the patient within 24 hours or the next available urgent visit appointment, the code is not reported; rather the encounter is considered part of the preservice work of the subsequent assessment and management service, procedure and visit. Likewise, if the telephone call refers to a service performed and reported by the qualified health care professional within the previous seven days (either qualified health care professional requested or unsolicited patient follow-up) or within the postoperative period of the previously completed procedure, then the service(s) are considered part of that previous service or procedure. (Do not report 98966-98969 if reporting 98966-98969 performed in the previous seven days.)

> (For telephone services provided by a physician, see 99441-99443)

98966   Telephone assessment and management service provided by a qualified nonphysician health care professional to an established patient, parent, or guardian not originating from a related assessment and management service provided within the previous 7 days nor leading to an assessment and management service or procedure within the next 24 hours or soonest available appointment; 5-10 minutes of medical discussion
→ *CPT Changes: An Insider's View* 2008

98967   11-20 minutes of medical discussion
→ *CPT Changes: An Insider's View* 2008

98968   21-30 minutes of medical discussion
→ *CPT Changes: An Insider's View* 2008

On-line Medical Evaluation

An on-line electronic medical evaluation is a non-face-to-face assessment and management service by a qualified health care professional to a patient using Internet resources in response to a patient's on-line inquiry. Reportable services involve the qualified health care professional's personal timely response to the patient's inquiry and must involve permanent storage (electronic or hard copy) of the encounter. This service is reported only once for the same episode of care during a seven-day period, although multiple qualified healthcare professionals could report their exchange with the same patient. If the on-line medical evaluation refers to an assessment and management service previously performed and reported by the qualified health care professional within the previous seven days (either qualified health care professional requested or unsolicited patient follow-up) or within the postoperative period of the previously completed procedure, then the service(s) are considered covered by the previous assessment and management office service or procedure. A reportable service encompasses the sum of communication (eg, related telephone calls, prescription provision, laboratory orders) pertaining to the on-line patient encounter.

(For an on-line medical evaluation provided by a physician, use 99444)

98969 Online assessment and management service provided by a qualified nonphysician health care professional to an established patient, guardian, or health care provider not originating from a related assessment and management service provided within the previous 7 days, using the Internet or similar electronic communications network

➜ *CPT Changes: An Insider's View* 2008

(Do not report 98969 when using 99339-99340, 99374-99380 for the same communication[s])

(Do not report 98969 for anticoagulation management when reporting 99363, 99364)

Special Services, Procedures and Reports

The procedures with code numbers 99000 through 99091 provide the reporting physician or other qualified healthcare professional with the means of identifying the completion of special reports and services that are an adjunct to the basic services rendered. The specific number assigned indicates the special circumstances under which a basic procedure is performed.

Code 99091 should be reported no more than once in a 30-day period to include the physician or health care provider time involved with data accession, review and interpretation, modification of care plan as necessary (including communication to patient and/or caregiver), and associated documentation.

If the services described by 99091 are provided on the same day the patient presents for an E/M service, these services should be considered part of the E/M service and not separately reported.

Do not report 99091 if it occurs within 30 days of care plan oversight services 99374-99380. Do not report 99091 if other more specific CPT codes exist (eg, 93014, 93227, 93233, 93272 for cardiographic services; 95250 for continuous glucose monitoring). Do not report 99091 for transfer and interpretation of data from hospital or clinical laboratory computers.

Codes 99050-99060 are reported in addition to an associated basic service. Typically only a single adjunct code from among 99050-99060 would be reported per patient encounter. However, there may be circumstances in which reporting multiple adjunct codes per patient encounter may be appropriate.

Miscellaneous Services

99000 Handling and/or conveyance of specimen for transfer from the physician's office to a laboratory

➜ *CPT Assistant* Winter 94:26, Feb 99:10, Oct 99:11, May 02:19, Aug 06:6, Sep 06:15, Jan 07:30

99001 Handling and/or conveyance of specimen for transfer from the patient in other than a physician's office to a laboratory (distance may be indicated)

➜ *CPT Assistant* Winter 94:26, May 02:19, Aug 06:6, Sep 06:15, Jan 07:30

99002 Handling, conveyance, and/or any other service in connection with the implementation of an order involving devices (eg, designing, fitting, packaging, handling, delivery or mailing) when devices such as orthotics, protectives, prosthetics are fabricated by an outside laboratory or shop but which items have been designed, and are to be fitted and adjusted by the attending physician

➜ *CPT Assistant* Winter 94:26, May 02:19, Aug 06:6, Sep 06:15, Jan 07:30

(For routine collection of venous blood, use 36415)

99024 Postoperative follow-up visit, normally included in the surgical package, to indicate that an evaluation and management service was performed during a postoperative period for a reason(s) related to the original procedure

➜ *CPT Assistant* Winter 94:26, Sep 97:10, Aug 98:5, May 02:19, Nov 03:13, Aug 06:6, Sep 06:15, Jan 07:30; *CPT Changes: An Insider's View* 2004

(As a component of a surgical "package," see **Surgery Guidelines**)

99026 Hospital mandated on call service; in-hospital, each hour

➜ *CPT Assistant* Jun 03:10, Aug 06:6, Sep 06:15, Jan 07:30; *CPT Changes: An Insider's View* 2003

99027 out-of-hospital, each hour

➜ *CPT Assistant* Jun 03:10, Aug 06:6, Sep 06:15, Jan 07:30; *CPT Changes: An Insider's View* 2003

(For physician standby services requiring prolonged physician attendance, use 99360, as appropriate. Time spent performing separately reportable procedure(s) or service(s) should not be included in the time reported as mandated on call service)

99050   Services provided in the office at times other than regularly scheduled office hours, or days when the office is normally closed (eg, holidays, Saturday or Sunday), in addition to basic service

➜ *CPT Assistant* Winter 94:27, May 02:19, Jun 03:10, May 06:18, Aug 06:6, Sep 06:15, Jan 07:30; *CPT Changes: An Insider's View* 2004, 2006

99051   Service(s) provided in the office during regularly scheduled evening, weekend, or holiday office hours, in addition to basic service

➜ *CPT Assistant* May 06:18, Aug 06:6, Sep 06:15, Jan 07:30; *CPT Changes: An Insider's View* 2006

99053   Service(s) provided between 10:00 PM and 8:00 AM at 24-hour facility, in addition to basic service

➜ *CPT Assistant* May 06:18, Aug 06:6, Sep 06:15, Jan 07:30; *CPT Changes: An Insider's View* 2006

99056   Service(s) typically provided in the office, provided out of the office at request of patient, in addition to basic service

➜ *CPT Assistant* Winter 94:27, May 02:19, May 06:18, Aug 06:6, Sep 06:15, Jan 07:30; *CPT Changes: An Insider's View* 2006

99058   Service(s) provided on an emergency basis in the office, which disrupts other scheduled office services, in addition to basic service

➜ *CPT Assistant* Winter 94:27, May 02:19, May 06:18, Aug 06:6, Sep 06:15, Jan 07:30; *CPT Changes: An Insider's View* 2006

99060   Service(s) provided on an emergency basis, out of the office, which disrupts other scheduled office services, in addition to basic service

➜ *CPT Assistant* May 06:18, Aug 06:6, Sep 06:15, Jan 07:30; *CPT Changes: An Insider's View* 2006

99070   Supplies and materials (except spectacles), provided by the physician over and above those usually included with the office visit or other services rendered (list drugs, trays, supplies, or materials provided)

➜ *CPT Assistant* Winter 94:28, May 98:10, Jun 99:10, Jun 00:11, Jul 01:2, May 02:19, Aug 02:11, Jun 05:1, Jul 06:1, Aug 06:6, Sep 06:15, Jan 07:30, 31, Feb 07:8, Sep 08:11

(For supply of spectacles, use the appropriate supply codes)

99071   Educational supplies, such as books, tapes, and pamphlets, provided by the physician for the patient's education at cost to physician

➜ *CPT Assistant* Winter 94:28, May 02:19, Aug 06:6, Sep 06:15, Jan 07:30

99075   Medical testimony

➜ *CPT Assistant* Winter 94:28, May 02:19, Aug 06:6, Sep 06:15, Jan 07:30

99078   Physician educational services rendered to patients in a group setting (eg, prenatal, obesity, or diabetic instructions)

➜ *CPT Assistant* Winter 94:28, Jan 98:12, May 02:19, Aug 06:6, Sep 06:15, Jan 07:30, Aug 07:9

99080   Special reports such as insurance forms, more than the information conveyed in the usual medical communications or standard reporting form

➜ *CPT Assistant* Winter 94:28, May 02:19, Aug 06:6, Sep 06:15, Jan 07:30

(Do not report 99080 in conjunction with 99455, 99456 for the completion of Workmen's Compensation forms)

99082   Unusual travel (eg, transportation and escort of patient)

➜ *CPT Assistant* May 02:19, Jan 03:24, Nov 03:14, Aug 06:6, Sep 06:15, Jan 07:30

99090   Analysis of clinical data stored in computers (eg, ECGs, blood pressures, hematologic data)

➜ *CPT Assistant* Winter 94:28, May 02:19, Jun 03:10, Aug 06:6, Sep 06:15, Jan 07:30, Feb 07:10, Jul 07:1, Apr 09:7; *CPT Changes: An Insider's View* 2002

(For physician/health care professional collection and interpretation of physiologic data stored/transmitted by patient/caregiver, see 99091)

(Do not report 99090 if other more specific CPT codes exist, eg, 93227, 93233, 93272 for cardiographic services; 95250 for continuous glucose monitoring, 97750 for musculoskeletal function testing)

99091   Collection and interpretation of physiologic data (eg, ECG, blood pressure, glucose monitoring) digitally stored and/or transmitted by the patient and/or caregiver to the physician or other qualified health care professional, requiring a minimum of 30 minutes of time

➜ *CPT Assistant* May 02:19, Jun 03:10, Aug 06:6, Sep 06:15, Jan 07:30, Apr 09:7; *CPT Changes: An Insider's View* 2002

Qualifying Circumstances for Anesthesia

(For explanation of these services, see **Anesthesia Guidelines**)

+ 99100   Anesthesia for patient of extreme age, younger than 1 year and older than 70 (List separately in addition to code for primary anesthesia procedure)

➜ *CPT Assistant* Apr 08:3

(For procedure performed on infants younger than 1 year of age at time of surgery, see 00326, 00561, 00834, 00836)

+ 99116   Anesthesia complicated by utilization of total body hypothermia (List separately in addition to code for primary anesthesia procedure)

➜ *CPT Assistant* Apr 08:3

+ 99135   Anesthesia complicated by utilization of controlled hypotension (List separately in addition to code for primary anesthesia procedure)
→ *CPT Assistant* Apr 08:3

+ 99140   Anesthesia complicated by emergency conditions (specify) (List separately in addition to code for primary anesthesia procedure)
→ *CPT Assistant* Mar 01:10, Apr 08:3

(An emergency is defined as existing when delay in treatment of the patient would lead to a significant increase in the threat to life or body part.)

Moderate (Conscious) Sedation

Moderate (conscious) sedation is a drug induced depression of consciousness during which patients respond purposefully to verbal commands, either alone or accompanied by light tactile stimulation. No interventions are required to maintain a patent airway, and spontaneous ventilation is adequate. Cardiovascular function is usually maintained.

Moderate sedation does not include minimal sedation (anxiolysis), deep sedation or monitored anesthesia care (00100-01999).

When providing moderate sedation, the following services are included and NOT reported separately:

- Assessment of the patient (not included in intraservice time);
- Establishment of IV access and fluids to maintain patency, when performed;
- Administration of agent(s);
- Maintenance of sedation;
- Monitoring of oxygen saturation, heart rate and blood pressure; and
- Recovery (not included in intraservice time).

Intraservice time starts with the administration of the sedation agent(s), requires continuous face-to-face attendance, and ends at the conclusion of personal contact by the physician providing the sedation.

Do not report 99143-99150 in conjunction with 94760-94762.

Do not report 99143-99145 in conjunction with codes listed in Appendix G. Do not report 99148-99150 in conjunction with codes listed in Appendix G when performed in the nonfacility setting.

When a second physician other than the healthcare professional performing the diagnostic or therapeutic services provides moderate sedation in the facility setting (eg, hospital, outpatient hospital/ambulatory surgery center, skilled nursing facility) for the procedures listed in Appendix G, the second physician reports 99148-99150.

However, for the circumstance in which these services are performed by the second physician in the nonfacility setting (eg, physician office, freestanding imaging center), codes 99148-99150 are not reported.

⊘ **99143**   Moderate sedation services (other than those services described by codes 00100-01999) provided by the same physician performing the diagnostic or therapeutic service that the sedation supports, requiring the presence of an independent trained observer to assist in the monitoring of the patient's level of consciousness and physiological status; younger than 5 years of age, first 30 minutes intra-service time
→ *CPT Assistant* Feb 06:9, May 06:19, 20, Feb 08:5; *CPT Changes: An Insider's View* 2006
→ *Clinical Examples in Radiology* Winter 06:18

⊘ **99144**   age 5 years or older, first 30 minutes intra-service time
→ *CPT Assistant* Feb 06:9, May 06:19, 20, Feb 08:5; *CPT Changes: An Insider's View* 2006
→ *Clinical Examples in Radiology* Winter 06:18, Summer 06:1-3, Fall 07:1,2, Spring 08:1,2, Summer 08:1, 2

+ 99145   each additional 15 minutes intra-service time (List separately in addition to code for primary service)
→ *CPT Assistant* Feb 06:9, May 06:19, 20, Feb 08:5; *CPT Changes: An Insider's View* 2006
→ *Clinical Examples in Radiology* Winter 06:18, Summer 06:1-3, Fall 07:1,2, Spring 08:1,2, Summer 08:1, 2

(Use 99145 in conjunction with 99143, 99144)

99148   Moderate sedation services (other than those services described by codes 00100-01999), provided by a physician other than the health care professional performing the diagnostic or therapeutic service that the sedation supports; younger than 5 years of age, first 30 minutes intra-service time
→ *CPT Assistant* Feb 06:9, May 06:19, 20; *CPT Changes: An Insider's View* 2006, 2008
→ *Clinical Examples in Radiology* Winter 06:18

99149   age 5 years or older, first 30 minutes intra-service time
→ *CPT Assistant* Feb 06:9, May 06:19, 20; *CPT Changes: An Insider's View* 2006, 2008
→ *Clinical Examples in Radiology* Winter 06:18

+ 99150   each additional 15 minutes intra-service time (List separately in addition to code for primary service)
→ *CPT Assistant* Feb 06:9, May 06:19, 20; *CPT Changes: An Insider's View* 2006
→ *Clinical Examples in Radiology* Winter 06:18

(Use 99150 in conjunction with 99148, 99149)

Other Services and Procedures

99170   Anogenital examination with colposcopic magnification in childhood for suspected trauma
→ *CPT Assistant* Nov 99:55, Apr 06:1

(For conscious sedation, use 99143-99150)

99172   Visual function screening, automated or semi-automated bilateral quantitative determination of visual acuity, ocular alignment, color vision by pseudoisochromatic plates, and field of vision (may include all or some screening of the determination[s] for contrast sensitivity, vision under glare)

➔ *CPT Assistant* Feb 01:7, Mar 05:1, 3; *CPT Changes: An Insider's View* 2001

(This service must employ graduated visual acuity stimuli that allow a quantitative determination of visual acuity [eg, Snellen chart]. This service may not be used in addition to a general ophthalmological service or an E/M service)

(Do not report 99172 in conjunction with 99173)

99173   Screening test of visual acuity, quantitative, bilateral

➔ *CPT Assistant* Nov 99:55, May 02:2, Mar 05:1, 3; *CPT Changes: An Insider's View* 2000

(The screening test used must employ graduated visual acuity stimuli that allow a quantitative estimate of visual acuity [eg, Snellen chart]. Other identifiable services unrelated to this screening test provided at the same time may be reported separately [eg, preventive medicine services]. When acuity is measured as part of a general ophthalmological service or of an E/M service of the eye, it is a diagnostic examination and not a screening test.)

(Do not report 99173 in conjunction with 99172)

99174   Ocular photoscreening with interpretation and report, bilateral

➔ *CPT Changes: An Insider's View* 2008

(Do not report 99174 in conjunction with 92002-92014, 99172, 99173)

99175   Ipecac or similar administration for individual emesis and continued observation until stomach adequately emptied of poison

(For diagnostic intubation, see 82926-82928, 89130-89141)

(For gastric lavage for diagnostic purposes, see 91055)

99183   Physician attendance and supervision of hyperbaric oxygen therapy, per session

➔ *CPT Assistant* Jan 03:23

(Evaluation and Management services and/or procedures [eg, wound debridement] provided in a hyperbaric oxygen treatment facility in conjunction with a hyperbaric oxygen therapy session should be reported separately)

▶(99185, 99186 have been deleted)◀

99190   Assembly and operation of pump with oxygenator or heat exchanger (with or without ECG and/or pressure monitoring); each hour

99191   45 minutes

99192   30 minutes

99195   Phlebotomy, therapeutic (separate procedure)

➔ *CPT Assistant* Apr 96:3, Jun 96:10

99199   Unlisted special service, procedure or report

➔ *CPT Assistant* Nov 99:55; *CPT Changes: An Insider's View* 2000

Home Health Procedures/Services

These codes are used by non-physician health care professionals. Physicians should utilize the home visit codes 99341-99350 and utilize CPT codes other than 99500-99600 for any additional procedure/service provided to a patient living in a residence.

The following codes are used to report services provided in a patient's residence (including assisted living apartments, group homes, nontraditional private homes, custodial care facilities, or schools).

Health care professionals who are authorized to use Evaluation and Management (E/M) Home Visit codes (99341-99350) may report 99500-99600 in addition to 99341-99350 if both services are performed. E/M services may be reported separately, using modifier 25, if the patient's condition requires a significant separately identifiable E/M service, above and beyond the home health service(s)/procedure(s) codes 99500-99600.

99500   Home visit for prenatal monitoring and assessment to include fetal heart rate, non-stress test, uterine monitoring, and gestational diabetes monitoring

➔ *CPT Assistant* Oct 03:7, Jan 07:30; *CPT Changes: An Insider's View* 2002

99501   Home visit for postnatal assessment and follow-up care

➔ *CPT Assistant* Oct 03:7, Jan 07:30; *CPT Changes: An Insider's View* 2002

99502   Home visit for newborn care and assessment

➔ *CPT Assistant* Oct 03:7, Jan 07:30; *CPT Changes: An Insider's View* 2002

99503   Home visit for respiratory therapy care (eg, bronchodilator, oxygen therapy, respiratory assessment, apnea evaluation)

➔ *CPT Assistant* Oct 03:7, Jan 07:30; *CPT Changes: An Insider's View* 2002

99504   Home visit for mechanical ventilation care

➔ *CPT Assistant* Oct 03:7, Jan 07:30; *CPT Changes: An Insider's View* 2002, 2003

99505   Home visit for stoma care and maintenance including colostomy and cystostomy

➔ *CPT Assistant* Oct 03:7, Jan 07:30; *CPT Changes: An Insider's View* 2002

99506   Home visit for intramuscular injections

➔ *CPT Assistant* Oct 03:7, Jan 07:30; *CPT Changes: An Insider's View* 2002

99507   Home visit for care and maintenance of catheter(s) (eg, urinary, drainage, and enteral)

➔ *CPT Assistant* Oct 03:7, Jan 07:30; *CPT Changes: An Insider's View* 2002

99509   Home visit for assistance with activities of daily living and personal care

➔ *CPT Assistant* Oct 03:7, Jan 07:30; *CPT Changes: An Insider's View* 2002

(To report self-care/home management training, see 97535)

(To report home medical nutrition assessment and intervention services, see 97802-97804)

(To report home speech therapy services, see 92507-92508)

99510   Home visit for individual, family, or marriage counseling

➔ *CPT Assistant* Oct 03:7, Jan 07:30; *CPT Changes: An Insider's View* 2002

99511   Home visit for fecal impaction management and enema administration

➔ *CPT Assistant* Oct 03:7, Jan 07:30; *CPT Changes: An Insider's View* 2002

99512   Home visit for hemodialysis

➔ *CPT Assistant* Oct 03:7, Jan 07:30; *CPT Changes: An Insider's View* 2002, 2004

(For home infusion of peritoneal dialysis, use 99601, 99602)

99600   Unlisted home visit service or procedure

➔ *CPT Assistant* Oct 03:7, Jan 07:30; *CPT Changes: An Insider's View* 2003

Home Infusion Procedures/Services

99601   Home infusion/specialty drug administration, per visit (up to 2 hours);

➔ *CPT Assistant* Nov 05:1; *CPT Changes: An Insider's View* 2004

+ 99602   each additional hour (List separately in addition to code for primary procedure)

➔ *CPT Assistant* Nov 05:1; *CPT Changes: An Insider's View* 2004

(Use 99602 in conjunction with 99601)

Medication Therapy Management Services

Medication therapy management service(s) (MTMS) describe face-to-face patient assessment and intervention as appropriate, by a pharmacist, upon request. MTMS is provided to optimize the response to medications or to manage treatment-related medication interactions or complications.

MTMS includes the following documented elements: review of the pertinent patient history, medication profile (prescription and nonprescription), and recommendations for improving health outcomes and treatment compliance. These codes are not to be used to describe the provision of product-specific information at the point of dispensing or any other routine dispensing-related activities.

99605   Medication therapy management service(s) provided by a pharmacist, individual, face-to-face with patient, with assessment and intervention if provided; initial 15 minutes, new patient

➔ *CPT Changes: An Insider's View* 2008

99606   initial 15 minutes, established patient

➔ *CPT Changes: An Insider's View* 2008

+ 99607   each additional 15 minutes (List separately in addition to code for primary service)

➔ *CPT Changes: An Insider's View* 2008

(Use 99607 in conjunction with 99605, 99606)

Category II Codes

The following section of *Current Procedural Terminology* (CPT) contains a set of supplemental tracking codes that can be used for performance measurement. It is anticipated that the use of Category II codes for performance measurement will decrease the need for record abstraction and chart review, and thereby minimize administrative burden on physicians, other health care professionals, hospitals, and entities seeking to measure the quality of patient care. These codes are intended to facilitate data collection about the quality of care rendered by coding certain services and test results that support nationally established performance measures and that have an evidence base as contributing to quality patient care.

The use of these codes is optional. The codes are not required for correct coding and may not be used as a substitute for Category I codes.

These codes describe clinical components that may be typically included in evaluation and management services or clinical services and, therefore, do not have a relative value associated with them. Category II codes may also describe results from clinical laboratory or radiology tests and other procedures, identified processes intended to address patient safety practices, or services reflecting compliance with state or federal law.

Category II codes described in this section make use of alphabetical characters as the 5th character in the string (ie, 4 digits followed by the letter **F**). These digits are not intended to reflect the placement of the code in the regular (Category I) part of the CPT codebook. To promote understanding of these codes and their associated measures, users are referred to Appendix H, which contains information about performance measurement exclusion modifiers, measures, and the measure's source.

Cross-references to the measures associated with each Category II code and their source are included for reference in Appendix H. In addition, acronyms for the related diseases or clinical condition(s) have been added at the end of each code descriptor to identify the topic or clinical category in which that code is included. A complete listing of the diseases/clinical conditions, and their acronyms are provided in alphabetical order in Appendix H. Users should review the complete measure(s) associated with each code prior to implementation.

Category II codes are reviewed by the Performance Measures Advisory Group (PMAG), an advisory body to the CPT Editorial Panel and the CPT/HCPAC Advisory Committee. The PMAG is comprised of performance measurement experts representing the Agency for Healthcare Research and Quality (AHRQ), the American Medical Association (AMA), the Centers for Medicare and Medicaid Services (CMS), The Joint Commission (TJC), the National Committee for Quality Assurance (NCQA), and the Physician Consortium for Performance Improvement® (PCPI). The PMAG may seek additional expertise and/or input from other national health care organizations, as necessary, for the development of tracking codes. These may include national medical specialty societies, other national health care professional associations, accrediting bodies, and federal regulatory agencies.

The most current listing of Category II codes, including guidelines, Code Change Proposal forms, and release and implementation dates for Category II codes may be accessed at http://www.ama-assn.org/go/cpt.

> (For blood pressure measured, use 2000F)

> (For tobacco use cessation intervention, pharmacologic therapy, use 4001F)

Modifiers

The following performance measurement modifiers may be used for Category II codes to indicate that a service specified in the associated measure(s) was considered but, due to either medical, patient, or system circumstance(s) documented in the medical record, the service was not provided. These modifiers serve as denominator exclusions from the performance measure. The user should note that not all listed measures provide for exclusions (see Appendix H for more discussion regarding exclusion criteria).

Category II modifiers should only be reported with Category II codes—they should not be reported with Category I or Category III codes. In addition, the modifiers in the Category II section should only be used where specified in the guidelines, reporting instructions, parenthetic notes, or code descriptor language listed in the Category II section (code listing and Appendix H).

1P Performance Measure Exclusion Modifier due to Medical Reasons

Reasons include:

- Not indicated (absence of organ/limb, already received/performed, other)

- Contraindicated (patient allergic history, potential adverse drug interaction, other)

Other medical reasons

2P Performance Measure Exclusion Modifier due to Patient Reasons

Reasons include:

- Patient declined
- Economic, social, or religious reasons
- Other patient reasons

3P Performance Measure Exclusion Modifier due to System Reasons

Reasons include:

- Resources to perform the services not available
- Insurance coverage/payor-related limitations
- Other reasons attributable to health care delivery system

Modifier 8P is intended to be used as a "reporting modifier" to allow the reporting of circumstances when an action described in a measure's numerator is not performed and the reason is not otherwise specified.

8P Performance measure reporting modifier—action not performed, reason not otherwise specified

Composite Codes

Composite codes combine several measures grouped within a single code descriptor to facilitate reporting for a clinical condition when all components are met. If only some of the components are met or if services are provided in addition to those included in the composite code, they may be reported individually using the corresponding CPT Category II codes for those services.

0001F Heart failure assessed (includes assessment of all the following components) (CAD, HF)[1]:

Blood pressure measured (2000F)[1]

Level of activity assessed (1003F)[1]

Clinical symptoms of volume overload (excess) assessed (1004F)[1]

Weight, recorded (2001F)[1]

Clinical signs of volume overload (excess) assessed (2002F)[1]

➜ *CPT Assistant* Oct 05:1; *CPT Changes: An Insider's View* 2006, 2007

(To report blood pressure measured, use 2000F)

0005F Osteoarthritis assessed (OA)[1]

Includes assessment of all the following components:

Osteoarthritis symptoms and functional status assessed (1006F)[1]

Use of anti-inflammatory or over-the-counter (OTC) analgesic medications assessed (1007F)[1]

Initial examination of the involved joint(s) (includes visual inspection, palpation, range of motion) (2004F)[1]

➜ *CPT Assistant* Oct 05:1, 6; *CPT Changes: An Insider's View* 2006, 2007

(To report tobacco use cessation intervention, use 4001F)

0012F Community-acquired bacterial pneumonia assessment (includes all of the following components) (CAP)[1]:

Co-morbid conditions assessed (1026F)[1]

Vital signs recorded (2010F)[1]

Mental status assessed (2014F)[1]

Hydration status assessed (2018F)[1]

➜ *CPT Changes: An Insider's View* 2007

0014F Comprehensive preoperative assessment performed for cataract surgery with intraocular lens (IOL) placement (includes assessment of all of the following components) (EC)[5]:

➜ *CPT Changes: An Insider's View* 2009

Dilated fundus evaluation performed within 12 months prior to cataract surgery (2020F)[5]

Pre-surgical (cataract) axial length, corneal power measurement and method of intraocular lens power calculation documented (must be performed within 12 months prior to surgery) (3073F)[5]

Preoperative assessment of functional or medical indication(s) for surgery prior to the cataract surgery with intraocular lens placement (must be performed within 12 months prior to cataract surgery) (3325F)[5]

➜ *CPT Changes: An Insider's View* 2009

0015F Melanoma follow up completed (includes assessment of all the following components) (ML)[5]:

➜ *CPT Changes: An Insider's View* 2009

History obtained regarding new or changing moles (1050F)[5]

Complete physical skin exam performed (2029F)[5]

Patient counseled to perform a monthly self skin examination (5005F)[5]

➜ *CPT Changes: An Insider's View* 2009

Footnotes

[1] Physician Consortium for Performance Improvement® (PCPI), www.physicianconsortium.org

[2] National Committee on Quality Assurance (NCQA), Health Employer Data Information Set (HEDIS®), www.ncqa.org

[3] The Joint Commission (TJC) ORYX Initiative Performance Measures, www.thejointcommission.org

[4] National Diabetes Quality Improvement Alliance (NDQIA), www.nationaldiabetesalliance.org

[5] Joint measure from the Physician Consortium for Performance Improvement, www.physicianconsortium.org and National Committee on Quality Assurance (NCQA), www.ncqa.org

[6] The Society of Thoracic Surgeons, www.sts.org, National Quality Forum, www.qualityforum.org

Patient Management

Patient management codes describe utilization measures or measures of patient care provided for specific clinical purposes (eg, prenatal care, pre- and post-surgical care).

0500F Initial prenatal care visit (report at first prenatal encounter with health care professional providing obstetrical care. Report also date of visit and, in a separate field, the date of the last menstrual period [LMP] (Prenatal)[2]

➔ *CPT Assistant* Oct 05:1, 6, 1, Aug 07:1; *CPT Changes: An Insider's View* 2005

0501F Prenatal flow sheet documented in medical record by first prenatal visit (documentation includes at minimum blood pressure, weight, urine protein, uterine size, fetal heart tones, and estimated date of delivery). Report also: date of visit and, in a separate field, the date of the last menstrual period [LMP] (Note: If reporting 0501F Prenatal flow sheet, it is not necessary to report 0500F Initial prenatal care visit) (Prenatal)[1]

➔ *CPT Assistant* Oct 05:6; *CPT Changes: An Insider's View* 2005

0502F Subsequent prenatal care visit (Prenatal)[2]

[Excludes: patients who are seen for a condition unrelated to pregnancy or prenatal care (eg, an upper respiratory infection; patients seen for consultation only, not for continuing care)]

➔ *CPT Assistant* Oct 05:6; *CPT Changes: An Insider's View* 2005, 2007

0503F Postpartum care visit (Prenatal)[2]

➔ *CPT Assistant* Oct 05:6; *CPT Changes: An Insider's View* 2005

0505F Hemodialysis plan of care documented (ESRD, P-ESRD)[1]

➔ *CPT Changes: An Insider's View* 2008

0507F Peritoneal dialysis plan of care documented (ESRD)[1]

➔ *CPT Changes: An Insider's View* 2008

0509F Urinary incontinence plan of care documented (GER)[5]

➔ *CPT Changes: An Insider's View* 2008

0513F Elevated blood pressure plan of care documented (CKD)[1]

➔ *CPT Changes: An Insider's View* 2009

0514F Plan of care for elevated hemoglobin level documented for patient receiving Erythropoiesis-Stimulating Agent therapy (ESA) (CKD)[1]

➔ *CPT Changes: An Insider's View* 2009

0516F Anemia plan of care documented (ESRD)[1]

➔ *CPT Changes: An Insider's View* 2009

0517F Glaucoma plan of care documented (EC)[5]

➔ *CPT Changes: An Insider's View* 2009

0518F Falls plan of care documented (GER)[5]

➔ *CPT Changes: An Insider's View* 2009

▲ **0519F** Planned chemotherapy regimen, including at a minimum: drug(s) prescribed, dose, and duration, documented prior to initiation of a new treatment regimen (ONC)[1]

➔ *CPT Changes: An Insider's View* 2009, 2010

▲ **0520F** Radiation dose limits to normal tissues established prior to the initiation of a course of 3D conformal radiation for a minimum of 2 tissue/organ (ONC)[1]

➔ *CPT Changes: An Insider's View* 2009, 2010

▲ **0521F** Plan of care to address pain documented (COA)[2] (ONC)[1]

➔ *CPT Changes: An Insider's View* 2009, 2010

0525F Initial visit for episode (BkP)[2]

➔ *CPT Changes: An Insider's View* 2009

0526F Subsequent visit for episode (BkP)[2]

➔ *CPT Changes: An Insider's View* 2009

● **0528F** Recommended follow-up interval for repeat colonoscopy of at least 10 years documented in colonoscopy report (End/Polyp)[5]

➔ *CPT Changes: An Insider's View* 2010

● **0529F** Interval of 3 or more years since patient's last colonoscopy, documented (End/Polyp)[5]

➔ *CPT Changes: An Insider's View* 2010

● **0535F** Dyspnea management plan of care, documented (Pall Cr)[5]

➔ *CPT Changes: An Insider's View* 2010

● **0540F** Glucorticoid Management Plan Documented (RA)[5]

➔ *CPT Changes: An Insider's View* 2010

● **0575F** HIV RNA control plan of care, documented (HIV)[5]

➔ *CPT Changes: An Insider's View* 2010

Patient History

Patient history codes describe measures for select aspects of patient history or review of systems.

1000F Tobacco use assessed (CAD, CAP, COPD, PV)[1] (DM)[4]

➔ *CPT Assistant* Oct 05:1, 6; *CPT Changes: An Insider's View* 2005, 2007

1002F Anginal symptoms and level of activity assessed (CAD)[1]

➔ *CPT Assistant* Oct 05:6; *CPT Changes: An Insider's View* 2005

1003F Level of activity assessed (HF)[1]

➔ *CPT Assistant* Oct 05:6; *CPT Changes: An Insider's View* 2006

1004F Clinical symptoms of volume overload (excess) assessed (HF)[1]

➔ *CPT Assistant* Oct 05:6; *CPT Changes: An Insider's View* 2006

Footnotes

[1] Physician Consortium for Performance Improvement, www.ama-assn.org/go/quality

[2] National Committee on Quality Assurance (NCQA), Health Employer Data Information Set (HEDIS®), www.ncqa.org

[3] The Joint Commission (TJC) ORYX Initiative Performance Measures, www.thejointcommission.org

[4] National Diabetes Quality Improvement Alliance (NDQIA), www.nationaldiabetesalliance.org

[5] Joint measure from the Physician Consortium for Performance Improvement, www.physicianconsortium.org and National Committee on Quality Assurance (NCQA), www.ncqa.org

[6] The Society of Thoracic Surgeons, www.sts.org, National Quality Forum, www.qualityforum.org

---

1005F   Asthma symptoms evaluated (includes physician documentation of numeric frequency of symptoms or patient completion of an asthma assessment tool/survey/questionnaire) (Asthma)[1]
➡ *CPT Assistant* Oct 05:6; *CPT Changes: An Insider's View* 2006

1006F   Osteoarthritis symptoms and functional status assessed (may include the use of a standardized scale or the completion of an assessment questionnaire, such as the SF-36, AAOS Hip & Knee Questionnaire) (OA)[1]

[Instructions: Report when osteoarthritis is addressed during the patient encounter]
➡ *CPT Assistant* Oct 05:6; *CPT Changes: An Insider's View* 2006

1007F   Use of anti-inflammatory or analgesic over-the-counter (OTC) medications for symptom relief assessed (OA)[1]
➡ *CPT Assistant* Oct 05:6; *CPT Changes: An Insider's View* 2006

1008F   Gastrointestinal and renal risk factors assessed for patients on prescribed or OTC non-steroidal anti-inflammatory drug (NSAID) (OA)[1]
➡ *CPT Assistant* Oct 05:6; *CPT Changes: An Insider's View* 2006

1015F   Chronic obstructive pulmonary disease (COPD) symptoms assessed (Includes assessment of at least 1 of the following: dyspnea, cough/sputum, wheezing), or respiratory symptom assessment tool completed (COPD)[1]
➡ *CPT Changes: An Insider's View* 2007

1018F   Dyspnea assessed, not present (COPD)[1]
➡ *CPT Changes: An Insider's View* 2007

1019F   Dyspnea assessed, present (COPD)[1]
➡ *CPT Changes: An Insider's View* 2007

1022F   Pneumococcus immunization status assessed (CAP, COPD)[1]
➡ *CPT Changes: An Insider's View* 2007

1026F   Co-morbid conditions assessed (eg, includes assessment for presence or absence of: malignancy, liver disease, congestive heart failure, cerebrovascular disease, renal disease, chronic obstructive pulmonary disease, asthma, diabetes, other co-morbid conditions) (CAP)[1]
➡ *CPT Changes: An Insider's View* 2007

1030F   Influenza immunization status assessed (CAP)[1]
➡ *CPT Changes: An Insider's View* 2007

1034F   Current tobacco smoker (CAD, CAP, COPD, PV)[1] (DM)[4]
➡ *CPT Changes: An Insider's View* 2007

1035F   Current smokeless tobacco user (eg, chew, snuff) (PV)[1]
➡ *CPT Changes: An Insider's View* 2007

1036F   Current tobacco non-user (CAD, CAP, COPD, PV)[1] (DM)[4]
➡ *CPT Changes: An Insider's View* 2007

1038F   Persistent asthma (mild, moderate or severe) (Asthma)[1]
➡ *CPT Changes: An Insider's View* 2007

1039F   Intermittent asthma (Asthma)[1]
➡ *CPT Changes: An Insider's View* 2007

1040F   DSM-IV™ criteria for major depressive disorder documented at the initial evaluation (MDD)[1]
➡ *CPT Changes: An Insider's View* 2008, 2009

1050F   History obtained regarding new or changing moles (ML)[5]
➡ *CPT Changes: An Insider's View* 2008

1055F   Visual functional status assessed (EC)[5]
➡ *CPT Changes: An Insider's View* 2008

1060F   Documentation of permanent OR persistent OR paroxysmal atrial fibrillation (STR)[5]
➡ *CPT Changes: An Insider's View* 2008

1061F   Documentation of absence of permanent AND persistent AND paroxysmal atrial fibrillation (STR)[5]
➡ *CPT Changes: An Insider's View* 2008

1065F   Ischemic stroke symptom onset of less than 3 hours prior to arrival (STR)[5]
➡ *CPT Changes: An Insider's View* 2008

1066F   Ischemic stroke symptom onset greater than or equal to 3 hours prior to arrival (STR)[5]
➡ *CPT Changes: An Insider's View* 2008

1070F   Alarm symptoms (involuntary weight loss, dysphagia, or gastrointestinal bleeding) assessed; none present (GERD)[5]
➡ *CPT Changes: An Insider's View* 2008

1071F   1 or more present (GERD)[5]
➡ *CPT Changes: An Insider's View* 2008

(1080F has been deleted. To report Surrogate decision maker or advance care plan documented in the medical record, report code 1123F or 1124F.)

1090F   Presence or absence of urinary incontinence assessed (GER)[5]
➡ *CPT Changes: An Insider's View* 2008

1091F   Urinary incontinence characterized (eg, frequency, volume, timing, type of symptoms, how bothersome) (GER)[5]
➡ *CPT Changes: An Insider's View* 2008

1100F   Patient screened for future fall risk; documentation of 2 or more falls in the past year or any fall with injury in the past year (GER)[5]
➡ *CPT Changes: An Insider's View* 2008

1101F   documentation of no falls in the past year or only 1 fall without injury in the past year (GER)[5]
➡ *CPT Changes: An Insider's View* 2008

Footnotes

[1] Physician Consortium for Performance Improvement® (PCPI), www.physicianconsortium.org
[2] National Committee on Quality Assurance (NCQA), Health Employer Data Information Set (HEDIS®), www.ncqa.org
[3] The Joint Commission (TJC) ORYX Initiative Performance Measures, www.thejointcommission.org
[4] National Diabetes Quality Improvement Alliance (NDQIA), www.nationaldiabetesalliance.org
[5] Joint measure from the Physician Consortium for Performance Improvement, www.physicianconsortium.org and National Committee on Quality Assurance (NCQA), www.ncqa.org
[6] The Society of Thoracic Surgeons, www.sts.org, National Quality Forum, www.qualityforum.org

1110F Patient discharged from an inpatient facility (eg, hospital, skilled nursing facility, or rehabilitation facility) within the last 60 days (GER)[5]

→ *CPT Changes: An Insider's View* 2008

1111F Discharge medications reconciled with the current medication list in outpatient medical record (COA)[2] (GER)[5]

→ *CPT Changes: An Insider's View* 2008

1116F Auricular or periauricular pain assessed (AOE)[1]

→ *CPT Changes: An Insider's View* 2009

1118F GERD symptoms assessed after 12 months of therapy (GERD)[5]

→ *CPT Changes: An Insider's View* 2009

1119F Initial evaluation for condition (HEP C)[1]

→ *CPT Changes: An Insider's View* 2009

1121F Subsequent evaluation for condition (HEP C)[1]

→ *CPT Changes: An Insider's View* 2009

1123F Advance Care Planning discussed and documented advance care plan or surrogate decision maker documented in the medical record (GER, Pall Cr)[5]

→ *CPT Changes: An Insider's View* 2009

1124F Advance Care Planning discussed and documented in the medical record – patient did not wish or was not able to name a surrogate decision maker or provide an advance care plan (GER, Pall Cr)[5]

→ *CPT Changes: An Insider's View* 2009, 2010

1125F Pain severity quantified; pain present (COA)[2] (ONC)[1]

→ *CPT Changes: An Insider's View* 2009

1126F no pain present (COA)[2] (ONC)[1]

→ *CPT Changes: An Insider's View* 2009, 2010

1127F New episode for condition (ML)[5]

→ *CPT Changes: An Insider's View* 2009

1128F Subsequent episode for condition (ML)[5]

→ *CPT Changes: An Insider's View* 2009

1130F Back pain and function assessed, including all of the following: Pain assessment AND functional status AND patient history, including notation of presence or absence of "red flags" (warning signs) AND assessment of prior treatment and response, AND employment status (BkP)[2]

→ *CPT Changes: An Insider's View* 2009

1134F Episode of back pain lasting 6 weeks or less (BkP)[2]

→ *CPT Changes: An Insider's View* 2009

1135F Episode of back pain lasting longer than 6 weeks (BkP)[2]

→ *CPT Changes: An Insider's View* 2009

1136F Episode of back pain lasting 12 weeks or less (BkP)[2]

→ *CPT Changes: An Insider's View* 2009

1137F Episode of back pain lasting longer than 12 weeks (BkP)[2]

→ *CPT Changes: An Insider's View* 2009

● **1150F** Documentation that a patient has a substantial risk of death within 1 year (Pall Cr)[5]

→ *CPT Changes: An Insider's View* 2010

● **1151F** Documentation that a patient does not have a substantial risk of death within one year (Pall Cr)[5]

→ *CPT Changes: An Insider's View* 2010

● **1152F** Documentation of advanced disease diagnosis, goals of care prioritize comfort (Pall Cr)[5]

→ *CPT Changes: An Insider's View* 2010

● **1153F** Documentation of advanced disease diagnosis, goals of care do not prioritize comfort (Pall Cr)[5]

→ *CPT Changes: An Insider's View* 2010

● **1157F** Advance care plan or similar legal document present in the medical record (COA)[2]

→ *CPT Changes: An Insider's View* 2010

● **1158F** Advance care planning discussion documented in the medical record (COA)[2]

→ *CPT Changes: An Insider's View* 2010

● **1159F** Medication list documented in medical record (COA)[2]

→ *CPT Changes: An Insider's View* 2010

● **1160F** Review of all medications by a prescribing practitioner or clinical pharmacist (such as, prescriptions, OTCs, herbal therapies and supplements) documented in the medical record (COA)[2]

→ *CPT Changes: An Insider's View* 2010

● **1170F** Functional status assessed (COA)[2] (RA)[5]

→ *CPT Changes: An Insider's View* 2010

● **1180F** All specified thromboembolic risk factors assessed (AFIB)[1]

→ *CPT Changes: An Insider's View* 2010

● **1220F** Patient screened for depression (SUD)[5]

→ *CPT Changes: An Insider's View* 2010

Footnotes

[1] Physician Consortium for Performance Improvement® (PCPI), www.physicianconsortium.org

[2] National Committee on Quality Assurance (NCQA), Health Employer Data Information Set (HEDIS®), www.ncqa.org

[3] The Joint Commission (TJC) ORYX Initiative Performance Measures, www.thejointcommission.org

[4] National Diabetes Quality Improvement Alliance (NDQIA), www.nationaldiabetesalliance.org

[5] Joint measure from the Physician Consortium for Performance Improvement, www.physicianconsortium.org and National Committee on Quality Assurance (NCQA), www.ncqa.org

[6] The Society of Thoracic Surgeons, www.sts.org, National Quality Forum, www.qualityforum.org

Physical Examination

Physical examination codes describe aspects of physical examination or clinical assessment.

2000F Blood pressure measured (CAD, CKD, HF, HTN)[1](DM)[2,4]
> *CPT Assistant* Oct 05:1, 6, Aug 07:1; *CPT Changes: An Insider's View* 2005, 2009

2001F Weight recorded (HF, PAG)[1]
> *CPT Assistant* Oct 05:6; *CPT Changes: An Insider's View* 2006

2002F Clinical signs of volume overload (excess) assessed (HF)[1]
> *CPT Assistant* Oct 05:6; *CPT Changes: An Insider's View* 2006

2004F Initial examination of the involved joint(s) (includes visual inspection, palpation, range of motion) (OA)[1]

[Instructions: Report only for initial osteoarthritis visit or for visits for new joint involvement]
> *CPT Assistant* Oct 05:6; *CPT Changes: An Insider's View* 2006

2010F Vital signs (temperature, pulse, respiratory rate, and blood pressure) documented and reviewed (CAP)[1] (EM)[5]
> *CPT Changes: An Insider's View* 2007, 2008

2014F Mental status assessed (CAP)[1] (EM)[5]
> *CPT Changes: An Insider's View* 2007, 2008

2018F Hydration status assessed (normal/mildly dehydrated/severely dehydrated) (CAP)[1]
> *CPT Changes: An Insider's View* 2007

2019F Dilated macular exam performed, including documentation of the presence or absence of macular thickening or hemorrhage AND the level of macular degeneration severity (EC)[5]
> *CPT Changes: An Insider's View* 2008

2020F Dilated fundus evaluation performed within 12 months prior to cataract surgery (EC)[5]
> *CPT Changes: An Insider's View* 2008, 2009

2021F Dilated macular or fundus exam performed, including documentation of the presence or absence of macular edema AND level of severity of retinopathy (EC)[5]
> *CPT Changes: An Insider's View* 2008

2022F Dilated retinal eye exam with interpretation by an ophthalmologist or optometrist documented and reviewed (DM)[2,4]
> *CPT Changes: An Insider's View* 2007, 2009

2024F 7 standard field stereoscopic photos with interpretation by an ophthalmologist or optometrist documented and reviewed (DM)[2,4]
> *CPT Changes: An Insider's View* 2007, 2009

2026F Eye imaging validated to match diagnosis from 7 standard field stereoscopic photos results documented and reviewed (DM)[2,4]
> *CPT Changes: An Insider's View* 2007, 2009

2027F Optic nerve head evaluation performed (EC)[5]
> *CPT Changes: An Insider's View* 2008

2028F Foot examination performed (includes examination through visual inspection, sensory exam with monofilament, and pulse exam – report when any of the 3 components are completed) (DM)[4]
> *CPT Changes: An Insider's View* 2007

2029F Complete physical skin exam performed (ML)[5]
> *CPT Changes: An Insider's View* 2008

2030F Hydration status documented, normally hydrated (PAG)[1]
> *CPT Changes: An Insider's View* 2008

2031F Hydration status documented, dehydrated (PAG)[1]
> *CPT Changes: An Insider's View* 2008

2035F Tympanic membrane mobility assessed with pneumatic otoscopy or tympanometry (OME)[1]
> *CPT Changes: An Insider's View* 2009

2040F Physical examination on the date of the initial visit for low back pain performed, in accordance with specifications (BkP)[2]
> *CPT Changes: An Insider's View* 2009

2044F Documentation of mental health assessment prior to intervention (back surgery or epidural steroid injection) or for back pain episode lasting longer than 6 weeks (BkP)[2]
> *CPT Changes: An Insider's View* 2009

● **2050F** Wound characteristics including size AND nature of wound base tissue AND amount of drainage prior to debridement documented (CWC)[5]
> *CPT Changes: An Insider's View* 2010

Diagnostic/Screening Processes or Results

Diagnostic/screening processes or results codes describe results of tests ordered (clinical laboratory tests, radiological or other procedural examinations, and conclusions of medical decision-making).

(Code 3000F has been deleted. To report blood pressure use the corresponding systolic codes (3074F, 3075F, 3077F) and diastolic codes (3078F, 3079F, 3080F)

Footnotes

[1] Physician Consortium for Performance Improvement® (PCPI), www.physicianconsortium.org

[2] National Committee on Quality Assurance (NCQA), Health Employer Data Information Set (HEDIS®), www.ncqa.org

[3] The Joint Commission (TJC) ORYX Initiative Performance Measures, www.thejointcommission.org

[4] National Diabetes Quality Improvement Alliance (NDQIA), www.nationaldiabetesalliance.org

[5] Joint measure from the Physician Consortium for Performance Improvement, www.physicianconsortium.org and National Committee on Quality Assurance (NCQA), www.ncqa.org

[6] The Society of Thoracic Surgeons, www.sts.org, National Quality Forum, www.qualityforum.org

(Code 3002F has been deleted. To report blood pressure use the corresponding systolic codes (3074F, 3075F, 3077F) and diastolic codes (3078F, 3079F, 3080F)

3006F Chest X-ray results documented and reviewed (CAP)[1]

> *CPT Assistant* Aug 07:1; *CPT Changes: An Insider's View* 2007

3011F Lipid panel results documented and reviewed (must include total cholesterol, HDL-C, triglycerides and calculated LDL-C) (CAD)[1]

> *CPT Changes: An Insider's View* 2007

3014F Screening mammography results documented and reviewed (PV)[1, 2]

> *CPT Changes: An Insider's View* 2007, 2009

● **3016F** Patient screened for unhealthy alcohol use using a systematic screening method (PV)[1]

> *CPT Changes: An Insider's View* 2010

3017F Colorectal cancer screening results documented and reviewed (PV)[1, 2]

> *CPT Changes: An Insider's View* 2009

● **3018F** Pre-procedure risk assessment AND depth of insertion AND quality of the bowel prep AND complete description of polyp(s) found, including location of each polyp, size, number and gross morphology AND recommendations for follow-up in final colonoscopy report documented (End/Polyp)[5]

> *CPT Changes: An Insider's View* 2010

3020F Left ventricular function (LVF) assessment (eg, echocardiography, nuclear test, or ventriculography) documented in the medical record (Includes quantitative or qualitative assessment results) (HF)[1]

> *CPT Changes: An Insider's View* 2007

3021F Left ventricular ejection fraction (LVEF) less than 40% or documentation of moderately or severely depressed left ventricular systolic function (CAD, HF)[1]

> *CPT Changes: An Insider's View* 2007

3022F Left ventricular ejection fraction (LVEF) greater than or equal to 40% or documentation as normal or mildly depressed left ventricular systolic function (CAD, HF)[1]

> *CPT Changes: An Insider's View* 2007

3023F Spirometry results documented and reviewed (COPD)[1]

> *CPT Changes: An Insider's View* 2007

3025F Spirometry test results demonstrate FEV_1/FVC less than 70% with COPD symptoms (eg, dyspnea, cough/sputum, wheezing) (CAP, COPD)[1]

> *CPT Changes: An Insider's View* 2007

3027F Spirometry test results demonstrate FEV_1/FVC greater than or equal to 70% or patient does not have COPD symptoms (COPD)[1]

> *CPT Changes: An Insider's View* 2007

3028F Oxygen saturation results documented and reviewed (includes assessment through pulse oximetry or arterial blood gas measurement) (CAP, COPD)[1] (EM)[5]

> *CPT Changes: An Insider's View* 2007

3035F Oxygen saturation less than or equal to 88 % or a PaO_2 less than or equal to 55 mm Hg (COPD)[1].

> *CPT Changes: An Insider's View* 2007

3037F Oxygen saturation greater than 88% or PaO_2 greater than 55 mmHg (COPD)[1]

> *CPT Changes: An Insider's View* 2007

3040F Functional expiratory volume (FEV_1) less than 40% of predicted value (COPD)[1]

> *CPT Changes: An Insider's View* 2007

3042F Functional expiratory volume (FEV_1) greater than or equal to 40% of predicted value (COPD)[1]

> *CPT Changes: An Insider's View* 2007

3044F Most recent hemoglobin A1c (HbA1c) level less than 7.0% (DM)[2,4]

> *CPT Changes: An Insider's View* 2008

3045F Most recent hemoglobin A1c (HbA1c) level 7.0 – 9.0 % (DM)[2,4]

> *CPT Changes: An Insider's View* 2008

3046F Most recent hemoglobin A1c level greater than 9.0% (DM)[4]

> *CPT Changes: An Insider's View* 2007

(Code 3047F has been deleted. To report most recent hemoglobin A1c level less than or equal to 9.0%, see codes 3044F-3045F)

3048F Most recent LDL-C less than 100 mg/dL (DM)[4]

> *CPT Changes: An Insider's View* 2007

3049F Most recent LDL-C 100-129 mg/dL (DM)[4]

> *CPT Changes: An Insider's View* 2007

3050F Most recent LDL-C greater than or equal to 130 mg/dL (DM)[4]

> *CPT Changes: An Insider's View* 2007

3060F Positive microalbuminuria test result documented and reviewed (DM)[2,4]

> *CPT Changes: An Insider's View* 2007

3061F Negative microalbuminuria test result documented and reviewed (DM)[2, 4]

> *CPT Changes: An Insider's View* 2007

3062F Positive macroalbuminuria test result documented and reviewed (DM)[2,4]

> *CPT Changes: An Insider's View* 2007

Footnotes

[1] Physician Consortium for Performance Improvement® (PCPI), www.physicianconsortium.org

[2] National Committee on Quality Assurance (NCQA), Health Employer Data Information Set (HEDIS®), www.ncqa.org

[3] The Joint Commission (TJC) ORYX Initiative Performance Measures, www.thejointcommission.org

[4] National Diabetes Quality Improvement Alliance (NDQIA), www.nationaldiabetesalliance.org

[5] Joint measure from the Physician Consortium for Performance Improvement, www.physicianconsortium.org and National Committee on Quality Assurance (NCQA), www.ncqa.org

[6] The Society of Thoracic Surgeons, www.sts.org, National Quality Forum, www.qualityforum.org

---

 ▲=Revised code   ●=New code   ►◄=Contains new or revised text   ⦸=Modifier 51 exempt

3066F Documentation of treatment for nephropathy (eg, patient receiving dialysis, patient being treated for ESRD, CRF, ARF, or renal insufficiency, any visit to a nephrologist) (DM)[2,4]

→ *CPT Changes: An Insider's View* 2007

3072F Low risk for retinopathy (no evidence of retinopathy in the prior year) (DM)[2,4]

→ *CPT Changes: An Insider's View* 2007

3073F Pre-surgical (cataract) axial length, corneal power measurement and method of intraocular lens power calculation documented within 12 months prior to surgery (EC)[5]

→ *CPT Changes: An Insider's View* 2008, 2009

3074F Most recent systolic blood pressure less than 130 mm Hg (DM)[2,4] (HTN, CKD)[1]

→ *CPT Changes: An Insider's View* 2008

3075F Most recent systolic blood pressure 130 - 139 mm Hg (DM)[2,4] (HTN, CKD)[1]

→ *CPT Changes: An Insider's View* 2008

(Code 3076F has been deleted. To report most recent systolic blood pressure less than 140 mm Hg, see codes 3074F-3075F)

3077F Most recent systolic blood pressure greater than or equal to 140 mm Hg (HTN, CKD)[1] (DM)[2,4]

→ *CPT Changes: An Insider's View* 2007

3078F Most recent diastolic blood pressure less than 80 mm Hg (HTN, CKD)[1] (DM)[2,4]

→ *CPT Changes: An Insider's View* 2007

3079F Most recent diastolic blood pressure 80-89 mm Hg (HTN, CKD)[1] (DM)[2,4]

→ *CPT Changes: An Insider's View* 2007

3080F Most recent diastolic blood pressure grreater than or equal to 90 mm Hg (HTN, CKD)[1] (DM)[2,4]

→ *CPT Changes: An Insider's View* 2007

3082F Kt/V less than 1.2 (Clearance of urea [Kt]/volume [V]) (ESRD, P-ESRD)[1]

→ *CPT Changes: An Insider's View* 2008

3083F Kt/V equal to or greater than 1.2 and less than 1.7 (Clearance of urea [Kt]/volume [V]) (ESRD, P-ESRD)[1]

→ *CPT Changes: An Insider's View* 2008

3084F Kt/V greater than or equal to 1.7 (Clearance of urea [Kt]/volume [V]) (ESRD, P-ESRD)[1]

→ *CPT Changes: An Insider's View* 2008

3085F Suicide risk assessed (MDD)[1]

→ *CPT Changes: An Insider's View* 2008

3088F Major depressive disorder, mild (MDD)[1]

→ *CPT Changes: An Insider's View* 2008

3089F Major depressive disorder, moderate (MDD)[1]

→ *CPT Changes: An Insider's View* 2008

3090F Major depressive disorder, severe without psychotic features (MDD)[1]

→ *CPT Changes: An Insider's View* 2008

3091F Major depressive disorder, severe with psychotic features (MDD)[1]

→ *CPT Changes: An Insider's View* 2008

3092F Major depressive disorder, in remission (MDD)[1]

→ *CPT Changes: An Insider's View* 2008

3093F Documentation of new diagnosis of initial or recurrent episode of major depressive disorder (MDD)[1]

→ *CPT Changes: An Insider's View* 2008

3095F Central dual-energy X-ray absorptiometry (DXA) results documented (OP)[5]

→ *CPT Changes: An Insider's View* 2008

3096F Central dual-energy X-ray absorptiometry (DXA) ordered (OP)[5]

→ *CPT Changes: An Insider's View* 2008

3100F Carotid imaging study report (includes direct or indirect reference to measurements of distal internal carotid diameter as the denominator for stenosis measurement) (STR, RAD)[5]

→ *CPT Changes: An Insider's View* 2008

(Code 3101F has been deleted)

(Code 3102F has been deleted)

3110F Presence or absence of hemorrhage and mass lesion and acute infarction documented in final CT or MRI report (STR)[5]

→ *CPT Changes: An Insider's View* 2008

→ *Clinical Examples in Radiology* Winter 08:6

3111F CT or MRI of the brain performed within 24 hours of arrival to the hospital (STR)[5]

→ *CPT Changes: An Insider's View* 2008

3112F CT or MRI of the brain performed greater than 24 hours after arrival to the hospital (STR)[5]

→ *CPT Changes: An Insider's View* 2008

→ *Clinical Examples in Radiology* Winter 08:6

3120F 12-Lead ECG Performed (EM)[5]

→ *CPT Changes: An Insider's View* 2008

3130F Upper gastrointestinal endoscopy performed (GERD)[5]

→ *CPT Changes: An Insider's View* 2008

3132F Documentation of referral for upper gastrointestinal endoscopy (GERD)[5]

→ *CPT Changes: An Insider's View* 2008

Footnotes

[1] Physician Consortium for Performance Improvement® (PCPI), www.physicianconsortium.org

[2] National Committee on Quality Assurance (NCQA), Health Employer Data Information Set (HEDIS®), www.ncqa.org

[3] The Joint Commission (TJC) ORYX Initiative Performance Measures, www.thejointcommission.org

[4] National Diabetes Quality Improvement Alliance (NDQIA), www.nationaldiabetesalliance.org

[5] Joint measure from the Physician Consortium for Performance Improvement, www.physicianconsortium.org and National Committee on Quality Assurance (NCQA), www.ncqa.org

[6] The Society of Thoracic Surgeons, www.sts.org, National Quality Forum, www.qualityforum.org

3140F Upper gastrointestinal endoscopy report indicates suspicion of Barrett's esophagus (GERD)[5]
➲ *CPT Changes: An Insider's View* 2008

3141F Upper gastrointestinal endoscopy report indicates no suspicion of Barrett's esophagus (GERD)[5]
➲ *CPT Changes: An Insider's View* 2008

3142F Barium swallow test ordered (GERD)[1]
➲ *CPT Changes: An Insider's View* 2008

(Code 3143F has been deleted. To report documentation of barium swallow study, use code 3142F)

3150F Forceps esophageal biopsy performed (GERD)[5]
➲ *CPT Changes: An Insider's View* 2008

3155F Cytogenetic testing performed on bone marrow at time of diagnosis or prior to initiating treatment (HEM)[1]
➲ *CPT Changes: An Insider's View* 2008

3160F Documentation of iron stores prior to initiating erythropoietin therapy (HEM)[1]
➲ *CPT Changes: An Insider's View* 2008

3170F Flow cytometry studies performed at time of diagnosis or prior to initiating treatment (HEM)[1]
➲ *CPT Changes: An Insider's View* 2008

3200F Barium swallow test not ordered (GERD)[5]
➲ *CPT Changes: An Insider's View* 2008

3210F Group A Strep Test Performed (PHAR)[2]
➲ *CPT Changes: An Insider's View* 2008

3215F Patient has documented immunity to Hepatitis A (HEP-C)[1]
➲ *CPT Changes: An Insider's View* 2009

3216F Patient has documented immunity to Hepatitis B (HEP-C) [1]
➲ *CPT Changes: An Insider's View* 2009

(3217F has been deleted)

3218F RNA testing for Hepatitis C documented as performed within 6 months prior to initiation of antiviral treatment for Hepatitis C (HEP-C)[1]
➲ *CPT Changes: An Insider's View* 2009

(3219F has been deleted)

3220F Hepatitis C quantitative RNA testing documented as performed at 12 weeks from initiation of antiviral treatment (HEP-C)[1]
➲ *CPT Changes: An Insider's View* 2009

3230F Documentation that hearing test was performed within 6 months prior to tympanostomy tube insertion (OME)[1]
➲ *CPT Changes: An Insider's View* 2009

● **3250F** Specimen site other than anatomic location of primary tumor (PATH)[1]
➲ *CPT Changes: An Insider's View* 2010

3260F pT category (primary tumor), pN category (regional lymph nodes), and histologic grade documented in pathology report (PATH) [1]
➲ *CPT Changes: An Insider's View* 2009

3265F Ribonucleic acid (RNA) testing for Hepatitis C viremia ordered or results documented (HEP C)[1]
➲ *CPT Changes: An Insider's View* 2009

3266F Hepatitis C genotype testing documented as performed prior to initiation of antiviral treatment for Hepatitis C (HEP C)[1]
➲ *CPT Changes: An Insider's View* 2009

3268F Prostate-specific antigen (PSA), AND primary tumor (T) stage, AND Gleason score documented prior to initiation of treatment (PRCA)[1]
➲ *CPT Changes: An Insider's View* 2009

3269F Bone scan performed prior to initiation of treatment or at any time since diagnosis of prostate cancer (PRCA)[1]
➲ *CPT Changes: An Insider's View* 2009

3270F Bone scan not performed prior to initiation of treatment nor at any time since diagnosis of prostate cancer (PRCA)[1]
➲ *CPT Changes: An Insider's View* 2009

3271F Low risk of recurrence, prostate cancer (PRCA)[1]
➲ *CPT Changes: An Insider's View* 2009

3272F Intermediate risk of recurrence, prostate cancer (PRCA)[1]
➲ *CPT Changes: An Insider's View* 2009

3273F High risk of recurrence, prostate cancer (PRCA)[1]
➲ *CPT Changes: An Insider's View* 2009

3274F Prostate cancer risk of recurrence not determined or neither low, intermediate nor high (PRCA)[1]
➲ *CPT Changes: An Insider's View* 2009

3278F Serum levels of calcium, phosphorus, intact Parathyroid Hormone (PTH) and lipid profile ordered (CKD)[1]
➲ *CPT Changes: An Insider's View* 2009

3279F Hemoglobin level greater than or equal to 13 g/dL (CKD, ESRD)[1]
➲ *CPT Changes: An Insider's View* 2009

3280F Hemoglobin level 11 g/dL to 12.9 g/dL (CKD, ESRD)[1]
➲ *CPT Changes: An Insider's View* 2009

3281F Hemoglobin level less than 11 g/dL (CKD, ESRD)[1]
➲ *CPT Changes: An Insider's View* 2009

Footnotes

[1] Physician Consortium for Performance Improvement® (PCPI), www.physicianconsortium.org

[2] National Committee on Quality Assurance (NCQA), Health Employer Data Information Set (HEDIS®), www.ncqa.org

[3] The Joint Commission (TJC) ORYX Initiative Performance Measures, www.thejointcommission.org

[4] National Diabetes Quality Improvement Alliance (NDQIA), www.nationaldiabetesalliance.org

[5] Joint measure from the Physician Consortium for Performance Improvement, www.physicianconsortium.org and National Committee on Quality Assurance (NCQA), www.ncqa.org

[6] The Society of Thoracic Surgeons, www.sts.org, National Quality Forum, www.qualityforum.org

---

▲ =Revised code   ● =New code   ► ◄ =Contains new or revised text   ⊘ =Modifier 51 exempt

3284F Intraocular pressure (IOP) reduced by a value of greater than or equal to 15% from the pre-intervention level (EC)[5]
> *CPT Changes: An Insider's View* 2009

3285F Intraocular pressure (IOP) reduced by a value less than 15% from the pre-intervention level (EC)[5]
> *CPT Changes: An Insider's View* 2009

3288F Falls risk assessment documented (GER)[5]
> *CPT Changes: An Insider's View* 2009

3290F Patient is D (Rh) negative and unsensitized (Pre-Cr)[1]
> *CPT Changes: An Insider's View* 2009

3291F Patient is D (Rh) positive or sensitized (Pre-Cr)[1]
> *CPT Changes: An Insider's View* 2009

3292F HIV testing ordered or documented and reviewed during the first or second prenatal visit (Pre-Cr)[1]
> *CPT Changes: An Insider's View* 2009

3300F American Joint Committee on Cancer (AJCC) stage documented and reviewed (ONC)[1]
> *CPT Changes: An Insider's View* 2009

3301F Cancer stage documented in medical record as metastatic and reviewed (ONC)[1]
> *CPT Changes: An Insider's View* 2009

▶(Codes 3302F-3312F have been deleted.

To report measures for cancer staging, see 3321F-3390F.)◀

3315F Estrogen receptor (ER) or progesterone receptor (PR) positive breast cancer (ONC)[1]
> *CPT Changes: An Insider's View* 2009

3316F Estrogen receptor (ER) and progesterone receptor (PR) negative breast cancer (ONC)[1]
> *CPT Changes: An Insider's View* 2009

3317F Pathology report confirming malignancy documented in the medical record and reviewed prior to the initiation of chemotherapy (ONC)[1]
> *CPT Changes: An Insider's View* 2009

3318F Pathology report confirming malignancy documented in the medical record and reviewed prior to the initiation of radiation therapy (ONC)[1]
> *CPT Changes: An Insider's View* 2009

3319F 1 of the following diagnostic imaging studies ordered: chest x-ray, CT, Ultrasound, MRI, PET, or nuclear medicine scans (ML)[5]
> *CPT Changes: An Insider's View* 2009, 2010

3320F None of the following diagnostic imaging studies ordered: chest X-ray, CT, Ultrasound, MRI, PET, or nuclear medicine scans (ML)[5]
> *CPT Changes: An Insider's View* 2009

● **3321F** AJCC Cancer Stage 0 or IA Melanoma, documented (ML)[5]
> *CPT Changes: An Insider's View* 2010

● **3322F** Melanoma greater than AJCC Stage 0 or IA (ML)[5]
> *CPT Changes: An Insider's View* 2010

3325F Preoperative assessment of functional or medical indication(s) for surgery prior to the cataract surgery with intraocular lens placement (must be performed within 12 months prior to cataract surgery) (EC)[5]
> *CPT Changes: An Insider's View* 2009

3330F Imaging study ordered (BkP)[2]
> *CPT Changes: An Insider's View* 2009

3331F Imaging study not ordered (BkP)[2]
> *CPT Changes: An Insider's View* 2009

3340F Mammogram assessment category of "incomplete: need additional imaging evaluation", documented (RAD)[5]
> *CPT Changes: An Insider's View* 2009

3341F Mammogram assessment category of "negative" documented (RAD)[5]
> *CPT Changes: An Insider's View* 2009, 2010

3342F Mammogram assessment category of "benign", documented (RAD)[5]
> *CPT Changes: An Insider's View* 2009

3343F Mammogram assessment category of "probably benign", documented (RAD)[5]
> *CPT Changes: An Insider's View* 2009

3344F Mammogram assessment category of "suspicious", documented (RAD)[5]
> *CPT Changes: An Insider's View* 2009

3345F Mammogram assessment category of "highly suggestive of malignancy", documented (RAD)[5]
> *CPT Changes: An Insider's View* 2009

3350F Mammogram assessment category of "known biopsy proven malignancy", documented (RAD)[5]
> *CPT Changes: An Insider's View* 2009

3351F Negative screen for depressive symptoms as categorized by using a standardized depression screening/assessment tool (MDD)[2]
> *CPT Changes: An Insider's View* 2009

3352F No significant depressive symptoms as categorized by using a standardized depression assessment tool (MDD)[2]
> *CPT Changes: An Insider's View* 2009

Footnotes

[1] Physician Consortium for Performance Improvement® (PCPI), www.physicianconsortium.org

[2] National Committee on Quality Assurance (NCQA), Health Employer Data Information Set (HEDIS®), www.ncqa.org

[3] The Joint Commission (TJC) ORYX Initiative Performance Measures, www.thejointcommission.org

[4] National Diabetes Quality Improvement Alliance (NDQIA), www.nationaldiabetesalliance.org

[5] Joint measure from the Physician Consortium for Performance Improvement, www.physicianconsortium.org and National Committee on Quality Assurance (NCQA), www.ncqa.org

[6] The Society of Thoracic Surgeons, www.sts.org, National Quality Forum, www.qualityforum.org

3353F   Mild to moderate depressive symptoms as categorized by using a standardized depression screening/assessment tool (MDD)[2]
➜ *CPT Changes: An Insider's View* 2009

3354F   Clinically significant depressive symptoms as categorized by using a standardized depression screening/assessment tool (MDD)[2]
➜ *CPT Changes: An Insider's View* 2009

● **3370F**   AJCC Breast Cancer Stage 0 documented (ONC)[1]
➜ *CPT Changes: An Insider's View* 2010

● **3372F**   AJCC Breast Cancer Stage I: T1mic, T1a or T1b (tumor size ≤ 1 cm) documented (ONC)[1]
➜ *CPT Changes: An Insider's View* 2010

● **3374F**   AJCC Breast Cancer Stage I: T1c (tumor size > 1 cm to 2 cm) documented (ONC)[1]
➜ *CPT Changes: An Insider's View* 2010

● **3376F**   AJCC Breast Cancer Stage II documented (ONC)[1]
➜ *CPT Changes: An Insider's View* 2010

● **3378F**   AJCC Breast Cancer Stage III documented (ONC)[1]
➜ *CPT Changes: An Insider's View* 2010

● **3380F**   AJCC Breast Cancer Stage IV documented (ONC)[1]
➜ *CPT Changes: An Insider's View* 2010

● **3382F**   AJCC colon cancer, Stage 0 documented (ONC)[1]
➜ *CPT Changes: An Insider's View* 2010

● **3384F**   AJCC colon cancer, Stage I documented (ONC)[1]
➜ *CPT Changes: An Insider's View* 2010

● **3386F**   AJCC colon cancer, Stage II documented (ONC)[1]
➜ *CPT Changes: An Insider's View* 2010

● **3388F**   AJCC colon cancer, Stage III documented (ONC)[1]
➜ *CPT Changes: An Insider's View* 2010

● **3390F**   AJCC colon cancer, Stage IV documented (ONC)[1]
➜ *CPT Changes: An Insider's View* 2010

● **3450F**   Dyspnea screened, no dyspnea or mild dyspnea (Pall Cr)[5]
➜ *CPT Changes: An Insider's View* 2010

● **3451F**   Dyspnea screened, moderate or severe dyspnea (Pall Cr)[5]
➜ *CPT Changes: An Insider's View* 2010

● **3452F**   Dyspnea not screened (Pall Cr)[5]
➜ *CPT Changes: An Insider's View* 2010

● **3455F**   TB screening performed and results interpreted within six months prior to initiation of first-time biologic disease modifying anti-rheumatic drug therapy for RA (RA)[5]
➜ *CPT Changes: An Insider's View* 2010

● **3470F**   Rheumatoid arthritis (RA) disease activity, low (RA)[5]
➜ *CPT Changes: An Insider's View* 2010

● **3471F**   Rheumatoid arthritis (RA) disease activity, moderate (RA)[5]
➜ *CPT Changes: An Insider's View* 2010

● **3472F**   Rheumatoid arthritis (RA) disease activity, high (RA)[5]
➜ *CPT Changes: An Insider's View* 2010

● **3475F**   Disease prognosis for rheumatoid arthritis assessed, poor prognosis documented (RA)[5]
➜ *CPT Changes: An Insider's View* 2010

● **3476F**   Disease prognosis for rheumatoid arthritis assessed, good prognosis documented (RA)[5]
➜ *CPT Changes: An Insider's View* 2010

● **3490F**   History of AIDS-defining condition (HIV)[5]
➜ *CPT Changes: An Insider's View* 2010

● **3491F**   HIV indeterminate (infants of undetermined HIV status born of HIV-infected mothers) (HIV)[5]
➜ *CPT Changes: An Insider's View* 2010

● **3492F**   History of nadir CD4+ cell count <350 cells/mm^3 (HIV)[5]
➜ *CPT Changes: An Insider's View* 2010

● **3493F**   No history of nadir CD4+ cell count <350 cells/mm^3 AND no history of AIDS-defining condition (HIV)[5]
➜ *CPT Changes: An Insider's View* 2010

● **3494F**   CD4+ cell count <200 cells/mm^3 (HIV)[5]
➜ *CPT Changes: An Insider's View* 2010

● **3495F**   CD4+ cell count 200 – 499 cells/mm^3 (HIV)[5]
➜ *CPT Changes: An Insider's View* 2010

● **3496F**   CD4+ cell count ≥500 cells/mm^3 (HIV)[5]
➜ *CPT Changes: An Insider's View* 2010

● **3497F**   CD4+ cell percentage <15% (HIV)[5]
➜ *CPT Changes: An Insider's View* 2010

● **3498F**   CD4+ cell percentage ≥15% (HIV)[5]
➜ *CPT Changes: An Insider's View* 2010

● **3500F**   CD4+ cell count or CD4+ cell percentage documented as performed (HIV)[5]
➜ *CPT Changes: An Insider's View* 2010

● **3502F**   HIV RNA viral load below limits of quantification (HIV)[5]
➜ *CPT Changes: An Insider's View* 2010

● **3503F**   HIV RNA viral load not below limits of quantification (HIV)[5]
➜ *CPT Changes: An Insider's View* 2010

● **3510F**   Documentation that tuberculosis (TB) screening test performed and results interpreted (HIV)[5]
➜ *CPT Changes: An Insider's View* 2010

● **3511F**   Chlamydia and gonorrhea screenings documented as performed (HIV)[5]
➜ *CPT Changes: An Insider's View* 2010

Footnotes
[1] Physician Consortium for Performance Improvement® (PCPI), www.physicianconsortium.org
[2] National Committee on Quality Assurance (NCQA), Health Employer Data Information Set (HEDIS®), www.ncqa.org
[3] The Joint Commission (TJC) ORYX Initiative Performance Measures, www.thejointcommission.org
[4] National Diabetes Quality Improvement Alliance (NDQIA), www.nationaldiabetesalliance.org
[5] Joint measure from the Physician Consortium for Performance Improvement, www.physicianconsortium.org and National Committee on Quality Assurance (NCQA), www.ncqa.org
[6] The Society of Thoracic Surgeons, www.sts.org, National Quality Forum, www.qualityforum.org

---

▲=Revised code   ●=New code   ▶ ◀=Contains new or revised text   ⊘=Modifier 51 exempt

● **3512F** Syphilis screening documented as performed (HIV)[5]
→ *CPT Changes: An Insider's View* 2010

● **3513F** Hepatitis B screening documented as performed (HIV)[5]
→ *CPT Changes: An Insider's View* 2010

● **3514F** Hepatitis C screening documented as performed (HIV)[5]
→ *CPT Changes: An Insider's View* 2010

● **3515F** Patient has documented immunity to Hepatitis C (HIV)[5]
→ *CPT Changes: An Insider's View* 2010

● **3550F** Low risk for thromboembolism (AFIB)[1]
→ *CPT Changes: An Insider's View* 2010

● **3551F** Intermediate risk for thromboembolism (AFIB)[1]
→ *CPT Changes: An Insider's View* 2010

● **3552F** High risk for thromboembolism (AFIB)[1]
→ *CPT Changes: An Insider's View* 2010

● **3555F** Patient had International Normalized Ratio (INR) measurement performed (AFIB)[1]
→ *CPT Changes: An Insider's View* 2010

● **3570F** Final report for bone scintigraphy study includes correlation with existing relevant imaging studies (eg, x-ray, MRI, CT) corresponding to the same anatomical region in question (NUC_MED)[1]
→ *CPT Changes: An Insider's View* 2010

● **3572F** Patient considered to be potentially at risk for fracture in a weight-bearing site (NUC_MED)[1]
→ *CPT Changes: An Insider's View* 2010

● **3573F** Patient not considered to be potentially at risk for fracture in a weight-bearing site (NUC_MED)[1]
→ *CPT Changes: An Insider's View* 2010

Therapeutic, Preventive, or Other Interventions

Therapeutic, preventive, or other interventions codes describe pharmacologic, procedural, or behavioral therapies, including preventive services such as patient education and counseling.

4000F Tobacco use cessation intervention, counseling (COPD, CAP, CAD)[1](DM)[4](PV)[2]
→ *CPT Assistant* Oct 05:1; *CPT Changes: An Insider's View* 2005

4001F Tobacco use cessation intervention, pharmacologic therapy (COPD, CAD, CAP, PV)[1] (DM)[4](PV)[2]
→ *CPT Assistant* Oct 05:6; *CPT Changes: An Insider's View* 2005

4002F Statin therapy, prescribed (CAD)[1]
→ *CPT Assistant* Oct 05:6; *CPT Changes: An Insider's View* 2005

4003F Patient education, written/oral, appropriate for patients with heart failure, performed (HF)[1]
→ *CPT Assistant* Oct 05:6; *CPT Changes: An Insider's View* 2006

4005F Pharmacologic therapy (other than minerals/vitamins) for osteoporosis prescribed (OP)[5]
→ *CPT Changes: An Insider's View* 2008

4006F Beta-blocker therapy prescribed (CAD, HF)[1]
→ *CPT Assistant* Oct 05:6; *CPT Changes: An Insider's View* 2005

(4007F has been deleted. To report age related eye disease study (AREDS) formulation prescribed or recommended, use code 4177F)

4009F Angiotensin converting enzyme (ACE) inhibitor or angiotensin receptor blocker (ARB) therapy prescribed (HF, CAD, CKD)[1], (DM)[2]
→ *CPT Assistant* Oct 05:6; *CPT Changes: An Insider's View* 2005, 2007

▲ **4011F** Oral antiplatelet therapy prescribed (CAD)[1]
→ *CPT Assistant* Oct 05:6; *CPT Changes: An Insider's View* 2005, 2010

4012F Warfarin therapy prescribed (HF)[1]
→ *CPT Assistant* Oct 05:6; *CPT Changes: An Insider's View* 2006

4014F Written discharge instructions provided to heart failure patients discharged home (Instructions include all of the following components: activity level, diet, discharge medications, follow-up appointment, weight monitoring, what to do if symptoms worsen) (HF)[3]

(Excludes patients less than 18 years of age)
→ *CPT Changes: An Insider's View* 2006, 2007, 2009

4015F Persistent asthma, preferred long term control medication or an acceptable alternative treatment, prescribed (Asthma)[1]

(Note: There are no medical exclusion criteria)
→ *CPT Changes: An Insider's View* 2006, 2007, 2009

(Do not report modifier 1P with 4015F)

(To report patient reasons for not prescribing, use modifier 2P)

4016F Anti-inflammatory/analgesic agent prescribed (OA)[1]

(Use for prescribed or continued medication[s], including over-the-counter medication[s])
→ *CPT Assistant* Oct 05:6; *CPT Changes: An Insider's View* 2006

4017F Gastrointestinal prophylaxis for NSAID use prescribed (OA)[1]
→ *CPT Assistant* Oct 05:6; *CPT Changes: An Insider's View* 2006

Footnotes

[1] Physician Consortium for Performance Improvement® (PCPI), www.physicianconsortium.org
[2] National Committee on Quality Assurance (NCQA), Health Employer Data Information Set (HEDIS®), www.ncqa.org
[3] The Joint Commission (TJC) ORYX Initiative Performance Measures, www.thejointcommission.org
[4] National Diabetes Quality Improvement Alliance (NDQIA), www.nationaldiabetesalliance.org
[5] Joint measure from the Physician Consortium for Performance Improvement, www.physicianconsortium.org and National Committee on Quality Assurance (NCQA), www.ncqa.org
[6] The Society of Thoracic Surgeons, www.sts.org, National Quality Forum, www.qualityforum.org

4018F Therapeutic exercise for the involved joint(s) instructed or physical or occupational therapy prescribed (OA)[1]
➔ *CPT Assistant* Oct 05:6; *CPT Changes: An Insider's View* 2006

4019F Documentation of receipt of counseling on exercise AND either both calcium and vitamin D use or counseling regarding both calcium and vitamin D use (OP)[5]
➔ *CPT Changes: An Insider's View* 2008

4025F Inhaled bronchodilator prescribed (COPD)[1]
➔ *CPT Changes: An Insider's View* 2007

4030F Long-term oxygen therapy prescribed (more than 15 hours per day) (COPD)[1]
➔ *CPT Changes: An Insider's View* 2007

4033F Pulmonary rehabilitation exercise training recommended (COPD)[1]
➔ *CPT Changes: An Insider's View* 2007

(Report 4033F with 1019F)

4035F Influenza immunization recommended (COPD)[1]
➔ *CPT Changes: An Insider's View* 2007

4037F Influenza immunization ordered or administered (COPD, PV, CKD, ESRD)[1]
➔ *CPT Changes: An Insider's View* 2007

4040F Pneumococcal vaccine administered or previously received (COPD)[1], (PV)[2]
➔ *CPT Changes: An Insider's View* 2007, 2009

4041F Documentation of order for cefazolin OR cefuroxime for antimicrobial prophylaxis (PERI 2)[5]
➔ *CPT Changes: An Insider's View* 2008

4042F Documentation that prophylactic antibiotics were neither given within 4 hours prior to surgical incision nor given intraoperatively (PERI 2)[5]
➔ *CPT Changes: An Insider's View* 2008

4043F Documentation that an order was given to discontinue prophylactic antibiotics within 48 hours of surgical end time, cardiac procedures (PERI 2)[5]
➔ *CPT Changes: An Insider's View* 2008

4044F Documentation that an order was given for venous thromboembolism (VTE) prophylaxis to be given within 24 hours prior to incision time or 24 hours after surgery end time (PERI 2)[5]
➔ *CPT Changes: An Insider's View* 2008

4045F Appropriate empiric antibiotic prescribed (CAP)[1], (EM)[5]
➔ *CPT Changes: An Insider's View* 2007, 2008

4046F Documentation that prophylactic antibiotics were given within 4 hours prior to surgical incision or given intraoperatively (PERI 2)[5]
➔ *CPT Changes: An Insider's View* 2008

4047F Documentation of order for prophylactic antibiotics to be given within 1 hour (if fluoroquinolone or vancomycin, 2 hours) prior to surgical incision (or start of procedure when no incision is required) (PERI 2)[5]
➔ *CPT Changes: An Insider's View* 2008

4048F Documentation that prophylactic antibiotic was given within 1 hour (if fluoroquinolone or vancomycin, 2 hours) prior to surgical incision (or start of procedure when no incision is required) (PERI 2)[5]
➔ *CPT Changes: An Insider's View* 2008

4049F Documentation that order was given to discontinue prophylactic antibiotics within 24 hours of surgical end time, non-cardiac procedure (PERI 2)[5]
➔ *CPT Changes: An Insider's View* 2008

4050F Hypertension plan of care documented as appropriate (HTN)[1]
➔ *CPT Changes: An Insider's View* 2007

4051F Referred for an arteriovenous (AV) fistula (ESRD, CKD)[1]
➔ *CPT Changes: An Insider's View* 2008

4052F Hemodialysis via functioning arteriovenous (AV) fistula (ESRD)[1]
➔ *CPT Changes: An Insider's View* 2008

4053F Hemodialysis via functioning arteriovenous (AV) graft (ESRD)[1]
➔ *CPT Changes: An Insider's View* 2008

4054F Hemodialysis via catheter (ESRD)[1]
➔ *CPT Changes: An Insider's View* 2008

4055F Patient receiving peritoneal dialysis (ESRD)[1]
➔ *CPT Changes: An Insider's View* 2008

4056F Appropriate oral rehydration solution recommended (PAG)[1]
➔ *CPT Changes: An Insider's View* 2008

4058F Pediatric gastroenteritis education provided to caregiver (PAG)[1]
➔ *CPT Changes: An Insider's View* 2008

4060F Psychotherapy services provided (MDD)[1]
➔ *CPT Changes: An Insider's View* 2008

4062F Patient referral for psychotherapy documented (MDD)[1]
➔ *CPT Changes: An Insider's View* 2008

4064F Antidepressant pharmacotherapy prescribed (MDD)[1]
➔ *CPT Changes: An Insider's View* 2008

4065F Antipsychotic pharmacotherapy prescribed (MDD)[1]
➔ *CPT Changes: An Insider's View* 2008

Footnotes

[1] Physician Consortium for Performance Improvement® (PCPI), www.physicianconsortium.org

[2] National Committee on Quality Assurance (NCQA), Health Employer Data Information Set (HEDIS®), www.ncqa.org

[3] The Joint Commission (TJC) ORYX Initiative Performance Measures, www.thejointcommission.org

[4] National Diabetes Quality Improvement Alliance (NDQIA), www.nationaldiabetesalliance.org

[5] Joint measure from the Physician Consortium for Performance Improvement, www.physicianconsortium.org and National Committee on Quality Assurance (NCQA), www.ncqa.org

[6] The Society of Thoracic Surgeons, www.sts.org, National Quality Forum, www.qualityforum.org

4066F Electroconvulsive therapy (ECT) provided (MDD)[1]
→ *CPT Changes: An Insider's View* 2008

4067F Patient referral for electroconvulsive therapy (ECT) documented (MDD)[1]
→ *CPT Changes: An Insider's View* 2008

4070F Deep vein thrombosis (DVT) prophylaxis received by end of hospital day 2 (STR)[5]
→ *CPT Changes: An Insider's View* 2008

4073F Oral antiplatelet therapy prescribed at discharge (STR)[5]
→ *CPT Changes: An Insider's View* 2008

4075F Anticoagulant therapy prescribed at discharge (STR)[5]
→ *CPT Changes: An Insider's View* 2008

4077F Documentation that tissue plasminogen activator (t-PA) administration was considered (STR)[5]
→ *CPT Changes: An Insider's View* 2008

4079F Documentation that rehabilitation services were considered (STR)[5]
→ *CPT Changes: An Insider's View* 2008

4084F Aspirin received within 24 hours before emergency department arrival or during emergency department stay (EM)[5]
→ *CPT Changes: An Insider's View* 2008

4090F Patient receiving erythropoietin therapy (HEM)[1]
→ *CPT Changes: An Insider's View* 2008

4095F Patient not receiving erythropoietin therapy (HEM)[1]
→ *CPT Changes: An Insider's View* 2008

4100F Bisphosphonate therapy, intravenous, ordered or received (HEM)[1]
→ *CPT Changes: An Insider's View* 2008

4110F Internal mammary artery graft performed for primary, isolated coronary artery bypass graft procedure (CABG)[6]
→ *CPT Changes: An Insider's View* 2008

4115F Beta blocker administered within 24 hours prior to surgical incision (CABG)[6]
→ *CPT Changes: An Insider's View* 2008

4120F Antibiotic prescribed or dispensed (URI, PHAR)[2], (A-BRONCH)[2]
→ *CPT Changes: An Insider's View* 2008

4124F Antibiotic neither prescribed nor dispensed (URI, PHAR)[2], (A-BRONCH)[2]
→ *CPT Changes: An Insider's View* 2008

4130F Topical preparations (including OTC) prescribed for acute otitis externa (AOE)[1]
→ *CPT Changes: An Insider's View* 2009

4131F Systemic antimicrobial therapy prescribed (AOE)[1]
→ *CPT Changes: An Insider's View* 2009

4132F Systemic antimicrobial therapy not prescribed (AOE)[1]
→ *CPT Changes: An Insider's View* 2009

4133F Antihistamines or decongestants prescribed or recommended (OME)[1]
→ *CPT Changes: An Insider's View* 2009

4134F Antihistamines or decongestants neither prescribed nor recommended (OME)[1]
→ *CPT Changes: An Insider's View* 2009

4135F Systemic corticosteroids prescribed (OME)[1]
→ *CPT Changes: An Insider's View* 2009

4136F Systemic corticosteroids not prescribed (OME)[1]
→ *CPT Changes: An Insider's View* 2009

● **4148F** Hepatitis A vaccine injection administered or previously received (HEP-C)[1]
→ *CPT Changes: An Insider's View* 2010

● **4149F** Hepatitis B vaccine injection administered or previously received (HEP-C)[1]
→ *CPT Changes: An Insider's View* 2010

4150F Patient receiving antiviral treatment for Hepatitis C (HEP-C)[1]
→ *CPT Changes: An Insider's View* 2009

4151F Patient not receiving antiviral treatment for Hepatitis C (HEP-C)[1]
→ *CPT Changes: An Insider's View* 2009

►(Code 4152F has been deleted.)◄

4153F Combination peginterferon and ribavirin therapy prescribed (HEP-C)[1]
→ *CPT Changes: An Insider's View* 2009

►(Code 4154F has been deleted.)◄

4155F Hepatitis A vaccine series previously received (HEP-C)[1]
→ *CPT Changes: An Insider's View* 2009

►(Code 4156F has been deleted.)◄

4157F Hepatitis B vaccine series previously received (HEP-C)[1]
→ *CPT Changes: An Insider's View* 2009

▲ **4158F** Patient counseled about risks of alcohol use (HEP-C)[1]
→ *CPT Changes: An Insider's View* 2009, 2010

4159F Counseling regarding contraception received prior to initiation of antiviral treatment (HEP-C)[1]
→ *CPT Changes: An Insider's View* 2009

Footnotes

[1] Physician Consortium for Performance Improvement, www.ama-assn.org/go/quality

[2] National Committee on Quality Assurance (NCQA), Health Employer Data Information Set (HEDIS®), www.ncqa.org

[3] The Joint Commission (TJC) ORYX Initiative Performance Measures, www.thejointcommission.org

[4] National Diabetes Quality Improvement Alliance (NDQIA), www.nationaldiabetesalliance.org

[5] Joint measure from the Physician Consortium for Performance Improvement, www.physicianconsortium.org and National Committee on Quality Assurance (NCQA), www.ncqa.org

[6] The Society of Thoracic Surgeons, www.sts.org, National Quality Forum, www.qualityforum.org

4163F Patient counseling at a minimum on all of the following treatment options for clinically localized prostate cancer: active surveillance, AND interstitial prostate brachytherapy, AND external beam radiotherapy, AND radical prostatectomy, provided prior to initiation of treatment (PRCA)[1]

→ *CPT Changes: An Insider's View* 2009

4164F Adjuvant (ie, in combination with external beam radiotherapy to the prostate for prostate cancer) hormonal therapy (gonadotropin-releasing hormone [GnRH] agonist or antagonist) prescribed/administered (PRCA)[1]

→ *CPT Changes: An Insider's View* 2009

4165F 3-dimensional conformal radiotherapy (3D-CRT) or intensity modulated radiation therapy (IMRT) received (PRCA)[1]

→ *CPT Changes: An Insider's View* 2009

4167F Head of bed elevation (30-45 degrees) on first ventilator day ordered (CRIT)[1]

→ *CPT Changes: An Insider's View* 2009

4168F Patient receiving care in the intensive care unit (ICU) and receiving mechanical ventilation, 24 hours or less (CRIT)[1]

→ *CPT Changes: An Insider's View* 2009

4169F Patient either not receiving care in the intensive care unit (ICU) OR not receiving mechanical ventilation OR receiving mechanical ventilation greater than 24 hours (CRIT)[1]

→ *CPT Changes: An Insider's View* 2009

4171F Patient receiving erythropoiesis-stimulating agents (ESA) therapy (CKD)[1]

→ *CPT Changes: An Insider's View* 2009

4172F Patient not receiving erythropoiesis-stimulating agents (ESA) therapy (CKD)[1]

→ *CPT Changes: An Insider's View* 2009

4174F Counseling about the potential impact of glaucoma on visual functioning and quality of life, and importance of treatment adherence provided to patient and/or caregiver(s) (EC)[5]

→ *CPT Changes: An Insider's View* 2009

4175F Best-corrected visual acuity of 20/40 or better (distance or near) achieved within the 90 days following cataract surgery (EC)[5]

→ *CPT Changes: An Insider's View* 2009

4176F Counseling about value of protection from UV light and lack of proven efficacy of nutritional supplements in prevention or progression of cataract development provided to patient and/or caregiver(s) (NMA No Measure Associated)

→ *CPT Changes: An Insider's View* 2009

4177F Counseling about the benefits and/or risks of the Age-Related Eye Disease Study (AREDS) formulation for preventing progression of age-related macular degeneration (AMD) provided to patient and/or caregiver(s) (EC)[5]

→ *CPT Changes: An Insider's View* 2009

4178F Anti-D immune globulin received between 26 and 30 weeks gestation (Pre-Cr)[1]

→ *CPT Changes: An Insider's View* 2009

4179F Tamoxifen or aromatase inhibitor (AI) prescribed (ONC)[1]

→ *CPT Changes: An Insider's View* 2009

▲ **4180F** Adjuvant chemotherapy referred, prescribed, or previously received for Stage III colon cancer (ONC)[1]

→ *CPT Changes: An Insider's View* 2009, 2010

4181F Conformal radiation therapy received (NMA-No Measure Assoc.)

→ *CPT Changes: An Insider's View* 2009

4182F Conformal radiation therapy not received (NMA-No Measure Assoc.)

→ *CPT Changes: An Insider's View* 2009

4185F Continuous (12-months) therapy with proton pump inhibitor (PPI) or histamine H2 receptor antagonist (H2RA) received (GERD)[5]

→ *CPT Changes: An Insider's View* 2009

4186F No continuous (12-months) therapy with either proton pump inhibitor (PPI) or histamine H2 receptor antagonist (H2RA) received (GERD)[5]

→ *CPT Changes: An Insider's View* 2009

4187F Disease modifying anti-rheumatic drug therapy prescribed or dispensed (RA)[2]

→ *CPT Changes: An Insider's View* 2009

4188F Appropriate angiotensin converting enzyme (ACE)/angiotensin receptor blockers (ARB) therapeutic monitoring test ordered or performed (AM)[2]

→ *CPT Changes: An Insider's View* 2009

4189F Appropriate digoxin therapeutic monitoring test ordered or performed (AM)[2]

→ *CPT Changes: An Insider's View* 2009

4190F Appropriate diuretic therapeutic monitoring test ordered or performed (AM)[2]

→ *CPT Changes: An Insider's View* 2009

4191F Appropriate anticonvulsant therapeutic monitoring test ordered or performed (AM)[2]

→ *CPT Changes: An Insider's View* 2009

● **4192F** Patient not receiving glucocorticoid therapy (RA)[5]

→ *CPT Changes: An Insider's View* 2010

Footnotes

[1] Physician Consortium for Performance Improvement® (PCPI), www.physicianconsortium.org

[2] National Committee on Quality Assurance (NCQA), Health Employer Data Information Set (HEDIS®), www.ncqa.org

[3] The Joint Commission (TJC) ORYX Initiative Performance Measures, www.thejointcommission.org

[4] National Diabetes Quality Improvement Alliance (NDQIA), www.nationaldiabetesalliance.org

[5] Joint measure from the Physician Consortium for Performance Improvement, www.physicianconsortium.org and National Committee on Quality Assurance (NCQA), www.ncqa.org

[6] The Society of Thoracic Surgeons, www.sts.org, National Quality Forum, www.qualityforum.org

---

● **4193F** Patient receiving <10 mg daily prednisone (or equivalent), or RA activity is worsening, or glucocorticoid use is for less than 6 months (RA)[5]
➔ *CPT Changes: An Insider's View* 2010

● **4194F** Patient receiving ≥10 mg daily prednisone (or equivalent) for longer than 6 months, and improvement or no change in disease activity (RA)[5]
➔ *CPT Changes: An Insider's View* 2010

● **4195F** Patient receiving first-time biologic disease modifying anti-rheumatic drug therapy for rheumatoid arthritis (RA)[5]
➔ *CPT Changes: An Insider's View* 2010

● **4196F** Patient not receiving first-time biologic disease modifying anti-rheumatic drug therapy for rheumatoid arthritis (RA)[5]
➔ *CPT Changes: An Insider's View* 2010

▲ **4200F** External beam radiotherapy as primary therapy to prostate with or without nodal irradiation (PRCA)[1]
➔ *CPT Changes: An Insider's View* 2009, 2010

▲ **4201F** External beam radiotherapy with or without nodal irradiation as adjuvant or salvage therapy for prostate cancer patient (PRCA)[1]
➔ *CPT Changes: An Insider's View* 2009, 2010

4210F Angiotensin converting enzyme (ACE) or angiotensin receptor blockers (ARB) medication therapy for 6 months or more (MM)[2]
➔ *CPT Changes: An Insider's View* 2009

4220F Digoxin medication therapy for 6 months or more (MM)[2]
➔ *CPT Changes: An Insider's View* 2009

4221F Diuretic medication therapy for 6 months or more (MM)[2]
➔ *CPT Changes: An Insider's View* 2009

4230F Anticonvulsant medication therapy for 6 months or more (MM)[2]
➔ *CPT Changes: An Insider's View* 2009

4240F Instruction in therapeutic exercise with follow-up by the physician provided to patients during episode of back pain lasting longer than 12 weeks (BkP)[2]
➔ *CPT Changes: An Insider's View* 2009

4242F Counseling for supervised exercise program provided to patients during episode of back pain lasting longer than 12 weeks (BkP)[2]
➔ *CPT Changes: An Insider's View* 2009

4245F Patient counseled during the initial visit to maintain or resume normal activities (BkP)[2]
➔ *CPT Changes: An Insider's View* 2009

4248F Patient counseled during the initial visit for an episode of back pain against bed rest lasting 4 days or longer (BkP)[2]
➔ *CPT Changes: An Insider's View* 2009

▲ **4250F** Active warming used intraoperatively for the purpose of maintaining normothermia, OR at least 1 body temperature equal to or greater than 36 degrees Centigrade (or 96.8 degrees Fahrenheit) recorded within the 30 minutes immediately before or the 15 minutes immediately after anesthesia end time (CRIT)[1]
➔ *CPT Changes: An Insider's View* 2009, 2010

● **4260F** Wound surface culture technique used (CWC)[5]
➔ *CPT Changes: An Insider's View* 2010

● **4261F** Technique other than surface culture of the wound exudate used (eg, Levine/deep swab technique, semi-quantitative or quantitative swab technique) OR wound surface culture technique not used (CWC)[5]
➔ *CPT Changes: An Insider's View* 2010

● **4265F** Use of wet to dry dressings prescribed or recommended (CWC)[5]
➔ *CPT Changes: An Insider's View* 2010

● **4266F** Use of wet to dry dressings neither prescribed nor recommended (CWC)[5]
➔ *CPT Changes: An Insider's View* 2010

● **4267F** Compression therapy prescribed (CWC)[5]
➔ *CPT Changes: An Insider's View* 2010

● **4268F** Patient education regarding the need for long term compression therapy including interval replacement of compression stockings received (CWC)[5]
➔ *CPT Changes: An Insider's View* 2010

● **4269F** Appropriate method of offloading (pressure relief) prescribed (CWC)[5]
➔ *CPT Changes: An Insider's View* 2010

● **4270F** Patient receiving potent antiretroviral therapy for 6 months or longer (HIV)[5]
➔ *CPT Changes: An Insider's View* 2010

● **4271F** Patient receiving potent antiretroviral therapy for less than 6 months or not receiving potent antiretroviral therapy (HIV)[5]
➔ *CPT Changes: An Insider's View* 2010

● **4274F** Influenza immunization administered or previously received (HIV)[5] (P-ESRD)[1]
➔ *CPT Changes: An Insider's View* 2010

● **4275F** Hepatitis B vaccine injection administered or previously received (HIV)[5]
➔ *CPT Changes: An Insider's View* 2010

● **4276F** Potent antiretroviral therapy prescribed (HIV)[5]
➔ *CPT Changes: An Insider's View* 2010

● **4279F** Pneumocystis jiroveci pneumonia prophylaxis prescribed (HIV)[5]
➔ *CPT Changes: An Insider's View* 2010

Footnotes

[1] Physician Consortium for Performance Improvement® (PCPI), www.physicianconsortium.org

[2] National Committee on Quality Assurance (NCQA), Health Employer Data Information Set (HEDIS®), www.ncqa.org

[3] The Joint Commission (TJC) ORYX Initiative Performance Measures, www.thejointcommission.org

[4] National Diabetes Quality Improvement Alliance (NDQIA), www.nationaldiabetesalliance.org

[5] Joint measure from the Physician Consortium for Performance Improvement, www.physicianconsortium.org and National Committee on Quality Assurance (NCQA), www.ncqa.org

[6] The Society of Thoracic Surgeons, www.sts.org, National Quality Forum, www.qualityforum.org

● **4280F**　Pneumocystis jiroveci pneumonia prophylaxis prescribed within 3 months of low CD4+ cell count or percentage (HIV)[5]

➔ *CPT Changes: An Insider's View* 2010

● **4290F**　Patient screened for injection drug use (HIV)[5]

➔ *CPT Changes: An Insider's View* 2010

● **4293F**　Patient screened for high-risk sexual behavior (HIV)[5]

➔ *CPT Changes: An Insider's View* 2010

● **4300F**　Patient receiving warfarin therapy for nonvalvular atrial fibrillation or atrial flutter (AFIB)[1]

➔ *CPT Changes: An Insider's View* 2010

● **4301F**　Patient not receiving warfarin therapy for nonvalvular atrial fibrillation or atrial flutter (AFIB)[1]

➔ *CPT Changes: An Insider's View* 2010

● **4305F**　Patient education regarding appropriate foot care AND daily inspection of the feet received (CWC)[5]

➔ *CPT Changes: An Insider's View* 2010

● **4306F**　Patient counseled regarding psychosocial AND pharmacologic treatment options for opioid addiction (SUD)[1]

➔ *CPT Changes: An Insider's View* 2010

● **4320F**　Patient counseled regarding psychosocial AND pharmacologic treatment options for alcohol dependence (SUD)[5]

➔ *CPT Changes: An Insider's View* 2010

Follow-up or Other Outcomes

Follow-up or other outcomes codes describe review and communication of test results to patients, patient satisfaction or experience with care, patient functional status, and patient morbidity and mortality.

5005F　Patient counseled on self-examination for new or changing moles (ML)[5]

➔ *CPT Changes: An Insider's View* 2008

5010F　Findings of dilated macular or fundus exam communicated to the physician managing the diabetes care (EC)[5]

➔ *CPT Changes: An Insider's View* 2008

5015F　Documentation of communication that a fracture occurred and that the patient was or should be tested or treated for osteoporosis (OP)[5]

➔ *CPT Changes: An Insider's View* 2008

▲ **5020F**　Treatment summary report communicated to physician(s) managing continuing care and to the patient within 1 month of completing treatment (ONC)[1]

➔ *CPT Changes: An Insider's View* 2009, 2010

5050F　Treatment plan communicated to provider(s) managing continuing care within 1 month of diagnosis (ML)[5]

➔ *CPT Changes: An Insider's View* 2009

5060F　Findings from diagnostic mammogram communicated to practice managing patient's on-going care within 3 business days of exam interpretation (RAD)[5]

➔ *CPT Changes: An Insider's View* 2009

5062F　Findings from diagnostic mammogram communicated to the patient within 5 days of exam interpretation (RAD)[5]

➔ *CPT Changes: An Insider's View* 2009

● **5100F**　Potential risk for fracture communicated to the referring physician within 24 hours of completion of the imaging study (NUC_MED)[1]

➔ *CPT Changes: An Insider's View* 2010

Patient Safety

Patient safety codes that describe patient safety practices.

6005F　Rationale (eg, severity of illness and safety) for level of care (eg, home, hospital) documented (CAP)[1]

➔ *CPT Assistant* Aug 07:1; *CPT Changes: An Insider's View* 2007

6010F　Dysphagia screening conducted prior to order for or receipt of any foods, fluids, or medication by mouth (STR)[5]

➔ *CPT Changes: An Insider's View* 2008

6015F　Patient receiving or eligible to receive foods, fluids, or medication by mouth (STR)[5]

➔ *CPT Changes: An Insider's View* 2008

6020F　NPO (nothing by mouth) ordered (STR)[5]

➔ *CPT Changes: An Insider's View* 2008

▲ **6030F**　All elements of maximal sterile barrier technique followed including: cap AND mask AND sterile gown AND sterile gloves AND a large sterile sheet AND hand hygiene AND 2% chlorhexidine for cutaneous antisepsis (or acceptable alternative antiseptics, per current guideline) (CRIT)[1]

➔ *CPT Changes: An Insider's View* 2009, 2010

6040F　Use of appropriate radiation dose reduction devices OR manual techniques for appropriate moderation of exposure, documented (RAD)[5]

➔ *CPT Changes: An Insider's View* 2009

Footnotes

[1] Physician Consortium for Performance Improvement, www.ama-assn.org/go/quality

[2] National Committee on Quality Assurance (NCQA), Health Employer Data Information Set (HEDIS®), www.ncqa.org

[3] The Joint Commission (TJC) ORYX Initiative Performance Measures, www.thejointcommission.org

[4] National Diabetes Quality Improvement Alliance (NDQIA), www.nationaldiabetesalliance.org

[5] Joint measure from the Physician Consortium for Performance Improvement, www.physicianconsortium.org and National Committee on Quality Assurance (NCQA), www.ncqa.org

[6] The Society of Thoracic Surgeons, www.sts.org, National Quality Forum, www.qualityforum.org

6045F   Radiation exposure or exposure time in final report for procedure using fluoroscopy, documented (RAD)[5]

➲ *CPT Changes: An Insider's View* 2009

Structural Measures

Structural measures codes are used to identify measures that address the setting or system of the delivered care. These codes also address aspects of the capabilities of the organization or health care professional providing the care.

7010F   Patient information entered into a recall system with the target date for the next exam specified (ML)[5]

➲ *CPT Changes: An Insider's View* 2009

7020F   Mammogram assessment category (eg, Mammography Quality Standards Act [MQSA], Breast Imaging Reporting and Data System [BI-RADS®], or FDA approved equivalent categories) entered into an internal database to allow for analysis of abnormal interpretation (recall) rate (RAD)[5]

➲ *CPT Changes: An Insider's View* 2009

7025F   Patient information entered into a reminder system with a target due date for the next mammogram (RAD)[5]

➲ *CPT Changes: An Insider's View* 2009

Footnotes

[1] Physician Consortium for Performance Improvement® (PCPI), www.physicianconsortium.org

[2] National Committee on Quality Assurance (NCQA), Health Employer Data Information Set (HEDIS®), www.ncqa.org

[3] The Joint Commission (TJC) ORYX Initiative Performance Measures, www.thejointcommission.org

[4] National Diabetes Quality Improvement Alliance (NDQIA), www.nationaldiabetesalliance.org

[5] Joint measure from the Physician Consortium for Performance Improvement, www.physicianconsortium.org and National Committee on Quality Assurance (NCQA), www.ncqa.org

[6] The Society of Thoracic Surgeons, www.sts.org, National Quality Forum, www.qualityforum.org

Category III Codes

The following section contains a set of temporary codes for emerging technology, services, and procedures. Category III codes allow data collection for these services/procedures. Use of unlisted codes does not offer the opportunity for the collection of specific data. If a Category III code is available, this code must be reported instead of a Category I unlisted code. This is an activity that is critically important in the evaluation of health care delivery and the formation of public and private policy. The use of the codes in this section allow physicians and other qualified health care professionals, insurers, health services researchers, and health policy experts to identify emerging technology, services, and procedures for clinical efficacy, utilization and outcomes.

The inclusion of a service or procedure in this section neither implies nor endorses clinical efficacy, safety or the applicability to clinical practice. The codes in this section may not conform to the usual requirements for CPT Category I codes established by the Editorial Panel. For Category I codes, the Panel requires that the service/procedure be performed by many health care professionals in clinical practice in multiple locations and that FDA approval, as appropriate, has already been received. The nature of emerging technology, services, and procedures is such that these requirements may not be met. For these reasons, temporary codes for emerging technology, services, and procedures have been placed in a separate section of the CPT codebook and the codes are differentiated from Category I CPT codes by the use of alphanumeric characters.

▶Services/procedures described in this section make use of alphanumeric characters. These codes have an alpha character as the 5th character in the string, preceded by four digits. The digits are not intended to reflect the placement of the code in the Category I section of CPT nomenclature. Codes in this section may or may not eventually receive a Category I CPT code. In either case, in general, a given Category III code will be archived five years from its date of publication or revision in the CPT code book unless it is demonstrated that a temporary code is still needed. Services/procedures described by Category III codes which have been archived after five years, without conversion, may be reported using the Category I unlisted code. New codes in this section are released semi-annually via the AMA/CPT internet site, to expedite dissemination for reporting. The full set of temporary codes for emerging technology, services, and procedures are published annually in the CPT codebook. Go to www.ama-assn.org/go/cpt for the most current listing.◀

0016T Destruction of localized lesion of choroid (eg, choroidal neovascularization), transpupillary thermotherapy
➲ *CPT Changes: An Insider's View* 2002

0017T Destruction of macular drusen, photocoagulation
➲ *CPT Changes: An Insider's View* 2002

0019T Extracorporeal shock wave involving musculoskeletal system, not otherwise specified, low energy
➲ *CPT Assistant* Jun 05:6, Mar 06:1; *CPT Changes: An Insider's View* 2002, 2006

(For application of high energy extracorporeal shock wave involving musculoskeletal system not otherwise specified, use 0101T)

(For application of high energy extracorporeal shock wave involving lateral humeral epicondyle, use 0102T)

(0024T has been deleted)

(For non-surgical septal reduction therapy, use 93799)

(0026T has been deleted)

(For lipoprotein, direct measurement, intermediate density lipoproteins [IDL] [remnant lipoprotein], use 84999)

(0027T has been deleted)

(For endoscopic lysis of epidural adhesions with direct visualization using mechnical means or solution injection [eg, normal saline], use 64999)

(0028T has been deleted)

(For dual energy x-ray absorptiometry [DXA] body composition study, use 76499)

(0029T has been deleted)

(For pulsed magnetic neuromodulation incontinence treatment, use 53899)

0030T Antiprothrombin (phospholipid cofactor) antibody, each Ig class
➲ *CPT Changes: An Insider's View* 2003

(0031T, 0032T have been deleted)

(For speculoscopy, including sampling, use 58999)

(0041T has been deleted)

(For urinalysis infectious agent detection, semi-quantitative analysis of volatile compounds, use 81099)

0042T Cerebral perfusion analysis using computed tomography with contrast administration, including post-processing of parametric maps with determination of cerebral blood flow, cerebral blood volume, and mean transit time

➜ *CPT Changes: An Insider's View* 2003

(0043T has been deleted)

(For carbon monoxide, expired gas analysis [eg, ETCO$_c$/hemolysis breath test], use 84999)

(0046T, 0047T have been deleted)

(For mammary duct[s] catheter lavage, use 19499)

0048T Implantation of a ventricular assist device, extracorporeal, percutaneous transseptal access, single or dual cannulation

➜ *CPT Assistant* Jul 04:7-8; *CPT Changes: An Insider's View* 2004

(0049T has been deleted)

(For prolonged extracorporeal percutaneous transseptal ventricular assist device, use 33999)

0050T Removal of a ventricular assist device, extracorporeal, percutaneous transseptal access, single or dual cannulation

➜ *CPT Assistant* Jul 04:7; *CPT Changes: An Insider's View* 2004

►(For replacement of a ventricular assist device, extracorporeal, percutaneous transseptal access, use 33999)◄

0051T Implantation of a total replacement heart system (artificial heart) with recipient cardiectomy

➜ *CPT Assistant* Jun 04:7; *CPT Changes: An Insider's View* 2004

(For implantation of heart assist or ventricular assist device, see 33975, 33976)

0052T Replacement or repair of thoracic unit of a total replacement heart system (artificial heart)

➜ *CPT Assistant* Jun 04:7; *CPT Changes: An Insider's View* 2004

(For replacement or repair of other implantable components in a total replacement heart system (artificial heart), use 0053T)

0053T Replacement or repair of implantable component or components of total replacement heart system (artificial heart), excluding thoracic unit

➜ *CPT Assistant* Jun 04:7; *CPT Changes: An Insider's View* 2004

(For replacement or repair of a thoracic unit of a total replacement heart system (artificial heart), use 0052T)

+ 0054T Computer-assisted musculoskeletal surgical navigational orthopedic procedure, with image-guidance based on fluoroscopic images (List separately in addition to code for primary procedure)

➜ *CPT Assistant* May 04:14, Jun 04:8; *CPT Changes: An Insider's View* 2004

+ 0055T Computer-assisted musculoskeletal surgical navigational orthopedic procedure, with image-guidance based on CT/MRI images (List separately in addition to code for primary procedure)

➜ *CPT Assistant* May 04:14, Jun 04:8; *CPT Changes: An Insider's View* 2004, 2005

(When CT and MRI are both performed, report 0055T only once)

(0056T has been deleted. To report, use 20985)

(0058T, 0059T have been deleted)

(For cryopreservation, ovarian reproductive tissue, oocytes, use 89240)

(0060T has been deleted)

(For electrical impedance breast scan, use 76499)

(0061T has been deleted)

(For destruction/reduction of malignant breast tumor, microwave phased array thermotherapy, use 19499)

►(0062T, 0063T have been deleted)◄

►(For percutaneous intradiscal annuloplasty, any method other than electrothermal, use 22899)◄

(For intradiscal electrothermal annuloplasty, see 22526, 22527)

►(0064T has been deleted. To report, use 94799)◄

(0065T has been deleted. To report, use 99174)

►(0066T has been deleted)◄

►(To report CT colon, screening, use 74263)◄

►(0067T has been deleted)◄

►(To report CT colon, diagnostic, see 74261-74262)◄

►(0068T-0070T have been deleted)◄

►(For acoustic heart sound recording and computer analysis, use 93799)◄

0071T Focused ultrasound ablation of uterine leiomyomata, including MR guidance; total leiomyomata volume less than 200 cc of tissue

➜ *CPT Assistant* Mar 05:1, 5, Dec 05:3; *CPT Changes: An Insider's View* 2005

0072T total leiomyomata volume greater or equal to 200 cc of tissue

➜ *CPT Assistant* Mar 05:1, 5, Dec 05:3; *CPT Changes: An Insider's View* 2005

(Do not report 0071T, 0072T in conjunction with 51702 or 77022)

0073T Compensator-based beam modulation treatment delivery of inverse planned treatment using 3 or more high resolution (milled or cast) compensator convergent beam modulated fields, per treatment session

➜ *CPT Assistant* Mar 05:1, 6, May 05:7; *CPT Changes: An Insider's View* 2005

(For treatment planning, use 77301)

(Do not report 0073T in conjunction with 77401-77416, 77418)

(0074T has been deleted. To report, see 98969, 99444)

0075T   Transcatheter placement of extracranial vertebral or intrathoracic carotid artery stent(s), including radiologic supervision and interpretation, percutaneous; initial vessel

➔ *CPT Assistant* May 05:7; *CPT Changes: An Insider's View* 2005

+ 0076T   each additional vessel (List separately in addition to code for primary procedure)

➔ *CPT Assistant* May 05:7; *CPT Changes: An Insider's View* 2005

(Use 0076T in conjunction with 0075T)

(When the ipsilateral extracranial vertebral or intrathoracic carotid arteriogram (including imaging and selective catheterization) confirms the need for stenting, then 0075T and 0076T include all ipsilateral extracranial vertebral or intrathoracic selective carotid catheterization, all diagnostic imaging for ipsilateral extracranial vertebral or intrathoracic carotid artery stenting, and all related radiologic supervision and interpretation. If stenting is not indicated, then the appropriate codes for selective catheterization and imaging should be reported in lieu of code 0075T or 0076T.)

▶(0077T has been deleted. To report, see 61107, 61210)◀

(0078T-0081T should be reported in accordance with the Endovascular Abdominal Aneurysm Repair guidelines established for 34800-34826)

0078T   Endovascular repair using prosthesis of abdominal aortic aneurysm, pseudoaneurysm or dissection, abdominal aorta involving visceral branches (superior mesenteric, celiac and/or renal artery[s])

➔ *CPT Assistant* May 05:7, Jun 05:6; *CPT Changes: An Insider's View* 2005, 2006

➔ *Clinical Examples in Radiology* Winter 06:20

(Do not report 0078T in conjunction with 34800-34805, 35081, 35102, 35452, 35454, 35472, 37205-37208)

(Report 0078T in conjunction with 35454, 37205-37208 when these procedures are performed outside the target zone of the endoprosthesis)

+ 0079T   Placement of visceral extension prosthesis for endovascular repair of abdominal aortic aneurysm involving visceral vessels, each visceral branch (List separately in addition to code for primary procedure)

➔ *CPT Assistant* May 05:7; *CPT Changes: An Insider's View* 2005

(Use 0079T in conjunction with 0078T)

(Do not report 0079T in conjunction with 34800-34805, 35081, 35102, 35452, 35454, 35472, 37205-37208)

(Report 0079T in conjunction with 35454, 37205-37208 when these procedures are performed outside the target zone of the endoprosthesis)

0080T   Endovascular repair of abdominal aortic aneurysm, pseudoaneurysm or dissection, abdominal aorta involving visceral vessels (superior mesenteric, celiac or renal), using fenestrated modular bifurcated prosthesis (2 docking limbs), radiological supervision and interpretation

➔ *CPT Assistant* May 05:7; *CPT Changes: An Insider's View* 2005

(Do not report 0080T in conjunction with 34800-34805, 35081, 35102, 35452, 35454, 35472, 37205-37208)

(Report 0080T in conjunction with 35454, 37205-37208 when these procedures are performed outside the target zone of the endoprosthesis)

+ 0081T   Placement of visceral extension prosthesis for endovascular repair of abdominal aortic aneurysm involving visceral vessels, each visceral branch, radiological supervision and interpretation (List separately in addition to code for primary procedure)

➔ *CPT Assistant* May 05:7; *CPT Changes: An Insider's View* 2005

(Use 0081T in conjunction with 0080T)

(Do not report 0081T in conjunction with 34800-34805, 35081, 35102, 35452, 35454, 35472, 37205-37208)

(Report 0081T in conjunction with 35454, 37205-37208 when these procedures are performed outside the target zone of the endoprosthesis)

(0082T, 0083T have been deleted. To report, see 77373, 77435)

▶(0084T has been deleted. To report, use 53855)◀

0085T   Breath test for heart transplant rejection

➔ *CPT Assistant* May 05:7; *CPT Changes: An Insider's View* 2005

▶(0086T has been deleted. To report use, 93799)◀

▶(0087T has been deleted. To report, use 89398)◀

(0088T has been deleted. To report, use 41530)

(0089T has been deleted. For actigraphy testing, use 95803)

(0090T has been deleted. To report total disc cervical arthroplasty, use 22856)

(To report total disc lumbar arthroplasty, use 22857)

+ 0092T   Total disc arthroplasty (artificial disc), anterior approach, including discectomy with end plate preparation (includes osteophytectomy for nerve root or spinal cord decompression and microdissection), each additional interspace, cervical (List separately in addition to code for primary procedure)

➔ *CPT Assistant* Jun 05:6, Feb 06:1; *CPT Changes: An Insider's View* 2006, 2009

(Use 0092T in conjunction with 22856)

(Do not report 0092T in conjunction with 22851 when performed at the same level)

(0093T has been deleted. To report removal of total disc cervical arthroplasty, use 22864)

(To report removal of total disc lumbar arthroplasty, use 22865)

+ 0095T   Removal of total disc arthroplasty (artificial disc), anterior approach, each additional interspace, cervical (List separately in addition to code for primary procedure)
➔ *CPT Assistant* Jun 05:6, Feb 06:1; *CPT Changes: An Insider's View* 2006, 2009

(Use 0095T in conjunction with 22864)

(0096T has been deleted. To report revision of total disc cervical arthroplasty, use 22861)

(To report revision of total disc lumbar arthroplasty, use 22862)

+ 0098T   Revision including replacement of total disc arthroplasty (artificial disc), anterior approach, each additional interspace, cervical (List separately in addition to code for primary procedure)
➔ *CPT Assistant* Jun 05:6, Feb 06:1; *CPT Changes: An Insider's View* 2006, 2009

(Use 0098T in conjunction with 22861)

(Do not report 0098T in conjunction with 0095T)

(Do not report 0098T in conjunction with 22851 when performed at the same level)

(For decompression, see 63001-63048)

0099T   Implantation of intrastromal corneal ring segments
➔ *CPT Assistant* Jun 05:6, Feb 06:1; *CPT Changes: An Insider's View* 2006

0100T   Placement of a subconjunctival retinal prosthesis receiver and pulse generator, and implantation of intra-ocular retinal electrode array, with vitrectomy
➔ *CPT Assistant* Jun 05:6, Feb 06:1; *CPT Changes: An Insider's View* 2006

0101T   Extracorporeal shock wave involving musculoskeletal system, not otherwise specified, high energy
➔ *CPT Assistant* Jun 05:6, Mar 06:1; *CPT Changes: An Insider's View* 2006

(For application of low energy musculoskeletal system extracorporeal shock wave, use 0019T)

0102T   Extracorporeal shock wave, high energy, performed by a physician, requiring anesthesia other than local, involving lateral humeral epicondyle
➔ *CPT Assistant* Jun 05:6, Mar 06:1; *CPT Changes: An Insider's View* 2006

(For application of low energy musculoskeletal system extracorporeal shock wave, use 0019T)

0103T   Holotranscobalamin, quantitative
➔ *CPT Assistant* Jun 05:6, Mar 06:1; *CPT Changes: An Insider's View* 2006

0104T   Inert gas rebreathing for cardiac output measurement; during rest
➔ *CPT Assistant* Jun 05:6, Mar 06:1; *CPT Changes: An Insider's View* 2006

0105T   during exercise
➔ *CPT Assistant* Jun 05:6, Mar 06:1; *CPT Changes: An Insider's View* 2006

0106T   Quantitative sensory testing (QST), testing and interpretation per extremity; using touch pressure stimuli to assess large diameter sensation
➔ *CPT Assistant* Jun 05:6, Mar 06:1; *CPT Changes: An Insider's View* 2006

0107T   using vibration stimuli to assess large diameter fiber sensation
➔ *CPT Assistant* Jun 05:6, Mar 06:1; *CPT Changes: An Insider's View* 2006

0108T   using cooling stimuli to assess small nerve fiber sensation and hyperalgesia
➔ *CPT Assistant* Jun 05:6, Mar 06:1; *CPT Changes: An Insider's View* 2006

0109T   using heat-pain stimuli to assess small nerve fiber sensation and hyperalgesia
➔ *CPT Assistant* Jun 05:6, Mar 06:1; *CPT Changes: An Insider's View* 2006

0110T   using other stimuli to assess sensation
➔ *CPT Assistant* Jun 05:6, Mar 06:1; *CPT Changes: An Insider's View* 2006

0111T   Long-chain (C20-22) omega-3 fatty acids in red blood cell (RBC) membranes
➔ *CPT Assistant* Jun 05:6, Mar 06:1; *CPT Changes: An Insider's View* 2006

(For very long chain fatty acids, use 82726)

(0115T-0117T have been deleted. To report, see 99605-99607)

0123T   Fistulization of sclera for glaucoma, through ciliary body
➔ *CPT Changes: An Insider's View* 2006

0124T   Conjunctival incision with posterior extrascleral placement of pharmacological agent (does not include supply of medication)
➔ *CPT Assistant* Jan 08:6; *CPT Changes: An Insider's View* 2006, 2009

(For suprachoroidal delivery of pharmacologic agent, use 0186T)

0126T   Common carotid intima-media thickness (IMT) study for evaluation of atherosclerotic burden or coronary heart disease risk factor assessment
➔ *CPT Changes: An Insider's View* 2006

0130T   Validated, statistically reliable, randomized, controlled, single-patient clinical investigation of FDA approved chronic care drugs, provided by a pharmacist, interpretation and report to the prescribing health care professional
➔ *CPT Changes: An Insider's View* 2006

(0133T has been deleted)

(0135T has been deleted. To report, use 50593)

(0137T has been deleted. For transperineal stereotactic template guided saturation prostate biopsies, use 55706)

0140T   Exhaled breath condensate pH
➔ *CPT Changes: An Insider's View* 2006

Pancreatic islet cells are transplanted by infusion into the portal vein. The portal vein may be cannulated percutaneously with imaging guidance, by laparoscopy, or by laparotomy. Codes 0141T-0143T include infusion of islet cells with monitoring and management of portal and systemic hemodynamics, monitoring and management of blood glucose and insulin therapy, immunotherapy infusion, antibiotic infusion, analgesic and sedative administration and monitoring, and all other therapeutic injections and infusions administered during the islet infusion. Codes 0141T-0143T also include typical postprocedural care. When reporting 0141T, percutaneous portal vein catheterization is reported separately (see codes 36481, 75887). Code 0142T includes diagnostic laparotomy (49000, 49002). Code 0143T includes diagnostic laparoscopy (49320).

0141T   Pancreatic islet cell transplantation through portal vein, percutaneous

➲ *CPT Assistant* Jun 07:7; *CPT Changes: An Insider's View* 2007

(For open approach, use 0142T)

(For laparoscopic approach, use 0143T)

(For percutaneous portal vein catheterization, use 36481)

(For radiological supervision and interpretation, use 75887)

0142T   Pancreatic islet cell transplantation through portal vein, open

➲ *CPT Assistant* Jun 07:7; *CPT Changes: An Insider's View* 2007

(For percutaneous approach, use 0141T)

(For laparoscopic approach, use 0143T)

(Do not report 0142T in conjunction with 49000, 49002)

0143T   Laparoscopy, surgical, pancreatic islet cell transplantation through portal vein

➲ *CPT Assistant* Jun 07:7; *CPT Changes: An Insider's View* 2007

(For percutaneous approach, use 0141T)

(For open approach, use 0142T)

(Do not report 0143T in conjunction with 49320)

▶(0144T-0151T have been deleted. To report, see 75571-75574)◀

(0152T has been deleted. To report, see 0174T, 0175T)

(0153T has been deleted. To report, use 34806)

(0154T has been deleted. To report, use 93982)

0155T   Laparoscopy, surgical; implantation or replacement of gastric stimulation electrodes, lesser curvature (ie, morbid obesity)

➲ *CPT Assistant* Mar 07:4, Apr 07:7; *CPT Changes: An Insider's View* 2007

0156T   revision or removal of gastric stimulation electrodes, lesser curvature (ie, morbid obesity)

➲ *CPT Assistant* Mar 07:4, Apr 07:7; *CPT Changes: An Insider's View* 2007

(For open approach, see 0157T, 0158T)

For laparoscopic or open insertion, revision or removal of antral gastric neurostimulator electrodes, see 43647, 43648, 43881, 43882)

(For insertion, revision or removal of gastric neurostimulator pulse generator, see 64590, 64595)

(For electronic analysis and programming of antral gastric neurostimulator pulse generator, see 95980-95982)

(For electronic analysis and programming of a gastric neurostimulator, lesser curvature, use 0162T)

0157T   Laparotomy, implantation or replacement of gastric stimulation electrodes, lesser curvature (ie, morbid obesity)

➲ *CPT Assistant* Apr 07:7; *CPT Changes: An Insider's View* 2007

0158T   Laparotomy, revision or removal of gastric stimulation electrodes, lesser curvature (ie, morbid obesity)

➲ *CPT Assistant* Apr 07:7; *CPT Changes: An Insider's View* 2007

(For laparoscopic approach, see 0155T, 0156T)

(For insertion of gastric neurostimulator pulse generator, use 64590)

(For revision or removal of gastric neurostimulator pulse generator, use 64595)

(For electronic analysis and programming of antral gastric neurostimulator pulse generator, see 95980-95982)

(For electronic analysis and programming of a gastric neurostimulator, lesser curvature, use 0162T)

+ 0159T   Computer-aided detection, including computer algorithm analysis of MRI image data for lesion detection/characterization, pharmacokinetic analysis, with further physician review for interpretation, breast MRI (List separately in addition to code for primary procedure)

➲ *CPT Assistant* Mar 07:7, Jul 07:6; *CPT Changes: An Insider's View* 2007

➲ *Clinical Examples in Radiology* Winter 07:9, Spring 07:8

(Use 0159T in conjunction with 77058, 77059)

(Do not report 0159T in conjunction with 76376, 76377)

0160T   Therapeutic repetitive transcranial magnetic stimulation treatment planning

➲ *CPT Assistant* Jul 07:6; *CPT Changes: An Insider's View* 2007

(Pre-treatment determination of optimal magnetic field strength via titration, treatment location determination and stimulation parameter and protocol programming in the therapeutic use of high power, focal magnetic pulses for the direct, noninvasive modulation of cortical neurons)

0161T Therapeutic repetitive transcranial magnetic stimulation treatment delivery and management, per session

→ *CPT Assistant* Jul 07:6; *CPT Changes: An Insider's View* 2007

(Treatment session using high power, focal magnetic pulses for the direct, noninvasive modulation of cortical neurons. Clinical evaluation, safety monitoring and treatment parameter review in the therapeutic use of high power, focal magnetic pulses for the direct, noninvasive modulation of cortical neurons)

(0162T has been deleted. To report, see 95980–95982)

+ 0163T Total disc arthroplasty (artificial disc), anterior approach, including discectomy to prepare interspace (other than for decompression), each additional interspace, lumbar (List separately in addition to code for primary procedure)

→ *CPT Assistant* Jun 07:1; *CPT Changes: An Insider's View* 2007, 2009

(Use 0163T in conjunction with 22857)

+ 0164T Removal of total disc arthroplasty, (artificial disc), anterior approach, each additional interspace, lumbar (List separately in addition to code for primary procedure)

→ *CPT Assistant* Jun 07:1; *CPT Changes: An Insider's View* 2007, 2009

(Use 0164T in conjunction with 22865)

+ 0165T Revision including replacement of total disc arthroplasty (artificial disc), anterior approach, each additional interspace, lumbar (List separately in addition to code for primary procedure)

→ *CPT Assistant* Jun 07:1; *CPT Changes: An Insider's View* 2007, 2009

(Use 0165T in conjunction with 22862)

(Do not report 0163T-0165T in conjunction with 22851, 49010, when performed at the same level)

(For decompression, see 63001-63048)

0166T Transmyocardial transcatheter closure of ventricular septal defect, with implant; without cardiopulmonary bypass

→ *CPT Assistant* Jul 07:6; *CPT Changes: An Insider's View* 2007

0167T with cardiopulmonary bypass

→ *CPT Assistant* Jul 07:6; *CPT Changes: An Insider's View* 2007

(Do not report 0166T, 0167T in conjunction with 32551, 33210, 33211)

(For ventricular septal defect closure via percutaneous transcatheter implant delivery, use 93581)

0168T Rhinophototherapy, intranasal application of ultraviolet and visible light, bilateral

→ *CPT Assistant* Jul 07:6; *CPT Changes: An Insider's View* 2007

0169T Stereotactic placement of infusion catheter(s) in the brain for delivery of therapeutic agent(s), including computerized stereotactic planning and burr hole(s)

→ *CPT Assistant* Jul 07:6, May 08:15, Jul 08:4; *CPT Changes: An Insider's View* 2007

(Do not report code 0169T in conjunction with 20660, 61107, 61795)

►(0170T has been deleted. To report, use 46707)◄

0171T Insertion of posterior spinous process distraction device (including necessary removal of bone or ligament for insertion and imaging guidance), lumbar; single level

→ *CPT Changes: An Insider's View* 2008

+ 0172T each additional level (List separately in addition to code for primary procedure)

→ *CPT Changes: An Insider's View* 2008

(Use 0172T in conjunction with 0171T)

+ 0173T Monitoring of intraocular pressure during vitrectomy surgery (List separately in addition to code for primary procedure)

→ *CPT Changes: An Insider's View* 2008

►(Use 0173T in conjunction with 67036, 67039-67043, 67108, 67112, 67113)◄

+ 0174T Computer-aided detection (CAD) (computer algorithm analysis of digital image data for lesion detection) with further physician review for interpretation and report, with or without digitization of film radiographic images, chest radiograph(s), performed concurrent with primary interpretation (List separately in addition to code for primary procedure)

→ *CPT Changes: An Insider's View* 2008

(Use 0174T in conjunction with 71010, 71020, 71021, 71022, 71030)

0175T Computer-aided detection (CAD) (computer algorithm analysis of digital image data for lesion detection) with further physician review for interpretation and report, with or without digitization of film radiographic images, chest radiograph(s), performed remote from primary interpretation

→ *CPT Changes: An Insider's View* 2008

(Do not report 0175T in conjunction with 71010, 71020, 71021, 71022, 71030)

0176T Transluminal dilation of aqueous outflow canal; without retention of device or stent

→ *CPT Changes: An Insider's View* 2008

0177T with retention of device or stent

→ *CPT Changes: An Insider's View* 2008

0178T Electrocardiogram, 64 leads or greater, with graphic presentation and analysis; with interpretation and report

→ *CPT Changes: An Insider's View* 2008

0179T tracing and graphics only, without interpretation and report

→ *CPT Changes: An Insider's View* 2008

0180T interpretation and report only

→ *CPT Changes: An Insider's View* 2008

(For electrocardiogram, routine, with at least 12 leads separately performed, see 93000-93010)

0181T   Corneal hysteresis determination, by air impulse stimulation, bilateral, with interpretation and report

➔ *CPT Changes: An Insider's View* 2008

0182T   High dose rate electronic brachytherapy, per fraction

➔ *CPT Changes: An Insider's View* 2008

▶(Do not report 0182T in conjunction with 77761-77763, 77776-77778, 77785-77787, 77789)◀

0183T   Low frequency, non-contact, non-thermal ultrasound, including topical application(s), when performed, wound assessment, and instruction(s) for ongoing care, per day

➔ *CPT Changes: An Insider's View* 2008

0184T   Excision of rectal tumor, transanal endoscopic microsurgical approach (ie, TEMS)

➔ *CPT Changes: An Insider's View* 2009

▶(For non-endoscopic excision of rectal tumor, see 45160, 45171, 45172)◀

(Do not report 0184T in conjunction with 45300-45327, 69990)

0185T   Multivariate analysis of patient-specific findings with quantifiable computer probability assessment, including report

➔ *CPT Changes: An Insider's View* 2009

(Do not report 0185T in conjunction with 99090)

0186T   Suprachoroidal delivery of pharmacologic agent (does not include supply of medication)

➔ *CPT Changes: An Insider's View* 2009

0187T   Scanning computerized ophthalmic diagnostic imaging, anterior segment, with interpretation and report, unilateral

➔ *CPT Changes: An Insider's View* 2009

Remote Real-Time Interactive Videoconferenced Critical Care Services

Remote real-time interactive video-conferenced critical care is the direct delivery by a physician(s) of medical care for a critically ill or critically injured patient from an off-site location. Remote real-time interactive video-conferenced critical care is intended to supplement on-site critical care services at times when a critically ill or injured patient requires additional critical care resources than are available on-site. (For definitions of critical illness or injury and critical care services, see **Critical Care Services** section).

In order to report remote real-time interactive video-conferenced critical care, the physician(s) in the remote location must have real-time access to the patient's medical record including progress notes, nursing notes, current medications, vital signs, clinical laboratory test results, other diagnostic test results, and radiographic images. The physician must have real-time capability to enter electronic orders; document the remote care services provided in the hospital medical record; videoconference with the on-site health care team in the patient room;

assess patients in their individual rooms, using high fidelity audio and video capabilities, including clear observation of the patient, monitors, ventilators, and infusion pumps; and speak to patients and family members.

The review and/or interpretation of all diagnostic information is included in reporting remote real-time interactive video-conferenced critical care when performed during the critical period by the physician(s) providing remote real-time interactive video-conferenced critical care and should not be reported separately.

The remote real-time interactive video-conferenced critical care codes 0188T and 0189T are used to report the total duration of time spent by a physician providing remote real-time interactive video-conferenced critical care services to a critically ill or critically injured patient, even if the time spent by the physician on that date is not continuous. For any given period of time spent providing remote real-time interactive video-conferenced critical care services, the physician must devote his or her full attention to the patient and, therefore, cannot provide services to any other patient during the same period of time.

Time spent with the individual patient should be recorded in the patient's record. The time that can be reported as remote real-time interactive video-conferenced critical care is the time spent engaged in work directly related to the individual patient's care. For example, time spent reviewing test results or imaging studies, discussing the critically ill patient's care with other medical staff or documenting remote real-time interactive video-conferenced critical care services in the medical record would be reported as remote real-time interactive video-conferenced critical care, even though it does not occur at the bedside. Also, when the patient is unable or lacks capacity to participate in discussions, time spent from the remote site with family members or surrogate decision makers obtaining a medical history, reviewing the patient's condition or prognosis, or discussing treatment or limitation(s) of treatment may be reported as remote real-time interactive video-conferenced critical care, provided that the conversation bears directly on the management of the patient.

Time spent in activities that occur away from the bedside when the physician does not have the real-time capabilities described above may not be reported as remote real-time interactive video-conferenced critical care because the physician is not immediately available to the patient. Time spent in activities that do not directly contribute to the treatment of the patient may not be reported as remote real-time interactive video-conferenced critical care, even if they are performed in the remote site (eg, participation in administrative meetings or telephone calls to discuss other patients). Only one physician may report either Critical Care Services (99291, 99292) or remote real-time interactive video-conferenced Critical Care for the same period of time. Do not report remote real-time interactive video-conferenced critical care if another physician reports Pediatric or Neonatal Critical Care or Intensive Care services (99468-99476).

Code 0188T is used to report the first 30 to 74 minutes of remote real-time interactive video-conferenced, critical care on a given date. It should be used only once per date even if the time spent by the physician is not continuous on that date. Remote real-time interactive video-conferenced, critical care of less than 30 minutes total duration on a given date should not be reported.

Code 0189T is used to report additional block(s) of time, of up to 30 minutes each, beyond the first 74 minutes (see table below).

The following examples illustrate the correct reporting of remote critical care services:

Total Duration of Critical Care	Codes
less than 30 minutes (less than 1/2 hour)	Do not report
30-74 minutes (1/2 hr. - 1 hr. 14 min.)	0188T X 1
75-104 minutes (1 hr. 15 min. - 1 hr. 44 min.)	0188T X 1 AND 0189T X 1
105-134 minutes (1 hr. 45 min. - 2 hr. 14 min.)	0188T X 1 AND 0189T X 2

0188T   Remote real-time interactive video-conferenced critical care, evaluation and management of the critically ill or critically injured patient; first 30-74 minutes
➔ *CPT Changes: An Insider's View* 2009

+ 0189T   each additional 30 minutes (List separately in addition to code for primary service)
➔ *CPT Changes: An Insider's View* 2009

(Use 0189T in conjunction with 0188T)

+ 0190T   Placement of intraocular radiation source applicator (List separately in addition to primary procedure)
➔ *CPT Changes: An Insider's View* 2009

(Use 0190T in conjunction with 67036)

(For application of the source by radiation oncologist, see Clinical Brachytherapy section)

0191T   Insertion of anterior segment aqueous drainage device, without extraocular reservoir; internal approach
➔ *CPT Changes: An Insider's View* 2009

0192T   external approach
➔ *CPT Changes: An Insider's View* 2009

0193T   Transurethral, radiofrequency micro-remodeling of the female bladder neck and proximal urethra for stress urinary incontinence
➔ *CPT Changes: An Insider's View* 2009

(Do not report 0193T in conjunction with 51701)

▶(0194T has been deleted. To report procalcitonin, use 84145)◀

0195T   Arthrodesis, pre-sacral interbody technique, including instrumentation, imaging (when performed), and discectomy to prepare interspace, lumbar; single interspace
➔ *CPT Changes: An Insider's View* 2009

+ 0196T   each additional interspace (List separately in addition to code for primary procedure)
➔ *CPT Changes: An Insider's View* 2009

(Use 0196T in conjunction with 0195T)

(Do not report 0195T, 0196T in conjunction with 22558, 22845, 22851, 76000, 76380, 76496, 76497)

● **0197T**   Intra-fraction localization and tracking of target or patient motion during delivery of radiation therapy (eg, 3D positional tracking, gating, 3D surface tracking), each fraction of treatment
➔ *CPT Changes: An Insider's View* 2010

● **0198T**   Measurement of ocular blood flow by repetitive intraocular pressure sampling, with interpretation and report
➔ *CPT Changes: An Insider's View* 2010

● **0199T**   Physiologic recording of tremor using accelerometer(s) and/or gyroscope(s) (including frequency and amplitude), including interpretation and report
➔ *CPT Changes: An Insider's View* 2010

⊙● **0200T**   Percutaneous sacral augmentation (sacroplasty), unilateral injection(s), including the use of a balloon or mechanical device, when used, 1 or more needles
➔ *CPT Changes: An Insider's View* 2010

⊙● **0201T**   Percutaneous sacral augmentation (sacroplasty), bilateral injections, including the use of a balloon or mechanical device, when used, 2 or more needles
➔ *CPT Changes: An Insider's View* 2010

▶(For radiological supervision and interpretation, see 72291, 72292)◀

▶(If bone biopsy is performed, see 20220, 20225)◀

● **0202T**   Posterior vertebral joint(s) arthroplasty (eg, facet joint[s] replacement), including facetectomy, laminectomy, foraminotomy, and vertebral column fixation, injection of bone cement, when performed, including fluoroscopy, single level, lumbar spine
➔ *CPT Changes: An Insider's View* 2010

▶(Do not report 0202T in conjunction with 22521, 22524, 22840, 22851, 22857, 63005, 63012, 63017, 63030, 63042, 63047, 63056 at the same level)◀

● **0203T** Sleep study, unattended, simultaneous recording; heart rate, oxygen saturation, respiratory analysis (eg, by airflow or peripheral arterial tone) and sleep time
➔ *CPT Changes: An Insider's View* 2010

►(Do not report 0203T in conjunction with 93012, 93014, 93041-93227, 93228, 93229, 93230-93272, 95803, 95806, 0204T)◄

►(For unattended sleep study that measures a minimum of heart rate, oxygen saturation, and respiratory analysis, use 0204T)◄

►(For unattended sleep study that measures heart rate, oxygen saturation, respiratory airflow, and respiratory effort, use 95806)◄

● **0204T** minimum of heart rate, oxygen saturation, and respiratory analysis (eg, by airflow or peripheral arterial tone)
➔ *CPT Changes: An Insider's View* 2010

►(Do not report 0204T in conjunction with 93012, 93014, 93041-93227, 93228, 93229, 93230-93272, 95806, 0203T)◄

►(For unattended sleep study that measures heart rate, oxygen saturation, respiratory analysis and sleep time, use 0203T)◄

►(For unattended sleep study that measures heart rate, oxygen saturation, respiratory airflow, and respiratory effort, use 95806)◄

+● **0205T** Intravascular catheter-based coronary vessel or graft spectroscopy (eg, infrared) during diagnostic evaluation and/or therapeutic intervention including imaging supervision, interpretation, and report, each vessel (List separately in addition to code for primary procedure)
➔ *CPT Changes: An Insider's View* 2010

►(Use 0205T in conjunction with 92980, 92982, 92995, 93508, 93510-93533)◄

● **0206T** Algorithmic analysis, remote, of electrocardiographic-derived data with computer probability assessment, including report
➔ *CPT Changes: An Insider's View* 2010

►(When a 12-lead ECG is performed, 93000-93010 may be reported, as appropriate)◄

● **0207T** Evacuation of meibomian glands, automated, using heat and intermittent pressure, unilateral
➔ *CPT Changes: An Insider's View* 2010

Notes

⊙=Moderate sedation   ✚=Add-on code   ✗=FDA approval pending   #=Resequenced code   ➡➡=See p xiii for details

Appendix A

Modifiers

This list includes all of the modifiers applicable to *CPT 2010* codes.

A modifier provides the means to report or indicate that a service or procedure that has been performed has been altered by some specific circumstance but not changed in its definition or code. Modifiers also enable health care professionals to effectively respond to payment policy requirements established by other entities.

(Modifier 21 has been deleted. To report prolonged physician services, see 99354-99357)

22 **Increased Procedural Services:** When the work required to provide a service is substantially greater than typically required, it may be identified by adding modifier 22 to the usual procedure code. Documentation must support the substantial additional work and the reason for the additional work (ie, increased intensity, time, technical difficulty of procedure, severity of patient's condition, physical and mental effort required). **Note:** This modifier should not be appended to an E/M service.
➔ *CPT Assistant* Jan 09:8, Apr 09:8, Jun 09:8,10 *CPT Changes: An Insider's View* 2008

23 **Unusual Anesthesia:** Occasionally, a procedure, which usually requires either no anesthesia or local anesthesia, because of unusual circumstances must be done under general anesthesia. This circumstance may be reported by adding modifier 23 to the procedure code of the basic service.

24 **Unrelated Evaluation and Management Service by the Same Physician During a Postoperative Period:** The physician may need to indicate that an evaluation and management service was performed during a postoperative period for a reason(s) unrelated to the original procedure. This circumstance may be reported by adding modifier 24 to the appropriate level of E/M service.

25 **Significant, Separately Identifiable Evaluation and Management Service by the Same Physician on the Same Day of the Procedure or Other Service:** It may be necessary to indicate that on the day a procedure or service identified by a CPT code was performed, the patient's condition required a significant, separately identifiable E/M service above and beyond the other service provided or beyond the usual preoperative and postoperative care associated with the procedure that was performed. A significant, separately identifiable E/M service is defined or substantiated by documentation that satisfies the relevant criteria for the respective E/M service to be reported (see **Evaluation and Management Services Guidelines** for instructions on determining level of E/M service). The E/M service may be prompted by the symptom or condition for which the procedure and/or service was provided. As such, different diagnoses are not required for reporting of the E/M services on the same date. This circumstance may be reported by adding modifier 25 to the appropriate level of E/M service. **Note:** This modifier is not used to report an E/M service that resulted in a decision to perform surgery. See modifier 57. For significant, separately identifiable non-E/M services, see modifier 59.
➔ *CPT Assistant* Feb 09:22, Mar 09:3, Apr 09:4; Jun 09:11 *CPT Changes: An Insider's View* 2008

26 **Professional Component:** Certain procedures are a combination of a physician component and a technical component. When the physician component is reported separately, the service may be identified by adding modifier 26 to the usual procedure number.
➔ *CPT Assistant* Jan 09:7, Apr 09:4, May 09:7

32 **Mandated Services:** Services related to *mandated* consultation and/or related services (eg, third party payer, governmental, legislative or regulatory requirement) may be identified by adding modifier 32 to the basic procedure.

47 **Anesthesia by Surgeon:** Regional or general anesthesia provided by the surgeon may be reported by adding modifier 47 to the basic service. (This does not include local anesthesia.) **Note:** Modifier 47 would not be used as a modifier for the anesthesia procedures.

50 **Bilateral Procedure:** Unless otherwise identified in the listings, bilateral procedures that are performed at the same operative session, should be identified by adding modifier 50 to the appropriate 5 digit code.
➔ *CPT Assistant* Apr 09:9

51 **Multiple Procedures:** When multiple procedures, other than E/M services, Physical Medicine and Rehabilitation services or provision of supplies (eg, vaccines), are performed at the same session by the same provider, the primary procedure or service may be reported as listed. The additional procedure(s) or service(s) may be identified by appending modifier 51 to the additional procedure or service code(s). **Note:** This modifier should not be appended to designated "add-on" codes (see Appendix D).
➔ *CPT Assistant* Feb 09:6, Mar 09:10, Apr 09:8 *CPT Changes: An Insider's View* 2008

52 **Reduced Services:** Under certain circumstances a service or procedure is partially reduced or eliminated at the physician's discretion. Under these circumstances the service provided can be identified by its usual procedure number and the addition of modifier 52, signifying that the service is reduced. This provides a means of reporting reduced services without disturbing the identification of the basic service. **Note:** For hospital outpatient reporting of a previously scheduled procedure/service that is partially reduced or cancelled as a result of extenuating circumstances or those that threaten the well-being of the patient prior to or after administration of anesthesia, see modifiers 73 and 74 (see modifiers approved for ASC hospital outpatient use).
➔ *CPT Assistant* Mar 09:11, Apr 09:5, May 09:8, Jun 09:10

53 **Discontinued Procedure:** Under certain circumstances, the physician may elect to terminate a surgical or diagnostic procedure. Due to extenuating circumstances or those that threaten the well being of the patient, it may be necessary to indicate that a surgical or diagnostic procedure was started but discontinued. This circumstance may be reported by adding modifier 53 to the code reported by the physician for the discontinued procedure. **Note:** This modifier is not used to report the elective cancellation of a procedure prior to the patient's anesthesia induction and/or surgical preparation in the operating suite. For outpatient hospital/ambulatory surgery center (ASC) reporting of a previously scheduled procedure/service that is partially reduced or cancelled as a result of extenuating circumstances or those that threaten the well being of the patient prior to or after administration of anesthesia, see modifiers 73 and 74 (see modifiers approved for ASC hospital outpatient use).

54 **Surgical Care Only:** When 1 physician performs a surgical procedure and another provides preoperative and/or postoperative management, surgical services may be identified by adding modifier 54 to the usual procedure number.

55 **Postoperative Management Only:** When 1 physician performed the postoperative management and another physician performed the surgical procedure, the postoperative component may be identified by adding modifier 55 to the usual procedure number.

56 **Preoperative Management Only:** When 1 physician performed the preoperative care and evaluation and another physician performed the surgical procedure, the preoperative component may be identified by adding modifier 56 to the usual procedure number.

57 **Decision for Surgery:** An evaluation and management service that resulted in the initial decision to perform the surgery may be identified by adding modifier 57 to the appropriate level of E/M service.

➲ *CPT Assistant* May 09:9

58 **Staged or Related Procedure or Service by the Same Physician During the Postoperative Period:** It may be necessary to indicate that the performance of a procedure or service during the postoperative period was: (a) planned or anticipated (staged); (b) more extensive than the original procedure; or (c) for therapy following a surgical procedure. This circumstance may be reported by adding modifier 58 to the staged or related procedure. **Note:** For treatment of a problem that requires a return to the operating/procedure room (eg, unanticipated clinical condition), see modifier 78.

➲ *CPT Changes: An Insider's View* 2008

59 **Distinct Procedural Service:** Under certain circumstances, it may be necessary to indicate that a procedure or service was distinct or independent from other non-E/M services performed on the same day. Modifier 59 is used to identify procedures/services, other than E/M services, that are not normally reported together, but are appropriate under the circumstances. Documentation must support a different session, different procedure or surgery, different site or

organ system, separate incision/excision, separate lesion, or separate injury (or area of injury in extensive injuries) not ordinarily encountered or performed on the same day by the same individual. However, when another already established modifier is appropriate it should be used rather than modifier 59. Only if no more descriptive modifier is available, and the use of modifier 59 best explains the circumstances, should modifier 59 be used. **Note:** Modifier 59 should not be appended to an E/M service. To report a separate and distinct E/M service with a non-E/M service performed on the same date, see modifier 25.

➲ *CPT Assistant* Feb 09:17, Apr 09:4,8, May 09:6, Jun 09:8 *CPT Changes: An Insider's View* 2008

62 **Two Surgeons:** When 2 surgeons work together as primary surgeons performing distinct part(s) of a procedure, each surgeon should report his/her distinct operative work by adding modifier 62 to the procedure code and any associated add-on code(s) for that procedure as long as both surgeons continue to work together as primary surgeons. Each surgeon should report the co-surgery once using the same procedure code. If additional procedure(s) (including add-on procedure(s) are performed during the same surgical session, separate code(s) may also be reported with modifier 62 added. **Note:** If a co-surgeon acts as an assistant in the performance of additional procedure(s) during the same surgical session, those services may be reported using separate procedure code(s) with modifier 80 or modifier 82 added, as appropriate.

63 **Procedure Performed on Infants less than 4 kg:** Procedures performed on neonates and infants up to a present body weight of 4 kg may involve significantly increased complexity and physician work commonly associated with these patients. This circumstance may be reported by adding modifier 63 to the procedure number. **Note:** Unless otherwise designated, this modifier may only be appended to procedures/services listed in the 20000-69990 code series. Modifier 63 should not be appended to any CPT codes listed in the **Evaluation and Management Services, Anesthesia, Radiology, Pathology/Laboratory, or Medicine** sections.

66 **Surgical Team:** Under some circumstances, highly complex procedures (requiring the concomitant services of several physicians, often of different specialties, plus other highly skilled, specially trained personnel, various types of complex equipment) are carried out under the "surgical team" concept. Such circumstances may be identified by each participating physician with the addition of modifier 66 to the basic procedure number used for reporting services.

76 **Repeat Procedure or Service by Same Physician:** It may be necessary to indicate that a procedure or service was repeated subsequent to the original procedure or service. This circumstance may be reported by adding modifier 76 to the repeated procedure/service.

➲ *CPT Assistant* Feb 09:6 *CPT Changes: An Insider's View* 2008

77 **Repeat Procedure by Another Physician:** The physician may need to indicate that a basic procedure or service performed by another physician had to be repeated. This situation may be reported by adding modifier 77 to the repeated procedure/service.

78 Unplanned Return to the Operating/Procedure Room by the Same Physician Following Initial Procedure for a Related Procedure During the Postoperative Period: It may be necessary to indicate that another procedure was performed during the postoperative period of the initial procedure (unplanned procedure following initial procedure). When this procedure is related to the first, and requires the use of an operating/procedure room, it may be reported by adding modifier 78 to the related procedure. (For repeat procedures, see modifier 76.)

➡ *CPT Changes: An Insider's View* 2008

79 Unrelated Procedure or Service by the Same Physician During the Postoperative Period: The physician may need to indicate that the performance of a procedure or service during the postoperative period was unrelated to the original procedure. This circumstance may be reported by using modifier 79. (For repeat procedures on the same day, see modifier 76.)

80 Assistant Surgeon: Surgical assistant services may be identified by adding modifier 80 to the usual procedure number(s).

81 Minimum Assistant Surgeon: Minimum surgical assistant services are identified by adding modifier 81 to the usual procedure number.

82 Assistant Surgeon (when qualified resident surgeon not available): The unavailability of a qualified resident surgeon is a prerequisite for use of modifier 82 appended to the usual procedure code number(s).

90 Reference (Outside) Laboratory: When laboratory procedures are performed by a party other than the treating or reporting physician, the procedure may be identified by adding modifier 90 to the usual procedure number.

91 Repeat Clinical Diagnostic Laboratory Test: In the course of treatment of the patient, it may be necessary to repeat the same laboratory test on the same day to obtain subsequent (multiple) test results. Under these circumstances, the laboratory test performed can be identified by its usual procedure number and the addition of modifier 91. **Note:** This modifier may not be used when tests are rerun to confirm initial results; due to testing problems with specimens or equipment; or for any other reason when a normal, one-time, reportable result is all that is required. This modifier may not be used when other code(s) describe a series of test results (eg, glucose tolerance tests, evocative/suppression testing). This modifier may only be used for laboratory test(s) performed more than once on the same day on the same patient.

➡ *CPT Assistant* May 09:6

92 Alternative Laboratory Platform Testing: When laboratory testing is being performed using a kit or transportable instrument that wholly or in part consists of a single use, disposable analytical chamber, the service may be identified by adding modifier 92 to the usual laboratory procedure code (HIV testing 86701-86703). The test does not

require permanent dedicated space, hence by its design may be hand carried or transported to the vicinity of the patient for immediate testing at that site, although location of the testing is not in itself determinative of the use of this modifier.

➡ *CPT Changes: An Insider's View* 2008

99 Multiple Modifiers: Under certain circumstances 2 or more modifiers may be necessary to completely delineate a service. In such situations modifier 99 should be added to the basic procedure, and other applicable modifiers may be listed as part of the description of the service.

Anesthesia Physical Status Modifiers

The Physical Status modifiers are consistent with the American Society of Anesthesiologists ranking of patient physical status, and distinguishing various levels of complexity of the anesthesia service provided. All anesthesia services are reported by use of the anesthesia five-digit procedure code (00100-01999) with the appropriate physical status modifier appended.

Example: 00100-P1

Under certain circumstances, when another established modifier(s) is appropriate, it should be used in addition to the physical status modifier.

Example: 00100-P4-53

Physical Status Modifier P1: A normal healthy patient

Physical Status Modifier P2: A patient with mild systemic disease

Physical Status Modifier P3: A patient with severe systemic disease

Physical Status Modifier P4: A patient with severe systemic disease that is a constant threat to life

Physical Status Modifier P5: A moribund patient who is not expected to survive without the operation

Physical Status Modifier P6: A declared brain-dead patient whose organs are being removed for donor purposes

Modifiers Approved for Ambulatory Surgery Center (ASC) Hospital Outpatient Use

CPT Level I Modifiers

25 Significant, Separately Identifiable Evaluation and Management Service by the Same Physician on the Same Day of the Procedure or Other Service: It may be necessary to indicate that on the day a procedure or service identified by a CPT code was performed, the patient's condition required a significant, separately identifiable E/M service above and beyond the other service provided or beyond the usual preoperative and postoperative care associated with the procedure that was performed. A significant, separately identifiable E/M service is defined or substantiated by documentation that satisfies the relevant criteria for the respective E/M service to be reported (see **Evaluation and Management Services Guidelines** for instructions on determining level of E/M service). The E/M service may be prompted by the symptom or condition for which the procedure and/or service was provided. As such, different diagnoses are not required for reporting of the E/M services on the same date. This circumstance may be reported by adding modifier 25 to the appropriate level of E/M service. **Note:** This modifier is not used to report an E/M service that resulted in a decision to perform surgery. See modifier 57. For significant, separately identifiable non-E/M services, see modifier 59.

27 **Multiple Outpatient Hospital E/M Encounters on the Same Date:** For hospital outpatient reporting purposes, utilization of hospital resources related to separate and distinct E/M encounters performed in multiple outpatient hospital settings on the same date may be reported by adding modifier 27 to each appropriate level outpatient and/or emergency department E/M code(s). This modifier provides a means of reporting circumstances involving evaluation and management services provided by physician(s) in more than one (multiple) outpatient hospital setting(s) (eg, hospital emergency department, clinic). **Note:** This modifier is not to be used for physician reporting of multiple E/M services performed by the same physician on the same date. For physician reporting of all outpatient evaluation and management services provided by the same physician on the same date and performed in multiple outpatient setting(s) (eg, hospital emergency department, clinic), see **Evaluation and Management, Emergency Department, or Preventive Medicine Services** codes.

50 **Bilateral Procedure:** Unless otherwise identified in the listings, bilateral procedures that are performed at the same operative session should be identified by adding modifier 50 to the appropriate 5 digit code.

52 **Reduced Services:** Under certain circumstances a service or procedure is partially reduced or eliminated at the physician's discretion. Under these circumstances the service provided can be identified by its usual procedure number and the addition of modifier 52, signifying that the service is reduced. This provides a means of reporting reduced services without disturbing the identification of the basic service. **Note:** For hospital outpatient reporting of a previously scheduled procedure/service that is partially reduced or cancelled as a result of extenuating circumstances or those that threaten the well-being of the patient prior to or after administration of anesthesia, see modifiers 73 and 74.

58 **Staged or Related Procedure or Service by the Same Physician During the Postoperative Period:** It may be necessary to indicate that the performance of a procedure or service during the postoperative period was: (a) planned or anticipated (staged); (b) more extensive than the original procedure; or (c) for therapy following a surgical procedure. This circumstance may be reported by adding modifier 58

to the staged or related procedure. **Note:** For treatment of a problem that requires a return to the operating/procedure room (eg, unanticipated clinical condition), see modifier 78.

59 **Distinct Procedural Service:** Under certain circumstances, it may be necessary to indicate that a procedure or service was distinct or independent from other non-E/M services performed on the same day. Modifier 59 is used to identify procedures/services, other than E/M services, that are not normally reported together, but are appropriate under the circumstances. Documentation must support a different session, different procedure or surgery, different site or organ system, separate incision/excision, separate lesion, or separate injury (or area of injury in extensive injuries) not ordinarily encountered or performed on the same day by the same individual. However, when another already established modifier is appropriate it should be used rather than modifier 59. Only if no more descriptive modifier is available, and the use of modifier 59 best explains the circumstances, should modifier 59 be used. **Note:** Modifier 59 should not be appended to an E/M service. To report a separate and distinct E/M service with a non-E/M service performed on the same date, see modifier 25.

73 **Discontinued Out-Patient Hospital/Ambulatory Surgery Center (ASC) Procedure Prior to the Administration of Anesthesia:** Due to extenuating circumstances or those that threaten the well being of the patient, the physician may cancel a surgical or diagnostic procedure subsequent to the patient's surgical preparation (including sedation when provided, and being taken to the room where the procedure is to be performed), but prior to the administration of anesthesia (local, regional block(s) or general). Under these circumstances, the intended service that is prepared for but cancelled can be reported by its usual procedure number and the addition of modifier 73. **Note:** The elective cancellation of a service prior to the administration of anesthesia and/or surgical preparation of the patient should not be reported. For physician reporting of a discontinued procedure, see modifier 53.

74 **Discontinued Out-Patient Hospital/Ambulatory Surgery Center (ASC) Procedure After Administration of Anesthesia:** Due to extenuating circumstances or those that threaten the well being of the patient, the physician may terminate a surgical or diagnostic procedure after the administration of anesthesia (local, regional block(s), general) or after the procedure was started (incision made, intubation started, scope inserted, etc). Under these circumstances, the procedure started but terminated can be reported by its usual procedure number and the addition of modifier 74. **Note:** The elective cancellation of a service prior to the administration of anesthesia and/or surgical preparation of the patient should not be reported. For physician reporting of a discontinued procedure, see modifier 53.

76 **Repeat Procedure or Service by Same Physician:** It may be necessary to indicate that a procedure or service was repeated subsequent to the original procedure or service. This circumstance may be reported by adding modifier 76 to the repeated procedure/service.

77 Repeat Procedure by Another Physician: The physician may need to indicate that a basic procedure or service performed by another physician had to be repeated. This situation may be reported by adding modifier 77 to the repeated procedure/service.

78 Unplanned Return to the Operating/Procedure Room by the Same Physician Following Initial Procedure for a Related Procedure During the Postoperative Period: It may be necessary to indicate that another procedure was performed during the postoperative period of the initial procedure (unplanned procedure following initial procedure). When this procedure is related to the first, and requires the use of an operating/procedure room, it may be reported by adding modifier 78 to the related procedure. (For repeat procedures, see modifier 76.)

79 Unrelated Procedure or Service by the Same Physician During the Postoperative Period: The physician may need to indicate that the performance of a procedure or service during the postoperative period was unrelated to the original procedure. This circumstance may be reported by using modifier 79. (For repeat procedures on the same day, see 76.)

91 Repeat Clinical Diagnostic Laboratory Test: In the course of treatment of the patient, it may be necessary to repeat the same laboratory test on the same day to obtain subsequent (multiple) test results. Under these circumstances, the laboratory test performed can be identified by its usual procedure number and the addition of modifier 91. **Note:** This modifier may not be used when tests are rerun to confirm initial results; due to testing problems with specimens or equipment; or for any other reason when a normal, one-time, reportable result is all that is required. This modifier may not be used when other code(s) describe a series of test results (eg, glucose tolerance tests, evocative/suppression testing). This modifier may only be used for laboratory test(s) performed more than once on the same day on the same patient.

Level II (HCPCS/National) Modifiers

E1 Upper left, eyelid

E2 Lower left, eyelid

E3 Upper right, eyelid

E4 Lower right, eyelid

F1 Left hand, second digit

F2 Left hand, third digit

F3 Left hand, fourth digit

F4 Left hand, fifth digit

F5 Right hand, thumb

F6 Right hand, second digit

F7 Right hand, third digit

F8 Right hand, fourth digit

F9 Right hand, fifth digit

FA Left hand, thumb

GG Performance and payment of a screening mammogram and diagnostic mammogram on the same patient, same day

GH Diagnostic mammogram converted from screening mammogram on same day

LC Left circumflex coronary artery

LD Left anterior descending coronary artery

LT Left side (used to identify procedures performed on the left side of the body)

QM Ambulance service provided under arrangement by a provider of services

QN Ambulance service furnished directly by a provider of services

RC Right coronary artery

RT Right side (used to identify procedures performed on the right side of the body)

T1 Left foot, second digit

T2 Left foot, third digit

T3 Left foot, fourth digit

T4 Left foot, fifth digit

T5 Right foot, great toe

T6 Right foot, second digit

T7 Right foot, third digit

T8 Right foot, fourth digit

T9 Right foot, fifth digit

TA Left foot, great toe

Appendix B

Summary of Additions, Deletions, and Revisions

►Appendix B shows the actual changes that were made to the code descriptors. New codes appear with a bullet (●) and are indicated as "Code Added." Revised codes are preceded with a triangle (▲). Within revised codes, the deleted language appears with a ~~strikethrough~~, while new text appears <u>underlined</u>. Codes with which conscious sedation would not be separately reported when performed at the same session by the same provider are denoted with the bullseye (⊙). The symbol (↗) is used to identify codes for vaccines that are pending FDA approval (see **Appendix K**). The symbol (#) is used to identify codes that have been resequenced (see **Appendix N**). CPT add-on codes are annotated by the symbol (✚) (see **Appendix D**). The symbol (⊘) is used to identify codes that are exempt from the use of modifier 51 (see **Appendix E**).◄

Evaluation and Management

▲ 99304   Initial nursing facility care, per day, for the evaluation and management of a patient, which requires these 3 key components:

■ **A detailed or comprehensive history;**

■ **A detailed or comprehensive examination; and**

■ **Medical decision making that is straightforward or of low complexity.**

Counseling and/or coordination of care with other providers or agencies are provided consistent with the nature of the problem(s) and the patientís and/or familyís needs.

Usually, the problem(s) requiring admission are of low severity. Physicians typically spend 25 minutes <u>at the bedside and on the patient's facility floor or unit.</u> ~~with the patient and/or family or caregiver.~~

▲ 99305   Initial nursing facility care, per day, for the evaluation and management of a patient, which requires these 3 key components:

■ **A comprehensive history;**

■ **A comprehensive examination; and**

■ **Medical decision making of moderate complexity.**

Counseling and/or coordination of care with other providers or agencies are provided consistent with the nature of the problem(s) and the patientís and/or familyís needs.

Usually, the problem(s) requiring admission are of moderate severity. Physicians typically spend 35 minutes <u>at the bedside and on the patient's facility floor or unit.</u> ~~with the patient and/or family or caregiver.~~

▲ 99306   Initial nursing facility care, per day, for the evaluation and management of a patient, which requires these 3 key components:

■ **A comprehensive history;**

■ **A comprehensive examination; and**

■ **Medical decision making of high complexity.**

Counseling and/or coordination of care with other providers or agencies are provided consistent with the nature of the problem(s) and the patientís and/or familyís needs.

Usually, the problem(s) requiring admission are of high severity. Physicians typically spend 45 minutes <u>at the bedside and on the patient's facility floor or unit.</u> ~~with the patient and/or family or caregiver.~~

▲ 99307   Subsequent nursing facility care, per day, for the evaluation and management of a patient, which requires at least 2 of these 3 key components:

■ **A problem focused interval history;**

■ **A problem focused examination;**

■ **Straightforward medical decision making.**

Counseling and/or coordination of care with other providers or agencies are provided consistent with the nature of the problem(s) and the patientís and/or familyís needs.

Usually, the patient is stable, recovering, or improving. Physicians typically spend 10 minutes <u>at the bedside and on the patient's facility floor or unit.</u> ~~with the patient and/or family or caregiver.~~

▲ 99308   Subsequent nursing facility care, per day, for the evaluation and management of a patient, which requires at least 2 of these 3 key components:

■ **An expanded problem focused interval history;**

■ **An expanded problem focused examination;**

■ **Medical decision making of low complexity.**

Counseling and/or coordination of care with other providers or agencies are provided consistent with the nature of the problem(s) and the patientís and/or familyís needs.

Usually, the patient is responding inadequately to therapy or has developed a minor complication. Physicians typically spend 15 minutes <u>at the bedside and on the patient's facility floor or unit.</u> ~~with the patient and/or family or caregiver.~~

▲ 99309   Subsequent nursing facility care, per day, for the evaluation and management of a patient, which requires at least 2 of these 3 key components:

■ **A detailed interval history;**

■ **A detailed examination;**

■ **Medical decision making of moderate complexity.**

Counseling and/or coordination of care with other providers or agencies are provided consistent with the nature of the problem(s) and the patientís and/or familyís needs.

Usually, the patient has developed a significant complication or a significant new problem. Physicians typically spend 25 minutes <u>at the bedside and on the patient's facility floor or unit.</u> ~~with the patient and/or family or caregiver.~~

▲ **99310** Subsequent nursing facility care, per day, for the evaluation and management of a patient, which requires at least 2 of these 3 key components:

■ **A comprehensive interval history;**

■ **A comprehensive examination;**

■ **Medical decision making of high complexity.**

Counseling and/or coordination of care with other providers or agencies are provided consistent with the nature of the problem(s) and the patientís and/or familyís needs.

The patient may be unstable or may have developed a significant new problem requiring immediate physician attention. Physicians typically spend 35 minutes <u>at the bedside and on the patient's facility floor or unit.</u> ~~with the patient and/or family or caregiver.~~

▲ **99318** Evaluation and management of a patient involving an annual nursing facility assessment, which requires these 3 key components:

■ **A detailed interval history;**

■ **A comprehensive examination; and**

■ **Medical decision making that is of low to moderate complexity.**

Counseling and/or coordination of care with other providers or agencies are provided consistent with the nature of the problem(s) and the patientís and/or familyís needs.

Usually, the patient is stable, recovering, or improving. Physicians typically spend 30 minutes <u>at the bedside and on the patient's facility floor or unit.</u> ~~with the patient and/or family or caregiver.~~

+ **99356** Grammatical Change

▲ **99358** **Prolonged evaluation and management service** before and/or after direct (face-to-face) patient care ~~(eg, review of extensive records and tests, communication with other professionals and/or the patient/family)~~; first hour ~~(List separately in addition to code(s) for other physician service(s) and/or inpatient or outpatient Evaluation and Management service)~~

+▲ **99359** each additional 30 minutes (List separately in addition to code for prolonged physician service)

99466 Grammatical Change

99468 Grammatical Change

99469 Grammatical Change

99477 Grammatical Change

Anesthesia

00528 Grammatical Change

00529 Grammatical Change

00541 Grammatical Change

00625 Grammatical Change

00626 Grammatical Change

~~01632~~ ~~radical resection~~

Surgery

~~14300~~ ~~Adjacent tissue transfer or rearrangement, more than 30 sq cm, unusual or complicated, any area~~

● **14301** Code added

+● **14302** Code added

+ **15787** Grammatical Change

16030 Grammatical Change

19120 Grammatical Change

+▲ **19295** Image guided placement, metallic localization clip, percutaneous, during breast biopsy<u>/aspiration</u> (List separately in addition to code for primary procedure)

20690 Grammatical Change

20692 Grammatical Change

20696 Grammatical Change

● **21011** Code added

● **21012** Code added

● **21013** Code added

● **21014** Code added

▲ **21015** Radical resection of tumor (eg, malignant neoplasm), soft tissue of face or scalp<u>; less than 2 cm</u>

● **21016** Code added

● **21552** Code added

● **21554** Code added

▲ **21555** Excision<u>,</u> tumor, soft tissue of neck or <u>anterior</u> thorax<u>,</u>~~;~~ subcutaneous<u>; less than 3 cm</u>

▲ **21556** Excision, tumor, soft tissue of neck or anterior thorax~~, deep~~, subfascial<u>,</u> <u>(eg,</u> intramuscular)<u>; less than 5 cm</u>

▲ **21557** Radical resection of tumor (eg, malignant neoplasm), soft tissue of neck or <u>anterior</u> thorax<u>; less than 5 cm</u>

● **21558** Code added

▲ **21930** Excision, tumor, soft tissue of back or flank<u>, subcutaneous; less than 3 cm</u>

● **21931** Code added

● **21932** Code added

● **21933** Code added

▲ **21935** Radical resection of tumor (eg, malignant neoplasm), soft tissue of back or flank<u>; less than 5 cm</u>

● **21936** Code added

22206 Grammatical Change

22210 Grammatical Change

22325 Grammatical Change

⊙▲ **22520** Percutaneous vertebroplasty, 1 vertebral body, unilateral or bilateral injection; thoracic

⊙▲ **22521** lumbar

22523 Grammatical Change

+⊙ **22527** Grammatical Change

+ **22840** Grammatical Change

▲ **22900** Excision, <u>tumor, soft tissue of</u> abdominal wall ~~tumor~~, subfascial (eg, ~~desmoid~~ <u>intramuscular); less than 5 cm</u>

● **22901** Code added

● **22902** Code added

● **22903** Code added

● **22904** Code added

● **22905** Code added

● **23071** Code added

● **23073** Code added

▲ **23075** Excision, tumor, soft tissue tumor, of shoulder area;, subcutaneous; less than 3 cm

▲ **23076** Excision, tumor, soft tissue of shoulder area, deep, subfascial, or (eg, intramuscular); less than 5 cm

▲ **23077** Radical resection of tumor (eg, malignant neoplasm), soft tissue of shoulder area; less than 5 cm

● **23078** Code added

▲ **23200** Radical resection for of tumor; clavicle

▲ **23210** scapula

▲ **23220** Radical resection of bone tumor, proximal humerus;

23221 with autograft (includes obtaining graft)

23222 with prosthetic replacement

● **24071** Code added

● **24073** Code added

▲ **24075** Excision, tumor, soft tissue of upper arm or elbow area;, subcutaneous; less than 3 cm

▲ **24076** Excision, tumor, soft tissue of upper arm or elbow area, deep (subfascial or (eg, intramuscular); less than 5 cm

▲ **24077** Radical resection of tumor (eg, malignant neoplasm), soft tissue of upper arm or elbow area; less than 5 cm

● **24079** Code added

▲ **24150** Radical resection for of tumor, shaft or distal humerus;

24151 with autograft (includes obtaining graft)

▲ **24152** Radical resection for of tumor, radial head or neck;

24153 with autograft (includes obtaining graft)

● **25071** Code added

● **25073** Code added

▲ **25075** Excision, tumor, soft tissue of forearm and/or wrist area;, subcutaneous; less than 3 cm

▲ **25076** Excision, tumor, soft tissue of forearm and/or wrist area, deep (subfascial or (eg, intramuscular); less than 3 cm

▲ **25077** Radical resection of tumor (eg, malignant neoplasm), soft tissue of forearm and/or wrist area; less than 3 cm

● **25078** Code added

▲ **25170** Radical resection for of tumor, radius or ulna

25210 Grammatical Change

25660 Grammatical Change

25670 Grammatical Change

● **26111** Code added

● **26113** Code added

▲ **26115** Excision, tumor or vascular malformation, soft tissue of hand or finger;, subcutaneous; less than 1.5 cm

▲ **26116** Excision, tumor, soft tissue, or vascular malformation, of hand or finger, deep (subfascial or (eg, intramuscular); less than 1.5 cm

▲ **26117** Radical resection of tumor (eg, malignant neoplasm), soft tissue of hand or finger; less than 3 cm

● **26118** Code added

▲ **26250** Radical resection of tumor, metacarpal (eg, tumor);

26255 with autograft (includes obtaining graft)

▲ **26260** Radical resection of tumor, proximal or middle phalanx of finger (eg, tumor);

26261 with autograft (includes obtaining graft)

▲ **26262** Radical resection of tumor, distal phalanx of finger (eg, tumor)

26498 Grammatical Change

● **27043** Code added

● **27045** Code added

▲ **27047** Excision, tumor, soft tissue of pelvis and hip area;, subcutaneous tissue; less than 3 cm

▲ **27048** Excision, tumor, soft tissue of pelvis and hip area, deep, subfascial, (eg, intramuscular); less than 5 cm

▲ **27049** Radical resection of tumor (eg, malignant neoplasm), soft tissue of pelvis and hip area (eg, malignant neoplasm); less than 5 cm

● **27059** Code added

▲ **27075** Radical resection of tumor or infection; wing of ilium, 1 pubic or ischial ramus or symphysis pubis

▲ **27076** ilium, including acetabulum, both pubic rami, or ischium and acetabulum

▲ **27077** innominate bone, total

▲ **27078** ischial tuberosity and greater trochanter of femur

27079 ischial tuberosity and greater trochanter of femur, with skin flaps

▲ **27327** Excision, tumor, soft tissue of thigh or knee area;, subcutaneous; less than 3 cm

▲ **27328** Excision, tumor, soft tissue of thigh or knee area, deep, subfascial, or (eg, intramuscular); less than 5 cm

▲ **27329** Radical resection of tumor (eg, malignant neoplasm), soft tissue of thigh or knee area; less than 5 cm

● **27337** Code added

● **27339** Code added

● **27364** Code added

▲ **27365** Radical resection of tumor, bone, femur or knee

27391 Grammatical Change

27394 Grammatical Change

27486 Grammatical Change

27496 Grammatical Change

▲ **27615** Radical resection of tumor (eg, malignant neoplasm), soft tissue of leg or ankle area; less than 5 cm

● **27616** Code added

▲ **27618** Excision, tumor, soft tissue of leg or ankle area;, subcutaneous tissue; less than 3 cm

▲ **27619** Excision, tumor, soft tissue of leg or ankle area, deep (subfascial or (eg, intramuscular); less than 5 cm

● **27632** Code added

● **27634** Code added

▲ 27640   Partial excision (craterization, saucerization, or diaphysectomy), bone (eg, osteomyelitis or exostosis); tibia

▲ 27641   fibula

▲ 27645   Radical resection of tumor, bone; tibia

▲ 27646   fibula

▲ 27647   talus or calcaneus

● 28039   Code added

● 28041   Code added

▲ 28043   Excision, tumor, soft tissue of foot or toe,; subcutaneous tissue; less than 1.5 cm

▲ 28045   Excision, tumor, soft tissue of foot or toe, deep, subfascial, (eg, intramuscular); less than 1.5 cm

▲ 28046   Radical resection of tumor (eg, malignant neoplasm), soft tissue of foot or toe; less than 3 cm

● 28047   Code added

▲ 28171   Radical resection of tumor, bone; tarsal (except talus or calcaneus)

▲ 28173   metatarsal

▲ 28175   phalanx of toe

   29044   Grammatical Change

   29220   low back

   29305   Grammatical Change

   29325   Grammatical Change

● 29581   Code added

   29876   Grammatical Change

▲ 30801   Cautery and/or aAblation, soft tissuemucosa of inferior turbinates, unilateral or bilateral, any method (eg, electrocautery, radiofrequency ablation, or tissue volume reduction); superficial

▲ 30802   intramural (ie, submucosal)

   31090   Grammatical Change

   31580   Grammatical Change

   31601   Grammatical Change

⊙▲ 31622   Bronchoscopy, rigid or flexible, includingwith or without fluoroscopic guidance, when performed; diagnostic, with or without cell washing, when performed (separate procedure)

⊙● 31626   Code added

+⊙● 31627   Code added

▲ 31641   Bronchoscopy (rigid or flexible), with destruction of tumor or relief of stenosis by any method other than excision (eg, laser therapy, cryotherapy)

▲ 31643   with placement of catheter(s) for intracavitary radioelement application

⊙▲ 31645   with therapeutic aspiration of tracheobronchial tree, initial (eg, drainage of lung abscess)

⊙▲ 31646   with therapeutic aspiration of tracheobronchial tree, subsequent

⊙▲ 31656   with injection of contrast material for segmental bronchography (fiberscope only)

   32482   Grammatical Change

● 32552   Code added

⊙● 32553   Code added

▲ 32560   Instillation, via chest tube/catheter, Chemical agent for pleurodesis (eg, talc for recurrent or persistent pneumothorax)

● 32561   Code added

● 32562   Code added

   32998   Grammatical Change

⊙▲ 33216   Insertion of a single transvenous electrode,; single chamber (1 electrode) permanent pacemaker or single chamber pacing cardioverter-defibrillator

⊙▲ 33217   Insertion of dual chamber (2 transvenous electrodes,) permanent pacemaker or dual chamber pacing cardioverter-defibrillator

⊙ 33220   Grammatical Change

⊙▲ 33223   Revision of skin pocket for single or dual chamber pacing cardioverter-defibrillator

   33511   Grammatical Change

   33512   Grammatical Change

   33513   Grammatical Change

   33514   Grammatical Change

   33516   Grammatical Change

+ 33518   Grammatical Change

+ 33519   Grammatical Change

+ 33521   Grammatical Change

+ 33522   Grammatical Change

+ 33523   Grammatical Change

+ 33530   Grammatical Change

   33534   Grammatical Change

   33535   Grammatical Change

   33536   Grammatical Change

   33766   Grammatical Change

● 33782   Code added

● 33783   Code added

● 33981   Code added

● 33982   Code added

● 33983   Code added

   34802   Grammatical Change

   34803   Grammatical Change

+ 35390   Grammatical Change

+ 35500   Grammatical Change

+ 35572   Grammatical Change

+ 35600   Grammatical Change

+ 35682   Grammatical Change

+ 35683   Grammatical Change

+ 35700   Grammatical Change

   36145   arteriovenous shunt created for dialysis (cannula, fistula, or graft)

⊙● 36147   Code added

+⊙● 36148   Code added

⊙▲ 36481   Percutaneous portal vein catheterization by any method

⊙ 36565   Grammatical Change

~~35834~~   ~~Plastic repair of arteriovenous aneurysm (separate procedure)~~

⊙▲ 37183   Revision of transvenous intrahepatic portosystemic shunt(s) (TIPS) (includes venous access, hepatic and portal vein catheterization, portography with hemodynamic evaluation, intrahepatic tract recanalization/dilatation, stent placement and all associated imaging guidance and documentation)

▲ 37760   Ligation of perforator veins, subfascial, radical (Linton type), including~~with or without~~ skin graft, when performed, open,1 leg

● 37761   Code added

37765   Grammatical Change

37785   Grammatical Change

40701   Grammatical Change

40702   Grammatical Change

41530   Grammatical Change

42508   Grammatical Change

▲ 42894   Resection of pharyngeal wall requiring closure with myocutaneous or fasciocutaneous flap or free muscle, skin, or fascial flap with microvascular anastamosis

● 43281   Code added

● 43282   Code added

43600   Grammatical Change

▲ 43761   Repositioning of ~~the~~a naso- or oro-gastric feeding tube, through the duodenum for enteric nutrition

● 43775   Code added

44100   Grammatical Change

44110   Grammatical Change

~~45170~~   ~~Excision of rectal tumor, transanal approach~~

● 45171   Code added

● 45172   Code added

▲ 46200   Fissurectomy, including ~~with or without~~ sphincterotomy, when performed

~~46210~~   ~~Cryptectomy; single~~

~~46211~~   ~~multiple (separate procedure)~~

▲ 46220   ~~Papillectomy or e~~Excision of single external papilla or tag, anus ~~(separate procedure)~~

▲ 46221   Hemorrhoidectomy, internal, by rubber band ligation(s)~~simple ligature (eg, rubber band)~~

▲ 46230   Excision of ~~external hemorrhoid tags and/or~~multiple external papillae or tags, anus

▲ 46250   Hemorrhoidectomy, external, ~~complete~~2 or more columns/groups

▲ 46255   Hemorrhoidectomy, internal and external, ~~simple~~single column/group;

▲ 46258   with fistulectomy, including ~~with or without~~fissurectomy, when performed

▲ 46260   Hemorrhoidectomy, internal and external, ~~complex or extensive~~2 or more columns/groups;

▲ 46262   with fistulectomy, including ~~with or without~~fissurectomy, when performed

▲ 46275   ~~submuscular~~intersphincteric

▲ 46280   ~~complex~~transsphincteric, suprasphincteric, extrasphincteric or multiple, including ~~with or without~~placement of seton, when performed

▲ 46320   ~~Enucleation or e~~Excision of thrombosed hemorrhoid, external ~~thrombotic hemorrhoid~~

● 46707   Code added

~~46937~~   ~~Cryosurgery of rectal tumor; benign~~

~~46938~~   ~~malignant~~

▲ 46945   Hemorrhoidectomy, internal, by L~~l~~igation ~~of internal hemorrhoids~~other than rubber band; single hemorrhoid column/group~~procedure~~

▲ 46946   ~~multiple procedures~~2 or more hemorrhoid columns/groups

47010   Grammatical Change

⊙ 47011   Grammatical Change

47144   Grammatical Change

47145   Grammatical Change

47370   Grammatical Change

47380   Grammatical Change

⊙▲ 47382   Ablation, 1 or more liver tumor(s), percutaneous, radiofrequency

⊙▲ 47525   Change of percutaneous biliary drainage catheter

⊙● 49411   Code added

⊙▲ 50200   Renal biopsy; percutaneous, by trocar or needle

50540   Grammatical Change

▲ 51726   Complex cystometrogram (~~eg~~ie, calibrated electronic equipment);

● 51727   Code added

● 51728   Code added

● 51729   Code added

~~51772~~   ~~Urethral pressure profile studies (UPP) (urethral closure pressure profile), any technique~~

~~51795~~   ~~Voiding pressure studies (VP); bladder voiding pressure, any technique~~

+▲ 51797   Voiding pressure studies, intra-abdominal ~~voiding pressure (AP)~~ (ie, rectal, gastric, intraperitoneal) (List separately in addition to code for primary procedure)

▲ 52282   Cystourethroscopy, with insertion of permanent urethral stent

● 53855   Code added

54322   Grammatical Change

54332   Grammatical Change

54336   Grammatical Change

▲ 55873   Cryosurgical ablation of the prostate (includes ultrasonic guidance and monitoring~~for interstitial cryosurgical probe placement~~)

▲ 55876   Placement of interstitial device(s) for radiation therapy guidance (eg, fiducial markers, dosimeter), percutaneous, prostate~~(via needle, any approach)~~, single or multiple

56605   Grammatical Change

● 57426   Code added

59850   Grammatical Change

59855   Grammatical Change

▲ 59897   Unlisted fetal invasive procedure, including ultrasound guidance, when performed

61460   Grammatical Change

61531   Grammatical Change

61886   Grammatical Change

63050   Grammatical Change

~~63660~~   ~~Revision or removal of spinal neurostimulator electrode percutaneous array(s) or plate/paddle(s)~~

● 63661   Code added

● 63662   Code added

● 63663   Code added

● 63664   Code added

~~64470~~   ~~Injection, anesthetic agent and/or steroid, paravertebral facet joint or facet joint nerve; cervical or thoracic, single level~~

~~64472~~   ~~cervical or thoracic, each additional level (List separately in addition to code for primary procedure)~~

~~64475~~   ~~lumbar or sacral, single level~~

~~64476~~   ~~lumbar or sacral, each additional level (List separately in addition to code for primary procedure)~~

● 64490   Code added

✚● 64491   Code added

✚● 64492   Code added

● 64493   Code added

✚● 64494   Code added

✚● 64495   Code added

64834   Grammatical Change

66982   Grammatical Change

Radiology

70160   Grammatical Change

▲ 72291   Radiological supervision and interpretation, percutaneous vertebroplasty, ~~or~~ vertebral augmentation, or sacral augmentation (sacroplasty), including cavity creation, per vertebral body or sacrum; under fluoroscopic guidance

▲ 72292   under CT guidance

● 74261   Code added

● 74262   Code added

● 74263   Code added

~~75558~~   ~~with flow/velocity quantification~~

~~75560~~   ~~with flow/velocity quantification and stress~~

~~75562~~   ~~with flow/velocity quantification~~

~~75564~~   ~~with flow/velocity quantification and stress~~

✚● 75565   Code added

● 75571   Code added

● 75572   Code added

● 75573   Code added

● 75574   Code added

~~75790~~   ~~Angiography, arteriovenous shunt (eg, dialysis patient), radiological supervision and interpretation~~

● 75791   Code added

▲ 77003   Fluoroscopic guidance and localization of needle or catheter tip for spine or paraspinous diagnostic or therapeutic injection procedures (epidural, transforaminal epidural, subarachnoid, ~~paravertebral facet joint, paravertebral facet joint nerve,~~ or sacroiliac joint), including neurolytic agent destruction

● 77338   Code added

⊙▲ 77371   Radiation treatment delivery, stereotactic radiosurgery (SRS), complete course of treatment of cranial lesion(s) consisting of 1 session; multi-source Cobalt 60 based

● 78451   Code added

● 78452   Code added

● 78453   Code added

● 78454   Code added

~~78460~~   ~~Myocardial perfusion imaging; (planar) single study, at rest or stress (exercise and/or pharmacologic), with or without quantification~~

~~78461~~   ~~multiple studies (planar), at rest and/or stress (exercise and/or pharmacologic), and redistribution and/or rest injection, with or without quantification~~

~~78464~~   ~~tomographic (SPECT), single study (including attenuation correction when performed), at rest or stress (exercise and/or pharmacologic), with or without quantification~~

~~78465~~   ~~tomographic (SPECT), multiple studies (including attenuation correction when performed), at rest and/or stress (exercise and/or pharmacologic) and redistribution and/or rest injection, with or without quantification~~

~~78478~~   ~~Myocardial perfusion study with wall motion, qualitative or quantitative study (List separately in addition to code for primary procedure)~~

~~78480~~   ~~Myocardial perfusion study with ejection fraction (List separately in addition to code for primary procedure)~~

78483   Grammatical Change

Pathology and Laboratory

▲ 80055   Obstetric panel

This panel must include the following:

Blood count, complete (CBC), automated and automated differential WBC count (85025 or 85027 and 85004)

OR

Blood count, complete (CBC), automated (85027) and appropriate manual differential WBC count (85007 or 85009)

Hepatitis B surface antigen (HBsAg) (87340)

Antibody, rubella (86762)

Syphilis test, non-treponemal antibody; qualitative (eg, VDRL, RPR, ART) (86592)

Antibody screen, RBC, each serum technique (86850)

Blood typing, ABO (86900) AND

Blood typing, Rh (D) (86901)

▲ 82306   ~~Calcifediol (25-OH-~~Vitamin D-~~3)~~; 25 hydroxy, includes fraction(s), if performed

82307 ~~Calciferol (Vitamin D)~~

▲ 82652 ~~Dihydroxyvitamin D,~~ 1, 25- dihydroxy, includes fraction(s), if performed

▲ 82784 Gammaglobulin (immunoglobulin); IgA, IgD, IgG, IgM, each

▲ 82785 IgE

▲ 82787 immunoglobulin subclasses (eg, IgG1, 2, 3, or 4), each

82951 Grammatical Change

82952 Grammatical Change

▲ 83516 Immunoassay for analyte other than infectious agent antibody or infectious agent antigen~~;~~ qualitative or semiquantitative~~;~~ multiple step method

▲ 83518 qualitative or semiquantitative, single step method (eg, reagent strip)

▲ 83519 ~~Immunoassay, analyte,~~ quantitative~~;~~ by ~~radiopharmaceutical technique~~ radioimmunoassay (eg, RIA)

▲ 83520 quantitative, not otherwise specified

▲ 83986 pH~~;~~ body fluid, ~~except blood~~not otherwise specified

● 83987 Code added

● 84145 Code added

● 84431 Code added

85046 Grammatical Change

85240 Grammatical Change

● 86305 Code added

● 86352 Code added

▲ 86592 Syphilis test, non-treponemal antibody; qualitative (eg, VDRL, RPR, ART)

▲ 86593 quantitative

● 86780 Code added

86781 ~~Treponema pallidum, confirmatory test (eg, FTA-abs)~~

● 86825 Code added

✚● 86826 Code added

▲ 87149 identification by nucleic acid (DNA or RNA) probe, direct probe technique, per culture or isolate, each organism probed

● 87150 Code added

● 87153 Code added

● 87493 Code added

▲ 88312 Special stains ~~(List separately in addition to code for primary service)~~; Group I for microorganisms (eg, Gridley, acid fast, methenamine silver), including interpretation and report, each

▲ 88313 Group II, all other (eg, iron, trichrome), except immunocytochemistry and immunoperoxidase stains, including interpretation and report, each

✚▲ 88314 histochemical staining with frozen section(s), including interpretation and report (List separately in addition to code for primary procedure)

● 88387 Code added

✚● 88388 Code added

● 88738 Code added

● 89398 Code added

Medicine

▲ 90378 Respiratory syncytial virus ~~immune globulin (RSV IgIM),~~ monoclonal antibody, recombinant, for intramuscular use, 50 mg, each

90379 ~~Respiratory syncytial virus immune globulin (RSV IgIV), human, for intravenous use~~

90471 Grammatical Change

90473 Grammatical Change

▲ 90669 Pneumococcal conjugate vaccine, ~~polyvalent~~7 valent, ~~when administered to children younger than 5 years,~~ for intramuscular use

✗● 90670 Code added

▲ 90738 Japanese encephalitis virus vaccine, inactivated, for intramuscular use

92533 Grammatical Change

● 92540 Code added

92543 Grammatical Change

● 92550 Code added

92569 ~~decay~~

● 92570 Code added

▲ 93279 Programming device evaluation (in person) with iterative adjustment of the implantable device to test the function of the device and select optimal permanent programmed values with physician analysis, review and report; single lead pacemaker system

▲ 93280 dual lead pacemaker system

▲ 93281 multiple lead pacemaker system

▲ 93282 single lead implantable cardioverter-defibrillator system

▲ 93283 dual lead implantable cardioverter-defibrillator system

▲ 93284 multiple lead implantable cardioverter-defibrillator system

▲ 93285 implantable loop recorder system

▲ 93286 Peri-procedural device evaluation (in person) and programming of device system parameters before or after a surgery, procedure, or test with physician analysis, review and report; single, dual, or multiple lead pacemaker system

▲ 93287 single, dual, or multiple lead implantable cardioverter-defibrillator system

⊘⊙ 93540 Grammatical Change

▲ 93701 Bioimpedance-derived physiologic cardiovascular analysis~~; thoracic, electrical~~

● 93750 Code added

⊙● 94011 Code added

⊙● 94012 Code added

⊙● 94013 Code added

▲ 95806 Sleep study, unattended, simultaneous recording of, ~~ventilation~~ heart rate, oxygen saturation, respiratory airflow, and respiratory effort~~, ECG~~ (eg, thoracoabdominal movement)~~or heart rate, and oxygen saturation, unattended by a technologist~~

95860 Grammatical Change

95870 Grammatical Change

⊘● 95905 Code added

	95921	Grammatical Change
	95923	Grammatical Change
	95937	Grammatical Change
+▲	96570	Photodynamic therapy by endoscopic application of light to ablate abnormal tissue via activation of photosensitive drug(s); first 30 minutes (List separately in addition to code for endoscopy or bronchoscopy procedures of lung and ~~esophagus~~gastrointestinal tract)
+▲	96571	each additional 15 minutes (List separately in addition to code for endoscopy or bronchoscopy procedures of lung and ~~esophagus~~gastrointestinal tract)
	96913	Grammatical Change
	97032	Grammatical Change
	97110	Grammatical Change
	97140	Grammatical Change
	~~99185~~	~~Hypothermia; regional~~
	~~99186~~	~~total body~~

Category II Codes

	0500F	Grammatical Change
	0501F	Grammatical Change
▲	0519F	Planned chemotherapy regimen, including at a minimum: drug(s) prescribed, dose, and duration, documented prior to initiation of ~~course of treatment~~a new treatment regimen (ONC)[1]
▲	0520F	~~Normal tissue dose constraints~~Radiation dose limits to normal tissues established ~~within 5 treatment days from~~prior to the initiation of a course of 3D conformal radiation for a minimum of ~~one~~2 tissue/organ (ONC)[1]
▲	0521F	Plan of care to address pain documented (COA)[2] (ONC)[1]
●	0528F	Code added
●	0529F	Code added
●	0535F	Code added
●	0540F	Code added
●	0575F	Code added
	1100F	Grammatical Change
	1101F	Grammatical Change
	1110F	Grammatical Change
	1111F	Grammatical Change
	1123F	Grammatical Change
	1124F	Grammatical Change
	1125F	Grammatical Change
	1126F	Grammatical Change
	1136F	Grammatical Change
●	1150F	Code added
●	1151F	Code added
●	1152F	Code added
●	1153F	Code added
●	1157F	Code added
●	1158F	Code added

●	1159F	Code added
●	1160F	Code added
●	1170F	Code added
●	1180F	Code added
●	1220F	Code added
	2024F	Grammatical Change
●	2050F	Code added
●	3016F	Code added
●	3018F	Code added
	3082F	Grammatical Change
	3083F	Grammatical Change
	3084F	Grammatical Change
	3095F	Grammatical Change
	3096F	Grammatical Change
●	3250F	Code added
	3290F	Grammatical Change
	3291F	Grammatical Change
	3292F	Grammatical Change
	~~3302F~~	~~AJCC Cancer Stage 0, documented (ONC)[4], (ML)[5]~~
	~~3303F~~	~~AJCC Cancer Stage IA, documented (ONC)[4], (ML)[5]~~
	~~3304F~~	~~AJCC Cancer Stage IB, documented (ONC)[4], (ML)[5]~~
	~~3305F~~	~~AJCC Cancer Stage IC, documented (ONC)[4], (ML)[5]~~
	~~3306F~~	~~AJCC Cancer Stage IIA, documented (ONC)[4], (ML)[5]~~
	~~3307F~~	~~AJCC Cancer Stage IIB, documented (ONC)[4], (ML)[5]~~
	~~3308F~~	~~AJCC Cancer Stage IIC, documented (ONC)[4], (ML)[5]~~
	~~3309F~~	~~AJCC Cancer Stage IIIA, documented (ONC)[4], (ML)[5]~~
	~~3310F~~	~~AJCC Cancer Stage IIIB, documented (ONC)[4], (ML)[5]~~
	~~3311F~~	~~AJCC Cancer Stage IIIC, documented (ONC)[4], (ML)[5]~~
	~~3312F~~	~~AJCC Cancer Stage IV, documented (ONC)[4], (ML)[5]~~
▲	3319F	1 of the following diagnostic imaging studies ordered: chest x-ray, CT, Ultrasound, MRI, PET, or nuclear medicine scans (ML)[5]
●	3321F	Code added
●	3322F	Code added
	3325F	Grammatical Change
	3341F	Grammatical Change
●	3370F	Code added
●	3372F	Code added
●	3374F	Code added
●	3376F	Code added
●	3378F	Code added
●	3380F	Code added
●	3382F	Code added
●	3384F	Code added
●	3386F	Code added
●	3388F	Code added

- 3390F — Code added
- 3450F — Code added
- 3451F — Code added
- 3452F — Code added
- 3455F — Code added
- 3470F — Code added
- 3471F — Code added
- 3472F — Code added
- 3475F — Code added
- 3476F — Code added
- 3490F — Code added
- 3491F — Code added
- 3492F — Code added
- 3493F — Code added
- 3494F — Code added
- 3495F — Code added
- 3496F — Code added
- 3497F — Code added
- 3498F — Code added
- 3500F — Code added
- 3502F — Code added
- 3503F — Code added
- 3510F — Code added
- 3511F — Code added
- 3512F — Code added
- 3513F — Code added
- 3514F — Code added
- 3515F — Code added
- 3550F — Code added
- 3551F — Code added
- 3552F — Code added
- 3555F — Code added
- 3570F — Code added
- 3572F — Code added
- 3573F — Code added
- ▲ 4011F — Oral antiplatelet therapy prescribed (~~eg, aspirin, clopidogrel/Plavix, or combination of aspirin and dipyridamole/Aggrenox~~) (CAD)[1]
- 4014F — Grammatical Change
- 4058F — Grammatical Change
- 4066F — Grammatical Change
- 4148F — Code added
- 4149F — Code added
- 4152F — ~~Documentation that combination peginterferon and ribavirin therapy considered (HEP-C)[1]~~
- 4154F — ~~Hepatitis A vaccine series recommended (HEP-C)[1]~~

- 4156F — ~~Hepatitis B vaccine series recommended (HEP-C)[1]~~
- ▲ 4158F — Patient ~~education regarding risk of alcohol consumption performed~~ counseled about risks of alcohol use (HEP-C)[1]
- 4176F — Grammatical Change
- 4178F — Grammatical Change
- ▲ 4180F — Adjuvant chemotherapy referred, prescribed, or previously received for Stage III~~A through Stage IIIC~~ colon cancer (ONC)[1]
- 4192F — Code added
- 4193F — Code added
- 4194F — Code added
- 4195F — Code added
- 4196F — Code added
- ▲ 4200F — External beam radiotherapy as primary therapy to prostate ~~only~~with or without nodal irradiation (PRCA)[1]
- ▲ 4201F — External beam radiotherapy with or without nodal irradiation as adjuvant or salvage therapy for prostate cancer ~~to region(s) other than prostate only~~patient (PRCA)[1]
- ▲ 4250F — Active warming used intraoperatively for the purpose of maintaining normothermia, OR at least 1 body temperature equal to or greater than 36 degrees Centigrade (or 96.8 degrees Fahrenheit) recorded within the 30 minutes immediately before or the ~~30~~15 minutes immediately after anesthesia end time (CRIT)[1]
- 4260F — Code added
- 4261F — Code added
- 4265F — Code added
- 4266F — Code added
- 4267F — Code added
- 4268F — Code added
- 4269F — Code added
- 4270F — Code added
- 4271F — Code added
- 4274F — Code added
- 4275F — Code added
- 4276F — Code added
- 4279F — Code added
- 4280F — Code added
- 4290F — Code added
- 4293F — Code added
- 4300F — Code added
- 4301F — Code added
- 4305F — Code added
- 4306F — Code added
- 4320F — Code added
- ▲ 5020F — Treatment summary report communicated to physician(s) managing continuing care and to the patient within 1 month of completing treatment (ONC)[1]
- 5060F — Grammatical Change
- 5062F — Grammatical Change

● **5100F**   Code added

▲ **6030F**   All elements of maximal sterile barrier technique <u>followed</u> including: cap AND mask AND sterile gown AND sterile gloves AND a large sterile sheet AND hand hygiene AND 2% chlorhexidine for cutaneous antisepsis, followed (or acceptable alternative antiseptics, per current guideline) (CRIT)[1]

Category III Codes

0062T   ~~Percutaneous intradiscal annuloplasty, any method except electrothermal, unilateral or bilateral including fluoroscopic guidance; single level~~

0063T   ~~1 or more additional levels (List separately in addition to 0062T for primary procedure)~~

0064T   ~~Spectroscopy, expired gas analysis (eg, nitric oxide/carbon dioxide test)~~

0066T   ~~Computed tomographic (CT) colonography (ie, virtual colonoscopy); screening~~

0067T   ~~diagnostic~~

0068T   ~~Acoustic heart sound recording and computer analysis; with interpretation and report~~

0069T   ~~acoustic heart sound recording and computer analysis only~~

0070T   ~~interpretation and report only~~

0077T   ~~Implanting and securing cerebral thermal perfusion probe, including twist drill or burr hole, to measure absolute cerebral tissue perfusion~~

0084T   ~~Insertion of a temporary prostatic urethral stent~~

0086T   ~~Left ventricular filling pressure indirect measurement by computerized calibration of the arterial waveform response to Valsalva maneuver~~

0087T   ~~Sperm evaluation, Hyaluronan sperm binding test~~

0144T   ~~Computed tomography, heart, without contrast material, including image postprocessing and quantitative evaluation of coronary calcium~~

0145T   ~~Computed tomography, heart, with contrast material(s), including noncontrast images, if performed, cardiac gating and 3D image postprocessing; cardiac structure and morphology~~

0146T   ~~computed tomographic angiography of coronary arteries (including native and anomalous coronary arteries, coronary bypass grafts), without quantitative evaluation of coronary calcium~~

0147T   ~~computed tomographic angiography of coronary arteries (including native and anomalous coronary arteries, coronary bypass grafts), with quantitative evaluation of coronary calcium~~

0148T   ~~cardiac structure and morphology and computed tomographic angiography of coronary arteries (including native and anomalous coronary arteries, coronary bypass grafts), without quantitative evaluation of coronary calcium~~

0149T   ~~cardiac structure and morphology and computed tomographic angiography of coronary arteries (including native and anomalous coronary arteries, coronary bypass grafts), with quantitative evaluation of coronary calcium~~

0150T   ~~cardiac structure and morphology in congenital heart disease~~

0151T   ~~Computed tomography, heart, with contrast material(s), including noncontrast images, if performed, cardiac gating and 3D image postprocessing, function evaluation (left and right ventricular function, ejection fraction and segmental wall motion) (List separately in addition to code for primary procedure)~~

0170T   ~~Repair of anorectal fistula with plug (eg, porcine small intestine submucosa [SIS])~~

0188T   Grammatical Change

0194T   ~~Procalcitonin (PCT)~~

● **0197T**   Code added

● **0198T**   Code added

● **0199T**   Code added

⊙● **0200T**   Code added

⊙● **0201T**   Code added

● **0202T**   Code added

● **0203T**   Code added

● **0204T**   Code added

✚● **0205T**   Code added

● **0206T**   Code added

● **0207T**   Code added

Appendix C

Clinical Examples

As described in *CPT 2010*, clinical examples of the CPT codes for Evaluation and Management (E/M) services are intended to be an important element of the coding system. The clinical examples, when used with the E/M descriptors contained in the full text of *CPT*, provide a comprehensive and powerful tool for physicians to report the services provided to their patients.

The American Medical Association is pleased to provide you with these clinical examples for *CPT 2010*. The clinical examples that are provided in this supplement are limited to Office or Other Outpatient Services, Hospital Inpatient Services, Consultations, Critical Care, Prolonged Services and Care Plan Oversight.

These clinical examples do not encompass the entire scope of medical practice. Inclusion or exclusion of any particular specialty group does not infer any judgment of importance or lack thereof; nor does it limit the applicability of the example to any particular specialty.

Of utmost importance is that these clinical examples are just that: examples. A particular patient encounter, depending on the specific circumstances, must be judged by the services provided by the physician for that particular patient. Simply because the patient's complaints, symptoms, or diagnoses match those of a particular clinical example, does not automatically assign that patient encounter to that particular level of service. The three components (history, examination, and medical decision making) must be met and documented in the medical record to report a particular level of service.

New Patient

Office or Other Outpatient Service

99201   Initial office visit for a 50-year-old male from out-of-town who needs a prescription refill for a nonsteroidal anti-inflammatory drug. (Anesthesiology)

Initial office visit for a 40-year-old female, new patient, requesting information about local pain clinics. (Anesthesiology/Pain Medicine)

Initial office visit for a 10-year-old girl for determination of visual acuity as part of a summer camp physical (does not include determination of refractive error). (Ophthalmology)

Initial office visit for an out-of-town patient requiring topical refill. (Dermatology)

Initial office visit for a 65-year-old male for reassurance about an isolated seborrheic keratosis on upper back. (Plastic Surgery)

Initial office visit for an out-of-state visitor who needs refill of topical steroid to treat lichen planus. (Dermatology)

Initial office visit for an 86-year-old male, out-of-town visitor, who needs prescription refilled for an anal skin preparation that he forgot. (General Surgery/Colon & Rectal Surgery)

Initial office visit for a patient with alveolar osteitis for repacking. (Oral & Maxillofacial Surgery)

Initial office visit for a patient with a pedunculated lesion of the neck which is unsightly. (Dermatology)

Initial office visit for a 10-year-old male, for limited subungual hematoma not requiring drainage. (Internal Medicine)

Initial office visit with an out-of-town visitor who needs a prescription refilled because she forgot her hay fever medication. (Allergy & Immunology/Internal Medicine)

Initial office visit with a 9-month-old female with diaper rash. (Pediatrics)

Initial office visit with a 10-year-old male with severe rash and itching for the past 24 hours, positive history for contact with poison oak 48 hours prior to the visit. (Family Medicine)

Initial office visit with a 5-year-old female to remove sutures from simple wound placed by another physician. (Plastic Surgery)

Initial office visit for a 22-year-old male with a small area of sunburn requiring first aid. (Dermatology/Family Medicine/Internal Medicine)

Initial office visit for the evaluation and management of a contusion of a finger. (Orthopaedic Surgery)

99202   Initial office visit for a 13-year-old patient with comedopapular acne of the face unresponsive to over-the-counter medications. (Family Medicine)

Initial office visit for a patient with a clinically benign lesion or nodule of the lower leg which has been present for many years. (Dermatology)

Initial office visit for a patient with a circumscribed patch of dermatitis of the leg. (Dermatology)

Initial office visit for a patient with papulosquamous eruption of elbows. (Dermatology)

Initial office visit for a 9-year-old patient with erythematous grouped, vesicular eruption of the lip of three day's duration. (Pediatrics)

Initial office visit for an 18-year-old male referred by an orthodontist for advice regarding removal of four wisdom teeth. (Oral & Maxillofacial Surgery)

Initial office visit for a 14-year-old male, who was referred by his orthodontist, for advice on the exposure of impacted maxillary cuspids. (Oral & Maxillofacial Surgery)

Initial office visit for a patient presenting with itching patches on the wrists and ankles. (Dermatology)

Initial office visit for a 30-year-old male for evaluation and discussion of treatment of rhinophyma. (Plastic Surgery)

Initial office visit for a 16-year-old male with severe cystic acne, new patient. (Dermatology)

Initial office evaluation for gradual hearing loss, 58-year-old male, history and physical examination, with interpretation of complete audiogram, air bone, etc. (Otolaryngology)

Initial evaluation and management of recurrent urinary infection in female. (Internal Medicine)

Initial office visit with a 10-year-old girl with history of chronic otitis media and a draining ear. (Pediatrics)

Initial office visit for a 10-year-old female with acute maxillary sinusitis. (Family Medicine)

Initial office visit for a patient with recurring episodes of herpes simplex who has developed a clustering of vesicles on the upper lip. (Internal Medicine)

Initial office visit for a 25-year-old patient with a single season allergic rhinitis. (Allergy & Immunology)

99203 Initial office visit of a 76-year-old male with a stasis ulcer of three month's duration. (Dermatology)

Initial office visit for a 30-year-old female with pain in the lateral aspect of the forearm. (Physical Medicine & Rehabilitation)

Initial office visit for a 15-year-old patient with a four-year history of moderate comedopapular acne of the face, chest, and back with early scarring. Discussion of use of systemic medication. (Dermatology)

Initial office visit for a patient with papulosquamous eruption of the elbow with pitting of nails and itchy scalp. (Dermatology)

Initial office visit for a 57-year-old female who complains of painful parotid swelling for one week's duration. (Oral & Maxillofacial Surgery)

Initial office visit for a patient with an ulcerated non-healing lesion or nodule on the tip of the nose. (Dermatology)

Initial office visit for a patient with dermatitis of the antecubital and popliteal fossae. (Dermatology)

Initial office visit for a 22-year-old female with irregular menses. (Family Medicine)

Initial office visit for a 50-year-old female with dyspepsia and nausea. (Family Medicine)

Initial office visit for a 53-year-old laborer with degenerative joint disease of the knee with no prior treatment. (Orthopaedic Surgery)

Initial office visit for a 60-year-old male with Dupuytren's contracture of one hand with multiple digit involvement. (Orthopaedic Surgery)

Initial office visit for a 33-year-old male with painless gross hematuria without cystoscopy. (Internal Medicine)

Initial office visit for a 55-year-old female with chronic blepharitis. There is a history of use of many medications. (Ophthalmology)

Initial office visit for an 18-year-old female with a two-day history of acute conjunctivitis. Extensive history of possible exposures, prior normal ocular history, and medication use is obtained. (Ophthalmology)

Initial office visit for a 14-year-old male with unilateral anterior knee pain. (Physical Medicine & Rehabilitation)

Initial office visit of an adult who presents with symptoms of an upper-respiratory infection that has progressed to unilateral purulent nasal discharge and discomfort in the right maxillary teeth. (Otolaryngology, Head & Neck Surgery)

Initial office visit of a 40-year-old female with symptoms of atopic allergies including eye and sinus congestion, often associated with infections. She would like to be tested for allergies. (Otolaryngology, Head & Neck Surgery)

Initial office visit of a 65-year-old with nasal stuffiness. (Otolaryngology, Head & Neck Surgery)

Initial office visit for initial evaluation of a 48-year-old man with recurrent low back pain radiating to the leg. (General Surgery)

Initial office visit for evaluation, diagnosis, and management of painless gross hematuria in a new patient, without cystoscopy. (Internal Medicine)

Initial office visit with couple for counseling concerning voluntary vasectomy for sterility. Spent 30 minutes discussing procedure, risks and benefits, and answering questions. (Urology)

Initial office visit of a 49-year-old male with nasal obstruction. Detailed exam with topical anesthesia. (Plastic Surgery)

Initial office visit for evaluation of a 13-year-old female with progressive scoliosis. (Physical Medicine & Rehabilitation)

Initial office visit for a 21-year-old female desiring counseling and evaluation of initiation of contraception. (Family Practice/Internal Medicine/Obstetrics & Gynecology)

Initial office visit for a 49-year-old male presenting with painless blood per rectum associated with bowel movement. (Colon & Rectal Surgery)

Initial office visit for a 19-year-old football player with three-day-old acute knee injury; now with swelling and pain. (Orthopaedic Surgery)

99204 Initial office visit for a 13-year-old female with progressive scoliosis. (Orthopaedic Surgery)

Initial office visit for a 34-year-old female with primary infertility for evaluation and counseling. (Obstetrics & Gynecology)

Initial office visit for a 6-year-old male with multiple upper respiratory infections. (Allergy & Immunology)

Initial office visit for a patient with generalized dermatitis of 80 percent of the body surface area. (Dermatology)

Initial office visit for an adolescent who was referred by school counselor because of repeated skipping school. (Psychiatry)

Initial office visit for a 50-year-old machinist with a generalized eruption. (Dermatology)

Initial office visit for a 45-year-old female who has been abstinent from alcohol and benzodiazepines for three months but complains of headaches, insomnia, and anxiety. (Psychiatry)

Initial office visit for a 60-year-old male with recent change in bowel habits, weight loss, and abdominal pain. (Abdominal Surgery/General Surgery)

Initial office visit for a 50-year-old male with an aortic aneurysm who is considering surgery. (General Surgery)

Initial office visit for a 17-year-old female with depression. (Internal Medicine)

Initial office visit of a 40-year-old with chronic draining ear, imbalance, and probable cholesteatoma. (Otolaryngology, Head & Neck Surgery)

Initial office visit for initial evaluation of a 63-year-old male with chest pain on exertion. (Cardiology/Internal Medicine)

Initial office visit for evaluation of a 70-year-old patient with recent onset of episodic confusion. (Internal Medicine)

Initial office visit for a 7-year-old female with juvenile diabetes mellitus, new to area, past history of hospitalization times three. (Pediatrics)

Initial office visit of a 50-year-old female with progressive solid food dysphagia. (Gastroenterology)

Initial office visit for a 34-year-old patient with primary infertility, including counseling. (Obstetrics & Gynecology)

Initial office visit for evaluation of a 70-year-old female with polyarthralgia. (Rheumatology)

Initial office visit for a patient with papulosquamous eruption involving 60 percent of the cutaneous surface with joint pain. Combinations of topical and systemic treatments discussed. (Dermatology)

99205 Initial office visit for a patient with disseminated lupus erythematosus with kidney disease, edema, purpura, and scarring lesions on the extremities plus cardiac symptoms. (Dermatology/General Surgery/Internal Medicine)

Initial office visit for a 25-year-old female with systemic lupus erythematosus, fever, seizures, and profound thrombocytopenia. (Rheumatology/Allergy & Immunology)

Initial office visit for an adult with multiple cutaneous blisters, denuded secondarily infected ulcerations, oral lesions, weight loss, and increasing weakness refractory to high dose corticosteroid. Initiation of new immunosuppressive therapy. (Dermatology)

Initial office visit for a 28-year-old male with systemic vasculitis and compromised circulation to the limbs. (Rheumatology)

Initial office visit for a 41-year-old female new to the area requesting rheumatologic care, on disability due to scleroderma and recent hospitalization for malignant hypertension. (Rheumatology)

Initial office visit for a 52-year-old female with acute four extremity weakness and shortness of breath one week post-flu vaccination. (Physical Medicine & Rehabilitation)

Initial office visit for a 60-year-old male with previous back surgery; now presents with back and pelvic pain, two-month history of bilateral progressive calf and thigh tightness and weakness when walking, causing several falls. (Orthopaedic Surgery)

Initial office visit for an adolescent referred from emergency department after making suicide gesture. (Psychiatry)

Initial office visit for a 49-year-old female with a history of headaches and dependence on opioids. She reports weight loss, progressive headache, and depression. (Psychiatry)

Initial office visit for a 50-year-old female with symptoms of rash, swellings, recurrent arthritic complaints, and diarrhea and lymphadenopathy. Patient has had a 25 lb weight loss and was recently camping in the Amazon. (Allergy & Immunology)

Initial office visit for a 34-year-old uremic Type I diabetic patient referred for ESRD modality assessment and planning. (Nephrology)

Initial office visit for a 75-year-old female with neck and bilateral shoulder pain, brisk deep tendon reflexes, and stress incontinence. (Physical Medicine & Rehabilitation)

Initial office visit for an 8-year-old male with cerebral palsy and spastic quadriparesis. (Physical Medicine & Rehabilitation)

Initial office visit for a 73-year-old male with known prostate malignancy, who presents with severe back pain and a recent onset of lower extremity weakness. (Physical Medicine & Rehabilitation)

Initial office visit for a 38-year-old male with paranoid delusions and a history of alcohol abuse. (Psychiatry)

Initial office visit for a 12-week-old with bilateral hip dislocations and bilateral club feet. (Orthopaedic Surgery)

Initial office visit for a 29-year-old female with acute orbital congestion, eyelid retraction, and bilateral visual loss from optic neuropathy. (Ophthalmology)

Initial office visit for a 70-year-old diabetic patient with progressive visual field loss, advanced optic disc cupping and neovascularization of retina. (Ophthalmology)

Initial office visit for a newly diagnosed Type I diabetic patient. (Endocrinology)

Initial office evaluation of a 65-year-old female with exertional chest pain, intermittent claudication, syncope and a murmur of aortic stenosis. (Cardiology)

Initial office visit for a 73-year-old male with an unexplained 20 lb weight loss. (Hematology/Oncology)

Initial office evaluation, patient with systemic lupus erythematosus, fever, seizures and profound thrombocytopenia. (Allergy & Immunology/Internal Medicine/Rheumatology)

Initial office evaluation and management of patient with systemic vasculitis and compromised circulation to the limbs. (Rheumatology)

Initial office visit for a 24-year-old homosexual male who has a fever, a cough, and shortness of breath. (Infectious Disease)

Initial outpatient evaluation of a 69-year-old male with severe chronic obstructive pulmonary disease, congestive heart failure, and hypertension. (Family Medicine)

Initial office visit for a 17-year-old female, who is having school problems and has told a friend that she is considering suicide. The patient and her family are consulted in regard to treatment options. (Psychiatry)

Initial office visit for a female with severe hirsutism, amenorrhea, weight loss and a desire to have children. (Endocrinology/Obstetrics & Gynecology)

Initial office visit for a 42-year-old male on hypertensive medication, newly arrived to the area, with diastolic blood pressure of 110, history of recurrent calculi, episodic headaches, intermittent chest pain and orthopnea. (Internal Medicine)

Established Patient

99211 Office visit for an 82-year-old female, established patient, for a monthly B12 injection with documented Vitamin B12 deficiency. (Geriatrics/Internal Medicine/Family Medicine)

Office visit for a 50-year-old male, established patient, for removal of uncomplicated facial sutures. (Plastic Surgery)

Office visit for an established patient who lost prescription for lichen planus. Returned for new copy. (Dermatology)

Office visit for an established patient undergoing orthodontics who complains of a wire which is irritating his/her cheek and asks you to check it. (Oral & Maxillofacial Surgery)

Office visit for a 50-year-old female, established patient, seen for her gold injection by the nurse. (Rheumatology)

Office visit for a 73-year-old female, established patient, with pernicious anemia for weekly B12 injection. (Gastroenterology)

Office visit for an established patient for dressing change on a skin biopsy. (Dermatology)

Office visit for a 19-year-old, established patient, for removal of sutures from a 2-cm laceration of forehead, which you placed four days ago in ER. (Plastic Surgery)

Office visit of a 20-year-old female, established patient, who receives an allergy vaccine injection and is observed for a reaction by the nurse. (Otolaryngology, Head & Neck Surgery)

Office visit for a 45-year-old male, established patient, with chronic renal failure for the administration of erythropoietin. (Nephrology)

Office visit for an established patient, a Peace Corps enlistee, who requests documentation that third molars have been removed. (Oral & Maxillofacial Surgery)

Office visit for a 69-year-old female, established patient, for partial removal of antibiotic gauze from an infected wound site. (Plastic Surgery)

Office visit for a 9-year-old, established patient, successfully treated for impetigo, requiring release to return to school. (Dermatology/Pediatrics)

Office visit for an established patient requesting a return-to-work certificate for resolving contact dermatitis. (Dermatology)

Office visit for an established patient who is performing glucose monitoring and wants to check accuracy of machine with lab blood glucose by technician who checks accuracy and function of patient machine. (Endocrinology)

Follow-up office visit for a 65-year-old female with a chronic indwelling percutaneous nephrostomy catheter seen for routine pericatheter skin care and dressing change. (Interventional Radiology)

Outpatient visit with 19-year-old male, established patient, for supervised drug screen. (Addiction Medicine)

Office visit with 12-year-old male, established patient, for cursory check of hematoma one day after venipuncture. (Internal Medicine)

Office visit with 31-year-old female, established patient, for return to work certificate. (Anesthesiology)

Office visit for a 42-year-old, established patient, to read tuberculin test results. (Allergy & Immunology)

Office visit for 14-year-old, established patient, to re-dress an abrasion. (Orthopaedic Surgery)

Office visit for a 45-year-old female, established patient, for a blood pressure check. (Obstetrics & Gynecology)

Office visit for a 23-year-old, established patient, for instruction in use of peak flow meter. (Allergy & Immunology)

Office visit for prescription refill for a 35-year-old female, established patient, with schizophrenia who is stable but has run out of neuroleptic and is scheduled to be seen in a week. (Psychiatry)

99212 Office visit for an 11-year-old, established patient, seen in follow-up for mild comedonal acne of the cheeks on topical desquamating agents. (Dermatology/Family Medicine/Pediatrics)

Office visit for a 10-year-old female, established patient, who has been swimming in a lake, now presents with a one-day history of left ear pain with purulent drainage. (Family Medicine)

Office visit for a child, established patient, with chronic secretory otitis media. (Otolaryngology, Head & Neck Surgery)

Office visit for an established patient seen in follow-up of clearing patch of localized contact dermatitis. (Family Medicine/Dermatology)

Office visit for an established patient returning for evaluation of response to treatment of lichen planus on wrists and ankles. (Dermatology)

Office visit for an established patient with tinea pedis being treated with topical therapy. (Dermatology)

Office visit for an established patient with localized erythematous plaque of psoriasis with topical hydration. (Dermatology)

Office visit for a 50-year-old male, established patient, recently seen for acute neck pain, diagnosis of spondylosis, responding to physical therapy and intermittent cervical traction. Returns for evaluation for return to work. (Neurology)

Office visit for an established patient with recurring episodes of herpes simplex who has developed a clustering of vesicles on the upper lip. (Oral & Maxillofacial Surgery)

Evaluation of a 50-year-old male, established patient, who has experienced a recurrence of knee pain after he discontinued NSAID. (Anesthesiology/Pain Medicine)

Office visit for an established patient with an irritated skin tag for reassurance. (Dermatology)

Office visit for a 40-year-old, established patient, who has experienced a systemic allergic reaction following administration of immunotherapy. The dose must be readjusted. (Allergy & Immunology)

Office visit for a 33-year-old, established patient, for contusion and abrasion of lower extremity. (Orthopaedic Surgery)

Office visit for a 22-year-old male, established patient, one month after I & D of "wrestler's ear." (Plastic Surgery)

Office visit for a 21-year-old, established patient, who is seen in follow-up after antibiotic therapy for acute bacterial tonsillitis. (Otolaryngology, Head & Neck Surgery)

Office visit for a 4-year-old, established patient, with tympanostomy tubes, check-up. (Otolaryngology, Head & Neck Surgery)

Office visit for an established patient who has had needle aspiration of a peritonsillar abscess. (Otolaryngology, Head & Neck Surgery)

Follow-up office examination for evaluation and treatment of acute draining ear in a 5-year-old with tympanotomy tubes. (Otolaryngology, Head & Neck Surgery)

Office visit, established patient, 6-year-old with sore throat and headache. (Family Medicine/Pediatrics)

Office evaluation for possible purulent bacterial conjunctivitis with one- to two-day history of redness and discharge, 16-year-old female, established patient. (Pediatrics/Internal Medicine/Family Medicine)

Office visit for a 65-year-old female, established patient, returns for three-week follow-up for resolving severe ankle sprain. (Orthopaedic Surgery)

Office visit, sore throat, fever, and fatigue in a 19-year-old college student, established patient. (Internal Medicine)

Office visit with a 33-year-old female, established patient, recently started on treatment for hemorrhoidal complaints, for re-evaluation. (Colon & Rectal Surgery)

Office visit with a 36-year-old male, established patient, for follow-up on effectiveness of medicine management of oral candidiasis. (Oral & Maxillofacial Surgery)

Office visit for a 27-year-old female, established patient, with complaints of vaginal itching. (Obstetrics & Gynecology)

Office visit for a 65-year-old, established patient, with eruptions on both arms from poison oak exposure. (Allergy & Immunology/Internal Medicine)

99213 Office visit for an established patient with new lesions of lichen planus in spite of topical therapies. (Dermatology)

Office visit for the quarterly follow-up of a 45-year-old male with stable chronic asthma requiring regular drug therapy. (Allergy & Immunology)

Office visit for a 13-year-old, established patient, with comedopapular acne of the face which has shown poor response to topical medication. Discussion of use of systemic medication. (Dermatology)

Office visit for a 62-year-old female, established patient, for follow-up for stable cirrhosis of the liver. (Internal Medicine/Family Medicine)

Office visit for a 3-year-old, established patient, with atopic dermatitis and food hypersensitivity for quarterly follow-up evaluation. The patient is on topical lotions and steroid creams as well as oral antihistamines. (Allergy & Immunology)

Office visit for an 80-year-old female, established patient, to evaluate medical management of osteoarthritis of the temporomandibular joint. (Rheumatology)

Office visit for a 70-year-old female, established patient, one year post excision of basal cell carcinoma of nose with nasolabial flap. Now presents with new suspicious recurrent lesion and suspicious lesion of the back. (Plastic Surgery)

Office visit for a 68-year-old female, established patient, with polymyalgia rheumatic, maintained on chronic low-dose corticosteroid, with no new complaints. (Rheumatology)

Office visit for a 3-year-old female, established patient, for earache and dyshidrosis of feet. (Pediatrics/Family Medicine)

Office visit for an established patient for 18-months postoperative follow-up of TMJ repair. (Oral & Maxillofacial Surgery)

Office visit for a 45-year-old male, established patient, being re-evaluated for recurrent acute prostatitis. (Urology)

Office visit for a 43-year-old male, established patient, with known reflex sympathetic dystrophy. (Anesthesiology)

Office visit for an established patient with an evenly pigmented superficial nodule of leg which is symptomatic. (Dermatology)

Office visit for an established patient with psoriasis involvement of the elbows, pitting of the nails, and itchy scalp. (Dermatology)

Office visit for a 27-year-old male, established patient, with deep follicular and perifollicular inflammation unable to tolerate systemic antibiotics due to GI upset, requires change of systemic medication. (Dermatology)

Office visit for a 16-year-old male, established patient, who is on medication for exercise-induced bronchospasm. (Allergy & Immunology)

Office visit for a 60-year-old, established patient, with chronic essential hypertension on multiple drug regimen, for blood pressure check. (Family Medicine)

Office visit for a 20-year-old male, established patient, for removal of sutures in hand. (Family Medicine)

Office visit for a 58-year-old female, established patient, with unilateral painful bunion. (Orthopaedic Surgery)

Office visit for a 45-year-old female, established patient, with known osteoarthritis and painful swollen knees. (Rheumatology)

Office visit for a 25-year-old female, established patient, complaining of bleeding and heavy menses. (Obstetrics & Gynecology)

Office visit for a 55-year-old male, established patient, with hypertension managed by a beta blocker/thiazide regime; now experiencing mild fatigue. (Nephrology)

Office visit for a 65-year-old female, established patient, with primary glaucoma for interval determination of intraocular pressure and possible adjustment of medication. (Ophthalmology)

Office visit for a 56-year-old male, established patient, with stable exertional angina who complains of new onset of calf pain while walking. (Cardiology)

Office visit for a 63-year-old female, established patient, with rheumatoid arthritis on auranofin and ibuprofen, seen for routine follow-up visit. (Rheumatology)

Office visit for an established patient with Graves' disease, three months post I-131 therapy, who presents with lassitude and malaise. (Endocrinology)

Office visit for the quarterly follow-up of a 63-year-old male, established patient, with chronic myofascial pain syndrome, effectively managed by doxepin, who presents with new onset urinary hesitancy. (Pain Medicine)

Office visit for the biannual follow-up of an established patient with migraine variant having infrequent, intermittent, moderate to severe headaches with nausea and vomiting, which are sometimes effectively managed by ergotamine tartrate and an antiemetic, but occasionally requiring visits to an emergency department. (Pain Medicine)

Office visit for an established patient after discharge from a pain rehabilitation program to review and adjust medication dosage. (Pain Medicine)

Office visit with 55-year-old male, established patient, for management of hypertension, mild fatigue, on beta blocker/thiazide regimen. (Family Medicine/Internal Medicine)

Outpatient visit with 37-year-old male, established patient, who is three years post total colectomy for chronic ulcerative colitis, presents for increased irritation at his stoma. (General Surgery)

Office visit for a 70-year-old diabetic hypertensive established patient with recent change in insulin requirement. (Internal Medicine/Nephrology)

Office visit with 80-year-old female, established patient, for follow-up osteoporosis, status-post compression fractures. (Rheumatology)

Office visit for an established patient with stable cirrhosis of the liver. (Gastroenterology)

Routine, follow-up office evaluation at a three-month interval for a 77-year-old female, established patient, with nodular small cleaved-cell lymphoma. (Hematology/Oncology)

Quarterly follow-up office visit for a 45-year-old male, established patient, with stable chronic asthma, on steroid and bronchodilator therapy. (Pulmonary Medicine)

Office visit for a 50-year-old female, established patient, with insulin-dependent diabetes mellitus and stable coronary artery disease, for monitoring. (Family Medicine/Internal Medicine)

99214 Office visit for an established patient now presenting with generalized dermatitis of 80% of the body surface area. (Dermatology)

Office visit for a 32-year-old female, established patient, with new onset right lower quadrant pain. (Family Medicine)

Office visit for reassessment and reassurance/counseling of a 40-year-old female, established patient, who is experiencing increased symptoms while on a pain management treatment program. (Pain Medicine)

Office visit for a 30-year-old, established patient, under management for intractable low back pain, who now presents with new onset right posterior thigh pain. (Pain Medicine)

Office visit for an established patient with frequent intermittent, moderate to severe headaches requiring beta blocker or tricyclic antidepressant prophylaxis, as well as four symptomatic treatments, but who is still experiencing headaches at a frequency of several times a month that are unresponsive to treatment. (Pain Medicine)

Office visit for an established patient with psoriasis with extensive involvement of scalp, trunk, palms, and soles with joint pain. Combinations of topical and systemic treatments discussed and instituted. (Dermatology)

Office visit for a 55-year-old male, established patient, with increasing night pain, limp, and progressive varus of both knees. (Orthopaedic Surgery)

Follow-up visit for a 15-year-old withdrawn patient with four-year history of papulocystic acne of the face, chest, and back with early scarring and poor response to past treatment. Discussion of use of systemic medication. (Dermatology)

Office visit for a 28-year-old male, established patient, with regional enteritis, diarrhea, and low-grade fever. (Internal Medicine)

Office visit for a 25-year-old female, established patient, following recent arthrogram and MR imaging for TMJ pain. (Oral & Maxillofacial Surgery)

Office visit for a 32-year-old female, established patient, with large obstructing stone in left mid-ureter, to discuss management options including urethroscopy with extraction or ESWL. (Urology)

Evaluation for a 28-year-old male, established patient, with new onset of low back pain. (Anesthesiology/Pain Medicine)

Office visit for a 28-year-old female, established patient, with right lower quadrant abdominal pain, fever, and anorexia. (Internal Medicine/Family Medicine)

Office visit for a 45-year-old male, established patient, four months follow-up of L4-5 discectomy, with persistent incapacitating low back and leg pain. (Orthopaedic Surgery)

Outpatient visit for a 77-year-old male, established patient, with hypertension, presenting with a three-month history of episodic substernal chest pain on exertion. (Cardiology)

Office visit for a 25-year-old female, established patient, for evaluation of progressive saddle nose deformity of unknown etiology. (Plastic Surgery)

Office visit for a 65-year-old male, established patient, with BPH and severe bladder outlet obstruction, to discuss management options such as TURP. (Urology)

Office visit for an adult diabetic established patient with a past history of recurrent sinusitis who presents with a one-week history of double vision. (Otolaryngology, Head & Neck Surgery)

Office visit for an established patient with lichen planus and 60% of the cutaneous surface involved, not responsive to systemic steroids, as well as developing symptoms of progressive heartburn and paranoid ideation. (Dermatology)

Office visit for a 52-year-old male, established patient, with a 12-year history of bipolar disorder responding to lithium carbonate and brief psychotherapy. Psychotherapy and prescription provided. (Psychiatry)

Office visit for a 63-year-old female, established patient, with a history of familial polyposis, status post-colectomy with sphincter sparing procedure, who now presents with rectal bleeding and increase in stooling frequency. (General Surgery)

Office visit for a 68-year-old male, established patient, with the sudden onset of multiple flashes and floaters in the right eye due to a posterior vitreous detachment. (Ophthalmology)

Office visit for a 55-year-old female, established patient, on cyclosporin for treatment of resistant, small vessel vasculitis. (Rheumatology)

Follow-up office visit for a 55-year-old male, two months after iliac angioplasty with new onset of contralateral extremity claudication. (Interventional Radiology)

Office visit for a 68-year-old male, established patient, with stable angina, two months post myocardial infarction, who is not tolerating one of his medications. (Cardiology)

Weekly office visit for 5FU therapy for an ambulatory established patient with metastatic colon cancer and increasing shortness of breath. (Hematology/Oncology)

Follow-up office visit for a 60-year-old male, established patient, whose post-traumatic seizures have disappeared on medication and who now raises the question of stopping the medication. (Neurology)

Office evaluation on new onset RLQ pain in a 32-year-old female, established patient. (Urology/General Surgery/Internal Medicine/Family Medicine)

Office evaluation of 28-year-old, established patient, with regional enteritis, diarrhea, and low-grade fever. (Family Medicine/Internal Medicine)

Office visit with 50-year-old female, established patient, diabetic, blood sugar controlled by diet. She now complains of frequency of urination and weight loss, blood sugar of 320, and negative ketones on dipstick. (Internal Medicine)

Follow-up office visit for a 45-year-old, established patient, with rheumatoid arthritis on gold, methotrexate, or immunosuppressive therapy. (Rheumatology)

Office visit for a 60-year-old male, established patient, two years post-removal of intracranial meningioma, now with new headaches and visual disturbance. (Neurosurgery)

Office visit for a 68-year-old female, established patient, for routine review and follow-up of non-insulin dependent diabetes, obesity, hypertension, and congestive heart failure. Complains of vision difficulties and admits dietary noncompliance. Patient is counseled concerning diet and current medications adjusted. (Family Medicine)

99215 Office visit for an established patient who developed persistent cough, rectal bleeding, weakness, and diarrhea plus pustular infection on skin. Patient on immunosuppressive therapy. (Dermatology)

Office visit for an established patient with disseminated lupus erythematosus, extensive edema of extremities, kidney disease, and weakness requiring monitored course on azathioprene, corticosteroid and complicated by acute depression. (Dermatology/Internal Medicine/Rheumatology)

Office visit for an established patient with progressive dermatomyositis and recent onset of fever, nasal speech, and regurgitation of fluids through the nose. (Dermatology)

Office visit for a 28-year-old female, established patient, who is abstinent from previous cocaine dependence, but reports progressive panic attacks and chest pains. (Psychiatry)

Office visit for an established adolescent patient with history of bipolar disorder treated with lithium; seen on urgent basis at family's request because of severe depressive symptoms. (Psychiatry)

Office visit for an established patient having acute migraine with new onset neurological symptoms and whose headaches are unresponsive to previous attempts at management with a combination of preventive and abortive medication. (Pain Medicine)

Office visit for an established patient with exfoliative lichen planus with daily fever spikes, disorientation, and shortness of breath. (Dermatology)

Office visit for a 25-year-old, established patient, two years post-burn with bilateral ectropion, hypertrophic facial burn scars, near absence of left breast, and burn syndactyly of both hands. Discussion of treatment options following examination. (Plastic Surgery)

Office visit for a 6-year-old, established patient, to review newly diagnosed immune deficiency with recommendations for therapy including IV immunoglobulin and chronic antibiotics. (Allergy & Immunology)

Office visit for a 36-year-old, established patient, three months status post-transplant, with new onset of peripheral edema, increased blood pressure, and progressive fatigue. (Nephrology)

Office visit for an established patient with Kaposi's sarcoma who presents with fever and widespread vesicles. (Dermatology)

Office visit for a 27-year-old female, established patient, with bipolar disorder who was stable on lithium carbonate and monthly supportive psychotherapy but now has developed symptoms of hypomania. (Psychiatry)

Office visit for a 25-year-old male, established patient with a history of schizophrenia who has been seen bi-monthly but is complaining of auditory hallucinations. (Psychiatry)

Office visit for a 62-year-old male, established patient, three years postoperative abdominal perineal resection, now with a rising carcinoembryonic antigen, weight loss, and pelvic pain. (Abdominal Surgery)

Office visit for a 42-year-old male, established patient, nine months postoperative emergency vena cava shunt for variceal bleeding, now presents with complaints of one episode of "dark" bowel movement, weight gain, tightness in abdomen, whites of eyes seem "yellow" and occasional drowsiness after eating hamburgers. (Abdominal Surgery)

Office visit for a 68-year-old male, established patient, with biopsy-proven rectal carcinoma, for evaluation and discussion of treatment options. (General Surgery)

Office visit for a 60-year-old, established patient, with diabetic nephropathy with increasing edema and dyspnea. (Endocrinology)

Office visit with 30-year-old male, established patient for three-month history of fatigue, weight loss, intermittent fever, and presenting with diffuse adenopathy and splenomegaly. (Family Medicine)

Office visit for restaging of an established patient with new lymphadenopathy one year post-therapy for lymphoma. (Hematology/Oncology)

Office visit for evaluation of recent onset syncopal attacks in a 70-year-old female, established patient. (Internal Medicine)

Follow-up visit, 40-year-old mother of three, established patient, with acute rheumatoid arthritis, anatomical Stage 3, ARA function Class 3 rheumatoid arthritis, and deteriorating function. (Rheumatology)

Follow-up office visit for a 65-year-old male, established patient, with a fever of recent onset while on outpatient antibiotic therapy for endocarditis. (Infectious Disease)

Office visit for a 75-year-old, established patient, with ALS (amyotrophic lateral sclerosis), who is no longer able to swallow. (Neurology)

Office visit for a 70-year-old female, established patient, with diabetes mellitus and hypertension, presenting with a two-month history of increasing confusion, agitation and short-term memory loss. (Family Medicine/Internal Medicine)

Hospital Inpatient Services

Initial Hospital Care

New or Established Patient

99221 Initial hospital visit following admission for a 42-year-old male for observation following an uncomplicated mandible fracture. (Plastic Surgery/Oral & Maxillofacial Surgery)

Initial hospital visit for a 40-year-old patient with a thrombosed synthetic arteriovenous conduit. (Nephrology)

Initial hospital visit for a healthy 24-year-old male with an acute onset of low back pain following a lifting injury. (Internal Medicine/Anesthesiology/Pain Medicine)

Initial hospital visit for a 69-year-old female with controlled hypertension, scheduled for surgery. (Internal Medicine/Cardiology)

Initial hospital visit for a 24-year-old healthy female with benign tumor of palate. (Oral & Maxillofacial Surgery)

Initial hospital visit for a 14-year-old female with infectious mononucleosis and dehydration. (Internal Medicine)

Initial hospital visit for a 62-year-old female with stable rheumatoid arthritis, admitted for total joint replacement. (Rheumatology)

Initial hospital visit for a 12-year-old patient with a laceration of the upper eyelid, involving the lid margin and superior canaliculus, admitted prior to surgery for IV antibiotic therapy. (Plastic Surgery)

Initial hospital visit for a 69-year-old female with controlled hypertension, scheduled for surgery. (Cardiology)

Hospital admission, examination, and initiation of treatment program for a 67-year-old male with uncomplicated pneumonia who requires IV antibiotic therapy. (Internal Medicine)

Hospital admission for an 18-month-old with 10% dehydration. (Pediatrics)

Hospital admission for a 12-year-old with a laceration of the upper eyelid involving the lid margin and superior canaliculus, admitted prior to surgery for IV antibiotic therapy. (Ophthalmology)

Hospital admission for a 32-year-old female with severe flank pain, hematuria and presumed diagnosis of ureteral calculus as determined by Emergency Department physician. (Urology)

Initial hospital visit for a patient with several large venous stasis ulcers not responding to outpatient therapy. (Dermatology)

Initial hospital visit for 21-year-old pregnant patient (nine-weeks gestation) with hyperemesis gravidarum. (Obstetrics & Gynecology)

Initial hospital visit for a 73-year-old female with acute pyelonephritis who is otherwise generally healthy. (Geriatrics)

Initial hospital visit for 62-year-old patient with cellulitis of the foot requiring bedrest and intravenous antibiotics. (Orthopaedic Surgery)

99222 Initial hospital visit for a 50-year-old patient with lower quadrant abdominal pain and increased temperature, but without septic picture. (General Surgery/Abdominal Surgery/Colon & Rectal Surgery)

Initial hospital visit for airway management, due to a benign laryngeal mass. (Otolaryngology, Head & Neck Surgery)

Initial hospital visit for a 66-year-old female with an L-2 vertebral compression fracture with acute onset of paralytic ileus; seen in the office two days previously. (Orthopaedic Surgery)

Initial hospital visit and evaluation of a 15-year-old male admitted with peritonsillar abscess or cellulitis requiring intravenous antibiotic therapy. (Otolaryngology, Head & Neck Surgery)

Initial hospital visit for a 42-year-old male with vertebral compression fracture following a motor vehicle accident. (Orthopaedic Surgery)

Initial hospital visit for a patient with generalized atopic dermatitis and secondary infection. (Dermatology)

Initial hospital visit for a 3-year-old patient with high temperature, limp, and painful hip motion of 18 hours' duration. (Pediatrics/Orthopaedic Surgery)

Initial hospital visit for a young adult, presenting with an acute asthma attack unresponsive to outpatient therapy. (Allergy & Immunology)

Initial hospital visit for an 18-year-old male who has suppurative sialoadenitis and dehydration. (Oral & Maxillofacial Surgery)

Initial hospital visit for a 65-year-old female for acute onset of thrombotic cerebrovascular accident with contralateral paralysis and aphasia. (Neurology)

Initial hospital visit for a 50-year-old male chronic paraplegic patient with pain and spasm below the lesion. (Anesthesiology)

Partial hospital admission for an adolescent patient from chaotic blended family, transferred from inpatient setting, for continued treatment to control symptomatic expressions of hostility and depression. (Psychiatry)

Initial hospital visit for a 15-year-old male with acute status asthmaticus, unresponsive to outpatient therapy. (Internal Medicine)

Initial hospital visit for a 61-year-old male with history of previous myocardial infarction, who now complains of chest pain. (Internal Medicine)

Initial hospital visit of a 15-year-old on medications for a sore throat over the last two weeks. The sore throat has worsened and patient now has dysphagia. The exam shows large necrotic tonsils with an adequate airway and small palpable nodes. The initial mono test was negative. (Otolaryngology, Head & Neck Surgery)

Initial hospital evaluation of a 23-year-old allergy patient admitted with eyelid edema and pain on fifth day of oral antibiotic therapy. (Otolaryngology, Head & Neck Surgery)

Hospital admission, young adult patient, failed previous therapy and now presents in acute asthmatic attack. (Family Medicine/Allergy & Immunology)

Hospital admission of a 62-year-old smoker, established patient, with bronchitis in acute respiratory distress. (Internal Medicine/Pulmonary Medicine)

Hospital admission, examination, and initiation of a treatment program for a 65-year-old female with new onset of right-sided paralysis and aphasia. (Neurology)

Hospital admission, examination, and initiation of treatment program for a 66-year-old chronic hemodialysis patient with fever and a new pulmonary infiltrate. (Nephrology)

Hospital admission for an 8-year-old febrile patient with chronic sinusitis and severe headache, unresponsive to oral antibiotics. (Allergy & Immunology)

Hospital admission for a 40-year-old male with submaxillary cellulitis and trismus from infected lower molar. (Oral & Maxillofacial Surgery)

99223 Initial hospital visit for a 45-year-old female, who has a history of rheumatic fever as a child and now has anemia, fever, and congestive heart failure. (Cardiology)

Initial hospital visit for a 50-year-old male with acute chest pain and diagnostic electrocardiographic changes of an acute anterior myocardial infarction. (Cardiology/Family Medicine/Internal Medicine)

Initial hospital visit of a 75-year-old with progressive stridor and dysphagia with history of cancer of the larynx treated by radiation therapy in the past. Exam shows a large recurrent tumor of the glottis with a mass in the neck. (Otolaryngology, Head & Neck Surgery)

Initial hospital visit for a 70-year-old male admitted with chest pain, complete heart block, and congestive heart failure. (Cardiology)

Initial hospital visit for an 82-year-old male who presents with syncope, chest pain, and ventricular arrhythmias. (Cardiology)

Initial hospital visit for a 75-year-old male with history of arteriosclerotic coronary vascular disease, who is severely dehydrated, disoriented, and experiencing auditory hallucinations. (Psychiatry)

Initial hospital visit for a 70-year-old male with alcohol and sedative-hypnotic dependence, admitted by family for severe withdrawal, hypertension, and diabetes mellitus. (Psychiatry)

Initial hospital visit for a persistently suicidal latency-aged child whose parents have requested admission to provide safety during evaluation, but are anxious about separation from her. (Psychiatry)

Initial psychiatric visit for an adolescent patient without previous psychiatric history, who was transferred from the medical ICU after a significant overdose. (Psychiatry)

Initial hospital visit for a 35-year-old female with severe systemic lupus erythematosus on corticosteroid and cyclophosphamide, with new onset of fever, chills, rash, and chest pain. (Rheumatology)

Initial hospital visit for a 52-year-old male with known rheumatic heart disease who presents with anasarca, hypertension, and history of alcohol abuse. (Cardiology)

Initial hospital visit for a 55-year-old female with a history of congenital heart disease; now presents with cyanosis. (Cardiology)

Initial hospital visit for a psychotic, hostile, violently combative adolescent, involuntarily committed, for seclusion and restraint in order to provide for safety on unit. (Psychiatry)

Initial hospital visit for a now subdued and sullen teenage male with six-month history of declining school performance, increasing self-endangerment, and resistance of parental expectations, including running away past weekend after physical fight with father. (Psychiatry)

Initial partial hospital admission for a 17-year-old female with history of borderline mental retardation who has developed auditory hallucinations. Parents are known to abuse alcohol, and Child Protective Services is investigating allegations of sexual abuse of a younger sibling. (Psychiatry)

Initial hospital visit of a 67-year-old male admitted with a large neck mass, dysphagia, and history of myocardial infarction three months before. (Otolaryngology, Head & Neck Surgery)

Initial hospital visit for a patient with suspected cerebrospinal fluid rhinorrhea which developed two weeks after head injury. (Otolaryngology, Head & Neck Surgery)

Initial hospital visit for a 25-year-old female with history of poly-substance abuse and psychiatric disorder. The patient appears to be psychotic with markedly elevated vital signs. (Psychiatry)

Initial hospital visit for a 70-year-old male with cutaneous T-cell lymphoma who has developed fever and lymphadenopathy. (Internal Medicine)

Initial hospital visit for a 62-year-old female with known coronary artery disease, for evaluation of increasing edema, dyspnea on exertion, confusion, and sudden onset of fever with productive cough. (Internal Medicine)

Initial hospital visit for a 3-year-old female with 36-hour history of sore throat and high fever; now with sudden onset of lethargy, irritability, photophobia, and nuchal rigidity. (Pediatrics)

Initial hospital visit for a 26-year-old female for evaluation of severe facial fractures (LeFort's II/III). (Plastic Surgery)

Initial hospital visit for a 55-year-old female for bilateral mandibular fractures resulting in flail mandible and airway obstruction. (Plastic Surgery)

Initial hospital visit for a 71-year-old patient with a red painful eye four days following uncomplicated cataract surgery due to endophthalmitis. (Ophthalmology)

Initial hospital visit for a 45-year-old patient involved in a motor vehicle accident who suffered a perforating corneoscleral laceration with loss of vision. (Ophthalmology)

Initial hospital visit for a 58-year-old male who has Ludwig's angina and progressive airway compromise. (Oral & Maxillofacial Surgery)

Initial hospital visit for a patient with generalized systemic sclerosis, receiving immunosuppressive therapy because of recent onset of cough, fever, and inability to swallow. (Dermatology)

Initial hospital visit for an 82-year-old male who presents with syncope, chest pain, and ventricular arrhythmias. (Cardiology)

Initial hospital visit for a 62-year-old male with history of previous myocardial infarction, comes in with recurrent, sustained ventricular tachycardia. (Cardiology)

Initial hospital visit for a chronic dialysis patient with infected PTFE fistula, septicemia, and shock. (Nephrology)

Initial hospital visit for a 1-year-old male, victim of child abuse, with central nervous system depression, skull fracture, and retinal hemorrhage. (Family Medicine/Neurology)

Initial hospital visit for a 25-year-old female with recent C4-5 quadriplegia, admitted for rehabilitation. (Physical Medicine & Rehabilitation)

Initial hospital visit for an 18-year-old male, post-traumatic brain injury with multiple impairment. (Physical Medicine & Rehabilitation)

Initial partial hospital admission for 16-year-old male, sullen and subdued, with six-month history of declining school performance, increasing self-endangerment, and resistance to parental expectations. (Psychiatry)

Initial hospital visit for a 16-year-old primigravida at 32-weeks gestation with severe hypertension (200/110), thrombocytopenia, and headache. (Obstetrics & Gynecology)

Initial hospital visit for a 49-year-old male with cirrhosis of liver with hematemesis, hepatic encephalopathy, and fever. (Gastroenterology)

Initial hospital visit for a 55-year-old female in chronic pain who has attempted suicide. (Psychiatry)

Initial hospital visit for a 70-year-old male, with multiple organ system disease, admitted with history of being aneuric and septic for 24 hours prior to admission. (Urology)

Initial hospital visit for a 3-year-old female with 36-hour history of sore throat and high fever, now with sudden onset of lethargy, irritability, photophobia, and nuchal rigidity. (Internal Medicine)

Initial hospital visit for a 78-year-old male, transfers from nursing home with dysuria and pyuria, increasing confusion, and high fever. (Internal Medicine)

Initial hospital visit for a 1-day-old male with cyanosis, respiratory distress, and tachypnea. (Cardiology)

Initial hospital visit for a 3-year-old female with recurrent tachycardia and syncope. (Cardiology)

Initial hospital visit for a thyrotoxic patient who presents with fever, atrial fibrillation, and delirium. (Endocrinology)

Initial hospital visit for a 50-year-old Type I diabetic who presents with diabetic ketoacidosis with fever and obtundation. (Endocrinology)

Initial hospital visit for a 40-year-old female with anatomical stage 3, ARA functional class 3 rheumatoid arthritis on methotrexate, corticosteroid, and nonsteroidal anti-inflammatory drugs. Patient presents with severe arthritis flare, new oral ulcers, abdominal pain, and leukopenia. (Rheumatology)

Initial hospital exam of a pediatric patient with high fever and proptosis. (Otolaryngology, Head & Neck Surgery)

Initial hospital visit for a 25-year-old patient admitted for the first time to the rehab unit, with recent C4-C5 quadriplegia. (Physical Medicine & Rehabilitation)

Hospital admission, examination, and initiation of treatment program for a previously unknown 58-year-old male who presents with acute chest pain. (Cardiology)

Hospital admission, examination, and initiation of induction chemotherapy for a 42-year-old patient with newly diagnosed acute myelogenous leukemia. (Hematology/Oncology)

Hospital admission following a motor vehicle accident of a 24-year-old male with fracture dislocation of C5-C6; neurologically intact. (Neurosurgery)

Hospital admission for a 78-year-old female with left lower lobe pneumonia and a history of coronary artery disease, congestive heart failure, osteoarthritis and gout. (Family Medicine)

Hospital admission, examination, and initiation of treatment program for a 65-year-old immunosuppressed male with confusion, fever, and a headache. (Infectious Disease)

Hospital admission for a 9-year-old with vomiting, dehydration, fever, tachypnea, and an admitting diagnosis of diabetic ketoacidosis. (Pediatrics)

Initial hospital visit for a 65-year-old male who presents with acute myocardial infarction, oliguria, hypotension, and altered state of consciousness. (Cardiology)

Initial hospital visit for a hostile/resistant adolescent patient who is severely depressed and involved in poly-substance abuse. Patient is experiencing significant conflict in his chaotic family situation and was suspended from school following an attack on a teacher with a baseball bat. (Psychiatry)

Initial hospital visit for 89-year-old female with fulminant hepatic failure and encephalopathy. (Gastroenterology)

Initial hospital visit for a 42-year-old female with rapidly progressing scleroderma, malignant hypertension, digital infarcts, and oligurea. (Rheumatology)

Subsequent Hospital Care

99231   Subsequent hospital visit for a 65-year-old female, post-open reduction and internal fixation of a fracture. (Physical Medicine & Rehabilitation)

Subsequent hospital visit for a 33-year-old patient with pelvic pain who is responding to pain medication and observation. (Obstetrics & Gynecology)

Subsequent hospital visit for a 21-year-old female with hyperemesis who has responded well to intravenous fluids. (Obstetrics & Gynecology)

Subsequent hospital visit to re-evaluate postoperative pain and titrate patient-controlled analgesia for a 27-year-old female. (Anesthesiology)

Follow-up hospital visit for a 35-year-old female, status post-epidural analgesia. (Anesthesiology/Pain Medicine)

Subsequent hospital visit for a 56-year-old male, post-gastrectomy, for maintenance of analgesia using an intravenous dilaudid infusion. (Anesthesiology)

Subsequent hospital visit for a 4-year-old on day three receiving medication for uncomplicated pneumonia. (Allergy & Immunology)

Subsequent hospital visit for a 30-year-old female with urticaria which has stabilized with medication. (Allergy & Immunology)

Subsequent hospital visit for a 76-year-old male with venous stasis ulcers. (Dermatology)

Subsequent hospital visit for a 24-year-old female with otitis externa, seen two days before in consultation, now to have otic wick removal. (Otolaryngology, Head & Neck Surgery)

Subsequent hospital visit for a 27-year-old with acute labyrinthitis. (Otolaryngology, Head & Neck Surgery)

Subsequent hospital visit for a 10-year-old male admitted for lobar pneumonia with vomiting and dehydration; is becoming afebrile and tolerating oral fluids. (Family Medicine/Pediatrics)

Subsequent hospital visit for a 62-year-old patient with resolving cellulitis of the foot. (Orthopaedic Surgery)

Subsequent hospital visit for a 25-year-old male admitted for supra-ventricular tachycardia and converted on medical therapy. (Cardiology)

Subsequent hospital visit for a 27-year-old male two days after open reduction and internal fixation for malar complex fracture. (Plastic Surgery)

Subsequent hospital visit for a 76-year-old male with venous stasis ulcers. (Geriatrics)

Subsequent hospital visit for a 67-year-old female admitted three days ago with bleeding gastric ulcer; now stable. (Gastroenterology)

Subsequent hospital visit for stable 33-year-old male, status post-lower gastrointestinal bleeding. (General Surgery/Gastroenterology)

Subsequent hospital visit for a 29-year-old auto mechanic with effort thrombosis of left upper extremity. (General Surgery)

Subsequent hospital visit for a 14-year-old female in middle phase of inpatient treatment, who is now behaviorally stable and making satisfactory progress in treatment. (Psychiatry)

Subsequent hospital visit for an 18-year-old male with uncomplicated asthma who is clinically stable. (Allergy & Immunology)

Subsequent hospital visit for a 55-year-old male with rheumatoid arthritis, two days following an uncomplicated total joint replacement. (Rheumatology)

Subsequent hospital visit for a 60-year-old dialysis patient with an access infection, now afebrile on antibiotic. (Nephrology)

Subsequent hospital visit for a 36-year-old female with stable post-rhinoplasty epistaxis. (Plastic Surgery)

Subsequent hospital visit for a 66-year-old female with L-2 vertebral compression fracture with resolving ileus. (Orthopaedic Surgery)

Subsequent hospital visit for a patient with peritonsillar abscess. (Otolaryngology, Head & Neck Surgery)

Subsequent hospital visit for an 18-year-old female responding to intravenous antibiotic therapy for ear or sinus infection. (Otolaryngology, Head & Neck Surgery)

Subsequent hospital visit for a 70-year-old male admitted with congestive heart failure who has responded to therapy. (Cardiology)

Follow-up hospital visit for a 32-year-old female with left ureteral calculus; being followed in anticipation of spontaneous passage. (Urology)

Subsequent hospital visit for a 4-year-old female, admitted for acute gastroenteritis and dehydration, requiring IV hydration; now stable. (Family Medicine)

Subsequent hospital visit for a 50-year-old Type II diabetic who is clinically stable and without complications requiring regulation of a single dose of insulin daily. (Endocrinology)

Subsequent hospital visit to reassesses the status of a 65-year-old patient post-open reduction and internal fixation of hip fracture, on the rehab unit. (Physical Medicine & Rehabilitation)

Subsequent hospital visit for a 78-year-old male with cholangiocarcinoma managed by biliary drainage. (Interventional Radiology)

Subsequent hospital visit for a 50-year-old male with uncomplicated myocardial infarction who is clinically stable and without chest pain. (Family Medicine/Cardiology/Internal Medicine)

Subsequent hospital visit for a stable 72-year-old lung cancer patient undergoing a five-day course of infusion chemotherapy. (Hematology/Oncology)

Subsequent hospital visit, two days post admission for a 65-year-old male with a CVA (cerebral vascular accident) and left hemiparesis, who is clinically stable. (Neurology/Physical Medicine and Rehabilitation)

Subsequent hospital visit for now stable, 33-year-old male, status post lower gastrointestinal bleeding. (General Surgery)

Subsequent visit on third day of hospitalization for a 60-year-old female recovering from an uncomplicated pneumonia. (Infectious Disease/Internal Medicine/Pulmonary Medicine)

Subsequent hospital visit for a 3-year-old patient in traction for a congenital dislocation of the hip. (Orthopaedic Surgery)

Subsequent hospital visit for a 4-year-old female, admitted for acute gastroenteritis and dehydration, requiring IV hydration; now stable. (Family Medicine/Internal Medicine)

Subsequent hospital visit for 50-year-old female with resolving uncomplicated acute pancreatitis. (Gastroenterology)

99232 Subsequent hospital visit for a patient with venous stasis ulcers who developed fever and red streaks adjacent to the ulcer. (Dermatology/Internal Medicine/Family Medicine)

Subsequent hospital visit for a 66-year-old male for dressing changes and observation. Patient has had a myocutaneous flap to close a pharyngeal fistula and now has a low-grade fever. (Plastic Surgery)

Subsequent hospital visit for a 54-year-old female admitted for myocardial infarction, but who is now having frequent premature ventricular contractions. (Internal Medicine)

Subsequent hospital visit for an 80-year-old patient with a pelvic rim fracture, inability to walk, and severe pain; now 36 hours post-injury, experiencing urinary retention. (Orthopaedic Surgery)

Subsequent hospital visit for a 17-year-old female with fever, pharyngitis, and airway obstruction, who after 48 hours develops a maculopapular rash. (Pediatrics/Family Medicine)

Follow-up hospital visit for a 32-year-old patient admitted the previous day for corneal ulcer. (Dermatology)

Follow-up visit for a 67-year-old male with congestive heart failure who has responded to antibiotics and diuretics, and has now developed a monoarthropathy. (Internal Medicine)

Follow-up hospital visit for a 58-year-old male receiving continuous opioids who is experiencing severe nausea and vomiting. (Pain Medicine)

Subsequent hospital visit for a patient after an auto accident who is slow to respond to ambulation training. (Physical Medicine & Rehabilitation)

Subsequent hospital visit for a 14-year-old with unstable bronchial asthma complicated by pneumonia. (Allergy & Immunology)

Subsequent hospital visit for a 50-year-old diabetic, hypertensive male with back pain not responding to conservative inpatient management with continued radiation of pain to the lower left extremity. (Orthopaedic Surgery)

Subsequent hospital visit for a 37-year-old female on day five of antibiotics for bacterial endocarditis, who still has low-grade fever. (Cardiology)

Subsequent hospital visit for a 54-year-old patient, post MI (myocardial infarction), who is out of the CCU (coronary care unit) but is now having frequent premature ventricular contractions on telemetry. (Cardiology/Internal Medicine)

Subsequent hospital visit for a patient with neutropenia, a fever responding to antibiotics, and continued slow gastrointestinal bleeding on platelet support. (Hematology/Oncology)

Subsequent hospital visit for a 50-year-old male admitted two days ago for sub-acute renal allograft rejection. (Nephrology)

Subsequent hospital visit for a 35-year-old drug addict, not responding to initial antibiotic therapy for pyelonephritis. (Urology)

Subsequent hospital visit of an 81-year-old male with abdominal distention, nausea, and vomiting. (General Surgery)

Subsequent hospital care for a 62-year-old female with congestive heart failure, who remains dyspneic and febrile. (Internal Medicine)

Subsequent hospital visit for a 73-year-old female with recently diagnosed lung cancer, who complains of unsteady gait. (Pulmonary Medicine)

Subsequent hospital visit for a 20-month-old male with bacterial meningitis treated one week with antibiotic therapy; has now developed a temperature of 101.0 degrees. (Pediatrics)

Subsequent hospital visit for 13-year-old male admitted with left lower quadrant abdominal pain and fever, not responding to therapy. (General Surgery)

Subsequent hospital visit for a 65-year-old male with hemiplegia and painful paretic shoulder. (Physical Medicine & Rehabilitation)

99233 Subsequent hospital visit for a 38-year-old male, quadriplegic with acute autonomic hyperreflexia, who is not responsive to initial care. (Physical Medicine & Rehabilitation)

Follow-up hospital visit for a teenage female who continues to experience severely disruptive, violent and life-threatening symptoms in a complicated multi-system illness. Family/social circumstances also a contributing factor. (Psychiatry)

Subsequent hospital visit for a 42-year-old female with progressive systemic sclerosis (scleroderma), renal failure on dialysis, congestive heart failure, cardiac arrhythmias, and digital ulcers. (Allergy & Immunology)

Subsequent hospital visit for a 50-year-old diabetic, hypertensive male with nonresponding back pain and radiating pain to the lower left extremity, who develops chest pain, cough, and bloody sputum. (Orthopaedic Surgery)

Subsequent hospital visit for a 64-year-old female, status post-abdominal aortic aneurysm resection, with non-responsive coagulopathy, who has now developed lower GI bleeding. (Abdominal Surgery/Colon & Rectal Surgery/General Surgery)

Follow-up hospital care of a patient with pansinusitis infection complicated by a brain abscess and asthma; no response to current treatment. (Otolaryngology, Head & Neck Surgery)

Subsequent hospital visit for a patient with a laryngeal neoplasm who develops airway compromise, suspected metastasis. (Otolaryngology, Head & Neck Surgery)

Subsequent hospital visit for a 49-year-old male with significant rectal bleeding, etiology undetermined, not responding to treatment. (Abdominal Surgery/General Surgery/Colon & Rectal Surgery)

Subsequent hospital visit for a 50-year-old male, post-aortocoronary bypass surgery; now develops hypotension and oliguria. (Cardiology)

Subsequent hospital visit for an adolescent patient who is violent, unsafe, and noncompliant, with multiple expectations for participation in treatment plan and behavior on the treatment unit. (Psychiatry)

Subsequent hospital visit for an 18-year-old male being treated for presumed PCP psychosis. Patient is still moderately symptomatic with auditory hallucinations and is insisting on signing out against medical advice. (Psychiatry)

Subsequent hospital visit for an 8-year-old female with caustic ingestion, who now has fever, dyspnea, and dropping hemoglobin. (Gastroenterology)

Follow-up hospital visit for a chronic renal failure patient on dialysis who develops chest pain and shortness of breath and a new onset pericardial friction rub. (Nephrology)

Subsequent hospital visit for a 44-year-old patient with electrical burns to the left arm with ascending infection. (Orthopaedic Surgery)

Subsequent hospital visit for a patient with systemic sclerosis who has aspirated and is short of breath. (Dermatology)

Subsequent hospital visit for a 65-year-old female, status postoperative resection of abdominal aortic aneurysm, with suspected ischemic bowel. (General Surgery)

Subsequent hospital visit for a 50-year-old male, post-aortocoronary bypass surgery, now develops hypotension and oliguria. (Cardiology)

Subsequent hospital visit for a 65-year-old male, following an acute myocardial infarction, who complains of shortness of breath and new chest pain. (Cardiology)

Subsequent hospital visit for a 65-year-old female with rheumatoid arthritis (stage 3, class 3) admitted for urosepsis. On the third hospital day, chest pain, dyspnea and fever develop. (Rheumatology)

Follow-up hospital care of a pediatric case with stridor, laryngomalacia, established tracheostomy, complicated by multiple medical problems in PICU. (Otolaryngology, Head & Neck Surgery)

Subsequent hospital visit for a 60-year-old female, four days post uncomplicated inferior myocardial infarction who has developed severe chest pain, dyspnea, diaphoresis and nausea. (Family Medicine)

Subsequent hospital visit for a patient with AML (acute myelogenous leukemia), fever, elevated white count and uric acid undergoing induction chemotherapy. (Hematology/Oncology)

Subsequent hospital visit for a 38-year-old quadriplegic male with acute autonomic hyperreflexia, who is not responsive to initial care. (Physical Medicine & Rehabilitation)

Subsequent hospital visit for a 65-year-old female postoperative resection of abdominal aortic aneurysm, with suspected ischemic bowel. (General Surgery)

Subsequent hospital visit for a 60-year-old female with persistent leukocytosis and a fever seven days after a sigmoid colon resection for carcinoma. (Infectious Disease)

Subsequent hospital visit for a chronic renal failure patient on dialysis, who develops chest pain, shortness of breath and new onset of pericardial friction rub. (Nephrology)

Subsequent hospital visit for a 65-year-old male with acute myocardial infarction who now demonstrates complete heart block and congestive heart failure. (Cardiology)

Subsequent hospital visit for a 25-year-old female with hypertension and systemic lupus erythematosus, admitted for fever and respiratory distress. On the third hospital day, the patient presented with purpuric skin lesions and acute renal failure. (Allergy & Immunology)

Subsequent hospital visit for a 55-year-old male with severe chronic obstructive pulmonary disease and bronchospasm; initially admitted for acute respiratory distress requiring ventilatory support in the ICU. The patient was stabilized, extubated and transferred to the floor, but has now developed acute fever, dyspnea, left lower lobe rhonchi and laboratory evidence of carbon dioxide retention and hypoxemia. (Family Medicine/Internal Medicine)

Subsequent hospital visit for 46-year-old female, known liver cirrhosis patient, with recent upper gastrointestinal hemorrhage from varices; now with worsening ascites and encephalopathy. (Gastroenterology)

Subsequent hospital visit for 62-year-old female admitted with acute subarachnoid hemorrhage, negative cerebral arteriogram, increased lethargy and hemiparesis with fever. (Neurosurgery)

Consultations

Office or Other Outpatient Consultations

New or Established Patient

99241 Initial office consultation for a 40-year-old female in pain from blister on lip following a cold. (Oral & Maxillofacial Surgery)

Initial office consultation for a 62-year-old construction worker with olecranon bursitis. (Orthopaedic Surgery)

Office consultation with 25-year-old postpartum female with severe symptomatic hemorrhoids. (Colon & Rectal Surgery)

Office consultation with 58-year-old male, referred for follow-up of creatinine level and evaluation of obstructive uropathy, relieved two months ago. (Nephrology)

Office consultation for 30-year-old female tennis player with sprain or contusion of the forearm. (Orthopaedic Surgery)

Office consultation for a 45-year-old male, requested by his internist, with asymptomatic torus palatinus requiring no further treatment. (Oral & Maxillofacial Surgery)

99242 Initial office consultation for a 20-year-old male with acute upper respiratory tract symptoms. (Allergy & Immunology)

Initial office consultation for a 29-year-old soccer player with painful proximal thigh/groin injury. (Orthopaedic Surgery)

Initial office consultation for a 66-year-old female with wrist and hand pain, numbness of finger tips, suspected median nerve compression by carpal tunnel syndrome. (Plastic Surgery)

Initial office consultation for a patient with a solitary lesion of discoid lupus erythematosus on left cheek to rule out malignancy or self-induced lesion. (Dermatology)

Office consultation for management of systolic hypertension in a 70-year-old male scheduled for elective prostate resection. (Geriatrics)

Office consultation with 27-year-old female, with old amputation, for evaluation of existing above-knee prosthesis. (Physical Medicine & Rehabilitation)

Office consultation with 66-year-old female with wrist and hand pain, and finger numbness, secondary to suspected carpal tunnel syndrome. (Orthopaedic Surgery)

Office consultation for 61-year-old female, recently on antibiotic therapy, now with diarrhea and leukocytosis. (Abdominal Surgery)

Office consultation for a patient with papulosquamous eruption of elbow with pitting of nails and itchy scalp. (Dermatology)

Office consultation for a 30-year-old female with single season allergic rhinitis. (Allergy & Immunology)

99243 Initial office consultation for a 60-year-old male with avascular necrosis of the left femoral head with increasing pain. (Orthopaedic Surgery)

Office consultation for a 31-year-old woman complaining of palpitations and chest pains. Her internist had described a mild systolic click. (Cardiology)

Office consultation for a 65-year-old female with persistent bronchitis. (Infectious Disease)

Office consultation for a 65-year-old man with chronic low-back pain radiating to the leg. (Neurosurgery)

Office consultation for 23-year-old female with Crohn's disease not responding to therapy. (Abdominal Surgery/Colon & Rectal Surgery)

Office consultation for 25-year-old patient with symptomatic knee pain and swelling, with torn anterior cruciate ligament and/or torn meniscus. (Orthopaedic Surgery)

Office consultation for a 67-year-old patient with osteoporosis and mandibular atrophy with regard to reconstructive alternatives. (Oral & Maxillofacial Surgery)

Office consultation for 39-year-old patient referred at a perimenopausal age for irregular menses and menopausal symptoms. (Obstetrics & Gynecology)

99244 Initial office consultation for a 28-year-old male, HIV+, with a recent change in visual acuity. (Ophthalmology)

Initial office consultation for a 15-year-old male with failing grades, suspected drug abuse. (Pediatrics)

Initial office consultation for a 36-year-old factory worker, status four months post-occupational low back injury and requires management of intractable low back pain. (Pain Medicine)

Initial office consultation for a 45-year-old female with a history of chronic arthralgia of TMJ and associated myalgia and sudden progressive symptomatology over last two to three months. (Oral & Maxillofacial Surgery)

Initial office consultation for evaluation of a 70-year-old male with appetite loss and diminished energy. (Psychiatry)

Initial office consultation for an elementary school-aged patient, referred by pediatrician, with multiple systematic complaints and recent onset of behavioral discontrol. (Psychiatry)

Initial office consultation for a 23-year-old female with developmental facial skeletal anomaly and subsequent abnormal relationship of jaw(s) to cranial base. (Oral & Maxillofacial Surgery)

Initial office consultation for a 45-year-old myopic patient with a one-week history of floaters and a partial retinal detachment. (Ophthalmology)

Initial office consultation for a 65-year-old female with moderate dementia, mild unsteadiness, back pain fatigue on ambulation, intermittent urinary incontinence. (Neurosurgery)

Initial office consultation for a 33-year-old female referred by endocrinologist with amenorrhea and galactorrhea, for evaluation of pituitary tumor. (Neurosurgery)

Initial office consultation for a 34-year-old male with new onset nephrotic syndrome. (Nephrology)

Initial office consultation for a 39-year-old female with intractable chest wall pain secondary to metastatic breast cancer. (Anesthesiology/Pain Medicine)

Initial office consultation for a patient with multiple giant tumors of jaws. (Oral & Maxillofacial Surgery)

Initial office consultation for a patient with a failed total hip replacement with loosening and pain upon walking. (Orthopaedic Surgery)

Initial office consultation for a 60-year-old female with three-year history of intermittent tic-like unilateral facial pain; now constant pain for six weeks without relief by adequate carbamazepine dosage. (Neurosurgery)

Initial office consultation for a 45-year-old male heavy construction worker with prior lumbar disc surgery two years earlier; now gradually recurring low back and unilateral leg pain for three months, unable to work for two weeks. (Neurosurgery)

Initial office consultation of a patient who presents with a 30-year history of smoking and right neck mass. (Otolaryngology, Head & Neck Surgery)

Office consultation with 38-year-old female, with inflammatory bowel disease, who now presents with right lower quadrant pain and suspected intra-abdominal abscess. (General Surgery/Colon & Rectal Surgery)

Office consultation with 72-year-old male with esophageal carcinoma, symptoms of dysphagia, and reflux. (Thoracic Surgery)

Office consultation for discussion of treatment options for a 40-year-old female with a 2-cm adenocarcinoma of the breast. (Radiation Oncology)

Office consultation for young patient referred by pediatrician because of patient's short attention span, easy distractibility, and hyperactivity. (Psychiatry)

Office consultation for 66-year-old female, history of colon resection for adenocarcinoma six years earlier, now with severe mid-back pain; X rays showing osteoporosis and multiple vertebral compression fractures. (Neurosurgery)

Office consultation for a patient with chronic pelvic inflammatory disease who now has left lower quadrant pain with a palpable pelvic mass. (Obstetrics & Gynecology)

Office consultation for a patient with long-standing psoriasis with acute onset of erythroderma, pustular lesions, chills, and fever. Combinations of topical and systemic treatments discussed and instituted. (Dermatology)

99245 Initial office consultation for a 35-year-old multiple-trauma male patient with complex pelvic fractures, for evaluation and formulation of management plan. (Orthopaedic Surgery)

Initial emergency room consultation for 10-year-old male in status epilepticus, recent closed head injury, information about medication not available. (Neurosurgery)

Initial emergency room consultation for a 23-year-old patient with severe abdominal pain, guarding, febrile, and unstable vital signs. (Obstetrics & Gynecology)

Office consultation for a 67-year-old female longstanding uncontrolled diabetic who presents with retinopathy, nephropathy, and a foot ulcer. (Endocrinology)

Office consultation for a 37-year-old male for initial evaluation and management of Cushing's disease. (Endocrinology)

Office consultation for a 60-year-old male who presents with thyrotoxicosis, exophthalmos, frequent premature ventricular contractions and congestive heart failure. (Endocrinology)

Initial office consultation for a 36-year-old patient, one year status post occupational herniated cervical disk treated by laminectomy, requiring management of multiple sites of intractable pain, depression, and narcotic dependence. (Pain Medicine)

Office consultation for a 58-year-old man with a history of MI and CHF who complains of the recent onset of rest angina and shortness of breath. The patient has a systolic blood pressure of 90 mmHG and is in Class IV heart failure. (Cardiology)

Emergency department consultation for a 1-year-old with a three-day history of fever with increasing respiratory distress who is thought to have cardiac tamponade by the ER physician. (Cardiology)

Office consultation in the emergency department for a 25-year-old male with severe, acute, closed head injury. (Neurosurgery)

Office consultation for a 23-year-old female with Stage II A Hodgkins disease with positive supraclavicular and mediastinal nodes. (Radiation Oncology)

Office consultation for a 27-year-old juvenile diabetic patient with severe diabetic retinopathy, gastric atony, nephrotic syndrome and progressive renal failure, now with a serum creatinine of 2.7, and a blood pressure of 170/114. (Nephrology)

Office consultation for independent medical evaluation of a patient with a history of complicated low back and neck problems with previous multiple failed back surgeries. (Orthopaedic Surgery)

Office consultation for an adolescent referred by pediatrician for recent onset of violent and self-injurious behavior. (Psychiatry)

Office consultation for a 6-year-old male for evaluation of severe muscle and joint pain and a diffuse rash. Patient was feeling well until 4 to 6 weeks earlier, when he developed arthralgia, myalgias, and a fever of 102 degrees for one week. (Rheumatology)

Inpatient Consultations

New or Established Patient

99251 Initial hospital consultation for a 27-year-old female with fractured incisor post-intubation. (Oral & Maxillofacial Surgery)

Initial hospital consultation for an orthopaedic patient on IV antibiotics who has developed an apparent candida infection of the oral cavity. (Oral & Maxillofacial Surgery)

Initial inpatient consultation for a 30-year-old female complaining of vaginal itching, post orthopaedic surgery. (Obstetrics & Gynecology)

Initial inpatient consultation for a 36-year-old male on orthopaedic service with complaint of localized dental pain. (Oral & Maxillofacial Surgery)

99252 Initial hospital consultation for a 45-year-old male, previously abstinent alcoholic, who relapsed and was admitted for management of gastritis. The patient readily accepts the need for further treatment. (Addiction Medicine)

Initial hospital consultation for a 35-year-old dialysis patient with episodic oral ulcerations. (Oral & Maxillofacial Surgery)

Initial inpatient preoperative consultation for a 43-year-old female with cholecystitis and well-controlled hypertension. (Cardiology)

Initial inpatient consultation for recommendation of antibiotic prophylaxis for a patient with a synthetic heart valve who will undergo urologic surgery. (Internal Medicine)

Initial inpatient consultation for possible drug induced skin eruption in 50-year-old male. (Dermatology)

Preoperative inpatient consultation for evaluation of hypertension in a 60-year-old male who will undergo a cholecystectomy. Patient had a normal annual check-up in your office four months ago. (Internal Medicine)

Initial inpatient consultation for 66-year-old patient with wrist and hand pain and finger numbness, secondary to carpal tunnel syndrome. (Orthopaedic Surgery/Plastic Surgery)

Initial inpatient consultation for a 66-year-old male smoker referred for pain management immediately status post-biliary tract surgery done via sub-costal incision. (Anesthesiology/Pain Medicine)

99253 Initial hospital consultation for a 50-year-old female with incapacitating knee pain due to generalized rheumatoid arthritis. (Orthopaedic Surgery)

Initial hospital consultation for a 60-year-old male with avascular necrosis of the left femoral heel with increasing pain. (Orthopaedic Surgery)

Initial hospital consultation for a 45-year-old female with compound mandibular fracture and concurrent head, abdominal and/or orthopaedic injuries. (Oral & Maxillofacial Surgery)

Initial hospital consultation for a 22-year-old female, paraplegic, to evaluate wrist and hand pain. (Orthopaedic Surgery)

Initial hospital consultation for a 40-year-old male with 10-day history of incapacitating unilateral sciatica, unable to walk now, not improved by bed rest. (Neurosurgery)

Initial hospital consultation, requested by pediatrician, for treatment recommendations for a patient admitted with persistent inability to walk following soft tissue injury to ankle. (Physiatry)

Initial hospital consultation for a 27-year-old previously healthy male who vomited during IV sedation and may have aspirated gastric contents. (Anesthesiology)

Initial hospital consultation for a 33-year-old female, post-abdominal surgery, who now has a fever. (Internal Medicine)

Initial inpatient consultation for a 57-year-old male, post lower endoscopy, for evaluation of abdominal pain and fever. (General Surgery)

Initial inpatient consultation for rehabilitation of a 73-year-old female one week after surgical management of a hip fracture. (Physical Medicine & Rehabilitation)

Initial inpatient consultation for diagnosis/management of fever following abdominal surgery. (Internal Medicine)

Initial inpatient consultation for a 35-year-old female with a fever and pulmonary infiltrate following cesarean section. (Pulmonary Medicine)

Initial inpatient consultation for a 42-year-old nondiabetic patient, postop cholecystectomy, now with an acute urinary tract infection. (Nephrology)

Initial inpatient consultation for 53-year-old female with moderate uncomplicated pancreatitis. (Gastroenterology)

Initial inpatient consultation for 45-year-old patient with chronic neck pain with radicular pain of the left arm. (Orthopaedic Surgery)

Initial inpatient consultation for 8-year-old patient with new onset of seizures who has a normal examination and previous history. (Neurology)

99254 Initial hospital consultation for a 15-year-old patient with painless swelling of proximal humerus with lytic lesion by X ray. (Orthopaedic Surgery)

Initial hospital consultation for evaluation of a 29-year-old female with a diffusely positive medical review of systems and history of multiple surgeries. (Psychiatry)

Initial hospital consultation for a 70-year-old diabetic female with gangrene of the foot. (Orthopaedic Surgery)

Initial inpatient consultation for a 47-year-old female with progressive pulmonary infiltrate, hypoxemia, and diminished urine output. (Anesthesiology)

Initial hospital consultation for a 13-month-old with spasmodic cough, respiratory distress, and fever. (Allergy & Immunology)

Initial hospital consultation for a patient with failed total hip replacement with loosening and pain upon walking. (Orthopaedic Surgery)

Initial hospital consultation for a 62-year-old female with metastatic breast cancer to the femoral neck and thoracic vertebra. (Orthopaedic Surgery)

Initial hospital consultation for a 39-year-old female with nephrolithiasis requiring extensive opioid analgesics, whose vital signs are now elevated. She initially denied any drug use, but today gives history of multiple substance abuse, including opioids and prior treatment for a personality disorder. (Psychiatry)

Initial hospital consultation for a 70-year-old female without previous psychiatric history, who is now experiencing nocturnal confusion and visual hallucinations following hip replacement surgery. (Psychiatry)

Initial inpatient consultation for evaluation of a 63-year-old in the ICU with diabetes and chronic renal failure who develops acute respiratory distress syndrome 36 hours after a mitral valve replacement. (Anesthesiology)

Initial inpatient consultation for a 66-year-old female with enlarged supraclavicular lymph nodes, found on biopsy to be malignant. (Hematology/Oncology)

Initial inpatient consultation for a 43-year-old female for evaluation of sudden painful visual loss, optic neuritis and episodic paresthesia. (Ophthalmology)

Initial inpatient consultation for evaluation of a 71-year-old male with hyponatremia (serum sodium 114) who was admitted to the hospital with pneumonia. (Nephrology)

Initial inpatient consultation for a 72-year-old male with emergency admission for possible bowel obstruction. (Internal Medicine/General Surgery)

Initial inpatient consultation for a 35-year-old female with fever, swollen joints, and rash of one-week duration. (Rheumatology)

99255 Initial inpatient consultation for a 76-year-old female with massive, life-threatening gastrointestinal hemorrhage and chest pain. (Gastroenterology)

Initial inpatient consultation for a 75-year-old female, admitted to intensive care with acute respiratory distress syndrome, who is hypersensitive, has a moderate metabolic acidosis, and a rising serum creatinine. (Nephrology)

Initial hospital consultation for patient with a history of complicated low back pain and neck problems with previous multiple failed back surgeries. (Orthopaedic Surgery/Neurosurgery)

Initial hospital consultation for a 66-year-old female, two days post-abdominal aneurysm repair, with oliguria and hypertension of one-day duration. (Nephrology/Internal Medicine)

Initial hospital consultation for a patient with shotgun wound to face with massive facial trauma and airway obstruction. (Oral & Maxillofacial Surgery)

Initial hospital consultation for patient with severe pancreatitis complicated by respiratory insufficiency, acute renal failure, and abscess formation. (General Surgery/Colon & Rectal Surgery)

Initial hospital consultation for a 35-year-old multiple-trauma male patient with complex pelvic fractures to evaluate and formulate management plan. (Orthopaedic Surgery)

Initial inpatient consultation for adolescent patient with fractured femur and pelvis who pulled out IVs and disconnected traction in attempt to elope from hospital. (Psychiatry)

Initial hospital consultation for a 16-year-old primigravida at 32-weeks gestation requested by a family practitioner for evaluation of severe hypertension, thrombocytopenia, and headache. (Obstetrics & Gynecology)

Initial hospital consultation for a 58-year-old insulin-dependent diabetic with multiple antibiotic allergies, now with multiple fascial plane abscesses and airway obstruction. (Oral & Maxillofacial Surgery)

Initial inpatient consultation for a 55-year-old male with known cirrhosis and ascites, now with jaundice, encephalopathy, and massive hematemesis. (Gastroenterology)

Initial hospital consultation for a 25-year-old male, seen in emergency room with severe, closed head injury. (Neurosurgery)

Initial hospital consultation for a 2-day-old male with single ventricle physiology and subaortic obstruction. Family counseling following evaluation for multiple, staged surgical procedures. (Thoracic Surgery)

Initial hospital consultation for a 45-year-old male admitted with subarachnoid hemorrhage and intracranial aneurysm on angiogram. (Neurosurgery)

Initial inpatient consultation for myxedematous patient who is hypoventilating and obtunded. (Endocrinology)

Initial hospital consultation for a 45-year-old patient with widely metastatic lung carcinoma, intractable back pain, and a history that includes substance dependence, NSAID allergy, and two prior laminectomies with fusion for low back pain. (Pain Medicine)

Initial hospital consultation for evaluation of treatment options in a 50-year-old patient with cirrhosis, known peptic ulcer disease, hypotension, encephalopathy, and massive acute upper gastrointestinal bleeding which cannot be localized by endoscopy. (Interventional Radiology)

Initial inpatient consultation in the ICU for a 70-year-old male who experienced a cardiac arrest during surgery and was resuscitated. (Cardiology)

Initial inpatient consultation for a patient with severe pancreatitis complicated by respiratory insufficiency, acute renal failure and abscess formation. (Gastroenterology)

Initial inpatient consultation for a 70-year-old cirrhotic male admitted with ascites, jaundice, encephalopathy, and massive hematemesis. (Gastroenterology)

Initial inpatient consultation in the ICU for a 51-year-old patient who is on a ventilator and has a fever two weeks after a renal transplantation. (Infectious Disease)

Initial inpatient consultation for evaluation and formulation of plan for management of multiple trauma patient with complex pelvic fracture, 35-year-old male. (General Surgery/Orthopaedic Surgery)

Initial inpatient consultation for a 50-year-old male with a history of previous myocardial infarction, now with acute pulmonary edema and hypotension. (Cardiology)

Initial inpatient consultation for 45-year-old male with recent, acute subarachnoid hemorrhage, hesitant speech, mildly confused, drowsy. High risk group for HIV+ status. (Neurosurgery)

Initial inpatient consultation for 36-year-old female referred by her internist to evaluate a patient being followed for abdominal pain and fever. The patient has developed diffuse abdominal pain, guarding, rigidity and increased fever. (Obstetrics & Gynecology)

Emergency Department Services

New or Established Patient

99281 Emergency department visit for a patient for removal of sutures from a well-healed, uncomplicated laceration. (Emergency Medicine)

Emergency department visit for a patient for tetanus toxoid immunization. (Emergency Medicine)

Emergency department visit for a patient with several uncomplicated insect bites. (Emergency Medicine)

99282 Emergency department visit for a 20-year-old student who presents with a painful sunburn with blister formation on the back. (Emergency Medicine)

Emergency department visit for a child presenting with impetigo localized to the face. (Emergency Medicine)

Emergency department visit for a patient with a minor traumatic injury of an extremity with localized pain, swelling, and bruising. (Emergency Medicine)

Emergency department visit for an otherwise healthy patient whose chief complaint is a red, swollen cystic lesion on his/her back. (Emergency Medicine)

Emergency department visit for a patient presenting with a rash on both legs after exposure to poison ivy. (Emergency Medicine)

Emergency department visit for a young adult patient with infected sclera and purulent discharge from both eyes without pain, visual disturbance or history of foreign body in either eye. (Emergency Medicine)

99283 Emergency department visit for a sexually active female complaining of vaginal discharge who is afebrile and denies experiencing abdominal or back pain. (Emergency Medicine)

Emergency department visit for a well-appearing 8-year-old who has a fever, diarrhea, and abdominal cramps, is tolerating oral fluids and is not vomiting. (Emergency Medicine)

Emergency department visit for a patient with an inversion ankle injury, who is unable to bear weight on the injured foot and ankle. (Emergency Medicine)

Emergency department visit for a patient who has a complaint of acute pain associated with a suspected foreign body in the painful eye. (Emergency Medicine)

Emergency department visit for a healthy, young adult patient who sustained a blunt head injury with local swelling and bruising without subsequent confusion, loss of consciousness or memory deficit. (Emergency Medicine)

99284 Emergency department visit for a 4-year-old who fell off a bike sustaining a head injury with brief loss of consciousness. (Emergency Medicine)

Emergency department visit for an elderly female who has fallen and is now complaining of pain in her right hip and is unable to walk. (Emergency Medicine)

Emergency department visit for a patient with flank pain and hematuria. (Emergency Medicine)

Emergency department visit for a female presenting with lower abdominal pain and a vaginal discharge. (Emergency Medicine)

99285 Emergency department visit for a patient with a complicated overdose requiring aggressive management to prevent side effects from the ingested materials. (Emergency Medicine)

Emergency department visit for a patient with a new onset of rapid heart rate requiring IV drugs. (Emergency Medicine)

Emergency department visit for a patient exhibiting active, upper gastrointestinal bleeding. (Emergency Medicine)

Emergency department visit for a previously healthy young adult patient who is injured in an automobile accident and is brought to the emergency department immobilized and has symptoms compatible with intra-abdominal injuries or multiple extremity injuries. (Emergency Medicine)

Emergency department visit for a patient with an acute onset of chest pain compatible with symptoms of cardiac ischemia and/or pulmonary embolus. (Emergency Medicine)

Emergency department visit for a patient who presents with a sudden onset of "the worst headache of her life," and complains of a stiff neck, nausea, and inability to concentrate. (Emergency Medicine)

Emergency department visit for a patient with a new onset of a cerebral vascular accident. (Emergency Medicine)

Emergency department visit for acute febrile illness in an adult, associated with shortness of breath and an altered level of alertness. (Emergency Medicine)

Critical Care Services

99291 First hour of critical care of a 65-year-old male with septic shock following relief of ureteral obstruction caused by a stone.

First hour of critical care of a 15-year-old with acute respiratory failure from asthma.

First hour of critical care of a 45-year-old who sustained a liver laceration, cerebral hematoma, flailed chest, and pulmonary contusion after being struck by an automobile.

First hour of critical care of a 65-year-old female who, following a hysterectomy, suffered a cardiac arrest associated with a pulmonary embolus.

First hour of critical care of a 6-month-old with hypovolemic shock secondary to diarrhea and dehydration.

First hour of critical care of a 3-year-old with respiratory failure secondary to pneumocystis carinii pneumonia.

Prolonged Services

Prolonged Physician Service With Direct (Face-to-Face) Patient Contact

Office or Other Outpatient

99354/ 99355 A 20-year-old female with history of asthma presents with acute bronchospasm and moderate respiratory distress. Initial evaluation shows respiratory rate 30, labored breathing and wheezing heard in all lung fields. Office treatment is initiated, which includes intermittent bronchial dilation and subcutaneous epinephrine. Requires intermittent physician face-to-face time with patient over a period of 2 to 3 hours. (Family Medicine/Internal Medicine)

Inpatient

99356 A 34-year-old primigravida presents to hospital in early labor. Admission history and physical reveals severe preeclampsia. Physician supervises management of preeclampsia, IV magnesium initiation and maintenance, labor augmentation with pitocin, and close maternal-fetal monitoring. Physician face-to-face involvement includes 40 minutes of continuous bedside care until the patient is stable, then is intermittent over several hours until the delivery. (Family Medicine/Internal Medicine/Obstetrics & Gynecology)

Prolonged Physician Service Without Direct Patient (Face-to-Face) Contact

99358/ 99359 An 85-year-old new patient with multiple complicated medical problems has moved to the area to live closer to her daughter. She is brought to the primary care office by her daughter and has been seen and examined by the physician. The physician indicated that past medical records would be obtained from the patient's prior physicians' and that he will communicate further with the daughter upon review of them.

Physician Standby Services

99360 A 24-year-old patient is admitted to OB unit attempting VBAC. Fetal monitoring shows increasing fetal distress. Patient's blood pressure is rising and labor progressing slowly. A primary care physician is requested by the OB/GYN to standby in the unit for possible cesarean delivery and neonatal resuscitation. (Family Medicine/Internal Medicine)

Care Plan Oversight Services

99375 First month of care plan oversight for terminal care of a 58-year-old female with advanced intraabdominal ovarian cancer. Care plan includes home oxygen, diuretics IV for edema and ascites control and pain control management involving IV morphine infusion when progressive ileus occurred. Physician phone contacts with nurse, family, and MSW. Discussion with MSW concerning plans to withdraw supportive measures per patient wishes. Documentation includes review and modification of care plan and certifications from nursing, MSW, pharmacy, and DME. (Family Medicine/Internal Medicine)

Appendix D

Summary of CPT Add-on Codes

This listing is a summary of CPT add-on codes for *CPT 2010*. The codes listed below are identified in *CPT 2010* with a ✚ symbol.

01953	15361	22841	33961	44139	63295	77051
01968	15366	22842	34806	44203	63308	77052
01969	15401	22843	34808	44213	63621	78020
11001	15421	22844	34813	44701	64480	78496
11008	15431	22845	34826	44955	64484	78730
11101	15787	22846	35306	47001	64491	83901
11201	15847	22847	35390	47550	64492	86826
11732	16036	22848	35400	48400	64494	87187
11922	17003	22851	35500	49326	64495	87904
13102	17312	26125	35572	49435	64623	88155
13122	17314	26861	35600	49568	64627	88185
13133	17315	26863	35681	49905	64727	88311
13153	19001	27358	35682	51797	64778	88314
14302	19126	27692	35683	56606	64783	88388
15003	19291	31620	35685	57267	64787	90466
15005	19295	31627	35686	58110	64832	90468
15101	19297	31632	35697	58611	64837	90472
15111	20930	31633	35700	59525	64859	90474
15116	20931	31637	36148	60512	64872	92547
15121	20936	32501	36218	61316	64874	92608
15131	20937	33141	36248	61517	64876	92627
15136	20938	33225	36476	61609	64901	92973
15151	20985	33257	36479	61610	64902	92974
15152	22103	33258	37185	61611	65757	92978
15156	22116	33259	37186	61612	66990	92979
15157	22208	33508	37206	61641	67225	92981
15171	22216	33517	37208	61642	67320	92984
15176	22226	33518	37250	61795	67331	92996
15201	22328	33519	37251	61797	67332	92998
15221	22522	33521	38102	61799	67334	93320
15241	22525	33522	38746	61800	67335	93321
15261	22527	33523	38747	61864	67340	93325
15301	22534	33530	43273	61868	69990	93352
15321	22585	33572	43635	62148	74301	93571
15331	22614	33768	44015	62160	75565	93572
15336	22632	33884	44121	63035	75774	93609
15341	22840	33924	44128	63043	75946	93613
				63044	75964	93621
				63048	75968	93622
				63057	75993	93623
				63066	75996	93662
				63076	76125	94645
				63078	76802	95873
				63082	76810	95874
				63086	76812	95920
				63088	76814	95962
				63091	76937	95967
				63103	77001	95973

95975	0174T
95979	0189T
96361	0190T
96366	0196T
96367	0205T
96368	
96370	
96371	
96375	
96376	
96411	
96415	
96417	
96423	
96570	
96571	
97546	
97811	
97814	
99100	
99116	
99135	
99140	
99145	
99150	
99292	
99354	
99355	
99356	
99357	
99359	
99467	
99602	
99607	
0054T	
0055T	
0076T	
0079T	
0081T	
0092T	
0095T	
0098T	
0159T	
0163T	
0164T	
0165T	
0172T	
0173T	

Appendix E

Summary of CPT Codes Exempt from Modifier 51

This listing is a summary of CPT codes that are exempt from the use of modifier 51. Procedures on this list are typically performed with another procedure but may be a stand alone procedure and not always be performed with other specified procedures. For add-on codes see Appendix D. This is not an exhaustive list of procedures that are typically exempt from multiple procedure reductions. The codes listed below are identified in *CPT 2010* with a ⊘ symbol.

17004

20697

20974

20975

31500

36620

44500

61107

93503

93539

93540

93544

93545

93555

93556

93600

93602

93603

93610

93612

93615

93616

93618

93631

94610

95900

95903

95904

95905

95992

99143

99144

Appendix F

Summary of CPT Codes Exempt from Modifier 63

The listing is a summary of CPT codes that are exempt from the use of modifier 63. The codes listed below are additionally identified in *CPT 2010* with the parenthetical instruction "(Do not report modifier 63 in conjunction with…)"

30540	36660	63700
30545	39503	63702
31520	43313	63704
33401	43314	63706
33403	43520	65820
33470	43831	
33472	44055	
33502	44126	
33503	44127	
33505	44128	
33506	46070	
33610	46705	
33611	46715	
33619	46716	
33647	46730	
33670	46735	
33690	46740	
33694	46742	
33730	46744	
33732	47700	
33735	47701	
33736	49215	
33750	49491	
33755	49492	
33762	49495	
33778	49496	
33786	49600	
33922	49605	
33960	49606	
33961	49610	
36415	49611	
36420	53025	
36450	54000	
36460	54150	
36510	54160	

Appendix G

Summary of CPT Codes That Include Moderate (Conscious) Sedation

The following list of procedures includes conscious sedation as an inherent part of providing the procedure. These codes are identified in the CPT codebook with a ⊙ symbol.

Since these services include moderate sedation, it is not appropriate for the same physician to report both the service and the sedation codes 99143-99145. It is expected that if conscious sedation is provided to the patient as part of one of these services, it is provided by the same physician who is providing the service.

In the unusual event when a second physician other than the health care professional performing the diagnostic or therapeutic services provides moderate sedation in the facility setting (eg, hospital, outpatient hospital/ambulatory surgery center, skilled nursing facility) for the procedures listed in Appendix G, the second physician can report 99148-99150. However, for the circumstance in which these services are performed by the second physician in the nonfacility setting (eg, physician office, freestanding imaging center), codes 99148-99150 would not be reported. Moderate sedation does not include minimal sedation (anxiolysis), deep sedation, or monitored anesthesia care (00100-01999).

The inclusion of a procedure on this list does not prevent separate reporting of an associated anesthesia procedure/service (CPT codes 00100-01999) when performed by a physician other than the health care professional performing the diagnostic or therapeutic procedure. In such cases the person providing anesthesia services shall be present for the purpose of continuously monitoring the patient and shall not act as a surgical assistant. When clinical conditions of the patient require such anesthesia services, or in the circumstances when the patient does not require sedation, the operating physician is not required to report the procedure as a reduced service using modifier 52.

				33212	37186	43263
				33213	37187	43264
				33214	37188	43265
				33216	37203	43267
				33217	37210	43268
				33218	37215	43269
				33220	37216	43271
				33222	43200	43272
				33223	43201	43273
				33233	43202	43453
				33234	43204	43456
				33235	43205	43458
				33240	43215	44360
				33241	43216	44361
				33244	43217	44363
				33249	43219	44364
				35470	43220	44365
				35471	43226	44366
				35472	43227	44369
				35473	43228	44370
				35474	43231	44372
				35475	43232	44373
				35476	43234	44376
				36147	43235	44377
				36148	43236	44378
				36481	43237	44379
				36555	43238	44380
				36557	43239	44382
				36558	43240	44383
				36560	43241	44385
				36561	43242	44386
				36563	43243	44388
				36565	43244	44389
				36566	43245	44390
				36568	43246	44391
				36570	43247	44392
				36571	43248	44393
				36576	43249	44394
				36578	43250	44397
				36581	43251	44500
19298	31622	31635	32553	36582	43255	44901
20982	31623	31645	33010	36583	43256	45303
22520	31624	31646	33011	36585	43257	45305
22521	31625	31656	33206	36590	43258	45307
22526	31626	31725	33207	36870	43259	45308
22527	31627	32201	33208	37183	43260	45309
31615	31628	32550	33210	37184	43261	45315
31620	31629	32551	33211	37185	43262	45317

45320	58823	93544
45321	66720	93545
45327	69300	93555
45332	77371	93556
45333	77600	93561
45334	77605	93562
45335	77610	93571
45337	77615	93572
45338	92953	93609
45339	92960	93613
45340	92961	93615
45341	92973	93616
45342	92974	93618
45345	92975	93619
45355	92978	93620
45378	92979	93621
45379	92980	93622
45380	92981	93624
45381	92982	93640
45382	92984	93641
45383	92986	93642
45384	92987	93650
45385	92995	93651
45386	92996	93652
45387	93312	94011
45391	93313	94012
45392	93314	94013
47011	93315	0200T
47382	93316	0201T
47525	93317	
48511	93318	
49021	93501	
49041	93505	
49061	93508	
49411	93510	
49440	93511	
49441	93514	
49442	93524	
49446	93526	
50021	93527	
50200	93528	
50382	93529	
50384	93530	
50385	93539	
50386	93540	
50387	93541	
50592	93542	
50593	93543	

Appendix H

Alphabetic Index of Performance Measures by Clinical Condition or Topic

The Alphabetic Index of Performance Measures by Clinical Condition/Topic (ie, Appendix H) has been removed from the CPT Codebook. Since this document is a dynamic, rapidly expanding source of information, the Alphabetic Index of Performance Measures by Clinical Topic has been transferred to be accessed solely on the AMA web site at www.ama-assn.org/go/cpt.

In addition, the revised codes for the publication cycle (ie, **the Update to List of Category II Codes**) will continue to be located on the AMA web site and also in the CPT Codebook for the following publication cycle (subsequent to its listing to the web).

Appendix I

Genetic Testing Code Modifiers

This listing of modifiers is intended for reporting with molecular laboratory procedures related to genetic testing. Genetic testing modifiers should be used in conjunction with CPT and HCPCS codes to provide diagnostic granularity of service to enable providers to submit complete and precise genetic testing information without altering test descriptors. These two-character modifiers are categorized by mutation. The first (numeric) character indicates the disease category and the second (alpha) character denotes gene type. Introductory guidelines in the molecular diagnostic and molecular cytogenetic code sections of the CPT codebook provide further guidance in interpretation and application of genetic testing modifiers.

Neoplasia (Solid Tumor, Excluding Sarcoma and Lymphoma)

0A	BRCA1 (hereditary breast/ovarian cancer)
0B	BRCA2 (hereditary breast cancer)
0C	Neurofibromin (neurofibromatosis, type 1)
0D	Merlin (neurofibromatosis, type 2)
0E	c-RET (multiple endocrine neoplasia, types 2A/B, familial medullary thyroid carcinoma)
0F	VHL (Von Hippel Lindau disease, renal carcinoma)
0G	SDHD (hereditary paraganglioma)
0H	SDHB (hereditary paraganglioma)
0I	ERRB2, commonly called Her-2/neu
0J	MLH1 (HNPCC, mismatch repair genes)
0K	MSH2, MSH6, or PMS2 (HNPCC, mismatch repair genes)
0L	APC (hereditary polyposis coli)
0M	Rb (retinoblastoma)
0N	TP53, commonly called p53
0O	PTEN (Cowden's syndrome)
0P	KIT, also called CD117 (gastrointestinal stromal tumor)
0Z	Solid tumor gene, not otherwise specified

Neoplasia (Sarcoma)

1A	WT1 or WT2 (Wilm's tumor)
1B	PAX3, PAX7, or FOXO1A (alveolar rhabdomyosarcoma)
1C	FLI1, ERG, ETV1, or EWSR1 (Ewing's sarcoma, desmoplastic round cell)
1D	DDIT3 or FUS (myxoid liposarcoma)
1E	NR4A3, RBF56, or TCF12 (myxoid chondrosarcoma)
1F	SSX1, SSX2, or SYT (synovial sarcoma)
1G	MYCN (neuroblastoma)
1H	COL1A1 or PDGFB (dermatofibrosarcoma protruberans)
1I	TFE3 or ASPSCR1 (alveolar soft parts sarcoma)
1J	JAZF1 or JJAZ1 (endometrial stromal sarcoma)
1Z	Sarcoma gene, not otherwise specified

Neoplasia (Lymphoid/Hematopoietic)

2A	RUNX1 or CBFA2T1, commonly called AML1 or ETO, genes associated with t(8;21) AML1—also ETO (acute myelogenous leukemia)
2B	BCR or ABL1, genes associated with t(9;22) (chronic myelogenous or acute leukemia) BCR—also ABL (chronic myeloid, acute lymphoid leukemia)
2C	PBX1 or TCF3, genes associated with t(1;19) (acute lymphoblastic leukemia) CGF1
2D	CBFB or MYH11, genes associated with inv 16 (acute myelogenous leukemia) CBF beta (leukemia)
2E	MLL (acute leukemia)
2F	PML or RARA, genes associated with t(15;17) (acute promyelocytic leukemia) PML/RAR alpha (promyelocytic leukemia)
2G	ETV6, commonly called TEL, gene associated with t(12;21) (acute leukemia) TEL (Leukemia)
2H	BCL2 (B cell lymphoma, follicle center cell origin) bcl-2 (Lymphoma)
2I	CCND1, commonly called BCL1, cyclin D1 (Mantle cell lymphoma, myeloma) bcl-1 (lymphoma)
2J	MYC (Burkitt lymphoma) c-myc (lymphoma)
2K	IgH (lymphoma/leukemia)
2L	IGK (lymphoma/leukemia)
2M	TRB, T cell receptor beta (lymphoma/leukemia)
2N	TRG, T cell receptor gamma (lymphoma/leukemia)

2O SIL or TAL1 (T cell leukemia)

2T BCL6 (B cell lymphoma)

2Q API1 or MALT1 (MALT lymphoma)

2R NPM or ALK, genes associated with t(2;5) (anaplastic large cell lymphoma)

2S FLT3 (Acute myelogenous leukemia)

2Z Lymphoid/hematopoietic neoplasia, not otherwise specified

Non-Neoplastic Hematology/Coagulation

3A F5, commonly called Factor V (Leiden, others) (hypercoagulable state)

3B FACC (Fanconi anemia)

3C FACD (Fanconi anemia)

3D HBB, beta globin (thalassemia, sickle cell anemia, other hemoglobinopathies)

3E HBA, commonly called alpha globin (thalassemia)

3F MTHFR (elevated homocystinemia)

3G F2, commonly called prothrombin (20210, others) (hypercoagulable state) prothrombin (factor II, 20210A) (hypercoagulable state)

3H F8, commonly called factor VIII (hemophilia A/VWF)

3I F9, commonly called factor IX (hemophilia B)

3K F13, commonly called factor XIII (bleeding or hypercoagulable state) beta globin

3Z Non-neoplastic hematology/coagulation, not otherwise specified

Histocompatiblity/Blood Typing/Identity/Microsatellite

4A HLA-A

4B HLA-B

4C HLA-C

4D HLA-D

4E HLA-DR

4F HLA-DQ

4G HLA-DP

4H Kell

4I Fingerprint for engraftment (post allogeneic progenitor cell transplant)

4J Fingerprint for donor allelotype (allogeneic transplant)

4K Fingerprint for recipient allelotype (allogeneic transplant)

4L Fingerprint for leukocyte chimerism (allogeneic solid organ transplant)

4M Fingerprint for maternal versus fetal origin

4N Microsatellite instability

4O Microsatellite loss (loss of heterozygosity)

4Z Histocompatiblity/blood typing, not otherwise specified

Neurologic, Non-Neoplastic

5A ASPA, commonly called Aspartoacylase A (Canavan disease)

5B FMR-1 (fragile X, FRAXA, syndrome)

5C FRDA, commonly called Frataxin (Freidreich ataxia)

5D HD, commonly called Huntington (Huntington's disease)

5E GABRA5, NIPA1, UBE3A, or ANCR GABRA (Prader Willi-Angelman syndrome)

5F GJB2, commonly called Connexin-26 (hereditary hearing loss) Connexin-32 (GJB2) (hereditary deafness)

5G GJB1, commonly called Connexin-32 (X-linked Charcot-Marie-Tooth disease)

5H SNRPN (Prader Willi-Angelman syndrome)

5I SCA1, commonly called Ataxin-1 (spinocerebellar ataxia, type 1)

5J SCA2, commonly called Ataxin-2 (spinocerebellar ataxia, type 2)

5K MJD, commonly called Ataxin-3 (spinocerebellar ataxia, type 3, Machado-Joseph disease)

5L CACNA1A (spinocerebellar ataxia, type 6)

5M ATXN7 Ataxin-7 (spinocerebellar ataxia, type 7)

5N PMP-22 (Charcot-Marie-Tooth disease, type 1A)

5O MECP2 (Rett syndrome)

5Z Neurologic, non-neoplastic, not otherwise specified

Muscular, Non-Neoplastic

6A DMD, commonly called dystrophin (Duchenne/Becker muscular dystrophy)

6B DMPK (myotonic dystrophy, type 1)

6C ZNF-9 (myotonic dystrophy, type 2)

6D SMN1/SMN2 (autosomal recessive spinal muscular atrophy)

6E MTTK, commonly called tRNAlys (myotonic epilepsy, MERRF)

6F MTTL1, commonly called tRNAleu (mitochondrial encephalomyopathy, MELAS)

6Z Muscular, not otherwise specified

Metabolic, Other

7A APOE, commonly called apolipoprotein E (cardiovascular disease or Alzheimer's disease)

7B NPC1 or NPC2, commonly called sphingomyelin phosphodiesterase (Nieman-Pick disease)

7C GBA, commonly called acid beta glucosidase (Gaucher disease)

7D HFE (hemochromatosis)

7E HEXA, commonly called hexosaminidase A (Tay-Sachs disease)

7F ACADM (medium chain acyl CoA dehydrogenase deficiency)

7Z Metabolic, other, not otherwise specified

Metabolic, Transport

8A CFTR (cystic fibrosis)

8B PRSS1 (hereditary pancreatitis)

8C Long QT syndrome, KCN (Jervell and Lange-Nielsen syndromes, types 1, 2, 5, and 6) and SCN (Brugada syndrome, SIDS and type 3)

8Z Metabolic, transport, not otherwise specified

Metabolic-Pharmacogenetics

9A TPMT, commonly called (thiopurine methyltransferase) (patients on antimetabolite therapy)

9B CYP2 genes, commonly called cytochrome p450 (drug metabolism)

9C ABCB1, commonly called MDR1 or p-glycoprotein (drug transport)

9D NAT2 (drug metabolism)

9L Metabolic-pharmacogenetics, not otherwise specified

Dysmorphology

9M FGFR1 (Pfeiffer and Kallman syndromes)

9N FGFR2 (Crouzon, Jackson-Weiss, Apert, Saethre-Chotzen syndromes)

9O FGFR3 (achondroplasia, hypochondroplasia, thanatophoric dysplasia, types I and II, Crouzon syndrome with acanthosis nigricans, Muencke syndromes)

9P TWIST (Saethre-Chotzen syndrome)

9Q DGCR, commonly called CATCH-22 (DiGeorge and 22q11 deletion syndromes)

9Z Dysmorphology, not otherwise specified

Appendix J

Electrodiagnostic Medicine Listing of Sensory, Motor, and Mixed Nerves

This summary assigns each sensory, motor, and mixed nerve with its appropriate nerve conduction study code in order to enhance accurate reporting of codes 95900, 95903, and 95904. Each nerve constitutes one unit of service.

Motor Nerves Assigned to Codes 95900 and 95903

I. Upper extremity, cervical plexus, and brachial plexus motor nerves
  A. Axillary motor nerve to the deltoid
  B. Long thoracic motor nerve to the serratus anterior
  C. Median nerve
    1. Median motor nerve to the abductor pollicis brevis
    2. Median motor nerve, anterior interosseous branch, to the flexor pollicis longus
    3. Median motor nerve, anterior interosseous branch, to the pronator quadratus
    4. Median motor nerve to the first lumbrical
    5. Median motor nerve to the second lumbrical
  D. Musculocutaneous motor nerve to the biceps brachii
  E. Radial nerve
    1. Radial motor nerve to the extensor carpi ulnaris
    2. Radial motor nerve to the extensor digitorum communis
    3. Radial motor nerve to the extensor indicis proprius
    4. Radial motor nerve to the brachioradialis
  F. Suprascapular nerve
    1. Suprascapular motor nerve to the supraspinatus
    2. Suprascapular motor nerve to the infraspinatus
  G. Thoracodorsal motor nerve to the latissimus dorsi
  H. Ulnar nerve
    1. Ulnar motor nerve to the abductor digiti minimi
    2. Ulnar motor nerve to the palmar interosseous
    3. Ulnar motor nerve to the first dorsal interosseous
    4. Ulnar motor nerve to the flexor carpi ulnaris
  I. Other
II. Lower extremity motor nerves
  A. Femoral motor nerve to the quadriceps
    1. Femoral motor nerve to vastus medialis
    2. Femoral motor nerve to vastus lateralis
    3. Femoral motor nerve to vastus intermedialis
    4. Femoral motor nerve to rectus femoris
  B. Ilioinguinal motor nerve
  C. Peroneal (fibular) nerve
    1. Peroneal motor nerve to the extensor digitorum brevis
    2. Peroneal motor nerve to the peroneus brevis
    3. Peroneal motor nerve to the peroneus longus
    4. Peroneal motor nerve to the tibialis anterior
  D. Plantar motor nerve
  E. Sciatic nerve
  F. Tibial nerve
    1. Tibial motor nerve, inferior calcaneal branch, to the abductor digiti minimi
    2. Tibial motor nerve, medial plantar branch, to the abductor hallucis
    3. Tibial motor nerve, lateral plantar branch, to the flexor digiti minimi brevis
  G. Other
III. Cranial nerves and trunk
  A. Cranial nerve VII (facial motor nerve)
    1. Facial nerve to the frontalis
    2. Facial nerve to the nasalis
    3. Facial nerve to the orbicularis oculi
    4. Facial nerve to the orbicularis oris
  B. Cranial nerve XI (spinal accessory motor nerve)
  C. Cranial nerve XII (hypoglossal motor nerve)
  D. Intercostal motor nerve
  E. Phrenic motor nerve to the diaphragm
  F. Recurrent laryngeal nerve
  G. Other
IV. Nerve Roots
  A. Cervical nerve root stimulation
    1. Cervical level 5 (CT)
    2. Cervical level 6 (C6)
    3. Cervical level 7 (C7)
    4. Cervical level 8 (C8)

B. Thoracic nerve root stimulation
1. Thoracic level 1 (T1)
2. Thoracic level 2 (T2)
3. Thoracic level 3 (T3)
4. Thoracic level 4 (T4)
5. Thoracic level 5 (T5)
6. Thoracic level 6 (T6)
7. Thoracic level 7 (T7)
8. Thoracic level 8 (T8)
9. Thoracic level 9 (T9)
10. Thoracic level 10 (T10)
11. Thoracic level 11 (T11)
12. Thoracic level 12 (T12)
C. Lumbar nerve root stimulation
1. Lumbar level 1 (L1)
2. Lumbar level 2 (L2)
3. Lumbar level 3 (L3)
4. Lumbar level 4 (L4)
5. Lumbar level 5 (L5)
D. Sacral nerve root stimulation
1. Sacral level 1 (S1)
2. Sacral level 2 (S2)
3. Sacral level 3 (S3)
4. Sacral level 4 (S4)

Sensory and Mixed Nerves Assigned to Code 95904

I. Upper extremity sensory and mixed nerves
A. Lateral antebrachial cutaneous sensory nerve
B. Medial antebrachial cutaneous sensory nerve
C. Medial brachial cutaneous sensory nerve
D. Median nerve
1. Median sensory nerve to the first digit
2. Median sensory nerve to the second digit
3. Median sensory nerve to the third digit
4. Median sensory nerve to the fourth digit
5. Median palmar cutaneous sensory nerve
6. Median palmar mixed nerve
E. Posterior antebrachial cutaneous sensory nerve
F. Radial sensory nerve
1. Radial sensory nerve to the base of the thumb
2. Radial sensory nerve to digit 1
G. Ulnar nerve
1. Ulnar dorsal cutaneous sensory nerve
2. Ulnar sensory nerve to the fourth digit
3. Ulnar sensory nerve to the fifth digit
4. Ulnar palmar mixed nerve
H. Intercostal sensory nerve
I. Other

II. Lower extremity sensory and mixed nerves
A. Lateral femoral cutaneous sensory nerve
B. Medial calcaneal sensory nerve
C. Medial femoral cutaneous sensory nerve
D. Peroneal nerve
1. Deep peroneal sensory nerve
2. Superficial peroneal sensory nerve, medial dorsal cutaneous branch
3. Superficial peroneal sensory nerve, intermediate dorsal cutaneous branch
E. Posterior femoral cutaneous sensory nerve
F. Saphenous nerve
1. Saphenous sensory nerve (distal technique)
2. Saphenous sensory nerve (proximal technique)
G. Sural nerve
1. Sural sensory nerve, lateral dorsal cutaneous branch
2. Sural sensory nerve
H. Tibial sensory nerve (digital nerve to toe 1)
I. Tibial sensory nerve (medial plantar nerve)
J. Tibial sensory nerve (lateral plantar nerve)
K. Other
III. Head and trunk sensory nerves
A. Dorsal nerve of the penis
B. Greater auricular nerve
C. Ophthalmic branch of the trigeminal nerve
D. Pudendal sensory nerve
E. Suprascapular sensory nerves
F. Other

The following table provides a reasonable maximum number of studies performed per diagnostic category necessary for a physician to arrive at a diagnosis in 90% of patients with that final diagnosis. The numbers in each column represent the number of studies recommended. The appropriate number of studies to be performed is based upon the physician's discretion.

Indication	Needle EMG (95860-95864, 95867-95870)	Type of Study/Maximum Number of Studies			
		Nerve Conduction Studies (95900, 95903, 95904)		Other EMG Studies (95934, 95936, 95937)	
		Motor NCS With and/or Without F wave	Sensory NCS	H-Reflex	Neuromuscular Junction Testing (Repetitive Stimulation)
Carpal Tunnel (Unilateral)	1	3	4	—	—
Carpal Tunnel (Bilateral)	2	4	6	—	—
Radiculopathy	2	3	2	2	—
Mononeuropathy	1	3	3	2	—
Polyneuropathy/Mononeuropathy Multiplex	3	4	4	2	—
Myopathy	2	2	2	—	2
Motor Neuronopathy (eg, ALS)	4	4	2	—	2
Plexopathy	2	4	6	2	—
Neuromuscular Junction	2	2	2	—	3
Tarsal Tunnel Syndrome (Unilateral)	1	4	4	—	—
Tarsal Tunnel Syndrome (Bilateral)	2	5	6	—	—
Weakness, Fatigue, Cramps, or Twitching (Focal)	2	3	4	—	2
Weakness, Fatigue, Cramps, or Twitching (General)	4	4	4	—	2
Pain, Numbness, or Tingling (Unilateral)	1	3	4	2	—
Pain, Numbness, or Tingling (Bilateral)	2	4	6	2	—

Appendix K

Product Pending FDA Approval

Some vaccine products have been assigned a CPT Category I code in anticipation of future approval from the Food and Drug Administration (FDA). Following is a list of the vaccine product codes pending FDA approval status that are identified in the CPT codebook with the (✔) symbol. Upon revision of the approval status by the FDA, notation of this revision will be provided via the AMA CPT "Category I Vaccine Codes" Internet listing (www.ama-assn.org/ama/pub/category/10902.html) and in subsequent publications of the CPT codebook.

90650

90661

90662

90663

90670

Appendix L

Vascular Families

Assignment of branches to first, second, and third order in this table makes the assumption that the starting point is catheterization of the aorta. This categorization would not be accurate, for instance, if a femoral or carotid artery were catheterized directly in an antegrade direction. Arteries highlighted in bold are those more commonly reported during arteriographic procedures.

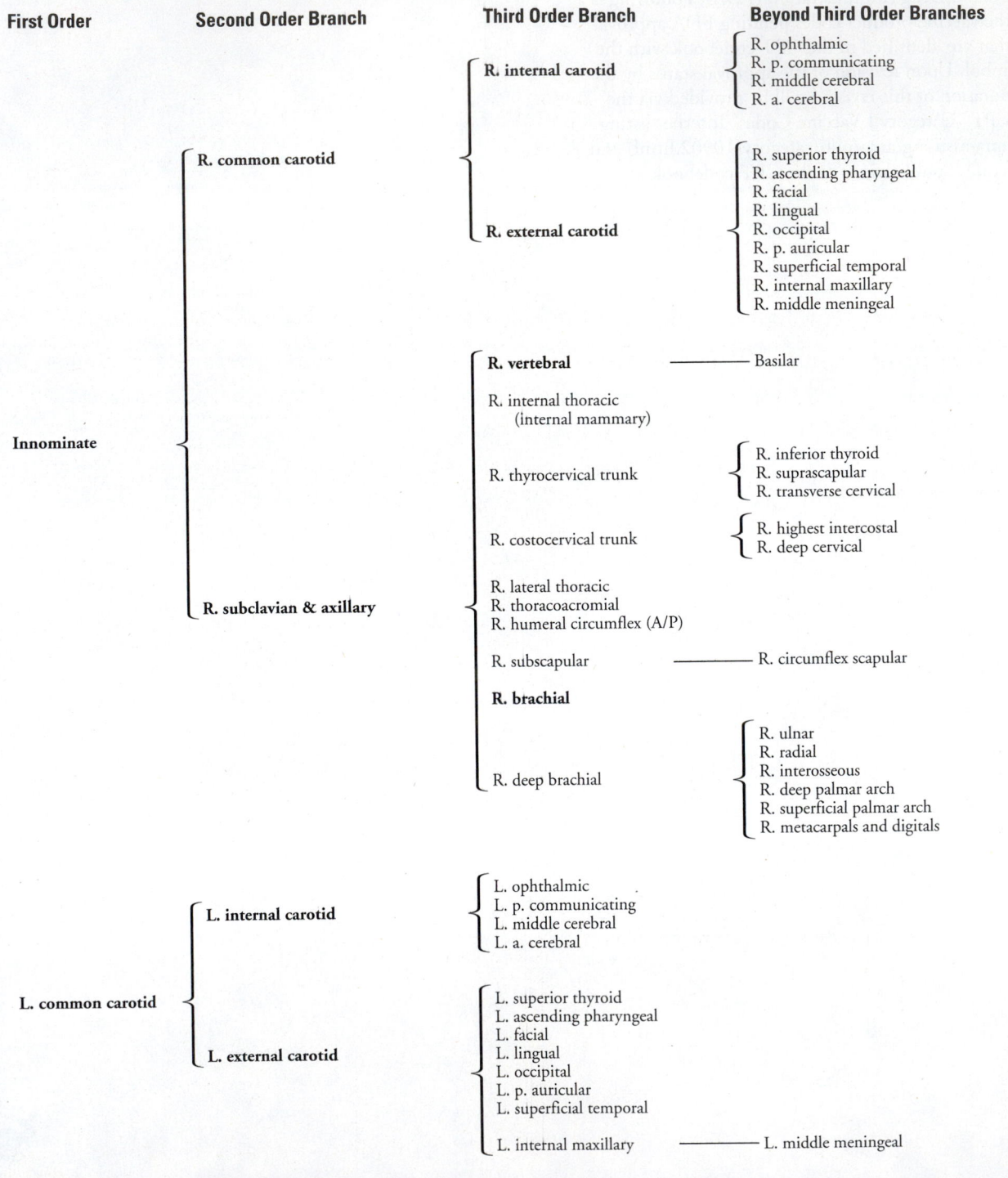

First Order	Second Order Branch	Third Order Branch	Beyond Third Order Branches
		R. internal carotid	R. ophthalmic R. p. communicating R. middle cerebral R. a. cerebral
	R. common carotid	**R. external carotid**	R. superior thyroid R. ascending pharyngeal R. facial R. lingual R. occipital R. p. auricular R. superficial temporal R. internal maxillary R. middle meningeal
Innominate		**R. vertebral** ——— Basilar	
		R. internal thoracic (internal mammary)	
		R. thyrocervical trunk	R. inferior thyroid R. suprascapular R. transverse cervical
		R. costocervical trunk	R. highest intercostal R. deep cervical
	R. subclavian & axillary	R. lateral thoracic R. thoracoacromial R. humeral circumflex (A/P)	
		R. subscapular ——— R. circumflex scapular	
		R. brachial	
		R. deep brachial	R. ulnar R. radial R. interosseous R. deep palmar arch R. superficial palmar arch R. metacarpals and digitals
L. common carotid	**L. internal carotid**	L. ophthalmic L. p. communicating L. middle cerebral L. a. cerebral	
	L. external carotid	L. superior thyroid L. ascending pharyngeal L. facial L. lingual L. occipital L. p. auricular L. superficial temporal	
		L. internal maxillary ——— L. middle meningeal	

R = right, L = left, A = anterior, P = posterior

First Order	Second Order Branch	Third Order Branch	Beyond Third Order Branches

L. subclavian & axillary

- **L. vertebral**
- L. internal thoracic (internal mammary)
- L. thyrocervical trunk
  - L. inferior thyroid
  - L. suprascapular
  - L. transverse cervical
- L. costocervical trunk
  - L. highest intercostal
  - L. deep cervical
- L. lateral thoracic
- L. thoracoacromial
- L. humeral circumflex (A/P)
- L. subscapular — L. circumflex scapular
- **L. brachial**
  - L. ulnar
  - L. radial
- L. deep brachial
  - L. interosseous
    - L. deep palmar arch
    - L. superficial palmar arch
    - L. metacarpals and digitals

Intercostals

Bronchials

Recurrent esophageal

Inferior phrenic —— Superior suprarenal

Celiac trunk

- L. gastric —— Esophageal branch
- Splenic
  - Dorsal pancreatic —— Inferior transverse pancreatic
  - Great pancreatic
  - Caudal pancreatic
  - Gastroepiploic
  - Short gastrics
- Common hepatic
  - Gastroduodenal
    - P. superior pancreaticoduodenal
    - A. superior pancreaticoduodenal
  - Proper Hepatic
    - L. hepatic
    - R. hepatic
    - Cystic
    - Gastroepiploic
    - Supraduodenal
    - Intermediate hepatic

Middle suprarenal

Superior mesenteric

- Middle colic
- Inferior pancreaticoduodenal
  - P. inferior pancreaticoduodenal
  - A. inferior pancreaticoduodenal
- Jejunal
- Ileocolic
- Appendicular
- P. cecal
- A. cecal
- Marginal
- R. colic

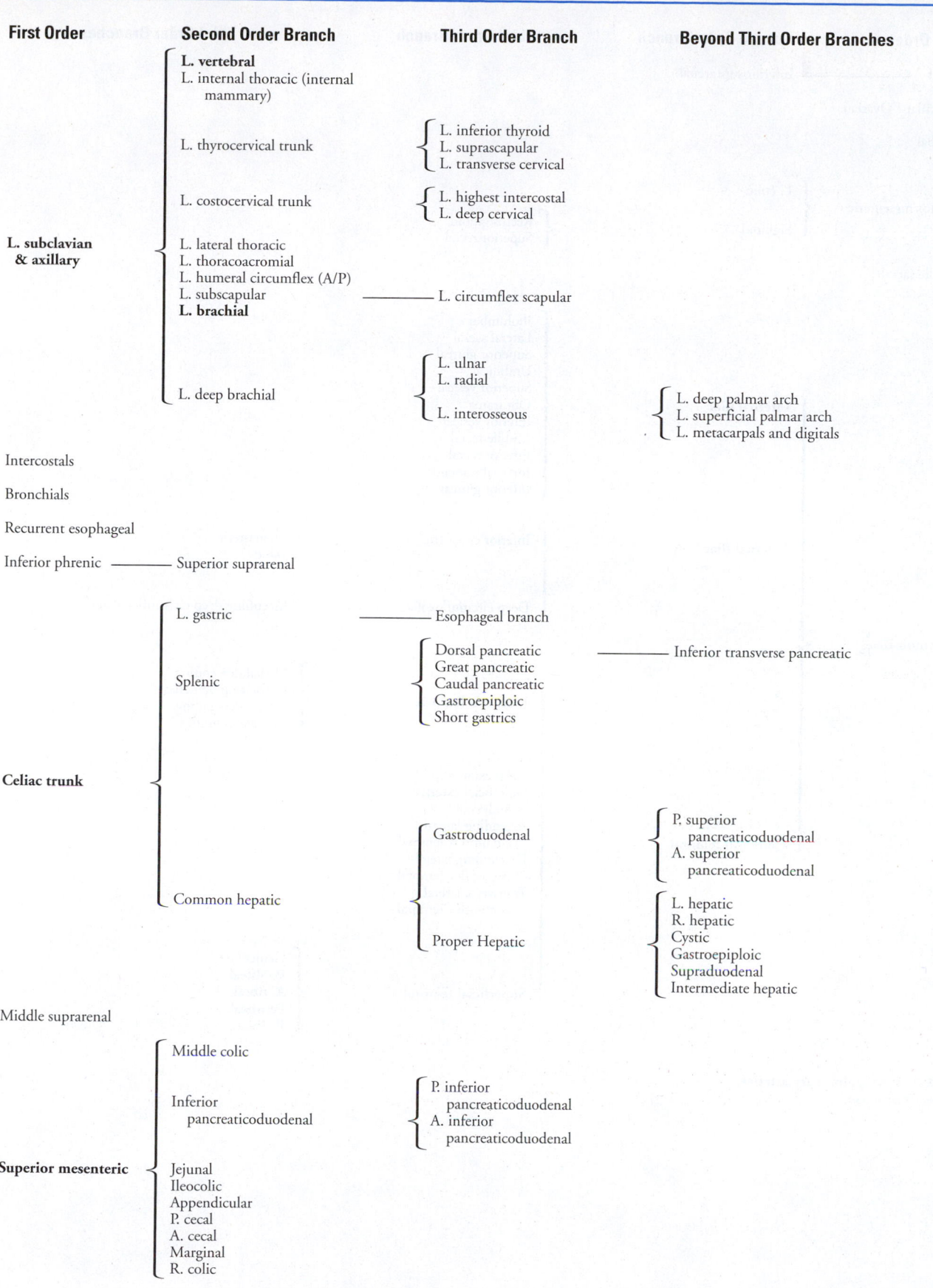

R = right, L = left, A = anterior, P = posterior

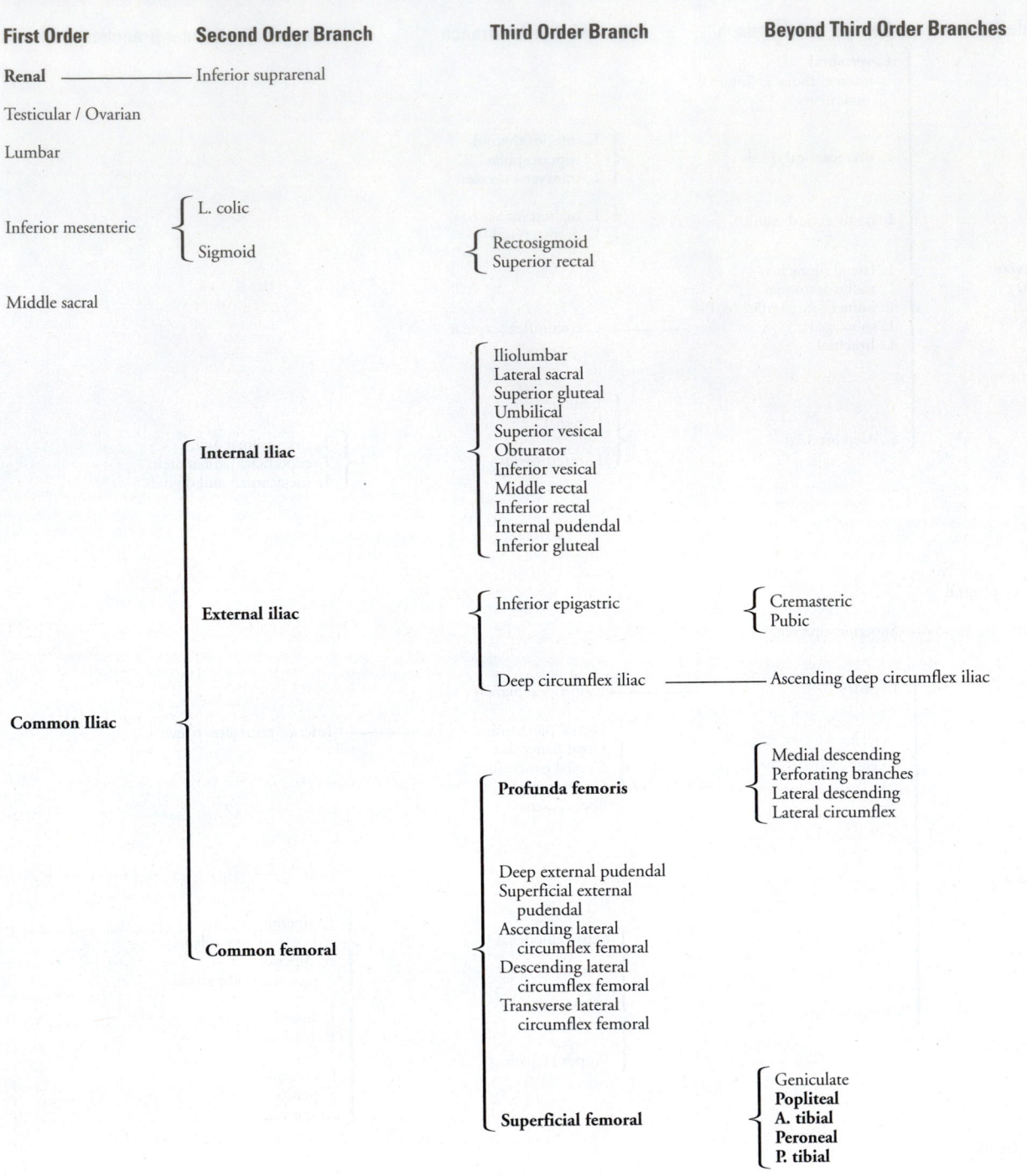

First Order — **Second Order Branch** — **Third Order Branch** — **Beyond Third Order Branches**

Renal —————— Inferior suprarenal

Testicular / Ovarian

Lumbar

Inferior mesenteric
{
L. colic

Sigmoid —— { Rectosigmoid / Superior rectal
}

Middle sacral

Common Iliac
{
Internal iliac — {
Iliolumbar
Lateral sacral
Superior gluteal
Umbilical
Superior vesical
Obturator
Inferior vesical
Middle rectal
Inferior rectal
Internal pudendal
Inferior gluteal
}

External iliac — {
Inferior epigastric — { Cremasteric / Pubic }

Deep circumflex iliac ————— Ascending deep circumflex iliac
}

Common femoral — {
Profunda femoris — {
Medial descending
Perforating branches
Lateral descending
Lateral circumflex
}

Deep external pudendal
Superficial external pudendal
Ascending lateral circumflex femoral
Descending lateral circumflex femoral
Transverse lateral circumflex femoral

Superficial femoral — {
Geniculate
Popliteal
A. tibial
Peroneal
P. tibial
}
}
}

R. & L. main pulmonary arteries
(venous selective)

Reference: Kadir S. *Atlas of Normal and Variant Angiographic Anatomy.* Philadephia, Pa: WB Saunders Co; 1991.
R = right, L = left, A = anterior, P = posterior

Appendix M

Summary of Crosswalked Deleted CPT Codes

This listing is a summary of crosswalked deleted and renumbered codes and descriptors with the associated CPT Assistant references for the deleted codes

Current Code(s)	Deleted/Former Code	Year Code Deleted	Citations Referencing Former Code— Applicable To Current Code(s)
89240	0058T	2009	Jun 04:8 CPT Changes: An Insider's View 2004
89240	0059T	2009	CPT Changes: An Insider's View 2004
41530	0088T	2009	May 05:7, Sep 05:9 CPT Changes: An Insider's View 2005
95803	0089T	2009	Jun 05:6, Feb 06:1 CPT Changes: An Insider's View 2006
22856	0090T	2009	Jun 05:6, Feb 06:1 CPT Changes: An Insider's View 2006, 2007
22864	0093T	2009	Jun 05:6, Feb 06:1 CPT Changes: An Insider's View 2006, 2007
22861	0096T	2009	Jun 05:6, Feb 06:1 CPT Changes: An Insider's View 2006, 2007
55706	0137T	2009	CPT Changes: An Insider's View 2006
95980-95982	0162T	2009	CPT Changes: An Insider's View 2007
1123F, 1124F	1080F	2009	CPT Changes: An Insider's View 2008
0054T, 0055T	20986	2009	CPT Changes: An Insider's View 2008
0054T, 0055T	20987	2009	CPT Changes: An Insider's View 2008
4177F	4007F	2009	CPT Changes: An Insider's View 2008
52214	52606	2009	Apr 01:4
52601	52612	2009	Apr 01:4
52601	52614	2009	Apr 01:4
52630	52620	2009	Apr 01:4
61796-61800, 63620, 63621	61793	2009	Nov 97:23, May 03:19, Apr 04:15, Jan 06:46
77785, 77786	77781	2009	Winter 90:10, Winter 91:23, Mar 99:3, Feb 02:7, Mar 02:2, Sep 05:1, Nov 05:15
77785-77787	77782	2009	Winter 90:10, Winter 91:23, Mar 99:3, Feb 02:7, Mar 02:2, Sep 05:1, Nov 05:15
77785-77787	77783	2009	Winter 90:10, Winter 91:23, Mar 99:3, Feb 02:7, Mar 02:2, Sep 05:1, Nov 05:15
77785-77787	77784	2009	Winter 90:10, Winter 91:23, Mar 99:3, Feb 02:7, Mar 02:2, Sep 05:1, Nov 05:15
88720	88400	2009	Aug 05:9
96360	90760	2009	Nov 05:1, Jul 06:4, Sep 06:14, Dec 06:14 CPT Changes: An Insider's View 2006, 2008
96361	90761	2009	Nov 05:1, Jul 06:4, Sep 06:14, Dec 06:14, Mar 07:10 CPT Changes: An Insider's View 2006, 2007
96365	90765	2009	Nov 05:1, Sep 06:14, Nov 06:22, Dec 06:14 CPT Changes: An Insider's View 2006
96366	90766	2009	Nov 05:1, Sep 06:14, Dec 06:14, Mar 07:10 CPT Changes: An Insider's View 2006, 2007
96367	90767	2009	Nov 05:1, Sep 06:14, Nov 06:22, Dec 06:14 CPT Changes: An Insider's View 2006
96368	90768	2009	Nov 05:1, Aug 06:11, Sep 06:14, Nov 06:22, Dec 06:14 CPT Changes: An Insider's View 2006
96369	90769	2009	CPT Changes: An Insider's View 2008
96370	90770	2009	CPT Changes: An Insider's View 2008
96371	90771	2009	CPT Changes: An Insider's View 2008
96372	90772	2009	Nov 05:1, Sep 06:14, Dec 06:14 CPT Changes: An Insider's View 2006
96373	90773	2009	Nov 05:1, Sep 06:14, Dec 06:14 CPT Changes: An Insider's View 2006
96374	90774	2009	Nov 05:1, Sep 06:14, Dec 06:14 CPT Changes: An Insider's View 2006

Current Code(s)	Deleted/Former Code	Year Code Deleted	Citations Referencing Former Code— Applicable To Current Code(s)
96375	90775	2009	Nov 05:1, Sep 06:14, Dec 06:14 CPT Changes: An Insider's View 2006
96376	90776	2009	CPT Changes: An Insider's View 2008
96379	90779	2009	Nov 05:1, Sep 06:14, Dec 06:14 CPT Changes: An Insider's View 2006
90951-90953, 90963, 90967	90918	2009	Fall 93:5, May 96:4, May 02:17, Jan 03:22
90954-90956, 90964, 90968	90919	2009	Fall 93:5, May 96:5, May 02:17, Jan 03:22
90957-90959, 90965, 90969	90920	2009	Fall 93:5, May 96:5, May 02:17, Jan 03:22
90960-90962, 90966, 90970	90921	2009	Fall 93:5, May 96:5, May 02:17, Jan 03:22
90951-90953, 90963, 90967	90922	2009	Fall 93:5, May 96:5, May 02:17, Jan 03:22
90954-90956, 90964, 90968	90923	2009	May 96:5, May 02:17, Jan 03:22
90957-90959, 90965, 90969	90924	2009	May 96:5, May 02:17, Jan 03:22
90960-90962, 90966, 90970	90925	2009	May 96:5, May 02:17, Jan 03:22
93285, 93291, 93298	93727	2009	Nov 99:50, Jul 00:5 CPT Changes: An Insider's View 2000
93280, 93288, 93294	93731	2009	Summer 94:23, Feb 98:11
93280, 93288, 93294	93732	2009	Summer 94:23, Feb 98:11, Mar 00:10
93293	93733	2009	Summer 94:23
93279, 93288, 93294	93734	2009	Summer 94:23, Feb 98:11
93279, 93288, 93294	93735	2009	Summer 94:23, Feb 98:11
93293	93736	2009	Summer 94:23
93282, 93289, 93292, 93295	93741	2009	Nov 99:50-51, Jul 00:5, Nov 00:9, Sep 05:8 CPT Changes: An Insider's View 2000, 2005
93282, 93289, 93292, 93295	93742	2009	Nov 99:50-51, Jul 00:5, Nov 00:9 CPT Changes: An Insider's View 2000, 2005
93283, 93289, 93295	93743	2009	Nov 99:50-51, Jul 00:5, Nov 00:9, Sep 05:8 CPT Changes: An Insider's View 2000
93283, 93289, 93295	93744	2009	Nov 99:50-51, Jul 00:5, Nov 00:9 CPT Changes: An Insider's View 2000
99466	99289	2009	May 05:1, Jul 06:4 CPT Changes: An Insider's View 2002, 2003
99467	99290	2009	CPT Changes: An Insider's View 2002
99471	99293	2009	Feb 03:15, Oct 03:2, Aug 04:7, 10, May 05:1, Nov 05:10, Jul 06:4, Apr 07:3 CPT Changes: An Insider's View 2003, 2004, 2005
99472	99294	2009	Feb 03:15, Oct 03:2, Aug 04:7, Nov 05:10, Jul 06:4, Apr 07:3 CPT Changes: An Insider's View 2003, 2004, 2005
99468	99295	2009	Summer 93:1, Nov 97:4-5, Mar 98:11, Nov 99:5-6, Dec 00:14, Feb 03:15, Oct 03:1, May 05:1, Nov 05:10, CPT Changes: An Insider's View 2000, 2003, 2004, 2005
99469	99296	2009	Summer 93:1, Nov 97:4-5, Mar 98:11, Nov 99:5-6, Dec 00:14, Feb 03:15, Oct 03:1, Nov 05:10, CPT Changes: An Insider's View 2000, 2003, 2004, 2005, 2008

Current Code(s)	Deleted/Former Code	Year Code Deleted	Citations Referencing Former Code— Applicable To Current Code(s)
99478	99298	2009	Nov 98:2-3, Nov 99:5-6, Aug 00:4, Dec 00:15, Oct 03:2, May 05:1, Nov 05:10; CPT Changes: An Insider's View 2000, 2003
99479	99299	2009	Oct 03:2, Nov 05:10; CPT Changes: An Insider's View 2003
99480	99300	2009	CPT Changes: An Insider's View 2006
99460	99431	2009	Apr 97:10, Nov 97:9, Sep 98:5, Apr 04:14, May 05:1
99461	99432	2009	Sep 98:5, May 99:11, Apr 04:14
99462	99433	2009	Sep 98:5, Apr 03:27
99463	99435	2009	Sep 98:5, Apr 04:14
99464	99436	2009	Nov 97:9-10, Sep 98:5, Nov 99:5-6, Aug 00:3, Aug 04:9, Nov 05:15
99465	99440	2009	Summer 93:3, Mar 96:10, Nov 97:9, Sep 98:5, Nov 99:5-6, Aug 00:3, Oct 03:3, Aug 04:9, Apr 07:3
20985-20987	0054T	2008	May 04:14, Jun 04:8 CPT Changes: An Insider's View 2004
20985-20987	0055T	2008	May 04:14, Jun 04:8 CPT Changes: An Insider's View 2004, 2005
20985-20987	0056T	2008	May 04:14, Jun 04:8 CPT Changes: An Insider's View 2004
99174	0065T	2008	Mar 05:1, 3-4 CPT Changes: An Insider's View 2005
99444	0074T	2008	May 05:7, Sep 05:6 CPT Changes: An Insider's View 2005
99605-99607	0115T	2008	CPT Changes: An Insider's View 2006
99605-99607	0116T	2008	CPT Changes: An Insider's View 2006
99605-99607	0117T	2008	CPT Changes: An Insider's View 2006
50593	0135T	2008	CPT Changes: An Insider's View 2006, Clinical Examples in Radiology Winter 06:18
34806	0153T	2008	CPT Changes: An Insider's View 2007, Clinical Examples in Radiology Winter 06:19
93982	0154T	2008	CPT Changes: An Insider's View 2007, Clinical Examples in Radiology Winter 06:19
01935, 01936	01905	2008	Mar 06:15 CPT Changes: An Insider's View 2002
24357-24359	24350	2008	
24357-24359	24351	2008	
24357-24359	24352	2008	
24357-24359	24354	2008	
24357-24359	24356	2008	
3044F-3045F	3047F	2008	CPT Changes: An Insider's View 2007
3074F-3075F	3076F	2008	CPT Changes: An Insider's View 2007
32421	32000	2008	Spring 91:4, Winter 92:20
32422	32002	2008	Nov 03:14
32560	32005	2008	
32550	32019	2008	CPT Changes: An Insider's View 2005
32551	32020	2008	Fall 92:13, Nov 03:14
36591	36540	2008	Jan 02:11, Nov 02:3, Apr 03:26, Nov 05:1 CPT Changes: An Insider's View 2001, 2003
36593	36550	2008	Nov 99:20, Nov 05:1 CPT Changes: An Insider's View 2000
49203-49205, 58957, 58958	49200	2008	CPT Changes: An Insider's View 2003
49203-49205, 58957, 58958	49201	2008	
51100	51000	2008	Nov 99:32-33, Aug 00:3, Oct 03:2
51101	51005	2008	
51102	51010	2008	
60300	60001	2008	

Current Code(s)	Deleted/Former Code	Year Code Deleted	Citations Referencing Former Code— Applicable To Current Code(s)
67041, 67042, 67043	67038	2008	Aug 03:15, Sep 05:12
75557-75564	75552	2008	Fall 95:2
75557-75564	75553	2008	Fall 95:2
75557-75564	75554	2008	Fall 95:2
75557-75564	75555	2008	Fall 95:2
75557-75564	75556	2008	Fall 95:2
78610	78615	2008	CPT Changes: An Insider's View 2002
86356, 86486	86586	2008	Jul 98:11
99365-99368	99361	2008	May 05:1
99365-99368	99362	2008	
99441-99443	99371	2008	Spring 94:34, May 00:11, May 05:1, Nov 05:10
99441-99443	99372	2008	Spring 94:34, May 00:11, Nov 05:10
99441-99443	99373	2008	Spring 94:34, May 00:11, Nov 05:10
0160T, 0161T	0018T	2007	CPT Changes: An Insider's View 2002
96904	0044T	2007	CPT Changes: An Insider's View 2003, 2004
96904	0045T	2007	Jul 04:7 CPT Changes: An Insider's View 2004
77371-77373	0082T	2007	CPT Changes: An Insider's View 2005
77371-77373	0083T	2007	CPT Changes: An Insider's View 2005
22857	0091T	2007	CPT Changes: An Insider's View 2006
22865	0094T	2007	CPT Changes: An Insider's View 2006
22862	0097T	2007	CPT Changes: An Insider's View 2006
19105	0120T	2007	CPT Changes: An Insider's View 2006
15002, 15004	15000	2007	Fall 93:7, Apr 97:4, Aug 97:6, Sep 97:2, Nov 98:5, Jan 99:4, Apr 99:10, May 99:10, Nov 02:7, Aug 03:14 CPT Changes: An Insider's View 2001, 2006
15003, 15005	15001	2007	Nov 98:5-6, Jan 99:4, May 99:10, Aug 03:14
15830, 15847, 17999	15831	2007	May 01:11 CPT Changes: An Insider's View 2007
17311	17304	2007	Winter 94:19, Mar 99:11, Jun 99:10, Nov 02:7, Nov 03:15, Feb 04:11, Jul 04:2 CPT Changes: An Insider's View 2003
17312, 17314	17305	2007	Winter 94:19, Mar 99:11, Jun 99:10, Nov 02:7, Feb 04:11, Jul 04:3
17312, 17314	17306	2007	Winter 94:19, Mar 99:11, Jun 99:10, Nov 02:7, Feb 04:11, Jul 04:4
17312, 17314	17307	2007	Winter 94:19, Mar 99:11, Jun 99:10, Nov 02:7, Nov 03:15, Feb 04:11, Jul 04:4
17315	17310	2007	Winter 94:19, Mar 99:11, Jun 99:10, Nov 02:7, Feb 04:11, May 04:14, Jul 04:4 CPT Changes: An Insider's View 2003
19300	19140	2007	Feb 96:9, Apr 05:13
19301	19160	2007	Apr 05:7 CPT Changes: An Insider's View 2005
19302	19162	2007	Jun 00:11, Apr 05:7
19303	19180	2007	Apr 05:7
19304	19182	2007	Apr 05:7
19305	19200	2007	Apr 05:7
19306	19220	2007	Apr 05:7
19307	19240	2007	Apr 05:7
25606	25611	2007	Fall 93:23, Oct 99:5
25607-25609	25620	2007	
26390	26504	2007	

Current Code(s)	Deleted/Former Code	Year Code Deleted	Citations Referencing Former Code— Applicable To Current Code(s)
27325	27315	2007	
27326	27320	2007	
28055	28030	2007	
33254-33256	33253	2007	
35302-35306	35381	2007	
35506	35507	2007	
35537, 35538	35541	2007	
35539, 35540	35546	2007	
35637, 35638	35641	2007	Dec 01:7
44799	44152	2007	
44799	44153	2007	
47719	47716	2007	
48105	48005	2007	
48548	48180	2007	
49402	49085	2007	
54150	54152	2007	Sep 96:11, Dec 96:10, May 98:11, Apr 03:27 CPT Changes: An Insider's View 2007
54865	54820	2007	Oct 01:8
55875	55859	2007	Apr 04:6
56442	56720	2007	
57558	57820	2007	
67346	67350	2007	
77001	75998	2007	Dec 04:12-13 CPT Changes: An Insider's View 2004 Clinical Examples in Radiology Inaugural 04:1-2, Winter 05:9
77002	76003	2007	Fall 93:14, Jul 01:7 CPT Changes: An Insider's View 2001 Clinical Examples in Radiology Spring 05:5-6
77003	76005	2007	Nov 99:32, 34, 41, Jan 00:2, Feb 00:6, Aug 00:8, Sep 02:11, Sep 04:5 CPT Changes: An Insider's View 2000
77071	76006	2007	Nov 98:21 CPT Changes: An Insider's View 2003
72291	76012	2007	Mar 01:2 CPT Changes: An Insider's View 2001, 2006
72292	76013	2007	Mar 01:2 CPT Changes: An Insider's View 2001
77072	76020	2007	
77073	76040	2007	
77074	76061	2007	
77075	76062	2007	
77076	76065	2007	
77077	76066	2007	CPT Changes: An Insider's View 2002
77078	76070	2007	Nov 97:24 CPT Changes: An Insider's View 2002, 2003
77079	76071	2007	CPT Changes: An Insider's View 2003
77080	76075	2007	Nov 97:24, Jun 03:11 CPT Changes: An Insider's View 2005
77081	76076	2007	Nov 97:24
77082	76077	2007	CPT Changes: An Insider's View 2005
77083	76078	2007	Nov 97:24 CPT Changes: An Insider's View 2002
77051	76082	2007	CPT Changes: An Insider's View 2004
77052	76083	2007	CPT Changes: An Insider's View 2004
77053	76086	2007	

Current Code(s)	Deleted/Former Code	Year Code Deleted	Citations Referencing Former Code— Applicable To Current Code(s)
77054	76088	2007	
77055	76090	2007	Jul 96:6, Jun 99:10 CPT Changes: An Insider's View 2004
77056	76091	2007	Jul 96:6 CPT Changes: An Insider's View 2004
77057	76092	2007	Jul 96:6, Jun 99:10 CPT Changes: An Insider's View 2004
77058	76093	2007	
77059	76094	2007	
77031	76095	2007	Apr 96:9, Nov 97:24, Jan 01:9 CPT Changes: An Insider's View 2001
77032	76096	2007	Jan 01:10 CPT Changes: An Insider's View 2001
77011	76355	2007	CPT Changes: An Insider's View 2002, 2003
77012	76360	2007	Fall 93:12, Fall 94:2, Jan 01:9-10, Mar 05:2 CPT Changes: An Insider's View 2001, 2002, 2003
77013	76362	2007	Oct 02:4 CPT Changes: An Insider's View 2002, 2004
77014	76370	2007	Fall 91:12 CPT Changes: An Insider's View 2002, 2003
77021	76393	2007	Jan 01:10, Mar 05:2 CPT Changes: An Insider's View 2001, 2002
77022	76394	2007	Oct 02:4, Mar 05:5 CPT Changes: An Insider's View 2002, 2004
77084	76400	2007	
76775, 76776	76778	2007	CPT Changes: An Insider's View 2002
76998	76986	2007	CPT Changes: An Insider's View 2001
78707-78709	78704	2007	
78701-78709	78715	2007	
78761	78760	2007	
92700	92573	2007	
94002, 94004	94656	2007	Fall 92:30, Spring 95:4, Summer 95:4, Feb 96:9, Aug 00:2, Oct 03:2
94003, 94004	94657	2007	Fall 92:30, Spring 95:4, Summer 95:4, Feb 96:9, Aug 00:2, Oct 03:2

Appendix N

Summary of Resequenced CPT Codes

This is a summary of CPT codes that do not appear in numeric sequence in the listing of CPT codes. Rather than deleting and renumbering, resequencing allows existing codes to be relocated to an appropriate location for the code concept, regardless of the numeric sequence. The codes listed below are identified in *CPT 2010* with a # symbol for location of the resequenced number within the family of related concepts. Numerically placed references (eg, **Code is out of numerical sequence. See…**) are used as navigational alerts to direct the user to the location of the out-of-sequence code.

21552	27337
21554	27339
23071	27632
23073	27634
24071	28039
24073	28041
25071	46220
25073	46320
26111	46945
26113	46946
27043	46947
27045	51797
27059	82652
27329	

Notes

Index

Instructions for the Use of the CPT Index

Main Terms

The index is organized by main terms. Each main term can stand alone, or be followed by up to three modifying terms. There are four primary classes of main entries:

1. Procedure or service.
   For example: Endoscopy; Anastomosis; Splint

2. Organ or other anatomic site.
   For example: Tibia; Colon; Salivary Gland

3. Condition.
   For example: Abscess; Entropion; Tetralogy of Fallot

4. Synonyms, Eponyms, and Abbreviations.
   For example: EEG; Bricker Operation; Clagett Procedure

Modifying Terms

A main term may be followed by a series of up to three indented terms that modify the main term. When modifying terms appear, one should review the list, as these subterms do have an effect on the selection of the appropriate code for the procedure.

Code Ranges

Whenever more than one code applies to a given index entry, a code range is listed. If several non-sequential codes apply, they will be separated by a comma. For example:

Esophagus
    Reconstruction 43300, 43310, 43313

If two or more sequential codes apply, they will be separated by a hyphen. For example:

Debridement
    Burns 01951-01953, 16020-16030

Conventions

As a space saving convention, certain words infer some meaning. This convention is primarily used when a procedure or service is listed as a subterm. For example:

Knee
    Incision (of)

In this example, the word in parentheses (of) does not appear in the index, but it is inferred. As another example:

Pancreas
    Anesthesia (for procedures on)

In this example, as there is no such entity as pancreas anesthesia, the words in parentheses are inferred. That is, anesthesia for procedures on the pancreas.

The alphabetic index is NOT a substitute for the main text of the CPT codebook. Even if only one code appears, the user must refer to the main text to ensure that the code selection is accurate.

Index

A

A Vitamin
See Vitamin, A

A-II
See Angiotensin II

Abbe-Estlander Procedure
See Reconstruction; Repair, Cleft Lip

Abdomen
Abdominal Aorta
   Angiography 75635
Abdominal Wall
   Removal
      Mesh............................11008
      Prosthesis 11008
   Repair
      Hernia 49491-49496, 49501,
              49507, 49521, 49590
   Tumor
      Excision 22900-22903
      Radical Resection 22904-22905
   Unlisted Services and Procedures 22999
Abscess
   Incision and Drainage 49020, 49040
      Open 49040
      Percutaneous 49021
Angiography 74175, 75635
Artery
   Ligation 37617
Biopsy 49000
Bypass Graft 35907
Cannula/Catheter
   Removal 49422
Celiotomy
   for Staging 49220
CT Scan 74150-74175, 75635
Cyst
   Destruction/Excision 49203-49205
Drainage
   Fluid 49080-49081
Ectopic Pregnancy 59130
Endometrioma
   Destruction/Excision 49203-49205
Exploration 49000-49002
   Blood Vessel 35840
   Staging 58960
Incision 49000
   Staging 58960
Incision and Drainage
   Pancreatitis 48000
Infraumbilical Panniculectomy 15830
Injection
   Air 49400
   Contrast Material 49400
Insertion
   Catheter 49419-49421, 49324
   Venous Shunt 49425
Intraperitoneal
   Catheter Exit Site 49436
   Catheter Insertion 49324, 49435
   Catheter Removal 49422
   Catheter Revision 49325
Shunt
   Ligation 49428
   Removal 49429

Laparotomy
   Staging 49220
Magnetic Resonance Imaging
(MRI) 74181-74183
Needle Biopsy
   Mass 49180
Peritoneocentesis 49080-49081
Radical Resection 51597
Radiation Therapy
   Placement of Guidance
   Devices 49410-49411
Repair
   Blood Vessel 35221
      with Other Graft 35281
      with Vein Graft 35251
   Hernia 49491-49525, 49560-49587
   Suture 49900
Revision
   Venous Shunt 49426
Suture 49900
Tumor
   Destruction/Excision 49203-49205
Ultrasound 76700-76705
Unlisted Services and Procedures 49999
Wound Exploration
   Penetrating 20102
X-ray 74000-74022

Abdominal
Aorta
   See Abdomen, Abdominal Aorta; Aorta,
   Abdominal
Aortic Aneurysm
   See Aorta, Abdominal, Aneurysm
Deliveries
   See Caesarean Delivery
Hysterectomy
   See Hysterectomy, Abdominal
Lymphangiogram
   See Lymphangiography, Abdomen
Paracentesis
   See Abdomen, Drainage
Radiographies
   See Abdomen, X-ray
Wall
   See Abdomen, Abdominal Wall
   Debridement
      Infected 11005-11006
   Reconstruction 49905
   Removal
      Mesh 11008
      Prosthesis 11008
   Surgery 22999
   Tumor
      Excision 22900-22903

Abdominohysterectomy
See Hysterectomy, Abdominal

Abdominopelvic Amputation
See Amputation, Interpelviabdominal

Abdominoplasty
See Panniculectomy
Excision 15830, 15847

Ablation
Anal
   Polyp 46615
   Tumor 46615
Bone
   Tumor 20982

Colon
   Tumor 45339
Cryosurgical
   Fibroadenoma 19105
   Renal Mass 50250
   Renal Tumor
      Percutaneous 50593
CT Scan Guidance 77013
Endometrial 58353-58356, 58563
Endometrium
   Ultrasound Guidance 58356
Heart
   Arrhythmogenic Focus 93650-93652
      See Cardiology; Diagnostic, Intracardiac
      Pacing and Mapping
   Atrioventricular Node Function 93650
Liver
   Tumor
      Laparoscopic 47370-47371
      Open 47380-47382
Lung
   Tumor
      Radiofrequency 32998
Magnetic Resonance Guidance 77022
Parenchymal Tissue
   CT Scan Guidance 77013
Prostate 55873
Pulmonary Tumor 32998
Radiofrequency 32998
Renal Cyst 50541
Renal Mass 50542
   Radiofrequency 50592
Renal Tumor
   Cryotherapy
      Percutaneous 50593
Tongue Base
   Radiofrequency 41530
Turbinate Mucosa 30801-30802
Ultrasound
   Guidance 76940
   Uterine Tumor 0071T-0072T
Uterine Tumor
   Ultrasound, Focused 0071T-0072T
Vein
   Endovenous 36475-36479

Abortion
See Obstetrical Care
Incomplete 59812
Induced
   by Dilation and Curettage 59840
   by Dilation and Evacuation 59841
   by Saline 59850-59851
   by Vaginal Suppositories 59855-59856
   with Hysterectomy 59100, 59852, 59857
Missed
   First Trimester 59820
   Second Trimester 59821
Septic 59830
Spontaneous 59812
Therapeutic
   by Saline 59850
      with Dilation and Curettage 59851
      with Hysterectomy 59852

Abrasion
Skin
   Chemical Peel 15788-15793
   Dermabrasion 15780-15783
   Lesion 15786-15787

Abscess

Abdomen 49040-49041
  Incision and Drainage
    Open 49040
    Percutaneous 49021
Anal
  Incision and Drainage 46045-46050
Ankle 27603
Appendix
  Incision and Drainage 44900
    Open 44900
    Percutaneous 44901
Arm, Lower 25028
  Excision 25145
  Incision and Drainage 25035
Arm, Upper
  Incision and Drainage 23930-23935
Auditory Canal, External 69020
Bartholin's Gland
  Incision and Drainage 56420
Bladder
  Incision and Drainage 51080
Brain
  Drainage 61150-61151
  Excision 61514, 61522
  Incision and Drainage 61320-61321
Breast
  Incision and Drainage 19020
Carpals
  Incision, Deep 25035
Clavicle
  Sequestrectomy 23170
Drainage
  with X-ray 75989
Ear, External
  Complicated 69005
  Simple 69000
Elbow
  Incision and Drainage 23930-23935
Epididymis
  Incision and Drainage 54700
Excision
  Olecranon Process 24138
  Radius 24136
  Ulna 24138
Eyelid
  Incision and Drainage 67700
Facial Bones
  Excision 21026
Finger 26010-26011
  Incision and Drainage 26034
Foot
  Incision 28005
Gums
  Incision and Drainage 41800
Hand
  Incision and Drainage 26034
Hematoma
  Incision and Drainage 27603
Hip
  Incision and Drainage 26990-26992
Humeral Head 23174
Humerus
  Excision 24134
  Incision and Drainage 23935
Kidney
  Incision and Drainage 50020
    Open 50020
    Percutaneous 50021
Leg, Lower
  Incision and Drainage 27603

Liver 47010
  Drainage
    Open 47010
    Injection 47015
    Repair 47300
  Localization
    Nuclear Medicine 78806-78807
Lung
  Percutaneous Drainage 32200-32201
Lymph Node
  Incision and Drainage 38300-38305
Lymphocele Drainage 49062
Mandible
  Excision 21025
Mouth
  Incision and Drainage 40800-40801,
             41005-41009, 41015-41018
Nasal Septum
  Incision and Drainage 30020
Neck
  Incision and Drainage 21501-21502
Ovarian
  Incision and Drainage 58820-58822
    Abdominal Approach 58822
    Vaginal Approach 58820
Ovary
  Drainage
    Percutaneous 58823
Palate
  Incision and Drainage 42000
Paraurethral Gland
  Incision and Drainage 53060
Parotid Gland Drainage 42300-42305
Pelvic
  Drainage
    Percutaneous 58823
Pelvis
  Incision and Drainage 26990-26992, 45000
Pericolic
  Drainage
    Percutaneous 58823
Perineum
  Incision and Drainage 56405
Perirenal or Renal
  Drainage 50020-50021
    Percutaneous 50021
Peritoneum
  Incision and Drainage
    Open 49020
    Percutaneous 49021
Prostate
  Incision and Drainage 55720-55725
  Transurethral Drainage 52700
Radius
  Incision, Deep 25035
Rectum
  Incision and Drainage 45005-45020,
               46040, 46060
Retroperitoneal 49060-49061
  Drainage
    Open 49060
    Percutaneous 49061
Salivary Gland
  Drainage 42300-42320
Scapula
  Sequestrectomy 23172
Scrotum
  Incision and Drainage 54700, 55100
Shoulder
  Drainage 23030
Skene's Gland
  Incision and Drainage 53060

Skin
  Incision and Drainage 10060-10061
  Puncture Aspiration 10160
Soft Tissue
  Incision 20000-20005
Spine
  Incision and Drainage 22010-22015
Subdiaphragmatic 49040-49041
Sublingual Gland
  Drainage 42310-42320
Submaxillary Gland
  Drainage 42310-42320
Subphrenic 49040-49041
Testis
  Incision and Drainage 54700
Thoracostomy 32551
Thorax
  Incision and Drainage 21501-21502
Throat
  Incision and Drainage 42700-42725
Tongue
  Incision and Drainage 41000-41006
Tonsil
  Incision and Drainage 42700
Ulna
  Incision, Deep 25035
Urethra
  Incision and Drainage 53040
Uvula
  Incision and Drainage 42000
Vagina
  Incision and Drainage 57010
Vulva
  Incision and Drainage 56405
Wrist
  Excision 25145
  Incision and Drainage 25028, 25035
X-ray 76080

Abscess, Nasal
See Nose, Abscess

Abscess, Parotid Gland
See Parotid Gland, Abscess

Absorptiometry
Dual Energy 3095F-3096F
  Bone
    Appendicular 77081
    Axial Skeleton 77080
    Vertebral 77082
Dual Photon
  Bone 78351
Radiographic
  Photodensity 77083
Single Photon
  Bone 78350

Absorption Spectrophotometry, Atomic
See Atomic Absorption Spectroscopy

Accessory Nerve, Spinal
See Nerves, Spinal Accessory

Accessory, Toes
See Polydactyly, Toes

ACE
See Angiotensin Converting Enzyme (ACE), Performance Measures

Acetabuloplasty 27120-27122

Acetabulum
Fracture
    Closed Treatment 27220-27222
    Open Treatment 27226-27228
    with Manipulation 27222
    without Manipulation 27220
Reconstruction 27120
    with Resection, Femoral Head 27122
Tumor
    Excision .27076

Acetaldehyde
Blood 82000

Acetaminophen
Urine 82003

Acetic Anhydrides 84600

Acetone
Blood or Urine 82009-82010

Acetone Body 82009-82010

Acetylcholinesterase
Blood or Urine 82013

AcG
See Clotting Factor

Achilles Tendon
Incision 27605-27606
Lengthening 27612
Repair 27650-27654

Achillotomy
See Tenotomy, Achilles Tendon

Acid
Gastric 82926-82928

Acid Diethylamide, Lysergic
See Lysergic Acid Diethylamide

Acid Fast Bacilli (AFB)
Culture 87116

Acid Fast Bacillus Culture
See Culture, Acid Fast Bacilli

Acid Fast Stain 88312

Acid Perfusion Test
Esophagus .91012, 91030

Acid Phosphatase 84060-84066

Acid Probes, Nucleic
See Nucleic Acid Probe

Acid Reflux Test
Esophagus 91034-91038

Acid, Adenylic
See Adenosine Monophosphate (AMP)

Acid, Aminolevulinic
See Aminolevulinic Acid (ALA)

Acid, Ascorbic
See Ascorbic Acid

Acid, Deoxyribonucleic
See Deoxyribonucleic Acid

Acid, Folic
See Folic Acid

Acid, Glycocholic
See Cholylglycine

Acid, Lactic
See Lactic Acid

Acid, N-Acetylneuraminic
See Sialic Acid

Acid, Phenylethylbarbituric
See Phenobarbital

Acid, Uric
See Uric Acid

Acidity/Alkalinity
See pH

Acids, Amino
See Amino Acids

Acids, Bile
See Bile Acids

Acids, Fatty
See Fatty Acid

Acids, Guanylic
See Guanosine Monophosphate

Acids, N-Acetylneuraminic
See Sialic Acid

Acne Surgery
Incision and Drainage
    Abscess 10060-10061
    Comedones 10040
    Cyst 10040
    Milia, Multiple 10040
    Pustules 10040

Acne Treatment
Abrasion .15786-15787
Chemical Peel 15788-15793
Cryotherapy 17340
Dermabrasion 15780-15783
Exfoliation
    Chemical 17360

Acoustic Evoked Brain Stem Potential
See Evoked Potential, Auditory Brainstem

Acoustic Neuroma
See Brain, Tumor, Excision; Brainstem; Mesencephalon; Skull Base Surgery

Acoustic Recording
Heart Sounds
    with Computer Analysis 93799

Acromioclavicular Joint
Arthrocentesis 20605
Arthrotomy 23044
    with Biopsy .23101
Dislocation 23540-23552
    Open Treatment 23550-23552
X-ray 73050

Acromion
Excision
    Shoulder 23130

Acromionectomy
Partial 23130

Acromioplasty 23415-23420
Partial 23130

ACTH
See Adrenocorticotropic Hormone (ACTH)

ACTH Releasing Factor
See Corticotropic Releasing Hormone (CRH)

Actigraphy
Sleep Study 95803

Actinomyces
Antibody 86602

Actinomycosis 86000

Actinomycotic Infection
See Actinomycosis

Actinotherapy 0168T, 96900
See Dermatology

Activated Factor X
See Thrombokinase

Activated Partial Thromboplastin Time
See Thromboplastin, Partial, Time

Activation, Lymphocyte
See Blastogenesis

Activities of Daily Living
See Physical Medicine/Therapy/Occupational Therapy

Activity, Glomerular Procoagulant
See Thromboplastin

Acupuncture
with Electrical Stimulation 97813-97814
without Electrical Stimulation 97810-97811

Acute Poliomyelitis
See Polio

Acylcarnitines 82016-82017

Adamantinoma, Pituitary
See Craniopharyngioma

Addam Operation
See Dupuytren's Contracture

Adductor Tenotomy of Hip
See Tenotomy, Hip, Adductor

Adenoidectomy
See Adenoids, Excision

Adenoids
Excision 42830-42836
    with Tonsils 42820-42821
Unlisted Services and Procedures 42999

Adenoma
Pancreas
    Excision 48120
Parathyroid
    Localization
        Injection Procedure 78808
Thyroid Gland Excision 60200

Adenosine 3'5' Monophosphate
See Cyclic AMP

Adenosine Diphosphate
Blood 82030

Adenosine Monophosphate (AMP)
Blood 82030

Adenovirus
Antibody 86603
Antigen Detection
    Enzyme Immunoassay 87301
    Immunofluorescense 87260

Adenovirus Vaccine
See Vaccines

Adenylic Acid
See Adenosine Monophosphate (AMP)

ADH
See Antidiuretic Hormone

Adhesions
Epidural 62263-62264
Eye
    Corneovitreal 65880
    Incision
        Anterior Segment 65860-65870
        Posterior Segment 65875
Intermarginal
    Construction 67880
        Transposition of Tarsal Plate 67882
Intestinal
    Enterolysis 44005
        Laparoscopic 44180
Intracranial
    Lysis 62161
Intrauterine
    Lysis 58559
Labial
    Lysis 56441
Lungs
    Lysis 32124
Pelvic
    Lysis 58660, 58662, 58740
Penile
    Lysis
        Post-circumcision 54162
Preputial
    Lysis 54450
Urethral
    Lysis 53500

Adipectomy
See Lipectomy

ADL
See Activities of Daily Living

Administration
Immunization
    Each Additional
    Vaccine/Toxoid 90472, 90474
        with Counseling 90466, 90468
    One Vaccine/Toxoid 90471, 90473
        with Counseling 90465, 90467

ADP
See Adenosine Diphosphate

ADP Phosphocreatine Phosphotransferase
See CPK

Adrenal Cortex Hormone
See Corticosteroids

Adrenal Gland
Biopsy 60540-60545
Excision
    Laparoscopy 60650
    Retroperitoneal Tumor 60545
Exploration 60540-60545
Nuclear Medicine
    Imaging 78075

Adrenal Medulla
See Medulla

Adrenalectomy 60540
Anesthesia 00866
Laparoscopic 50545

Adrenalin
See Catecholamines
Blood 82383
Urine 82384

Adrenaline-Noradrenaline
Testing 82382-82384

Adrenocorticotropic Hormone (ACTH) 80400-80406, 80412, 80418, 82024
Blood or Urine 82024
Stimulation Panel 80400-80406

Adrenogenital Syndrome ...56805, 57335

Adult T Cell Leukemia Lymphoma Virus I
See HTLV I

Advanced Life Support
See Emergency Department Services
Physician Direction 99288

Advancement
Genioglossus 21199
Tendon
    Foot 28238

Advancement Flap
See Skin, Adjacent Tissue Transfer

Aerosol Inhalation
See Pulmonology, Therapeutic
Pentamidine 94642

AFB
See Acid Fast Bacilli (AFB)

Afferent Nerve
See Sensory Nerve

AFP
See Alpha-Fetoprotein

After Hours Medical Services 99050

Agents, Anticoagulant
See Clotting Inhibitors

Agglutinin
Cold 86156-86157
Febrile 86000

Aggregation
Platelet 85576

AHG
See Clotting Factor

AICD (Pacing Cardioverter-Defibrillator)
See Defibrillator, Heart; Pacemaker, Heart

Aid, Hearing
See Hearing Aid

AIDS Antibodies
See Antibody, HIV

AIDS Virus
See HIV-1

Akin Operation
See Bunion Repair

ALA
See Aminolevulinic Acid (ALA)

Alanine 2 Oxoglutarate Aminotransferase
See Transaminase, Glutamic Pyruvic

Alanine Amino (ALT) 84460

Alanine Transaminase
See Transaminase, Glutamic Pyruvic

Albarran Test
See Water Load Test

Albumin
Ischemia modified 82045
Serum, Plasma or Whole Blood 82040
Urine 82042-82044

Alcohol
Breath 82075
Ethyl
    Blood 82055
    Urine 82055
Ethylene Glycol 82693
Use–See Performance Measures–Preventive Care & Screening–Interventions–Unhealthy Alcohol Use: Sceening

Alcohol Dehydrogenase
See Antidiuretic Hormone

Alcohol, Isopropyl
See Isopropyl Alcohol

Alcohol, Methyl
See Methanol

Aldolase
Blood 82085

Aldosterone
Blood 82088
Suppression Evaluation 80408
Urine 82088

Alimentary Canal
See Gastrointestinal Tract

Alkaline Phosphatase 84075-84080
Leukocyte 85540
WBC 85540

Alkaloids
See Specific Drug
Urine 82101

Anesthesia Local

See Anesthesia, Local

Repair

- Achilles Tendon 27650-27654
- Ligament 27695-27698
- Tendon 27612, 27680-27687

Strapping 29540

Synovium

- Excision 27625-27626

Tenotomy 27605-27606

Tumor

- Excision 27618-27619, 27630-27634
- Radical Resection 27615-27616

Unlisted Services and Procedures 27899

X-ray 73600-73610

- with Contrast 73615

Ankylosis (Surgical)
See Arthrodesis

Annuloplasty
Percutaneous, Intradiscal 22526-22527

Anogenital Region
See Perineum

Anoplasty
Stricture 46700-46705

Anorectal
Biofeedback 90911

Repair

- Fistula 46706-46707

Anorectal Exam (Surgical) 45990

Anorectal Myectomy
See Myomectomy, Anorectal

Anorectovaginoplasty 46744-46746

Anoscopy
Ablation

- Polyp 46615
- Tumor 46615

Biopsy 46606

Dilation 46604

Exploration 46600

Hemorrhage 46614

Removal

- Foreign Body 46608
- Polyp 46610-46612
- Tumor 46610-46612

Antebrachium
See Forearm

Antecedent, Plasma Thromboplastin
See Plasma Thromboplastin, Antecedent

Antepartum Care
Cesarean Delivery 59510

- Previous 59610, 59618

Vaginal Delivery 59425-59426

Anterior Ramus of Thoracic Nerve
See Intercostal Nerve

Anthrax Vaccine
See Vaccines

Anthrogon
See Follicle Stimulating Hormone (FSH)

Anti Australia Antigens
See Antibody, Hepatitis B

Anti D Immunoglobulin
See Immune Globulins, Rho (D)

Anti-Human Globulin Consumption Test
See Coombs Test

Anti-Phospholipid Antibody
See Antibody, Phospholipid

Antiactivator, Plasmin
See Alpha-2 Antiplasmin

Antibiotic Administration
Injection 96372-96379

Prescribed or Dispensed 4120F-4124F

Antibiotic Sensitivity 87181-87184, 87188
Enzyme Detection 87185

Minimum Bactericidal Concentration 87187

Minimum Inhibitory Concentration 87186

Antibodies, Thyroid-Stimulating
See Immunoglobulin, Thyroid Stimulating

Antibodies, Viral
See Viral Antibodies

Antibody
See Antibody Identification; Microsomal Antibody

Actinomyces 86602

Adenovirus 86603

Antinuclear 86038-86039

Antiphosphatidylserine (Phospholipid) 86148

Antiprothrombin 0030T

Antistreptolysin O 86060-86063

Aspergillus 86606

Bacterium 86609

Bartonella 86611

Beta 2 Glycoprotein I 86146

Blastomyces 86612

Blood Crossmatch 86920-86923

Bordetella 86615

Borrelia 86618-86619

Brucella 86622

Campylobacter 86625

Candida 86628

Cardiolipin 86147

Chlamydia 86631-86632

Coccidioides 86635

Coxiella Burnetii 86638

Cryptococcus 86641

Cyclic Citrullinated Peptide (CCP) 86200

Cytomegalovirus 86644-86645

Cytotoxic Screen 86807-86808

Deoxyribonuclease 86215

Deoxyribonucleic Acid (DNA) 86225-86226

Diphtheria 86648

Ehrlichia 86666

Encephalitis 86651-86654

Enterovirus 86658

Epstein-Barr Virus 86663-86665

Fluorescent 86255-86256

Francisella Tularensis 86668

Fungus 86671

Giardia Lamblia 86674

Growth Hormone 86277

Helicobacter Pylori 86677

Helminth 86682

Hemophilus Influenza 86684

Hepatitis

- Delta Agent 86692

Hepatitis A 86708-86709

Hepatitis B

- Core 86704
- IgM 86705
- Surface 86706

Hepatitis Be 86707

Hepatitis C 86803-86804

Herpes Simplex 86694-86696

Heterophile 86308-86310

Histoplasma 86698

HIV 86689, 86701-86703

HIV-1 . . . . 86701, 86703

HIV-2 86702-86703

HTLV-I 86687, 86689

HTLV-II 86688

Influenza Virus 86710

Insulin 86337

Intrinsic Factor 86340

Islet Cell 86341

Legionella 86713

Leishmania 86717

Leptospira 86720

Listeria Monocytogenes 86723

Lyme Disease 86617

Lymphocytic Choriomeningitis 86727

Lymphogranuloma Venereum 86729

Microsomal 86376

Mucormycosis 86732

Mumps 86735

Mycoplasma 86738

Neisseria Meningitidis 86741

Nocardia 86744

Nuclear Antigen 86235

Other Virus 86790

Parvovirus 86747

Phospholipid 86147

Phospholipid Cofactor 0030T

Plasmodium 86750

Platelet 86022-86023

Protozoa 86753

Red Blood Cell 86850-86870

Respiratory Syncytial Virus 86756

Rickettsia 86757

Rotavirus 86759

Rubella 86762

Rubeola 86765

Salmonella 86768

Shigella 86771

Sperm 89325

Streptokinase 86590

Tetanus 86774

Thyroglobulin 86800

Toxoplasma 86777-86778

Treponema Pallidum 86780

Trichinella 86784

Varicella-Zoster 86787

West Nile Virus 86788-86789

White Blood Cell 86021

Yersinia 86793

Antibody Identification
Leukocyte Antibodies 86021

Platelet 86022-86023

Red Blood Cell

- Pretreatment 86970-86972

Serum

- Pretreatment 86975-86978

Antibody Neutralization Test
See Neutralization Test

Antibody Receptor
See FC Receptor

Antibody Screening 86807-86808

Anticoagulant
See Clotting Inhibitors

Anticoagulant Management 99363-99364

Antidiabetic Hormone
See Glucagon

Antidiuretic Hormone Measurement
Vasopressin 84588

AntiDNA Autoantibody
See Antinuclear Antibodies (ANA)

Antigen
Allergen Immunotherapy 95144
Carcinoembryonic 82378
Prostate Specific 84152-84153

Antigen Bronchial Provocation Tests
See Bronchial Challenge Test

Antigen Detection
Direct Fluorescence 87265-87272, 87276,
                   87278, 87280, 87285-87290
  Bordetella 87265
  Chlamydia Trachomatis 87270
  Cryptosporidium 87272
  Cytomegalovirus 87271
  Enterovirus 87267
  Giardia 87269
  Influenza A 87276
  Legionella Pneumophila 87278
  Not Otherwise Specified 87299
  Respiratory Syncytial Virus 87280
  Treponema Pallidum 87285
  Varicella-Zoster 87290
Enzyme Immunoassay 87301-87451
  Adenovirus 87301
  Aspergillus 87305
  Chlamydia Trachomatis 87320
  Clostridium Difficile 87324
  Cryptococcus Neoformans 87327
  Cryptosporidium 87328
  Cytomegalovirus 87332
  Entamoeba Histolytica Dispar Group ...87336
  Entamoeba Histolytica Group 87337
  Escherichia coli 0157 87335
  Giardia 87329
  Helicobacter Pylori 87338-87339
  Hepatitis B Surface Antigen (HBsAg) ...87340
  Hepatitis B Surface Antigen
  (HBsAg) Neutralization 87341
  Hepatitis Be Antigen (HBeAg) 87350
  Hepatitis Delta Agent 87380
  Histoplasma capsulatum 87385
  HIV-1 87390
  HIV-2 87391
  Influenza A 87400
  Influenza B 87400
  Multiple Step Method 87301-87449
    Polyvalent 87451
  Not Otherwise Specified 87449, 87451
  Respiratory Syncytial Virus 87420
  Rotavirus 87425
  Shigella-like Toxin 87427
  Single Step Method 87450

Streptococcus, Group A 87430
Immunoassay
  Direct Optical
    Clostridium Difficile Toxin A 87803
    Influenza 87804
    Respiratory Syncytial Virus 87807
    Streptococcus, Group B 87802
    Trichomonas Vaginalis 87808
Immunofluorescence 87260-87300
  Adenovirus 87260
  Herpes Simplex 87273-87274
  Influenza B 87275
  Legionella Micdadei 87277
  Not Otherwise Specified 87299
  Parainfluenza Virus 87279
  Pneumocystis Carinii 87281
  Polyvalent 87300
  Rubeola 87283

Antigen, Australia
See Hepatitis Antigen, B Surface

Antigen, CD4
See CD4

Antigen, CD8
See CD8

Antigens, CD142
See Thromboplastin

Antigens, CD143
See Angiotensin Converting Enzyme (ACE)

Antigens, E
See Hepatitis Antigen, Be

Antigens, Hepatitis
See Hepatitis Antigen

Antigens, Hepatitis B
See Hepatitis Antigen, B

Antihemophilic Factor B
See Christmas Factor

Antihemophilic Factor C
See Plasma Thromboplastin, Antecedent

Antihemophilic Globulin (AHG) 85240

Antihuman Globulin 86880-86886

Antimony 83015

Antinuclear Antibodies (ANA) 86038-86039

Antiplasmin, Alpha-2 85410

Antiplatelet Therapy
See Performance Measures

Antiprotease, Alpha 1
See Alpha-1 Antitrypsin

Antiprothrombin Antibody 0030T

Antistreptococcal Antibody 86215

Antistreptokinase Titer 86590

Antistreptolysin O 86060-86063

Antithrombin III 85300-85301

Antithrombin VI
See Fibrin Degradation Products

Antitoxin Assay 87230

Antiviral Antibody
See Viral Antibodies

Antrostomy
Sinus
  Maxillary 31256-31267

Antrotomy
Sinus
  Maxillary 31020-31032
Transmastoid 69501

Antrum of Highmore
See Sinus, Maxillary

Antrum Puncture
Sinus
  Maxillary 31000
  Sphenoid 31002

Anus
See Hemorrhoids; Rectum
Ablation 46615
Abscess
  Incision and Drainage 46045-46050
Biofeedback 90911
Biopsy
  Endoscopy 46606
Crypt
  Excision 46999
Dilation
  Endoscopy 46604
Endoscopy
  Biopsy 46606
  Dilation 46604
  Exploration 46600
  Hemorrhage 46614
  Removal
    Foreign Body 46608
    Polyp 46610, 46612
    Tumor 46610, 46612
Excision
  Tag 46220, 46230
Exploration
  Endoscopy 46600
  Surgical 45990
Fissure
  Destruction 46940-46942
  Excision 46200
Fistula
  Excision 46270-46285
  Repair 46706
Hemorrhage
  Endoscopic Control 46614
Hemorrhoids
  Clot Excision 46320
  Destruction 46930
  Excision 46250-46262
  Injection 46500
  Ligation 46221, 46945-46946
  Stapling 46947
  Suture 46945-46946
Imperforated
  Repair 46715-46742
Incision
  Septum 46070
  Sphincterotomy 46200

Catheterization .... .36120
Embolectomy .... .34101
Exploration .... .24495
Exposure .... .34834
Thrombectomy .... .34101
Thromboendarterectomy .... .35321
Brachiocephalic
    Angioplasty .... .35458
    Atherectomy .... .35484, 35494
    Catheterization 36215-36218
Bypass Graft
    with Composite Graft 35681-35683
Cannulization
    for Extra Corporeal Circulation .... .36823
    to Vein 36810-36815
Carotid
    Aneurysm 35001-35002, 61697-61705
        Vascular Malformation or Carotid
        Cavernous Fistula 61705-61710
    Angiography 75660-75680
    Bypass Graft ... .33891, 35501-35510, 35526,
                35601-35606, 35626, 35642
    Catheterization .... .36100
    Decompression .. .61590-61591, 61595-61596
    Embolectomy .... .34001
    Exploration .... .35701
    Ligation 37600-37606, 61611-61612
    Stenosis
        Imaging Study Measurement .... .3100F
    Thrombectomy .... .34001
    Thromboendarterectomy .... .35301, 35390
    Transection 61611-61612
    Transposition .... .33889
Carotid, Common
    Intima-Media Thickness (IMT) Study ... .0126T
Celiac
    Aneurysm 35121-35122
    Bypass Graft .... .35531, 35631
    Embolectomy .... .34151
    Thrombectomy .... .34151
    Thromboendarterectomy .... .35341
Chest
    Ligation .... .37616
Coronary
    Angiography .... .93556
    Atherectomy 92995-92996
    Bypass 33517-33519
        Arterial 33533-33536
    Bypass Venous Graft 33510-33517, 35523
        Internal Mammary Artery Graft ...... .4110F
    Graft 33503-33505
    Ligation .... .33502
    Repair 33500-33507
    Thrombectomy
        Percutaneous .... .92973
Digital
    Sympathectomy .... .64820
Ethmoidal
    Ligation .... .30915
Extra Corporeal Circulation
    for Regional Chemotherapy
    of Extremity .... .36823
Extracranial
    Vascular Studies
        Non-Invasive, Physiologic .... .93875
Extremities
    Vascular Studies 93922-93923
Extremity
    Bypass Graft Revision 35879-35884
    Catheterization .... .36140
    Ligation .... .37618

Femoral
    Aneurysm 35141-35142
    Angioplasty .... .35456
    Atherectomy .... .35483, 35493
    Bypass Graft .... .35521, 35533, 35551-35558,
                35566, 35621, 35646-35647,
                35651-35661, 35666, 35700
    Bypass Graft Revision 35883-35884
    Bypass In-Situ 35583-35585
    Embolectomy .... .34201
    Exploration .... .35721
    Exposure 34812-34813
    Thrombectomy .... .34201
    Thromboendarterectomy 35371-35372
Great Vessel
    Repair 33770-33781
Head
    Angiography .... .75650
Hepatic
    Aneurysm 35121-35122
Iliac
    Aneurysm 35131-35132, 75954
    Angioplasty .... .35454
    Atherectomy .... .35482, 35492
    Bypass Graft .... .35563, 35632-35634, 35663
    Embolectomy 34151-34201
    Exposure .... .34820, 34833
    Graft .... .34900
    Occlusion Device .... .34808
    Thrombectomy 34151-34201
    Thromboendarterectomy .... .35351,
                                35361-35363
Ilio-celiac
    Bypass Graft .... .35632
Iliofemoral
    Bypass Graft 35548-35549, 35565
    Thromboendarterectomy ...... .35355, 35363
    X-ray with Contrast .... .75630
Ilio-mesenteric
    Bypass Graft .... .35633
Iliorenal
    Bypass Graft .... .35634
Innominate
    Aneurysm 35021-35022
    Embolectomy 34001-34101
    Thrombectomy 34001-34101
    Thromboendarterectomy .... .35311
Leg
    Angiography 75710-75716
    Catheterization 36245-36248
Mammary
    Angiography .... .75756
Maxillary
    Ligation .... .30920
Mesenteric
    Aneurysm 35121-35122
    Bypass Graft .... .35531, 35631
    Embolectomy .... .34151
    Thrombectomy .... .34151
    Thromboendarterectomy .... .35341
Middle Cerebral Artery, Fetal
    Vascular Studies .... .76821
Neck
    Angiography .... .75650
    Ligation .... .37615
Nose
    Incision 30915-30920
Other Angiography .... .75774
Other Artery
    Exploration .... .35761

Pelvic
    Angiography .... .75736
    Catheterization 36245-36248
Peripheral Arterial Rehabilitation .... .93668
Peroneal
    Bypass Graft 35566-35571, 35666-35671
    Bypass In-Situ 35585-35587
    Embolectomy .... .34203
    Thrombectomy .... .34203
    Thromboendarterectomy 35305-35306
Popliteal
    Aneurysm 35151-35152
    Angioplasty .... .35456
    Atherectomy .... .35483, 35493
    Bypass Graft 35551-35556, 35571, 35623,
                35651, 35656, 35671, 35700
    Bypass In-Situ .... .35583, 35587
    Embolectomy .... .34203
    Exploration .... .35741
    Thrombectomy .... .34203
    Thromboendarterectomy .... .35303
Pulmonary
    Anastomosis .... .33606
    Angiography 75741-75746
    Repair .... .33690, 33925-33926
Radial
    Aneurysm .... .35045
    Embolectomy .... .34111
    Sympathectomy .... .64821
    Thrombectomy .... .34111
Rehabilitation .... .93668
Reimplantation
    Carotid .... .35691, 35694-35695
    Subclavian 35693-35695
    Vertebral 35691-35693
    Visceral .... .35697
Renal
    Aneurysm 35121-35122
    Angiography 75722-75724
    Angioplasty .... .35450
    Atherectomy .... .35480, 35490
    Bypass Graft 35535-35536, 35560,
                    35631-35636
    Embolectomy .... .34151
    Thrombectomy .... .34151
    Thromboendarterectomy .... .35341
Repair
    Aneurysm 61697-61708
    Angioplasty 75962-75968
Revision
    Hemodialysis Graft or Fistula
        with Thrombectomy .... .36833
        without Thrombectomy .... .36832
Spine
    Angiography .... .75705
Splenic
    Aneurysm 35111-35112
    Bypass Graft .... .35536, 35636
Subclavian
    Aneurysm 35001-35002, 35021-35022
    Angioplasty .... .35458
    Bypass Graft ... .35506, 35511-35516, 35526,
                35606-35616, 35626, 35645
    Embolectomy 34001-34101
    Thrombectomy 34001-34101
    Thromboendarterectomy .... .35301, 35311
    Transposition .... .33889
    Unlisted Services and Procedures ..... .37799
Superficial Femoral
    Thromboendarterectomy .... .35302
Superficial Palmar Arch
    Sympathectomy .... .64823

B

for Spine Surgery
　　Local 20936
　　Morselized 20937
　　Structural 20938
Osteochondral
　　Knee 27416
　　Talus 28446
Skin
　　Dermal 15130-15136
　　Epidermal 15110-15116, 15150-15157
　　Harvesting
　　　for Tissue Culture 15040

Autologous Blood Transfusion
See Autotransfusion

Autologous Transplantation
See Autograft

Autonomic Nervous System Function
See Neurology, Diagnostic; Neurophysiologic Testing

Autoprothrombin C
See Thrombokinase

Autoprothrombin I
See Proconvertin

Autoprothrombin II
See Christmas Factor

Autoprothrombin III
See Stuart-Prower Factor

Autopsy
Coroner's Exam 88045
Forensic Exam 88040
Gross and Micro Exam 88020-88029
Gross Exam 88000-88016
Organ 88037
Regional 88036
Unlisted Services and Procedures 88099

Autotransfusion
Blood 86890-86891

Autotransplant
See Autograft

Autotransplantation
Renal 50380

AV Fistula
See Arteriovenous Fistula

AV Shunt
See Arteriovenous Shunt

Avulsion
Nails 11730-11732
Nerve 64732-64772

Axillary Arteries
See Artery, Axillary

Axillary Nerve
Injection
　　Anesthetic 64417

Axis, Dens
See Odontoid Process

B Antibodies, Hepatitis
See Antibody, Hepatitis B

B Antigens, Hepatitis
See Hepatitis Antigen, B

B Complex Vitamins
B-12 Absorption 78270-78272

B-Cells
Count 86355

B-DNA
See Deoxyribonucleic Acid

b-Hexosaminidase 83080

B-1 Vitamin
See Thiamine

B-6 Vitamin
See Vitamin, B-6

B-12 Vitamin
See Cyanocobalamin

Bacillus Calmette Guerin Vaccine
See BCG Vaccine

Back/Flank
Biopsy 21920-21925
Repair
　　Hernia 49540
Tumor
　　Excision 21930-21933
　　Radical Resection 21935-21936
Wound Exploration
　　Penetrating 20102

Backbone
See Spine

Bacteria Culture
Additional Methods 87077
Aerobic 87040-87071
Anaerobic 87073-87076
Blood 87040
Other Source 87070-87075
Screening 87081
Stool 87045-87046
Urine 87086-87088

Bacterial Endotoxins 87176

Bacterial Overgrowth Breath Test 91065

Bactericidal Titer, Serum 87197

Bacterium
Antibody 86609

BAER
See Evoked Potential, Auditory Brainstem

Baker Tube
Intestine Decompression 44021

Baker's Cyst 27345

Balanoplasty
See Penis, Repair

Balkan Grippe
See Q Fever

Balloon Angioplasties, Coronary
See Percutaneous Transluminal Angioplasty

Balloon Angioplasty
See Angioplasty

Balloon Assisted Device
Aorta 33967-33974

Band, Pulmonary Artery
See Banding, Artery, Pulmonary

Banding
Artery
　　Fistula 37607
　　Pulmonary 33690

Bank, Blood
See Blood Banking

Bankart Procedure
See Capsulorrhaphy, Anterior

Barany Caloric Test
See Caloric Vestibular Test

Barbiturates
Blood or Urine 82205

Bardenheurer Operation
See Ligation, Artery, Chest

Bariatric Surgery 43644-43645,
　　43770-43775, 43842-43848, 43886-43888

Barium 83015

Barium Enema 74270-74280

Barker Operation
See Talus, Excision

Barr Bodies 88130

Barr Procedure
See Tendon, Transfer, Leg, Lower

Bartholin's Gland
Abscess
　　Incision and Drainage 56420
Cyst
　　Repair 56440
Excision 56740
Marsupialization 56440

Bartonella
Antibody 86611

Bartonella Detection 87470-87472

Basic Life Services 99450

Basic Proteins, Myelin
See Myelin Basic Protein

Basilar Arteries
See Artery, Basilar

Batch-Spittler-McFaddin Operation
See Disarticulation, Knee

BCG Vaccine 90585-90586
See Vaccines

Be Antigens, Hepatitis
See Hepatitis Antigen, Be

Bed Sores
See Debridement; Pressure Ulcer (Decubitus);
Skin Graft and Flap

Bekesy Audiometry
See Audiometry, Bekesy

Belsey IV Procedure
See Fundoplasty

Bender-Gestalt Test 96101-96103

Benedict Test for Urea
See Urinalysis, Qualitative

Benign Cystic Mucinous Tumor
See Ganglion

Benign Neoplasm of Cranial Nerves
See Cranial Nerve

Bennett Fracture
See Phalanx; Thumb, Fracture

Bennett Procedure
See Repair, Leg, Upper, Muscle; Revision

Benzidine Test
See Blood, Feces

Benzodiazepine
Assay 80154

Benzoyl Cholinesterase
See Cholinesterase

Bernstein Test
See Acid Perfusion Test, Esophagus

Beryllium 83015

Beta 2 Glycoprotein I Antibody ..86146

Beta Blocker Therapy
See Performance Measures

Beta Glucosidase 82963

Beta Hypophamine
See Antidiuretic Hormone

Beta Lipoproteins
See Lipoprotein, LDL

Beta Test
See Psychiatric Diagnosis

Beta-2-Microglobulin
Blood 82232
Urine 82232

Beta-hydroxydehydrogenase 80406

Bethesda System 88164-88167

Bicarbonate 82374

Biceps Tendon
Insertion 24342

Bichloride, Methylene
See Dichloromethane

Bicuspid Valve
See Mitral Valve

Bifrontal Craniotomy 61557

Bilaminate Skin Substitute/Neodermis
See Tissue
Repair
 See Tissue, Culture
 Repair; Tissue, Culture, Skin Grafts

Bile Acids 82239
Blood 82240

Bile Duct
See Gallbladder
Anastomosis
 with Intestines 47760, 47780-47785
Biopsy
 Endoscopy 47553
Catheterization 75982
Change Catheter Tube 75984
Cyst
 Excision 47715
Destruction
 Calculi (Stone) 43265
Dilation
 Endoscopy 43271, 47555-47556
Drainage
 Transhepatic 75980
Endoscopy
 Biopsy 47553
 Cannulation 43273
 Destruction
  Calculi (Stone) 43265
  Tumor 43272
 Dilation 43271, 47555-47556
 Exploration 47552
 Intraoperative 47550
 Removal
  Calculi (Stone) 43264, 47554
  Foreign Body 43269
  Stent 43269
 Specimen Collection 43260
 Sphincter Pressure 43263
 Sphincterotomy 43262
 Tube Placement 43267-43268
Exploration
 Atresia 47700
 Endoscopy 47552
Incision
 Sphincter 43262, 47460
Incision and Drainage 47420-47425
Insertion
 Catheter 47510, 47525, 75982
  Revision 47530
 Stent 47511, 47801
Nuclear Medicine
 Imaging 78223
Reconstruction
 Anastomosis 47800
Removal
 Calculi (Stone) 43264, 47420-47425
  Percutaneous 47630
 Foreign Body 43269
 Stent 43269
Repair 47701
 Gastrointestinal Tract 47785
 with Intestines 47760, 47780
Tube Placement
 Nasobiliary 43267
 Stent 43268

Tumor
 Destruction 43271
 Excision 47711-47712
Unlisted Services and Procedures 47999
X-ray
 Guide Dilation 74360
 with Contrast 74300-74320
  Calculus Removal 74327
  Guide Catheter 74328, 74330

Bile Duct, Common, Cystic Dilatation
See Cyst, Choledochal

Bilirubin
Blood 82247-82248
Feces 82252
Total
 Direct 82247-82248
 Transcutaneous 88720

Billroth I or II
See Gastrectomy, Partial

Bilobectomy 32482

Bimone
See Testosterone

Binding Globulin, Testosterone-Estradiol
See Globulin, Sex Hormone Binding

Binet Test 96101-96103

Binet-Simon Test 96101-96103

Binocular Microscopy 92504

Biofeedback
See Training, Biofeedback
Anorectal 90911
Psychiatric Treatment 90875-90876

Biofeedback Training
See Training, Biofeedback

Bioimpedance
Cardiovascular Analysis 93701

Biological Skin Grafts
See Allograft, Skin

Biometry
Eye 76516-76519, 92136

Biopsies, Needle
See Needle Biopsy

Biopsy
See Brush Biopsy; Needle Biopsy
Abdomen 49000
Adrenal Gland 60540-60545
Anal
 Endoscopy 46606
Ankle 27613-27614, 27620
Arm, Lower 25065-25066
Arm, Upper 24065-24066
Artery
 Temporal 37609
Auditory Canal, External 69105
Back/Flank 21920-21925
Bile Duct
 Endoscopy 47553
Bladder 52354
 Cystourethroscope 52204
 Cystourethroscopy 52224, 52250

Biopsy, Skin
See Skin, Biopsy

Biopsy, Vein
See Vein, Biopsy

Biostatistics
See Biometry

Biosterol
See Vitamin, A

Biotinidase 82261

Birthing Room
Newborn Care 99460, 99463
    Attendance at Delivery 99464
    Resuscitation 99465

Bischof Procedure
See Laminectomy, Surgical

Bismuth .83015

Bizzozero's Corpuscle/Cell
See Blood, Platelet

Bladder
Abscess
    Incision and Drainage 51080
Anastomosis 51960
Aspiration 51100-51102
Biopsy 52204
Catheterization 51045, 51701-51703
Change Tube 51705-51710
Creation
    Stoma 51980
Cyst
    Urachal
      Excision 51500
Destruction
    Endoscopic 52214-52224, 52354
Dilation
    Ureter 52260-52265, 52341-52342,
              52344-52345
Diverticulum
    Excision .51525
    Incision 52305
    Resection 52305
Endoscopy .52000
    Biopsy 52204, 52354
    Catheterization 52005, 52010
    Destruction 52214-52224, 52400

Bronchopulmonary Lavage
See Lung, Lavage

Bronchoscopy
Ablation
　　Photodynamic Therapy 96570-96571
Alveolar Lavage 31624
Aspiration 31645-31646
Biopsy 31625-31629, 31632-31633
Brushing/Protected Brushing 31623
Catheter Placement
　　Intracavitary Radioelement 31643
Computer-assisted Navigation 31627
Dilation 31630-31631, 31636-31638
Exploration 31622
Fiducial Marker Placement 31626
Fracture 31630
Injection 31656
Needle Biopsy 31629, 31633
Removal
　　Foreign Body 31635
　　Tumor 31640, 31641
Stenosis 31641
Stent Placement 31631, 31636-31637
Stent Revision 31638
Ultrasound 31620
X-ray, Contrast 31656

Bronchospasm Evaluation
See Pulmonology, Diagnostic, Spirometry

Bronkodyl
See Theophylline

Brow Ptosis
Repair 67900

Brucella
Brucella 86000
Antibody 86622

Bruise
See Hematoma

Brunschwig Operation 58240
See Hip; Pelvis, Exenteration

Brush Biopsy
See Biopsy; Needle Biopsy
Bronchi 31717

Brush Border ab
See Antibody, Heterophile

Bucca
See Cheek

Buccal Mucosa
See Mouth, Mucosa

Bulbourethral Gland
Excision 53250

Bulla
Incision and Drainage
　　Puncture Aspiration 10160
Lung
　　Excision-Plication 32141
　　　Endoscopic 32655

BUN
See Blood Urea Nitrogen; Urea Nitrogen

Bunion Repair 28296-28299
Chevron Procedure 28296
Concentric Procedure 28296

Joplin Procedure .28294
Keller Procedure .28292
Lapidus Procedure 28297
Mayo Procedure .28292
McBride Procedure 28292
Mitchell Procedure 28296
Silver Procedure .28290
with Implant 28293

Burgess Amputation
See Disarticulation, Ankle

Burkitt Herpesvirus
See Epstein-Barr Virus

Burns
Allograft 15300-15336
Debridement 01951-01953, 15002-15005,
　　　　　　　　　　　　　　16020-16030
Dressings .16020-16030
Escharotomy 16035-16036
Excision 01951-01953
Initial Treatment .16000
Tissue Culture Skin Grafts 15100-15157
Xenograft .15400-15431

Burr Hole
Anesthesia 00214
Skull
　　Biopsy, Brain 61140
　　Catheterization 61210
　　Drainage
　　　Abscess 61150-61151
　　　Cyst 61150-61151
　　　Hematoma 61154-61156
　　Exploration
　　　Infratentorial 61253
　　　Supratentorial 61250
　　for Implant of Neurostimulator
　　Array .61863-61868
　　Injection, Contrast Media 61120
　　Insertion
　　　Catheter .61210
　　　Reservoir .61210

Burrow's Operation
See Skin, Adjacent Tissue Transfer

Bursa
Ankle 27604
Arm, Lower 25031
Elbow
　　Excision 24105
　　Incision and Drainage 23931
Femur
　　Excision 27062
Foot
　　Incision and Drainage 28001
Hip
　　Incision and Drainage 26991
Injection .20600-20610
Ischial
　　Excision 27060
Joint
　　Aspiration 20600-20610
　　Drainage 20600-20610
　　Injection 20600-20610
Knee
　　Excision 27340
Leg, Lower 27604
Palm
　　Incision and Drainage 26025-26030

Pelvis
　　Incision and Drainage 26991
Shoulder
　　Drainage 23031
Wrist 25031
　　Excision 25115-25116

Bursectomy
See Excision, Bursa

Bursitis, Radiohumeral
See Tennis Elbow

Bursocentesis
See Aspiration, Bursa

Button
Nasal Septal Prosthesis
　　Insertion 30220

Butyrylcholine Esterase
See Cholinesterase

Bypass Graft
Aortobi-iliac 35538, 35638
Aortobifemoral 35540
Aortofemoral 35539
Aortoiliac 35537, 35637
Axillary Artery 35516-35522, 35533,
　　　　　　　　　　35616-35623, 35650, 35654
Brachial Artery 35510, 35512, 35522-35525
Carotid Artery 33891, 35501-35510, 35526,
　　　　　　　　　35601-35606, 35626, 35642
Celiac Artery 35531, 35631
Coronary Artery
　　Angiography .93556
　　Arterial 33533-33536
　　Venous Graft 33510-33516
Excision
　　Abdomen 35907
　　Extremity 35903
　　Neck 35901
　　Thorax 35905
Femoral Artery 35521, 35533, 35551-35558,
　　　　　　　　　　35566, 35621, 35646-35647,
　　　　　　　　　　35651-35661, 35666, 35700
Harvest
　　Endoscopic .33508
　　Upper Extremity Vein 35500
Hepatorenal
　　Venous Graft 35535
Iliac Artery 35563
Ilio-celiac Artery .35632
Iliofemoral Artery 35548-35549, 35565, 35665
Ilio-mesenteric Artery 35633
Iliorenal Artery 35634
Mesenteric Artery 35531, 35631
Peroneal Artery 35566-35571, 35666-35671
Peroneal-Tibial
　　Venous Graft 35570
Placement
　　Vein Patch 35685
Popliteal Artery 35551-35558, 35571, 35623,
　　　　　　　　　　35651, 35656, 35671, 35700
Renal Artery 35536, 35560, 35631-35636
Reoperation 35700
Repair
　　Abdomen 35907
　　Extremity 35903
　　Lower Extremity
　　　with Composite Graft 35681-35683
　　Neck 35901
　　Thorax 35905

Revascularization
　Extremity 35903
　Neck 35901
　Thorax 35905
Revision
　Lower Extremity
　　Femoral Artery 35883-35884
　　　with Angioplasty 35879
　　　with Vein Interposition 35881
Secondary Repair .35870
Splenic Artery 35536, 35636
Subclavian Artery 35506, 35511-35516, 35526,
　　　　　　　　　35606-35616, 35626, 35645
Thrombectomy 37184-37186
　Other than Hemodialysis Graft
　or Fistula 35875-35876
Tibial Artery . . .35566-35571, 35623, 35666-35671
Tibial/Peroneal Trunk-Tibial
　Venous Graft 35570
Tibial-Tibial
　Venous Graft 35570
Vertebral Artery 35508, 35515, 35642-35645
with Composite Graft 35681

Bypass In-Situ
Femoral Artery 35583-35585
Peroneal Artery 35585-35587
Popliteal Artery 35583, 35587
Tibial Artery 35585-35587
Ventricular Restoration 33548

Bypass, Cardiopulmonary
See Cardiopulmonary Bypass

C

C-13
Urea Breath Test 83013-83014
Urease Activity 83013-83014

C-14
Urea Breath Test 78267-78268
Urease Activity 83013-83014

C-Peptide 80432, 84681

C-Reactive Protein 86140-86141

C-Section
See Cesarean Delivery

C Vitamin
See Ascorbic Acid

CABG
See Coronary Artery Bypass Graft (CABG)

Cadmium
Urine 82300

**Caffeine Halothane Contracture
Test (CHCT)** 89049

Calcaneal Spur
See Heel Spur

Calcaneus
Craterization 28120

Cyst
　Excision 28100-28103
Diaphysectomy .28120
Excision .28118-28120
Fracture
　Open Treatment 28415-28420
　Percutaneous Fixation 28406
　with Manipulation 28405-28406
　without Manipulation 28400
Repair
　Osteotomy 28300
Saucerization 28120
Tumor
　Excision 28100-28103
　Radical Resection 27647
X-ray 73650

Calcareous Deposits
Subdeltoid
　Removal 23000

Calcifediol
See Vitamin D

Calciferol
See Vitamin D

Calcification
See Calcium, Deposits

Calciol
See Vitamin, D-3

Calcitonin
Blood or Urine .82308
Stimulation Panel 80410

Calcium
Blood
　Infusion Test 82331
Deposits
　See Removal, Calculi (Stone); Removal,
　Foreign Bodies
Ionized 82330
Total 82310
Urine 82340

**Calcium-Binding Protein,
Vitamin K-Dependent**
See Osteocalcin

**Calcium-Pentagastrin
Stimulation** 80410

Calculus
Analysis 82355-82370
Destruction
　Bile Duct 43265
　Pancreatic Duct 43265
Removal
　Bile Duct 43264, 47554, 74327
　Bladder 51050, 52310-52318, 52352
　Kidney 50060-50081, 50130, 50561,
　　　　　　　　　　50580, 52352
　Pancreatic Duct 43264
　Ureter 50610-50630, 50961, 50980,
　　　　　　　　51060-51065, 52320-52325, 52352
　Urethra 52310-52315, 52352

Calculus of Kidney
See Calculus, Removal, Kidney

Caldwell-Luc Procedure
See Sinus/Sinuses, Maxillary; Sinusotomy;
Sternum, Fracture
Orbital Floor Blowout Fracture 21385
Sinusotomy 31030-31032

Caliper
Application/Removal 20660

Callander Knee Disarticulation
See Disarticulation, Knee

Callosum, Corpus
See Corpus Callosum

Calmette Guerin Bacillus Vaccine
See BCG Vaccine

Caloric Vestibular Test 92533

Calprotectin
Fecal 83993

Calycoplasty 50405

Camey Enterocystoplasty 50825

CAMP
See Cyclic AMP

Campbell Procedure 27422

Campylobacter
Antibody 86625

Campylobacter Pylori
See Helicobacter Pylori

Canal, Ear
See Auditory Canal

Canal, Semicircular
See Semicircular Canal

Canalith Repositioning 95992

Canaloplasty 69631, 69635

Candida
Antibody 86628
Skin Test 86485

Cannulation 36821
Arterial .36620-36625
Endoscopic
　Common Bile Duct 43273
　Pancreatic Duct 43273
Sinus
　Maxillary 31000
　Sphenoid 31002
Thoracic Duct .38794

Cannulation, Renoportal
See Anastomosis, Renoportal

Cannulization
See Catheterization
Arteriovenous 36147-36148, 36810-36815
Declotting 36593, 36860-36861
ECMO 36822
External
　Declotting 36860-36861
Vas Deferens 55200
Vein to Vein 36800

Canthocystostomy
See Conjunctivorhinostomy

Canthopexy
Lateral 21282
Medial 21280

Canthoplasty 67950

Canthorrhaphy 67880-67882

Canthotomy .67715

Canthus
Reconstruction 67950

Cap, Cervical
See Cervical Cap

Capsule
See Capsulodesis
Elbow
   Arthrotomy 24006
   Excision 24006
Foot 28264
Interphalangeal Joint
   Excision .26525
   Incision 26525
Knee 27435
Metacarpophalangeal Joint
   Excision .26520
   Incision 26520
Metatarsophalangeal Joint
   Release 28289
Shoulder
   Incision 23020
Wrist
   Excision .25320

Capsulectomy
Breast
   Periprosthetic 19371

Capsulodesis
Metacarpophalangeal Joint 26516-26518

Capsulorrhaphy
Anterior 23450-23462
Multi-Directional Instability 23466
Posterior 23465
Wrist 25320

Capsulotomy
Breast
   Periprosthetic 19370
Foot 28260-28262
Hip
   with Release, Flexor Muscles 27036
Interphalangeal Joint 28272
Knee 27435
Metacarpophalangeal Joint 26520
Metatarsophalangeal Joint 28270
Toe 28270-28272
Wrist 25085

Captopril 80416-80417

Carbamazepine
Assay .80156-80157

Carbazepin
See Carbamazepine

Carbinol
See Methanol

**Carbohydrate Deficient
Transferrin** 82373

Carbon Dioxide
Blood or Urine .82374

Carbon Tetrachloride 84600

Carboxycathepsin
See Angiotensin Converting Enzyme (ACE)

Carboxyhemoglobin . . .82375-82376, 88740

Carbuncle
Incision and Drainage 10060-10061

Carcinoembryonal Antigen
See Antigen, Carcinoembryonic

Carcinoembryonic Antigen 82378

Cardiac
See Coronary
Muscle
   See Myocardium
Neoplasm
   See Heart, Tumor
Pacemaker
   See Heart, Pacemaker
Septal Defect
   See Septal Defect

Cardiac Arrhythmia, Tachycardia
See Tachycardia

Cardiac Atria
See Atria

Cardiac Catheterization
Combined Left and Right Heart 93526-93529
Combined Right and Retrograde Left
   Congenital Cardiac Anomalies 93531
Combined Right and Transseptal Left
   Congenital Cardiac Anomalies . . .93532-93533
for Angiography 93508, 93541-93543
for Biopsy 93505
for Dilution Studies 93561-93562
Imaging 93555-93556
Injection 93539-93545
   See Catheterization, Cardiac
Left Heart 93510-93524
Pacemaker 33210
Right
   Congenital Cardiac Anomalies 93530
Right Heart 93501-93503

Cardiac Electroversion
See Cardioversion

Cardiac Event Recorder
Implantation 33282
Removal 33284

**Cardiac Magnetic Resonance
Imaging (CMRI)**
Complete Study 75554
Limited Study .75555
Morphology 75553
Velocity Flow Mapping 75556

Cardiac Massage
Thoracotomy 32160

Cardiac Output
Indicator Dilution 93561-93562
Inert Gas Rebreathing 0104T-0105T

Cardiac Rehabilitation 93797-93798

Cardiac Transplantation
See Heart, Transplantation

Cardiectomy
Donor .33930, 33940

Cardioassist 92970-92971

Cardiolipin Antibody 86147

Cardiology
See Defibrillator, Heart; Electrocardiography;
Pacemaker, Heart
Diagnostic
  Acoustic Recording with Computer Analysis
  Atrial Electrogram
    Esophageal Recording 93615-93616
  Bioimpedance Analysis 93701
  Cardiovascular Monitor, Implantable
    Data Analysis 93290, 93297, 93299
  Cardioverter-Defibrillator, Implantable
    Data Analysis 93289, 93295-93296
    Evaluation of Programming . . .93282-93284,
      93287, 93289, 93292, 93295-93296,
              93640-93642
  Echocardiography
    Doppler 93303-93321, 93662
    Intracardiac 93662
    Transesophageal 93318
    Transthoracic . . .93303-93317, 93350-93352
  Electrocardiogram
    Evaluation 0178T-0180T, 93000, 93010,
                93014, 93660
    Microvolt T-wave Alternans 93025
    Monitoring 93224-93237
    Rhythm 93040-93042
    Tracing .93005
    Transmission 93012
    Patient-Activated 93268, 93272
  Ergonovine Provocation Test 93024
  Intracardiac Pacing and Mapping 93631
    3-D Mapping 93613
    Follow-up Study 93624
    Stimulation and Pacing 93623
  Intracardiac Pacing and Recording
    Arrhythmia Induction 93618-93624
    Bundle of His 93600, 93619-93620
    Comprehensive 93619-93622
    Intra-Atrial 93602, 93610
    Right Ventricle 93603
    Tachycardia Sites 93609
    Ventricular 93612
  Intravascular Ultrasound 92978-92979
  Loop Recorder, Implantable
    Data Analysis 93291, 93298-93299
    Evaluation of Device Programming . . .93285,
            93291, 93298-93299
  Pacemaker Testing 93642
    Antitachycardia System 93724
    Data Analysis 93288, 93293-93294
    Evaluation of Device
      Programming 93279-93281, 93286,
        93288, 93290, 93293-93294, 93296
  Perfusion Imaging 78460-78461
    See Nuclear Medicine
  Stress Tests
    Cardiovascular 93015-93018
    Drug Induced 93024
    Multiple Gated Acquisition (MUGA) . .78473
  Tilt Table Evaluation 93660

Bladder 51701-51703
　　Irrigation 51700
Declotting 36593
Exchange
　　Intravascular 37209, 75900
　　Peritoneal 49423
Intracatheter
　　Irrigation 99507
　　Obstruction Clearance 36596
Pericatheter
　　Obstruction
　　　Clearance 36595
Placement
　　Brain
　　　Stereotactic 0169T
　　Breast
　　　for Interstitial Radioelement
　　　Application 19296-19298, 20555, 41019
　　Bronchus
　　　for Intracavitary Radioelement
　　　Application 31643
Removal
　　Central Venous 36589
　　Peritoneum 49422
　　Spinal Cord 62355
Repair
　　Central Venous 36575
Replacement
　　Central Venous 36580-36581, 36584
Repositioning 36597

Catheterization
See Catheter
Abdomen 49420-49421
Abdominal Artery 36245-36248
Aorta 36160-36215
Arterial
　　Cutdown 36625
　　Intracatheter/Needle 36100-36140
　　Percutaneous 36620
Arteriovenous Shunt 36147-36148
Bile Duct 47530
　　Change 47525
　　Percutaneous 47510
Bladder 51010, 51045
Brachiocephalic Artery 36215-36218
Brain 61210
　　Replacement 62160, 62194, 62225
　　Stereotactic 0169T
Bronchography 31710
Cardiac
　　Combined Left and Right Heart ...93526-93529
　　Combined Right and Retrograde Left for
　　Congenital Cardiac Anomalies 93531
　　Combined Right and Transseptal Left for
　　Congenital Cardiac Anomalies ...93532-93533
　　Flow Directed 93503
　　for Biopsy 93505
　　for Dilution Studies 93561-93562
　　Imaging 93555-93556
　　Injection 93539-93545
　　Left Heart 93510-93524
　　Pacemaker 33210
　　Right Heart 36013, 93501
　　for Congenital Cardiac Anomalies 93530
Central 36555-36566
Cerebral Artery 36215
Cystourethroscopy
　　Ejaculatory Duct 52010
　　Ureteral 52005
Ear, Middle 69405
Eustachian Tube 69405

Fallopian Tube 58345, 74742
Intracardiac
　　Ablation 93650-93652
Jejunum
　　for Enteral 44015
Kidney
　　Drainage 50392
　　with Ureter 50393
Legs 36245-36248
Nasotracheal 31720
Newborn
　　Umbilical Vein 36510
Pelvic Artery 36245-36248
Peripheral 36568-36571
Placement
　　Arterial Coronary Conduit
　　　without Concomitant Left Heart
　　　Catheterization 93508
　　Coronary Artery
　　　without Concomitant Left Heart
　　　Catheterization 93508
　　Venous Coronary Bypass Graft
　　　without Concomitant Left Heart
　　　Catheterization 93508
Pleural Cavity 32550-32552
Portal Vein 36481
Pulmonary Artery 36013-36015
Radioelement Application 55875
Removal
　　Fractured Catheter 75961
　　Obstructive Material
　　　Intracatheter 36596
　　　Pericatheter 36595
Salivary Duct 42660
Skull 61107
Spinal Cord 62350-62351
Thoracic Artery 36215-36218
Tracheobronchi 31725
Umbilical Artery 36660
Umbilical Vein 36510
Ureter
　　Endoscopic 50553, 50572, 50953,
　　　　　　　　　　　　　　　　50972, 52005
　　Injection 50394, 50684
　　Manometric Studies 50396, 50686
Uterus
　　Radiology 58340
Vena Cava 36010
Venous
　　Central Line 36555-36556, 36568-36569,
　　　　　　　　　　　　　　　36580, 36584
　　First Order 36011
　　Intracatheter/Needle 36000
　　Organ Blood 36500
　　Second Order 36012
　　Umbilical Vein 36510
Ventricular 61020-61026, 61210-61215

Cauda Equina
See Spinal Cord
Decompression 63005-63011, 63017,
　　　　63047-63048, 63055-63057, 63087-63091
Exploration 63005-63011, 63017

Cauterization
Anal Fissure 46940-46942
Cervix 57522
　　Cryocautery 57511
　　Electro or Thermal 57510
　　Laser Ablation 57513
Chemical
　　Granulation Tissue 17250

Everted Punctum 68705
Nasopharyngeal Hemorrhage 42970
Nose
　　Hemorrhage 30901-30906
Skin Lesion 11055-11057, 17000-17004
Skin Tags 11200-11201
Turbinate Mucosa
　　Electrocautery 30801-30802

Cavernitides, Fibrous
See Peyronie Disease

Cavernosography
Corpora 54230

Cavernosometry 54231

Cavities, Pleural
See Pleural Cavity

Cavus Foot Correction 28309

CBC
See Blood Cell Count; Complete Blood Count (CBC)

CCL4
See Carbon Tetrachloride

CCU Visit
See Critical Care Services

CD142 Antigens
See Thromboplastin

CD143 Antigens
See Angiotensin Converting Enzyme (ACE)

CD4 86360

CD8 86360

CEA
See Carcinoembryonic Antigen

Cecil Repair
See Urethroplasty

Cecostomy 44300
Contrast 49465
Insertion of Tube 49442
Laparoscopic 44188
Obstructive Material Removal 49460
Radiological Evaluation of Tube 49465
Tube Replacement 49450

Celiac Plexus
Destruction 64680
Injection
　　Anesthetic 64530
　　Neurolytic 64680

Celiac Trunk Artery
See Artery, Celiac

Celioscopy
See Endoscopy, Peritoneum

Celiotomy 49000
Abdomen
　　for Staging 49220

Cell Count
Body Fluid 89050-89051

Cell, Blood
See Blood Cell

Open Treatment 21360-21366
Reconstruction 21270
Fascia Graft 15840
Muscle Graft 15841-15845
Muscle Transfer 15845

Cheilectomy
Metatarsophalangeal Joint Release 28289

Cheiloplasty
See Lip, Repair

Cheiloschisis
See Cleft Lip

Cheilotomy
See Incision, Lip

Chemical Cauterization
Granulation Tissue 17250

Chemical Exfoliation 17360

Chemical Peel 15788-15793

Chemiluminescent Assay 82397

Chemistry Tests
Clinical
Unlisted Services and Procedures 84999

Chemocauterization
Corneal Epithelium 65435
with Chelating Agent 65436

Chemodenervation
Anal Sphincter 46505
Eccrine Glands
Axillae 64650
Other Area 64653
Electrical Stimulation for Guidance 95873
Extraocular Muscle 67345
Extremity Muscle 64614
Facial Muscle .64612
Neck Muscle .64613
Needle Electromyography for Guidance 95874
Trunk Muscle .64614

Chemonucleolysis 62292

Chemosurgery
Destruction of Benign Lesions 17110-17111
Skin Lesion 17000-17004, 17110-17111,
17270, 17280

Chemotaxis Assay 86155

Chemotherapy
Arterial Catheterization 36640
Bladder Instillation 51720
CNS 61517, 96450
Extracorporeal Circulation
Extremity 36823
Home Infusion Procedures 99601-99602
Intra-Arterial 96420-96425
Intralesional 96405-96406
Intramuscular 96401-96402
Intravenous 96409-96415, 96417
Infusion Pump 96416
Kidney Instillation 50391
Peritoneal Cavity 96445
Pleural Cavity .96440
Pump Services
Implantable 96522
Maintenance 95990-95991
Portable 96521

Reservoir Filling 96542
Subcutaneous 96401-96402
Unlisted Services and Procedures 96549
Ureteral Instillation 50391

Chest
See Mediastinum; Thorax
Angiography .71275
Artery
Ligation .37616
CT Scan 71250-71275
Exploration
Blood Vessel 35820
Magnetic Resonance Imaging
(MRI) 71550-71552
Repair
Blood Vessel 35211-35216
with Other Graft 35271-35276
with Vein Graft 35241-35246
Ultrasound 76604
Wound Exploration
Penetrating 20101
X-ray .71010-71035
Complete (Four Views)
with Fluoroscopy 71034
Insertion Pacemaker 71090
Partial (Two Views)
with Fluoroscopy 71023
Stereo .71015
with Computer-aided Detection . . .0174T-0175T
with Fluoroscopy 71090

Chest Cavity
Bypass Graft .35905
Endoscopy
Exploration 32601-32606
Surgical 32650-32665

Chest Wall
See Pulmonology, Therapeutic
Manipulation 94667-94668
Reconstruction 49904
Trauma .32820
Repair 32905
Closure .32810
Fistula 32906
Tumor
Excision 19260-19272
Unlisted Services and Procedures 32999

Chest Wall Fistula
See Fistula, Chest Wall

Chest, Funnel
See Pectus Excavatum

Chevron Procedure 28296

Chiari Osteotomy of the Pelvis
See Osteotomy, Pelvis

Chicken Pox Vaccine 90716

Child Procedure
See Excision, Pancreas, Partial

Chin
Repair
Augmentation 21120
Osteotomy 21121-21123

Chinidin
See Quinidine

Chiropractic Manipulation
See Manipulation, Chiropractic

Chiropractic Treatment
Spinal
Extraspinal 98940-98943

Chlamydia
Antibody 86631-86632
Antigen Detection
Direct Fluorescence 87270
Direct Optical 87810
Enzyme Immunoassay 87320
Culture 87110

Chloramphenicol 82415

Chloride
Blood 82435
Other Source 82438
Spinal Fluid .82438
Urine 82436

Chloride, Methylene
See Dichloromethane

Chlorinated Hydrocarbons 82441

Chlorohydrocarbon
See Chlorinated Hydrocarbons

Chlorpromazine 84022

Choanal Atresia
Repair 30540-30545

Cholangiography
Injection 47500-47505
Intraoperative 74300-74301
Percutaneous 74320
with Laparoscopy 47560-47561
Postoperative 74305
Repair
with Bile Duct Exploration 47700
with Cholecystectomy . . .47563, 47605, 47620

Cholangiopancreatography 43260
See Bile Duct; Pancreatic Duct
Repair
See Bile Duct; Pancreatic Duct
with Biopsy 43261
with Surgery 43262-43267, 43269

Cholangiostomy
See Hepaticostomy

Cholangiotomy
See Hepaticostomy

Cholecalciferol
See Vitamin, D-3

Cholecystectomy 47562-47564,
47600-47620
Any Method 47562-47564
with Cholangiography . . .47563, 47605, 47620
with Exploration Common
Duct 47564, 47610

Cholecystenterostomy 47570,
47720-47741

Cholecystography 74290-74291

Cholecystotomy 47480, 48001
Percutaneous 47490

Colonography

CT Scan
Diagnostic 74261-74262
Screening 74263

Colonoscopy

Biopsy 45380, 45392
Collection Specimen 45380
  via Colotomy 45355
Destruction
  Lesion 45383
  Tumor 45383
Dilation 45386
Hemorrhage Control 45382
Injection
  Submucosal 45381
Placement
  Stent 45387
Removal
  Foreign Body 45379
  Polyp 45384-45385
  Tumor 45384-45385
Surveillance Intervals 0528F-0529F
Ultrasound 45391-45392
via Stoma 44388-44390
  Biopsy 44389
  Destruction
    of Lesion 44393
    of Tumor 44393
  Exploration 44388
  Hemorrhage 44391
  Placement
    Stent 44397
  Removal
    Foreign Body 44390
    Polyp 44392, 44394
    Tumor 44392, 44394

Color Vision Examination 92283

Colorrhaphy 44604

Colostomy 44320, 45563

Abdominal
  Establishment 50810
Colostomy 44188
Home Visit 99505
Intestine, Large
  with Suture 44605
Laparoscopic 44188
Perineal
  Establishment 50810
Revision 44340
  Paracolostomy Hernia 44345-44346

Colotomy .44025

Colpectomy

Partial 57106
Total 57110
with Hysterectomy 58275-58280
  with Repair of Enterocele 58280

Colpo-Urethrocystopexy 58152,
                                58267, 58293
Marshall-Marchetti-Krantz Procedure58152, 58267,
                                58293
Pereyra Procedure 58267, 58293

Colpoceliocentesis

See Colpocentesis

Colpocentesis 57020

Colpocleisis 57120

Colpocleisis Complete

See Vagina, Closure

Colpohysterectomies

See Excision, Uterus, Vaginal

Colpoperineorrhaphy 57210

Colpopexy

Extra-Peritoneal 57282
Intra-Peritoneal 57283
Laparoscopic 57425
Open 57280

Colpoplasty

See Repair, Vagina

Colporrhaphy

Anterior 57240, 57289
  with Insertion of Mesh 57267
  with Insertion of Prosthesis 57267
Anteroposterior 57260-57265
  with Enterocele Repair 57265
  with Insertion of Mesh 57267
  with Insertion of Prosthesis 57267
Nonobstetrical 57200
Posterior 57250
  with Insertion of Mesh 57267
  with Insertion of Prosthesis 57267

Colposcopy

Biopsy 56821, 57421, 57454-57455, 57460
  Endometrium 58110
Cervix 57421, 57452-57461
Exploration .57452
Loop Electrode Biopsy 57460
Loop Electrode Conization 57461
Perineum 99170
Vagina 57420-57421
Vulva 56820
  Biopsy 56821

Colpotomy

Drainage
  Abscess .57010
Exploration .57000

Colprosterone

See Progesterone

Column Chromatography/Mass
Spectrometry 82541-82544

Columna Vertebralis

See Spine

Combined Heart-Lung
Transplantation

See Transplantation, Heart-Lung

Combined Right and Left Heart
Cardiac Catheterization

See Cardiac Catheterization, Combined Left and
Right Heart

Comedones

Removal 10040

Commissurotomy

Right Ventricle 33476-33478

Common Sensory Nerve

Repair/Suture 64834

Common Truncus

See Truncus Arteriosus

Communication Device

Non-Speech-Generating 92605-92606
Speech-Generating 92606-92609

Community/Work Reintegration

Training 97537
  See Physical Medicine/Therapy/Occupational
  Therapy

Compatibility Test

Blood 86920, 86923

Complement

Antigen 86160
Fixation Test 86171
Functional Activity 86161
Hemolytic
  Total 86162
Total 86162

Complete Blood Count
(CBC) 85025-85027

See Blood Cell Count

Complete Colectomy

See Colectomy, Total

Complete Pneumonectomy

See Pneumonectomy, Completion

Complete Transposition of Great
Vessels

See Transposition, Great Arteries

Complex, Factor IX

See Christmas Factor

Complex, Vitamin B

See B Complex Vitamins

Component Removal, Blood

See Apheresis

Composite Graft 15760-15770,
                                35681-35683

Compound B

See Corticosterone

Compound F

See Cortisol

Compression, Nerve, Median

See Carpal Tunnel Syndrome

Computed Tomographic Scintigraphy

See Emission Computerized Tomography

Computed Tomography (CT)

See CT Scan; Specific Anatomic Site

Computer Analysis

Acoustic Recording
  Heart Sounds
Probability Assessment 0185T

Computer-Aided Detection

Chest X-ray .0152T
Lesion
  Chest Radiograph 0174T-0175T
Mammography 77051-77052
  Magnetic Resonance Imaging (MRI) 0159T

Contracture of Palmar Fascia
See Dupuytren's Contracture

Contralateral Ligament
Repair
  Knee 27405

Contrast Aortogram
See Aortography

Contrast Bath Therapy 97034
See Physical Medicine/Therapy/Occupational Therapy

Contrast Material
Injection
  via Peritoneal Catheter 49424

Contrast Phlebogram
See Venography

Contusion
See Hematoma

Converting Enzyme, Angiotensin
See Angiotensin Converting Enzyme (ACE)

Coombs Test 86880, 86885-86886

Copper 82525

Coprobilinogen
Feces 84577

Coproporphyrin 84120

Coracoacromial Ligament Release 23415

Coracoid Process Transfer 23462

Cord, Spermatic
See Spermatic Cord

Cord, Spinal
See Spinal Cord

Cord, Vocal
See Vocal Cords

Cordectomy 31300

Cordocenteses
See Cordocentesis

Cordocentesis 59012

Cordotomy 63194-63199

Corectomy
See Excision, Iris

Coreoplasty 66762

Cornea
Biopsy 65410
Curettage 65435-65436
  with Chelating Agent 65436
Epithelium
  Excision 65435-65436
    with Chelating Agent 65436
Hysteresis Determination 0181T
Lesion
  Destruction 65450
  Excision 65400
    with Graft 65426
    without Graft 65420

Pachymetry 76514
Prosthesis 65770
Pterygium
  Excision 65420
Puncture 65600
Relaxing Incisions 65772-65775
Repair
  Astigmatism 65772-65775
  Wedge Resection 65775
  with Glue 65286
  Wound
    Nonperforating 65275
    Perforating 65280-65285
    Tissue Glue 65286
Reshape
  Epikeratoplasty 65765
  Keratomileusis 65760
  Keratoprosthesis 65767
Scraping
  Smear 65430
Tattoo 65600
Thickness Measurement 76514
Transplantation
  Autograft or Homograft
    Allograft Preparation 65757
    Endothelial 65756
    Lamellar 65710
    Penetrating 65730-65755
    for Aphakia 65750

Coronary
Atherectomy
  Percutaneous 92995-92996
Thrombectomy
  Percutaneous 92973

Coronary Angioplasty, Transluminal Balloon
See Percutaneous Transluminal Angioplasty

Coronary Artery
Insertion
  Stent 92980-92981
Ligation 33502
Placement
  Radiation Delivery Device 92974
Repair 33500-33507

Coronary Artery Bypass Graft (CABG) 33503-33505, 33510-33516
Arterial 33533-33536
Arterial Graft 33548
  Spectroscopy
    Catheter Based 0205T
Arterial-Venous 33517-33523
Beta Blocker Administered 4115F
Harvest
  Upper Extremity Artery 35600
Internal Mammary Artery Graft 4110F
Reoperation 33530
Venous 33510-33516

Coronary Endarterectomy 33572

Coroner's Exam 88045

Coronoidectomy
Temporomandibular Joint 21070

Corpectomy 63101-63103

Corpora Cavernosa
Corpus Spongiosum Shunt 54430
Glans Penis Fistulization 54435

Injection 54235
Irrigation
  Priapism 54220
Saphenous Vein Shunt 54420
X-ray with Contrast 74445

Corpora Cavernosa, Plastic Induration
See Peyronie Disease

Corpora Cavernosography 74445

Corpus Callosum
Transection 61541

Corpus Vertebrae (Vertebrale)
See Vertebral Body

Correction of Cleft Palate
See Cleft Palate, Repair

Correction of Lid Retraction
See Repair, Eyelid, Retraction

Correction of Malrotation of Duodenum
See Ladd Procedure

Correction of Syndactyly
See Syndactyly, Repair

Correction of Ureteropelvic Junction
See Pyeloplasty

Cortex Decortication, Cerebral
See Decortication

Cortical Mapping
Transection
  by Electric Stimulation 95961-95962

Corticoids
See Corticosteroids

Corticoliberin
See Corticotropic Releasing Hormone (CRH)

Corticosteroid Binding Globulin
See Transcortin

Corticosteroid Binding Protein
See Transcortin

Corticosteroids
Blood 83491
Urine 83491

Corticosterone
Blood or Urine 82528

Corticotropic Releasing Hormone (CRH) 80412

Cortisol 80400-80406, 80418-80420, 80436, 82530
Stimulation 80412
Total 82533

Cortisol Binding Globulin 84449

Costectomy
See Resection, Ribs

Costen Syndrome
See Temporomandibular Joint (TMJ)

Costotransversectomy 21610

Shunt
    Cerebrospinal Fluid 62200
    Subarachnoid
        Lumbar-Peritoneal 63740
    Subarachnoid-Subdural 62190
    Ventriculo 62220
Sigmoid Bladder 50810
Speech Prosthesis 31611
Stoma
    Bladder 51980
    Kidney 50395
    Renal Pelvis .50395
    Tympanic Membrane 69433-69436
    Ureter 50860
Ventral Hernia .39503

CRF
See Corticotropic Releasing Hormone (CRH)

CRH
See Corticotropic Releasing Hormone (CRH)

Cricoid Cartilage Split
Larynx 31587

Cricothyroid Membrane
Incision 31605

Cristobalite
See Silica

Critical Care Services 99291-99292
See Emergency Department Services; Prolonged
Attendance
Evaluation and Management 99291-99292
Gastric Intubation 91105
Interfacility Transport 99466-99467
Ipecac Administration for Poison 99175
Neonatal
    Initial 99468
    Low Birth Weight Infant 99478-99479
    Subsequent 99469
Pediatric
    Initial 99471, 99475
    Interfacility Transport 99466-99467
    Subsequent 99472, 99476
Remote
    Video-Conferenced Evaluation and
    Management 0188T-0189T

Cross Finger Flap 15574

Crossmatch 86825-86826, 86920-86923

Crossmatching, Tissue
See Tissue, Typing

Cruciate Ligament
Arthroscopic Repair 29888-29889
Repair 27407-27409
    Knee
        with Collateral Ligament 27409

Cryoablation
See Cryosurgery

Cryofibrinogen 82585

Cryofixation
See Cryopreservation

Cryoglobulin .82595

Cryopreservation
Cells 38207-38209, 88240-88241
Embryo 89258

for Transplantation 32850, 33930, 33940,
   44132, 47133, 47140, 48550, 50300-50320, 50547
Freezing and Storage 38207, 88240
Sperm 89259
Testes 89335
Thawing
    Embryo 89352
    Oocytes 89353
    Reproductive Tissue 89354
    Sperm 89356

Cryosurgery 17000-17286, 47371, 47381
See Cryotherapy; Destruction
Fibroadenoma .0120T
    Breast 19105
Labyrinthotomy 69801
Lesion
    Kidney 50250
    Mouth 40820
    Penis 54056, 54065
    Vagina 57061-57065
    Vulva 56501-56515

Cryotherapy
Ablation
    Renal Tumor 50593
Acne 17340
Destruction
    Ciliary Body 66720
Lesion
    Cornea 65450
    Retina 67208, 67227
Retinal Detachment
    Prophylaxis 67141
    Repair 67101, 67113
Trichiasis
    Correction .67825

Cryptectomy 46999

Cryptococcus
Antibody 86641
Antigen Detection
    Enzyme Immunoassay 87327

Cryptococcus Neoformans
Antigen Detection
    Enzyme Immunoassay 87327

Cryptorchism
See Testis, Undescended

Cryptosporidium
Antigen Detection
    Direct Fluorescence 87272
    Enzyme Immunoassay 87328

Crystal Identification
Any Body Fluid 89060
Tissue 89060

CSF
See Cerebrospinal Fluid Leak

CT Scan
3-D Rendering 76376-76377
Bone
    Density Study 77078-77079
Brain 3111F-3112F
Drainage 75989
Follow-up Study 76380
Guidance
    Localization 77011
    Needle Placement 77012

    Parenchymal Tissue Ablation 77013
    Radiation Therapy 77014
    Vertebroplasty 72292
    Visceral Tissue Ablation 76362
Heart
    Evaluation
        Angiography 75574
        for Coronary Calcium 75571
        for Structure and
        Morphology 75572-75573
    Hemorrhage Documented 3110F
    Infarction Documented 3110F
    Lesion Documented 3110F
Unlisted Services and Procedures 76497
with Contrast .70460
    Abdomen 74160
    Arm 73201
    Brain 0042T, 70460
    Cerebral Blood Flow/Volume 0042T
    Ear 70481
    Face 70487
    Head 70460
    Leg 73701
    Maxilla 70487
    Neck 70491
    Orbit 70481
    Pelvis 72193
    Sella Turcica 70481
    Spine
        Cervical .72126
        Lumbar .72132
        Thoracic 72129
    Thorax 71260
without and with Contrast
    Abdomen 74170-74175, 75635
    Arm 73202-73206
    Brain 70470, 70496
    Chest 71275
    Ear 70482
    Face 70488
    Head 70470, 70496
    Leg 73702-73706, 75635
    Maxilla 70488
    Neck 70492, 70498
    Orbit 70482
    Pelvis 72191, 72194
    Sella Turcica 70482
    Spine
        Cervical .72127
        Lumbar .72133
        Thoracic 72130
    Thorax 71270-71275
without Contrast 70450
    Abdomen 74150
    Arm 73200
    Brain 70450
    Colon
        Colonography 74261-74263
    Ear 70480
    Face 70486
    Head 70450
    Leg 73700
    Maxilla 70486
    Neck 70490
    Orbit 70480
    Pelvis 72192
    Sella Turcica 70480
    Spine
        Cervical .72125
        Lumbar .72131
        Thoracic 72128
    Thorax 71250

CT Scan, Radionuclide
See Emission Computerized Tomography

Cuff, Rotator
See Rotator Cuff

Culdocentesis
See Colpocentesis

Culture
Acid Fast Bacilli 87116
Amniotic Fluid
    Chromosome Analysis 88235
Bacteria
    Additional Methods 87077
    Aerobic 87040-87070
    Anaerobic 87073-87076
    Blood 87040
    Other 87070-87073
    Screening 87081
    Stool 87045-87046
    Urine 87086-87088
Bone Marrow
    Chromosome Analysis 88237
Chlamydia 87110
Chorionic Villus
    Chromosome Analysis 88235
Fertilized Oocytes
    for In Vitro Fertilization 89250
        Co-Culture of Embryo 89251
Fungus
    Blood 87103
    Hair 87101
    Identification 87106
    Nail 87101
    Other 87102
    Skin 87101
Lymphocyte
    Chromosome Analysis 88230
Mold 87107
Mycobacteria 87116-87118
Mycoplasma 87109
Oocyte/Embryo 89250
    Co-Culture of Oocyte/Embryo 89251
    Extended Culture 89272
Pathogen
    by Kit 87084
Skin
    Chromosome Analysis 88233
Tissue
    Toxin/Antitoxin 87230
    Virus 87252-87253
Tubercle Bacilli 87116
Typing 87140-87158
Unlisted Services and Procedures 87999
Yeast 87106

Curettage
See Dilation and Curettage
Cervix
    Endocervical 57454, 57456, 57505
Cornea 65435-65436
    Chelating Agent 65436
Hydatidiform Mole 59870
Postpartum 59160

Curettage and Dilatation
See Dilation and Curettage

Curettage, Uterus
See Uterus, Curettage

Curettement
Skin Lesion 11055-11057, 17004,
                 17110, 17270, 17280

Curietherapy
See Brachytherapy

Custodial Care
See Domiciliary Services; Nursing Facility Services

Cutaneolipectomy
See Lipectomy

Cutaneous Electrostimulation, Analgesic
See Application, Neurostimulation

Cutaneous Tag
See Skin, Tags

Cutaneous Tissue
See Integumentary System

Cutaneous-Vesicostomy
See Vesicostomy, Cutaneous

CVS
See Biopsy, Chorionic Villus

Cyanacobalamin
See Cyanocobalamin

Cyanide
Blood 82600
Tissue 82600

Cyanocobalamin 82607-82608

Cyclic AMP 82030

Cyclic GMP 83008

Cyclic Somatostatin
See Somatostatin

Cyclocryotherapy
See Cryotherapy, Destruction, Ciliary Body

Cyclodialysis
Destruction
    Ciliary Body 66740

Cyclophotocoagulation
Destruction
    Ciliary Body 66710-66711

Cyclosporine
Assay 80158

Cyst
Abdomen
    Destruction/Excision 49203-49205
Ankle
    Capsule 27630
    Tendon Sheath 27630
Bartholin's Gland
    Excision 56740
    Repair 56440
Bile Duct 47715
Bladder
    Excision 51500
Bone
    Drainage 20615
    Injection 20615

Brain
    Drainage ...61150-61151, 61156, 62161-62162
    Excision 61516, 61524, 62162
Branchial Cleft
    Excision 42810-42815
Breast
    Incision and Drainage 19020
    Puncture Aspiration 19000-19001
Calcaneus 28100-28103
Carpal 25130-25136
Choledochal 47715
Ciliary Body
    Destruction 66770
Clavicle
    Excision 23140-23146
Conjunctiva 68020
Dermoid
    Nose
        Excision 30124-30125
Drainage
    Contrast Injection 49424
    with X-ray 76080
Excision
    Cheekbone 21030
    Clavicle 23140
        with Allograft 23146
        with Autograft 23145
    Femur 27355-27358
    Ganglion
        See Ganglion
    Humerus
        with Allograft 23156
        with Autograft 23155
    Hydatid
        See Echinococcosis
    Lymphatic
        See Lymphocele
    Maxilla 21030
    Mediastinum 32662
    Olecranon Process
        with Allograft 24126
        with Autograft 24125
    Pericardial 32661
    Pilonidal 11770-11772
    Radius
        with Allograft 24126
        with Autograft 24125
    Scapula 23140
        with Allograft 23146
        with Autograft 23145
    Ulna
        with Allograft 24126
        with Autograft 24125
    Zygoma 21030
Facial Bones
    Excision 21030
Femur 27065-27067
Fibula 27635-27638
Ganglion
    Aspiration/Injection 20612
Gums
    Incision and Drainage 41800
Hip 27065-27067
Humerus
    Excision 23150-23156, 24110
    with Allograft 24116
    with Autograft 24115
Ileum 27065-27067
Incision and Drainage 10060-10061
    Pilonidal 10080-10081

Cyst, Ovary

See Ovary, Cyst

Cystatin C

Cystatins, Kininogen

See Kininogen

Cystectomy

Cystic Hygroma

See Hygroma

Cystine

Cystitis

Cystography

Cystolithotomy

Cystometrogram

Cystoplasty

Cystorrhaphy

Cystoscopy

Cystoscopy, with Biopsy

See Biopsy, Bladder, Cystourethroscopy

Cystostomy

Cystotomy

Cystourethrogram, Retrograde

See Urethrocystography, Retrograde

Cystourethropexy

See Vesicourethropexy

Cystourethroplasty

Cystourethroscopy

Pelvis/Buttock
    Fasciotomy 27027
        with Debridement 27057
Skull 61322-61323, 61340-61345
Spinal Cord 63001-63017, 63045-63103
    Cauda Equina 63005
    Osteophytectomy 22856
Tarsal Tunnel Release 28035
Volvulus .45321, 45337
with Nasal/Sinus Endoscopy
    Optic Nerve .31294
    Orbit Wall 31292-31293
Wrist 25020-25025

Decortication
Lung
    Endoscopic 32651-32652
    Partial 32225
    Total 32220
    with Parietal Pleurectomy 32320

Decubiti
See Pressure Ulcer (Decubitus)

Decubitus Ulcers
See Debridement; Pressure Ulcer (Decubitus);
Skin Graft and Flap

Deetjeen's Body
See Blood, Platelet

Defect, Coagulation
See Coagulopathy

Defect, Heart Septal
See Septal Defect

Defect, Septal Closure, Atrial
See Heart, Repair, Atrial Septum

Deferens, Ductus
See Vas Deferens

Defibrillation
See Cardioversion

Defibrillator, Heart
See Pacemaker, Heart
Cardioverter-Defibrillator, Implantable
    Data Analysis 93289, 93295-93296
    Evaluation of Programming 93282-93284,
                    93287, 93289, 93292,
            93295-93296, 93640-93642
    Electrode Insertion 33216-33217,
                    33224-33225, 33249
    Pulse Generator 33240
Removal Single/Dual Chamber
    Electrodes 33243-33244
    Pulse Generator 33241
Repair .33218-33220
Repositioning
    Electrodes 33215, 33226
Revise Pocket Chest 33223
Wearable Device 93745

Deformity, Boutonniere
See Boutonniere Deformity

Deformity, Sprengel's
See Sprengel's Deformity

Degenerative, Articular Cartilage, Patella
See Chondromalacia Patella

Degradation Products, Fibrin
See Fibrin Degradation Products

Dehydroepiandrosterone 82626

Dehydroepiandrosterone Sulfate 82627

Dehydrogenase, 6-Phosphogluconate
See Phosphogluconate-6, Dehydrogenase

Dehydrogenase, Alcohol
See Antidiuretic Hormone

Dehydrogenase, Glucose-6-Phosphate
See Glucose-6-Phosphate, Dehydrogenase

Dehydrogenase, Glutamate
See Glutamate Dehydrogenase

Dehydrogenase, Isocitrate
See Isocitric Dehydrogenase

Dehydrogenase, Lactate
See Lactic Dehydrogenase

Dehydrogenase, Malate
See Malate Dehydrogenase

Dehydroisoandrosterone Sulfate
See Dehydroepiandrosterone Sulfate

Delay of Flap
Skin Graft .15600-15630

Deligation
Ureter 50940

Deliveries, Abdominal
See Cesarean Delivery

Delivery
See Cesarean Delivery; Vaginal Delivery

Delorme Operation
See Pericardiectomy

Denervation
Hip
    Femoral 27035
    Obturator 27035
    Sciatic 27035

Denervation, Sympathetic
See Excision, Nerve, Sympathetic

Denis-Browne Splint 29590

Dens Axis
See Odontoid Process

Denver Developmental Screening Test 96101-96103

Denver Krupic Procedure
See Aqueous Shunt, to Extraocular Reservoir

Denver Shunt
Patency Test 78291

Denver-Krupin Procedure 66180

Deoxycorticosterone
See Desoxycorticosterone

Deoxycortisol 80436, 82634

Deoxyephedrine
See Methamphetamine

Deoxyribonuclease
Antibody 86215

Deoxyribonuclease I
See DNAse

Deoxyribonucleic Acid
Antibody 86225-86226
Extraction 83890-83891

Depilation
See Removal, Hair

Depletion
Plasma 38214
Platelet 38213
T-Cell 38210
Tumor Cell 38211

Deposit Calcium
See Calcium, Deposits

Depth Electrode
Insertion 61760

Derma-Fat-Fascia Graft 15770

Dermabrasion 15780-15783

Dermatology
Actinotherapy 96900
Examination of Hair
    Microscopic 96902
Ultraviolet A Treatment 96912
Ultraviolet B Treatment 96910
Ultraviolet Light Treatment 96900, 96913
Unlisted Services and Procedures 96999

Dermatoplasty
Septal 30620

Dermoid
See Cyst, Dermoid

Derrick-Burnet Disease
See Q Fever

Descending Abdominal Aorta
See Aorta, Abdominal

Desipramine
Assay 80160

Desmotomy
See Ligament, Release

Desoxycorticosterone 82633

Desoxycortone
See Desoxycorticosterone

Desoxyephedrine
See Methamphetamine

Desoxynorephedrin
See Amphetamine

Desoxyphenobarbital
See Primidone

Desquamation
See Exfoliation

Open Treatment 28615
Percutaneous Fixation 28606
Temporomandibular Joint
  Closed Treatment 21480-21485
  Open Treatment 21490
Thumb
  Closed Treatment 26641-26645
  Open Treatment 26665
  Percutaneous Fixation 26650
  with Fracture 26645
    Open Treatment 26665
    Percutaneous Fixation 26650
  with Manipulation 26641-26650
Tibiofibular Joint
  Closed Treatment 27830-27831
  Open Treatment 27832
Vertebra
  Additional Segment
    Open Treatment 22328
  Cervical
    Open Treatment 22326
    Closed Treatment 22305
      with Manipulation, Casting and/or
      Bracing 22315
      without Manipulation 22310
  Lumbar
    Open Treatment 22325
  Thoracic
    Open Treatment 22327
Wrist
  Closed Treatment 25660, 25675, 25680
  Intercarpal .25660
    Open Treatment 25670
  Open Treatment 25670, 25685
  Percutaneous Fixation 25671
  Radiocarpal 25660
    Open Treatment 25670
  Radioulnar
    Closed Treatment 25675
    Open Treatment 25676
    Percutaneous Fixation 25671
  with Fracture
    Closed Treatment 25680
    Open Treatment 25685
  with Manipulation 25660, 25675, 25680

Dislocation, Radiocarpal Joint
See Radiocarpal Joint, Dislocation

Disorder
Blood Coagulation
  See Coagulopathy
Penis
  See Penis
Retinal
  See Retina

Displacement Therapy
Nose 30210

Dissection
Hygroma, Cystic
  Axillary/Cervical 38550-38555
Lymph Nodes 38542

Dissection, Neck, Radical
See Radical Neck Dissection

Distention
See Dilation

Diverticula, Meckel's
See Diverticulum, Meckel's

Diverticulectomy
. 44800
Esophagus 43130-43135

Diverticulectomy, Meckel's
See Meckel's Diverticulum, Excision

Diverticulum
Bladder
  See Bladder, Diverticulum
Meckel's
  Excision .44800
Repair
  Urethra 53400-53405

Division
Muscle
  Foot 28250
Plantar Fascia
  Foot 28250

Division, Isthmus, Horseshoe Kidney
See Symphysiotomy, Horseshoe Kidney

Division, Scalenus Anticus Muscle
See Muscle Division, Scalenus Anticus

Dl-Amphetamine
See Amphetamine

DMO
See Dimethadione

DNA
Antibody 86225-86226

DNA Endonuclease
See DNAse

DNA Probe
See Cytogenetics Studies; Nucleic Acid Probe

DNAse
Antibody 86215

Domiciliary Services
See Nursing Facility Services
Assisted Living 99339-99340
Discharge Services 99315-99316
Established Patient 99334-99337
New Patient 99324-99328

Donor Procedures
Conjunctival Graft 68371
Heart Excision 33940
Heart/Lung Excision 33930
Liver Segment 47140-47142
Stem Cells
  Donor Search 38204

Dopamine
See Catecholamines
Blood 82383-82384
Urine 82382, 82384

Doppler Echocardiography
. . . . .76827-76828, 93306-93308, 93320-93350
Extracranial 93875
Intracardiac 93662
Transesophageal 93318
Transthoracic 93303-93317

Doppler Scan
Arterial Studies
  Extremities 93922-93924

Fetal
  Middle Cerebral Artery 76821
  Umbilical Artery 76820
Extremities 93965
Intracranial Arteries 93886-93893

Dorsal Vertebra
See Vertebra, Thoracic

Dose Plan
See Dosimetry

Dosimetry
Radiation Therapy 77300, 77331
  Brachytherapy 77326-77328
  Intensity Modulation 77301, 77338
  Teletherapy 77305-77321

Double-Stranded DNA
See Deoxyribonucleic Acid

Doxepin
Assay 80166

DPH
See Phenytoin

Drainage
See Excision; Incision; Incision and Drainage;
Paracentesis
Abdomen
  Abdomen Fluid 49080-49081
Abscess
  Appendix 44900-44901
    Percutaneous 44901
  Brain 61150-61151
  Eyelid 67700
  Liver 47010-47011
  Ovary
    Percutaneous 58823
  Pelvic
    Percutaneous 58823
  Pericolic
    Percutaneous 58823
  Perirenal or Renal 50020-50021
    Percutaneous 50021
  Prostate .52700
  Retroperitoneal 49060-49061
    Percutaneous 49061
  Subdiaphragmatic or
  Subphrenic 49040-49041
    Percutaneous 49040-49041
  with X-ray 75989
Amniotic Fluid
  Diagnostic Aspiration 59000
  Therapeutic Aspiration 59001
Bile Duct
  Transhepatic 75980
Brain Fluid 61070
Bursa 20600-20610
Cerebrospinal Fluid 61000-61020, 61050, 61070, 62272
Cervical Fluid 61050
Cisternal Fluid 61050
Cyst
  Bone 20615
  Brain 61150-61151, 62161-62162
  Breast 19000-19001
  Ganglion 20612
  Liver 47010-47011
    Percutaneous 47011
  Salivary Gland 42409
  Sublingual Gland 42409

Removal
    Foreign Body 44010
X-ray 74260

Duplex Scan
See Vascular Studies
Arterial Studies
    Aorta .93978-93979
    Extracranial 93880-93882
    Lower Extremity 93925-93926
    Penile .93980-93981
    Upper Extremity 93930-93931
    Visceral 93975-93979
Hemodialysis Access 93990
Venous Studies
    Extremity 93970-93971
    Penile .93980-93981

Dupuy-Dutemp Operation
See Reconstruction, Eyelid; Revision

Dupuytren's Contracture . . .26040-26045

Durand-Nicolas-Favre Disease
See Lymphogranuloma Venereum

Dust, Angel
See Phencyclidine

Duvries Operation
See Tenoplasty

Dwyer Procedure
See Osteotomy, Calcaneus

DXA
See Dual X-ray Absorptiometry (DXA)

Dynamometry
See Osteotomy, Calcaneus
Venous Studies
  See Osteotomy, Calcaneus
    with Ophthalmoscopy 92260

E

E Antigens
See Hepatitis Antigen, Be

E B Virus
See Epstein-Barr Virus

E Vitamin
See Tocopherol

E1
See Estrone

E2
See Estradiol

E3
See Estriol

Ear
Collection of Blood 36415-36416
Drum 69420-69421, 69433-69436,
               69450, 69610-69620
  See Tympanic Membrane

External
  Abscess Incision and Drainage
    Complicated 69005
    Simple .69000
  Biopsy 69100
  Excision
    Partial .69110
    Total 69120
  Hematoma
    Incision and Drainage 69000-69005
  Reconstruction 69300
  Unlisted Services and Procedures 69399
Inner
  CT Scan 70480-70482
  Excision
    Labyrinth 69905-69910
  Exploration
    Endolymphatic Sac 69805-69806
  Incision 69820
    Labyrinth 69801-69802
    Semicircular Canal 69840
  Insertion
    Cochlear Device 69930
  Semicircular Canal 69820
  Unlisted Services and Procedures 69949
  Vertigo
    See Canalith Repositioning
Middle
  Catheterization 69405
  CT Scan 70480-70482
  Exploration 69440
  Inflation
    with Catheterization 69400
    without Catheterization 69401
  Insertion
    Catheter 69405
  Lesion
    Excision 69540
  Reconstruction
    Tympanoplasty with Antrotomy or
    Mastoidotomy 69635-69637
    Tympanoplasty with
    Mastoidectomy 69641-69646
    Tympanoplasty without
    Mastoidectomy 69631-69633
  Removal
    Ventilating Tube 69424
  Repair
    Oval Window 69666
    Round Window 69667
  Revision
    Stapes .69662
  Tumor
    Excision 69550-69554
  Unlisted Services and Procedures 69799
Outer
  CT Scan 70480-70482

Ear Canal
See Auditory Canal

Ear Cartilage
Graft
  to Face 21235

Ear Lobes
Pierce 69090

Ear Protector Attenuation 92596
See Hearing Aid Services

Ear Wax
See Cerumen

Ear, Nose, and Throat
See Hearing Aid Services; Otorhinolaryngology, Diagnostic
Audiologic Function Tests
  Acoustic Reflex 92568
  Acoustic Reflex Decay 92570
  Audiometry
    Bekesy 92560-92561
    Comprehensive 92557
    Conditioning Play 92582
    Evoked Response 92585-92586
    Groups .92559
    Pure Tone 92552-92553
    Select Picture 92583
    Speech 92555-92556
  Brainstem Evoked Response 92585-92586
  Central Auditory Function 92620-92621
  Ear Protector Evaluation 92596
  Electrocochleography 92584
  Filtered Speech 92571
  Hearing Aid Evaluation 92590-92595
  Loudness Balance 92562
  Screening Test 92551
  Sensorineural Acuity 92575
  Short Increment Sensitivity Index (SISI) . . .92564
  Staggered Spondaic Word Test 92572
  Stenger Test 92565, 92577
  Synthetic Sentence Test 92576
  Tone Decay 92563
  Tympanometry 92550, 92567, 92570
Audiometry
  Evoked Otoacoustic Emissions . . .92587-92588
  Visual Reinforcement 92579
Binocular Microscopy 92504
Diagnostic Analysis
  Auditory Brainstem Implant 92640
Facial Nerve Function Study 92516
Hearing, Language and Speech Evaluation . . .92506
Laryngeal Function Study 92520
Nasal Function Study 92512
Nasopharyngoscopy 92511
Vestibular Function Tests
  Additional Electrodes 92547
  Caloric Tests 92533, 92543
  Foveal Stimulation 92540
  Nystagmus
    Optokinetic 92534, 92540, 92544
    Positional 92532, 92540, 92542
    Spontaneous 92531, 92540-92541
  Peripheral Stimulation 92540
  Posturography 92548
  Torsion Swing Test 92546
  Tracking Tests 92545

Ebstein Anomaly Repair 33468

Eccrine Glands
Chemodenervation
  Axillae 64650
  Feet 64999
  Hands 64999
  Other Area 64653

ECG
See Electrocardiography

Echinococcosis 86171, 86280

Echocardiography
Cardiac .93320-93350
  Intracardiac 93662
  Transesophageal 93318

Endovascular Repair 0078T, 0079T, 0080T, 0081T, 33880-33891, 34800-34805, 34812-34826, 34833-34900
Angiography 75952-75959

Endovascular Therapy
Ablation
    Vein 36475-36479
Occlusion 61623

Enema
Home Visit for Fecal Impaction 99511
Intussusception 74283
Therapeutic
    for Intussusception 74283

Energies, Electromagnetic
See Irradiation

ENT
See Ear, Nose, and Throat; Otorhinolaryngology, Diagnostic
Therapeutic
    See Otorhinolaryngology

Entamoeba Histolytica
Antigen Detection
    Enzyme Immunoassay 87336-87337

Enterectomy 44120-44121, 44126-44128, 44137, 44202
Donor 44132-44133
with Enterostomy 44125

Enterocele
Repair 57556
    Hysterectomy
      with Colpectomy 58280

Enterocystoplasty 51960
Camey 50825

Enteroenterostomy
See Anastomosis, Intestines

Enterolysis 44005
Laparoscopic 44180

Enteropancreatostomy
See Anastomosis, Pancreas to Intestines

Enterorrhaphy 44602-44603, 44615

Enterostomy 44300
Closure 44625-44626
with Enterectomy
    Intestine, Small 44125

Enterotomy 44615

Enterovirus
Antibody 86658

Entropion
Repair 67921-67924
    Excision Tarsal Wedge 67923
    Suture 67921
    Thermocauterization 67922

Enucleation
Eye
    with Implant 65103
      Muscles Attached 65105
    without Implant 65101
Pleural 32540

Enucleation, Cyst, Ovarian
See Cystectomy, Ovarian

Enucleation, Prostate
See Prostate, Enucleation

Environmental Intervention
for Psychiatric Patients 90882

Enzyme Activity
Non-Radioactive Substrate 82657
Infectious Agent 87905
Radioactive Substrate 82658

Enzyme, Angiotensin Converting
See Angiotensin Converting Enzyme (ACE)

Enzyme, Angiotensin-Forming
See Renin

EOG
See Electro-oculography

Eosinocyte
See Eosinophils

Eosinophils
Nasal Smear 89190

Epiandrosterone 82666

Epicondylitides, Lateral Humeral
See Tennis Elbow

Epicondylitis, Radiohumeral
See Tennis Elbow

Epidemic Parotitis
See Mumps

Epididymectomy
Bilateral 54861
Unilateral 54860

Epididymis
Abscess
    Incision and Drainage 54700
Anastomosis
    to Vas Deferens
      Bilateral 54901
      Unilateral 54900
Biopsy 54800, 54865
Epididymography 74440
Excision
    Bilateral 54861
    Unilateral 54860
Exploration
    Biopsy 54865
Hematoma
    Incision and Drainage 54700
Lesion
    Excision
      Local 54830
      Spermatocele 54840
Needle Biopsy 54800
Spermatocele
    Excision 54840
Unlisted Services and Procedures 55899
X-ray with Contrast 74440

Epididymograms 55300

Epididymography 74440

Epididymoplasty
See Repair, Epididymis

Epididymovasostomy
Bilateral 54901
Unilateral 54900

Epidural
Electrode
    Insertion 61531
    Removal 61535
Injection 62281-62282, 62310-62319, 64479-64484
Lysis 62263-62264

Epidural Anesthesia
See Anesthesia, Epidural

Epidurography 72275

Epigastric
Hernia Repair 49572

Epiglottidectomy 31420

Epiglottis
Excision 31420

Epikeratoplasty 65767

Epilation
See Removal, Hair

Epinephrine
See Catecholamines
Blood 82383-82384
Urine 82384

Epiphyseal Arrest
Femur ..20150, 27185, 27475, 27479-27485, 27742
Fibula 20150, 27477-27485, 27730-27742
Radius 20150, 25450-25455
Tibia ..20150, 27477-27485, 27730, 27734-27742
Ulna 20150, 25450-25455

Epiphyseal Separation
Radius
    Closed Treatment 25600
    Open Treatment 25607-25609

Epiphysiodesis
See Epiphyseal Arrest

Epiphysis
See Bone; Specific Bone

Epiploectomy 49255

Episiotomy 59300

Epispadias
Penis
    Reconstruction 54385
Repair 54380-54390
    with Exstrophy of Bladder 54390
    with Incontinence 54380-54390

Epistaxis 30901-30906
with Nasal/Sinus Endoscopy 31238

EPO
See Erythropoietin

Epstein-Barr Virus
Antibody 86663-86665

Equina, Cauda
See Cauda Equina

ERCP
See Bile Duct; Cholangiopancreatography; Pancreatic Duct

ERG
See Electroretinography

Ergocalciferol
See Vitamin D

Ergocalciferols
See Vitamin D

Ergonovine Provocation Test 93024

Erythrocyte
See Red Blood Cell (RBC)

Erythrocyte ab
See Antibody, Red Blood Cell

Erythrocyte Count
See Red Blood Cell (RBC), Count

Erythropoietin 82668

Escharotomy
Burns 16035-16036

Escherichia coli 0157
Antigen Detection
    Enzyme Immunoassay 87335

ESD
See Endoscopy, Gastrointestinal, Upper

Esophageal Acid Infusion Test
See Acid Perfusion Test

Esophageal Polyp
See Polyp, Esophagus

Esophageal Tumor
See Tumor, Esophagus

Esophageal Varices
Ligation 43205, 43400
Transection/Repair 43401

Esophagectomy
Partial 43116-43124
Total 43107-43113, 43124

Esophagoenterostomy
with Total Gastrectomy 43620

Esophagogastroduodenoscopies
See Endoscopy, Gastrointestinal, Upper

Esophagogastromyotomy
See Esophagomyotomy

Esophagogastrostomy 43320

Esophagojejunostomy 43340-43341

Esophagomyotomy 32665, 43330-43331
with Fundoplasty 43279

Esophagorrhaphy
See Esophagus, Suture

Esophagoscopies
See Endoscopy, Esophagus

Esophagostomy 43350-43352
Closure 43420-43425

Esophagotomy 43020, 43045

Esophagotracheal Fistula
See Fistula, Tracheoesophageal

Esophagus
Acid Perfusion Test 91030
Acid Reflux Tests 91034-91038
Balloon Distension
    Provocation Study 91040
Biopsy
    Endoscopy 43202
    Forceps 3150F
Cineradiography 74230
Dilation 43450-43458
    Endoscopic 43220-43226, 43248-43249
    Surgical 43510
Endoscopy
    Biopsy 43202
    Dilation 43220-43226
    Exploration 43200
    Hemorrhage 43227
    Injection 43201, 43204
    Insertion Stent 43219
    Needle Biopsy 43232
    Removal
        Foreign Body 43215
        Polyp 43216-43217, 43228
        Tumor 43216, 43228
    Ultrasound 43231-43232
    Vein Ligation 43205
Excision
    Diverticula 43130-43135
    Partial 43116-43124
    Total 43107-43113, 43124
Exploration
    Endoscopy 43200
Hemorrhage 43227
Incision 43020, 43045
    Muscle 43030
Injection
    Sclerosing Agent 43204
    Submucosal 43201
Insertion
    Stent 43219
    Tamponade 43460
    Tube 43510
Intubation with Specimen Collection 91000
Lesion
    Excision 43100-43101
Ligation 43405
Motility Study 78258, 91010-91012
Needle Biopsy
    Endoscopy 43232
Nuclear Medicine
    Imaging (Motility) 78258
    Reflux Study 78262
Reconstruction 43300, 43310, 43313
    Creation
        Stoma 43350-43352
    Esophagostomy 43350
    Fistula 43305, 43312, 43314
    Gastrointestinal 43360-43361
Removal
    Foreign Bodies ..43020, 43045, 43215, 74235
    Lesion 43216
    Polyp 43216-43217, 43228
Repair 43300, 43310, 43313
    Esophagogastric Fundoplasty 43324-43325
    Laparoscopic 43280
    Esophagogastrostomy 43320
    Esophagojejunostomy 43340-43341

Fistula 43305, 43312, 43314, 43420-43425
Muscle 43330-43331
Paraesophageal Hernia
    Laparoscopic 43281-43282
Pre-existing Perforation 43405
Varices 43401
Wound 43410-43415
Suture 43405
    Wound 43410-43415
Ultrasound
    Endoscopy 43231-43232
Unlisted Services and Procedures ..43289, 43499
Vein
    Ligation 43205, 43400
Video 74230
X-ray 74220

Esophagus Neoplasm
See Tumor, Esophagus

Esophagus, Varix
See Esophageal Varices

Established Patient
Domiciliary or Rest Home Visit 99334-99337
Emergency Department Services ...99281-99285
Home Services 99347-99350
Hospital Inpatient Services 99221-99239
Hospital Observation Services 99217-99220
Inpatient Consultations 99251-99255
Office and/or Other Outpatient
Consultations 99241-99245
Office Visit 99211-99215
Online Medical Evaluation 98969, 99444
Outpatient Visit 99211-99215
Telephone Services ...98966-98968, 99441-99443

Establishment
Colostomy
    Abdominal 50810
    Perineal 50810

Estes Operation
See Ovary, Transposition

Estlander Procedure 40525

Estradiol 82670
Response 80414

Estriol
Blood or Urine 82677

Estrogen
Blood or Urine 82671-82672
Receptor 84233

Estrone
Blood or Urine 82679

Ethanediols
See Ethylene Glycol

Ethanol
Blood 82055
Breath 82075
Urine 82055

Ethchlorovynol
See Ethchlorvynol

Ethchlorvinol
See Ethchlorvynol

Bladder Neck Contracture
    Postoperative 52640
Bone
    Facial 21026
    Mandible 21025
    Postoperative
        Femur 20150
        Fibula 20150
        Radius 20150
        Tibia 20150
        Ulna 20150
Bone Abscess
    Facial 21026
    Mandible 21025
Brain
    Amygdala 61566
    Epileptogenic Focus 61536
    Hemisphere 61542-61543
    Hippocampus 61566
    Other Lobe 61323, 61539-61540
    Temporal Lobe 61537-61538
Brain Lobe
    See Lobectomy, Brain
Breast
    Biopsy 19100-19103
    Chest Wall Tumor 19260-19272
    Cyst .19120-19126
    Lactiferous Duct Fistula 19112
    Lesion 19120-19126
        by Needle Localization 19125-19126
    Mastectomy 19300-19307
    Nipple Exploration 19110
Bulbourethral Gland 53250
Bullae
    Lung 32141
        Endoscopic 32655
Burns 01951-01953, 15002-15005
Bursa
    Elbow 24105
    Femur 27062
    Ischial 27060
    Knee 27340
    Wrist .25115-25116
Bypass Graft 35901-35907
Calcaneus 28118-28120
Calculi (Stone)
    Parotid Gland 42330, 42340
    Salivary Gland 42330-42340
    Sublingual Gland 42330
    Submandibular Gland 42330-42335
Carotid Artery .60605
Carpal 25145, 25210-25215
Cartilage
    Knee Joint 27332-27333
    Shoulder Joint 23101
    Temporomandibular Joint 21060
    Wrist 25107
Caruncle
    Urethra 53265
Cataract
    Secondary 66830
Cervix
    Radical 57531
    Stump
        Abdominal Approach 57540-57545
        Vaginal Approach 57550-57556
    Total 57530
Chalazion
    Multiple
        Different Lids 67805
        Same Lid .67801

    Single 67800
    with Anesthesia 67808
Chest Wall
    Tumor 19260-19272
Choroid Plexus 61544
Clavicle
    Partial 23120, 23180
    Sequestrectomy 23170
    Total 23125
    Tumor
        Radical Resection 23200
Coccyx 27080
Colon
    Excision
        Partial 44140-44147, 44160
           with Anastomosis 44140
        Total 44150-44158
    Laparoscopic
        with Anastomosis 44204, 44207-44208
        with Colostomy 44206, 44208
        with Ileocolostomy 44205
Condyle
    Temporomandibular Joint 21050
Constricting Ring
    Finger 26596
Cornea
    Epithelium 65435
        with Chelating Agent 65436
    Scraping 65430
Coronoidectomy 21070
Cowper's Gland 53250
Cranial Bone
    Tumor 61563-61564
Cyst
    See Ganglion Cyst
    Bile Duct 47715
    Bladder 51500
    Brain 61516, 61524, 62162
    Branchial 42810-42815
    Calcaneus 28100-28103
    Carpal 25130-25136
    Cheekbone .21030
    Clavicle 23140
        with Allograft 23146
        with Autograft 23145
    Facial Bones 21030
    Femur 27065-27067, 27355-27358
    Fibula 27635-27638
    Finger 26160
    Foot 28090
    Hand 26160
    Hip .27065-27067
    Humerus 23150, 24110
        with Allograft 23156, 24116
        with Autograft 23155, 24115
    Ileum 27065-27067
    Kidney 50280-50290
    Knee 27345-27347
    Lung 32140
    Mandible 21040, 21046-21047
    Maxilla 21030, 21048-21049
    Mediastinal .39200
    Mediastinum 32662
    Metacarpal 26200-26205
    Metatarsal 28104-28107
    Mullerian Duct 55680
    Nose 30124-30125
    Olecranon 24120
    Olecranon Process
        with Allograft 24126
        with Autograft 24125

    Ovarian 58925
        See Cystectomy, Ovarian
    Pericardial 33050
        Endoscopic 32661
    Phalanges 26210-26215
        Toe 28108
    Pilonidal 11770-11772
    Pubis 27066-27067
    Radius 24120, 25120-25126
        with Allograft 24126
        with Autograft 24125
    Salivary Gland 42408
    Scapula 23140
        with Allograft 23146
        with Autograft 23145
    Seminal Vesicle 55680
    Sublingual Gland 42408
    Talus 28100-28103
    Tarsal 28104-28107
    Thyroglossal Duct 60280-60281
    Thyroid Gland 60200
    Tibia 27635-27638
    Toe 28092
    Ulna 24120, 25120-25126
        with Allograft 24126
        with Autograft 24125
    Urachal
        Bladder 51500
    Vaginal 57135
Destruction of the Vestibule of the Mouth
    See Mouth, Vestibule of, Excision, Destruction
Diverticulum, Meckel's
    See Meckel's Diverticulum, Excision
Ear, External
    Partial 69110
    Total 69120
Elbow Joint 24155
Electrode 57522
Embolectomy/Thrombectomy
    Aortoiliac Artery 34151-34201
    Axillary Artery 34101
    Brachial Artery 34101
    Carotid Artery 34001
    Celiac Artery 34151
    Femoral Artery 34201
    Heart 33310-33315
    Iliac Artery 34151-34201
    Innominate Artery 34001-34101
    Mesentery Artery 34151
    Peroneal Artery 34203
    Popliteal Artery 34203
    Radial Artery 34111
    Renal Artery .34151
    Subclavian Artery 34001-34101
    Tibial Artery .34203
    Ulnar Artery .34111
Embolism
    Pulmonary Artery 33910-33916
Empyema
    Lung 32540
    Pleural 32540
Epididymis
    Bilateral 54861
    Unilateral 54860
Epiglottis 31420
Esophagus
    Diverticula 43130-43135
    Partial 43116-43124
    Total 43107-43113, 43124
Eye
    See Enucleation, Eye

Peritrochanteric 27244
   Closed Treatment 27238
   Open Treatment 27269, 27267-27628
   Treatment with Implant 27244
   with Implant 27245
   with Manipulation 27240
Proximal End, Head
   Closed Treatment 27267-27268
Shaft 27500, 27502, 27506-27507
Subtrochanteric 27244
   Closed Treatment 27238
   Treatment with Implant 27244
   with Implant 27245
   with Manipulation 27240
Supracondylar 27501-27503, 27509,
                   27511-27513
   Open Treatment 27511, 27513
Transcondylar 27501-27503, 27509,
                   27511-27513
   Open Treatment 27511, 27513
Trochanteric
   Closed Treatment 27246
   Open Treatment 27248
   with Manipulation 27503
   without Manipulation 27501
Halo 20663
Lesion
   Excision .27062
Osteoplasty
   Lengthening 27466-27468
   Shortening 27465, 27468
Osteotomy
   without Fixation 27448
Prophylactic Treatment 27187, 27495
Realignment .27454
Reconstruction 27468
   at Knee 27442-27443, 27446
   Lengthening 27466-27468
   Shortening 27465, 27468
Repair .27470-27472
   Epiphysis 27181, 27475, 27742
   Arrest 27185
   Muscle Transfer 27110
   Osteotomy 27140, 27151-27156,
           27161-27165, 27450-27454
   with Graft 27170
Saucerization 27070, 27360
Tumor
   Excision . . .27065-27067, 27355-27358, 27365
X-ray 73550

Fenestration Procedure
Semicircular Canal 69820
   Revision .69840
Tracheostomy 31610

Fenestration, Pericardium
See Pericardiostomy

Fern Test 89060
See Smear and Stain, Wet Mount

Ferric Chloride
Urine 81005

Ferrihemoglobin
See Methemoglobin

Ferritin
Blood or Urine 82728

Ferroxidase
See Ceruloplasmin

Fertility Control
See Contraception

Fertility Test
Semen Analysis 89300-89322
Sperm Analysis 89331
   Cervical Mucus Penetration Test 89330
   Hamster Penetration 89329
Sperm Evaluation 89331

Fertilization
Assisted
   Oocyte
      Microtechnique 89280-89281
Oocyte
   with Co-Culture 89251

Fertilization in Vitro
See In Vitro Fertilization

Fetal Biophysical Profile 76818-76819

Fetal Contraction Stress Test 59020

Fetal Hemoglobin 85461

Fetal Lung Maturity Assessment; Lecithin Sphingomyelin Ratio 83661

Fetal Monitoring
See Monitoring, Fetal

Fetal Non-Stress Test 59025
Ultrasound 76818

Fetal Procedure
Amnioinfusion 59070
Cord Occlusion 59072
Fluid Drainage 59074
Shunt Placement 59076
Unlisted Fetal Invasive Procedure 59897
Unlisted Laparoscopy Procedure 59898
Unlisted Procedure, Maternity Care and
Delivery 59899

Fetal Testing
Amniotic Fluid
   Lung Maturity 83661, 83663-83664
Heart 76825-76826
   Doppler
      Complete 76827
      Follow-up or Repeat Study 76828
Hemoglobin 83030-83033, 85460
Ultrasound 76801-76828
   Heart 76825
   Middle Cerebral Artery 76821
   Umbilical Artery 76820

Fetuin
See Alpha-Fetoprotein

Fever, Australian Q
See Q Fever

Fever, Japanese River
See Scrub Typhus

Fibrillation
Atrial 33254-33256, 33265-33266
   Documentation 1060F-1061F

Fibrillation, Heart
See Heart, Fibrillation

Fibrin Degradation Products 85362-85380

Fibrin Deposit
Removal 32150

Fibrin Stabilizing Factor 85290-85291

Fibrinase
See Plasmin

Fibrinogen 85384-85385

Fibrinolysin
See Plasmin

Fibrinolysins 85390

Fibrinolysis
Alpha-2 Antiplasmin 85410
Assay 85396
   Activity .85397
   ADAMTS-13 85397
Plasmin 85400
Plasminogen 85420-85421
Plasminogen Activator 85415
Pleural Cavity
   Instillation of Agent 32561-32562

Fibroadenoma
Ablation
   Cryosurgical 19105
Excision 19120-19126

Fibroblastoma, Arachnoidal
See Meningioma

Fibrocutaneous Tags 11200-11201

Fibromatosis, Dupuytren's
See Dupuytren's Contracture

Fibromatosis, Penile
See Peyronie Disease

Fibromyoma
See Leiomyomata

Fibronectin, Fetal 82731

Fibrosis, Penile
See Peyronie Disease

Fibrosis, Retroperitoneal
See Retroperitoneal Fibrosis

Fibrous Cavernitides
See Peyronie Disease

Fibrous Dysplasia 21029, 21181-21184

Fibula
See Ankle; Knee; Tibia
Bone Graft with Microvascular
Anastomosis .20955
Craterization 27360, 27641
Cyst
   Excision 27635-27638
Diaphysectomy 27360, 27641
Excision 27360, 27641
   Epiphyseal Bar 20150
Fracture
   Malleolus 27786-27814
   Shaft 27780-27784
   Proximal
      Open Treatment 27784
Incision 27607
Osteoplasty
   Lengthening 27715

Skeletal
   Humeral Epycondyle
      Percutaneous 24566
Spinal
   Insertion 22841-22847
   Prosthetic 22851
   Reinsertion 22849

Fixation Test, Complement
See Complement, Fixation Test

Fixation, External
See External Fixation

Fixation, Kidney
See Nephropexy

Fixation, Rectum
See Proctopexy

Fixation, Tongue
See Tongue, Fixation

Flank
See Back/Flank

Flap
See Skin Graft and Flap
Free
   Breast Reconstruction 19364
Grafts 15570-15738, 15842
Latissimus Dorsi
   Breast Reconstruction 19361
Omentum 49905
   Free
      with Microvascular Anastomosis 49906
Transverse Rectus Abdominis Myocutaneous
   Breast Reconstruction 19367-19369

Flatfoot Correction 28735

Flea Typhus
See Murine Typhus

Fletcher Factor 85292

Flow Cytometry 88182-88189
Diagnostic/Pretreatment 3170F

Flow-Volume Loop
See Pulmonology, Diagnostic
Pulmonary 94375

Flu Vaccines 90645-90648, 90655-90663

Fluid Collection
Incision and Drainage
   Skin 10140

Fluid, Amniotic
See Amniotic Fluid

Fluid, Body
See Body Fluid

Fluid, Cerebrospinal
See Cerebrospinal Fluid

Fluorescein
Angiography, Ocular 92287
Intravenous Injection
   Vascular Flow Check, Graft 15860

Fluorescein Angiography
See Angiography, Fluorescein

Fluorescent In Situ
Hybridization 88365

Fluoride
Blood 82735
Urine 82735

Fluoroscopy
Bile Duct
   Calculus Removal 74327
   Guide Catheter 74328, 74330
Chest
   Bronchoscopy 31622-31646
   Complete (Four Views) 71034
   Partial (Two Views) 71023
Drain Abscess .75989
GI Tract
   Guide Intubation 74340
Hourly .76000-76001
Introduction
   GI Tube 74340
Larynx 70370
Nasogastric 43752
Needle Biopsy .77002
Orogastric 43752
Pancreatic Duct
   Guide Catheter 74329-74330
Pharynx 70370
Renal
   Guide Catheter 74475
Spine/Paraspinous
   Guide Catheter/Needle 77003
Unlisted Services and Procedures 76496
Ureter
   Guide Catheter 74480
Venous Access Device 36598, 77001
Vertebra
   Osteoplasty 77291

Flurazepam
Blood or Urine .82742

Flush Aortogram 75722-75724

FNA
See Fine Needle Aspiration

Foam Stability Test 83662

Fold, Vocal
See Vocal Cords

Foley Operation Pyeloplasty
See Pyeloplasty

Foley Y-Pyeloplasty 50400-50405

Folic Acid 82747
Blood 82746

Follicle Stimulating Hormone
(FSH) 80418, 80426, 83001

Folliculin
See Estrone

Follitropin
See Follicle Stimulating Hormone (FSH)

Follow-up Inpatient Consultations
See Consultation, Follow-up Inpatient

Follow-up Services
See Hospital Services; Office and/or Other
Outpatient Services
Post-Op 99024

Fontan Procedure
See Repair, Heart, Anomaly; Revision

Food Allergy Test 95075
See Allergy Tests

Foot
See Metatarsal; Tarsal
Amputation 28800-28805
Bursa
   Incision and Drainage 28001
Capsulotomy 28260-28264
Cast 29450
Fasciectomy 28060
   Radical 28060-28062
Fasciotomy 28008
   Endoscopic .29893
Incision 28002-28005
Joint
   See Talotarsal Joint; Tarsometatarsal Joint
   Magnetic Resonance Imaging
   (MRI) 73721-73723
Lesion
   Excision 28080, 28090
Magnetic Resonance Imaging (MRI) . . .73718-73720
Nerve
   Destruction
      Neurolytic 64632
   Excision 28055
   Incision 28035
Neurectomy 28055
Neuroma
   Excision 28080
   Injection of Anesthetic or Steroid . . .64455
   Morton's
      Destruction 64632
      Injection 64455
Reconstruction
   Cleft Foot 28360
Removal
   Foreign Body 28190-28193
Repair
   Muscle 28250
   Tendon 28200-28230, 28234-28238
Replantation 20838
Sesamoid
   Excision 28315
Splint 29590
Strapping 29540, 29590
Suture
   Tendon 28200-28210
Tendon Sheath
   Excision 28086-28088
Tenotomy 28230, 28234
Tumor
   Excision 28039-28045
   Radical Resection 28046-28047
Unlisted Services and Procedures 28899
X-ray 73620-73630

Foot Abscess
See Abscess, Foot

Foot Navicular Bone
See Navicular

Forearm 20805
See Arm, Lower

Gall Bladder
See Gallbladder

Gallbladder
See Bile Duct
Anastomosis
    with Intestines 47720-47741
Excision 47562-47564, 47600-47620
Exploration 47480
Incision 47490
Incision and Drainage 47480
Nuclear Medicine
    Imaging 78223
Removal
    Calculi (Stone) 47480
Repair
    with Gastroenterostomy 47741
    with Intestines 47720-47740
Unlisted Services and Procedures 47999
X-ray with Contrast 74290-74291

Galvanocautery
See Electrocautery

Galvanoionization
See Iontophoresis

Gamete Intrafallopian Transfer (GIFT) 58976

Gamete Transfer
In Vitro Fertilization 58976

Gamma Camera Imaging
See Nuclear Medicine

Gamma Glutamyl Transferase 82977

Gamma Seminoprotein
See Antigen, Prostate Specific

Gammacorten
See Dexamethasone

Gammaglobulin
Blood 82784-82787

Gamulin Rh
See Immune Globulins, Rho (D)

Ganglia, Trigeminal
See Gasserian Ganglion

Ganglion
See Gasserian Ganglion
Cyst
    Aspiration/Injection 20612
    Drainage 20612
    Wrist
        Excision 25111-25112
Injection
    Anesthetic 64505, 64510

Ganglion Cervicothoracicum
See Stellate Ganglion

Ganglion Pterygopalatinum
See Sphenopalatine Ganglion

Ganglion, Gasser's
See Gasserian Ganglion

Gardner Operation
See Meningocele Repair

Gardnerella Vaginalis Detection 87510-87512

Gasser Ganglion
See Gasserian Ganglion

Gasserian Ganglion
Sensory Root
    Decompression 61450
    Section 61450
Stereotactic 61790

Gastrectomy
Longitudinal 43775
Partial 43631-43635, 43845
    with Gastrojejunostomy 43632
Sleeve 43775
Total 43621-43622
    with Esophagoenterostomy 43620
with Gastroduodenostomy 43631

Gastric Acid 82926-82928

Gastric Analysis Test 91052

Gastric Electrodes
Implantation
    Laparoscopic
        Neurostimulator 43647
        Stimulation 0155T
    Open
        Neurostimulator 43881
        Stimulation 0157T
Removal
    Laparoscopic
        Neurostimulator 43648
        Stimulation 0156T
    Open
        Neurostimulator 43882
        Stimulation 0158T
Replacement
    Laparoscopic
        Neurostimulator 43647
        Stimulation 0155T
    Open
        Neurostimulator 43881
        Stimulation 0157T
Revision
    Laparoscopic
        Neurostimulator 43648
        Stimulation 0156T
    Open
        Neurostimulator 43882
        Stimulation 0158T

Gastric Intubation 89130-89141, 91105

Gastric Lavage, Therapeutic 91105

Gastric Tests
Manometry 91020

Gastric Ulcer Disease
See Stomach, Ulcer

Gastrin 82938-82941

Gastrocnemius Recession
Leg, Lower 27687

Gastroduodenostomy 43810, 43850-43855

Gastroenterology, Diagnostic
Breath Hydrogen Test 91065
Esophagus Tests
    Acid Perfusion 91030
    Acid Reflux 91034-91038
    Balloon Distension Provocation Study . . .91040
    Intubation with Specimen Collection . . .91000
    Motility Study 91010-91012
Gastric Tests
    Manometry 91020
Gastroesophageal Reflux Test
    See Acid Reflux
Intestine
    Bleeding Tube 91100
Manometry 91020
Rectum
    Sensation, Tone, and Compliance Test . . .91120
Rectum/Anus
    Manometry 91122
Stomach
    Intubation with Specimen Prep 91055
    Stimulation of Secretion 91052
Unlisted Services and Procedures 91299

Gastroenterostomy
for Obesity 43644-43645, 43842-43848

Gastroesophageal Reflux Test 91034-91038

Gastrointestinal Endoscopies
See Endoscopy, Gastrointestinal

Gastrointestinal Exam
Nuclear Medicine
    Blood Loss Study 78278
    Protein Loss Study 78282
    Shunt Testing 78291
    Unlisted Services and Procedures 78299

Gastrointestinal Tract
Imaging
    Intraluminal 91110-91111
Reconstruction 43360-43361
Upper
    Dilation 43249
X-ray .74240-74245
    Guide Dilator 74360
    Guide Intubation 74340
    with Contrast 74246-74249

Gastrointestinal, Upper
Biopsy
    Endoscopy 43239
Dilation
    Endoscopy 43245
    Esophagus 43248
Endoscopy
    Catheterization 43241
    Destruction
        Lesion 43258
    Dilation 43245
    Drainage
        Pseudocyst 43240
    Exploration 43234-43235
    Hemorrhage 43255
    Inject Varices 43243
    Injection 43236
    Needle Biopsy 43238, 43242
    Removal
        Foreign Body 43247
        Lesion 43251

Glaucoma
Cryotherapy 66720
Cyclophotocoagulation 66710-66711
Diathermy 66700
Fistulization of Sclera 66150
Provocative Test 92140

Glaucoma Drainage Implant
See Aqueous Shunt

Glenn Procedure 33766-33767

Glenohumeral Joint
Arthrotomy 23040
   with Biopsy 23100
   with Synovectomy 23105
Exploration 23107
Removal
   Foreign or Loose Body 23107

Glenoid Fossa
Reconstruction 21255

GLN
See Glutamine

Globulin
Antihuman .86880-86886
Immune 90281-90399
Sex Hormone Binding 84270

Globulin, Corticosteroid-Binding
See Transcortin

Globulin, Rh Immune
See Immune Globulins, Rho (D)

Globulin, Thyroxine-Binding
See Thyroxine Binding Globulin

Glomerular Procoagulant Activity
See Thromboplastin

Glomus Caroticum
See Carotid Body

Glossectomies
See Excision, Tongue

Glossopexy
See Tongue, Fixation

Glossorrhaphy
See Suture, Tongue

Glucagon 82943
Tolerance Panel 80422-80424
Tolerance Test 82946

Glucose 80422-80424, 80430-80435,
95250-95251
Blood Test 82947-82950, 82962
Body Fluid 82945
Interstitial Fluid
   Continuous Monitoring 95250-95251
Tolerance Test 82951-82952
   with Tolbutamide 82953

Glucose Phosphate Isomerase
See Phosphohexose Isomerase

Glucose Phosphate Isomerase Measurement
See Phosphohexose Isomerase

Glucose-6-Phosphate
Dehydrogenase 82955-82960

Glucosidase 82963

Glucuronide Androstanediol 82154

Glue
Cornea Wound 65286
Sclera Wound 65286

Glukagon
See Glucagon

Glutamate Dehydrogenase
Blood 82965

Glutamate Pyruvate Transaminase
See Transaminase, Glutamic Pyruvic

Glutamic Alanine Transaminase
See Transaminase, Glutamic Pyruvic

Glutamic Aspartic Transaminase
See Transaminase, Glutamic Oxaloacetic

Glutamic Dehydrogenase
See Glutamate Dehydrogenase

Glutamine 82975

Glutamyltransferase, Gamma 82977

Glutathione 82978

Glutathione Reductase 82979

Glutethimide .82980

Glycanhydrolase, N-Acetylmuramide
See Lysozyme

Glycated Hemoglobins
See Glycohemoglobin

Glycated Protein 82985

Glycerol Phosphoglycerides
See Phosphatidylglycerol

Glycerol, Phosphatidyl
See Phosphatidylglycerol

Glycerophosphatase
See Alkaline Phosphatase

Glycinate, Theophylline Sodium
See Theophylline

Glycocholic Acid
See Cholylglycine

Glycohemoglobin 83036

Glycol, Ethylene
See Ethylene Glycol

Glycols, Ethylene
See Ethylene Glycol

Glycosaminoglycan
See Mucopolysaccharides

GMP
See Guanosine Monophosphate

GMP, Cyclic
See Cyclic GMP

Goeckerman Treatment 96910-96913

Gol-Vernet Operation
See Pyelotomy, Exploration

Gold
Assay 80172

Goldwaite Procedure 27422

Golfer's Elbow
See Tennis Elbow

Gonadectomy, Female
See Oophorectomy

Gonadectomy, Male
See Excision, Testis

Gonadotropin
Chorionic 84702-84704
FSH 83001
ICSH 83002
LH 83002

Gonadotropin Panel 80426

Gonioscopy 92020

Goniotomy 65820

Gonococcus
See Neisseria Gonorrhoeae

Goodenough Harris Drawing
Test 96101-96103

GOTT
See Transaminase, Glutamic Oxaloacetic

GPUT
See Galactose-1-Phosphate, Uridyl Transferase

Graft
See Bone Graft; Bypass Graft
Anal 46753
Aorta 33840-33851, 33860-33877
Artery
   Coronary 33503-33505
Bone
   See Bone Marrow, Transplantation
   Harvesting 20900-20902
   Microvascular/Anastomosis . . .20955-20962
   Osteocutaneous Flap with
     Microvascular Anastomosis 20969-20973
   Vascular Pedicle 25430
Bone and Skin 20969-20973
Cartilage
   Costochondral 20910
   Ear to Face 21235
   Harvesting 20910-20912
     See Cartilage Graft
   Rib to Face 21230
Conjunctiva 65782
   Harvesting 68371
Cornea
   with Lesion Excision 65426
Cornea Transplant
   Allograft Preparation 65757
   Endothelial 65756
     in Aphakia 65750
     in Pseudophakia 65755
   Lamellar
     Anterior 65710
   Penetrating 65730

H

Haloperidol
Assay 80173

Halstead-Reitan Neurospychological Battery 96118

Halsted Mastectomy
See Mastectomy, Radical

Halsted Repair
See Hernia, Repair, Inguinal

Ham Test
See Hemolysins

Hammertoe Repair 28285-28286

Hamster Penetration Test 89329

Hand
See Carpometacarpal Joint; Intercarpal Joint
Amputation
  at Metacarpal 25927
  at Wrist 25920
    Revision 25922
  Revision 25924, 25929-25931
Arthrodesis
  Carpometacarpal Joint 26843-26844
  Intercarpal Joint 25820-25825
Bone
  Incision and Drainage 26034
Cast 29085
Decompression 26035-26037
Fracture
  Carpometacarpal 26641-26650
  Interphalangeal 26740-26746
  Metacarpal 26600-26615
  Metacarpophalangeal 26740-26746
  Phalangeal 26720-26735, 26750-26765
Insertion
  Tendon Graft 26392
Magnetic Resonance Imaging (MRI) . . .73218-73223
Reconstruction
  Tendon Pulley 26500-26502
Removal
  Implantation 26320
    Tube/Rod 26390-26392, 26416
Repair
  Blood Vessel 35207
  Cleft Hand 26580
  Muscle 26591-26593
  Tendon
    Extensor 26410-26416, 26426-26428,
                26433-26437
    Flexor 26350-26358, 26440
    Profundus 26370-26373
Replantation .20808
Strapping 29280
Tendon
  Excision .26390
  Extensor 26415
Tenotomy 26450, 26460
Tumor
  Excision 26115-26116
  Radical Resection 26117-26118, 26250
Unlisted Services and Procedures 26989
X-ray 73120-73130

Hand Abscess
See Abscess, Hand

Hand Phalange
See Finger, Bone

Hand(s) Dupuytrens Contracture(s)
See Dupuytren's Contracture

Handling
Device 99002
Radioelement 77790
Specimen 99000-99001

Hanganutziu Deicher Antibodies
See Antibody, Heterophile

Haptoglobin 83010-83012

Hard Palate
See Palate

Harelip Operation
See Cleft Lip, Repair

Harii Procedure 25430

Harrington Rod
Insertion 22840
Removal 22850

Hartmann Procedure
Laparoscopic .44206
Open 44143

Harvest of Upper Extremity Artery for Coronary Artery Bypass 35600

Harvesting
Bone Graft 20900-20902
Bone Marrow 38230
Cartilage Graft 20910-20912
Conjunctival Graft 68371
Eggs
  In Vitro Fertilization 58970
Endoscopic
  Vein for Bypass Graft 33508
Fascia Lata Graft 20920-20922
Intestines 44132-44133
Kidney 50300-50320, 50547
Liver 47133, 47140-47142
Lower Extremity Vein
  for Vascular Reconstruction 35572
Skin
  for Tissue Culture 15040
Stem Cell 38205-38206
Tendon Graft 20924
Tissue Grafts 20926
Upper Extremity Artery
  for Coronary Artery Bypass Graft 35600
Upper Extremity Vein
  for Bypass Graft 35500

Hauser Procedure 27420

Hayem's Elementary Corpuscle
See Blood, Platelet

Haygroves Procedure
See Reconstruction, Acetabulum; Revision

HBcAb
See Antibody, Hepatitis

HBeAb
See Antibody, Hepatitis

HBeAg
See Hepatitis Antigen, Be

HBsAb
See Antibody, Hepatitis

HBsAg (Hepatitis B Surface Antigen)
See Hepatitis Antigen, B Surface

HCG
See Chorionic Gonadotropin

HCO₃
See Bicarbonate

HCV Antibodies
See Antibody, Hepatitis C

HDL
See Lipoprotein

Head
Angiography 70496, 70544-70546
CT Scan 70450-70470, 70496
Excision 21011-21070
Fracture and/or Dislocation 21310-21497
Incision 21010, 61316, 62148
Introduction or Removal 21076-21116
Lipectomy, Suction Assisted 15876
Magnetic Resonance Angiography
(MRA) .70544-70546
Nerve
  Graft 64885-64886
Other Procedures 21299, 21499
Repair/Revision and/or
Reconstruction 21120-21296
Ultrasound Exam 76506, 76536
Unlisted Services and Procedures 21499
X-ray 70350

Head Rings, Stereotactic
See Stereotactic Frame

Headbrace
Application 21100
Application/Removal 20661

Heaf Test
See TB Test

Health Behavior
See Evaluation and Management, Health Behavior

Health Risk Assessment Instrument
See Preventive Medicine

Hearing Aid
Bone Conduction
  Implantation 69710
  Removal 69711
  Repair 69711
  Replacement 69710

Hearing Aid Check 92592-92593

Hearing Aid Services
Electroacoustic Test 92594-92595
Examination 92590-92591

Hearing Tests
See Audiologic Function Tests

Hearing Therapy 92507-92508,
                           92601-92604

Heart
Ablation .33250-33266
Allograft Preparation 33933
Angiography
  Injection 93542-93543
  See Cardiac Catheterization; Injection

Huggin Operation
See Orchiectomy, Simple

Huhner Test 89300, 89320

Human Chorionic Gonadotropin
See Chorionic Gonadotropin

Human Chorionic Somatomammotropin
See Lactogen, Human Placental

Human Cytomegalovirus Group
See Cytomegalovirus

Human Epididymis Protein 86305

Human Growth Hormone (HGH) 80418, 80428-80430

Human Herpes Virus 4
See Epstein-Barr Virus

Human Immunodeficiency Virus
See HIV

Human Immunodeficiency Virus 1
See HIV-1

Human Immunodeficiency Virus 2
See HIV-2

Human Papillomavirus
See Vaccine

Human Papillomavirus Detection 87620-87622

Human Placental Lactogen
See Lactogen, Human Placental

Human T Cell Leukemia Virus I
See HTLV I

Human T Cell Leukemia Virus I Antibodies
See Antibody, HTLV I

Human T Cell Leukemia Virus II
See HTLV II

Human T Cell Leukemia Virus II Antibodies
See Antibody, HTLV II

Humeral Epicondylitides, Lateral
See Tennis Elbow

Humeral Fracture
See Fracture, Humerus

Humerus
See Arm, Upper; Shoulder
Abscess
    Incision and Drainage 23935
Craterization 23184, 24140
Cyst
    Excision 23150, 24110
      with Allograft 23156, 24116
      with Autograft 23155, 24115
Diaphysectomy 23184, 24140
Excision 23174, 23184, 23195,
         24134, 24140, 24150

Fracture
  Closed Treatment 24500-24505
    with Manipulation 23605
    without Manipulation 23600
  Condyle
    Closed Treatment 24576-24577
    Open Treatment 24579
    Percutaneous Fixation 24582
  Epicondyle
    Closed Treatment 24560-24565
    Open Treatment 24575
    Skeletal Fixation
      Percutaneous 24566
  Greater Tuberosity Fracture
    Closed Treatment with
    Manipulation 23625
    Closed Treatment without
    Manipulation 23620
    Open Treatment 23630
  Open Treatment 23615-23616
  Shaft 24500-24505, 24516
    Open Treatment 24515
  Supracondylar
    Closed Treatment 24530-24535
    Open Treatment 24545-24546
    Percutaneous Fixation 24538
  Transcondylar
    Closed Treatment 24530-24535
    Open Treatment 24545-24546
    Percutaneous Fixation 24538
  with Dislocation 23665-23670
Osteomyelitis 24134
Pinning, Wiring 23491, 24498
Prophylactic Treatment 23491, 24498
Radical Resection 23220, 24150, 24152
Repair 24430
  Nonunion, Malunion 24430-24435
  Osteoplasty 24420
  Osteotomy 24400-24410
  with Graft 24435
Resection Head 23195
Saucerization 23184, 24140
Sequestrectomy 23174, 24134
Tumor
  Excision 23150, 23220, 24110,
             24071-24076
    with Allograft 23156, 24116
    with Autograft 23155, 24115
X-ray 73060

Hummelshein Operation
See Strabismus, Repair

Humor Shunt, Aqueous
See Aqueous Shunt

HVA
See Homovanillic Acid

Hybridization Probes, DNA
See Nucleic Acid Probe

Hydatid Disease
See Echinococcosis

Hydatid Mole
See Hydatidiform Mole

Hydatidiform Mole
Evacuation and Curettage 59870
Excision 59100

Hydration 96360-96361
Rehydration Oral Solution 4056F
Status 2030F-2031F

Hydrocarbons, Chlorinated
See Chlorinated Hydrocarbons

Hydrocele
Aspiration 55000
Excision
  Bilateral
    Tunica Vaginalis 55041
  Unilateral
    Spermatic Cord 55500
    Tunica Vaginalis 55040
Repair 55060

Hydrochloric Acid, Gastric
See Acid, Gastric

Hydrochloride, Vancomycin
See Vancomycin

Hydrocodon
See Dihydrocodeinone

Hydrogen Ion Concentration
See pH

Hydrolase, Acetylcholine
See Acetylcholinesterase

Hydrolase, Triacylglycerol
See Lipase

Hydrolases, Phosphoric Monoester
See Phosphatase

Hydrotherapy (Hubbard Tank) 97036
See Physical Medicine/Therapy/Occupational Therapy

Hydrotubation 58350

Hydroxyacetanilide
See Acetaminophen

Hydroxycorticosteroid 83491

Hydroxyindolacetic Acid 83497
Urine 83497

Hydroxypregnenolone 80406, 84143

Hydroxyprogesterone 80402-80406,
            83498-83499

Hydroxyproline 83500-83505

Hydroxytyramine
See Dopamine

Hygroma
Cystic
  Axillary/Cervical
    Excision 38550-38555

Hymen
Excision 56700
Incision 56442

Hymenal Ring
Revision 56700

Hymenectomy 56700

Hymenotomy 56442

Incision and Drainage

Incisional Hernia Repair
See Hernia, Repair, Incisional

Incomplete Abortion
See Abortion, Incomplete

Induced Abortion
See Abortion

Induced Hyperthermia
See Thermotherapy

Induced Hypothermia
See Hypothermia

Induratio Penis Plastica
See Peyronie Disease

Infant, Newborn, Intensive Care
See Intensive Care, Neonatal

Infantile Paralysis
See Polio

Infection, Actinomyces
See Actinomycosis

Infection, Bone
See Osteomyelitis

Infection, Filarioidea
See Filariasis

Infection, Postoperative Wound
See Postoperative Wound Infection

Infection, Wound
See Wound, Infection

Inspiratory Positive Pressure Breathing

Instillation

Instillation, Bladder

Instrumentation

Insufflation, Eustachian Tube

Insulin

Insulin C-Peptide Measurement

Insulin Like Growth Factors

Insurance

Integumentary System

Integumentum Commune

Intelligence Test

Intensive Care

Intercarpal Joint

Intercostal Nerve

Interdental Fixation

Interdental Papilla

Intestinovesical Fistula
See Fistula, Enterovesical

Intima-Media Thickness (IMT) Study
Artery

Intimectomy
See Endarterectomy

Intra Arterial Injections
See Injection, Intraarterial

Intra-Abdominal Voiding Pressure Studies

Intra-Osseous Infusion
See Infusion, Intraosseous

Intracapsular Extraction of Lens
See Extraction, Lens, Intracapsular

Intracardiac Echocardiography

Intracranial

Intracranial Arterial Perfusion

Intracranial Neoplasm, Acoustic Neuroma
See Brain, Tumor, Excision

Intracranial Neoplasm, Craniopharyngioma
See Craniopharyngioma

Intracranial Neoplasm, Meningioma
See Meningioma

Intrafallopian Transfer, Gamete
See GIFT

Intraluminal Angioplasty
See Angioplasty

Intramuscular Injection
See Injection, Intramuscular

Intraocular Lens

Intratracheal Intubation
See Insertion, Endotracheal Tube

Intrauterine Contraceptive Device
See Intrauterine Device (IUD)

Intrauterine Device (IUD)

Intrauterine Synechiae
See Adhesions, Intrauterine

Intravascular Sensor
Pressure

Intravascular Stent
See Transcatheter, Placement, Intravascular Stents

Intravascular Ultrasound

Intravenous Infusion

Intravenous Injection
See Injection, Intravenous

Intravenous Pyelogram
See Urography, Intravenous

Intravenous Therapy
See Injection, Chemotherapy

Intravesical Instillation
See Bladder, Instillation

Intravitreal Injection

Intrinsic Factor

Introduction
Breast

Intubation
See Insertion

Intubation Tube
See Endotracheal Tube

Intussusception

Invagination, Intestinal
See Intussusception

Inversion, Nipple
See Nipples, Inverted

Iodide Test
See Nuclear Medicine, Thyroid, Uptake

Iodine Test
See Starch Granules, Feces

Ionization, Medical
See Iontophoresis

Iontophoreses
See Iontophoresis

Iontophoresis

IP
See Allergen Immunotherapy

Ipecac Administration

IPPB
See Intermittent Positive Pressure Breathing;
Pulmonology, Therapeutic

Iridectomy
by Laser Surgery 66761
Peripheral for Glaucoma 66625
with Corneoscleral or Corneal Section 66600
with Sclerectomy with Punch or Scissors . . .66160
with Thermocauterization 66155
with Transfixion as for Iris Bombe 66605
with Trephination 66150

Iridencleisis 66165

Iridodialysis 66680

Iridoplasty 66762

Iridotasis 66165

Iridotomy
by Laser Surgery 66761
by Stab Incision 66500
Excision
    Optical 66635
    Peripheral 66625
    with Corneoscleral or Corneal Section . . .66600
    with Cyclectomy 66605
Incision
    Stab 66500
    with Transfixion as for Iris Bombe 66505
Optical 66635
Peripheral 66625
Sector 66630

Iris
Cyst
    Destruction 66770
Excision
    Iridectomy
        Optical 66635
        Peripheral .66625
        Sector 66630
        with Corneoscleral or Corneal
        Section 66600
        with Cyclectomy 66605
Incision
    Iridotomy
        Stab 66500
        with Transfixion as for Iris Bombe 66505
Lesion
    Destruction 66770
Repair
    with Ciliary Body 66680
        Suture 66682
Revision
    Laser Surgery .66761
    Photocoagulation 66762
Suture
    with Ciliary Body 66682

Iron 83540

Iron Binding Capacity 83550

Iron Hematoxylin Stain 88312

Iron Stain 85536, 88313

Irradiation
Blood Products 86945

Irrigation
Bladder 51700
Catheter
    Brain 62194, 62225
Corpora Cavernosa
    Priapism 54220

Penis
    Priapism 54220
Peritoneal
    See Peritoneal Lavage
Rectum
    for Fecal Impaction 91123
Shunt
    Spinal Cord 63744
Sinus
    Maxillary 31000
    Sphenoid 31002
Vagina 57150
Venous Access Device 96523

Irving Sterilization
See Ligation, Fallopian Tube, Oviduct

Ischemic Stroke
Onset 1065F-1066F
Tissue Plasminogen Activator (tPA)
    Documentation That Administration
    Was Considered 4077F

Ischial
Bursa
    Excision 27060
Tumor
    Radical Resection 27075, 27078

Ischiectomy .15941

Island Pedicle Flaps 15740

Islands of Langerhans
See Islet Cell

Islet Cell
Antibody 86341
Transplantation 0141T-0143T

Isocitrate Dehydrogenase
See Isocitric Dehydrogenase

Isocitric Dehydrogenase
Blood 83570

Isolation
Sperm .89260-89261

Isomerase, Glucose 6 Phosphate
See Phosphohexose Isomerase

Isopropanol
See Isopropyl Alcohol

Isopropyl Alcohol 84600

Isthmusectomy
Thyroid Gland 60210-60225

IUD
See Intrauterine Device (IUD)

IV
See Injection, Chemotherapy; Intravenous Therapy

IV Infusion Therapy
See Allergen Immunotherapy; Chemotherapy;
Infusion; Injection, Chemotherapy

IV Injection
See Injection, Intravenous

IV, Coagulation Factor
See Calcium

IVC Filter
Placement 75940

IVF
See Artificial Insemination; In Vitro Fertilization

Ivy Bleeding Time 85002

IX Complex, Factor
See Christmas Factor

J

Jaboulay Operation
See Gastroduodenostomy

Jaboulay Operation Gastroduodenostomy
See Gastroduodenostomy

Jannetta Procedure
See Decompression, Cranial Nerve; Section

Japanese Encephalitis Virus
See Vaccine

Japanese, River Fever
See Scrub Typhus

Jatene Type 33770-33781

Jaw Joint
See Facial Bones; Mandible; Maxilla

Jaws
Muscle Reduction 21295-21296
X-ray
    for Orthodontics 70355

Jejunostomy
Catheterization .44015
Contrast 49465
Insertion
    Catheter 44015
    Percutaneous 49441
Laparoscopic 44186-44187
Non-Tube 44187, 44310
Obstructive Material Removal 49460
Replacement 49451
with Pancreatic Drain 48001

Jejunum
Creation
    Stoma
Laparoscopic 44186
Transfer
    with Microvascular Anastomosis
        Free 43496

Johannsen Procedure 53400

Joint
See Specific Joint
Acromioclavicular
    See Acromioclavicular Joint
Arthrocentesis 20600-20610
Aspiration 20600-20610
Dislocation
    See Dislocation

Drainage 20600-20610
Finger
   See Intercarpal Joint
Fixation (Surgical)
   See Arthrodesis
Foot
   See Foot, Joint
Hip
   See Hip Joint
Injection 20600-20610
Intertarsal
   See Intertarsal Joint
Knee
   See Knee Joint
Ligament
   See Ligament
Metacarpophalangeal
   See Metacarpophalangeal Joint
Metatarsophalangeal
   See Metatarsophalangeal Joint
Nuclear Medicine
   Imaging 78300, 78315
Radiology
   Stress Views 77071
Replacement
   Vertebral 0202T
Sacroiliac
   See Sacroiliac Joint
Shoulder
   See Glenohumeral Joint
Sternoclavicular
   See Sternoclavicular Joint
Survey 77077
Temporomandibular
   See Temporomandibular Joint (TMJ)
   Dislocation Temporomandibular
     See Dislocation, Temporomandibular Joint
   Implant
     See Prosthesis, Temporomandibular Joint
Wrist
   See Radiocarpal Joint

Joint Syndrome, Temporomandibular
See Temporomandibular Joint (TMJ)

Jones and Cantarow Test
See Blood Urea Nitrogen; Urea Nitrogen, Clearance

Jones Procedure 28760

Joplin Procedure 28294

Jugal Bone
See Cheekbone

Jugular Vein
See Vein, Jugular

K

K-Wire Fixation
Tongue 41500

Kader Operation
See Incision, Stomach, Creation, Stoma; Incision and Drainage

Kala Azar Smear 87207

Kallidin I /Kallidin 9
See Bradykinin

Kallikrein HK3
See Antigen, Prostate Specific

Kallikreinogen
See Fletcher Factor

Kasai Procedure 47701

Kedani Fever
See Scrub Typhus

Keel
Insertion/Removal
   Laryngoplasty 31580

Kelikian Procedure 28280

Keller Procedure 28292

Kelly Urethral Plication 57220

Keratectomy
Partial
   for Lesion 65400

Keratomileusis 65760

Keratophakia 65765

Keratoplasty
Endothelial 65756
   Allograft Preparation 65757
Lamellar
   Anterior 65710
Penetrating 65730
   in Aphakia 65750
   in Pseudophakia 65755

Keratoprosthesis 65770

Keratotomy
Radial 65771

Ketogenic Steroids 83582

Ketone Body
Acetone 82009-82010

Ketosteroids 83586-83593

Kidner Procedure 28238

Kidney
Abscess
   Incision and Drainage 50020
     Open 50020
     Percutaneous 50021
Anesthesia 00862
Biopsy 50200-50205
   Endoscopic 50555-50557, 52354
Catheterization
   Endoscopic 50572
Cyst
   Ablation 50541
   Aspiration 50390
   Excision 50280-50290
   Injection 50390
   X-ray 74470
Destruction
   Calculus 50590
   Endoscopic 50557, 50576, 52354
Dilation 50395

Endoscopy
   Biopsy 50555, 50574-50576, 52354
   Catheterization 50553, 50572
   Destruction 50557, 50576, 52354
   Dilation
     Intra-Renal Stricture 52343, 52346
     Ureter 50553
   Excision
     Tumor 52355
   Exploration 52351
   Lithotripsy 52353
   Removal
     Calculus 50561, 50580, 52352
     Foreign Body 50561, 50580
   via Incision 50562-50580
   via Stoma 50551-50561
Excision
   Donor 50300-50320, 50547
   Partial 50240
   Recipient 50340
   Transplantation 50370
   with Ureters 50220-50236
Exploration 50010, 50045, 50120
Incision 50010, 50045
Incision and Drainage 50040, 50125
Injection
   Drugs 50391
   Radiologic 50394
Insertion
   Catheter 50392-50393
   Guide 50395
   Intracatheter 50392
   Stent 50393
   Tube 50398
Instillation
   Drugs 50391
Lithotripsy 50590
Manometry
   Pressure 50396
Mass
   Ablation 50542
     Cryosurgical 50250
     Radiofrequency 50592
Needle Biopsy 50200
Nuclear Medicine
   Function Study 78725
   Imaging 78700-78710
   Unlisted Services and Procedures 78799
Removal
   Calculus 50060-50081, 50130, 50561
   Foreign Body 50561, 50580
   Tube
     Nephrostomy 50389
Repair
   Blood Vessels 50100
   Fistula 50520-50526
   Horseshoe Kidney 50540
   Renal Pelvis 50400-50405
   Wound 50500
Solitary 50405
Suture
   Fistula 50520-50526
   Horseshoe Kidney 50540
Transplantation
   Allograft Preparation 50323-50329
   Anesthesia
     Donor 00862
     Recipient 00868
   Donor 00862
   Donor Nephrectomy 50300-50320, 50547
   Implantation of Graft 50360
   Recipient Nephrectomy 50340, 50365

Reimplantation Kidney 50380
Removal Transplant Renal Autograft 50370
Tumor
  Ablation
    Cryotherapy 0135T, 50593
Ultrasound 76770-76776
X-ray with Contrast
  Guide Catheter .74475

Kidney Stone
See Calculus, Removal, Kidney

Killian Operation
See Sinusotomy, Frontal

Kinase, Creatine
See CPK

Kineplasty
See Cineplasty

Kinetic Therapy 97530
See Physical Medicine/Therapy/Occupational
Therapy

Kininase A
See Angiotensin Converting Enzyme (ACE)

Kininogen 85293

Kininogen, High Molecular Weight
See Fitzgerald Factor

Kleihauer-Betke Test 85460

Kloramfenikol
See Chloramphenicol

Knee
See Femur; Fibula; Patella; Tibia
Abscess 27301
Arthrocentesis 20610
Arthrodesis 27580
Arthroplasty 27440-27445, 27447
  Revision 27486-27487
Arthroscopy
  Diagnostic 29870
  Surgical 29866-29868, 29871-29889
Arthrotomy 27310, 27330-27335, 27403
Autogaft, Osteochondral, Open 27416
Biopsy 27323-27324, 27330-27331
  Synovium 27330
Bone
  Drainage 27303
Bursa 27301
  Excision 27340
Cyst
  Excision 27345-27347
Disarticulation 27598
Dislocation 27550-27552, 27560-27562
  Open Treatment 27556-27558, 27566
Drainage 27310
Excision
  Cartilage 27332-27333
  Ganglion 27347
  Lesion 27347
  Synovium 27334-27335
Exploration 27310, 27331
Fasciotomy 27305, 27496-27499
Fracture .27520-27524
  Arthroscopic Treatment 29850-29851
Fusion 27580
Hematoma 27301
Incision
  Capsule 27435

Injection
  X-ray 27370
Magnetic Resonance Imaging (MRI) . . .73721-73723
Manipulation 27570
Meniscectomy 27332-27333
Reconstruction 27437-27438
  Ligament 27427-27429
  with Prosthesis 27445
Removal
  Foreign Body 27310, 27331, 27372
  Loose Body .27331
  Prosthesis 27488
Repair
  Ligament 27405-27409
    Collateral 27405
    Collateral and Cruciate 27409
    Cruciate 27407-27409
  Meniscus 27403
  Tendon 27380-27381
Replacement 27447
Retinacular
  Release 27425
Strapping 29530
Suture
  Tendon 27380-27381
Transplantation
  Chondrocytes 27412
  Meniscus 29868
  Osteochondral
    Allograft 27415, 29867
    Autograft 27412, 29866
Tumor
  Excision 27327-27328, 27337-27339
  Radical Resection 27329, 27364-27365
Unlisted Services and Procedures 27599
X-ray 73560-73564
  Arthrography 73580
  Bilateral 73565
X-ray with Contrast
  Arthrography 73580

Knee Joint
Arthroplasty 27446

Knee Prosthesis
See Prosthesis, Knee

Kneecap
Excision 27350
Repair
  Instability 27420-27424

Knock-Knee Repair 27455-27457

Kocher Operation 23650-23680
See Clavicle; Scapula; Shoulder, Dislocation,
Closed Treatment

Kocher Pylorectomy
See Gastrectomy, Partial

Kock Pouch 44316
Formation 50825

Kock Procedure 44316

KOH
See Hair, Nails, Tissue, Examination for Fungi

Kraske Procedure 45116

Kroenlein Procedure 67420

Krukenberg Procedure 25915

Kuhlmann Test 96101-96103

Kyphectomy
More than Two Segments 22819
Up to Two Segments 22818

Kyphoplasty 22523-22525

L

L Ascorbic Acid
See Ascorbic Acid

L Aspartate 2 Oxoglutarate Aminotransferase
See Transaminase, Glutamic Oxaloacetic

L Glutamine
See Glutamine

L-Alanine
See Aminolevulinic Acid (ALA)

L-Leucylnaphthylamidase
See Leucine Aminopeptidase

L/S Ratio
Amniotic Fluid 83661

Labial Adhesions
Lysis 56441

Labyrinth
See Ear, Inner

Labyrinthectomy 69905
with Mastoidectomy 69910
with Skull Base Surgery 61596

Labyrinthotomy
with Mastoidectomy 69802
with/without Cryosurgery 69801

Laceration Repair
See Specific Site

Lacrimal Duct
Balloon 68816
Canaliculi
  Repair 68700
Dilation 68816
Exploration 68810
  Canaliculi 68840
  Stent 68815
  with Anesthesia 68811
Insertion
  Stent 68815
Nasolacrimal Duct Probing 68816
Removal
  Dacryolith 68530
  Foreign Body 68530
X-ray with Contrast 70170

Lacrimal Gland
Biopsy 68510
Close Fistula 68770
Excision
  Partial 68505
  Total 68500

Proctectomy
  Complete 45395
    with Creation of Colonic Reservoir 45397
Proctopexy
  for Prolapse 45400-45402
Prostatectomy 55866
Pyeloplasty 50544
Rectum
  Resection 45395-45397
  Unlisted 45499
Removal
  Fallopian Tube 58661
  Leiomyomata 58545-58546
  Ovaries 58661
  Spleen 38120
  Testis 54690
Resection
  Intestines
    with Anastomosis 44202-44203
    Rectum 45395-45397
Salpingostomy 58673
Splenectomy 38120-38129
Splenic Flexure
  Mobilization 44213
Stomach 43647-43659
  Gastric Bypass 43644-43645
  Gastric Restrictive Procedures ...43770-43775,
                    43848, 43886-43888
  Gastroenterostomy 43644-43645
  Roux-En-Y 43644
Transplantation
  Islet Cell 0143T
Unlisted Services and Procedures
  Abdomen, Omentum, and Peritoneum ...49329
  Appendix 44979
  Biliary Tract 47579
  Bladder 51999
  Esophagus 43289
  Hernioplasty, Herniorrhaphy,
  Herniotomy 49659
  Intestine 44238
  Liver 47379
  Lymphatic System 38589
  Maternity Care and Delivery 59898-59899
  Oviduct, Ovary 58679
  Rectum 45499
  Renal 50549
  Spermatic Cord 55559
  Spleen 38129
  Stomach 43659
  Testis 54699
  Ureter 50949
  Uterus 58578-58579
Ureterolithotomy 50945
Ureteroneocystostomy 50947-50948
Urethral Suspension 51990
Vaginal Hysterectomy 58550-58554
Vaginal Suspension 57425
Vagus Nerves
  Transection 43651-43652
with X-ray 47560

Laparotomy
Electrode Implantation
  Gastric 43881, 0157T
Electrode Removal
  Gastric 43882, 0158T
Electrode Replacement
  Gastric 43881, 0157T
Electrode Revision
  Gastric 43882, 0158T
Exploration 47015, 49000-49002

Hemorrhage Control 49002
Second Look 58960
Staging 49220, 58960
with Biopsy 49000

Laparotomy, Exploratory
See Abdomen, Exploration

Lapidus Procedure 28297

Large Bowel
See Anus; Rectum

Laroyenne Operation
See Vagina, Abscess, Incision and Drainage

Laryngeal Function Study 92520

Laryngeal Sensory
Testing 92614-92617

Laryngectomy 31360-31382
Partial 31367-31382
Subtotal 31367-31368

Laryngocele
Removal 31300

Laryngofissure 31300

Laryngography 70373
Instillation

Laryngopharyngectomy
See Excision, Larynx, with Pharynx

Laryngopharynx
See Hypopharynx

Laryngoplasty
Burns 31588
Cricoid Split 31587
Laryngeal Stenosis 31582
Laryngeal Web 31580
Open Reduction of Fracture 31584

Laryngoscopy
Diagnostic 31505
Direct 31515-31571
Exploration 31505, 31520-31526, 31575
Fiberoptic 31575-31579
  with Stroboscopy 31579
Indirect 31505-31513
Newborn 31520
Operative 31530-31561

Laryngotomy 31300
Diagnostic 31320

Larynx
Aspiration
  Endoscopy 31515
Biopsy
  Endoscopy 31510, 31535-31536, 31576
Dilation
  Endoscopic 31528-31529
Electromyography
  Needle 95865
Endoscopy
  Direct 31515-31571
  Excision 31545-31546
  Exploration 31505, 31520-31526, 31575
  Fiberoptic 31575-31579
    with Stroboscopy 31579
  Indirect 31505-31513
  Operative 31530-31561

Excision
  Lesion 31512, 31578
    Endoscopic 31545-31546
  Partial 31367-31382
  Total 31360-31365
  with Pharynx 31390-31395
Exploration
  Endoscopic 31505, 31520-31526, 31575
Fracture 31584
Insertion
  Obturator 31527
Nerve
  Destruction 31595
Reconstruction
  Burns 31588
  Cricoid Split 31587
  Other 31588
  Stenosis 31582
  Web 31580
Removal
  Foreign Body
    Endoscopic 31511, 31530-31531, 31577
  Lesion
    Endoscopic 31512, 31545-31546, 31578
Repair
  Reinnervation Neuromuscular Pedicle ...31590
Stroboscopy 31579
Tumor
  Excision 31300
    Endoscopic 31540-31541
Unlisted Services and Procedures 31599
Vocal Cord(s)
  Injection 31513, 31570-31571
X-ray 70370
  with Contrast 70373

Laser Surgery
Anus 46614, 46917
Cautery
  Esophagus 43227
  Hemorrhoids 46930
Lacrimal Punctum 68760
Lens, Posterior 66821
Lesion
  Mouth 40820
  Nose 30117-30118
  Penis 54057
  Skin 17000-17111, 17260-17286
Myocardium 33140-33141
Prostate 52647-52648
Spine
  Discectomy 62287
Tumors
  Urethra and Bladder 52234
Urethra and Bladder 52214

Laser Treatment 17000-17286,
                    96920-96922

See Destruction

Lateral Epicondylitis
See Tennis Elbow

Latex Fixation 86403-86406

LATS
See Thyrotropin Releasing Hormone (TRH)

Latzko Operation
See Repair, Vagina, Fistula; Revision

LAV
See HIV

LAV Antibodies
See Antibody, HIV

LAV-2
See HIV-2

Lavage
Colon .... .44701
Lung
   Bronchial .... .31624
   Total .... .32997
Peritoneal .... .49080

LCM
See Lymphocytic Choriomeningitis

LD
See Lactate Dehydrogenase

LDH 83615-83625

LDL
See Lipoprotein, LDL

Lead .... .83655

Leadbetter Procedure .... .53431

Lecithin-Sphingomyelin Ratio .... .83661

Lecithinase C
See Tissue, Typing

Lee and White Test .... .85345

LEEP Procedure .... .57460

LeFort Procedure
Vagina .... .57120

LeFort I Procedure
Midface Reconstruction 21141-21147,
                                21155, 21160
Palatal or Maxillary Fracture 21421-21423

LeFort II Procedure
Midface Reconstruction 21150-21151
Nasomaxillary Complex Fracture 21345-21348

LeFort III Procedure
Craniofacial Separation 21431-21436
Midface Reconstruction 21154-21159

Left Atrioventricular Valve
See Mitral Valve

Left Heart Cardiac Catheterization
See Cardiac Catheterization, Left Heart

Leg
Cast
   Rigid Total Contact .... .29445
Lower
  See Ankle; Fibula; Knee; Tibia
   Abscess
     Incision and Drainage .... .27603
   Amputation .... .27598, 27880-27882
     Revision 27884-27886
   Angiography .... .73706
   Artery
     Ligation .... .37618
   Biopsy 27613-27614
   Bursa
     Incision and Drainage .... .27604
   Bypass Graft .... .35903
   Cast 29405-29435, 29450

CT Scan 73700-73706
Decompression 27600-27602
Exploration
   Blood Vessel .... .35860
Fasciotomy 27600-27602, 27892-27894
Hematoma
   Incision and Drainage .... .27603
Lesion
   Excision .... .27630
Magnetic Resonance Imaging
(MRI) 73718-73720
Neurectomy 27325-27326
Repair
   Blood Vessel .... .35226
   Blood Vessel with Other Graft ...... .35286
   Blood Vessel with Vein Graft .... .35256
   Fascia .... .27656
   Tendon 27658-27692
Splint .... .29515
Strapping
   Unna Boot .... .29580
   Venous Wound Compression .... .29581
Suture
   Tendon 27658-27665
Tumor
   Excision 27618-27619, 27632-27634
   Radical Resection 27615-27616
Ultrasound .... .76880
Unlisted Services and Procedures ..... .27899
Unna Boot .... .29580
X-ray .... .73592
Upper
  See Femur
   Abscess .... .27301
   Amputation 27590-27592
     at Hip 27290-27295
     Revision 27594-27596
   Angiography .... .73706, 75635
   Artery
     Ligation .... .37618
   Biopsy 27323-27324
   Bursa .... .27301
   Bypass Graft .... .35903
   Cast 29345-29355, 29365, 29450
   Cast Brace .... .29358
   CT Scan 73700-73706, 75635
   Exploration
     Blood Vessel .... .35860
   Fasciotomy .... .27305, 27496-27499,
                       27892-27894
   Halo Application .... .20663
   Hematoma .... .27301
   Magnetic Resonance Imaging
   (MRI) 73718-73720
   Neurectomy 27325-27326
   Removal
     Cast .... .29705
     Foreign Body .... .27372
   Repair
     Blood Vessel with Other Graft ...... .35286
     Blood Vessel with Vein Graft .... .35256
     Muscle 27385-27386, 27400, 27430
     Tendon 27393-27400
   Splint .... .29505
   Strapping .... .29580
   Suture
     Muscle 27385-27386
   Tenotomy 27306-27307, 27390-27392
   Tumor
     Excision 27327-27328, 27337-27339
   Ultrasound .... .76880
   Unlisted Services and Procedures ..... .27599

   Unna Boot .... .29580
   X-ray .... .73592
Wound Exploration
   Penetrating .... .20103

Leg Length Measurement X-ray
See Scanogram

Legionella
Antibody .... .86713
Antigen 87277-87278, 87540-87542

Legionella Micdadei
Antigen Detection
   Immunofluorescence .... .87277

Legionella Pneumophila
Antigen Detection
   Direct Fluorescence .... .87278

Leiomyomata
Embolization .... .37210
Removal .... .58140, 58545-58546, 58561

Leishmania
Antibody .... .86717

Lengthening, Tendon
See Tendon, Lengthening

Lens
Extracapsular .... .66940
Incision .... .66821
Intracapsular .... .66920
   Dislocated .... .66930
Intraocular
   Exchange .... .66986
   Reposition .... .66825
Laser .... .66821
Prosthesis
   Insertion .... .66983
     Manual or Mechanical Technique .... .66982,
                            66984
     Not Associated with Concurrent Cataract
     Removal .... .66985
Removal
   Lens Material
     Aspiration Technique .... .66840
     Extracapsular .... .66940
     Intracapsular 66920-66930
     Pars Plana Approach .... .66852
     Phacofragmentation Technique ...... .66850

Lens Material
Aspiration Technique .... .66840
Pars Plana Approach .... .66852
Phacofragmentation Technique .... .66850

Leptomeningioma
See Meningioma

Leptospira
Antibody .... .86720

Leriche Operation .... .64809
See Sympathectomy, Thoracolumbar

Lesion
See Tumor
Anal
   Destruction 46900-46917, 46924
   Excision .... .45108, 46922
Ankle
   Tendon Sheath .... .27630

Arm, Lower
  Tendon Sheath
    Excision 25110
Auditory Canal, External
  Excision
    Exostosis 69140
    Radical with Neck Dissection 69155
    Radical without Neck Dissection 69150
    Soft Tissue 69145
Bladder
  Destruction 51030
Brain
  Excision 61534, 61536,
          61600-61608, 61615-61616
Brainstem
  Excision 61575-61576
Breast
  Excision 19120-19126
Carotid Body
  Excision 60600-60605
Chemotherapy 96405-96406
  Destruction 67220-67225
Choroid
  Destruction 0016T
Ciliary Body
  Destruction 66770
Colon
  Destruction 44393, 45383
  Excision 44110-44111
Conjunctiva
  Destruction 68135
  Excision 68110-68130
    Over 1 cm 68115
    with Adjacent Sclera 68130
  Expression 68040
Cornea
  Destruction 65450
  Excision 65400
    of Pterygium 65420-65426
Cranium 77432
Destruction
  Ureter 52341-52342, 52344-52345, 52354
Ear, Middle
  Excision 69540
Epididymis
  Excision 54830
Esophagus
  Ablation 43228
  Excision 43100-43101
  Removal 43216
Excision 59100
  Bladder 52224
  Urethra 52224, 53265
Eye
  Excision 65900
Eyelid
  Destruction 67850
  Excision
    Multiple, Different Lids 67805
    Multiple, Same Lid 67801
    Single 67800
    Under Anesthesia 67808
    without Closure 67840
Facial
  Destruction 17000-17004, 17280-17286
Femur
  Excision 27062
Finger
  Tendon Sheath 26160
Foot
  Excision 28080, 28090

Gums
  Destruction 41850
  Excision 41822-41828
Hand Tendon Sheath 26160
Intestines
  Excision 44110
Intestines, Small
  Destruction 44369
  Excision 44111
Iris
  Destruction 66770
Larynx
  Excision 31545-31546
Leg, Lower
  Tendon Sheath 27630
Lymph Node
  Incision and Drainage 38300-38305
Mesentery
  Excision 44820
Mouth
  Destruction 40820
  Excision 40810-40816, 41116
  Vestibule
    Destruction 40820
    Repair 40830
Nerve
  Excision 64774-64792
Nose
  Intranasal
    External Approach 30118
    Internal Approach 30117
Orbit
  Excision 61333, 67412
Palate
  Destruction 42160
  Excision 42104-42120
Pancreas
  Excision 48120
Pelvis
  Destruction 58662
Penis
  Destruction
    Cryosurgery 54056
    Electrodesiccation 54055
    Extensive 54065
    Laser Surgery 54057
    Simple 54050-54060
    Surgical Excision 54060
  Excision 54060
    Penile Plague 54110-54112
Pharynx
  Destruction 42808
  Excision 42808
Radiosurgery
  Cranial 61796-61800
Rectum
  Excision 45108
Removal
  Larynx 31512, 31578
Resection 52354
Retina
  Destruction
    Extensive 67227-67228
    Localized 0017T, 67208-67210
    Radiation by Implantation of Source 67218
Sciatic Nerve
  Excision 64786
Sclera
  Excision 66130
Skin
  Abrasion 15786-15787
  Biopsy 11100-11101

Destruction
  Benign 17110-17111, 17250
  Malignant 17260-17286
  Premalignant 17000-17004
Excision
  Benign 11400-11471
  Malignant 11600-11646
Injection 11900-11901
Paring or Curettement 11055-11057
Shaving 11300-11313
Skin Tags
  Removal 11200-11201
Skull
  Excision ...61500, 61600-61608, 61615-61616
Spermatic Cord
  Excision 55520
Spinal Cord
  Destruction 62280-62282
  Excision 63265-63273
Stomach
  Excision 43611
Testis
  Excision 54512
Toe
  Excision 28092
Tongue
  Excision 41110-41114
Uvula
  Destruction 42145
  Excision 42104-42107
Vagina
  Destruction 57061-57065
Vulva
  Destruction
    Extensive 56515
    Simple 56501
Wrist Tendon
  Excision 25110

Leu 2 Antigens
See CD8

Leucine Aminopeptidase 83670

Leukemia Lymphoma Virus I Antibodies, Human T Cell
See Antibody, HTLV-I

Leukemia Lymphoma Virus I, Adult T Cell
See HTLV I

Leukemia Lymphoma Virus II Antibodies, Human T Cell
See Antibody, HTLV-II

Leukemia Virus II, Hairy Cell Associated, Human T Cell
See HTLV II

Leukoagglutinins 86021

Leukocyte
See White Blood Cell
Alkaline Phosphatase 85540
Antibody 86021
Count 85032, 85048, 89055
Histamine Release Test 86343
Phagocytosis 86344
Transfusion 86950

Levarterenol
See Noradrenalin

Excision
Extensive 47122
Partial ...47120, 47125-47130, 47140-47142
Total 47133
Injection 47015
Radiologic 47505
X-ray 47500
Lobectomy 47125-47130
Partial 47120
Needle Biopsy 47000-47001
Nuclear Medicine
Function Study 78220
Imaging 78201-78216
Vascular Flow 78206
Repair
Abscess 47300
Cyst 47300
Wound 47350-47362
Suture
Wound 47350-47362
Transplantation 47135-47136
Allograft Preparation 47143-47147
Trisegmentectomy....................47122
Unlisted Services and Procedures ...47379, 47399

Living Activities, Daily
See Activities of Daily Living

Lobectomy
Brain 61323, 61537-61540
Contralateral Subtotal
Thyroid Gland 60212, 60225
Liver 47120-47130
Lung 32480-32482
Sleeve 32486
Parotid Gland 42410-42415
Segmental 32663
Sleeve 32486
Temporal Lobe 61537-61538
Thyroid Gland Partial 60210-60212
Total 60220-60225
Total 32663

Lobotomy
Frontal 61490

Local Excision Mastectomies
See Breast, Excision, Lesion

Local Excision of Lesion or Tissue of Femur
See Excision, Lesion, Femur

Localization of Nodule
Radiographic
Breast..........................77032

Log Hydrogen Ion Concentration
See pH

Long Acting Thyroid Stimulator
See Thyrotropin Releasing Hormone (TRH)

Long-Term Care Facility Visits
See Nursing Facility Services

Longmire Operation
See Anastomosis, Hepatic Duct to Intestines

Loopogram
See Urography, Antegrade

Loose Body
Removal

Ankle 27620
Carpometacarpal Joint 26070
Elbow 24101
Interphalangeal Joint 28020
Toe 28024
Knee Joint 27331
Metatarsophalangeal Joint 28022
Tarsometatarsal Joint 28020
Toe 28022
Wrist 25101

Lord Procedure
See Anal Sphincter, Dilation

Louis Bar Syndrome
See Ataxia Telangiectasia

Low Birth Weight Intensive Care Services 99478-99480

Low Density Lipoprotein
See Lipoprotein, LDL

Low Frequency Ultrasound 0183T

Low Vision Aids
See Spectacle Services
Fitting 92354-92355

Lower Extremities
See Extremity, Lower

Lower GI Series
See Barium Enema

LRH
See Luteinizing Releasing Factor

LSD
See Lysergic Acid Diethylamide

LTH
See Prolactin

Lumbar
See Spine
Decompression, Disc
Percutaneous 62287

Lumbar Plexus
Decompression 64714
Injection
Anesthetic 64449
Neuroplasty 64714
Release 64714
Repair/Suture 64862

Lumbar Puncture
See Spinal Tap

Lumbar Spine Fracture
See Fracture, Vertebra, Lumbar

Lumbar Sympathectomy
See Sympathectomy, Lumbar

Lumbar Vertebra
See Vertebra, Lumbar

Lumen Dilation 74360

Lumpectomy 19301-19302

Lunate
Arthroplasty
with Implant 25444

Dislocation
Closed Treatment 25690
Open Treatment 25695

Lung
Ablation 32998
Abscess
Incision and Drainage
Open 32200
Percutaneous 32200-32201
Aspiration 32420
Biopsy 32095-32100
Bullae
Excision 32141
Endoscopic 32655
Cyst
Incision and Drainage
Open 32200
Removal 32140
Decortication
Endoscopic 32651-32652
Partial 32225
Total 32220
with Parietal Pleurectomy 32320
Empyema
Excision 32540
Excision
Bronchus Resection 32486
Completion 32488
Donor
Heart-Lung 33930
Lung 32850
Emphysematous 32491
Empyema 32540
Lobe 32480-32482
Segment 32484
Total 32440-32445
Tumor 32503-32504
Wedge Resection 32500
Endoscopic 32657
Foreign Body
Removal 32151
Hemorrhage 32110
Lavage
Bronchial 31624
Total 32997
Lysis
Adhesions 32124
Needle Biopsy 32405
Nuclear Medicine
Imaging, Perfusion 78580-78585
Imaging, Ventilation 78586-78594
Unlisted Services and Procedures 78599
Placement
Interstitial Device 32553
Pneumocentesis 32420
Pneumolysis 32940
Pneumothorax......................32960
Puncture 32420
Removal
Bronchoplasty 32501
Completion Pneumonectomy 32488
Extrapleural 32445
Single Lobe 32480
Single Segment 32484
Sleeve Lobectomy 32486
Sleeve Pneumonectomy 32442
Total Pneumonectomy 32440-32445
Two Lobes 32482
Volume Reduction 32491
Wedge Resection 32500

Labial 56441
Lung 32124
Nose 30560
Ovary 58740
Oviduct 58740
Penile
    Post-Circumcision 54162
Ureter 50715-50725
Urethra 53500
Uterus 58559
Euglobulin 85360
Labial
    Adhesions .56441
Nose
    Intranasal Synechia 30560

Lysozyme 85549

M

Macrodactylia
Repair 26590

Macroscopic Evaluation . . .88387-88388

Magnesium 83735

Magnet Operation
See Ciliary Body; Cornea; Eye, Removal, Foreign
Body; Iris; Lens; Retina; Sclera; Vitreous

Magnetic Resonance
Unlisted Services and Procedures 76498

Magnetic Resonance Angiography (MRA)
Abdomen 74185
Arm 73225
Chest 71555
Head 70544-70546
Leg 73725
Neck 70547-70549
Pelvis 72198
Spine 72159

Magnetic Resonance Imaging (MRI)
3-D Rendering 76376-76377
Abdomen 74181-74183
Ankle 73721-73723
Arm 73218-73220, 73223
Bone Marrow Study 77084
Brain 70551-70555
    Intraoperative 70557-70559
Breast 77058-77059
    with Computer-aided Detection 0159T
Chest 71550-71552
Elbow 73221
Face 70540-70543
Finger Joint 73221
Foot 73718-73719
Foot Joints 73721-73723
Guidance
    Needle Placement 77021
    Parenchymal Tissue Ablation 77022
Hand 73218-73220, 73223
Heart 75557-75565

Joint
    Lower Extremity 73721-73723
    Upper Extremity 73221-73223
Knee 73721-73723
Leg .73718-73720
Neck 70540-70543
Orbit 70540-70543
Pelvis 72195-72197
Spectroscopy .76390
Spine
    Cervical 72141-72142, 72156-72158
    Lumbar 72148-72158
    Thoracic 72146-72147, 72156-72158
Temporomandibular Joint (TMJ) 70336
Toe .73721-73723
Unlisted 76498
Wrist 73221

Magnetic Resonance Spectroscopy 76390

Magnetic Stimulation
Transcranial 0160T, 0161T

Magnetoencephalography (MEG) 95965-95967

Magnuson Procedure 23450

MAGPI Operation 54322

MAGPI Procedure
See Hypospadias, Repair

Major Vestibular Gland
See Bartholin's Gland

Malar Area
Augmentation .21270
Bone Graft 21210
Fracture
    Open Treatment 21360-21366
    with Bone Graft 21366
    with Manipulation 21355
Reconstruction 21270

Malar Bone
See Cheekbone

Malaria Antibody 86750

Malaria Smear 87207

Malate Dehydrogenase 83775

Maldescent, Testis
See Testis, Undescended

Male Circumcision
See Circumcision

Malformation, Arteriovenous
See Arteriovenous Malformation

Malic Dehydrogenase
See Malate Dehydrogenase

Malignant Hyperthermia Susceptibility
Caffeine Halothane Contracture
Test (CHCT) 89049

Malleolus
See Ankle; Fibula; Leg, Lower; Tibia; Tibiofibular
Joint

Mallet Finger Repair 26432

Maltose
Tolerance Test 82951-82952

Malunion Repair
Femur
    with Graft 27472
    without Graft 27470
Metatarsal 28322
Tarsal Joint 28320

Mammalian Oviduct
See Fallopian Tube

Mammaplasty
See Breast, Reconstruction; Mammoplasty

Mammary Abscess
See Abscess, Breast

Mammary Arteries
See Artery, Mammary

Mammary Duct
X-ray with Contrast 77053-77054

Mammary Ductogram
Injection 19030

Mammary Stimulating Hormone
See Prolactin

Mammillaplasty
See Nipples, Reconstruction

Mammogram
Breast
    Localization Nodule 77032

Mammography 77055-77057
Magnetic Resonance Imaging (MRI)
    with Computer-Aided Detection 0159T
Screening 77057
with Computer-Aided Detection 77051-77052

Mammoplasty
Augmentation 19324-19325
Reduction 19318

Mammotomy
See Incision, Breast; Incision and Drainage, Breast;
Mastotomy

Mammotropic Hormone, Pituitary
See Prolactin

Mammotropic Hormone, Placental
See Lactogen, Human Placental

Mammotropin
See Prolactin

Mandated Services
On Call Services 99027

Mandible
See Facial Bones; Maxilla; Temporomandibular
Joint (TMJ)
Abscess
    Excision 21025
Bone Graft 21215
Cyst
    Excision 21040, 21046-21047

with Tympanoplasty 69604, 69641-69646
  Cochlear Device Implantation 69930
  Complete 69502
    Revision .69601
  Ossicular Chain Reconstruction 69605
  Radical 69511
    Modified .69505
    Revision 69602-69603
  Simple 69501
  with Labyrinthectomy 69910
  with Labyrinthotomy 69802
  with Petrous Apicectomy 69530

Mastoidotomy 69635-69637
with Tympanoplasty 69635
  Ossicular Chain Reconstruction 69636
    and Synthetic Prosthesis 69636

Mastoids
Polytomography 76101-76102
X-ray 70120-70130

Mastopexy .19316

Mastotomy 19020

Maternity Care
See Abortion; Cesarean Delivery; Ectopic
Pregnancy; Obstetrical Care

**Maternity Care and
Delivery** 59612-59622, 59898

Maxilla
See Facial Bones; Mandible
Bone Graft 21210
CT Scan 70486-70488
Cyst
    Excision 21048-21049
Excision 21030, 21032-21034
Fracture
    Closed Treatment 21345, 21421
    Open Treatment . .21346-21348, 21422-21423
    with Fixation 21345-21347
Osteotomy 21206
Reconstruction
    with Implant 21245-21246, 21248-21249
Tumor
    Excision 21048-21049

Maxillary Arteries
See Artery, Maxillary

Maxillary Sinus
See Sinus/Sinuses, Maxillary

Maxillary Torus Palatinus
Tumor Excision 21032

Maxillectomy 31225-31230

Maxillofacial Fixation
Application
    Halo Type Appliance 21100

Maxillofacial Impressions
Auricular Prosthesis 21086
Definitive Obturator Prosthesis 21080
Facial Prosthesis 21088
Interim Obturator Prosthesis 21079
Mandibular Resection Prosthesis 21081
Nasal Prosthesis 21087
Oral Surgical Splint 21085
Orbital Prosthesis 21077
Palatal Augmentation Prosthesis 21082

Palatal Lift Prosthesis 21083
Speech Aid Prosthesis 21084
Surgical Obturator Prosthesis 21076

Maxillofacial Procedures
Unlisted Services and Procedures 21299

Maxillofacial Prosthetics 21076-21089
Unlisted Services and Procedures 21089

Maydl Operation 45563, 50810
See Colostomy

Mayo Hernia Repair
See Hernia, Repair, Umbilicus

Mayo Procedure 28292

Maze Procedure
    Endoscopic 33265-33266
    Open 33254-33256

McBride Procedure 28292

McBurney Operation
See Hernia, Repair, Inguinal

McCannel Procedure 66682

McKissock Surgery
See Breast, Reduction

McVay Operation
See Hernia, Repair, Inguinal

Measles Uncomplicated
See Rubeola

Measles Vaccine
See Vaccines

Measles, German
See Rubella

Meat Fibers
Feces 89160

Meatoplasty 69310

Meatotomy 53020-53025
Cystourethroscopy 52281
Infant 53025
Prostate
    Laser Coagulation 52647
    Laser Vaporization 52648
Transurethral Electrosurgical Resection
    Prostate 52601
Ureter 52290
Ureteral
    Cystourethroscopy 52290-52305

Meckel's Diverticulum
Excision 44800
Unlisted Services and Procedures 44899

Median Nerve
Decompression 64721
Neuroplasty 64721
Release 64721
Repair/Suture
    Motor Thenar 64835
Transposition .64721

Median Nerve Compression
See Carpal Tunnel Syndrome

Mediastinal Cyst
See Cyst, Mediastinal; Mediastinum, Cyst

Mediastinoscopy 39400

Mediastinotomy
Cervical Approach 39000
Transthoracic Approach 39010

Mediastinum
See Chest; Thorax
Cyst
    Excision 32662, 39200
Endoscopy
    Biopsy 39400
    Exploration 39400
Exploration 39000-39010
Incision and Drainage 39000-39010
Needle Biopsy 32405
Removal
    Foreign Body 39000-39010
Tumor
    Excision 32662, 39220
Unlisted Procedures 39499

**Medical Disability Evaluation
Services** 99455-99456

Medical Genetics 96040
Genetic Counseling 96040

**Medical Team
Conference** 99366-99368

Medical Testimony 99075

Medication Therapy Management
Pharmacist Provided 99605-99607

Medicine, Preventive
See Preventive Medicine

Medicine, Pulmonary
See Pulmonology

Medulla
Tractotomy 61470

Medullary Tract
Incision 61470
Section 61470

Meibomian Cyst
See Chalazion

**Membrane Oxygenation,
Extracorporeal**
See Extracorporeal Membrane Oxygenation

Membrane, Mucous
See Mucosa

Membrane, Tympanic
See Ear, Drum

Meninges
Tumor
    Excision 61512, 61519

Meningioma
Excision 61512, 61519
Tumor
    Excision 61512, 61519

Meningitis, Lymphocytic Benign
See Lymphocytic Choriomeningitis

Micro-Ophthalmia
Orbit Reconstruction 21256

Microalbumin
Urine 82043-82044

Microbiology 87001-87999

Microdissection 88380-88381

Microfluorometries, Flow
See Flow Cytometry

Microglobulin, Beta 2
Blood 82232
Urine 82232

Micrographic Surgery
Mohs Technique 17311-17315

Micrographic Surgery, Mohs
See Mohs Micrographic Surgery

Micropigmentation
Correction .11920-11922

Microscope, Surgical
See Operating Microscope

Microscopic Evaluation
Hair 96902

Microscopies, Electron
See Electron Microscopy

Microscopy
Ear Exam 92504

Microsomal Antibody 86376

Microsomia, Hemifacial
See Hemifacial Microsomia

Microsurgery
Operating Microscope 69990

Microvascular Anastomosis
Bone Graft
    Fibula 20955
    Other 20962
Fascial Flap, Free 15758
Muscle Flap, Free 15756
Osteocutaneous Flap with 20969-20973
Skin Flap, Free .15757

Microvite A
See Vitamin, A

Microwave Therapy 97024
See Physical Medicine/Therapy/Occupational
Therapy

Midbrain
See Brain; Brainstem; Mesencephalon; Skull Base
Surgery

Midcarpal Medioccipital Joint
Arthrotomy 25040

**Middle Cerebral Artery
Velocimetry** 76821

Middle Ear
See Ear, Middle

Midface
Reconstruction
    Forehead Advancement 21159-21160
    with Bone Graft 21145-21160, 21188
    without Bone Graft 21141-21143

**Migration Inhibitory Factor
(MIF)** 86378

Mile Operation
See Colectomy, Total, with Proctectomy

Milia, Multiple
Removal 10040

Miller Procedure 28737

Miller-Abbott Intubation . . .44500, 74340

Minerva Cast 29035
Removal 29710

**Minimum Inhibitory
Concentration** 87186

**Minimum Lethal
Concentration** 87187

**Minnesota Multiphasic Personality
Inventory**
See MMPI

Miscarriage
Incomplete Abortion 59812
Missed Abortion
    First Trimester 59820
    Second Trimester 59821
Septic Abortion .59830

Missed Abortion
See Abortion

Mitchell Procedure 28296

Mitogen Blastogenesis 86353

Mitral Valve
Incision 33420-33422
Repair .33420-33427
    Incision 33420-33422
Replacement 33430

Mitrofanoff Operation 50845
See Appendico-Vesicostomy

Miyagawanella
See Chlamydia

MLC
See Lymphocyte, Culture

MMPI 96101-96103
Computer-Assisted 96103

MMR Shots .90707
See Vaccines

Mobilization
Splenic Flexure .44139
    Laparoscopic 44213
Stapes 69650

Moderate Sedation
See Sedation

Modified Radical Mastectomy
See Mastectomy, Modified Radical

**Mohs Micrographic
Surgery** .17311-17315

Molar Pregnancy
See Hydatidiform Mole

Mold
Culture 87107

Mole, Carneous
See Abortion

Mole, Hydatid
See Hydatidiform Mole

Molecular Cytogenetics 88271-88275
Interpretation and Report 88291

Molecular Diagnostics 83890-83914
Amplification 83898-83901, 83908
Cell Lysis 83907
Dot/Slot Production 83893
Enzymatic Digestion 83892
Extraction 83890-83891
Interpretation 83912
Macroscopic Evaluation 88387-88388
Molecular Isolation (Extraction) 83890
Mutation Identification 83904-83906
    Enzymatic Ligation 83914
Mutation Scanning 83903
Nucleic Acid Amplification . . .83900-83901, 83908
Nucleic Acid Extraction 83890-83891, 83907
Nucleic Acid Probe 83896
Nucleic Acid Transfer 83897
Polymerase Reaction Chain 83898
Reverse Transcription 83902
RNA Stabilization 83913
Separation 83894
Separation and Identification
    High Resolution Technique 83909

Molecular Oxygen Saturation
See Oxygen Saturation

Molecular Probes 88384-88386
Multiple
    Array-Based Evaluation 88384-88386

Molluscum Contagiosum
Destruction 17110-17111, 54050-54065

Molteno Procedure 66180

Monilia
See Candida

Monitoring
Blood Pressure, 24 Hour 93784-93790
Cardiovascular Device
    Evaluation and Programming
        Cardioverter-Defibrillator 93282-93284,
                93287, 93289-93290, 93292,
                        93295, 93296
        Loop Recorder . . .93285, 93291, 93298-93299
        Pacemaker 93279-93281, 93294, 93296
Electrocardiogram . . .93224-93237, 93268-93272
    See Electrocardiography
Electroencephalogram 95812-95813,
                95950-95953, 95956
    with Drug Activation 95954
    with Physical Activation 95954
    with WADA Activation 95958

Muscle
See Specific Muscle
Abdomen
    See Abdominal Wall
Biopsy 20200-20206
Debridement
    Infected 11004-11006
    Nonviable 27057
Heart
    See Myocardium
Neck
    See Neck Muscle
Removal
    Foreign Body 20520-20525
Repair
    Extraocular 67346
    Forearm 25260-25274
    Wrist 25260-25274
Revision
    Arm, Upper 24330-24331
Transfer
    Arm, Upper 24301, 24320
    Elbow 24301
    Femur 27110
    Hip 27100-27105, 27111
    Shoulder 23395-23397, 24301, 24320

Muscle Compartment Syndrome
Detection 20950

Muscle Denervation
See Denervation

Muscle Division
Scalenus Anticus 21700-21705
Sternocleidomastoid 21720-21725

Muscle Flaps 15731-15738
Free 15756

Muscle Grafts 15841-15845

Muscle Testing
Dynamometry, Eye 92260
Extraocular Multiple Muscles 92265
Manual .95831-95834

Muscle, Oculomotor
See Eye Muscles

Muscles
Repair
    Extraocular 65290, 67346

Musculo-Skeletal System
See Musculoskeletal System

Musculoplasty
See Muscle, Repair

Musculoskeletal System
Computer-Assisted Surgical
Navigation 0054T-0055T, 20985
Unlisted Services and Procedures 20999,
    24999, 25999, 26989, 27299, 27599, 27899
Unlisted Services and Procedures, Head 21499

Musculotendinous (Rotator) Cuff
Repair .23410-23412

Mustard Procedure
See Repair, Great Arteries; Revision

Myasthenia Gravis
Tensilon Test 95857

Myasthenic, Gravis
See Myasthenia Gravis

Mycobacteria
Culture 87116
    Identification 87118
Detection 87550-87562
Sensitivity Studies 87190

Mycoplasma
Antibody 86738
Culture 87109
Detection 87580-87582

Mycota
See Fungus

Myectomy, Anorectal
See Myomectomy, Anorectal

Myelencephalon
See Medulla

Myelin Basic Protein
Cerebrospinal Fluid 83873

Myelography
Brain 70010
Spine
    Cervical 72240
    Lumbosacral 72265
    Thoracic 72255
    Total 72270

Myelomeningocele
Repair .63704-63706

Myeloperoxidase (MPO) 83876

Myelotomy 63170

Myocardial
Perfusion Imaging 78451-78454
    See Nuclear Medicine
Positron Emission Tomography (PET) 78459

Myocardial Imaging 78466-78469
Perfusion Study
    Positron Emission Tomography
    (PET) 78491-78492
    Single Photon Emission Computed
    Tomography (SPECT) 78451-78452
Repair
    Postinfarction 33542

Myocutaneous
Flaps 15731-15738, 15756

Myofascial Pain Dysfunction
Syndrome
See Temporomandibular Joint (TMJ)

Myofibroma
See Leiomyomata

Myoglobin 83874

Myomectomy
Anorectal 45108
Uterus 58140-58146, 58545-58546

Myoplasty
See Muscle, Repair

Myotomy
Esophagus 43030
Hyoid 21685

Myringoplasty 69620

Myringostomy
See Myringotomy

Myringotomy 69420-69421

Myxoid Cyst
See Ganglion

N

N. Meningitidis
See Neisseria Meningitidis

Naffziger Operation
See Decompression, Orbit; Section

Nagel Test
See Color Vision Examination

Nail Bed
Reconstruction 11762
Repair 11760

Nail Fold
Excision
    Wedge 11765

Nail Plate Separation
See Nails, Avulsion

Nails
Avulsion 11730-11732
Biopsy 11755
Debridement 11720-11721
Drainage 10060-10061
Evacuation
    Hematoma, Subungual 11740
Excision 11750-11752
KOH Examination 87220
Removal 11730-11732, 11750-11752
Trimming 11719

Narcosynthesis
Diagnostic and Therapeutic 90865

Nasal Abscess
See Nose, Abscess

Nasal Area
Bone Graft 21210

Nasal Bleeding
See Epistaxis

Nasal Bone
Fracture
    Closed Treatment 21310-21320
    Open Treatment 21325-21335
    with Manipulation 21315-21320
    without Manipulation 21310
X-ray 70160

Nasal Deformity
Repair .40700-40761

Neoplastic Growth
See Tumor

Nephelometry 83883

Nephrectomy
Donor 50300-50320, 50547
Laparoscopic 50545-50548
Partial 50240
   Laparoscopic 50543
Recipient 50340
with Ureters 50220-50236, 50546, 50548

Nephrolith
See Calculus, Removal, Kidney

Nephrolithotomy 50060-50075

Nephropexy 50400-50405

Nephroplasty
See Kidney, Repair

Nephropyeloplasty
See Pyeloplasty

Nephrorrhaphy 50500

Nephroscopy
See Endoscopy, Kidney

Nephrostogram 50394

Nephrostolithotomy
Percutaneous 50080-50081

Nephrostomy 50040
Change Tube 50398
Endoscopic 50562-50570
Percutaneous 52334
with Drainage 50040
X-ray with Contrast
   Guide Dilation 74485

Nephrostomy Tract
Establishment 50395

Nephrotomogram
See Nephrotomography

Nephrotomography 74415

Nephrotomy 50040-50045
with Exploration 50045

Nerve
Cranial
   See Cranial Nerve
Facial
   See Facial Nerve
Intercostal
   See Intercostal Nerve
Lingual
   See Lingual Nerve
Median
   See Median Nerve
Obturator
   See Obturator Nerve
Peripheral
   See Peripheral Nerve
Phrenic
   See Phrenic Nerve
Sciatic
   See Sciatic Nerve
Spinal
   See Spinal Nerve

Tibial
   See Tibial Nerve
Ulnar
   See Ulnar Nerve
Vestibular
   See Vestibular Nerve

Nerve Conduction
Motor Nerve 95900-95903
Preconfigured Electrode Array 0197T
Sensory Nerve or Mixed 95904-95905

Nerve Root
See Cauda Equina; Spinal Cord
Decompression 22856, 63020-63048,
                     63055-63103
Incision 63185-63190
Section 63185-63190

Nerve Stimulation, Transcutaneous
See Application, Neurostimulation

Nerve Teasing 88362

Nerve II, Cranial
See Optic Nerve

Nerve V, Cranial
See Trigeminal Nerve

Nerve VII, Cranial
See Facial Nerve

Nerve X, Cranial
See Vagus Nerve

Nerve XI, Cranial
See Accessory Nerve

Nerve XII, Cranial
See Hypoglossal Nerve

Nerves
Anastomosis
   Facial to Hypoglossal 64868
   Facial to Phrenic 64870
   Facial to Spinal Accessory 64866
Avulsion 64732-64772
Biopsy 64795
Decompression 64702-64727
Destruction 64600-64681
   Laryngeal, Recurrent 31595
Foot
   Excision 28055
   Incision 28035
Graft 64885-64907
Implantation
   Electrode 64553-64581
   to Bone 64787
   to Muscle 64787
Incision 43640-43641, 64732-64772
Injection
   Anesthetic 01991-01992, 64400-64530
   Neurolytic Agent 64600-64681
Insertion
   Electrode 64553-64581
Lesion
   Excision 64774-64792
Neurofibroma
   Excision 64788-64792
Neurolemmoma
   Excision 64788-64792
Neurolytic
   Internal 64727

Neuroma
   Destruction 64632
   Excision 64774-64786
   Injection 64455
Neuroplasty 64702-64721
Removal
   Electrode 64585
Repair
   Graft 64885-64911
   Microdissection 69990
   Suture 64831-64876
Spinal Accessory
   Incision 63191
   Section 63191
Suture 64831-64876
Sympathectomy
   Excision 64802-64818
Transection 43640-43641, 64732-64772
Transposition 64718-64721
Unlisted Services and Procedures 64999

Nervous System
Nuclear Medicine
   Unlisted Services and Procedures 78699

Nesidioblast
See Islet Cell

Neural Conduction
See Nerve Conduction

Neural Ganglion
See Ganglion

Neurectomy
Foot 28055
Gastrocnemius 27326
Hamstring Muscle 27325
Leg, Lower 27326
Leg, Upper 27325
Popliteal 27326
Tympanic 69676

Neuroendoscopy
Intracranial 62160-62165

Neurofibroma
Cutaneous Nerve
   Excision 64788
Extensive
   Excision 64792
Peripheral Nerve
   Excision 64790

Neurolemmoma
Cutaneous Nerve
   Excision 64788
Extensive
   Excision 64792
Peripheral Nerve
   Excision 64790

Neurologic System
See Nervous System

Neurology
Brain Cortex Magnetic Stimulation ...0160T-0161T
Brain Mapping 96020
Brain Surface Electrode Stimulation ...95961-95962
Central Motor
   Transcranial Motor Stimulation ...95928-95929
Cognitive Performance 96125

Noble Procedure
See Repair; Suture

Nocardia
Antibody 86744

Nocturnal Penile Rigidity Test 54250

Nocturnal Penile Tumescence Test
54250

Node Dissection, Lymph
See Dissection, Lymph Nodes

Node, Lymph
See Lymph Nodes

Nodes
See Lymph Nodes

Non-Invasive Vascular Imaging
See Vascular Studies

Non-Office Medical Services 99056
Emergency Care 99060

Non-Stress Test, Fetal 59025

Nonunion Repair
Femur
   with Graft 27472
   without Graft 27470
Metatarsal 28322
Tarsal Joint 28320

Noradrenalin
Blood 82383-82384
Urine 82384

Norchlorimipramine
See Imipramine

Norepinephrine
See Catecholamines
Blood 82383-82384
Urine 82384

Nortriptyline
Assay 80182

Norwood Procedure 33611-33612, 33619
See Repair, Heart, Ventricle; Revision

Nose
Abscess
   Incision and Drainage 30000-30020
Actinotherapy
   Intranasal 0168T
Artery
   Incision .30915-30920
Biopsy
   Intranasal 30100
Dermoid Cyst
   Excision
      Complex 30125
      Simple 30124
Displacement Therapy 30210
Endoscopy
   Diagnostic 31231-31235
   Surgical 31237-31294
Excision
   Rhinectomy 30150-30160
Fracture
   Closed Treatment 21345
   Open Treatment 21325-21336,
      21338-21339, 21346-21347

Percutaneous Treatment 21340
   with Fixation 21330, 21340, 21345-21347
Hematoma
   Incision and Drainage 30000-30020
Hemorrhage
   Cauterization 30901-30906
Insertion
   Septal Prosthesis 30220
Intranasal
   Actinotherapy 0168T
   Lesion
      External Approach 30118
      Internal Approach 30117
   Phototherapy .0168T
Lysis of Adhesions 30560
Phototherapy
   Intranasal 0168T
Polyp
   Excision
      Extensive .30115
      Simple 30110
Reconstruction
   Cleft Lip/Cleft Palate 30460-30462
   Dermatoplasty 30620
   Primary 30400, 30420
   Secondary 30430-30450
   Septum 30520
Removal
   Foreign Body .30300
      Anesthesia 30310
      Lateral Rhinotomy 30320
Repair
   Adhesions 30560
   Cleft Lip 40700-40761
   Fistula 30580-30600, 42260
   Rhinophyma 30120
   Septum 30540-30545, 30630
   Synechia 30560
   Vestibular Stenosis 30465
Skin
   Excision 30120
   Surgical Planing 30120
Submucous Resection Turbinate
   Excision 30140
Turbinate
   Excision 30130-30140
   Fracture 30930
   Injection 30200
Turbinate Mucosa
   Cauterization 30801-30802
Unlisted Services and Procedures 30999

Nose Bleed 30901-30906
See Hemorrhage, Nasal

NTD 86384
See Nitroblue Tetrazolium Dye Test

Nuclear Antigen
Antibody 86235

Nuclear Imaging
See Nuclear Medicine

Nuclear Magnetic Resonance Imaging
See Magnetic Resonance Imaging (MRI)

Nuclear Magnetic Resonance Spectroscopy
See Magnetic Resonance Spectroscopy

Nuclear Medicine
Adrenal Gland Imaging 78075
Bile Duct
   Imaging 78223
Bladder
   Residual Study 78730
Blood
   Bone
      Density Study 78350-78351
      Imaging 78300-78320
      SPECT 78320
      Ultrasound 76977
      Unlisted Services and Procedures 78399
   Flow Imaging .78445
   Iron
      Red Cells .78140
   Platelet Survival 78190-78191
   Red Cell Survival 78130-78135
   Red Cells 78120-78121
   Unlisted Services and Procedures 78199
   Whole Blood Volume 78122
Bone Marrow
   Imaging 78102-78104
Brain
   Blood Flow 78610
   Cerebrospinal Fluid 78630-78650
   Imaging 78600-78609
      Vascular Flow 78610
Endocrine System
   Unlisted Services and Procedures 78099
Esophagus
   Imaging (Motility) 78258
   Reflux Study .78262
Gallbladder
   Imaging 78223
Gastric Mucosa
   Imaging 78261
Gastrointestinal
   Blood Loss Study 78278
   Protein Loss Study 78282
   Shunt Testing 78291
   Unlisted Services and Procedures 78299
Genitourinary System
   Unlisted Services and Procedures 78799
Heart
   Blood Flow 78414
   Blood Pool Imaging 78472-78473,
         78481-78483, 78494-78496
   Myocardial Imaging 78459, 78466-78469
   Myocardial Perfusion 78451-78454
   Shunt Detection 78428
   Unlisted Services and Procedures 78499
Hepatic Duct
   Imaging 78223
Inflammatory Process 78805-78807
   Injection Procedure 78808
Intestines
   Imaging 78290
Kidney
   Function Study 78725
   Imaging 78700-78707, 78710
   Vascular Flow 78701-78709
Lacrimal Gland Tear Flow 78660
Liver
   Function Study 78220
   Imaging 78201-78216
   Vascular Flow 78206
Lung
   Imaging Perfusion 78580-78585
   Imaging Ventilation 78586-78594
   Unlisted Services and Procedures 78599

Nucleases, DNA
See DNAse

Nucleic Acid Probe 83896

Nucleolysis, Intervertebral Disc
See Chemonucleolysis

Nucleotidase 83915

Nursemaid Elbow 24640

Nursing Facility Discharge Services
See Discharge Services, Nursing Facility

Nursing Facility Services

Nuss Procedure

Nutrition Therapy

Nystagmus Tests
See Vestibular Function Tests

O

O₂ Saturation
See Oxygen Saturation

Ober-Yount Procedure 27025
See Fasciotomy, Hip

Obliteration

Oblongata, Medulla
See Medulla

Observation 99234-99236
See Evaluation and Management; Hospital Services

Obstetrical Care

Spontaneous .59812
Therapeutic 59840-59852
Antepartum Care 59425-59426
Cesarean Delivery 59618-59622
Only 59514
Postpartum Care 59515
Routine 59510
with Hysterectomy 59525
Curettage
Hydatidiform Mole 59870
Evacuation
Hydatidiform Mole 59870
External Cephalic Version 59412
Miscarriage
Surgical Completion 59812-59821
Placenta Delivery 59414
Postpartum Care 59430, 59514
Septic Abortion 59830
Total (Global) 59400, 59610, 59618
Unlisted Services and Procedures 59898-59899
Vaginal
after Cesarean 59610-59614
Vaginal Delivery 59409-59410
Delivery after Cesarean 59610-59614

Obstruction
See Occlusion

Obstruction Clearance
Venous Access Device 36595-36596

Obstruction Colon
See Colon, Obstruction

Obturator Nerve
Avulsion 64763-64766
Incision 64763-64766
Transection 64763-64766

Obturator Prosthesis 21076
Definitive .21080
Insertion
Larynx 31527
Interim 21079

Occipital Nerve, Greater
Avulsion 64744
Incision 64744
Injection
Anesthetic 64405
Transection 64744

Occlusion
Extracranial
Intracranial 61623
Fallopian Tube
Oviduct 58565, 58615
Penis
Vein 37790
Umbilical Cord 59072

Occlusive Disease of Artery
See Repair, Artery; Revision

Occult Blood 82270-82272
by Hemoglobin Immunoassay 82274

Occupational Therapy
Evaluation 97003-97004

Ocular Implant
See Orbital Implant
Insertion
in Scleral Shell 65130

Muscles, Attached 65140
Muscles, Not Attached 65135
Modification 65125
Reinsertion 65150
with Foreign Material 65155
Removal 65175

Ocular Muscle
See Eye Muscles

Ocular Orbit
See Orbit

Ocular Photoscreening 99174

Ocular Prostheses
See Prosthesis, Ocular

Oculomotor Muscle
See Eye Muscles

Oddi Sphincter
See Sphincter of Oddi

Odontoid Dislocation
Open Treatment/Reduction 22318
with Grafting 22319

Odontoid Fracture
Open Treatment/Reduction 22318
with Grafting 22319

Odontoid Process
Excision 22548

Oesophageal Neoplasm
See Tumor, Esophagus

Oesophageal Varices
See Esophageal Varices

Oesophagus
See Esophagus

Oestradiol
See Estradiol

Office and/or Other Outpatient Services
See History and Physical Consultation
Established Patient 99211-99215
New Patient 99201-99205
Normal Newborn 99432
Office Visit
Established Patient 99211-99215
New Patient 99201-99205
Outpatient Visit
Established Patient 99211-99215
New Patient 99201-99205
Prolonged Services 99354-99355

Office Medical Services
After Hours 99050
Emergency Care 99058
Extended Hours 99051

Office or Other Outpatient Consultations
See Consultation, Office and/or Other Outpatient

Olecranon
See Elbow; Humerus; Radius; Ulna
Bursa
Arthrocentesis 20605
Cyst
Excision 24125-24126

Tumor
Cyst 24120
Excision 24125-24126

Olecranon Process
Craterization 24147
Diaphysectomy 24147
Excision 24147
Abscess .24138
Fracture
See Elbow; Humerus; Radius
Closed Treatment 24670-24675
Open Treatment 24685
Osteomyelitis 24138, 24147
Saucerization 24147
Sequestrectomy 24138

Oligoclonal Immunoglobulins . . .83916

Omentectomy 49255, 58950-58958
Laparotomy 58960
Oophorectomy 58943
Resection Ovarian Malignancy 58950-58952
Resection Peritoneal Malignancy 58950-58958
Resection Tubal Malignancy 58950-58958

Omentum
Excision 49255, 58950-58958
Flap .49904-49905
Free
with Microvascular Anastomosis 49906
Omentopexy 49326
Unlisted Services and Procedures 49999

Omphalectomy 49250

Omphalocele
Repair 49600-49611

Omphalomesenteric Duct
Excision 44800

Omphalomesenteric Duct, Persistent
See Diverticulum, Meckel's

Oncoprotein
Des-gamma-carboxyprothrombin (DCP) 83951
HER-2/neu .83950

Online Internet Assessment and Management
Nonphysician 98969
Physician 99444

One Stage Prothrombin Time 85610-85611
See Prothrombin Time

Onychectomy
See Excision, Nails

Onychia
Drainage 10060-10061

Oocyte
Assisted Fertilization
Microtechnique 89280-89281
Biopsy 89290-89291
Culture
Extended 89272
Less than 4 Days 89250
with Co-Culture 89251
Identification
Follicular Fluid 89254
Insemination 89268

Orbitotomy
with Bone Flap
　for Exploration .67450
　Lateral Approach 67420
　with Drainage .67440
　with Removal Foreign Body 67430
　with Removal of Bone for
　Decompression 67445
with Removal Foreign Body 67413
with Removal of Bone for Decompression . . .67414
without Bone Flap
　for Exploration .67400
　with Drainage Only 67405
　with Removal Lesion 67412

Orchidectomies
See Excision, Testis

Orchidopexy
See Orchiopexy

Orchidoplasty
See Repair, Testis

Orchiectomy
Laparoscopic 54690
Partial 54522
Radical
　Abdominal Exploration 54535
　　Inguinal Approach 54530
Simple 54520

Orchiopexy
Abdominal Approach 54650
Inguinal Approach 54640
Intra-Abdominal Testis 54692

Orchioplasty
See Repair, Testis

Organ Grafting
See Transplantation

Organ or Disease-Oriented Panel
Electrolyte 80051
General Health Panel 80050
Hepatic Function Panel 80076
Hepatitis Panel 80074
Lipid Panel 80061
Metabolic
　Basic 80047, 80048
　Comprehensive 80053
Obstetric Panel 80055
Renal Function 80069

Organ System, Neurologic
See Nervous System

Organic Acids 83918-83921

Ormond Disease
See Retroperitoneal Fibrosis

Orogastric Tube
Placement 43752

Oropharynx
Biopsy 42800

Orthodontic Cephalogram 70350

Orthomyxoviridae
See Influenza Virus

Orthomyxovirus
See Influenza Virus

Orthopantogram 70355

Orthopedic Cast
See Cast

Orthopedic Surgery
Computer Assisted Navigation 20985-20987
Stereotaxis
　Computer Assisted 20985-20987

Orthoptic Training 92065

Orthoroentgenogram 77073

Orthosis
See Orthotics

Orthotics
Check-Out 97762
Management and Training 97760

Os Calcis Fracture
See Calcaneus, Fracture

Osmolality
Blood 83930
Urine 83935

Osseous Survey 77074-77076

Osseous Tissue
See Bone

Ossicles
Excision
　Stapes
　　with Footplate Drill Out 69661
　　without Foreign Material 69660-69661
Reconstruction
　Ossicular Chain
　　Tympanoplasty with Antrotomy or
　　Mastoidotomy 69636-69637
　　Tympanoplasty with
　　Mastoidectomy 69642, 69644, 69646
　　Tympanoplasty without
　　Mastoidectomy 69632-69633
Release
　Stapes 69650
Replacement
　with Prosthesis 69633, 69637

Ostectomy
Metacarpal 26250
Metatarsal 28288
Phalanges
　Finger .26260-26262
Pressure Ulcer
　Ischial 15941, 15945
　Sacral 15933, 15935, 15937
　Trochanteric 15951, 15953, 15958
Scapula 23190
Sternum 21620

Osteocalcin .83937

Osteocartilaginous Exostoses
See Exostosis

Osteochondroma
See Exostosis

Osteocutaneous Flap
with Microvascular Anastomosis 20969-20973

Osteoma
Sinusotomy
　Frontal 31075

Osteomyelitis 20000-20005
Elbow
　Incision and Drainage 23935
Excision
　Clavicle 23180
　Facial 21026
　Humerus, Proximal 23184
　Mandible 21025
　Scapula 23182
Femur/Knee
　Incision and Drainage 27303
Finger
　Incision 26034
Hand Incision 26034
Hip
　Incision, Deep 26992
Humerus 24134
　Incision and Drainage 23935
Incision
　Foot 28005
　Shoulder 23035
　Thorax 21510
Olecranon Process 24138, 24147
Pelvis
　Incision, Deep 26992
Radius .24136, 24145
Sequestrectomy
　Clavicle 23170
　Humeral Head 23174
　Scapula 23172
　Skull 61501

**Osteopathic
Manipulation** 98925-98929

Osteoplasty
Carpal Bone 25394
Facial Bones
　Augmentation 21208
　Reduction 21209
Femoral Neck 27179
Femur 27179
　Lengthening 27466-27468
　Shortening 27465, 27468
Fibula
　Lengthening .27715
Humerus 24420
Metacarpal 26568
Phalanges, Finger 26568
Radius 25390-25393
Tibia
　Lengthening .27715
Ulna 25390-25393
Vertebra .72291-72292
　Lumbar 22521-22522
　Thoracic 22520, 22522

Osteotomy
Calcaneus 28300
Chin 21121-21123
Clavicle .23480-23485
Femur 27140, 27151
　Femoral Neck 27161
　for Slipped Epiphysis 27181
　with Fixation .27165
　with Open Reduction of Hip 27156
　with Realignment 27454
　without Fixation 27448-27450

Insertion 33206-33208
   Electrode 33210-33211, 33216-33217,
                     33224-33225
   Pulse Generator Only 33212-33213
Removal 33233-33237
   via Thoracotomy 33236-33237
Repair
   Electrode 33218-33220
Replacement
   Catheter 33210
   Electrode 33210-33211
   Insertion 33206-33208
   Pulse Generator 33212-33213
Repositioning
   Electrode 33215, 33226
Revise Pocket
   Chest 33222
Telephonic Analysis 93293
Upgrade 33214

Pachymetry
Eye 76514

Packing
Nasal Hemorrhage 30901-30906

Pain Management
Epidural/Intrathecal 62350-62351,
             62360-62362, 99601-99602
Intravenous Therapy . . .96365-96368, 96374-96379

Palate
Abscess
   Incision and Drainage 42000
Biopsy 42100
Excision .42120, 42145
Fracture
   Closed Treatment 21421
   Open Treatment 21422-21423
Lesion
   Destruction 42160
   Excision 42104-42120
Prosthesis
   Augmentation 21082
   Impression 42280
   Insertion 42281
   Lift 21083
Reconstruction
   Lengthening 42226-42227
Repair
   Cleft Palate 42200-42225
   Laceration 42180-42182
   Vomer Flap 42235
Unlisted Services and Procedures 42299

Palate, Cleft
See Cleft Palate

Palatoplasty 42200-42225

Palatoschisis
See Cleft Palate

Palm
Bursa
   Incision and Drainage 26025-26030
Fasciectomy 26121-26125
Fasciotomy 26040-26045
Tendon
   Excision 26170
Tendon Sheath
   Excision 26145
   Incision and Drainage 26020

Palsy, Seventh Nerve
See Facial Nerve Paralysis

Pancreas
Anastomosis
   with Intestines 48520-48540, 48548
Anesthesia 00794
Biopsy 48100
   Needle Biopsy 48102
Cyst
   Anastomosis 48520-48540
   Repair 48500
Debridement
   Peripancreatic Tissue 48105
Excision
   Ampulla of Vater 48148
   Duct 48148
   Partial 48140-48146, 48150, 48154, 48160
   Peripancreatic Tissue 48105
   Total .48155-48160
Lesion
   Excision 48120
Needle Biopsy 48102
Placement
   Drainage 48000-48001
Pseudocyst
   Drainage
      Open 48510
      Percutaneous 48511
Removal
   Calculi (Stone) 48020
Removal Transplanted Allograft 48556
Repair
   Cyst 48500
Resection 48105
Suture 48545
Transplantation 48160, 48550, 48554-48556
   Allograft Preparation 48550-48552
   Islet Cell 0141T, 0142T, 0143T
Unlisted Services and Procedures 48999
X-ray with Contrast 74300-74305
   Injection Procedure 48400

Pancreas, Endocrine Only
See Islet Cell

Pancreatectomy
Donor 48550
Partial 48140-48146, 48150-48154, 48160
Total 48155-48160
with Transplantation 48160

Pancreatic DNAse
See DNAse

Pancreatic Duct
Destruction
   Calculi (Stone) 43265
Dilation
   Endoscopy 43271
Endoscopy 43273
   Collection
      Specimen .43260
   Destruction
      Calculi (Stone) 43265
      Tumor 43272
   Dilation 43271
   Removal (Endoscopic)
      Calculi (Stone) 43264
      Foreign Body 43269
      Stent 43269
   Sphincter Pressure 43263

Sphincterotomy .43262
Tube Placement 43267-43268
Incision
   Sphincter 43262
Removal
   Calculi (Stone) 43264
   Foreign Body .43269
   Stent 43269
Tube Placement
   Nasopancreatic 43267
   Stent 43268
Tumor
   Destruction 43272
X-ray with Contrast
   Guide Catheter 74329-74330

Pancreatic Elastase 1 (PE1) 82656

Pancreatic Islet Cell AB
See Antibody, Islet Cell

Pancreaticojejunostomy 48548

Pancreatography
Injection Procedure 48400
Intraoperative 74300-74301
Postoperative 74305

Pancreatorrhaphy 48545

Pancreatotomy
See Incision, Pancreas

Pancreozymin-Secretin Test 82938

Panel
See Blood Tests; Organ or Disease-Oriented Panel

Panniculectomy
See Lipectomy

Pap Smears 88141-88155, 88164-88167,
                     88174-88175

Paper, Chromatography
See Chromatography, Paper

Papilla, Interdental
See Gums

Papilloma
Destruction
   Anus .46900-46924
   Penis .54050-54065

PAPP D
See Lactogen, Human Placental

Para-Tyrosine
See Tyrosine

Paracentesis
Abdomen .49080-49081
Eye
   with Aqueous Aspiration 65800
   with Aqueous Release 65805
   with Discission of Anterior Hyaloid
   Membrane 65810
   with Removal
      Blood 65815
      Vitreous 65810
Thorax 32421-32422

Paracervical Nerve
Injection
   Anesthetic 64435

Persistent, Omphalomesenteric Duct
See Diverticulum, Meckel's

Personal Care
See Self Care

Personality Test 96101-96103
Computer-Assisted 96103

Pessary
Insertion 57160

Pesticides
Chlorinated Hydrocarbons 82441

PET
See Positron Emission Tomography

Petrous Temporal
Excision
    Apex 69530

Peyronie Disease
Injection 54200
Surgical Exposure 54205
with Graft 54110-54112

pH
See Blood
Exhaled Breath Condensate 0140T, 83987
Other Fluid 83986
Urine 83986

Phacoemulsification
Removal
    Extracapsular Cataract 66982, 66984
    Secondary Membranous Cataract 66850

Phagocytosis
White Blood Cells 86344

Phalangectomy
Toe 28150
    Partial 28160

Phalanges (Hand)
See Finger, Bone

Phalanx, Finger
Craterization 26235-26236
Cyst
    Excision 26210-26215
Diaphysectomy 26235-26236
Excision 26235-26236
    Radical
        for Tumor 26260-26262
Fracture
    Articular
        Closed Treatment 26740
        Open Treatment 26746
        with Manipulation 26742
    Distal 26755-26756
        Closed Treatment 26750
        Open Treatment 26765
        Percutaneous Fixation 26756
    Open Treatment 26735
        Distal 26765
    Shaft 26720-26727
        Open Treatment 26735
Incision and Drainage 26034
Ostectomy
    Radical
        for Tumor 26260-26262
Repair
    Lengthening 26568

Nonunion 26546
Osteotomy 26567
Saucerization 26235-26236
Thumb
    Fracture
        Shaft 26720-26727
Tumor
    Excision 26210-26215

Phalanx, Great Toe
See Phalanx, Toe
Fracture 28490
    Open Treatment 28505
    with Manipulation 28495-28496
    Percutaneous Fixation 28496
    without Manipulation 28490

Phalanx, Toe
Condyle
    Excision 28126
Craterization 28124
Cyst
    Excision 28108
Diaphysectomy 28124
Excision 28124, 28150-28160
Fracture
    Open Treatment 28525
    with Manipulation 28515
    without Manipulation 28510
Repair
    Osteotomy 28310-28312
Saucerization 28124
Tumor
    Excision 28108
    Radical Resection 28175

Pharmaceutic Preparations
See Drug

Pharmacotherapies
See Chemotherapy

Pharyngeal Tonsil
See Adenoids

Pharyngectomy
Partial 42890

Pharyngolaryngectomy 31390-31395

Pharyngoplasty 42950

Pharyngorrhaphy
See Suture, Pharynx

Pharyngostomy 42955

Pharyngotomy
See Incision, Pharynx

Pharyngotympanic Tube
See Eustachian Tube

Pharynx
See Nasopharynx; Throat
Biopsy 42800-42806
Cineradiography 70371, 74230
Creation
    Stoma 42955
Excision 42145
    Partial 42890
    Resection 42892-42894
    with Larynx 31390-31395
Hemorrhage 42960-42962

Lesion
    Destruction 42808
    Excision 42808
Reconstruction 42950
Removal
    Foreign Body 42809
Repair
    with Esophagus 42953
Unlisted Services and Procedures 42999
Video Study 70371, 74230
X-ray 70370, 74210

Phencyclidine 83992

Phenobarbital 82205
Assay 80184

Phenothiazine 84022

Phenotype Analysis
by Nucleic Acid
    Infectious Agent
        HIV-1 Drug Resistance 87903-87904

Phenotype Prediction
by Genetic Database
    HIV-1 Drug Susceptibility 87900

Phenylalanine 84030

Phenylalanine-Tyrosine Ratio ...84030

Phenylketones 84035

Phenylketonuria
See Phenylalanine

Phenytoin
Assay 80185-80186

Pheochromocytoma 80424

Pheresis
See Apheresis

Phlebectasia
See Varicose Vein

Phlebectomy
Varicose Veins 37765-37766

Phlebographies
See Venography

Phleborrhaphy
See Suture, Vein

Phlebotomy
Therapeutic 99195

Phoria
See Strabismus

Phosphatase
Alkaline 84075, 84080
    Blood 84078
Forensic Examination 84061

Phosphatase Acid 84060
Blood 84066

Phosphate, Pyridoxal
See Pyridoxal Phosphate

Phosphatidyl Glycerol
See Phosphatidylglycerol

Incision
Empyema 32035-32036
Pneumothorax 32551
Instillation of Agent for Fibrinolysis ..32561-32562
Instillation of Agent for Pleurodesis 32560
Puncture and Drainage 32421-32422
Thoracostomy 32035-32036

Pleural Endoscopies
See Thoracoscopy

Pleural Scarification
for Repeat Pneumothorax 32215

Pleural Tap
See Thoracentesis

Pleurectomy
Anesthesia 00542
Parietal 32310-32320
Endoscopic 32656

Pleuritis, Purulent
See Abscess, Thorax

Pleurocentesis
See Thoracentesis

Pleurodesis
Endoscopic 32650
Intillation of Agent 32560

Pleurosclerosis
See Pleurodesis

Pleurosclerosis, Chemical
See Pleurodesis, Chemical

Plexectomy, Choroid
See Choroid Plexus, Excision

Plexus
Brachialis
See Brachial Plexus
Cervicalis
See Cervical Plexus
Choroid
See Choroid Plexus
Coeliacus
See Celiac Plexus
Lumbalis
See Lumbar Plexus

PLGN
See Plasminogen

Plication, Sphincter, Urinary Bladder
See Bladder, Repair, Neck

Pneumocentesis
Lung 32420

Pneumocisternogram
See Cisternography

Pneumococcal Vaccine
See Vaccines

Pneumocystis Carinii
Antigen Detection
Immunofluorescence 87281

Pneumogastric Nerve
See Vagus Nerve

Pneumogram
Pediatric 94772

Pneumolysis 32940

Pneumonectomy 32440-32500
Completion 32488
Donor 32850, 33930
Sleeve 32442
Total 32440-32445

Pneumonology
See Pulmonology

Pneumonolysis 32940
Intrapleural 32652
Open Intrapleural 32124

Pneumonostomy 32200-32201

Pneumonotomy
See Incision, Lung

Pneumoperitoneum 49400

Pneumoplethysmography
Ocular 93875

Pneumothorax
Pleurodesis 32560
Pleural Scarification for Repeat 32215
Therapeutic
Injection Intrapleural Air 32960
Thoracentesis with Tube Insertion 32422

Polio
Antibody 86658
Vaccine 90712-90713

Poliovirus Vaccine
See Vaccines

Pollicization
Digit 26550

Polya Gastrectomy
See Gastrectomy, Partial

Polydactylism
See Polydactyly; Supernumerary Digit

Polydactyly
Digit
Reconstruction 26587
Repair 26587
Toe 28344

Polymerase Chain Reaction 83898

Polyp
Antrochoanal
Removal 31032
Esophagus
Ablation 43228
Nose
Excision
Endoscopic 31237-31240
Extensive 30115
Simple 30110
Sphenoid Sinus
Removal 31051
Urethra
Excision 53260

Polypectomy
Nose
Endoscopic 31237
Uterus 58558

Polypeptide, Vasoactive Intestinal
See Vasoactive Intestinal Peptide

Polysomnography 95808-95811

Polyuria Test
See Water Load Test

Pomeroy's Operation
See Tubal Ligation

Pooling
Blood Products 86965

Popliteal Arteries
See Artery, Popliteal

Popliteal Synovial Cyst
See Baker's Cyst

Poradenitistras
See Lymphogranuloma Venereum

PORP (Partial Ossicular Replacement Prosthesis) ...69633, 69637

Porphobilinogen
Urine 84106-84110

Porphyrin Precursors 82135

Porphyrins
Feces 84126-84127
Urine 84119-84120

Port Film 77417

Portal Vein
See Vein, Hepatic Portal

Portoenterostomies, Hepatic
See Hepaticoenterostomy

Portoenterostomy 47701

Positional Nystagmus Test
See Nystagmus Tests, Positional

Positive End Expiratory Pressure
See Pressure Breathing, Positive

Positive-Pressure Breathing, Inspiratory
See Intermittent Positive Pressure Breathing (IPPB)

Positron Emission Tomography (PET)
Brain 78608-78609
Heart 78459
Myocardial Imaging
Perfusion Study 78491-78492

Post-Op Visit 99024

Postauricular Fistula
See Fistula, Postauricular

Postcaval Ureter
See Retrocaval Ureter

Postmortem
See Autopsy

Postop Vas Reconstruction
See Vasovasorrhaphy

Postoperative Wound Infection
Incision and Drainage 10180

Radical Vaginal Hysterectomy

Radical Vulvectomy

Radio-Cobalt B-12 Schilling Test

Radioactive Colloid Therapy 79300

Radioactive Substance

Radiocarpal Joint

Radiocinematographies

Radioelement

Radioelement Substance

Radiography

Radioimmunosorbent Test

Radioisotope Brachytherapy

Radioisotope Scan

Radiological Marker

Radiology

Radionuclide CT Scan

Radionuclide Imaging

Radionuclide Therapy

Radionuclide Tomography, Single-Photon Emission-Computed

Radiopharmaceutical Localization

Radiopharmaceutical Therapy

Radiotherapeutic

Radiotherapies

Radiotherapy, Surface

Radioulnar Joint

Radius

Ramstedt Operation

Ramus Anterior, Nervus Thoracicus

Range of Motion Test

Rectal Bleeding
See Hemorrhage, Rectum

Rectal Prolapse
See Procidentia, Rectum

Rectal Sphincter

Rectocele

Rectopexy
See Proctopexy

Rectoplasty
See Proctoplasty

Rectorrhaphy
See Rectum, Suture

Rectovaginal Fistula
See Fistula, Rectovaginal

Rectovaginal Hernia
See Rectocele

Rectum
See Anus

Red Blood Cell (RBC)

Sedimentation Rate
  Automated 85652
  Manual 85651
Sequestration 78140
Sickling 85660
Survival Test 78130-78135
Volume Determination 78120-78121

Red Blood Cell ab
See Antibody, Red Blood Cell

Reductase, Glutathione
See Glutathione Reductase

Reductase, Lactic Cytochrome
See Lactic Dehydrogenase

Reduction
Forehead 21137-21139
Lung Volume 32491
Mammoplasty 19318
Masseter Muscle/Bone 21295-21296
Osteoplasty
  Facial Bones 21209
Pregnancy
  Multifetal 59866
Skull
  Craniomegalic 62115-62117
Ventricular Septum
  Non-Surgical 93733

Reflex Test
Blink Reflex 95933
H-Reflex 95934-95936

Reflux Study 78262
Gastroesophageal 91034-91038

Refraction 92015

Rehabilitation
Artery
  Occlusive Disease 93668
Auditory
  Post-Lingual Hearing Loss 92633
  Pre-Lingual Hearing Loss 92630
  Status Evaluation 92626-92627
Cardiac 93797-93798
Services Considered
  Documentation 4079F

Rehabilitation Facility
Discharge Services 1110F-1111F

Rehabilitative
See Rehabilitation

Reimplantation
Arteries
  Aorta
    Prosthesis 35697
  Carotid 35691, 35694-35695
  Subclavian 35693-35695
  Vertebral 35691-35693
  Visceral 35697
Kidney 50380
Ovary 58825
Pulmonary Artery 33788
Ureter, to Bladder 50780-50785
Ureters 51565

Reinnervation
Larynx
  Neuromuscular Pedicle 31590

Reinsch Test 83015

Reinsertion
Drug Delivery Implant 11983
Implantable Contraceptive Capsules ...11977
Spinal Fixation Device 22849

Relative Density
See Specific Gravity

Release
Carpal Tunnel 64721
Elbow Contracture
  with Radical Release of Capsule 24149
Flexor Muscles
  Hip 27036
Muscle
  Knee 27422
Nerve 64702-64726
  Neurolytic 64727
Retina
  Encircling Material 67115
Spinal Cord 63200
Stapes 69650
Tarsal Tunnel 28035
Tendon 24332, 25295

Release-Inhibiting Hormone, Somatotropin
See Somatostatin

Removal
Adjustable Gastric Restrictive
Device 43772-43774
Allograft
  Intestinal 44137
Artificial Intervertebral Disc
  Cervical Interspace 0095T, 22864
  Lumbar Interspace 0164T, 22865
Balloon
  Intra-Aortic 33974
Balloon Assist Device
  Intra-Aortic 33968, 33971
Blood Clot
  Eye 65930
Blood Component
  Apheresis 36511-36516
Breast
  Capsules 19371
  Implants 19328-19330
  Modified Radical 19307
  Partial 19300-19302
  Radical 19305-19306
  Simple, Complete 19303
  Subcutaneous 19304
Calcareous Deposits
  Subdeltoid 23000
Calculi (Stone)
  Bile Duct 43264, 47420-47425
    Percutaneous 47554, 47630
  Bladder 51050, 52310-52318, 52352
  Gallbladder 47480
  Hepatic Duct 47400
  Kidney 50060-50081, 50130,
                    50561, 50580, 52352
  Pancreas 48020
  Pancreatic Duct 43264
  Salivary Gland 42330-42340
  Ureter 50610-50630, 50961, 50980,
                  51060-51065, 52320-52330, 52352
  Urethra 52310-52315, 52352
Cardiac Event Recorder 33284
Cast 29700-29715

Cataract
  Dilated Fundus Evaluation 2021F
  with Replacement
    Extracapsular 66982, 66984
    Intracapsular 66983
    Not Associated with Concurrent 66983
Catheter
  Central Venous 36589
  Fractured 75961
  Peritoneum 49422
  Pleural Cavity 32552
  Spinal Cord 62355
Cerclage
  Cervix 59871
Cerumen
  Auditory Canal, External 69210
Clot
  Pericardium 33020
    Endoscopic 32658
Comedones 10040
Contraceptive Capsules 11976-11977
Cranial Tongs 20665
Cyst 10040
Dacryolith
  Lacrimal Duct 68530
  Lacrimal Gland 68530
Defibrillator
  Heart 33244
    Pulse Generator Only 33241
    via Thoracotomy 33243
Drug Delivery Implant 11982-11983
Ear Wax
  Auditory Canal, External 69210
Electrode
  Brain 61535, 61880
  Heart 33238
  Nerve 64585
  Spinal Cord 63661-63664
  Stomach 0156T, 0158T, 43648, 43882
Embolus
  See Embolectomy
External Fixation System 20694
Eye
  Bone 67414, 67445
  Ocular Contents
    with Implant 65093
    without Implant 65091
  Orbital Contents Only 65110
  with Bone 65112
  with Implant
    Muscles Attached 65105
    Muscles, Not Attached 65103
  with Muscle or Myocutaneous Flap 65114
  without Implant 65101
Fallopian Tube
  Laparoscopy 58661
  with Hysterectomy 58542, 58544, 58548
Fat
  Lipectomy 15876-15879
Fecal Impaction
  Rectum 45915
Fibrin Deposit 32150
Fixation Device 20670-20680
Foreign Body 65205-65265
  Anal 46608
  Ankle Joint 27610, 27620
  Arm
    Lower 25248
    Upper 24200-24201
  Auditory Canal, External 69200
    with Anesthesia 69205
  Bile Duct 43269

Cystocele 57240, 57260,
       57284-57285, 57423
Enterocele 57265
Fistula 46715-46716, 51900
   Rectovaginal 57300-57307
   Transvesical and Vaginal Approach . . .57330
   Urethrovaginal 57310-57311
   Vesicovaginal 57320-57330
Hysterectomy 58267, 58293
Incontinence 57284-57285, 57288, 57423
Pereyra Procedure 57289
Postpartum 59300
Prolapse 57282, 57284
Rectocele 57250-57260
Suspension 57280-57284
   Laparoscopic 57423, 57425
Wound 57200-57210
Vaginal Wall Prolapse
   See Colporrhaphy
Vas Deferens
   Suture 55400
Vein
   Angioplasty 35460, 35476, 75978
   Femoral 34501
   Graft 34520
   Pulmonary 33730
   Transposition 34510
Vulva
   Postpartum 59300
Wound
   Complex 13100-13160
   Intermediate 12031-12057
   Simple 12001-12021
Wound Dehiscence
   Complex 13160
   Simple 12020-12021
Wrist 25260-25263, 25270, 25447
   Bone 25440
   Carpal Bone 25431
   Cartilage .25107
   Removal
     Implant 25449
   Secondary 25265, 25272-25274
   Tendon 25280-25316
   Tendon Sheath 25275
   Total Replacement 25446

Repeat Surgeries
See Reoperation

Replacement
Adjustable Gastric Band 43773
Aortic Valve .33405-33413
Arthroplasties, Hip
   See Arthroplasty, Hip
Artificial Heart
   Intracorporeal 0052T, 0053T
Cecostomy Tube 49450
Cerebrospinal Fluid Shunt 62160, 62194,
     62225-62230
Colonic Tube 49450
Contact Lens
   See Contact Lens Services
Duodenostomy Tube 49451
Elbow
   Total 24363
Electrode
   Heart 33210-33211, 33216-33217
   Stomach 0155T, 0157T, 43647
Eye
   Drug Delivery System 67121
Gastro-Jejunostomy Tube 49452

Gastrostomy Tube 43760, 49450
Hearing Aid
   Bone Conduction 69710
Hip 27130-27132
   Revision 27134-27138
Implant
   Bone
     for External Speech Processor/Cochlear
     Stimulator 69717-69718
Intervertebral Disc
   Cervical Interspace 0098T, 22861
   Lumbar Interspace 0165T, 22862
Jejunostomy Tube 49451
Knee
   Total 27447
Mitral Valve .33430
Nephrostomy Tube
   See Nephrostomy, Change Tube
Nerve 64726
Neurostimulator
   Pulse Generator/Receiver
     Intracranial 61885
     Peripheral Nerve 64590
     Spinal 63685
Ossicles
   with Prosthesis 69633, 69637
Ossicular Replacement
   See TORP (Total Ossicular Replacement
   Prosthesis)
Pacemaker 33206-33208
   Catheter 33210
   Electrode 33210-33211, 33216-33217
Pacing Cardioverter-Defibrillator
   Leads 33243-33244
   Pulse Generator Only 33241
Penile
   Prosthesis 54410-54411, 54416-54417
Prosthesis
   Skull 62143
   Urethral Sphincter 53448
Pulmonary Valve 33475
Pulse Generator
   Brain 61885
   Peripheral Nerve 64590
   Spinal Cord 63685
Receiver
   Brain 61885
   Peripheral Nerve 64590
   Spinal Cord 63685
Skin
   Acellular Dermal Matrix 15170-15176
Skull Plate 62143
Spinal Cord
   Reservoir .62360
Stent
   Ureteral 50382, 50387
Subcutaneous Port
   for Gastric Restrictive Procedure 43888
Tissue Expanders
   Skin 11970
Total Replacement
   See Hip, Total Replacement
Total Replacement Heart System
   Intracorporeal 0052T, 0053T
Tricuspid Valve 33465
Ureter
   with Intestines 50840
Venous Access Device 36582-36583, 36585
   Catheter 36578
Venous Catheter
   Central 36580-36581, 36584

Ventricular Assist Device
   Extracorporeal 33981
   Intracorporeal 33982-33983

Replantation
Arm, Upper .20802
Digit 20816-20822
Foot 20838
Forearm 20805
Hand 20808
Thumb 20824-20827

Report Preparation
Extended, Medical 99080
Psychiatric 90889

Reposition
Toe to Hand 26551-26556

Repositioning
Central Venous Catheter 36597
Electrode
   Heart 33215-33217, 33226
Gastrostomy Tube 43761
Heart
   Defibrillator
     Leads 33215-33216, 33226, 33249
Intraocular Lens 66825
Tricuspid Valve 33468

Reproductive Tissue
Cryopreserved
   Preparation
     Thawing 89354
Storage 89344

Reprogramming
Shunt
   Brain 62252

Reptilase Test 85635

Reptilase Time
See Thrombin Time

Resection
Aortic Valve
   Stenosis 33415
Bladder Diverticulum 52305
Bladder Neck
   Transurethral 52500
Brain Lobe
   See Lobectomy, Brain
Chest Wall 19260-19272
Diaphragm 39560-39561
Endaural
   See Ear, Inner, Excision
Humeral Head 23195
Intestines, Small
   Laparoscopic 44202-44203
Lung .32503-32504
Mouth
   with Tongue Excision 41153
Myocardium
   Aneurysm .33542
   Septal Defect 33545
Nasal Septum Submucous
   See Nasal Septum, Submucous Resection
Nose
   Septum 30520
Ovary, Wedge
   See Ovary, Wedge Resection
Palate 42120

Electrode
    Stomach 0156T, 0158T
External Fixation System 20693
Eye
    Aqueous Shunt 66185
Gastric Restrictive Procedure
    Other than Adjustable Gastric Restrictive
    Device 43848
Gastrostomy Tube 44373
Hip Replacement
    See Replacement, Hip, Revision
Hymenal Ring 56700
Ileostomy
    See Ileostomy, Revision
Infusion Pump
    Intraarterial 36261
    Intravenous 36576-36578, 36582-36583
Iris
    Iridoplasty 66762
    Iridotomy 66761
Jejunostomy Tube 44373
Lower Extremity Arterial Bypass 35879-35881
Pacemaker Site
    Chest 33222
Rhytidectomy 15824-15829
Semicircular Canal
    Fenestration 69840
Shunt
    Intrahepatic Portosystemic 37183
Sling 53442
Stapedectomy
    See Stapedectomy, Revision
Stomach
    for Obesity 43848
Subcutaneous Port
    for Gastric Restrictive Procedure 43886
Tracheostomy
    Scar 31830
Urinary-Cutaneous Anastomosis 50727-50728
Vagina
    Prosthetic Graft 57295-57296, 57426
    Sling
        Stress Incontinence 57287
Venous Access Device 36576-36578,
                 36582, 36583, 36585
Ventricle
    Ventriculomyectomy 33416
    Ventriculomyotomy 33416

Rh (D)
See Blood Typing

Rh Immune Globulin
See Immune Globulins, Rho (D)

Rheumatoid Factor 86430-86431

Rhinectomy
Partial 30150
Total 30160

Rhinomanometry 92512

Rhinopharynx
See Nasopharynx

Rhinophototherapy 0168T

Rhinophyma
Repair 30120

Rhinoplasty
Cleft Lip/Cleft Palate 30460-30462

Primary 30400-30420
Secondary 30430-30450

Rhinoscopy
See Endoscopy, Nose

Rhinotomy
Lateral 30118, 30320

Rhizotomy 63185-63190

Rho Variant Du 86905

Rhytidectomy 15824-15829

Rhytidoplasties
See Face Lift

Rib
Antibody 86756
Antigen Detection
    by Immunoassay
        with Direct Optical Observation
    Direct Fluorescense 87280
    Enzyme Immunoassay 87420
Excision 21600-21616, 32900
Fracture
    Closed Treatment 21800
    External Fixation 21810
    Open Treatment 21805
Graft
    to Face 21230
Resection 19260-19272, 32900
X-ray 71100-71111

Riboflavin 84252

Richardson Operation Hysterectomy
See Hysterectomy, Abdominal, Total

Richardson Procedure 53460

Rickettsia
Antibody 86757

Ridell Operation
See Sinusotomy, Frontal

Ridge, Alveolar
See Alveolar Ridge

Right Atrioventricular Valve
See Tricuspid Valve

Right Heart Cardiac Catheterization
See Cardiac Catheterization, Right Heart

Ripstein Operation
See Proctopexy

Risk Factor Reduction Intervention
See Performance Measures, Preventive Medicine

Risser Jacket 29010-29015
Removal 29710

Rocky Mountain Spotted Fever 86000

Roentgen Rays
See X-ray

Roentgenographic
See X-ray

Roentgenography
See Radiology, Diagnostic

Ropes Test 83872

Rorschach Test 96101

**Ross Information Processing
Assessment** 96125

Ross Procedure 33413

Rotation Flap
See Skin, Adjacent Tissue Transfer

Rotator Cuff
Repair 23410-23420

Rotavirus
Antibody 86759
Antigen Detection
    Enzyme Immunoassay 87425

Rotavirus Vaccine
3 Dose 90680
2 Dose 90681

Round Window
Repair Fistula 69667

Round Window Fistula
See Fistula, Round Window

Roux-En-Y Procedure 43621,
             43633-43634, 43644, 43846,
         47740-47741, 47780-47785, 48540

RPR 86592-86593

RSV
See Immune Globulins; Respiratory Syncytial Virus

RT3
See Triiodothyronine, Reverse

Rubbing Alcohol
See Isopropyl Alcohol

Rubella
Antibody 86762
Vaccine 90706-90710

Rubella HI Test
See Hemagglutination Inhibition Test

Rubella/Mumps
See Vaccines

Rubeola
Antibody 86765
Antigen Detection
    Immunofluorescence 87283

Rubeolla
See Rubeola

**Russell Viper Venom
Time** 85612-85613

S

Sac, Endolymphatic
See Endolymphatic Sac

Saccomanno Technique 88108

Schlatter Operation Total Gastrectomy
See Excision, Stomach, Total

Schlicter Test 87197
See Bactericidal Titer, Serum

Schocket Procedure 66180
See Aqueous Shunt

Schuchard Procedure
Osteotomy
　Maxilla 21206

Schwannoma, Acoustic
See Brain, Tumor, Excision

Sciatic Nerve
Decompression 64712
Injection
　Anesthetic 64445-64446
Lesion
　Excision 64786
Neuroma
　Excision 64786
Neuroplasty 64712
Release 64712
Repair/Suture 64858

Scintigraphy
See Nuclear Medicine
Computed Tomographic
　See Emission Computerized Tomography

Scissoring
Skin Tags 11200-11201

Sclera
Excision
　Sclerectomy with Punch or Scissors 66160
Fistulization
　for Glaucoma 0123T
　Iridencleisis or Iridotasis 66165
　Sclerectomy with Punch or Scissors with
　　Iridectomy 66160
　Thermocauterization with Iridectomy ...66155
　Trabeculectomy ab Externo in Absence of
　　Previous Surgery 66170
　Trephination with Iridectomy 66150
Incision
　Fistulization
　　Iridencleisis or Iridotasis 66165
　　Sclerectomy with Punch or Scissors
　　with Iridectomy 66160
　　Thermocauterization with
　　　Iridectomy 66155
　　Trabeculectomy ab Externo in Absence
　　of Previous Surgery 66170
　　Trephination with Iridectomy 66150
Lesion
　Excision 66130
Repair
　Reinforcement
　　with Graft 67255
　　without Graft 67250
　Staphyloma
　　with Graft 66225
　　without Graft 66220
　with Glue 65286
　Wound
　　Operative 66250
　　Tissue Glue 65286

Scleral Buckling Operation
See Retina, Repair, Detachment

Scleral Ectasia
See Staphyloma, Sclera

Sclerectomy 66160

Sclerotherapy
Venous 36468-36471

Sclerotomy
See Incision, Sclera

Screening, Drug
See Drug Screen
Alcohol and/or Substance Abuse 99408-99409

Scribner Cannulization 36810

Scrotal Varices
See Varicocele

Scrotoplasty 55175-55180

Scrotum
Abscess
　Incision and Drainage 54700, 55100
Excision 55150
Exploration 55110
Hematoma
　Incision and Drainage 54700
Removal
　Foreign Body 55120
Repair 55175-55180
Ultrasound 76870
Unlisted Services and Procedures 55899

Scrub Typhus 86000

Second Look Surgery
See Reoperation

Section
See Decompression
Cesarean
　See Cesarean Delivery
Cranial Nerve 61460
　Spinal Access 63191
Dentate Ligament 63180-63182
Gasserian Ganglion
　Sensory Root 61450
Medullary Tract 61470
Mesencephalic Tract 61480
Nerve Root 63185-63190
Spinal Accessory Nerve 63191
Spinal Cord Tract 63194-63199
Tentorium Cerebelli 61440
Vestibular Nerve
　Transcranial Approach 69950
　Translabyrinthine Approach 69915

Sedation
Moderate 99143-99150
　with Independent Observation ...99143-99145

Seddon-Brookes Procedure 24320

Sedimentation Rate
Blood Cell
　Automated 85652
　Manual 85651

Segmentectomy
Breast 19301-19302
Lung 32484

Seidlitz Powder Test
See X-ray, with Contrast

Selective Cellular Enhancement Technique 88112

Selenium 84255

Self Care
See Physical Medicine/Therapy/Occupational Therapy
Training 97535, 98960-98962, 99509

Sella Turcica
CT Scan 70480-70482
X-ray 70240

Semen
See Sperm

Semen Analysis 89300-89322
Sperm Analysis 89331
　Antibodies 89325
with Sperm Isolation 89260-89261

Semenogelase
See Antigen, Prostate Specific

Semicircular Canal
Incision
　Fenestration 69820
　Revised 69840

Semilunar
Bone
　See Lunate
Ganglion
　See Gasserian Ganglion

Seminal Vesicle
Cyst
　Excision 55680
Excision 55650
Incision 55600-55605
Mullerian Duct
　Excision 55680
Unlisted Services and Procedures 55899

Seminal Vesicles
Vesiculography 74440
X-ray with Contrast 74440

Seminin
See Antigen, Prostate Specific

Semiquantitative 81005

Sengstaken Tamponade
Esophagus 43460

Senning Procedure 33774-33777
See Repair, Great Arteries; Revision

Senning Type 33774-33777

Sensitivity Study
Antibiotic
　Agar 87181
　Disc 87184
　Enzyme Detection 87185
　Macrobroth 87188
　MIC 87186
　Microtiter 87186
　MLC 87187
　Mycobacteria 87190

Shoulder Joint
See Clavicle; Scapula
Arthroplasty
　　with Implant 23470-23472
Arthrotomy
　　with Biopsy 23100-23101
　　with Synovectomy 23105-23106
Dislocation
　　Open Treatment 23660
　　with Greater Tuberosity Fracture
　　　　Closed Treatment 23665
　　　　Open Treatment 23670
　　with Surgical or Anatomical Neck Fracture
　　　　Closed Treatment with
　　　　Manipulation 23675
　　　　Open Treatment 23680
Excision
　　Torn Cartilage 23101
Exploration 23040-23044
Incision and Drainage 23040-23044
Removal
　　Foreign Body 23040-23044
X-ray 73050

Shunt(s)
Aqueous
　　to Extraocular Reservoir 66180
　　　　Revision 66185
Arteriovenous
　　See Arteriovenous Shunt
Brain
　　Creation 62180-62223
　　Removal 62256-62258
　　Replacement 62160, 62194,
　　　　　　　　　　　　　　　62225-62230, 62258
　　Reprogramming 62252
Cerebrospinal Fluid
　　See Cerebrospinal Fluid Shunt
Creation
　　Arteriovenous
　　　　Direct 36821
　　　　ECMO 36822
　　　　Thomas Shunt 36835
　　　　Transposition 36818-36820
　　　　with Bypass Graft 35686
　　　　with Graft 36825-36830
　　Cerebrospinal Fluid 62200
　　Thomas Shunt 36835
Fetal 59076
Great Vessel
　　Aorta
　　　　Pulmonary 33924
　　Aorta to Pulmonary Artery
　　　　Ascending 33755
　　　　Descending 33762
　　Central 33764
　　Subclavian Pulmonary Artery 33750
　　Vena Cava to Pulmonary Artery . . .33766-33768
Intra-Atrial 33735-33737
LeVeen
　　See LeVeen Shunt
Nonvascular
　　X-ray 75809
Peritoneal
　　Venous
　　　　Injection 49427
　　　　Ligation 49428
　　　　Removal 49429
　　X-ray 75809
Pulmonary Artery
　　See Pulmonary Artery, Shunt

Revision
　　Arteriovenous 36832
Spinal Cord
　　Creation 63740-63741
　　Irrigation 63744
　　Removal 63746
　　Replacement 63744
Superior Mesenteric-Caval
　　See Anastomosis, Caval to Mesenteric
Ureter to Colon 50815
Ventriculocisternal with Valve
　　See Ventriculocisternostomy

Shuntogram 75809

Sialic Acid 84275

Sialodochoplasty 42500-42505

Sialogram
See Sialography

Sialography 70390

Sickling
Electrophoresis 83020

Siderocytes 85536

Siderophilin
See Transferrin

Sigmoid
See Colon-Sigmoid

Sigmoid Bladder
Cystectomy 51590

Sigmoidoscopy
Ablation
　　Polyp 45339
　　Tumor 45339
Biopsy 45331
Collection
　　Specimen .45331
Exploration 45330, 45335
Hemorrhage Control 45334
Injection
　　Submucosal 45335
Needle Biopsy 45342
Placement
　　Stent 45345
Removal
　　Foreign Body 45332
　　Polyp 45333, 45338
　　Tumor 45333, 45338
Repair
　　Volvulus 45337
Ultrasound 45341-45342

Signal-Averaged Electrocardiography
See Electrocardiogram

Silica 84285

Silicon Dioxide
See Silica

Silicone
Contouring Injections 11950-11954

Silver Operation
See Keller Procedure

Silver Procedure 28290

Simple Mastectomies
See Mastectomy

Single Photon Absorptiometry
See Absorptiometry, Single Photon

Single Photon Emission Computed Tomography
See SPECT

Sinu, Sphenoid
See Sinus/Sinuses, Sphenoid

Sinus/Sinuses
Ethmoid
　　Excision 31200-31205
　　　　with Nasal/Sinus Endoscopy . . .31254-31255
　　Repair of Cerebrospinal Leak 31290
Ethmoidectomy
　　Excision 31254
Frontal
　　Destruction 31080-31085
　　Exploration 31070-31075
　　　　with Nasal/Sinus Endoscopy 31276
　　Fracture
　　　　Open Treatment 21343-21344
　　Incision 31070-31087
Injection 20500
　　Diagnostic 20501
Maxillary
　　Antrostomy 31256-31267
　　Excision 31225-31230
　　Exploration 31020-31032
　　　　with Nasal/Sinus Endoscopy 31233
　　Incision 31020-31032, 31256-31267
　　Irrigation 31000
　　Skull Base .61581
　　Surgery 61581
Multiple
　　Incision 31090
Paranasal
　　Incision 31090
Pilonidal
　　See Cyst, Pilonidal
Sinus of Valsalva
　　Repair 33702-33722
Sinus Venosus
　　Repair 33645
Sphenoid
　　Biopsy 31050-31051
　　Exploration 31050-31051
　　　　with Nasal/Sinus Endoscopy 31235
　　Incision 31050-31051
　　　　with Nasal/Sinus Endoscopy . .31287-31288
　　Irrigation 31002
　　Repair of Cerebrospinal Leak 31291
　　Sinusotomy 31050-31051
　　Skull Base Surgery 61580-61581
Unlisted Services and Procedures 31299
X-ray .70210-70220

Sinusectomy, Ethmoid
See Sinus/Sinuses; Ethmoidectomy

Sinusoidal Rotational Testing
See Ear, Nose, and Throat

Sinusoscopy
Sinus
　　Maxillary 31233
　　Sphenoid 31235

Stoma
Creation
- Bladder 51980
- Kidney 50551-50561
- Stomach
  - Neonatal 43831
  - Temporary 43830-43831
- Ureter 50860

Ureter
- Endoscopy via 50951-50961

Stomach
Anastomosis
- with Duodenum 43810, 43850-43855
- with Jejunum 43820-43825, 43860-43865

Biopsy .43600-43605

Creation
- Stoma
  - Temporary 43830-43831
  - Temporary Stoma
    - Laparoscopic 43653

Electrode
- Removal 0156T, 0158T, 43882

Electrogastrography 91132-91133

Excision
- Partial 43631-43635, 43845
- Total 43620-43622

Exploration 43500

Gastric Bypass 43644-43645, 43846
- Revision 43848

Gastric Restrictive Procedures 43770-43775, 43848, 43886-43888

Implantation
- Electrodes 0155T, 0157T, 43647, 43881

Incision 43830-43832
- Exploration 43500
- Pyloric Sphincter 43520
- Removal
  - Foreign Body 43500

Intubation with Specimen Prep 91055

Laparoscopy 0155T-0156T, 43647-43648

Nuclear Medicine
- Blood Loss Study 78278
- Emptying Study 78264
- Imaging .78261
- Protein Loss Study 78282
- Reflux Study 78262
- Vitamin B-12 Absorption 78270-78272

Reconstruction
- for Obesity 43644-43645, 43842-43847
- Roux-En-Y 43644, 43846

Removal
- Foreign Body 43500

Repair 48547
- Fistula 43880
- Fundoplasty 43324-43325
  - Laparoscopic 43280-43282
- Laceration 43501-43502
- Stoma 43870
- Ulcer 43501

Replacement
- Electrodes 0155T, 0157T, 43647, 43881

Specimen Collection 89130-89141

Stimulation of Secretion 91052

Suture
- Fistula 43880
- for Obesity 43842-43843
- Stoma 43870
- Ulcer 43840
- Wound 43840

Tumor
- Excision 43610-43611

Ulcer
- Excision .43610

Unlisted Services and Procedures . . .43659, 43999

Stomatoplasty
See Mouth, Repair

Stone, Kidney
See Calculus, Removal, Kidney

Stookey-Scarff Procedure
See Ventriculocisternostomy

Stool Blood
See Blood, Feces

Storage
- Embryo 89342
- Oocyte 89346
- Reproductive Tissue 89344
- Sperm 89343

Strabismus
Chemodenervation 67345

Repair
- Adjustable Sutures 67335
- Extraocular Muscles 67340
- One Horizontal Muscle 67311
- One Vertical Muscle 67314
- Posterior Fixation Suture
  - Technique 67334, 67335
- Previous Surgery, Not Involving Extraocular
  - Muscles 67331
- Release Extensive Scar Tissue 67343
- Superior Oblique Muscle 67318
- Transposition 67320
- Two Horizontal Muscles 67312
- Two or More Vertical Muscles 67316

Strapping
See Cast; Splint
- Ankle 29540
- Chest 29200
- Elbow 29260
- Finger 29280
- Foot 29540, 29590
- Hand 29280
- Hip 29520
- Knee 29530
- Leg, Lower
  - Venous Wound Compression 29581
- Shoulder .29240
- Thorax 29200
- Toes 29550
- Unlisted Services and Procedures 29799
- Unna Boot 29580
- Wrist 29260

Strassman Procedure 58540

Strayer Procedure
Leg, Lower 27687

Streptococcus pneumoniae Vaccine
See Vaccines

Streptococcus, Group A
Antigen Detection
- Enzyme Immunoassay 87430
- Nucleic Acid 87650-87652

Direct Optical Observation (rapid test) . . .87880

Streptococcus, Group B
by Immunoassay
- with Direct Optical Observation 87802

Streptokinase, Antibody 86590

Stress Tests
- Cardiovascular 93015-93024
- Multiple Gated Acquisition
  - (MUGA) 78472-78473
- Myocardial Perfusion Imaging 78451-78454
- Pulmonary 94620-94621
  - *See* Pulmonology, Diagnostic

Stricture
Repair
- Urethra 53400-53405

Urethra
- *See* Urethral Stenosis

Stricturoplasty
Intestines .44615

Stroboscopy
Larynx 31579

STS 86592-86593
See Syphilis Test

Stuart-Prower Factor 85260

Study, Color Vision
See Color Vision Examination

Sturmdorf Procedure 57520

Styloid Process
Radial
- Excision .25230

Styloidectomy
Radial 25230

Stypven Time
See Russell Viper Venom Time

Subacromial Bursa
Arthrocentesis 20610

Subclavian Arteries
See Artery, Subclavian

Subcutaneous Infusion
See Infusion, Subcutaneous

Subcutaneous Injection
See Injection, Subcutaneous

Subcutaneous Mastectomies
See Mastectomy, Subcutaneous

Subcutaneous Tissue
Excision 15830-15839, 15847

Subdiaphragmatic Abscess
See Abscess, Subdiaphragmatic

Subdural Electrode
- Insertion 61531-61533
- Removal .61535

Subdural Hematoma
See Hematoma, Subdural

Subdural Puncture 61105-61108

Subdural Tap 61000-61001

Sublingual Gland
Abscess
- Incision and Drainage 42310-42320

Calculi (Stone)
Excision 42330
Cyst
Drainage 42409
Excision 42408
Excision 42450

Subluxation
Elbow 24640

Submandibular Gland
Calculi (Stone)
Excision 42330-42335
Excision 42440

Submaxillary Gland
Abscess
Incision and Drainage 42310-42320

Submucous Resection of Nasal Septum
See Nasal Septum, Submucous Resection

Subperiosteal Implant
Reconstruction
Mandible 21245-21246
Maxilla 21245-21246

Subphrenic Abscess
See Abscess, Subdiaphragmatic

Subtrochanteric Fracture
See Femur, Fracture, Subtrochanteric

Sucrose Hemolysis Test
See Red Blood Cell (RBC), Fragility, Osmotic

Suction Lipectomies
See Liposuction

Sudiferous Gland
See Sweat Glands

Sugar Water Test
See Red Blood Cell (RBC), Fragility, Osmotic

Sugars 84375-84379

Sugiura Procedure
See Esophagus, Repair, Varices

Sulfate
Chondroitin
See Chondroitin Sulfate
DHA
See Dehydroepiandrosterone Sulfate
Urine 84392

Sulfation Factor
See Somatomedin

Sulphates
See Sulfate

Sumatran Mite Fever
See Scrub Typhus

Superficial Musculoaponeurotic System (SMAS) Flap
Rhytidectomy 15829

Supernumerary Digit
Reconstruction 26587
Repair 26587

Supply
See Chemotherapy

Educational Materials 99071
Low Vision Aids
See Spectacle Services
Materials 99070
Prosthesis
Breast 19396

Suppositories, Vaginal
See Pessary

Suppression 80400-80408

Suppression/Testing
See Evocative/Suppression Test

Suppressor T Lymphocyte Marker
See CD8

Suppurative Hidradenitides
See Hidradenitis, Suppurative

Suprahyoid
Lymphadenectomy 38700

Supraorbital
Nerve
Avulsion 64732
Incision 64732
Transection 64732
Reconstruction
Forehead 21179-21180
Rim 21179-21180

Suprapubic Prostatectomies
See Prostatectomy, Suprapubic

Suprarenal
Gland
See Adrenal Gland
Vein
See Vein, Adrenal

Suprascapular Nerve
Injection
Anesthetic 64418

Suprasellar Cyst
See Craniopharyngioma

Surface CD4 Receptor
See CD4

Surface Radiotherapy
See Application, Radioelement, Surface

Surgeries
Breast-Conserving
See Breast, Excision, Lesion
Conventional
See Celiotomy
Laser
See Laser Surgery
Mohs
See Mohs Micrographic Surgery
Repeat
See Reoperation

Surgical
Avulsion
See Avulsion
Cataract Removal
See Cataract, Excision
Collapse Therapy; Thoracoplasty
See Thoracoplasty
Diathermy
See Electrocautery

Galvanism
See Electrolysis
Incision
See Incision
Microscopes
See Operating Microscope
Pathology
See Pathology, Surgical
Planing
Nose
Skin 30120
Pneumoperitoneum
See Pneumoperitoneum
Removal, Eye
See Enucleation, Eye
Revision
See Reoperation
Services
Post-Op Visit 99024

Surveillance
See Monitoring

Suspension
Aorta 33800
Kidney
See Nephropexy
Muscle
Hyoid 21685
Tongue Base 41512
Vagina
See Colpopexy

Suture
See Repair
Abdomen 49900
Aorta 33320-33322
Bile Duct
Wound 47900
Bladder
Fistulization 44660-44661, 45800-45805,
51880-51925
Vesicouterine 51920-51925
Vesicovaginal 51900
Wound 51860-51865
Cervix 57720
Colon
Diverticula 44604-44605
Fistula 44650-44661
Plication .44680
Stoma 44620-44625
Ulcer 44604-44605
Wound 44604-44605
Esophagus
Wound 43410-43415
Eyelid 67880
Closure of 67875
with Transposition of Tarsal Plate 67882
Wound
Full Thickness 67935
Partial Thickness 67930
Facial Nerve
Intratemporal
Lateral to Geniculate Ganglion 69740
Medial to Geniculate Ganglion 69745
Foot
Tendon 28200-28210
Gastroesophageal 43405
Great Vessel 33320-33322
Hemorrhoids 46945-46946
Hepatic Duct
See Hepatic Duct, Repair

Intestine
Large
    Diverticula 44605
    Ulcer 44605
    Wound 44605
Intestines
Large
    Diverticula 44604
    Ulcer 44604
    Wound 44604
Small
    Diverticula 44602-44603
    Fistula 44640-44661
    Plication 44680
    Ulcer 44602-44603
    Wound 44602-44603
Stoma 44620-44625
Iris
with Ciliary Body 66682
Kidney
Fistula 50520-50526
Horseshoe 50540
Wound 50500
Leg, Lower
Tendon 27658-27665
Leg, Upper
Muscle 27385-27386
Liver
Wound 47350-47361
Mesentery 44850
Nerve 64831-64876
Pancreas 48545
Pharynx
Wound 42900
Rectum
Fistula 45800-45825
Prolapse 45540-45541
Removal
Anesthesia 15850-15851
Spleen
See Splenorrhapy
Stomach
Fistula 43880
Laceration 43501-43502
Stoma 43870
Ulcer 43501, 43840
Wound 43840
Tendon
Foot 28200-28210
Knee 27380-27381
Testis
Injury 54670
Suspension 54620-54640
Thoracic Duct
Abdominal Approach 38382
Cervical Approach 38380
Thoracic Approach 38381
Throat
Wound 42900
Tongue
Base Suspension 41512
to Lip 41510
Trachea
Fistula
    with Plastic Repair 31825
    without Plastic Repair 31820
Stoma
    with Plastic Repair 31825
    without Plastic Repair 31820
Wound
    Cervical 31800
    Intrathoracic 31805

Ulcer 44604-44605
Ureter 50900
Deligation 50940
Fistula 50920-50930
Urethra
Fistula 45820-45825, 53520
Stoma 53520
to Bladder 51840-51841
Wound 53502-53515
Uterus
Fistula 51920-51925
Rupture 58520, 59350
Suspension 58400-58410
Vagina
Cystocele 57240, 57260
Enterocele 57265
Fistula
    Rectovaginal 57300-57307
    Transvesical and Vaginal Approach ...57330
    Urethrovaginal 57310-57311
    Vesicovaginal 51900, 57320-57330
Rectocele 57250-57260
Suspension 57280, 57283
Wound 57200-57210
Vas Deferens 55400
Vein
Femoral 37650
Iliac 37660
Vena Cava 37620
Wound 44604-44605

Swallowing
Evaluation 92610-92613, 92616-92617
Imaging 74230
Treatment 92526

Swanson Procedure 28309

Sweat Collection
Iontophoresis 89230

Sweat Glands
Excision
Axillary 11450-11451
Inguinal 11462-11463
Perianal 11470-11471
Perineal 11470-11471
Umbilical 11470-11471

Sweat Test 82435
See Chloride, Blood

Swenson Procedure 45120

Syme Procedure 27888

Sympathectomy
Artery
Digital 64820
Radial 64821
Superficial Palmar Arch 64823
Ulnar 64822
Cervical 64802
Cervicothoracic 64804
Digital Artery
with Magnification 64820
Lumbar 64818
Presacral 58410
Thoracic 32664
Thoracolumbar 64809
with Rib Excision 21616

Sympathetic Nerve
Excision 64802-64818
Injection
Anesthetic 64508, 64520-64530

Sympathins
See Catecholamines

Symphysiotomy
Horseshoe Kidney 50540

Symphysis, Pubic
See Pubic Symphysis

Syncytial Virus, Respiratory
See Respiratory Syncytial Virus

Syndactylism, Toes
See Webbed, Toe

Syndactyly
Repair 26560-26562

Syndesmotomy
See Ligament, Release

Syndrome
Adrenogenital
    See Adrenogenital Syndrome
Ataxia-Telangiectasia
    See Ataxia Telangiectasia
Bloom
    See Bloom Syndrome
Carpal Tunnel
    See Carpal Tunnel Syndrome
Costen's
    See Temporomandibular Joint (TMJ)
Erb -Goldflam
    See Myasthenia Gravis
Ovarian Vein
    See Ovarian Vein Syndrome
Synechiae, Intrauterine
    See Adhesions, Intrauterine
Treacher Collins
    See Treacher-Collins Syndrome
Urethral
    See Urethral Syndrome

Syngesterone
See Progesterone

Synostosis (Cranial)
See Craniosynostosis

Synovectomy
Arthrotomy with
    Glenohumeral Joint 23105
    Sternoclavicular Joint 23106
Elbow 24102
Excision
    Carpometacarpal Joint 26130
    Finger Joint 26135-26140
    Hip Joint 27054
    Interphalangeal Joint 26140
    Knee Joint 27334-27335
    Metacarpophalangeal Joint 26135
    Palm 26145
Wrist 25105, 25118-25119
    Radical 25115-25116

Tattoo
Cornea 65600
Skin 11920-11922

TB Test
Antigen Response 86480
Skin Test 86580

TBG
See Thyroxine Binding Globulin

TBS
See Bethesda System

TCT
See Thrombin Time

Td Shots
See Tetanus Immunization; Vaccines

Team Conference
Case Management Services 99366-99368

Tear Duct
See Lacrimal Duct

Tear Gland
See Lacrimal Gland

Technique
Pericardial Window
    See Pericardiostomy
Projective
    See Projective Test

Teeth
X-ray 70300-70320

Telangiectasia
Chromosome Analysis 88248
Injection 36468

Telangiectasia, Cerebello-Oculocutaneous
See Ataxia Telangiectasia

Telephone
Evaluation and Management
    Nonphysician 98966-98968
    Physician .99441-99443
Pacemaker Analysis 93293
Transmission of ECG 93012

Teletherapy
Dose Plan 77305-77321

Temperature Gradient Studies 93740

Temporal Arteries
See Artery, Temporal

Temporal Bone
Electromagnetic Bone Conduction Hearing Device
    Implantation/Replacement 69710
    Removal/Repair 69711
Excision 69535
Resection 69535
Tumor
    Removal 69970
Unlisted Services and Procedures 69979

Temporal, Petrous
Excision
    Apex 69530

Temporomandibular Joint (TMJ)
Arthrocentesis 20605
Arthrography 70328-70332
    Injection 21116
Arthroplasty .21240-21243
Arthroscopy
    Diagnostic 29800
    Surgical 29804
Arthrotomy 21010
Cartilage
    Excision 21060
Condylectomy 21050
Coronoidectomy 21070
Dislocation
    Closed Treatment 21480-21485
    Open Treatment 21490
Injection
    Radiologic 21116
Magnetic Resonance Imaging (MRI) 70336
Manipulation 21073
Meniscectomy 21060
Prostheses
    See Prosthesis, Temporomandibular Joint
Reconstruction
    See Reconstruction, Temporomandibular Joint
X-ray with Contrast 70328-70332

Tenago Procedure 53431

Tendinosuture
See Suture, Tendon

Tendon
Achilles
    See Achilles Tendon
Arm, Upper
    Revision 24320
Excision
    Finger 26180
    Forearm 25109
    Palm 26170
    Wrist 25109
Finger
    Excision 26180
Forearm
    Excision 25109
    Repair 25260-25274
Graft
    Harvesting 20924
Insertion
    Biceps Tendon 24342
Lengthening
    Ankle 27685-27686
    Arm, Upper 24305
    Elbow 24305
    Finger .26476, 26478
    Forearm 25280
    Hand 26476, 26478
    Leg, Lower 27685-27686
    Leg, Upper 27393-27395
    Toe 28240
    Wrist 25280
Palm
    Excision 26170
Release
    Arm, Lower 25295
    Arm, Upper 24332
    Wrist 25295
Shortening
    Ankle 27685-27686
    Finger .26477, 26479

Hand .26477, 26479
Leg, Lower 27685-27686
Transfer
    Arm, Lower 25310-25312, 25316
    Arm, Upper 24301
    Elbow 24301
    Finger .26497-26498
    Hand 26480-26489
    Leg, Lower 27690-27692
    Leg, Upper 27400
    Pelvis 27098
    Thumb 26490-26492, 26510
    Wrist 25310-25312, 25316
Transplant
    Leg, Upper 27396-27397
Wrist
    Excision 25109
    Repair 25260-25274

Tendon Origin
Insertion
    Injection 20551

Tendon Pulley Reconstruction of Hand
See Hand, Reconstruction, Tendon Pulley

Tendon Sheath
Arm
    Lower
        Repair 25275
Finger
    Incision 26055
    Incision and Drainage 26020
    Lesion 26160
Foot
    Excision 28086-28088
Hand Lesion 26160
Injection 20550
Palm
    Incision and Drainage 26020
Removal
    Foreign Body 20520-20525
Wrist
    Excision, Radical 25115-25116
    Incision 25000-25001
    Repair 25275

Tenectomy, Tendon Sheath
See Excision, Lesion, Tendon Sheath

Tennis Elbow
Tenotomy 24357-24359

Tenodesis
Biceps Tendon
    Arthroscopic 29828
    at Elbow 24340
    Shoulder 23430
Finger 26471-26474
Wrist 25300-25301

Tenolysis
Ankle 27680-27681
Arm, Lower 25295
Arm, Upper 24332
Finger
    Extensor 26445-26449
    Flexor 26440-26442
Foot 28220-28226
Hand Extensor 26445-26449
    Flexor 26440-26442
Leg, Lower .27680-27681
Wrist 25295

Therapeutic

Abortion
See Abortion, Therapeutic
Apheresis
See Apheresis, Therapeutic
Drug Assay
See Drug Assay
Mobilization
See Mobilization
Photopheresis
See Photopheresis
Radiology
See Radiology, Therapeutic

Therapies

Cold
See Cryotherapy
Exercise
See Exercise Therapy
Family
See Psychotherapy, Family
Language
See Language Therapy
Milieu
See Environmental Intervention
Occupational
See Occupational Therapy
Photodynamic
See Photochemotherapy
Photoradiation
See Actinotherapy
Physical
See Physical Medicine/Therapy/Occupational
Therapy
Speech
See Speech Therapy
Tocolytic
See Tocolysis
Ultraviolet
See Actinotherapy

Therapy

ACE Inhibitor Therapy
See Performance Measures
Beta Blocker Therapy
See Performance Measures
Desensitization
See Allergen Immunotherapy
Hemodialysis
See Hemodialysis
Hot Pack
See Hot Pack Treatment
Pharmacologic; for Cessation of Tobacco Use
See Performance Measures
Radiation
Brachytherapy .0182T
See Irradiation
Speech
See Speech Therapy
Statin Therapy, Prescribed
See Performance Measures

Thermocauterization

Ectropion
Repair 67922
Lesion
Cornea 65450

Thermocoagulation

See Electrocautery

Thermographies

See Thermogram

Thermography, Cerebral

See Thermogram, Cephalic

Thermotherapy

Prostate 53850-53852
Microwave .53850
Radiofrequency 53852

Thiamine 84425

Thiersch Operation 15050

See Pinch Graft

Thiersch Procedure 46753

Thigh

Fasciotomy 27025
See Femur; Leg, Upper

Thin Layer Chromatographies

See Chromatography, Thin-Layer

Thiocyanate .84430

Third Disease

See Rubella

Thompson Procedure 27430

Thoracectomy

See Thoracoplasty

Thoracentesis 32421-32422

Thoracic

Anterior Ramus
See Intercostal Nerve
Arteries
See Artery, Thoracic
Cavity
See Chest Cavity
Duct
See Lymphatics
Cannulation .38794
Ligation 38380
Abdominal Approach 38382
Thoracic Approach 38381
Suture
Abdominal Approach 38382
Cervical Approach 38380
Thoracic Approach 38381
Empyema
See Abscess, Thorax
Surgery
Video-Assisted
See Thoracoscopy
Vertebra
See Vertebra, Thoracic
Wall
See Chest Wall

Thoracocentesis

See Thoracentesis

Thoracoplasty 32905

with Closure Bronchopleural Fistula 32906

Thoracoscopy

Diagnostic 32601-32606
with Biopsy 32602, 32604, 32606
without Biopsy 32601, 32603, 32605
Surgical .32650-32665
with Control Traumatic Hemorrhage 32654
with Creation Pericardial Window 32659
with Esophagomyotomy 32665

with Excision Mediastinal Cyst, Tumor
and/or Mass .32662
with Excision Pericardial Cyst, Tumor
and/or Mass .32661
with Excision-Plication of Bullae 32655
with Lobectomy 32663
with Parietal Pleurectomy 32656
with Partial Pulmonary Decortication . . .32651
with Pleurodesis 32650
with Removal Intrapleural Foreign
Body 32653
with Removal of Clot/Foreign Body 32658
with Sternum Reconstruction 21743
with Thoracic Sympathectomy 32664
with Total Pericardiectomy 32660
with Total Pulmonary Decortication 32652
with Wedge Resection of Lung 32657

Thoracostomy

Empyema .32035-32036
Tube, with/without Water Seal 32551

Thoracotomy

Cardiac Massage 32160
for Post-Op Complications 32120
Hemorrhage 32110
Removal
Bullae 32141
Cyst 32140
Defibrillator 33243
Electrodes 33238
Foreign Body
Intrapleural 32150
Intrapulmonary 32151
Pacemaker 33236-33237
with Biopsy 32095-32100
with Excision-Plication of Bullae 32141
with Lung Repair 32110
with Open Intrapleural Pneumolysis . . .32124
Transmyocardial Laser
Revascularization 33140, 33141

Thorax

See Chest; Chest Cavity; Mediastinum
Angiography 71275
Biopsy 21550
CT Scan .71250-71275
Incision
Empyema 32035-32036
Incision and Drainage
Abscess 21501-21502
Deep 21510
Hematoma 21501-21502
Strapping 29200
Tube Thoracostomy 32551
Tumor
Excision 21552-21558
Excision/Resection 21557-21558
Unlisted Services and Procedures, Surgery . . .21899

Three Glass Test

See Urinalysis, Glass Test

Three-Day Measles

See Rubella

Throat

See Pharynx
Abscess
Incision and Drainage 42700-42725
Biopsy 42800-42806
Hemorrhage 42960-42962
Reconstruction .42950

Total 60240, 60271
   Cervical Approach 60271
   for Malignancy
      Limited Neck Dissection 60252
      Radical Neck Dissection 60254
   Removal All Thyroid Tissue 60260
   Sternal Split/Transthoracic Approach . . .60270

Thyrolingual Cyst
See Cyst, Thyroglossal Duct

Thyrotomy 31300

Thyrotropin Receptor Ab
See Thyrotropin Releasing Hormone (TRH)

Thyrotropin Releasing Hormone (TRH) 80438-80439

Thyroxine
Free 84439
Neonatal 84437
Total 84436
True 84436

Thyroxine Binding Globulin 84442

Tibia
See Ankle
Arthroscopy Surgical 29891-29892
Craterization 27360, 27640
Cyst
   Excision .27635-27638
Diaphysectomy 27360, 27640
Excision 27360, 27640
   Epiphyseal Bar 20150
Fracture
   Arthroscopic Treatment 29855-29856
     Plafond 29892
   Closed Treatment 27824-27825
   Distal 27824-27828
   Intercondylar 27538-27540
   Malleolus 27760-27766, 27808-27814
   Open Treatment 27535-27536,
                27758-27759, 27826-27828
   Plateau .29855-29856
     Closed Treatment 27530-27536
   Shaft 27752-27759
   with Manipulation 27825
   without Manipulation 27824
Incision 27607
Osteoplasty
   Lengthening .27715
Prophylactic Treatment 27745
Reconstruction .27418
   at Knee 27440-27443, 27446
Repair 27720-27725
   Epiphysis 27477-27485, 27730-27742
   Osteochondritis Dissecans
     Arthroscopy 29892
   Osteotomy 27455-27457, 27705,
                    27709-27712
   Pseudoarthrosis 27727
Saucerization 27360, 27640
Tumor
   Excision .27635-27638
   Radical Resection 27645
X-ray 73590

Tibial
Arteries
   See Artery, Tibial

Nerve
   Repair/Suture
     Posterior .64840

Tibiofibular Joint
Arthrodesis 27871
Dislocation 27830-27832
Disruption
   Open Treatment 27829
Fusion 27871

TIG
See Immune Globulins, Tetanus

Time
Bleeding
   See Bleeding Time
Prothrombin
   See Prothrombin Time
Reptilase
   See Thrombin Time

Tinnitus
Assessment 92625

Tissue
Crystal Identification 89060
Culture
   Chromosome Analysis 88230-88239
   Homogenization 87176
   Non-neoplastic Disorder 88230, 88237
   Skin Grafts 15100-15101, 15120-15121
     Harvesting 15040
   Solid Tumor 88239
   Toxin/Antitoxin 87230
   Virus 87252-87253
Dissection, Macroscopic 88387-88388
Examination, Macroscopic 88387-88388
Enzyme Activity 82657
Examination for Ectoparasites 87220
Examination for Fungi 87220
Expander
   Breast Reconstruction with 19357
   Insertion
     Skin 11960
   Removal
     Skin 11971
   Replacement
     Skin 11970
Grafts
   Harvesting .20926
Granulation
   See Granulation Tissue
Homogenization 87176
Hybridization In Situ 88365-88368
Mucosal
   See Mucosa
Preparation
   Drug Analysis 80103
   Macroscopic 88387-88388
Skin Harvest for Culture 15040
Soft
   Abscess 20000-20005
   Tumor
     See Tumor, Excision
     See Tumor, Radical Resection
Transfer
   Adjacent
     Eyelids 67961
     Skin .14000-14350
   Facial Muscles 15845

   Finger Flap 14350
   Toe Flap 14350
Typing
   Culture 87140-87158
   Human Leukocyte Antigen (HLA)
     Antibodies 86812-86817
     Crossmatch 86825-86826
   Lymphocyte Culture 86821-86822

Tissue Culture
from Skin Harvest 15040
Skin Grafts 15150-15157, 15340-15366

Tissue Factor
See Thromboplastin

TLC
See Chromatography, Thin-Layer
Screen 84375

TMJ
See Temporomandibular Joint (TMJ)
Manipulation, Therapeutic
   See Manipulation, Temporomandibular Joint
Prostheses
   See Prosthesis, Temporomandibular Joint

Tobacco
See Performance Measures

Tobramycin
Assay 80200

Tocolysis 59412

Tocopherol .84446

Toe
See Interphalangeal Joint, Toe;
Metatarsophalangeal Joint; Phalanx
Amputation 28810-28825
Capsulotomy 28270-28272
Fasciotomy 28008
Fracture
   See Fracture, Phalanges, Toe
Lesion
   Excision 28092
Reconstruction
   Angle Deformity 28313
   Extra Toes .28344
   Hammertoe 28285-28286
   Macrodactyly 28340-28341
   Syndactyly .28345
   Webbed Toe 28345
Repair
   Bunion 28290-28299
   Muscle 28240
   Tendon 28232-28234, 28240
   Webbed 28280
   Webbed Toe 28345
Tenotomy 28010-28011, 28232-28234
Unlisted Services and Procedures 28899

Toe Flap
Tissue Transfer .14350

Toes
Arthrocentesis .20600
Dislocation
   See Specific Joint
Magnetic Resonance Imaging
(MRI) 73721-73723
Reconstruction
   Extra Digit .26587

Wound
　Suture
　　Cervical 31800
　　Intrathoracic 31805

Tracheal
Stent
　Placement 31631
Tubes
　See Endotracheal Tube

Trachelectomy 57530
Radical 57531

Tracheloplasty
See Cervicoplasty

Trachelorrhaphy 57720

Tracheo-Esophageal Fistula
See Fistula, Tracheoesophageal

Tracheobronchoscopy
through Tracheostomy 31615

Tracheoplasty
Cervical 31750
Intrathoracic 31760
Tracheopharyngeal Fistulization 31755

Tracheostoma
Revision 31613-31614

Tracheostomy
Emergency 31603-31605
Planned 31600-31601
Revision
　Scar 31830
Surgical Closure
　with Plastic Repair 31825
　without Plastic Repair 31820
Tracheobronchoscopy through 31615
with Flaps 31610

Tracheotomy
Tube Change 31502

Tracking Tests (Ocular) 92545
See Ear, Nose, and Throat

Tract, Urinary
See Urinary Tract

Traction Therapy
See Physical Medicine/Therapy/Occupational
Therapy
Manual 97140
Mechanical 97012

Tractotomy
Medulla 61470
Mesencephalon .61480

Training
Activities of Daily Living 97535, 99509
Biofeedback 90901-90911
Cognitive Skills .97532
Community/Work Reintegration 97537
Home Management 97535, 99509
Orthoptic/Pleoptic 92065
Orthotics 97760
Prosthetics 97761
Self Care 97535, 98960-98962, 99509
Sensory Integration 97533
Walking (Physical Therapy) 97116
Wheelchair Management 97542

TRAM Flap
Breast Reconstruction 19367-19369

Trans-Scaphoperilunar
Fracture/Dislocation
　Closed Treatment 25680
　Open Treatment 25685

Transaminase
Glutamic Oxaloacetic 84450
Glutamic Pyruvic 84460

Transanal Endoscopic Microsurgery (TEMS)
See Bladder, Neck

Transcatheter
Biopsy 37200
Closure
　Percutaneous
　　Heart 93580-93581
　Transmyocardial
　　Heart 0166T, 0167T
Embolization
　Percutaneous 37204
　Cranial 61624-61626
Occlusion
　Percutaneous 37204
　Cranial 61624-61626
Placement
　Intravascular Stents 0075T-0076T,
　　　　　　　　　　　37205-37208, 37215-37216
　Sensor, Aneurysmal Sac 34806
Therapy
　Embolization 75894
　Infusion 37201-37202, 75896-75898
Perfusion
　Cranial 61624-61626
　Retrieval 75961

Transcatheter Foreign Body
Retrieval 37203

Transcortin 84449

Transcranial
Doppler Study (TCP) 93886-93893
Stimulation, Motor 95928-95929

Transcutaneous Testing
Bilirubin 88720
Carboxyhemoglobin 88740
Hemoglobin (Hgb) 88738
Methemoglobin .88741

Transcutaneous Electric Nerve Stimulation
See Application, Neurostimulation

Transdermal Electrostimulation
See Application, Neurostimulation

Transection
Artery
　Carotid 61610, 61612
Blood Vessel
　Kidney 50100
Brain
　Subpial 61567
Carotid
　with Skull Base Surgery 61609
Nerve .64732-64772
　Vagus 43640-43641
Pulmonary Artery 33922

Transesophageal
Doppler Echocardiography 93312-93318

Transfer
Blastocyst
　See Embryo Transfer
Gamete Intrafallopian
　See GIFT
Jejunum
　with Microvascular Anastomosis
　　Free 43496
Preparation
　Embryo 89255
　　Cryopreserved 89352
Surgical
　See Transposition
Tendon
　See Tendon, Transfer
Toe to Hand 26551-26556

Transferase
Aspartate Amino 84450
Glutamic Oxaloacetic 84450

Transferrin 84466

Transformation
Lymphocyte 86353

Transfusion
Blood 36430
　Exchange 36450-36455
　Fetal 36460
　Push
　　Infant 36440
Blood Parts
　Exchange 36511-36516
Unlisted Services and Procedures 86999
White Blood Cells 86950

Transfusion of, Blood, Autologous
See Autotransfusion

Transluminal
Angioplasty
　Arterial 75962-75968
Atherectomies
　See Artery, Atherectomy
Coronary Balloon Dilatation
　See Percutaneous Transluminal Angioplasty

Transmyocardial Laser Revascularization 33140, 33141

Transosteal Bone Plate
Reconstruction
　Mandible 21244

Transpeptidase, Gamma-Glutamyl
See Gamma Glutamyl Transferase

Transplant
See Graft
Bone
　See Bone Graft
Hair
　See Hair, Transplant

Transplantation
See Graft
Allogenic
　See Homograft
Autologous
　See Autograft

Triolean Hydrolase
See Lipase

Trioxopurine
See Uric Acid

Tripcellim
See Trypsin

Trisegmentectomy 47122

Trocar Biopsy
Bone Marrow 38221

Trochanteric Femur Fracture
See Femur, Fracture, Trochanteric

Trophoblastic Tumor GTT
See Hydatidiform Mole

Troponin 84484
Qualitative 84512
Quantitative 84484

Truncal Vagotomies
See Vagotomy, Truncal

Truncus Arteriosus
Repair 33786

Truncus Brachiocephalicus
See Artery, Brachiocephalic

Trunk, Brachiocephalic
See Artery, Brachiocephalic

Trypanosomiases
See Trypanosomiasis

Trypanosomiasis 86171, 86280

Trypsin
Duodenum 84485
Feces 84488-84490

Trypsin Inhibitor, Alpha 1-Antitrypsin
See Alpha-1 Antitrypsin

Trypure
See Trypsin

Tsalicylate Intoxication
See Salicylate

TSH
See Thyroid Stimulating Hormone

TSI
See Thyroid Stimulating Immunoglobulin

Tsutsugamushi Disease
See Scrub Typhus

TT
See Thrombin Time

TT-3
See Triiodothyronine, True

TT-4
See Thyroxine, True

Tuba Auditoria (Auditiva)
See Eustachian Tube

Tubal Embryo Stage Transfer
See Embryo Transfer

Tubal Ligation 58600
Laparoscopic .58670
with Cesarean Delivery 58611

Tubal Occlusion
See Fallopian Tube, Occlusion; Occlusion
Create Lesion

Tubal Pregnancy 59121
with Salpingectomy and/or Oophorectomy . . .59120

Tube Change
Colonic 49450
Duodenostomy 49451
Gastro-Jejunostomy 49452
Gastrostomy 43760, 49446
Jejunostomy 49451
Tracheostomy .31502

Tube Placement
Cecostomy Tube 44300, 49442
Duodenostomy Tube 49441
Endoscopic
    Bile Duct, Pancreatic Duct 43268
    Jejunostomy Tube
        Percutaneous 49441
    Nasobiliary, Nasopancreatic
        for Drainage 43267
Enterostomy Tube 44300
Gastrostomy Tube 43246, 49440
Nasogastric Tube 43752
Orogastric Tube 43752

Tube, Fallopian
See Fallopian Tube

Tubectomy
See Excision, Fallopian Tube

Tubed Pedicle Flap
Formation 15570-15576

Tubercle Bacilli
Culture 87116

Tubercleplasty
Tibia
    Anterior 27418

Tuberculin Test
See Skin, Tests, Tuberculosis

Tuberculosis
Antigen Response Test 86480
Culture 87116
Skin Test 86580

**Tuberculosis Vaccine
(BCG)** 90585-90586

Tubes
Colonic
    See Colon
Duodenostomy
    See Duodenostomy
Endotracheal
    See Endotracheal Tube
Gastrostomy
    See Gastrostomy Tube
Jejunostomy
    See Jejunostomy

Tudor 'Rabbit Ear'
See Urethra, Repair

Tuffier Vaginal Hysterectomy
See Hysterectomy, Vaginal

Tumor
See Craniopharyngioma
Abdomen
    Destruction/Excision 49203-49205
Abdominal Wall
    Excision 22900-22903
    Radical Resection 22904, 22905
Acetabulum
    Excision .27076
Ankle
    Excision 27618-27619, 27632-27634
    Radical Resection 27615-27616
Arm, Lower
    Excision 25071-25076
    Radical Resection 25077-25078
Arm, Upper
    Excision 24071-24076
    Radical Resection 24077, 24079
Back/Flank
    Excision 21930-21933
    Radical Resection 21935, 21936
Bile Duct
    Destruction 43272
    Extrahepatic 47711
    Intrahepatic 47712
Bladder 52234-52240
    Excision 51530, 52355
Bone
    Ablation 20982
Brain 61510
    Excision 61518, 61520-61521,
                61526-61530, 61545, 62164
Breast
    Excision 19120-19126
Bronchi
    Excision 31640
Calcaneus
    Excision 28100-28103
    Radical Resection 27647
Carpal 25130-25136
Cheekbone 21030, 21034
Chest Wall
    Excision 19260-19272
Clavicle
    Excision 23140, 23200
        with Allograft 23146
        with Autograft 23145
Coccyx 49215
Colon
    Destruction 44393, 45383
Cranial Bone
    Reconstruction 21181-21184
Destruction
    Chemosurgery 17311-17315
    Urethra 53220
Ear, Middle
    Extended 69554
    Transcanal 69550
    Transmastoid 69552
Elbow
    Excision 24071-24076
    Radical Resection 24077, 24079
Esophagus
    Ablation 43228
Excision
    Femur 27355-27358
Face or Scalp
    Excision 21011-21014
    Radical Resection 21015, 21016

Tunica Vaginalis
Hydrocele
    Aspiration 55000
    Excision 55040-55041
    Repair 55060

Turbinate
Excision 30130-30140
Fracture
    Therapeutic 30930
Injection 30200
Submucous Resection
    Nose Excision 30140

Turbinate Mucosa
Cauterization 30801-30802

Turcica, Sella
See Sella Turcica

Turnbuckle Jacket 29020-29025
Removal 29715

TURP
See Prostatectomy, Transurethral

Tylectomy
See Breast, Excision, Lesion

Tylenol
Urine 82003

Tympanic Membrane
Create Stoma 69433-69436
Incision 69420-69421
Reconstruction 69620
Repair 69450, 69610

Tympanic Nerve
Excision 69676

Tympanolysis 69450

Tympanomastoidectomy
See Tympanoplasty

Tympanometry 92550, 92567, 92570
See Audiologic Function Tests

Tympanoplasty
See Myringoplasty
Radical or Complete 69645
    with Ossicular Chain Reconstruction ...69646
    with Antrotomy or Mastoidotomy 69635
      with Ossicular Chain Reconstruction ...69636
        and Synthetic Prosthesis 69637
with Mastoidectomy 69641
    with Intact or Reconstructed Wall 69643
      and Ossicular Chain Reconstruction ...69644
    with Ossicular Chain Reconstruction ...69642
without Mastoidectomy 69631
    with Ossicular Chain Reconstruction ...69632
      and Synthetic Prosthesis 69633

Tympanostomy 69433-69436

Tympanotomy
See Myringotomy

Typhoid Vaccine 90690-90693
AKD 90693
H-P 90692
Oral 90690
Polysaccharide 90691

Typhus
Endemic
    See Murine Typhus
Mite-Borne
    See Scrub Typhus
Sao Paulo
    See Rocky Mountain Spotted Fever
Tropical
    See Scrub Typhus

Typing, Blood
See Blood Typing

Typing, HLA
See HLA Typing

Typing, Tissue
See Tissue, Typing

Tyrosine 84510

Tzank Smear 88160-88161

U

UDP Galactose Pyrophosphorylase
See Galactose-1-Phosphate, Uridyl Transferase

UFR
See Uroflowmetry

Ulcer
Anal
    See Anus, Fissure
Decubitus
    See Debridement; Pressure Ulcer (Decubitus);
    Skin Graft and Flap
Pinch Graft 15050
Pressure 15920-15999
Stomach
    Excision 43610

Ulcerative, Cystitis
See Cystitis, Interstitial

Ulna
See Arm, Lower; Elbow; Humerus; Radius
Arthrodesis
    Radioulnar Joint
      with Resection 25830
Arthroplasty
    with Implant 25442
Centralization or Wrist 25335
Craterization 24147, 25150-25151
Cyst
    Excision 24125-24126, 25120-25126
Diaphysectomy 24147, 25150-25151
Excision 24147
    Abscess 24138
    Complete 25240
    Epiphyseal Bar 20150
    Partial 25145-25151, 25240
Fracture
    Closed Treatment 25530-25535
    Olecranon 24670-24675
    Open Treatment 24685, 25545
    Shaft 25530-25545
      Open Treatment 25574

Styloid
    Closed Treatment 25650
    Open Treatment 25652
    Percutaneous Fixation 25651
with Dislocation
    Closed Treatment 24620
    Open Treatment 24635
with Manipulation 25535
with Radius 25560-25565
    Open Treatment 25575
without Manipulation 25530
Incision and Drainage 25035
Osteoplasty 25390-25393
Prophylactic Treatment 25491-25492
Reconstruction
    Radioulnar 25337
Repair
    Epiphyseal Arrest 25450-25455
    Malunion or Nonunion 25400, 25415
    Osteotomy 25360, 25370-25375
      and Radius 25365
    with Graft 25405, 25420-25426
Saucerization 24147, 25150-25151
Sequestrectomy 24138, 25145
Tumor
    Cyst 24120
    Excision ...24125-24126, 25120-25126, 25170

Ulnar Arteries
See Artery, Ulnar

Ulnar Nerve
Decompression 64718
Neuroplasty 64718-64719
Reconstruction 64718-64719
Release 64718-64719
Repair/Suture
    Motor 64836
Transposition 64718-64719

Ultrasonic
See Ultrasound

Ultrasonic Cardiography
See Echocardiography

Ultrasonic Procedure 52325

Ultrasonography
See Echography

Ultrasound
See Echocardiography; Echography
3-D Rendering 76376-76377
Abdomen 76700-76705
Arm 76880
Artery
    Intracranial 93886-93893
    Middle Cerebral 76821
    Umbilical 76820
Bladder 51798
Bone Density Study 76977
Breast 76645
Bronchi
    Endoscopy 31620
Chest 76604
Colon
    Endoscopic 45391-45392
Colon-Sigmoid
    Endoscopic 45341-45342
Computer-Assisted Surgical Navigation
    Intraoperative 20986
    Preoperative 20987

Infant
- Cutdown 36420
- Percutaneous 36400-36406
- Routine 36415

Venography
- Adrenal 75840-75842
- Arm 75820-75822
- Epidural 75872
- Hepatic Portal 75885-75887
- Injection 36005
- Jugular 75860
- Leg 75820-75822
- Liver 75889-75891
- Neck 75860
- Nuclear Medicine 78445, 78457-78458
- Orbit 75880
- Renal 75831-75833
- Sagittal Sinus 75870
- Vena Cava 75825-75827
- Venous Sampling 75893

Venorrhaphy
See Suture, Vein

Venotomy
See Phlebotomy

Venous Access Device
- Blood Collection 36591-36592
- Declotting 36593
- Fluoroscopic Guidance 77001
- Insertion
  - Central 36560-36566
  - Peripheral 36570-36571
- Irrigation 96523
- Obstruction Clearance 36595-36596
  - Guidance 75901-75902
- Removal 36590
- Repair 36576
- Replacement 36582-36583, 36585
  - Catheter Only 36578

Venous Blood Pressure
See Blood Pressure, Venous

Venovenostomy
See Anastomosis, Vein

Ventilating Tube
- Insertion 69433
- Removal 69424

Ventilation Assist 94002-94005, 99504
See Pulmonology, Therapeutic

Ventricular Puncture .61020-61026, 61105-61120

Ventriculocisternostomy 62180, 62200-62201

Ventriculography
Anesthesia
- Brain 00214
- Cardiac 01920
- Nuclear Imaging 78635

Ventriculomyectomy 33416

Ventriculomyotomy 33416

Vermiform Appendix
See Appendix

Vermilionectomy 40500

Verruca Plana
See Warts, Flat

Verruca(e)
See Warts

Version, Cephalic
See Cephalic Version

Vertebra
See Intervertebral Disc; Spinal Cord; Spine; Vertebral Body; Vertebral Process
Additional Segment
- Excision 22103, 22116
Arthrodesis
- Anterior 22548-22585
- Exploration 22830
- Lateral Extracavitary 22532-22534
- Posterior 22590-22802
- Spinal Deformity
  - Anterior Approach 22808-22812
  - Posterior Approach 22800-22804
Aspiration 62267
Cervical
- Excision
  - for Tumor 22100, 22110
- Fracture 23675-23680
Decompression 62287
Fracture/Dislocation
- Additional Segment
  - Open Treatment 22328
- Cervical
  - Open Treatment 22326
- Lumbar
  - Open Treatment 22325
- Thoracic
  - Open Treatment 22327
Kyphectomy 22818-22819
Lumbar
- Distraction Device 0171T-0172T
- Excision
  - for Tumor 22102, 22114
- Foraminotomy 0202T
Osteoplasty
- CT Scan 72292
- Fluoroscopy 72291
- Lumbar 22521-22522
- Thoracic 22520-22522
Osteotomy
- Additional Segment
  - Anterior Approach 22226
  - Posterior/Posterolateral Approach ..22216
- Cervical
  - Anterior Approach 22220
  - Posterior/Posterolateral Approach ..22210
- Lumbar
  - Anterior Approach 22224
  - Posterior/Posterolateral Approach ..22214
- Thoracic
  - Anterior Approach 22222
  - Posterior/Posterolateral Approach ..22212

Vertebrae
See Vertebra
Arthrodesis
- Anterior 22548-22585
- Lateral Extracavitary 22532-22534
- Spinal Deformity 22818-22819

Vertebral
Arteries
See Artery, Vertebral
Body
- Biopsy 20250-20251
- Excision
  - Decompression 63081-63103
  - Lesion 63300-63308
  - with Skull Base Surgery 61597
- Fracture/Dislocation
  - Closed Treatment 22305
  - without Manipulation 22310
- Kyphectomy 22818-22819
- Repair
  - Injection
    - Lumbar 22521
    - Thoracic.....................22520
Column
See Spine
Corpectomy 63081-63103, 63300-63308
Fracture
See Fracture, Vertebra
Joint Replacement
- Lumbar Spine 0202T
Process
- Fracture/Dislocation
  - Closed Treatment
    - with Manipulation, Casting and/or Bracing 22315

Very Low Density Lipoprotein
See Lipoprotein, Blood

Vesication
See Bulla

Vesicle, Seminal
See Seminal Vesicle

Vesico-Psoas Hitch 50785

Vesicostomy
Cutaneous 51980

Vesicourethropexy 51840-51841

Vesicovaginal Fistula
See Fistula, Vesicovaginal

Vesiculectomy 55650

Vesiculogram, Seminal
See Vesiculography

Vesiculography 55300, 74440

Vesiculotomy 55600-55605
Complicated 55605

Vessel, Blood
See Blood Vessels

Vessels Transposition, Great
See Transposition, Great Arteries

Vestibular Function Tests
See Ear, Nose, and Throat
- Additional Electrodes 92547
- Caloric Test 92533
- Caloric Vestibular Tests 92543
- Foveal Stimulation 92540
- Nystagmus
  - Optokinetic 92534, 92540, 92544
  - Positional 92532, 92540, 92542
  - Spontaneous 92531, 92540-92541

W

X-ray Tomography, Computed
See CT Scan

Xa, Coagulation Factor
See Thrombokinase

Xenoantibodies
See Antibody, Heterophile

Xenografts, Skin
See Heterograft, Skin

Xenotransplantation
See Heterograft

Xerography
See Xeroradiography

XI, Coagulation Factor
See Plasma Thromboplastin, Antecedent

XI, Cranial Nerve
See Accessory Nerve

XII, Coagulation Factor
See Hageman Factor

XII, Cranial Nerve
See Hypoglossal Nerve

XIII, Coagulation Factor
See Fibrin Stabilizing Factor

Y

Yacoub Procedure
See Ascending Aorta Graft

YHrium-Aluminum-Garnet (YAG) Laser
See Eye, Incision

Z

Zinc Manganese Leucine Aminopeptidase
See Leucine Aminopeptidase

Zygoma
See Cheekbone